California Contractors License Law & Reference Book

2023 Edition

With Rules and Regulations

Contractors State License Board
STATE OF CALIFORNIA
Gavin Christopher Newsom, *Governor*

ISBN: 978-1-66334-953-8

© 2023 California Contractors State License Board

© 2023 Matthew Bender & Company, Inc., a member of the LexisNexis Group.

All rights reserved.

LexisNexis, the knowledge burst logo, and Michie are trademarks of Reed Elsevier Properties Inc., used under license. Matthew Bender is a registered trademark of Matthew Bender Properties Inc.

The California regulations appearing in this publication have been extracted from Barclays Official California Code of Regulations, copyright © 2022, State of California.

This material may not be commercially reproduced or sold in printed or electronic form without written permission of Thomson/West, and is subject to the following disclaimer:

THOMSON/WEST MAKES NO WARRANTY OR REPRESENTATION WHATSOEVER, EXPRESS OR IMPLIED, WITH RESPECT TO THE MERCHANTABILITY OR FITNESS FOR ANY PARTICULAR PURPOSE WITH RESPECT TO THE INFORMATION CONTAINED IN THIS PUBLICATION; AND

THOMSON/WEST ASSUMES NO LIABILITY WHATSOEVER WITH RESPECT TO ANY USE OF THIS PUBLICATION OR ANY PORTION THEREOF OR WITH RESPECT TO ANY DAMAGES WHICH MAY RESULT FROM SUCH USE.

 **LexisNexis**

Matthew Bender & Company, Inc.
Editorial Offices
9443 Springboro Pike
Miamisburg, OH 45342
800-833-9844
www.lexisnexis.com

(Pub. 29700)

TABLE OF CONTENTS

Section I. The California Contractor License

Section II. Home Improvement

Section V. The Department of Consumer Affairs

Page

Section VI. The Contractors State License Board; License Law, Rules and Regulations, and Related Laws

Page

Page

ABOUT THIS BOOK

The *California Contractors License Law & Reference Book* begins with several narrative chapters that describe required licensing and legal processes affecting contractors. California contracting laws, rules, and regulations are detailed in the later chapters; laws and regulations are those in effect on January 1, 2023, unless otherwise noted.

SUMMARY OF RECENT CHANGES TO CONSTRUCTION OR CONTRACTORS' LAW

Effective January 1, 2023

Unless indicated otherwise

AB 1747 (Quirk)

Amends Sections 7099.2 and 7110 of the Business and Professions Code, relating to CSLB.

This bill increases the civil penalty from $5,000 to $30,000 for every violation of Business and Professions Code section 7110. In addition to building permit violations, the bill addresses the failure to comply with certain health and safety laws, water laws, safe excavation requirements, pest control requirements, illegal dumping, and other state laws related to building and insurance requirements.

(Chapter 757, Statutes of 2022)

AB 2105 (Smith)

Amend Section 7137 of the Business and Professions Code, relating to CSLB.

This bill requires the board to grant a 50% fee reduction for an initial license or registration fee to an applicant who provides specified documentation to the board that the applicant is a veteran who has served as an active-duty member of the United States Armed Forces, including the National Guard or Reserve components, and was not dishonorably discharged. This bill applies to initial license fees for contractors and registration fees for home improvement salespersons.

(Chapter 156, Statutes of 2022)

AB 2374 (Bauer-Kahan)

Amends Section 374.3 of the Penal Code, relating to crimes.

This bill requires courts to notify the Contractors State License Board or other Department of Consumer Affairs board or bureau when a licensee is convicted of an illegal dumping crime in order for the board to publish it on their website. This bill increases the fines a court may impose for this crime. This bill also requires the court to order a person convicted of dumping commercial quantities of waste to remove, or pay for the removal of, the waste matter that was illegally dumped.

(Chapter 784, Statutes of 2022)

AB 2916 (McCarty)

Amends Section 7124.6 of the Business and Professions Code, relating to CSLB.

The bill updates the CSLB Letter of Admonishment (LOA) program to allow the Board to determine whether it should be disclosed for one or two years, rather than the current one year. In making that determination, the Board is required to consider gravity of the violation, the good faith of the licensee or applicant being charged, and the history of previous violations should be considered.

(Chapter 293, Statutes of 2022)

SB 216 (Dodd)

Amends, repeals, and adds Section 7125 of the Business and Professions Code, relating to professions and vocations.

This bill requires contractors who possess a C-8, C-20, C-22, or D-49 license to hold valid workers' compensation insurance as of January 1, 2023. Additionally, this bill requires that by January 1, 2026, all contractors, except for joint ventures without employees, hold valid workers' compensation insurance, whether or not they have employees.

(Chapter 978, Statutes of 2022)

SB 1076 (Archuleta)

Amends Section 105254 of and adds Section 105250.5 to the Health and Safety Code, relating to lead-based paint.

This bill requires the Department of Public Health to review and revise regulations governing lead-related construction work, including training and certification for workers and accreditation for trainers in lead-safe work practices, to comply with existing state regulations and the United States Environmental Protection Agency's

Lead Renovation, Repair, and Painting Rule. This bill also requires the Department of Public Health to provide the Contractors State License Board with educational and outreach materials and for the Board to make the materials available to contractors and consumers on its website.

(Chapter 507, Statutes of 2022)

SB 1237 (Newman)

Amends Section 114.3 of the Business and Professions Code, relating to professions and vocations.

The bill updates current law that requires Department of Consumer Affairs boards, including CSLB, waive renewal fees for a licensee who is called to active duty as a member of the U.S. Armed Forces or California National Guard if the licensee or registrant is stationed outside of California. The bill expands the definition of "called to active duty" to align with definitions elsewhere in federal and state law and extends existing law to licensees on active duty during a "state of insurrection" or a "state of extreme emergency."

(Chapter 386, Statutes of 2022)

SB 1443 (Roth)

Amends Business and Professions Code sections 7000.5 and 7011, relating to CSLB.

This bill amends various Business and Professions Code sections and affects the sunset review of multiple Department of Consumer Affairs boards and bureaus. As it relates to the Contractors State License Board, this bill amends the statutory sunset date of CSLB from January 1, 2024, to January 1, 2025.

(Chapter 625, Statutes of 2022)

SB 1495 (Committee on Business, Professions and Economic Development)

Amends Business and Professions Code section 7086.10, as it relates to CSLB.

This bill amends various Business and Professions Code sections related to the Department of Consumer Affairs, including the Contractors State License Board. Existing law provides that when a restitution claim payment is made under the CSLB Solar Energy System Restitution Program (SESRP), CSLB will disclose that fact on the public license detail of the contractor involved for seven years. This bill clarifies that the public disclosure will only apply to contractors whose licenses are revoked or pending revocation.

(Chapter 511, Statutes of 2022)

SECTIONS AFFECTED BY 2022 LEGISLATION

Business & Professions Code

Section Affected		Type of Change	Chapter Number	Page
101	Composition of department	Amended	414	167
114.3	Waiver of fees and requirements for active duty members of armed forces and national guard	Amended	386	176
7000.5	Contractors' State License Board; Members; Effect of repeal	Amended	625	280
7011	Registrar of contractors	Amended	625	284
7058.7	Hazardous substance certification examination	Amended	258	325
7086.10	Notice of licensee subject of program payment	Amended	511	386
7099.2	Regulations for assessment of civil penalties; Factors; Maximum amount; Letter of admonishment	Amended	757	391
7110	Disregard or violation of statutes	Amended	757	402
7124.6	Public access to complaints against licensees; Disclaimer; Limitations of disclosure	Amended	293	414
7125	Reports to registrar; Exemptions [Repealed effective January 1, 2026]	Amended	978	416
7125	Reports to registrar; Exemptions [Operative effective January 1, 2026]	Added	978	418
7137	Fee schedule	Amended	156	423

Civil Code

Section Affected		Type of Change	Chapter Number	Page
1770	Unlawful acts and practices	Amended	324	670
2782.6	Exception for professional engineer or geologist; "Hazardous materials"	Amended	258	684

Code of Civil Procedure

Section Affected		Type of Change	Chapter Number	Page
995.710	Deposit of money, certificates, accounts, bonds, or notes	Amended	452	737

Government Code

Section Affected		Type of Change	Chapter Number	Page
11343	Procedure	Amended	48	797
12944	Discrimination by licensing board	Amended	48	802
12944	Discrimination by licensing board	Amended	630	802

Health and Safety Code

Section Affected		Type of Change	Chapter Number	Page
25281	Definitions	Amended	258	828
105250.5	Review and amendment of regulations governing lead-related construction work; Certifications or accreditation fees	Added	507	843
105254	Types of lead construction work requiring certification	Amended	507	844

Labor Code

Section Affected		Type of Change	Chapter Number	Page
1771.4	Requirements for public works projects; Compliance	Amended	824	911
4600	Medical treatment provided by employer; Liability for reasonable expense; Medical provider network; Predesignation of personal physician; Expenses incurred in submitting to examination; Qualified interpreter	Amended	609	988
4610	Employers to establish utilization review process; Criteria; Administrative penalties	Amended	292	1001
4616	Establishment of medical provider network; Goal; Requirements; Regulations	Amended	609	1016
5402	Employer's knowledge of injury equivalent to service; When presumed compensable; Authorization for treatment; Liability limit	Amended	835	1063

Penal Code

Section Affected		Type of Change	Chapter Number	Page
	Illegal dumping on roads, right-of-way, or private or public property; Use of own property; Mandatory fine; Removal of waste; Punishment for dumping in commercial			
374.3	quantities	Amended	784	1075
	Investigators, inspectors, and other			
830.3	employees of specified agencies	Amended	452	1087

Public Contract Code

Section Affected		Type of Change	Chapter Number	Page
6980	Citation of chapter	Added	875	1112
	Legislative findings and			
6981	declarations; Intent	Added	875	1112
6982	Definitions	Added	875	1114
	Legislative intent; High road jobs standards; Development of policies, procedures, and requirements applicable to covered public			
6983	contracts	Added	875	1115
6984	Compliance; Reporting requirements	Added	875	1116
	Legislative declarations regarding effects of climate change; Labor			
6985	peace agreement	Added	875	1117
6986	Repeal of chapter	Added	875	1119
	Applicability to contracts entered into on or after January 1, 2012 relating to construction of public work of improvement; Retention proceeds withheld from payments;			
7201	Limitations.	Amended	121	1120
	Payments upon contracts; Progress payments; Substantially complex			
10261	projects will include a description	Amended	121	1125
10261	[Section repealed 2023.]	Repealed	121	1125
	Extension or renewal of contracts awarded without competitive			
10295.8	bidding; Report	Added	543	1127
	Use of proceeds; Contracts [Repealed			
10298.5	effective January 1, 2028]	Added	310	1127

Public Utilities Code

Section Affected		Type of Change	Chapter Number	Page
130232	Competitive bidding for contracts; Bid requirements	Amended	460	1141

Unemployment Insurance Code

Section Affected		Type of Change	Chapter Number	Page
1095	Purposes for which director must permit use of information in their possession	Amended	48	1172
1095	Purposes for which director must permit use of information in their possession	Amended	49	1172
1095	Purposes for which director must permit use of information in their possession	Amended	569	1172
1095	Purposes for which director must permit use of information in their possession	Amended	983	1172

California Code of Regulations, Title 16

Section Affected		Type of Change	Register Number	Page
823	Definitions: Bona Fide Employee; Direct Supervision and Control.	Repealed	2022-22	609
832	Specialty Contractors Classified	Amended	2022-13	505
832.49	Class C-49—Tree and Palm Contractor	Added	2022-13	517
858.2	Application for Approval of Blanket Performance and Payment Bond	Amended	2022-36	528

CSLB HISTORY & BACKGROUND

The Contractors State License Board (CSLB) was established in 1929 as the Contractors License Bureau under the Department of Professional and Vocational Standards. Today, CSLB is part of the Department of Consumer Affairs.

A 15-member board appoints CSLB's executive officer, or registrar of contractors, and directs administrative policy for the board's operations. CSLB's board includes nine public members (eight non-contractors and one local building official), five contractors, and one labor representative. The governor makes 11 appointments and four are made by the Legislature. The board holds regularly scheduled public meetings at various locations in the state. These meetings provide the public with an opportunity for input on agenda items and other issues.

CSLB licenses and regulates contractors in 44 license classifications that constitute the construction industry. Currently, there are nearly 285,000 contractor licenses in the state. The registrar oversees approximately 400 employees who work at the headquarters office in Sacramento and field offices throughout the state.

Headquarters staff receive and process applications for new contractor licenses, additional classifications, changes of license records, and license renewals. Staff also review and maintain records of disciplinary actions initiated by the field offices, provide verified certificates of licensure used in court or other legal actions, and provide other support services.

Headquarters directs the activities of field offices and initiates all disciplinary actions resulting from investigations. Field office staff investigate consumer complaints against contractors. The Statewide Investigative Fraud Team (SWIFT) addresses unlicensed activity.

CSLB's website, www.cslb.ca.gov or www.CheckTheLicenseFirst.com, provides the ability to look up a contractor by license number, name, or business name, and obtain the licensee's contact information, license status, CSLB legal actions (if any), classifications held, business type, and bond and workers' compensation insurance information. Home Improvement Salesperson registrations also are listed on the website's license look-up page.

Identical information is available through CSLB's automated public information line, (800) 321-CSLB (2752), which operates 24 hours per day. Also available is recorded information on licensing and examination procedures, complaint procedures and how to obtain information on a complaint that has been referred for legal action, the location and hours of CSLB offices, and current topics, such as recently passed laws or regulations. Callers also can order forms, applications, and other publications.

The "Find My Licensed Contractor" feature on CSLB's website allows users to search for licensed contractors in a specific classification by geographic area based on zip code or city. The randomly displayed results link to the license record and can be downloaded as either a PDF or a Word file.

CSLB aims to protect those whose homes and property are directly affected by disasters, such as wildfires, floods, mudflows, earthquakes, and pipeline explosions. CSLB offers materials at Local Assistance and Disaster Recovery Centers as well as monitors a Disaster Hotline, (800) 962-1125, to aid those in need.

CSLB offers a variety of publications and guides to help consumers make informed choices when contracting for home repairs and improvements. Speakers can be provided for groups interested in learning more about CSLB. Check the website for details or write to CSLB Public Affairs, P.O. Box 26000, Sacramento, CA 95826.

CSLB MISSION

The Contractors State License Board protects consumers by regulating the construction industry through policies that promote the health, safety, and general welfare of the public in matters relating to construction.

The Contractors State License Board accomplishes this by:

- Ensuring that construction is performed in a safe, competent, and professional manner;

- Licensing contractors and enforcing licensing laws;

- Requiring licensure for any person practicing or offering to practice construction contracting;

- Enforcing the laws, regulations, and standards governing construction contracting in a fair and uniform manner;

- Providing resolution to disputes that arise from construction activities; and

- Educating consumers so they can make informed choices.

CONTRACTORS STATE LICENSE BOARD OFFICES

Headquarters
9821 Business Park Drive
Sacramento, CA 95827
(800) 321-CSLB (2752)

Mailing Address
P.O. Box 26000,
Sacramento, CA 95826

Website
www.cslb.ca.gov
www.CheckTheLicenseFirst.com

Northern Region

9821 Business Park Drive
Sacramento, CA 95827
Legal Action Disclosure (916) 255-4041
Case Management (916) 255-4027
SWIFT (Unlicensed Activity)
  (916) 255-2924

Bakersfield Branch Office*
5800 District Blvd., Suite 300
Bakersfield, CA 93313
(800) 321-CSLB (2752)

Fresno Investigative Center
1277 East Alluvial, Suite 106
Fresno, CA 93720
(800) 321-CSLB (2752)

Sacramento Investigative Center
P.O. Box 269115
Sacramento, CA 95826-9115
(800) 321-CSLB (2752)

Sacramento Intake & Mediation Center
P.O. Box 269116
Sacramento, CA 95826-9116
(800) 321-CSLB (2752)
Fax (916) 255-4449

San Francisco Investigative Center
301 Junipero Serra Blvd, Suite 206
San Francisco, CA 94127
(800) 321- CSLB (2752)

Southern Region

12501 East Imperial Hwy, Suite 600
Norwalk, CA 90650
Legal Action Disclosure (562) 345-7656
Case Management (562) 345-7656
SWIFT (Unlicensed Activity)
  (562) 345-7600

Norwalk Intake & Mediation Center
12501 East Imperial Hwy, Suite 620
Norwalk, CA 90650
(800) 321-CSLB (2752)
Fax (562) 466-6064

Norwalk Investigative Center
12501 East Imperial Hwy, Suite 630
Norwalk, CA 90650
(800) 321-CSLB (2752)

Orange County Investigative Center
12501 East Imperial Hwy, Suite 640
Norwalk, CA 90650
(800) 321-CSLB (2752)

San Bernardino Investigative Center
1845 Business Center Drive, Suite 206
San Bernardino, CA 92408-3467
(800) 321-CSLB (2752)

San Diego Investigative Center
9246 Lightwave Ave., Suite 130
San Diego, CA 92123
(800) 321-CSLB (2752)

Santa Rosa Branch Office *
50 D Street, Room 400
Santa Rosa, CA 95404
(800) 321-CSLB (2752)

Valencia Investigative Center
25360 Magic Mountain Parkway, Suite 200
Santa Clarita, CA 91355
(800) 321-CSLB (2752)

West Covina Investigative Center
100 N. Barranca St., Suite 300
West Covina, CA 91791
(800) 321-CSLB (2752)

---

* Limited office hours

REFERENCE SECTIONS

The following sections contain general information about obtaining and maintaining a contractor license, how to operate a business, and other information that may be of interest. Please note, though we attempt to make this reference section accurate as of the date of publication, it is not a definitive statement of the law.
Laws and statutes begin with Chapter 11.

SECTION I.

THE CALIFORNIA CONTRACTOR LICENSE

Chapter

Chapter 1.

Becoming a California Licensed Contractor

GENERAL REQUIREMENTS

1. Who can become a licensed contractor in California?

An individual must:

- Be at least 18 years old; and
- Have either a valid Social Security number or individual taxpayer identification number; and
- Have the knowledge, experience, and skills to manage the daily activities of a construction business (including field supervision) or be represented by someone else with that background who serves as the "qualifier."

The qualifier must have at least four years of experience within the past ten years as a journeyperson, foreperson, supervising employee, or contractor in the trade being applied for.

The experience listed on the application must be verifiable, and people with first-hand knowledge of that experience must certify the accuracy of the information provided to CSLB on the "Certification of Work Experience" form. (Please see the section on "Applying for a License" for more information about the responsibilities of a qualifier.)

2. Who does CSLB license?

CSLB issues licenses to five types of business entities:

> Sole Owner
> Partnership
> Corporation
> Joint Venture

Limited Liability Company (LLC)

3. Who must be licensed as a contractor?

Any construction work that costs $500 or more in labor and/or material must be done by a state-licensed contractor. It is illegal to divide a job into smaller parts to get around the $500 limit.

Contractors, including subcontractors, specialty contractors, and people engaged in the business of home improvement must be licensed before submitting bids.

4. Is anyone exempt from the requirement to have a contractor license?

Yes. Exemptions include:

- Work on a project where the combined cost (labor and materials, whether purchased by the contractor or the consumer) is *less* than $500.

- Government or other public personnel working on public projects.

- Officers of a court acting within the scope of their office.

- Public utilities working under specified conditions.

- Oil and gas operations performed by an owner or lessee.

- Someone who sells installed carpets who holds a retail furniture dealer's license and contracts with a licensed carpet installer to install the carpet and certifies this to the buyer before the installation.

- Security alarm company operators (licensed by the Bureau of Security and Investigative Services) who install, maintain, monitor, sell, alter, or service alarm systems (fire alarm company operators must be licensed by CSLB).

- Individuals who install satellite antenna systems on residential structures or property (these installers must be registered with the Bureau of Household Goods and Services).

- Owner-builders who:

    1.) Engage in home improvement and: 1) the worksite is their principal residence for 12 months prior to completion of the work; and 2) the work is performed prior to sale of the home; and 3) they do not act as the owner-builder on more than two structures during any three-year period.

2.) Engage in the construction of new single-family residences and: 1) they do the work themselves or hire employees (paid in wages) to complete the work and do not sell the home for one year after completion; or 2) they hire properly licensed subcontractor(s) to perform the work in their specialty trade and do not sell more than four homes in a calendar year.

5. Do I need to live in California to get and keep a CSLB-issued contractor license?

No.

6. Does California recognize contractor licenses issued by other states or countries?

No. To work as a contractor in California, you must apply for and be issued a license by CSLB.

However, CSLB does have "reciprocity" agreements with Arizona, Louisiana, and Nevada. Under certain conditions the CSLB Registrar may waive the written trade exam for a contractor licensed from one of these states; CSLB evaluates requests for reciprocity on a case-by-case basis. Applicants still must take and pass the CSLB law and business exam and undergo certification of relevant work experience.

7. What happens if I contract without a license?

Contracting for work valued at $500 or more without a license can lead to misdemeanor charges. Unlicensed contractors face a first offense sentence of up to six months in jail, and/or a $5,000 fine, and potential administrative fines of $200 to $15,000. Subsequent violations can result in increased criminal penalties and fines. In addition, you may face felony charges if you contract without a license when one is required in a state or federally declared disaster area.

WORK EXPERIENCE REQUIREMENTS

8. What kind of work experience is required for a California contractor license?

The license qualifier must have four years of at least journey-level work experience in the past ten years immediately prior to filing the application in the classification being applied for. Credit is given only for experience as a journeyperson, foreperson, supervising employee, or contractor.

A journeyperson is an experienced worker, not a trainee, who can perform the trade without supervision or someone who has completed an apprenticeship program.

Someone other than the applicant must verify work experience claims, such as an employer, fellow employee, other journeyperson, contractor, union representative, building inspector, architect, engineer, business associate, or homeowner or client if the applicant is/was self-employed.

The person who verifies the experience must have observed the relevant work done during the time period in question and complete and sign the "Certification of Work Experience" form, which is included with the application. Be prepared to provide documentation of any experience listed on the form whenever CSLB requests it.

9. Are there educational requirements for a license?

No. There are no specific educational or course requirements to get a California contractor license. CSLB is not affiliated with any license preparation schools and cannot make recommendations about them. CSLB does have free study guides for the exams available at www.cslb.ca.gov (search: study guides).

10. May I substitute any education, technical training, or apprenticeship training for the required work experience?

Yes. CSLB may grant credit toward the work experience requirement for a completed apprenticeship program, or technical training or completed education at an accredited school. You will need to provide written documentation, including copies of apprenticeship completion certificates and official transcripts with the application. No credit is given for high school course work. All documents are reviewed on a case-by-case basis.

11. Can I use my armed services experience toward getting a contractor license?

Yes. The Military Veterans Application Assistance Program helps those transitioning from military service to civilian employment meet the minimum requirements for a contractor license. This program offers expedited processing of veterans' applications by specially trained staff, including the evaluation of any transferable military experience and training, as well as education.

You will be asked to provide evidence of the qualifier's current or previous military service with the application:

- Military orders; or

- Certificate of Release or Discharge from Active Duty (DD 214); or

- Copy of Enlisted Record Brief (ERB); or

- Copy of Officer Record Brief (ORB); or

- Verification of Military Experience and Training (DD 2586); or

- Copy of Joint Service Transcripts (military transcripts); and/or

- Sealed, official educational transcripts of civilian education.

You can obtain copies of service records from www.archives.gov/veterans/military-service-records.

12. Does CSLB offer assistance to military spouses/domestic partners who want a California contractor license?

Yes. The Military Spouse/Domestic Partner Application Assistance Program expedites applications from those who meet both of the following requirements:

1) Submits satisfactory evidence that they are married to, in a domestic partnership with, or in another legal union with an active-duty member of the U.S. armed forces who is assigned to a duty station in California under official active-duty orders; and

2) Holds a current and valid contractor license in another state, district, or territory of the U.S. in the classification or trade being applied for.

   CSLB will also waive the application fee and original license fee for individuals who meet the two criteria above.

LICENSE CLASSIFICATIONS

13. What are the contractor license classifications?

CSLB issues licenses in particular construction trades. Each trade is recognized as a "classification." At least four years of verifiable experience is required for each classification being applied for.

CSLB issues licenses for the following classifications:

- **Class "A" - General Engineering Contractor**

The principal business is in connection with fixed works that require specialized engineering knowledge and skill.

- **Class "B" - General Building Contractor**
  The principal business deals with any structure built, being built, or to be built, that requires as part of its construction at least two unrelated building trades or crafts; however, framing or carpentry projects may be performed without limitation. "B" General Building contractors may take a contract for projects that involve one trade only if the contractor holds the appropriate specialty license or subcontracts with an appropriately licensed specialty contractor to perform the work.

- **Class "B-2" - Residential Remodeling Contractor**
  The principal business is in connection with any existing residential wood frame structure with nonstructural projects requiring at least three unrelated building trades or crafts.

- **Class "C" - Specialty Contractor**
  For contractors whose construction work requires special skill and whose principal contracting business involves the use of specialized building trades or crafts. Manufacturers are considered contractors if engaged in onsite construction, alteration, or repair.

Classification	Code
Insulation and Acoustical	C-2
Boiler, Hot-Water Heating and Steam Fitting	C-4
Framing and Rough Carpentry	C-5
Cabinet, Millwork and Finish Carpentry	C-6
Low Voltage Systems	C-7
Concrete	C-8
Drywall	C-9
Electrical	C-10
Elevator	C-11
Earthwork and Paving	C-12
Fencing	C-13
Flooring and Floor Covering	C-15

Classification	Code
Fire Protection	C-16
Glazing	C-17
Warm-Air Heating, Ventilating and Air- Conditioning	C-20
Building Moving/Demolition	C-21
Asbestos Abatement	C-22
Ornamental Metal	C-23
Landscaping	C-27
Lock and Security Equipment	C-28
Masonry	C-29
Construction Zone Traffic Control	C-31
Parking and Highway Improvement	C-32
Painting and Decorating	C-33
Pipeline	C-34
Lathing and Plastering	C-35
Plumbing	C-36
Refrigeration	C-38
Roofing	C-39
Sanitation System	C-42
Sheet Metal	C-43
Sign	C-45
Solar	C-46
General Manufactured Housing	C-47
Reinforcing Steel	C-50
Structural Steel	C-51
Swimming Pool	C-53
Ceramic and Mosaic Tile	C-54
Water Conditioning	C-55
Well Drilling	C-57
Welding	C-60
Limited Specialty*	C-61

*A C-61 Limited Specialty license is only allowed when the work performed does not fit within any other established classification. If

the scope of work falls within either an already recognized primary
("A"-Engineering or "B"-General Building) or specialty classification,
CSLB will assign that classification.

Applicants for a C-61 Limited Specialty license must pass CSLB's
written law and business exam, but no trade exam is required.
Following is a list of limited specialty classifications:

Classification	Code
Concrete-Related Services	D-6
Drilling, Blasting, and Oil Field Work	D-9
Elevated Floors	D-10
Synthetic Products	D-12
Hardware, Locks, and Safes	D-16
Machinery and Pumps	D-21
Metal Products	D-24
Doors, Gates, and Activating Devices	D-28
Paperhanging	D-29
Pile Driving and Pressure Foundation Jacking	D-30
Pole Installation and Maintenance	D-31
Prefabricated Equipment	D-34
Pool and Spa Maintenance	D-35
Sand and Water Blasting	D-38
Scaffolding	D-39
Service Station Equipment and Maintenance	D-40
Siding and Decking	D-41
Non-Electrical Sign Installation	D-42
Tree Service	D-49
Suspended Ceilings	D-50
Waterproofing and Weatherproofing (under relevant class)	D-51
Window Coverings	D-52
Wood Tanks	D-53
Trenching Only	D-56
Hydroseed Spraying	D-59
Air and Water Balancing	D-62
Construction Clean-Up	D-63
Non-Specialized**	D-64
Weatherization and Energy Conservation	D-65

**The D-64 subcategory is only allowed if CSLB determines that the work performed is outside the scope of any already recognized classification.

14. What contractor classifications are currently authorized by CSLB to perform solar energy projects?

Only the license classifications below are currently approved to perform solar projects.

"A" – General Engineering contractors are authorized to perform active solar energy projects that require specialized engineering.

"B"– General Building contractors are authorized to perform active solar energy projects in connection with a structure as defined by Business & Professions Code §7057, since an active solar energy system constitutes the use of two unrelated building trades or crafts.

C-4 – Boiler, Hot-Water Heating and Steam Fitting contractors are authorized to perform projects that include solar heating equipment associated with systems authorized by this classification.

C-10 – Electrical contractors are authorized to perform any solar projects that generate, transmit, transform, or utilize electrical energy in any form for any purpose.

C-36 – Plumbing contractors are authorized to perform any project using solar equipment to heat water or fluids to a suitable temperature.

C-46 – Solar contractors install, modify, maintain, and repair thermal and photovoltaic solar energy systems. A C-46 licensee shall not undertake or perform building or construction trades, crafts, or skills, except when required to install a thermal or photovoltaic solar energy system.

C-53 – Swimming Pool contractors are authorized to install solar heating in swimming pool projects.

C-61/D-35 – Pool and Spa Maintenance contractors are authorized to repair existing solar systems that heat pools.

Check with your local utility company, the California Public Utilities Commission, or the California Energy Commission about authorized contractor classifications and any certification(s) that may be necessary to participate in local, state, or federal energy rebate programs.

15. Are there any special requirements for contractors who work with asbestos or other hazardous substances?

Yes. Contractors who work with asbestos or other hazardous substances are regulated by the United States Department of Labor's Federal Occupational Safety and Health Administration and the California Department of Industrial Relations' Division of Occupational Safety and Health (DOSH), as well as by CSLB. Contractors working in these areas are subject to a number of certification, registration, reporting, and safety requirements.

Asbestos

CSLB issues a C-22 Asbestos Abatement license and a separate Asbestos Certification. C-22 licensees may contract for asbestos abatement with no limitations; those who are certified may only perform abatement work within the license classification they hold.

To receive either a C-22 license or an Asbestos Certification a contractor must:

- Take and pass an EPA-accredited asbestos abatement training course.
- Register with the Asbestos Contractors' Registration Unit of DOSH.
- Submit an application and all required paperwork to CSLB.
- Demonstrate four years of relevant journey-level work experience, and
- Pass the appropriate exam(s).

Other Hazardous Waste

Contractors who perform hazardous substance removal work must be certified by CSLB and:

- Complete an "Application for Hazardous Substance Removal and Remedial Actions;" and
- Pass a CSLB certification exam.

Any contractor with an "A" General Engineering, "B" General Building, C-36 Plumbing, C-12 Earthwork and Paving, C-57 Well Drilling (Water) or, in some cases, the C-61/D-40 Limited Specialty–Service Station Equipment and Maintenance license is eligible for the hazardous waste certification.

Underground Storage Tanks

Contractors who install or remove underground storage tanks <u>must</u> hold the Hazardous Substance Removal and Remedial Actions certification. CSLB policy currently limits certified contractors doing underground storage tank work as follows:

- "A"-General Engineering contractors may install and/or remove underground storage tanks for any purpose at any location.

- "B"-General Building contractors may, in the course of work performed under a contract that meets the requirements for the "B" classification (*see above*), install and/or remove an underground storage tank if they have a Hazardous Substance Removal and Remedial Actions certification.

- C-36 Plumbing contractors may install and/or remove any underground storage tank that provides service to a building, including storage tanks for service stations.

16. Are there any special requirements to obtain a C-47 General Manufactured Housing classification?

Yes, before CSLB issues a C-47 – General Manufactured Housing contractor classification, applicants must complete a federally approved initial installer training. In addition, applicants must provide a certificate of completion from the training with their application. The training must be completed by a qualified trainer approved by the U.S. Department of Housing and Urban Development (HUD). (See 16 CCR section 825.5)

APPLYING FOR A LICENSE

17. How do I apply for a contractor license?

- Complete an "Application for Original Contractor License." You can fill it out on CSLB's website: www.cslb.ca.gov (search: application) and then print it; or download and print a blank application and complete it using blue or black ink; or request a paper copy at any CSLB office or by calling 800-321-CSLB (2752).

- Carefully read the general information and follow the instructions included with the application.

- Identify a qualifier for the license. (Please see below for more information about the responsibilities of a qualifier.)

- Be aware that you must submit certifications to support the work experience listed on the application. CSLB will not accept work experience certifications after the application has been reviewed and accepted.

- Be sure to sign and date the application before sending it in.

- Proofread the application for any missing information. If CSLB needs to return an incomplete application, the license may be delayed, or the application denied or considered abandoned if corrections are not made within 90 days of CSLB notifying you of the problem.

- Applicants requesting special testing accommodations should complete an "Accommodation Request for Examination" available at www.cslb.ca.gov (search: accommodation request) and include it with the application.

- If the qualifier needs to take one or both licensing exams:

   o You may apply for only one classification at a time. After CSLB issues your license, you may apply for any additional classifications.

   o Submit the application, the non-refundable application processing fee of $450, and all required application documents (do not submit any bonds or the initial license fee with your application) to:

      Contractors State License Board
      P.O. Box 26000
      Sacramento, CA 95826

   o After the qualifier passes the exam(s), CSLB will send information about how to submit the $200 initial licensing fee for sole owners (or a $350 initial licensing fee for all other license entities) and other required documents (bonds, proof of workers' compensation insurance, etc.) before we can issue a license. Please submit all of the required documents together to avoid delays. CSLB cannot issue a license until you meet all issuance requirements.

- <u>If the qualifier does not need to take an exam:</u>

  o You may submit an original application for more than one classification at a time if you meet the statutory requirements for a waiver.

  o Submit an application and the application fees. (You have the option to submit the $450 application processing fee and $200 or $350 initial license fee, in addition to $150 for each additional classification at this time) to:

  > Contractors State License Board
  > P.O. Box 26000
  > Sacramento, CA 95826

- The following items are required before CSLB can issue an active license:

  o A contractor bond, or equivalent, in the business name of the applicant. Also, if appropriate, a bond of qualifying individual or exemption statement for each responsible managing officer or responsible managing employee (the bond of qualifying individual must be in the names of the qualifying individuals and the business). Learn more about bonds at www.cslb.ca.gov (search: bonds).

  o Proof of workers' compensation insurance or exemption (if you have no employees, you must submit an exemption certificate). Learn more about workers' compensation at www.cslb.ca.gov (search: workers' compensation).

If the license is qualified by a responsible managing employee, the qualifier is considered an employee and workers' compensation insurance is required. An exemption certificate should <u>not</u> be submitted.

All C-39 Roofing contractors must carry workers' compensation insurance, regardless of whether they have employees. Senate Bill 216 (Chapter 978, Statutes of 2022) extends this requirement to C-8 Concrete, C-20 Warm-Air Heating, Ventilating and Air-Conditioning, C-22 Asbestos Abatement, and D-49 Tree Service contractors.

18. Who is the qualifier?

A "qualifier" is the person listed in CSLB records who meets the experience and exam requirements for the license. A qualifier is required for every classification on each license CSLB issues.

19. What is the qualifier required to do?

The qualifier for a license must take and pass all required exams, as well as undergo a criminal background check. After the license is issued, the qualifier is responsible for exercising supervision and control of the employer's (or principal's) construction operations.

20. Who can be a qualifier?

- Sole ownership license: Either the owner or a Responsible Managing Employee (RME) may serve as a qualifier.

- Partnership license: Either one of the general partners (who shall be designated the qualifying partner) or an RME may serve as the qualifier.

- Corporate license: Either one of the current officers listed in CSLB records for the license (who shall be designated the responsible managing officer, or RMO) or an RME may serve as the qualifier.

- Limited liability company license: A responsible managing member, responsible managing manager, RMO, or RME may serve as the qualifier.

If the qualifier is an RME, they must be a *bona fide* employee of the firm and may not be the qualifier on any other active CSLB license. The RME must be permanently employed by the firm and actively engaged in the operation of the contracting business at least 32 hours per week or 80 percent of the total business operating hours per week, whichever is less.

21. Can the same person serve as the qualifier for more than one active license?

Yes. But only if one of the following conditions exists:

- There is common ownership of at least 20 percent of the equity of each firm for which they act as the qualifier; or

- The additional firm is a subsidiary of, or a joint venture with, the first firm (the parent company must have a CSLB license); or

Section I

- In the case of partnerships, corporations, or LLCs the majority of partners, officers, or members/managers are the same for each firm.

Even if one of the above conditions exists, a person may act as the qualifier for no more than three firms in any one-year period.

22. Will a criminal conviction prevent someone from obtaining a contractor license or serving as a qualifier?

Not necessarily. CSLB may deny a license if the criminal conviction is substantially related to the duties, functions, and qualifications of a contractor. However, even under such circumstances, CSLB may issue a license if the individual has demonstrated sufficient rehabilitation.

23. Will CSLB acknowledge receipt of my application?

Yes. CSLB will send a letter of acknowledgment, which will have two important numbers: 1) a nine-digit application fee number; and 2) a four-digit personal identification number (PIN). The letter will also include instructions about how to use these numbers to check the status of your application.

The application fee number also will appear on other documents related to the application. Please keep a record of this number and use it in all inquiries about the pending application.

24. How long does it take to complete the license application process?

Processing times continually change because of the many factors (i.e., type of application, workload, staff vacancies, etc.) that affect the time it takes to process an application. (Visit www.cslb.ca.gov and search "Processing Times" for dates we are currently working on for each document type.)

If no exam is required and you meet all license requirements, CSLB can issue a license shortly after the application is processed.

If an exam is required, CSLB will send a Notice to Schedule an Examination so the applicant can schedule an exam with the private vendor, PSI Exams, after the application is processed and considered acceptable, which means no corrections or additional information are required.

After you pass the exam, additional time is required to complete application processing and you must meet all license requirements before CSLB can issue a license.

25. Does CSLB expedite license applications?

Yes. CSLB expedites license applications from veterans and military spouses/domestic partners (see question 12 above). CSLB also expedites license applicants for refugees, those who have been granted asylum, and, under certain circumstances, those with a special immigrant visa.

26. How will I know if the initial review of my application is complete?

After CSLB reviews and accepts your application, you will receive a "Notice to Schedule an Examination." If the exam is waived, you will instead receive a request for additional documents and payment of the initial license fee.

A randomly selected percentage of applications undergo additional investigation of work experience claims. If your application is selected for further review and even though you may take and pass the exams, CSLB cannot issue the license until this process is complete, the work experience claims verified, and you meet all additional issuance requirements.

27. How can I check the status of my application?

Each week CSLB updates information on its website (www.cslb.ca.gov) and through its automated phone system (800-321-CSLB) about the application date staff are currently processing, which will give you a good idea of when your application will likely be processed.

Additionally, you can use your PIN and application fee number to check the status of your application.

28. What happens if my application is not accepted?

CSLB will return the application if it is insufficient or incomplete. You must provide any missing information, make any necessary corrections, and return the application to CSLB within 90 days from the date it was returned.

If you do not return the corrected application to CSLB within 90 days, it becomes void. A voided application cannot be reinstated; you will need to submit a new application and the appropriate processing fee if you wish to get a license.

29. If my application is not accepted, can CSLB refund my application fee?

No. The $450 fee is for processing your application, whether or not it is accepted. Since CSLB files each application for processing as soon as it arrives, we cannot refund the fee.

30. Are there any other requirements to get a license?

Yes. You must be fingerprinted and complete an asbestos open book exam before CSLB can issue a license.

Fingerprinting

All license applicants must submit a full set of fingerprints for a criminal background check. Fingerprints will be compared to California Department of Justice and Federal Bureau of Investigation records to determine if a criminal history exists.

After submitting an application, CSLB will send each person listed on the application instructions about how to submit fingerprints. For more information, visit CSLB's website: www.cslb.ca.gov (search: fingerprint).

Asbestos Open Book Exam

Before CSLB can issue a license, every applicant must take an open book exam on asbestos abatement standards. The exam can be taken on CSLB's website: www.cslb.ca.gov (search: asbestos open book). Or, paper copies can be requested by calling 800-321-CSLB (2752).

LICENSING EXAMINATIONS

31. Is there an exam requirement for a contractor license?

Yes. The qualifier for a contractor license must pass both the law and business exam, and a specific trade exam, unless they meet the criteria for a waiver (see "Applying for a License" above). No trade exam is required for the C-61 Limited Specialty license.

Accommodation Request for Examination

In accordance with the Americans with Disabilities Act (ADA), CSLB accommodates applicants who may require an accommodation to take the exam(s). The applicant must notify CSLB about the need for accommodation; CSLB is not required to provide accommodation if it is unaware of specific needs. To request accommodation, submit the "Special Accommodation Request for Examination" available at www.cslb.ca.gov (search: accommodation request) or in any CSLB office.

32. What if the qualifier needs a translator?

If the qualifier has difficulty understanding or reading English, CSLB may allow the use of a translator to read the exam. CSLB must approve in advance the translator you choose. To request use of a translator, please check the appropriate box on the application form and CSLB will send additional information.

33. Under what circumstances will CSLB grant an exam waiver?

The registrar <u>may</u> waive the trade exam if the qualifier meets one of the following conditions:

- The person is currently the qualifier for a license in good standing (current and not under suspension) in the same classification being applied for; or

- The person has been a qualifier within the past five years for a license in good standing in the same classification being applied for; or

- Within the last five years, the person has passed both the law and business exam and the trade exam in the same classification being applied for.

Other waiver provisions defined in Business and Professions Code sections 7065.1, 7065.2, and 7065.3 may also be granted.

34. If I think I am eligible for an exam waiver, do I need to complete the experience section of the application?

Yes. Even if you think you are eligible for an exam waiver, you must complete the work experience section of the application to document a minimum of four years journey-level work out of the previous ten years.

Someone other than the applicant must verify all experience claims, such as an employer, fellow employee, other journeyperson, contractor, union representative, building inspector, architect, engineer, business associate, or homeowner or client if the applicant is/was self-employed. This person must have observed the work.

35. How will I find out if I need to take the exam?

If the qualifier needs to take the exam, CSLB will send a "Notice to Schedule an Examination."

36. How soon after submitting the application will CSLB send the "Notice to Schedule an Examination?"

CSLB sends a "Notice to Schedule an Examination" after the application is processed and found acceptable; many factors can affect how long this takes. You can check the status of your application either through CSLB's website (www.cslb.ca.gov) or its automated phone system (800-321-CSLB) using your PIN and application fee number.

37. Where can I take the exam?

PSI Exams administers CSLB exams at locations around California. Once an application has been approved, the applicant can schedule their own exams at the location and date of their choice. More information can be found by contacting PSI Exams at (877) 392-6422 or psiexams.com.

38. What are the major parts of the examination?

All qualifiers must pass: 1) the law and business exam; and 2) a specific trade or certification exam in the classification applied for. (No trade exam is required for the C-61 Limited Specialty classification.)

39. What does the law and business examination cover?

The law and business exam consists of multiple-choice questions related to business management and California construction law.

40. How can I prepare for the law and business exam?

You can find information about the exam topics in the "Law and Business Examination Study Guide" available by calling CSLB at 800-321-CSLB (2752) or on the CSLB website www.cslb.ca.gov (search: study guides).

41. What does the trade exam cover?

Exams are developed with the assistance of licensed contractors and most include questions that refer to accompanying booklets containing blueprints and/or drawings. Exams are updated every five to seven years.

42. How can I prepare for the trade exam?

The study guides for each exam are available on CSLB's website: www.cslb.ca.gov (search: study guides) or by calling 800-321-CSLB (2752). The study guide lists the topic areas covered by the exam, includes sample questions, shows how each content area is weighted, and recommends resource materials to study.

43. What should the qualifier bring to the examination site?

Refer to PSI Exams' Candidate Information Bulletin for what you need to bring to the examination site.

44. What are the exams like?

All exams are taken on a computer and consist of multiple-choice questions. Visit ww.cslb.ca.gov and search "What to Expect on Test Day" for an informational video.

45. What is involved with computer-based testing?

Exams are taken using an easy-to-use computer-based system that guides the applicant through an on-screen tutorial.

46. How long does the examination take?

You will be given 3½ hours to complete each exam.

47. What kind of feedback will I receive?

Test results will be shared before the qualifier leaves the test center. Successful candidates are told that they have passed but are not given detailed information about their score.

Unsuccessful candidates will see on the computer once they finish the exam how well they performed on each section of the exam. These sections are described in greater detail in the study guide for that particular exam, so candidates can review these areas when preparing to retake the exam.

48. If I fail to appear for an exam may I reschedule?

Yes. If you fail to appear for an exam, you must pay a non-refundable $100 rescheduling fee. You may reschedule the exam as many times as needed within 18 months, as long as you pay the rescheduling fee each time. After 18 months, the application is considered void and you will have to submit a new application with new fees.

You may cancel and reschedule an examination appointment without forfeiting your fee if your cancellation notice is received two days prior to the scheduled examination date. You need to call PSI at (877) 392-6422.

49. If I fail one or both exam(s) may I retake them?

Yes. If you fail the law and business exam and/or the trade exam, you must pay a non-refundable $100 fee each time you reschedule. You have 18 months after CSLB accepts your application to pass the exams. After 18 months, the application is considered void and you will have to submit a new application with new fees. Any void date extensions are at the discretion of CSLB.

Exam results are good for five years. If you pass one exam and fail the other, you only have to retake and pass the one you failed within five years.

50. May I review the test questions after the exams?

No. However, you may type a comment about a question during the exam at any time before it is scored. You also may contact CSLB for a "Request for Examination Appeal" form after the exam. Once CSLB staff review your appeal request, you will receive a letter informing you of the outcome.

51. Are there penalties for disclosing the contents of a state examination?

Yes. Conduct that violates exam security includes:

- Providing information about test questions to any school, person, or business.

- Removing exam materials from the test site (including taking notes or recording anything electronically).

- Communicating with other test takers during an exam.

- Copying or permitting your answers to be copied.

- Possessing any written material other than test materials provided by CSLB.

- Taking the exam on behalf of another applicant.

Penalties for violating exam security include:

- Automatic exam failure.

- Forfeiture of any fees already paid.

- Prosecution on misdemeanor charges that can result in a $500 fine; payment of damages of up to $10,000, plus the costs of litigation; and a county jail sentence.

- Inability to apply for any CSLB license for one year from the exam date.

ISSUING A LICENSE

52. After the qualifier passes the exam(s), are there additional requirements before CSLB will issue a license?

Yes. After passing the exams, the qualifier will receive a letter from CSLB outlining the additional requirements before CSLB can issue a license. These include:

- A $200 initial licensing fee for sole owners or a $350 initial licensing fee for all other license entities.

- Completion of the asbestos open book exam and submission to CSLB of the results (active and inactive licenses).

- Every first-time applicant listed (each owner, officer, partner, member, manager, or responsible managing employee) must submit fingerprints for the mandatory criminal background check (active and inactive licenses).

- A $25,000 contractor's bond or cashier's check (active licenses only).

- Proof of current and valid workers' compensation insurance if any of the following apply (active licenses only):

  o   You hire any employee(s) who reside in California; or

  o   You employ home improvement salesperson(s); or

  o   Your qualifier is a responsible managing employee (RME); or

  o   You hold a C-8 Concrete, C-20 Warm-Air Heating, Ventilating and Air-Conditioning, C-22 Asbestos Abatement, C-39 Roofing, or D-49 Tree Service classification.

- Submission of an "Exemption from Workers' Compensation" if you do not have employees, the qualifier is not a responsible managing employee, and you do not hold a C-8, C-20, C-22, C-39, or D-49 classification (active licenses only).

- A $25,000 bond of qualifying individual or cashier's check for every responsible managing employee and all responsible managing officers who own less than 10 percent of the voting stock or equity of the corporation or

LLC they serve as the qualifier for (corporate and LLC licenses only).

- A $100,000 LLC/worker bond in addition to the $25,000 contractor bond (LLC licenses only).

- Liability insurance, with an aggregate limit of $1 million, for licenses with five or fewer persons listed as personnel; plus an additional $100,000 for each additional personnel listed on the license; not to exceed $5 million total (LLC licenses only).

53. What is the difference between an active and an inactive license?

Active License:

The holder of an active license can contract for work in the classification(s) that appear on the license.

The licensee must have a current contractor bond, a bond of qualifying individual (if required), and workers' compensation insurance, if required by law. An active LLC license has additional requirements – a $100,000 LLC/worker bond and liability insurance.

Inactive License (Renewed, but Inactive):

The holder may not bid or contract for work.

Neither the contractor bond nor bond of qualifying individual is required. Also, the licensee does not need to have either workers' compensation or proof of exemption from workers' compensation insurance coverage on file with CSLB.

54. What will I receive to show that I'm licensed?

CSLB will send a wall certificate that shows the name of the person or company on the license; the license number, classification, date of issue, and expiration date; and a plastic pocket license card showing the same information.

State law requires that you display the wall certificate in your main office or chief place of business and provide proof that you have a contractor license when asked. You should carry your pocket license card with you, especially in situations where you may solicit business or talk to potential customers. CSLB encourages consumers to ask to see a contractor's pocket license card.

It takes approximately 5 to 10 business days from the time CSLB issues the license to receive your wall certificate and pocket license card.

55. How long is a license valid?

A contractor license is initially issued, whether active or inactive, for a two-year period. It will expire two years from the last day of the month in which it was issued. For example, if the license was issued on January 15, 2022, it will expire on January 31, 2024.

After the initial two-year license period, active licenses are renewed for two years; inactive licenses for four years.

FINANCIAL REQUIREMENTS

56. Are there any bond requirements for a contractor license?

Yes. You must file a $25,000 contractor license surety bond or cashier's check with CSLB.

If applicable, you must also submit a separate $25,000 bond of qualifying individual or cash deposit for the responsible managing employee or responsible managing officer. However, a bond of qualifying individual is not required if the RMO certifies that they own 10 percent or more of the voting stock or equity of the corporation for which they serve as the qualifier.

If you have a limited liability company (LLC) license, whether the license is issued as active or inactive, you must file a $100,000 surety bond (in addition to the $25,000 contractor bond) for the benefit of any employee or worker damaged by the LLC's failure to pay wages, interest on wages, or fringe benefits, as well as other contributions.

57. Where do I obtain bonds?

You may purchase bonds from your insurance agent or from one of the private holding companies licensed by the California Department of Insurance. CSLB does not issue bonds. Copies of the approved bond form and information about the option of a cashier's check is available at www.cslb.ca.gov (search: bonds) or by calling 800-321-CSLB (2752).

58. What is the total fee amount for a contractor license?

Fees are subject to change. As of this printing, the total fee amount for a contractor license for one classification is $650 for sole owners and $800 for all other license entities. This includes both the nonrefundable application processing fee of $450 and the two-year initial license fee of $200 for sole owners and $350 for all other license entities.

Current fees are printed on the application forms and notices that CSLB sends. You may also check www.cslb.ca.gov (search: fees) or call CSLB (800-321-2752) to verify the current fees.

Chapter 2.

Your Existing License:
Maintaining and Changing It

BONDS

Contractors are required to maintain a surety bond for the benefit of consumers who may be harmed as a result of defective construction or other license law violations, and for the benefit of employees who have not been paid wages due to them.

Contractor Bond

The contractor bond is executed by a surety in favor of the State of California for the benefit of specific categories of people damaged if a contractor violates contractors' state license law. The list of beneficiaries can be found in Business and Professions (B&P) Code section ($)7071.5.

Before an active contractor license can be issued or renewed, or an inactive license made active, the licensee must have a current contractor bond, or cashier's check (see below), on file with CSLB. The contractor bond required is $25,000 for all classifications. If a license is inactive, no contractor bond is required.

Bond of Qualifying Individual

A qualifying individual must have a $25,000 bond or cashier's check on file for:

1. Each responsible managing employee (RME).

2. Each responsible managing officer (RMO), unless the RMO owns 10 percent or more of the voting stock of the corporation.

3. Each responsible managing member or officer unless they own 10 percent or more of the membership interest in the limited liability company (LLC).

If the license is inactive the bond of qualifying individual is not needed.

Limited Liability Surety Bond

A $100,000 surety bond (in addition to the $25,000 contractor bond) is required for the issuance, reissuance, reinstatement, reactivation, or renewal of a limited liability company license for the benefit of any employee or worker damaged by the LLC's failure to pay wages,

27

interest on wages, or fringe benefits, as well as other contributions (not required for inactive LLC licenses). *(See B&P Code §7071.8.)*

General Requirements for Bonds

The following requirements must be met before CSLB can accept your bond:

- The business name and license number on the bond must correspond exactly to the information in CSLB's records.

- The license number on the bond of qualifying individual must match that of the firm for which the individual is to serve as the qualifier.

- Contractor bonds must be in the correct amount of $25,000.

- A bond of qualifying individual must be in the correct amount of $25,000.

- Bonds must be written by a surety company licensed through the California Department of Insurance and have the signature of the attorney in fact.

- Bonds must be written on a form approved by the California Attorney General's Office.

- Bonds must be filed with CSLB within 90 days of their effective date.

NOTE: Bonds are not transferable – they cannot be transferred from one license to another or from one license qualifier to another.

Approved Alternative to Contractor Bonds – Cashier's Check

Instead of filing a surety bond with CSLB, a contractor may prefer to use a cashier's check.

- Cashier's checks are not transferable – they cannot be transferred from one license to another or from one licensed qualifier to another.

- Cashier's checks are retained by CSLB for three years after the end of the license period that they cover.

- If CSLB is notified of a complaint relative to a claim against the cashier's check, the cashier's check shall not be released until the complaint has been adjudicated.

General Requirements for Cashier's Checks

The following requirements must be met before CSLB can accept your cashier's check in lieu of a bond:

- The cashier's check must state: Payable to the Contractors State License Board.

- Cashier's check in lieu of a contractor bond must list the business name and license number and exactly match the information in CSLB's records.

- Cashier's check in lieu of a contractor bond must be in the correct amount of $25,000.

- Cashier's check in lieu of a bond of qualifying individual, must list the business name, license number, and name of the qualifying individual and exactly match the information in CSLB's records.

- Cashier's check in lieu of a bond of qualifying individual must be in the correct amount of $25,000.

It is the contractor's responsibility to make sure the bond or cashier's check is timely and meets CSLB requirements. Failure to have a required bond or cashier's check on file may result in license suspension and a gap in licensure.

The registrar may reinstate your license following a suspension for failing to have a required bond or cashier's check. However, the suspension may result in a gap in licensure.

Maintaining Bonds

The following guidelines will help you avoid problems with the bonds filed for your license:

- Keep your required bonds, or bond exemptions current at all times.

- Renew your bonds promptly. To avoid a period of suspension, make sure that the effective date of the new bond is the same as the cancellation date of the old bond. To allow for processing time, arrange for a new bond four weeks before your old one expires.

- Only one bond is in effect at a time. A second bond filed for the same period cancels out the first bond.

- CSLB does not return any bond that has been accepted or processed for an active license.

- Keep accurate records on your agent, surety company, bond numbers, effective dates, and terms of the bond(s).

Suspensions

CSLB will suspend your license if any of the following occur:

- Your surety company cancels one or more of your required bonds.

- The voting stock of the responsible managing officer (RMO) for a corporate license or the membership interest in a limited liability license is no longer at least 10 percent of the total voting stock of the corporation *(see B&P Code §7071.9).*

  Suspension is effective from the date ownership or membership interest terminated unless a bond of qualifying individual is filed and backdated to the date their percentage of the stock or membership interest fell below 10 percent.

- A judgment or payment of claim reduces the amount of any required bond *(see B&P Code §7071.11.).*

- You fail to maintain a disciplinary bond in full force and effect for the required length of time or a cashier's check.

A suspended license can be reinstated if the surety company sends a "Rescission of Cancelation Notice" to CSLB, or if you obtain a new bond and submit it to CSLB within 90 days of the date that the new bond becomes effective, or within 90 days of the date the old bond is canceled.

JUDGMENTS AND OUTSTANDING LIABILITIES

Civil Court Judgments

A contractor is required to report a construction-related civil court judgment to CSLB within 90 days of the judgment date. Once received, CSLB enters the information on the contractor license record and sends a notice to the contractor. The notice gives the contractor 90 days from the notice date to resolve the judgment. After 90 days, if the unsatisfied final judgment is not resolved, the contractor license is automatically suspended and remains suspended until the judgment is resolved.

If the contractor fails to report the judgment within 90 days, CSLB will automatically suspend their contractor license when it is reported. The license will remain suspended until the judgment is resolved.

NOTE: Anyone can report a construction-related judgment against a contractor by sending a copy of the judgment to the CSLB Judgment Unit at the Sacramento headquarters office. Most of the judgments received by CSLB are sent by the person to whom the contractor owes money.

Once an unsatisfied final judgment is entered on a contractor's license record, it can affect any other license that a person is on or any license they apply for. For example, if a contractor has a sole owner license and a corporate license, an unresolved judgment against the corporation will result in the suspension of both the corporate and sole owner license.

In addition, any other licenses for the qualifier or personnel of record on the license subject to suspension will also be suspended, if these individuals were associated with the license at the time of the activities on which the judgment is based.

A private arbitration decision is considered the same as a judgment (*B&P Code §7071.17*).

Frequently Asked Questions About Judgments:

I was never served or notified of this suit or judgment—what can I do? The judgment wasn't fair, the judge wouldn't listen to me—what can I do?

Whether the suit or judgment was properly served or was fair is for the court to decide. CSLB cannot override a decision made by the court in a civil judgment. If you believe you were not properly served or treated fairly, you may wish to consult an attorney. With a small claims judgment, you can speak with staff from the small claims court in which the judgment was filed.

Can I appeal the court decision?

There are many factors that determine when and why an appeal can be filed, so you should consult an attorney. In the case of a small claims judgment, you can speak with staff from the small claims court where the judgment was filed.

I filed an appeal. Why are you suspending my license?

Before appeal information can be entered on your license records, you must submit a copy of the court-endorsed appeal with proof of a Stay of Enforcement document.

What type of proof do you need to show that I paid the judgment?

Any of the following can be used as proof of payment:

- An acknowledgment of Satisfaction of Judgment.

- A notarized, signed statement from the judgment creditor which confirms the judgment has been paid in full.

- A copy of the front and back of a canceled payment check.

CSLB will contact the judgment creditor to verify payment, so include that person's telephone number. If you cannot contact the person who holds the judgment, consult an attorney. In the case of a small claims judgment, you can speak with staff from the small claims court where the judgment was filed.

I can't pay the full amount of the judgment. Can I make payments?

You can make payments only if you work out an agreement with the judgment creditor. The judgment creditor is not required to accept payments. If you reach an agreement, it should state the amount owed, the monthly payment amount, the date the payment is due each month, and when a payment will be considered late. All parties must sign the agreement. Once you have a written agreement, submit a copy to CSLB's Judgment Unit. When CSLB receives a copy, it will lift the suspension. However, if CSLB is notified by the judgment creditor that you failed to make payments CSLB will immediately suspend your license.

I filed for bankruptcy. What happens now?

You must provide CSLB with proof of the bankruptcy filing and confirm that you named the judgment creditor in the bankruptcy. To comply with this requirement, submit a copy of the bankruptcy filing to CSLB, which must include the page from the creditors list on which the judgment creditor appears.

This judgment isn't construction-related. What can I do?

The applicable section of law (*B&P Code §7071.17*) states that the judgment must be "substantially related ... to the qualifications, functions, or duties of the license." CSLB broadly interprets this section of law to mean that if the judgment relates to your construction business in any way, it is considered construction-related. It does not mean that you had to necessarily contract with the judgment creditor to build something. If you did not pay your office rent, your office utility bills, your material supplier, subcontractor, employee, or any other bill incurred by your business, CSLB will consider it construction-related.

Very few judgments received by CSLB are not construction-related. If you feel confident that your judgment is not construction-related, you should provide CSLB with documentation that will support your statement.

NOTE: Do not wait until the last few days before the suspension occurs to try to resolve the judgment. It is often difficult to gather all necessary paperwork at the last minute. Preventing your license from being suspended is a top priority with CSLB; however, sometimes problems arise that cannot be immediately resolved. To avoid delay, promptly submit all necessary documents to the CSLB Judgment Unit. Once acceptable documentation has been received and the matter has been cleared, CSLB will send you a confirmation notice.

Outstanding Liabilities

The state Board of Equalization, Employment Development Department, Department of Industrial Relations, or Franchise Tax Board can notify CSLB of outstanding final liabilities owed by a contractor to those departments. When CSLB receives such a notification, a letter is sent to the contractor notifying them that they have 60 days to resolve the outstanding liability or the license will be suspended. If CSLB does not receive any information about a resolution at the end of the 60-day period it will suspend the license until the outstanding liability is resolved. The same procedure will be followed if a check submitted to CSLB by a licensee is dishonored (*B&P Code §7145.5*).

WORKERS' COMPENSATION INSURANCE COVERAGE

General Requirements

All contractors are required to submit proof of workers' compensation insurance coverage as a condition of licensure, to maintain a license, activate an inactive license, or renew a license, unless they are exempt from this requirement (*see B&P Code §7125*).

Exemptions

Contractors who do not have employees working for them (except C-8 Concrete, C-20 Warm-Air Heating, Ventilating and Air-Conditioning, C-22 Asbestos Abatement, C-39 Roofing, and D-49 Tree Service licensees) are exempt from the requirement for workers' compensation insurance, but they must file a certification of this exemption with the registrar. Neither insurance coverage nor the exemption is required for an inactive license.

NOTE: All C-39 Roofing contractors must have a Certificate of Workers' Compensation Insurance or a Certificate of Self-Insurance on file with CSLB (*B&P Code §7125*). Senate Bill 216 (Chapter 978, Statutes of 2022) extends this requirement to C-8 Concrete, C-20 Warm-Air Heating, Ventilating and Air-Conditioning, C-22 Asbestos Abatement, and D-49 Tree Service contractors.

LIABILITY INSURANCE COVERAGE FOR LIMITED LIABILITY COMPANIES

Liability insurance is required for limited liability companies (LLCs) with the aggregate limit of $1 million required for licensees with five or fewer persons listed as members of the personnel of record; an additional $100,000 is required for each additional member of the personnel of record, not to exceed $5 million total (see B&P Code §7071.19).

ADDING A CLASSIFICATION TO AN EXISTING LICENSE

Under what conditions may I add a classification to my license?

You may add a classification to your existing license only if it is renewed and in good standing.

How many classifications may I apply for at a time?

In most cases, you must file a separate "Application for Additional Classification" for each classification you are requesting. However, all of the C-61 (Limited Specialty) classifications you request may be applied for on the same application.

What are the requirements to add a classification to my license?

To add a classification to your license, you must:

- Select a qualifier (who may be the licensee) for the new classification you are applying for.

- Have the qualifier describe, in detail, four years of experience within the last ten years as a journeyperson, foreperson, supervisor, or contractor in the classification for which they are to serve as the qualifier.

- Provide verification for the claimed experience.

- Submit the required application processing fee with the application.

- Take and pass the trade exam for the new classification, unless the qualifier meets the criteria for and is granted a waiver (see below). Each qualifier also must pass the CSLB law and business examination if they have not done so previously.

- File any required bonds.

- Inactivate their individual license, if the qualifier is an RME.

Under what conditions can I qualify for a waiver of an examination?

- *See Questions 32 and 33 in Chapter 1.*

CHANGES IN PERSONNEL

What should I do if any of the official personnel listed on the records for my license leave the firm?

Sole Owner

A sole owner license is not transferable. If a contracting business is purchased from the holder of a sole owner license, the contractor license is not part of the purchase. The new owner must apply for and obtain their own license before they can contract legally.

Partner

If a general or qualifying partner leaves the business, the existing license is canceled. The remaining partners may request a one-year continuance of the license to complete projects in progress. The request for a continuance must be submitted to CSLB within 90 days of the date the partner left. Except for those cases where the partner died, the remaining partners cannot contract for any new projects under that license.

The remaining partners must apply for a new license if they choose to remain in business beyond the one-year limit of the continuance.

NOTE: Do not wait until the one-year continuance is about to expire before applying for a new license. Timely processing of your new license is important. To avoid a lapse in licensure, submit the necessary applications as soon as possible.

A limited partner may be added or deleted from a license by submitting an "Application to Add New Limited Partner to an Existing Partnership License" form.

Corporate Officers

If any of the officers listed in CSLB records for a corporate license leave your business, you must report the change to CSLB within 90 days by submitting a "Disassociation Request." To add personnel, you must complete and submit an "Application to Add New Personnel to an Existing Corporation or Limited Liability Company License." The status of your license is not affected by adding officers or having any of them leave unless the person who leaves has been serving as a qualifier. (See *Qualifier* below.)

Limited Liability Company (LLC) Personnel

If any of the members, managers, or officers listed in CSLB records for an LLC license leave your business, you must report this change to CSLB within 90 days by submitting a "Disassociation Request." To add personnel, you must complete and submit an "Application to Add New Personnel to an Existing Corporation or Limited Liability Company License." If you are adding personnel, the amount of your LLC liability insurance must be sufficient for the total number of personnel of record as required by law.

The status of your license is not affected by adding members, managers, or officers, or having any of them leave unless the person who leaves has been serving as a qualifier. (See *Qualifier below.*)

Qualifier (Responsible Managing Officer, Employee, Member, or Manager)

If an RMO, RME, responsible managing member, or responsible managing manager leaves a business (disassociates), you must notify CSLB in writing within 90 days of the date of disassociation. Use a "Disassociation Notice" form. You must specify:

- Name of the qualifier who left.
- Date of disassociation.
- Name of the business.
- Contractor license number.

One of the remaining official personnel listed in CSLB records for that license, or the qualifier who is disassociating, must sign the notification of disassociation or your letter.

If you intend to continue to conduct business in the classification for which the qualifier was responsible, **you must replace them within 90 days of the date of disassociation.** Failure to do so will result in suspension of your license or removal of the classification from your license.

To replace a qualifying individual, you must file an "Application for Replacing the Qualifying Individual" **or** an "Application for Limited Liability Company (LLC) Replacing the Qualifying Individual" and submit the required application fee. This application also can serve as the notice of disassociation. You should act quickly because, within those 90 days, CSLB must process your application and, if necessary, the new qualifier must pass the CSLB law and business exam and/or trade exam(s).

The requirements for a qualifier and the criteria for a waiver of the exams are described in Chapter 1.

Right to Petition

You may petition the registrar for reconsideration if you dispute the date of disassociation on which the suspension was based. You may also petition if you can show good cause for your failure to notify the registrar within 90 days of the date of disassociation. CSLB must receive your petition within 90 days from the date of the board's notice that you must replace the qualifier or CSLB will suspend the license *(see B&P Code §7068.2 and §7076)*.

Changes in the Bond Exemption Status of a Responsible Managing Officer of a Corporation, or Officer, Member or Manager of an LLC

If the RMO's share of the voting stock of the corporation, or the RMO's, responsible managing member's, or responsible managing manager's membership interest of a limited liability company falls below 10 percent they will no longer be eligible for exemption from the bond requirements. You must report the change in exemption status and file a "Bond of Qualifying Individual" form within 90 days of the change.

Exemption that Allows an Individual to Serve as the Qualifier for More Than One License

A person is allowed to serve as the qualifier for more than one license, **but for no more than three firms in any one-year period** if any of the following conditions exist:

- There is common ownership of at least 20 percent of the equity of each firm involved.

- The other licenses are subsidiaries of, or participants in a joint venture with the first.

- The majority of partners, officers, or managers are the same.

If this common ownership no longer exists, the qualifier must disassociate from each license for which the exemption status no longer applies *(see B&P Code §7068.1)*.

CHANGES IN BUSINESS NAME OR ADDRESS

Report changes in business name or address as soon as possible, but no later than 90 days after the change.

Business Name

Report a change in business name by completing an "Application to Change Business Name and/or Address" and submitting the $100 fee. Note the following conditions:

- The form must be signed by an owner, partner, officer, member, or manager of the firm.

- If you hold a corporate license or limited liability company (LLC) license, you must first register the name change with the California Secretary of State. Include a certified copy of the "Amendment of Articles of Incorporation" (for a corporation) or "Statement of Information" (for an LLC), as appropriate, when you submit the information to CSLB.

- The new business name must not conflict with the type of business entity or the classification held.

  For example, if John Smith applies for a C-36 Plumbing license:

Acceptable	Unacceptable
John Smith Plumbing	John Smith Plumbing Inc.
River City Plumbing	River City Plumbing Partners
JS Plumbing	JS Floors & Tile

Business Address

Report a change of the official address of your business by completing the "Application to Change Business Name and/or Address." The form must be signed by the owner, a partner, officer, member, or manager of the firm.

Please remember to immediately submit a change of address form to CSLB when your business address changes. Many licensees do not receive their renewal notice in the mail because they did not provide CSLB their new address, and as a result, fail to renew on time.

CHANGES IN BUSINESS TYPE

New License Necessary if Business Type Changes

CSLB issues licenses to five types of business entities: sole ownership, partnership, corporation, joint venture, and limited liability company. Licenses are associated with the business and not necessarily the qualifier. Therefore, licenses are not transferable from one business entity to another, even if the qualifier is the same for both. A new license is required whenever the business entity type is changed. For example, if a contractor with a sole ownership business decides to incorporate, or a partnership is split into multiple sole ownership businesses, a new license is required in each case.

Whenever a business entity type changes and a new license is not issued, that business faces all the legal risks of an unlicensed contractor.

How do I get a license for my new business?

To obtain a license for your new business, you must submit an "Application for Original License" (available at www.cslb.ca.gov). Use the "Application for Original License-Examination Waiver (7065)" if you took the exam for the previous license and are applying for the classification previously held.

No exam will be required if the qualifier passed the exam for that same classification in the preceding five years or served as the qualifier on a license in the same classification that was in good standing at any time during the preceding five years.

You also must pay all required fees, post new bonds, provide proof of workers' compensation insurance, or file a workers' compensation exemption statement, and provide proof of liability insurance coverage, if applicable, for the new business.

Can I keep my old license number?

Only in some cases will the same license number be reissued. In some instances, CSLB will reissue the original license number if a sole ownership business is being incorporated or changed to a limited liability company, and the qualifier on the sole ownership business owns 51 percent or more of the voting stock or equity of the new corporation, or of the membership interests of the LLC. In this situation, you must submit a "Request for License Number Reissuance" form with your application asking that your sole ownership license be reissued to the corporation or LLC. In other instances, CSLB must issue a new license number.

Can the license number be changed back to a sole ownership license after it has been used as a corporate or LLC license?

No. Once your license number is reissued to a corporation or LLC, it cannot be changed back to a sole ownership license. CSLB will issue a new license number if you apply for a sole ownership license.

Information about new license requirements can be found at www.cslb.ca.gov. You also can call (800) 321-CSLB (2752).

INACTIVATING AND REACTIVATING A LICENSE

What is an inactive license?

An inactive license is "on hold." While your license is inactive, you cannot practice as a contractor or submit a bid for work. You do not need to maintain a bond or workers' compensation or liability insurance coverage, nor do you need to have a qualifier on your license. As long as you continue to renew your inactive license you will receive informational bulletins and a license renewal application every four years at the address listed in CSLB records.

It is not necessary to inactivate your license because of bond suspension or temporary work stoppages. However, you may be required to inactivate your license if you apply to serve as the qualifier for another license and you do not meet one of the conditions of B&P Code section 7068.1 *(see "Exemption that Allows an Individual to Serve as the Qualifier for More Than One License" above)*.

How do I inactivate my license?

To inactivate your license:

- Request the "Application to Inactivate State Contractor's License" form by telephone, in writing from any CSLB office, or online at www.cslb.ca.gov. There is no fee. (There is a fee to reactivate a license.) If the period of inactivity will be short, read the section describing how to reactivate a license before you decide to inactivate your license.

- Have the owner; a partner; an officer of your corporation; a member, manager, or officer of your limited liability company; or a member of the joint venture license who is listed in CSLB records for your license sign the application.

- Return your current pocket license with the application. If you have lost your pocket license, check the box on the application and enclose the replacement fee indicated. You will be sent a pocket license stamped "Inactive."

Is an inactive license subject to renewal requirements?

Yes. Every four years, a renewal application will be sent to the business address listed in CSLB records. You must notify CSLB in writing of any change of address. There is no limit on the number of times your contractor license can be renewed on inactive status.

What should I do if I want to resume contracting?

If you want to resume contracting and your license is inactive, you must reactivate your license before you begin contracting *(see B&P Code §7076.5 and CCR §867)*.

How do I reactivate my license?

To reactivate an inactive license, request an "Application to Reactivate" by telephone, via CSLB's website, or in writing from

CSLB's Sacramento headquarters office, complete the application, and meet the following conditions:

- Meet all bond requirements, including any disciplinary bond, contractor bond, LLC surety bond, or bond of qualifying individual. Attach all required bonds to the application. Do not send bonds separately.

- Submit proof of workers' compensation insurance or exemption.

- For limited liability company licenses only, submit proof of liability insurance in the amount required for the number of personnel on the license.

- The application must be signed by **all** qualifying partners, responsible managing employees, responsible managing members, responsible managing managers, and responsible managing officers.

    If applying to reactivate a:

    Sole ownership license, the **owner** must sign.

    Partnership license, all **partners** must sign.

    Corporate license, **one corporate officer** must sign.

    Limited liability company, **one member, manager, or officer** must sign.

    Joint venture license, the **qualifier of each entity** must sign.

- Comply with any special requirements for the qualifier, such as the need to disassociate from any other license for which they currently serve as the qualifier or the need to inactivate their individual license, unless they can provide verification of common ownership of at least 20 percent of the equity of every business for which they serve as the qualifier.

- Submit the required fee.

What other conditions must I consider when reactivating a license?

If there has been a change in the form of your business (for example, you have formed a partnership, corporation, or limited liability company), or if a partner has joined or left your business, you will need a new license.

If you hold a corporate license and wish to make any additions to the list of officers, you must complete and submit an "Application to Report New Officers of a Corporation." To delete officers, complete and submit a "Disassociation Request." To change the qualifier, request the "Application to Replace the Qualifying Individual." For changes to the personnel of LLCs, you must complete and submit the comparable LLC forms.

Before a license can be activated, contractors must submit proof of workers' compensation insurance coverage, and liability insurance coverage, if applicable, or file an exemption.

What is the effective date of reactivation?

Your license will be reactivated on the date that the required fee, an acceptable application, and other required documents are received and processed by CSLB. After CSLB processes your reactivation application, your license will be active for two years from the end of the month in which it was reactivated *(see B&P Code §7076.5 and CCR §867)*.

How do I order a new wall or pocket license?

Official personnel for the license may order a new or an additional wall or pocket license by completing and sending CSLB the "Order Wall Certificate or Pocket License" form available at www.cslb.ca.gov. Specify the license number and whether you are requesting the wall or pocket license. The form must be signed by current personnel listed on the license (owner, partners, officers, managers, members, or RMEs). A fee is required for each copy.

RENEWING YOUR LICENSE

Active licenses expire every two years. Inactive licenses expire every four years. Check your current pocket license for the expiration date.

How do I renew my license?

About 60 days before your license is due to expire, CSLB will send you a renewal application. It is important to notify CSLB of any change of address. **It is your responsibility to make sure your license is renewed even if you don't receive the renewal form. You may not contract for work with an expired license.**

Online Renewal Option (All Single Qualifier Licensees)

All single qualifier licensees may renew online at www.cslb.ca.gov and pay using a credit card. There is a 2.99% processing fee for this service. Once the process is complete, your license record is immediately updated.

Paper Renewal Option (All Other Licensees)

When you receive the renewal application, complete it, and promptly return it to CSLB. Keep the following things in mind as you complete your application:

- Because processing times vary, CSLB encourages you to submit your renewal as early as possible.

- The application and requirements must be submitted and approved as "accepted."

- You must submit the required fee.

- The renewal application must be completed and signed.

- Your renewed license may be either active or inactive. If you renew the license as inactive, you do not need to maintain any bonds or designate a qualifier. If you wish to change the license from inactive to active at the time of renewal, see the section above, *"How do I reactivate my license?"*

What happens if I don't renew my license by the expiration date?

You cannot legally contract for work with an expired license.

CSLB must receive an acceptable license renewal form prior to the expiration date of the license. If you renew your license after the expiration date or if you send a form not considered acceptable, your renewal will be considered delinquent, and the license record will show a break in license status. **During any such period, the contractor will be considered unlicensed.** In addition, if the license is expired, you will need to pay an additional delinquent fee of 50 percent of the renewal fee.

If you submit a completed application for renewal within 90 days of your expiration, you will have no break in licensure.

You may renew an expired license within five years after its expiration. After five years, it becomes void, and if you wish to contract, you must apply for a new license and meet the exam or waiver requirements again.

May I renew my license if it is suspended?

If you wish to contract for work, you must clear the suspension before your license can be renewed as active. However, you may not contract for work with an inactive or suspended license and you will not be issued a wall or pocket license. A suspended license may be renewed as either active or inactive *(see B&P Code §§7140-7145 and CCR §853).*

CANCELATION OF A LICENSE

Under what circumstances is a license canceled?

A license is canceled if any of the following occur:

- Individual license: death of the owner.

- Partnership license: death or disassociation of a general or qualifying partner.

- Corporate or limited liability company license: notification by the licensee of merger, dissolution, or surrender of the right to do business in California.

- Joint venture license: cancelation, revocation, or withdrawal of any of the businesses that formed the joint venture.

A corporation or limited liability company license also will be canceled 60 days after CSLB discovers that the corporation or LLC has merged, dissolved, or surrendered the right to do business.

A licensee may also voluntarily request to cancel a license at any time. **Remember: It is illegal to contract with a canceled license.**

How do I cancel my license?

You must notify CSLB in writing within 90 days of the event that prompted the cancelation request. There is no fee for cancelation. Return your wall certificate and your current pocket license with the written request for cancelation.

Depending on the type of license you hold, your request for cancelation must meet the following requirements:

- The owner of a **sole owner** license must sign the request for voluntary cancelation. In the case of the owner's death, a family member or administrator of the estate must sign the request, state the date of death, and provide a copy of the death certificate.

- If a **partnership** license must be canceled due to the disassociation of a partner, a general partner must sign the request and state the date of disassociation; in the case of a partner's death, a remaining partner must sign the request, state the date of death, and provide a copy of the death certificate.

- To cancel a **corporate** license, two officers listed on the license, or the remaining officer if only one officer remains, must sign the request and state the date of the event causing cancelation, or enclose a copy of the corporate minutes documenting the dissolution or merger, or enclose a copy of the dissolution papers issued by the California Secretary of State.

- To cancel a **limited liability company** license, two members, managers, or officers listed on the license, or the remaining officer if only one remains, must sign the request and state the date of the event causing cancelation, or enclose a copy of the dissolution papers issued by the California Secretary of State.

- To cancel a **joint venture** license, one of the official personnel (other than an RME) listed in CSLB's records for the license of any of the businesses forming the joint venture must sign the request and state the date of the event causing the cancelation.

What is the effective date of a license cancelation?

The effective date of cancelation of a license is usually either the date CSLB receives the request or the date of the event causing the cancelation.

NOTE: A cancelation is not effective until it has been accepted by CSLB. The board may decide not to cancel a license if disciplinary action is pending.

If an event occurs that makes a license subject to cancelation, can a business continue to operate temporarily?

Yes. Under certain circumstances, the registrar may grant a continuance for up to one year. There are restrictions on who may apply for the continuance and on one's right to enter into new contracts. If granted a continuance, this is a temporary period for the business to reorganize. If a business wants to operate beyond the temporary period, it must submit an application as soon as possible.

Who may apply for a continuance?

The rules on who may apply for a continuance vary depending on the type of license:

- <u>Sole Ownership</u>
  If the licensee dies, a member of his or her immediate family may apply to continue the family business.

- <u>Partnership</u>
  The remaining partners, as listed in CSLB records, may apply.

- <u>Joint Venture</u>
  The remaining businesses listed in CSLB records as those who formed the joint venture may apply.

NOTE: Since corporate and limited liability company licenses are granted to the corporation or LLC as a whole, the status of the license is not affected if one of the officers, members, or managers leaves. Therefore, continuances are not granted for corporate or LLC licenses.

How do I apply for a continuance?

To apply for a continuance, submit a written request to CSLB as soon as possible but no later than 90 days from the date of a death or disassociation, stating why a continuance is necessary.

What does a continuance allow me to do?

Under a continuance of a sole owner or of a partnership license (when one of the partners has died), you may continue normal business operations and enter into new contracts during the period for which the continuance is granted.

Under a continuance of a joint venture license or of a partnership license (when one of the partners has disassociated), you may conduct business only on those contracts entered into before the event necessitating cancelation occurred. You may not enter into new contracts.

Can a continuance be extended?

Yes. The registrar may approve an extension to the one-year provision if additional time is necessary to complete projects contracted for or begun before the disassociation or death. A license extended under these circumstances is subject to all provisions, including those relating to renewal and bond requirements.

Chapter 3.

Access to Licensee Information

AVAILABLE DOCUMENTS, COMPLAINT RECORDS, FEES

You may obtain license information by checking CSLB's website, www.cslb.ca.gov, or by calling the 24/7 automated, toll-free line (800) 321-CSLB (2752). CSLB's website is generally unavailable from 8:30 p.m. Sunday to 6:30 a.m. Monday for maintenance.

Callers can enter the contractor license number to learn if a contractor license is valid and the contractor has disclosable complaints.

Visit CSLB's website for general information regarding licensing, consumer assistance services (such as selecting a contractor during a state of emergency), consumer complaint services, online publications, license status information, and finding a licensed contractor by their zip code or city.

To obtain written information or copies of documents in CSLB's possession, send a written request to CSLB, P.O. Box 26000, Sacramento, CA 95826. Provide the full name, business name, or contractor license number, and specify exactly what kind of information you are seeking. CSLB provides copies of records with personal and confidential information deleted.

INFORMATION REGARDING INDIVIDUAL LICENSE RECORDS

CSLB will provide the following information after receiving a written request and the appropriate fees. *(See chart on following pages.)*

- Report of current bond information

- Report of current license status

- Records search and certified report of license history (past 10 years only unless a specific time period is requested)

- Records search and certified report of no license history (past 10 years only unless supporting documents are submitted to justify the need for more than 10 years)

- Records search and certified report of home improvement salesperson registration

- Copies of documents (personal and confidential information deleted)

- Disclosure of complaints resulting in legal action and a history of legal actions taken by CSLB against current license holders

- Disclosure of open complaints that meet the criteria of B&P Code section 7124.6, in that they: "... have been referred for investigation after a determination by board enforcement staff that a probable violation has occurred, and have been reviewed by a supervisor, and [the complaints] regard allegations that if proven would present a risk of harm to the public and would be appropriate for suspension or revocation of the contractor's license or criminal prosecution."

INFORMATION REGARDING ACCESSING LARGE QUANTITIES OF LICENSE INFORMATION

CSLB offers a no-cost publicly accessible website feature to search and download custom and statewide license information.

Information includes:

- A complete list of contractors filtered by license classifications (up to ten) in up to ten different counties,

- A full license list of all contractors statewide:

  o Master License List – Provides complete public information for all licensees

  o Workers' Compensation List – Provides public information on all licensees that carry workers' compensation insurance policies

  o Personnel List – Provides public information on all personnel directly associated with a license

Public Sales Custom Order Form

With this form, you may order license information within specified parameters, including license status, license classification(s), geographical locations, etc. The information provided is in Text File Format, and includes contractor license number, business name, address and telephone number, license classification(s), business county, bond company, and workers' compensation insurance information. **No email addresses are provided.**

Record layout may be viewed by visiting www.cslb.ca.gov, selecting the "Online Services" tab on the main menu, choosing "Public Sales Order Form" from the list. There is a **$245 non-refundable fee** for this service.

Full File/Update File Order Form - DVD or email

CSLB license information is available in Text File Format on DVD or via email. Available files include:

License Master Full File*, License Master Update File, Business Principal Full File, Business Principal Update File, Action Code Full File, Action Code Update File, Workers' Compensation Full File, Workers' Compensation Update File, Complaint Disclosure/Legal Action Full File, and Complaint Disclosure/Legal Action Update File.

* Full Files may require the use of software to read large files.

Telephone numbers are provided on the license master file only. There is a **$235 non-refundable fee** for each file.

To obtain an order form, call (800) 321-2752, or download the form at www.cslb.ca.gov. Go to the "Online Services" section, click on the "Request Applications, Forms, Guides" tab, then select "Forms and Applications." Under "Forms," go to "Full File/Update File Order Form."

Submit the completed form to:

> Contractors State License Board
> Attn: Data Services Unit
> P. O. Box 26000
> Sacramento, CA 95826

Fees must be paid in advance by check or money order. DO NOT SEND CASH. If you have questions about ordering, call the CSLB Help Desk at (916) 255-3975.

INFORMATION REGARDING PENDING APPLICATION RECORDS

CSLB provides a website page that allows users to download the Pending Application Master Postlist and Pending Application Personnel File on a daily basis.

The Pending Application Master Postlist includes application number, business type, business name and address, license classification(s), and examinee name (if an exam is required). **No telephone numbers are provided**.

The **Pending Application Personnel File** includes application number, personnel name, position, and license classification(s). **No telephone numbers are provided**.

To access this information, visit www.cslb.ca.gov, select the "Online Services" tab on the main menu, then choose "Applicant Posting List" from the list.

If you have questions about accessing this data, call the CSLB Help Desk at (916) 255-3975.

INFORMATION REGARDING LEGAL ACTION AGAINST CONTRACTORS

CSLB can provide public information on complaints that have been investigated and referred for legal action, or that concluded in legal action administered by the board against a license. The fact that a complaint against a contractor has been referred for legal action does not necessarily mean the contractor has violated contractors' state license law; no conclusions or judgments as to the validity of the charges are assumed.

You may obtain a "Request for Disclosure of Contractor's License Information" form from the CSLB website.

CSLB's website and toll-free line also provide the following:

- General license information, including business name, license number, license classification(s), address of record, and official personnel listed for a license.

- Bond information, including bond amount, bond identification number, and name of bonding company.

- Workers' compensation insurance information, including the workers' compensation insurance carrier, policy number, effective date, and expiration date.

DOCUMENTS AVAILABLE FROM CSLB

<u>PLEASE NOTE</u>: All fees are current as of this publication. For verification of current fees, check www.cslb.ca.gov or contact CSLB at (800) 321-CSLB (2752).

TYPE OF INFORMATION	PROVIDES	DISTRIBUTION/ AVAILABLE	FEE
BOND STATUS LETTER Submit a "Request for Current Bond Information" form	Current bond(s) information; names/addresses of surety companies that provide bonds; issuance, renewal, and expiration/ cancellation dates; entity status; business name of contractor, address, and classification(s) held	Public; Available at: www.cslb.ca.gov (800) 321-CSLB	$8 each
CERTIFIED COPY of WALL OR POCKET LICENSE of a currently renewed license Submit a "Wall and/or Pocket Certificate" form (also used to change a business name and/or address)	Replacement copy	Members of the licensed entity; Available at: www.cslb.ca.gov	$25 each
CERTIFIED COPY of HOME IMPROVEMENT SALESPERSON REGISTRATION Pocket Card of a currently renewed registration Submit a "Changing HIS Address or Request for Pocket Registration Card" form	Replacement copy	Registered salesperson; Available at: www.cslb.ca.gov	$25 each
PHOTOCOPIES of DOCUMENTS Submit a "Request for Copies" form	Copy with all personal or confidential information deleted	Public; Available at: www.cslb.ca.gov (800) 321-CSLB	10¢ per page

TYPE OF INFORMATION	PROVIDES	DISTRIBUTION/ AVAILABLE	FEE
CERTIFIED COPIES of PHOTOCOPIED DOCUMENTS Submit a "Request for Copies" form	Board certification of authenticity, currency, and accuracy	Public; Available at: www.cslb.ca.gov (800) 321-CSLB	$2 certification fee per license PLUS 10¢ per page copied
GENERAL STATUS LETTER Submit a "Request for General Status Letter" form	Current license information excluding bond status: NOT certified	Public; Available at: www.cslb.ca.gov (800) 321-CSLB	$8 each
CERTIFIED LICENSE HISTORY Admissible as *prima facie* evidence of the facts stated (used primarily for court actions) Submit "Request for Certified License History" form **six-to-eight weeks IN ADVANCE** of need	Certified history of license ("record") or absence of license ("No-record" / "Certificate of Non-licensee") for a given time period. Includes: classification(s) held; license personnel, any disciplinary actions on bond but NO OTHER bond information UNLESS specially requested, and the standing of the license at all times during the period covered by the certificate.	Public; Available at: www.cslb.ca.gov (800) 321-CSLB	$67 each
CERTIFIED REGISTRATION HISTORY Home Improvement Salesperson Submit a "Request for Home Improvement Salesperson Registration Information" form **six-to-eight weeks IN ADVANCE** of need	Certified history of Home Improvement Salesperson Registration. A "record" certificate includes the registration number, effective date, business name, and the license number of the contractor with whom the salesperson is registered. If the person is not registered, a "no-record" certificate is issued.	Public; Available at: www.cslb.ca.gov	$67 each

TYPE OF INFORMATION	PROVIDES	DISTRIBUTION/ AVAILABLE	FEE
ELECTRONIC MEDIA Submit a "Full File/ Update File Order" form Information is available in Text File Format on DVD or via email. Full Files are produced twice a year. Update Files, showing the past month's activity, are produced monthly.	Four different file formats are available: • License file • Business principal file (all personnel of record for each license) • Workers' compensation file • Action codes or complaint disclosure/legal action file	Public; available at: www.cslb.ca.gov	$235 each file, non-refundable
SPECIAL INFORMATION REQUEST Submit a "Public Sales Custom Order" form	Specially compiled list of contractors, according to a variety of criteria that you select. With this service, you can specify geographic area, license classification, license status, etc. The information provided is in Text File Format, and includes the business name, business address and telephone number, license number, and license classification(s).	Public; available at: www.cslb.ca.gov	$245, nonrefund-able

TYPE OF INFORMATION	PROVIDES	DISTRIBUTION/ AVAILABLE	FEE
INTERNET ACCESS TO PENDING APPLICATION RECORDS	Downloads of the Pending Application MASTER and PERSONNEL Posting List on a daily basis. Available information includes the name, address, personnel, and classification(s) for all applications posted by CSLB.	Public; Access this information at: https://www2.cslb. ca.gov/OnlineServ ices/CheckApplica tionII/ApplicantRe quest.aspx For help, call the CSLB Help Desk at (916) 255-3975	No fee

Chapter 4.

Enforcement Procedures: Complaints and Citations

Complaints against contractors may be filed with CSLB by homeowners, other contractors, subcontractors, material suppliers, or employees. Public agencies also may file complaints.

Most complaints made against contractors involve poor workmanship; abandonment of a project; failure to pay subcontractors, suppliers, or employees; building code violations; lack of reasonable diligence in executing a construction project; use of false, misleading, or deceptive advertising; and violations of the law governing home improvement contracts.

COMPLAINTS AGAINST LICENSED CONTRACTORS

When a complaint is made against a licensed contractor, CSLB reviews it to determine if it falls within CSLB's jurisdiction. CSLB sends a confirmation to the person who filed the complaint and also sends a notice to the licensed contractor to determine if the complaint can be resolved without further board involvement.

If the complaint has not been resolved after the contractor has been notified, a CSLB representative may contact the complainant and respondent (the licensee) to request additional information and, if necessary, documentation. If appropriate, CSLB will attempt mediation. If mediation is unsuccessful, CSLB may recommend settlement through its arbitration program, recommend that the complainant contact the surety company that issued the contractor's bond, file a claim in small claims court, or file a civil suit in superior court.

If CSLB finds that it's warranted, it may conduct an investigation to determine if there are violations of contractors state license law. An investigation may involve interviewing the complainant, the contractor, and any other parties who can furnish relevant information.

What happens if a violation is established?

If a violation is established but it is an isolated or minor one, CSLB may send the licensee an advisory notice. The advisory notice informs the licensee that CSLB is aware of the violation and that a future occurrence of the same violation may result in more stringent board actions.

For some violations, CSLB may issue a letter of admonishment, which may require the licensee to submit a corrective action plan showing compliance with the law, and is publicly disclosable on the license record for one or two years.

If a more serious violation is established, the registrar of contractors may issue a citation, which can include an order to correct a project, make restitution to an injured party, and pay a civil penalty of up to $8,000 for most violations, and up to $30,000 for serious violations. *(See B&P §7099.2(b) regarding $30,000 citations for violations of B&P §§ 7110, 7114, 7118, and 7125.4.)*

If the licensee complies with the citation orders, CSLB takes no further action. If the licensee contests all or any part of the citation, an informal citation conference may be held to resolve the citation. If the matter is not settled, a hearing can be set before an administrative law judge of the State of California. At the hearing, the licensee can argue against the citation orders. If the licensee prevails at this hearing, CSLB takes no further action. If, however, the licensee does not prevail and does not comply with a final citation order, the license may be suspended and then revoked.

For flagrant violations of law, the registrar will take administrative action by filing an accusation with the state attorney general stating the board's intent to suspend or revoke the license. The licensee may be provided the opportunity to resolve the matter at an informal settlement conference. If the matter is not settled, the licensee is given an opportunity to defend themselves at a hearing before an administrative law judge.

The following procedures may be used to decide a case:

- The licensee may choose to have a hearing before an administrative law judge. The recommendation of this judge is used by the registrar in determining the appropriate action to take.

- The licensee and the registrar may negotiate a settlement of the case. This settlement is known as a "stipulation."

- If the licensee fails to respond to the accusation, the case will be considered in default. The registrar will decide on the appropriate action to take against the licensee.

The decision of the registrar may include various remedies:

- **Revocation of the License**

   The licensee's right to contract is taken away. The license shall not be reinstated or reissued for one to five years from the effective date of the decision.

   None of the official personnel listed in CSLB records for a revoked license and who have been found to have known about, or participated in, the acts or omissions constituting grounds for the revocation may apply for a license until the penalty period is over. The licensee also must show that they have complied with all provisions of the decision and settled any loss caused by the act or omission that resulted in the revocation of the license and must file a disciplinary bond in the amount set by the registrar.

- **Suspension of the License**

   The licensee is not entitled to operate during the period of suspension. A disciplinary bond must be filed before the license will be reinstated or reissued.

- **Stay of Suspension or Revocation (Probation)**

   The licensee must abide by certain terms and conditions to keep the suspension or revocation from going into effect. They also must file a disciplinary bond to remain in business during this period. Suspension or revocation of the license will result if any of the terms of the agreement are violated.

- **Recovery of Investigation and Enforcement Costs**

   The licensee, to maintain good and clear standing or as a condition for renewal and reinstatement of their license, must pay the costs as ordered or as stipulated.

- **Dismissal with No Penalties**

   Matters that have been dismissed are not disclosed to the public.

- **Injunction against Unlawful Activity**

   Upon establishing that a blatant violation of the law has occurred, CSLB may go to court to request an injunction to immediately stop the unlawful activity.

- **Criminal Charges**

   If a blatant violation of the law has occurred, CSLB may refer the complaint to the local office of the district attorney for a possible criminal filing.

Section I

Complaint Disclosure

Once CSLB has determined that a probable violation of law has occurred, which, if proven, would present a risk of harm to the public—and for which suspension or revocation of the contractor's license would be appropriate—the date, nature, and status of the complaint will be disclosed to the public. A disclaimer stating that the complaint is, at this time, only an allegation will accompany this disclosure.

Citations will be disclosed to the public from date of issuance and for five years from the date of compliance.

Accusations that result in suspension or stayed revocation of the contractor license shall be disclosed from the date the accusation is filed and for seven years after the accusation has been settled, including the terms and conditions of probation. All revocations that are not stayed shall be disclosed indefinitely from the effective date of the revocation.

ADDRESSING COMPLAINTS AGAINST UNLICENSED CONTRACTORS

In California, it is a misdemeanor to engage in the business or act in the capacity of a contractor without a contractor license unless the contractor meets the criteria for exemption specified in Business and Professions Code sections 7040 through 7054.5.

When a complaint is filed against an unlicensed contractor, CSLB will verify that the accused individual or firm contracted without a license and will, with sufficient evidence, determine the amount of financial injury involved.

How does CSLB process complaints against unlicensed contractors?

When the board receives a complaint against an unlicensed contractor, it may issue an administrative citation or file a criminal action with the local district attorney's office. In some cases, it may initiate injunction proceedings against the non-licensee through the Office of the Attorney General or the district attorney.

- **Citation**

   The registrar may issue a citation to an unlicensed contractor when there is probable cause to believe that the person is acting in the capacity of a contractor or engaging in the business of contracting without a license in good standing (current and not under suspension) with CSLB. The citation includes an **order of abatement** to cease and desist and a **civil penalty** of up to $15,000. Unless the board receives a written appeal within 15 working days after the citation is served, the citation becomes a final order of the registrar. The civil penalty is paid to CSLB.

If the citation is appealed, an informal settlement conference may be held to resolve the citation. If the matter is not settled, an administrative law judge will hear the appeal. The administrative law judge submits a decision to uphold, modify, or dismiss the citation. The decision is sent to the registrar for adoption.

If the cited unlicensed contractor continues to contract without a license, the registrar may refer the case to the local district attorney for criminal action.

- **Criminal Action**

  CSLB may refer investigations to the local prosecutor to file criminal charges. If criminal charges are filed, the unlicensed contractor appears in local court, which renders a final decision on the case. The court may order a fine, probation, restitution, a jail sentence, or all of these.

- **Injunction**

  The registrar may apply for an injunction with the superior court of either the county in which an alleged practice or transaction took place, or the county in which the unlicensed person maintains a business or residence. An injunction restrains an unlicensed person from acting in the capacity or engaging in the business of contracting without a license in good standing with CSLB.

How does CSLB process complaints against unregistered salespersons?

The same citation process used for complaints against unlicensed contractors is used for complaints against unregistered home improvement salespersons. Disciplinary action also can be taken against the licensed contractor who employs the unregistered salesperson.

Statewide Investigative Fraud Team

In addition to the complaint process, CSLB established the Statewide Investigative Fraud Team (SWIFT), an arm of the Enforcement Division that focuses on the underground economy and unlicensed contractors who prosper at the expense of consumers and legitimate businesses. SWIFT has the authority to visit any jobsite without cause or complaint, ask contractors to produce proof of licensure in good standing, and cite those who are not properly licensed. *(See B&P Code §7011.4 and §7099.)*

SECTION II.
HOME IMPROVEMENT

Chapter 5.

Home Improvement

Home improvement is the repairing, remodeling, altering, converting, or modernizing of, or adding to, residential property and includes, but is not limited to, the construction, erection, replacement, or improvement of driveways, swimming pools (including spas and hot tubs), terraces, patios, awnings, storm windows, solar energy systems, landscaping, fences, porches, garages, fallout shelters, basements, and other improvements of the structures or land adjacent to a dwelling. Home improvement is also the installation of home improvement goods or the furnishing of home improvement services.

HOME IMPROVEMENT CONTRACTOR

A home improvement contractor, including a swimming pool contractor, is a contractor licensed by the Contractors State License Board (CSLB) who is engaged in the business of home improvement either full-time or part-time.

HOME IMPROVEMENT CONTRACTS

The home improvement business in California constitutes a large portion of the state's construction industry. Problems can occur because of a general misunderstanding of basic requirements and the agreement between the owner and contractor. Special legal requirements specifically for home improvement contracts were enacted to eliminate as many of these problems as possible.

In 2004, through SB 30, and in 2005, through AB 316, the Legislature made significant additions to the information contractors must provide to the buyer of home improvements. The idea behind the legislation is to use the contract itself to inform homeowners of the most important contract requirements to help them better understand the process. The availability of this simple consumer protection information is intended to reduce the number of disputes between contractors and homeowners and, therefore, the number of complaints that homeowners make to CSLB.

SB 30, which took effect in 2005, maintained many of the existing home improvement contract provisions and added some new requirements as well. Among the requirements: any changes made to contracts must be in writing, be legible, be easy to understand, and inform a consumer of their right to cancel or rescind the contract; and a home improvement contract must contain various information, notices, and disclosures for the protection of the consumer. SB 30 also created a "service and repair contract" to be used by licensed contractors for jobs of $750 or less, provided that the contract meets all four of the new requirements. The bill enacted various disclosure requirements applicable to the service and repair contract. SB 30 provided that any violation of the provisions subjected the contractor to discipline.

SB 1113 postponed implementation of the SB 30 provisions until 2006. The bill also revised and recast some of the provisions and made other related changes in other provisions of law. SB 1113 took effect immediately as an emergency statute.

AB 316 revised and recast the service and repair contract requirements and set forth information, notices, and disclosures required to be included as part of the contract. In addition, a service and repair contract that does not meet specified requirements is subject to the requirements applicable to a home improvement contract regardless of the aggregate contract price.

AB 2471, effective January 1, 2021, extends the right to cancel home improvement contracts, service and repair contracts, Property Assessed Clean Energy assessment contracts, and seminar sales contracts from three business days to five business days for those 65 years and older.

SB 1189, effective January 1, 2021, and in part, includes in the definition of home improvement the reconstruction, restoration, or rebuilding of residential property damaged or destroyed by a disaster for which a state of emergency has been declared by either the governor or the president.

SB 757, effective January 1, 2022, clarifies that a contract for a residential solar energy system is considered home improvement when installed on a residential building or property, for the purposes of the home improvement contract requirements.

In drawing up contracts, contractors should pay strict attention to the requirements for print typeface and point size of the notices and disclosures. For example, unless a larger print typeface is specified, text in any printed form shall be in at least 10-point type and the headings shall be in at least 10-point boldface type.

For more detailed information on home improvement contract requirements, visit www.cslb.ca.gov (search: home improvement contract).

HOME WARRANTIES

Home warranties generally are not transferrable, except as provided for home roof warranties. Home Roof Warranties of the California Civil Code provides:

> For any contract subject to this chapter that is entered into on or after January 1, 1994, the warranty obligations shall inure to the benefit of, and shall be directly enforceable by, all subsequent purchasers and transferees of the residential structure, without limitation, unless the contract contains a clear and conspicuous provision limiting transferability of the warranty (*Civil Code §1797.62*).

HOME IMPROVEMENT SALESPERSON REGISTRATION

Anyone who solicits, sells, negotiates, or executes home improvement contracts for a licensed contractor outside of the contractor's normal place of business, regardless of the dollar amount of these contracts, must be registered with CSLB as a Home Improvement Salesperson (HIS).

In 2016, the HIS registration process underwent an important change. **SB 561** allows home improvement salespersons to file a single registration with CSLB, while still permitting them to represent multiple employers. This new law removed the previous requirement that an HIS register separately with CSLB for each contractor that employed them.

In addition to the single registration, the new law requires licensees to notify CSLB in writing prior to employing an already registered HIS, and to notify CSLB in writing when employment of a registered HIS ends. These notification forms are available on CSLB's website: www.cslb.ca.gov (search: HIS forms).

Who is exempt from the HIS registration requirement?

Salespersons who only sell goods or negotiate contracts at a fixed business establishment where the goods or services are exhibited or offered for sale are not considered home improvement salespersons.

The official personnel listed in CSLB's records for the contractor license also are exempt from registration requirements. This includes individual contractors, qualifiers, partners, officers of the corporation, and responsible managing officers, members, managers or employees of an LLC.

Other exemptions from the registration requirements include people who contact prospective buyers for the exclusive purpose of scheduling appointments for a registered home improvement salesperson, and *bona fide* service or repair people who are employed by a licensed contractor and whose repair or service calls are limited to the service or repair initially requested by the buyer.

What are the qualifications for a home improvement salesperson?

A home improvement salesperson must be at least 18 years old. There are no educational, residency, or experience requirements.

How do I apply for registration?

Complete an online easy-fill "Application for Registration as a Home Improvement Salesperson" by visiting www.cslb.ca.gov or obtain a copy of the application by downloading it from www.cslb.ca.gov or by calling (800) 321-CSLB (2752).

Then:

- Follow all instructions on the application.

- Submit the required nonrefundable, nontransferable application fee of $200 and your application to the CSLB headquarters office.

May I begin working as an HIS as soon as I have submitted my registration application and fee to CSLB?

No. CSLB must review your application and issue a registration number before you may legally work as a home improvement salesperson.

How long will it take to become registered?

CSLB's processing times vary depending on its workload, staff vacancies, etc. CSLB's website includes a processing time chart that lists the date of documents currently being processed, including HIS applications and renewals. The chart is updated weekly and helps keep applicants informed of current processing times. Visit www.cslb.ca.gov (search: processing times).

When does my HIS registration expire?

The HIS registration expires two years from the last day of the month in which it was issued. CSLB will mail a renewal application to your address of record several weeks before your registration expires. Upon verification of the renewal, a new registration certificate will be mailed showing the new expiration date.

What if my address has changed since my registration was issued or last renewed?

If your address has changed since your registration was issued or last renewed, it is your responsibility to notify CSLB in writing within 90 days of the change.

If you have not received an advance notification of renewal, notify CSLB. This should be done no later than three weeks before your registration expires.

Is a contract sold or negotiated by an unregistered salesperson enforceable?

According to B&P Code section 7154, a contractor who employs an unregistered person to negotiate home improvement contracts is subject to disciplinary action by the registrar. Furthermore, B&P Code section 7153 states that it is a misdemeanor for a person to act as a home improvement salesperson without being registered. In addition to possible criminal action, the same section provides that an administrative citation may be issued to any unregistered person who engages in the HIS occupation.

For additional information, refer to B&P Code sections 7150 through 7173 in Chapter 12 of this book.

REGISTRAR-APPROVED JOINT CONTROL AGREEMENTS

California Business & Professions Code provides for the use of a joint control agreement approved by the registrar of contractors "covering full performance and completion of the contract" as an alternative to certain contract requirements. When a joint control is used, a schedule of payments is not required in the contract.

A joint control is a builder's construction control service, which acts as an escrow holder of a consumer's money. A joint control company manages the disbursement of funds to prevent the contractor from being paid more than the value of the work already completed. A joint control also safeguards the consumer's property from mechanics liens by requiring the contractor to supply lien releases as progress payments are made.

A joint control normally includes an analysis of the contract and building plans or specifications, breakdown of costs, and the preparation of an account from which the funds will be disbursed through scheduled progress payments. An addendum *(see following page)* must be incorporated into joint control agreements for it to be considered approved by the registrar.

CSLB does not license joint control companies, nor does CSLB have legal jurisdiction over joint control company activities, nor does it maintain lists of approved joint control companies nor monitor their activities. Registrar approval is implicit if the addendum is used. Responsibility for incorporating the addendum in agreements rests solely with the joint control companies. Contractors and consumers should compare any joint control agreement with the following addendum to ensure that the agreement supplies the services required for approval.

NOTE: The last paragraph in the joint control addendum pertains to home improvement contracts other than swimming pool contracts. **The same down payment provisions apply to swimming pools as to other home improvement projects: $1,000 or 10 percent of the total contract price, whichever is less.**

JOINT CONTROL ADDENDUM

Addendum to Control Agreement/Escrow Instructions

This addendum is hereby incorporated into and becomes a part of the Control Agreement attached hereto, dated _____.

1. Should any of the terms or provisions of the contract between Owner and Contractor or of the contract into which this Addendum is incorporated conflict with any of the terms or provisions of this Addendum, then the terms of this Addendum shall prevail.

2. Control agrees to control and disburse funds in the following manner:

   a) Supplier or subcontractor submits to contractor duplicate copies of invoices requesting payment;

   b) If payment is justified, based on work completed, Control accepts disbursement order or voucher in favor of payee for net amount;

   c) After signing by the contractor and the payee concerned, order for payment (together with copies of invoices, unconditional lien releases and/or other substantiating data) is delivered or mailed to the Control for payment.

3. Prior to issuing payment, Control agrees to verify:

   a) That all vouchers have authorized signatures;

   b) That adequate unconditional lien releases have been submitted in writing; and

   c) That sufficient funds are on hand to pay the specific invoice(s) submitted.

4. Prior to issuing final payment, Control agrees to verify that project has passed final inspection by local building authorities, unless the scope of the contracted project does not require a final inspection.

5. After verification of the above, checks shall be made payable to the supplier or subcontractor, or to the prime contractor and supplier or subcontractor, jointly.

6. Control agrees that in no event shall it disburse payments in excess of 100 percent of the value of the work

performed on the project at any time, excluding finance charges.

7. The funds from this account shall be used only for the project described in the contract. Control warrants that work and material paid for by Control has been provided.

8. If this agreement is terminated for any reason prior to disbursement of all monies payable under the contract between Owner and Contractor, all subsequent disbursements to Contractor shall conform to the requirements of Business and Professions Code section 7159.

NOTE: B&P Code section 7159 requires that all change orders be in writing and signed by all parties.

SO AGREED this _____ day of _____, 20_____.

_____   _____
CONTROL   OWNER

_____   _____
CONTRACTOR   OWNER

Contractors who furnish a joint control as part of the terms of a home improvement contract should be aware that the law prohibits them from having any financial or other interest in the joint control company. Also, it is the contractor's responsibility to determine if the above addendum is included in the control agreement.

If an approved joint control or bond covering the complete contract is not included with a home improvement contract, the contractor may not require a down payment in excess of $1,000 or 10 percent of the total contract price, whichever is less. The contract also must contain a schedule of payments stated in dollars and cents, specifically corresponding to the work or services to be performed or the materials and equipment to be supplied. Also, no payments other than the down payment can exceed the value of the work (excluding finance charges) performed at any time on the project.

MECHANICS LIEN WARNING

The "Mechanics Lien Warning" replaced the previously used "Notice to Owner." This notice describes, in non-technical language, pertinent provisions of the state's mechanics lien laws that specify the rights and responsibilities of both the property owner and the contractor.

The Mechanics Lien Warning must be a part of any home improvement contract, including swimming pool contracts. This notice is not required for a contract that meets the service and repair contract requirements.

Anyone who helps improve property but is not paid for work performed or materials supplied, may record what is called a mechanics lien against that property. A mechanics lien is a claim, like a mortgage or home equity loan, made against the property and recorded with the county recorder.

Even if the contractor is paid in full, unpaid subcontractors, suppliers, and laborers who helped improve the property may record mechanics liens and sue the property owner in court to foreclose a lien. If a court finds the lien valid, the property owner could be forced to pay additional money or have a court officer sell the home to pay the lien. Liens also can affect personal credit records.

20-DAY PRELIMINARY NOTICE

To preserve their right to record a lien, each subcontractor and material supplier **must provide the property owner with a document called a "20-Day Preliminary Notice."** This notice is not a lien. The notice lets the property owner know that the person who is sending the notice has the *right* to record a lien on the property if they are not paid.

The Preliminary Notice can be sent up to 20 days after the subcontractor starts work or the supplier provides material. The prime contractor and laborers do not send 20-Day Preliminary Notices; contractor law assumes the property owner already knows they are improving the property.

A list of all contractors, subcontractors, and material suppliers who work on a project can be provided to the property owner to help avoid confusion.

PAYING WITH JOINT CHECKS

Joint checks are a protective method to make sure the subcontractor or material supplier is paid. When the contractor tells the property owner that it is time to pay for the work of a subcontractor or supplier who has sent the property owner a Preliminary Notice, a joint check payable to both the contractor and the subcontractor or material supplier is written to confirm payment.

For other ways to prevent liens, visit www.cslb.ca.gov (search: prevent liens).

The Notice of Mechanics Lien must be served on the owner or person believed to be the owner of the property, on the construction lender, or on the original contractor, <u>and</u> a "proof of service affidavit" to that person(s) must be completed and signed by the person serving the Notice of Mechanics Lien. <u>Failure to serve the mechanics lien and confirm a proof of service affidavit makes the mechanics lien unenforceable.</u>

SECTION III.

BUSINESS MANAGEMENT

Chapter 6.

Managing a Business

This chapter will show how good management and accounting techniques can be applied to the construction industry. The numbers used in the examples were chosen to illustrate the average successful small contracting business.

THE CONTRACTOR MANAGER

Statistics show that 90 percent of bankruptcies and business closures result from poor management. The specific reasons include an inability to plan, manage, and control business affairs; insufficient on-the-job supervisory experience or the inability to manage employees; and lack of knowledge about business practices. Hard work is not enough.

The main duties of the contractor, who is also a manager, are to plan and direct the major activities of the business; coordinate employee work and materials; and train, direct, and advise employees in supervisory and non-supervisory positions.

PRINCIPLES OF MANAGEMENT

The most difficult part of changing roles from employee to manager may be in developing a clear understanding of what is important for successful management. Management theory has been divided into two different areas: functional and behavioral.

The Functional Areas of Management Include:

- **Planning**

    Good planning is one of the most important, but most neglected, management duties. Large amounts of information from within the business must be put together with information from outside the business to schedule business activities. Planning is essential to make sure that resources,

71

money, people, and equipment are available to the business in the right amounts and at the right time.

- **Decision-Making/Delegation**

  Employees should be trained and encouraged to assume responsibility for routine decision-making. The manager's responsibility is to make sure that these decisions fit together with the plans for the project and the business as a whole.

- **Standardization**

  For the greatest efficiency, it is important to standardize methods for routine, ongoing operations. After you determine the best method, it should be adopted as the pattern for similar operations in the future. Standardization also makes it easier for decisions to be made at lower levels.

- **Controls**

  Controls are established to inform the manager when the actual business outcome is different from what was expected. Controls should be designed to warn the manager before the differences become too great. The manager can both check on the progress of the business and evaluate overall performance by comparing results with plans. Effective controls must be established and rigidly enforced. The manager can then adapt to change rather than resist it.

ESTABLISHING YOUR BUSINESS

Forms of Business

The legal form of the business will determine the available sources of financing, the extent of personal liability, the extent of control, and the tax liabilities. The legal form may change as the business grows and should be reviewed as financing requirements change.

- **Sole Ownership**

  Sole ownership (often called personal ownership or sole proprietorship) is the simplest form of business organization and relies primarily on the financial resources available to an individual. The owner has sole responsibility and complete control. They must obtain all the financing and are personally liable for any claims against the business.

  For tax purposes, business income is reported as personal income. *(See Chapter 2 for information about maintaining a sole ownership license.)*

- **General Partnership**

    General partnerships use the financial and personal resources of two or more individuals who share in the ownership and operation of the business. A general partnership requires registration of the name of the business. Consult a lawyer to formalize the rights and responsibilities of the partners regarding management and profit-sharing.

    Under most circumstances, a partnership agreement terminates with the death or withdrawal of a partner or the addition of a new partner. Some partnership agreements avoid termination by entering into a prior written agreement allowing the partnership to continue. However, when a contractor license is issued to a general partnership and a general partner leaves for any reason or the partnership wants to add another general partner, the license is canceled. (*See Chapter 2 for a discussion of partnership and ways to continue as a partnership for a short period of time after cancelation.*)

    The partnership is not an entity separate from the partners. Each partner may be personally liable to the extent of their personal assets and may be legally responsible for the negligent acts of the other partner(s). For tax purposes, an individual's share of the partnership income is taxed as personal income.

- **Limited Partnership**

    The limited partnership allows investors to join in a partnership without taking full responsibility for the business. The limited partner risks only their original investment. In this case, there must be at least one general partner who runs the business and who remains fully responsible for the liabilities of the business. (*See Chapter 2 for a discussion of what to do if a limited partner leaves the partnership.*)

- **Corporation**

    A corporation is a separate legal entity created by the government. It can make contracts, be held legally liable, and is taxed. The corporation may raise capital by selling stock to private investors or to the public. Stockholders are usually not liable for claims against the corporation beyond their original investment. Creditors may claim only the corporate assets, although corporate officers may be personally liable.

    You can begin the process of incorporations by filing articles of incorporation with the Secretary of State. The corporation has no fixed life. The death of a stockholder or sale of one's personal investment will not disrupt the business.

- **"S" Chapter Corporation**

  "S" corporations must meet certain restrictions and can report the business income as individual income. This benefit is designed to remove tax considerations from the decision regarding the form of business organization for the small business. The business can operate in corporate form to reduce the owner's liability but is taxed like a partnership. Since the corporation is not taxed separately, only an information return similar to the partnership tax return needs to be filed.

- **Limited Liability Company**

  A California limited liability company (LLC) generally offers liability protection similar to that of a corporation but is taxed differently. Domestic LLCs may be managed by one or more managers or one or more members. In addition to filing the applicable documents with the Secretary of State, an operating agreement among the members as to the affairs of the LLC and the conduct of its business is required. The LLC does not file the operating agreement with the Secretary of State but maintains it at the office where the LLC's records are kept.

  To form an LLC in California, Articles of Organization (Form LLC-1) must be filed with the California Secretary of State's office.

Taxes and Permits

The owner(s) of the business is required to pay taxes and fees at the federal, state, and local levels. If the business is a sole ownership or partnership, estimated federal and state income taxes must be prepaid or paid quarterly.

A federal Employer Identification Number (EIN) must be requested from the Internal Revenue Service, and the federal income and Social Security taxes withheld from employee wages must be paid quarterly, monthly, or semimonthly, as required.

The contractor must register with the Employment Development Department, obtain a state EIN, and pay state payroll and unemployment insurance taxes for employees who earn over $100 in a calendar quarter.

California requires a Seller's Permit for businesses that sell tangible personal property. The State Board of Equalization can require a deposit of the estimated sales tax for the first six months. The contractor must collect the required sales tax from the customer unless the tax on materials was already paid at the time of purchase.

Before starting a job, determine if city or county permits are required. In addition, the contractor must be familiar with zoning laws and building codes.

Bonds

A requirement for bonding is generally mandatory for large jobs financed by institutional lenders, such as savings and loans, insurance companies, or commercial banks. In addition, many owners and lenders, as well as other contractors, impose bonding requirements. Bonds can be obtained from bonding companies for a percentage of the contract price, usually in the one to two percent range. This requirement is a cost of doing business that should be recognized when the bid is submitted. Bonds may be classified as follows:

- **Performance bonds** guarantee the project's completion according to the building plans and specifications. If the job is abandoned or the work is unacceptable, the bonding company has the option to hire another contractor to complete the work or settle for damages.

- **Payment bonds** assure the property owner that no liens for labor and materials will be filed against the property.

- **Contract bonds** guarantee both job completion and payment of all labor and materials.

In general, unless the bonding company has taken responsibility for completing the project, the bonding company will not have to pay more than the face amount of the bond.

The new contractor should be aware that bonding requirements may exclude the new business from bidding on desired jobs. Bonding companies will not take risks without verifying the technical and resource capabilities of the bonded contractor.

Contractor License Bonds

Contractor license bonds are different from performance, payment, and contract bonds. Each licensed contractor is required to carry a contractor bond. Unlike payment, performance, and contract bonds, which are usually written to cover specific projects, a contractor license bond is written to cover any project the contractor agrees to perform. As of January 1, 2022, the contractor license bond amount is $25,000. The bond for qualifying individuals is $25,000.

Limited Liability Company Surety Bond

A $100,000 surety bond (in addition to the $25,000 contractor bond) is required for the issuance, reissuance, reinstatement, reactivation, and renewal of an LLC license for the benefit of any employee or worker damaged by the LLC's failure to pay wages, interest on wages, or fringe benefits, as well as other contributions. (*See B&P Code §7071.6.5.*)

Commercial General Liability Insurance

Commercial general liability (CGL) insurance can shift the risk of liability for accidents and mistakes from the contractor to the insurance company. As the International Risk Management Institute explains in its *Guide to Construction Insurance*, commercial general liability insurance protects "the insured contractor from liability to members of the public (other than employees) for bodily injury, property damage, or personal injury caused by virtually any activity."

The insurance company:

- Provides a claim-handling process.
- Defends the contractor against insurance claims.
- Pays claims for covered damages.
- Pays for immediately necessary medical treatment, even when the contractor is not ultimately found liable.

Contractors' state license law does not require contractors to carry CGL insurance unless their business entity is a limited liability company (see below). Even though it is not universally required by licensing law, commercial property owners routinely require the contractors they hire to carry CGL insurance.

On the other hand, when a homeowner hires a contractor to perform home improvement work, they rarely require the contractor to carry CGL insurance. Most homeowners assume that a contractor would not work on the house without being insured. To alert homeowners to the value of CGL insurance, the California Code of Regulations (CCR) section 872(a), requires home improvement contractors to:

- Disclose in writing if they do or do not carry commercial general liability insurance.
- If they do carry CGL insurance, provide the homeowner with the name and telephone number of the insurance company, in writing, so the homeowner can verify coverage.

$1 Million Liability Insurance Minimum

Liability insurance with the aggregate limit of $1 million for licensees with five or fewer persons listed as members of the personnel of record is required for a limited liability company; plus, an additional $100,000 in insurance is required for each additional member of the personnel of record, not to exceed $5 million total. (*See B&P Code §7071.19*).

For more information about the risks covered by insurance, see "Risk Management" on page 106.

Workers' Compensation Insurance

California workers' compensation law establishes a no-fault insurance plan purchased by the employer-contractor and administered by the state to:

- Limit the employer-contractor's liability and possibly avoid costly lawsuits.

- Guarantee that an injured worker receives prompt and complete medical treatment and specific benefits for job-related injury or illness. Under some circumstances, an employer-contractor can be sued for damages.

   For example, the harmed parties may sue if an employee is injured when the employer is illegally uninsured, or if the employer conceals the existence of an employee's injury and its connection with employment. Check with the Department of Industrial Relations, www.dir.ca.gov, for more information.

Employer Liability

For a work-incurred injury or illness, an employer-contractor is required to provide weekly benefit payments (indemnity) and necessary medical and hospital treatment. This liability of the employer extends to employed relatives on the same basis as any other employee.

If the employer has one or more employees, even part-time, they are required to insure for workers' compensation claims. An "owner-operator" or "independent contractor" should pay particular attention to Labor Code §2750.5.

Workers' Compensation Insurance Coverage

The employer-contractor may provide insurance protection in one of three ways:

- A standard approved policy of workers' compensation insurance available through any licensed carrier; or

- Securing a permit from the Director of the state Department of Industrial Relations to become a self-insurer *(Labor Code §3700)*; or

- Participating in a collectively bargained alternative dispute resolution program recognized by the Division of Workers' Compensation *(Labor Code §3201.5)*.

In general, if a contractor carries compensation insurance, the compensation insurance company assumes the obligation of the contractor under the workers' compensation laws. Some exceptions include penalties based on:

- The contractor's serious and willful misconduct *(Labor Code §4553)*.

- Injury to an illegally employed person under 16 years of age *(Labor Code §4557)*.

- Instances where the employer discriminates against an employee because an industrial injury claim was filed *(Labor Code §132a)*.

Reporting Name of Insurer

Every licensed contractor must report, in writing, the name and address of the insurer carrying workers' compensation on their employee to CSLB within 90 days after the issuance of any policy. The insurer can submit this information to CSLB electronically using the online submission system on CSLB's website: www.cslb.ca.gov. If you don't have employees, you must file an exemption from the workers' compensation requirement unless your classification requires you to carry workers' compensation insurance

Reporting Occupational Injury or Illness

- An employer-contractor MUST file a complete report of every employee occupational injury or occupational illness that results in lost time beyond the date of injury or illness, or which requires medical treatment beyond first aid, with the Department of Industrial Relations through its Division of Labor Statistics and Research or, if an insured employer, with the insurer *(Labor Code §6409.1)*.

  The report filed shall be the original of the form required by the Division of Labor Statistics and Research. A report shall be filed concerning each injury and illness that has, or is alleged to have, arisen out of and in the course of employment, within five days after the employer obtains knowledge of the injury or illness. Each report of occupational injury or occupational illness must indicate the Social Security number of the injured employee *(Labor Code §6409.1)*.

The insured employer must file with their insurer a complete report of every injury or illness to each employee. If a report is not filed with the insurance carrier, the Workers' Compensation Appeals Board may issue an order directing the insured employer to report the injury or illness within five days. Failure of the employer to comply with this order may be punished as contempt *(Labor Code §3760)*.

- In every case involving a serious injury or illness, or death, IN ADDITION TO the report described above, the employer must report immediately by telephone or email to the Division of Occupational Safety and Health *(Labor Code §6409.1)*.

Employee Notification and Posting Requirements

Every employer-contractor subject to the provisions of the workers' compensation laws MUST:

- Give every new employee, either at the time of hiring or by the end of their first pay period, written notice of the employee's right to receive workers' compensation benefits should they be injured on the job while working for the employer. The content of the notice must be approved by the Administrative Director of the Division of Workers' Compensation and must contain the information listed in Section 9880 of CCR Title 8. *The notice shall be available in both English and Spanish when there are Spanish-speaking employees (Labor Code §3551).*

- Post conspicuously, in a location frequented by employees, a Notice to Employees poster. *The Notice to Employees must be posted in English (and Spanish where there are Spanish-speaking employees).* The Notice to Employees poster must contain the information listed in Section 9881 of CCR Title 8 or the employer may post the Administrative Director's approved Notice to Employees poster provided in Section 9881.1 of CCR Title 8 (DWC 7 (8/1/04)). Failure to keep such a notice conspicuously posted is punishable as a misdemeanor *(Labor Code §3550)*.

- Post information regarding protections and obligations of employees under occupational safety and health laws, and related citations *(Labor Code §6408)*. *(See Chapter 7 in this book for details.)*

- Give any employee who is a victim of workplace crime written notification that the employee is eligible for workers' compensation *(Labor Code §3553)*.

- The contractor or their insurance company should notify an employee, in case of an injury, of a physician who will provide professional care.

Benefits to Which Workers May Be Entitled

- **Medical Treatment**

  Employers are required to authorize medical treatment consistent with the American College of Occupational and Environmental Medicine's (ACOEM) Occupational Medicine Practice Guidelines, Second Edition, or the treatment utilization schedule adopted by the Administrative Director to cure or relieve the injured worker from the effects of their injury. Within one working day of receiving the employee's claim form, the employer must authorize treatment for the alleged industrial injury and must continue to provide the treatment until the date that liability for the claim is either accepted or rejected by the employer. Until the date the claim is accepted or rejected, liability for medical treatment is limited to $10,000 *(Labor Code §§4600, 4604.5, 4610, 5307.27, and 5402)*.

- **Supplemental Job Displacement Benefit**

  The worker may be entitled to a supplemental job displacement benefit if they cannot return to work for the employer within 60 days following the end of the temporary disability period. The amount of the benefit is based on the employee's permanent disability level and must be used for retraining, skill enhancement, or job placement assistance *(Labor Code §4658.5)*.

- **Temporary Disability**

  The worker is also entitled to temporary disability payments while recovering from the injury. These weekly payments begin after the third day of disability and are based upon two-thirds of the weekly earnings, *up to a legal maximum*. The compensation insurance company should be able to provide information on current rates. Where temporary disability extends beyond 14 days or requires overnight hospitalization, the three-day waiting period is eliminated *(Labor Code §§4453, 4650, 4652, and 4653)*.

- **Permanent Disability**

  If a permanent disability arises out of an industrial injury, the worker is entitled to compensation based on the rated degree of disability. Benefits are based on the earning of the disabled worker, and the range of benefit amounts is set by state law *(Labor Code §4453)*.

- **Death Benefits**

  If the injury causes death, a benefit is payable to those dependent on the deceased for support at the time of injury. In addition, burial expenses are allowed up to a prescribed amount *(Labor Code §§4701 and 4702)*.

- **Compensation for Serious and Willful Employer Misconduct**

  The amount of compensation otherwise recoverable can be increased one-half, together with costs and expenses not to exceed $250, where the employee is injured by reason of the serious or willful misconduct of the employer or their managing representative, partner, executive, managing officer, or general superintendent. The insurance company is not liable for the increase and is not permitted to cover it under the insurance policy *(Labor Code §§4550 and 4553; Insurance Code §11661)*.

Penalties for Noncompliance

- Failure to secure payment of compensation as required by law is a misdemeanor *(Labor Code §3700.5)*.

- A contractor's license may be suspended or revoked by the registrar of contractors if the contractor fails to secure the payment of compensation *(Business and Professions Code §7110)*.

- The Department of Industrial Relations' Division of Labor Standards Enforcement also may take action against a contractor who has failed to secure the payment of compensation. This may include:

  o Issuing a "Stop Order," prohibiting the use of employee labor until insurance is provided *(Labor Code §3710.1)*.

  o Obtaining a restraining order in superior court against the contractor *(Labor Code §3712)*.

  o Issuing a penalty assessment order

    (Penalties for an uninsured contractor may be either the greater of twice the amount the contractor would have paid

in premiums during the period they were uninsured, or
$1,000 per employee employed during that same period. If
the contractor's uninsured status is discovered following
the filing of a claim for compensation, the penalty shall be
either $2,000 for each employee employed on the date of
injury in non-compensable cases, or $10,000 for each
employee in compensable cases (*Labor Code §3722*).

    o Recording a lien against the real property and personal
       property of the contractor as a security interest (*Labor
       Code §3727*).

- If a contractor willfully fails to provide compensation insurance
  for an employee and an injury occurs, the contractor must pay
  the disability compensation plus a penalty of 10 percent and
  attorney fees. They must also supply all necessary medical
  treatment. In addition, they are liable for damages in a civil
  action, with a legal presumption that the injury was caused by
  the employer's negligence. Contributory negligence of the
  employee is no defense (*Labor Code §§3706, 3708, 4554, and
  4555*).

- Every employer, and every employee having direction,
  management control, or custody of employment of any other
  employee, who willfully violates any occupational safety or
  health standard that causes the death of any employee or the
  prolonged impairment of the body of any employee shall, upon
  conviction, be punished by a fine and or imprisonment (*Labor
  Code §6425*).

Additional Information

- Department of Industrial Relations
  Division of Workers' Compensation
  1515 Clay Street, 6th Floor
  Oakland, California 94612
  (510) 622-2866

- Visit the Division's website: www.dir.ca.gov/dwc.

- Call (800) 736-7401 for recorded messages.

- The Division of Workers' Compensation publishes an
  Employer's Guide that can be requested by calling one of the
  numbers listed above.

FINANCIAL RESPONSIBILITY AND CONTROL

Records

State and federal agencies frequently specify that certain records must be maintained and made available for government audits and to substantiate tax reporting. For a description of the records specifically required under contractors' state license law, see Business and Professions Code section 7111.

Accurate accounting records must be kept to provide the base to construct financial statements. The information summarized in these statements highlights the total operational costs, individual job costs, and other costs that affect your ability to make a profit. Accurate records also provide information on cash receipts and a basis for control of disbursements. The contractor can, by reviewing these records, determine the cash flow requirements of other jobs that they have completed to help estimate the costs of future jobs.

Understand the Fundamental Terms of Accounting

- **Cash Basis of Accounting**

  Under the cash basis of accounting, revenue is recognized when cash is actually received, and expenses are deductible in the year paid (unless they should be taken in a different period to clearly reflect income).

  A cash basis of accounting may be appropriate where no prepaid expenses (e.g., insurance, rent), depreciable assets, or inventories exist, and where revenue is received during the accounting period.

  Information regarding cash flow, as provided by the cash basis of accounting method, can be valuable in judging the ability of the business to pay its debts, to finance replacement of productive assets, and to expand the scope of business operations. However, a strict cash method neither records receivables nor payables since these items have not been received or disbursed. This failure to match income and expenses for a given accounting period restricts the information available to the manager using a cash basis of accounting.

  Additionally, where depreciation and inventories are utilized, the accrual method is necessary to accurately reflect expenses and income. For federal income tax purposes, the accrual method is required when inventories are utilized.

The net increase or decrease in cash during a given period is not very useful in evaluating a company's operating performance because, although progress payments come in during the course of a job, final profit cannot be determined until after the job is completed. For these reasons, the cash basis of accounting is not recommended for contractors.

- **Accrual Basis of Accounting**

The accrual basis of accounting recognizes revenues when earned and expenses when incurred, regardless of when payment is received or made. Thus, this method allows the matching of revenues and associated expenses for individual periods of time.

In a contracting business that has qualifying long-term projects, the accrual basis of accounting is often further modified using two methods: 1) the **percentage of completion**; and 2) the **completed contract**.

1) The percentage of completion method will report profits and losses regularly on the basis of actual work accomplished on each job. For example, if the work performed in a given year is estimated to represent 50 percent of total performance under contract, then 50 percent of the total estimated revenue and profit is considered earned.

2) The completed contract method allows for the gross income and related costs for each contract to be reported in the year in which such a contract is completed.

- **Financial Statements**

The balance sheet and income statement summarize the firm's internal data. These statements, in turn, provide the information for ratio analysis that highlights the strengths and exposes the weaknesses of the company.

- **Balance Sheet**

The balance sheet is a statement of financial condition of an individual business at a certain point in time. The balance sheet is often referred to as a "snap shot." The accountant will usually provide two balance sheets, one for the current year just ending and another for the prior year. An example of a balance sheet for a corporation is shown on the next page. This balance sheet lets the reader compare where the company stood at the end of each of the past two years.

The balance sheet is a statement of the company's resources, financial obligations, and ownership investment. The balance sheet is divided into two sides: on the left are the assets; on the right are the company's liabilities and stockholders' equity (the owners' investment). Both sides are always equal or in balance. The company's assets include its cash, physical goods, and its financial claims on others. Liabilities represent the claims others have on the company. The stockholder's equity section includes the original investment of the owners. Since this example is a corporation, the equity section includes undistributed profits earned by the corporation to date (additional investment of earnings held by the corporation).

The following section briefly describes some of the important features of a balance sheet:

Typical Construction Company, Inc.
Balance Sheet
December 31, 2022

Assets	Current Year	Prior Year	Liabilities and Stockholders' Equity	Current Year	Prior Year
Current Assets			**Liabilities**		
Cash	$10,000	$15,000	Current Liabilities		
Retention	$40,000	$35,000	Accounts payable	$80,000	$60,000
Accounts Receivable	$70,000	$50,000	Notes payable	$25,000	$30,000
Total current assets	**$120,000**	**$100,000**	Accrued expenses payable	$20,000	$20,000
			Accrued payroll	$20,000	$18,000
Inventories			Misc taxes payable	$5,000	$10,000
Construction in progress	$200,000	$160,000	Federal income taxes payable	$30,000	$12,000
Less: partial billings or contracts	-$120,000	-$100,000	**Total, current liabilities**	**$180,000**	**$150,000**
Costs or contracts in excess of billings	**$80,000**	**$60,000**	Long-term liabilities		
Raw Materials	$30,000	$30,000	Bank loan, truck and equipment; 14% due	$100,000	$90,000
Total Inventories	**$110,000**	**$90,000**	**Total, Liabilities**	**$280,000**	**$240,000**
Prepaid Expenses (permits and licenses, etc.)	$20,000	$25,000			
Total, Current Assets	**$250,000**	**$215,000**	**Stockholders' Equity**		
			Common stock, $5 par value, authorized, issued and outstanding 10,000 shares	$50,000	$50,000
Property, plant and equipment					
Leasehold improvements	$4,000	$4,000	Retained earnings	$70,000	$60,000
Office furniture and fixtures	$2,000	$2,000			
Small tools	$10,000	$10,000	**Total, Stockholders' Equity**	**$120,000**	**$110,000**
Construction equipment	$154,000	$130,000	**Total, Liabilities and Stockholders' Equity**	**$400,000**	**$350,000**
Less: accumulated depreciation	-$20,000	-$15,000			
Net property, plant and equipment	**$150,000**	**$131,000**			
Other Assets		$4,000			
Total Assets	**$400,000**	**$350,000**			

ASSETS (left columns)

Assets are categorized as either current or fixed and are listed in order of declining liquidity. (Liquidity refers to the speed with which an item can be converted into cash or, put another way, the ability of the organization to pay its current debt.) Current assets are the first items listed on the left side of the balance sheet. These are the assets that are either cash or capable of being converted into cash in the normal course of business, generally within one year from the date of the balance sheet. In addition to cash (money on hand and deposits in the bank), the other items that will be turned into cash include retentions, accounts receivable, inventories, and prepaid expenses. After current assets, the balance sheet lists fixed assets.

All of these are briefly described below:

- **Cash**: Immediately available or liquid funds.

- **Retention**: A specified amount, usually 10 percent, withheld from progress payments to the contractor pending satisfactory completion and final acceptance of the project. This amount you have already earned even though you have not yet been paid.

- **Accounts Receivable**: The amounts due from customers (other than retentions) in payment for construction projects.

- **Inventory**: Includes all materials, labor, and direct and indirect overhead on jobs currently in progress. (For an example of direct and indirect costs, refer to the Internal Revenue Code Sections 263A [capitalization and inclusion in inventory costs of certain expenses] and 451 [general rule for taxable year of inclusion]).

- **Prepaid Expenses**: Goods or services the company buys and pays for before use. Examples are insurance premiums and office supplies.

- **Property, Plant, and Equipment**: Sometimes called fixed assets or plant and equipment, this group of assets includes physical resources a contractor owns or acquires for use in operations and has no intention to resell. Regardless of their current market value, fixed assets are valued at their original cost less accumulated depreciation. Sometimes property, plant, and equipment may be leased rather than owned. The value of the leased property is often included with the fixed assets and the lease payments are included with the liabilities.

- **Other Assets**: Resources not included under current assets, or under "Property, Plant, and Equipment" are placed here.

Section III

Examples include scrap materials or equipment held for resale and long-term receivables.

LIABILITIES (right columns)

Liabilities, like assets, are broken down into two major categories: current liabilities and long-term liabilities. Liabilities represent obligations to pay money, pay other assets or render future services to others. The relationship of current and fixed assets and current and long-term liabilities will become apparent when you learn how to analyze the information presented in the financial statements.

Current Liabilities: This item includes debts of the company that become due within one year of the balance sheet date. Current assets are the source from which these payments are usually made. Management must be aware of this relationship and maintain sufficient current assets or control the amount of current liabilities to avoid becoming delinquent in its bills. In our example, Typical Construction Company, Inc. has $180,000 of current liabilities composed of the following items:

- **Accounts Payable**: Money owed to suppliers and subcontractors.

- **Notes Payable**: Balance of the principal owed on a written promissory note.

- **Accrued Expenses Payable**: Money owed for interest, services, insurance premiums, and other fees that are not included under accounts payable. Thus, expenses that have been incurred but are not due for payment on the date of the balance sheet are grouped under accrued expenses payable.

- **Accrued Payroll**: Salaries and wages that the contractor currently owes to employees.

- **Miscellaneous Taxes Payable**: Amounts estimated by the accountant to have been incurred during the accounting period and are owed to local and state governmental agencies.

- **Federal Income Taxes Payable**: Amount of liability for taxes owed to the federal government.

  <u>NOTE:</u> Different organizational forms will have different tax obligations.

LONG-TERM LIABILITIES

Long-term liabilities are notes or mortgages due one year beyond the balance sheet date. In our sample balance sheet, Typical Construction Company, Inc. owed $100,000 on a bank loan due more than a year in the future. This loan was secured by using certain equipment as collateral.

Stockholders' Equity (right column): The stockholders' equity section of the balance sheet, also called net worth or equity, represents the claim of the owners on the assets of the business. Different organizational forms use different names for this section of the balance sheet, but basically this is the original investment of the owners. Our example is a corporation, and the stockholders' equity section has two accounts.

Capital Stock: The total amount invested in the business by the contractor in exchange for shares of common stock at par value. Par value is arbitrarily established and need not be the same as the current market price of that share of stock.

Retained Earnings: Total corporation earnings from its beginning, minus the total dividends declared (distributions to owners) since the corporation was founded. This account represents additional investment by the owners who were willing to forego a larger distribution of the company's earnings.

INCOME STATEMENT

The income statement summarizes the operations of the company over a period of time. For the Typical Construction Company, Inc. (see next page) the period of time is one year. The balance sheets presented for Typical were year-end balance sheets with the income statement summarizing the operations during the intervening time period. Income statements are often prepared to cover shorter operational periods (e.g., quarter or month).

Basically, the income statement shows business revenue, expenses, and the resulting profit or loss for a given accounting period. Since the revenues are matched against the related costs and expenses, the difference between the two is how much the corporation makes or loses. This profit or loss is often called the "bottom line" because it is an important indicator of performance, and it is also the last line of the income statement.

Note, however, that this is only one performance indicator that financial statements report. The relationships of the various expense categories to total revenue presented in this statement must be understood if the company is to be effectively managed.

The components of this income statement are illustrated as follows:

Typical Construction Company, Inc.
Income Statement
for the year ending December 31, 2022

	Current Year	Prior Year
Sales of Residences	$1,250,000	$1,000,000
Cost of Operations		
Cost of Sales	1,030,000	850,000
General and administrative expenses	91,000	75,000
Operating expenses	23,900	22,000
Total operating expenses	1,145,000	947,000
Income Before Provision for Federal Income Tax	105,000	53,000
Provision for Federal Income Tax	30,000	12,000
Net Profit for year	$75,000	$41,000

Income: The revenue amount reflects all the billings made to customers for completed projects, as well as work in progress. This is an example of the accrual basis previously discussed. In our example for Typical Construction Company, Inc., the sales of residences for the current year were $1,250,000, which represents amounts billed for completed projects and work in progress.

Cost of Operations: Cost of operations in the contracting business is comprised of all costs and expenses associated with running the business, with the exception that federal income taxes are shown on another line. By totaling all the costs of operations and subtracting these from the revenue, the operating profit of the company can be found. In our example, Typical Construction Company, Inc., the total cost of operations for the current year is $1,145,000, which, when subtracted from the net sales, leaves an operating profit of $105,000. This represents the amount of profit earned by the contractor without taking into consideration federal income taxes.

Within the Cost of Operations section of the Income Statement are several important amounts:

Direct Labor: The actual cost for labor payroll for all jobs worked on during the period covered by the income statement.

The amount of direct labor and the percentage of direct labor to the total cost of any particular project should be closely monitored by management. Direct labor expense is an important variable in determining the ultimate profit of the company. The labor percentage is also a direct measurement of the efficiency of the workers and the performance of supervision.

Direct Labor Burden: This includes all payroll taxes, insurance, and employee benefits associated with the labor payroll. If the workers belong to a union, the direct labor burden will include union benefit assessments and, in some cases, association fees.

Materials Used: This includes the cost of all materials used on the job, and is usually the largest single expense item on the income statement. Since materials comprise such a large part of the total cost of contracting, this account should be carefully controlled and every effort made to ensure that purchasing is done efficiently.

Other Direct Costs: These costs include all items, other than those listed above, that are directly chargeable to individual jobs. For example, permits, bonds, insurance, and equipment rentals would be included here.

General and Administrative Expenses: This figure on the income statement is comprised of all items of expense of a general nature that cannot be specifically attributed to individual construction projects.

Whether individual expenses will be listed separately or combined with others will vary among accountants and contractors.

Pretax Income: To get this figure, the total operating expenses were subtracted from the sales of residences. This figure is called Income Before Provision for Federal Income Tax for those corporations that are subject to federal taxation. Certain corporations, as well as sole ownerships and partnerships, do not pay taxes on income; the income is reported on the owner's personal tax returns. This is another example of how the organizational form the contractor initially chooses will influence the content of the financial statements.

Net Profit for Year: This figure is often called net income and represents the sum of all revenues minus all expenses including taxes, if applicable. Net profit or income is commonly referred to as the "bottom line."

Statement of Changes in Financial Position

The Statement of Changes in Financial Position, also called the Statement of Sources and Applications of Funds, is a third major financial statement. It shows how funds were obtained and where funds were used. We do not show an example of this statement because in many small operations it is not used. However, if a contracting company is going to be audited by certified public accountants for the purpose of presenting financial statements to creditors or others, a Statement of Changes in Financial Position may be necessary.

Financial Analysis and Ratios

While the figures listed in the financial statements are meaningful and important taken alone, they become even more valuable when compared with other information. For example, comparing any balance sheet item for the current year with the prior year immediately provides added information. Did the figure increase? Decrease? If so, by how much in absolute dollars? How much in percentage terms?

The comparison of financial relationships is often done in three ways.

1. The first method is the comparison of current financial data with prior years. Very often, businesses will compare three to five years of key items, such as revenue and net income. This type of comparison gives the reader an idea as to the trends over time.

2. The second method is to compare the current financial data with that of other businesses within the same industry. Sources for industry data are provided by organizations, such as Robert Morris Associates, Dun and Bradstreet, Inc., and Standard and Poor's, and are available on many websites that offer financial information. This information also can be found at large local libraries and at local California State University libraries.

3. The third method used in interpreting financial statements is ratio analysis. The relationship between any two figures within the current financial data is called a ratio. For example, if current assets are $100,000 and current liabilities are $50,000, the relationship of current assets to current liabilities ($100,000/$50,000) may be shown as 2 to 1, or 2:1 (ratio). The bank loan officer who is to recommend the establishment of a line of credit (short-term loan) would be interested in the current ratio and quick ratio, as the bank

would expect the contractor to repay the loan in the near term.

Current Ratio

One very important kind of information that can be readily determined from the balance sheet is the ability of the company to pay debts when due (sometimes referred to as liquidity). The difference between the total current assets and the total current liabilities is called **working capital**.

One way of looking at working capital is that it represents the amount that is free and clear if all current debts are paid off. A comfortable amount of working capital gives a company the ability to meet its obligations and take advantage of opportunities.

What is a comfortable amount of working capital? To help answer this question, the current ratio provides additional helpful information. To calculate the current ratio, divide total current assets by total current liabilities. In the example of Typical Construction Company, Inc., the figures are:

$$\frac{\text{Current Assets } \$250,000}{\text{Current Liabilities } \$180,000} = \quad 1.39$$

Therefore, for each $1 of current liabilities there is $1.39 in current assets to back it up.

Quick Ratio

The quick ratio is another, more conservative way of testing the adequacy of the current liquidity of the company. Instead of using current assets, quick assets are substituted because these are quickly converted into cash. One simple method of determining the quick assets is total current assets minus inventories. In our example:

Current Assets	$250,000
−Inventories	−$110,000
Quick Assets	$140,000

Quick Ratio:

$$\frac{\text{Quick Assets}}{\text{Current Liabilities}} \qquad \frac{\$140,000}{\$180,000} \quad = \quad .78$$

For the above analysis, we can see that we have $.78 of assets that may readily be converted into cash for each $1 of current liabilities that will require cash payments shortly.

The long-term creditors (banks or insurance companies) would be interested in the ratio of total liabilities to net worth. This measure indicates the relative proportions of the contractor's assets supplied by creditors and owners. In the event that the company defaulted on its debts, this ratio indicates the degree of safety for the creditors.

Net sales to net working capital, net sales to total assets, and net income to net worth are all measures of the efficiency of the company's use of its resources. These measures are important indicators to management. Net sales to net working capital (low ratio) might be attributed either to an excess of working capital or to inadequate sales. Management should examine each ratio, keeping in mind that if the ratios reflect a weakness, the manager then must analyze the problem area and develop possible solutions, e.g., more vigorous collection effort to reduce the size of receivables.

Keep in mind that the ratios also are interdependent. When the receivables are reduced, the cash generated by the collection effort may be used to reduce long-term liabilities and improve the debt ratio. Management must not focus its attention narrowly. The broad perspective created by knowledge of business principles is essential for success.

FINANCIAL MANAGEMENT

The financial management section focuses first on the need for financial resources; second, on the sources; and finally, on how to best determine if those financial resources are being fully utilized.

Capitalization

Capitalization refers to the total of financial resources made available to the owner. These financial resources are used to acquire the physical assets necessary to conduct the business. As you assess your financial requirements, the more obvious needs to finance the tools, vehicles, and other equipment (physical resources) used daily in the business are recognized first. The need for additional financing of office expenses, licenses, payroll expenses, bonding, rentals, etc. is critical for the business because of the differences between when you must pay and when you get paid.

The amount of working capital required depends on the type of contracting business. The progress payments required under contracts for custom building and remodeling may be used to meet payroll expenses and material costs. The typical contract provides for three or more payments, 90 percent during the construction phase and the final 10 percent upon completion and expiration of the lien period. This final 10 percent is the "retention." The contractor cannot collect more than the percentage already completed. The contractor must be aware that differences in the timing of expenditures and receipts may limit their capacity to finance the business, particularly if the company commits itself to new jobs before final payments on completed jobs have been received.

The significance of "retention" must not be underestimated. Retention usually exceeds profits and therefore represents a claim on working capital. Retention payments to the individual contractor may be held up through no fault of the contractor. The total project must be accepted before retentions are released. The problem is even greater for the subcontractor who completes their phase early in the project and must contend with a long waiting period. Since these funds are not available for use elsewhere in the business, the contractor must often finance the costs through borrowing.

Speculative builders require larger amounts of capital than custom builders. Consequently, speculative builders often must provide substantial financial resources to qualify for loan commitments.

Sources of Financing

The new business owner typically lacks the needed financial resources. Two types of external financing are available—**equity funds** and **debt**. Equity funds are supplied by investors who acquire some control of the business and a share of future profits. These funds remain in the business. Debt represents borrowed dollars that require both the repayment of the original amount and periodic interest payments. The owner does not normally give up control of the business.

EQUITY FUNDS

The typical sources of these funds are acquaintances of the new owner-contractor. Equity funds are sometimes available from private venture capital companies, small business investment corporations that are funded by the federal Small Business Administration, and minority enterprise small business investment companies. These sources are usually restricted to businesses with a proven track record in a growing industry.

DEBT

Long-Term

Banks may offer long-term financing to contractors with good credit ratings, technical knowledge, and capacity for repayment as evidenced by financial planning in the form of projected balance sheets, income statements, and cash budgets.

The Small Business Administration (SBA) does not make direct loans, but it does guarantee repayment of a loan. For more information, visit www.sba.gov.

Short-Term

The operating business may want to establish a line of credit with a bank to meet some of its short-term needs for working capital. Through the line of credit, commercial banks can provide the working capital necessary to complete the awarded contract, with the loan requiring repayment when the contractor is paid.

The bank loan officer will normally require balance sheets and income statements on the business for the current period, as well as over several prior years. The contractor is advised to have these reports prepared by a certified public accountant so that they meet professional accounting standards. The lender will expect to be provided with information on the contract up for bid, as well as all uncompleted contracts. The loan officer will evaluate:

> **Character**: Includes experience with similar jobs and locations; business reputation with lenders, suppliers, and subcontractors; and reasonableness of bid.

> **Capacity**: Requires an evaluation of current workload, availability of equipment, and financial resources available to withstand any reasonable loss. The financial strengths of the awarding agency, and subcontractors and suppliers also are important considerations.

> **Certainty**: What are the chances that repayment will be affected by unexpected losses on existing business? Are completion dates realistic? Is there a chance that penalties will be assessed for delays?

Bank loans to speculative builders may include funds necessary to provide offsite improvements, as well as the construction of buildings. Funding also may be arranged to acquire land for future development.

OPERATIONS MANAGEMENT

Job Selection

The planning involved in job selection requires knowledge of the general level of business activity in the local area, the need for new construction, costs of materials and labor, the contractor's current financial resources, the contractor's technical expertise, and any new architectural or structural advances.

Bidding and Estimation (Planning)

Accurate bidding requires that the contractor map out the entire construction process. The time spent on this detailed work ensures the accuracy of cost estimates necessary for the contractor to make a profit. Careful review of the job requires on-site inspection (walk the job), review of plans and specifications, identification of equipment required and the financing method (purchase, lease, rental), and the need for subcontractors.

Materials required are determined from takeoffs (quantity and measurements taken from plans) that are converted to costs on the estimation form. Prices should be obtained from published price lists and quotes from suppliers and subcontractors. It is important to include sales tax and freight costs. Cash discounts should not be included unless the contractor is certain that sufficient financial resources will be available so that accounts payable may be repaid during the discount period.

Labor costs are calculated according to work classification. These costs include not only the hourly wage rate, but also payroll taxes, health and welfare benefits, vacation pay, and required insurance.

Other direct costs that must be examined include permits and other fees; interest, loan commitment fees, points, and other charges on borrowed funds; equipment owned or rented; and any additional insurance that may be required.

Fuel and lubricant expenses, general maintenance, and small tools represent indirect costs that may be charged to the project and should not be overlooked.

The contractor also must identify the overhead expenses. Overhead normally includes such expenses as office rental, supplies and wages, advertising, bad debts, storage charges, and any other general administrative costs.

When all the costs have been totaled, the contractor must add profit. The contractor will seriously jeopardize the business by omitting the allowance for profit, especially if the bid has a low margin and there is any chance of underestimation. Insufficient profits threaten both capitalization (losses reduce retained earnings) and cash flow (payments to vendors may exceed receipts) to the extent that bankruptcy and/or dissolution may be the result.

Common pitfalls that can be avoided include the following: Bidding on projects for which the plans and specifications are not completely understood, insufficient planning so that hurried analysis becomes necessary, overextension of the managerial and/or financial resources of the company, and bidding against the competition and not on the job itself. It is easier to avoid financial difficulty by not bidding on a job for which you lack the capability than to try to salvage the job after a poor bid has been accepted.

The Construction Process (Coordination and Control)

The estimate that is the basis for the bid becomes a budget for the project. Without extensive planning and scheduling, lack of coordination can result in added costs that quickly reduce the profits.

If the estimation has been done properly, the job was broken down into a job schedule to arrive at the number of labor hours required. Actual construction, however, requires that materials and labor be brought together at the proper time. Two methods of production scheduling may be used to accomplish this coordination.

The **bar chart** (Figure 6.A) is a fundamental scheduling technique that shows graphically the starting and finishing times for the individual tasks that make up the job. This scheduling approach is simple but overlooks some interrelated tasks.

The **critical path** method (Figure 6.B) is a more complex tool that better interrelates the tasks. This technique derives its name from the key path through the network that considers all the tasks to be completed.

Any delay in one of these tasks will result in overall delay of the project. This procedure, therefore, identifies the tasks on which the manager must focus attention to ensure completion of the project on time.

FIGURE 6.A
Building a New Home: Construction Schedule

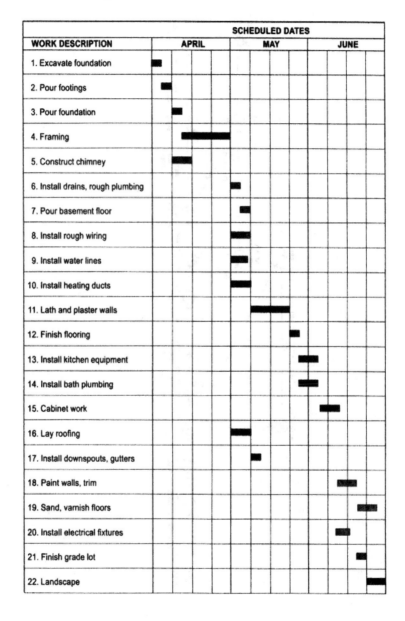

FIGURE 6.B
Building a New Home: Critical Path Analysis

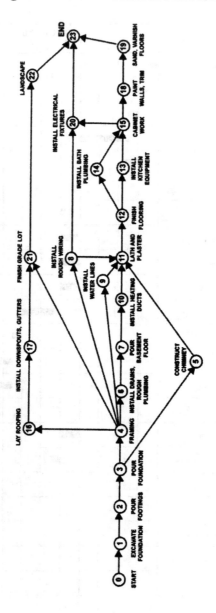

Controlling Costs

Contractors typically have a small permanent payroll that consists of a foreperson and skilled journeypersons. This force can be expanded by union hiring halls, which means that the contractor must be knowledgeable about the union's master labor contract. The work of the various subcontractors must be scheduled and coordinated with the overall job. The small contractor must expect to spend most of the day at the site, coordinating these activities and resolving conflicts. Subcontractors should be chosen on the basis of their ability to perform, as well as cost, since untimely delays quickly eliminate the potential savings of the lowest bid.

Purchasing is an essential part of the job because of the high cost of carrying an inventory of materials. As with subcontractors, reliability is equally important as price. The contractor will typically develop trade relations with a limited number of suppliers. Costs are best controlled by checking with other suppliers if prices increase significantly, by verifying order quantities, by taking cash discounts when offered, and by not overstocking.

Risk Management

Businesses operate under conditions of uncertainty. Unexpected property and casualty losses can severely damage the business's prospects. Insurance is a means of reducing the company's exposure to risk. The contractor should consult an insurance agent or broker to design a comprehensive insurance package to meet the company's specific needs. This package could include:

- Workers' compensation insurance.
- Fire insurance.
- Liability insurance.
- Automobile insurance.
- Fidelity bonds.
- Business interruption insurance.
- Employee health and life insurance.
- "Key person" insurance.

If the contractor lacks sufficient funds for total coverage, a planned approach to risk management becomes necessary. Principles that should be followed include:

Section III

- Covering the largest loss exposure first; property and liability insurance should be reviewed yearly to reflect changes in valuation and take current court judgments into account.

- Using deductibles to significantly reduce costs.

- Reviewing coverage yearly to reflect changes in the business.

- Taking time to understand the implications of any changes in the insurer's contracts.

Marketing Management

Personal contacts represent the major source of business for the new contractor. Small and medium-sized contracting businesses rely on referrals. The extent of the marketing effort is limited by the sources available to the contractor.

LEGAL CONSIDERATIONS AND REMEDIES

A continuing relationship with an attorney familiar with the construction business can be helpful. Printed standard forms of agreements used in the industry are available from the contractor's particular trade association, the American Institute of Architects, or the Associated General Contractors of America. It is a good idea to have an attorney double-check the contract for compliance with all regulatory agency requirements.

In addition to helping with the interpretation of contracts, the attorney can help in choosing the form of business organization; making sure all necessary documents are filed with city, county, and state governments; and helping resolve any differences that might occur between the contractor and other business parties.

There are typically four types of contractual agreements between the builder and owner with which the contractor should be familiar. These are the lump-sum, the cost-plus, the unit-price, and the guaranteed-maximum cost contract. Each of these contract types specifies different terms and obligations with which the contractor must be familiar.

In addition, the contractor has to be aware of the proper filing methods, the number of days for filing, and other documents, such as lien release notices, lien claims, and notices of completion. It is essential for the contractor to be familiar with the California mechanics lien law.

Disputes

At the outset, you should be aware that there is no good lawsuit. You will never be fully compensated for your out-of-pocket expenses, much less for the physical, emotional, and business disruption that a lawsuit can create. Therefore, you should do everything within reason to settle your differences. This can be done in a number of ways:

Get It in Writing

Besides the statutory requirement that certain contracts be in writing, it is extremely important that a contract of any significance at all be in writing. First, a written document will not be forgotten like a verbal agreement and is more likely to keep the parties aware of their rights and responsibilities.

Second, if there is a dispute and an arbitrator or judge is asked to interpret the agreement, they are more likely to find in accordance with your true intent if that intent is in writing.

Extras

"Changes" or "extras" added to a contract tend to contribute to disputes. To determine if something is in addition to or outside the scope of the original agreement, you must be able to accurately determine what the original agreement states. If the original agreement is well defined and in writing, it will be much easier to determine if something is added or changed.

Once you determine that a request is different than what was agreed to (whether more or less), document that fact in writing. You should also immediately negotiate the effect of the change, such as cost and time. Tell your customer what is going on and allow the customer to determine if the change is worth it. If you and your customer agree to the change, make sure both parties sign the written change order.

Communication

Whenever possible you should communicate with your customer and encourage your customer to communicate with you. Frequent "punch lists" are a good idea. A walk-through near the end of the job to determine the items that are left to be completed is recommended. Correct any deficiencies quickly.

It is a good idea to document the progress of the project and keep your customer up to date.

Closely allied with the communication of progress is frequent billing. By invoicing regularly, you will minimize your business's cash demands while keeping your customer informed. Let your customer know what is going on; and, if

there is a problem, face it head-on before it becomes
insurmountable.

Even if you have done everything you could, you may still find
yourself involved in a dispute. You have various options:

Settlement

Lawsuits are costly, time-consuming, and disruptive. If at all
possible, you should attempt to settle your differences.

Small Claims

If you are owed money and cannot settle your dispute, you
might consider filing suit in small claims court rather than
courts of greater jurisdiction. Although you cannot foreclose
on a mechanics lien in small claims court, you may get a
monetary judgment of up to $10,000 (see CCP §116.221).
Aside from the fact that if a defendant loses they have an
automatic right of appeal, small claims judgments are as
valid and binding as courts of greater jurisdiction.

Small claims courts are fast and economical. Your claim can
usually be heard within one month and the entire cost should
be minimal. You and your customer must represent
yourselves. Neither you nor your customer may be
represented by an attorney. For information about small
claims court topics, such as filing a complaint and collecting a
judgment, see the California Courts website:
https://www.courts.ca.gov/selfhelp-smallclaims.htm. If the
defendant loses in small claims court, there is an automatic
right of appeal. But even that appeal is usually within a
month or two.

Arbitration

Another option for settling disputes is arbitration. CSLB has
its own arbitration program, but many contractors choose to
bring their disputes to private arbitrators.

Arbitration is different from court proceedings in a number of
ways. Usually, both parties must agree to arbitration and can
often have a say in choosing the arbitrator.

Either side may present its own case or use an attorney.

Because of its more informal nature, some of the protections
afforded in court, such as the rules of evidence, are not always
followed. Arbitrators tend to allow much more evidence than
would be allowed in court. Most arbitration decisions are

binding (the arbitrator's decision is final). Finally, there are very few grounds for appeal of an arbitration decision.

If you want potential disputes to be solved via *private* arbitration you must use the arbitration notice in Business and Professions Code section 7191. If the parties to the contract agree to such a notice, they will not be allowed access to CSLB's arbitration program (unless both parties later sign a waiver of the contractual arbitration clause).

CSLB Arbitration Program

To help resolve complaints filed with the board, CSLB offers two free arbitration programs: a mandatory program for disputes involving alleged damages of less than $15,000, and a voluntary program for disputes involving alleged damages of between $15,000 and $50,000. When the alleged damages are less than $15,000, CSLB can order the contractor to a mandatory CSLB arbitration meeting.

To qualify for CSLB arbitration, disputes must comply with certain criteria:

- The contractor's license must be in good standing (current and not under suspension) at the time of the alleged violation.

- The contractor cannot have a record of prior violations.

- The parties cannot have previously agreed to private arbitration in the contract or elsewhere.

Mechanics Liens

Mechanics liens and "stop notices" are briefly touched on in this portion of the book; these two avenues are discussed in greater detail in the next portion. However, you should note that, as a contractor (one who enhances the value of property), you are entitled to a lien on the property and may be entitled to a lien on any construction funds. The manner in which these liens are perfected is very technical and the time limits are short. You should be thoroughly familiar with the manner and means of perfecting your lien rights, such as giving the preliminary notice, recording the mechanics lien, filing a stop notice, and filing suit to foreclose. These remedies can be utilized by anyone who improves the property.

Filing Suit

Regardless of your mechanics lien rights, as with any other businessperson, you can file suit for breach of the construction contract if someone does not fulfill their obligation. Certainly, if the customer does not pay you money when it is due, you can sue them. In the event that you have been unsuccessful in resolving the dispute and have not availed yourself of the mechanics lien rights due to the strict statutory requirements, you can still file suit. The seller of any product or service is entitled to compensation. You, as a contractor, also are entitled to your money.

If you are a corporation, you cannot represent yourself in court and must obtain the services of an attorney. In the event that you are a partnership or a sole proprietor, you can represent yourself in court and are not required to have an attorney represent you.

CALIFORNIA MECHANICS LIENS AND STOP NOTICES

Mechanics Liens

In California, mechanics liens are provided for in Article 14, Section 3 of the California Constitution:

> Mechanics, persons furnishing materials, artisans, and laborers of every class, shall have a lien upon the property upon which they have bestowed labor or furnished materials for the value of such labor done and materials furnished; and the Legislature shall provide, by law, for the speedy and efficient enforcement of such liens.

The manner in which mechanics lien rights are perfected is based on statutes. The California Supreme Court has held that mechanics lien rights are constitutional.

The list of people who may claim liens as provided by the Constitution, as well as the California Civil Code, is as follows: mechanics; persons furnishing materials; contractors; subcontractors; lessors of equipment; artisans; architects; registered engineers; licensed land surveyors; machinists; builders; teamsters; draymen; and all persons and laborers performing labor on or bestowing skill or other necessary services to, furnishing material or leasing equipment to be used or consumed in, or furnishing appliances, teams, or power contributing to a work of improvement. This does not mean that these people must have a contract directly with the owner. However, they must have a contract with the agent of the owner and every contractor, subcontractor, architect, builder, or other person having charge of a work of improvement and held to be an agent of the owner.

A material supplier is not the agent of the owner and, therefore, a material supplier's supplier is not entitled to a statutory lien. Further, to perfect your lien, the work and/or materials, etc. must be incorporated into the structure. That is to say, it has to be installed.

Stop Notices

A mechanics lien is a lien on property. A stop notice is a lien on funds. You may use one or the other, or both. However, it should be noted that in public works, you cannot file a mechanics lien; therefore, your only remedy may be a stop notice. Since the stop notice is a lien on funds, it may be preferable to a mechanics lien in some instances.

Other Remedies

Even though you may be one of the people protected by the mechanics lien laws in California, you are not precluded from other remedies. You can still sue on a contract theory or on any other legal theory available. So, even if you have not availed yourself of the mechanics lien rights, you still have alternative legal remedies.

Procedure

The mechanics lien laws and stop notice requirements are relatively complicated and must be adhered to very strictly. Listed below is a procedural checklist to help you complete each step necessary in a timely manner.

Mechanics Lien and Stop Notice Checklist

I. Prior to Serving the Notices

Before serving the notices, it is important to do all of the following:

- ☐ Obtain the legal description of the property.

- ☐ Determine the name of the owner and the extent of the owner's interest in the property.

- ☐ Determine if the owner is the one requesting the improvement. (If not, what is the interest of the person requesting it and are there any others who claim an interest in the property, such as lenders, etc.).

- ☐ Determine if you are a prime contractor, subcontractor, laborer, or material supplier.

- ☐ Determine the name of the construction lender (if any).

- ☐ Consider the effect of a bond or joint control.

II. Subcontractors and Material Suppliers

A. Within 20 days from first furnishing labor or materials, serve a "Preliminary 20-day Notice" on the owner, the original contractor, and construction lender. No matter how many deliveries you make, or the time span over which you furnish labor or materials, only one Preliminary Notice is required.

The notice must include specific wording to inform a property owner of a new responsibility to notify anyone else who served a Preliminary Notice.

NOTE: You may also file the Preliminary 20-day Notice with the county recorder in the county in which the property is located. The county recorder will then notify you when a Notice of Completion or Notice of Cessation is recorded on the property.

The most common method for serving a notice is to use first class certified or registered mail, return receipt requested, postage prepaid, addressed to the residence or place of business of the person being served, or at the address shown by the building permit, or at an address contained on a recorded mortgage or trust deed. Be sure to keep post office receipts for later use if you need to file a claim and prove it in court. A Preliminary Notice also may be served by personal delivery or by leaving it with a "person in charge" at the residence or place of business of the person you wish to serve (must be an adult).

B. After the work is completed or ceases, the following apply:

1. If the owner records a Notice of Completion after completion of work of improvement (this requires signature of owner or owner's agent), you should not do additional work under the contract. (While this notice provision is designed to primarily protect the owner, it might serve to increase the funds accessible to satisfy your claim and indicate that you have performed your contractual obligations.)

2. Labor must have ceased for at least 30 days before the owner is entitled to record a Notice of Cessation. If the owner files a Notice of Cessation of labor or a Notice of Completion, then:

    (a) Within 30 days of the owner recording either a Notice of Cessation or Completion, the subcontractor must record a Claim of Lien with the county recorder. Also at this time, serve stop notices (see below).

        NOTE: An owner who files a Notice of Cessation or a Notice of Completion must notify any potential lien claimants within 10 days of recording the notices.

This notification is designed to let you, the potential lien claimant, know that the time for filing a Claim of Lien has been reduced. This provision does not apply to a residential property of four or fewer units.

(b) File Lien Foreclosure Action within 90 days of recording a Claim of Lien and record a *lis pendens* at the same time. You must also file an action on the stop notice at this time, if applicable. If you want more than 90 days in which to foreclose, then after recording the lien but before 90 days elapses, give credit to the owner and record a notice of the fact and terms of credit. Within 90 days after your offer expires, you must foreclose. You can keep granting extensions by the above procedure, but you must foreclose within one year after work is completed. The action should be brought to trial within two years after commencement.

3. If no Notice of Completion or Notice of Cessation is recorded and either:

(a) Labor ceases and the owner or agent uses work of improvement, or

(b) The owner or agent accepts improvement, then:

(1) Within 90 days of any of the above acts, record a Claim of Lien. Also, at this time, serve stop notices (see below).

(2) Within 90 days of recording the lien, file a Lien Foreclosure Action and record a *lis pendens* at the same time. If you want to extend the time in which to file a foreclosure action, after you record the Claim of Lien but before 90 days elapse, give credit to the owner and record a notice of the fact and terms of credit. The extension will be for 90 days after the credit expires, but even with extensions you must foreclose within one year after the work is completed. The action should be brought to trial within two years after commencement.

4. Stop Notices:

(a) Serve stop notices on the owner, bonded stop notices on the construction lender, or anyone holding funds.

Section III

(b) If no mechanics lien has been recorded, and a surety payment bond has been recorded, then the notice must be served on the surety.

(c) File suit on the notice at the same time that you file a Lien Foreclosure Action.

III. Prime Contractors

A. Within 10 days after completion, you may record a Notice of Completion. (While this notice provision is designed to primarily protect the owner, it might serve to increase the funds accessible to satisfy your claim and indicate that you have performed your contractual obligations.) Do not do additional work under the contract. This notice requires the signature of the owner or the owner's agent.

B. Within 60 days of recording the above, record the Claim of Lien.

C. Within 90 days of recording the lien, file a Lien Foreclosure Action and record a *lis pendens* at the same time. If you want to extend the time in which to file a foreclosure action, after you record the Claim of Lien but before 90 days elapse, give credit to the owner and record a notice of the fact and terms of credit. The extension will be for 90 days after the credit expires, but even with extensions you must foreclose within one year after the work is completed. The action should be brought to trial within two years after commencement.

D. If the owner records a Notice of Cessation of Labor or a Notice of Completion, do the following:

NOTE: Labor must have ceased for at least 30 days before the owner is entitled to record the Notice of Cessation.

1. Within 60 days of recording a Notice of Cessation or a Notice of Completion, the contractor must record a Claim of Lien.

2. Within 90 days of recording the Claim of Lien, file a Lien Foreclosure Action, and record a *lis pendens*. If you want more than 90 days in which to foreclose, then after recording the lien but before the first 90 days elapse, give credit to the owner and record a notice of fact and terms of credit. Within 90 days after your "offer" expires, you must foreclose. You can keep granting extensions by the above procedure, but you must foreclose within one year after work is completed. The action should be brought to trial within two years after commencement.

E. If no Notice of Completion or Cessation is recorded, and either:

   1. Labor ceases and owner or agent uses the work of improvement; or

   2. Owner or agent accepts improvement, then:

      (a) Within 90 days of any of the above acts, record a Claim of Lien.

      (b) File a Lien Foreclosure Action within 90 days of recording Claim of Lien and record a *lis pendens* at the same time. If you want more than 90 days in which to foreclose, then after recording the lien but before the first 90 days elapse, extend credit to the owner and record a notice of the fact and terms of credit. Within 90 days after your offer expires, you must foreclose. You can keep granting extensions by the above procedure, but you must foreclose within one year after work is completed. The action should be brought to trial within two years after commencement.

NOTE: Per AB 457, which took effect in 2011, the definitions of "claim of lien" and "mechanics lien" are the same. This law also requires that a Notice of Mechanics Lien be served on the owner or person believed to be the owner of the property or on the construction lender or original contractor, and that a "proof of service affidavit" to the above mentioned party or parties be completed and signed by the person serving the Notice of Mechanics Lien. Failure to serve the mechanics lien and confirm a proof of service affidavit will cause the mechanics lien to be unenforceable. These requirements are detailed at the following link: http://www.leginfo.ca.gov/pub/09-10/bill/asm/ab_0451-0500/ab_457_bill_20090806_chaptered.html

GLOSSARY OF TERMS
ASSOCIATED WITH MECHANICS LIENS

Awarding Authority is the owner or the agent of the owner who awards an original building or construction contract, also known as the prime contract. This term is usually used with public works.

Bonded Stop Notice is a bond that accompanies a stop notice to a construction lender and must be in a sum equal to 1 ¼ times the amount of the claim. The bond, along with the stop notice, must be delivered by certified or registered mail or in person, to the persons responsible for administering or holding construction funds. Should the claimant lose their action (lawsuit on the bond), then the claimant must pay all costs that may be awarded against the owner or contractor or construction lenders. This is the reason for the bond on the stop notice.

Claimant is the person claiming or asserting the right or demand (the person claiming mechanics lien or stop notice rights).

Claim of Lien (mechanics lien) is a written statement signed and verified by the claimant or by the claimant's agent that must state the following:

1. The amount of claimant's demand (after deducting credits and offsets).

2. The name of the owner or reputed owner, if known.

3. The kind of labor, services, equipment, or materials furnished by the claimant.

4. The name of the person who employed the claimant or to whom the claimant furnished the labor, services, equipment, or materials (the contractor who hired you if you are a subcontractor or the owner who hired you if you are the prime contractor).

5. A description of the site sufficient for identification.

Defendant is the person who defends themselves or who denies a claim. A defendant is the person against whom relief or recovery is sought in an action or suit.

Lien Foreclosure Action is a lawsuit to foreclose the mechanics lien.

Lis Pendens is a notice that a lawsuit is pending and that the lawsuit affects real property. It warns everyone who might acquire the property that they may be bound by an adverse judgment.

Notice of Cessation is a written notice, signed and verified by the owner or their agent, stating:

1. Approximate date when labor on the job stopped.

2. Confirmation that no further labor has been performed since the recording of the notice.

3. Name and address of the owner.

4. Nature of the interest or estate of the owner.

5. Street address of the site, if any, or a description of the site sufficient for identification.

6. Name of the original contractor, if any, for the work of improvement.

Notice of Completion is a written notice, signed and verified by the owner or their agent, stating:

1. Date that the job was finished.

2. Name and address of the owner.

3. Nature of the interest or estate of the owner.

4. Street address of the site, if any, or a description of the site sufficient for identification.

5. Name of the original contractor, if any, for the contract covering the portion of the work of improvement completed.

The Notice of Completion must be recorded in the Office of the County Recorder of the county in which the site is located within 10 days after completion of the project. If the Notice of Completion is recorded, then the time within which you have to record your mechanics lien is 60 days if you are a prime contractor and 30 days if you are a subcontractor. If this notice is not filed in a timely manner, you have a 90-day period within which to record the claim.

Notice of Non-Responsibility is a written notice, as described below, which is signed and verified by a person or that person's agent who owns or claims to have an interest in the property being improved and who has not caused the work of improvement. For example, the owner completes this notice when their tenant is requiring the work of improvement without the owner's direction. This notice must contain:

1. Description of the site sufficient for identification.

2. Name and nature of the title or interest of the person giving the notice.

3. Name of the purchaser or person holding the lease (lessee), if known.

4. Statement by the person giving the notice that they will NOT be responsible for any claims arising from the work of improvement.

Within 10 days of discovering the work of improvement, the person asserting non-responsibility must post this notice in a conspicuous place on the site and must record the notice in the Office of the County Recorder of the county in which the site is located.

Original Contractor, also known as prime contractor, is usually a general contractor.

Owner includes any person(s) having some title or interest in a parcel of real property.

Payment Bond is a bond usually procured by the owner or contractor in an amount sufficient to pay all claims of claimants. The bond gives the claimant the right to recover in any suit brought on the bond. Usually the bond is used to protect against mechanics liens and substitutes the bond as security instead of the real property.

Prime Contractor see "Original Contractor" above.

Stop Notice is a written notice, signed and verified by the claimant or the claimant's agent, that puts a lender or anyone else holding construction funds on notice that there is money due and owed to the claimant. It must state the following:

1. Type of labor, services, equipment, or materials furnished or agreed to be furnished by the claimant.

2. Name of the person to or for whom the labor, services, etc. were furnished.

3. Amount, based on value as near as possible, of the work or equipment already completed or furnished and the amount of the whole work agreed to be done or furnished.

If involving a private work of improvement, the notice must be delivered to the owner personally or left at their residence or place of business with a person in charge or delivered to their architect, if any; and, if the notice is served upon a construction lender holding construction funds and maintaining branch offices, it must be delivered to the manager or other responsible person at the office or branch administering or holding the construction funds.

If involving any public work for the state, the notice must be filed with the director of the department that initiated the contract.

If involving any other public work, the notice must be filed in the office of the controller, auditor, or other public disbursing officer whose duty it is to make payments under the provisions of the contract or with the commissioners, managers, trustees, officers, board of supervisors, board of trustees, common council, or other body by whom the contract was awarded.

Any stop notice may be served by registered or certified mail with the same effect as personal service.

The stop notice obligates the person holding construction funds to withhold sufficient funds to satisfy the amount in the stop notice. If the person holding the funds does not withhold sufficient funds to satisfy the stop notice, then the lender or whoever else is holding the funds may be responsible to the claimant directly.

To bind a construction lender, the stop notice must be bonded. The bond that accompanies a stop notice to any construction lender must be in the sum equal to 1 ¼ times the amount of the claim. The bond must be delivered along with the stop notice in person or by certified or registered mail to the persons responsible for administering or holding the construction funds.

Should the claimant lose in their action (lawsuit on the bond), then the claimant must pay all costs that may be awarded against the owner or contractor or construction lender. That is the reason for the bond on the stop notice.

Subcontractor is any person who does not have a contract directly with an owner. The subcontractor has a contract with and from the prime contractor or another subcontractor. A subcontractor is usually a specialty contractor but can also be a general contractor.

EXPERT ADVISORS

The new contractor must be prepared to seek out and utilize the expertise of specialists in business affairs, just as the contractor has come to rely upon skilled specialists in the building trades. If the business is to be organized as a partnership or corporation, an attorney, preferably one who specializes in drawing up partnership agreements or incorporation papers, should be consulted. The local bar association may be a good source for recommendations.

The accounting records should be prepared by a certified public accountant (CPA) whose practice specializes in building trade industry clients, if at all possible. The CPA or tax lawyer should be consulted for specialized tax problems.

The U.S. Small Business Administration (SBA) along with its resource partners, Service Corps of Retired Executives (SCORE), Small Business Development Centers (SBDC), and Small Business Information Centers (BIC), offer a wide variety of services to individuals wanting to start or expand their business. Services include one-on-one counseling, workshops, training, business seminars, and SBA's guaranteed loan programs designed to help with your business financing needs. Contact them at:

U.S. Small Business Administration
(800) U ASK SBA (827-5722)
www.sba.gov
Email: answerdesk@sba.gov

BIDDING ON GOVERNMENT CONTRACTS

Contractors bidding in California should know that there are a variety of federal, state, and local governmental agencies, as well as public utilities and private corporations, which may require a bidder to take specific steps to achieve established minority, women, and disabled veteran business enterprise (DVBE) goals. For information on fulfilling these goals on bids for certain government contracts, check with the following agencies:

California Department of General Services,
Procurement Division
Office of Small Business and DVBE Certification (OSDC)
707 Third Street
West Sacramento, CA 95605

Phone: (916) 376-5000
Email: OSDSHelp@dgs.ca.gov
Website: http://www.dgs.ca.gov/pd/

The U.S. Department of Commerce Minority Business Development Agency (MBDA) provides direct business development services to minority businesses through a network of Minority Business Development Centers (MBDCs) located in most major cities throughout the country. Services may include identification of contracting opportunities, preparation of bid proposals, identification of lending sources, preparation of loan applications, etc.

As per Presidential Executive Order 11625, the following ethnic groups are among those eligible for assistance from MBDA-funded organizations: African-Americans, Puerto Ricans, Spanish-speaking Americans, Native Americans, Eskimos, Aleuts, Hasidic Jews, Asian-Pacific Islanders, and Asian Indians. For more information, visit http://www.mbda.gov.

Section III

SECTION IV.

CONSTRUCTION STANDARDS AND SAFETY REGULATIONS

Chapter 7.

Safety and Health in Construction

According to the California Division of Labor Statistics and Research, the construction industry has one of the highest occupational injury rates of any major industry in the state.

Following is a description of many of the general safety and health requirements and practices that affect contractors in California. In addition, there are many safety and health requirements that apply to specific construction trades and activities.

It is your responsibility to be informed about the local, state, and federal laws and regulations that affect your business, as well as which regulatory agencies have or share jurisdiction in your area.

RESPONSIBLE AGENCIES

Regulatory and advisory roles pertaining to construction safety and health in California are performed by several state agencies. The following agencies are those with whom contractors and their employees are most likely to be involved.

California Department of Industrial Relations, Division of Occupational Safety and Health (DOSH)

DOSH, within the Department of Industrial Relations, is given the authority to implement and enforce the Cal/OSHA program according to the provisions of California Labor Law. The Cal/OSHA program is approved, monitored, and partially funded by federal OSHA in accordance with the Federal Occupational Safety and Health Act of 1970. To ensure that working conditions are safe and healthful and that employers meet their obligations to provide such conditions,

Section IV

DOSH enforces occupational safety and health regulations, responds to employees' complaints, makes routine inspections of workplaces, and investigates serious and fatal job-related injuries and illnesses.

DOSH works to ensure safe and healthful working conditions for California employees through standards enforcement, consultation service to employers, occupational safety and health research, and by providing information and publications.

Cal/OSHA Consultation Service

The Cal/OSHA Consultation Service provides free on-site consultation. Its goal is to help employers develop solutions to their occupational safety and health problems so that they can voluntarily comply with safety and health standards. The Consultation Service staff identifies workplace hazards and helps employers develop and improve the company's Injury and Illness Prevention Program (IIPP), as per Title 8 California Code of Regulations (*T8 CCR §3203*).

When the Consultation Service staff visits a jobsite and reviews the contractor's IIPP, they not only identify occupational hazards, but also point out areas where the safety orders require specific actions and recommend ways to achieve compliance.

In contrast to DOSH, the Consultation Service staff do not issue citations or penalties. Instead, they give the contractor a report that outlines the conditions found and describes the need for corrective action.

Occupational Safety and Health Standards Board

The Occupational Safety and Health Standards Board adopts, amends, or repeals California safety and health standards. (State standards must be at least as strict as the federal OSHA standards.) The Standards Board also has the authority to grant petitions to adopt or amend regulations, and to grant variances to employers.

To keep current on any proposed or new construction safety orders, such as washing facilities at construction jobsites, visit the website at www.dir.ca.gov/OSHSB.

Occupational Safety and Health Appeals Board

The Occupational Safety and Health Appeals Board hears and makes decisions on appeals concerning citations, orders, civil penalties, and abatement dates issued by DOSH. Employers, employees, and employee representatives may participate in proceedings of the Appeals Board.

Other Agencies Share Responsibility

The following agencies share additional responsibilities in the area of hazardous substances: California Department of Public Health, Department of Toxic Substances Control, California Environmental Protection Agency, State Allocation Board, Office of Public School Construction, California Department of Resources Recycling and Recovery, Department of Fish and Wildlife, California Highway Patrol, California Department of Forestry and Fire Protection, U.S. Environmental Protection Agency, and regional air emissions control boards.

NOTE: CSLB may take action against a contractor who has violated regulations under the jurisdiction of other agencies.

CONSTRUCTION SAFETY LEGAL REQUIREMENTS

Every employer and employee must comply with all applicable occupational safety and health standards, rules, regulations, and orders. The bulk of the legal requirements governing employer responsibilities and employee rights can be found in the California Labor Code and Title 8 of the California Code of Regulations (CCR). Title 8 regulations that pertain to most construction contractors can be found in the Construction Safety Orders (beginning with section 1500) and the General Industry Safety Orders (beginning with section 3200).

Title 8 regulations also include many other safety orders that encompass regulations that govern more limited trades and activities, such as the Electrical Safety Orders and Compressed Air Safety Orders. Title 8 includes requirements for permits, safe work practices, operations, and equipment. In some cases, detailed specifications that apply to construction work are included.

Many of the employer responsibilities and employee rights are detailed in the Cal/OSHA poster, *Safety and Health Protection on the Job*. **Each construction contractor is required to post at least one copy of this poster and the Code of Safe Practices** at each location where employees report to work each day, or, if the employees do not usually work at or report to a single establishment, at the location(s) from which the employees operate to carry out their activities *(Labor Code §6408(a); T8 CCR §340)*. The notice must be posted in a conspicuous place where notices to employees are customarily posted.

MULTIPLE EMPLOYER WORKSITES

Construction and non-construction worksites may have multiple employers (*T8 CCR §§336.10-336.11*). When multiple employers are involved, DOSH has developed the following enforcement criteria to categorize employers into four types:

- *Exposing Employer*: the employer whose employees were exposed to the hazard.

- *Creating Employer*: the employer who actually created the hazard.

- *Controlling Employer*: the employer who was responsible, by contract or who has the authority for ensuring that the hazardous condition is corrected.

- *Correcting Employer*: the employer who had the responsibility for actually correcting the hazard.

NOTE: DOSH may cite the creating, controlling, or correcting employers regardless of whether or not their own employees were exposed to the hazard.

DOSH may determine if the available information indicates that the exposing employer meets each of the following five criteria for an affirmative defense:

1) The employer did not create the hazard.

2) The employer did not have the responsibility or the authority to have the hazard corrected.

3) The employer did not have the ability to correct or remove the hazard.

4) The employer can demonstrate that the creating, controlling, and/or correcting employers, as appropriate, were specifically notified or were aware of the hazards to which the employees were exposed.

5) The employer took appropriate feasible steps to protect the employees from the hazard; instructed them to recognize the hazard; and, where necessary, informed them of how to avoid dangers associated with it, including removing the employees from the job if the hazard was extreme and there was no other way to protect them from the hazard.

INJURY AND ILLNESS PREVENTION PROGRAM (IIPP)

Accidents are costly. These costs may include:

- Productive time lost by the injured employee.

- Productive time lost by employees and supervisors attending to the accident victim.

- Clean-up and start-up of operations interrupted by the accident.

- Time to hire or to retrain other individuals to replace the injured employee until their return.

- Time and costs for repair or replacement of any damaged equipment or materials.

- Costs of continuing all or part of the employee's wages, in addition to compensation.

- Reduced morale among employees, and perhaps lower efficiency.

- Increased workers' compensation insurance rates.

- Costs of completing paperwork generated by the incident.

- Costs of legal representation in civil and criminal cases.

In California, every employer is required to provide a safe and healthful workplace for their employees by doing everything reasonably necessary to protect their lives, safety, and health (*Labor Code §§6400, 6401, 6401.7, 6402, and 6403*). The key to accomplishing this goal is the requirement that every employer have and maintain an effective IIPP. Senate Bill 198 placed strict guidelines for such a program into law in 1989. The regulations required by that law, and other related laws, can be found in *T8 CCR §§1509, 1510, 1511, 1512, 1514, and 3203*.

Professional consultants from the Cal/OSHA Consultation Service are available to provide free assistance to employers and employees on how to set up an effective IIPP at your jobsite. These consultants can also provide safety and health training to employees at your jobsite.

Required IIPP Elements

Your IIPP must be a written plan that includes procedures and is put into practice and documented. Some of the requirements are:

- **Management commitment to safety and health**

  This commitment should be evident from strong organizational policies, procedures, incentives, and disciplinary actions that ensure employee compliance with safe and healthful work practices. Management commitment also is demonstrated by

Section IV

the allocation of company resources—financial, material, and personnel—for identifying and controlling hazards, purchasing protective equipment, and training employees in safety and health.

- **Identify the person(s) with program implementation authority and responsibility**

- **System for communicating with employees**

Communicate with employees in a way readily understandable by all affected employees on matters related to occupational safety and health. Employees should be encouraged to report unsafe conditions with the assurance that management will take action to correct the problem and that the employee need not fear reprisal for reporting the problem.

   o   As part of this communication system, every construction contractor must adopt a written Code of Safe Practices. The contents must include language equivalent to the applicable general statements included in Plate A-3 of the appendix to the Construction Safety Orders in Title 8. In addition, each employer should include other safety guidelines that fit the operations more exactly. The Code of Safe Practices must be posted at a conspicuous location at each jobsite office or be provided to each supervisory employee, who shall have it readily available.

- **System for identifying, evaluating, and controlling existing or potential workplace hazards**

   o   No employee shall be required or knowingly permitted to work in an unsafe place, unless for the purpose of making it safe, and then, only after proper precautions have been taken to protect the employee while doing such work.

   o   Prior to starting work, the employer must survey the jobsite to determine what hazards may be involved and what safeguards will be necessary to ensure that the work is performed safely.

   o   Periodic, scheduled inspections must be conducted to identify unsafe conditions and work practices. The frequency of inspections should be determined by the type and magnitude of the hazards, the proficiency of the employees, how recently any changes in equipment or procedures were introduced, and the history of workplace injuries and illnesses.

o   Occupational illnesses and accidents must be investigated. The investigatory procedures must include a written report of each event.

o   The employer shall permit only qualified persons to operate equipment and machinery.

o   Every employer must provide and require employees to use safety devices. Employers must adopt and require the use of methods and procedures that are reasonably adequate to make the work and workplace safe.

- **Develop, maintain, and document training programs for supervisors and employees**

  Every employer program should provide information about general safe work practices, plus specific instruction with regard to hazards unique to a job assignment.

  o   When employees are first hired, they must be given instructions regarding job hazards, safety precautions, and the employer's Code of Safe Practices.

  o   Employees given new job assignments must be given training for this work.

  o   Supervisors must conduct "toolbox" or "tailgate" safety meetings with their crews at least every 10 working days.

  o   Where employees may be subjected to known or new jobsite hazards, such as flammable liquids, gases, poisons, caustics, harmful plants and animals, toxic materials, confined spaces, etc., they must be instructed in the recognition of the hazard, in the procedures for protecting themselves from injury, and in the first aid procedure in the event of injury.

  NOTE: Specific requirements pertaining to exposure to hazardous substances are discussed below.

  o   Employees need instruction when new protective equipment or different work practices are to be used for existing hazards.

- **Ensure the availability of emergency medical services for employees**

  Every employer must have a suitable number of appropriately trained and available staff to render first aid. A first aid kit must be present at each workplace.

Section IV

Keep in mind that safety regulations and codes establish minimum standards.

EMPLOYEE COMPLAINT RIGHTS AND PROTECTIONS

Employees or their representatives who believe that unsafe or unhealthful conditions exist in their workplace have the right to file a complaint with any DOSH office. DOSH must investigate good faith complaints of serious violations within three working days of receiving the complaint. Complaints of non-serious violations must be investigated within 14 calendar days (*Labor Code §6309*).

The name of the person making the complaint will be kept confidential by DOSH (*Labor Code §6309*). Employees may not be fired or otherwise punished for filing a good faith complaint with DOSH or for cooperating in any investigation of unsafe working conditions or work practices (*Labor Code §6310*). Employees have a right to refuse to perform work that would violate any labor code provision or occupational safety or health regulation, where the violation would create a real and apparent hazard to the employee or other employees. No employee may be laid off or discharged for refusing to perform such work (*Labor Code §6311*).

INJURY AND ILLNESS REPORTING
AND RECORDKEEPING REQUIREMENTS

In addition to the documentation of safety inspections and employee training described above, employers must file reports and maintain records of occupational injuries or illnesses. There are specific requirements for the form and content of this information.

Reporting Requirements

- Employers must report immediately by telephone or other method to the nearest DOSH district office any work-related fatality or serious injury or illness suffered by an employee. "Immediately" means as soon as practically possible, but not longer than eight hours after the employer knows of, or, with diligent inquiry would have known of, the incident (*T8 CCR §342*). "Serious injury or illness," in general, means any employment-related injury or illness that requires inpatient hospitalization for a period in excess of 24 hours for other than medical observation, or in which an employee suffers a loss of any member of the body or suffers any serious degree of permanent disfigurement (*T8 CCR §330*).

- Employers must file a complete report of every occupational injury or illness that results in absence from work for a full day or shift beyond the date of the injury or illness, or which requires medical treatment beyond first aid (*Labor Code §5401(a); Labor Code §6409.1; T8 CCR §14001*).

The report must be made within five days of the incident, using Form 5020, "Employer's Report of Occupational Injury or Illness," published by the Department of Industrial Relations, Division of Labor Statistics and Research. In the event an employer has filed a report of injury or illness, and the employee subsequently dies as a result of the reported injury or illness, the employer must file an amended report, which indicates the death. This amended report must be filed within five days after the employer is notified or learns of the death. Self-insured employers must report directly to the Division. Employers who are insured by a workers' compensation insurance carrier must file the report with the carrier.

NOTE: Insured employers are required to file a report with their carriers of EVERY work-related illness or injury (*Labor Code §3760*).

Recordkeeping Requirements

Records of accidents, work-related injuries, illnesses, and property losses serve a valuable purpose. As stated above, occupational illnesses, accidents, and near misses must be investigated. Standard investigatory procedures must include a written report of each incident. Records of scheduled periodic hazard identification inspections must be maintained, as well as safety training that employees and supervisors have received. When all of these records are reviewed together, causes of the injuries and accidents can be identified. An employer may determine they need different or additional inspection and/or training practices that will more likely prevent similar illnesses or accidents from recurring.

Employers must keep records when injuries or illnesses occur on the Cal/OSHA Form 300, "Log of Work-Related Injuries and Illnesses." The only exception applies to employers who had no more than ten employees for all shifts combined during any 24-hour period during the previous calendar year. Employees, former employees, and their representatives shall have access to the Form 300 log.

For more details on this regulation, see Title 8 CCR Sections 14300–14300.48.

Section IV

PERMITS

Permits must be obtained from DOSH before an employer undertakes the following kinds of work (*T8 CCR §341*):

- Construction of trenches or excavations that are five feet or more deep, into which a person is required to descend.

- Construction of any building, structure, falsework, or scaffolding more than three stories high. (One story is 12 feet in height. A tower crane erected on a construction project is considered, for the purposes of these requirements, a structure.).

- Demolition of any building, structure, or the dismantling of falsework, or scaffolding more than three stories high or the equivalent height (36 feet).

- Underground use of diesel engines for work in mines and tunnels.

The contractor should contact the local DOSH office to obtain information regarding who must obtain the permit, when the permit must be obtained, the fees charged to obtain the permit, and any additional requirements the employer must comply with before the permit can be granted.

Annual permits may be obtained for the erection and dismantling of scaffolds, falsework, vertical shoring systems, and construction of excavations or trenches (*T8 CCR §341.1*).

DOSH may conduct an investigation or require a safety conference prior to issuing the permit. Employees or their representatives are to be included in any required pre-job safety conference (*T8 CCR §341.1*).

Permits must be posted at or near each place of employment requiring a permit (*T8 CCR §341.4*).

An employer who is denied a permit by DOSH may appeal that denial to the Director of the Department of Industrial Relations (*T8 CCR §341.2*).

DOSH may at any time, upon a showing of good cause and after notice and an opportunity to be heard, revoke or suspend a permit (*T8 CCR §341.5*). The employer may appeal the revocation or suspension to the Director.

VARIANCES

Permanent Variance

An employer may apply to the DOSH Standards Board for a permanent variance from a California occupational safety and health standard, order, or special order, if the employer demonstrates that an equivalent method, device, or process can be used that will provide equal or better safety for employees. Applications are considered at variance hearings conducted by the Standards Board. Rules of procedure are contained in Chapter 3.5 of Title 8 of the California Code of Regulations.

Temporary Variance

DOSH may grant a temporary variance to employers if the employer files a proper application and establishes that (*Labor Code §6450–§6457*):

- They are unable to comply with a standard by its effective date because of the unavailability of professional or technical personnel or of materials and equipment needed to comply with the standard or because necessary construction or alteration of facilities cannot be completed by the effective date.

- They are taking all available steps to safeguard employees against the hazards covered by the standard.

- They have an effective program for coming into compliance with the standard as quickly as it can be put into practice.

A temporary variance of up to one year may be granted only after notice is given to employees and a hearing is held by DOSH. The temporary order may be renewed up to two times, for a maximum of 180 days each time. Anyone adversely affected by the granting or denial of a temporary variance may appeal that action to the Standards Board.

INVESTIGATIONS OF UNSAFE CONDITIONS

Employers may be subject to an inspection (without advance notice) in response to one or more of the DOSH criteria: imminent danger, fatality or serious accident, investigations of serious injuries or illness, employee complaint, public complaint, high hazards list, permits, etc. Also, firms in industries with higher-than-average potential risk are scheduled for inspections. During the inspection, employees may be interviewed, and photographs may be taken. An employee representative must have an opportunity to accompany a DOSH investigator on worksite inspections (*Labor Code §6314*).

Section IV

The employer is protected from having to reveal trade secrets as a result of an inspection or subsequent proceedings (*Labor Code §§6322 and 6396*).

When, in the opinion of DOSH, a place of employment or piece of equipment is in a dangerous condition, is not properly guarded, or is dangerously placed so as to constitute an imminent hazard to employees, DOSH may prohibit entry into the area or use of the equipment (other than, with DOSH approval, to eliminate the dangerous condition). DOSH will attach a conspicuous notice stating the limitations. The notice must remain in place until removed by DOSH after the area or equipment is made safe and the required safeguards or safety devices are provided (*Labor Code §6325*).

As a result of the investigation, the employer may receive a citation, notice, special order, information memorandum, or an order to take special action for any alleged violation of standards, rules, orders, or regulations. Violations will be classified as serious, general, or regulatory, and may be designated as repeat or willful. Citations will have financial penalty assessments.

Any citation (or copy of a citation) issued for safety and health violations must be posted at or near the place of violation where it is readily observable by affected employees for a period of three working days or until the condition is corrected, whichever is longer (*Labor Code §6318; T8 CCR §332.4*).

The employer may contest any citations, penalties, and abatement (correction) requirements through both formal and informal proceedings (*Labor Code §6319*).

Penalties will be based on the gravity and severity of the violation (*Labor Code §6319, §6423-6435*).

Penalties may be adjusted, based on:

- The size of the business.
- The good faith of the employer, including timely abatement.
- The employer's history of previous violations.

Employers who do not have an Injury and Illness Prevention Program shall receive no adjustment for either good faith or a positive history (*Labor Code §6428*).

The law contains other misdemeanor provisions related to such matters as revealing trade secrets and unauthorized advance notice of an inspection.

If, after inspection or investigation, DOSH issues a citation for a serious violation, it may conduct a reinspection at the end of the period fixed for abatement of the violation (*Labor Code §6320*).

HAZARDOUS SUBSTANCES

Information and Training

All employers who use hazardous substances and whose employees might be exposed under either normal work conditions or reasonably foreseeable emergency conditions resulting from workplace operations (e.g., equipment failure, rupture of containers, failure of control equipment, etc.) must provide their employees with information and training about these substances, the hazards of these substances, and how to handle these substances under normal and emergency conditions.

Manufacturers of these substances must prepare safety data sheets (SDS), and the manufacturers or sellers of these substances must provide the SDS to anyone who purchases them.

Employers and employees can find out what hazards are associated with particular substances or chemicals in the workplace, the recommended exposure levels, and the precautions to take in using these substances or chemicals by writing to:

HESIS (Hazard Evaluation System and
Information Service)
850 Marina Bay Parkway
Bldg. P, 3rd Floor
Richmond, CA 94804
(510) 620-5757

Employers must notify any employee who has been or is being exposed to toxic substances or harmful physical agents in concentrations at levels exceeding those prescribed by applicable standards, orders, or special orders, and inform any employee so exposed of corrective action being taken (*Labor Code §6408(e)*).

Employers must allow employees to observe monitoring or measuring of exposure to hazards (*Labor Code §6408(c)*).

Employees must have access to their medical records and exposure records to potentially toxic materials or harmful physical agents (*Labor Code §6408(d); T8 CCR §3204*).

Hazardous Substance Removal Work and Remedial Actions

NOTE: The removal of hazardous substances and related remedial actions do not include asbestos-related work, as defined in Labor

Code §6501.8, or work related to a hazardous substance spill on a highway (*B&P Code §7058.7*).

Contractors must have passed an approved hazardous substance removal certification exam before removing hazardous substances or taking related remedial actions (as defined in Chapter 6.8 of Division 20 of the Health and Safety Code) in cases that involve digging into the surface of the earth and removing the material from:

- A site listed pursuant to section 25356 of the Health and Safety Code.

- A site listed as a hazardous waste site by the Department of Toxic Substances Control.

- A site listed on the National Priorities List compiled pursuant to the Comprehensive Environmental Response, Compensation, and Liability Act of 1980 (42 U.S.C. section 9601 et seq.).

CSLB may require currently certified licensees to pass additional updated, approved hazardous substance removal certification exams based on new public or occupational health and safety information (*B&P Code §7058.7; Labor Code §142.7*).

Contractors must also comply with the "Hazardous Waste Operations and Emergency Response Standards" (*Labor Code §142.7; T8 CCR §5192*). These require:

- Specific work practices.

- The certification of employees and supervisors involved in hazardous substance removal work.

- The designation of a qualified person who shall be responsible for scheduling any air sampling, laboratory calibration of sampling equipment, evaluation of soil or other contaminated materials sampling results, and for conducting any equipment testing and evaluating the results of the tests.

- Holding a safety and health conference for all hazardous substance removal jobs before the start of actual work. The conference shall include representatives of the owner or contracting agency, the contractor, the employer, employees, and employee representatives. It shall include a discussion of the employer's safety and health program and the means that the employer intends to use to provide a safe and healthy place of employment.

Any contractor who engages in hazardous substance work, or any contractor or employer who either knowingly or negligently enters into a contract with another person to do hazardous substance work, when that person is required to be but is not certified pursuant to B&P Code §7058.7, is subject to penalty (*B&P Code §7028.1 and 7118.6*).

Lead in Construction Work

This section applies to all construction work where an employee may be exposed to lead. Construction work, in general, is defined as work for construction, alteration, and/or repair, including painting and decoration (*T8 CCR §1532.1*). Lead is defined as metallic lead, all inorganic lead compounds, and organic lead soaps.

Employers shall provide a written lead-work pre-job notification to the nearest DOSH District office as per T8 CCR §1532.1 (p)(1)-(p)(4) when work is planned that includes any of the tasks listed in subsection (d)(2). Also, employers are responsible for being knowledgeable about the permissible exposure limit (PEL); exposure assessment; methods of compliance; respiratory protection; protective work clothing and equipment; housekeeping procedures; and hygiene facilities, practices, and establishing regulated areas. The employer must also know the medical surveillance program and medical removal protection practices. Lastly, the employer is to display appropriate signs and allow employees to observe monitoring procedures.

The employer is required to provide employee information, training, and certification as per T8 CCR §1532.1(l). As required by T8 CCR §1532.1(l)(3), the employer shall ensure that all employees and supervisors that perform any lead-related construction work are trained by an accredited training provider and are then certified by the California Department of Health Services.

CARCINOGEN CONTROL

Employers in California must meet strict standards for the occupational health and safety of employees who handle carcinogenic (cancer-causing) substances on their jobs—for example, asbestos. These standards are part of the "Construction Safety Orders and General Industry Safety Orders" in Title 8 of the California Code of Regulations. Due to the extent and complexity of the many code requirements, contractors are urged to read the regulations themselves, including sections 1529, 1532, 1535, 8358, or Article 110 sections 5200-5220.

Registration Required for Carcinogen Use

Businesses involved in the use of carcinogens must inform DOSH as per T8 CCR §5203. Report of use must be mailed to:

Cal/OSHA Asbestos and Carcinogen Unit
1750 Howe Avenue, Suite 460
Sacramento, CA 95825
https://www.dir.ca.gov/dosh/asbestos.html

Requirements for Asbestos-Related Work

Asbestos is the most common carcinogen in construction and demolition work. Persons engaged in insulation, plasterboard, siding, and ceiling plasterwork risk higher-than-usual exposure to asbestos. Failure to adopt safe work practices for handling asbestos has caused many employees to develop asbestos-related disabilities and fatal diseases. It is your responsibility to familiarize yourself with the laws pertaining to asbestos.

The owner of a commercial or industrial building or structure, an employer, or a contractor who engages in, or contracts for, asbestos-related work must make a good faith effort to determine if asbestos is present before work begins. The contractor or employer must first ask the owner of a building or structure built prior to 1978 if asbestos is present. Failure to do so may result in a penalty (*Labor Code §§6501.9 and 6505.5*). Similar requirements exist in T8 CCR §1529(k)(1) and (2), "Communication of Hazards and Duties of Building and Facility Owners."

If DOSH has reasonable cause to believe that any workplace contains asbestos, and if there appears to be inadequate protection for employees at that workplace from the hazards of airborne asbestos fibers, DOSH may issue an order prohibiting use (*Labor Code §6325.5*).

"Asbestos-related work" means any activity which, by disturbing asbestos-containing construction materials, may release asbestos fibers into the air and which is not related to its manufacture, the mining or excavation of asbestos-bearing ore or materials, or the installation or repair of automotive materials containing asbestos (*Labor Code §6501.8*).

"Asbestos-containing construction material" means any manufactured construction material that contains more than one-tenth of one percent (0.1%) asbestos by weight (*T8 CCR §341.6*).

Asbestos Abatement

A contractor may not engage in asbestos-related work that involves 100 square feet or more of surface area of asbestos-containing materials unless the qualifier for the license holds an asbestos certification or a C-22 Asbestos Abatement classification and is registered by DOSH. Exceptions include contractors involved with the installation, maintenance, and repair of asbestos cement pipe or sheets, vinyl asbestos floor materials, or asbestos bituminous or resinous materials (*B&P Code §§7058.5 and 7065.01, and T16 CCR §7058.5*).

Any contractor who engages in asbestos-related work, or any contractor or employer who either knowingly or negligently enters into a contract with another person to do asbestos-related work, when that person is required to be but is not certified pursuant to B&P Code §7058.5, or does not hold the C-22 Asbestos Abatement license pursuant to T16 CCR §832.22, or is not registered by DOSH, is subject to penalty (*B&P Code §§7028.1 and 7118.5*). A contractor who *is not* certified for asbestos-related work or does not hold the C-22 Asbestos Abatement license may bid on a project involving this work if a separate contractor who is properly certified or licensed by CSLB and registered by DOSH performs the asbestos-related work.

Asbestos Abatement Registration

All contractors who perform asbestos-related work must be registered with DOSH. In addition, the State of California, a city, city and county, county, district, or public utility subject to the jurisdiction of the Public Utilities Commission shall be required to apply for a registration through the designated chief executive officer of that body. No registration fees shall be required, however, of any public agencies (*Labor Code §6508.5*).

DOSH registration applications, applications for renewal, and information can be obtained from the Asbestos Contractors' Registration Unit (ACRU) at:

ACRU-DOSH
P.O. Box 420603
San Francisco, CA 94142
Email: ACRU@dir.ca.gov
https://www.dir.ca.gov/dosh/acru/acruhome.htm

If the removal of asbestos-containing materials involves less than 100 square feet of surface area, CSLB does not require certification/licensure as an asbestos abatement contractor and DOSH does not require registration. However, a contractor is still doing asbestos-related work and must file a carcinogen "Report of Use" from the Occupational Control Unit of DOSH, and they (including others involved with the project) must also complete 40 hours of asbestos training. This training must be provided by a DOSH-approved asbestos trainer. In addition, contractors must follow the OSHA worker protection rules (*Title 8, California Code of Regulations, section 1529*).

Notification and Posting of Asbestos-Related Work

When an employer will be conducting separate jobs or phases of work that require asbestos removal registration, or where the work process may differ or is performed at noncontiguous locations, written notice must be provided to the nearest DOSH enforcement district office prior to commencement of any work (*Labor Code §6501.5; T8 CCR §341.7*). Furthermore, the employer must post a sign readable at 20 feet at the location where any asbestos-related work is to be conducted which states, "Danger–Asbestos. Cancer and Lung Hazard. Keep Out."

Asbestos-Related Work in Schools

When asbestos-related work is done in elementary or secondary schools, either public or private, additional standards must be met as per Title 40, Code of Federal Regulations (CFR) Part 763, Asbestos Hazard Emergency Response Act (AHERA).

Local education agencies are required to use only AHERA-accredited persons to perform the following tasks:

- Inspecting for asbestos-containing materials in school buildings.

- Preparing management plans concerning the presence of asbestos-containing materials in schools.

- Designing and drafting specifications for asbestos abatement projects.

- Supervising and conducting the abatement work.

Persons seeking accreditation must complete a training course approved by DOSH and pass an examination for that course. There are separate course requirements for inspectors, management planners, project designers, asbestos abatement contractors and supervisors, and for asbestos abatement workers.

Renovation and Demolition Work

Renovation and demolition jobs are subject to the National Emission Standards for Hazardous Air Pollutants (NESHAP), which are enforced by the federal Environmental Protection Agency and local air quality and air pollution districts. Before a renovation or demolition job begins on a site that may include asbestos-containing materials, one of these agencies must be notified. There are strict penalties for violations of the NESHAP requirements.

Disposal of Asbestos

The California Department of Toxic Substances Control, Hazardous Waste Management Branch, enforces the requirements governing the disposal of waste that contains asbestos. These requirements include the following (*Health and Safety Code §25143.7*):

- If a landfill is used, it must meet waste disposal requirements issued by the regional water quality control board that allows the disposal of such waste.

- The waste must be handled and disposed of in accordance with the Toxic Substances Control Act (*Title 15, United States Code, Chapter 53*) and all other applicable laws and regulations.

CONFINED SPACES

Safety and health practices for confined spaces are outlined in Title 8 of the California Code of Regulations Sections 5156, 5157, and 5158 (*Labor Code §142.3*). A permit-required confined space (*T8 CCR §5157*) is defined as a space large enough and so configured that an employee can bodily enter and perform assigned work; has limited or restricted means for entry or exit; and is not designed for continuous employee occupancy. In other confined space operations (*T8 CCR §5158*), confined space is defined by the concurrent existence of conditions where the existing ventilation is insufficient to remove dangerous air contamination, oxygen enrichment and/or oxygen deficiency that may exist or develop; and where ready access or egress for the removal of a suddenly disabled employee is difficult due to the location or size of the openings.

EXCAVATIONS AND TRENCHES

For regulations relating to permits for excavations and trenches, refer to the California Code of Regulations Title 8, Chapter 3.2, Article 2, Section 341 of the California Occupational Safety and Health Regulations (Cal/OSHA).

For definitions, general requirements, and information pertaining to excavations and trenching safety orders, see Title 8 of the California Code of Regulations, §1504, §1539–§1547 and Labor Code §142.3.

HOW TO OBTAIN ADDITIONAL INFORMATION

WHAT YOU NEED	WHERE TO GET IT
Browse and order free DOSH publications	www.dir.ca.gov/dosh/puborder.asp
California Occupational Safety and Health Standards— *Title 8 California Code of Regulations, Industrial Relations*. The entire Title 8 and the Safety Orders for each industry are available for purchase.	Barclays Official CA Code of Regulations P.O. Box 2006 San Francisco, CA 94126 (800) 888-3600, or, www.dir.ca.gov
Information concerning California Occupational Safety and Health requirements Free on-site consultation to discuss particular problems and obtain assistance and advice DOSH workplace posters	Cal/OSHA Consultation Services Offices (see list on the next page) or order posters online at: www.dir.ca.gov/wpnodb.html
Recordkeeping and Reporting Requirements *Log and Summary of Occupational Injuries and Illnesses (OSHA Form 300)* *California Work Injuries and Illnesses— Annual Report* *Work Injuries and Illnesses—Quarterly Report*	Department of Industrial Relations Division of Labor Statistics and Research P.O. Box 420603 San Francisco, CA 94142 (415) 703-3020 Statistics@dir.ca.gov Website: https://www.dir.ca.gov/oprl/ContactUs_O DResearch.htm

Chapter 8.

Regional Notification Centers: Underground Service Alert

What is a Regional Notification Center?

A regional notification center is an association of owners and operators of subsurface installations (water, gas, electric, telephone, sewer, oil lines, etc.). Damage to these underground structures may result in the disruption of essential public services and pose a threat to workers, the public, and environmental safety. The purpose of the center is to provide a single telephone number that excavators can use to give the center's members advance notification of their intent to excavate. The operators of the underground installations are then responsible for providing information about the locations of the facility, marking or staking the approximate location of their facility, or advising the excavator of clearance. Operators are only responsible for facilities they own; operators are not responsible for facilities they do not own.

Contacting a Regional Notification Center is a Requirement— Not an Option.

California Government Code Sections 4216-4216.9 require anyone planning to excavate to contact the appropriate regional notification center at least two working days (but not more than 14 calendar days) before beginning excavation. The center will issue an inquiry identification number to the excavator as confirmation of the call.

NOTE: An excavation permit is not valid without this identification number.

Who Must Comply:

- Any person or entity who plans to disturb the surface of the ground by digging, drilling, boring, etc.

Exempt Persons:

- An owner of private property who contracts with a California state-licensed contractor or subcontractor for an excavation project that does not require an excavation permit;

- An owner of private property (who is not a licensed contractor or subcontractor) who, as a part of improving their principal residence, does work that does not require an excavation permit.

- Any person or private entity that leases or rents power-operated or power-driven excavating or boring equipment to a contractor or subcontractor licensed pursuant to contractors' state license law, regardless of whether an equipment operator is provided for that piece of equipment, if the signed rental agreement contains the following provision:

> "It is the sole responsibility of the lessee or renter to follow the requirements of the regional notification center law pursuant to Article 2 (commencing with Section 4216) of Chapter 3.1 of Division 5 of Title 1 of the Government Code. By signing this contract, the lessee or renter accepts all liabilities and responsibilities contained in the regional notification center law."

Steps Required for Compliance:

- Every contractor or subcontractor excavating at a jobsite must have their own Underground Service Alert (USA) identification (ticket) number for the excavation work they are performing.

- Excluding emergency situations, parties planning excavation activities must contact the appropriate regional notification center not less than two working days, nor more than 14 calendar days, prior to the start of work.

THE REGIONAL NOTIFICATION CENTER CALL IS FREE: 811/(800) 640-5137.

- Upon notification, the center will issue an identification (ticket) number. The ticket number will be valid for 28 calendar days. If work is to continue past 28 calendar days, the ticket number must be revalidated by again notifying the center before the ticket number expires.

- At the site, excavators must clearly mark the boundaries of the work area, usually with white paint.

- Within these boundary markings, operators of underground installations must then provide information about their facilities, mark or stake the location of their lines clearly using the appropriate color to show what type of installation is present, or advise of clearance.

- If, during the course of the job, the operator's markings become no longer visible, the excavator must contact the regional center and request that the operator re-mark the lines within two working days.

- Using the operator's markings, an excavator must determine the exact location of underground facilities with hand tools or a vacuum device before any power equipment may be used.

- After January 1, 2023, all new subsurface installations must be mapped using a geographic information system and maintained as permanent records of the operator.

- An excavator must notify the regional notification center within 48 hours of discovering or causing damage.

Helpful Hints

- Provide the beginning date and time of your excavation.

- Give your name, company's name, company's mailing address, email address, telephone number where you can be contacted, nature of work (grading, drilling, etc.), whom the work is being done for, name of the foreman, permit name and number, if excavation has been outlined in white paint, and a description of the excavation site.

- When describing your excavation site, give the address or description where you will be digging (including side of street, the intersection corner, footage, and total distances or other tie-in measurements), and nearest intersecting street, city, and county.

Penalties

- Any operator or excavator who negligently violates any portion of Government Code sections 4216–4216.9 is subject to a fine not to exceed $10,000.

- Any operator or excavator who knowingly and willfully violates any portion of Government Code sections 4216–4216.9 is subject to a fine not to exceed $50,000.

- Any operator or excavator who knowingly and willfully violates any of the provisions of this article in a way that results in damage to a gas or hazardous liquid pipeline subsurface installation and that results in the escape of any flammable, toxic, or corrosive gas or liquid is subject to a civil penalty in an amount not to exceed one hundred thousand dollars ($100,000).

- An excavator also may be subject to third party claims for damages arising from the excavation work.

- Violation of Government Code sections 4216–4216.9 could result in disciplinary action and possible revocation of your contractor license by CSLB.

REGIONAL NOTIFICATION CENTERS

Underground Service Alert of Northern California and Nevada: 811
www.usanorth811.org

Serves the following counties in Northern California:

Alameda, Alpine, Amador, Butte, Calaveras, Colusa, Contra Costa, Del Norte, El Dorado, Fresno, Glenn, Humboldt, Kern, Kings, Lake, Lassen, Madera, Marin, Mariposa, Mendocino, Merced, Modoc, Mono, Monterey, Napa, Nevada, Placer, Plumas, Sacramento, San Benito, San Francisco, San Joaquin, San Luis Obispo, San Mateo, Santa Clara, Santa Cruz, Shasta, Sierra, Siskiyou, Solano, Sonoma, Stanislaus, Sutter, Tehama, Trinity, Tulare, Tuolumne, Yolo, and Yuba

Serves the entire state of Nevada

Service: Monday–Friday, 6 a.m.–7 p.m., excluding holidays

Underground Service Alert of Southern California—

811
www.digalert.org

Serves the following counties in Southern California:

Imperial, Inyo, Los Angeles, Orange, Riverside, San Bernardino, San Diego, Santa Barbara, and Ventura

Service: Monday–Friday, 6 a.m.–7 p.m., excluding holidays

Chapter 9.

Preservation of Native American Remains

California has one of the largest Native American populations in the United States. With approximately 115 federally recognized tribes and more applying for recognition, California Native American lands include reservations and rancherias in over half of California's counties. Historically, Native American land holdings encompassed the entire state of California.

Several laws provide for the protection and sensitive treatment of these human remains and associated burial goods (Health and Safety Code section 7050.5; Public Resources Code sections 5097.9-5097.991). The intent of the law is to provide protection to Native American burials and associated grave goods from vandalism and inadvertent destruction.

REPORTING REQUIREMENT

In the event of discovery or recognition of any human remains in any location other than a dedicated cemetery, there shall be no further excavation or disturbance of the site or nearby area. Upon the discovery of human remains or burial artifacts at any site other than a dedicated cemetery, the following actions must be taken immediately:

1. Stop work immediately at that site and any nearby area reasonably suspected to have remains and contact the county coroner.

2. The coroner has two working days to examine the remains after being notified by the person responsible for the excavation. If the remains are Native American, the coroner has 24 hours to notify the Native American Heritage Commission.

3. The Native American Heritage Commission will immediately notify the person it believes to be the most likely descendant of the deceased Native American.

4. The most likely descendant has 24 hours to make recommendations to the owner or representative for the treatment and disposition, with proper dignity, of the remains and grave goods.

5. If the owner doesn't accept the descendant's recommendations, the owner or the descendant may request mediation by the Native American Heritage Commission.

6. If mediation fails to provide measures acceptable to the landowner, the landowner or their authorized representative shall reinter the human remains and items associated with Native American burials, with appropriate dignity, and in a location on the property not subject to further subsurface disturbance.

PENALTIES

It is a felony to obtain or possess Native American remains or associated grave goods. (*See Public Resource Code §§5097.94, 5097.98, and 5097.99.*) Any person who knowingly or willfully removes, obtains, or possesses any Native American remains or associated burial artifacts, without authority of law, is guilty of a felony, punishable by imprisonment in state prison.

ADDITIONAL INFORMATION

To learn more about the protection and preservation of Native American burial grounds, human remains, and associated grave goods, contact the Native American Heritage Commission at:

Native American Heritage Commission
1550 Harbor Boulevard, Suite 100
West Sacramento, CA 95691
(916) 373-3710
Email: nahc@nahc.ca.gov
Website: www.nahc.ca.gov

Chapter 10.

Construction of Wells

LICENSE REQUIRED FOR WATER WELLS

Section 13750.5 of the California Water Code states:

> No person shall undertake to dig, bore, or drill a water well, cathodic protection well, groundwater monitoring well, or geothermal heat exchange well, to deepen or re-perforate such a well, or to abandon or destroy such a well, unless the person responsible for that construction, alteration, destruction, or abandonment possesses a C-57 Water Well contractor license.

REPORTING REQUIREMENTS

Water Wells, Cathodic Protection Wells, and Monitoring Wells

California Water Code sections 13751 through 13754 require persons who construct, alter (including, but not limited to, drilling, deepening, re-perforation, or abandonment), or destroy a water well, cathodic protection well, monitoring well, or geothermal heat exchange well, to file a report of completion, called the "Well Completion Report, DWR 188," with the California Department of Water Resources (DWR) within 60 days after completion of the work. Earlier versions of the form were called "Water Well Driller's Report." All of these reports are also called "well logs" or "driller's logs."

This requirement also applies to persons who convert—for use as a water well, cathodic protection well, or monitoring well—any oil or gas well originally constructed under the jurisdiction of the California Department of Conservation.

The State of California and other agencies use the information provided by these reports to evaluate groundwater resources, to protect groundwater quality, and to conserve water supplies

NOTE: Failure to file the Well Completion Report is a misdemeanor (*Water Code §13754*) and constitutes cause for disciplinary action against your contractor license (*Business and Professions Code section 7110*).

How and where to file

Drillers submit their well completion reports to DWR with the Online System of Well Completion Reports (OSWCR). OSWCR users create an account based on their C-57 license that DWR will validate. Upon approval, users will be able to submit Well Completion Reports.

More information is available on the DWR website: www.water.ca.gov

WELL STANDARDS

Standards for construction, modification, rehabilitation, and destruction of water wells, monitoring wells, and cathodic protection wells are published by DWR in Bulletin 74, the California Well Standards. The current Standards are contained in Bulletin 74-81 *Water Well Standards: State of California,* and the draft supplemental Bulletin 74-90 *California Well Standards: Water Wells, Monitoring Wells, Cathodic Protection Wells.*

Counties and other local jurisdictions may have adopted local well ordinances with standards in addition to the statewide standards contained in Bulletin 74-90. The designated local enforcing agency, which is usually the county Department of Environmental Health, should be contacted whenever work on a well is being planned to ensure compliance with local ordinances. Many of these local agencies require permits for any work on a well and charge a fee for that permit.

Questions about well standards should be directed to the local enforcing agency or to DWR at (916) 653-5791.

LAW SECTIONS

SECTION V.

THE DEPARTMENT OF CONSUMER AFFAIRS

Chapter 11.

Laws Governing the Department of Consumer Affairs

The Department of Consumer Affairs includes 40 regulatory entities—among them the Contractors State License Board—which regulate various services and industries in the state. Some of the other boards and bureaus under the department's purview include the Medical Board of California, the Structural Pest Control Board, and the Bureau of Automotive Repair. The department's mission, through its regulatory boards, is "to promote and protect the interests of California consumers by serving as guardian and advocate for their health, safety, privacy, and economic well being; enhancing public participation in regulatory decision-making; promoting legal and ethical standards of professional conduct; identifying marketplace trends so that the Department's programs and policies are contemporary, relevant, and responsive; partnering with business and consumer groups in California and the nation; and working with law enforcement to combat fraud and enforce consumer protection laws vigorously and fairly." The laws governing the department and the CSLB are part of California's Business and Professions Code. What follows are selected sections from the codes that relate, in general or in specifics, to the purpose and function of the department.

Section V

BUSINESS & PROFESSIONS CODE

GENERAL PROVISIONS

§ 7.5. "Conviction"; When action by board following establishment of conviction may be taken; Prohibition against denial of licensure; Application of section

(a) A conviction within the meaning of this code means a judgment following a plea or verdict of guilty or a plea of nolo contendere or finding of guilt. Any action which a board is permitted to take following the establishment of a conviction may be taken when the time for appeal has elapsed, or the judgment of conviction has been affirmed on appeal or when an order granting probation is made suspending the imposition of sentence. However, a board may not deny a license to an applicant who is otherwise qualified pursuant to subdivision (b) or (c) of Section 480.

(b) (1) Nothing in this section shall apply to the licensure of persons pursuant to Chapter 4 (commencing with Section 6000) of Division 3.

(2) This section does not in any way modify or otherwise affect the existing authority of the following entities in regard to licensure:

(A) The State Athletic Commission.

(B) The Bureau for Private Postsecondary Education.

(C) The California Horse Racing Board.

(c) Except as provided in subdivision (b), this section controls over and supersedes the definition of conviction contained within individual practice acts under this code.

(d) This section shall become operative on July 1, 2020.

Added Stats 2018 ch 995 § 2 (AB 2138), effective January 1, 2019, operative July 1, 2020.

§ 8. Governing provisions

Unless the context otherwise requires, the general provisions hereinafter set forth shall govern the construction of this code.

Enacted Stats 1937.

§ 9. Effect of headings

Division, part, chapter, article and section headings contained herein shall not be deemed to govern, limit, modify, or in any manner affect the scope, meaning, or intent of the provisions of this code.

Enacted Stats 1937.

§ 10. Authority of deputies

Whenever, by the provisions of this code, a power is granted to a public officer or a duty imposed upon such an officer, the power may be exercised or duty performed by a deputy of the officer or by a person authorized pursuant to law by the officer, unless it is expressly otherwise provided.

Enacted Stats 1937.

§ 12.5. Violation of regulation adopted pursuant to code provision; Issuance of citation

Whenever in any provision of this code authority is granted to issue a citation for a violation of any provision of this code, that authority also includes the authority to issue a citation for the violation of any regulation adopted pursuant to any provision of this code.

Added Stats 1986 ch 1379 § 1.

§ 14.1. Legislative intent

The Legislature hereby declares its intent that the terms "man" or "men" where appropriate shall be deemed "person" or "persons" and any references to the terms "man" or "men" in sections of this code be changed to "person" or "persons" when such code sections are being amended for any purpose. This act is declaratory and not amendatory of existing law.

Added Stats 1976 ch 1171 § 1.

§ 14.2. "Spouse" to include registered domestic partner

"Spouse" includes "registered domestic partner," as required by Section 297.5 of the Family Code.

Added Stats 2016 ch 50 § 1 (SB 1005), effective January 1, 2017.

§ 22. "Board"

"Board," as used in any provision of this code, refers to the board in which the administration of the provision is vested, and unless otherwise expressly provided, shall include "bureau," "commission," "committee," "department," "division," "examining committee," "program," and "agency."

Enacted Stats 1937. Amended Stats 1947 ch 1350 § 1; Stats 1980 ch 676 § 1; Stats 1991 ch 654 § 1 (AB 1893); Stats 1999 ch 656 § 1 (SB 1306); Stats 2004 ch 33 § 1 (AB 1467), effective April 13, 2004; Stats 2010 ch 670 § 1 (AB 2130), effective January 1, 2011.

§ 23.5. "Director"

"Director," unless otherwise defined, refers to the Director of Consumer Affairs.

Wherever the laws of this state refer to the Director of Professional and Vocational Standards, the reference shall be construed to be to the Director of Consumer Affairs.

Added Stats 1939 ch 30 § 2. Amended Stats 1971 ch 716 § 2.

§ 23.6. "Appointing power"

"Appointing power," unless otherwise defined, refers to the Director of Consumer Affairs.

Added Stats 1945 ch 1276 § 1. Amended Stats 1971 ch 716 § 3.

§ 23.7. "License"

Unless otherwise expressly provided, "license" means license, certificate, registration, or other means to engage in a business or profession regulated by this code or referred to in Section 1000 or 3600.

Added Stats 1994 ch 26 § 1 (AB 1807), effective March 30, 1994.

§ 23.8. "Licensee"

"Licensee" means any person authorized by a license, certificate, registration, or other means to engage in a business or profession regulated by this code or referred to in Sections 1000 and 3600.

Any reference to licentiate in this code shall be deemed to refer to licensee.

Added Stats 1961 ch 2232 § 1. Amended Stats 2019 ch 351, § 1 (AB 496), effective January 1, 2020.

§ 23.9. Licensing eligibility of prison releasees

Notwithstanding any other provision of this code, any individual who, while imprisoned in a state prison or other correctional institution, is trained, in the course of a rehabilitation program approved by the particular licensing agency concerned and provided by the prison or other correctional institution, in a particular skill, occupation, or profession for which a state license, certificate, or other evidence of proficiency is required by this code shall not, when released from the prison or institution, be denied the right to take the next regularly scheduled state examination or any examination thereafter required to obtain the license, certificate, or other evidence of proficiency and shall not be denied such license, certificate, or other evidence of proficiency, because of that individual's imprisonment or the conviction from which the imprisonment resulted, or because the individual obtained the individual's training in prison or in the correctional institution, if the licensing agency, upon recommendation of the Adult Authority or the Department of the Youth Authority, as the case may be, finds that the individual is a fit person to be licensed.

Added Stats 1967 ch 1690 § 1, as B & P C § 23.8. Amended and Renumbered by Stats 1971 ch 582 § 1; Stats 2019 ch 351 § 2 (AB 496), effective January 1, 2020.

§ 26. Rules and regulations regarding building standards

Wherever, pursuant to this code, any state department, officer, board, agency, committee, or commission is authorized to adopt rules and regulations, such rules and regulations which are building standards, as defined in Section 18909 of the Health and Safety Code, shall be adopted pursuant to the provisions of Part 2.5 (commencing with Section 18901) of Division 13 of the Health and Safety Code unless the provisions of Sections 18930, 18933, 18938, 18940, 18943, 18944, and 18945 of the Health and Safety Code are expressly excepted in the provision of this code under which the authority to adopt the specific building standard is delegated. Any building standard adopted in violation of this section shall have no force or effect. Any building standard adopted prior to January 1, 1980, pursuant to this code and not expressly excepted by statute from such provisions of the State Building Standards Law shall remain in effect only until January 1, 1985, or until adopted, amended, or superseded by provisions published in the State Building Standards Code, whichever occurs sooner.

Added Stats 1979 ch 1152 § 1.

§ 27. Information to be provided on internet; Entities in Department of Consumer Affairs required to comply

(a) Each entity specified in subdivisions (c), (d), and (e) shall provide on the internet information regarding the status of every license issued by that entity in accordance with the California Public Records Act (Chapter 3.5 (commencing with Section 6250) of Division 7 of Title 1 of the Government Code) and the Information Practices Act of 1977 (Chapter 1 (commencing with Section 1798) of Title 1.8 of Part 4 of Division 3 of the Civil Code). The public information to be provided on the internet shall include information on suspensions and revocations of licenses issued by the entity and other related enforcement action, including accusations filed pursuant to the Administrative Procedure Act (Chapter 3.5 (commencing with Section 11340) of Part 1 of Division 3 of Title 2 of the Government Code) taken by the entity relative to persons, businesses, or facilities subject to licensure or regulation by the entity. The information may not include personal information, including home telephone number, date of birth, or social security number. Each entity shall disclose a licensee's address of record. However, each entity shall allow a licensee to provide a post office box number or other alternate address, instead of the licensee's home address, as the address of record. This section shall not preclude an entity from also requiring a licensee, who has provided a post office box number or other alternative mailing address as the licensee's address of record, to provide a physical business address or residence address only for the entity's internal administrative use and not for disclosure as the licensee's address of record or disclosure on the internet.

(b) In providing information on the internet, each entity specified in subdivisions (c) and (d) shall comply with the Department of Consumer Affairs' guidelines for access to public records.

(c) Each of the following entities within the Department of Consumer Affairs shall comply with the requirements of this section:

(1) The Board for Professional Engineers, Land Surveyors, and Geologists shall disclose information on its registrants and licensees.

(2) The Bureau of Automotive Repair shall disclose information on its licensees, including auto repair dealers, smog stations, lamp and brake stations, smog check technicians, and smog inspection certification stations.

(3) The Bureau of Household Goods and Services shall disclose information on its licensees, registrants, and permitholders.

(4) The Cemetery and Funeral Bureau shall disclose information on its licensees, including cemetery brokers, cemetery salespersons, cemetery managers, crematory managers, cemetery authorities, crematories, cremated remains disposers, embalmers, funeral establishments, and funeral directors.

(5) The Professional Fiduciaries Bureau shall disclose information on its licensees.

(6) The Contractors State License Board shall disclose information on its licensees and registrants in accordance with Chapter 9 (commencing with Section 7000) of Division 3. In addition to information related to licenses as specified in subdivision (a), the board shall also disclose information provided to the board by the Labor Commissioner pursuant to Section 98.9 of the Labor Code.

(7) The Bureau for Private Postsecondary Education shall disclose information on private postsecondary institutions under its jurisdiction, including disclosure of notices to comply issued pursuant to Section 94935 of the Education Code.

(8) The California Board of Accountancy shall disclose information on its licensees and registrants.

(9) The California Architects Board shall disclose information on its licensees, including architects and landscape architects.

(10) The State Athletic Commission shall disclose information on its licensees and registrants.

(11) The State Board of Barbering and Cosmetology shall disclose information on its licensees.

(12) The Acupuncture Board shall disclose information on its licensees.

(13) The Board of Behavioral Sciences shall disclose information on its licensees and registrants.

(14) The Dental Board of California shall disclose information on its licensees.

(15) The California State Board of Optometry shall disclose information on its licensees and registrants.

(16) The Board of Psychology shall disclose information on its licensees, including psychologists and registered psychological associates.

(17) The Veterinary Medical Board shall disclose information on its licensees, registrants, and permitholders.

(d) The State Board of Chiropractic Examiners shall disclose information on its licensees.

(e) The Structural Pest Control Board shall disclose information on its licensees, including applicators, field representatives, and operators in the areas of fumigation, general pest and wood destroying pests and organisms, and wood roof cleaning and treatment.

(f) "Internet" for the purposes of this section has the meaning set forth in paragraph (6) of subdivision (f) of Section 17538.

Added Stats 1997 ch 661 § 1 (SB 492). Amended Stats 1998 ch 59 § 1 (AB 969); Stats 1999 ch 655 § 1 (SB 1308); Stats 2000 ch 927 § 1 (SB 1889); Stats 2001 ch 159 § 1 (SB 662); Stats 2003 ch 849 § 1 (AB 1418); Stats 2009 ch 308 § 1 (SB 819), effective January 1, 2010, ch 310 § 1.5 (AB 48), effective January 1, 2010; Stats 2011 ch 381 § 2 (SB 146), effective January 1, 2012, ch 712 § 1 (SB 706), effective January 1, 2012; Stats 2014 ch 316 § 1 (SB 1466), effective January 1, 2015; Stats 2015 ch 689 § 1 (AB 266), effective January 1, 2016; Stats 2016 ch 32 § 1 (SB 837), effective June 27, 2016; Stats 2016 ch 489 § 1 (SB 1478), effective January 1, 2017; Stats 2017 ch 429 § 1 (SB 547), effective January 1, 2018. Stats 2018 ch 578 § 1 (SB 1483), effective January 1, 2019. Stats 2018 ch 599 § 1 (AB 3261), effective January 1, 2019. Stats 2018 ch 703 § 1.3 (SB 1491), effective January 1, 2019 (ch 703 prevails); Stats 2019 ch 351 § 4 (AB 496), effective January 1, 2020; Stats 2020 ch 312 § 1 (SB 1474), effective January 1, 2021; Stats 2021 ch 70 § 1 (AB 141), effective July 12, 2021; Stats 2021 ch 188 § 1 (SB 826), effective January 1, 2022; Stats 2021 ch 630 § 1 (AB 1534), effective January 1, 2022; Stats 2021 ch 647 § 1.3 (SB 801), effective January 1, 2022 (ch 647 prevails).

§ 29.5. Additional qualifications for licensure

In addition to other qualifications for licensure prescribed by the various acts of boards under the department, applicants for licensure and licensees renewing their licenses shall also comply with Section 17520 of the Family Code.

Added Stats 1991 ch 542 § 1 (SB 1161). Amended Stats 2003 ch 607 § 1 (SB 1077).

—See *Family Code Section 17520, Compliance with Support Orders by Applicants for Professional Licenses, in Appendix.*

§ 30. Provision of federal employer identification number or social security number by licensee

(a) (1) Notwithstanding any other law, any board, as defined in Section 22, the State Bar of California, and the Department of Real Estate shall, at the time of issuance of the license, require that the applicant provide its federal employer identification number, if the applicant is a partnership, or the applicant's social security number for all other applicants.

(2) (A) In accordance with Section 135.5, a board, as defined in Section 22, the State Bar of California, and the Department of Real Estate shall require either the individual taxpayer identification number or social security number if the applicant is an individual for a license or certificate, as defined in subparagraph (2) of subdivision (e), and for purposes of this subdivision.

(B) In implementing the requirements of subparagraph (A), a licensing board shall not require an individual to disclose either citizenship status or immigration status for purposes of licensure.

(C) A licensing board shall not deny licensure to an otherwise qualified and eligible individual based solely on the individual's citizenship status or immigration status.

(D) The Legislature finds and declares that the requirements of this subdivision are consistent with subsection (d) of Section 1621 of Title 8 of the United States Code.

(b) A licensee failing to provide the federal employer identification number, or the individual taxpayer identification number or social security number shall be reported by the licensing board to the Franchise Tax Board. If the licensee fails to provide that information after notification pursuant to paragraph (1) of subdivision (b) of Section 19528 of the Revenue and Taxation Code, the licensee shall be subject to the penalty provided in paragraph (2) of subdivision (b) of Section 19528 of the Revenue and Taxation Code.

(c) In addition to the penalty specified in subdivision (b), a licensing board shall not process an application for an initial license unless the applicant provides its federal employer identification number, or individual taxpayer identification number or social security number where requested on the application.

(d) A licensing board shall, upon request of the Franchise Tax Board or the Employment Development Department, furnish to the board or the department, as applicable, the following information with respect to every licensee:

(1) Name.

(2) Address or addresses of record.

(3) Federal employer identification number if the licensee is a partnership, or the licensee's individual taxpayer identification number or social security number for all other licensees.

(4) Type of license.

(5) Effective date of license or a renewal.

(6) Expiration date of license.

(7) Whether license is active or inactive, if known.

(8) Whether license is new or a renewal.

(e) For the purposes of this section:

(1) "Licensee" means a person or entity, other than a corporation, authorized by a license, certificate, registration, or other means to engage in a business or profession regulated by this code or referred to in Section 1000 or 3600.

(2) "License" includes a certificate, registration, or any other authorization needed to engage in a business or profession regulated by this code or referred to in Section 1000 or 3600.

(3) "Licensing board" means any board, as defined in Section 22, the State Bar of California, and the Department of Real Estate.

(f) The reports required under this section shall be filed on magnetic media or in other machine-readable form, according to standards furnished by the Franchise Tax Board or the Employment Development Department, as applicable.

(g) Licensing boards shall provide to the Franchise Tax Board or the Employment Development Department the information required by this section at a time that the board or the department, as applicable, may require.

(h) Notwithstanding Division 10 (commencing with Section 7920.000) of Title 1 of the Government Code, a federal employer identification number, individual taxpayer identification number, or social security number furnished pursuant to this section shall not be deemed to be a public record and shall not be open to the public for inspection.

(i) A deputy, agent, clerk, officer, or employee of a licensing board described in subdivision (a), or any former officer or employee or other individual who, in the course of their employment or duty, has or has had access to the information required to be furnished under this section, shall not disclose or make known in any manner that information, except as provided pursuant to this section, to the Franchise Tax Board, the Employment Development Department, the Office of the Chancellor of the California Community Colleges, a collections agency contracted to collect funds owed to the State Bar by licensees pursuant to Sections 6086.10 and 6140.5, or as provided in subdivisions (j) and (k).

(j) It is the intent of the Legislature in enacting this section to utilize the federal employer identification number, individual taxpayer identification number, or social security number for the purpose of establishing the identification of persons affected by state tax laws, for purposes of compliance with Section 17520 of the Family Code, for purposes of measuring employment outcomes of students who participate in career technical education programs offered by the California Community Colleges, and for purposes of collecting funds owed to the State Bar by licensees pursuant to Section 6086.10 and Section 6140.5 and, to that end, the information furnished pursuant to this section shall be used exclusively for those purposes.

(k) If the board utilizes a national examination to issue a license, and if a reciprocity agreement or comity exists between the State of California and the state requesting release of the individual taxpayer identification number or social security number, any deputy, agent, clerk, officer, or employee of any licensing board described in subdivision (a) may release an individual taxpayer identification number or social security number to an examination or licensing entity, only for the purpose of verification of licensure or examination status.

(*l*) For the purposes of enforcement of Section 17520 of the Family Code, and notwithstanding any other law, a board, as defined in Section 22, the State Bar of California, and the Department of Real Estate shall at the time of issuance of the license require that each licensee provide the individual taxpayer identification number or social security number of each individual listed on the license and any person who qualifies for the license. For the purposes of this subdivision, "licensee" means an entity that is issued a license by any board, as defined in Section 22, the State Bar of California, the Department of Real Estate, and the Department of Motor Vehicles.

(m) The department shall, upon request by the Office of the Chancellor of the California Community Colleges, furnish to the chancellor's office, as applicable, the following information with respect to every licensee:

(1) Name.

(2) Federal employer identification number if the licensee is a partnership, or the licensee's individual taxpayer identification number or social security number for all other licensees.

(3) Date of birth.

(4) Type of license.

(5) Effective date of license or a renewal.

(6) Expiration date of license.

(n) The department shall make available information pursuant to subdivision (m) only to allow the chancellor's office to measure employment outcomes of students who participate in career technical education programs offered by the California Community Colleges and recommend how these programs may be improved. Licensure information made available by the department pursuant to this section shall not be used for any other purpose.

(o) The department may make available information pursuant to subdivision (m) only to the extent that making the information available complies with state and federal privacy laws.

(p) The department may, by agreement, condition or limit the availability of licensure information pursuant to subdivision (m) in order to ensure the security of the information and to protect the privacy rights of the individuals to whom the information pertains.

(q) All of the following apply to the licensure information made available pursuant to subdivision (m):

(1) It shall be limited to only the information necessary to accomplish the purpose authorized in subdivision (n).

(2) It shall not be used in a manner that permits third parties to personally identify the individual or individuals to whom the information pertains.

(3) Except as provided in subdivision (n), it shall not be shared with or transmitted to any other party or entity without the consent of the individual or individuals to whom the information pertains.

(4) It shall be protected by reasonable security procedures and practices appropriate to the nature of the information to protect that information from unauthorized access, destruction, use, modification, or disclosure.

Section V

(5) It shall be immediately and securely destroyed when no longer needed for the purpose authorized in subdivision (n).

(r) The department or the chancellor's office may share licensure information with a third party who contracts to perform the function described in subdivision (n), if the third party is required by contract to follow the requirements of this section.

Added Stats 2017 ch 828 § 2 (SB 173), effective January 1, 2018, operative July 1, 2018. Amended Stats 2018 ch 659 § 1 (AB 3249), effective January 1, 2019. Stats 2018 ch 838 § 2.5 (SB 695), effective January 1, 2019 (ch 838 prevails); Stats 2019 ch 351 § 6 (AB 496), effective January 1, 2020; Stats 2021 ch 615 § 2 (AB 474), effective January 1, 2022.

§ 31. Compliance with judgment or order for support upon issuance or renewal of license

(a) As used in this section, "board" means any entity listed in Section 101, the entities referred to in Sections 1000 and 3600, the State Bar, the Department of Real Estate, and any other state agency that issues a license, certificate, or registration authorizing a person to engage in a business or profession.

(b) Each applicant for the issuance or renewal of a license, certificate, registration, or other means to engage in a business or profession regulated by a board who is not in compliance with a judgment or order for support shall be subject to Section 17520 of the Family Code.

(c) "Compliance with a judgment or order for support" has the meaning given in paragraph (4) of subdivision (a) of Section 17520 of the Family Code.

(d) Each licensee or applicant whose name appears on a list of the 500 largest tax delinquencies pursuant to Section 7063 or 19195 of the Revenue and Taxation Code shall be subject to Section 494.5.

(e) Each application for a new license or renewal of a license shall indicate on the application that the law allows the California Department of Tax and Fee Administration and the Franchise Tax Board to share taxpayer information with a board and requires the licensee to pay the licensee's state tax obligation and that the licensee's license may be suspended if the state tax obligation is not paid.

(f) For purposes of this section, "tax obligation" means the tax imposed under, or in accordance with, Part 1 (commencing with Section 6001), Part 1.5 (commencing with Section 7200), Part 1.6 (commencing with Section 7251), Part 1.7 (commencing with Section 7280), Part 10 (commencing with Section 17001), or Part 11 (commencing with Section 23001) of Division 2 of the Revenue and Taxation Code.

Added Stats 1991 ch 110 § 4 (SB 101). Amended Stats 1991 ch 542 § 3 (SB 1161); Stats 2010 ch 328 § 1 (SB 1330), effective January 1, 2011; Stats 2011 ch 455 § 1 (AB 1424), effective January 1, 2012; Stats 2013 ch 352 § 2 (AB 1317), effective September 26, 2013, operative July 1, 2013; Stats 2019 ch 351 § 7 (AB 496), effective January 1, 2020.

§ 35. Provision in rules and regulations for evaluation experience obtained in armed services

It is the policy of this state that, consistent with the provision of high-quality services, persons with skills, knowledge, and experience obtained in the armed services of the United States should be permitted to apply this learning and contribute to the employment needs of the state at the maximum level of responsibility and skill for which they are qualified. To this end, rules and regulations of boards provided for in this code shall provide for methods of evaluating education, training, and experience obtained in the armed services, if applicable to the requirements of the business, occupation, or profession regulated. These rules and regulations shall also specify how this education, training, and experience may be used to meet the licensure requirements for the particular business, occupation, or profession regulated. Each board shall consult with the Department of Veterans Affairs and the Military Department before adopting these rules and regulations. Each board shall perform the duties required by this section within existing budgetary resources of the agency within which the board operates.

Added Stats 1994 ch 987 § 1 (SB 1646), effective September 28, 1994. Amended Stats 1995 ch 91 § 1 (SB 975); Stats 2010 ch 214 § 1 (AB 2783), effective January 1, 2011.

§ 40. State Board of Chiropractic Examiners or Osteopathic Medical Board of California expert consultant agreements

(a) Subject to the standards described in Section 19130 of the Government Code, any board, as defined in Section 22, the State Board of Chiropractic Examiners, or the Osteopathic Medical Board of California may enter into an agreement with an expert consultant to do any of the following:

(1) Provide an expert opinion on enforcement-related matters, including providing testimony at an administrative hearing.

(2) Assist the board as a subject matter expert in examination development, examination validation, or occupational analyses.

(3) Evaluate the mental or physical health of a licensee or an applicant for a license as may be necessary to protect the public health and safety.

(b) An executed contract between a board and an expert consultant shall be exempt from the provisions of Part 2 (commencing with Section 10100) of Division 2 of the Public Contract Code.

(c) Each board shall establish policies and procedures for the selection and use of expert consultants.

(d) Nothing in this section shall be construed to expand the scope of practice of an expert consultant providing services pursuant to this section.

Added Stats 2011 ch 339 § 1 (SB 541), effective September 26, 2011.

DIVISION 1

DEPARTMENT OF CONSUMER AFFAIRS

Chapter 1

The Department

Chapter 2

The Director of Consumer Affairs

Section V

Chapter 3

Funds of the Department

Chapter 4

Consumer Affairs

Article 1

General Provisions and Definitions

Article 2

Director and Employees

Section V

Chapter 7

Licensee

Chapter 8

Dispute Resolution Programs

Article 1

Legislative Purpose

Article 3

Establishment and Administration of Programs

Article 4

Application Procedures

Article 6

Funding

Chapter 1

The Department

§ 100. Establishment

There is in the state government, in the Business, Consumer Services, and Housing Agency, a Department of Consumer Affairs.

Enacted Stats 1937. Amended Stats 1969 ch 138 § 5; Stats 1971 ch 716 § 4; Stats 1984 ch 144 § 1. See this section as modified in Governor's Reorganization Plan No. 2 § 1 of 2012. Amended Stats 2012 ch 147 § 1 (SB 1039), effective January 1, 2013, operative July 1, 2013 (ch 147 prevails).

§ 101. Composition of department

The department is comprised of the following:
(a) The Dental Board of California.
(b) The Medical Board of California.
(c) The California State Board of Optometry.
(d) The California State Board of Pharmacy.
(e) The Veterinary Medical Board.
(f) The California Board of Accountancy.
(g) The California Architects Board.
(h) The State Board of Barbering and Cosmetology.
(i) The Board for Professional Engineers, Land Surveyors, and Geologists.
(j) The Contractors State License Board.
(k) The Bureau for Private Postsecondary Education.
(l) The Bureau of Household Goods and Services.
(m) The Board of Registered Nursing.
(n) The Board of Behavioral Sciences.
(o) The State Athletic Commission.
(p) The Cemetery and Funeral Bureau.
(q) The Bureau of Security and Investigative Services.
(r) The Court Reporters Board of California.
(s) The Board of Vocational Nursing and Psychiatric Technicians.
(t) The Landscape Architects Technical Committee.
(u) The Division of Investigation.
(v) The Bureau of Automotive Repair.
(w) The Respiratory Care Board of California.

Section V

(x) The Acupuncture Board.

(y) The Board of Psychology.

(z) The Podiatric Medical Board of California.

(aa) The Physical Therapy Board of California.

(ab) The Arbitration Review Program.

(ac) The Physician Assistant Board.

(ad) The Speech-Language Pathology and Audiology and Hearing Aid Dispensers Board.

(ae) The California Board of Occupational Therapy.

(af) The Osteopathic Medical Board of California.

(ag) The California Board of Naturopathic Medicine.

(ah) The Dental Hygiene Board of California.

(ai) The Professional Fiduciaries Bureau.

(aj) The State Board of Chiropractic Examiners.

(ak) The Bureau of Real Estate Appraisers.

(al) The Structural Pest Control Board.

(am) Any other boards, offices, or officers subject to its jurisdiction by law.

Added Stats 2017 ch 823 § 4 (SB 173), effective January 1, 2018, operative July 1, 2018. Amended Stats 2018 ch 578 § 2 (SB 1483), effective January 1, 2019; Stats 2018 ch 858 § 1.5 (SB 1482), effective January 1, 2019 (ch 858 prevails); Stats 2019 ch 351 § 8 (AB 496), effective January 1, 2020; Stats 2020 ch 312 § 2 (SB 1474), effective January 1, 2021; Stats 2021 ch 70 § 2 (AB 141), effective July 27, 2021; Stats 2021 ch 630 § 2 (AB 1534), effective January 1, 2022; Stats 2022 ch 414 § 1 (AB 2685), effective January 1, 2023.

§ 101.1. [Section repealed 2011.]

Added Stats 1994 ch 908 § 2 (SB 2036). Amended Stats 1999 ch 983 § 1 (SB 1307). Repealed Stats 2010 ch 670 § 2 (AB 2130), effective January 1, 2011. The repealed section related to legislative intent regarding existing and proposed consumer-related boards.

§ 101.6. Purpose

The boards, bureaus, and commissions in the department are established for the purpose of ensuring that those private businesses and professions deemed to engage in activities which have potential impact upon the public health, safety, and welfare are adequately regulated in order to protect the people of California.

To this end, they establish minimum qualifications and levels of competency and license persons desiring to engage in the occupations they regulate upon determining that such persons possess the requisite skills and qualifications necessary to provide safe and effective services to the public, or register or otherwise certify persons in order to identify practitioners and ensure performance according to set and accepted professional standards. They provide a means for redress of grievances by investigating allegations of unprofessional conduct, incompetence, fraudulent action, or unlawful activity brought to their attention by members of the public and institute disciplinary action against persons licensed or registered under the provisions of this code when such action is warranted. In addition, they conduct periodic checks of licensees, registrants, or otherwise certified persons in order to ensure compliance with the relevant sections of this code.

Added Stats 1980 ch 375 § 1.

§ 101.7. Meetings of boards; Regular and special

(a) Notwithstanding any other provision of law, boards shall meet at least two times each calendar year. Boards shall meet at least once each calendar year in northern California and once each calendar year in southern California in order to facilitate participation by the public and its licensees.

(b) The director has discretion to exempt any board from the requirement in subdivision (a) upon a showing of good cause that the board is not able to meet at least two times in a calendar year.

(c) The director may call for a special meeting of the board when a board is not fulfilling its duties.

(d) An agency within the department that is required to provide a written notice pursuant to subdivision (a) of Section 11125 of the Government Code, may provide that notice by regular mail, email, or by both regular mail and email. An agency shall give a person who requests a notice the option of receiving the notice by regular mail, email, or by both regular mail and email. The agency shall comply with the requester's chosen form or forms of notice.

(e) An agency that plans to webcast a meeting shall include in the meeting notice required pursuant to subdivision (a) of Section 11125 of the Government Code a statement of the board's intent to webcast the meeting. An agency may webcast a meeting even if the agency fails to include that statement of intent in the notice.

Added Stats 2007 ch 354 § 1 (SB 1047), effective January 1, 2008. Amended Stats 2014 ch 395 § 1 (SB 1243), effective January 1, 2015; Stats 2018 ch 571 § 1 (SB 1480), effective January 1, 2019; Stats 2019 ch 351 § 9 (AB 496), effective January 1, 2020.

§ 102. Assumption of duties of board created by initiative

Upon the request of any board regulating, licensing, or controlling any professional or vocational occupation created by an initiative act, the Director of Consumer Affairs may take over the duties of the board under the same conditions and in the same manner as provided in this code for other boards of like character. Such boards shall pay a proportionate cost of the administration of the department on the same basis as is charged other boards included within the department. Upon request from any such board which has adopted the provisions of Chapter 5 (commencing with Section 11500) of Part 1 of Division 3 of Title 2 of the Government Code as rules of procedure in proceedings before it, the director shall assign hearing officers for such proceedings in accordance with Section 110.5.

Enacted Stats 1937. Amended Stats 1945 ch 869 § 1; Stats 1971 ch 716 § 6.

§ 102.3. Interagency agreement to delegate duties of certain repealed boards; Technical committees for regulation of professions under delegated authority; Renewal of agreement

(a) The director may enter into an interagency agreement with an appropriate entity within the Department of Consumer Affairs as provided for in Section 101 to delegate the duties, powers, purposes, responsibilities, and jurisdiction that have been succeeded and vested with the department, of a board, as defined in Section 477, which became inoperative and was repealed in accordance with Chapter 908 of the Statutes of 1994.

(b) (1) Where, pursuant to subdivision (a), an interagency agreement is entered into between the director and that entity, the entity receiving the delegation of authority may establish a technical committee to regulate, as directed by the entity, the profession subject to the authority that has been delegated. The entity may delegate to the technical committee only those powers that it received pursuant to the interagency agreement with the director. The technical committee shall have only those powers that have been delegated to it by the entity.

(2) Where the entity delegates its authority to adopt, amend, or repeal regulations to the technical committee, all regulations adopted, amended, or repealed by the technical committee shall be subject to the review and approval of the entity.

(3) The entity shall not delegate to a technical committee its authority to discipline a licensee who has violated the provisions of the applicable chapter of the Business and Professions Code that is subject to the director's delegation of authority to the entity.

(c) An interagency agreement entered into, pursuant to subdivision (a), shall continue until such time as the licensing program administered by the technical committee has undergone a review by the Assembly Committee on Business and Professions and the Senate Committee on Business, Professions and Economic Development to evaluate and determine whether the licensing program has demonstrated a public need for its continued existence. Thereafter, at the director's discretion, the interagency agreement may be renewed.

Added Stats 1997 ch 475 § 1 (AB 1546). Amended Stats 2004 ch 33 § 2 (AB 1467), effective April 13, 2004; Stats 2019 ch 351 § 10 (AB 496), effective January 1, 2020.

§ 103. Compensation and reimbursement for expenses

Each member of a board, commission, or committee created in the various chapters of Division 2 (commencing with Section 500) and Division 3 (commencing with Section 5000), and in Chapter 2 (commencing with Section 18600) and Chapter 3 (commencing with Section 19000) of Division 8, shall receive the moneys specified in this section when authorized by the respective provisions.

Each such member shall receive a per diem of one hundred dollars ($100) for each day actually spent in the discharge of official duties, and shall be reimbursed for traveling and other expenses necessarily incurred in the performance of official duties.

The payments in each instance shall be made only from the fund from which the expenses of the agency are paid and shall be subject to the availability of money.

Notwithstanding any other provision of law, no public officer or employee shall receive per diem salary compensation for serving on those boards, commissions, or committees on any day when the officer or employee also received compensation for the officer or employee's regular public employment.

Added Stats 1959 ch 1645 § 1. Amended Stats 1978 ch 1141 § 1; Stats 1985 ch 502 § 1; Stats 1987 ch 850 § 1; Stats 1993 ch 1264 § 1 (SB 574); Stats 2019 ch 351 § 11 (AB 496), effective January 1, 2020.

§ 105.5. Tenure of members of boards, etc., within department

Notwithstanding any other provision of this code, each member of a board, commission, examining committee, or other similarly constituted agency within the department shall hold office until the appointment and qualification of that member's successor or until one year shall have elapsed since the expiration of the term for which the member was appointed, whichever first occurs.

Added Stats 1967 ch 524 § 1. Amended Stats 2019 ch 351 § 12 (AB 496), effective January 1, 2020.

§ 106. Removal of board members

The appointing authority has power to remove from office at any time any member of any board appointed by the appointing authority for continued neglect of duties required by law, or for incompetence, or unprofessional or dishonorable conduct. Nothing in this section shall be construed as a limitation or restriction on the power of the appointing authority conferred on the appointing authority by any other provision of law to remove any member of any board.

Enacted Stats 1937. Amended Stats 1945 ch 1276 § 3; Stats 2019 ch 351 § 13 (AB 496), effective January 1, 2020.

§ 106.5. Removal of member of licensing board for disclosure of examination information

Notwithstanding any other provision of law, the Governor may remove from office a member of a board or other licensing entity in the department if it is shown that such member has knowledge of the specific questions to be asked on the licensing entity's next examination and directly or indirectly discloses any such question or questions in advance of or during the examination to any applicant for that examination.

The proceedings for removal shall be conducted in accordance with the provisions of Chapter 5 of Part 1 of Division 3 of Title 2 of the Government Code, and the Governor shall have all the powers granted therein.

Added Stats 1977 ch 482 § 1.

§ 107. Executive officers

Pursuant to subdivision (e) of Section 4 of Article VII of the California Constitution, each board may appoint a person exempt from civil service, who shall be designated as an executive officer unless the licensing act of the particular board designates the person as a registrar, and may fix that person's salary, with the approval of the Department of Human Resources pursuant to Section 19825 of the Government Code.

Enacted Stats 1937. Amended Stats 1984 ch 47 § 2, effective March 21, 1984; Stats 1987 ch 850 § 2. See this section as modified in Governor's Reorganization Plan No. 1 § 1 of 2011; Amended Stats 2012 ch 665 § 1 (SB 1308), effective January 1, 2013; Stats 2019 ch 351 § 14 (AB 496), effective January 1, 2020; Stats 2020 ch 370 § 1 (SB 1371), effective January 1, 2021.

§ 107.5. Official seals

If any board in the department uses an official seal pursuant to any provision of this code, the seal shall contain the words "State of California" and "Department of Consumer Affairs" in addition to the title of the board, and shall be in a form approved by the director.

Added Stats 1967 ch 1272 § 1. Amended Stats 1971 ch 716 § 7.

§ 108. Status and powers of boards

Each of the boards comprising the department exists as a separate unit, and has the functions of setting standards, holding meetings, and setting dates thereof, preparing and conducting examinations, passing upon applicants, conducting investigations of violations of laws under its jurisdiction, issuing citations and holding hearings for the revocation of licenses, and the imposing of penalties following those hearings, insofar as these powers are given by statute to each respective board.

Enacted Stats 1937. Amended Stats 2008 ch 179 § 1 (SB 1498), effective January 1, 2009.

§ 108.5. Witness fees and expenses

In any investigation, proceeding, or hearing that any board, commission, or officer in the department is empowered to institute, conduct, or hold, any witness appearing at the investigation, proceeding, or hearing whether upon a subpoena or voluntarily, may be paid the sum of twelve dollars ($12) per day for every day in actual attendance at the investigation, proceeding, or hearing and for the witness's actual, necessary, and reasonable expenses and those sums shall be a legal charge against the funds of the respective board, commission, or officer; provided further, that no witness appearing other than at the instance of the board, commission, or officer may be compensated out of the fund.

The board, commission, or officer shall determine the sums due to any witness and enter the amount on its minutes.

Added Stats 1943 ch 1035 § 1. Amended Stats 1957 ch 1908 § 6; Stats 1970 ch 1061 § 1; Stats 2019 ch 351 § 15 (AB 496), effective January 1, 2020.

§ 109. Review of decisions; Investigations

(a) The decisions of any of the boards comprising the department with respect to setting standards, conducting examinations, passing candidates, and revoking licenses, are not subject to review by the director, but are final within the limits provided by this code which are applicable to the particular board, except as provided in this section.

(b) The director may initiate an investigation of any allegations of misconduct in the preparation, administration, or scoring of an examination which is administered by a board, or in the review of qualifications which are a part of the licensing process of any board. A request for investigation shall be made by the director to the Division of Investigation through the chief of the division or to any law enforcement agency in the jurisdiction where the alleged misconduct occurred.

(c) The director may intervene in any matter of any board where an investigation by the Division of Investigation discloses probable cause to believe that the conduct or activity of a board, or its members or employees constitutes a violation of criminal law.

The term "intervene," as used in paragraph (c) of this section may include, but is not limited to, an application for a restraining order or injunctive relief as specified in Section 123.5, or a referral or request for criminal prosecution. For purposes of this section, the director

Section V

shall be deemed to have standing under Section 123.5 and shall seek representation of the Attorney General, or other appropriate counsel in the event of a conflict in pursuing that action.

Enacted Stats 1937. Amended Stats 1991 ch 1013 § 1 (SB 961).

§ 110. Records and property

The department shall have possession and control of all records, books, papers, offices, equipment, supplies, funds, appropriations, land and other property—real or personal—now or hereafter held for the benefit or use of all of the bodies, offices or officers comprising the department. The title to all property held by any of these bodies, offices or officers for the use and benefit of the state, is vested in the State of California to be held in the possession of the department. Except as authorized by a board, the department shall not have the possession and control of examination questions prior to submission to applicants at scheduled examinations.

Enacted Stats 1937. Amended Stats 1996 ch 829 § 1 (AB 3473).

§ 111. Commissioners on examination

Unless otherwise expressly provided, any board may, with the approval of the appointing power, appoint qualified persons, who shall be designated as commissioners on examination, to give the whole or any portion of any examination. A commissioner on examination need not be a member of the board but shall have the same qualifications as one and shall be subject to the same rules.

Added Stats 1937 ch 474. Amended Stats 1947 ch 1350 § 3; Stats 1978 ch 1161 § 1; Stats 2019 ch 351 § 16 (AB 496), effective January 1, 2020.

§ 112. Publication and sale of directories of authorized persons

Notwithstanding any other provision of this code, no agency in the department, with the exception of the Board for Professional Engineers and Land Surveyors, shall be required to compile, publish, sell, or otherwise distribute a directory. When an agency deems it necessary to compile and publish a directory, the agency shall cooperate with the director in determining its form and content, the time and frequency of its publication, the persons to whom it is to be sold or otherwise distributed, and its price if it is sold. Any agency that requires the approval of the director for the compilation, publication, or distribution of a directory, under the law in effect at the time the amendment made to this section at the 1970 Regular Session of the Legislature becomes effective, shall continue to require that approval. As used in this section, "directory" means a directory, roster, register, or similar compilation of the names of persons who hold a license, certificate, permit, registration, or similar indicia of authority from the agency.

Added Stats 1937 ch 474. Amended Stats 1968 ch 1345 § 1; Stats 1970 ch 475 § 1; Stats 1998 ch 59 § 3 (AB 969).

§ 113. Conferences; Traveling expenses

Upon recommendation of the director, officers, and employees of the department, and the officers, members, and employees of the boards, committees, and commissions comprising it or subject to its jurisdiction may confer, in this state or elsewhere, with officers or employees of this state, its political subdivisions, other states, or the United States, or with other persons, associations, or organizations as may be of assistance to the department, board, committee, or commission in the conduct of its work. The officers, members, and employees shall be entitled to their actual traveling expenses incurred in pursuance hereof, but when these expenses are incurred with respect to travel outside of the state, they shall be subject to the approval of the Governor and the Director of Finance.

Added Stats 1937 ch 474. Amended Stats 1941 ch 885 § 1; Stats 2000 ch 277 § 1 (AB 2697); Stats 2001 ch 159 § 2 (SB 662).

§ 114. Reinstatement of expired license of licensee serving in military

(a) Notwithstanding any other provision of this code, any licensee or registrant of any board, commission, or bureau within the department whose license expired while the licensee or registrant was on active duty as a member of the California National Guard or the United States Armed Forces, may, upon application, reinstate their license or registration without examination or penalty, provided that all of the following requirements are satisfied:

(1) The licensee or registrant's license or registration was valid at the time they entered the California National Guard or the United States Armed Forces.

(2) The application for reinstatement is made while serving in the California National Guard or the United States Armed Forces, or not later than one year from the date of discharge from active service or return to inactive military status.

(3) The application for reinstatement is accompanied by an affidavit showing the date of entrance into the service, whether still in the service, or date of discharge, and the renewal fee for the current renewal period in which the application is filed is paid.

(b) If application for reinstatement is filed more than one year after discharge or return to inactive status, the applicant, in the discretion of the licensing agency, may be required to pass an examination.

Section V

(c) If application for reinstatement is filed and the licensing agency determines that the applicant has not actively engaged in the practice of the applicant's profession while on active duty, then the licensing agency may require the applicant to pass an examination.

(d) Unless otherwise specifically provided in this code, any licensee or registrant who, either part time or full time, practices in this state the profession or vocation for which the licensee or registrant is licensed or registered shall be required to maintain their license in good standing even though the licensee or registrant is in military service.

For the purposes in this section, time spent by a licensee in receiving treatment or hospitalization in any veterans' facility during which the licensee is prevented from practicing the licensee's profession or vocation shall be excluded from said period of one year.

Added Stats 1951 ch 185 § 2. Amended Stats 1953 ch 423 § 1; Stats 1961 ch 1253 § 1; Stats 2010 ch 389 § 1 (AB 2500), effective January 1, 2011; Stats 2011 ch 296 § 1 (AB 1023), effective January 1, 2012; Stats 2019 ch 351 § 17 (AB 496), effective January 1, 2020.

§ 114.3. Waiver of fees and requirements for active duty members of armed forces and national guard

(a) Notwithstanding any other law, every board, as defined in Section 22, within the department shall waive the renewal fees, continuing education requirements, and other renewal requirements as determined by the board, if any are applicable, for a licensee or registrant called to active duty as a member of the United States Armed Forces or the California National Guard if all of the following requirements are met:

(1) The licensee or registrant possessed a current and valid license with the board at the time the licensee or registrant was called to active duty.

(2) The renewal requirements are waived only for the period during which the licensee or registrant is on active duty service.

(3) Written documentation that substantiates the licensee or registrant's active duty service is provided to the board.

(b) For purposes of this section, the phrase "called to active duty" shall have the same meaning as "active duty" as defined in Section 101 of Title 10 of the United States Code and shall additionally include individuals who are on active duty in the California National Guard, whether due to proclamation of a state of insurrection pursuant to Section 143 of the Military and Veterans Code or due to a proclamation of a state extreme emergency or when the California National Guard is otherwise on active duty pursuant to Section 146 of the Military and Veterans Code.

(c) (1) Except as specified in paragraph (2), the licensee or registrant shall not engage in any activities requiring a license during the period that the waivers provided by this section are in effect.

(2) If the licensee or registrant will provide services for which the licensee or registrant is licensed while on active duty, the board shall convert the license status to military active and no private practice of any type shall be permitted.

(d) In order to engage in any activities for which the licensee or registrant is licensed once discharged from active duty, the licensee or registrant shall meet all necessary renewal requirements as determined by the board within six months from the licensee's or registrant's date of discharge from active duty service.

(e) After a licensee or registrant receives notice of the licensee or registrant's discharge date, the licensee or registrant shall notify the board of their discharge from active duty within 60 days of receiving their notice of discharge.

(f) A board may adopt regulations to carry out the provisions of this section.

(g) This section shall not apply to any board that has a similar license renewal waiver process statutorily authorized for that board.

Added Stats 2012 ch 742 § 1 (AB 1588), effective January 1, 2013. Amended Stats 2019 ch 351 § 18 (AB 496), effective January 1, 2020; Stats 2022 ch 386 § 1 (SB 1237), effective January 1, 2023.

§ 114.5. Military service; Posting of information on Web site about application of military experience and training towards licensure

(a) Each board shall inquire in every application for licensure if the individual applying for licensure is serving in, or has previously served in, the military.

(b) If a board's governing law authorizes veterans to apply military experience and training towards licensure requirements, that board shall post information on the board's Internet Web site about the ability of veteran applicants to apply military experience and training towards licensure requirements.

Added Stats 2013 ch 693 § 1 (AB 1057), effective January 1, 2014. Amended Stats 2016 ch 174 § 1 (SB 1348), effective January 1, 2017.

§ 115. Applicability of Section 114

The provisions of Section 114 of this code are also applicable to a licensee or registrant whose license or registration was obtained while in the armed services.

Added Stats 1951 ch 1577 § 1.

§ 115.4. Licensure process expedited for honorably discharged veterans of Armed Forces

(a) Notwithstanding any other law, on and after July 1, 2016, a board within the department shall expedite, and may assist, the initial licensure process for an applicant who supplies satisfactory evidence to the board that the applicant has served as an active duty member of the Armed Forces of the United States and was honorably discharged.

(b) A board may adopt regulations necessary to administer this section.

Added Stats 2014 ch 657 § 1 (SB 1226), effective January 1, 2015.

§ 115.5. Board required to expedite licensure process for certain applicants; Adoption of regulations [Repealed]

Added Stats 2012 ch 399 § 1 (AB 1904), effective January 1, 2013. Amended Stats 2019 ch 351 § 19 (AB 496), effective January 1, 2020; Stat 2021 ch 367 § 1 (SB 607), effective September 28, 2021; Repealed July 1, 2022.

§ 115.5. Requirements for expedited licensure process [Operative July 1, 2022]

(a) A board within the department shall expedite the licensure process and waive the licensure application fee and the initial or original license fee charged by the board for an applicant who meets both of the following requirements:

(1) Supplies evidence satisfactory to the board that the applicant is married to, or in a domestic partnership or other legal union with, an active duty member of the Armed Forces of the United States who is assigned to a duty station in this state under official active duty military orders.

(2) Holds a current license in another state, district, or territory of the United States in the profession or vocation for which the applicant seeks a license from the board.

(b) A board may adopt regulations necessary to administer this section.

(c) This section shall become operative on July 1, 2022.

Added Stats 2012 ch 399 § 1 (AB 1904), effective January 1, 2013. Amended Stats 2019 ch 351 § 19 (AB 496), effective January 1, 2020; Stat 2021 ch 367 § 1 (SB 607), effective September 28, 2021; Repealed July 1, 2022; Stat 2021 ch 367 § 2 (SB 607), operative July 1, 2021.

§ 115.6. Temporary licensure process for spouses of active duty members of Armed Forces [Repealed effective July 1, 2023]

(a) A board within the department shall, after appropriate investigation, issue the following eligible temporary licenses to an applicant if the applicant meets the requirements set forth in subdivision (c):

(1) Registered nurse license by the Board of Registered Nursing.

(2) Vocational nurse license issued by the Board of Vocational Nursing and Psychiatric Technicians of the State of California.

(3) Psychiatric technician license issued by the Board of Vocational Nursing and Psychiatric Technicians of the State of California.

(4) Speech-language pathologist license issued by the Speech-Language Pathology and Audiology and Hearing Aid Dispensers Board.

(5) Audiologist license issued by the Speech-Language Pathology and Audiology and Hearing Aid Dispensers Board.

(6) Veterinarian license issued by the Veterinary Medical Board.

(7) All licenses issued by the Board for Professional Engineers, Land Surveyors, and Geologists.

(8) All licenses issued by the Medical Board of California.

(9) All licenses issued by the Podiatric Medical Board of California.

(b) The board may conduct an investigation of an applicant for purposes of denying or revoking a temporary license issued pursuant to this section. This investigation may include a criminal background check.

(c) An applicant seeking a temporary license pursuant to this section shall meet the following requirements:

(1) The applicant shall supply evidence satisfactory to the board that the applicant is married to, or in a domestic partnership or other legal union with, an active duty member of the Armed Forces of the United States who is assigned to a duty station in this state under official active duty military orders.

(2) The applicant shall hold a current, active, and unrestricted license that confers upon the applicant the authority to practice, in another state, district, or territory of the United States, the profession or vocation for which the applicant seeks a temporary license from the board.

(3) The applicant shall submit an application to the board that shall include a signed affidavit attesting to the fact that the applicant meets all of the requirements for the temporary license and that the information submitted in the application is accurate, to the best of the applicant's knowledge. The application shall also include written verification from the applicant's original licensing jurisdiction stating that the applicant's license is in good standing in that jurisdiction.

Section V

(4) The applicant shall not have committed an act in any jurisdiction that would have constituted grounds for denial, suspension, or revocation of the license under this code at the time the act was committed. A violation of this paragraph may be grounds for the denial or revocation of a temporary license issued by the board.

(5) The applicant shall not have been disciplined by a licensing entity in another jurisdiction and shall not be the subject of an unresolved complaint, review procedure, or disciplinary proceeding conducted by a licensing entity in another jurisdiction.

(6) The applicant shall, upon request by a board, furnish a full set of fingerprints for purposes of conducting a criminal background check.

(d) A board may adopt regulations necessary to administer this section.

(e) A temporary license issued pursuant to this section may be immediately terminated upon a finding that the temporary licenseholder failed to meet any of the requirements described in subdivision (c) or provided substantively inaccurate information that would affect the person's eligibility for temporary licensure. Upon termination of the temporary license, the board shall issue a notice of termination that shall require the temporary licenseholder to immediately cease the practice of the licensed profession upon receipt.

(f) An applicant seeking a temporary license as a civil engineer, geotechnical engineer, structural engineer, land surveyor, professional geologist, professional geophysicist, certified engineering geologist, or certified hydrogeologist pursuant to this section shall successfully pass the appropriate California-specific examination or examinations required for licensure in those respective professions by the Board for Professional Engineers, Land Surveyors, and Geologists.

(g) A temporary license issued pursuant to this section shall expire 12 months after issuance, upon issuance of an expedited license pursuant to Section 115.5, or upon denial of the application for expedited licensure by the board, whichever occurs first.

(h) This section shall remain in effect only until July 1, 2023, and as of that date is repealed.

Added Stats 2021 ch 639 § 1 (AB 107), effective January 1, 2022.

§ 115.6. Temporary licensure process for spouses of active duty members of Armed Forces [Operative July 1, 2023]

(a) (1) Except as provided in subdivision (j), a board within the department shall, after appropriate investigation, issue a temporary license to practice a profession or vocation to an applicant who meets the requirements set forth in subdivisions (c) and (d).

(2) Revenues from fees for temporary licenses issued by the California Board of Accountancy shall be credited to the Accountancy Fund in accordance with Section 5132.

(b) The board may conduct an investigation of an applicant for purposes of denying or revoking a temporary license issued pursuant to this section. This investigation may include a criminal background check.

(c) An applicant seeking a temporary license pursuant to this section shall meet the following requirements:

(1) The applicant shall supply evidence satisfactory to the board that the applicant is married to, or in a domestic partnership or other legal union with, an active duty member of the Armed Forces of the United States who is assigned to a duty station in this state under official active duty military orders.

(2) The applicant shall hold a current, active, and unrestricted license that confers upon the applicant the authority to practice, in another state, district, or territory of the United States, the profession or vocation within the same scope for which the applicant seeks a temporary license from the board.

(3) The applicant shall submit an application to the board that shall include a signed affidavit attesting to the fact that the applicant meets all of the requirements for the temporary license, and that the information submitted in the application is accurate, to the best of the applicant's knowledge. The application shall also include written verification from the applicant's original licensing jurisdiction stating that the applicant's license is in good standing in that jurisdiction.

(4) The applicant shall not have committed an act in any jurisdiction that would have constituted grounds for denial, suspension, or revocation of the license under this code at the time the act was committed. A violation of this paragraph may be grounds for the denial or revocation of a temporary license issued by the board.

(5) The applicant shall not have been disciplined by a licensing entity in another jurisdiction and shall not be the subject of an unresolved complaint, review procedure, or disciplinary proceeding conducted by a licensing entity in another jurisdiction.

(6) (A) The applicant shall, upon request by a board, furnish a full set of fingerprints for purposes of conducting a criminal background check.

(B) The board shall request a fingerprint-based criminal history information check from the Department of Justice in accordance with subdivision (u) of Section 11105 of the Penal Code and the Department of Justice shall furnish state or federal criminal history information in accordance with subdivision (p) of Section 11105 of the Penal Code.

(d) The applicant shall pass a California law and ethics examination if otherwise required by the board for the profession or vocation for which the applicant seeks licensure.

(e) Except as specified in subdivision (g), a board shall issue a temporary license pursuant to this section within 30 days of receiving documentation that the applicant has met the requirements specified in subdivisions (c) and (d) if the results of the criminal background check do not show grounds for denial.

(f) (1) A temporary license issued pursuant to this section may be immediately terminated upon a finding that the temporary licenseholder failed to meet any of the requirements described in subdivision (c) or (d) or provided substantively inaccurate information that would affect the person's eligibility for temporary licensure. Upon termination of the temporary license, the board shall issue a notice of termination that shall require the temporary licenseholder to immediately cease the practice of the licensed profession upon receipt.

(2) Notwithstanding any other law, if, after notice and an opportunity to be heard, a board finds that a temporary licenseholder engaged in unprofessional conduct or any other act that is a cause for discipline by the board, the board shall revoke the temporary license.

(g) An applicant seeking a temporary license as a civil engineer, geotechnical engineer, structural engineer, land surveyor, professional geologist, professional geophysicist, certified engineering geologist, or certified hydrogeologist pursuant to this section shall successfully pass the appropriate California-specific examination or examinations required for licensure in those respective professions by the Board for Professional Engineers, Land Surveyors, and Geologists. The board shall issue a temporary license pursuant to this subdivision within 30 days of receiving documentation that the applicant has met the requirements specified in this subdivision and subdivisions (c) and (d) if the results of the criminal background check do not show grounds for denial.

(h) A temporary license issued pursuant to this section is nonrenewable and shall expire 12 months after issuance, upon issuance or denial of a standard license, upon issuance or denial of a license by endorsement, or upon issuance or denial of an expedited license pursuant to Section 115.5, whichever occurs first.

(i) A board shall submit to the department for approval, if necessary to implement this section, draft regulations necessary to administer this section. These regulations shall be adopted pursuant to the Administrative Procedure Act (Chapter 3.5 (commencing with Section 11340) of Part 1 of Division 3 of Title 2 of the Government Code).

(j) (1) This section shall not apply to a board that has a process in place by which an out-of-state licensed applicant in good standing who is married to, or in a domestic partnership or other legal union with, an active duty member of the Armed Forces of the United

States is able to receive expedited, temporary authorization to practice while meeting state-specific requirements for a period of at least one year or is able to receive an expedited license by endorsement with no additional requirements superseding those described in subdivisions (c) and (d).

(2) This section shall apply only to the extent that it does not amend an initiative or violate constitutional requirements.

(k) This section shall become operative on July 1, 2023.

Added Stats 2021 ch 639 § 2 (AB 107), operative July 1, 2023.

§ 115.8. Annual report on military, veteran, and spouse licensure

The Department of Consumer Affairs shall compile information on military, veteran, and spouse licensure into an annual report for the Legislature, which shall be submitted in conformance with Section 9795 of the Government Code. The report shall include all of the following:

(a) The number of applications for a temporary license submitted by active duty servicemembers, veterans, or military spouses per calendar year, pursuant to Section 115.6.

(b) The number of applications for expedited licenses submitted by veterans and active duty spouses pursuant to Sections 115.4 and 115.5.

(c) The number of licenses issued and denied per calendar year pursuant to Sections 115.4, 115.5, and 115.6.

(d) The number of licenses issued pursuant to Section 115.6 that were suspended or revoked per calendar year.

(e) The number of applications for waived renewal fees received and granted pursuant to Section 114.3 per calendar year.

(f) The average length of time between application and issuance of licenses pursuant to Sections 115.4, 115.5, and 115.6 per board and occupation.

Added Stats 2021 ch 639 § 3 (AB 107), effective January 1, 2022.

§ 115.9. Publishing information on licensing options available to military spouses

The department and each board within the department shall publish information pertinent to all licensing options available to military spouses on the home page of the internet website of the department or board, as applicable, including, but not limited to, the following:

(a) The process for expediting applications for military spouses.

(b) The availability of temporary licensure, the requirements for obtaining a temporary license, and length of time a temporary license is active.

Section V

(c) The requirements for full, permanent licensure by endorsement or credential for out-of-state applicants.

Added Stats 2021 ch 639 § 4 (AB 107), effective January 1, 2022.

§ 118. Effect of withdrawal of application; Effect of suspension, forfeiture, etc., of license

(a) The withdrawal of an application for a license after it has been filed with a board in the department shall not, unless the board has consented in writing to such withdrawal, deprive the board of its authority to institute or continue a proceeding against the applicant for the denial of the license upon any ground provided by law or to enter an order denying the license upon any such ground.

(b) The suspension, expiration, or forfeiture by operation of law of a license issued by a board in the department, or its suspension, forfeiture, or cancellation by order of the board or by order of a court of law, or its surrender without the written consent of the board, shall not, during any period in which it may be renewed, restored, reissued, or reinstated, deprive the board of its authority to institute or continue a disciplinary proceeding against the licensee upon any ground provided by law or to enter an order suspending or revoking the license or otherwise taking disciplinary action against the licensee on any such ground.

(c) As used in this section, "board" includes an individual who is authorized by any provision of this code to issue, suspend, or revoke a license, and "license" includes "certificate," "registration," and "permit."

Added Stats 1961 ch 1079 § 1.

§ 119. Misdemeanors pertaining to use of licenses

Any person who does any of the following is guilty of a misdemeanor:

(a) Displays or causes or permits to be displayed or has in the person's possession either of the following:

(1) A canceled, revoked, suspended, or fraudulently altered license.

(2) A fictitious license or any document simulating a license or purporting to be or have been issued as a license.

(b) Lends the person's license to any other person or knowingly permits the use thereof by another.

(c) Displays or represents any license not issued to the person as being the person's license.

(d) Fails or refuses to surrender to the issuing authority upon its lawful written demand any license, registration, permit, or certificate which has been suspended, revoked, or canceled.

(e) Knowingly permits any unlawful use of a license issued to the person.

(f) Photographs, photostats, duplicates, manufactures, or in any way reproduces any license or facsimile thereof in a manner that it could be mistaken for a valid license, or displays or has in the person's possession any such photograph, photostat, duplicate, reproduction, or facsimile unless authorized by this code.

(g) Buys or receives a fraudulent, forged, or counterfeited license knowing that it is fraudulent, forged, or counterfeited. For purposes of this subdivision, "fraudulent" means containing any misrepresentation of fact.

As used in this section, "license" includes "certificate," "permit," "authority," and "registration" or any other indicia giving authorization to engage in a business or profession regulated by this code or referred to in Section 1000 or 3600.

Added Stats 1965 ch 1083 § 1. Amended Stats 1990 ch 350 § 1 (SB 2084) (ch 1207 prevails), ch 1207 § 1 (AB 3242); Stats 1994 ch 1206 § 1 (SB 1775); Stats 2000 ch 568 § 1 (AB 2888); Stats 2019 ch 351 § 22 (AB 496), effective January 1, 2020.

§ 121. Practice during period between renewal and receipt of evidence of renewal

No licensee who has complied with the provisions of this code relating to the renewal of the licensee's license prior to expiration of such license shall be deemed to be engaged illegally in the practice of the licensee's business or profession during any period between such renewal and receipt of evidence of such renewal which may occur due to delay not the fault of the applicant.

As used in this section, "license" includes "certificate," "permit," "authorization," and "registration," or any other indicia giving authorization, by any agency, board, bureau, commission, committee, or entity within the Department of Consumer Affairs, to engage in a business or profession regulated by this code or by the board referred to in the Chiropractic Act or the Osteopathic Act.

Added Stats 1979 ch 77 § 1. Amended Stats 2019 ch 351 § 24 (AB 496), effective January 1, 2020.

§ 121.5. Application of fees to licenses or registrations lawfully inactivated

Except as otherwise provided in this code, the application of delinquency fees or accrued and unpaid renewal fees for the renewal of expired licenses or registrations shall not apply to licenses or registrations that have lawfully been designated as inactive or retired.

Added Stats 2001 ch 435 § 1 (SB 349).

§ 122. Fee for issuance of duplicate certificate

Except as otherwise provided by law, the department and each of the boards, bureaus, committees, and commissions within the department may charge a fee for the processing and issuance of a duplicate copy of any certificate of licensure or other form evidencing licensure or renewal of licensure. The fee shall be in an amount sufficient to cover all costs incident to the issuance of the duplicate certificate or other form but shall not exceed twenty-five dollars ($25).

Added Stats 1986 ch 951 § 1.

§ 123. Conduct constituting subversion of licensing examination; Penalties and damages

It is a misdemeanor for any person to engage in any conduct which subverts or attempts to subvert any licensing examination or the administration of an examination, including, but not limited to:

(a) Conduct which violates the security of the examination materials; removing from the examination room any examination materials without authorization; the unauthorized reproduction by any means of any portion of the actual licensing examination; aiding by any means the unauthorized reproduction of any portion of the actual licensing examination; paying or using professional or paid examination-takers for the purpose of reconstructing any portion of the licensing examination; obtaining examination questions or other examination material, except by specific authorization either before, during, or after an examination; or using or purporting to use any examination questions or materials which were improperly removed or taken from any examination for the purpose of instructing or preparing any applicant for examination; or selling, distributing, buying, receiving, or having unauthorized possession of any portion of a future, current, or previously administered licensing examination.

(b) Communicating with any other examinee during the administration of a licensing examination; copying answers from another examinee or permitting one's answers to be copied by another examinee; having in one's possession during the administration of the licensing examination any books, equipment, notes, written or printed materials, or data of any kind, other than the examination materials distributed, or otherwise authorized to be in one's possession during the examination; or impersonating any examinee or having an impersonator take the licensing examination on one's behalf.

Nothing in this section shall preclude prosecution under the authority provided for in any other provision of law.

In addition to any other penalties, a person found guilty of violating this section, shall be liable for the actual damages sustained by the agency administering the examination not to exceed ten thousand dollars ($10,000) and the costs of litigation.

(c) If any provision of this section or the application thereof to any person or circumstances is held invalid, that invalidity shall not affect other provisions or applications of the section that can be given effect without the invalid provision or application, and to this end the provisions of this section are severable.

Added Stats 1989 ch 1022 § 1. Amended Stats 1991 ch 647 § 1 (SB 879).

§ 123.5. Enjoining violations

Whenever any person has engaged, or is about to engage, in any acts or practices which constitute, or will constitute, a violation of Section 123, the superior court in and for the county wherein the acts or practices take place, or are about to take place, may issue an injunction, or other appropriate order, restraining such conduct on application of a board, the Attorney General or the district attorney of the county.

The proceedings under this section shall be governed by Chapter 3 (commencing with Section 525) of Title 7 of Part 2 of the Code of Civil Procedure.

The remedy provided for by this section shall be in addition to, and not a limitation on, the authority provided for in any other provision of law.

Added Stats 1983 ch 95 § 2, as B & P C § 497. Amended and Renumbered by Stats 1989 ch 1022 § 4.

§ 124. Manner of notice

Notwithstanding subdivision (c) of Section 11505 of the Government Code, whenever written notice, including a notice, order, or document served pursuant to Chapter 3.5 (commencing with Section 11340), Chapter 4 (commencing with Section 11370), or Chapter 5 (commencing with Section 11500), of Part 1 of Division 3 of Title 2 of the Government Code, is required to be given by any board in the department, the notice may be given by regular mail addressed to the last known address of the licensee or by personal service, at the option of the board.

Added Stats 1961 ch 1253 § 2. Amended Stats 1994 ch 26 § 4 (AB 1807), effective March 30, 1994; Stats 1995 ch 938 § 1 (SB 523), operative July 1, 1997; Stats 2019 ch 351 § 25 (AB 496), effective January 1, 2020.

§ 125. Misdemeanor offenses by licensees

Any person, licensed under Division 1 (commencing with Section 100), Division 2 (commencing with Section 500), or Division 3 (commencing with Section 5000) is guilty of a misdemeanor and subject to the disciplinary provisions of this code applicable to them, who conspires with a person not so licensed to violate any provision of this code, or who, with intent to aid or assist that person in violating those provisions does either of the following:

(a) Allows their license to be used by that person.

(b) Acts as their agent or partner.

Added Stats 1949 ch 308 § 1. Amended Stats 1994 ch 1206 § 2 (SB 1775); Stats 2019 ch 351 § 26 (AB 496), effective January 1, 2020.

§ 125.3. Direction to licensee violating licensing act to pay costs of investigation and enforcement

(a) Except as otherwise provided by law, in any order issued in resolution of a disciplinary proceeding before any board within the department or before the Osteopathic Medical Board, upon request of the entity bringing the proceeding, the administrative law judge may direct a licensee found to have committed a violation or violations of the licensing act to pay a sum not to exceed the reasonable costs of the investigation and enforcement of the case.

(b) In the case of a disciplined licensee that is a corporation or a partnership, the order may be made against the licensed corporate entity or licensed partnership.

(c) A certified copy of the actual costs, or a good faith estimate of costs where actual costs are not available, signed by the entity bringing the proceeding or its designated representative shall be prima facie evidence of reasonable costs of investigation and prosecution of the case. The costs shall include the amount of investigative and enforcement costs up to the date of the hearing, including, but not limited to, charges imposed by the Attorney General.

(d) The administrative law judge shall make a proposed finding of the amount of reasonable costs of investigation and prosecution of the case when requested pursuant to subdivision (a). The finding of the administrative law judge with regard to costs shall not be reviewable by the board to increase the cost award. The board may reduce or eliminate the cost award, or remand to the administrative law judge if the proposed decision fails to make a finding on costs requested pursuant to subdivision (a).

(e) If an order for recovery of costs is made and timely payment is not made as directed in the board's decision, the board may enforce the order for repayment in any appropriate court. This right of enforcement shall be in addition to any other rights the board may have as to any licensee to pay costs.

(f) In any action for recovery of costs, proof of the board's decision shall be conclusive proof of the validity of the order of payment and the terms for payment.

(g) (1) Except as provided in paragraph (2), the board shall not renew or reinstate the license of any licensee who has failed to pay all of the costs ordered under this section.

(2) Notwithstanding paragraph (1), the board may, in its discretion, conditionally renew or reinstate for a maximum of one year the license of any licensee who demonstrates financial hardship and who enters into a formal agreement with the board to reimburse the board within that one-year period for the unpaid costs.

(h) All costs recovered under this section shall be considered a reimbursement for costs incurred and shall be deposited in the fund of the board recovering the costs to be available upon appropriation by the Legislature.

(i) Nothing in this section shall preclude a board from including the recovery of the costs of investigation and enforcement of a case in any stipulated settlement.

(j) This section does not apply to any board if a specific statutory provision in that board's licensing act provides for recovery of costs in an administrative disciplinary proceeding.

(k) Notwithstanding the provisions of this section, the Medical Board of California shall not request nor obtain from a physician and surgeon, investigation and prosecution costs for a disciplinary proceeding against the licensee. The board shall ensure that this subdivision is revenue neutral with regard to it and that any loss of revenue or increase in costs resulting from this subdivision is offset by an increase in the amount of the initial license fee and the biennial renewal fee, as provided in subdivision (e) of Section 2435.

Added Stats 1992 ch 1289 § 1 (AB 2743), effective January 1, 1993. Amended Stats 2001 ch 728 § 1 (SB 724); Stats 2005 ch 674 § 2 (SB 231), effective January 1, 2006; Stats 2006 ch 223 § 2 (SB 1438), effective January 1, 2007; Stats 2019 ch 351 § 27 (AB 496), effective January 1, 2020.

§ 125.5. Enjoining violations; Restitution orders

(a) The superior court for the county in which any person has engaged or is about to engage in any act which constitutes a violation of a chapter of this code administered or enforced by a board within the department may, upon a petition filed by the board with the approval of the director, issue an injunction or other appropriate order restraining such conduct. The proceedings under this section shall be governed by Chapter 3 (commencing with Section 525) of Title 7 of Part 2 of the Code of Civil Procedure. As used in this section, "board" includes commission, bureau, division, agency and a medical quality review committee.

(b) The superior court for the county in which any person has engaged in any act which constitutes a violation of a chapter of this code administered or enforced by a board within the department may, upon a petition filed by the board with the approval of the director, order such person to make restitution to persons injured as a result of such violation.

(c) The court may order a person subject to an injunction or restraining order, provided for in subdivision (a) of this section, or subject to an order requiring restitution pursuant to subdivision (b), to reimburse the petitioning board for expenses incurred by the board in its investigation related to its petition.

(d) The remedy provided for by this section shall be in addition to, and not a limitation on, the authority provided for in any other section of this code.

Added Stats 1972 ch 1238 § 1. Amended Stats 1973 ch 632 § 1; Stats 2d Ex Sess 1975 ch 1 § 2; Stats 1982 ch 517 § 1.

§ 125.6. Unlawful discrimination by licensees

(a) (1) With regard to an applicant, every person who holds a license under the provisions of this code is subject to disciplinary action under the disciplinary provisions of this code applicable to that person if, because of any characteristic listed or defined in subdivision (b) or (e) of Section 51 of the Civil Code, the person refuses to perform the licensed activity or aids or incites the refusal to perform that licensed activity by another licensee, or if, because of any characteristic listed or defined in subdivision (b) or (e) of Section 51 of the Civil Code, the person makes any discrimination, or restriction in the performance of the licensed activity.

(2) Nothing in this section shall be interpreted to prevent a physician or health care professional licensed pursuant to Division 2 (commencing with Section 500) from considering any of the characteristics of a patient listed in subdivision (b) or (e) of Section 51 of the Civil Code if that consideration is medically necessary and for the sole purpose of determining the appropriate diagnosis or treatment of the patient.

(3) Nothing in this section shall be interpreted to apply to discrimination by employers with regard to employees or prospective employees, nor shall this section authorize action against any club license issued pursuant to Article 4 (commencing with Section 23425) of Chapter 3 of Division 9 because of discriminatory membership policy.

(4) The presence of architectural barriers to an individual with physical disabilities that conform to applicable state or local building codes and regulations shall not constitute discrimination under this section.

(b) (1) Nothing in this section requires a person licensed pursuant to Division 2 (commencing with Section 500) to permit an individual to participate in, or benefit from, the licensed activity of the licensee where that individual poses a direct threat to the health or safety of others. For this purpose, the term "direct threat" means a significant risk to the health or safety of others that cannot be eliminated by a modification of policies, practices, or procedures or by the provision of auxiliary aids and services.

(2) Nothing in this section requires a person licensed pursuant to Division 2 (commencing with Section 500) to perform a licensed activity for which the person is not qualified to perform.

(c) (1) "Applicant," as used in this section, means a person applying for licensed services provided by a person licensed under this code.

(2) "License," as used in this section, includes "certificate," "permit," "authority," and "registration" or any other indicia giving authorization to engage in a business or profession regulated by this code.

Added Stats 1974 ch 1350 § 1. Amended Stats 1977 ch 293 § 1; Stats 1980 ch 191 § 1; Stats 1992 ch 913 § 2 (AB 1077); Stats 2007 ch 568 § 2 (AB 14), effective January 1, 2008; Stats 2019 ch 351 § 28 (AB 496), effective January 1, 2020.

§ 125.7. Restraining orders

In addition to the remedy provided for in Section 125.5, the superior court for the county in which any licensee licensed under Division 2 (commencing with Section 500), or any initiative act referred to in that division, has engaged or is about to engage in any act that constitutes a violation of a chapter of this code administered or enforced by a board referred to in Division 2 (commencing with Section 500), may, upon a petition filed by the board and accompanied by an affidavit or affidavits in support thereof and a memorandum of points and authorities, issue a temporary restraining order or other appropriate order restraining the licensee from engaging in the business or profession for which the person is licensed or from any part thereof, in accordance with this section.

(a) If the affidavits in support of the petition show that the licensee has engaged or is about to engage in acts or omissions constituting a violation of a chapter of this code and if the court is satisfied that permitting the licensee to continue to engage in the business or profession for which the license was issued will endanger the public health, safety, or welfare, the court may issue an order temporarily restraining the licensee from engaging in the profession for which he or she is licensed.

(b) The order may not be issued without notice to the licensee unless it appears from facts shown by the affidavits that serious injury would result to the public before the matter can be heard on notice.

(c) Except as otherwise specifically provided by this section, proceedings under this section shall be governed by Chapter 3 (commencing with Section 525) of Title 7 of Part 2 of the Code of Civil Procedure.

(d) When a restraining order is issued pursuant to this section, or within a time to be allowed by the superior court, but in any case not more than 30 days after the restraining order is issued, an accusation shall be filed with the board pursuant to Section 11503 of the Government Code or, in the case of a licensee of the State Department of Health Services, with that department pursuant to Section 100171 of the Health and Safety Code. The accusation shall be served upon the licensee as provided by Section 11505 of the Government Code. The licensee shall have all of the rights and privileges available as specified in Chapter 5 (commencing with Section 11500) of Part 1 of Division 3 of Title 2 of the Government Code. However, if the licensee requests a hearing on the accusation, the board shall provide the licensee with a hearing within 30 days of the request and a decision within 15 days of the date the decision is received from the administrative law judge, or the court may nullify the restraining order previously issued. Any restraining order issued pursuant to this section shall be dissolved by operation of law at the time the board's decision is subject to judicial review pursuant to Section 1094.5 of the Code of Civil Procedure.

(e) The remedy provided for in this section shall be in addition to, and not a limitation upon, the authority provided by any other provision of this code.

Added Stats 1977 ch 292 § 1. Amended Stats 1982 ch 517 § 2; Stats 1994 ch 1206 § 3 (SB 1775); Stats 1997 ch 220 § 1 (SB 68), effective August 4, 1997; Stats 1998 ch 878 § 1.5 (SB 2239).

§ 125.8. Temporary order restraining licensee engaged or about to engage in violation of law

In addition to the remedy provided for in Section 125.5, the superior court for the county in which any licensee licensed under Division 3 (commencing with Section 5000) or Chapter 2 (commencing with Section 18600) or Chapter 3 (commencing with Section 19000) of Division 8 has engaged or is about to engage in any act which constitutes a violation of a chapter of this code administered or enforced by a board referred to in Division 3 (commencing with Section 5000) or Chapter 2 (commencing with Section 18600) or Chapter 3 (commencing with Section 19000) of Division 8 may, upon a petition filed by the board and accompanied by an affidavit or affidavits in support thereof and a memorandum of points and authorities, issue a temporary restraining order or other appropriate order restraining the licensee from engaging in the business or profession for which the person is licensed or from any part thereof, in accordance with the provisions of this section.

(a) If the affidavits in support of the petition show that the licensee has engaged or is about to engage in acts or omissions constituting a violation of a chapter of this code and if the court is satisfied that permitting the licensee to continue to engage in the business or profession for which the license was issued will endanger the public health, safety, or welfare, the court may issue an order temporarily restraining the licensee from engaging in the profession for which he is licensed.

(b) Such order may not be issued without notice to the licensee unless it appears from facts shown by the affidavits that serious injury would result to the public before the matter can be heard on notice.

(c) Except as otherwise specifically provided by this section, proceedings under this section shall be governed by Chapter 3 (commencing with Section 525) of Title 7 of Part 2 of the Code of Civil Procedure.

(d) When a restraining order is issued pursuant to this section, or within a time to be allowed by the superior court, but in any case not more than 30 days after the restraining order is issued, an accusation shall be filed with the board pursuant to Section 11503 of the Government Code. The accusation shall be served upon the licensee as provided by Section 11505 of the Government Code. The licensee shall have all of the rights and privileges available as specified in Chapter 5 (commencing with Section 11500) of Part 1 of Division 3 of Title 2 of the Government Code; however, if the licensee requests a hearing on the accusation, the board must provide the licensee with a hearing within 30 days of the request and a decision within 15 days of the date of the conclusion of the hearing, or the court may nullify the restraining order previously issued. Any restraining order issued pursuant to this section shall be dissolved by operation of law at such time the board's decision is subject to judicial review pursuant to Section 1094.5 of the Code of Civil Procedure.

Added Stats 1977 ch 443 § 1. Amended Stats 1982 ch 517 § 3.

§ 125.9. System for issuance of citations to licensees; Contents; Fines

(a) Except with respect to persons regulated under Chapter 11 (commencing with Section 7500), any board, bureau, or commission within the department, the State Board of Chiropractic Examiners, and the Osteopathic Medical Board of California, may establish, by regulation, a system for the issuance to a licensee of a citation which may contain an order of abatement or an order to pay an administrative fine assessed by the board, bureau, or commission where the licensee is in violation of the applicable licensing act or any regulation adopted pursuant thereto.

(b) The system shall contain the following provisions:

(1) Citations shall be in writing and shall describe with particularity the nature of the violation, including specific reference to the provision of law determined to have been violated.

(2) Whenever appropriate, the citation shall contain an order of abatement fixing a reasonable time for abatement of the violation.

(3) In no event shall the administrative fine assessed by the board, bureau, or commission exceed five thousand dollars ($5,000) for each inspection or each investigation made with respect to the violation, or five thousand dollars ($5,000) for each violation or count if the violation involves fraudulent billing submitted to an insurance company, the Medi-Cal program, or Medicare. In assessing a fine, the board, bureau, or commission shall give due consideration to the appropriateness of the amount of the fine with respect to factors such as the gravity of the violation, the good faith of the licensee, and the history of previous violations.

(4) A citation or fine assessment issued pursuant to a citation shall inform the licensee that if the licensee desires a hearing to contest the finding of a violation, that hearing shall be requested by written notice to the board, bureau, or commission within 30 days of the date of issuance of the citation or assessment. If a hearing is not requested pursuant to this section, payment of any fine shall not constitute an admission of the violation charged. Hearings shall be held pursuant to Chapter 5 (commencing with Section 11500) of Part 1 of Division 3 of Title 2 of the Government Code.

(5) Failure of a licensee to pay a fine or comply with an order of abatement, or both, within 30 days of the date of assessment or order, unless the citation is being appealed, may result in disciplinary action being taken by the board, bureau, or commission. Where a citation is not contested and a fine is not paid, the full amount of the assessed fine shall be added to the fee for renewal of the license. A license shall not be renewed without payment of the renewal fee and fine.

(c) The system may contain the following provisions:

(1) A citation may be issued without the assessment of an administrative fine.

(2) Assessment of administrative fines may be limited to only particular violations of the applicable licensing act.

(d) Notwithstanding any other provision of law, if a fine is paid to satisfy an assessment based on the finding of a violation, payment of the fine and compliance with the order of abatement, if applicable, shall be represented as satisfactory resolution of the matter for purposes of public disclosure.

(e) Administrative fines collected pursuant to this section shall be deposited in the special fund of the particular board, bureau, or commission.

Added Stats 1986 ch 1379 § 2. Amended Stats 1987 ch 1088 § 1; Stats 1991 ch 521 § 1 (SB 650); Stats 1995 ch 381 § 4 (AB 910), effective August 4, 1995, ch 708 § 1 (SB 609); Stats 2000 ch 197 § 1 (SB 1636); Stats 2001 ch 309 § 1 (AB 761), ch 728 § 1.2 (SB 724); Stats 2003 ch 788 § 1 (SB 362); Stats 2012 ch 291 § 1 (SB 1077), effective January 1, 2013; Stats 2019 ch 351 § 29 (AB 496), effective January 1, 2020; Stats 2020 ch 312 § 3 (SB 1474), effective January 1, 2021.

§ 126. Submission of reports to Governor

Notwithstanding any other provision of this code, any board, commission, examining committee, or other similarly constituted agency within the department required prior to the effective date of this section to submit reports to the Governor under any provision of this code shall not be required to submit such reports.

Added Stats 1967 ch 660 § 1.

§ 127. Submission of reports to director

Notwithstanding any other provision of this code, the director may require such reports from any board, commission, examining committee, or other similarly constituted agency within the department as the director deems reasonably necessary on any phase of their operations.

Added Stats 1967 ch 660 § 2. Amended Stats 2019 ch 351 § 30 (AB 496), effective January 1, 2020.

§ 128. Sale of equipment, supplies, or services for use in violation of licensing requirements

Notwithstanding any other provision of law, it is a misdemeanor to sell equipment, supplies, or services to any person with knowledge that the equipment, supplies, or services are to be used in the performance of a service or contract in violation of the licensing requirements of this code.

The provisions of this section shall not be applicable to cash sales of less than one hundred dollars ($100).

For the purposes of this section, "person" includes, but is not limited to, a company, partnership, limited liability company, firm, or corporation.

For the purposes of this section, "license" includes certificate or registration.

A violation of this section shall be punishable by a fine of not less than one thousand dollars ($1,000) and by imprisonment in the county jail not exceeding six months.

Added Stats 1971 ch 1052 § 1. Amended Stats 1994 ch 1010 § 1 (SB 2053).

§ 128.5. Reduction of license fees in event of surplus funds

(a) Notwithstanding any other provision of law, if at the end of any fiscal year, an agency within the Department of Consumer Affairs, except the agencies referred to in subdivision (b), has unencumbered funds in an amount that equals or is more than the agency's operating budget for the next two fiscal years, the agency shall reduce license or other fees, whether the license or other fees be fixed by stat-

Section V

ute or may be determined by the agency within limits fixed by statute, during the following fiscal year in an amount that will reduce any surplus funds of the agency to an amount less than the agency's operating budget for the next two fiscal years.

(b) Notwithstanding any other provision of law, if at the end of any fiscal year, the California Architects Board, the Board of Behavioral Sciences, the Veterinary Medical Board, the Court Reporters Board of California, the Medical Board of California, the Board of Vocational Nursing and Psychiatric Technicians, or the Bureau of Security and Investigative Services has unencumbered funds in an amount that equals or is more than the agency's operating budget for the next two fiscal years, the agency shall reduce license or other fees, whether the license or other fees be fixed by statute or may be determined by the agency within limits fixed by statute, during the following fiscal year in an amount that will reduce any surplus funds of the agency to an amount less than the agency's operating budget for the next two fiscal years.

Added Stats 1972 ch 938 § 2, effective August 16, 1972, as B & P C § 128. Amended Stats 1973 ch 863 § 3. Amended and Renumbered by Stats 1978 ch 1161 § 4. Amended Stats 1987 ch 850 § 3; Stats 1989 ch 886 § 2; Stats 1993 ch 1263 § 2 (AB 936); Stats 1994 ch 26 § 5 (AB 1807), effective March 30, 1994; Stats 1995 ch 60 § 2 (SB 42), effective July 6, 1995; Stats 1997 ch 759 § 2 (SB 827); Stats 2000 ch 1054 § 1 (SB 1863); Stats. 2009, Ch. 308 (SB 819).

§ 129. Handling of complaints; Reports to Legislature

(a) As used in this section, "board" means every board, bureau, commission, committee, and similarly constituted agency in the department that issues licenses.

(b) Each board shall, upon receipt of any complaint respecting an individual licensed by the board, notify the complainant of the initial administrative action taken on the complainant's complaint within 10 days of receipt. Each board shall notify the complainant of the final action taken on the complainant's complaint. There shall be a notification made in every case in which the complainant is known. If the complaint is not within the jurisdiction of the board or if the board is unable to dispose satisfactorily of the complaint, the board shall transmit the complaint together with any evidence or information it has concerning the complaint to the agency, public or private, whose authority in the opinion of the board will provide the most effective means to secure the relief sought. The board shall notify the complainant of this action and of any other means that may be available to the complainant to secure relief.

(c) The board shall, when the board deems it appropriate, notify the person against whom the complaint is made of the nature of the complaint, may request appropriate relief for the complainant, and may meet and confer with the complainant and the licensee in order to mediate the complaint. Nothing in this subdivision shall be construed as authorizing or requiring any board to set or to modify any fee charged by a licensee.

(d) It shall be the continuing duty of the board to ascertain patterns of complaints and to report on all actions taken with respect to those patterns of complaints to the director and to the Legislature at least once per year. The board shall evaluate those complaints dismissed for lack of jurisdiction or no violation and recommend to the director and to the Legislature at least once per year the statutory changes it deems necessary to implement the board's functions and responsibilities under this section.

(e) It shall be the continuing duty of the board to take whatever action it deems necessary, with the approval of the director, to inform the public of its functions under this section.

(f) Notwithstanding any other law, upon receipt of a child custody evaluation report submitted to a court pursuant to Chapter 6 (commencing with Section 3110) of Part 2 of Division 8 of the Family Code, the board shall notify the noncomplaining party in the underlying custody dispute, who is a subject of that report, of the pending investigation.

Added Stats 1972 ch 1041 § 1. Amended Stats 2014 ch 283 § 1 (AB 1843), effective January 1, 2015; Stats 2019 ch 351 § 31 (AB 496), effective January 1, 2020.

§ 130. Terms of office of agency members

(a) Notwithstanding any other law, the term of office of any member of an agency designated in subdivision (b) shall be for a term of four years expiring on June 1.

(b) Subdivision (a) applies to the following boards or committees:

(1) The Medical Board of California.

(2) The Podiatric Medical Board of California.

(3) The Physical Therapy Board of California.

(4) The Board of Registered Nursing, except as provided in subdivision (c) of Section 2703.

(5) The Board of Vocational Nursing and Psychiatric Technicians.

(6) The California State Board of Optometry.

(7) The California State Board of Pharmacy.

(8) The Veterinary Medical Board.

(9) The California Architects Board.

(10) The Landscape Architect Technical Committee.

(11) The Board for Professional Engineers and Land Surveyors.

(12) The Contractors State License Board.

(13) The Board of Behavioral Sciences.

(14) The Court Reporters Board of California.

(15) The State Athletic Commission.

(16) The Osteopathic Medical Board of California.

(17) The Respiratory Care Board of California.

(18) The Acupuncture Board.

(19) The Board of Psychology.

(20) The Structural Pest Control Board.

Added Stats 1969 ch 465 § 1. Amended Stats 1971 ch 716 § 8; Stats 1978 ch 1161 § 5; Stats 1983 ch 150 § 2; Stats 1986 ch 655 § 1; Stats 1987 ch 850 § 4; Stats 1989 ch 886 § 3; Stats 1990 ch 1256 § 2 (AB 2649); Stats 1991 ch 359 § 2 (AB 1332); Stats 1994 ch 26 § 6 (AB 1807), effective March 30, 1994, ch 1274 § 1.3 (SB 2039); Stats 1995 ch 60 § 3 (SB 42), effective July 6, 1995; Stats 1997 ch 759 § 3 (SB 827); Stats 1998 ch 59 § 4 (AB 969), ch 970 § 1 (AB 2802), ch 971 § 1 (AB 2721); Stats 2000 ch 1054 § 2 (SB 1863); Stats 2001 ch 159 § 3 (SB 662); Stats 2009–2010 4th Ex Sess ch 18 § 2 (ABX4 20), effective October 23, 2009; Stats 2012 ch 4 § 1 (SB 98), effective February 14, 2012. See this section as modified in Governor's Reorganization Plan No. 2 § 3 of 2012; Amended Stats 2013 ch 352 § 4 (AB 1317), effective September 26, 2013, operative July 1, 2013; Stats 2019 ch 351 § 32 (AB 496), effective January 1, 2020; Stats 2020 ch 312 § 4 (SB 1474), effective January 1, 2021; Stats 2021 ch 630 § 3 (AB 1534), effective January 1, 2022.

§ 131. Maximum number of terms

Notwithstanding any other provision of law, no member of an agency designated in subdivision (b) of Section 130 or member of a board, commission, committee, or similarly constituted agency in the department shall serve more than two consecutive full terms.

Added Stats 1970 ch 1394 § 1, operative July 1, 1971. Amended Stats 1987 ch 850 § 5.

§ 134. Proration of license fees

When the term of any license issued by any agency in the department exceeds one year, initial license fees for licenses which are issued during a current license term shall be prorated on a yearly basis.

Added Stats 1974 ch 743 § 1. Amended Stats 1978 ch 1161 § 6.

§ 135. Reexamination of applicants

No agency in the department shall, on the basis of an applicant's failure to successfully complete prior examinations, impose any additional limitations, restrictions, prerequisites, or requirements on any applicant who wishes to participate in subsequent examinations except that any examining agency which allows an applicant conditional credit for successfully completing a divisible part of an examination may require that an applicant be reexamined in those parts successfully completed if such applicant has not successfully completed all parts of the examination within a required period of time established by the examining agency. Nothing in this section, however, requires the exemption of such applicant from the regular fees and requirements normally associated with examinations.

Added Stats 1974 ch 743 § 2.

§ 135.4. Refugees, asylees, and special immigrant visa holders; professional licensing; initial licensure process

(a) Notwithstanding any other law, a board within the department shall expedite, and may assist, the initial licensure process for an applicant who supplies satisfactory evidence to the board that they have been admitted to the United States as a refugee under Section 1157 of Title 8 of the United States Code, have been granted asylum by the Secretary of Homeland Security or the Attorney General of the United States pursuant to Section 1158 of Title 8 of the United States Code, or they have a special immigrant visa (SIV) that has been granted a status under Section 1244 of Public Law 110-181, under Public Law 109-163, or under Section 602(b) of Title VI of Division F of Public Law 111-8.

(b) Nothing in this section shall be construed as changing existing licensure requirements. A person applying for expedited licensure under subdivision (a) shall meet all applicable statutory and regulatory licensure requirements.

(c) A board may adopt regulations necessary to administer this section.

Added Stats 2020 ch 186 § 1 (AB 2113), effective January 1, 2021.

§ 135.5. Licensure and citizenship or immigration status

(a) The Legislature finds and declares that it is in the best interests of the State of California to provide persons who are not lawfully present in the United States with the state benefits provided by all licensing acts of entities within the department, and therefore enacts this section pursuant to subsection (d) of Section 1621 of Title 8 of the United States Code.

(b) Notwithstanding subdivision (a) of Section 30, and except as required by subdivision (e) of Section 7583.23, no entity within the department shall deny licensure to an applicant based on his or her citizenship status or immigration status.

(c) Every board within the department shall implement all required regulatory or procedural changes necessary to implement this section no later than January 1, 2016. A board may implement the provisions of this section at any time prior to January 1, 2016.

Added Stats 2014 ch 752 § 2 (SB 1159), effective January 1, 2015.

§ 136. Notification of change of address; Punishment for failure to comply

(a) Each person holding a license, certificate, registration, permit, or other authority to engage in a profession or occupation issued by a board within the department shall notify the issuing board at its principal office of any change in the person's mailing address within 30 days after the change, unless the board has specified by regulations a shorter time period.

(b) Except as otherwise provided by law, failure of a licensee to comply with the requirement in subdivision (a) constitutes grounds for the issuance of a citation and administrative fine, if the board has the authority to issue citations and administrative fines.

Added Stats 1994 ch 26 § 7 (AB 1807), effective March 30, 1994. Amended Stats 2019 ch 351 § 34 (AB 496), effective January 1, 2020.

§ 137. Regulations requiring inclusion of license numbers in advertising, etc.

Any agency within the department may promulgate regulations requiring licensees to include their license numbers in any advertising, soliciting, or other presentments to the public.

However, nothing in this section shall be construed to authorize regulation of any person not a licensee who engages in advertising, solicitation, or who makes any other presentment to the public on behalf of a licensee. Such a person shall incur no liability pursuant to this section for communicating in any advertising, soliciting, or other presentment to the public a licensee's license number exactly as provided by the licensee or for failure to communicate such number if none is provided by the licensee.

Added Stats 1974 ch 743 § 3. Amended Stats 2019 ch 351 § 35 (AB 496), effective January 1, 2020.

§ 138. Notice that practitioner is licensed; Evaluation of licensing examination

Every board in the department, as defined in Section 22, shall initiate the process of adopting regulations on or before June 30, 1999, to require its licensees, as defined in Section 23.8, to provide notice to their clients or customers that the practitioner is licensed by this state. A board shall be exempt from the requirement to adopt regulations pursuant to this section if the board has in place, in statute or regulation, a requirement that provides for consumer notice of a practitioner's status as a licensee of this state.

Added Stats 1998 ch 879 § 1 (SB 2238). Amended Stats 1999 ch 67 § 1 (AB 1105), effective July 6, 1999; Stats 2019 ch 351 § 36 (AB 496), effective January 1, 2020.

§ 139. Policy for examination development and validation, and occupational analysis

(a) The Legislature finds and declares that occupational analyses and examination validation studies are fundamental components of licensure programs. It is the intent of the Legislature that the policy developed by the department pursuant to subdivision (b) be used by the fiscal, policy, and sunset review committees of the Legislature in their annual reviews of these boards, programs, and bureaus.

(b) Notwithstanding any other provision of law, the department shall develop, in consultation with the boards, programs, bureaus, and divisions under its jurisdiction, and the Osteopathic Medical Board of California and the State Board of Chiropractic Examiners, a policy regarding examination development and validation, and occupational analysis. The department shall finalize and distribute this policy by September 30, 1999, to each of the boards, programs, bureaus, and divisions under its jurisdiction and to the Osteopathic Medical Board of California and the State Board of Chiropractic Examiners. This policy shall be submitted in draft form at least 30 days prior to that date to the appropriate fiscal, policy, and sunset review committees of the Legislature for review. This policy shall address, but shall not be limited to, the following issues:

(1) An appropriate schedule for examination validation and occupational analyses, and circumstances under which more frequent reviews are appropriate.

(2) Minimum requirements for psychometrically sound examination validation, examination development, and occupational analyses, including standards for sufficient number of test items.

(3) Standards for review of state and national examinations.

(4) Setting of passing standards.

(5) Appropriate funding sources for examination validations and occupational analyses.

(6) Conditions under which boards, programs, and bureaus should use internal and external entities to conduct these reviews.

(7) Standards for determining appropriate costs of reviews of different types of examinations, measured in terms of hours required.

(8) Conditions under which it is appropriate to fund permanent and limited term positions within a board, program, or bureau to manage these reviews.

(c) Every regulatory board and bureau, as defined in Section 22, and every program and bureau administered by the department, the Osteopathic Medical Board of California, and the State Board of Chiropractic Examiners, shall submit to the director on or before December 1, 1999, and on or before December 1 of each subsequent year, its method for ensuring that every licensing examination administered by or pursuant to contract with the board is subject to periodic evaluation. The evaluation shall include (1) a description of the occupational analysis serving as the basis for the examination; (2) sufficient item analysis data to permit a psychometric evaluation of the items; (3) an assessment of the appropriateness of prerequisites for admittance to the examination; and (4) an estimate of the costs and personnel required to perform these functions. The evaluation shall be revised and a new evaluation submitted to the director whenever, in the judgment of the board, program, or bureau, there is a substantial change in the examination or the prerequisites for admittance to the examination.

(d) The evaluation may be conducted by the board, program, or bureau, the Office of Professional Examination Services of the department, the Osteopathic Medical Board of California, or the State Board of Chiropractic Examiners or pursuant to a contract with a qualified private testing firm. A board, program, or bureau that provides for development or administration of a licensing examination pursuant to contract with a public or private entity may rely on an occupational analysis or item analysis conducted by that entity. The department shall compile this information, along with a schedule specifying when examination validations and occupational analyses shall be performed, and submit it to the appropriate fiscal, policy, and sunset review committees of the Legislature by September 30 of each year. It is the intent of the Legislature that the method specified in this report be consistent with the policy developed by the department pursuant to subdivision (b).

Added Stats 1999 ch 67 § 2 (AB 1105), effective July 6, 1999. Amended Stats. 2009, Ch. 307 (SB 821)

§ 139.5. Quarterly internet website posting requirements

Beginning July 1, 2021, each board, as defined in Section 22, within the department that issues a license shall do both of the following on at least a quarterly basis:

(a) Prominently display on its internet website one of the following:

(1) The current average timeframes for processing initial and renewal license applications.

(2) The combined current average timeframe for processing both initial and renewal license applications.

(b) Prominently display on its internet website one of the following:

(1) The current average timeframes for processing each license type that the board administers.

(2) The combined current average timeframe for processing all license types that the board administers.

Added Stats 2020 ch 131 § 1 (SB 878), effective January 1, 2021.

§ 140. Disciplinary action; Licensee's failure to record cash transactions in payment of employee wages

Any board, as defined in Section 22, which is authorized under this code to take disciplinary action against a person who holds a license may take disciplinary action upon the ground that the licensee has failed to record and preserve for not less than three years, any and all cash transactions involved in the payment of employee wages by a licensee. Failure to make these records available to an authorized representative of the board may be made grounds for disciplinary action. In any action brought and sustained by the board which involves a violation of this section and any regulation adopted thereto, the board may assess the licensee with the actual investigative costs incurred, not to exceed two thousand five hundred dollars ($2,500). Failure to pay those costs may result in revocation of the license. Any moneys collected pursuant to this section shall be deposited in the respective fund of the board.

Added Stats 1984 ch 1490 § 2, effective September 27, 1984.

§ 141. Disciplinary action by foreign jurisdiction; Grounds for disciplinary action by state licensing board

(a) For any licensee holding a license issued by a board under the jurisdiction of the department, a disciplinary action taken by another state, by any agency of the federal government, or by another country for any act substantially related to the practice regulated by the California license, may be a ground for disciplinary action by the respective state licensing board. A certified copy of the record of the disciplinary action taken against the licensee by another state, an agency of the federal government, or another country shall be conclusive evidence of the events related therein.

(b) Nothing in this section shall preclude a board from applying a specific statutory provision in the licensing act administered by that board that provides for discipline based upon a disciplinary action taken against the licensee by another state, an agency of the federal government, or another country.

Added Stats 1994 ch 1275 § 2 (SB 2101).

§ 143. Proof of license as condition of bringing action for collection of compensation

(a) No person engaged in any business or profession for which a license is required under this code governing the department or any board, bureau, commission, committee, or program within the department, may bring or maintain any action, or recover in law or equity in any action, in any court of this state for the collection of compensation for the performance of any act or contract for which a li-

Section V

cense is required without alleging and proving that he or she was duly licensed at all times during the performance of that act or contract, regardless of the merits of the cause of action brought by the person.

(b) The judicial doctrine of substantial compliance shall not apply to this section.

(c) This section shall not apply to an act or contract that is considered to qualify as lawful practice of a licensed occupation or profession pursuant to Section 121.

Added Stats 1990 ch 1207 § 1.5 (AB 3242).

§ 143.5. Provision in agreements to settle certain causes of action prohibited; Adoption of regulations; Exemptions

(a) No licensee who is regulated by a board, bureau, or program within the Department of Consumer Affairs, nor an entity or person acting as an authorized agent of a licensee, shall include or permit to be included a provision in an agreement to settle a civil dispute, whether the agreement is made before or after the commencement of a civil action, that prohibits the other party in that dispute from contacting, filing a complaint with, or cooperating with the department, board, bureau, or program within the Department of Consumer Affairs that regulates the licensee or that requires the other party to withdraw a complaint from the department, board, bureau, or program within the Department of Consumer Affairs that regulates the licensee. A provision of that nature is void as against public policy, and any licensee who includes or permits to be included a provision of that nature in a settlement agreement is subject to disciplinary action by the board, bureau, or program.

(b) Any board, bureau, or program within the Department of Consumer Affairs that takes disciplinary action against a licensee or licensees based on a complaint or report that has also been the subject of a civil action and that has been settled for monetary damages providing for full and final satisfaction of the parties may not require its licensee or licensees to pay any additional sums to the benefit of any plaintiff in the civil action.

(c) As used in this section, "board" shall have the same meaning as defined in Section 22, and "licensee" means a person who has been granted a license, as that term is defined in Section 23.7.

(d) Notwithstanding any other law, upon granting a petition filed by a licensee or authorized agent of a licensee pursuant to Section 11340.6 of the Government Code, a board, bureau, or program within the Department of Consumer Affairs may, based upon evidence and legal authorities cited in the petition, adopt a regulation that does both of the following:

(1) Identifies a code section or jury instruction in a civil cause of action that has no relevance to the board's, bureau's, or program's en-

forcement responsibilities such that an agreement to settle such a cause of action based on that code section or jury instruction otherwise prohibited under subdivision (a) will not impair the board's, bureau's, or program's duty to protect the public.

(2) Exempts agreements to settle such a cause of action from the requirements of subdivision (a).

(e) This section shall not apply to a licensee subject to Section 2220.7.

Added Stats 2012 ch 561 § 1 (AB 2570), effective January 1, 2013.

§ 144. Requirement of fingerprints for criminal record checks; Applicability

(a) Notwithstanding any other law, an agency designated in subdivision (b) shall require an applicant to furnish to the agency a full set of fingerprints for purposes of conducting criminal history record checks. Any agency designated in subdivision (b) may obtain and receive, at its discretion, criminal history information from the Department of Justice and the United States Federal Bureau of Investigation.

(b) Subdivision (a) applies to the following:

(1) California Board of Accountancy.

(2) State Athletic Commission.

(3) Board of Behavioral Sciences.

(4) Court Reporters Board of California.

(5) Dental Board of California.

(6) California State Board of Pharmacy.

(7) Board of Registered Nursing.

(8) Veterinary Medical Board.

(9) Board of Vocational Nursing and Psychiatric Technicians of the State of California.

(10) Respiratory Care Board of California.

(11) Physical Therapy Board of California.

(12) Physician Assistant Board.

(13) Speech-Language Pathology and Audiology and Hearing Aid Dispensers Board.

(14) Medical Board of California.

(15) California State Board of Optometry.

(16) Acupuncture Board.

(17) Cemetery and Funeral Bureau.

(18) Bureau of Security and Investigative Services.

(19) Division of Investigation.

(20) Board of Psychology.

(21) California Board of Occupational Therapy.

(22) Structural Pest Control Board.

(23) Contractors State License Board.

Section V

(24) Naturopathic Medicine Committee.

(25) Professional Fiduciaries Bureau.

(26) Board for Professional Engineers, Land Surveyors, and Geologists.

(27) Podiatric Medical Board of California.

(28) Osteopathic Medical Board of California.

(29) California Architects Board, beginning January 1, 2021.

(30) Landscape Architects Technical Committee, beginning January 1, 2022.

(31) Bureau of Household Goods and Services with respect to household movers as described in Chapter 3.1 (commencing with Section 19225) of Division 8.

(c) For purposes of paragraph (26) of subdivision (b), the term "applicant" shall be limited to an initial applicant who has never been registered or licensed by the board or to an applicant for a new licensure or registration category.

Added Stats 1997 ch 758 § 2 (SB 1346). Amended Stats 2000 ch 697 § 1.2 (SB 1046), operative January 1, 2001; Stats 2001 ch 159 § 4 (SB 662), Stats 2001 ch 687 § 2 (AB 1409) (ch 687 prevails); Stats 2002 ch 744 § 1 (SB 1953), Stats 2002 ch 825 § 1 (SB 1952); Stats 2003 ch 485 § 2 (SB 907), Stats 2003 ch 789 § 1 (SB 364), Stats 2003 ch 874 § 1 (SB 363); Stats 2004 ch 909 § 1.2 (SB 136), effective September 30, 2004; Stats 2009 ch 308 § 4 (SB 819), effective January 1, 2010; Stats 2011 ch 448 § 1 (SB 543), effective January 1, 2012; Stats 2015 ch 719 § 1 (SB 643), effective January 1, 2016; Stats 2016 ch 32 § 3 (SB 837), effective June 27, 2016; Stats 2017 ch 775 § 3 (SB 798), effective January 1, 2018; Stats 2018 ch 6 § 1 (AB 106), effective March 13, 2018; Stats 2019 ch 351 § 37 (AB 496), effective January 1, 2020; Stats 2019 ch 376 § 1 (SB 608), effective January 1, 2020; Stats 2019 ch 865 § 1.3 (AB 1519), effective January 1, 2020 (ch 865 prevails); Stats 2020 ch 312 § 5 (SB 1474), effective January 1, 2021; Stats 2021 ch 70 § 3 (AB 141), effective July 12, 2021; Stats 2021 ch 188 § 2 (SB 826), effective January 1, 2022; Stats 2021 ch 630 § 4.5 (AB 1534), effective January 1, 2022 (ch 630 prevails).

Chapter 2

The Director of Consumer Affairs

§ 150. Designation

The department is under the control of a civil executive officer who is known as the Director of Consumer Affairs.

Enacted Stats 1937. Amended Stats 1971 ch 716 § 9.

§ 151. Appointment and tenure; Salary and traveling expenses

The director is appointed by the Governor and holds office at the Governor's pleasure. The director shall receive the annual salary provided for by Chapter 6 (commencing with Section 11550) of Part 1 of Division 3 of Title 2 of the Government Code, and the director's necessary traveling expenses.

Enacted Stats 1937. Amended Stats 1943 ch 1029 § 1; Stats 1945 ch 1185 § 2; Stats 1947 ch 1442 § 1; Stats 1951 ch 1613 § 14; Stats 1984 ch 144 § 2, ch 268 § 0.1, effective June 30, 1984; Stats 1985 ch 106 § 1; Stats 2019 ch 351 § 38 (AB 496), effective January 1, 2020.

§ 152. Departmental organization

For the purpose of administration, the reregistration and clerical work of the department is organized by the director, subject to the approval of the Governor, in such manner as the director deems necessary to properly segregate and conduct the work of the department.

Enacted Stats 1937. Amended Stats 2019 ch 351 § 39 (AB 496), effective January 1, 2020; Stats 2020 ch 370 § 2 (SB 1371), effective January 1, 2021.

§ 152.5. Extension of renewal dates

For purposes of distributing the reregistration work of the department uniformly throughout the year as nearly as practicable, the boards in the department may, with the approval of the director, extend by not more than six months the date fixed by law for the renewal of any license, certificate or permit issued by them, except that in such event any renewal fee which may be involved shall be prorated in such manner that no person shall be required to pay a greater or lesser fee than would have been required had the change in renewal dates not occurred.

Added Stats 1959 ch 1707 § 1.

§ 152.6. Establishment of license periods and renewal dates

Notwithstanding any other provision of this code, each board within the department shall, in cooperation with the director, establish such license periods and renewal dates for all licenses in such manner as best to distribute the renewal work of all boards throughout each year and permit the most efficient, and economical use of personnel and equipment. To the extent practicable, provision shall be made for the proration or other adjustment of fees in such manner that no person shall be required to pay a greater or lesser fee than the person would have been required to pay if the change in license periods or renewal dates had not occurred.

As used in this section "license" includes "certificate," "permit," "authority," "registration," and similar indicia of authority to engage in a business or profession, and "board" includes "board," "bureau," "commission," "committee," and an individual who is authorized to renew a license.

Added Stats 1968 ch 1248 § 1. Amended Stats 2019 ch 351 § 40 (AB 496), effective January 1, 2020.

§ 153. Investigations

The director may investigate the work of the boards in the department and may obtain a copy of all records and full and complete data in all official matters in possession of the boards and their members, officers, or employees, other than examination questions prior to submission to applicants at scheduled examinations.

Enacted Stats 1937. Amended Stats 2019 ch 351 § 41 (AB 496), effective January 1, 2020.

§ 154. Matters relating to employees of boards

Any and all matters relating to employment, tenure or discipline of employees of any board, agency or commission, shall be initiated by said board, agency or commission, but all such actions shall, before reference to the State Personnel Board, receive the approval of the appointing power.

To effect the purposes of Division 1 of this code and each agency of the department, employment of all personnel shall be in accord with Article XXIV of the Constitution, the law and rules and regulations of the State Personnel Board. Each board, agency or commission, shall select its employees from a list of eligibles obtained by the appointing power from the State Personnel Board. The person selected by the board, agency or commission to fill any position or vacancy shall thereafter be reported by the board, agency or commission, to the appointing power.

Enacted Stats 1937. Amended Stats 1945 ch 1276 § 4.

§ 154.5. Legal assistance for experts aiding in investigations of licensees

If a person, not a regular employee of a board under this code, including the Board of Chiropractic Examiners and the Osteopathic Medical Board of California, is hired or under contract to provide expertise to the board in the evaluation of an applicant or the conduct of a licensee, and that person is named as a defendant in a civil action arising out of the evaluation or any opinions rendered, statements made, or testimony given to the board or its representatives, the board shall provide for representation required to defend the defendant in that civil action. The board shall not be liable for any judgment rendered against the person. The Attorney General shall be utilized in the action and his or her services shall be a charge against the board.

Added Stats 1986 ch 1205 § 1, as B & P C § 483. Amended and Renumbered by Stats 1987 ch 850 § 8. Amended Stats 1991 ch 359 § 3 (AB 1332).

§ 155. Employment of investigators; Inspectors as employees or under contract

(a) In accordance with Section 159.5, the director may employ such investigators, inspectors, and deputies as are necessary properly to investigate and prosecute all violations of any law, the enforcement of which is charged to the department or to any board, agency, or commission in the department.

(b) It is the intent of the Legislature that inspectors used by boards, bureaus, or commissions in the department shall not be required to be employees of the Division of Investigation, but may either be employees of, or under contract to, the boards, bureaus, or commissions. Contracts for services shall be consistent with Article 4.5 (commencing with Section 19130) of Chapter 6 of Part 2 of Division 5 of Title 2 of the Government Code. All civil service employees currently employed as inspectors whose functions are transferred as a result of this section shall retain their positions, status, and rights in accordance with Section 19994.10 of the Government Code and the State Civil Service Act (Part 2 (commencing with Section 18500) of Division 5 of Title 2 of the Government Code).

(c) Nothing in this section limits the authority of, or prohibits, investigators in the Division of Investigation in the conduct of inspections or investigations of any licensee, or in the conduct of investigations of any officer or employee of a board or the department at the specific request of the director or his or her designee.

Enacted Stats 1937. Amended Stats 1945 ch 1276 § 5; Stats 1971 ch 716 § 10; Stats 1985 ch 1382 § 1.

§ 156. Contractual authority

(a) The director may, for the department and at the request and with the consent of a board within the department on whose behalf the contract is to be made, enter into contracts pursuant to Chapter 3 (commencing with Section 11250) of Part 1 of Division 3 of Title 2 of the Government Code or Chapter 2 (commencing with Section 10290) of Part 2 of Division 2 of the Public Contract Code for and on behalf of any board within the department.

(b) In accordance with subdivision (a), the director may, in his or her discretion, negotiate and execute contracts for examination purposes, which include provisions that hold harmless a contractor where liability resulting from a contract between a board in the department and the contractor is traceable to the state or its officers, agents, or employees.

(c) The director shall report progress on release 3 entities' transition to a new licensing technology platform to all the appropriate committees of the Legislature by December 31 of each year. Progress reports shall include updated plans and timelines for completing all of the following:

(1) Business process documentation.

(2) Cost benefit analyses of information technology options.

(3) Information technology system development and implementation.

(4) Any other relevant steps needed to meet the IT needs of release 3 entities.

(5) Any other information as the Legislature may request.

Added Stats 1953 ch 864 § 1. Amended Stats 1984 ch 144 § 3; Stats 1988 ch 1448 § 1; Stats 2017 ch 429 § 2 (SB 547), effective January 1, 2018.

§ 156.1. Retention of records by providers of services related to treatment of alcohol or drug impairment

(a) Notwithstanding any other law, individuals or entities contracting with the department or any board within the department for the provision of services relating to the treatment and rehabilitation of licensees impaired by alcohol or dangerous drugs shall retain all records and documents pertaining to those services until such time as these records and documents have been reviewed for audit by the department. These records and documents shall be retained for three years from the date of the last treatment or service rendered to that licensee, after which time the records and documents may be purged and destroyed by the contract vendor. This provision shall supersede any other law relating to the purging or destruction of records pertaining to those treatment and rehabilitation programs.

(b) Unless otherwise expressly provided by statute or regulation, all records and documents pertaining to services for the treatment and rehabilitation of licensees impaired by alcohol or dangerous drugs provided by any contract vendor to the department or to any board within the department shall be kept confidential and are not subject to discovery or subpoena.

(c) With respect to all other contracts for services with the department, or any board within the department other than those set forth in subdivision (a), the director or chief deputy director may request an examination and audit by the department's internal auditor of all performance under the contract. For this purpose, all documents and records of the contract vendor in connection with such performance shall be retained by the vendor for a period of three years after final payment under the contract. Nothing in this section shall affect the authority of the State Auditor to conduct any examination or audit under the terms of Section 8546.7 of the Government Code.

Added Stats 1991 ch 654 § 3 (AB 1893). Amended Stats 2003 ch 107 § 1 (AB 569); Stats 2010 ch 517 § 1 (SB 1172), effective January 1, 2011; Stats 2019 ch 351 § 42 (AB 496), effective January 1, 2020.

§ 156.5. Leases for examination or meeting purposes

The director may negotiate and execute for the department and for its component agencies, rental agreements for short-term hiring of space and furnishings for examination or meeting purposes. The director may, in his or her discretion, negotiate and execute contracts for that space which include provisions which hold harmless the provider of the space where liability resulting from use of the space under the contract is traceable to the state or its officers, agents, or employees. Notwithstanding any other provision of law, the director may, in his or her discretion, advance payments as deposits to reserve and hold examination or meeting space. Any such agreement is subject to the approval of the legal office of the Department of General Services.

Added Stats 1967 ch 1235 § 1. Amended Stats 1988 ch 1448 § 1.5.

§ 157. Expenses in criminal prosecutions and unprofessional conduct proceedings

Expenses incurred by any board or on behalf of any board in any criminal prosecution or unprofessional conduct proceeding constitute proper charges against the funds of the board.

Added Stats 1937 ch 474.

§ 158. Refunds to applicants

With the approval of the Director of Consumer Affairs, the boards and commissions comprising the department or subject to its jurisdiction may make refunds to applicants who are found ineligible to take the examinations or whose credentials are insufficient to entitle them to certificates or licenses.

Notwithstanding any other law, any application fees, license fees, or penalties imposed and collected illegally, by mistake, inadvertence, or error shall be refunded. Claims authorized by the department shall be filed with the State Controller, and the Controller shall draw a warrant against the fund of the agency in payment of the refund.

Added Stats 1937 ch 474. Amended Stats 1945 ch 1378 § 1; Stats 1971 ch 716 § 11; Stats 2019 ch 351 § 43 (AB 496), effective January 1, 2020.

§ 159. Administration of oaths

The members and the executive officer of each board, agency, bureau, division, or commission have power to administer oaths and affirmations in the performance of any business of the board, and to certify to official acts.

Added Stats 1947 ch 1350 § 5.

Section V

§ 159.5. Division of Investigation; Appointments; Health Quality Investigation Unit

(a) (1) There is in the department the Division of Investigation. The division is in the charge of a person with the title of chief of the division.

(2) Except as provided in Section 160, investigators who have the authority of peace officers, as specified in subdivision (a) of Section 160 and in subdivision (a) of Section 830.3 of the Penal Code, shall be in the division and shall be appointed by the director.

(b) (1) There is in the Division of Investigation the Health Quality Investigation Unit. The primary responsibility of the unit is to investigate violations of law or regulation within the jurisdiction of the Medical Board of California, the Podiatric Medical Board of California, the Board of Psychology, the Osteopathic Medical Board of California, the Physician Assistant Board, or any entities under the jurisdiction of the Medical Board of California.

(2) The Medical Board of California shall not be charged an hourly rate for the performance of investigations by the unit.

Added Stats 1971 ch 716 § 12. Amended Stats 1985 ch 1382 § 2; Stats 2010 ch 719 § 2 (SB 856), effective October 19, 2010; Stats 2013 ch 515 § 1 (SB 304), effective January 1, 2014; Stats 2019 ch 351 § 44 (AB 496), effective January 1, 2020.

§ 161. Availability of public records at charge sufficient to pay costs

The department, or any board in the department, may, in accordance with the California Public Records Act (Division 10 (commencing with Section 7920.000) of Title 1 of the Government Code) and the Information Practices Act of 1977 (Chapter 1 (commencing with Section 1798) of Title 1.8 of Part 4 of Division 3 of the Civil Code), make available to the public copies of any part of its respective public records, or compilations, extracts, or summaries of information contained in its public records, at a charge sufficient to pay the actual cost thereof. That charge shall be determined by the director with the approval of the Department of General Services.

Added Stats 1949 ch 704 § 1. Amended Stats 1963 ch 590 § 1; Stats 1965 ch 371 § 9; Stats 2019 ch 351 § 45 (AB 496), effective January 1, 2020; Stats 2021 ch 615 § 3 (AB 474), effective January 1, 2022.

§ 162. Evidentiary effect of certificate of records officer as to license, etc.

The certificate of the officer in charge of the records of any board in the department that any person was or was not on a specified date, or during a specified period of time, licensed, certified or registered under the provisions of law administered by the board, or that the license, certificate or registration of any person was revoked or under suspension, shall be admitted in any court as prima facie evidence of the facts therein recited.

Added Stats 1949 ch 355 § 1.

§ 163. Fee for certification of records, etc.

Except as otherwise expressly provided by law, the department and each board in the department shall charge a fee of two dollars ($2) for the certification of a copy of any record, document, or paper in its custody or for the certification of any document evidencing the content of any such record, document or paper.

Added Stats 1961 ch 1858 § 1. Amended Stats 1963 ch 590 § 2.

§ 163.5. Delinquency fees; Reinstatement fees

Except as otherwise provided by law, the delinquency, penalty, or late fee for any licensee within the Department of Consumer Affairs shall be 50 percent of the renewal fee for such license in effect on the date of the renewal of the license, but not less than twenty-five dollars ($25) nor more than one hundred fifty dollars ($150).

A delinquency, penalty, or late fee shall not be assessed until 30 days have elapsed from the date that the licensing agency mailed a notice of renewal to the licensee at the licensee's last known address of record. The notice shall specify the date for timely renewal, and that failure to renew in a timely fashion shall result in the assessment of a delinquency, penalty, or late fee.

In the event a reinstatement or like fee is charged for the reinstatement of a license, the reinstatement fee shall be 150 percent of the renewal fee for such license in effect on the date of the reinstatement of the license, but not more than twenty-five dollars ($25) in excess of the renewal fee, except that in the event that such a fee is fixed by statute at less than 150 percent of the renewal fee and less than the renewal fee plus twenty-five dollars ($25), the fee so fixed shall be charged.

Added Stats 1974 ch 743 § 4. Amended Stats 1985 ch 587 § 1.

§ 163.6. [Section repealed 1992.]

Added Stats 1985 ch 587 § 2. Inoperative June 30, 1991. Repealed, operative January 1, 1992, by its own terms. The repealed section related to reduction in license renewal fees to offset increase in revenue.

§ 164. Form and content of license, certificate, permit, or similar indicia of authority

The form and content of any license, certificate, permit, or similar indicia of authority issued by any agency in the department, including any document evidencing renewal of a license, certificate, permit, or similar indicia of authority, shall be determined by the director after consultation with and consideration of the views of the agency concerned.

Added Stats 1971 ch 716 § 15. Amended Stats 1987 ch 850 § 6.

§ 165. Prohibition against submission of fiscal impact analysis relating to pending legislation without prior submission to director for comment

Notwithstanding any other provision of law, no board, bureau, committee, commission, or program in the Department of Consumer Affairs shall submit to the Legislature any fiscal impact analysis relating to legislation pending before the Legislature until the analysis has been submitted to the Director of Consumer Affairs, or his or her designee, for review and comment. The boards, bureaus, committees, commissions, and programs shall include the comments of the director when submitting any fiscal impact analysis to the Legislature. This section shall not be construed to prohibit boards, bureaus, committees, commissions, and programs from responding to direct requests for fiscal data from Members of the Legislature or their staffs. In those instances it shall be the responsibility of boards, bureaus, committees, commissions, and programs to also transmit that information to the director, or his or her designee, within five working days.

Added Stats 1984 ch 268 § 0.2, effective June 30, 1984.

§ 166. Development of guidelines for mandatory continuing education programs

The director shall, by regulation, develop guidelines to prescribe components for mandatory continuing education programs administered by any board within the department.

(a) The guidelines shall be developed to ensure that mandatory continuing education is used as a means to create a more competent licensing population, thereby enhancing public protection. The guidelines shall require mandatory continuing education programs to address, at least, the following:

(1) Course validity.

(2) Occupational relevancy.

(3) Effective presentation.

(4) Actual attendance.

(5) Material assimilation.

(6) Potential for application.

(b) The director shall consider educational principles, and the guidelines shall prescribe mandatory continuing education program formats to include, but not be limited to, the following:

(1) The specified audience.

(2) Identification of what is to be learned.

(3) Clear goals and objectives.

(4) Relevant learning methods (participatory, hands-on, or clinical setting).

(5) Evaluation, focused on the learner and the assessment of the intended learning outcomes (goals and objectives).

(c) Any board within the department that, after January 1, 1993, proposes a mandatory continuing education program for its licensees shall submit the proposed program to the director for review to assure that the program contains all the elements set forth in this section and complies with the guidelines developed by the director.

(d) Any board administering a mandatory continuing education program that proposes to amend its current program shall do so in a manner consistent with this section.

(e) Any board currently administering a mandatory continuing education program shall review the components and requirements of the program to determine the extent to which they are consistent with the guidelines developed under this section. The board shall submit a report of their findings to the director. The report shall identify the similarities and differences of its mandatory continuing education program. The report shall include any board-specific needs to explain the variation from the director's guidelines.

(f) Any board administering a mandatory continuing education program, when accepting hours for credit which are obtained out of state, shall ensure that the course for which credit is given is administered in accordance with the guidelines addressed in subdivision (a).

(g) Nothing in this section or in the guidelines adopted by the director shall be construed to repeal any requirements for continuing education programs set forth in any other provision of this code.

Added Stats 1992 ch 1135 § 2.2 (SB 2044). Amended Stats 1994 ch 146 § 1 (AB 3601).

Section V

Chapter 3

Funds of the Department

§ 200.1. Fund accruals exempt from transfer

(a) Any accruals that occur on or after September 11, 1993, to any funds or accounts within the Professions and Vocations Fund that realize increased revenues to that fund or account as a result of legislation enacted on or after September 11, 1993, and that have not been transferred pursuant to Sections 13.50, 13.60, and 13.70 of the Budget Act of 1993 on the effective date of the act that enacted this section, shall be exempt from the transfers contained in Sections 13.50, 13.60, and 13.70 of the Budget Act of 1993. These funds shall include, but not be limited to, all of the following:

(1) Athletic Commission Fund.

(2) Bureau of Home Furnishings and Thermal Insulation Fund.

(3) Contractors License Fund.

(4) Private Investigator Fund.

(5) Respiratory Care Fund.

(6) Vocational Nursing and Psychiatric Technicians Fund.

(b) Subdivision (a) shall not apply to the Contingent Fund of the Medical Board of California.

Added Stats 1994 ch 26 § 10 (AB 1807), effective March 30, 1994. Amended Stats 1997 ch 759 § 4 (SB 827); Stats 2020 ch 312 § 6 (SB 1474), effective January 1, 2021.

§ 201. Levy for administrative expenses

A charge for the estimated administrative expenses of the department, not to exceed the available balance in any appropriation for any one fiscal year, may be levied in advance on a pro rata share basis against any of the funds of any of the boards, bureaus, commissions, divisions, and agencies, at the discretion of the director and with the approval of the Department of Finance.

Enacted Stats 1937. Amended Stats 1947 ch 1350 § 4; Stats 1965 ch 371 § 10; Stats 1974 ch 1221 § 1.

§ 202.5. Itemized statement of services and changes from Department of Justice

Prior to payment to the Department of Justice of any charges for legal services rendered to any board within the department, the Department of Justice shall submit to the board an itemized statement of the services and charges. The itemized statement shall include detailed information regarding the services performed and the amount of time billed for each of those services.

Added Stats 1994 ch 1273 § 1 (SB 2038).

§ 205. Professions and Vocations Fund [Repealed]

Added Stats 2015 ch 510 § 2.3 (AB 179), effective January 1, 2016, operative July 1, 2016. Amended Stats 2016 ch 800 § 1 (SB 1196), effective January 1, 2017; Stats 2017 ch 421 § 6 (SB 19), effective January 1, 2018, operative July 1, 2018; Stats 2017 ch 669 § 3.5 (AB 1705), effective January 1, 2018, operative July 1, 2018 (ch 669 prevails); Stats 2019 ch 865 § 2 (AB 1519), effective January 1, 2020, repealed July 1, 2022; Stats 2020 ch 312 § 7 (SB 1474), effective January 1, 2021, repealed July 1, 2022.

§ 205. Professions and Vocations Fund

(a) There is in the State Treasury the Professions and Vocations Fund. The fund shall consist of the following special funds:

(1) Accountancy Fund.

(2) California Architects Board Fund.

(3) Athletic Commission Fund.

(4) Barbering and Cosmetology Contingent Fund.

(5) Cemetery and Funeral Fund.

(6) Contractors License Fund.

(7) State Dentistry Fund.

(8) Home Furnishings and Thermal Insulation Fund.

(9) California Architects Board-Landscape Architects Fund.

(10) Contingent Fund of the Medical Board of California.

(11) Optometry Fund.

(12) Pharmacy Board Contingent Fund.

(13) Physical Therapy Fund.

(14) Private Investigator Fund.

(15) Private Security Services Fund.

(16) Professional Engineer's, Land Surveyor's, and Geologist's Fund.

(17) Consumer Affairs Fund.

(18) Behavioral Sciences Fund.

(19) Licensed Midwifery Fund.

(20) Court Reporters' Fund.

(21) Veterinary Medical Board Contingent Fund.

(22) Vocational Nursing and Psychiatric Technicians Fund.

(23) Electronic and Appliance Repair Fund.

(24) Acupuncture Fund.

(25) Physician Assistant Fund.

(26) Board of Podiatric Medicine Fund.

(27) Psychology Fund.

(28) Respiratory Care Fund.

(29) Speech-Language Pathology and Audiology and Hearing Aid Dispensers Fund.

(30) Board of Registered Nursing Fund.

(31) Animal Health Technician Examining Committee Fund.

Section V

(32) State Dental Hygiene Fund.

(33) Structural Pest Control Fund.

(34) Structural Pest Control Eradication and Enforcement Fund.

(35) Structural Pest Control Research Fund.

(36) Household Movers Fund.

(b) For accounting and recordkeeping purposes, the Professions and Vocations Fund shall be deemed to be a single special fund, and each of the several special funds therein shall constitute and be deemed to be a separate account in the Professions and Vocations Fund. Each account or fund shall be available for expenditure only for the purposes as are now or may hereafter be provided by law.

(c) This section shall become operative on July 1, 2022.

Added Stats 2019 ch 865 § 3 (AB 1519), effective January 1, 2020, operative July 1, 2022. Amended Stats 2020 ch 121 § 1 (AB 896), effective September 24, 2020, operative July 1, 2022; Stats 2020 ch 312 § 8.5 (SB 1474), effective January 1, 2021, operative July 1, 2022.

§ 206. Dishonored check tendered for payment of fine, fee, or penalty

Notwithstanding any other provision of law, any person tendering a check for payment of a fee, fine, or penalty that was subsequently dishonored, shall not be granted a license, or other authority that they were seeking, until the applicant pays the amount outstanding from the dishonored payment together with the applicable fee, including any delinquency fee. The board may require the person whose check was returned unpaid to make payment of all fees by cashier's check or money order.

Added Stats 1994 ch 26 § 12 (AB 1807), effective March 30, 1994.

§ 210. BreEZe system vendor contract

(a) (1) The department may enter into a contract with a vendor for the BreEZe system, the integrated, enterprisewide enforcement case management and licensing system described in the department's strategic plan, no sooner than 30 days after notification in writing to the chairpersons of the Appropriations Committees of each house of the Legislature and the Chairperson of the Joint Legislative Budget Committee.

(2) The amount of BreEZe system vendor contract funds, authorized pursuant to this section, shall be consistent with the project costs approved by the office of the State Chief Information Officer based on its review and approval of the most recent BreEZe Special Project Report to be submitted by the department prior to contract award at the conclusion of procurement activities.

(3) Paragraph (2) shall apply to all Budget Act items for the department that have an appropriation for the BreEZe system.

(b) (1) If the department enters into a contract with a vendor for the BreEZe system pursuant to subdivision (a), the department shall, by December 31, 2014, submit to the Legislature, the Senate Committee on Business, Professions and Economic Development, the Assembly Committee on Business and Professions, and the budget committees of each house, a report analyzing the workload of licensing personnel employed by boards within the department participating in the BreEZe system.

(2) A report to the Legislature pursuant to this subdivision shall be submitted in compliance with Section 9795 of the Government Code.

(3) This subdivision shall become inoperative on December 1, 2018, pursuant to Section 10231.5 of the Government Code.

(c) (1) Notwithstanding any other provision of law, upon the request of the Department of Consumer Affairs, the Department of Finance may augment the budgets of the boards, bureaus, commissions, committees, programs, and divisions that comprise the Department of Consumer Affairs, as defined in Section 101, for expenditure of non-General Fund moneys to pay BreEZe project costs. The augmentation may be made no sooner than 30 days after notification in writing to the chairpersons of the committees in each house of the Legislature that consider appropriations and the Chairperson of the Joint Legislative Budget Committee, or no sooner than whatever lesser time the chairperson of the joint committee may in each instance determine. The amount of funds augmented pursuant to the authority of this subdivision shall be consistent with project cost increases approved by the Secretary of California Technology based on the secretary's review and approval of the most recent BreEZe Special Project Report to be submitted at the conclusion of procurement activities. This subdivision shall apply to all Budget Act items for the boards, bureaus, commissions, committees, programs, and divisions that comprise the Department of Consumer Affairs, as defined in Section 101, that have an appropriation for the BreEZe system in the Budget Act of 2011.

(2) This subdivision shall become inoperative upon enactment of the Budget Act of 2012.

Added Stats 2010 ch 719 § 4 (SB 856), effective October 19, 2010. Amended Stats 2011 ch 448 § 3 (SB 543), effective January 1, 2012; Stats 2019 ch 351 § 46 (AB 496), effective January 1, 2020.

Section V

Chapter 4

Consumer Affairs

Article 1

General Provisions and Definitions

§ 300. Citation of chapter

This chapter may be cited as the Consumer Affairs Act

Added Stats 1970 ch 1394 § 3, operative July 1, 1971.

§ 301. Declaration of intent

It is the intent of the Legislature and the purpose of this chapter to promote and protect the interests of the people as consumers. The Legislature finds that vigorous representation and protection of consumer interests are essential to the fair and efficient functioning of a free enterprise market economy. The Legislature declares that government advances the interests of consumers by facilitating the proper functioning of the free enterprise market economy through (a) educating and informing the consumer to insure rational consumer choice in the marketplace; (b) protecting the consumer from the sale of goods and services through the use of deceptive methods, acts, or practices which are inimical to the general welfare of consumers; (c) fostering competition; and (d) promoting effective representation of consumers' interests in all branches and levels of government.

Added Stats 1970 ch 1394 § 3, operative July 1, 1971. Amended Stats 1975 ch 1262 § 1.

§ 302. Definitions

As used in this chapter, the following terms have the following meanings:

(a) "Department" means the Department of Consumer Affairs.

(b) "Director" means the Director of the Department of Consumer Affairs.

(c) "Consumer" means any individual who seeks or acquires, by purchase or lease, any goods, services, money, or credit for personal, family, or household purposes.

(d) "Person" means an individual, partnership, corporation, limited liability company, association, or other group, however organized.

(e) "Individual" does not include a partnership, corporation, association, or other group, however organized.

(f) "Division" means the Division of Consumer Services.

(g) "Interests of consumers" is limited to the cost, quality, purity, safety, durability, performance, effectiveness, dependability, availability, and adequacy of choice of goods and services offered or furnished to consumers and the adequacy and accuracy of information relating to consumer goods, services, money, or credit (including labeling, packaging, and advertising of contents, qualities, and terms of sales).

Added Stats 1970 ch 1394 § 3, operative July 1, 1971. Amended Stats 1972 ch 808 § 1; Stats 1975 ch 1262 § 2; Stats 1994 ch 1010 § 2 (SB 2053).

§ 303. Division of Consumer Services; Chief [Repealed]

Added Stats 1972 ch 808 § 2. Amended Stats 2017 ch 561 § 1 (AB 1516), effective January 1, 2018. Repealed Stats 2017 ch 429 § 3 (SB 429), effective January 1, 2018 (ch 429 prevails). The repealed section related to the chief of the Division of Consumer Services.

Article 2

Director and Employees

§ 305. Administration of chapter

The director shall administer and enforce the provisions of this chapter. Every power granted or duty imposed upon the director under this chapter may be exercised or performed in the name of the director by a deputy or assistant director or the chief of the department's Division of Consumer Services, subject to such conditions and limitations as the director may prescribe.

Added Stats 1970 ch 1394 § 3, operative July 1, 1971. Amended Stats 1971 ch 114 § 1, effective June 2, 1971, operative July 1, 1971.

§ 306. Employment matters

The director, in accordance with the State Civil Service Act, may appoint and fix the compensation of such clerical or other personnel as may be necessary to carry out the provisions of this chapter. All such personnel shall perform their respective duties under the supervision and the direction of the director.

Added Stats 1970 ch 1394 § 3, operative July 1, 1971.

§ 307. Experts and consultants

The director may contract for the services of experts and consultants where necessary to carry out the provisions of this chapter and may provide compensation and reimbursement of expenses for such experts and consultants in accordance with state law.

Added Stats 1975 ch 1262 § 3.

§ 308. Notice of vacancy of department chief or executive officer of any bureau or board

The director shall notify the appropriate policy committees of the Legislature within 60 days after the position of chief or executive officer of any bureau or board within the department becomes vacant pursuant to Section 1770 of the Government Code.

Added Stats 2021 ch 376 § 1 (AB 830), effective September 28, 2021.

Article 3

Powers and Duties

§ 310. Director's powers and duties

The director shall have the following powers and it shall be his duty to:

(a) Recommend and propose the enactment of such legislation as necessary to protect and promote the interests of consumers.

(b) Represent the consumer's interests before federal and state legislative hearings and executive commissions.

(c) Assist, advise, and cooperate with federal, state, and local agencies and officials to protect and promote the interests of consumers.

(d) Study, investigate, research, and analyze matters affecting the interests of consumers.

(e) Hold public hearings, subpoena witnesses, take testimony, compel the production of books, papers, documents, and other evidence, and call upon other state agencies for information.

(f) Propose and assist in the creation and development of consumer education programs.

(g) Promote ethical standards of conduct for business and consumers and undertake activities to encourage public responsibility in the production, promotion, sale and lease of consumer goods and services.

(h) Advise the Governor and Legislature on all matters affecting the interests of consumers.

(i) Exercise and perform such other functions, powers and duties as may be deemed appropriate to protect and promote the interests of consumers as directed by the Governor or the Legislature.

(j) Maintain contact and liaison with consumer groups in California and nationally.

Added Stats 1970 ch 1394 § 3, operative July 1, 1971. Amended Stats 1975 ch 1262 § 4.

§ 311. Interdepartmental committee

The director may create an interdepartmental committee to assist and advise him in the implementation of his duties. The members of such committee shall consist of the heads of state departments, or their designees. Members of such committee shall serve without compensation but shall be reimbursed for the expenses actually and necessarily incurred by them in the performance of their duties.

Added Stats 1970 ch 1394 § 3, operative July 1, 1971.

§ 312. Report to Governor and Legislature

The director shall submit to the Governor and the Legislature on or before January 1, 2003, and annually thereafter, a report of programmatic and statistical information regarding the activities of the department and its constituent entities. The report shall include information concerning the director's activities pursuant to Section 326, including the number and general patterns of consumer complaints and the action taken on those complaints.

Added Stats 1970 ch 1394 § 3, operative July 1, 1971. Amended Stats 1975 ch 1262 § 5; Stats 1998 ch 829 § 1 SB 1652); Stats 2002 ch 405 § 3 (AB 2973).

§ 313.2. Adoption of regulations in conformance with Americans with Disabilities Act

The director shall adopt regulations to implement, interpret, and make specific the provisions of the Americans with Disabilities Act (P.L. 101–336), as they relate to the examination process for professional licensing and certification programs under the purview of the department.

Added Stats 1992 ch 1289 § 3 (AB 2743).

§ 313.5. Publication of consumer information bibliography

The director shall periodically publish a bibliography of consumer information available in the department library and elsewhere. Such bibliography shall be sent to subscribers upon payment of a reasonable fee therefor.

Added Stats 1972 ch 1251 § 2. Amended Stats 1975 ch 1262 § 7.

Article 3.6

Uniform Standards Regarding Substance-Abusing Healing Arts Licensees

§ 315.2. Cease practice order

(a) A board, as described in Section 315, shall order a licensee of the board to cease practice if the licensee tests positive for any substance that is prohibited under the terms of the licensee's probation or diversion program.

(b) An order to cease practice under this section shall not be governed by the provisions of Chapter 5 (commencing with Section 11500) of Part 1 of Division 3 of Title 2 of the Government Code.

(c) A cease practice order under this section shall not constitute disciplinary action.

(d) This section shall have no effect on the Board of Registered Nursing pursuant to Article 3.1 (commencing with Section 2770) of Chapter 6 of Division 2.

Added Stats 2010 ch 517 § 2 (SB 1172), effective January 1, 2011.

§ 315.4. Cease practice order for violation of probation or diversion program

(a) A board, as described in Section 315, may adopt regulations authorizing the board to order a licensee on probation or in a diversion program to cease practice for major violations and when the board orders a licensee to undergo a clinical diagnostic evaluation pursuant to the uniform and specific standards adopted and authorized under Section 315.

(b) An order to cease practice under this section shall not be governed by the provisions of Chapter 5 (commencing with Section 11500) of Part 1 of Division 3 of Title 2 of the Government Code.

(c) A cease practice order under this section shall not constitute disciplinary action.

(d) This section shall have no effect on the Board of Registered Nursing pursuant to Article 3.1 (commencing with Section 2770) of Chapter 6 of Division 2.

Added Stats 2010 ch 517 § 3 (SB 1172), effective January 1, 2011.

Article 4

Representation of Consumers

§ 320. Intervention in administrative or judicial proceedings

Whenever there is pending before any state commission, regulatory agency, department, or other state agency, or any state or federal court or agency, any matter or proceeding which the director finds may affect substantially the interests of consumers within California, the director, or the Attorney General, may intervene in such matter or proceeding in any appropriate manner to represent the interests of consumers. The director, or any officer or employee designated by the director for that purpose, or the Attorney General, may thereafter present to such agency, court, or department, in conformity with the rules of practice and procedure thereof, such evidence and argument as he shall determine to be necessary, for the effective protection of the interests of consumers.

Added Stats 1970 ch 1394 § 3, operative July 1, 1971. Amended Stats 1975 ch 1262 § 8.

§ 321. Commencement of legal proceedings

Whenever it appears to the director that the interests of the consumers of this state are being damaged, or may be damaged, by any person who engaged in, or intends to engage in, any acts or practices in violation of any law of this state, or any federal law, the director or any officer or employee designated by the director, or the Attorney General, may commence legal proceedings in the appropriate forum to enjoin such acts or practices and may seek other appropriate relief on behalf of such consumers.

Added Stats 1975 ch 1262 § 9.

Article 5

Consumer Complaints

§ 325. Actionable complaints

It shall be the duty of the director to receive complaints from consumers concerning (a) unfair methods of competition and unfair or deceptive acts or practices undertaken by any person in the conduct of any trade or commerce; (b) the production, distribution, sale, and lease of any goods and services undertaken by any person which may endanger the public health, safety, or welfare; (c) violations of provisions of this code relating to businesses and professions licensed by any agency of the department, and regulations promulgated pursuant thereto; (d) student concerns related to the Bureau for Private Postsecondary Education's performance of its responsibilities, including concerns that arise related to the Bureau for Private Postsecondary Education's handling of a complaint or its administration of the Student Tuition Recovery Fund, established in Article 14 (commencing with Section 94923) of Chapter 8 of Part 59 of Division 10 of Title 3 of the Education Code; and (e) other matters consistent with the purposes of this chapter, whenever appropriate.

Added Stats 1970 ch 1394 § 3, operative July 1, 1971. Amended Stats 2016 ch 593 § 1 (SB 1192), effective January 1, 2017.

§ 325.3. Consumer complaints on paging services

In addition to the duties prescribed by Section 325, it shall be the duty of the director to receive complaints from consumers concerning services provided by the entities described in paragraph (2) of subdivision (b) of Section 234 of the Public Utilities Code.

Added Stats 1995 ch 357 § 1 (AB 202).

§ 326. Proceedings on receipt of complaint

(a) Upon receipt of any complaint pursuant to Section 325, the director may notify the person against whom the complaint is made of the nature of the complaint and may request appropriate relief for the consumer.

(b) The director shall also transmit any valid complaint to the local, state or federal agency whose authority provides the most effective means to secure the relief.

The director shall, if appropriate, advise the consumer of the action taken on the complaint and of any other means which may be available to the consumer to secure relief.

(c) If the director receives a complaint or receives information from any source indicating a probable violation of any law, rule, or order of any regulatory agency of the state, or if a pattern of complaints from consumers develops, the director shall transmit any complaint he or she considers to be valid to any appropriate law enforcement or regulatory agency and any evidence or information he or she may have concerning the probable violation or pattern of complaints or request the Attorney General to undertake appropriate legal action. It shall be the continuing duty of the director to discern patterns of complaints and to ascertain the nature and extent of action taken with respect to the probable violations or pattern of complaints.

Added Stats 1970 ch 1394 § 3, operative July 1, 1971. Amended Stats 1978 ch 1161 § 8; Stats 1989 ch 1360 § 1.

Article 7

Personal Information and Privacy Protection

§ 350. [Section repealed 2008.]

Added Stats 2000 ch 984 § 1 (SB 129). Amended Stats 2001 ch 159 § 5 (SB 662). Repealed Stats 2007 ch 183 § 1 (SB 90), effective January 1, 2008. The repealed section related to the office of privacy protection.

§ 352. [Section repealed 2008.]

Added Stats 2000 ch 984 § 1 (SB 129). Amended Stats 2004 ch 227 § 1 (SB 1102), effective August 16, 2004, operation contingent. Repealed Stats 2007 ch 183 § 2 (SB 90), effective January 1, 2008. The repealed section related to commencement of activities under the article and funding for such.

Chapter 6

Public Members

§ 450. Qualifications generally

In addition to the qualifications provided in the respective chapters of this code, a public member or a lay member of any board shall not be, nor shall they have been within the period of five years immediately preceding their appointment, any of the following:

(a) An employer, or an officer, director, or substantially full-time representative of an employer or group of employers, of any licensee of a board, except that this subdivision shall not preclude the appointment of a person who maintains infrequent employer status with a licensee, or maintains a client, patient, or customer relationship with a licensee that does not constitute more than 2 percent of the practice or business of the licensee.

(b) A person maintaining a contractual relationship with a licensee of a board that would constitute more than 2 percent of the practice or business of the licensee, or an officer, director, or substantially full-time representative of that person or group of persons.

(c) An employee of a licensee of a board, or a representative of the employee, except that this subdivision shall not preclude the appointment of a person who maintains an infrequent employee relationship or renders professional or related services to a licensee if the employment or service does not constitute more than 2 percent of the employment or practice of the member of the board.

Added Stats 1961 ch 2232 § 2. Amended Stats 2019 ch 351 § 48 (AB 496), effective January 1, 2020.

§ 450.3. Conflicting pecuniary interests

No public member shall either at the time of their appointment or during their tenure in office have any financial interest in any organization subject to regulation by the board, commission, or committee of which they are a member.

Added Stats 1972 ch 1032 § 1. Amended Stats 2019 ch 351 § 49 (AB 496), effective January 1, 2020.

§ 450.4. [Section repealed 2003.]

Added Stats 1976 ch 1188 § 1. Repealed Stats 2003 ch 563 § 1 (AB 827). The repealed section related to expertise required by board members.

§ 450.5. Prior industrial and professional pursuits

A public member, or a lay member, at any time within five years immediately preceding his or her appointment, shall not have been engaged in pursuits which lie within the field of the industry or profession, or have provided representation to the industry or profession, regulated by the board of which he or she is a member, nor shall he or she engage in those pursuits or provide that representation during his or her term of office.

Added Stats 1961 ch 2232 § 2. Amended Stats 2003 ch 563 § 2 (AB 827).

§ 450.6. Age

Notwithstanding any other section of law, a public member may be appointed without regard to age so long as the public member has reached the age of majority prior to appointment.

Added Stats 1976 ch 1188 § 1.3.

§ 451. Delegation of duties

If any board shall as a part of its functions delegate any duty or responsibility to be performed by a single member of such board, such delegation shall not be made solely to any public member or any lay member of the board in any of the following instances:

(a) The actual preparation of, the administration of, and the grading of, examinations.

(b) The inspection or investigation of licentiates, the manner or method of practice or doing business, or their place of practice or business.

Nothing in this section shall be construed as precluding a public member or a lay member from participating in the formation of policy relating to the scope of the activities set forth in subdivisions (a) and (b) or in the approval, disapproval or modification of the action of its individual members, nor preclude such member from participating as a member of a subcommittee consisting of more than one member of the board in the performance of any duty.

Added Stats 1961 ch 2232 § 2.

§ 452. "Board"

"Board," as used in this chapter, includes a board, advisory board, commission, examining committee, committee or other similarly constituted body exercising powers under this code.

Added Stats 1961 ch 2232 § 2. Amended Stats 1976 ch 1188 § 1.5.

Chapter 7

Licensee

§ 460. Powers of local governmental entities

(a) No city or county shall prohibit a person or group of persons, authorized by one of the agencies in the Department of Consumer Affairs by a license, certificate, or other such means to engage in a particular business, from engaging in that business, occupation, or profession or any portion thereof.

(b) No city, county, or city and county shall prohibit a healingarts professional licensed with the state under Division 2 (commencing with Section 500) from engaging in any act or performing any procedure that falls within the professionally recognized scopeof practice of that licensee.

(1) This subdivision shall not be construed to prohibit the enforcement of a local ordinance in effect prior to January 1, 2010, related to any act or procedure that falls within the professionally recognized scope of practice of a healing arts professional licensed under Division 2 (commencing with Section 500).

(2) This subdivision shall not be construed to prevent a city, county, or city and county from adopting or enforcing any local ordinance governing zoning, business licensing, or reasonable health and safety requirements for establishments or businesses of a healing arts professional licensed under Division 2 (commencing with Section500).

(c) Nothing in this section shall prohibit any city, county, or city and county from levying a business license tax solely forrevenue purposes, nor any city or county from levying a license taxsolely for the purpose of covering the cost of regulation.

Added Stats 1967 ch 1095 § 1. Amended Stats 1971 ch 716 § 24; Stats. 2009, Ch. 16.

§ 461. Asking applicant to reveal arrest record prohibited

No public agency, state or local, shall, on an initial application form for any license, certificate or registration, ask for or require the applicant to reveal a record of arrest that did not result in a conviction or a plea of nolo contendere. A violation of this section is a misdemeanor.

This section shall apply in the case of any license, certificate or registration provided for by any law of this state or local government, including, but not limited to, this code, the Corporations Code, the Education Code, and the Insurance Code.

Added Stats 1975 ch 883 § 1.

Section V

§ 462. Inactive category of licensure

(a) Any of the boards, bureaus, commissions, or programs within the department may establish, by regulation, a system for an inactive category of licensure for persons who are not actively engaged in the practice of their profession or vocation.

(b) The regulation shall contain the following provisions:

(1) The holder of an inactive license issued pursuant to this section shall not engage in any activity for which a license is required.

(2) An inactive license issued pursuant to this section shall be renewed during the same time period in which an active license is renewed. The holder of an inactive license need not comply with any continuing education requirement for renewal of an active license.

(3) The renewal fee for a license in an active status shall apply also for a renewal of a license in an inactive status, unless a lesser renewal fee is specified by the board.

(4) In order for the holder of an inactive license issued pursuant to this section to restore his or her license to an active status, the holder of an inactive license shall comply with all the following:

(A) Pay the renewal fee.

(B) If the board requires completion of continuing education for renewal of an active license, complete continuing education equivalent to that required for renewal of an active license, unless a different requirement is specified by the board.

(c) This section shall not apply to any healing arts board as specified in Section 701.

Added Stats 1994 ch 26 § 14 (AB 1807), effective March 30, 1994.

§ 464. Retired category of licensure

(a) Any of the boards within the department may establish, by regulation, a system for a retired category of licensure for persons who are not actively engaged in the practice of their profession or vocation.

(b) The regulation shall contain the following:

(1) A retired license shall be issued to a person with either an active license or an inactive license that was not placed on inactive status for disciplinary reasons.

(2) The holder of a retired license issued pursuant to this section shall not engage in any activity for which a license is required, unless the board, by regulation, specifies the criteria for a retired licensee to practice his or her profession or vocation.

(3) The holder of a retired license shall not be required to renew that license.

(4) The board shall establish an appropriate application fee for a retired license to cover the reasonable regulatory cost of issuing a retired license.

(5) In order for the holder of a retired license issued pursuant to this section to restore his or her license to an active status, the holder of that license shall meet all the following:

(A) Pay a fee established by statute or regulation.

(B) Certify, in a manner satisfactory to the board, that he or she has not committed an act or crime constituting grounds for denial of licensure.

(C) Comply with the fingerprint submission requirements established by regulation.

(D) If the board requires completion of continuing education for renewal of an active license, complete continuing education equivalent to that required for renewal of an active license, unless a different requirement is specified by the board.

(E) Complete any other requirements as specified by the board by regulation.

(c) A board may upon its own determination, and shall upon receipt of a complaint from any person, investigate the actions of any licensee, including a person with a license that either restricts or prohibits the practice of that person in his or her profession or vocation, including, but not limited to, a license that is retired, inactive, canceled, revoked, or suspended.

(d) Subdivisions (a) and (b) shall not apply to a board that has other statutory authority to establish a retired license.

Added Stats 2016 ch 473 § 1 (AB 2859), effective January 1, 2017.

Chapter 8

Dispute Resolution Programs

Article 1

Legislative Purpose

§ 465.5. Legislative intent

It is the intent of the Legislature to permit counties to accomplish all of the following:

(a) Encouragement and support of the development and use of alternative dispute resolution techniques.

(b) Encouragement and support of community participation in the development, administration, and oversight of local programs designed to facilitate the informal resolution of disputes among members of the community.

(c) Development of structures for dispute resolution that may serve as models for resolution programs in other communities.

(d) Education of communities with regard to the availability and benefits of alternative dispute resolution techniques.

(e) Encouragement of courts, prosecuting authorities, public defenders, law enforcement agencies, and administrative agencies to work in cooperation with, and to make referrals to, dispute resolution programs.

At the time that the state assumes the responsibility for the funding of California trial courts, consideration shall be given to the Dispute Resolution Advisory Council's evaluation of the effectiveness of alternative dispute resolution programs and the feasibility of the operation of a statewide program of grants, with the intention of funding alternative dispute resolution programs on a statewide basis.

Added Stats 1986 ch 1313 § 1.

Article 3

Establishment and Administration of Programs

§ 467. Dispute Resolution Advisory Council

(a) There is in the Division of Consumer Services of the Department of Consumer Affairs a Dispute Resolution Advisory Council. The advisory council shall complete the duties required by this chapter no later than January 1, 1989.

(b) The advisory council shall consist of seven persons, five of whom shall be appointed by the Governor. One member shall be appointed by the Senate Rules Committee, and one member shall be appointed by the Speaker of the Assembly. At least four of the persons appointed to the advisory council shall be active members of the State Bar of California, and at least four persons appointed to the advisory council shall have a minimum of two years of direct experience in utilizing dispute resolution techniques. The members of the advisory council shall reflect the racial, ethnic, sexual, and geographic diversity of the State of California.

(c) The members of the advisory council shall not receive a salary for their services but shall be reimbursed for their actual and necessary travel and other expenses incurred in the performance of their duties.

Added Stats 1986 ch 1313 § 1. Amended Stats 1987 ch 28 § 1, effective May 28, 1987.

§ 467.1. Contract requirements; County programs

(a) A program funded pursuant to this chapter shall be operated pursuant to contract with the county and shall comply with all of the requirements of this chapter and the rules and regulations of the advisory council.

(b) Counties may establish a program of grants to public entities and nonpartisan nonprofit corporations for the establishment and continuance of programs to be operated under the requirements of this chapter and the standards developed by the advisory council. The board of supervisors of a county in which, because of the county's size, the distribution authorized by Section 470.5 is insufficient to establish a county program may enter into an agreement with the board of supervisors of one or more other such counties to establish a program authorized by this chapter on a regional basis.

Added Stats 1986 ch 1313 § 1. Amended Stats 1987 ch 28 § 2, effective May 28, 1987; Stats 2005 ch 75 § 2 (AB 145), effective July 19, 2005, operative January 1, 2006.

§ 467.2. Eligibility for program funding

A program shall not be eligible for funding under this chapter unless it meets all of the following requirements:

(a) Compliance with this chapter and the applicable rules and regulations of the advisory council.

(b) Provision of neutral persons adequately trained in conflict resolution techniques as required by the rules and regulations promulgated by the advisory council pursuant to Section 471.

(c) Provision of dispute resolution, on a sliding scale basis, and without cost to indigents.

(d) Provision that, upon consent of the parties, a written agreement or an award resolving a dispute will be issued setting out a settlement of the issues involved in the dispute and the future responsibilities of each party.

(e) Provision of neutral procedures applicable equally to all participants without any special benefit or consideration given to persons or entities providing funding for the programs.

(f) Provision that participation in the program is voluntary and that the parties are not coerced to enter dispute resolution.

(g) Provision of alternative dispute resolution is the primary purpose of the program.

(h) Programs operated by counties that receive funding under this chapter shall be operated primarily for the purposes of dispute resolution, consistent with the purposes of this chapter.

Added Stats 1986 ch 1313 § 1.

§ 467.3. Provision of written statement to parties; Contents

Programs funded pursuant to this chapter shall provide persons indicating an intention to utilize the dispute resolution process with a written statement prior to the dispute resolution proceeding, in language easy to read and understand, stating all of the following:

(a) The nature of the dispute.

(b) The nature of the dispute resolution process.

Section V

(c) The rights and obligations of the parties, including, but not limited to, all of the following:

(1) The right to call and examine witnesses.

(2) The right of the parties to be accompanied by counsel, who may participate as permitted under the rules and procedures of the program.

(d) The procedures under which the dispute resolution will be conducted.

(e) If the parties enter into arbitration, whether the dispute resolution process will be binding.

Added Stats 1986 ch 1313 § 1.

§ 467.4. Agreements resolving disputes; Enforcement; Admissibility in evidence; Tolling statute of limitations

(a) An agreement resolving a dispute entered into with the assistance of a program shall not be enforceable in a court nor shall it be admissible as evidence in any judicial or administrative proceeding, unless the consent of the parties or the agreement includes a provision that clearly states the intention of the parties that the agreement or any resulting award shall be so enforceable or admissible as evidence.

(b) The parties may agree in writing to toll the applicable statute of limitations during the pendency of the dispute resolution process.

Added Stats 1986 ch 1313 § 1.

§ 467.5. Communications during mediation proceedings

Notwithstanding the express application of Chapter 2 (commencing with Section 1115) of Division 9 of the Evidence Code to mediations, all proceedings conducted by a program funded pursuant to this chapter, including, but not limited to, arbitrations and conciliations, are subject to Chapter 2 (commencing with Section 1115) of Division 9 of the Evidence Code.

Added Stats 1988 ch 188 § 2. Amended Stats 1997 ch 772 § 1 (AB 939).

§ 467.6. Statistical records; Anonymity of parties

Each program shall maintain those statistical records required by Section 471.5, and as may be required by the county. The records shall maintain the confidentiality and anonymity of the parties.

Added Stats 1986 ch 1313 § 1.

§ 467.7. Withdrawal from dispute resolution; Criminal complaints; Waiver of right to counsel

(a) Unless the parties have agreed to a binding award, nothing in this chapter shall be construed to prohibit any person who voluntarily enters the dispute resolution process from revoking his or her consent, withdrawing from dispute resolution, and seeking judicial or administrative redress.

(b) In cases in which a criminal complaint has been filed by a prosecutor, other than for an infraction, the advice of counsel shall be obtained before any dispute resolution process is initiated. Nothing in this subdivision shall be construed to preclude a defendant from knowingly and voluntarily waiving the right to counsel. A defendant who indicates a desire to waive the right to counsel shall be encouraged to consult with the public defender or private counsel before waiving that right.

Added Stats 1986 ch 1313 § 1.

Article 4

Application Procedures

§ 468.1. Selection of programs

Programs shall be selected for funding by a county from the applications submitted therefor.

Added Stats 1986 ch 1313 § 1.

§ 468.2. Applications; Required information

Applications submitted for funding shall include, but need not be limited to, all of the following information:

(a) Evidence of compliance with Sections 467.2, 467.3, and 467.4.

(b) A description of the proposed community area of service, cost of the principal components of operation, and any other characteristics, as determined by rules of the advisory council.

(c) A description of available dispute resolution services and facilities within the defined geographical area.

(d) A description of the applicant's proposed program, by type and purpose, including evidence of community support, the present availability of resources, and the applicant's administrative capability.

(e) A description of existing or planned cooperation between the applicant and local human service and justice system agencies.

(f) A demonstrated effort on the part of the applicant to show the manner in which funds that may be awarded under this program may be coordinated or consolidated with other local, state, or federal funds available for the activities described in Sections 467.2, 467.3, and 467.4.

(g) An explanation of the methods to be used for selecting and training mediators and other facilitators used in the dispute resolution process.

(h) Such additional information as may be required by the county.

Added Stats 1986 ch 1313 § 1.

§ 468.3. Funding priorities; Criteria

Data supplied by each applicant shall be used to assign relative funding priority on the basis of criteria developed by the advisory council. The criteria may include, but shall not be limited to, all of the following, in addition to the criteria set forth in Section 468.2:

(a) Unit cost, according to the type and scope of the proposed program.

(b) Quality and validity of the program.

(c) Number of participants who may be served.

(d) Administrative capability.

(e) Community support factors.

Added Stats 1986 ch 1313 § 1.

Article 6

Funding

§ 470.1. Acceptance of funds by grant recipients

(a) A grant recipient may accept funds from any public or private source for the purposes of this chapter.

(b) A county and its representatives may inspect, examine, and audit the fiscal affairs of the programs and the projects funded under this chapter.

(c) Programs shall, whenever reasonably possible, make use of public facilities at free or nominal costs.

Added Stats 1986 ch 1313 § 1.

§ 470.2. County's share of funding

A county's share of the funding pursuant to this chapter shall not exceed 50 percent of the approved estimated cost of the program.

Added Stats 1986 ch 1313 § 1.

§ 470.3. [Section repealed 2006.]

Added Stats 1986 ch 1313 § 1. Amended Stats 1987 ch 28 § 3, effective May 28, 1987, ch 1431 § 1; Stats 1992 ch 685 § 2 (SB 1707), effective September 12, 1992; Stats 1998 ch 931 § 1 (SB 2139), effective September 28, 1998. Repealed Stats 2005 ch 75 § 3 (AB 145), effective July 19, 2005, operative January 1, 2006. The repealed section related to fees for support of programs.

§ 470.5. Monthly distributions from filing fees for support of dispute resolution programs

(a) On and after January 1, 2006, as described in Section 68085.1 of the Government Code, the Administrative Office of the Courts shall make monthly distributions from superior court filing fees for the support of dispute resolution programs under this chapter in each county that has acted to establish a program. The amount distributed in each county shall be equal to the following:

(1) From each first paper filing fee collected by the court as provided under Section 70611 or 70612, subdivision (a) of Section 70613, subdivision (a) of Section 70614, or Section 70670 of the Government Code, and each first paper or petition filing fee collected by the court in a probate matter as provided under Section 70650, 70651, 70652, 70653, or 70655 of the Government Code, the same amount as was required to be collected for the support of dispute resolution programs in that county as of December 31, 2005, when a fee was collected for the filing of a first paper in a civil action under Section 26820.4 of the Government Code.

(2) From each first paper filing fee in a limited civil case collected by the court as provided under subdivision (b) of Section 70613 or subdivision (b) of Section 70614 of the Government Code, and each first paper or petition filing fee collected by the court in a probate matter as provided under Section 70654, 70656, or 70658 of the Government Code, the same amount as was required to be collected for the support of dispute resolution programs in that county as of December 31, 2005, when a fee was collected for the filing of a first paper in a civil action under Section 72055 of the Government Code where the amount demanded, excluding attorney's fees and costs, was ten thousand dollars ($10,000) or less.

(b) Distributions under this section shall be used only for the support of dispute resolution programs authorized by this chapter. The county shall deposit the amounts distributed under this section in an account created and maintained for this purpose by the county. Records of these distributions shall be available for inspection by the public upon request.

(c) After January 1, 2006, a county that does not already have a distribution from superior court filing fees under this section and that establishes a dispute resolution program authorized by this chapter may approve a distribution under this section. A county that already has a distribution under this section may change the amount of the distribution. The total amount to be distributed for the support of dispute resolution programs under this section may not exceed eight dollars ($8) per filing fee.

(d) The county may make changes under subdivision (c) to be effective January 1 or July 1 of any year, on and after January 1, 2006. The county shall provide the Administrative Office of the Courts with a copy of the action of the board of supervisors that establishes the change at least 15 days before the date that the change goes into effect.

Added Stats 2005 ch 75 § 4 (AB 145), effective July 19, 2005, operative January 1, 2006.

§ 470.6. Carry over of moneys and fees

A county may carry over moneys received from distributions under Section 470.5 and from the fees for the support of dispute resolution programs authorized by this chapter that were added to fees for filing a first paper in a civil action in superior court under the laws in effect before January 1, 2006.

Added Stats 2005 ch 75 § 5 (AB 145), effective July 19, 2005, operative January 1, 2006.

Article 7

Rules and Regulations

§ 471.3. Statewide uniformity with guidelines contained in rules and regulations

The rules and regulations adopted by the advisory council pursuant to Section 471 shall be formulated to promote statewide uniformity with the guidelines contained in those rules and regulations.

Added Stats 1987 ch 28 § 6, effective May 28, 1987.

§ 471.5. Annual provision of statistical data

Each program funded pursuant to this chapter shall annually provide the county with statistical data regarding its operating budget; the number of referrals, categories, or types of cases referred to the program; the number of persons served by the program; the number of disputes resolved; the nature of the disputes resolved; rates of compliance; the number of persons utilizing the process more than once; the duration of and the estimated costs of the hearings conducted by the programs; and any other information that the county may require. The data shall maintain the confidentiality and anonymity of the persons employing the dispute resolution process.

Added Stats 1986 ch 1313 § 1. Amended Stats 1987 ch 56 § 1.

DIVISION 1.2

JOINT COMMITTEE ON BOARDS, COMMISSIONS, AND CONSUMER PROTECTION

Chapter 1

Review of Boards under the Department of Consumer Affairs

§ 473.   [Section repealed 2011.]
§ 473.1.   [Section repealed 2011.]
§ 473.15. [Section repealed 2011.]
§ 473.16. [Section repealed 2011.]
§ 473.17. [Section repealed 2000.]
§ 473.2.   [Section repealed 2011.]
§ 473.3.   [Section repealed 2011.]
§ 473.4.   [Section repealed 2011.]
§ 473.5.   [Section repealed 2011.]
§ 473.6.   [Section repealed 2011.]

§ 473. [Section repealed 2011.]

Added Stats 1994 ch 908 § 5 (SB 2036). Amended Stats 1998 ch 991 § 2 (SB 1980); Stats 2003 ch 874 § 2 (SB 363); Stats 2004 ch 33 § 3 (AB 1467), effective April 13, 2004. Repealed Stats 2010 ch 670 § 3 (AB 2130), effective January 1, 2011. The repealed section related to the establishment of the Joint Committee on Boards, Commissions, and Consumer Protection, powers and duties, designation of staff, and termination of Committee.

§ 473.1. [Section repealed 2011.]

Added Stats 1994 ch 908 § 5 (SB 2036). Amended Stats 1997 ch 78 § 3.5 (AB 71); Stats 2000 ch 393 § 1 (SB 2028); Stats 2002 ch 825 § 2 (SB 1952); Stats 2003 ch 789 § 3 (SB 364); Stats 2009 ch 310 § 5 (AB 48), effective January 1, 2010. Repealed Stats 2010 ch 670 § 3 (AB 2130), effective January 1, 2011. The repealed section related to applicability of chapter "Review of Boards under the Department of Consumer Affairs."

§ 473.15. [Section repealed 2011.]

Added Stats 1997 ch 759 § 6 (SB 827). Amended Stats 2000 ch 199 § 1 (SB 2034); Stats 2002 ch 681 § 1 (SB 1954), ch 1012 § 1.5 (SB 2025), effective September 27, 2002; Stats 2004 ch 33 § 4 (AB 1467), effective April 13, 2004; Stats 2005 ch 659 § 0.5 (SB 248), effective January 1, 2006; Stats 2006 ch 658 § 4 (SB 1476), effective January 1, 2007. Repealed Stats 2010 ch 670 § 3 (AB 2130), effective January 1, 2011. The repealed section related to review of specified boards by committee and legislative intent.

§ 473.16. [Section repealed 2011.]

Added Stats 2005 ch 674 § 3 (SB 231), effective January 1, 2006. Repealed Stats 2010 ch 670 § 3 (AB 2130), effective January 1, 2011. The repealed section related to examination and report of Medical Board of California's composition, initial and biennial fees, and report of findings.

§ 473.17. [Section repealed 2000.]

Added Stats ch 736 § 1 (SB 1981). Repealed Stats 2000 ch 393 § 3 (SB 2028). The repealed section related to review of referral of cases by specified boards to Licensing and Health Quality Enforcement Sections of Attorney General's office.

§ 473.2. [Section repealed 2011.]

Added Stats 1994 ch 908 § 5 (SB 2036). Amended Stats 2000 ch 393 § 4 (SB 2028); Stats 2003 ch 789 § 4 (SB 364); Stats 2004 ch 33 § 5 (AB 1467), effective April 13, 2004. Repealed Stats 2010 ch 670 § 3 (AB 2130), effective January 1, 2011. The repealed section related to submission of analysis and report to committee concerning the board.

§ 473.3. [Section repealed 2011.]

Added Stats 1994 ch 908 § 5 (SB 2036). Amended Stats 1997 ch 78 § 3.7 (AB 71); Stats 2000 ch 393 § 5 (SB 2028); Stats 2001 ch 399 § 1 (AB 1720); Stats 2003 ch 789 § 5 (SB 364); Stats 2004 ch 33 § 6 (AB 1467), effective April 13, 2004. Repealed Stats 2010 ch 670 § 3 (AB 2130), effective January 1, 2011. The repealed section related to public hearings prior to termination, continuation, or reestablishment of any board, the review of the Bureau for Private Postsecondary and Vocational Education and Bureau of Automotive Repair.

§ 473.4. [Section repealed 2011.]

Added Stats 1994 ch 908 § 5 (SB 2036). Amended Stats 2004 ch 33 § 7 (AB 1467), effective April 13, 2004. Repealed Stats 2010 ch 670 § 3 (AB 2130), effective January 1, 2011. The repealed section related to the evaluation of boards and regulatory programs and determination of need for continued existence.

§ 473.5. [Section repealed 2011.]

Added Stats 1994 ch 908 § 5 (SB 2036). Amended Stats 2000 ch 393 § 6 (SB 2028); Stats 2004 ch 33 § 8 (AB 1467), effective April 13, 2004. Repealed Stats 2010 ch 670 § 3 (AB 2130), effective January 1, 2011. The repealed section related to report of findings and preliminary recommendations by Joint Committee on Boards, Commissions, and Consumer Protection.

§ 473.6. [Section repealed 2011.]

Added Stats 1997 ch 759 § 7 (SB 827). Amended Stats 2002 ch 1012 § 2 (SB 2025), effective September 27, 2002; Stats 2004 ch 33 § 9 (AB 1467), effective April 13, 2004, ch 909 § 1.5 (SB 136), effective September 30, 2004. Repealed Stats 2010 ch 670 § 3 (AB 2130), effective January 1, 2011. The repealed section related to the referral of proposals to create new licensure categories, change requirements, or create new licensing board to Joint Committee.

DIVISION 1.5

DENIAL, SUSPENSION AND REVOCATION OF LICENSES

Chapter 1

General Provisions

Chapter 2

Denial of Licenses

Chapter 3

Suspension and Revocation of Licenses

Chapter 4

Public Reprovals

Section V

Chapter 5

Examination Security

Chapter 1

General Provisions

§ 475. Applicability of division

(a) Notwithstanding any other provisions of this code, the provisions of this division shall govern the denial of licenses on the grounds of:

(1) Knowingly making a false statement of material fact, or knowingly omitting to state a material fact, in an application for a license.

(2) Conviction of a crime.

(3) Commission of any act involving dishonesty, fraud or deceit with the intent to substantially benefit himself or another, or substantially injure another.

(4) Commission of any act which, if done by a licentiate of the business or profession in question, would be grounds for suspension or revocation of license.

(b) Notwithstanding any other provisions of this code, the provisions of this division shall govern the suspension and revocation of licenses on grounds specified in paragraphs (1) and (2) of subdivision (a).

(c) A license shall not be denied, suspended, or revoked on the grounds of a lack of good moral character or any similar ground relating to an applicant's character, reputation, personality, or habits.

Added Stats 1972 ch 903 § 1. Amended Stats 1974 ch 1321 § 1; Stats 1992 ch 1289 § 5 (AB 2743).

§ 476. Exemptions

(a) Except as provided in subdivision (b), nothing in this division shall apply to the licensure or registration of persons pursuant to Chapter 4 (commencing with Section 6000) of Division 3, or pursuant to Division 9 (commencing with Section 23000) or pursuant to Chapter 5 (commencing with Section 19800) of Division 8.

(b) Section 494.5 shall apply to the licensure of persons authorized to practice law pursuant to Chapter 4 (commencing with Section 6000) of Division 3, and the licensure or registration of persons pursuant to Chapter 5 (commencing with Section 19800) of Division 8 or pursuant to Division 9 (commencing with Section 23000).

Added Stats 1972 ch 903 § 1. Amended Stats 1983 ch 721 § 1; Stats 2011 ch 455 § 2 (AB 1424), effective January 1, 2012.

§ 477. "Board"; "License"

As used in this division:

(a) "Board" includes "bureau," "commission," "committee," "department," "division," "examining committee," "program," and "agency."

(b) "License" includes certificate, registration or other means to engage in a business or profession regulated by this code.

Added Stats 1972 ch 903 § 1. Amended Stats 1974 ch 1321 § 2; Stats 1983 ch 95 § 1; Stats 1991 ch 654 § 5 (AB 1893).

§ 478. "Application"; "Material"

(a) As used in this division, "application" includes the original documents or writings filed and any other supporting documents or writings including supporting documents provided or filed contemporaneously, or later, in support of the application whether provided or filed by the applicant or by any other person in support of the application.

(b) As used in this division, "material" includes a statement or omission substantially related to the qualifications, functions, or duties of the business or profession.

Added Stats 1992 ch 1289 § 6 (AB 2743).

Chapter 2

Denial of Licenses

§ 480. Grounds for denial by board; Effect of obtaining certificate of rehabilitation

(a) Notwithstanding any other provision of this code, a board may deny a license regulated by this code on the grounds that the applicant has been convicted of a crime or has been subject to formal discipline only if either of the following conditions are met:

(1) The applicant has been convicted of a crime within the preceding seven years from the date of application that is substantially related to the qualifications, functions, or duties of the business or profession for which the application is made, regardless of whether the applicant was incarcerated for that crime, or the applicant has been convicted of a crime that is substantially related to the qualifications, functions, or duties of the business or profession for which the application is

made and for which the applicant is presently incarcerated or for which the applicant was released from incarceration within the preceding seven years from the date of application. However, the preceding seven-year limitation shall not apply in either of the following situations:

(A) The applicant was convicted of a serious felony, as defined in Section 1192.7 of the Penal Code or a crime for which registration is required pursuant to paragraph (2) or (3) of subdivision (d) of Section 290 of the Penal Code.

(B) The applicant was convicted of a financial crime currently classified as a felony that is directly and adversely related to the fiduciary qualifications, functions, or duties of the business or profession for which the application is made, pursuant to regulations adopted by the board, and for which the applicant is seeking licensure under any of the following:

(i) Chapter 6 (commencing with Section 6500) of Division 3.

(ii) Chapter 9 (commencing with Section 7000) of Division 3.

(iii) Chapter 11.3 (commencing with Section 7512) of Division 3.

(iv) Licensure as a funeral director or cemetery manager under Chapter 12 (commencing with Section 7600) of Division 3.

(v) Division 4 (commencing with Section 10000).

(2) The applicant has been subjected to formal discipline by a licensing board in or outside California within the preceding seven years from the date of application based on professional misconduct that would have been cause for discipline before the board for which the present application is made and that is substantially related to the qualifications, functions, or duties of the business or profession for which the present application is made. However, prior disciplinary action by a licensing board within the preceding seven years shall not be the basis for denial of a license if the basis for that disciplinary action was a conviction that has been dismissed pursuant to Section 1203.4, 1203.4a, 1203.41, 1203.42, or 1203.425 of the Penal Code or a comparable dismissal or expungement.

(b) Notwithstanding any other provision of this code, a person shall not be denied a license on the basis that the person has been convicted of a crime, or on the basis of acts underlying a conviction for a crime, if that person has obtained a certificate of rehabilitation under Chapter 3.5 (commencing with Section 4852.01) of Title 6 of Part 3 of the Penal Code, has been granted clemency or a pardon by a state or federal executive, or has made a showing of rehabilitation pursuant to Section 482.

(c) Notwithstanding any other provision of this code, a person shall not be denied a license on the basis of any conviction, or on the basis of the acts underlying the conviction, that has been dismissed pursuant to Section 1203.4, 1203.4a, 1203.41, 1203.42, or 1203.425 of the Penal Code, or a comparable dismissal or expungement. An applicant who has a conviction that has been dismissed pursuant to Section 1203.4, 1203.4a, 1203.41, or 1203.42 of the Penal Code shall provide proof of the dismissal if it is not reflected on the report furnished by the Department of Justice.

(d) Notwithstanding any other provision of this code, a board shall not deny a license on the basis of an arrest that resulted in a disposition other than a conviction, including an arrest that resulted in an infraction, citation, or a juvenile adjudication.

(e) A board may deny a license regulated by this code on the ground that the applicant knowingly made a false statement of fact that is required to be revealed in the application for the license. A board shall not deny a license based solely on an applicant's failure to disclose a fact that would not have been cause for denial of the license had it been disclosed.

(f) A board shall follow the following procedures in requesting or acting on an applicant's criminal history information:

(1) A board issuing a license pursuant to Chapter 3 (commencing with Section 5500), Chapter 3.5 (commencing with Section 5615), Chapter 10 (commencing with Section 7301), Chapter 20 (commencing with Section 9800), or Chapter 20.3 (commencing with Section 9880), of Division 3, or Chapter 3 (commencing with Section 19000) or Chapter 3.1 (commencing with Section 19225) of Division 8 may require applicants for licensure under those chapters to disclose criminal conviction history on an application for licensure.

(2) Except as provided in paragraph (1), a board shall not require an applicant for licensure to disclose any information or documentation regarding the applicant's criminal history. However, a board may request mitigating information from an applicant regarding the applicant's criminal history for purposes of determining substantial relation or demonstrating evidence of rehabilitation, provided that the applicant is informed that disclosure is voluntary and that the applicant's decision not to disclose any information shall not be a factor in a board's decision to grant or deny an application for licensure.

(3) If a board decides to deny an application for licensure based solely or in part on the applicant's conviction history, the board shall notify the applicant in writing of all of the following:

(A) The denial or disqualification of licensure.

(B) Any existing procedure the board has for the applicant to challenge the decision or to request reconsideration.

(C) That the applicant has the right to appeal the board's decision.

(D) The processes for the applicant to request a copy of the applicant's complete conviction history and question the accuracy or completeness of the record pursuant to Sections 11122 to 11127 of the Penal Code.

(g) (1) For a minimum of three years, each board under this code shall retain application forms and other documents submitted by an applicant, any notice provided to an applicant, all other communications received from and provided to an applicant, and criminal history reports of an applicant.

(2) Each board under this code shall retain the number of applications received for each license and the number of applications requiring inquiries regarding criminal history. In addition, each licensing authority shall retain all of the following information:

(A) The number of applicants with a criminal record who received notice of denial or disqualification of licensure.

(B) The number of applicants with a criminal record who provided evidence of mitigation or rehabilitation.

(C) The number of applicants with a criminal record who appealed any denial or disqualification of licensure.

(D) The final disposition and demographic information, consisting of voluntarily provided information on race or gender, of any applicant described in subparagraph (A), (B), or (C).

(3) (A) Each board under this code shall annually make available to the public through the board's internet website and through a report submitted to the appropriate policy committees of the Legislature deidentified information collected pursuant to this subdivision. Each board shall ensure confidentiality of the individual applicants.

(B) A report pursuant to subparagraph (A) shall be submitted in compliance with Section 9795 of the Government Code.

(h) "Conviction" as used in this section shall have the same meaning as defined in Section 7.5.

(i) This section does not in any way modify or otherwise affect the existing authority of the following entities in regard to licensure:

(1) The State Athletic Commission.

(2) The Bureau for Private Postsecondary Education.

(3) The California Horse Racing Board.

(j) This section shall become operative on July 1, 2020.

Added Stats 2018 ch 995 § 4 (AB 2138), effective January 1, 2019, operative July 1, 2020. Amended Stats 2019 ch 359 § 1 (AB 1521), effective January 1, 2020, operative July 1, 2020; Stats 2019 ch 578 § 2.5 (AB 1076), effective January 1, 2020, operative July 1, 2020 (ch 578 prevails).

§ 480.2. Grounds for denial of license by Bureau for Private Postsecondary Education, State Athletic Commission, and California Horse Racing Board

(a) The Bureau for Private Postsecondary Education, the State Athletic Commission, and the California Horse Racing Board may deny a license regulated by it on the grounds that the applicant has one of the following:

(1) Been convicted of a crime.

(2) Done any act involving dishonesty, fraud, or deceit with the intent to substantially benefit themselves or another, or substantially injure another.

(3) (A) Done any act that if done by a licentiate of the business or profession in question, would be grounds for suspension or revocation of license.

(B) The Bureau for Private Postsecondary Education, the State Athletic Commission, and the California Horse Racing Board may deny a license pursuant to this subdivision only if the crime or act is substantially related to the qualifications, functions, or duties of the business or profession for which the application is made.

(b) Notwithstanding any other provision of this code, a person shall not be denied a license solely on the basis that the person has been convicted of a felony if that person has obtained a certificate of rehabilitation under Chapter 3.5 (commencing with Section 4852.01) of Title 6 of Part 3 of the Penal Code or that the person has been convicted of a misdemeanor if the person has met all applicable requirements of the criteria of rehabilitation developed by the Bureau for Private Postsecondary Education, the State Athletic Commission, and the California Horse Racing Board to evaluate the rehabilitation of a person when considering the denial of a license under paragraph (1) of subdivision (f).

(c) Notwithstanding any other provisions of this code, a person shall not be denied a license by the Bureau for Private Postsecondary Education, the State Athletic Commission, or the California Horse Racing Board solely on the basis of a conviction that has been dismissed pursuant to Section 1203.4, 1203.4a, 1203.41, or 1203.425 of the Penal Code. An applicant who has a conviction that has been dismissed pursuant to Section 1203.4, 1203.4a, or 1203.41 of the Penal Code shall provide proof of the dismissal.

(d) The Bureau for Private Postsecondary Education, the State Athletic Commission, and the California Horse Racing Board may deny a license regulated by it on the ground that the applicant knowingly made a false statement of fact that is required to be revealed in the application for the license.

(e) The Bureau for Private Postsecondary Education, the State Athletic Commission, and the California Horse Racing Board shall develop criteria to aid it, when considering the denial, suspension, or revocation of a license, to determine whether a crime or act is substantially related to the qualifications, functions, or duties of the business or profession it regulates.

(f) (1) The Bureau for Private Postsecondary Education, the State Athletic Commission, and the California Horse Racing Board shall develop criteria to evaluate the rehabilitation of a person either when:

(A) Considering the denial of a license under this section.

Section V

(B) Considering suspension or revocation of a license under Section 490.

(2) The Bureau for Private Postsecondary Education, the State Athletic Commission, and the California Horse Racing Board shall take into account all competent evidence of rehabilitation furnished by the applicant or licensee.

(g) Except as otherwise provided by law, following a hearing requested by an applicant pursuant to subdivision (b) of Section 485, the Bureau for Private Postsecondary Education, the State Athletic Commission, and the California Horse Racing Board may take any of the following actions:

(1) Grant the license effective upon completion of all licensing requirements by the applicant.

(2) Grant the license effective upon completion of all licensing requirements by the applicant, immediately revoke the license, stay the revocation, and impose probationary conditions on the license, which may include suspension.

(3) Deny the license.

(4) Take other action in relation to denying or granting the license as the Bureau for Private Postsecondary Education, the State Athletic Commission, or the California Horse Racing Board, in its discretion, may deem proper.

(h) Notwithstanding any other law, in a proceeding conducted by the Bureau for Private Postsecondary Education, the State Athletic Commission, or the California Horse Racing Board to deny an application for a license or to suspend or revoke a license or otherwise take disciplinary action against a person who holds a license, upon the ground that the applicant or the licensee has been convicted of a crime substantially related to the qualifications, functions, and duties of the licensee in question, the record of conviction of the crime shall be conclusive evidence of the fact that the conviction occurred, but only of that fact, and the Bureau for Private Postsecondary Education, the State Athletic Commission, and the California Horse Racing Board may inquire into the circumstances surrounding the commission of the crime in order to fix the degree of discipline or to determine if the conviction is substantially related to the qualifications, functions, and duties of the licensee in question.

(i) Notwithstanding Section 7.5, a conviction within the meaning of this section means a plea or verdict of guilty or a conviction following a plea of nolo contendere. Any action that the Bureau for Private Postsecondary Education, the State Athletic Commission, or the California Horse Racing Board is permitted to take following the establishment of a conviction may be taken when the time for appeal has elapsed, the judgment of conviction has been affirmed on appeal, or when an order granting probation is made suspending the imposition of sentence, irrespective of a subsequent order under the provisions of Section 1203.4, 1203.4a, 1203.41, or 1203.425 of the Penal Code.

(j) This section shall become operative on July 1, 2020.

Added Stats 2018 ch 995 § 5 (AB 2138), effective January 1, 2019, operative July 1, 2020. Amended Stats 2019 ch 578 § 3 (AB 1076), effective January 1, 2020, operative July 1, 2020.

§ 481. Crime and job-fitness criteria

(a) Each board under this code shall develop criteria to aid it, when considering the denial, suspension, or revocation of a license, to determine whether a crime is substantially related to the qualifications, functions, or duties of the business or profession it regulates.

(b) Criteria for determining whether a crime is substantially related to the qualifications, functions, or duties of the business or profession a board regulates shall include all of the following:

(1) The nature and gravity of the offense.

(2) The number of years elapsed since the date of the offense.

(3) The nature and duties of the profession in which the applicant seeks licensure or in which the licensee is licensed.

(c) A board shall not deny a license based in whole or in part on a conviction without considering evidence of rehabilitation submitted by an applicant pursuant to any process established in the practice act or regulations of the particular board and as directed by Section 482.

(d) Each board shall post on its Internet Web site a summary of the criteria used to consider whether a crime is considered to be substantially related to the qualifications, functions, or duties of the business or profession it regulates consistent with this section.

(e) This section does not in any way modify or otherwise affect the existing authority of the following entities in regard to licensure:

(1) The State Athletic Commission.

(2) The Bureau for Private Postsecondary Education.

(3) The California Horse Racing Board.

(f) This section shall become operative on July 1, 2020.

Added Stats 2018 ch 995 § 7 (AB 2138), effective January 1, 2019, operative July 1, 2020.

§ 482. Rehabilitation criteria

(a) Each board under this code shall develop criteria to evaluate the rehabilitation of a person when doing either of the following:

(1) Considering the denial of a license by the board under Section 480.

(2) Considering suspension or revocation of a license under Section 490.

(b) Each board shall consider whether an applicant or licensee has made a showing of rehabilitation if either of the following are met:

(1) The applicant or licensee has completed the criminal sentence at issue without a violation of parole or probation.

(2) The board, applying its criteria for rehabilitation, finds that the applicant is rehabilitated.

(c) This section does not in any way modify or otherwise affect the existing authority of the following entities in regard to licensure:

(1) The State Athletic Commission.

(2) The Bureau for Private Postsecondary Education.

(3) The California Horse Racing Board.

(d) This section shall become operative on July 1, 2020.

Added Stats 2018 ch 995 § 9 (AB 2138), effective January 1, 2019, operative July 1, 2020.

§ 484. Attestation to good moral character of applicant

No person applying for licensure under this code shall be required to submit to any licensing board any attestation by other persons to his good moral character.

Added Stats 1972 ch 903 § 1. Amended Stats 1974 ch 1321 § 9.

§ 485. Procedure upon denial

Upon denial of an application for a license under this chapter or Section 496, the board shall do either of the following:

(a) File and serve a statement of issues in accordance with Chapter 5 (commencing with Section 11500) of Part 1 of Division 3 of Title 2 of the Government Code.

(b) Notify the applicant that the application is denied, stating (1) the reason for the denial, and (2) that the applicant has the right to a hearing under Chapter 5 (commencing with Section 11500) of Part 1 of Division 3 of Title 2 of the Government Code if written request for hearing is made within 60 days after service of the notice of denial. Unless written request for hearing is made within the 60-day period, the applicant's right to a hearing is deemed waived.

Service of the notice of denial may be made in the manner authorized for service of summons in civil actions, or by registered mail addressed to the applicant at the latest address filed by the applicant in writing with the board in his or her application or otherwise. Service by mail is complete on the date of mailing.

Added Stats 1972 ch 903 § 1. Amended Stats 1997 ch 758 § 2.3 (SB 1346).

§ 486. Contents of decision or notice

Where the board has denied an application for a license under this chapter or Section 496, it shall, in its decision, or in its notice under subdivision (b) of Section 485, inform the applicant of the following:

(a) The earliest date on which the applicant may reapply for a license which shall be one year from the effective date of the decision, or service of the notice under subdivision (b) of Section 485, unless the board prescribes an earlier date or a later date is prescribed by another statute.

(b) That all competent evidence of rehabilitation presented will be considered upon a reapplication.

Along with the decision, or the notice under subdivision (b) of Section 485, the board shall serve a copy of the criteria relating to rehabilitation formulated under Section 482.

Added Stats 1972 ch 903 § 1. Amended Stats 1974 ch 1321 § 9.5; Stats 1997 ch 758 § 2.4 (SB 1346).

§ 487. Hearing; Time

If a hearing is requested by the applicant, the board shall conduct such hearing within 90 days from the date the hearing is requested unless the applicant shall request or agree in writing to a postponement or continuance of the hearing. Notwithstanding the above, the Office of Administrative Hearings may order, or on a showing of good cause, grant a request for, up to 45 additional days within which to conduct a hearing, except in cases involving alleged examination or licensing fraud, in which cases the period may be up to 180 days. In no case shall more than two such orders be made or requests be granted.

Added Stats 1972 ch 903 § 1. Amended Stats 1974 ch 1321 § 10; Stats 1986 ch 220 § 1, effective June 30, 1986.

§ 488. Hearing request

(a) Except as otherwise provided by law, following a hearing requested by an applicant pursuant to subdivision (b) of Section 485, the board may take any of the following actions:

(1) Grant the license effective upon completion of all licensing requirements by the applicant.

(2) Grant the license effective upon completion of all licensing requirements by the applicant, immediately revoke the license, stay the revocation, and impose probationary conditions on the license, which may include suspension.

(3) Deny the license.

(4) Take other action in relation to denying or granting the license as the board in its discretion may deem proper.

(b) This section does not in any way modify or otherwise affect the existing authority of the following entities in regard to licensure:

(1) The State Athletic Commission.

(2) The Bureau for Private Postsecondary Education.

(3) The California Horse Racing Board.

(c) This section shall become operative on July 1, 2020.

Added Stats 2018 ch 995 § 11 (AB 2138), effective January 1, 2019, operative July 1, 2020.

§ 489. Denial of application without a hearing

Any agency in the department which is authorized by law to deny an application for a license upon the grounds specified in Section 480 or 496, may without a hearing deny an application upon any of those grounds, if within one year previously, and after proceedings conducted in accordance with Chapter 5 (commencing with Section 11500) of Part 1 of Division 3 of Title 2 of the Government Code, that agency has denied an application from the same applicant upon the same ground.

Added Stats 1955 ch 1151 § 1, as B & P C § 116. Amended Stats 1978 ch 1161 § 2. Renumbered by Stats 1989 ch 1104 § 1. Amended Stats 1997 ch 758 § 2.5 (SB 1346).

Chapter 3

Suspension and Revocation of Licenses

§ 490. Grounds for suspension or revocation; Discipline for substantially related crimes; Conviction; Legislative findings

(a) In addition to any other action that a board is permitted to take against a licensee, a board may suspend or revoke a license on the ground that the licensee has been convicted of a crime, if the crime is substantially related to the qualifications, functions, or duties of the business or profession for which the license was issued.

(b) Notwithstanding any other provision of law, a board may exercise any authority to discipline a licensee for conviction of a crime that is independent of the authority granted under subdivision (a) only if the crime is substantially related to the qualifications, functions, or duties of the business or profession for which the licensee's license was issued.

(c) A conviction within the meaning of this section means a plea or verdict of guilty or a conviction following a plea of nolo contendere. An action that a board is permitted to take following the establishment of a conviction may be taken when the time for appeal has elapsed, or the judgment of conviction has been affirmed on appeal, or when an order granting probation is made suspending the imposition of sentence, irrespective of a subsequent order under Section 1203.4 of the Penal Code.

(d) The Legislature hereby finds and declares that the application of this section has been made unclear by the holding in Petropoulos v. Department of Real Estate (2006) 142 Cal.App.4th 554, and that the holding in that case has placed a significant number of statutes and regulations in question, resulting in potential harm to the consumers of California from licensees who have been convicted of crimes. Therefore, the Legislature finds and declares that this section establishes an independent basis for a board to impose discipline upon a licensee, and that the amendments to this section made by Chapter 33 of the Statutes of 2008 do not constitute a change to, but rather are declaratory of, existing law.

Added Stats 1974 ch 1321 § 13. Amended Stats 1979 ch 876 § 3; Stats 1980 ch 548 § 1; Stats 1992 ch 1289 § 7 (AB 2743); Stats 2008 ch 33 § 2 (SB 797) (ch 33 prevails), effective June 23, 2008, ch 179 § 3 (SB 1498), effective January 1, 2009; Stats 2010 ch 328 § 2 (SB 1330), effective January 1, 2011.

§ 490.5. Suspension of license for failure to comply with child support order

A board may suspend a license pursuant to Section 17520 of the Family Code if a licensee is not in compliance with a child support order or judgment.

Added Stats 1994 ch 906 § 1 (AB 923), operative January 1, 1996. Amended Stats 2010 ch 328 § 3 (SB 1330), effective January 1, 2011.

§ 491. Procedure upon suspension or revocation

Upon suspension or revocation of a license by a board on one or more of the grounds specified in Section 490, the board shall:

(a) Send a copy of the provisions of Section 11522 of the Government Code to the ex-licensee.

(b) Send a copy of the criteria relating to rehabilitation formulated under Section 482 to the ex-licensee.

Added Stats 1972 ch 903 § 1. Amended Stats 1974 ch 1321 § 14; Stats 1975 ch 678 § 1.

§ 493. Evidentiary effect of record of conviction of crime substantially related to licensee's qualifications, functions, and duties

(a) Notwithstanding any other law, in a proceeding conducted by a board within the department pursuant to law to deny an application for a license or to suspend or revoke a license or otherwise take disciplinary action against a person who holds a license, upon the ground that the applicant or the licensee has been convicted of a crime substantially related to the qualifications, functions, and duties of the licensee in question, the record of conviction of the crime shall be conclusive evidence of the fact that the conviction occurred, but only of that fact.

(b) (1) Criteria for determining whether a crime is substantially related to the qualifications, functions, or duties of the business or profession the board regulates shall include all of the following:

(A) The nature and gravity of the offense.

(B) The number of years elapsed since the date of the offense.

(C) The nature and duties of the profession.

(2) A board shall not categorically bar an applicant based solely on the type of conviction without considering evidence of rehabilitation.

(c) As used in this section, "license" includes "certificate," "permit," "authority," and "registration."

(d) This section does not in any way modify or otherwise affect the existing authority of the following entities in regard to licensure:

(1) The State Athletic Commission.

(2) The Bureau for Private Postsecondary Education.

(3) The California Horse Racing Board.

(e) This section shall become operative on July 1, 2020.

Added Stats 2018 ch 995 § 13 (AB 2138), effective January 1, 2019, operative July 1, 2020.

§ 494. Interim suspension or restriction order

(a) A board or an administrative law judge sitting alone, as provided in subdivision (h), may, upon petition, issue an interim order suspending any licentiate or imposing license restrictions, including, but not limited to, mandatory biological fluid testing, supervision, or remedial training. The petition shall include affidavits that demonstrate, to the satisfaction of the board, both of the following:

(1) The licentiate has engaged in acts or omissions constituting a violation of this code or has been convicted of a crime substantially related to the licensed activity.

(2) Permitting the licentiate to continue to engage in the licensed activity, or permitting the licentiate to continue in the licensed activity without restrictions, would endanger the public health, safety, or welfare.

(b) No interim order provided for in this section shall be issued without notice to the licentiate unless it appears from the petition and supporting documents that serious injury would result to the public before the matter could be heard on notice.

(c) Except as provided in subdivision (b), the licentiate shall be given at least 15 days' notice of the hearing on the petition for an interim order. The notice shall include documents submitted to the board in support of the petition. If the order was initially issued without notice as provided in subdivision (b), the licentiate shall be entitled to a hearing on the petition within 20 days of the issuance of the interim order without notice. The licentiate shall be given notice of the hearing within two days after issuance of the initial interim order, and shall receive all documents in support of the petition. The failure of the board to provide a hearing within 20 days following the issuance of the interim order without notice, unless the licentiate waives his or her right to the hearing, shall result in the dissolution of the interim order by operation of law.

(d) At the hearing on the petition for an interim order, the licentiate may:

(1) Be represented by counsel.

(2) Have a record made of the proceedings, copies of which shall be available to the licentiate upon payment of costs computed in accordance with the provisions for transcript costs for judicial review contained in Section 11523 of the Government Code.

(3) Present affidavits and other documentary evidence.

(4) Present oral argument.

Section V

(e) The board, or an administrative law judge sitting alone as provided in subdivision (h), shall issue a decision on the petition for interim order within five business days following submission of the matter. The standard of proof required to obtain an interim order pursuant to this section shall be a preponderance of the evidence standard. If the interim order was previously issued without notice, the board shall determine whether the order shall remain in effect, be dissolved, or modified.

(f) The board shall file an accusation within 15 days of the issuance of an interim order. In the case of an interim order issued without notice, the time shall run from the date of the order issued after the noticed hearing. If the licentiate files a Notice of Defense, the hearing shall be held within 30 days of the agency's receipt of the Notice of Defense. A decision shall be rendered on the accusation no later than 30 days after submission of the matter. Failure to comply with any of the requirements in this subdivision shall dissolve the interim order by operation of law.

(g) Interim orders shall be subject to judicial review pursuant to Section 1094.5 of the Code of Civil Procedure and shall be heard only in the superior court in and for the Counties of Sacramento, San Francisco, Los Angeles, or San Diego. The review of an interim order shall be limited to a determination of whether the board abused its discretion in the issuance of the interim order. Abuse of discretion is established if the respondent board has not proceeded in the manner required by law, or if the court determines that the interim order is not supported by substantial evidence in light of the whole record.

(h) The board may, in its sole discretion, delegate the hearing on any petition for an interim order to an administrative law judge in the Office of Administrative Hearings. If the board hears the noticed petition itself, an administrative law judge shall preside at the hearing, rule on the admission and exclusion of evidence, and advise the board on matters of law. The board shall exercise all other powers relating to the conduct of the hearing but may delegate any or all of them to the administrative law judge. When the petition has been delegated to an administrative law judge, he or she shall sit alone and exercise all of the powers of the board relating to the conduct of the hearing. A decision issued by an administrative law judge sitting alone shall be final when it is filed with the board. If the administrative law judge issues an interim order without notice, he or she shall preside at the noticed hearing, unless unavailable, in which case another administrative law judge may hear the matter. The decision of the administrative law judge sitting alone on the petition for an interim order is final, subject only to judicial review in accordance with subdivision (g).

(i) Failure to comply with an interim order issued pursuant to subdivision (a) or (b) shall constitute a separate cause for disciplinary action against any licentiate, and may be heard at, and as a part of, the noticed hearing provided for in subdivision (f). Allegations of noncompliance with the interim order may be filed at any time prior to the rendering of a decision on the accusation. Violation of the interim order is established upon proof that the licentiate was on notice of the interim order and its terms, and that the order was in effect at the time of the violation. The finding of a violation of an interim order made at the hearing on the accusation shall be reviewed as a part of any review of a final decision of the agency.

If the interim order issued by the agency provides for anything less than a complete suspension of the licentiate from his or her business or profession, and the licentiate violates the interim order prior to the hearing on the accusation provided for in subdivision (f), the agency may, upon notice to the licentiate and proof of violation, modify or expand the interim order.

(j) A plea or verdict of guilty or a conviction after a plea of nolo contendere is deemed to be a conviction within the meaning of this section. A certified record of the conviction shall be conclusive evidence of the fact that the conviction occurred. A board may take action under this section notwithstanding the fact that an appeal of the conviction may be taken.

(k) The interim orders provided for by this section shall be in addition to, and not a limitation on, the authority to seek injunctive relief provided in any other provision of law.

(l) In the case of a board, a petition for an interim order may be filed by the executive officer. In the case of a bureau or program, a petition may be filed by the chief or program administrator, as the case may be.

(m) "Board," as used in this section, shall include any agency described in Section 22, and any allied health agency within the jurisdiction of the Medical Board of California. Board shall also include the Osteopathic Medical Board of California and the State Board of Chiropractic Examiners. The provisions of this section shall not be applicable to the Medical Board of California, the Board of Podiatric Medicine, or the State Athletic Commission.

Added Stats 1993 ch 840 § 1 (SB 842). Amended Stats 1994 ch 1275 § 4 (SB 2101).

§ 494.5. Agency actions when licensee is on certified list; Definitions; Collection and distribution of certified list information; Timing; Notices; Challenges by applicants and licensees; Release forms; Interagency agreements; Fees; Remedies; Inquiries and disclosure of information; Severability

(a) (1) Except as provided in paragraphs (2), (3), and (4), a state governmental licensing entity shall refuse to issue, reactivate, reinstate, or renew a license and shall suspend a license if a licensee's name is included on a certified list.

(2) The Department of Motor Vehicles shall suspend a license if a licensee's name is included on a certified list. Any reference in this section to the issuance, reactivation, reinstatement, renewal, or denial of a license shall not apply to the Department of Motor Vehicles.

(3) The State Bar of California may recommend to refuse to issue, reactivate, reinstate, or renew a license and may recommend to suspend a license if a licensee's name is included on a certified list. The word "may" shall be substituted for the word "shall" relating to the issuance of a temporary license, refusal to issue, reactivate, reinstate, renew, or suspend a license in this section for licenses under the jurisdiction of the California Supreme Court.

(4) The Department of Alcoholic Beverage Control may refuse to issue, reactivate, reinstate, or renew a license, and may suspend a license, if a licensee's name is included on a certified list.

(b) For purposes of this section:

(1) "Certified list" means either the list provided by the State Board of Equalization or the list provided by the Franchise Tax Board of persons whose names appear on the lists of the 500 largest tax delinquencies pursuant to Section 7063 or 19195 of the Revenue and Taxation Code, as applicable.

(2) "License" includes a certificate, registration, or any other authorization to engage in a profession or occupation issued by a state governmental licensing entity. "License" includes a driver's license issued pursuant to Chapter 1 (commencing with Section 12500) of Division 6 of the Vehicle Code. "License" excludes a vehicle registration issued pursuant to Division 3 (commencing with Section 4000) of the Vehicle Code.

(3) "Licensee" means an individual authorized by a license to drive a motor vehicle or authorized by a license, certificate, registration, or other authorization to engage in a profession or occupation issued by a state governmental licensing entity.

(4) "State governmental licensing entity" means any entity listed in Section 101, 1000, or 19420, the office of the Attorney General, the Department of Insurance, the Department of Motor Vehicles, the State Bar of California, the Department of Real Estate, and any other

state agency, board, or commission that issues a license, certificate, or registration authorizing an individual to engage in a profession or occupation, including any certificate, business or occupational license, or permit or license issued by the Department of Motor Vehicles or the Department of the California Highway Patrol. "State governmental licensing entity" shall not include the Contractors State License Board.

(c) The State Board of Equalization and the Franchise Tax Board shall each submit its respective certified list to every state governmental licensing entity. The certified lists shall include the name, social security number or taxpayer identification number, and the last known address of the persons identified on the certified lists.

(d) Notwithstanding any other law, each state governmental licensing entity shall collect the social security number or the federal taxpayer identification number from all applicants for the purposes of matching the names of the certified lists provided by the State Board of Equalization and the Franchise Tax Board to applicants and licensees.

(e) (1) Each state governmental licensing entity shall determine whether an applicant or licensee is on the most recent certified list provided by the State Board of Equalization and the Franchise Tax Board.

(2) If an applicant or licensee is on either of the certified lists, the state governmental licensing entity shall immediately provide a preliminary notice to the applicant or licensee of the entity's intent to suspend or withhold issuance or renewal of the license. The preliminary notice shall be delivered personally or by mail to the applicant's or licensee's last known mailing address on file with the state governmental licensing entity within 30 days of receipt of the certified list. Service by mail shall be completed in accordance with Section 1013 of the Code of Civil Procedure.

(A) The state governmental licensing entity shall issue a temporary license valid for a period of 90 days to any applicant whose name is on a certified list if the applicant is otherwise eligible for a license.

(B) The 90-day time period for a temporary license shall not be extended. Only one temporary license shall be issued during a regular license term and the term of the temporary license shall coincide with the first 90 days of the regular license term. A license for the full term or the remainder of the license term may be issued or renewed only upon compliance with this section.

(C) In the event that a license is suspended or an application for a license or the renewal of a license is denied pursuant to this section, any funds paid by the applicant or licensee shall not be refunded by the state governmental licensing entity.

(f) (1) A state governmental licensing entity shall refuse to issue or shall suspend a license pursuant to this section no sooner than 90 days and no later than 120 days of the mailing of the preliminary notice described in paragraph (2) of subdivision (e), unless the state governmental licensing entity has received a release pursuant to subdivision (h). The procedures in the administrative adjudication provisions of the Administrative Procedure Act (Chapter 4.5 (commencing with Section 11400) and Chapter 5 (commencing with Section 11500) of Part 1 of Division 3 of Title 2 of the Government Code) shall not apply to the denial or suspension of, or refusal to renew, a license or the issuance of a temporary license pursuant to this section.

(2) Notwithstanding any other law, if a board, bureau, or commission listed in Section 101, other than the Contractors State License Board, fails to take action in accordance with this section, the Department of Consumer Affairs shall issue a temporary license or suspend or refuse to issue, reactivate, reinstate, or renew a license, as appropriate.

(g) Notices shall be developed by each state governmental licensing entity. For an applicant or licensee on the State Board of Equalization's certified list, the notice shall include the address and telephone number of the State Board of Equalization, and shall emphasize the necessity of obtaining a release from the State Board of Equalization as a condition for the issuance, renewal, or continued valid status of a license or licenses. For an applicant or licensee on the Franchise Tax Board's certified list, the notice shall include the address and telephone number of the Franchise Tax Board, and shall emphasize the necessity of obtaining a release from the Franchise Tax Board as a condition for the issuance, renewal, or continued valid status of a license or licenses.

(1) The notice shall inform the applicant that the state governmental licensing entity shall issue a temporary license, as provided in subparagraph (A) of paragraph (2) of subdivision (e), for 90 calendar days if the applicant is otherwise eligible and that upon expiration of that time period, the license will be denied unless the state governmental licensing entity has received a release from the State Board of Equalization or the Franchise Tax Board, whichever is applicable.

(2) The notice shall inform the licensee that any license suspended under this section will remain suspended until the state governmental licensing entity receives a release along with applications and fees, if applicable, to reinstate the license.

(3) The notice shall also inform the applicant or licensee that if an application is denied or a license is suspended pursuant to this section, any moneys paid by the applicant or licensee shall not be refunded by the state governmental licensing entity. The state governmental licensing entity shall also develop a form that the applicant or licensee shall use to request a release by the State Board of Equalization or the Franchise Tax Board. A copy of this form shall be included with every notice sent pursuant to this subdivision.

(h) If the applicant or licensee wishes to challenge the submission of their name on a certified list, the applicant or licensee shall make a timely written request for release to the State Board of Equalization or the Franchise Tax Board, whichever is applicable. The State Board of Equalization or the Franchise Tax Board shall immediately send a release to the appropriate state governmental licensing entity and the applicant or licensee, if any of the following conditions are met:

(1) The applicant or licensee has complied with the tax obligation, either by payment of the unpaid taxes or entry into an installment payment agreement, as described in Section 6832 or 19008 of the Revenue and Taxation Code, to satisfy the unpaid taxes.

(2) The applicant or licensee has submitted a request for release not later than 45 days after the applicant's or licensee's receipt of a preliminary notice described in paragraph (2) of subdivision (e), but the State Board of Equalization or the Franchise Tax Board, whichever is applicable, will be unable to complete the release review and send notice of its findings to the applicant or licensee and state governmental licensing entity within 45 days after the State Board of Equalization's or the Franchise Tax Board's receipt of the applicant's or licensee's request for release. Whenever a release is granted under this paragraph, and, notwithstanding that release, the applicable license or licenses have been suspended erroneously, the state governmental licensing entity shall reinstate the applicable licenses with retroactive effect back to the date of the erroneous suspension and that suspension shall not be reflected on any license record.

(3) The applicant or licensee is unable to pay the outstanding tax obligation due to a current financial hardship. "Financial hardship" means financial hardship as determined by the State Board of Equalization or the Franchise Tax Board, whichever is applicable, where the applicant or licensee is unable to pay any part of the outstanding liability and the applicant or licensee is unable to qualify for an installment payment arrangement as provided for by Section 6832 or Section 19008 of the Revenue and Taxation Code. In order to establish the existence of a financial hardship, the applicant or licensee shall submit any information, including information related to reasonable business and personal expenses, requested by the State Board of Equalization or the Franchise Tax Board, whichever is applicable, for purposes of making that determination.

(i) An applicant or licensee is required to act with diligence in responding to notices from the state governmental licensing entity and the State Board of Equalization or the Franchise Tax Board with the recognition that the temporary license will lapse or the license suspension will go into effect after 90 days and that the State Board of Equalization or the Franchise Tax Board must have time to act within that period. An applicant's or licensee's delay in acting, without good cause, which directly results in the inability of the State Board

Section V

of Equalization or the Franchise Tax Board, whichever is applicable, to complete a review of the applicant's or licensee's request for release shall not constitute the diligence required under this section which would justify the issuance of a release. An applicant or licensee shall have the burden of establishing that they diligently responded to notices from the state governmental licensing entity or the State Board of Equalization or the Franchise Tax Board and that any delay was not without good cause.

(j) The State Board of Equalization or the Franchise Tax Board shall create release forms for use pursuant to this section. When the applicant or licensee has complied with the tax obligation by payment of the unpaid taxes, or entry into an installment payment agreement, or establishing the existence of a current financial hardship as defined in paragraph (3) of subdivision (h), the State Board of Equalization or the Franchise Tax Board, whichever is applicable, shall mail a release form to the applicant or licensee and provide a release to the appropriate state governmental licensing entity. Any state governmental licensing entity that has received a release from the State Board of Equalization and the Franchise Tax Board pursuant to this subdivision shall process the release within five business days of its receipt. If the State Board of Equalization or the Franchise Tax Board determines subsequent to the issuance of a release that the licensee has not complied with their installment payment agreement, the State Board of Equalization or the Franchise Tax Board, whichever is applicable, shall notify the state governmental licensing entity and the licensee in a format prescribed by the State Board of Equalization or the Franchise Tax Board, whichever is applicable, that the licensee is not in compliance and the release shall be rescinded. The State Board of Equalization and the Franchise Tax Board may, when it is economically feasible for the state governmental licensing entity to develop an automated process for complying with this subdivision, notify the state governmental licensing entity in a manner prescribed by the State Board of Equalization or the Franchise Tax Board, whichever is applicable, that the licensee has not complied with the installment payment agreement. Upon receipt of this notice, the state governmental licensing entity shall immediately notify the licensee on a form prescribed by the state governmental licensing entity that the licensee's license will be suspended on a specific date, and this date shall be no longer than 30 days from the date the form is mailed. The licensee shall be further notified that the license will remain suspended until a new release is issued in accordance with this subdivision.

(k) The State Board of Equalization and the Franchise Tax Board may enter into interagency agreements with the state governmental licensing entities necessary to implement this section.

(l) Notwithstanding any other law, a state governmental licensing entity, with the approval of the appropriate department director or governing body, may impose a fee on a licensee whose license has been suspended pursuant to this section. The fee shall not exceed the amount necessary for the state governmental licensing entity to cover its costs in carrying out the provisions of this section. Fees imposed pursuant to this section shall be deposited in the fund in which other fees imposed by the state governmental licensing entity are deposited and shall be available to that entity upon appropriation in the annual Budget Act.

(m) The process described in subdivision (h) shall constitute the sole administrative remedy for contesting the issuance of a temporary license or the denial or suspension of a license under this section.

(n) Any state governmental licensing entity receiving an inquiry as to the licensed status of an applicant or licensee who has had a license denied or suspended under this section or who has been granted a temporary license under this section shall respond that the license was denied or suspended or the temporary license was issued only because the licensee appeared on a list of the 500 largest tax delinquencies pursuant to Section 7063 or 19195 of the Revenue and Taxation Code. Information collected pursuant to this section by any state agency, board, or department shall be subject to the Information Practices Act of 1977 (Chapter 1 (commencing with Section 1798) of Title 1.8 of Part 4 of Division 3 of the Civil Code). Any state governmental licensing entity that discloses on its internet website or other publication that the licensee has had a license denied or suspended under this section or has been granted a temporary license under this section shall prominently disclose, in bold and adjacent to the information regarding the status of the license, that the only reason the license was denied, suspended, or temporarily issued is because the licensee failed to pay taxes.

(o) Any rules and regulations issued pursuant to this section by any state agency, board, or department may be adopted as emergency regulations in accordance with the rulemaking provisions of the Administrative Procedure Act (Chapter 3.5 (commencing with Section 11340) of Part 1 of Division 3 of Title 2 of the Government Code). The adoption of these regulations shall be deemed an emergency and necessary for the immediate preservation of the public peace, health, and safety, or general welfare. The regulations shall become effective immediately upon filing with the Secretary of State.

(p) The State Board of Equalization, the Franchise Tax Board, and state governmental licensing entities, as appropriate, shall adopt regulations as necessary to implement this section.

(q) (1) Neither the state governmental licensing entity, nor any officer, employee, or agent, or former officer, employee, or agent of a state governmental licensing entity, may disclose or use any information obtained from the State Board of Equalization or the Franchise Tax Board, pursuant to this section, except to inform the public of the denial, refusal to renew, or suspension of a license or the issuance of a temporary license pursuant to this section. The release or other use of information received by a state governmental licensing entity pursuant to this section, except as authorized by this section, is punishable as a misdemeanor. This subdivision may not be interpreted to prevent the State Bar of California from filing a request with the Supreme Court of California to suspend a member of the bar pursuant to this section.

(2) A suspension of, or refusal to renew, a license or issuance of a temporary license pursuant to this section does not constitute denial or discipline of a licensee for purposes of any reporting requirements to the National Practitioner Data Bank and shall not be reported to the National Practitioner Data Bank or the Healthcare Integrity and Protection Data Bank.

(3) Upon release from the certified list, the suspension or revocation of the applicant's or licensee's license shall be purged from the state governmental licensing entity's internet website or other publication within three business days. This paragraph shall not apply to the State Bar of California.

(r) If any provision of this section or the application thereof to any person or circumstance is held invalid, that invalidity shall not affect other provisions or applications of this section that can be given effect without the invalid provision or application, and to this end the provisions of this section are severable.

(s) All rights to review afforded by this section to an applicant shall also be afforded to a licensee.

(t) Unless otherwise provided in this section, the policies, practices, and procedures of a state governmental licensing entity with respect to license suspensions under this section shall be the same as those applicable with respect to suspensions pursuant to Section 17520 of the Family Code.

(u) No provision of this section shall be interpreted to allow a court to review and prevent the collection of taxes prior to the payment of those taxes in violation of the California Constitution.

(v) This section shall apply to any licensee whose name appears on a list of the 500 largest tax delinquencies pursuant to Section 7063 or 19195 of the Revenue and Taxation Code on or after July 1, 2012.

Added Stats 2011 ch 455 § 3 (AB 1424), effective January 1, 2012. Amended Stats 2012 ch 327 § 1 (SB 937), effective January 1, 2013; Stats 2020 ch 312 § 9 (SB 1474), effective January 1, 2021.

§ 494.6. Suspension under Labor Code Section 244

(a) A business license regulated by this code may be subject to suspension or revocation if the licensee has been determined by the Labor Commissioner or the court to have violated subdivision (b) of Section 244 of the Labor Code and the court or Labor Commissioner has taken into consideration any harm such suspension or revocation would cause to employees of the licensee, as well as the good faith efforts of the licensee to resolve any alleged violations after receiving notice.

(b) Notwithstanding subdivision (a), a licensee of an agency within the Department of Consumer Affairs who has been found by the Labor Commissioner or the court to have violated subdivision (b) of Section 244 of the Labor Code may be subject to disciplinary action by his or her respective licensing agency.

(c) An employer shall not be subject to suspension or revocation under this section for requiring a prospective or current employee to submit, within three business days of the first day of work for pay, an I-9 Employment Eligibility Verification form.

Added Stats 2013 ch 577 § 1 (SB 666), effective January 1, 2014.

Chapter 4

Public Reprovals

§ 495. Public reproval of licentiate or certificate holder for act constituting grounds for suspension or revocation of license or certificate; Proceedings

Notwithstanding any other provision of law, any entity authorized to issue a license or certificate pursuant to this code may publicly reprove a licentiate or certificate holder thereof, for any act that would constitute grounds to suspend or revoke a license or certificate. Any proceedings for public reproval, public reproval and suspension, or public reproval and revocation shall be conducted in accordance with Chapter 5 (commencing with Section 11500) of Part 1 of Division 3 of Title 2 of the Government Code, or, in the case of a licensee or certificate holder under the jurisdiction of the State Department of Health Services, in accordance with Section 100171 of the Health and Safety Code.

Added Stats 1977 ch 886 § 1. Amended Stats 1997 ch 220 § 2 (SB 68), effective August 4, 1997.

Chapter 5

Examination Security

§ 496. Grounds for denial, suspension, or revocation of license

A board may deny, suspend, revoke, or otherwise restrict a license on the ground that an applicant or licensee has violated Section 123 pertaining to subversion of licensing examinations.

Added Stats 1989 ch 1022 § 3.

§ 498. Fraud, deceit or misrepresentation as grounds for action against license

A board may revoke, suspend, or otherwise restrict a license on the ground that the licensee secured the license by fraud, deceit, or knowing misrepresentation of a material fact or by knowingly omitting to state a material fact.

Added Stats 1992 ch 1289 § 8 (AB 2743).

§ 499. Action against license based on licentiate's actions regarding application of another

A board may revoke, suspend, or otherwise restrict a license on the ground that the licensee, in support of another person's application for license, knowingly made a false statement of a material fact or knowingly omitted to state a material fact to the board regarding the application.

Added Stats 1992 ch 1289 § 9 (AB 2743).

SECTION VI.

THE CONTRACTORS STATE LICENSE BOARD; LICENSE LAW, RULES AND REGULATIONS, AND RELATED LAWS

Chapter 12.

Contractors' State License Law

BUSINESS & PROFESSIONS CODE

DIVISION 3

PROFESSIONS AND VOCATIONS GENERALLY

Chapter 9

Contractors

Article 1

Administration

269

Article 2

Application of Chapter

Section VI

Section VI

Article 6

Records

Article 6.2

Arbitration

Article 6.5

Solar Energy System Restitution Program
[Repealed effective June 30, 2024]

Article 7

Disciplinary Proceedings

Article 7.5

Workers' Compensation Insurance Reports

Article 8

Revenue

Article 8.5

The Construction Management Education Sponsorship Act of 1991

Article 9

Renewal of Licenses

Article 10

Home Improvement Business

Article 11

Asbestos Consultants

Section VI

Chapter 9

Contractors

Article 1

Administration

§ 7000. Citation of chapter

This chapter constitutes, and may be cited as, the Contractors State
License Law.

Added Stats 1961 ch 1822 § 2. Amended Stats 1984 ch 193 § 1; Stats 2020 ch 312 § 46
(SB 1474), effective January 1, 2021.

§ 7000.2. Requiring contractors to show proof of compliance with local business tax requirements prior to permit issuance; Limit on business taxes

Nothing in this code shall be interpreted to prohibit cities, counties, and cities and counties from requiring contractors to show proof that they are in compliance with local business tax requirements of the entity prior to issuing any city, county, or city and county permit. Nothing in this code shall be interpreted to prohibit cities, counties, and cities and counties from denying the issuance of a permit to a licensed contractor who is not in compliance with local business tax requirements.

Any business tax required or collected as part of this process shall not exceed the amount of the license tax or license fee authorized by Section 37101 of the Government Code or Section 16000 of the Business and Professions Code.

Added Stats 1992 ch 325 § 1 (AB 2710).

§ 7000.5. Contractors' State License Board; Members; Effect of repeal [Repealed effective January 1, 2025]

(a) There is in the Department of Consumer Affairs a Contractors State License Board, which consists of 15 members.

(b) Notwithstanding any other provision of law, the repeal of this section renders the board subject to review by the appropriate policy committees of the Legislature.

(c) This section shall remain in effect only until January 1, 2025, and as of that date is repealed.

Added Stats 1939 ch 37 § 1, as B & P C § 7000. Amended Stats 1961 ch 1821 § 61; Amended and renumbered by Stats 1961 ch 1822 § 3; Amended Stats 1963 ch 1098 § 1; Stats 1971 ch 716 § 98; Stats 1972 ch 1314 § 1; Stats 1975 ch 1153 § 1; Stats 1982 ch 676 § 40; Stats 1994 ch 908 § 48 (SB 2036); Stats 1997 ch 812 § 1 (SB 857), ch 813 § 1 (SB 825); Stats 1999 ch 656 § 5 (SB 1306); Stats 2000 ch 1005 § 1 (SB 2029); Stats 2002 ch 744 § 2 (SB 1953); Stats 2004 ch 33 § 24 (AB 1467), effective April 13, 2004; Stats 2005 ch 675 § 10 (SB 232), effective January 1, 2006; Stats 2006 ch 658 § 105 (SB 1476), effective January 1, 2007; Stats 2008 ch 385 § 7 (SB 963), effective January 1, 2009; Stats 2010 ch 695 § 37 (SB 294), effective January 1, 2011, repealed January 1, 2012; Stats 2011 ch 448 § 21 (SB 543), effective January 1, 2012, repealed January 1, 2016; Stats 2015 ch 656 § 6 (SB 467), effective January 1, 2016, repealed January 1, 2020. Amended Stats 2019 ch 378 § 1 (SB 610), effective January 1, 2020, repealed January 1, 2024; Stats 2020 ch 312 § 47 (SB 1474), effective January 1, 2021, repealed January 1, 2024; Stats 2022 ch 625 § 15 (SB 1443), effective January 1, 2023, repealed January 1, 2025.

§ 7000.6. Priority of board; Protection of the public

Protection of the public shall be the highest priority for the Contractors State License Board in exercising its licensing, regulatory, and disciplinary functions. Whenever the protection of the public is inconsistent with other interests sought to be promoted, the protection of the public shall be paramount.

Added Stats 2002 ch 744 § 3 (SB 1953). Amended Stats 2020 ch 312 § 48 (SB 1474), effective January 1, 2021.

§ 7001. Members of board; Qualifications; Public member

All members of the board, except the public members, shall be contractors actively engaged in the contracting business, have been so engaged for a period of not less than five years preceding the date of their appointment and shall so continue in the contracting business during the term of their office. No one, except a public member, shall be eligible for appointment who does not at the time hold an unexpired license to operate as a contractor.

The public members shall not be licentiates of the board.

Added Stats 1939 ch 37 § 1. Amended Stats 1961 ch 1821 § 62; Stats 1971 ch 716 § 99; Stats 2000 ch 1005 § 2 (SB 2029).

§ 7002. Board members; Kinds of contractors and qualifications; Definitions

(a) One member of the board shall be a general engineering contractor, two members shall be general building contractors, two members shall be specialty contractors, one member shall be a member of a labor organization representing the building trades, one member shall be an active local building official, and eight members shall be public members, one of whom shall be from a statewide senior citizen organization.

(b) No public member shall be a current or former licensee of the board or a close family member of a licensee or be currently or formerly connected with the construction industry or have any financial interest in the business of a licensee of the board. Each public member shall meet all of the requirements for public membership on a board as set forth in Chapter 6 (commencing with Section 450) of Division 1. Notwithstanding the provisions of this subdivision and those of Section 450, a representative of a labor organization shall be eligible for appointment to serve as a public member of the board.

(c) Each contractor member of the board shall be of recognized standing in his or her branch of the contracting business and hold an unexpired license to operate as a contractor. In addition, each contractor member shall, as of the date of his or her appointment, be actively engaged in the contracting business and have been so engaged for a period of not less than five years. Each contractor member shall remain actively engaged in the contracting business during the entire term of his or her membership on the board.

(d) Each member of the board shall be at least 30 years of age and of good character. In addition, each member shall have been a citizen and resident of the State of California for at least five years next preceding his or her appointment.

(e) For the purposes of construing this article, the terms "general engineering contractor," "general building contractor," and "specialty contractor" shall have the meanings given in Article 4 (commencing with Section 7055) of this chapter.

Added Stats 1939 ch 37 § 1. Amended 1941 ch 971 § 1; Stats 1961 ch 1821 § 63; Stats 1963 ch 1098 § 2; Stats 1971 ch 716 § 100; Stats 1972 ch 1314 § 2; Stats 1973 ch 319 § 32; Stats 1975 ch 1153 § 2; Stats 1976 ch 1188 § 39; Stats 1991 ch 1160 § 1 (AB 2190); Stats 1994 ch 279 § 1 (AB 203); Stats 2000 ch 1005 § 3 (SB 2029).

§ 7003. Terms, vacancies, and appointment of successors

Except as otherwise provided, an appointment to fill a vacancy caused by the expiration of the term of office shall be for a term of four years and shall be filled, except for a vacancy in the term of a public member, by a member from the same branch of the contracting business as was the branch of the member whose term has expired. A vacancy in the term of a public member shall be filled by another public member. Each member shall hold office until the appointment and qualification of his or her successor or until the office is deemed to be vacant pursuant to Section 1774 of the Government Code, whichever first occurs.

Vacancies occurring in the membership of the board for any cause shall be filled by appointment for the balance of the unexpired term.

No person shall serve as a member of the board for more than two consecutive terms.

The Governor shall appoint four of the public members, including the public member who is from a statewide senior citizen organization, the local building official, the member of a labor organization representing the building trades, and the five contractor members qualified as provided in Section 7002. The Senate Rules Committee and the Speaker of the Assembly shall each appoint two public members.

Added Stats 1939 ch 37 § 1. Amended Stats 1955 ch 1532 § 1; Stats 1961 ch 1821 § 64; Stats 1963 ch 1098 § 3; Stats 1971 ch 716 § 101; Stats 1972 ch 1314 § 3; Stats 1973 ch 319 § 33; Stats 1975 ch 1153 § 3; Stats 1976 ch 1188 § 40; Stats 1982 ch 676 § 41; Stats 1991 ch 1160 § 2 (AB 2190); Stats 1994 ch 279 § 2 (AB 203); Stats 1999 ch 983 § 5 (SB 1307); Stats 2000 ch 1005 § 4 (SB 2029).

—See Government Code 1774, Vacancies; Appointments and Reappointments by the Governor and Senate, in Appendix.

§ 7005. Removal of members; Grounds

The Governor may remove any member of the board for misconduct, incompetency or neglect of duty.

Added Stats 1939 ch 37 § 1.

§ 7006. Meetings of board; Regular and special

The board shall meet at least once each calendar quarter for the purpose of transacting business as may properly come before it. The board shall make every effort to make all regularly scheduled quarterly meetings of the board available as a webcast when the appropriate resources are available.

Special meetings of the board may be held at times as the board may provide in its bylaws. Four members of the board may call a special meeting at any time.

Added Stats 1939 ch 37 § 1. Amended Stats 2001 ch 728 § 52 (SB 724); Stats 2019 ch 378 § 2 (SB 610), effective January 1, 2020.

§ 7007. Quorum; Notice of meetings

Eight members constitute a quorum at a board meeting.

Due notice of each meeting and the time and place thereof shall be given each member in the manner provided by the bylaws.

Added Stats 1939 ch 37 § 1. Amended Stats 1961 ch 1821 § 65; Stats 1972 ch 1314 § 4; Stats 1975 ch 1153 § 4; Stats 2000 ch 1005 § 5 (SB 2029).

§ 7008. Appointment of committees; Making of rules and regulations

The board may appoint such committees and make such rules and regulations as are reasonably necessary to carry out the provisions of this chapter. Such rules and regulations shall be adopted in accordance with the provisions of the Administrative Procedure Act.

Added Stats 1939 ch 37 § 1. Amended Stats 1957 ch 2084 § 20; Stats 1983 ch 891 § 1.

§ 7009. Administration of oaths and taking of proofs

Any member or committee of the board may administer oaths and may take testimony and proofs concerning all matters within the jurisdiction of the board.

Added Stats 1939 ch 37 § 1.

Section VI

§ 7010. Functions and duties of board

The board is vested with all functions and duties relating to the administration of this chapter, except those functions and duties vested in the director under the provisions of Division I of this code.

Added Stats 1939 ch 37 § 1.

§ 7011. Registrar of contractors [Repealed effective January 1, 2025]

(a) The board, by and with the approval of the director, shall appoint a registrar of contractors and fix the registrar's compensation.

(b) The registrar shall be the executive officer and secretary of the board and shall carry out all of the administrative duties as provided in this chapter and as delegated to the registrar by the board.

(c) For the purpose of administration of this chapter, there may be appointed a deputy registrar, a chief reviewing and hearing officer, and, subject to Section 159.5, other assistants and subordinates as may be necessary.

(d) Appointments shall be made in accordance with the provisions of civil service laws.

(e) This section shall remain in effect only until January 1, 2025, and as of that date is repealed.

Added Stats 1939 ch 37 § 1. Amended Stats 1947 ch 1406 § 1; Stats 1951 ch 1613 § 16; Stats 1963 ch 1587 § 1; Stats 1971 ch 716 § 102; Stats 1994 ch 908 § 49 (SB 2036); Stats 1997 ch 812 § 2 (SB 857), ch 813 § 2 (SB 825); Stats 1999 ch 656 § 6 (SB 1306); Stats 2001 ch 615 § 9 (SB 26), effective October 9, 2001; Stats 2002 ch 744 § 4 (SB 1953); Stats 2005 ch 675 § 11 (SB 232), effective January 1, 2006; Stats 2006 ch 658 § 106 (SB 1476), effective January 1, 2007; Stats 2008 ch 385 § 8 (SB 963), effective January 1, 2009; Stats 2010 ch 695 § 38 (SB 294), effective January 1, 2011, repealed January 1, 2012; Stats 2011 ch 448 § 22 (SB 543), effective January 1, 2012, repealed January 1, 2016; Stats 2015 ch 656 § 7 (SB 467), effective January 1, 2016, repealed January 1, 2020; Stats 2019 ch 378 § 3 (SB 610), effective January 1, 2020, repealed January 1, 2024; Stats 2022 ch 625 § 16 (SB 1443), effective January 1, 2023, repealed January 1, 2025.

§ 7011.3. Prohibition against double penalty for same offense

The registrar shall not assess a civil penalty against a licensed contractor who has been assessed a specified civil penalty by the Labor Commissioner under Section 1020 or 1022 of the Labor Code for the same offense.

Added Stats 1982 ch 327 § 5, effective June 30, 1982.

§ 7011.4. Enforcement division for licensing provisions and workers' compensation insurance; Special investigators

(a) Notwithstanding Section 7011, there is in the Contractors State License Board, a separate enforcement division that shall rigorously enforce this chapter prohibiting all forms of unlicensed activity and shall enforce the obligation to secure the payment of valid and current workers' compensation insurance in accordance with Section 3700.5 of the Labor Code.

(b) Persons employed as special investigators of the Contractors State License Board and designated by the Director of Consumer Affairs shall have the authority to issue a written notice to appear in court pursuant to Chapter 5C (commencing with Section 853.5) of Title 3 of Part 2 of the Penal Code. An employee so designated is not a peace officer and does not have the power of arrest.

(c) When participating in the activities of the Joint Enforcement Strike Force on the Underground Economy pursuant to Section 329 of the Unemployment Insurance Code, the enforcement division shall have free access to all places of labor.

Added Stats 1989 ch 1363 § 1. Amended Stats 1994 ch 413 § 1 (SB 1694); Stats 2004 ch 865 § 4 (SB 1914); Stats 2012 ch 85 § 1 (AB 2554), effective January 1, 2013; Stats 2014 ch 392 § 1 (SB 315), effective January 1, 2015; Stats 2015 ch 389 § 2 (SB 560), effective January 1, 2016; Stats 2020 ch 312 § 49 (SB 1474), effective January 1, 2021; Stats 2021 ch 188 § 6 (SB 826), effective January 1, 2022.

—See Government Code Section 11181, Powers in Connection with Investigations and Actions, in Appendix.

§ 7011.5. Investigators as peace officers

Persons employed as investigators of the Special Investigations Unit of the Contractors State License Board and designated by the Director of Consumer Affairs have the authority of peace officers while engaged in exercising the powers granted or performing the duties imposed upon them in investigating the laws administered by the Contractors State License Board or commencing directly or indirectly any criminal prosecution arising from any investigation conducted under these laws. All persons herein referred to shall be deemed to be acting within the scope of employment with respect to all acts and matters in this section set forth.

Added Stats 1982 ch 1277 § 1. Amended Stats 2020 ch 312 § 50 (SB 1474), effective January 1, 2021.

§ 7011.7. Reviewing and investigating complaints

(a) The registrar shall review and investigate complaints filed in a manner consistent with this chapter and the Budget Act. It is the in-

Section VI

tent of the Legislature that complaints be reviewed and investigated as promptly as resources allow.

(b) The board shall set as a goal the improvement of its disciplinary system so that an average of no more than six months elapses from the receipt of a complaint to the completion of an investigation.

(c) Notwithstanding subdivision (a), the goal for completing the review and investigation of complaints that, in the opinion of the board, involve complex fraud issues or complex contractual arrangements, should be no more than one year.

Added Stats 1983 ch 1301 § 1, operative January 1, 1984. Amended Stats 1989 ch 1132 § 1, effective September 29, 1989; Stats 2000 ch 1005 § 6 (SB 2029).

§ 7011.8. False complaints against contractors; Penalties

(a) Any person subject to licensure under this chapter who reports to, or causes a complaint to be filed with, the Contractors State License Board that a person licensed by that entity has engaged in professional misconduct, knowing the report or complaint to be false, may be issued a citation by the registrar.

(b) The board may notify the appropriate district attorney or city attorney that a person subject to licensure under this chapter has made or filed what the entity believes to be a false report or complaint against a licensee.

Added Stats 1992 ch 437 § 1 (AB 2966). Amended Stats 2001 ch 745 § 5 (SB 1191), effective October 12, 2001; Stats 2012 ch 661 § 10 (SB 1576), effective January 1, 2013; Stats 2020 ch 312 § 51 (SB 1474), effective January 1, 2021.

§ 7012. Cooperation in enforcement of legislation relating to construction industry; Assistants

The registrar, with the approval of the board and the director, may, when funds are available, cooperate in the enforcement of governmental legislation relating to the construction industry, and, except as provided by Section 159.5, shall appoint such assistants as may be necessary therefor.

Added Stats 1939 ch 37 § 1. Amended Stats 1971 ch 716 § 103.

§ 7013. Review of registrar's acts or decisions by board; Application of section

The board may in its discretion review and sustain or reverse by a majority vote any action or decision of the registrar.

This section shall apply to any action, decision, order, or proceeding of the registrar conducted in accordance with the provisions of Chapter 5 (commencing with Section 11500) of Part 1 of Division 3 of Title 2 of the Government Code.

Added Stats 1939 ch 37 § 1. Amended Stats 1961 ch 941 § 1; Stats 1979 ch 410 § 1.

§ 7013.5. Transcript of witness as evidence

In all application, citation, or disciplinary proceedings pursuant to this chapter and conducted in accordance with the provisions of Chapter 5 (commencing with Section 11500) of Part 1 of Division 3 of Title 2 of the Government Code, the testimony of a witness given in any contested civil or criminal action or special proceeding, in any state or before any governmental body or agency, to which the licensee or person complained against is a party, or in whose behalf the action or proceeding is prosecuted or defended, may be received in evidence, so far as relevant and material to the issues in the proceedings, by means of a duly authenticated transcript of that testimony and without proof of the unavailability of the witness; provided that the registrar may order the production of and testimony by that witness, in lieu of or in addition to receiving a transcript of his or her testimony and may decline to receive in evidence the transcript of testimony, in whole or in part, when it appears that the testimony was given under circumstances that did not require or allow an opportunity for full cross-examination.

Added Stats 2003 ch 607 § 30 (SB 1077).

§ 7014. Equipment and records; Procurement

The board may procure equipment and records necessary to carry out the provisions of this chapter.

Added Stats 1939 ch 37 § 1.

§ 7015. Seal of board

The board shall adopt a seal for its own use. The seal shall have the words "Contractors State License Board, State of California, Department of Consumer Affairs," and the care and custody thereof shall be in the hands of the registrar.

Added Stats 1939 ch 37 § 1. Amended Stats 1972 ch 1138 § 1; Stats 2020 ch 312 § 52 (SB 1474), effective January 1, 2021.

§ 7016. Per diem and expenses of members of board

Each member of the board shall receive a per diem and expenses as provided in Section 103.

Added Stats 1959 ch 1645 § 27.

Section VI

§ 7017.3. Report on complaints and case aging statistics

The Contractors State License Board shall report annually to the Legislature, not later than October 1 of each year, the following statistical information for the prior fiscal year. The following data shall be reported on complaints filed with the board against licensed contractors, registered home improvement salespersons, and unlicensed persons acting as licensees or registrants:

(a) The number of complaints received by the board categorized by source, such as public, trade, profession, government agency, or board-initiated, and by type of complaint, such as licensee or nonlicensee.

(b) The number of complaints closed prior to referral for field investigation, categorized by the reason for the closure, such as settled, referred for mandatory arbitration, or referred for voluntary arbitration.

(c) The number of complaints referred for field investigation categorized by the type of complaint, such as licensee or nonlicensee.

(d) The number of complaints closed after referral for field investigation categorized by the reason for the closure, such as settled, referred for mandatory arbitration, or referred for voluntary arbitration.

(e) For the board's Intake/Mediation Center and the board's Investigation Center closures, respectively, the total number of complaints closed prior to a field investigation per consumer services representative, and the total number of complaints closed after referral for a field investigation per investigator and special investigator. Additionally, the board shall report the total number of complaints closed by other board staff during the year.

(f) The number of complaints pending at the end of the fiscal year grouped in 90-day increments, and the percentage of total complaints pending, represented by the number of complaints in each grouping.

(g) The number of citations issued to licensees categorized by the type of citation such as order of correction only or order of correction and fine, and the number of citations issued to licensees that were vacated or withdrawn.

(h) The number of citations issued to nonlicensees and the number of these citations that were vacated or withdrawn.

(i) The number of complaints referred to a local prosecutor for criminal investigation or prosecution, the number of complaints referred to the Attorney General for the filing of an accusation, and the number of complaints referred to both a local prosecutor and the Attorney General, categorized by type of complaint, such as licensee and nonlicensee.

(j) Actions taken by the board, including, but not limited to, the following:

(1) The number of disciplinary actions categorized by type, such as revocations or suspensions, categorized by whether the disciplinary action resulted from an accusation, failure to comply with a citation, or failure to comply with an arbitration award.

(2) The number of accusations dismissed or withdrawn.

(k) For subdivisions (g) and (j), the number of cases containing violations of Sections 7121 and 7121.5, and paragraph (5) of subdivision (a) of Section 7159.5, categorized by section.

(*l*) The number of interim suspension orders sought, the number of interim suspension orders granted, the number of temporary restraining orders sought, and the number of temporary restraining orders granted.

(m) The amount of cost recovery ordered and the amount collected.

(n) Case aging data, including data for each major stage of the enforcement process, including the following:

(1) The average number of days from the filing of a complaint to its closure by the board's Intake/Mediation Center prior to the referral for an investigation categorized by the type of complaint, such as licensee or nonlicensee.

(2) The average number of days from the referral of a complaint for an investigation to its closure by the Investigation Center categorized by the type of complaint, such as licensee or nonlicensee.

(3) The average number of days from the filing of a complaint to the referral of the completed investigation to the Attorney General.

(4) The average number of days from the referral of a completed investigation to the Attorney General to the filing of an accusation by the Attorney General.

(5) The average number of days from the filing of an accusation to the first hearing date or date of a stipulated settlement.

(6) The average number of days from the receipt of the administrative law judge's proposed decision to the registrar's final decision.

Added Stats 2002 ch 744 § 5 (SB 1953). Amended Stats 2006 ch 106 § 1 (AB 2457), effective January 1, 2007; Stats 2007 ch 130 § 28 (AB 299), effective January 1, 2008; Stats 2020 ch 312 § 53 (SB 1474), effective January 1, 2021; Stats 2021 ch 188 § 7 (SB 826), effective January 1, 2022.

—*See Civil Code Section 3097, Preliminary 20-Day Notice (Private Work), in Appendix.*

§ 7018. Contractor license search by ZIP Code or geographic location

The board shall maintain the current contractor license check search function on their internet website that permits consumers to search for a licensed contractor by either ZIP Code or geographic location.

Added Stats 2016 ch 270 § 1 (AB 2486), effective January 1, 2017. Amended Stats 2019 ch 378 § 4 (SB 610), effective January 1, 2020.

§ 7019. Contract with licensed professionals for site investigation of consumer complaints

(a) If funding is made available for that purpose, the board may contract with licensed professionals, as appropriate, for the site investigation of consumer complaints.

(b) The board may contract with other professionals, including, but not limited to, interpreters and manufacturer's representatives, whose skills or expertise are required to aid in the investigation or prosecution of a licensee, registrant, applicant for a license or registration, or those subject to licensure or registration by the board.

(c) The registrar shall determine the rate of reimbursement for those individuals providing assistance to the board pursuant to this section. All reports shall be completed on a form prescribed by the registrar.

(d) As used in this section, "licensed professionals" means, but is not limited to, engineers, architects, landscape architects, geologists, and accountants licensed, certificated, or registered pursuant to this division.

Added Stats 1987 ch 1264 § 2, effective September 28, 1987. Amended Stats 1991 ch 1160 § 4 (AB 2190); Stats 2002 ch 1013 § 59 (SB 2026).

§ 7019.1. [Section repealed 2001.]

Added Stats 1997 ch 812 § 2 (SB 857), operative until July 1, 2000. Repealed, operative January 1, 2001, by its own terms. The repealed section related to copy of opinion.

—See *Unemployment Insurance Code Section 329, Joint Enforcement Strike Force on the Underground Economy,* in Appendix.

—See also *Labor Code Section 106, Authority of the Labor Commissioner,* in the Appendix.

§ 7020. Computerized enforcement tracking system for consumer complaints

The board shall maintain a computerized enforcement tracking system for consumer complaints.

Added Stats 1987 ch 1264 § 3, effective September 28, 1987. Amended Stats 1991 ch 1160 § 5 (AB 2190).

§ 7021. Interagency agreement for information to protect the public

The board may enter into an interagency agreement with any other state or local agency the board deems to be in possession of any information relevant to its priority to protect the public described in Section 7000.6.

Added Stats 2016 ch 372 § 1 (SB 465), effective January 1, 2017.

Article 2
Application of Chapter

§ 7025. "Members of the personnel of record"; "Person"; "Qualifying person"; "Qualifying individual"; "Qualifier"

(a) "Members of the personnel of record" as used in this chapter means every person listed in the records of the registrar as then associated with a licensee.

(b) "Person" as used in this chapter includes an individual, a firm, partnership, corporation, limited liability company, association or other organization, or any combination thereof.

(c) "Qualifying person," "qualifying individual," or "qualifier," as used in this chapter, means a person who qualifies for a license pursuant to Section 7068.

Added Stats 1939 ch 37 § 1. Amended Stats 2010 ch 698 § 2 (SB 392), effective January 1, 2011.

§ 7026. "Contractor"; "Roadway"

"Contractor," for the purposes of this chapter, is synonymous with "builder" and, within the meaning of this chapter, a contractor is any person who undertakes to or offers to undertake to, or purports to have the capacity to undertake to, or submits a bid to, or does himself or herself or by or through others, construct, alter, repair, add to, subtract from, improve, move, wreck or demolish any building, highway, road, parking facility, railroad, excavation or other structure, project, development or improvement, or to do any part thereof, including the erection of scaffolding or other structures or works in connection therewith, or the cleaning of grounds or structures in connection therewith, or the preparation and removal of roadway construction zones, lane closures, flagging, or traffic diversions, or the installation, repair, maintenance, or calibration of monitoring equipment for underground storage tanks, and whether or not the performance of work herein described involves the addition to, or fabrication into, any structure, project, development or improvement herein described of any material or article of merchandise. "Contractor" includes subcontractor and specialty contractor. "Roadway" includes, but is not limited to, public or city streets, highways, or any public conveyance.

Added Stats 1939 ch 37 § 1. Amended Stats 1939 ch 1091 § 1; Stats 1941 ch 971 § 2; Stats 1949 ch 90 § 1; Stats 1963 ch 972 § 1; Stats 1969 ch 761 § 1; Stats 1970 ch 340 § 1; Stats 1973 ch 892 § 1; Stats 1977 ch 429 § 1; Stats 1999 ch 708 § 1 (AB 1206); Stats 2001 ch 728 § 53 (SB 724).

§ 7026.1. "Contractor"

(a) The term "contractor" includes all of the following:

(1) Any person not exempt under Section 7053 who maintains or services air-conditioning, heating, or refrigeration equipment that is a fixed part of the structure to which it is attached.

(2) (A) Any person, consultant to an owner-builder, firm, association, organization, partnership, business trust, corporation, or company, who or which undertakes, offers to undertake, purports to have the capacity to undertake, or submits a bid to construct any building or home improvement project, or part thereof.

(B) For purposes of this paragraph, a consultant is a person, other than a public agency or an owner of privately owned real property to be improved, who meets either of the following criteria as it relates to work performed pursuant to a home improvement contract as defined in Section 7151.2:

(i) Provides or oversees a bid for a construction project.

(ii) Arranges for and sets up work schedules for contractors and subcontractors and maintains oversight of a construction project.

(3) A temporary labor service agency that, as the employer, provides employees for the performance of work covered by this chapter. The provisions of this paragraph shall not apply if there is a properly licensed contractor who exercises supervision in accordance with Section 7068.1 and who is directly responsible for the final results of the work. Nothing in this paragraph shall require a qualifying individual, as provided in Section 7068, to be present during the supervision of work covered by this chapter. A contractor requesting the services of a temporary labor service agency shall provide his or her license number to that temporary labor service agency.

(4) Any person not otherwise exempt by this chapter, who performs tree removal, tree pruning, stump removal, or engages in tree or limb cabling or guying. The term contractor does not include a person performing the activities of a nurseryperson who in the normal course of routine work performs incidental pruning of trees, or guying of planted trees and their limbs. The term contractor does not include a gardener who in the normal course of routine work performs incidental pruning of trees measuring less than 15 feet in height after planting.

(5) Any person engaged in the business of drilling, digging, boring, or otherwise constructing, deepening, repairing, reperforating, or abandoning any water well, cathodic protection well, or monitoring well.

(b) The term "contractor" or "consultant" does not include a common interest development manager, as defined in Section 11501, and a common interest development manager is not required to have a contractor's license when performing management services, as defined in subdivision (d) of Section 11500.

Added Stats 1971 ch 1365 § 1. Amended Stats 1991 ch 1160 § 6 (AB 2190); Stats 2003 ch 759 § 1 (AB 544); Stats 2004 ch 183 § 10 (AB 3082); Stats 2012 ch 371 § 1 (AB 2237), effective January 1, 2013; Stats 2013 ch 319 § 6 (SB 822), effective January 1, 2014.

§ 7026.2. Definitions

(a) For the purposes of this chapter, "contractor" includes any person engaged in the business of the construction, installation, alteration, repair, or preparation for moving of a mobilehome or mobilehome accessory buildings and structures upon a site for the purpose of occupancy as a dwelling.

(b) "Contractor" does not include the manufacturer of the mobilehome or mobilehome accessory building or structure if it is constructed at a place other than the site upon which it is installed for the purpose of occupancy as a dwelling, and does not include the manufacturer when the manufacturer is solely performing work in compliance with the manufacturer's warranty. "Contractor" includes the manufacturer if the manufacturer is engaged in onsite construction, alteration, or repair of a mobilehome or mobilehome accessory buildings and structures pursuant to specialized plans, specifications, or models, or any work other than in compliance with the manufacturer's warranty.

(c) "Contractor" does not include a seller of a manufactured home or mobilehome who holds a retail manufactured home or mobilehome dealer's license under Chapter 7 (commencing with Section 18045) of Part 2 of Division 13 of the Health and Safety Code, if the installation of the manufactured home or mobilehome is to be performed by a licensed contractor and the seller certifies that fact in writing to the buyer prior to the performance of the installation. The certification shall include the name, business address, and contractor's license number of the licensed contractor by whom the installation will be performed.

(d) For the purposes of this chapter, the following terms have the following meanings:

(1) "Mobilehome" means a vehicle defined in Section 18008 of the Health and Safety Code.

(2) "Mobilehome accessory building or structure" means a building or structure defined in Section 18008.5 of the Health and Safety Code.

(3) "Manufactured home" means a structure defined in Section 18007 of the Health and Safety Code.

Section VI

Added Stats 1969 ch 761 § 2 as § 7027. Amended Stats 1970 ch 340 § 2; Stats 1973 ch 892 § 2; Stats 1983 ch 891 § 1.5; Stats 1986 ch 851 § 1. Renumbered by Stats 1991 ch 1160 § 17 (AB 2190).

—*See California Water Code Section 13750.5, License Required for Water Wells, in the Appendix.*

§ 7026.3. Persons who install or contract for the installation of carpet

For the purpose of this chapter, "contractor" includes any person who installs or contracts for the installation of carpet wherein the carpet is attached to the structure by any conventional method as determined by custom and usage in the trade; except that a seller of installed carpet who holds a retail furniture dealer's license under Chapter 3 (commencing with Section 19000) of Division 8 shall not be required to have a contractor's license if the installation of the carpet is performed by a licensed contractor and the seller so certifies in writing to the buyer prior to the performance of the installation, which certification shall include the name, business address, and contractor's license number of the licensed contractor by whom the installation will be performed.

Added Stats 1991 ch 1160 § 9 (AB 2190).

§ 7026.11. Permissible scope of work for the General Manufactured Housing Contractor (C-47) license classification

Notwithstanding any other provision of law, the permissible scope of work for the General Manufactured Housing Contractor (C-47) license classification set forth in Section 832.47 of Division 8 of Title 16 of the California Code of Regulations shall include manufactured homes, as defined in Section 18007 of the Health and Safety Code, mobilehomes, as defined in Section 18008 of the Health and Safety Code, and multifamily manufactured homes, as defined in Section 18008.7 of the Health and Safety Code.

Added Stats 2007 ch 540 § 1 (SB 538), effective January 1, 2008.

§ 7026.12. Installations of fire protection systems

Except as provided in Section 7026.13, the installation of a fire protection system, excluding an electrical alarm system, shall be performed only by either of the following:

(a) A contractor holding a fire protection contractor classification, as defined in the regulations of the board.

(b) An owner-builder of an owner-occupied, single-family dwelling, if not more than two single-family dwellings on the same parcel are constructed within one year, plans are submitted to, and approved by, the city, county, or city and county authority, and the city, county, or city and county authority inspects and approves the installation.

Added Stats 1988 ch 1035 § 1. Amended Stats 1994 ch 185 § 1 (AB 2646); Stats 2013 ch 377 § 1 (AB 433), effective January 1, 2014.

§ 7026.13. [Section repealed 2017.]

Added Stats 2013 ch 377 § 2 (AB 433), effective January 1, 2014, repealed January 1, 2017. The repealed section related to exception for installations of residential fire protection systems.

§ 7027. Advertising as contractor

Any person who advertises or puts out any sign or card or other device that would indicate to the public that he or she is a contractor, or who causes his or her name or business name to be included in a classified advertisement or directory under a classification for construction or work of improvement covered by this chapter is subject to the provisions of this chapter regardless of whether his or her operations as a builder are otherwise exempted.

Added Stats 1957 ch 948 § 1, as B & P C § 7026.6. Amended Stats 1978 ch 771 § 1. Amended and renumbered by Stats 1991 ch 1160 § 12 (AB 2190); Stats 2011 ch 432 § 8 (SB 944), effective January 1, 2012.

§ 7027.1. Advertising by unlicensed person; Penalties

(a) It is a misdemeanor for any person to advertise for construction or work of improvement covered by this chapter unless that person holds a valid license under this chapter in the classification so advertised, except that a licensed building or engineering contractor may advertise as a general contractor.

(b) "Advertise," as used in this section, includes, but not by way of limitation, the issuance of any card, sign, or device to any person, the causing, permitting, or allowing of any sign or marking on or in any building or structure, or in any newspaper, magazine, or by airwave or any electronic transmission, or in any directory under a listing for construction or work of improvement covered by this chapter, with or without any limiting qualifications.

(c) A violation of this section is punishable by a fine of not less than seven hundred dollars ($700) and not more than one thousand dollars ($1,000), which fine shall be in addition to any other punishment imposed for a violation of this section.

(d) If upon investigation, the registrar has probable cause to believe that an unlicensed individual is in violation of this section, the registrar may issue a citation pursuant to Section 7028.7 or 7099.10.

Section VI

Added Stats 1957 ch 948 § 2, as B & P C § 7026.7. Amended Stats 1978 ch 771 § 2; Stats 1986 ch 518 § 1. Amended and renumbered by Stats 1991 ch 1160 § 13 (AB 2190). Amended Stats 1994 ch 413 § 2 (SB 1694); Stats 1998 ch 599 § 2 (SB 597).

§ 7027.2. Advertising by person not licensed

Notwithstanding any other provision of this chapter, a person who is not licensed pursuant to this chapter may advertise for construction work or a work of improvement covered by this chapter only if the aggregate contract price for labor, material, and all other items on a project or undertaking is less than five hundred dollars ($500), and he or she states in the advertisement that he or she is not licensed under this chapter.

Added Stats 1978 ch 771 § 3, as B & P C § 7026.8. Amended and renumbered by Stats 1991 ch 1160 § 14 (AB 2190); Stats 2014 ch 392 § 2 (SB 315), effective January 1, 2015.

§ 7027.3. Penalties for fraudulent use of incorrect license number

Any person, licensed or unlicensed, who willfully and intentionally uses, with intent to defraud, a contractor's license number that does not correspond to the number on a currently valid contractor's license held by that person, is punishable by a fine not exceeding ten thousand dollars ($10,000), or by imprisonment in state prison, or in county jail for not more than one year, or by both that fine and imprisonment. The penalty provided by this section is cumulative to the penalties available under all other laws of this state. If, upon investigation, the registrar has probable cause to believe that an unlicensed individual is in violation of this section, the registrar may issue a citation pursuant to Section 7028.7.

Added Stats 1984 ch 815 § 1, as B & P C § 7026.10. Amended Stats 1987 ch 930 § 1, effective September 22, 1987. Amended and renumbered by Stats 1991 ch 1160 § 15 (AB 2190). Amended Stats 2001 ch 728 § 54 (SB 724).

§ 7027.4. Advertising as insured or bonded; Requirements; Cause for discipline

(a) It is a cause for discipline for any contractor to advertise that he or she is "insured" or has insurance without identifying in the advertisement the type of insurance, including, for example, "commercial general liability insurance" or "workers' compensation insurance" that is carried by the contractor. The contractor may abbreviate the title of the type of insurance.

(b) It is cause for discipline for a contractor to advertise that he or she is "bonded" if the reference is to a contractor's license bond required pursuant to Section 7071.6 or to a disciplinary bond required pursuant to Section 7071.8.

(c) "Advertise," as used in this section, includes, but is not limited to, the issuance of any card, sign, or device to any person, the causing, permitting, or allowing of any sign or marking on or in any building or structure or business vehicle or in any newspaper, magazine, or by airwave or any electronic transmission, or in any directory under a listing for construction or work of improvement covered by this chapter, for the direct or indirect purpose of performing or offering to perform services that require a contractor's license.

Added Stats 2003 ch 607 § 31 (SB 1077).

§ 7027.5. Authority for landscape contractor to design systems or facilities; Prime contract for pool, spa, hot tub, outdoor cooking center, outdoor fireplace, or rainwater capture system; Subcontracting work outside of the field and scope of activities

(a) A landscape contractor working within the classification for which the license is issued may design systems or facilities for work to be performed and supervised by that contractor.

(b) Notwithstanding any other provision of this chapter, a landscape contractor working within the classification for which the license is issued may enter into a prime contract for the construction of any of the following:

(1) A swimming pool, spa, or hot tub, provided that the improvements are included within the landscape project that the landscape contractor is supervising and the construction of any swimming pool, spa, or hot tub is subcontracted to a single licensed contractor holding a Swimming Pool (C-53) classification, as set forth in Section 832.53 of Title 16 of the California Code of Regulations, or performed by the landscape contractor if the landscape contractor also holds a Swimming Pool (C-53) classification. The contractor constructing the swimming pool, spa, or hot tub may subcontract with other appropriately licensed contractors for the completion of individual components of the construction.

(2) An outdoor cooking center, provided that the improvements are included within a residential landscape project that the contractor is supervising. For purposes of this subdivision, "outdoor cooking center" means an unenclosed area within a landscape that is used for the cooking or preparation of food or beverages.

(3) An outdoor fireplace, provided that it is included within a residential landscape project that the contractor is supervising and is not attached to a dwelling.

(4) A rainwater capture system, as defined in Section 10573 of the Water Code, used exclusively for landscape irrigation or as a water

supply for a fountain, pond, or similar decorative water feature in a landscaping project.

(c) (1) Work performed in connection with a landscape project specified in paragraph (2), (3), or (4) of subdivision (b) that is outside of the field and scope of activities authorized to be performed under the Landscape Contractor (C-27) classification, as set forth in Section 832.27 of Title 16 of the California Code of Regulations, may only be performed by a landscape contractor if the landscape contractor also either holds an appropriate specialty license classification to perform the work or is licensed as a General Building contractor. If the landscape contractor neither holds an appropriate specialty license classification to perform the work nor is licensed as a General Building contractor, the work shall be performed by a Specialty contractor holding the appropriate license classification or by a General Building contractor performing work in accordance with the requirements of subdivision (b) of Section 7057.

(2) Notwithstanding paragraph (1), a landscape contractor performing work under the Landscape Contractor (C-27) classification, as set forth in Section 832.27 of Title 16 of the California Code of Regulations, may design and install all exterior components of a rainwater capture system, as defined in Section 10573 of the Water Code, that are not a part of, or attached to, a structure.

(d) A violation of this section shall be cause for disciplinary action.

(e) Nothing in this section authorizes a landscape contractor to engage in or perform activities that require a license pursuant to the Professional Engineers Act (Chapter 7 (commencing with Section 6700)).

Added Stats 1983 ch 699 § 12. Amended Stats 2003 ch 34 § 1 (AB 341); Stats 2007 ch 107 § 1 (AB 711), effective January 1, 2008; Stats 2008 ch 179 § 17 (SB 1498), effective January 1, 2009; Stats 2012 ch 537 § 1 (AB 1750), effective January 1, 2013.

§ 7028. Engaging in business without license; Fine and punishment; Statute of limitations

(a) Unless exempted from this chapter, it is a misdemeanor for a person to engage in the business of, or act in the capacity of, a contractor within this state under either of the following conditions:

(1) The person is not licensed in accordance with this chapter.

(2) The person performs acts covered by this chapter under a license that is under suspension for failure to pay a civil penalty or to comply with an order of correction, pursuant to Section 7090.1, or for failure to resolve all outstanding final liabilities, pursuant to Section 7145.5.

(b) A first conviction for the offense described in this section is punishable by a fine not exceeding five thousand dollars ($5,000) or by imprisonment in a county jail not exceeding six months, or by both that fine and imprisonment.

(c) If a person has been previously convicted of the offense described in this section, unless the provisions of subdivision (d) are applicable, the court shall impose a fine of 20 percent of the contract price, or 20 percent of the aggregate payments made to, or at the direction of, the unlicensed person, or five thousand dollars ($5,000), whichever is greater, and, unless the sentence prescribed in subdivision (d) is imposed, the person shall be confined in a county jail for not less than 90 days, except in an unusual case where the interests of justice would be served by imposition of a lesser sentence or a fine. If the court imposes only a fine or a jail sentence of less than 90 days for second or subsequent convictions under this section, the court shall state the reasons for its sentencing choice on the record.

(d) A third or subsequent conviction for the offense described in this section is punishable by a fine of not less than five thousand dollars ($5,000) nor more than the greater amount of ten thousand dollars ($10,000) or 20 percent of the contract price, or 20 percent of the aggregate payments made to, or at the direction of, the unlicensed person, and by imprisonment in a county jail for not more than one year or less than 90 days. The penalty provided by this subdivision is cumulative to the penalties available under all other laws of this state.

(e) A person who violates this section is subject to the penalties prescribed in subdivision (d) if the person was named on a license that was previously revoked and, either in fact or under law, was held responsible for any act or omission resulting in the revocation.

(f) If the unlicensed person engaging in the business of or acting in the capacity of a contractor has agreed to furnish materials and labor on an hourly basis, "the contract price" for the purposes of this section means the aggregate sum of the cost of materials and labor furnished and the cost of completing the work to be performed.

(g) Notwithstanding any other law, an indictment for any violation of this section by an unlicensed person shall be found, or information or a complaint shall be filed, within four years from the date of the contract proposal, contract, completion, or abandonment of the work, whichever occurs last.

(h) For any conviction under this section, a person who utilized the services of the unlicensed person is a victim of crime and is eligible, pursuant to subdivision (f) of Section 1202.4 of the Penal Code, for restitution for economic losses, regardless of whether he or she had knowledge that the person was unlicensed.

(i) The changes made to this section by the act adding this subdivision are declaratory of existing law.

Added Stats 1939 ch 37 § 1. Amended Stats 1963 ch 1883 § 1; Stats 1969 ch 1583 § 4; Stats 1972 ch 125 § 1; Stats 1982 ch 607 § 1; Stats 1989 ch 366 § 1; Stats 1995 ch 467 § 1 (SB 1061); Stats 1996 ch 145 § 1 (AB 2958); Stats 2003 ch 706 § 1 (SB 443); Stats 2004 ch 183 § 11 (AB 3082); Stats 2005 ch 205 § 1 (SB 488), effective January 1, 2006; Stats 2008 ch 33 § 13 (SB 797), effective June 23, 2008; Stats 2009 ch 319 § 1 (AB 370), effective January 1, 2010; Stats 2010 ch 328 § 15 (SB 1330), effective January 1, 2011; Stats 2014 ch 392 § 3 (SB 315), effective January 1, 2015.

Section VI

§ 7028.1. Penalties against uncertified contractors performing asbestos-related work

It is a misdemeanor for any contractor, whether licensed or unlicensed, to perform or engage in asbestos-related work, as defined in Section 6501.8 of the Labor Code, without certification pursuant to Section 7058.5 of this code, or to perform or engage in a removal or remedial action, as defined in subdivision (d) of Section 7058.7, or, unless otherwise exempted by this chapter, to bid for the installation or removal of, or to install or remove, an underground storage tank, without certification pursuant to Section 7058.7. A contractor in violation of this section is subject to one of the following penalties:

(a) Conviction of a first offense is punishable by a fine of not less than one thousand dollars ($1,000) or more than three thousand dollars ($3,000), and by possible revocation or suspension of any contractor's license.

(b) Conviction of a subsequent offense requires a fine of not less than three thousand dollars ($3,000) or more than five thousand dollars ($5,000), or imprisonment in the county jail not exceeding one year, or both the fine and imprisonment, and a mandatory action to suspend or revoke any contractor's license.

Added Stats 1985 ch 1587 § 1, effective October 2, 1985. Amended Stats 1986 ch 1443 § 1, effective September 30, 1986, ch 1451 § 1.4, effective September 30, 1986; Stats 1990 ch 1366 § 1 (SB 2004), effective September 26, 1990; Stats 1991 ch 1160 § 18 (AB 2190); Stats 1993 ch 589 § 10 (AB 2211); Stats 1996 ch 712 § 1 (SB 1557); Stats 2004 ch 865 § 7 (SB 1914).

§ 7028.2. Complaints; Disposition of penalties

A criminal complaint pursuant to this chapter may be brought by the Attorney General or by the district attorney or prosecuting attorney of any city, in any county in the state with jurisdiction over the contractor or employer, by reason of the contractor's or employer's act, or failure to act, within that jurisdiction. Any penalty assessed by the court shall be paid to the office of the prosecutor bringing the complaint.

Added Stats 1985 ch 1587 § 2, effective October 2, 1985. Amended Stats 1986 ch 1451 § 1.5, effective September 30, 1986; Stats 1989 ch 366 § 2; Stats 1998 ch 931 § 8 (SB 2139), effective September 28, 1998.

§ 7028.3. Injunction against violations

In addition to all other remedies, when it appears to the registrar, either upon complaint or otherwise, that a licensee has engaged in, or is engaging in, any act, practice, or transaction which constitutes a violation of this chapter whereby another person may be substantially injured, or that any person, who does not hold a state contractor's license in any classification, has engaged in, or is engaging in, any act, practice, or transaction which constitutes a violation of this chapter, whether or not there is substantial injury, the registrar may, either through the Attorney General or through the district attorney of the county in which the act, practice, or transaction is alleged to have been committed, apply to the superior court of that county or any other county in which such person maintains a place of business or resides, for an injunction restraining such person from acting in the capacity of a contractor without a license in violation of this chapter, or from acting in violation of this chapter when another person may be substantially injured, and, upon a proper showing, a temporary restraining order, a preliminary injunction, or a permanent injunction shall be granted.

Added Stats 1965 ch 942 § 1. Amended Stats 1969 ch 698 § 1, ch 1583 § 7; Stats 1982 ch 517 § 17.

§ 7028.4. Injunction against continuing violation by person not holding state contractor's license

In addition to the remedies set forth in Section 7028.3, on proper showing by (1) a licensed contractor, or an association of contractors, (2) a consumer affected by the violation, (3) a district attorney, or (4) the Attorney General, of a continuing violation of this chapter by a person who does not hold a state contractor's license in any classification, an injunction shall issue by a court specified in Section 7028.3 at the request of any such party, prohibiting such violation. The plaintiff in any such action shall not be required to prove irreparable injury.

Added Stats 1969 ch 1583 § 8. Amended Stats 1971 ch 442 § 1.

§ 7028.5. Specified individuals acting as contractor without license

It is unlawful for a person who is or has been a partner, officer, director, manager, responsible managing employee, responsible managing member, responsible managing manager, or responsible managing officer of, or an individual who is listed in the personnel of record of, a licensed partnership, corporation, limited liability company, firm, association or other organization to individually engage in the business or individually act in the capacity of a contractor within this state without having a license in good standing to so engage or act.

Added Stats 1941 ch 971 § 3. Amended Stats 2010 ch 698 § 3 (SB 392), effective January 1, 2011.

Section VI

§ 7028.6. Authority to issue citations

The Registrar of Contractors is hereby empowered to issue citations containing orders of abatement and civil penalties against persons acting in the capacity of or engaging in the business of a contractor within this state without having a license in good standing to so act or engage.

Added Stats 1981 ch 1124 § 1. Amended Stats 1998 ch 633 § 1 (SB 2217); Stats 2010 ch 415 § 17 (SB 1491), effective January 1, 2011.

§ 7028.7. Issuance of citation

(a) If upon inspection or investigation, either upon complaint or otherwise, the registrar has probable cause to believe that a person is acting in the capacity of or engaging in the business of a contractor or salesperson within this state without having a license or registration in good standing to so act or engage, and the person is not otherwise exempted from this chapter, the registrar shall issue a citation to that person.

(b) Within 72 hours of receiving notice that a public entity is intending to award, or has awarded, a contract to an unlicensed contractor, the registrar shall give written notice to the public entity that a citation may be issued if a contract is awarded to an unlicensed contractor. If after receiving the written notice from the registrar that the public entity has awarded or awards the contract to an unlicensed contractor, the registrar may issue a citation to the responsible officer or employee of the public entity as specified in Section 7028.15.

(c) Each citation shall be in writing and shall describe with particularity the basis of the citation. Notwithstanding Sections 125.9 and 148, each citation shall contain an order of abatement and an assessment of a civil penalty in an amount not less than two hundred dollars ($200) nor more than fifteen thousand dollars ($15,000).

(d) With the approval of the Contractors State License Board, the registrar shall prescribe procedures for the issuance of a citation under this section. The board shall adopt regulations covering the assessment of a civil penalty that shall give due consideration to the gravity of the violation, and any history of previous violations.

(e) The sanctions authorized under this section shall be separate from, and in addition to, all other remedies either civil or criminal.

Added Stats 1986 ch 995 § 3, operative January 1, 1988. Amended Stats 1990 ch 774 § 1 (SB 1079), effective September 11, 1990; Stats 1991 ch 785 § 1 (AB 800); Stats 1992 ch 606 § 1 (AB 3240); Stats 2001 ch 728 § 55 (SB 724); Stats 2009 ch 307 § 69 (SB 821), effective January 1, 2010; Stats 2010 ch 415 § 18 (SB 1491), effective January 1, 2011; Stats 2020 ch 312 § 54 (SB 1474), effective January 1, 2021.

§ 7028.8. Service of citation

Service of a citation issued under Section 7028.7 may be made by certified mail at the last known business address or residence address of the person cited.

Added Stats 1981 ch 1124 § 3.

§ 7028.9. Limitations period

A citation under Section 7028.7 shall be issued by the registrar within four years after the act or omission that is the basis for the citation or within 18 months after the date of the filing of the complaint with the registrar, whichever is later.

Added Stats 1981 ch 1124 § 4. Amended Stats 1996 ch 145 § 2 (AB 2958); Stats 2010 ch 415 § 19 (SB 1491), effective January 1, 2011.

§ 7028.10. Appeal to registrar

Any person served with a citation under Section 7028.7 may appeal to the registrar within 15 working days after service of the citation with respect to violations alleged, scope of the order of abatement, or amount of civil penalty assessed.

Added Stats 1981 ch 1124 § 5. Amended Stats 1985 ch 1281 § 1.

§ 7028.11. Citation as final order

If within 15 working days after service of the citation, the person cited fails to notify the registrar that he or she intends to appeal the citation, the citation shall be deemed a final order of the registrar and not subject to review by any court or agency. The 15-day period may be extended by the registrar for good cause.

Added Stats 1981 ch 1124 § 6. Amended Stats 1985 ch 1281 § 2.

§ 7028.12. Hearing; Decision

If the person cited under Section 7028.7 timely notifies the registrar that he or she intends to contest the citation, the registrar shall afford an opportunity for a hearing. The registrar shall thereafter issue a decision, based on findings of fact, affirming, modifying, or vacating the citation or directing other appropriate relief. The proceedings under this section shall be conducted in accordance with the provisions of Chapter 5 (commencing with Section 11500) of Part 1 of Division 3 of Title 2 of the Government Code, and the registrar shall have all the powers granted therein.

Added Stats 1981 ch 1124 § 7.

Section VI

§ 7028.13. Application for court order; Collection of civil penalty; Assignment of rights to civil penalty; Time limit for collection of penalty

(a) After the exhaustion of the review procedures provided for in Sections 7028.10 to 7028.12, inclusive, the registrar may apply to the appropriate superior court for a judgment in the amount of the civil penalty and an order compelling the cited person to comply with the order of abatement. The application, which shall include a certified copy of the final order of the registrar, shall constitute a sufficient showing to warrant the issuance of the judgment and order. If the cited person did not appeal the citation, a certified copy of the citation and proof of service, and a certification that the person cited is not or was not a licensed contractor or applicant for a license at the time of issuance of the citation, shall constitute a sufficient showing to warrant the issuance of the judgment and order.

(b) Notwithstanding any other provision of law, the registrar may delegate the collection of the civil penalty for any citation issued to any person or entity legally authorized to engage in collections. Costs of collection shall be borne by the person cited. The registrar shall not delegate the authority to enforce the order of abatement.

(c) Notwithstanding any other provision of law, the registrar shall have the authority to assign the rights to the civil penalty, or a portion thereof, for adequate consideration. The assignee and the registrar shall have all the rights afforded under the ordinary laws of assignment of rights and delegation of duties. The registrar shall not assign the order of abatement. The assignee may apply to the appropriate superior court for a judgment based upon the assigned rights upon the same evidentiary showing as set forth in subdivision (a).

(d) Notwithstanding any other provision of law, including subdivisions (a) and (b) of Section 340 of the Code of Civil Procedure, the registrar or his or her designee or assignee shall have four years from the date of the final order to collect civil penalties except that the registrar or his or her designee or assignee shall have 10 years from the date of the judgment to enforce civil penalties on citations that have been converted to judgments through the process described in subdivisions (a) and (c).

Added Stats 1981 ch 1124 § 8. Amended Stats 2001 ch 728 § 56 (SB 724); Stats 2005 ch 280 § 2 (SB 1112), effective January 1, 2006.

§ 7028.14. Waiver of part of civil penalty on issuance of license

Notwithstanding any other provision of the law, the registrar may waive part of the civil penalty if the person against whom the civil penalty is assessed satisfactorily completes all the requirements for, and is issued, a contractor's license. Any outstanding injury to the public shall be satisfactorily settled prior to issuance of the license.

Added Stats 1989 ch 1174 § 1.

§ 7028.15. License required to submit bid to public agency; Exceptions

(a) It is a misdemeanor for any person to submit a bid to a public agency in order to engage in the business or act in the capacity of a contractor within this state without having a license therefor, except in any of the following cases:

(1) The person is particularly exempted from this chapter.

(2) The bid is submitted on a state project governed by Section 10164 of the Public Contract Code or on any local agency project governed by Section 20103.5 of the Public Contract Code.

(b) If a person has been previously convicted of the offense described in this section, the court shall impose a fine of 20 percent of the price of the contract under which the unlicensed person performed contracting work, or four thousand five hundred dollars ($4,500), whichever is greater, or imprisonment in the county jail for not less than 10 days nor more than six months, or both.

In the event the person performing the contracting work has agreed to furnish materials and labor on an hourly basis, "the price of the contract" for the purposes of this subdivision means the aggregate sum of the cost of materials and labor furnished and the cost of completing the work to be performed.

(c) This section shall not apply to a joint venture license, as required by Section 7029.1. However, at the time of making a bid as a joint venture, each person submitting the bid shall be subject to this section with respect to his or her individual licensure.

(d) This section shall not affect the right or ability of a licensed architect, land surveyor, or registered professional engineer to form joint ventures with licensed contractors to render services within the scope of their respective practices.

(e) Unless one of the foregoing exceptions applies, a bid submitted to a public agency by a contractor who is not licensed in accordance with this chapter shall be considered nonresponsive and shall be rejected by the public agency. Unless one of the foregoing exceptions applies, a local public agency shall, before awarding a contract or issuing a purchase order, verify that the contractor was properly licensed when the contractor submitted the bid. Notwithstanding any other provision of law, unless one of the foregoing exceptions applies, the registrar may issue a citation to any public officer or employee of a public entity who knowingly awards a contract or issues a purchase order to a contractor who is not licensed pursuant to this chapter. The amount of civil penalties, appeal, and finality of such citations shall

Section VI

be subject to Sections 7028.7 to 7028.13, inclusive. Any contract awarded to, or any purchase order issued to, a contractor who is not licensed pursuant to this chapter is void.

(f) Any compliance or noncompliance with subdivision (e) of this section, as added by Chapter 863 of the Statutes of 1989, shall not invalidate any contract or bid awarded by a public agency during which time that subdivision was in effect.

(g) A public employee or officer shall not be subject to a citation pursuant to this section if the public employee, officer, or employing agency made an inquiry to the board for the purposes of verifying the license status of any person or contractor and the board failed to respond to the inquiry within three business days. For purposes of this section, a telephone response by the board shall be deemed sufficient.

Added Stats 1989 ch 863 § 1. Amended Stats 1990 ch 321 § 1 (SB 929), effective July 16, 1990; Stats 1991 ch 785 § 2 (AB 800); Stats 1992 ch 294 § 1 (AB 2347).

—*See Public Contract Code Section 10164, License Required for Award of Contract on State Project; 10262 Payment to Subcontractors, and 20103.5, Public Works Contracts: Bidder or Contract Not Licensed; Penalties, in Appendix.*

§ 7028.16. Punishment for engaging in business without license with respect to structures damaged by natural disaster for which state of emergency has been declared

A person who engages in the business or acts in the capacity of a contractor, without having a license therefor, in connection with the offer or performance of repairs or improvements to a residential or nonresidential structure or property, or by adding to, or subtracting from, grounds in connection therewith, for damage or destruction caused by a natural disaster for which a state of emergency is proclaimed by the Governor pursuant to Section 8625 of the Government Code, or for which an emergency or major disaster is declared by the President of the United States, shall be punished by a fine up to ten thousand dollars ($10,000), or by imprisonment pursuant to subdivision (h) of Section 1170 of the Penal Code for 16 months, or for two or three years, or by both that fine and imprisonment, or by a fine up to one thousand dollars ($1,000), or by imprisonment in a county jail not exceeding one year, or by both that fine and imprisonment. In addition, a person who utilized the services of the unlicensed contractor is a victim of crime regardless of whether that person had knowledge that the contractor was unlicensed.

Added Stats 1st Ex Sess 1989-1990 ch 36 § 3, effective September 22, 1990. Amended Stats 2009 ch 319 § 2 (AB 370), effective January 1, 2010; Stats 2011 ch 15 § 18 (AB 109), effective April 4, 2011, operative October 1, 2011; Stats 2020 ch 364 § 1 (SB 1189), effective January 1, 2021.

—See Penal Code Sections 670, State of Emergency; Fraud of Owners or Lessees of Residential Structures; Penalties; 667.16, Enhanced Sentence for Fraud in Repairing Natural Disaster Damage; 551, Insurance Fraud, in Appendix.

§ 7028.17. Failure of unlicensed person to comply with citation; Distribution of fines

(a) The failure of an unlicensed individual to comply with a citation after it is final is a misdemeanor.

(b) Notwithstanding Section 1462.5 or 1463 of the Penal Code or any other provision of law, any fine collected upon conviction in a criminal action brought under this section shall be distributed as follows:

(1) If the action is brought by a district attorney, any fine collected shall be paid to the treasurer of the county in which the judgment was entered to be designated for use by the district attorney.

(2) If the action is brought by a city attorney or city prosecutor, any fine collected shall be paid to the treasurer of the city in which the judgment was entered, to be designated for use by the city attorney.

Added Stats 1988 ch 725 § 1, as B & P C § 7099.85. Amended Stats 1989 ch 366 § 3. Amended and renumbered by Stats 1991 ch 1160 § 30 (AB 2190).

§ 7029. Issuance and suspension of joint venture license

A joint venture license is a license issued to any combination of individuals, corporations, limited liability companies, partnerships, or other joint ventures, each of which holds a current, active license in good standing. A joint venture license may be issued in any classification in which at least one of the entities is licensed. An active joint venture license shall be automatically suspended by operation of law during any period in which any member of the entity does not hold a current, active license in good standing.

Added Stats 1983 ch 891 § 3. Amended Stats 1984 ch 1174 § 1; Stats 2010 ch 698 § 4 (SB 392), effective January 1, 2011.

§ 7029.1. Unlawfully acting in joint venture without license

(a) Except as provided in this section, it is unlawful for any two or more licensees, each of whom has been issued a license to act separately in the capacity of a contractor within this state, to be awarded a contract jointly or otherwise act as a contractor without first having secured a joint venture license in accordance with the provisions of this chapter.

(b) Prior to obtaining a joint venture license, contractors licensed in accordance with this chapter may jointly bid for the performance of work covered by this section. If a combination of licensees submit a bid for the performance of work for which a joint venture license is required, a failure to obtain that license shall not prevent the imposition of any penalty specified by law for the failure of a contractor who submits a bid to enter into a contract pursuant to the bid.

(c) A violation of this section constitutes a cause for disciplinary action.

Added Stats 1983 ch 891 § 4. Amended Stats 1987 ch 930 § 3, effective September 22, 1987; Stats 2003 ch 607 § 32 (SB 1077).

§ 7029.5. Display of name, business address and business license number on commercial vehicles

Every C-36 plumbing contractor, C-45 sign contractor, and C-57 well-drilling contractor licensed under this chapter shall have displayed on each side of each motor vehicle used in his or her business, for which a commercial vehicle registration fee has been paid pursuant to Article 3 (commencing with Section 9400) of Chapter 6 of Division 3 of the Vehicle Code, his or her name, permanent business address, and contractor's license number, all in letters and numerals not less than 1½ inches high.

The identification requirements of this section shall also apply to any drill rig used for the drilling of water wells.

Failure to comply with this section constitutes a cause for disciplinary action.

Added Stats 1972 ch 681 § 1, operative July 1, 1973, as B & P C § 7029.6. Amended and renumbered by Stats 1991 ch 1160 § 20 (AB 2190); Stats 2011 ch 432 § 9 (SB 944), effective January 1, 2012.

§ 7029.6. Display of business name and contractors' license number

Except for contractors identified in Section 7029.5, every contractor licensed under this chapter shall have displayed, in or on each motor vehicle used in his or her construction business, for which a commercial vehicle registration fee has been paid pursuant to Article 3 (commencing with Section 9400) of Chapter 6 of Division 3 of the Vehicle Code, his or her business name and contractors' license number in a clearly visible location in print type of at least 72-point font or three-quarters of an inch in height and width.

Added Stats 2003 ch 118 § 1 (AB 1538).

§ 7030. Licensee's statement on contracts; Notice requirements; Exceptions

(a) Except for contractors writing home improvement contracts pursuant to Section 7151.2 and contractors writing service and repair contracts pursuant to Section 7159.10, every person licensed pursuant to this chapter shall include the following statement in at least 10-point type on all written contracts with respect to which the person is a prime contractor:

"Contractors are required by law to be licensed and regulated by the Contractors State License Board which has jurisdiction to investigate complaints against contractors if a complaint regarding a patent act or omission is filed within four years of the date of the alleged violation. A complaint regarding a latent act or omission pertaining to structural defects must be filed within 10 years of the date of the alleged violation. Any questions concerning a contractor may be referred to the Registrar, Contractors State License Board, P.O. Box 26000, Sacramento, CA 95826."

(b) Every person licensed pursuant to this chapter shall include the following statement in at least 12-point type in all home improvement contracts written pursuant to Section 7151.2 and service and repair contracts written pursuant to Section 7159.10:

"Information about the Contractors State License Board (CSLB): CSLB is the state consumer protection agency that licenses and regulates construction contractors.

Contact CSLB for information about the licensed contractor you are considering, including information about disclosable complaints, disciplinary actions and civil judgments that are reported to CSLB.

Use only licensed contractors. If you file a complaint against a licensed contractor within the legal deadline (usually four years), CSLB has authority to investigate the complaint. If you use an unlicensed contractor, CSLB may not be able to help you resolve your complaint. Your only remedy may be in civil court, and you may be liable for damages arising out of any injuries to the unlicensed contractor or the unlicensed contractor's employees.

For more information:

Visit CSLB's internet website at www.cslb.ca.gov

Call CSLB at 800-321-CSLB (2752)

Write CSLB at P.O. Box 26000, Sacramento, CA 95826."

(c) Failure to comply with the notice requirements set forth in subdivision (a) or (b) of this section is cause for disciplinary action.

Added Stats 2005 ch 48 § 5 (SB 1113), effective July 18, 2005, operative January 1, 2006. Amended Stats 2011 ch 432 § 10 (SB 944), effective January 1, 2012; Stats 2020 ch 312 § 55 (SB 1474), effective January 1, 2021.

§ 7030.1. Disclosure

(a) A contractor, who has his or her license suspended or revoked two or more times within an eight-year period, shall disclose either in capital letters in 10-point roman boldface type or in contrasting red print in at least 8-point roman boldface type, in a document provided prior to entering into a contract to perform work on residential property with four or fewer units, any disciplinary license suspension, or license revocation during the last eight years resulting from any violation of this chapter by the contractor, whether or not the suspension or revocation was stayed.

(b) The disclosure notice required by this section may be provided in a bid, estimate, or other document prior to entering into a contract.

(c) A violation of this section is subject to the following penalties:

(1) A penalty of one thousand dollars ($1,000) shall be assessed for the first violation.

(2) A penalty of two thousand five hundred dollars ($2,500) shall be assessed for the second violation.

(3) A penalty of five thousand dollars ($5,000) shall be assessed for a third violation in addition to a one-year suspension of license by operation of law.

(4) A fourth violation shall result in the revocation of license in accordance with this chapter.

Added Stats 1996 ch 282 § 3 (AB 2494).

§ 7030.5. Inclusion of license number in contracts, bids, and advertising

Every person licensed pursuant to this chapter shall include his license number in: (a) all construction contracts; (b) subcontracts and calls for bid; and (c) all forms of advertising, as prescribed by the registrar of contractors, used by such a person.

Added Stats 1972 ch 124 § 1, operative July 1, 1973. Amended Stats 1973 ch 153 § 1, effective July 6, 1973, operative July 1, 1973.

§ 7031. Allegation and proof of license in action on contract; Recovery of compensation paid to unlicensed contractor; Substantial compliance; Exceptions

(a) Except as provided in subdivision (e), no person engaged in the business or acting in the capacity of a contractor, may bring or maintain any action, or recover in law or equity in any action, in any court of this state for the collection of compensation for the performance of any act or contract where a license is required by this chapter without alleging that they were a duly licensed contractor at all times during the performance of that act or contract regardless of the merits of the cause of action brought by the person, except that this prohibition shall not apply to contractors who are each individually licensed under this chapter but who fail to comply with Section 7029.

(b) Except as provided in subdivision (e), a person who utilizes the services of an unlicensed contractor may bring an action in any court of competent jurisdiction in this state to recover all compensation paid to the unlicensed contractor for performance of any act or contract.

(c) A security interest taken to secure any payment for the performance of any act or contract for which a license is required by this chapter is unenforceable if the person performing the act or contract was not a duly licensed contractor at all times during the performance of the act or contract.

(d) If licensure or proper licensure is controverted, then proof of licensure pursuant to this section shall be made by production of a verified certificate of licensure from the Contractors State License Board which establishes that the individual or entity bringing the action was duly licensed in the proper classification of contractors at all times during the performance of any act or contract covered by the action. Nothing in this subdivision shall require any person or entity controverting licensure or proper licensure to produce a verified certificate. When licensure or proper licensure is controverted, the burden of proof to establish licensure or proper licensure shall be on the licensee.

(e) The judicial doctrine of substantial compliance shall not apply under this section where the person who engaged in the business or acted in the capacity of a contractor has never been a duly licensed contractor in this state. However, notwithstanding subdivision (b) of Section 143, the court may determine that there has been substantial compliance with licensure requirements under this section if it is shown at an evidentiary hearing that the person who engaged in the business or acted in the capacity of a contractor (1) had been duly licensed as a contractor in this state prior to the performance of the act or contract, (2) acted reasonably and in good faith to maintain proper licensure, and (3) acted promptly and in good faith to remedy the failure to comply with the licensure requirements upon learning of the failure.

(f) The exceptions to the prohibition against the application of the judicial doctrine of substantial compliance found in subdivision (e) shall apply to all contracts entered into on or after January 1, 1992, and to all actions or arbitrations arising therefrom, except that the amendments to subdivisions (e) and (f) enacted during the 1994 portion of the 1993-94 Regular Session of the Legislature shall not apply to either of the following:

(1) Any legal action or arbitration commenced prior to January 1, 1995, regardless of the date on which the parties entered into the contract.

(2) Any legal action or arbitration commenced on or after January 1, 1995, if the legal action or arbitration was commenced prior to January 1, 1995, and was subsequently dismissed.

Section VI

Added Stats 1939 ch 37 § 1. Amended Stats 1957 ch 845 § 1; Stats 1961 ch 1325 § 1; Stats 1965 ch 681 § 1; Stats 1989 ch 368 § 1; Stats 1991 ch 632 § 1 (AB 1382); Stats 1992 ch 229 § 1 (AB 2413); Stats 1993 ch 797 § 1 (AB 628); Stats 1994 ch 550 § 1 (SB 1844); Stats 2001 ch 226 § 1 (AB 678); Stats 2003 ch 289 § 1 (AB 1386); Stats 2016 ch 244 § 1 (AB 1793), effective January 1, 2017; Stats 2020 ch 312 § 56 (SB 1474), effective January 1, 2021.

§ 7031.5. Applicant's statement as to license required by city or county permit regulations; Penalty for violation

Each county or city which requires the issuance of a permit as a condition precedent to the construction, alteration, improvement, demolition or repair of any building or structure shall also require that each applicant for such a permit file as a condition precedent to the issuance of a permit a statement which he has prepared and signed stating that the applicant is licensed under the provisions of this chapter, giving the number of the license and stating that it is in full force and effect, or, if the applicant is exempt from the provisions of this chapter, the basis for the alleged exemption.

Any violation of this section by any applicant for a permit shall be subject to a civil penalty of not more than five hundred dollars ($500).

Added Stats 1963 ch 1140 § 1. Amended Stats 1977 ch 1052 § 1.

§ 7032. Construction of chapter; Complaints to registrar against licensees

Nothing in this chapter shall limit the power of a city or county to regulate the quality and character of installations made by contractors through a system of permits and inspections which are designed to secure compliance with and aid in the enforcement of applicable state and local building laws, or to enforce other local laws necessary for the protection of the public health and safety. Nothing in this chapter shall limit the power of a city or county to adopt any system of permits requiring submission to and approval by the city or county of plans and specifications for an installation prior to the commencement of construction of the installation.

Cities or counties may direct complaints to the registrar against licensees based upon determinations by city or county enforcement officers of violations by such licensees of codes the enforcement of which is the responsibility of the complaining city or county. Such complaints shall to the extent determined to be necessary by the registrar be given priority in processing over other complaints.

Nothing contained in this section shall be construed as authorizing a city or county to enact regulations relating to the qualifications necessary to engage in the business of contracting.

Added Stats 1959 ch 1403 § 1, effective July 1, 1959. Amended Stats 1961 ch 198 § 1.

§ 7033. Requirement of filing by licensee or applicant statement as to license, or exemption and proof thereof

Every city or city and county which requires the issuance of a business license as a condition precedent to engaging, within the city or city and county, in a business which is subject to regulation under this chapter, shall require that each licensee and each applicant for issuance or renewal of such license shall file, or have on file, with such city or city and county, a signed statement that such licensee or applicant is licensed under the provisions of this chapter and stating that the license is in full force and effect, or, if such licensee or applicant is exempt from the provisions of this chapter, he shall furnish proof of the facts which entitle him to such exemption.

Added Stats 1965 ch 1082 § 1.

—*See Government Code Section 37101.7, Licensing for Revenue by Cities, in Appendix.*

§ 7034. Insertion of void or unenforceable provisions in contract prohibited

(a) No contractor that is required to be licensed under this chapter shall insert in any contract, or be a party, with a subcontractor that is licensed under this chapter to any contract which contains, a provision, clause, covenant, or agreement which is void or unenforceable under Section 2782 of the Civil Code.

(b) No contractor that is required to be licensed under this chapter shall require a waiver of lien rights from any subcontractor, employee, or supplier in violation of Section 8122 of the Civil Code.

Added Stats 1976 ch 411 § 1. Amended Stats 1979 ch 1013 § 3; Stats 2010 ch 697 § 1 (SB 189), effective January 1, 2011, operative July 1, 2012.

—*See Civil Code Sections 2782 Construction Contracts; Invalidity of Provisions to Indemnify Promissee Against Liability; Exceptions and 2782.6 Exception for Professional Engineer or Geologist; "Hazardous Materials" Defined, in Appendix.*

Article 3
Exemptions

§ 7040. United States, State, and subdivisions

(a) This chapter does not apply to an authorized representative of the United States government, the State of California, or any incorporated town, city, county, irrigation district, reclamation district or other municipal or political corporation or subdivision of this state when the entity or its representative is acting within the scope of the entity's or representative's official capacity.

Section VI

(b) Nothing in this section authorizes the entity or its authorized representative thereof either to enter into or authorize a contract with an unlicensed contractor for work that is required by this chapter to be performed by a licensed contractor.

Added Stats 1939 ch 37 § 1. Amended Stats 1986 ch 1230 § 1; Stats 1995 ch 467 § 2 (SB 1061); Stats 2019 ch 378 § 5 (SB 610), effective January 1, 2020.

—See *Public Contract Code Section 6100 License Required for Award of Contract,* in *Appendix.*

§ 7041. Court officers

This chapter does not apply to officers of a court when they are acting within the scope of their office.

Added Stats 1939 ch 37 § 1.

§ 7042. Public utilities in their own business operations

This chapter does not apply to public utilities operating under the regulation of the State Railroad Commission on construction, maintenance and development work incidental to their own business.

Added Stats 1939 ch 37 § 1.

§ 7042.1. Adoption fees; Deferral, waiver, or reduction

(a) Notwithstanding any other provisions of this chapter, gas heat, or electrical corporations and their subsidiaries that are regulated as public utilities by the Public Utilities Commission shall not conduct work for which a contractor's license is required, except under any one or more of the following conditions:

(1) The work is performed upon the gas, heat, or electrical corporation's properties.

(2) The work is performed through a contract with a contractor or contractors licensed pursuant to this chapter or the work is performed for low-income citizens pursuant to a program authorized by order of the Public Utilities Commission.

(3) The work is undertaken by the gas, heat, or electrical corporation in furtherance of the generation, transmission, or distribution of electricity, gas, or steam, whether within or without the service area of the corporation, if any work performed within a structure and beyond a customer's utility meter is necessary to protect the public safety or to avoid interruption of service.

(4) The work is otherwise exempt from the provisions of this chapter.

(5) The work is performed to comply with programs or procedures ordered or authorized by the Public Utilities Commission not inconsistent with the objectives expressed in Chapter 984 of the Statutes of 1983.

(b) For the purposes of this section, the following terms have the following meanings:

(1) "Gas, heat, or electrical corporation properties" means properties which a gas, heat, or electrical corporation owns or leases, or over which it has been granted an easement for utility purposes, or facilities which a gas, heat, or electrical corporation owns or operates for utility purposes.

(2) "Subsidiaries" means subsidiaries of a gas, heat, or electrical corporation regulated as public utilities by the Public Utilities Commission which carry out activities solely for utility purposes.

(c) It is the intention of the Legislature in enacting this section that public utility regulations be clearly based on the principle that the energy conservation industry should be allowed to develop in a competitive manner, as declared in Chapter 984 of the Statutes of 1983.

Added Stats 1984 ch 1136 § 1. Amended Stats 1989 ch 29 § 1.

—See *Labor Code Section 3099 Electrician Competency and Training Standards, in Appendix.*

§ 7042.5. Application of chapter; Underground trenching operations; Cable television corporation defined

This chapter does not apply to public utilities operating under the regulation of the Public Utilities Commission on construction, maintenance, and development work incidental to their own business, or to those activities of a cable television corporation subject to regulation pursuant to Section 768.5 of the Public Utilities Code, except underground trenching by a cable television corporation within the public streets, other than that necessary solely for the connection of its distribution system to, or within the properties of, subscribers or potential subscribers.

As used in this section, a cable television corporation is a corporation or person that transmits television programs by cable to subscribers for a fee.

Added Stats 1983 ch 1230 § 1. Amended Stats 1984 ch 945 § 1.

§ 7043. Oil or gas drilling and operation

This chapter does not apply to any construction, repair or operation incidental to the discovering or producing of petroleum or gas, or the drilling, testing, abandoning or other operation of any petroleum or gas well, when performed by an owner or lessee.

Added Stats 1939 ch 37 § 1.

§ 7044. Property owner making own improvements

(a) This chapter does not apply to any of the following:

(1) An owner who builds or improves a structure on his or her property, provided that both of the following conditions are met:

(A) None of the improvements are intended or offered for sale.

(B) The property owner personally performs all of the work or any work not performed by the owner is performed by the owner's employees with wages as their sole compensation.

(2) An owner who builds or improves a structure on his or her property, provided that both of the following conditions are met:

(A) The owner directly contracts with licensees who are duly licensed to contract for the work of the respective trades involved in completing the project.

(B) For projects involving single-family residential structures, no more than four of these structures are intended or offered for sale in a calendar year. This subparagraph shall not apply if the owner contracts with a general contractor for the construction.

(3) A homeowner improving his or her principal place of residence or appurtenances thereto, provided that all of the following conditions exist:

(A) The work is performed prior to sale.

(B) The homeowner has actually resided in the residence for the 12 months prior to completion of the work.

(C) The homeowner has not availed himself or herself of the exemption in this paragraph on more than two structures more than once during any three-year period.

(4) A nonprofit corporation providing assistance to an owner-builder, as defined in subdivision (a) of Section 50692 of the Health and Safety Code, who is participating in a mutual self-help housing program, as defined in Section 50078 of the Health and Safety Code.

(b) In all actions brought under this chapter, both of the following shall apply:

(1) Except as provided in paragraph (2), proof of the sale or offering for sale of a structure by or for the owner-builder within one year after completion of the structure constitutes a rebuttable presumption affecting the burden of proof that the structure was undertaken for purposes of sale.

(2) Proof of the sale or offering for sale of five or more structures by the owner-builder within one year after completion constitutes a conclusive presumption that the structures were undertaken for purposes of sale.

Added Stats 1981 ch 1124 § 10. Amended Stats 1988 ch 1035 § 1.3; Stats 2009 ch 307 § 70 (SB 821), effective January 1, 2010; Stats 2016 ch 714 § 1 (SB 944), effective January 1, 2017.

§ 7044.01. Remedies; Violations; Fees and costs

In addition to all other remedies, any licensed contractor or association of contractors, labor organization, consumer affected by the violation, district attorney, or the Attorney General shall be entitled to seek injunctive relief prohibiting any violation of this chapter by an owner-builder who is neither licensed nor exempted from licensure under this chapter. The plaintiff in that action shall not be required to prove irreparable injury and shall be entitled to attorney's fees and all costs incurred in the prosecution of the action, provided the plaintiff is the prevailing party. The defendant in that action shall be entitled to attorney's fees and all costs incurred in the defense against the action, provided the defendant is the prevailing party.

Enacted by Stats. 2009, Ch. 307.

§ 7044.1. Real estate licensee acting within scope of license

This chapter does not apply to a real estate licensee acting within the course and scope of his or her license pursuant to the Real Estate Law (Part 1 (commencing with Section 10000) of Division 4). However, nothing in this section shall authorize a real estate licensee or a property manager to act in the capacity of a contractor unless licensed by the board.

Added Stats 1994 ch 361 § 1 (AB 2636).

§ 7044.2. Inapplicability of chapter

This chapter does not apply to an admitted surety insurer whenever that surety insurer engages a contractor to undertake the completion of a contract on which a performance or completion bond was issued by the surety insurer, provided all actual construction work is performed by duly licensed contractors.

Added Stats 1996 ch 287 § 1 (SB 2002). Amended Stats 1997 ch 17 § 7 (SB 947).

§ 7045. Sale or installation of products not part of structure

This chapter does not apply to the sale or installation of any finished products, materials, or articles of merchandise that do not become a fixed part of the structure, nor shall it apply to a material supplier or manufacturer furnishing finished products, materials, or articles of merchandise who does not install or contract for the installation of those items. The term "finished products" shall not include installed carpets or mobilehomes or mobilehome accessory structures, as defined in Section 7026.2.

This chapter shall apply to the installation of home improvement goods, as defined in Section 7151.

Added Stats 1939 ch 37 § 1. Amended Stats 1961 ch 1585 § 1; Stats 1967 ch 687 § 1; Stats 1969 ch 761 § 3; Stats 1970 ch 340 § 3; Stats 1973 ch 892 § 3; Stats 1979 ch 1012 § 1; Stats 1981 ch 916 § 1; Stats 1991 ch 1160 § 23 (AB 2190); Stats 1993 ch 589 § 11 (AB 2211).

§ 7046. Personal property work; Mobilehome accessory buildings or structures

This chapter does not apply to any construction, alteration, improvement, or repair of personal property. The term "personal property" shall not include mobilehomes or mobilehome accessory structures as defined in Section 7026.2.

Added Stats 1939 ch 37 § 1. Amended Stats 1969 ch 761 § 4; Stats 1970 ch 340 § 4; Stats 1973 ch 892 § 4; Stats 1991 ch 1160 § 24 (AB 2190).

§ 7048. Contracts aggregating less than specified amount; When exemption not applicable

This chapter does not apply to any work or operation on one undertaking or project by one or more contracts, the aggregate contract price which for labor, materials, and all other items, is less than five hundred dollars ($500), that work or operations being considered of casual, minor, or inconsequential nature.

This exemption does not apply in any case wherein the work of construction is only a part of a larger or major operation, whether undertaken by the same or a different contractor, or in which a division of the operation is made in contracts of amounts less than five hundred dollars ($500) for the purpose of evasion of this chapter or otherwise.

This exemption does not apply to a person who advertises or puts out any sign or card or other device which might indicate to the public that he or she is a contractor or that he or she is qualified to engage in the business of a contractor.

Added Stats 1939 ch 37 § 1. Amended Stats 1945 ch 1361 § 1; Stats 1977 ch 416 § 1; Stats 1986 ch 293 § 1; Stats 1998 ch 633 § 3 (SB 2217); Stats 2004 ch 865 § 8 (SB 1914).

§ 7049. Ditch work and agricultural or fire prevention work

This chapter does not apply to any construction or operation incidental to the construction and repair of irrigation and drainage ditches of regularly constituted irrigation districts, reclamation districts, or to farming, dairying, agriculture, viticulture, horticulture, or stock or poultry raising, or clearing or other work upon the land in rural districts for fire prevention purposes, except when performed by a licensee under this chapter.

The provisions of this chapter do apply to the business of drilling, digging, boring, or otherwise constructing, deepening, repairing, reperforating, or abandoning water wells.

Added Stats 1939 ch 37 § 1. Amended 1959 ch 1691 § 2.

§ 7051. Application of chapter to certain licensees or registrants

This chapter does not apply to a licensed architect or a registered civil or professional engineer acting solely in his or her professional capacity or to a licensed structural pest control operator acting within the scope of his or her license or a licensee operating within the scope of the Geologist and Geophysicist Act.

Added Stats 1949 ch 90 § 4. Amended Stats 1955 ch 1532 § 4; Stats 1994 ch 26 § 206 (AB 1807), effective March 30, 1994.

§ 7052. People furnishing material or supplies

This chapter does not apply to any person who only furnishes materials or supplies without fabricating them into, or consuming them in the performance of, the work of the contractor.

Added Stats 1949 ch 90 § 5.

§ 7053. Employees

Except as provided in Article 10 (commencing with Section 7150), this chapter does not apply to any person who engages in the activities herein regulated as an employee who receives wages as his or her sole compensation, does not customarily engage in an independently established business, and does not have the right to control or discretion as to the manner of performance so as to determine the final results of the work performed.

Added Stats 1949 ch 90 § 6. Amended Stats 1970 ch 227 § 1; Stats 1974 ch 434 § 1; Stats 1982 ch 1427 § 2.

§ 7054. Inapplicability of chapter to licensed alarm company operators

This chapter does not apply to any person who performs work in the installation, maintenance, monitoring, selling, alteration, or servicing of alarm systems, as defined in Section 7590.1, and who holds an alarm company operator's license issued pursuant to Chapter 11.6 (commencing with Section 7590).

Added Stats 1982 ch 1210 § 1. Amended Stats 1991 ch 1160 § 25 (AB 2190); Stats 2018 ch 406 § 2 (SB 904), effective January 1, 2019.

Section VI

§ 7054.5. Application of licensing provisions to installation of satellite antenna systems on residential structures

The licensing provisions of this chapter do not apply to any person registered under Chapter 20 (commencing with Section 9800) if that person's activities consist only of installing satellite antenna systems on residential structures or property.

Added Stats 1987 ch 422 § 1.

—*See Business & Professions Code Sections 7590.1, Definitions; 5537 Licensed Contractor Exemptions from the Architect Act 5537.2 Exemptions and 6737.5, Exemptions for the Provisions of the Engineers Act, in Appendix.*

Article 4
Classifications

§ 7055. Branches of contracting business

For the purpose of classification, the contracting business includes any or all of the following branches:
(a) General engineering contracting.
(b) (1) General building contracting.
(2) Residential remodeling contracting.
(c) Specialty contracting.

Added Stats 1945 ch 1159 § 1. Amended Stats 2020 ch 364 § 2 (SB 1189), effective January 1, 2021.

§ 7056. General engineering contractor

A general engineering contractor is a contractor whose principal contracting business is in connection with fixed works requiring specialized engineering knowledge and skill, including the following divisions or subjects: irrigation, drainage, water power, water supply, flood control, inland waterways, harbors, docks and wharves, shipyards and ports, dams and hydroelectric projects, levees, river control and reclamation works, railroads, highways, streets and roads, tunnels, airports and airways, sewers and sewage disposal plants and systems, waste reduction plants, bridges, overpasses, underpasses and other similar works, pipelines and other systems for the transmission of petroleum and other liquid or gaseous substances, parks, playgrounds and other recreational works, refineries, chemical plants and similar industrial plants requiring specialized engineering knowledge and skill, powerhouses, powerplants and other utility plants and installations, mines and metallurgical plants, land leveling and earthmoving projects, excavating, grading, trenching, paving and surfacing work and cement and concrete works in connection with the above-mentioned fixed works.

Added Stats 1945 ch 1159 § 2. Amended Stats 1951 ch 1606 § 1; Stats 2011 ch 296 § 12 (AB 1023), effective January 1, 2012.

§ 7057. General building contractor

(a) Except as provided in this section, a general building contractor is a contractor whose principal contracting business is in connection with any structure built, being built, or to be built, for the support, shelter, and enclosure of persons, animals, chattels, or movable property of any kind, requiring in its construction the use of at least two unrelated building trades or crafts, or to do or superintend the whole or any part thereof.

This does not include anyone who merely furnishes materials or supplies under Section 7045 without fabricating them into, or consuming them in the performance of, the work of the general building contractor.

(b) A general building contractor may take a prime contract or a subcontract for a framing or carpentry project. However, a general building contractor shall not take a prime contract for any project involving trades other than framing or carpentry unless the prime contract requires at least two unrelated building trades or crafts other than framing or carpentry, or unless the general building contractor holds the appropriate license classification or subcontracts with an appropriately licensed contractor to perform the work. A general building contractor shall not take a subcontract involving trades other than framing or carpentry, unless the subcontract requires at least two unrelated trades or crafts other than framing or carpentry, or unless the general building contractor holds the appropriate license classification. The general building contractor shall not count framing or carpentry in calculating the two unrelated trades necessary in order for the general building contractor to be able to take a prime contract or subcontract for a project involving other trades.

(c) A general building contractor shall not contract for any project that includes a fire protection system as provided for in Section 7026.12 or 7026.13, or the "C-57" Well Drilling classification as provided for in Section 13750.5 of the Water Code, unless the general building contractor holds the appropriate license classification, or subcontracts with the appropriately licensed contractor.

Added Stats 1945 ch 1159 § 3. Amended Stats 1997 ch 812 § 2 (SB 857); Stats 2002 ch 1013 § 60 (SB 2026); Stats 2013 ch 377 § 3 (AB 433), effective January 1, 2014.

§ 7057.5. Residential remodeling contractor

(a) A residential remodeling contractor is a contractor whose principal contracting business is in connection with any project to make improvements to, on, or in an existing residential wood frame structure, and the project requires the use of at least three unrelated building trades or crafts for a single contract.

(b) (1) A residential remodeling contractor may take a prime contract for trades or crafts which may include, but is not limited to, the following:

(A) Drywall.

(B) Finish carpentry.

(C) Flooring.

(D) Insulation.

(E) Painting.

(F) Plastering.

(G) Roof repair.

(H) Siding.

(I) Tiling.

(J) Installing, repairing, or replacing electrical fixtures, such as dimmers, fans, lights, outlets, and switches.

(K) Installing, repairing, or replacing plumbing fixtures, such as faucets, sinks, toilets, and tubs.

(L) Installing, repairing, or replacing mechanical fixtures, such as air filters, air delivery and return grills, and preassembled exhaust fans.

(2) A residential remodeling contractor shall not take a contract unless the contract includes three or more unrelated trades or crafts.

(3) Subject to the limit described in paragraph (2), a residential remodeling contractor may self-perform its contract or may subcontract any of the trades or crafts to appropriately licensed subcontractor or subcontractors.

(c) A residential remodeling contractor shall conduct its contracting activity in accordance with the following restrictions:

(1) A residential remodeling contractor shall not contract for a project that includes the following trades or crafts unless the contractor holds the appropriate license classification or subcontracts with an appropriately licensed contractor:

(A) C-16 Fire Protection.

(B) C-22 Asbestos Abatement.

(C) C-57 Well Drilling.

(2) A residential remodeling contractor shall not contract to make structural changes to load bearing portions of an existing structure, including, but not limited to, footings, foundations, load bearing walls, partitions, and roof structures.

(3) (A) The residential remodeling contractor shall not contract to install, replace, substantially alter, or extend electrical, mechanical, or plumbing systems or their component parts, or the mechanisms or devices that are part of those systems, unless the residential remodeling contractor holds the appropriate license classification or subcontracts with an appropriately licensed contractor.

(B) The residential remodeling contractor may contract to make minor alterations to existing electrical, mechanical, or plumbing systems to effectuate the purpose of installing, repairing, or replacing electrical, mechanical and plumbing fixtures, provided that the contract requires the use of at least three unrelated building trades or crafts.

(C) The board may adopt regulations to further define what activity constitutes the minor alterations described in subparagraph (B), and to further define the electrical, mechanical, or plumbing systems, or their component parts, or the mechanisms or devices that are part of those systems, that are subject to the restriction described in subparagraph (A).

(d) This contractor classification may be cited as the B-2 Residential Remodeling Contractor.

Added Stats 2020 ch 364 § 3 (SB 1189), effective January 1, 2021.

§ 7058. "Specialty contractor"

(a) A specialty contractor is a contractor whose operations involve the performance of construction work requiring special skill and whose principal contracting business involves the use of specialized building trades or crafts.

(b) A specialty contractor includes a contractor whose operations include the business of servicing or testing fire extinguishing systems.

(c) A specialty contractor includes a contractor whose operations are concerned with the installation and laying of carpets, linoleum, and resilient floor covering.

(d) A specialty contractor includes a contractor whose operations are concerned with preparing or removing roadway construction zones, lane closures, flagging, or traffic diversions on roadways, including, but not limited to, public streets, highways, or any public conveyance.

Added Stats 1945 ch 1159 § 4. Amended Stats 1959 ch 2175 § 1; Stats 1963 ch 1320 § 1; Stats 1967 ch 687 § 2; Stats 1985 ch 253 § 1; Stats 1991 ch 1160 § 26 (AB 2190); Stats 1999 ch 708 § 2 (AB 1206); Stats 2007 ch 354 § 15 (SB 1047), effective January 1, 2008.

§ 7058.1. [Section repealed 2002.]

Added Stats 1999 ch 708 § 3 (AB 1206). Repealed Stats 2002 ch 1013 § 61 (SB 2026). The repealed section related to requirements for exemption from testing.

Section VI

§ 7058.5. Classification or certification of contractors performing asbestos-related work

A contractor shall not engage in asbestos-related work, as defined in Section 6501.8 of the Labor Code, that involves 100 square feet or more of surface area of asbestos containing materials, unless the contractor holds a C-22 Asbestos Abatement classification or the qualifier for the license passes an asbestos certification examination. Additional updated asbestos certification examinations may be required based on new health and safety information. The decision on whether to require an updated certification examination shall be made by the Contractors State License Board, in consultation with the Division of Occupational Safety and Health in the Department of Industrial Relations and the Division of Environmental and Occupational Disease Control in the State Department of Public Health.

No asbestos certification examination shall be required for contractors involved with the installation, maintenance, and repair of asbestos cement pipe or sheets, vinyl asbestos floor materials, or asbestos bituminous or resinous materials.

"Asbestos," as used in this section, has the same meaning as defined in Section 6501.7 of the Labor Code.

(b) The Contractors State License Board shall make available to all applicants, either on the board's internet website or, if requested, in hard copy, a booklet containing information relative to handling and disposal of asbestos, together with an open book examination concerning asbestos-related work. All applicants for an initial contractor license shall complete the open book examination and, prior to the issuance of a contractor's license, submit it to the board electronically or by mail if the applicant elects to use the hard-copy format.

Added Stats 1985 ch 1587 § 3, effective October 2, 1985. Amended Stats 1986 ch 1451 § 2, effective September 30, 1986; Stats 1987 ch 930 § 4, effective September 22, 1987; Stats 1991 ch 1160 § 27 (AB 2190); Stats 2010 ch 415 § 20 (SB 1491), effective January 1, 2011; Stat 2021 ch 188 § 8 (SB 826), effective January 1, 2022.

§ 7058.6. Registration with Division of Occupational Safety and Health as condition of asbestos certification; Certification examination; Proof of current registration

(a) The board shall not issue an asbestos certification, as required by Section 7058.5, unless the contractor is registered with the Division of Occupational Safety and Health of the Department of Industrial Relations pursuant to Section 6501.5 of the Labor Code. The board may issue an asbestos certification to a contractor who is not registered, provided the contractor in a written statement acknowledges that they do not perform asbestos-related work. The board shall notify both the division and the contractor, in writing, of the contractor's passage of the certification examination, for the purpose of allowing the contractor to satisfy the requirement of paragraph (1) of subdivision (a) of Section 6501.5 of the Labor Code. The contractor shall register with the division within 90 days from the date the contractor is notified of the passage of the certification examination. The board may require a reexamination if the contractor fails to register within 90 days following issuance of the notification. Applicable test fees shall be paid for any reexamination required under this section.

(b) Any contractor who is certified to engage in asbestos-related work shall present proof of current registration with the division pursuant to Section 6501.5 of the Labor Code upon application for renewal of the contractor's license, if the contractor engages in asbestos-related work, as defined in Section 6501.8 of the Labor Code.

(c) A contractor who is not certified pursuant to this section may bid on and contract to perform a project involving asbestos-related work as long as the asbestos-related work is performed by a contractor who holds the C-22 Asbestos Abatement classification or is certified and registered pursuant to this section and Section 6501.5 of the Labor Code.

(d) The board shall obtain and periodically update the list of contractors certified to engage in asbestos-related work who are registered pursuant to Section 6501.5 of the Labor Code.

Added Stats 1988 ch 1003 § 1.5, operative July 1, 1989. Amended Stats 1995 ch 467 § 3 (SB 1061); Stats 2011 ch 432 § 11 (SB 944), effective January 1, 2012; Stats 2021 ch 188 § 9 (SB 826), effective January 1, 2022.

§ 7058.7. Hazardous substance certification examination [Effective January 1, 2023; Operative January 1, 2024]

(a) No contractor may engage in a removal or remedial action, as defined in subdivision (d), unless the qualifier for the license has passed an approved hazardous substance certification examination.

(b) (1) The Contractors State License Board, the Division of Occupational Safety and Health of the Department of Industrial Relations, and the Department of Toxic Substances Control shall jointly select an advisory committee, which shall be composed of two representatives of hazardous substance removal workers in California, two general engineering contractors in California, and two representatives of insurance companies in California who shall be selected by the Insurance Commissioner.

(2) The Contractors State License Board shall develop a written test for the certification of contractors engaged in hazardous substance removal or remedial action, in consultation with the Division of Occupational Safety and Health, the State Water Resources Control Board, the Department of Toxic Substances Control, and the advisory committee.

(c) The Contractors State License Board may require additional updated approved hazardous substance certification examinations of licensees currently certified based on new public or occupational health and safety information. The Contractors State License Board, in consultation with the Department of Toxic Substances Control and the State Water Resources Control Board, shall approve other initial and updated hazardous substance certification examinations and determine whether to require an updated certification examination of all current certificate holders.

(d) For purposes of this section "removal or remedial action" has the same meaning as found in Part 2 (commencing with Section 78000) of Division 45 of the Health and Safety Code, if the action requires the contractor to dig into the surface of the earth and remove the dug material and the action is at a site listed pursuant to Article 5 (commencing with Section 78760) of Chapter 4 of Part 2 of Division 45 of the Health and Safety Code or any other site listed as a hazardous substance release site by the Department of Toxic Substances Control or a site listed on the National Priorities List compiled pursuant to the Comprehensive Environmental Response, Compensation, and Liability Act of 1980 (42 U.S.C. Sec. 9601 et seq.). "Removal or remedial action" does not include asbestos-related work, as defined in Section 6501.8 of the Labor Code, or work related to a hazardous substance spill on a highway.

(e) (1) A contractor may not install or remove an underground storage tank, unless the contractor has passed the hazardous substance certification examination developed pursuant to this section.

(2) A contractor who is not certified may bid on or contract for the installation or removal of an underground tank, if the work is performed by a contractor who is certified pursuant to this section.

(3) For purposes of this subdivision, "underground storage tank" has the same meaning as defined in subdivision (y) of Section 25281 of the Health and Safety Code.

Added Stats 1986 ch 1443 § 2, effective September 30, 1986. Amended Stats 1990 ch 1366 § 2 (SB 2004), effective September 26, 1990; Stats 1992 ch 1289 § 42.5 (AB 2743), ch 1290 § 1 (AB 3188), effective September 30, 1992; Stats 1993 ch 168 § 1 (AB 427); Stats 2002 ch 999 § 1 (AB 2481); Stats 2020 ch 312 § 57 (SB 1474), effective January 1, 2021; Stats 2022 ch 258 § 1 (AB 2327), effective January 1, 2023, operative effective 1/1/2024.

—See Health and Safety Code Section 25281 Definitions in Appendix.

—See Labor Code Sections 6501.5 Asbestos Certification, 6501.7 Asbestos: Definitions and 6501.8 Asbestos-Related Work Containing Construction Material, in Appendix.

—See also Health and Safety Code Sections 25914 Asbestos and Hazardous Removal Contracts Intent, 25914.1 Definitions, 25914.2 Need for Separate Contract; Emergency Conditions and 25914.3 Certification Requirements: Bids, in Appendix

§ 7058.8. Information to public regarding removal or encapsulation of asbestos-containing materials

The board shall make available to the public upon request information about contracting for the removal or encapsulation of asbestos-containing materials in a building including all of the following:

(a) Steps to take when contracting with a company to remove asbestos.

(b) Existing laws and regulations pertaining to asbestos-related work in California.

(c) Basic health information as contained in the United States Environmental Protection Agency publication, "Guidance for Controlling Asbestos-Containing Materials in Buildings."

(d) A current list of contractors who are certified pursuant to Section 7058.5 to engage in asbestos-related work and who are registered pursuant to Section 6501.5 of the Labor Code.

Added Stats 1988 ch 1003 § 2, operative July 1, 1989. Amended Stats 2011 ch 432 § 12 (SB 944), effective January 1, 2012.

§ 7059. Rules and regulations affecting classification of contractors; Contracts involving two or more crafts; Public works contracts

(a) The board may adopt reasonably necessary rules and regulations to effect the classification of contractors in a manner consistent with established usage and procedure as found in the construction business, and may limit the field and scope of the operations of a licensed contractor to those in which he or she is classified and qualified to engage, as defined by Sections 7055, 7056, 7057, and 7058. A licensee may make application for classification and be classified in more than one classification if the licensee meets the qualifications prescribed by the board for such additional classification or classifications. The application shall be in a form as prescribed by the registrar and shall be accompanied by the application fee fixed by this chapter. No license fee shall be charged for an additional classification or classifications.

Nothing contained in this section shall prohibit a specialty contractor from taking and executing a contract involving the use of two or more crafts or trades, if the performance of the work in the crafts or trades, other than in which he or she is licensed, is incidental and supplemental to the performance of the work in the craft for which the specialty contractor is licensed.

(b) In public works contracts, as defined in Section 1101 of the Public Contract Code, the awarding authority shall determine the license classification necessary to bid and perform the project. In no case shall the awarding authority award a prime contract to a specialty

Section VI

contractor whose classification constitutes less than a majority of the project. When a specialty contractor is authorized to bid a project, all work to be performed outside of his or her license specialty, except work authorized by subdivision (a), shall be performed by a licensed subcontractor in compliance with the Subletting and Subcontracting Fair Practices Act (Chapter 4 (commencing with Section 4100) of Part 1 of Division 2 of the Public Contract Code).

Added Stats 1939 ch 37 § 1. Amended Stats 1941 ch 971 § 9; Stats 1945 ch 1159 § 5; Stats 1957 ch 2084 § 21; Stats 1966 ch 4 § 1; Stats 1983 ch 891 § 5; Stats 1987 ch 485 § 1.

§ 7059.1. Misleading or incompatible use of name styles

(a) A licensee shall not use any business name that indicates the licensee is qualified to perform work in classifications other than those issued for that license, or any business name that is incompatible with the type of business entity licensed.

(b) A licensee shall not conduct business under more than one name for each license. Nothing in this section shall prevent a licensee from obtaining a business name change as otherwise provided by this chapter.

Added Stats 1983 ch 891 § 6. Amended Stats 2001 ch 728 § 57 (SB 724).

Article 5
Licensing

§ 7065. Investigation, classification, and examinations

(a) Under rules and regulations adopted by the board and approved by the director, the registrar shall investigate, classify, and qualify applicants for contractors' licenses by written examination. This examination shall include questions designed to show that the applicant has the necessary degree of knowledge required by Section 7068 and shall include pertinent questions relating to the laws of this state and the contracting business and trade.

(b) Contractors' licenses are to be issued to individual owners, partnerships, corporations, and limited liability companies in accordance with this chapter.

(1) Every person who is an officer, member, responsible manager, or director of a corporation or limited liability company seeking licensure under this chapter shall be listed on the application as a member of the personnel of record.

(2) Every person who is a member of a partnership seeking licensure under this chapter shall be listed on the application as a member of the personnel record.

(c) An applicant shall qualify for licensure in accordance with this subdivision as follows:

(1) An individual owner may qualify by examination for a contractor's license upon the appearance of the owner or a qualifying individual appearing as a responsible managing employee on behalf of the owner.

(2) A partnership may qualify by examination for a contractor's license upon the appearance of a partner or a qualifying individual appearing as a responsible managing employee on behalf of the partnership.

(3) A corporation may qualify by examination for a contractor's license upon the appearance of a qualifying individual appearing either as a responsible managing officer or a responsible managing employee on behalf of the corporation.

(4) A limited liability company may qualify by examination for a contractor's license upon the appearance of a qualifying individual appearing as a responsible managing officer, a responsible managing manager, a responsible managing member, or a responsible managing employee on behalf of the company.

(d) No examination shall be required of a qualifying individual if, within the five-year period immediately preceding the application for licensure, the qualifying individual has either personally passed the written examination for the same classification being applied for, or has served as the qualifying individual for a licensee whose license was in good standing at any time during the five-year period immediately preceding the application for licensure and in the same classification being applied for.

(e) The registrar may contract with a public or private organization to conduct or administer the examination. The registrar may also contract with a public or private organization for materials or services related to the examination.

Added Stats 1939 ch 37 § 1. Amended Stats 1979 ch 1013 § 4; Stats 1980 ch 138 § 1, effective May 30, 1980; Stats 1981 ch 1122 § 1; Stats 1982 ch 378 § 1, ch 1347 § 2; Stats 1989 ch 350 § 1; Stats 2010 ch 698 § 5 (SB 392), effective January 1, 2011; Stats 2011 ch 296 § 13 (AB 1023), effective January 1, 2012; Stats 2020 ch 295 § 1 (AB 3087), effective January 1, 2021.

—*See Government Code Section 12944, Discrimination by "Licensing Board," in Appendix.*

§ 7065.01. Examination not required for limited specialty license classification

Notwithstanding Section 7065, no trade examination shall be required of an applicant for the limited specialty license classification.

Added Stats 2002 ch 311 § 2 (AB 264).

§ 7065.05. Review and revision of examination contents

The board shall periodically review and, if needed, revise the contents of qualifying examinations to insure that the examination questions are timely and relevant to the business of contracting. The board shall, in addition, construct and conduct examinations in such a manner as to preclude the possibility of any applicant having prior knowledge of any specific examination question.

Added Stats 1979 ch 1013 § 5. Amended Stats 2000 ch 1005 § 8 (SB 2029); Stats 2005 ch 280 § 3 (SB 1112), effective January 1, 2006.

§ 7065.06. Revision to landscaping contractor examination

(a) Before the board revises the examination for a landscaping contractor (C-27), the board shall confer with the Department of Water Resources and the California Landscape Contractors Association to determine whether any updates or revisions to the examination are needed to reflect new and emerging landscape irrigation efficiency practices.

(b) The board shall ensure that the examination includes questions that are specific to water use efficiency and sustainable practices to help ensure that the state's water efficiency needs identified in the California Water Plan, described in Section 10004 of the Water Code, are sufficiently supported.

(c) The board shall ensure that the reference study material for the examination continues to include the most current version of the Model Water Efficient Landscape Ordinance (23 Cal. Code Regs. 490, et seq.) and shall add other collateral material specific to water use efficiency and sustainability.

Added Stats 2018 ch 867 § 2 (AB 2371), effective January 1, 2019.

§ 7065.1. Waiver of examination

Notwithstanding Section 7065, the registrar may waive the examination for a contractor's license under any of the following circumstances:

(a) The qualifying individual has, for five of the seven years immediately preceding the application for licensure, been listed on the official records of the board as a member of the personnel of any licensee who held a license, which was active and in good standing, in the same classification being applied for, and who during the period listed on the license has been actively engaged in a licensee's construction activities in the same classification within which the applicant applies for a license.

(b) The qualifying individual is an immediate member of the family of a licensee whose individual license was active and in good standing for five of the seven years immediately preceding the application for licensure, and the qualifying individual is able to show all of the following:

(1) The qualifying individual has been actively engaged in the licensee's business for five of the seven years immediately preceding the application for licensure.

(2) The license is required to continue the existing family business in the event of the absence or death of the licensee.

(3) An application is made for a new license in the same classifications in which the licensee is or was licensed.

(c) The qualifying individual is an employee of a corporation or a limited liability company seeking to replace its former qualifying individual and has been employed by that corporation or limited liability company under the following conditions:

(1) For five of the seven years immediately preceding the application for licensure, the qualifying individual has been continually employed by the corporation or limited liability company in a supervisory capacity in the same classifications being applied for.

(2) For five of the seven years immediately preceding the application for licensure, the corporation or limited liability company has held an active license in good standing in the same classifications being applied for.

(3) The corporation or limited liability company has not requested a waiver under this subdivision within the past five years.

For purposes of this section, employees of a corporation or limited liability company shall include, but not be limited to, the officers of a corporation and the officers and managers of a limited liability company.

Added Stats 1981 ch 1122 § 3. Amended Stats 1982 ch 378 § 2; Stats 1986 ch 27 § 1; Stats 1990 ch 1456 § 1 (SB 2476); Stats 1992 ch 746 § 1 (AB 2424); Stats 2010 ch 698 § 6 (SB 392), effective January 1, 2011.

§ 7065.2. Waiver of examination

Notwithstanding Section 7065, the registrar may waive the examination for a contractor's license if the applicant has previously held a valid contractor's license in this state and has been acting in the capacity of a contractor for the United States government in a position exempt from licensure under this chapter.

Added Stats 1987 ch 630 § 1.

§ 7065.3. Additional classification without examination under specified conditions

Notwithstanding Section 7065, upon a conclusive showing by a licensee that he or she possesses experience satisfactory to the registrar in the classification applied for, an additional classification may be added, without further examination, under all of the following conditions:

(a) For five of the seven years immediately preceding the application, the qualifying individual of the licensee has been listed as a member of the personnel of any licensee whose license was active and in good standing, and who during the period listed on a license was actively engaged in the licensee's construction activities.

(b) The qualifying individual for the applicant has had within the last 10 years immediately preceding the filing of the application, not less than four years experience as a journeyman, foreman, supervising employee, or contractor in the classification within which the licensee intends to engage in the additional classification as a contractor.

(c) The application is, as determined by the registrar, for a classification that is closely related to the classification or classifications in which the licensee is licensed, or the qualifying individual is associated with a licensed general engineering contractor or licensed general building contractor and is applying for a classification that is a significant component of the licensed contractor's construction business as determined by the registrar. This section shall not apply to an applicant who is licensed solely within the limited-specialty classifications.

Pursuant to Section 7065, the registrar shall conduct a comprehensive investigation of no less than 3 percent of applications filed under this section to ensure that the applicants met the experience requirements of this section.

Added Stats 1990 ch 1456 § 3 (SB 2476). Amended Stats 2013 ch 319 § 7 (SB 822), effective January 1, 2014.

§ 7065.4. Reciprocity

The registrar may accept the qualifications of an applicant who is licensed as a contractor in a similar classification in another state if that state accepts the qualifications of a contractor licensed in this state for purposes of licensure in that other state, and if the board ascertains, on a case-by-case basis, that the professional qualifications and conditions of good standing for licensure and continued licensure are at least the same or greater in that state as in California. The registrar may waive the trade examination for that applicant if the applicant provides written certification from that other state in which he or she is licensed, that the applicant's license has been in good standing for the previous five years.

Added Stats 1990 ch 1326 § 2 (AB 3480), effective September 25, 1990.

§ 7065.5. Minor not to be licensed unless guardian appointed

No license shall be issued to a minor, nor to any partnership a partner of which is a minor, nor to any corporation any officer, director or responsible managing employee of which is a minor, nor to any limited liability company any officer, manager, or responsible managing employee of which is a minor, nor to any other kind of business organization in which a minor holds a responsible official position, unless the minor shall first have had a guardian appointed by a court of competent jurisdiction.

Added Stats 1941 ch 971 § 10. Amended Stats 2010 ch 698 § 7 (SB 392), effective January 1, 2011.

§ 7066. Application; Form and contents; Fee

To obtain an original license, an applicant shall submit to the registrar an application in writing containing the statement that the applicant desires the issuance of a license under the terms of this chapter.

The application shall be made on a form prescribed by the registrar in accordance with the rules and regulations adopted by the board and shall be accompanied by the fee fixed by this chapter.

Added Stats 1939 ch 37 § 1.

§ 7066.5. Blank forms

Any person may obtain blank license application forms from the board or may cause to be printed forms used by or approved by the Registrar of Contractors.

Added Stats 1984 ch 1252 § 1. Amended Stats 2011 ch 432 § 13 (SB 944), effective January 1, 2012.

§ 7067.5. [Section repealed 2016.]

Added Stats 1965 ch 636 § 1. Amended Stats 1969 ch 735 § 1; Stats 1974 ch 435 § 1; Stats 1979 ch 1013 § 6. Repealed Stats 2015 ch 656 § 8 (SB 467), effective January 1, 2016. The repealed section related to financial solvency, requirements to license applicants, and financial statements of licensees.

§ 7067.6. Application form; Signatures required

(a) Every application form for an original license, for renewal thereof, for reinstatement or for reissuance, including both active and inactive licenses, shall be signed by both the applicant and by the person qualifying on behalf of an individual or firm as referred to in Section 7068.1.

(b) (1) Notwithstanding any other law, the board may implement a system that provides for the electronic transmission of an application described in subdivision (a) and the acceptance of a digital or electronic signature as part of the filing of those applications.

(2) The board by regulation may specify the form and manner of these transmissions and acceptances, including, but not limited to, the adoption of any protocols necessary to ensure the validity and security of any information, signature, data, or document transmitted electronically or digitally. Upon the effective date of the regulations, the electronic submission of an initial license application or a renewal application, including a digital or electronic signature, shall satisfy the requirements of this article.

Added Stats 1963 ch 1016 § 1. Amended Stats 2015 ch 281 § 1 (SB 561), effective January 1, 2016.

§ 7068. Qualifications

(a) The board shall require an applicant to show the degree of knowledge and experience in the classification applied for, and the general knowledge of the building, safety, health, and lien laws of the state and of the administrative principles of the contracting business that the board deems necessary for the safety and protection of the public.

(b) An applicant shall qualify in regard to their experience and knowledge in one of the following ways:

(1) If an individual, they shall qualify by personal appearance or by the appearance of their responsible managing employee who is qualified for the same license classification as the classification being applied for.

(2) If a partnership or a limited partnership, it shall qualify by the appearance of a general partner or by the appearance of a responsible managing employee who is qualified for the same license classification as the classification being applied for.

(3) If a corporation, or any other combination or organization, it shall qualify by the appearance of a responsible managing officer or responsible managing employee who is qualified for the same license classification as the classification being applied for.

(4) If a limited liability company, it shall qualify by the appearance of a responsible managing officer, a responsible managing manager, responsible managing member, or a responsible managing employee who is qualified for the same license classification as the classification being applied for.

(c) (1) For purposes of this chapter, "a responsible managing employee" means an individual who is a bona fide employee of the applicant and is actively engaged in the classification of work for which that responsible managing employee is the qualifying person on behalf of the applicant.

(2) For purposes of this subdivision, the following definitions apply:

(A) "Bona fide employee of the applicant" means an employee who is permanently employed by the applicant.

(B) "Actively engaged" means working 32 hours per week, or 80 percent of the total hours per week that the applicant's business is in operation, whichever is less.

(d) The board shall, in addition, require an applicant who qualifies by means of a responsible managing employee under either paragraph (1) or (2) of subdivision (b) to show their general knowledge of the building, safety, health, and lien laws of the state and of the administrative principles

of the contracting business as the board deems necessary for the safety and protection of the public.

(e) Except in accordance with Section 7068.1, no person qualifying on behalf of an individual or firm under paragraph (1), (2), (3), or (4) of subdivision (b) shall hold any other active contractor's license while acting in the capacity of a qualifying individual pursuant to this section.

(f) At the time of application for renewal of a license, the current qualifying individual shall file a statement with the registrar, on a form prescribed by the registrar, verifying their capacity as a qualifying individual to the licensee.

(g) Statements made by or on behalf of an applicant as to the applicant's experience in the classification applied for shall be verified by a qualified and responsible person. In addition, the registrar shall, as specified by board regulation, randomly review a percentage of such statements for their veracity.

(h) The registrar shall review experience gained by applicants from other states to determine whether all of that experience was gained in a lawful manner in that state.

Added Stats 1939 ch 37 § 1. Amended Stats 1941 ch 971 § 11; Stats 1957 ch 720 § 1; Stats 1959 ch 407 § 1; Stats 1963 ch 1017 § 1; Stats 1967 ch 1368 § 1; Stats 1979 ch 1013 § 7; Stats 1980 ch 138 § 2, effective May 30, 1980; Stats 1986 ch 995 § 4; Stats 1989 ch 1174 § 2; Stats 1991 ch 1160 § 28 (AB 2190); Stats 2004 ch 865 § 9 (SB 1914); Stats 2010 ch 698 § 8 (SB 392), effective January 1, 2011; Stats 2021 ch 376 § 5 (AB 830), effective September 28, 2021.

—See Unemployment Code Section 1095, Permissible Uses for EDD Data, in Appendix.

§ 7068.1. Duty of individual qualifying on behalf of another; Acting as qualifying individual for additional person or firm; Violation as cause for disciplinary action and misdemeanor

(a) The person qualifying on behalf of an individual or firm under paragraph (1), (2), (3), or (4) of subdivision (b) of Section 7068 shall be responsible for exercising supervision and control of their employer's or principal's construction operations to secure compliance with this chapter and the rules and regulations of the board. This person shall not act in the capacity of the qualifying person for an additional individual or firm unless one of the following conditions exists:

(1) There is a common ownership of at least 20 percent of the equity of each individual or firm for which the person acts in a qualifying capacity.

(2) The additional firm is a subsidiary of or a joint venture with the first. "Subsidiary," as used in this subdivision, means any firm at least 20 percent of the equity of which is owned by the other firm.

(3) With respect to a firm under paragraph (2), (3), or (4) of subdivision (b) of Section 7068, the majority of the partners, officers, or managers are the same.

(b) Notwithstanding paragraphs (1) to (3), inclusive, of subdivision (a), a qualifying individual may act as the qualifier for no more than three firms in any one-year period.

(c) The following definitions shall apply for purposes of this section:

(1) "Firm" means a partnership, a limited partnership, a corporation, a limited liability company, or any other combination or organization described in Section 7068.

(2) "Person" is limited to natural persons, notwithstanding the definition of "person" in Section 7025.

(3) "Supervision or control" means direct supervision or control or monitoring and being available to assist others to whom direct supervision and control has been delegated.

(4) "Direct supervision or control" means any of the following:

(A) Supervising construction.

(B) Managing construction activities by making technical and administrative decisions.

(C) Checking jobs for proper workmanship.

(D) Supervision on construction sites.

(d) The board shall require every applicant or licensee qualifying by the appearance of a qualifying individual to submit detailed information on the qualifying individual's duties and responsibilities for supervision and control of the applicant's construction operations, including, but not limited to, an employment duty statement prepared by the qualifier's employer or principal. Failure of an applicant or licensee to provide information required by this subdivision constitutes a violation of this section.

(e) Violation of this section shall constitute a cause for disciplinary action and shall be punishable as a misdemeanor by imprisonment in a county jail not to exceed six months, by a fine of not less than three thousand dollars ($3,000), but not to exceed five thousand dollars ($5,000), or by both the fine and imprisonment.

Added Stats 1959 ch 407 § 2. Amended Stats 1961 ch 1777 § 1; Stats 1963 ch 1016 § 2; Stats 1967 ch 1368 § 2; Stats 1979 ch 1013 § 8; Stats 1991 ch 145 § 1 (AB 425); Stats 2006 ch 106 § 2 (AB 2457), effective January 1, 2007; Stats 2010 ch 698 § 9 (SB 392), effective January 1, 2011; Stats 2011 ch 296 § 14 (AB 1023), effective January 1, 2012;

Stats 2013 ch 180 § 1 (SB 262), effective January 1, 2014; Stats 2021 ch 376 § 6 (AB 830), effective September 28, 2021.

§ 7068.2. Disassociation of responsible managing officer; Notice; Replacement; Petition of licensee; Failure to notify registrar

(a) If the responsible managing officer, responsible managing employee, responsible managing member, or responsible managing manager disassociates from the licensed entity, the licensee or the qualifier shall notify the registrar in writing within 90 days after the date of disassociation. The licensee shall have 90 days after the date of disassociation in which to replace the qualifier. Upon failure to replace the qualifier within 90 days after the date of disassociation, the license shall be automatically suspended or the classification removed at the end of the 90 days.

(b) To replace a responsible managing officer, responsible managing employee, responsible managing member, or responsible managing manager, the licensee shall file an application as prescribed by the registrar, accompanied by the fee fixed by this chapter, designating an individual to qualify as required by this chapter.

(c) Upon failure of the licensee or the qualifier to notify the registrar of the disassociation of the qualifier within 90 days after the date of disassociation, the license shall be automatically suspended or the classification removed and the qualifier removed from the license effective the date the written notification is received at the board's headquarters office.

(d) The person qualifying on behalf of a licensee under Section 7068 shall be responsible for the licensee's construction operations until the date of disassociation or the date the board receives the written notification of disassociation, whichever is later.

(e) (1) Upon a showing of good cause by the licensee, the registrar may review and accept a petition for one 90-day extension to replace the qualifier immediately following the initial 90-day period described in subdivision (a) only under one or more of the following circumstances:

(A) If the licensee is disputing the date of disassociation.

(B) If the responsible managing officer, employee, member, or manager has died.

(C) If there has been a delay in processing the application to replace the qualifier that is out of the applicant's control and it is the responsibility of the board or another state or federal agency that is relied upon in the application process.

(2) This petition shall be received within 90 days after the date of disassociation or death or delay. The petition shall only be considered if an application to replace the qualifier as prescribed by the registrar

is on file with the board. Under the circumstances described in sub-paragraphs (A) and (B) of paragraph (1), the licensee shall have no more than a total of 180 days after the date of disassociation or death in which to replace the qualifier.

(f) Failure of the licensee or the qualifier to notify the registrar of the qualifier's disassociation within 90 days after the date of disassociation shall constitute grounds for disciplinary action.

Added Stats 1983 ch 891 § 9. Amended Stats 1984 ch 1174 § 3; Stats 1987 ch 930 § 5, effective September 22, 1987; Stats 2010 ch 698 § 10 (SB 392), effective January 1, 2011; Stats 2011 ch 168 § 1 (AB 1091), effective January 1, 2012; Stats 2012 ch 162 § 2 (SB 1171), effective January 1, 2013.

§ 7068.5. Taking qualifying examination on behalf of applicant for contractor's license; Misdemeanor

It is a misdemeanor for any person other than the examinee named in the application to take the qualifying examination on behalf of an applicant for a contractor's license.

Added Stats 1961 ch 491 § 1.

§ 7068.7. Obtaining examination for another; Misdemeanor

Any person who obtains and provides for another the qualifying examination, or any part thereof, when not authorized to do so, is guilty of a misdemeanor.

Added Stats 1979 ch 1013 § 9.

§ 7069. Grounds for denial of license; Fingerprints of applicants; Criminal history and subsequent arrest information

(a) An applicant, and each officer, director, partner, manager, associate, and responsible managing employee thereof, shall not have committed acts or crimes that are grounds for denial of licensure under Section 480.

(b) As part of an application for a contractor's license, the board shall require an applicant to furnish a full set of fingerprints for purposes of conducting a criminal history record check. Fingerprints furnished pursuant to this subdivision shall be submitted in an electronic format if readily available. Requests for alternative methods of furnishing fingerprints are subject to the approval of the registrar. The board shall use the fingerprints furnished by an applicant to obtain criminal history information on the applicant from the Department of Justice and the United States Federal Bureau of Investigation, and the board may obtain any subsequent arrest information that is available.

Added Stats 1939 ch 37 § 1. Amended Stats 1941 ch 971 § 12; Stats 1955 ch 1547 § 1; Stats 1978 ch 1161 § 362; Stats 2002 ch 744 § 6 (SB 1953); Stats 2003 ch 874 § 20 (SB 363); Stats 2004 ch 909 § 27.3 (SB 136), effective September 30, 2004; Stats 2007 ch 240 § 1 (AB 936), effective January 1, 2008; Stats 2010 ch 698 § 11 (SB 392), effective January 1, 2011.

§ 7069.1. Arrest of licensee or home improvement salesperson

(a) Upon notification of an arrest of a member of the personnel of a licensee or a home improvement salesperson, the registrar, by first-class mail to the last official address of record, may require the arrestee to provide proof of the disposition of the matter.

(b) The proof required by this section shall be satisfactory for carrying out the purposes of this chapter, and at the registrar's discretion may include, but is not limited to, certified court documents, certified court orders, or sentencing documents. Any proof required by this section shall be received by the registrar within 90 days of the date of the disposition, or within 90 days of the registrar's demand for information if that date is later.

(c) Failure to comply with the provisions of this section constitutes cause for disciplinary action.

Added Stats 2004 ch 586 § 1 (AB 2216).

§ 7070. Showing that no license was refused or revoked

An applicant shall show that he or she has never been denied a license or had a license revoked for reasons that would preclude the granting of the license applied for. Where the board has denied an application for license under this chapter or Chapter 2 (commencing with Section 480) of Division 1.5, it shall, in its decision, or in its notice under subdivision (b) of Section 485, inform the applicant of the earliest date that the applicant may reapply for a license, which shall be one year from the effective date of the decision or service of notice under subdivision (b) of Section 485, unless the board prescribes an earlier date.

Added Stats 1939 ch 37 § 1. Amended Stats 1997 ch 334 § 1 (SB 299).

§ 7071. Refusal to corporation, partnership, or limited liability company for member's lack of qualifications

No license shall be issued to a corporation, partnership, limited liability company, or other combination or organization if a responsible officer or director of the corporation, or other combination or organization, or a partner of the partnership, or a manager or officer of the limited liability company, or any member of an organization seeking licensure under this chapter does not meet the qualifications required

Section VI

of an applicant other than those qualifications relating to knowledge and experience.

Added Stats 1939 ch 37 § 1. Amended Stats 1955 ch 1267 § 1; Stats 2010 ch 698 § 12 (SB 392), effective January 1, 2011; Stats 2011 ch 296 § 15 (AB 1023), effective January 1, 2012.

§ 7071.3. Entry into armed forces by licensee; Designation of manager to act for such entrant; Renewal fee and duration of license

Notwithstanding any other provision of this code, the holder of a current valid license under this chapter who has entered or enters the armed forces of the United States may designate a responsible managing person or persons to act for him while in the armed forces and until one year after his discharge therefrom, after which time the authority to so act for the licensee shall terminate. The renewal fee shall be paid for any such licensee so designating others to act for him.

Any license shall remain in full force and effect for 30 days after the entrance of the licensee into the armed forces, but he shall prior to the expiration of such 30-day period provide the registrar with the name or names of the persons so designated to conduct his business. The registrar may qualify such persons in any manner he may adopt. Persons so designated shall not have committed acts or crimes constituting grounds for denial of licensure under Section 480.

Persons so designated committing any of the acts or crimes constituting grounds for denial of licensure under Section 480 shall be removed from the business of such licensee after a hearing as provided in this chapter.

Added Stats 1945 ch 452 § 1, effective May 24, 1945. Amended Stats 1961 ch 1636 § 1, operative October 1, 1962; Stats 1978 ch 1161 § 363.

§ 7071.4. Licensee; Bond

(a) Each person licensed under the provisions of this chapter and subject to any of the bonding provisions of this article shall maintain the requisite bond as executed by an admitted surety insurer or as deposited with the registrar pursuant to paragraph (1) of subdivision (a) of Section 995.710 of the Code of Civil Procedure in the appropriate amount. Notwithstanding Article 7 (commencing with Section 995.710) of Chapter 2 of Title 14 of Part 2 of the Code of Civil Procedure, no other method of deposit, including, but not limited to, a certificate of deposit, shall satisfy a bond requirement under this article.

(b) All existing alternatives in lieu of a bond currently filed with the registrar shall be replaced for a surety bond or the deposit prescribed by paragraph (1) of subdivision (a) of Section 995.710 of the Code of Civil Procedure by January 1, 2020.

(c) (1) If the board is notified, in writing, of a civil action against the deposit authorized under this section, the deposit or any portion thereof shall not be released for any purpose, except as determined by the court.

(2) If any deposit authorized under this section is insufficient to pay, in full, all claims that have been adjudicated under any action filed in accordance with this section, the amount of the deposit shall be distributed to all claimants in proportion to the amount of their respective claims.

(d) Notwithstanding subdivision (a), this section shall not apply to the bond equivalents described in Section 7159.5 of this chapter.

(e) (1) This section shall be operative on and after January 1, 2019, upon which date the registrar shall thereafter no longer accept alternatives in lieu of a bond, other than as provided in this section.

(2) Notwithstanding any other law, in order to comply with the bonding provisions of this article, a person shall only be required to provide information consistent with the requirements for an applicant under Section 30.

(f) All alternatives in lieu of a bond filed with the registrar before January 1, 2019, and any lawful money or cashier's check deposited pursuant to paragraph (1) of subdivision (a) of Section 995.710 of the Code of Civil Procedure after January 1, 2019, shall be subject to the following limitations periods:

(1) Any action, other than an action to recover wages or fringe benefits, against a deposit given in lieu of a contractor's bond or bond of a qualifying individual filed by an active licensee shall be brought within three years after the expiration of the license period during which the act or omission occurred, or within three years of the date the license of the active licensee was inactivated, canceled, or revoked by the board, whichever occurs first.

(2) Any action, other than an action to recover wages or fringe benefits, against a deposit given in lieu of a disciplinary bond filed by an active licensee pursuant to Section 7071.8 shall be brought within three years after the expiration of the license period during which the act or omission occurred, or within three years of the date the license of the active licensee was inactivated, canceled, or revoked by the board, or within three years after the last date for which a deposit given in lieu of a disciplinary bond filed pursuant to Section 7071.8 was required, whichever date is first.

(3) A claim to recover wages or fringe benefits shall be brought within six months from the date that the wage or fringe benefit delinquencies were discovered, but in no event shall a civil action thereon be brought later than two years from the date the wage or fringe benefit contributions were due.

(g) In any case in which a claim is filed against an alternative given in lieu of a bond filed with the registrar before January 1, 2019, or deposited with the registrar pursuant to subdivision (a), by any employee or by an employee organization on behalf of an employee, concerning wages or fringe benefits based upon the employee's employment, claims for the nonpayment shall be filed with the Labor Commissioner. The Labor Commissioner shall, pursuant to the authority vested by Section 96.5 of the Labor Code, conduct hearings to determine whether or not the wages or fringe benefits should be paid to the complainant. Upon a finding by the commissioner that the wages or fringe benefits should be paid to the complainant, the commissioner shall notify the registrar of the findings. The registrar shall not make payment from the deposit on the basis of findings by the commissioner for a period of 10 days following determination of the findings. If, within the period, the complainant or the contractor files written notice with the registrar and the commissioner of an intention to seek judicial review of the findings pursuant to Section 11523 of the Government Code, the registrar shall not make payment if an action is actually filed, except as determined by the court. If, thereafter, no action is filed within 60 days following determination of findings by the commissioner, the registrar shall make payment from the deposit to the complainant.

(h) Legal fees may not be charged by the board against any alternative given in lieu of a bond filed with the registrar before January 1, 2019, or deposited with the registrar pursuant to subdivision (a).

Added Stats 2018 ch 925 § 1 (AB 3126), effective January 1, 2019. Amended Stats 2020 ch 312 § 58 (SB 1474), effective January 1, 2021.

§ 7071.5. Contractor's bond

The contractor's bond required by this article shall be executed by an admitted surety in favor of the State of California, in a form acceptable to the registrar and filed with the registrar by the licensee or applicant. The contractor's bond shall be for the benefit of the following:

(a) A homeowner contracting for home improvement upon the homeowner's personal family residence damaged as a result of a violation of this chapter by the licensee.

(b) A property owner contracting for the construction of a single-family dwelling who is damaged as a result of a violation of this chapter by the licensee. That property owner shall only recover under this subdivision if the single-family dwelling is not intended for sale or offered for sale at the time the damages were incurred.

(c) A person damaged as a result of a willful and deliberate violation of this chapter by the licensee, or by the fraud of the licensee in the execution or performance of a construction contract.

(d) An employee of the licensee damaged by the licensee's failure to pay wages.

(e) A person or entity, including a laborer described in subdivision (b) of Section 8024 of the Civil Code, to which a portion of the compensation of an employee of a licensee is paid by agreement with that employee or the collective bargaining agent of that employee, damaged as the result of the licensee's failure to pay fringe benefits for its employees, including, but not limited to, employer payments described in Section 1773.1 of the Labor Code and regulations thereunder (without regard to whether the work was performed on a private or public work). Damage to a person or entity under this subdivision is limited to actual employer payments required to be made on behalf of employees of the licensee, as part of the overall compensation of those employees, which the licensee fails to pay.

Added Stats 1967 ch 1604 § 6, operative July 1, 1969. Amended Stats 1979 ch 1013 § 10, ch 1138 § 1.5; Stats 1980 ch 27 § 1.5, effective March 5, 1980; Stats 1982 ch 517 § 18; Stats 1999 ch 795 § 1 (SB 914); Stats 2008 ch 157 § 1 (SB 1432), effective January 1, 2009; Stats 2010 ch 697 § 2 (SB 189), effective January 1, 2011, operative July 1, 2012.

—*See Code of Civil Procedure, Bond and Undertaking Law Sections 995.010 to 996.560 in Appendix.*

§ 7071.6. [Section repealed 2023]

Added Stats 2002 ch 1123 § 2 (SB 1919), operative January 1, 2004. Amended Stats 2005 ch 280 § 4 (SB 1112), effective January 1, 2006; Stats 2007 ch 354 § 16 (SB 1047), effective January 1, 2008; Stats 2015 ch 656 § 9 (SB 467), effective January 1, 2016; Stats 2019 ch 378 § 6 (SB 610), effective January 1, 2020; Stats 2021 ch 367 § 16 (SB 607), repealed January 1, 2023.

§ 7071.6. Bond as condition precedent to license [Operative January 1, 2023]

(a) The board shall require as a condition precedent to the issuance, reinstatement, reactivation, renewal, or continued maintenance of a license, that the applicant or licensee file or have on file a contractor's bond in the sum of twenty-five thousand dollars ($25,000).

(b) Excluding the claims brought by the beneficiaries specified in subdivision (a) of Section 7071.5, the aggregate liability of a surety on claims brought against a bond required by this section shall not exceed the sum of seven thousand five hundred dollars ($7,500). The bond proceeds in excess of seven thousand five hundred dollars ($7,500) shall be reserved exclusively for the claims of the beneficiaries specified in subdivision (a) of Section 7071.5. However, nothing in this section shall be construed so as to prevent any beneficiary specified in subdivision (a) of Section 7071.5 from claiming or recovering the full measure of the bond required by this section.

Section VI

(c) A bond shall not be required of a holder of a license that has been inactivated on the official records of the board during the period the license is inactive.

(d) Notwithstanding any other law, as a condition precedent to licensure, the board may require an applicant to post a contractor's bond in twice the amount required pursuant to subdivision (a) until the time that the license is renewed, under the following conditions:

(1) The applicant has either been convicted of a violation of Section 7028 or has been cited pursuant to Section 7028.7.

(2) If the applicant has been cited pursuant to Section 7028.7, the citation has been reduced to a final order of the registrar.

(3) The violation of Section 7028, or the basis for the citation issued pursuant to Section 7028.7, constituted a substantial injury to the public.

(e) This section shall become operative on January 1, 2023.

Added Stats 2002 ch 1123 § 2 (SB 1919), operative January 1, 2004. Amended Stats 2005 ch 280 § 4 (SB 1112), effective January 1, 2006; Stats 2007 ch 354 § 16 (SB 1047), effective January 1, 2008; Stats 2015 ch 656 § 9 (SB 467), effective January 1, 2016; Stats 2019 ch 378 § 6 (SB 610), effective January 1, 2020; Stats 2021 ch 367 § 16 (SB 607), repealed January 1, 2023; Stats 2021 ch 367 § 16 (SB 607), operative January 1, 2023.

§ 7071.6.5. Surety bond as condition precedent to license

(a) The board shall require, as a condition precedent to the issuance, reissuance, reinstatement, reactivation, renewal, or continued valid use of a limited liability company license, that the applicant or licensee file or have on file a surety bond in the sum of one hundred thousand dollars ($100,000).

(b) The bond required by this section shall be executed by an admitted surety in favor of the State of California, in a form acceptable to the registrar and filed with the registrar, electronically or otherwise, by the applicant or licensee.

(c) The bond required by this section shall be for the benefit of any employee damaged by his or her employer's failure to pay wages, interest on wages, or fringe benefits and is intended to serve as an additional safeguard for workers employed by or contracted to work for a limited liability company.

(d) If an applicant or licensee subject to subdivision (a) is also a party to a collective bargaining agreement, the bond required by this section shall also cover, in addition to the coverage described in subdivision (c), welfare fund contributions, pension fund contributions, and apprentice program contributions.

(e) The bond required by this section shall not be applicable to a licensee whose license has been inactivated on the official records of the board during the period the license is inactive.

Added Stats 2010 ch 698 § 13 (SB 392), effective January 1, 2011.

§ 7071.7. Acceptance of bond as of effective date; Retroactive reinstatement of license

(a) Except as provided in subdivision (b), the registrar shall accept a bond required by Section 7071.6, 7071.6.5, 7071.8, or 7071.9 as of the effective date shown on the bond, if the bond is received by the registrar within 90 days after that date, and shall reinstate the license to which the bond pertains, if otherwise eligible, retroactive to the effective date of the bond.

(b) Notwithstanding subdivision (a), the registrar shall accept a bond as of the effective date shown on the bond, even if the bond is not received by the registrar within 90 days after that date, upon a showing by the licensee, on a form acceptable to the registrar, that the failure to have a bond on file was due to circumstances beyond the control of the licensee. The registrar shall reinstate the license to which the bond pertains, if otherwise eligible, retroactive to the effective date of the bond.

Added Stats 1986 ch 27 § 2. Amended Stats 2010 ch 698 § 14 (SB 392), effective January 1, 2011.

§ 7071.8. [Section repealed 2023]

Added 1941 ch 882 § 1, as B & P C § 7071.5. Amended Stats 1961 ch 1125 § 1; Stats 1963 ch 1972 § 1; Stats 1965 ch 1022 § 1, ch 1025 § 1. Amended and renumbered Stats 1967 ch 1604 § 1, operative July 1, 1969. Amended Stats 1968 ch 482 § 2, operative July 1, 1969; Stats 1974 ch 434 § 2; Stats 1982 ch 517 § 20; Stats 1986 ch 79 § 1; Stats 1992 ch 294 § 2 (AB 2347); Stats 1994 ch 192 § 1 (AB 3475); Stats 2010 ch 698 § 15 (SB 392), effective January 1, 2011; Stats 2021 ch 367 § 18 (SB 607), repealed effective January 1, 2023.

§ 7071.8. Bond required for restoration of suspended or revoked license [Operative January 1, 2023]

(a) This section applies to an application for a license, for renewal or restoration of a license, an application to change officers or members of a corporation or a limited liability company, or for continued valid use of a license which has been disciplined, whether or not the disciplinary action has been stayed, made by any of the following persons or firms:

(1) A person whose license has been suspended or revoked as a result of disciplinary action, or a person who was a qualifying individual for a licensee at any time during which cause for disciplinary action occurred resulting in suspension or revocation of the licensee's license, whether or not the qualifying individual had knowledge or participated in the prohibited act or omission.

(2) A person who was an officer, director, manager, partner, or member of the personnel of record of a licensee at any time during which cause for disciplinary action occurred resulting in suspension or revocation of the licensee's license and who had knowledge of or participated in the act or omission which was the cause for the disciplinary action.

(3) A partnership, corporation, limited liability company, firm, or association of which an existing or new officer, director, manager, partner, qualifying person, or member of the personnel of record has had a license suspended or revoked as a result of disciplinary action.

(4) A partnership, corporation, limited liability company, firm, or association of which a member of the personnel of record, including, but not limited to, an officer, director, manager, partner, or qualifying person was, likewise, a manager, officer, director, or partner of a licensee at any time during which cause for disciplinary action occurred resulting in suspension or revocation of the license, and who had knowledge of or participated in the act or omission which was the cause for the disciplinary action.

(b) The board shall require as a condition precedent to the issuance, reissuance, renewal, or restoration of a license to the applicant, or to the approval of an application to change officers of a corporation or a limited liability company, or removal of suspension, or to the continued valid use of a license which has been suspended or revoked, but which suspension or revocation has been stayed, that the applicant or licensee file or have on file a contractor's bond in a sum to be fixed by the registrar based upon the seriousness of the violation, but which sum shall not be less than twenty-five thousand dollars ($25,000) nor more than 10 times that amount required by Section 7071.6.

(c) The bond is in addition to, may not be combined with, and does not replace any other type of bond required by this chapter. The bond shall remain on file with the registrar for a period of at least two years and for any additional time that the registrar determines. The bond period shall run only while the license is current, active, and in good standing, and shall be extended until the license has been current, active, and in good standing for the required period. Each applicant or licensee shall be required to file only one disciplinary contractor's bond of the type described in this section for each application or license subject to this bond requirement.

(d) This section shall become operative on January 1, 2023.

Added 1941 ch 882 § 1, as B & P C § 7071.5. Amended Stats 1961 ch 1125 § 1; Stats 1963 ch 1972 § 1; Stats 1965 ch 1022 § 1, ch 1025 § 1. Amended and renumbered Stats 1967 ch 1604 § 1, operative July 1, 1969. Amended Stats 1968 ch 482 § 2, operative July 1, 1969; Stats 1974 ch 434 § 2; Stats 1982 ch 517 § 20; Stats 1986 ch 79 § 1; Stats 1992 ch 294 § 2 (AB 2347); Stats 1994 ch 192 § 1 (AB 3475); Stats 2010 ch 698 § 15 (SB 392), effective January 1, 2011; Stats 2021 ch 367 § 18 (SB 607), repealed effective January 1, 2023; Stats 2021 ch 367 § 18 (SB 607), operative January 1, 2023.

§ 7071.9. [Section repealed 2023]

Added Stats 1967 ch 1604 § 7, operative July 1, 1970. Amended Stats 1968 ch 482 § 3, operative July 1, 1970; Stats 1971 ch 669 § 2; Stats 1972 ch 7 § 2, effective February 29, 1972, operative March 4, 1972; Stats 1973 ch 319 § 36, Stats 1979 ch 1013 § 12; Stats 1980 ch 27 § 3, effective March 5, 1980; Stats 1982 ch 517 § 21; Stats 1986 ch 27 § 3; Stats 1993 ch 1264 § 6.4 (SB 574); Stats 2004 ch 865 § 10 (SB 1914); Stats 2007 ch 354 § 17 (SB 1047), effective January 1, 2008; Stats 2010 ch 698 § 16 (SB 392), effective January 1, 2011; Stat. 2021 ch 367 § 20 (SB 607) Repealed January 1, 2023.

§ 7071.9. Requirement of qualifying individual's bond as condition precedent to license [Operative January 1, 2023]

(a) If the qualifying individual, as referred to in Sections 7068 and 7068.1, is neither the proprietor, a general partner, nor a joint licensee, the qualifying individual shall file or have on file a qualifying individual's bond as provided in Section 7071.10 in the sum of twenty-five thousand dollars ($25,000). This bond is in addition to, and shall not be combined with, any contractor's bond required by Sections 7071.5 to 7071.8, inclusive, and is required for the issuance, reinstatement, reactivation, or continued valid use of a license.

(b) Excluding the claims brought by the beneficiaries specified in paragraph (1) of subdivision (a) of Section 7071.10, the aggregate liability of a surety on claims brought against the bond required by this section shall not exceed the sum of seven thousand five hundred dollars ($7,500). The bond proceeds in excess of seven thousand five hundred dollars ($7,500) shall be reserved exclusively for the claims of the beneficiaries specified in paragraph (1) of subdivision (a) of Section 7071.10. However, nothing in this section shall be construed to prevent any beneficiary specified in paragraph (1) of subdivision (a) of Section 7071.10 from claiming or recovering the full measure of the bond required by this section. This bond is in addition to, and shall not be combined with, any contractor's bond required by Sections 7071.5 to 7071.8, inclusive, and is required for the issuance, reinstatement, reactivation, or continued valid use of a license.

(c) The responsible managing officer of a corporation shall not be required to file or have on file a qualifying individual's bond, if the responsible managing officer owns 10 percent or more of the voting stock of the corporation and certifies to that fact on a form prescribed by the registrar.

(d) The qualifying individual for a limited liability company shall not be required to file or have on file a qualifying individual's bond if the qualifying individual owns at least a 10-percent membership interest in the limited liability company and certifies to that fact on a form prescribed by the registrar.

(e) This section shall become operative on January 1, 2023.

Added Stats 1967 ch 1604 § 7, operative July 1, 1970. Amended Stats 1968 ch 482 § 3, operative July 1, 1970; Stats 1971 ch 669 § 2; Stats 1972 ch 7 § 2, effective February 29, 1972, operative March 4, 1972; Stats 1973 ch 319 § 36, Stats 1979 ch 1013 § 12; Stats 1980 ch 27 § 3, effective March 5, 1980; Stats 1982 ch 517 § 21; Stats 1986 ch 27 § 3; Stats 1993 ch 1264 § 6.4 (SB 574); Stats 2004 ch 865 § 10 (SB 1914); Stats 2007 ch 354 § 17 (SB 1047), effective January 1, 2008; Stats 2010 ch 698 § 16 (SB 392), effective January 1, 2011; Stat. 2021 ch 367 § 20 (SB 607) Repealed January 1, 2023; Stat. 2021 ch 367 § 21 (SB 607) Operative January 1, 2023.

§ 7071.10. Qualifying individual's bond

The qualifying individual's bond required by this article shall be executed by an admitted surety insurer in favor of the State of California, in a form acceptable to the registrar and filed with the registrar by the qualifying individual. The qualifying individual's bond shall not be required in addition to the contractor's bond when, as set forth under paragraph (1) of subdivision (b) of Section 7068, the individual proprietor has qualified for the license by his or her personal appearance, or the qualifier is a general partner as set forth under paragraph (2) of subdivision (b) of Section 7068. The qualifying individual's bond shall be for the benefit of the following persons:

(a) A homeowner contracting for home improvement upon the homeowner's personal family residence damaged as a result of a violation of this chapter by the licensee.

(b) A property owner contracting for the construction of a single-family dwelling who is damaged as a result of a violation of this chapter by the licensee. That property owner shall only recover under this subdivision if the single-family dwelling is not intended for sale or offered for sale at the time the damages were incurred.

(c) A person damaged as a result of a willful and deliberate violation of this chapter by the licensee, or by the fraud of the licensee in the execution or performance of a construction contract.

(d) An employee of the licensee damaged by the licensee's failure to pay wages.

(e) A person or entity, including a laborer described in subdivision (b) of Section 8024 of the Civil Code, to which a portion of the compensation of an employee of a licensee is paid by agreement with that employee or the collective bargaining agent of that employee, that is damaged as the result of the licensee's failure to pay fringe benefits for its employees including, but not limited to, employer payments described in Section 1773.1 of the Labor Code and regulations adopted thereunder (without regard to whether the work was performed on a public or private work). Damage to a person or entity under this subdivision is limited to employer payments required to be made on behalf of employees of the licensee, as part of the overall compensation of those employees, which the licensee fails to pay.

Added Stats 1967 ch 1604 § 8, operative July 1, 1969. Amended Stats 1968 ch 482 § 4, operative July 1, 1969; Stats 1979 ch 1013 § 13, ch 1138 § 2.5; Stats 1982 ch 517 § 22; Stats 1999 ch 795 § 2 (SB 914); Stats 2008 ch 157 § 2 (SB 1432), effective January 1, 2009; Stats 2010 ch 697 § 3 (SB 189), effective January 1, 2011, operative July 1, 2012.

§ 7071.11. Aggregate liability of surety on claim for wages and benefits; Renewal of license contingent on satisfaction of claims and debts; Limitations periods; Notice of payment; Protest of settlement; Accord; Legal fees not to be charged

(a) The aggregate liability of a surety on a claim for wages and fringe benefits brought against a bond required by this article, other than a bond required by Section 7071.8, shall not exceed the sum of four thousand dollars ($4,000). If a bond required by this article is insufficient to pay all claims in full, the sum of the bond shall be distributed to all claimants in proportion to the amount of their respective claims.

(b) No license may be renewed, reissued, or reinstated while a judgment or admitted claim in excess of the amount of the bond remains unsatisfied.

(c) Except for claims covered by subdivision (d), any action against a bond required under this article, excluding the judgment bond specified under Section 7071.17, shall be brought in accordance with the following:

(1) Within two years after the expiration of the license period during which the act or omission occurred. The provisions of this paragraph shall be applicable only if the license has not been inactivated, canceled, or revoked during the license period for which the bond was posted and accepted by the registrar as specified under Section 7071.7.

(2) If the license has been inactivated, canceled, or revoked, an action shall be brought within two years of the date the license of the active licensee would have expired had the license not been inactivated, canceled, or revoked. For the provisions of this paragraph to be applicable, the act or omission for which the action is filed must have occurred prior to the date the license was inactivated, canceled, or revoked.

(3) An action against a disciplinary bond filed by an active licensee pursuant to Section 7071.8 shall be brought in accordance with the provisions of paragraph (1) or (2), as applicable, or within two years after the last date for which a disciplinary bond filed pursuant to Section 7071.8 was required, whichever date is first.

(d) A claim to recover wages or fringe benefits shall be brought within six months from the date that the wage or fringe benefit delinquencies were discovered, but in no event shall a civil action thereon be brought later than two years from the date the wage or fringe benefit contributions were due.

(e) Whenever the surety makes payment on a claim against a bond required by this article, whether or not payment is made through a court action or otherwise, the surety shall, within 30 days of the payment, provide notice to the registrar. The notice required by this subdivision shall provide the following information by declaration on a form prescribed by the registrar:

(1) The name and license number of the contractor.

(2) The surety bond number.

(3) The amount of payment.

(4) The statutory basis upon which the claim is made.

(5) The names of the person or persons to whom payments have been made.

(6) Whether or not the payments were the result of a good faith action by the surety.

The notice shall also clearly indicate whether or not the licensee filed a protest in accordance with this section.

(f) Prior to the settlement of a claim through a good faith payment by the surety, a licensee shall have not less than 15 days in which to provide a written protest. This protest shall instruct the surety not to make payment from the bond on the licensee's account upon the specific grounds that the claim is opposed by the licensee, and provide the surety a specific and reasonable basis for the licensee's opposition to payment.

(1) Whenever a licensee files a protest in accordance with this subdivision, the board shall investigate the matter and file disciplinary action as set forth under this chapter if there is evidence that the surety has sustained a loss as the result of a good faith payment made for the purpose of mitigating any damages incurred by any person or entity covered under Section 7071.5.

(2) A licensee that fails to file a protest as specified in this subdivision shall have 90 days from the date of notification by the board to submit proof of payment of the actual amount owed to the surety and, if applicable, proof of payment of any judgment or admitted claim in excess of the amount of the bond or, by operation of law, the license shall be suspended at the end of the 90 days. A license suspension pursuant to this subdivision shall be disclosed indefinitely as a failure to settle outstanding final liabilities in violation of this chapter. The disclosure specified by this subdivision shall also be applicable to all licenses covered by the provisions of subdivision (g).

(g) During any period in which a surety remains unreimbursed for a loss or expense sustained on a bond issued pursuant to this article, the license for which the bond was issued, and any other license on which any member of the licensee's personnel of record has also been listed, may not be renewed, reissued, or reinstated while the licensee was subject to suspension or disciplinary action under this section.

(h) The licensee may provide the board with a notarized copy of an accord, reached with the surety to satisfy the debt in lieu of full payment. By operation of law, failure to abide by the accord shall result in the automatic suspension of a license to which this section applies. A license that is suspended for failure to abide by the accord may only be renewed or reinstated when proof of satisfaction of all debts is made.

(i) Legal fees may not be charged against the bond by the board.

Added Stats 1963 ch 1972 § 2, as B & P C § 7071.6. Amended Stats 1965 ch 1022 § 2. Amended and renumbered by Stats 1967 ch 1604 § 2, operative July 1, 1969. Amended Stats 1968 ch 482 § 5, operative July 1, 1969; Stats 1972 ch 7 § 3, effective February 29, 1972, operative March 4, 1972; Stats 1974 ch 201 § 1; Stats 1977 ch 280 § 1, effective July 7, 1977; Stats 1979 ch 1013 § 14, ch 1138 § 3.5; Stats 1980 ch 27 § 3.5, effective March 5, 1980; Stats 1982 ch 517 § 23; Stats 1986 ch 1353 § 1, operative July 1, 1987; Stats 1990 ch 1326 § 3 (AB 3480), effective September 25, 1990; Stats 1993 ch 1264 § 7 (SB 574); Stats 1999 ch 795 § 3 (SB 914); Stats 2001 ch 728 § 58 (SB 724); Stats 2002 ch 311 § 3 (AB 264); Stats 2004 ch 865 § 11 (SB 1914); Stats 2005 ch 280 § 5 (SB 1112), effective January 1, 2006; Stats 2008 ch 157 § 3 (SB 1432), effective January 1, 2009; Stats 2010 ch 698 § 17 (SB 392), effective January 1, 2011.

—See Code of Civil Procedure, Bond and Undertaking Law Sections 995.010 to 996.560 in Appendix.

§ 7071.12. [Section repealed 2019.]

Added Stats 1982 ch 517 § 24.5. Amended Stats 2005 ch 280 § 6 (SB 1112), effective January 1, 2006. Repealed Stats 2018 ch 925 § 2 (AB 3126), effective January 1, 2019.

§ 7071.13. Reference to bond in advertising, soliciting, or other presentments as ground for suspension of license

Any reference by a contractor in his advertising, soliciting, or other presentments to the public to any bond required to be filed pursuant to this chapter is a ground for the suspension of the license of such contractor.

Added Stats 1963 ch 1972 § 4, as B & P C § 7071.8. Renumbered Stats 1967 ch 1604 § 4, operative July 1, 1969.

§ 7071.14. Prohibited discrimination in denying license bond; Liability for damages

No licensee or applicant for a license under this chapter shall be denied a contractor's license bond solely because of his race, religious creed, color, national origin, ancestry, or sex. Whoever denies a contractor's license bond solely on the grounds specified herein is liable for each and every such offense for the actual damages, and two hundred fifty dollars ($250) in addition thereto, suffered by the licensee or applicant for a license.

Added Stats 1971 ch 669 § 4.

§ 7071.15. Revocation or suspension of license for failure to maintain bond

If a licensee fails to maintain a sufficient bond required by this article, the license is subject to suspension or revocation pursuant to Section 996.020 of the Code of Civil Procedure.

Added Stats 1983 ch 18 § 1.5, effective April 21, 1983.

§ 7071.17. Bond required where applicant or licensee has unsatisfied final judgment for failure to pay contractor, subcontractor, consumer, materials supplier, or employee; Notice of unsatisfied final judgments; Suspension for noncompliance; Reinstatement; Disqualification from serving as personnel of record for other licensee; Disciplinary action

(a) Notwithstanding any other provision of law, the board shall require, as a condition precedent to accepting an application for licensure, renewal, reinstatement, or to change officers or other personnel of record, that an applicant, previously found to have failed or refused to pay a contractor, subcontractor, consumer, materials supplier, or employee based on an unsatisfied final judgment, file or have on file with the board a bond sufficient to guarantee payment of an amount equal to the unsatisfied final judgment or judgments. The applicant shall have 90 days from the date of notification by the board to file the bond or the application shall become void and the applicant shall reapply for issuance, reinstatement, or reactivation of a license. The board may not issue, reinstate, or reactivate a license until the bond is filed with the board. The bond required by this section is in addition to the contractor's bond. The bond shall be on file for a minimum of one year, after which the bond may be removed by submitting proof of satisfaction of all debts. The applicant may provide the board with a notarized copy of any accord, reached with any individual holding an unsatisfied final judgment, to satisfy a debt in lieu of filing the bond. The board shall include on the license application for issuance, reinstatement, or reactivation, a statement, to be made under penalty of perjury, as to whether there are any unsatisfied judgments against the applicant on behalf of contractors, subcontractors, consumers, materials suppliers, or the applicant's employees. Notwithstanding any other provision of law, if it is found that the applicant falsified the statement then the license will be retroactively suspended to the date of issuance and the license will stay suspended until the bond, satisfaction of judgment, or notarized copy of any accord applicable under this section is filed.

(b) (1) Notwithstanding any other provision of law, all licensees shall notify the registrar in writing of any unsatisfied final judgment imposed on the licensee. If the licensee fails to notify the registrar in writing within 90 days, the license shall be automatically suspended on the date that the registrar is informed, or is made aware of the unsatisfied final judgment.

(2) The suspension shall not be removed until proof of satisfaction of the judgment, or in lieu thereof, a notarized copy of an accord is submitted to the registrar.

(3) If the licensee notifies the registrar in writing within 90 days of the imposition of any unsatisfied final judgment, the licensee shall, as a condition to the continual maintenance of the license, file or have on file with the board a bond sufficient to guarantee payment of an amount equal to all unsatisfied judgments applicable under this section.

(4) The licensee has 90 days from the date of notification by the board to file the bond or at the end of the 90 days the license shall be automatically suspended. In lieu of filing the bond required by this section, the licensee may provide the board with a notarized copy of any accord reached with any individual holding an unsatisfied final judgment.

(c) By operation of law, failure to maintain the bond or failure to abide by the accord shall result in the automatic suspension of any license to which this section applies.

(d) A license that is suspended for failure to comply with the provisions of this section can only be reinstated when proof of satisfaction of all debts is made, or when a notarized copy of an accord has been filed as set forth under this section.

(e) This section applies only with respect to an unsatisfied final judgment that is substantially related to the construction activities of a licensee licensed under this chapter, or to the qualifications, functions, or duties of the license.

(f) Except as otherwise provided, this section does not apply to an applicant or licensee when the financial obligation covered by this section has been discharged in a bankruptcy proceeding.

(g) Except as otherwise provided, the bond shall remain in full force in the amount posted until the entire debt is satisfied. If, at the time of renewal, the licensee submits proof of partial satisfaction of the financial obligations covered by this section, the board may authorize the bond to be reduced to the amount of the unsatisfied portion of the outstanding judgment. When the licensee submits proof of satisfaction of all debts, the bond requirement may be removed.

(h) The board shall take the actions required by this section upon notification by any party having knowledge of the outstanding judgment upon a showing of proof of the judgment.

(i) For the purposes of this section, the term "judgment" also includes any final arbitration award where the time to file a petition for a trial de novo or a petition to vacate or correct the arbitration award has expired, and no petition is pending.

(j) (1) If a judgment is entered against a licensee or any personnel of record of a licensee, then a qualifying person or personnel of record of the licensee at the time of the activities on which the judgment is based shall be automatically prohibited from serving as a qualifying individual or other personnel of record on any license until the judgment is satisfied.

(2) The prohibition described in paragraph (1) shall cause the license of any other existing renewable licensed entity with any of the same personnel of record as the judgment debtor licensee or with any of the same judgment debtor personnel to be suspended until the license of the judgment debtor is reinstated, the judgment is satisfied, or until those same personnel of record disassociate themselves from the renewable licensed entity.

(k) For purposes of this section, lawful money or cashier's check deposited pursuant to paragraph (1) of subdivision (a) of Section 995.710 of the Code of Civil Procedure, may be submitted in lieu of the bond.

(l) Notwithstanding subdivision (f), the failure of a licensee to notify the registrar of an unsatisfied final judgment in accordance with this section is cause for disciplinary action.

Added Stats 1995 ch 467 § 6 (SB 1061). Amended Stats 1997 ch 469 § 1 (AB 772); Stats 2003 ch 363 § 1 (AB 1382); Stats 2010 ch 698 § 18 (SB 392), effective January 1, 2011; Stats 2017 ch 506 § 1 (AB 1278), effective January 1, 2018; Stats 2018 ch 925 § 3 (AB 3126), effective January 1, 2019; Stats 2019 ch 378 § 7 (SB 610), effective January 1, 2020; Stats 2020 ch 370 § 10 (SB 1371), effective January 1, 2021.

—*See Code of Civil Procedure Section 116.220 Jurisdiction of Small Claims Court, in Appendix.*

—*See Code of Civil Procedure, Bond and Undertaking Law Sections 995.010 to 996.560 in Appendix.*

§ 7071.18. Report to registrar of convictions; Study of judgments, arbitration awards, settlements for construction defects in rental residential units; Contents of study

(a) Notwithstanding any other law, a licensee shall report to the registrar in writing the occurrence of any of the following within 90 days after the licensee obtains knowledge of the event:

(1) The conviction of the licensee for any felony.

(2) The conviction of the licensee for any other crime that is substantially related to the qualifications, functions, and duties of a licensed contractor.

(b) (1) The board shall consult with licensees, consumers, and other interested stakeholders in order to prepare a study of judgments, arbitration awards, and settlements that were the result of claims for construction defects for rental residential units and, by January 1, 2018, shall report to the Legislature the results of this study to determine if the board's ability to protect the public as described in Section 7000.6 would be enhanced by regulations requiring licensees to report judgments, arbitration awards, or settlement payments of those claims. Participation by licensees and consumers shall be voluntary. The study shall include, but not be limited to, criteria used by insurers or others to differentiate between settlements that are for nuisance value and those that are not, whether settlement information or other information can help identify licensees who may be subject to an enforcement action, if there is a way to separate subcontractors from general contractors when identifying licensees who may be subject to an enforcement action, whether reporting should be limited to settlements resulting from construction defects that resulted in death or injury, the practice of other boards within the department, and any other criteria considered reasonable by the board. The board shall submit the report to the Legislature in accordance with Section 9795 of the Government Code.

(2) Records or documents obtained by the board during the course of implementing this subdivision that are exempt from public disclosure under the California Public Records Act (Chapter 3.5 (commencing with Section 6250) of Division 7 of Title 1 of the Government Code) shall remain exempt from disclosure pursuant to that act.

Added Stats 2016 ch 372 § 2 (SB 465), effective January 1, 2017.

§ 7071.19. Insurance as condition precedent to license; Aggregate limit of liability; Compliance with financial security requirements; Duties of registrar

(a) As a condition of the issuance, reinstatement, reactivation, or continued valid use of a license under this chapter, in addition to any bond required under this article, a limited liability company shall, in accordance with this section, maintain a policy or policies of insurance against liability imposed on or against it by law for damages arising out of claims based upon acts, errors, or omissions arising out of the contracting services it provides.

(b) The total aggregate limit of liability under the policy or policies of insurance required under this section shall be as follows:

Section VI

(1) For a limited liability company licensee with five or fewer persons listed on the members of the personnel of record, the aggregate limit shall not be less than one million dollars ($1,000,000).

(2) For a limited liability company licensee with more than five persons listed on the members of the personnel of record, an additional one hundred thousand dollars ($100,000) of insurance shall be obtained for each person listed on the personnel of record of the licensee except that the maximum amount of insurance is not required to exceed five million dollars ($5,000,000) in any one designated period, less amounts paid in defending, settling, or discharging claims as set forth under this section.

(c) The policy or policies required by this section may be issued on a claims-made or occurrence basis, and shall cover: (1) in the case of a claims-made policy, claims initially asserted in the designated period, and (2) in the case of an occurrence policy, occurrences during the designated period. For purposes of this section, "designated period" means a policy year or any other period designated in the policy that is not greater than 12 months. Any policy or policies secured to satisfy the requirements of this section shall be written by an insurer or insurers duly licensed by this state or an eligible surplus line insurer, with the insurance procured pursuant to Section 1765.1 of the Insurance Code, and may be in a form reasonably available in the commercial insurance market and may be subject to those terms, conditions, exclusions, and endorsements that are typically contained in those policies. A policy or policies of insurance maintained pursuant to this section may be subject to a deductible or self-insured retention.

(d) The impairment or exhaustion of the aggregate limit of liability by amounts paid under any policy in connection with the settlement, discharge, or defense of claims applicable to a designated period shall not require the licensee to acquire additional insurance coverage for that designated period. However, the aggregate limit of liability coverage (coverage limit) required by this section shall be reinstated by not later than the commencement date of the next designated period, and the license of any licensee that fails to comply with this provision shall be suspended by operation of law until the date that the licensee complies with the coverage limit requirements of this section. In addition, the amount to which any coverage limit is depleted may be reported on the license record.

(e) Upon the dissolution and winding up of the company, the company shall, with respect to any insurance policy or policies then maintained pursuant to this section, maintain or obtain an extended reporting period endorsement or equivalent provision in the maximum total aggregate limit of liability required to comply with this section for a minimum of three years if reasonably available from the insurer.

(f) Prior to the issuance, reinstatement, or reactivation of a limited liability company license as provided under this chapter, the applicant or licensee shall, in the manner prescribed by the registrar, submit the information and documentation required by this section and requested by the registrar, demonstrating compliance with the financial security requirements specified by this section.

(g) For any insurance policy secured by a licensee in satisfaction of this section, a Certificate of Liability Insurance, signed by an authorized agent or employee of the insurer, shall be submitted electronically or otherwise to the registrar. The insurer issuing the certificate, or, in the case of a surplus line policy, the surplus line broker, shall report to the registrar the following information for any policy required under this section: name, license number, policy number, dates that coverage is scheduled to commence and lapse, the date and amount of any payment of claims, and cancellation date if applicable.

(h) Upon the issuance, reinstatement, or reactivation of a license under this section, the registrar may post the following information to the licensee's license record on the Internet:

(1) The name of the insurer or insurers providing the liability policy or policies submitted by the licensee for the most recent designated period.

(2) Any policy numbers and the sum of the aggregate limit of liability provided by each.

Added Stats 2010 ch 698 § 19 (SB 392), effective January 1, 2011. Amended Stats 2013 ch 114 § 1 (AB 1236), effective January 1, 2014.

§ 7071.20. Licensee; Reporting requirement

(a) A licensee shall report to the registrar in writing within 90 days after the licensee has knowledge of any civil action resulting in a final judgment, executed settlement agreement, or final arbitration award in which the licensee is named as a defendant or cross-defendant, filed on or after January 1, 2019, that meets all of the following criteria:

(1) The action alleges fraud, deceit, negligence, breach of contract or express or implied warranty, misrepresentation, incompetence, recklessness, wrongful death, or strict liability by the act or omission of a licensee while acting in the capacity of a contractor, whether as a general contractor or as a specialty contractor.

(2) The amount or value of the judgment, settlement payment, or arbitration award for which the licensee is named as a defendant or cross-defendant, is one million dollars ($1,000,000) or greater, not including investigative costs or prior repairs performed by the licensee.

(3) The action is the result of a claim for damages to a property or person that allegedly resulted in a failure or condition that creates a

substantial risk of a failure in the load bearing portions of a multi-family rental residential structure.

(4) The action is the result of a claim for damages to a property or person that was allegedly caused by a licensee's construction, repair, alteration to, subtraction from, improvement of, moving, wrecking, or demolishing of, any part of a multifamily rental residential structure, either personally or by or through others.

(5) The action, if a civil action, has been designated by a court of competent jurisdiction as a "complex case" pursuant to rules 3.400 to 3.403, inclusive, of the California Rules of Court because it involves a claim of construction defect or insurance coverage arising out of a construction defect claim, pursuant to paragraph (2) or (7) of subdivision (c) of Rule 3.400 of the California Rules of Court.

(b) This section shall not apply to residential construction subject to any part of Title 7 (commencing with Section 895) of Part 2 of Division 2 of the Civil Code.

(c) In an action that meets the criteria of this section, in which more than one contractor is named as a defendant or cross-defendant, all contractors who are apportioned any liability either by the court or pursuant to an agreement between parties, shall report the action pursuant to subdivision (a). This subdivision does not apply to a contractor who is named as a defendant or cross-defendant, but is assigned liability of less than fifteen thousand dollars ($15,000) in the action.

(d) The reports required by this section shall be signed by the licensee and shall set forth the license number of the licensee and the facts that constitute the reportable event. If the reportable event involves the action of a court, the report shall also set forth the following:

(1) The title of the matter.

(2) The court or agency name.

(3) The docket number.

(4) The claim or file number.

(5) The date on which the reportable event occurred.

(e) (1) The registrar or a designee shall review the reports required by this section. The registrar or designee shall return the report to the licensee and take no further action if, upon review, the registrar or a designee finds any of the following:

(A) The facts of the reportable event would not substantiate an allegation that a licensee has violated this chapter.

(B) There are reasonable grounds to believe that the public interest is sufficiently served by the existing resolution or disposition of the reportable event as reached by the parties to the action or by the court.

(C) Disciplinary action is unnecessary.

(2) Any report returned to a licensee pursuant to this subdivision shall be deemed to be a complaint resolved in favor of the licensee

and the facts underlying the event as reported by the licensee shall not be subject to further review by the board, except upon receipt of an independent complaint involving the same underlying facts.

(3) If additional information is necessary to make the determination required by paragraph (1), the registrar or designee shall keep and regard the report as a complaint that shall be subject to Sections 7090 and 7091. The disclosure of any complaint referred to investigation pursuant to this section shall comply with the public disclosure provisions of Section 7124.6.

(f) Failure of a licensee to report to the registrar in the time and manner required by this section shall be grounds for disciplinary action. Criminal penalties shall not be imposed for a violation of this section.

(g) Except as provided in paragraphs (1) and (2) of subdivision (e), nothing in this section is intended to limit the registrar's authority on his or her motion, or upon the verified written complaint of another, to investigate the actions of a contractor as specified in Section 7090.

Added Stats 2018 ch 514 § 1 (SB 1465), effective January 1, 2019.

§ 7071.21. Licensee insurer; Reporting requirement

(a) An insurer providing a licensee commercial general liability insurance, construction defect insurance, or professional liability insurance shall report to the registrar within 30 days of all or a portion of the insurer's payment of a civil action judgment, settlement payment, or arbitration award, that meets all of the requirements of Section 7071.20, against the licensee all of the following:

(1) The name and license number of the licensee.

(2) The claim or file number.

(3) The amount or value of the judgment, settlement payment, or arbitration award.

(4) The amount paid by the insurer.

(5) The identity of the payee.

(b) (1) The registrar or a designee shall review the reports required by this section. The registrar or designee shall return the report to the licensee and take no further action if, upon review, the registrar or a designee finds any of the following:

(A) The facts of the reportable event would not substantiate an allegation that a licensee has violated this chapter.

(B) There are reasonable grounds to believe that the public interest is sufficiently served by the existing resolution or disposition of the reportable event as reached by the parties to the action or by the court.

(C) Disciplinary action is unnecessary.

(2) Any report returned to a licensee pursuant to this subdivision shall be deemed to be a complaint resolved in favor of the licensee

and the facts underlying the event as reported by the licensee shall not be subject to further review by the board, except upon receipt of an independent complaint involving the same underlying facts.

(3) If additional information is necessary to make the determination required by paragraph (1), the registrar or designee shall keep and regard the report as a complaint that shall be subject to Sections 7090 and 7091. The disclosure of any complaint referred to investigation pursuant to this section shall comply with the public disclosure provisions of Section 7124.6.

(c) Except as provided in paragraphs (1) and (2) of subdivision (b), nothing in this section is intended to limit the registrar's authority on his or her motion, or upon the verified written complaint of another, to investigate the actions of a contractor as specified in Section 7090.

Added Stats 2018 ch 514 § 2 (SB 1465), effective January 1, 2019.

§ 7071.22. Licensee reports; Not confidentiality violation

(a) Sections 7071.20 and 7071.21 shall apply if a party to the civil action, judgment, settlement payment, or arbitration award is or was a licensee, as defined in Section 7096, or was a member of the personnel of the record, a person, or a qualifying person, as those terms are defined in Section 7025.

(b) Notwithstanding any other law, a licensee or person providing a report to the registrar pursuant to Section 7071.20 or 7071.21 shall not be considered to have violated a confidential settlement agreement or other confidential agreement.

(c) The board may adopt regulations to further the purposes of Sections 7071.20 and 7071.21, specifically with regard to the reporting requirements of those sections.

Added Stats 2018 ch 514 § 3 (SB 1465), effective January 1, 2019.

§ 7072. Issuance of license

Following receipt of the application fee and an application furnishing complete information in the manner required by the registrar, and after such examination and investigation as he may require, the registrar, within 15 days after approval of the application, shall notify the applicant that a license may be issued to him on payment of the initial license fee provided in Article 8 (commencing at Section 7135), and, when the initial license fee is paid, shall issue a license to him permitting him to engage in business as a contractor under the terms of this chapter.

Added Stats 1939 ch 37 § 1. Amended Stats 1961 ch 1636 § 3, operative October 1, 1962; Stats 1970 ch 340 § 5.

§ 7072.5. Issuance of pocket card

(a) Upon the issuance of a license, a plasticized pocket card of a size, design, and content as may be determined by the registrar shall be issued at no cost to each licensee, or to the partners, managers, officers, or responsible managing officers of licensees licensed as other than individuals, which card shall be evidence that the licensee is duly licensed pursuant to this chapter. All cards issued shall be surrendered upon the suspension, revocation, or denial of renewal of the license, and shall be mailed or delivered to the board within five days of the suspension, revocation, or denial.

(b) When a person to whom a card is issued terminates his or her position, office, or association with a licensee that is licensed as other than an individual, that person shall surrender his or her card to the licensee and within five days thereafter the card shall be mailed or delivered by the licensee to the board for cancellation.

Added Stats 1988 ch 1495 § 1. Amended Stats 2006 ch 106 § 3 (AB 2457), effective January 1, 2007; Stats 2010 ch 698 § 20 (SB 392), effective January 1, 2011.

§ 7073. Grounds and procedures for denial of application; Rehabilitation and reapplication; Probationary license in lieu of denial

(a) The registrar may deny any application for a license or supplemental classification where the applicant has failed to comply with any rule or regulation adopted pursuant to this chapter or where there are grounds for denial under Section 480. Procedures for denial of an application shall be conducted in accordance with Section 485.

(b) When the board has denied an application for a license on grounds that the applicant has committed a crime substantially related to qualifications, functions, or duties of a contractor, it shall, in its decision or in its notice under subdivision (b) of Section 485, inform the applicant of the earliest date on which the applicant may reapply for a license. The board shall develop criteria, similar to the criteria developed to evaluate rehabilitation, to establish the earliest date on which the applicant may reapply. The date set by the registrar shall not be more than five years from the effective date of the decision or service of notice under subdivision (b) of Section 485.

(c) The board shall inform an applicant that all competent evidence of rehabilitation shall be considered upon reapplication.

(d) Along with the decision or notice under subdivision (b) of Section 485, the board shall serve a copy of the criteria for rehabilitation formulated under Section 482.

(e) In lieu of denying licensure as authorized under this section, the registrar may issue an applicant a probationary license with terms and conditions. During the probationary period, if information is brought to the attention of the registrar regarding any act or omission of the licensee constituting grounds for discipline or denial of licensure for which the registrar determines that revocation of the probationary license would be proper, the registrar shall notify the applicant to show cause within 30 days why the probationary license should not be revoked. The proceedings shall be conducted in accordance with the provisions of Chapter 5 (commencing with Section 11500) of Part 1 of Division 3 of Title 2 of the Government Code, and the registrar shall have all the powers granted therein. A probationary license shall not be renewed during any period in which any proceeding brought pursuant to this section is pending.

Added Stats 1983 ch 891 § 11. Amended Stats 2004 ch 586 § 2 (AB 2216); Stats 2005 ch 280 § 7 (SB 1112), effective January 1, 2006.

§ 7074. When application becomes void; Disposition of application; Fee for reapplication

(a) Except as otherwise provided by this section, an application for an original license, for an additional classification, or for a change of qualifier shall become void when:

(1) The applicant or the examinee for the applicant has failed to achieve a passing grade in the qualifying examination within 18 months after the application has been deemed acceptable by the board.

(2) The applicant for an original license, after having been notified to do so, fails to pay the initial license fee within 90 days from the date of the notice.

(3) The applicant, after having been notified to do so, fails to file within 90 days from the date of the notice any bond or lawful money or cashier's check deposited pursuant to paragraph (1) of subdivision (a) of Section 995.710 of the Code of Civil Procedure or other documents that may be required for issuance or granting pursuant to this chapter.

(4) After filing, the applicant withdraws the application.

(5) The applicant fails to return the application rejected by the board for insufficiency or incompleteness within 90 days from the date of original notice or rejection.

(6) The application is denied after disciplinary proceedings conducted in accordance with the provisions of this code.

(b) The void date on an application may be extended up to 90 days or one examination may be rescheduled without a fee upon documented evidence by the applicant that the failure to complete the application process or to appear for an examination was due to a medical emergency or other circumstance beyond the control of the applicant.

(c) An application voided pursuant to this section shall remain in the possession of the registrar for the period as he or she deems necessary and shall not be returned to the applicant. Any reapplication for a license shall be accompanied by the fee fixed by this chapter.

Added Stats 1983 ch 891 § 13. Amended Stats 2001 ch 728 § 59 (SB 724); Stats 2016 ch 634 § 4 (SB 1479), effective January 1, 2017. Stats 2018 ch 925 § 4 (AB 3126), effective January 1, 2019.

§ 7075. Display of license

The license shall be displayed in the licensee's main office or chief place of business. Satisfactory evidence of the possession of a license and the current renewal thereof shall be provided by the licensee upon demand.

Added Stats 1939 ch 37 § 1. Amended Stats 1961 ch 1636 § 4, operative October 1, 1962; Stats 1963 ch 1016 § 3; Stats 1971 ch 716 § 104; Stats 1990 ch 1326 § 4 (AB 3480), effective September 25, 1990.

§ 7075.1. Nontransferability of license

(a) No license, regardless of type or classification, shall be transferable to any other person or entity under any circumstances.

(b) A license number may be reissued after cancellation, revocation, suspension, or expiration beyond the renewal period specified in Section 7141, only under the following circumstances:

(1) To an individual upon application.

(2) To a partnership upon application if there is no change in the partners or partnership structure.

(3) To a corporation upon application if there is no change in the status of the corporation as registered with the Secretary of State.

(4) To a limited liability company upon application if there is no change in the status of the company as registered with the Secretary of State.

(c) A license number may be reissued or reassigned to a different entity only under the following conditions:

(1) To a corporation when the parent corporation has merged or created a subsidiary, the subsidiary has merged into the parent corporation, or the corporation has changed its filing status with the Secretary of State from a domestic corporation to a foreign corporation or from a foreign corporation to a domestic corporation, and the new entity is being formed to continue the business of the formerly licensed corporation.

(2) To a limited liability company when the parent limited liability company has merged or created a subsidiary, the subsidiary has merged into the parent limited liability company, or the limited liability company has changed its filing status with the Secretary of State

from a domestic limited liability company to a foreign limited liability company or from a foreign limited liability company to a domestic limited liability company, and the new entity is being formed to continue the business of the formerly licensed limited liability company.

(3) To an individual when the individual is an immediate family member of a licensed individual who is deceased or absent and the license is required to continue an existing family contracting business.

(4) To a corporation or limited liability company when created by immediate members of an individual licensee's family to continue an existing deceased or absent individual licensee's contracting business.

(5) To a corporation or limited liability company when the corporation or limited liability company is formed by an individual licensee and the individual licensee maintains ownership directly or indirectly of shares or membership interests evidencing more than 50 percent of the voting power.

(6) To a limited liability company that is formed by a corporation to continue the business of the corporation subsequent to the cancellation of the corporate entity's license, provided the personnel listed for each entity are the same.

(d) For purposes of this section, an immediate family member of a deceased or absent licensed individual is either a spouse, father, mother, brother, sister, son, daughter, stepson, stepdaughter, grandson, granddaughter, son-in-law, or daughter-in-law.

Added Stats 1990 ch 1326 § 4.5 (AB 3480), effective September 25, 1990. Amended Stats 1992 ch 746 § 2 (AB 2424); Stats 2010 ch 698 § 21 (SB 392), effective January 1, 2011; Stats 2017 ch 573 § 29 (SB 800), effective January 1, 2018.

§ 7076. Events resulting in cancellation of license; Continuance of license

(a) An individual license shall be canceled upon the death of a person licensed as an individual. An immediate member of the family of the deceased licensee may request a continuance of the license to complete projects in progress and undertake new work for a reasonable amount of time to be determined by rules of the board. The request for a continuance must be made in writing and received at the board's headquarters office within 90 days after the death. Approval of the continuance of an individual license may be contingent upon meeting the bond requirements of Sections 7071.5 and 7071.6 within 90 days of notification by the board of that requirement. The immediate member of the family must apply for and obtain his or her own license to continue contracting after the continuance expires.

(b) A partnership license shall be canceled upon the death of a general partner. The remaining partner or partners shall notify the registrar in writing within 90 days of the death of a general partner.

Failure to notify the registrar within 90 days of the death is grounds for disciplinary action.

The remaining general partner or partners may request a continuance of the license to complete projects in progress and undertake new work for a reasonable amount of time to be determined by rules of the board. The request for a continuance must be made in writing and received at the board's headquarters office within 90 days after the death. The remaining general partner or partners must apply for and obtain a new license to continue contracting after the continuance expires.

(c) A partnership license shall be canceled upon the disassociation of a general partner or upon the dissolution of the partnership. The disassociating partner or the remaining partner or partners shall notify the registrar in writing within 90 days of the disassociation of a general partner or dissolution of the partnership. Failure to notify the registrar of the disassociation or dissolution within 90 days shall cause the license to be canceled effective the date the written notification is received at the board's headquarters office. Failure to notify the registrar within 90 days of the disassociation or dissolution is grounds for disciplinary action. The remaining general partner or partners may request a continuance of the license to complete projects contracted for or in progress prior to the date of disassociation or dissolution for a reasonable length of time to be determined by rules of the board. The request for a continuance must be made in writing and received at the board's headquarters office within 90 days after the disassociation or dissolution. The remaining general partner or partners must apply for and obtain a new license to undertake new work and to continue contracting after the continuance expires.

(d) The general partner or partners shall notify the registrar in writing within 90 days of the death of a limited partner. Failure to notify the registrar within 90 days of the death is grounds for disciplinary action.

The death of a limited partner will not affect the partnership license unless the partnership license has only one limited partner. In this case, the license will be canceled upon the death of the limited partner unless a new limited partner is added to the license within 90 days of the death.

If the license is canceled, the remaining general partner or partners may request a continuance of the license to complete projects in progress and to undertake new work for a reasonable amount of time to be determined by rules of the board. The request for a continuance must be made in writing and received at the board's headquarters office within 90 days after the death. The remaining general partner or partners must apply for and obtain a new license to continue contracting after the continuance expires.

(e) The general partner or partners shall notify the registrar in writing within 90 days of the disassociation of a limited partner. Failure to notify the registrar of the disassociation, within 90 days, shall cause the disassociation to be effective the date the written notification is received at the board's headquarters office. Failure to notify the registrar within 90 days of the disassociation is grounds for disciplinary action.

The disassociation of a limited partner will not affect the partnership license unless the partnership license has only one limited partner. In this case, the license will be canceled upon the disassociation of the limited partner unless a new limited partner is added to the license within 90 days of the disassociation. If the license is canceled, the remaining general partner or partners may request a continuance of the license to complete projects contracted for or in progress prior to the date of disassociation for a reasonable amount of time to be determined by rules of the board. The request for a continuance must be made in writing and received at the board's headquarters office within 90 days after the disassociation. The remaining general partner or partners must apply for and obtain a new license to undertake new work and to continue contracting after the continuance expires.

(f) A joint venture license shall be canceled upon the cancellation, revocation, or disassociation of any of its entity licenses or upon the dissolution of the joint venture. The registrar shall be notified in writing within 90 days of the disassociation of a joint venture entity or dissolution of the joint venture. Failure to notify the registrar of the disassociation or dissolution within 90 days shall cause the license to be canceled effective the date the written notification is received at the board's headquarters office. Failure to notify the registrar within 90 days of the disassociation or dissolution is grounds for disciplinary action.

Any remaining entity or entities may request a continuance of the license to complete projects contracted for or in progress prior to the date of disassociation or dissolution for a reasonable amount of time to be determined by rules of the board. The request for a continuance must be made in writing and received at the board's headquarters office within 90 days of the disassociation or dissolution. The remaining entity or entities must apply for and obtain a new license to undertake new work and to continue contracting after the continuance expires.

(g) Any individual, partnership, or joint venture license continued in accordance with this section is subject to all other provisions of this chapter.

(h) A corporation license shall be canceled upon the corporation's dissolution, merger, or surrender of its right to do business in this state. The corporation shall notify the registrar in writing within 90 days of the dissolution, merger, or surrender. Failure to notify the registrar of the dissolution, merger, or surrender within 90 days shall cause the license to be canceled effective the date written notification is received at the board's headquarters office. If the corporation fails to notify the board of the dissolution, merger, or surrender, the corporation license shall be canceled 60 days after the board's discovery when researching the corporate records of the Secretary of State. Failure to notify the registrar within 90 days of the dissolution, merger, or surrender is grounds for disciplinary action.

(i) A limited liability company license shall be canceled upon the company's dissolution, merger, or surrender of its right to do business in this state. The limited liability company shall notify the registrar in writing within 90 days of the dissolution, merger, or surrender. Failure to notify the registrar of the dissolution, merger, or surrender within 90 days shall cause the license to be canceled effective the date written notification is received at the board's headquarters office. If the limited liability company fails to notify the board of the dissolution, merger, or surrender, the limited liability company license shall be canceled 60 days after the board's discovery when researching the records of the Secretary of State. Failure to notify the registrar within 90 days of the dissolution, merger, or surrender is grounds for disciplinary action.

(j) The registrar shall review and accept the petition of a licensee who disputes the date of cancellation upon a showing of good cause. This petition shall be received within 90 days of the board's official notice of cancellation.

Added Stats 1995 ch 467 § 8 (SB 1061). Amended Stats 2010 ch 698 § 22 (SB 392), effective January 1, 2011; Stats 2012 ch 661 § 11 (SB 1576), effective January 1, 2013.

§ 7076.1. Voluntary surrender of license

Upon the voluntary surrender of a license by a licensee, the registrar shall order the license canceled. Cancellation will be effected upon receipt of the request by the registrar. No refund will be made of any fee which a licensee may have paid prior to the surrender of the license.

To reinstate a canceled license the licensee must pay all of the fees and meet all of the qualifications and requirements set forth in this chapter for obtaining an original license.

Added Stats 1975 ch 329 § 1.

§ 7076.2. Suspension for failure to be registered and in good standing after notice; Personal liability

(a) Notwithstanding any other provision of law, the failure of a contractor licensed to do business as a corporation or limited liability company in this state to be registered and in good standing with the

Secretary of State after notice from the registrar shall result in the automatic suspension of the license by operation of law. The registrar shall notify the licensee in writing of its failure to be registered and in good standing with the Secretary of State and that the licensee shall be suspended 30 days from the date of the notice if the licensee does not provide proof satisfactory to the registrar that it is properly registered and in good standing with the Secretary of State. Reinstatement may be made at any time following the suspension by providing proof satisfactory to the registrar that the license is properly registered and in good standing.

(b) Where the license of a limited liability company is suspended pursuant to subdivision (a), each person within the company identified in Section 7028.5 shall be personally liable up to one million dollars ($1,000,000) each for damages resulting to third parties in connection with the company's performance, during the period of suspension, of any act or contract where a license is required by this chapter. This personal liability shall not apply where there has been substantial compliance with the licensure requirements, as described in subdivision (e) of Section 7031.

Added Stats 1995 ch 467 § 9 (SB 1061). Amended Stats 2010 ch 698 § 23 (SB 392), effective January 1, 2011.

§ 7076.5. Inactive license certificate; Reinstatement; Holder not entitled to practice

(a) A contractor may inactivate his or her license by submitting a form prescribed by the registrar accompanied by the current active license certificate. When the current license certificate has been lost, the licensee shall pay the fee prescribed by law to replace the license certificate. Upon receipt of an acceptable application to inactivate, the registrar shall issue an inactive license certificate to the contractor. The holder of an inactive license shall not be entitled to practice as a contractor until his or her license is reactivated.

(b) Any licensed contractor who is not engaged in work or activities which require a contractor's license may apply for an inactive license.

(c) Inactive licenses shall be valid for a period of four years from their due date.

(d) During the period that an existing license is inactive, no bonding requirement pursuant to Section 7071.6, 7071.8 or 7071.9 or qualifier requirement pursuant to Section 7068 shall apply. An applicant for license having met the qualifications for issuance may request that the license be issued inactive unless the applicant is subject to the provisions of Section 7071.8.

(e) The board shall not refund any of the renewal fee which a licensee may have paid prior to the inactivation of his or her license.

(f) An inactive license shall be renewed on each established renewal date by submitting the renewal application and paying the inactive renewal fee.

(g) An inactive license may be reactivated by submitting an application acceptable to the registrar, by paying the full renewal fee for an active license and by fulfilling all other requirements of this chapter. No examination shall be required to reactivate an inactive license.

(h) The inactive status of a license shall not bar any disciplinary action by the board against a licensee for any of the causes stated in this chapter.

Added Stats 1983 ch 891 § 18. Amended Stats 1987 ch 875 § 1.

§ 7077. Original license probationary; Revocation

Every original license, except an additional classification issued pursuant to Section 7059, shall be a probationary license until such time as the license is renewed. If information is brought to the attention of the registrar, during such probationary period, regarding any act or omission of the licensee constituting grounds for denial, revocation, or suspension of an application or license, such that, in the registrar's discretion, it would be proper to revoke the probationary license, the registrar shall forthwith notify the applicant to show cause within not more than 30 days, why the probationary license should not be revoked. The proceedings shall be conducted in accordance with the provisions of Chapter 5 (commencing with Section 11500) of Part 1 of Division 3 of Title 2 of the Government Code, and the registrar shall have all the powers granted therein. A probationary license shall not be renewed during the pendency of any proceedings brought pursuant to this section.

Added Stats 1979 ch 1013 § 15.

Article 6

Records

§ 7080.5. Public posting following acceptance of application

When an application has been accepted by the registrar, the name and address of the applicant, every classification for which the applicant has applied, and the names and titles of all personnel who have signed the application shall be publicly posted by the registrar, on the day following acceptance, in the office of the Contractors State License Board in Sacramento.

Added Stats 1984 ch 1252 § 2. Amended Stats 2020 ch 312 § 59 (SB 1474), effective January 1, 2021.

§ 7081. List of contractors

Whenever funds are available for the purpose, the registrar shall publish a list of the names and addresses of contractors, registered under this chapter and of the licenses issued, suspended or revoked, and such further information with respect to this chapter and its administration as he deems proper.

He may furnish the lists to such public works and building departments, public officials or public bodies, and other persons interested in or allied with the building and construction industry in this or any other State as he deems advisable and, at such intervals as he deems necessary whenever funds are available.

Copies of the lists may also be furnished by the registrar upon request to any firm or individual upon payment of a reasonable fee fixed by the registrar.

Added Stats 1939 ch 37 § 1.

§ 7082. Publication and distribution of information of industry

Whenever funds are available for the purpose, the registrar may publish and disseminate to licentiates of the board, and public officials or other persons interested in or allied with the building and construction industry, such information with relation to the administration and enforcement of this chapter as he deems necessary to carry out its purposes.

Added Stats 1939 ch 37 § 1.

§ 7083. Notification by licensees of changes in recorded information

(a) Notwithstanding any other law, licensees shall notify the registrar, on a form prescribed by the registrar, in writing within 90 days of any change to information recorded under this chapter. This notification requirement shall include, but not be limited to, changes in business address, personnel, business name, qualifying individual bond exemption pursuant to Section 7071.9, or exemption to qualify multiple licenses pursuant to Section 7068.1.

(b) Failure of the licensee to notify the registrar of any change to information within 90 days shall cause the change to be effective the date the written notification is received at the board's headquarters office.

(c) Failure to notify the registrar of the changes within the 90 days is grounds for disciplinary action.

Added Stats 1983 ch 891 § 21. Amended Stats 1984 ch 1174 § 5; Stats 1986 ch 27 § 4; Stats 1990 ch 1326 § 7 (AB 3480), effective September 25, 1990; Stats 2004 ch 865 § 12 (SB 1914); Stats 2015 ch 430 § 5 (AB 181), effective January 1, 2016.

§ 7083.1. Notification of registrar of change of address of licensee whose license is expired, suspended, or cancelled

A licensee whose license is expired or suspended, and is renewable under Section 7141, or whose license is canceled, shall notify the registrar in writing of a change of address of record within 90 days, and shall maintain a current address of record during the five-year period immediately following the expiration or cancellation of the license.

Added Stats 1987 ch 930 § 6, effective September 22, 1987. Amended Stats 2007 ch 240 § 2 (AB 936), effective January 1, 2008.

§ 7084. Rules and regulations to carry out article

The registrar, with the approval of the director may adopt and promulgate the rules and regulations he deems necessary to carry out the provisions of this article.

Added Stats 1939 ch 37 § 1.

Article 6.2

Arbitration

§ 7085. Referral to arbitration; Conditions

(a) After investigating any verified complaint alleging a violation of Section 7107, 7109, 7110, 7113, 7119, or 7120, and any complaint arising from a contract involving works of improvement and finding a possible violation, the registrar may, with the concurrence of both the licensee and the complainant, refer the alleged violation, and any dispute between the licensee and the complainant arising thereunder, to arbitration pursuant to this article, provided the registrar finds that:

(1) There is evidence that the complainant has suffered or is likely to suffer material damages as a result of a violation of Section 7107, 7109, 7110, 7113, 7119, or 7120, and any complaint arising from a contract involving works of improvement.

(2) There are reasonable grounds for the registrar to believe that the public interest would be better served by arbitration than by disciplinary action.

(3) The licensee does not have a history of repeated or similar violations.

(4) The licensee was in good standing at the time of the alleged violation.

(5) The licensee does not have any outstanding disciplinary actions filed against him or her.

Section VI

(6) The parties have not previously agreed to private arbitration of the dispute pursuant to contract or otherwise.

(7) The parties have been advised of the provisions of Section 2855 of the Civil Code.

For the purposes of paragraph (1), "material damages" means damages greater than the amount of the bond required under subdivision (a) of Section 7071.6, but less than fifty thousand dollars ($50,000).

(b) In all cases in which a possible violation of the sections set forth in paragraph (1) of subdivision (a) exists and the contract price, or the demand for damages is equal to or less than the amount of the bond required under Section 7071.6, but, regardless of the contract price, the complaint shall be referred to arbitration, utilizing the criteria set forth in paragraphs (2) to (6), inclusive, of subdivision (a).

Added Stats 1979 ch 1013 § 16. Amended Stats 1987 ch 1311 § 1, effective September 28, 1987; Stats 1989 ch 1132 § 2, effective September 29, 1989; Stats 1992 ch 597 § 1 (AB 497); Stats 1998 ch 492 § 1 (SB 1792); Stats 2002 ch 312 § 1 (AB 728); Stats 2004 ch 865 § 13 (SB 1914); Stats 2005 ch 280 § 8 (SB 1112), effective January 1, 2006.

§ 7085.2. Arbitrator's award deemed award of registrar

An arbitrator may render an award and that award shall be deemed to be an order of the registrar.

Added Stats 1987 ch 1311 § 2, effective September 28, 1987.

§ 7085.3. Notice; Consequences of election; Right to retain counsel; Agreement to arbitrate

Once the registrar determines that arbitration pursuant to subdivision (a) of Section 7085 would be a suitable means of resolving the dispute, the registrar shall notify the complainant and the licensee of this decision. The registrar shall also notify the complainant of the consequences of selecting administrative arbitration over judicial remedies and advise the parties of their rights to retain counsel at their own expense. The registrar shall forward an "agreement to arbitrate" to the complainant and the licensee. This agreement shall be returned to the registrar within 30 calendar days of the date that the agreement is mailed by the registrar. The return of this agreement by the parties shall authorize the registrar to proceed with administrative arbitration.

Added Stats 1979 ch 1013 § 16. Amended Stats 1987 ch 1311 § 3, effective September 28, 1987; Stats 1989 ch 1132 § 3, effective September 29, 1989.

§ 7085.4. Referral of agreement to arbitrate to arbitrator or arbitration association; Notification of complainant and licensee

(a) For cases that the registrar determines to refer to arbitration under subdivision (a) of Section 7085, once the complainant and the licensee authorize the registrar to proceed with administrative arbitration, the registrar shall refer the agreement to arbitrate to an arbitrator or an arbitration association approved by the board.

(b) Once the registrar determines that a complaint must be referred to arbitration pursuant to subdivision (b) of Section 7085, the registrar shall notify the complainant and the licensee of that decision. The registrar shall inform the parties of the consequences of administrative arbitration over judicial remedies and shall advise the parties of their right to retain counsel at their own expense if they so choose. The registrar shall forward a notice to arbitrate to the complainant and the licensee. This notice shall be returned to the registrar within 30 calendar days of the date that the notice is mailed by the registrar. The complainant's failure to return an executed copy of the notice shall result in the closure of the complaint.

Notwithstanding Section 7085.5, a licensee's failure to return an executed copy of the notice shall not prohibit the registrar from referring the dispute to arbitration or bar the registrar from issuing an order enforcing any award resulting therefrom, pursuant to Section 7085.6, whether the award resulted from a contested hearing or a noncontested hearing.

Added Stats 1979 ch 1013 § 16. Amended Stats 1987 ch 1311 § 4, effective September 28, 1987; Stats 1989 ch 1132 § 4, effective September 29, 1989.

§ 7085.5. Rules of conduct for arbitrations; court procedure and exclusion of liability

Arbitrations of disputes arising out of cases filed with or by the board shall be conducted in accordance with the following rules:

(a) All "agreements to arbitrate" shall include the names, addresses, and telephone numbers of the parties to the dispute, the issue in dispute, and the amount in dollars or any other remedy sought. The appropriate fee shall be paid by the board from the Contractors License Fund.

(b) (1) The board or appointed arbitration association shall appoint an arbitrator in the following manner: immediately after the filing of the agreement to arbitrate, the board or appointed arbitration association shall submit simultaneously to each party to the dispute, an identical list of names of persons chosen from the panel. Each party to the dispute shall have seven days from the mailing date in which to cross off any names to which it objects, number the remaining names to indicate the order of preference, and return the list to the board or appointed arbitration association. If a party does not return the list within the time specified, all persons named in the list are acceptable. From among the persons who have been approved on both lists, and in accordance with the designated order of mutual preference, the board or appointed arbitration association shall appoint an arbitrator to serve. If the parties fail to agree on any of the parties named, if acceptable arbitrators are unable to act, or if, for any other reason, the appointment cannot be made from the submitted lists, the board or appointed arbitration association shall have the power to make the appointment from among other members of the panel without the submission of any additional lists. Each dispute shall be heard and determined by one arbitrator unless the board or appointed arbitration association, in its discretion, directs that a greater number of arbitrators be appointed.

(2) In all cases in which a complaint has been referred to arbitration pursuant to subdivision (b) of Section 7085, the board or the appointed arbitration association shall have the power to appoint an arbitrator to hear the matter.

(3) The board shall adopt regulations setting minimum qualification standards for listed arbitrators based upon relevant training, experience, and performance.

(c) No person shall serve as an arbitrator in any arbitration in which that person has any financial or personal interest in the result of the arbitration. Prior to accepting an appointment, the prospective arbitrator shall disclose any circumstances likely to prevent a prompt hearing or to create a presumption of bias. Upon receipt of that information, the board or appointed arbitration association shall immediately replace the arbitrator or communicate the information to the parties for their comments. Thereafter, the board or appointed arbitration association shall determine whether the arbitrator should be disqualified and shall inform the parties of its decision, which shall be conclusive.

(d) The board or appointed arbitration association may appoint another arbitrator if a vacancy occurs, or if an appointed arbitrator is unable to serve in a timely manner.

(e) (1) The board or appointed arbitration association shall provide the parties with a list of the times and dates, and locations of the hearing to be held. The parties shall notify the arbitrator, within seven calendar days of the mailing of the list, of the times and dates convenient to each party. If the parties fail to respond to the arbitrator within the seven-day period, the arbitrator shall fix the time, place, and location of the hearing. An arbitrator may, at the arbitrator's sole discretion, make an inspection of the construction site which is the subject of the arbitration. The arbitrator shall notify the parties of the time and date set for the inspection. Any party who so desires may be present at the inspection.

(2) The board or appointed arbitration association shall fix the time, place, and location of the hearing for all cases referred to arbitration pursuant to subdivision (b) of Section 7085. An arbitrator may, at the arbitrator's sole discretion, make an inspection of the construction site which is the subject of the arbitration. The arbitrator shall notify the parties of the time and date set for the inspection. Any party who desires may be present at the inspection.

(f) Any person having a direct interest in the arbitration is entitled to attend the hearing. The arbitrator shall otherwise have the power to require the exclusion of any witness, other than a party or other essential person, during the testimony of any other witness. It shall be discretionary with the arbitrator to determine the propriety of the attendance of any other person.

(g) Hearings shall be adjourned by the arbitrator only for good cause.

(h) A record is not required to be taken of the proceedings. However, any party to the proceeding may have a record made at its own expense. The parties may make appropriate notes of the proceedings.

(i) The hearing shall be conducted by the arbitrator in any manner which will permit full and expeditious presentation of the case by both parties. Consistent with the expedited nature of arbitration, the arbitrator shall establish the extent of, and schedule for, the production of relevant documents and other information, the identification of any witnesses to be called, and a schedule for any hearings to elicit facts solely within the knowledge of one party. The complaining party shall present its claims, proofs, and witnesses, who shall submit to questions or other examination. The defending party shall then present its defenses, proofs, and witnesses, who shall submit to questions or other examination. The arbitrator has discretion to vary this procedure but shall afford full and equal opportunity to the parties for the presentation of any material or relevant proofs.

(j) The arbitration may proceed in the absence of any party who, after due notice, fails to be present. The arbitrator shall require the attending party to submit supporting evidence in order to make an award. An award for the attending party shall not be based solely on the fact that the other party has failed to appear at the arbitration hearing.

(k) The arbitrator shall be the sole judge of the relevancy and materiality of the evidence offered and conformity to legal rules of evidence shall not be required.

(l) The arbitrator may receive and consider documentary evidence. Documents to be considered by the arbitrator may be submitted prior to the hearing. However, a copy shall be simultaneously transmitted to all other parties and to the board or appointed arbitration association for transmittal to the arbitrator or board appointed arbitrator.

(m) The arbitrator shall specifically inquire of the parties whether they have any further proofs to offer or witnesses to be heard. Upon receiving negative replies, the arbitrator shall declare the hearing closed and minutes thereof shall be recorded. If briefs are to be filed, the hearing shall be declared closed as of the final date set by the arbitrator for the receipt of briefs. If documents are to be filed as requested by the arbitrator and the date set for their receipt is later than that set for the receipt of briefs, the later date shall be the date of closing the hearings. The time limit within which the arbitrator is required to make the award shall commence to run, in the absence of other agreements by the parties, upon the closing of the hearings.

(n) The hearing may be reopened on the arbitrator's own motion.

(o) Any party who proceeds with the arbitration after knowledge that any provision or requirement of these rules has not been complied with, and who fails to state their objections to the arbitrator in writing, within 10 calendar days of close of hearing, shall be deemed to have waived their right to object.

(p) (1) Except as provided in paragraph (2), any papers or process necessary or proper for the initiation or continuation of an arbitration under these rules and for any court action in connection therewith, or for the entry of judgment on an award made thereunder, may be served upon any party (A) by regular mail addressed to that party or their attorney at the party's last known address, or (B) by personal service.

(2) Notwithstanding paragraph (1), in all cases referred to arbitration pursuant to subdivision (b) of Section 7085 in which the contractor fails or refuses to return an executed copy of the notice to arbitrate within the time specified, any papers or process specified in paragraph (1) to be sent to the contractor, including the notice of hearing, shall be mailed by certified mail to the contractor's address of record.

(q) The award shall be made promptly by the arbitrator, and unless otherwise agreed by the parties, no later than 30 calendar days from the date of closing the hearing, closing a reopened hearing, or if oral hearing has been waived, from the date of transmitting the final statements and proofs to the arbitrator.

The arbitrator may for good cause extend any period of time established by these rules, except the time for making the award. The arbitrator shall notify the parties of any extension and the reason therefor.

(r) (1) The arbitrator may grant any remedy or relief that the arbitrator deems just and equitable and within the scope of the board's referral and the requirements of the board. The arbitrator, in their sole discretion, may award costs or expenses.

(2) The amendments made in paragraph (1) during the 2003-04 Regular Session shall not be interpreted to prevent an arbitrator from awarding a complainant all direct costs and expenses for the completion or repair of the project.

(s) The award shall become final 30 calendar days from the date the arbitration award is issued. The arbitrator, upon written application of a party to the arbitration, may correct the award upon the following grounds:

(1) There was an evident miscalculation of figures or an evident mistake in the description of any person, things, or property referred to in the award.

(2) There is any other clerical error in the award, not affecting the merits of the controversy.

An application for correction of the award shall be made within 10 calendar days of the date of service of the award by serving a copy of the application on the arbitrator, and all other parties to the arbitration. Any party to the arbitration may make a written objection to the application for correction by serving a copy of the written objection on the arbitrator, the board, and all other parties to the arbitration, within 10 calendar days of the date of service of the application for correction.

The arbitrator shall either deny the application or correct the award within 30 calendar days of the date of service of the original award by mailing a copy of the denial or correction to all parties to the arbitration. Any appeal from the denial or correction shall be filed with a court of competent jurisdiction and a true copy thereof shall be filed with the arbitrator or appointed arbitration association within 30 calendar days after the award has become final. The award shall be in writing, and shall be signed by the arbitrator or a majority of them. If no appeal is filed within the 30-calendar day period, it shall become a final order of the registrar.

(t) Service of the award by certified mail shall be effective if a certified letter containing the award, or a true copy thereof, is mailed by the arbitrator or arbitration association to each party or to a party's attorney of record at their last known address, address of record, or by personally serving any party. Service may be proved in the manner authorized in civil actions.

(u) The board shall pay the expenses of one expert witness appointed by the board when the services of an expert witness are requested by either party involved in arbitration pursuant to this article and the case involves workmanship issues that are itemized in the complaint and have not been repaired or replaced. Parties who choose to present the findings of another expert witness as evidence shall pay for those services. Payment for expert witnesses appointed by the board shall be limited to the expert witness costs for inspection of the problem at the construction site, preparation of the expert witness' report, and expert witness fees for appearing or testifying at a hearing. All requests for payment to an expert witness shall be submitted on a form that has been approved by the registrar. All requests for payment to an expert witness shall be reviewed and approved by the board prior to payment. The registrar shall advise the parties that names of industry experts may be obtained by requesting this information from the registrar.

(v) The arbitrator shall interpret and apply these rules insofar as they relate to their powers and duties.

(w) The following shall apply as to court procedure and exclusion of liability:

(1) The board, the appointed arbitration association, or any arbitrator in a proceeding under these rules is not a necessary party in judicial proceedings relating to the arbitration.

(2) Parties to these rules shall be deemed to have consented that judgment upon the arbitration award may be entered in any federal or state court having jurisdiction thereof.

(3) The board, the appointed arbitration association, or any arbitrator is not liable to any party for any act or omission in connection with any arbitration conducted under these rules.

Added Stats 1987 ch 1311 § 5, effective September 28, 1987. Amended Stats 1988 ch 160 § 3; Stats 1989 ch 1132 § 5, effective September 29, 1989; Stats 1998 ch 492 § 2 (SB 1792); Stats 2003 ch 363 § 2 (AB 1382); Stats 2020 ch 312 § 60 (SB 1474), effective January 1, 2021.

§ 7085.6. Failure to comply with award as grounds for automatic suspension; Appeal; Reinstatement; Delay in revocation for good cause; Dissociation from other licensee

(a)(1) The failure of a licensee to comply with an arbitration award rendered under this article shall result in the automatic suspension of a license by operation of law.

(2) The registrar shall notify the licensee by certified mail of the failure to comply with the arbitrator's award, and that the license shall be automatically suspended 30 calendar days from the date of that notice.

(3) The licensee may appeal the suspension for noncompliance within 15 calendar days after service of the notice by written notice to the registrar.

(4) Reinstatement may be made at any time following the suspension by complying with the arbitrator's award and the final order of the registrar. If no reinstatement of the license is made within 90 days of the date of the automatic suspension, the license and any other contractor's license issued to the licensee shall be automatically revoked by operation of law for a period to be determined by the registrar pursuant to Section 7102.

(5) The registrar may delay, for good cause, the revocation of a contractor's license for failure to comply with the arbitration award. The delay in the revocation of the license shall not exceed one year. When seeking a delay of the revocation of his or her license, a licensee shall apply to the registrar in writing prior to the date of the revocation of the licensee's license by operation of law and state the reasons that establish good cause for the delay. The registrar's power to grant a delay of the revocation shall expire upon the effective date of the revocation of the licensee's license by operation of law.

(b) The licensee shall be automatically prohibited from serving as an officer, director, associate, partner, manager, or qualifying individual of another licensee, for the period determined by the registrar and the employment, election, or association of that person by another licensee shall constitute grounds for disciplinary action. A qualifier disassociated pursuant to this section shall be replaced within 90 days from the date of disassociation. Upon failure to replace the qualifier within 90 days of the disassociation, the license of the other licensee shall be automatically suspended or the qualifier's classification removed at the end of the 90 days.

Added Stats 1979 ch 1013 § 16. Amended Stats 1987 ch 1311 § 6, effective September 28, 1987; Stats 1988 ch 1619 § 2, effective September 30, 1988; Stats 2003 ch 363 § 3 (AB 1382); Stats 2010 ch 698 § 24 (SB 392), effective January 1, 2011.

§ 7085.7. Enforcement of award

A complainant may enforce an arbitrator's award in accordance with Chapter 2 (commencing with Section 1285) of Title 9 of Part 3 of the Code of Civil Procedure.

Added Stats 1987 ch 1311 § 8, effective September 28, 1987.

§ 7085.9. Disclosure to public of complaint referred to arbitration

Notwithstanding any other provision of law, a complaint referred to arbitration pursuant to Section 7085 is not subject to disclosure to the public until such time as an investigation into an alleged violation of Section 7085.6 has been initiated by the registrar.

Added Stats 1988 ch 1035 § 2.

Article 6.5
Solar Energy System Restitution Program
[Repealed effective June 30, 2024]

§ 7086. Administration upon appropriation [Repealed effective June 30, 2024]

The board shall administer the Solar Energy System Restitution Program upon appropriation of one-time resources by the Legislature for the purpose of providing restitution to consumers pursuant to this article.

Added Stats 2021 ch 77 § 1 (AB 137), effective July 16, 2021, repealed June 30, 2024.

§ 7086.1. Definitions [Repealed effective June 30, 2024]

For purposes of this article, the following definitions apply:

(a) "Program" means the Solar Energy System Restitution Program established pursuant to this article.

(b) "Consumer" means any of the following:

(1) A natural person who owns a single-family residence in this state and who contracted with a licensed or unlicensed contractor on or after January 1, 2016, for the installation of a solar energy system on that residence.

(2) A tenant or leaseholder of a single-family residence in this state owned by a natural person who contracted with a licensed or unlicensed contractor on or after January 1, 2016, for the installation of a solar energy system on the owner's residence.

(3) A natural person who purchases a single-family residence from a prior owner of the residence who contracted with a licensed or unlicensed contractor on or after January 1, 2016, for the installation of the solar energy system.

(c) "Solar energy system" has the same meaning as that term is defined in subdivision (g) of Section 7169.

(d) "Financial loss or injury" means an economic loss or expense suffered by a consumer resulting from fraud, misrepresentation, or another unlawful act committed by a residential solar energy system contractor that has not been and will not be fully reimbursed from any other source.

Added Stats 2021 ch 77 § 1 (AB 137), effective July 16, 2021, repealed June 30, 2024.

§ 7086.2. Scope of article [Repealed effective June 30, 2024]

(a) This article governs the administration of the program and operates independently of, and does not affect or relate to the licensing, regulation, and discipline of, contractors.

(b) This article does not limit the authority of the registrar to take disciplinary action against a contractor.

Added Stats 2021 ch 77 § 1 (AB 137), effective July 16, 2021, repealed June 30, 2024.

§ 7086.3. Awards limited to eligible claimants [Repealed effective June 30, 2024]

The registrar or their designee shall only award moneys appropriated to the program to consumers who are eligible claimants pursuant to this article.

Added Stats 2021 ch 77 § 1 (AB 137), effective July 16, 2021, repealed June 30, 2024.

§ 7086.4. Eligilbity criteria [Repealed effective June 30, 2024]

Except as provided in Section 7086.5, a consumer is an eligible claimant only if they meet one of the following criteria:

(a) The consumer has filed a complaint against a licensed contractor investigated pursuant to Article 7 (commencing with Section 7090), that resulted in one or more of the following:

(1) Issuance of an administrative citation that includes a payment of a specified sum to an injured party as prescribed by Section 7099 and that is not under appeal.

(2) Filing of accusation to suspend or revoke the license.

(3) Determination by the registrar or their designee that a probable violation of this chapter has occurred that if proven, would present a risk of harm to the public and would be appropriate for suspension, revocation, or criminal prosecution.

(b) The consumer has obtained a judgment in any civil court of competent jurisdiction for recovery of damages against a licensed or unlicensed contractor, proceedings in connection with the judgment have terminated, including appeals, and the consumer has not received the specified sum or restitution amount as of the date they claim eligibility.

(c) The consumer is the identified victim of a licensed or unlicensed contractor in a criminal case before a California superior court, with an established financial injury or restitution order, proceedings in connection with the judgment have terminated, including appeals, and the consumer has not received the specified sum or restitution amount as of the date they claim eligibility.

Added Stats 2021 ch 77 § 1 (AB 137), effective July 16, 2021, repealed June 30, 2024.

§ 7086.5. Exceptions to ineligibility under Section § 7086.4 [Repealed effective June 30, 2024]

(a) If any consumer alleges financial harm because of the contract for the installation of a solar energy system on their residence, but the board's authority to discipline the contractor has lapsed due to a limitations period specified in Section 7091, then the registrar or their designee may consider whether the consumer who is unable to claim eligibility under Section 7086.4 is nonetheless eligible to receive restitution pursuant to the program. In all those cases, the following apply:

(1) The registrar or their designee may elect to refer the consumer to arbitration process prescribed in Section 7085.5 for the arbitrator to render an award pursuant to the program.

(2) The arbitration shall commence for the sole purpose of determining whether a financial loss occurred, and whether an amount may justifiably be paid to the consumer pursuant to the program. Discipline of the contractor shall not be at issue in any case referred to arbitration under this subdivision and the contractor need not to appear. Any payment amount for the attending consumer shall not be based solely on the fact that the contractor has failed to appear at the arbitration hearing.

(3) The arbitrator has the sole discretion to request the documentation or testimony from the consumer necessary to support payment pursuant to the program, as well as sole discretion to determine whether an award shall be issued pursuant to the program based on the information provided.

(4) The registrar or their designee, or any arbitrator, is not liable to any party for any act or omission in connection with any arbitration conducted under this section.

(5) The arbitrator shall render an award no later than 30 calendar days from the date of closing the hearing, closing a reopened hearing, or if oral hearing has been waived, from the date of transmitting the final statements and proofs to the arbitrator.

(6) A determination on payment to an eligible claimant shall consider all matters relevant to the consumer seeking restitution, including the financial condition of the moneys appropriated to the program, the amount of money being sought, whether the claim appears to be supported by the documentation, whether the claimant has received full or partial payment of their loss from another source, and if there is more than one claimant, the equitable division of available money appropriated to the program among the claimants.

(7) A determination or decision regarding claimant eligibility and payment pursuant to the program and all related issues under this subdivision are final and are not subject to judicial review.

(b) The registrar or their designee may refer a consumer to the arbitration process described in Section 7085.5 for resolution of any claim by a consumer that does not explicitly meet the criteria in subdivision (a) of Section 7086.4.

Added Stats 2021 ch 77 § 1 (AB 137), effective July 16, 2021, repealed June 30, 2024.

§ 7086.6. "Solar Energy System Restitution Program Claim" form; Additional information; Denial [Repealed effective June 30, 2024]

(a) A consumer may claim eligibility for payment pursuant to the program by filing a form with the registrar entitled "Solar Energy System Restitution Program Claim" that shall be provided by the board. A consumer seeking restitution shall include, without limitation:

(1) The name, address, and telephone number of the consumer and which criteria under Section 7086.4 or 7086.5 the consumer claims eligibility.

(2) The name, address, license number, and telephone number, if known, of the contractor who installed the solar energy system.

(3) A description of the facts concerning the loss caused by the contractor, the nature and extent of the claimed loss, and the date on which, or the period during which, the alleged loss occurred.

(4) A copy of the contract, and any or all other relevant documentation specified in Section 7086.7, as applicable, supporting the grounds under which the consumer claims eligibility.

(5) A statement confirming whether the consumer has previously recovered a portion of their loss from sources other than an award pursuant to the program, and if so, in what amount, from what source, and the date that recovery occurred.

(b) The registrar or their designee may request from the consumer any additional information or documentation not specified in this section that the registrar or their designee deems necessary to determine eligibility.

(c) A claim that appears to include false or altered information shall be automatically denied and shall not be considered for restitution pursuant to the program. The denial of the claim shall be the exclusive remedy for filing false information.

(d) Any information or documentation distributed by the board about the program shall include a notice that restitution payments are only available as long as there are appropriated moneys available for payment.

Added Stats 2021 ch 77 § 1 (AB 137), effective July 16, 2021, repealed June 30, 2024.

§ 7086.7. Documentation required for payment [Repealed effective June 30, 2024]

(a) For all claimants deemed eligible pursuant to subdivision (a) of Section 7086.4, a document stamped with the seal of the Contractors State License Board reflecting the complaint number, name of the contractor, name of the special investigator, date of the contract, violation or violations alleged, the specified sum to an injured party amount, the consumer's name, and any other information the registrar deems relevant to include shall be sufficient documentation upon which to make payment to the consumer pursuant to the program.

(b) For all claimants deemed eligible pursuant to subdivision (b) of Section 7086.4, a certified copy of the civil court judgment with the dollar amount of damages shall be sufficient documentation upon which to make payment to the consumer pursuant to the program.

(c) For all claimants deemed eligible pursuant to subdivision (c) of Section 7086.4, a certified minute order or other document of the court of relevant jurisdiction that includes the certified copy of an order of financial injury or restitution amount shall be sufficient documentation upon which to make payment to the consumer pursuant to the program.

(d) For all claimants deemed eligible pursuant to paragraph (1) of subdivision (a) of Section 7086.5, the award of the arbitrator, stamped with the seal of the Contractors State License Board reflecting the complaint number, name of the contractor, name of the arbitrator, date of the contract, violations alleged, the specified sum to an injured party amount, the consumer's name, and any other information the registrar deems relevant to include shall be sufficient documentation upon which to make payment to the consumer pursuant to the program.

Added Stats 2021 ch 77 § 1 (AB 137), effective July 16, 2021, repealed June 30, 2024.

§ 7086.8. Payment limitations; Expenditures [Repealed effective June 30, 2024]

(a) If the registrar or their designee determines that a consumer is eligible for restitution pursuant to this article, the amount paid to a consumer shall not exceed forty thousand dollars ($40,000).

(b) If the registrar or their designee has determined that the injured person has recovered a portion of their loss from sources other than the program at the time they claim eligibility, the board shall deduct the amount recovered from the other sources from the amount payable upon the consumer's claim and direct the difference to be paid.

(c) Subject to appropriation by the Legislature, the board may expend up to one million dollars ($1,000,000) from the moneys appropriated to the program to employ or contract with persons as necessary for the performance of the duties required to administer this article.

Added Stats 2021 ch 77 § 1 (AB 137), effective July 16, 2021, repealed June 30, 2024.

§ 7086.9. Approval and disbursement timelines; Annual accounting statement [Repealed effective June 30, 2024]

(a) The registrar or their designee shall not approve a claim seeking payment pursuant to the program until at least 90 days after the date of the action described in Section 7086.4 or 7086.5 on which the consumer bases their claim of eligibility.

(b) If the registrar or their designee approves payment pursuant to the program to an eligible claimant, the board will forward a copy of the approval of the eligible claim to the accounting office of the Department of Consumer Affairs.

(c) The accounting office shall not commence procedures for the disbursement of money pursuant to an approval of payment from the board until 90 days after the date on which the registrar or their designee approved the eligible claim.

(d) The accounting office shall, on or before February 1 of each year, prepare and submit to the board a statement of the condition of the moneys appropriated to the program that is prepared in accordance with generally accepted accounting principles.

Added Stats 2021 ch 77 § 1 (AB 137), effective July 16, 2021, repealed June 30, 2024.

§ 7086.10. Notice of licensee subject of program payment [Repealed effective June 30, 2024]

(a) For any licensee whose license is revoked or pending revocation whose actions have caused the payment of an award to a consumer pursuant to the program, the board shall display a notice on the public license detail on the board's internet website stating that the licensee was the subject of a payment pursuant to the program.

(b) The notice specified in subdivision (a) shall remain on the board's internet website until seven years after the date of the payment.

(c) This section shall operate independently of, and is not subject to, Section 7124.6.

Added Stats 2021 ch 77 § 1 (AB 137), effective July 16, 2021, repealed June 30, 2024. Amended Stats 2022 ch 11 § 38 (SB 1495), effective January 1, 2023.

§ 7086.11. Repeal of article [Repealed effective June 30, 2024]

This article shall remain in effect until June 30, 2024, and as of that date is repealed.

Added Stats 2021 ch 77 § 1 (AB 137), effective July 16, 2021, repealed June 30, 2024.

Section VI

Article 7

Disciplinary Proceedings

§ 7090. Investigation, suspension, revocation; Construction without permit as violation; Burden of proof

The registrar may upon his or her own motion and shall upon the verified complaint in writing of any person, investigate the actions of any applicant, contractor, or home improvement salesperson within the state and may deny the licensure or the renewal of licensure of, or cite, temporarily suspend, or permanently revoke any license or registration if the applicant, licensee, or registrant, is guilty of or commits any one or more of the acts or omissions constituting causes for disciplinary action.

The registrar may proceed to take disciplinary action as in this article provided against an applicant or a person licensed or registered under the provisions of this chapter even though the grounds or cause for such disciplinary action arose upon projects or while the applicant, licensee, or registrant was acting in a capacity or under circumstances or facts which, under the provisions of Sections 7044, 7045, 7046, and 7048, would otherwise exempt the person or his or her operations from the provisions of this chapter.

Notwithstanding any provision of this chapter, if the registrar finds that any contractor licensed or registered under the provisions of this chapter has willfully and deliberately violated any state or local law relating to the issuance of building permits, other than failure to obtain a county or city permit for repair, maintenance, and adjustment of equipment where such repair, maintenance, or adjustment is valued at less than five hundred dollars ($500) for labor or materials, or where the repair of a part or component part of mechanical equipment consists of replacing such part or component part of mechanical equipment in need of repair with the identical part or component part, the registrar shall take disciplinary action against the contractor's license in accordance with this chapter.

For the purpose of this section, there shall be a rebuttable presumption affecting the burden of proof that construction performed without a permit is a willful and deliberate violation.

For the purposes of this section, with respect to administrative proceedings or hearings to suspend or revoke a contractor's license, the registrar at all times shall have the burden of proof to establish by clear and convincing evidence that he or she is entitled to the relief sought in the petition.

Added Stats 1939 ch 37 § 1. Amended Stats 1941 ch 971 § 15; Stats 1972 ch 1138 § 3.5; Stats 1974 ch 717 § 1; Stats 1975 ch 772 § 1; Stats 1984 ch 1174 § 6; Stats 1997 ch 334 § 2 (SB 299); Stats 2010 ch 698 § 25 (SB 392), effective January 1, 2011.

§ 7090.1. Automatic suspension of license for failure to pay civil penalty or comply with order of correction; Contest of determination; Reinstatement; Delay in revocation for good cause; Dissociation from other licensee

(a)(1) Notwithstanding any other provisions of law, the failure to pay a civil penalty, or to comply with an order of correction or an order to pay a specified sum to an injured party in lieu of correction once the order has become final, shall result in the automatic suspension of a license by operation of law 30 days after noncompliance with the terms of the order.

(2) The registrar shall notify the licensee in writing of the failure to comply with the final order and that the license shall be suspended 30 days from the date of the notice.

(3) The licensee may contest the determination of noncompliance within 15 days after service of the notice, by written notice to the registrar. Upon receipt of the written notice, the registrar may reconsider the determination and after reconsideration may affirm or set aside the suspension.

(4) Reinstatement may be made at any time following the suspension by complying with the final order of the citation. If no reinstatement of the license is made within 90 days of the date of the automatic suspension, the cited license and any other contractors' license issued to the licensee shall be automatically revoked by operation of law for a period to be determined by the registrar pursuant to Section 7102.

(5) The registrar may delay, for good cause, the revocation of a contractor's license for failure to comply with the final order of the citation. The delay in the revocation of the license shall not exceed one year. When seeking a delay of the revocation of his or her license, a licensee shall apply to the registrar in writing prior to the date of the revocation of the licensee's license by operation of law and state the reasons that establish good cause for the delay. The registrar's power to grant a delay of the revocation shall expire upon the effective date of the revocation of the licensee's license by operation of law.

(b) The cited licensee shall also be automatically prohibited from serving as an officer, director, associate, partner, manager, or qualifying individual of another licensee, for the period determined by the registrar, and the employment, election, or association of that person by a licensee shall constitute grounds for disciplinary action. A qualifier disassociated pursuant to this section shall be replaced within 90 days of the date of disassociation. Upon failure to replace the qualifier within 90 days of the prohibition, the license of the other licensee shall be automatically suspended or the qualifier's classification removed at the end of the 90 days.

Added Stats 1984 ch 1174 § 7. Amended Stats 1986 ch 27 § 5; Stats 1987 ch 831 § 1; Stats 1988 ch 1619 § 3, effective September 30, 1988; Stats 2003 ch 363 § 4 (AB 1382); Stats 2004 ch 865 § 14 (SB 1914); Stats 2010 ch 698 § 26 (SB 392), effective January 1, 2011.

§ 7090.5. Effect of correction of condition caused by fraudulent act

In the event a licensee commits a fraudulent act which is a ground for disciplinary action under Section 7116 of this article, the correction of any condition resulting from such act shall not in and of itself preclude the registrar from taking disciplinary action under this article.

If the registrar finds a licensee has engaged in repeated acts which would be grounds for disciplinary action under this article, and if by correction of conditions resulting from those acts the licensee avoided disciplinary action as to each individual act, the correction of those conditions shall not in and of itself preclude the registrar from taking disciplinary action under this article.

Added Stats 1953 ch 576 § 1. Amended Stats 1978 ch 985 § 1.

§ 7091. Filing complaints and disciplinary actions

(a) (1) A complaint against a licensee alleging commission of any patent acts or omissions that may be grounds for legal action shall be filed in writing with the registrar within four years after the act or omission alleged as the ground for the disciplinary action.

(2) A disciplinary action against a licensee relevant to this subdivision shall be filed or a referral to the arbitration program outlined in Section 7085 shall be referred within four years after the patent act or omission alleged as the ground for disciplinary action or arbitration or within 18 months from the date of the filing of the complaint with the registrar, whichever is later.

(b) (1) A complaint against a licensee alleging commission of any latent acts or omissions that may be grounds for legal action pursuant to subdivision (a) of Section 7109 regarding structural defects, as defined by regulation, shall be filed in writing with the registrar within 10 years after the act or omission alleged as the ground for the disciplinary action.

(2) A disciplinary action against a licensee relevant to this subdivision shall be filed within 10 years after the latent act or omission alleged as the ground for disciplinary action or within 18 months from the date of the filing of the complaint with the registrar, whichever is later. As used in this subdivision "latent act or omission" means an act or omission that is not apparent by reasonable inspection.

(c) A disciplinary action alleging a violation of Section 7112 shall be filed within two years after the discovery by the registrar or by the board of the alleged facts constituting the fraud or misrepresentation prohibited by the section.

(d) With respect to a licensee who has been convicted of a crime and, as a result of that conviction is subject to discipline under Section 7123, the disciplinary action shall be filed within two years after the discovery of the conviction by the registrar or by the board.

(e) A disciplinary action regarding an alleged breach of an express, written warranty issued by the contractor shall be filed not later than 18 months from the expiration of the warranty.

(f) The proceedings under this article shall be conducted in accordance with the provisions of Chapter 5 (commencing with Section 11500) of Part 1 of Division 3 of Title 2 of the Government Code, and the registrar shall have all the powers granted therein.

(g) Nothing in this section shall be construed to affect the liability of a surety or the period of limitations prescribed by law for the commencement of actions against a surety or lawful money or cashier's check deposited pursuant to paragraph (1) of subdivision (a) of Section 995.710 of the Code of Civil Procedure.

Added Stats 1939 ch 37 § 1. Amended Stats 1945 ch 886 § 2; Stats 1955 ch 1532 § 5; Stats 1963 ch 1258 § 1; Stats 1980 ch 865 § 1, ch 1210 § 2; Stats 1987 ch 1264 § 5, effective September 28, 1987; Stats 1994 ch 1135 § 2 (AB 3302); Stats 2001 ch 728 § 60 (SB 724); Stats 2002 ch 312 § 3 (AB 728); Stats 2007 ch 85 § 1 (AB 243), effective January 1, 2008; Stats 2018 ch 925 § 5 (AB 3126), effective January 1, 2019.

§ 7095. Decision of registrar

The decision may:

(a) Provide for the immediate complete suspension by the licensee of all operations as a contractor during the period fixed by the decision.

(b) Permit the licensee to complete any or all contracts shown by competent evidence taken at the hearing to be then uncompleted.

(c) Impose upon the licensee compliance with such specific conditions as may be just in connection with his operations as a contractor disclosed at the hearing and may further provide that until such conditions are complied with no application for restoration of the suspended or revoked license shall be accepted by the registrar.

Added Stats 1939 ch 37 § 1.

§ 7096. "Licensee"

For the purposes of this chapter, the term "licensee" shall include an individual, partnership, corporation, limited liability company, joint venture, or any combination or organization licensed under this chapter, and shall also include any named responsible managing officer, responsible managing manager, responsible managing member,

Section VI

or personnel of that licentiate whose appearance has qualified the licentiate under the provisions of Section 7068.

Added Stats 1957 ch 1712 § 1. Amended Stats 1995 ch 467 § 10 (SB 1061); Stats 2010 ch 698 § 27 (SB 392), effective January 1, 2011.

§ 7097. Suspension of additional license issued following suspension of any license

Notwithstanding the provisions of Sections 7121 and 7122, when any license has been suspended by a decision of the registrar pursuant to an accusation or pursuant to subdivision (b) of Section 7071.17, Section 7085.6 or 7090.1, any additional license issued under this chapter in the name of the licensee or for which the licensee furnished qualifying experience and appearance under the provisions of Section 7068, may be suspended by the registrar without further notice.

Added Stats 1957 ch 1712 § 2. Amended Stats 1995 ch 467 § 11 (SB 1061).

§ 7098. Revocation of additional license issued following revocation of license

Notwithstanding the provisions of Sections 7121 and 7122, when any license has been revoked under the provisions of this chapter, any additional license issued under this chapter in the name of the licensee or for which the licensee furnished qualifying experience and appearance under the provisions of Section 7068, may be revoked by the registrar without further notice.

Added Stats 1957 ch 1712 § 3. Amended Stats 1995 ch 467 § 12 (SB 1061).

§ 7099. Citation

If, upon investigation, the registrar has probable cause to believe that a licensee, or an applicant for a license under this chapter, has committed any acts or omissions which are grounds for denial, revocation, or suspension of license, he or she may, in lieu of proceeding pursuant to this article, issue a citation to the licensee or applicant. Each citation shall be in writing and shall describe with particularity the nature of the violation, including a reference to the provisions alleged to have been violated. In addition, each citation may contain an order of correction fixing a reasonable time for correction of the violation or an order, against the licensee only, for payment of a specified sum to an injured party in lieu of correction, and may contain an assessment of a civil penalty.

Added Stats 1979 ch 1013 § 17. Amended Stats 1983 ch 891 § 22; Stats 1984 ch 606 § 1; Stats 1985 ch 1281 § 3; Stats 1986 ch 27 § 6; Stats 1987 ch 930 § 7, effective September 22, 1987.

§ 7099.1. Regulations for order of correction

The board shall promulgate regulations covering the formulation of an order of correction which gives due consideration to the time required to correct and the practical feasibility of correction.

Added Stats 1979 ch 1013 § 18.

§ 7099.2. Regulations for assessment of civil penalties; Factors; Maximum amount; Letter of admonishment

(a) The board shall promulgate regulations covering the assessment of civil penalties under this article that give due consideration to the appropriateness of the penalty with respect to the following factors:

(1) The gravity of the violation.

(2) The good faith of the licensee or applicant for licensure being charged.

(3) The history of previous violations.

(b) Notwithstanding Section 125.9, and except as otherwise provided by this chapter, a civil penalty shall not be assessed in an amount greater than eight thousand dollars ($8,000). Notwithstanding Section 125.9, a civil penalty not to exceed thirty thousand dollars ($30,000) may be assessed for a violation of Section 7110, 7114, 7118, or 7125.4

Added Stats 1979 ch 1013 § 19. Amended Stats 1984 ch 606 § 1.5; Stats 1992 ch 606 § 2 (AB 3240); Stats 1996 ch 282 § 4 (AB 2494); Stats 2003 ch 363 § 5 (AB 1382); Stats 2010 ch 415 § 21 (SB 1491), effective January 1, 2011; Stats 2017 ch 308 § 2 (SB 486), effective January 1, 2018; Stats 2020 ch 312 § 61 (SB 1474), effective January 1, 2021; Stats 2021 ch 94 § 1 (AB 569), effective January 1, 2022; Stats 2022 ch 757 § 1 (AB 1747),effective January 1, 2023.

§ 7099.3. Appeal to registrar

Any licensee or applicant for licensure served with a citation pursuant to Section 7099, may appeal to the registrar within 15 working days from service of the citation with respect to violations alleged by the registrar, correction periods, amount of penalties, and the reasonableness of the change required by the registrar to correct the condition.

Added Stats 1979 ch 1013 § 20. Amended Stats 1983 ch 891 § 23; Stats 1984 ch 606 § 2.

§ 7099.4. Time to contest citation

If within 15 working days from service of the citation issued by the registrar, the licensee or applicant for licensure fails to notify the registrar that he or she intends to contest the citation, the citation shall be deemed a final order of the registrar and not be subject to review by any court or agency. The 15-day period may be extended by the registrar for cause.

Added Stats 1979 ch 1013 § 21. Amended Stats 1983 ch 891 § 24; Stats 1984 ch 606 § 3.

§ 7099.5. Hearing

If a licensee or applicant for licensure notifies the registrar that he or she intends to contest a citation issued under Section 7099, the registrar shall afford an opportunity for a hearing. The registrar shall thereafter issue a decision, based on findings of fact, affirming, modifying, or vacating the citation or penalty, or directing other appropriate relief. The proceedings under this section shall be conducted in accordance with the provisions of Chapter 5 (commencing with Section 11500) of Part 1 of Division 3 of Title 2 of the Government Code, and the registrar shall have all the powers granted therein.

Added Stats 1979 ch 1013 § 22. Amended Stats 1984 ch 606 § 4.

§ 7099.6. Failure to comply with citation as ground for denial, suspension, or revocation of license

(a) The failure of a licensee to comply with a citation after it is final is a ground for suspension or revocation of license.

(b) The failure of an applicant for licensure to comply with a citation after it is final is a ground for denial of license.

Added Stats 1979 ch 1013 § 23. Amended Stats 1984 ch 606 § 5; Stats 1986 ch 1205 § 2.

§ 7099.7. Bond exempt from payment of civil penalty

No order for payment of a civil penalty shall be made against any bond required pursuant to Sections 7071.5 to 7071.8.

Added Stats 1979 ch 1013 § 24.

§ 7099.8. Request for administrative hearing; Request for informal citation conference; Informal citation conference procedures

(a) Notwithstanding any other law, if a person cited pursuant to Section 7028.7 or 7099 wishes to contest the citation, that person shall, within 15 days after service of the citation, file in writing a request for an administrative hearing as provided pursuant to Section 7028.12 or 7099.5.

(b) (1) In addition to, or instead of, requesting an administrative hearing pursuant to subdivision (a), the person cited pursuant to Section 7028.7 or 7099 may, within 15 days after service of the citation, contest the citation by submitting a written request for an informal citation conference to the chief of the enforcement division or a designee.

(2) Upon receipt of a written request for an informal citation conference, the chief of the enforcement division or a designee shall, within 60 days of the request, hold an informal citation conference with the person requesting the conference. The cited person may be accompanied and represented by an attorney or other authorized representative.

(3) If an informal citation conference is held, the request for an administrative hearing shall be deemed withdrawn and the chief of the enforcement division, or a designee, may affirm, modify, or dismiss the citation at the conclusion of the informal citation conference. If so affirmed or modified, the citation originally issued shall be considered withdrawn and an affirmed or modified citation, including reasons for the decision, shall be issued. The affirmed or modified citation shall be mailed to the cited person and that person's counsel, if any, within 10 days of the date of the informal citation conference.

(4) If a cited person wishes to contest a citation affirmed or modified pursuant to paragraph (3), the person shall, within 30 days after service of the modified or affirmed citation, contest the affirmed or modified citation by submitting a written request for an administrative hearing to the chief of the enforcement division or a designee. An informal citation conference shall not be held for affirmed or modified citations.

(c) The citation conference is informal and shall not be subject to the Administrative Procedure Act (Chapter 4.5 (commencing with Section 11400) of, or Chapter 5 (commencing with Section 11500) of Part 1 of, Division 3 of Title 2 of the Government Code).

Added Stats 2018 ch 110 § 1 (SB 1042), effective January 1, 2019. Amended Stats 2019 ch 497 § 12 (AB 991), effective January 1, 2020.

§ 7099.9. Letter of admonishment

(a) If, upon investigation, the registrar has probable cause to believe that a licensee, registrant, or applicant has committed acts or omissions that are grounds for denial, suspension, or revocation of a license or registration, the registrar, or their designee, may issue a letter of admonishment to an applicant, licensee, or registrant in lieu of issuing a citation. Nothing in this article shall in any way limit the registrar's discretionary authority or ability to issue a letter of admonishment as prescribed by this subdivision.

(b) The letter of admonishment shall be in writing and shall describe in detail the nature and facts of the violation, including a reference to the statutes or regulations violated. The letter of admonishment shall inform the licensee, registrant, or applicant that within

30 days of service of the letter of admonishment the licensee, registrant, or applicant may do either of the following:

(1) Submit a written request for an office conference to the registrar to contest the letter of admonishment. Upon a timely request, the registrar, or their designee, shall hold an office conference with the licensee, registrant, or applicant and, if applicable, their legal counsel or authorized representative.

(A) No individual other than the legal counsel or authorized representative of the licensee, registrant, or applicant may accompany the licensee, registrant, or applicant to the office conference.

(B) Prior to or at the office conference, the licensee, registrant, or applicant may submit to the registrar declarations and documents pertinent to the subject matter of the letter of admonishment.

(C) The office conference is intended to be informal and shall not be subject to the Administrative Procedure Act (Chapter 4.5 (commencing with Section 11400) or Chapter 5 (commencing with Section 11500) of Part 1 of Division 3 of Title 2 of the Government Code).

(D) After the office conference, the registrar, or their designee, may affirm, modify, or withdraw the letter of admonishment. Within 14 calendar days from the date of the office conference, the registrar, or their designee, shall personally serve or send the written decision by certified mail to the licensee's, registrant's, or applicant's address of record. This decision shall be deemed the final administrative decision concerning the letter of admonishment.

(E) Judicial review of the decision may be had by filing a petition for a writ of mandate in accordance with the provisions of Section 1094.5 of the Code of Civil Procedure within 30 days after the date the decision was personally served or sent by certified mail. The judicial review shall extend to the question of whether or not there was a prejudicial abuse of discretion in the issuance of the letter of admonishment or in the decision after the office conference.

(2) Comply with the letter of admonishment and, if required, submit a written corrective action plan to the registrar documenting compliance. If an office conference is not requested pursuant to this section, compliance with the letter of admonishment shall not constitute an admission of the violation noted in the letter of admonishment.

(c) The letter of admonishment shall be served upon the licensee, registrant, or applicant personally or by certified mail at their address of record with the board. If the licensee, registrant, or applicant is served by certified mail, service shall be effective upon deposit in the United States mail.

(d) The licensee, registrant, or applicant shall maintain and have readily available a copy of the letter of admonishment and corrective action plan, if any, for at least one year from the date of issuance of the letter of admonishment.

(e) Nothing in this subdivision shall in any way limit the board's authority or ability to do either of the following:

(1) Issue a citation pursuant to Section 125.9, 148, or 7099.

(2) Institute disciplinary proceedings pursuant to this article.

(f) The issuance of a letter of admonishment shall not be construed as a disciplinary action or discipline for purposes of licensure or the reporting of discipline for licensure.

(g) The board shall not issue a letter of admonishment when any one of the following factors is present:

(1) The licensee, registrant, or applicant was unlicensed at the time of the violation.

(2) The licensee, registrant, or applicant has a history of the same or similar violations.

(3) The violation resulted in financial harm to another.

(4) The victim is an elder or dependent adult as defined in Section 368 of the Penal Code.

(5) The violation is related to the repair of damage caused by a natural disaster.

(h) The board may adopt regulations to further define the circumstances under which a letter of admonishment may be issued.

Added Stats 2020 ch 312 § 62 (SB 1474), effective January 1, 2021; Stats 2021 ch 94 § 1 (AB 569), effective January 1, 2022.

§ 7099.10. Citation; Hearing; Disconnection of telephone service

(a) If, upon investigation, the registrar has probable cause to believe that a licensee, an applicant for a license, or an unlicensed individual acting in the capacity of a contractor who is not otherwise exempted from the provisions of this chapter, has violated Section 7027.1 by advertising for construction or work of improvement covered by this chapter in an alphabetical or classified directory, without being properly licensed, the registrar may issue a citation under Section 7099 containing an order of correction which requires the violator to cease the unlawful advertising and to notify the telephone company furnishing services to the violator to disconnect the telephone service furnished to any telephone number contained in the unlawful advertising, and that subsequent calls to that number shall not be referred by the telephone company to any new telephone number obtained by that person.

(b) If the person to whom a citation is issued under subdivision (a) notifies the registrar that he or she intends to contest the citation, the registrar shall afford an opportunity for a hearing, as specified in Section 7099.5, within 90 days after receiving the notification.

(c) If the person to whom a citation and order of correction is issued under subdivision (a) fails to comply with the order of correction after the order is final, the registrar shall inform the Public Utilities Commission of the violation, and the Public Utilities Commission shall require the telephone corporation furnishing services to that person to disconnect the telephone service furnished to any telephone number contained in the unlawful advertising.

(d) The good faith compliance by a telephone corporation with an order of the Public Utilities Commission to terminate service issued pursuant to this section shall constitute a complete defense to any civil or criminal action brought against the telephone corporation arising from the termination of service.

Added Stats 1986 ch 518 § 2. Amended Stats 1991 ch 1160 § 32 (AB 2190); Stats 1992 ch 294 § 3 (AB 2347).

§ 7099.11. Advertising to promote services for asbestos removal; Notice to comply; Citation

(a) No person shall advertise, as that term is defined in Section 7027.1, to promote his or her services for the removal of asbestos unless he or she is certified to engage in asbestos-related work pursuant to Section 7058.5, and registered for that purpose pursuant to Section 6501.5 of the Labor Code. Each advertisement shall include that person's certification and registration numbers and shall use the same name under which that person is certified and registered.

(b) The registrar shall issue a notice to comply with the order of correction provisions of subdivision (a) of Section 7099.10, to any person who is certified and registered, as described in subdivision (a), and who fails to include in any advertisement his or her certification and registration numbers.

(c) The registrar shall issue a citation pursuant to Section 7099 to any person who fails to comply with the notice required by subdivision (b), or who advertises to promote his or her services for the removal of asbestos but does not possess valid certification and registration numbers as required by subdivision (a), or who fails to use in that advertisement the same name under which he or she is certified and registered.

Citations shall be issued and conducted pursuant to Sections 7099 to 7099.10, inclusive.

Added Stats 1988 ch 1003 § 1, operative July 1, 1989, as § 7030.6. Amended and renumbered by Stats 1991 ch 1160 § 22 (AB 2190). Amended Stats 1992 ch 294 § 4 (AB 2347).

§ 7100. Continuance of business pending review

In any proceeding for review by a court, the court may in its discretion, upon the filing of a proper bond by the licensee in an amount to be fixed by the court, but not less than one thousand dollars ($1,000) or an amount the court finds is sufficient to protect the public, whichever is greater, guaranteeing the compliance by the licensee with specific conditions imposed upon him by the registrar's decision, if any, permit the licensee to continue to do business as a contractor pending entry of judgment by the court in the case. There shall be no stay of the registrar's decision pending an appeal or review of any such proceeding unless the appellant or applicant for review shall file a bond in all respects conditioned as, and similar to, the bond required to stay the effect of the registrar's decision in the first instance.

Added Stats 1939 ch 37 § 1. Amended Stats 1945 ch 886 § 3; Stats 1949 ch 753 § 1; Stats 1979 ch 1013 § 27.

§ 7102. Reinstatement or reissuance of license

After suspension of a license upon any of the grounds set forth in this chapter, the registrar may reinstate the license upon proof of compliance by the contractor with all provisions of the decision as to reinstatement or, in the absence of a decision or any provisions of reinstatement, in the sound discretion of the registrar.

After revocation of a license upon any of the grounds set forth in this chapter, the license shall not be reinstated or reissued and a license shall not be issued to any member of the personnel of the revoked licensee found to have had knowledge of or participated in the acts or omissions constituting grounds for revocation, within a minimum period of one year and a maximum period of five years after the final decision of revocation and then only on proper showing that all loss caused by the act or omission for which the license was revoked has been fully satisfied and that all conditions imposed by the decision of revocation have been complied with.

The board shall promulgate regulations covering the criteria to be considered when extending the minimum one-year period. The criteria shall give due consideration to the appropriateness of the extension of time with respect to the following factors:

(a) The gravity of the violation.

(b) The history of previous violations.

(c) Criminal convictions.

When any loss has been reduced to a monetary obligation or debt, however, the satisfaction of the monetary obligation or debt as a prerequisite for the issuance, reissuance, or reinstatement of a license shall not be required to the extent the monetary obligation or debt was discharged in a bankruptcy proceeding. However, any nonmonetary condition not discharged in a bankruptcy proceeding shall be complied with prior to the issuance, the reissuance, or reinstatement of the license.

Added Stats 1939 ch 37 § 1. Amended Stats 1961 ch 1635 § 5, operative October 1, 1962; Stats 1975 ch 818 § 1; Stats 1983 ch 891 § 25; Stats 1987 ch 831 § 2; Stats 1995 ch 467 § 13 (SB 1061); Stats 2006 ch 123 § 1 (AB 2658), effective January 1, 2007.

§ 7103. Effect of disciplinary action by another state

The revocation, suspension, or other disciplinary action of a license to act as a contractor by another state shall constitute grounds for disciplinary action in this state if the individual is a licensee, or applies for a license, in this state. A certified copy of the revocation, suspension, or other disciplinary action by the other state is conclusive evidence of that action.

Added Stats 1994 ch 1135 § 2 (AB 3302).

§ 7104. Notice to complainant of resolution of complaint

When the board resolves a complaint, the board shall notify the complainant in writing of its action and the reasons for taking that action. The board shall provide the same notice in writing to the contractor provided that the contractor is licensed and the notification would not jeopardize an action or investigation that involves the contractor.

Added Stats 1994 ch 1135 § 4 (AB 3302).

§ 7106. Revocation or suspension of license incident to court action

The suspension or revocation of license as in this chapter provided may also be embraced in any action otherwise proper in any court involving the licensee's performance of his legal obligation as a contractor.

Added Stats 1939 ch 37 § 1.

§ 7106.5. Effect of expiration, cancellation, forfeiture, revocation, or suspension of license on jurisdiction of registrar

The expiration, cancellation, forfeiture, revocation, or suspension of a license by operation of law or by order or decision of the registrar or a court of law, or the voluntary surrender of a license by a licensee, shall not deprive the registrar of jurisdiction to proceed with any investigation of or action or disciplinary proceeding against the license, or to render a decision suspending or revoking the license.

Added Stats 1941 ch 971 § 16. Amended Stats 1961 ch 1636 § 6, operative October 1, 1962; Stats 2002 ch 1013 § 61.3 (SB 2026); Stats 2012 ch 85 § 2 (AB 2554), effective January 1, 2013.

§ 7107. Abandonment of contract

Abandonment without legal excuse of any construction project or operation engaged in or undertaken by the licensee as a contractor constitutes a cause for disciplinary action.

Added Stats 1939 ch 37 § 1.

§ 7108. Diversion or misapplication of funds or property

Diversion of funds or property received for prosecution or completion of a specific construction project or operation, or for a specified purpose in the prosecution or completion of any construction project or operation, or failure substantially to account for the application or use of such funds or property on the construction project or operation for which such funds or property were received constitutes a cause for disciplinary action.

Added Stats 1939 ch 37 § 1. Amended Stats 1959 ch 97 § 1.

—*See Penal Code Section 484b, Wrongful Diversion of Public Funds, a Public Offense, in Appendix.*

§ 7108.5. Failure to pay subcontractors

(a) A prime contractor or subcontractor shall pay to any subcontractor, not later than seven days after receipt of each progress payment, unless otherwise agreed to in writing, the respective amounts allowed the contractor on account of the work performed by the subcontractors, to the extent of each subcontractor's interest therein. In the event that there is a good faith dispute over all or any portion of the amount due on a progress payment from the prime contractor or subcontractor to a subcontractor, the prime contractor or subcontractor may withhold no more than 150 percent of the disputed amount.

(b) Any violation of this section shall constitute a cause for disciplinary action and shall subject the licensee to a penalty, payable to the subcontractor, of 2 percent of the amount due per month for every month that payment is not made.

(c) In any action for the collection of funds wrongfully withheld, the prevailing party shall be entitled to his or her attorney's fees and costs.

(d) The sanctions authorized under this section shall be separate from, and in addition to, all other remedies, either civil, administrative, or criminal.

(e) This section applies to all private works of improvement and to all public works of improvement, except where Section 10262 of the Public Contract Code applies.

Added Stats 2009 ch 307 § 73 (SB 821), effective January 1, 2010. Amended Stats 2010 ch 328 § 16 (SB 1330), effective January 1, 2011; Stats 2011 ch 700 § 1 (SB 293), effective January 1, 2012.

—See Public Contract Code Section 10262, in the Appendix.

§ 7108.6. Failure to pay transportation charges submitted by dump truck carrier

A licensed contractor is required to pay all transportation charges submitted by a duly authorized motor carrier of property in dump truck equipment by the 20th day following the last day of the calendar month in which the transportation was performed, if the charges, including all necessary documentation, are submitted by the fifth day following the last day of the calendar month in which the transportation was performed. The payment shall be made unless otherwise agreed to in writing by the contractor and by the duly authorized motor carrier of property in dump truck equipment. In the event that there is a good faith dispute over a portion of the charges claimed, the contractor may withhold payment of up to 150 percent of the disputed amount or an amount otherwise agreed to by the parties. A violation of this section constitutes a cause for disciplinary action under Section 7120 and shall also subject the contractor licensee to a penalty, payable to the carrier, of 2 percent of the amount due per month for every month that payment is outstanding. In an action for the collection of moneys not paid in accordance with this section, the prevailing party shall be entitled to his or her attorney's fees and costs.

This section applies to all private works of improvement and to all public works of improvement.

Added Stats 1984 ch 1494 § 1. Amended Stats 1995 ch 37 § 1 (AB 311); Stats 1996 ch 712 § 3 (SB 1557).

§ 7109. Departure from accepted trade standards; Departure from plans or specifications

(a) A willful departure in any material respect from accepted trade standards for good and workmanlike construction constitutes a cause for disciplinary action, unless the departure was in accordance with plans and specifications prepared by or under the direct supervision of an architect.

(b) A willful departure from or disregard of plans or specifications in any material respect, which is prejudicial to another, without the consent of the owner or his or her duly authorized representative and without the consent of the person entitled to have the particular construction project or operation completed in accordance with such plans or specifications, constitutes a cause for disciplinary action.

Added Stats 1939 ch 37 § 1. Amended Stats 1963 ch 1611 § 1; Stats 1988 ch 1619 § 4, effective September 30, 1988.

—See Business & Professions Code Section 8556 Removal and Replacement of Pest Damage Areas; Application of Wood Preservatives: Contracting for Performance of Soil Treatment Pest Control Work, in Appendix.

§ 7109.5. Violation of safety provisions

(a) Violation of any safety provision in, or authorized by, Article 12 (commencing with Section 3420) of Group 3 of Subchapter 7 of Chapter 4 of Division 1 of Title 8 of the California Code of Regulations constitutes a cause for disciplinary action without regard to whether death or serious injury to an employee resulted from the violation.

(b) Violation of any safety provision in, or authorized by, Division 5 (commencing with Section 6300) of the Labor Code resulting in death or serious injury to an employee constitutes a cause for disciplinary action.

Added Stats 1963 ch 1083 § 2. Amended Stats 2020 ch 128 § 1 (AB 2210), effective January 1, 2021.

§ 7110. Disregard or violation of statutes

Willful or deliberate disregard and violation of the building laws of the state, or of any political subdivision thereof, or of any of the following references to or provisions of law, constitutes a cause for disciplinary action against a licensee:

(a) Section 8550 or 8556.

(b) Sections 1689.5 to 1689.15, inclusive, of the Civil Code.

(c) The safety laws or labor laws or compensation insurance laws or Unemployment Insurance Code of the state.

(d) The Subletting and Subcontracting Fair Practices Act (Chapter 4 (commencing with Section 4100) of Part 1 of Division 2 of the Public Contract Code).

(e) Any provision of the Health and Safety Code or Water Code, relating to the digging, boring, or drilling of water wells.

(f) Any provision of Article 2 (commencing with Section 4216) of Chapter 3.1 of Division 5 of Title 1 of the Government Code.

(g) Section 374.3 of the Penal Code or any substantially similar law or ordinance that is promulgated by a local government agency as defined in Section 82041 of the Government Code.

(h) Any state or local law relating to the issuance of building permits.

Added Stats 2021 ch 46 § 2 (AB 246), effective January 1, 2022. Amended Stats 2022 ch 757 § 2 (AB 1747), effective January 1, 2023.

—See Public Contract Code Sections 4107 and 4110.

§ 7110.1. Requiring or causing execution of release

The requiring of an execution of release of any claim or the causing of the execution of any such release in violation of Section 206.5 of the Labor Code is a cause for disciplinary action.

Added Stats 1959 ch 1066 § 2.

—See Labor Code Section 206.5, Violation: Release of Claim for Wages, in Appendix.

§ 7110.5. Initiation of action against contractor after receipt of Labor Commissioner's finding of willful violation of Labor Code or transmission of citations.

Upon receipt of a certified copy of the Labor Commissioner's finding of a willful or deliberate violation of the Labor Code by a licensee, pursuant to Section 98.9 of the Labor Code, or upon transmission to the Contractors' State License Board of copies of any citations or other actions taken by the Division of Occupational Safety and Health pursuant to Article 12 (commencing with Section 3420) of Group 3 of Subchapter 7 of Chapter 4 of Division 1 of Title 8 of the Code of California Regulations, the registrar shall initiate disciplinary action against the licensee within 18 months from the date of the registrar's receipt of the violation.

Added Stats 1978 ch 1247 § 1. Amended Stats 2005 ch 280 § 9 (SB 1112), effective January 1, 2006; Stats 2014 ch 392 § 4 (SB 315), effective January 1, 2015; Stats 2020 ch 128 § 2 (AB 2210), effective January 1, 2021.

§ 7111. Failure to make and keep records for inspection; Disciplinary action

(a) Failure to make and keep records showing all contracts, documents, records, receipts, and disbursements by a licensee of all of his or her transactions as a contractor, and failure to have those records available for inspection by the registrar or his or her duly authorized representative for a period of not less than five years after completion of any construction project or operation to which the records refer, or refusal by a licensee to comply with a written request of the registrar to make the records available for inspection constitutes a cause for disciplinary action.

(b) Failure of a licensee, applicant, or registrant subject to the provisions of this chapter, who without lawful excuse, delays, obstructs, or refuses to comply with a written request of the registrar or designee for information or records, to provide that information or make available those records, when the information or records are required in the attempt to discharge any duty of the registrar, constitutes a cause for disciplinary action.

Added Stats 1939 ch 37 § 1. Amended Stats 1959 ch 98 § 1; Stats 1988 ch 1035 § 3; Stats 1991 ch 1160 § 33 (AB 2190).

§ 7111.1. Failure to respond to request to cooperate in investigation of complaint

The failure of, or refusal by, a licensee to respond to a written request of the registrar to cooperate in the investigation of a complaint against that licensee constitutes a cause for disciplinary action.

Added Stats 1984 ch 1174 § 8.

§ 7112. Omission or misrepresentation of material fact by applicant

Omission or misrepresentation of a material fact by an applicant or a licensee in obtaining, or renewing a license, or in adding a classification to an existing license constitutes a cause for disciplinary action.

Added Stats 1939 ch 37 § 1. Amended Stats 2001 ch 728 § 61 (SB 724).

§ 7112.1. Expungement of classification due to omission or misrepresentation

Any classification that has been added to an existing license record as a result of an applicant or licensee omitting or misrepresenting a material fact shall be expunged from the license record pursuant to a final order of the registrar evidencing a violation of Section 7112.

Added Stats 2001 ch 728 § 62 (SB 724).

§ 7113. Failure to complete project for contract price

Failure in a material respect on the part of a licensee to complete any construction project or operation for the price stated in the contract for such construction project or operation or in any modification of such contract constitutes a cause for disciplinary action.

Added Stats 1939 ch 37 § 1.

§ 7113.5. Avoidance or settlement of obligations for less than full amount

The avoidance or settlement by a licensee for less than the full amount of the lawful obligations of the licensee incurred as a contractor, whether by (a) composition, arrangement, or reorganization with creditors under state law, (b) composition, arrangement, or reorganization with creditors under any agreement or understanding, (c) receivership as provided in Chapter 5 (commencing at Section 564) of Title 7 of Part 2 of the Code of Civil Procedure, (d) assignment for the benefit of creditors, (e) trusteeship, or (f) dissolution, constitutes a cause for disciplinary action.

This section shall not apply to an individual settlement of the obligation of a licensee by the licensee with a creditor that is not a part of or in connection with a settlement with other creditors of the licensee.

No disciplinary action shall be commenced against a licensee for discharge of or settling in bankruptcy under federal law, the licensee's lawful obligations incurred as a contractor for less than the full amount of the obligations, so long as the licensee satisfies all of those lawful obligations, to the extent the obligations are not discharged under federal law.

Added Stats 1959 ch 1361 § 1. Amended Stats 1961 ch 1636 § 7, operative October 1, 1962; Stats 1963 ch 991 § 1; Stats 1975 ch 818 § 2; Stats 1980 ch 135 § 1; Stats 2006 ch 123 § 2 (AB 2658), effective January 1, 2007; Stats 2009. Ch. 500 (AB 1059).

§ 7114. Aiding, abetting, or conspiring with unlicensed person to evade law

(a) Aiding or abetting an unlicensed person to evade the provisions of this chapter or combining or conspiring with an unlicensed person, or allowing one's license to be used by an unlicensed person, or acting as agent or partner or associate, or otherwise, of an unlicensed person with the intent to evade the provisions of this chapter constitutes a cause for disciplinary action.

(b) A licensee who is found by the registrar to have violated subdivision (a) shall, in accordance with the provisions of this article, be subject to the registrar's authority to order payment of a specified sum to an injured party, including, but not limited to, payment for any injury resulting from the acts of the unlicensed person.

Added Stats 1939 ch 37 § 1. Amended Stats 1975 ch 329 § 2; Stats 2007 ch 299 § 1 (SB 354), effective January 1, 2008; Stats 2013 ch 319 § 8 (SB 822), effective January 1, 2014.

§ 7114.1. False certification of qualifications

Any licensee whose signature appears on a falsified certificate in support of an examinee's experience qualifications, or otherwise certifying to false or misleading experience claims by an applicant, which have been submitted to obtain a contractor's license shall be subject to disciplinary action.

Added Stats 1983 ch 891 § 26.

§ 7114.2. Administrative remedies authorized for misuse of contractor license

Any licensed or unlicensed person who commits any act prohibited by Section 119 is subject to the administrative remedies authorized by this chapter. Unless otherwise expressly provided, the remedies authorized under this section shall be separate from, and in addition to, all other available remedies, whether civil or criminal.

Added Stats 2013 ch 163 § 1 (SB 261), effective January 1, 2014.

§ 7115. Material failure to comply with chapter, rules, or regulations

Failure in any material respect to comply with the provisions of this chapter, or any rule or regulation adopted pursuant to this chapter, or to comply with the provisions of Section 7106 of the Public Contract Code, constitutes a cause for disciplinary action.

Added Stats 1939 ch 37 § 1. Amended Stats 1983 ch 891 § 27; Stats 1984 ch 1174 § 9; Stats 1990 ch 485 § 1 (SB 2290); Stats 1991 ch 1160 § 34 (AB 2190).

§ 7116. Wilful or fraudulent act injuring another

The doing of any wilful or fraudulent act by the licensee as a contractor in consequence of which another is substantially injured constitutes a cause for disciplinary action.

Added Stats 1939 ch 37 § 1.

§ 7116.5. Causes for discipline

It is a cause for discipline for a licensee to do any of the following:

(a) Engage in any conduct that subverts or attempts to subvert an investigation of the board.

(b) Threaten or harass any person or licensee for providing evidence in any possible or actual disciplinary action, arbitration, or other legal action.

(c) Discharge an employee primarily because of the employee's attempt to comply with or aid in compliance with the provisions of this chapter.

Added Stats 2003 ch 607 § 33 (SB 1077).

§ 7117. Acting as contractor under unlicensed name or personnel

Acting in the capacity of a contractor under any license issued hereunder except: (a) in the name of the licensee as set forth upon the license, or (b) in accordance with the personnel of the licensee as set

Section VI

forth in the application for such license, or as later changed as provided in this chapter, constitutes a cause for disciplinary action.

Added Stats 1939 ch 37 § 1.

§ 7117.5. Acting as contractor under inactive or suspended license

(a) Acting in the capacity of a contractor under any license which has been made inactive, as provided in Section 7076.5, constitutes a cause for disciplinary action.

(b) Acting in the capacity of a contractor under any license that has been suspended for any reason constitutes a cause for disciplinary action.

(c) Acting in the capacity of a contractor under any license that has expired constitutes a cause for disciplinary action if the license is subject to renewal pursuant to Section 7141. The actions authorized under this section shall be separate from, and in addition to, all other remedies either civil or criminal.

Added Stats 1961 ch 2099 § 2. Amended Stats 1984 ch 1174 § 10; Stats 1995 ch 467 § 15 (SB 1061).

§ 7117.6. Acting as contractor in unauthorized classification

Acting in the capacity of a contractor in a classification other than that currently held by the licensee constitutes a cause for disciplinary action.

Added Stats 1983 ch 891 § 28.

§ 7118. Entering into contract with unlicensed contractor

Entering into a contract with a contractor while such contractor is not licensed as provided in this chapter constitutes a cause for disciplinary action.

Added Stats 1939 ch 37 § 1. Amended Stats 1975 ch 329 § 3.

§ 7118.4. Asbestos inspections; Disclosure requirements

(a) If a contractor has made an inspection for the purpose of determining the presence of asbestos or the need for related remedial action with knowledge that the report has been required by a person as a condition of making a loan of money secured by the property, or is required by a public entity as a condition of issuing a permit concerning the property, the contractor shall disclose orally and in writing if it is owned or has any common ownership, or any financial relationship whatsoever, including, but not limited to, commissions or referral fees, with an entity in the business of performing the corrective work.

(b) This section does not prohibit a contractor that has contracted to perform corrective work after the report of another company has indicated the presence of asbestos or the need for related remedial action from making its own inspection prior to performing that corrective work or from making an inspection to determine whether the corrective measures were successful and, if not, thereafter performing additional corrective work.

(c) A violation of this section is grounds for disciplinary action.

(d) A violation of this section is a misdemeanor punishable by a fine of not less than three thousand dollars ($3,000) and not more than five thousand dollars ($5,000), or by imprisonment in the county jail for not more than one year, or both.

(e) For the purpose of this section, "asbestos" has the meaning set forth in Section 6501.7 of the Labor Code.

Added Stats 1988 ch 1491 § 1.

§ 7118.5. Sanctions against contractor hiring uncertified person to perform asbestos-related work

Any contractor, applicant for licensure, or person required to be licensed, who, either knowingly or negligently, or by reason of a failure to inquire, enters into a contract with another person who is required to be, and is not, certified pursuant to Section 7058.5 to engage in asbestos-related work, as defined in Section 6501.8 of the Labor Code, is subject to the following penalties:

(a) Conviction of a first offense is an infraction punishable by a fine of not less than one thousand dollars ($1,000) or more than three thousand dollars ($3,000), and by possible revocation or suspension of any contractor's license.

(b) Conviction of a subsequent offense is a misdemeanor requiring revocation or suspension of any contractor's license, and a fine of not less than three thousand dollars ($3,000) or more than five thousand dollars ($5,000), or imprisonment in the county jail for not more than one year, or both the fine and imprisonment.

Added Stats 1988 ch 1003 § 4, operative July 1, 1989. Amended Stats 1991 ch 1160 § 35 (AB 2190).

§ 7118.6. Sanctions for contracting with uncertified person to perform removal or remedial action

Any contractor who, either knowingly or negligently, or by reason of a failure to inquire, enters into a contract with another person who is required to be, and is not certified pursuant to Section 7058.7 to engage in a removal or remedial action, as defined in Section 7058.7, is subject to the following penalties:

(a) Conviction of a first offense is an infraction punishable by a fine of not less than one thousand dollars ($1,000) or more than three thousand dollars ($3,000), and by possible revocation or suspension of any contractor's license.

(b) Conviction of a subsequent offense is a misdemeanor requiring revocation or suspension of any contractor's license, and a fine of not less than three thousand dollars ($3,000) or more than five thousand dollars ($5,000), or imprisonment in the county jail for not more than one year, or both the fine and imprisonment.

Added Stats 1986 ch 1443 § 3, effective September 30, 1986. Amended Stats 1991 ch 1160 § 36 (AB 2190).

§ 7119. Failure to prosecute work diligently

Wilful failure or refusal without legal excuse on the part of a licensee as a contractor to prosecute a construction project or operation with reasonable diligence causing material injury to another constitutes a cause for disciplinary action.

Added Stats 1939 ch 37 § 1.

§ 7120. Failure to pay for materials or services; False denial of liability

Wilful or deliberate failure by any licensee or agent or officer thereof to pay any moneys, when due for any materials or services rendered in connection with his operations as a contractor, when he has the capacity to pay or when he has received sufficient funds therefor as payment for the particular construction work, project, or operation for which the services or materials were rendered or purchased constitutes a cause for disciplinary action, as does the false denial of any such amount due or the validity of the claim thereof with intent to secure for himself, his employer, or other person, any discount upon such indebtedness or with intent to hinder, delay, or defraud the person to whom such indebtedness is due.

Added Stats 1939 ch 37 § 1.

§ 7121. Participation in certain acts as disqualification from employment, election or association by licensee; Disciplinary action

A person who has been denied a license for a reason other than failure to document sufficient satisfactory experience for a supplemental classification for an existing license, or who has had his or her license revoked, or whose license is under suspension, or who has failed to renew his or her license while it was under suspension, or who has been a partner, officer, director, manager, or associate of any partnership, corporation, limited liability company, firm, or association whose application for a license has been denied for a reason other than failure to document sufficient satisfactory experience for a supplemental classification for an existing license, or whose license has been revoked, or whose license is under suspension, or who has failed to renew a license while it was under suspension, and while acting as a partner, officer, director, manager, or associate had knowledge of or participated in any of the prohibited acts for which the license was denied, suspended, or revoked, shall be prohibited from serving as an officer, director, associate, partner, manager, qualifying individual, or member of the personnel of record of a licensee, and the employment, election, or association of this type of person by a licensee in any capacity other than as a nonsupervising bona fide employee shall constitute grounds for disciplinary action.

Added Stats 1941 ch 971 § 18. Amended Stats 1983 ch 891 § 29; Stats 2003 ch 363 § 6 (AB 1382); Stats 2004 ch 865 § 15 (SB 1914); Stats 2010 ch 698 § 28 (SB 392), effective January 1, 2011.

§ 7121.1. Responsibility of disassociated partner, officer, director, manager, or associate for compliance with citation

Notwithstanding any other provision of this chapter, the disassociation of a partner, officer, director, manager, or associate from the license of a partnership, corporation, limited liability company, firm, or association whose license has been cited pursuant to Section 7099 shall not relieve the partner, officer, director, manager, or associate from responsibility for complying with the citation if he or she had knowledge of, or participated in, any of the prohibited acts for which the citation was issued. Section 7121 shall apply to a partner, officer, director, manager, or associate of a licensee that fails to comply with a citation after it is final.

Added Stats 1994 ch 192 § 2 (AB 3475). Amended Stats 2010 ch 698 § 29 (SB 392), effective January 1, 2011.

§ 7121.5. Effect of participation by qualifying individual in acts for which license suspended, revoked, or not renewed

A person who was the qualifying individual on a revoked license, or of a license under suspension, or of a license that was not renewed while it was under suspension, shall be prohibited from serving as an officer, director, associate, partner, manager, or qualifying individual of a licensee, whether or not the individual had knowledge of or participated in the prohibited acts or omissions for which the license was revoked, or suspended, and the employment, election, or association of that person by a licensee shall constitute grounds for disciplinary action.

Added Stats 1983 ch 891 § 30. Amended Stats 2010 ch 698 § 30 (SB 392), effective January 1, 2011.

§ 7121.6. Restricted activities for specified individuals

(a) An individual who meets all of the following criteria shall not perform any act regulated under this chapter for or on behalf of a licensee, other than as a bona fide nonsupervising employee:

(1) The individual was listed as an officer, director, owner, manager, partner, or associate of a license that was revoked.

(2) The individual had knowledge of or participated in any act or omission for which the license was revoked.

(3) The individual is not eligible for reinstatement for licensure under Section 7102.

(b) An individual who meets all of the following criteria shall not perform any act regulated under this chapter for or on behalf of a licensee, other than as a bona fide nonsupervising employee:

(1) The individual furnished the qualifications for licensure, as set forth under Section 7068, and that license was revoked.

(2) The individual served in the capacity of the qualifying individual during the commission or omission of any of the acts that resulted in the revocation of the license, whether or not he or she had knowledge of or participated in those acts.

(3) The individual is not eligible for reinstatement for licensure under Section 7102.

(c) A violation of this section is a misdemeanor punishable by a fine of not less than four thousand five hundred dollars ($4,500), by imprisonment in a county jail for not less than 90 days nor more than one year, or by both the fine and imprisonment. The penalty provided by this subdivision is cumulative to the penalties available under other laws of this state.

(d) Notwithstanding any other provision of law to the contrary, an indictment for any violation of this section shall be found or an information or complaint filed within four years from the performance of any act that is prohibited under this section.

Added Stats 2006 ch 171 § 1 (AB 2897), effective January 1, 2007. Amended Stats 2010 ch 698 § 31 (SB 392), effective January 1, 2011.

§ 7121.65. Notification of license revocation required

Prior to becoming employed in any capacity by an entity that is subject to licensure under this chapter, an individual who is described in subdivision (a) or (b) of Section 7121.6 shall provide the prospective employer with written notice of the license revocation.

Added Stats 2006 ch 171 § 2 (AB 2897), effective January 1, 2007.

§ 7121.7. Employment of individuals with revoked licenses

(a) A qualifying individual, officer, partner, or other person named on a license shall not knowingly employ an individual who is described in subdivision (a) or (b) of Section 7121.6, except as a bona fide nonsupervising employee.

(b) A violation of this section is a misdemeanor punishable by a fine of not less than four thousand five hundred dollars ($4,500), by imprisonment in a county jail for not less than 30 days nor more than one year, or by both the fine and imprisonment.

(c) Notwithstanding any other provision of law to the contrary, an indictment for any violation of this section shall be found or an information or complaint filed within four years from the performance of any act that is prohibited under this section.

Added Stats 2006 ch 171 § 3 (AB 2897), effective January 1, 2007.

§ 7121.8. "Bona fide nonsupervising employee"

For purposes of this article, "bona fide nonsupervising employee" means a person who is exempt from the provisions of this chapter under Section 7053, and who does not otherwise meet the test of an independent contractor, as set forth under Section 2750.5 of the Labor Code.

Added Stats 2006 ch 171 § 4 (AB 2897), effective January 1, 2007.

§ 7122. When act or omission of individual or business entity constitutes cause for disciplinary action against licensee

The performance by an individual, partnership, corporation, limited liability company, firm, or association of an act or omission constituting a cause for disciplinary action, likewise constitutes a cause for disciplinary action against a licensee other than the individual qualifying on behalf of the individual or entity, if the licensee was a partner, officer, director, manager, or associate of that individual, partnership, corporation, limited liability company, firm, or association at the time the act or omission occurred, and had knowledge of or participated in the prohibited act or omission.

Added Stats 1947 ch 1285. Amended Stats 1959 ch 407 § 5; Stats 2010 ch 698 § 32 (SB 392), effective January 1, 2011.

§ 7122.1. Responsibility of disassociated qualifying individual for compliance with citation; Applicability of § 7122.5

Notwithstanding Section 7068.2 or any other provision of this chapter, the disassociation of a qualifying individual from a license after the act or omission has occurred that resulted in a citation pursuant to Section 7099 shall not relieve the qualifying individual from responsibility for complying with the citation. Section 7122.5 shall apply to a qualifying individual of a licensee that fails to comply with a citation after it is final.

Added Stats 1994 ch 192 § 3 (AB 3475). Amended Stats 2003 ch 363 § 7 (AB 1382); Stats 2010 ch 698 § 33 (SB 392), effective January 1, 2011.

§ 7122.2. Responsibility for compliance with arbitration award following disassociation

(a) Notwithstanding Section 7068.2 or any other provisions of this chapter, the disassociation of a qualifying individual from a license that has been referred to arbitration pursuant to Section 7085 shall not relieve the qualifying individual from the responsibility of complying with an arbitration award rendered as a result of acts or omissions committed while acting as the qualifying individual for the license as provided under Sections 7068 and 7068.1.

(b) Section 7122.5 shall apply to a qualifying individual of a licensee that fails to comply with an arbitration award once it is rendered.

Added Stats 2002 ch 312 § 4 (AB 728). Amended Stats 2005 ch 385 § 1 (AB 316), effective January 1, 2006; Stats 2010 ch 698 § 34 (SB 392), effective January 1, 2011.

§ 7122.5. Immateriality of licensee's knowledge or participation

The performance by an individual, partnership, corporation, limited liability company, firm, or association of an act or omission constituting a cause for disciplinary action, likewise constitutes a cause for disciplinary action against a licensee who at the time that the act or omission occurred was the qualifying individual of that individual, partnership, corporation, limited liability company, firm, or association, whether or not he or she had knowledge of or participated in the prohibited act or omission.

Added Stats 1959 ch 407 § 6. Amended Stats 2010 ch 698 § 35 (SB 392), effective January 1, 2011.

§ 7123. Criminal conviction as cause for discipline

A conviction of a crime substantially related to the qualifications, functions and duties of a contractor constitutes a cause for disciplinary action. The record of the conviction shall be conclusive evidence thereof.

Added Stats 1955 ch 1532 § 2. Amended Stats 1978 ch 1161 § 365.

§ 7123.5. Disciplinary action for violation of overpricing following emergency or major disaster

If a contractor is convicted of violating Section 396 of the Penal Code or any substantially similar local ordinance in connection with the sale, or offer for sale, of repair or reconstruction services, as defined in Section 396 of the Penal Code, the Contractors State License Board shall take disciplinary action against the contractor, which shall include a suspension of at least six months or the permanent revocation of the contractor's license.

Added Stats 1993–94 1st Ex Sess ch 52 § 1 (AB 36 X), effective November 30, 1994. Amended Stats 2020 ch 312 § 63 (SB 1474), effective January 1, 2021.

—See Penal Code Section 396, Unlawful Price Increase Following a Declared State of Emergency, in Appendix.

§ 7124. What constitutes conviction; When license may be ordered suspended or revoked, or issuance refused

A plea or verdict of guilty or a conviction following a plea of nolo contendere is deemed to be a conviction within the meaning of this article. The board may order the license suspended or revoked, or may decline to issue a license, when the time for appeal has elapsed, or the judgment of conviction has been affirmed on appeal or when an order granting probation is made suspending the imposition of sentence, irrespective of a subsequent order under the provisions of Section 1203.4 of the Penal Code allowing such person to withdraw his plea of guilty and to enter a plea of not guilty, or setting aside the verdict of guilty, or dismissing the accusation, information or indictment.

Added Stats 1955 ch 1532 § 3.

§ 7124.5. [Section repealed 2004.]

Added Stats 1979 ch 188 § 2, effective June 29, 1979. Repealed Stats 2004 ch 865 § 16 (SB 1914). The repealed section related to public disclosure of complaints against licensees.

§ 7124.6. Public access to complaints against licensees; Disclaimer; Limitations of disclosure

(a) The registrar shall make available to members of the public the date, nature, and status of all complaints on file against a licensee that do either of the following:

(1) Have been referred for accusation.

(2) Have been referred for investigation after a determination by board enforcement staff that a probable violation has occurred, and have been reviewed by a supervisor, and regard allegations that if proven would present a risk of harm to the public and would be ap-

Section VI

propriate for suspension or revocation of the contractor's license or criminal prosecution.

(b) The board shall create a disclaimer that shall accompany the disclosure of a complaint that shall state that the complaint is an allegation. The disclaimer may also contain any other information the board determines would be relevant to a person evaluating the complaint.

(c)(1) A complaint resolved in favor of the contractor shall not be subject to disclosure.

(2) A complaint resolved by issuance of a letter of admonishment pursuant to Section 7099.9 shall not be deemed resolved in favor of the contractor for the purposes of this section. A letter of admonishment issued to a licensee shall be disclosed for a period of either one year or two years from the date of service described in subdivision (c) of Section 7099.9. For the limited purposes of this paragraph, the determination regarding the one- or two-year disclosure shall be made based on the factors enumerated in subdivision (a) of Section 7099.2.

(d) Except as described in subdivision (e), the registrar shall make available to members of the public the date, nature, and disposition of all legal actions.

(e) Disclosure of legal actions shall be limited as follows:

(1) (A) Citations shall be disclosed from the date of issuance and for five years after the date of compliance if no additional disciplinary actions have been filed against the licensee during the five-year period. If additional disciplinary actions were filed against the licensee during the five-year period, all disciplinary actions shall be disclosed for as long as the most recent disciplinary action is subject to disclosure under this section. At the end of the specified time period, those citations shall no longer be disclosed.

(B) Any disclosure pursuant to this paragraph shall also appear on the license record of any other license that includes a qualifier that is listed as one of the members of personnel of record of the license that was issued the citation.

(C) The disclosure described in subparagraph (B) shall be for the period of disclosure of the citation.

(2) Accusations that result in suspension, stayed suspension, or stayed revocation of the contractor's license shall be disclosed from the date the accusation is filed and for seven years after the accusation has been settled, including the terms and conditions of probation if no additional disciplinary actions have been filed against the licensee during the seven-year period. If additional disciplinary actions were filed against the licensee during the seven-year period, all disciplinary actions shall be posted for as long as the most recent disciplinary action is subject to disclosure under this section. At the end of the specified time period, those accusations shall no longer be disclosed.

(3) All revocations that are not stayed shall be disclosed indefinitely from the effective date of the revocation.

Added Stats 2001 ch 494 § 2 (SB 135), operative July 1, 2002. Amended Stats 2003 ch 607 § 34 (SB 1077); Stats 2016 § 1 (SB 1209), effective January 1, 2017. Stats 2017 ch 308 § 3 (SB 486), effective January 1, 2018; Stats 2019 ch 378 § 8 (SB 610), effective January 1, 2020; Stats 2021 ch 3188 § 10 (SB 826), effective January 1, 2022; Stats 2022 ch 293 § 1 (AB 2916).

Article 7.5

Workers' Compensation Insurance Reports

§ 7125. Reports to registrar; Exemptions [Repealed effective January 1, 2026]

(a) Except as provided in subdivision (b), the board shall require as a condition precedent to the issuance, reinstatement, reactivation, renewal, or continued maintenance of a license, that the applicant or licensee have on file at all times a current and valid Certificate of Workers' Compensation Insurance or Certification of Self-Insurance in the applicant's or licensee's business name. A Certificate of Workers' Compensation Insurance shall be issued and filed, electronically or otherwise, by an insurer duly licensed to write workers' compensation insurance in this state. A Certification of Self-Insurance shall be issued and filed by the Director of Industrial Relations. If reciprocity conditions exist, as provided in Section 3600.5 of the Labor Code, the registrar shall require the information deemed necessary to ensure compliance with this section.

(b) This section does not apply to an applicant or licensee who meets both of the following conditions:

(1) Has no employees provided that the applicant or licensee files a statement with the board on a form prescribed by the registrar before the issuance, reinstatement, reactivation, or continued maintenance of a license, certifying that the applicant or licensee does not employ any person in any manner so as to become subject to the workers' compensation laws of California or is not otherwise required to provide for workers' compensation insurance coverage under California law.

(2) Does not hold a C-8 license, as defined in Section 832.08 of Title 16 of the California Code of Regulations, a C-20 license, as defined in Section 832.20 of Title 16 of the California Code of Regulations, a C-22 license, as defined in Section 832.22 of Title 16 of the California Code of Regulations, a C-39 license, as defined in Section 832.39 of Title 16 of the California Code of Regulations, or a D-49 license, a subcategory of a C-61 license, as defined in Section 832.61 of Title 16 of the California Code of Regulations.

Section VI

(c) This section does not apply to an applicant or licensee organized as a joint venture pursuant to Section 7029 that has no employees, provided that the applicant or licensee files the statement prescribed by subparagraph (1) of subdivision (b).

(d) A Certificate of Workers' Compensation Insurance, Certification of Self-Insurance, or exemption certificate is not required of a holder of a license that has been inactivated on the official records of the board during the period the license is inactive.

(e) (1) The insurer, including the State Compensation Insurance Fund, shall report to the registrar the following information for any policy required under this section: name, license number, policy number, dates that coverage is scheduled to commence and lapse, and cancellation date if applicable.

(2) A workers' compensation insurer shall also report to the registrar a licensee whose workers' compensation insurance policy is canceled by the insurer if all of the following conditions are met:

(A) The insurer has completed a premium audit or investigation.

(B) A material misrepresentation has been made by the insured that results in financial harm to the insurer.

(C) No reimbursement has been paid by the insured to the insurer.

(3) Willful or deliberate disregard and violation of workers' compensation insurance laws constitutes a cause for disciplinary action by the registrar against the licensee.

(f) (1) For any license that, on January 1, 2013, is active and includes a C-39 classification in addition to any other classification, the registrar shall, in lieu of the automatic license suspension otherwise required under this article, remove the C-39 classification from the license unless a valid Certificate of Workers' Compensation Insurance or Certification of Self-Insurance is received by the registrar.

(2) For any licensee whose license, after January 1, 2013, is active and has had the C-39 classification removed as provided in paragraph (1), and who is found by the registrar to have employees and to lack a valid Certificate of Workers' Compensation Insurance or Certification of Self-Insurance, that license shall be automatically suspended as required under this article.

(g) (1) For any licensee whose license, after July 1, 2023, is active and includes a C-8, C-20, C-22, or D-49 classification, in addition to any other classification, the registrar shall, in lieu of the automatic license suspension otherwise required under this article, remove the C-8, C-20, C-22, or D-49 classification from the license unless a valid Certificate of Workers' Compensation Insurance or Certification of Self-Insurance is received by the registrar.

(2) For any licensee whose license, after July 1, 2023, is active and has had the C-8, C-20, C-22, or D-49 classification removed, as provided in paragraph (1), and who is found by the registrar to have employees and to lack a valid Certificate of Workers' Compensation In-

surance or Certification of Self-Insurance, that license shall be automatically suspended as required under this article.

(h) The information reported pursuant to paragraph (2) of subdivision (e) shall be confidential, and shall be exempt from disclosure under the California Public Records Act (Division 10 (commencing with Section 7920.000) of Title 1 of the Government Code).

(i) This section shall remain in effect only until January 1, 2026, and as of that date is repealed, unless a later enacted statute that is enacted before January 1, 2026, deletes or extends that date.

Added Stats 1943 ch 132 § 1. Amended Stats 1990 ch 1386 § 3 (AB 2282); Stats 1991 ch 1160 § 38 (AB 2190); Stats 1995 ch 467 § 16 (SB 1061); Stats 1996 ch 331 § 1 (AB 3355); Stats 2002 ch 311 § 4 (AB 264); Stats 2006 ch 38 § 1 (AB 881), effective January 1, 2007, repealed January 1, 2011; Stats 2010 ch 423 § 1 (AB 2305), effective January 1, 2011, repealed January 1, 2013; Stats 2011 ch 686 § 1 (AB 878), effective January 1, 2012, repealed January 1, 2013; Stats 2012 ch 389 § 1 (AB 2219), effective January 1, 2013; Stat 2022 ch 978 § 1 (SB 216), effective January 1, 2023, repealed effective January 1, 2026.

§ 7125. Reports to registrar; Exemptions [Operative effective January 1, 2026]

(a) Except as provided in subdivision (b), the board shall require as a condition precedent to the issuance, reinstatement, reactivation, renewal, or continued maintenance of a license, that the applicant or licensee have on file at all times a current and valid Certificate of Workers' Compensation Insurance or Certification of Self-Insurance in the applicant's or licensee's business name. A Certificate of Workers' Compensation Insurance shall be issued and filed, electronically or otherwise, by an insurer duly licensed to write workers' compensation insurance in this state. A Certification of Self-Insurance shall be issued and filed by the Director of Industrial Relations. If reciprocity conditions exist, as provided in Section 3600.5 of the Labor Code, the registrar shall require the information deemed necessary to ensure compliance with this section.

(b) This section does not apply to an applicant or licensee organized as a joint venture pursuant to Section 7029 that has no employees, provided that the applicant or licensee files a statement with the board on a form prescribed by the registrar before the issuance, reinstatement, reactivation, or continued maintenance of a license, certifying that the applicant or licensee does not employ any person in any manner so as to become subject to the workers' compensation laws of California or is not otherwise required to provide for workers' compensation insurance coverage under California law.

(c) A Certificate of Workers' Compensation Insurance or Certification of Self-Insurance is not required of a holder of a license that has been inactivated on the official records of the board during the period the license is inactive.

(d) (1) The insurer, including the State Compensation Insurance Fund, shall report to the registrar the following information for any policy required under this section: name, license number, policy number, dates that coverage is scheduled to commence and lapse, and cancellation date if applicable.

(2) A workers' compensation insurer shall also report to the registrar a licensee whose workers' compensation insurance policy is canceled by the insurer if all of the following conditions are met:

(A) The insurer has completed a premium audit or investigation.

(B) A material misrepresentation has been made by the insured that results in financial harm to the insurer.

(C) Reimbursement has not been paid by the insured to the insurer.

(3) Willful or deliberate disregard and violation of workers' compensation insurance laws constitutes a cause for disciplinary action by the registrar against the licensee.

(e) The information reported pursuant to paragraph (2) of subdivision (d) shall be confidential, and shall be exempt from disclosure under the

California Public Records Act (Division 10 (commencing with Section 7920.000) of Title 1 of the Government Code).

(f) This section shall become operative on January 1, 2026.

Added Stats 1943 ch 132 § 1. Amended Stats 1990 ch 1386 § 3 (AB 2282); Stats 1991 ch 1160 § 38 (AB 2190); Stats 1995 ch 467 § 16 (SB 1061); Stats 1996 ch 331 § 1 (AB 3355); Stats 2002 ch 311 § 4 (AB 264); Stats 2006 ch 38 § 1 (AB 881), effective January 1, 2007, repealed January 1, 2011; Stats 2010 ch 423 § 1 (AB 2305), effective January 1, 2011, repealed January 1, 2013; Stats 2011 ch 686 § 1 (AB 878), effective January 1, 2012, repealed January 1, 2013; Stats 2012 ch 389 § 1 (AB 2219), effective January 1, 2013; Stat 2022 ch 978 § 1 (SB 216), effective January 1, 2023, repealed effective January 1, 2026; Stat 2022 ch 978 § 2 (SB 216), effective January 1, 2023, operative January 1, 2026.

§ 7125.1. Time limit for acceptance of certificate

(a) The registrar shall accept a certificate required by Section 7125 as of the effective date shown on the certificate, if the certificate is received by the registrar within 90 days after that date, and shall reinstate the license to which the certificate pertains, if otherwise eligible, retroactive to the effective date of the certificate.

(b) Notwithstanding subdivision (a), the registrar shall accept the certificate as of the effective date shown on the certificate, even if the certificate is not received by the registrar within 90 days after that date, upon a showing by the licensee, on a form acceptable to the registrar, that the failure to have a certificate on file was due to circumstances beyond the control of the licensee. The registrar shall reinstate the license to which the certificate pertains, if otherwise eligible, retroactive to the effective date of the certificate.

Added Stats 1995 ch 467 § 18 (SB 1061).

§ 7125.2. Suspension of license for failure to maintain workers' compensation insurance

The failure of a licensee to obtain or maintain workers' compensation insurance coverage, if required under this chapter, shall result in the automatic suspension of the license by operation of law in accordance with the provisions of this section, but this suspension shall not affect, alter, or limit the status of the licensee as an employer for purposes of Section 3716 of the Labor Code.

(a) The license suspension imposed by this section is effective upon the earlier of either of the following:

(1) On the date that the relevant workers' compensation insurance coverage lapses.

(2) On the date that workers' compensation coverage is required to be obtained.

(b) A licensee who is subject to suspension under paragraph (1) of subdivision (a) shall be provided a notice by the registrar that includes all of the following:

(1) The reason for the license suspension and the effective date.

(2) A statement informing the licensee that a pending suspension will be posted to the license record for not more than 45 days prior to the posting of any license suspension periods required under this article.

(3) The procedures required to reinstate the license.

(c) Reinstatement may be made at any time following the suspension by showing proof of compliance as specified in Sections 7125 and 7125.1.

(d) In addition, with respect to an unlicensed individual acting in the capacity of a contractor who is not otherwise exempted from the provisions of this chapter, a citation may be issued by the registrar under Section 7028.7 for failure to comply with this article and to maintain workers' compensation insurance. An opportunity for a hearing as specified in Section 7028.10 will be granted if requested within 15 working days after service of the citation.

Added Stats 1995 ch 467 § 20 (SB 1061). Amended Stats 2002 ch 311 § 5 (AB 264).

§ 7125.3. Periods of licensure

A contractor shall be considered duly licensed during all periods in which the registrar is required to accept the certificate prescribed by Section 7125, provided the licensee has otherwise complied with the provisions of this chapter.

Added Stats 2002 ch 311 § 6 (AB 264).

SECTION VI. LICENSE LAW, RULES, REGULATIONS, AND RELATED LAWS

§ 7125.4. Causes for disciplinary action; Misdemeanor

(a) The filing of the exemption certificate prescribed by this article that is false, or the employment of a person subject to coverage under the workers' compensation laws after the filing of an exemption certificate without first filing a Certificate of Workers' Compensation Insurance or Certification of Self-Insurance in accordance with the provisions of this article, or the employment of a person subject to coverage under the workers' compensation laws without maintaining coverage for that person, constitutes cause for disciplinary action.

(b) Any qualifier for a license who, under Section 7068.1, is responsible for assuring that a licensee complies with the provisions of this chapter is also guilty of a misdemeanor for committing or failing to prevent the commission of any of the acts that are cause for disciplinary action under this section.

Added Stats 2002 ch 311 § 7 (AB 264). Amended Stats 2005 ch 205 § 2 (SB 488), effective January 1, 2006; Stats 2015 ch 389 § 3 (SB 560), effective January 1, 2016.

§ 7125.5. Renewal of license; Exemption for workers' compensation insurance; Recertification; Retroactive renewal

(a) At the time of renewal, all active licensees with an exemption for workers' compensation insurance on file with the board, submitted pursuant to subdivision (b) of Section 7125, shall either recertify the licensee's exemption by completing a recertification statement on the license renewal form, as provided by the board, or shall provide a current and valid Certificate of Workers' Compensation Insurance or Certificate of Self-Insurance, whichever is applicable.

(b) The license shall not be renewed unless a licensee with an exemption for workers' compensation insurance on file with the board recertifies the exemption status or provides a current and valid Certificate of Workers' Compensation Insurance or Certificate of Self-Insurance in conjunction with the license renewal.

(c) If the documentation required by subdivision (a) is not provided with the license renewal but is received within 30 days after notification by the board of the renewal rejection, the registrar shall grant a retroactive renewal pursuant to Section 7141.5 back to the date of the postmark of the otherwise acceptable renewal. A renewal that is still incomplete for any reason after 30 days after notification of rejection shall not be eligible for retroactive renewal under this subdivision.

Added Stats 2011 ch 546 § 1 (AB 397), effective January 1, 2012.

§ 7126. Misdemeanor violations

(a) Any licensee or agent or officer thereof, who violates, or omits to comply with, any of the provisions of this article is guilty of a misdemeanor.

(b) Any person not licensed in accordance with this chapter who is acting as a contractor and who violates, or omits to comply with, Section 3700 of the Labor Code is guilty of a misdemeanor.

(c) Prosecution of any offense under this section shall be commenced within two years after commission of the offense as provided in Section 802 of the Penal Code.

Added Stats 1943 ch 132 § 1. Amended Stats 2018 ch 323 § 1 (AB 2705), effective January 1, 2019.

—*See also Health and Safety Code Section 19825, Declaration of Worker's Compensation Required on Building Permits, in Appendix*

§ 7127. Stop order; Failure to observe; Protest

(a)(1) If an employer subject to licensure under this chapter has failed to secure the payment of compensation as required by Section 3700 of the Labor Code, and whether that employer is or is not licensed under this chapter, the registrar may, in addition to any other administrative remedy, issue and serve on that employer a stop order prohibiting the use of employee labor. The stop order shall become effective immediately upon service. An employee affected by the work stoppage shall be paid by the employer for his or her time lost, not exceeding 10 days, pending compliance by the employer.

(2) Failure of any employer, officer, or any person having direction, management, or control of any place of employment or of employees to observe a stop order issued and served upon him or her pursuant to this section is a misdemeanor punishable by imprisonment in the county jail not exceeding 60 days or by a fine not exceeding ten thousand dollars ($10,000), or both.

(b) An employer who is subject to this section may protest the stop order by making and filing with the registrar a written request for a hearing within 20 days after service of the stop order. The hearing shall be held within five days from the date of filing the request. The registrar shall notify the employer of the time and place of the hearing by mail. At the conclusion of the hearing, the stop order shall be immediately affirmed or dismissed, and within 24 hours thereafter the registrar shall issue and serve on all parties to the hearing by registered or certified mail a written notice of findings and findings. A writ of mandate may be taken from the findings to the appropriate superior court. Such writ must be taken within 45 days after the mailing of the notice of findings and findings.

Added Stats 2010 ch 643 § 1 (SB 1254), effective January 1, 2011.

Section VI

Article 8
Revenue

§ 7135. Disposition of fees and penalties; Appropriation

(a) The fees and civil penalties received under this chapter shall be deposited in the Contractors License Fund. All moneys in the fund are hereby appropriated for the purposes of this chapter.

(b) It is the intent of the Legislature that the board shall use moneys appropriated from the fund to improve its administrative and investigative oversight activities and capacity.

Added Stats 1939 ch 37 § 1. Amended Stats 1979 ch 1013 § 28; Stats 1986 ch 137 § 1; Stats 2020 ch 312 § 64 (SB 1474), effective January 1, 2021.

§ 7135.1. Funds to enforce unlicensed activity provisions

It is the intent of the Legislature that, each fiscal year the board shall designate, if appropriated in the Budget Act and to the extent that it does not conflict with the control language of the Budget Act, no less than 20 percent of the annual amount collected as a result of the fees increased by statutes enacted during the 1993 portion of the 1993–94 Regular Session to be used to enforce the provision of this chapter relative to unlicensed activity.

Added Stats 1993 ch 1188 § 1 (SB 148).

§ 7136. Percentage to be transferred to Consumer Affairs Fund

The director shall designate a sum not to exceed 10 percent of the total income of the Contractors State License Board for each fiscal year to be transferred to the Consumer Affairs Fund as the board's share of the cost of administration of the department.

Added Stats 1939 ch 37 § 1. Amended Stats 1971 ch 716 § 105; Stats 1984 ch 193 § 2; Stats 2020 ch 312 § 65 (SB 1474), effective January 1, 2021.

§ 7137. Fee schedule

(a) The board may set fees by regulation. These fees shall be set according to the following schedule:

(1) Application fees shall be set as follows:

(A) The application fee for an original license in a single classification shall be four hundred fifty dollars ($450) and may be increased to not more than five hundred sixty-three dollars ($563).

(B) The application fee for each additional classification applied for in connection with an original license shall be one hundred fifty dollars ($150) and may be increased to not more than one hundred eighty-eight dollars ($188).

(C) The application fee for each additional classification pursuant to Section 7059 shall be two hundred thirty dollars ($230) and may be increased to not more than two hundred eighty-eight dollars ($288).

(D) The application fee to replace a responsible managing officer, responsible managing manager, responsible managing member, or responsible managing employee pursuant to Section 7068.2 shall be two hundred thirty dollars ($230) and may be increased to not more than two hundred eighty-eight dollars ($288).

(E) The application fee to add personnel, other than a qualifying individual, to an existing license shall be one hundred twenty-five dollars ($125) and may be increased to not more than one hundred fifty-seven dollars ($157).

(F) The application fee for an asbestos certification examination shall be one hundred twenty-five dollars ($125) and may be increased to not more than one hundred fifty-seven dollars ($157).

(G) The application fee for a hazardous substance removal or remedial action certification examination shall be one hundred twenty-five dollars ($125) and may be increased to not more than one hundred fifty-seven dollars ($157).

(2) Examination scheduling fees shall be set as follows:

(A) The fee for rescheduling an examination for an applicant who has applied for an original license, additional classification, a change of responsible managing officer, responsible managing manager, responsible managing member, or responsible managing employee, or for an asbestos certification or hazardous substance removal certification, shall be one hundred dollars ($100) and may be increased to not more than one hundred twenty-five dollars ($125).

(B) The fee for scheduling or rescheduling an examination for a licensee who is required to take the examination as a condition of probation shall be one hundred dollars ($100) and may be increased to not more than one hundred twenty-five dollars ($125).

(3) Initial license and registration fees shall be set as follows:

(A) The initial license fee for an active or inactive license for an individual owner shall be two hundred dollars ($200) and may be increased to not more than two hundred fifty dollars ($250).

(B) The initial license fee for an active or inactive license for a partnership, corporation, limited liability company, or joint venture shall be three hundred fifty dollars ($350) and may be increased to not more than four hundred thirty-eight dollars ($438).

(C) The registration fee for a home improvement salesperson shall be two hundred dollars ($200) and may be increased to not more than two hundred fifty dollars ($250).

(D) (i) The board shall grant a 50-percent reduction in the fees prescribed by this paragraph to an applicant who is a veteran of the

United States Armed Forces, including the National Guard or Reserve components, and was not dishonorably discharged.

(ii) To demonstrate discharge grade at the time of the board's request for the initial license or registration fee, the applicant shall provide the board a copy of a current and valid driver's license or identification card issued by this state or another state with the word "Veteran" printed on its face or a copy of their DD214 long form.

(4) License and registration renewal fees shall be set as follows:

(A) The renewal fee for an active license for an individual owner shall be four hundred fifty dollars ($450) and may be increased to not more than five hundred sixty-three dollars ($563).

(B) The renewal fee for an inactive license for an individual owner shall be three hundred dollars ($300) and may be increased to not more than three hundred seventy-five dollars ($375).

(C) The renewal fee for an active license for a partnership, corporation, limited liability company, or joint venture shall be seven hundred dollars ($700) and may be increased to not more than eight hundred seventy-five dollars ($875).

(D) The renewal fee for an inactive license for a partnership, corporation, limited liability company, or joint venture shall be five hundred dollars ($500) and may be increased to not more than six hundred twenty-five dollars ($625).

(E) The renewal fee for a home improvement salesperson registration shall be two hundred dollars ($200) and may be increased to not more than two hundred fifty dollars ($250).

(5) The delinquency fee is an amount equal to 50 percent of the renewal fee, if the license is renewed after its expiration.

(6) Miscellaneous fees shall be set as follows:

(A) In addition to any other fees charged to C-10 contractors, the board shall charge a fee of twenty dollars ($20), to be assessed with the renewal fee for an active license, which shall be used by the board to enforce provisions of the Labor Code related to electrician certification.

(B) The service fee to deposit with the registrar lawful money or cashier's check pursuant to paragraph (1) of subdivision (a) of Section 995.710 of the Code of Civil Procedure for purposes of compliance with any provision of Article 5 (commencing with Section 7065) shall be one hundred dollars ($100), which shall be used by the board only to process each deposit filed with the registrar, to cover the reasonable costs to the registrar for holding money or cashier's checks in trust in interest bearing deposit or share accounts, and to offset the costs of processing payment of lawful claims against a deposit in a civil action.

(C) The fee for the processing and issuance of a duplicate copy of any certificate of licensure or other form evidencing licensure or renewal of licensure pursuant to Section 122 shall be twenty-five dollars ($25).

(D) The fee to change the business name of a license as it is recorded under this chapter shall be one hundred dollars ($100) and may be increased to not more than one hundred twenty-five dollars ($125).

(E) The service charge for a dishonored check authorized by Section 6157 of the Government Code shall be twenty-five dollars ($25) for each check.

(b) The board shall, by regulation, establish criteria for the approval of expedited processing of applications. Approved expedited processing of applications for licensure or registration, as required by other provisions of law, shall not be subject to this subdivision.

Added Stats 2016 ch 799 § 37 (SB 1039), effective January 1, 2017, operative July 1, 2017. Amended Stats 2018 ch 925 § 6 (AB 3126), effective January 1, 2019; Stats 2019 ch 378 § 9 (SB 610), effective January 1, 2020; Stats 2020 ch 312 § 66 (SB 1474), effective January 1, 2021; Stats 2021 ch 367 § 22 (SB 607), effective September 28, 2021; Stats 2022 ch 156 § 1 (AB 2105), effective effective January 1, 2023.

§ 7137.5. Transfer of funds for use of Uniform Construction Cost Accounting Commission; Recommendation; Reimbursement

The sum of ten thousand dollars ($10,000) shall be transferred from the Contractors License Fund to the Controller for the exclusive use of the California Uniform Construction Cost Accounting Commission.

The commission shall prepare a recommendation to the Legislature for a local public agency source to fund the commission beginning July 1, 1991, which will provide revenue supported by the contract activities represented by the commission's authority.

Upon adoption of this funding program, the commission shall reimburse the Contractors License Fund in the amount of ten thousand dollars ($10,000).

Added Stats 1990 ch 1326 § 8 (AB 3480), effective September 25, 1990. Amended Stats 2020 ch 312 § 67 (SB 1474), effective January 1, 2021.

§ 7138. Earned fee; Nonrefundability when application is filed

Notwithstanding any other provision of law, a fee paid in connection with a service or application covered by Section 7137 shall accrue to the Contractors License Fund as an earned fee and shall not be refunded.

Added Stats 1963 ch 160 § 3. Amended Stats 1966 ch 4 § 6; Stats 1974 ch 423 § 2; Stats 1982 ch 1615 § 3, effective September 30, 1982; Stats 2003 ch 607 § 35 (SB 1077); Stats 2010 ch 698 § 37 (SB 392), effective January 1, 2011; Stats 2020 ch 312 § 68 (SB 1474), effective January 1, 2021.

Section VI

—*See Unemployment Insurance Code Section 10501, Job Training Program: Waiver of Fees, in Appendix.*

§ 7138.1. Reserve fund level

Notwithstanding Section 7137, the board shall fix fees to be collected pursuant to that section in order to generate revenues sufficient to maintain the board's reserve fund at a level not to exceed approximately six months of annual authorized board expenditures.

Added Stats 1996 ch 528 § 1 (SB 1597). Amended Stats 2002 ch 744 § 9 (SB 1953).

Article 8.5

The Construction Management Education Sponsorship Act of 1991

§ 7139. Title of article

This article shall be known as the Construction Management Education Sponsorship Act of 1991.

Added Stats 1991 ch 1158 § 1 (AB 2158).

§ 7139.1. Legislative findings and declarations

The Legislature hereby finds and declares all of the following:

(a) There is a demand and increasing need for construction management education programs and resources within the postsecondary education system that prepare graduates for the management of construction operations and companies regulated by the Contractors State License Law and enforced by the Contractors State License Board.

(b) Although construction management programs do exist within the state university system, these programs are woefully underfunded and insufficiently funded to provide training on state-of-the-art management information systems for either graduates or extension programs for continuing education of licensed contractors. Construction industry associations have provided some assistance through direct grants and scholarships, but the industrywide service of these programs and the need for additional assistance mandates broad based industrywide support.

(c) It is the intent of the Legislature that by enabling contractors to designate a portion of their licensure fee and providing a format for contractors to contribute funds to construction management education, this article will receive broad based industry support. In addition, this article allows the contractor to demonstrate the importance of construction management education. This assistance will enable greater development of construction management curricula and will improve the overall quality of construction by providing construction management training to California licensed contractors and their current and future management personnel.

Added Stats 1991 ch 1158 § 1 (AB 2158). Amended Stats 2020 ch 312 § 69 (SB 1474), effective January 1, 2021.

§ 7139.2. Creation of account

(a) There is hereby created the Construction Management Education Account (CMEA) as a separate account in the Contractors License Fund for the purposes of construction management education. Funds in the account shall be available for the purposes of this article upon appropriation by the Legislature.

(b) The Contractors State License Board shall allow a contractor to make a contribution to the Construction Management Education Account at the time of the contractor license fee payment. The license fee form shall clearly display this alternative on its face and shall clearly inform the licensee that this provision is a contribution to the Construction Management Education Account and is in addition to the fees.

(c) The board may accept grants from federal, state, or local public agencies, or from private foundations or individuals, in order to assist it in carrying out its duties, functions, and powers under this article. Grant moneys shall be deposited into the Construction Management Education Account.

Added Stats 1991 ch 1158 § 1 (AB 2158). Amended Stats 2003 ch 807 § 15 (SB 1080); Stats 2020 ch 312 § 70 (SB 1474), effective January 1, 2021.

§ 7139.3. Grant awards

(a) The board may award grants to qualified public postsecondary educational institutions for the support of courses of study in construction management.

(b) Any organization of contractors, or organization of contractor organizations, incorporated under Division 2 (commencing with Section 5000) of the Corporations Code may request the board to award grants pursuant to subdivision (a) directly to qualified public postsecondary educational institutions of its choice. However, the total amount of money that may be awarded to one public postsecondary educational institution pursuant to subdivision (a) may not exceed an amount equal to 25 percent of the total funds available under this article.

(c) The board shall establish an advisory committee to recommend grant awards. The advisory committee shall be known as the Construction Management Education Account Advisory Committee and

Section VI

shall consist of 11 members, with at least one representative from each of the following: Associated General Contractors of California, Associated Builders and Contractors, California Building Industry Association, National Electrical Contractors Association, Plumbing-Heating-Cooling Contractor's Association, Southern California Contractor's Association, Associated General Contractors of San Diego, Engineering and Utility Contractors Association, Engineering Contractors Association, California Sheet Metal and Air Conditioning Contractor's Association, and one member representing the California State University and University of California construction management programs accredited by the American Council for Construction Education. Advisory committee member terms shall be for three years and the representatives shall be appointed by each identified group. Members of the advisory committee shall not receive per diem or reimbursement for traveling and other expenses pursuant to Section 103.

(d) The mission of the Construction Management Education Account Advisory Committee is to maintain, and increase the quality and availability of, education programs for the construction industry. The primary focus is to provide financial resources not now available to accredited construction management programs in California colleges and universities to maintain and upgrade facilities and provide greater access by the industry to modern construction standards and management practices. The advisory committee shall do all of the following:

(1) Confirm the qualifications of programs applying for grants.

(2) Award less than full grants when the account has insufficient funds to award full grants to all qualifying programs.

(3) Receive and review year-end reports of use and impact of funds.

(4) Affirm applications for American Council for Construction Education accreditation and, when funds are available, award grants to complete the accreditation process.

(5) Promote close ties between feeder junior colleges and four-year construction management programs.

(6) Support development of new educational programs with specific emphasis on outreach to the construction industry at large.

Added Stats 1991 ch 1158 § 1 (AB 2158). Amended Stats 1994 ch 647 § 1 (AB 2934).

§ 7139.4. Postsecondary programs; Qualifications

Qualified public postsecondary educational institutions shall provide postsecondary construction management programs at the baccalaureate or higher level that either award or provide one of the following:

(a) A bachelor of science construction management degree accredited by the American Council for Construction Education.

(b) A degree with an American Council for Construction Education accredited option, including, but not limited to, engineering technology and industrial technology.

(c) A bachelor of science or higher degree program documenting placement of more than 50 percent of their graduates with California licensed contractors. The placement of a person who holds a master or doctorate degree in the faculty of a construction program shall be counted as though placed with a California licensed contractor.

(d) The development of a construction management curriculum to meet the American Council for Construction Education criteria.

Added Stats 1991 ch 1158 § 1 (AB 2158).

§ 7139.5. Amounts of grants

Grants shall be made pursuant to this article to public postsecondary educational institutions that meet the qualifications specified in Section 7139.4 in the following amounts:

(a) Three thousand dollars ($3,000) per graduate during the past academic year for institutions qualifying under subdivision (a) of Section 7139.4.

(b) Three thousand dollars ($3,000) per graduate during the past academic year for institutions qualifying under subdivision (b) of Section 7139.4.

(c) Three thousand dollars ($3,000) per graduate placed with California licensed contractors during the past academic year for institutions qualifying under subdivision (c) of Section 7139.4. These funds shall be used for the purpose of becoming accredited by the American Council for Construction Education and shall be available for up to three years. The board may continue to provide this grant to an institution that in its judgment is meeting the intent of this act and is continuing its development towards accreditation.

(d) Institutions qualifying under subdivision (d) of Section 7139.4 may receive a grant in an amount up to twenty-five thousand dollars ($25,000) per year for up to two years. Thereafter, these institutions may receive grants based upon the criteria described in subdivisions (a) to (c), inclusive. The board may continue to award a grant to an institution that in its judgment is meeting the intent of this article and is continuing its development towards accreditation.

Added Stats 1991 ch 1158 § 1 (AB 2158).

§ 7139.6. Purposes for which grants may be used

(a) The grants issued pursuant to Sections 7139.3 and 7139.5 may be used for all of the following:

(1) Instructional materials and support, equipment, curriculum development, and delivery.

Section VI

(2) Support and development of outreach, continuing education, and cooperative education or internship programs.

(3) Administrative and clerical support positions.

(4) Faculty recruitment and development, to include support for postgraduate work leading to advanced degrees, visiting lecturer compensation and expenses, teaching assistant positions, and faculty positions.

(b) Grant moneys may also be used to support general classroom and laboratory operating expenses and related administrative supplies, including, but not limited to, reference materials, testing equipment, and equipment maintenance. The list of support items in this subdivision and subdivision (a) are intended to be descriptive rather than limiting. "Support" does not include faculty salary supplements.

Added Stats 1991 ch 1158 § 1 (AB 2158).

§ 7139.7. [Section repealed 2013.]

Added Stats 1991 ch 1158 § 1 (AB 2158). Repealed Stats 2012 ch 728 § 14 (SB 71), effective January 1, 2013. The repealed section related to an annual report on the condition of the grant program.

§ 7139.8. Report by president of institution receiving grant

The president of each public postsecondary educational institution receiving a grant under this article shall submit, with its respective request for a grant each year following the initial year for which grants are issued, a report to the board delineating the amount of the past grant awarded from the Construction Management Education Account to that institution and the utilization of those funds. The report shall include, but not be limited to, the following:

(a) The number of graduates placed with the California licensed contractors during the previous academic year.

(b) The expected enrollment in construction management courses in the upcoming academic year.

(c) Continuing education and extension courses offered during the previous academic year and their enrollments.

Added Stats 1991 ch 1158 § 1 (AB 2158).

§ 7139.9. Allocation for administration

The board may allocate up to fifteen thousand dollars ($15,000) per year from the Construction Management Education Account for the administration of this article.

Added Stats 1991 ch 1158 § 1 (AB 2158).

§ 7139.10. Intent of Legislature

It is the intent of the Legislature that state funding for the grants authorized to be awarded under this section be provided only from the Contractors' License Fund to the extent that funds are available in that fund and that no other state funding be provided for those grants.

Added Stats 1991 ch 1158 § 1 (AB 2158).

Article 9

Renewal of Licenses

§ 7140. Expiration of licenses; Renewal of unexpired licenses

All licenses issued under the provisions of this chapter shall expire two years from the last day of the month in which the license is issued, or two years from the date on which the renewed license last expired.

To renew a license which has not expired, the licensee shall, before the time at which the license would otherwise expire, apply for renewal on a form prescribed by the registrar and pay the renewal fee prescribed by this chapter. Renewal of an unexpired license shall continue the license in effect for the two-year period following the expiration date of the license, when it shall expire if it is not again renewed.

Added stats 1941 ch 971 § 20; Amended Stats 1961 ch 1636 § 9, operative October 1, 1962; Stats 1978 ch 1161 § 367; Stats 1981 ch 583 § 1; Stats 1991 ch 1160 § 39 (AB 2190).

§ 7141. Time for renewal; Effect; Failure to renew

(a) Except as otherwise provided in this chapter, a license that has expired may be renewed at any time within five years after its expiration by filing an application for renewal on a form prescribed by the registrar and payment of the appropriate renewal fee. Renewal under this section shall be effective on the date an acceptable renewal application is filed with the board. The licensee shall be considered unlicensed and there will be a break in the licensing time between the expiration date and the date the renewal becomes effective. Except as provided in subdivision (b), if the license is renewed after the expiration date, the licensee shall also pay the delinquency fee prescribed by this chapter.

(b) An incomplete renewal application that had originally been submitted on or before the license expiration date shall be returned to the licensee by the registrar with an explanation of the reasons for its rejection. If a corrected and acceptable renewal application is not re-

Section VI

turned within 30 days after the license expiration date, the delinquency fee shall apply. The 30 day grace period shall apply only to the delinquency fee. The license shall reflect an expired status for any period between the expiration date and the date of submission of a correct and acceptable renewal application.

(c) If so renewed, the license shall continue in effect through the date provided in Section 7140 that next occurs after the effective date of the renewal, when it shall expire if it is not again renewed.

(d) If a license is not renewed within five years, the licensee shall make an application for a license pursuant to Section 7066.

Added Stats 1941 ch 971 § 20. Amended Stats 1961 ch 1636 § 10, operative October 1, 1962; Stats 1970 ch 856 § 1; Stats 1972 ch 1138 § 4.7; Stats 1983 ch 891 § 31; Stats 1999 ch 982 § 3.9 (AB 1678); Stats 2002 ch 1013 § 62 (SB 2026); Stats 2003 ch 607 § 36 (SB 1077); Stats 2013 ch 319 § 9 (SB 822), effective January 1, 2014.

§ 7141.5. Retroactive issuance of license after failure to renew

The registrar shall grant the retroactive renewal of a license if, within 90 days of the expiration of the license, the otherwise eligible licensee submits a completed application for renewal on a form prescribed by the registrar, and pays the appropriate renewal fee and delinquency fee prescribed by this chapter. For the purposes of this section, an application shall be deemed submitted if it is delivered to the board's headquarters or postmarked within 90 days of the expiration of the license.

Added Stats 1972 ch 1138 § 5. Amended Stats 1975 ch 329 § 4; Stats 1983 ch 891 § 32; Stats 1984 ch 1174 § 11; Stats 2020 ch 312 § 71 (SB 1474), effective January 1, 2021.

§ 7143. Renewal of suspended license

A license that is suspended for any reason which constitutes a basis for suspension under this chapter, is subject to expiration and shall be renewed as provided in this chapter, but this renewal does not entitle the licensee, while the license remains suspended, and until it is reinstated, to engage in any activity to which the license relates, or in any other activity or conduct in violation of the order or judgment by which the license was suspended.

Added Stats 1941 ch 971 § 20. Amended Stats 1961 ch 1636 § 12, operative October 1, 1962; Stats 1972 ch 1138 § 7; Stats 1987 ch 930 § 8, effective September 22, 1987; Stats 2003 ch 363 § 8 (AB 1382).

§ 7143.5. Application for new license by person prohibited from renewing

A person who, by reason of the provisions of Section 7141, is not entitled to renew his license, may apply for and obtain a new license only if he pays all of the fees and meets all of the qualifications and requirements set forth in this chapter for obtaining an original license.

Added Stats 1961 ch 1636 § 13, operative October 1, 1962. Amended Stats 1972 ch 1138 § 8.

§ 7144. Reinstatement of revoked license

A revoked license shall be considered as having expired as of the date of revocation and shall not be renewed. To reinstate a revoked license a licensee may apply for reinstatement of the license only if he pays all of the fees and meets all of the qualifications and requirements set forth in this chapter for obtaining an original license.

Added Stats 1941 ch 971 § 20. Amended Stats 1961 ch 1636 § 14, operative October 1, 1962; Stats 1974 ch 433 § 3.

§ 7145. Incompleteness of application as grounds for refusal to renew license; Abandonment of application; Petition

The registrar may refuse to renew a license for the failure or refusal by the licensee to complete the renewal application prescribed by the registrar. If a licensee fails to return an application for renewal which was rejected for insufficiency or incompleteness within 90 days from the original date of rejection, the application and fee shall be deemed abandoned. Any application abandoned may not be reinstated. However, the applicant may file another application accompanied by the required fee.

The registrar may review and accept the petition of a licensee who disputes the invalidation of his or her application for renewal upon a showing of good cause. This petition shall be received within 90 days from the date the renewal application is deemed abandoned.

Added Stats 1941 ch 971 § 20. Amended Stats 1970 ch 524 § 2; Stats 1984 ch 1174 § 12.

§ 7145.5. Failure to resolve outstanding liabilities as grounds for refusal to renew license

(a) The registrar may refuse to issue, reinstate, reactivate, or renew a license or may suspend a license for the failure of a licensee to resolve all outstanding final liabilities, which include taxes, additions to tax, penalties, interest, and any fees that may be assessed by the board, the Department of Industrial Relations, the Employment Development Department, the Franchise Tax Board, or the State Board of Equalization.

(1) Until the debts covered by this section are satisfied, the qualifying person and any other personnel of record named on a license that has been suspended under this section shall be prohibited from serving in any capacity that is subject to licensure under this chapter, but

shall be permitted to act in the capacity of a nonsupervising bona fide employee.

(2) The license of any other renewable licensed entity with any of the same personnel of record that have been assessed an outstanding liability covered by this section shall be suspended until the debt has been satisfied or until the same personnel of record disassociate themselves from the renewable licensed entity.

(b) The refusal to issue a license or the suspension of a license as provided by this section shall be applicable only if the registrar has mailed a notice preliminary to the refusal or suspension that indicates that the license will be refused or suspended by a date certain. This preliminary notice shall be mailed to the licensee at least 60 days before the date certain.

(c) In the case of outstanding final liabilities assessed by the Franchise Tax Board, this section shall be operative within 60 days after the Contractors' State License Board has provided the Franchise Tax Board with the information required under Section 30, relating to licensing information that includes the federal employer identification number, individual taxpayer identification number, or social security number.

(d) All versions of the application for contractors' licenses shall include, as part of the application, an authorization by the applicant, in the form and manner mutually agreeable to the Franchise Tax Board and the board, for the Franchise Tax Board to disclose the tax information that is required for the registrar to administer this section. The Franchise Tax Board may from time to time audit these authorizations.

(e) In the case of outstanding final liabilities assessed by the State Board of Equalization, this section shall not apply to any outstanding final liability if the licensee has entered into an installment payment agreement for that liability with the State Board of Equalization and is in compliance with the terms of that agreement.

Added Stats 1990 ch 1386 § 6 (AB 2282). Amended Stats 2006 ch 122 § 1 (AB 2456), effective January 1, 2007; Stats 2007 ch 130 § 29 (AB 299), effective January 1, 2008; Stats 2011 ch 734 § 1 (AB 1307), effective January 1, 2012; Stats 2017 ch 573 § 30 (SB 800), effective January 1, 2018.

Article 10
Home Improvement Business

§ 7150. "Person"

(a) "Person" as used in this article is limited to natural persons, notwithstanding the definition of person in Section 7025.

(b) "Senior citizen" means an individual who is 65 years of age or older.

Added Stats 1961 ch 1021 § 1. Amended Stats 1972 ch 1138 § 9; Stats 2020 ch 158 § 1 (AB 2471), effective January 1, 2021.

§ 7150.1. "Home improvement contractor"

A home improvement contractor, including a swimming pool contractor, is a contractor as defined and licensed under this chapter who is engaged in the business of home improvement either full time or part time. A home improvement contractor shall satisfy all requirements imposed by this article.

Added Stats 1969 ch 1583 § 1 as § 7026.2. Amended and renumbered Stats 1972 ch 1138 § 1.1. Amended Stats 1991 ch 1160 § 40 (AB 2190). Amended Stats 1997 ch 888 § 1 (AB 1213).

§ 7150.2. [Section repealed 2004.]

Added Stats 1997 ch 888 § 2 (AB 1213). Repealed, operative January 1, 2004, by its own terms. The repealed section related to certification for home improvement contractors.

§ 7150.3. [Section repealed 2004.]

Added Stats 1997 ch 888 § 3 (AB 1213). Repealed, operative January 1, 2004, by its own terms. The repealed section related to qualification for home improvement contractor.

§ 7151. "Home improvement"; "Home improvement goods or services"

(a) "Home improvement" means the repairing, remodeling, altering, converting, or modernizing of, or adding to, residential property, as well as the reconstruction, restoration, or rebuilding of a residential property that is damaged or destroyed by a natural disaster for which a state of emergency is proclaimed by the Governor pursuant to Section 8625 of the Government Code, or for which an emergency or major disaster is declared by the President of the United States, and shall include, but not be limited to, the construction, erection, installation, replacement, or improvement of driveways, swimming pools, including spas and hot tubs, terraces, patios, awnings, storm windows, solar energy systems, landscaping, fences, porches, garages, fallout shelters, basements, and other improvements of the structures or land which is adjacent to a dwelling house. "Home improvement" shall also mean the installation of home improvement goods or the furnishing of home improvement services.

(b) For purposes of this chapter, "home improvement goods or services" means goods and services, as defined in Section 1689.5 of the

Civil Code, which are bought in connection with the improvement of real property. Such home improvement goods and services include, but are not limited to, carpeting, texture coating, fencing, air conditioning or heating equipment, and termite extermination. Home improvement goods include goods which are to be so affixed to real property as to become a part of real property whether or not severable therefrom.

(c) For purposes of this article, "solar energy system" means a solar energy device to be installed on a residential building or residential property that has the primary purpose of providing for the collection and distribution of solar energy for the generation of electricity, that produces at least one kilowatt, and not more than five megawatts, alternating current rated peak electricity, and that meets or exceeds the eligibility criteria established pursuant to Section 25782 of the Public Resources Code.

Added Stats 1961 ch 1021 § 1. Amended Stats 1969 ch 1583 § 10; Stats 1979 ch 1012 § 2; Stats 1980 ch 138 § 3, effective May 30, 1980; Stats 1981 ch 916 § 2; Stats 1982 ch 1210 § 2; Stats 1991 ch 1160 § 41 (AB 2190); Stats 2020 ch 364 § 4 (SB 1189), effective January 1, 2021; Stats 2021 ch 249 § 1 (SB 757), effective January 1, 2022.

§ 7151.2. "Home improvement contract"

"Home improvement contract" means an agreement, whether oral or written, or contained in one or more documents, between a contractor and an owner or between a contractor and a tenant, regardless of the number of residence or dwelling units contained in the building in which the tenant resides, if the work is to be performed in, to, or upon the residence or dwelling unit of the tenant, for the performance of a home improvement as defined in Section 7151, and includes all labor, services, and materials to be furnished and performed thereunder. "Home improvement contract" also means an agreement, whether oral or written, or contained in one or more documents, between a salesperson, whether or not he or she is a home improvement salesperson, and (a) an owner or (b) a tenant, regardless of the number of residence or dwelling units contained in the building in which the tenant resides, which provides for the sale, installation, or furnishing of home improvement goods or services.

Added Stats 1969 ch 1583 § 11. Amended Stats 1979 ch 1012 § 3; Stats 1991 ch 1160 § 42 (AB 2190).

—See Civil Code Sections 1689.5, Home Solicitation Contract;1689.6, Cancellation of Home Solicitation Contract;1689.7, Form of Notice of Cancellation; 1689.8 Contract which provides for Lien; 1689.9, Exemptions: 1689.10, After Cancellation, Seller to Return Downpayment; 1689.11, Buyer to Return Goods; 1689.12, Invalidity of Waiver of Statute; 1689.13, Notice Not Required for Emergency Situations; 1689.14, Void Contracts, in Appendix.

§ 7152. "Home improvement salesperson"

(a) "Home improvement salesperson" is a person who is registered under this chapter and engaged in the business of soliciting, selling, negotiating, or executing contracts for home improvements, for the sale, installation or furnishing of home improvement goods or services, or of swimming pools, spas, or hot tubs on behalf of a home improvement contractor licensed under this chapter.

(b) A home improvement salesperson shall register with the board in order to engage in the business of, or act in the capacity of, a home improvement salesperson.

(c) Subject to the provisions of Section 7154, a home improvement salesperson may be employed by one, or more than one, home improvement contractor. However, prior to engaging in any activity described in subdivision (a) of this section, a home improvement salesperson shall identify to the owner or tenant the business name and license number of the contractor they are representing for the purposes of that transaction. Failure to do so is a cause of disciplinary action within the meaning of Section 7155.

(d) The following shall not be required to be registered as home improvement salespersons:

(1) An officer of record of a corporation licensed pursuant to this chapter, or a manager, member, or officer of record of a limited liability company licensed pursuant to this chapter.

(2) A general partner listed on the license record of a partnership licensed pursuant to this chapter.

(3) A qualifying person, as defined in Section 7025.

(4) A salesperson whose sales are all made pursuant to negotiations between the parties if the negotiations are initiated by the prospective buyer at or with a general merchandise retail establishment that operates from a fixed location where goods or services are offered for sale.

(5) A person who contacts the prospective buyer for the exclusive purpose of scheduling appointments for a registered home improvement salesperson.

(6) A bona fide service repairperson who is in the employ of a licensed contractor and whose repair or service call is limited to the service, repair, or emergency repair initially requested by the buyer of the service.

(e) The exemption to registration provided under paragraphs (1), (2), and (3) of subdivision (c) shall apply only to those individuals who, at the time of the sales transaction, are listed as personnel of record for the licensee responsible for soliciting, negotiating, or contracting for a service or improvement that is subject to regulation under this article.

Added Stats 1972 ch 1138 § 11. Amended Stats 1973 ch 115 § 1, effective June 26, 1973; Stats 1979 ch 1012 § 4; Stats 1980 ch 138 § 4, effective May 30, 1980; Stats 1982 ch 585 § 1; Stats 1985 ch 1281 § 4; Stats 1991 ch 1160 § 43 (AB 2190); Stats 2006 ch 106 § 4 (AB 2457), effective January 1, 2007; Stats 2010 ch 698 § 38 (SB 392), effective January 1, 2011; Stats 2015 ch 281 § 2 (SB 561), effective January 1, 2016; Stats 2021 ch 249 § 2 (SB 757), effective January 1, 2022.

—See *Civil Code Sections 1804.3, Security Interest in Goods Paid For Not Sold; Security Interest unreal Property for Sale of Unattached Goods; 1805.6, Undelivered Goods; 1810.10, Finance Charge, in Appendix.*

§ 7153. Selling without registration

(a) It is a misdemeanor for any person to engage in the occupation of salesperson for one or more home improvement contractors within this state without having, at the time of the sales transaction, a current and valid home improvement salesperson registration issued by the registrar. If, upon investigation, the registrar has probable cause to believe that a salesperson is in violation of this section, the registrar may issue a citation pursuant to Section 7028.7.

It is a misdemeanor for any person to engage in the occupation of salesperson of home improvement goods or services within this state without having, at the time of the sales transaction, a current and valid home improvement salesperson registration issued by the registrar.

(b) Any security interest taken by a contractor, to secure any payment for the performance of any act or conduct described in Section 7151 that occurs on or after January 1, 1995, is unenforceable if the person soliciting the act or contract was not a duly registered salesperson or was not exempt from registration pursuant to Section 7152 at the time the homeowner signs the home improvement contract solicited by the salesperson.

Added Stats 1972 ch 1138 § 13. Amended Stats 1979 ch 1012 § 5; Stats 1994 ch 888 § 1 (AB 3269); Stats 2001 ch 728 § 63 (SB 724); Stats 2015 ch 281 § 3 (SB 561), effective January 1, 2016.

§ 7153.1. Salesperson's application for registration; Grounds for denial; Fingerprints of applicants; Criminal history and subsequent arrest information

(a) The home improvement salesperson shall submit to the registrar an application in writing containing the statement that he or she desires the issuance of a registration under the terms of this article.

The application shall be made on a form prescribed by the registrar and shall be accompanied by the fee fixed by this chapter.

(b) The registrar may refuse to register the applicant under the grounds specified in Section 480.

(c) As part of an application for a home improvement salesperson, the board shall require an applicant to furnish a full set of fingerprints for purposes of conducting criminal history record checks. Fingerprints furnished pursuant to this subdivision shall be submitted in an electronic format where readily available. Requests for alternative methods of furnishing fingerprints are subject to the approval of the registrar. The board shall use the fingerprints furnished by an applicant to obtain criminal history information on the applicant from the Department of Justice and the United States Federal Bureau of Investigation, including any subsequent arrest information available.

Added Stats 1972 ch 1138 § 14. Amended Stats 1978 ch 1161 § 368; Stats 2002 ch 744 § 10 (SB 1953); Stats 2003 ch 789 § 18 (SB 364); Stats 2004 ch 909 § 27.5 (SB 136), effective September 30, 2004; Stats 2007 ch 240 § 3 (AB 936), effective January 1, 2008.

§ 7153.2. Expiration of registrations

All home improvement salesperson registrations issued under the provisions of this article shall expire two years from the last day of the month in which the registration was issued, or two years from the date on which the renewed registration last expired.

Added Stats 1972 ch 1138 § 15. Amended Stats 1983 ch 891 § 33; Stats 1991 ch 1160 § 44 (AB 2190); Stats 2015 ch 281 § 4 (SB 561), effective January 1, 2016.

§ 7153.3. Renewal of registration; Delinquent renewal penalty; Abandonment of application; Petition

(a) To renew a home improvement salesperson registration, which has not expired, the registrant shall before the time at which the registration would otherwise expire, apply for renewal on a form prescribed by the registrar and pay a renewal fee prescribed by this chapter. Renewal of an unexpired registration shall continue the registration in effect for the two-year period following the expiration date of the registration, when it shall expire if it is not again renewed.

(b) An application for renewal of registration is delinquent if the application is not postmarked or received via electronic transmission as authorized by Section 7156.6 by the date on which the registration would otherwise expire. A registration may, however, still be renewed at any time within three years after its expiration upon the filing of an application for renewal on a form prescribed by the registrar and the payment of the renewal fee prescribed by this chapter and a delinquent renewal penalty equal to 50 percent of the renewal fee. If a registration is not renewed within three years, the person shall make a new application for registration pursuant to Section 7153.1.

(c) (1) The registrar may refuse to renew a registration for failure by the registrant to complete the application for renewal of registration. If a registrant fails to return the application rejected for insufficiency or incompleteness within 90 days from the original date of rejection, the application and fee shall be deemed abandoned. Any application abandoned may not be reinstated. However, the person may file a new application for registration pursuant to Section 7153.1.

(2) The registrar may review and accept the petition of a person who disputes the abandonment of his or her renewal application upon a showing of good cause. This petition shall be received within 90 days of the date the application for renewal is deemed abandoned.

(d) This section shall become operative on July 1, 2017.

Added Stats 2016 ch 799 § 39 (SB 1039), effective January 1, 2017, operative July 1, 2017.

§ 7154. Notification of employment of registered salesperson; Notification when registered salesperson ceases employment; Discipline for failure to report regarding employment of registered salesperson; Discipline for employment of unregistered salesperson

(a) A home improvement contractor licensed under this chapter shall notify the registrar in writing, on a form prescribed by the registrar, about the employment of a registered home improvement salesperson, pursuant to the terms of this article. This notification requirement shall include, but not be limited to, the name and registration number of the home improvement salesperson who is employed by the contractor. The form shall be submitted prior to the home improvement salesperson beginning work for the contractor.

(b) A home improvement contractor shall notify the registrar in writing, on a form prescribed by the registrar, when a registered home improvement salesperson ceases to be employed by the contractor. This notification requirement shall include, but not be limited to, the name and registration number of the home improvement salesperson who had been employed by the contractor. The form shall be submitted within 90 days after the home improvement salesperson ceases to be employed by the contractor.

(c) A home improvement contractor who employs a registered home improvement salesperson to sell home improvement contracts, but who fails to report to the registrar pursuant to subdivision (a) or (b), is subject to disciplinary action by the registrar.

(d) A home improvement contractor who employs a person to sell home improvement contracts while that person is not registered by the registrar as a home improvement salesperson as provided in this article, is subject to disciplinary action by the registrar.

Added Stats 1972 ch 1138 § 18. Amended Stats 2015 ch 281 § 6 (SB 561), effective January 1, 2016.

§ 7155. Discipline of salesman

Violation of any provision of this chapter by a home improvement salesperson constitutes cause for disciplinary action. The registrar may suspend or revoke the registration of the home improvement salesperson if he or she is found to be in violation. The disciplinary proceedings shall be conducted in accordance with Chapter 5 (commencing with Section 11500) of Part 1 of Division 3 of Title 2 of the Government Code.

Added Stats 1972 ch 1138 § 20. Amended Stats 2011 ch 296 § 16 (AB 1023), effective January 1, 2012.

§ 7155.5. Discipline of contractor for salesperson's violations

Violations of any provisions of this chapter by a home improvement salesperson likewise constitute cause for disciplinary action against the contractor, by whom he or she was employed at the time the violation occurred, whether or not the contractor had knowledge of or participated in the act or omission constituting violations of this chapter.

Added Stats 1972 ch 1138 § 21. Amended Stats 1997 ch 812 § 5 (SB 857), ch 813 § 3 (SB 825); Stats 2015 ch 281 § 7 (SB 561), effective January 1, 2016.

§ 7156. Misdemeanors; Grounds for discipline

It shall be a misdemeanor and a cause for disciplinary action to commit any of the following acts:

(a) For any home improvement salesperson to fail to account for or to remit to their employing contractor any payment received in connection with any home improvement transaction or any other transaction involving a work of improvement.

(b) For any person to use a contract form in connection with any home improvement transaction or any other transaction involving a work of improvement if the form fails to disclose the name of the contractor principal by whom the person is employed.

(c) For any home improvement salesperson to assist, recommend, select, or otherwise guide an owner or tenant in the selection of a contractor for the performance or sale of home improvement goods or services if notification of employment by the home improvement contractor, as required by subdivision (a) of Section 7154, has not been received by the Board.

Added Stats 1969 ch 1583 § 2 as § 7026.8. Amended and Renumbered Stats 1972 ch 1138 § 1.2; Stats 1997 ch 812 § 6 (SB 857), ch 813 § 4 (SB 825); Stats 2015 ch 281 § 8 (SB 561), effective January 1, 2016; Stats 2021 ch 249 § 3 (SB 757), effective January 1, 2022.

Section VI

§ 7156.6. Electronic transmission of applications, renewals, and notices

(a) Notwithstanding any other law, the board may implement a system that provides for the electronic transmission of an initial application or renewal application for the registration required by this article and the electronic transmission of the notices required by Section 7154.

(b) The board by regulation may specify the form and manner of these transmissions, including the adoption of any protocols necessary to ensure the validity and security of any information, data, or document transmitted electronically. Upon the effective date of the regulations, the electronic submission of an initial registration application, a renewal application, or the electronic transmission of a notice required by Section 7154 shall satisfy the requirements of this article.

Added Stats 2015 ch 281 § 9 (SB 561), effective January 1, 2016.

§ 7157. Prohibited inducements

(a) Except as otherwise provided in subdivision (b), as a part of or in connection with the inducement to enter into any home improvement contract or other contract, which may be performed by a contractor, no person may promise or offer to pay, credit, or allow to any owner, compensation or reward for the procurement or placing of home improvement business with others.

(b) A contractor or his or her agent or salesperson may give tangible items to prospective customers for advertising or sales promotion purposes where the gift is not conditioned upon obtaining a contract for home improvement work if the gift does not exceed a value of five dollars ($5) and only one such gift is given in connection with any one transaction.

(c) No salesperson or contractor's agent may accept any compensation of any kind, for or on account of a home improvement transaction, or any other transaction involving a work of improvement, from any person other than the contractor whom he or she represents with respect to the transaction, nor shall the salesperson or agent make any payment to any person other than his or her employer on account of the sales transaction.

(d) No contractor shall pay, credit, or allow any consideration or compensation of any kind to any other contractor or salesperson other than a licensee for or on account of the performance of any work of improvement or services, including, but not limited to, home improvement work or services, except: (1) where the person to or from whom the consideration is to be paid is not subject to or is exempted from the licensing requirements of this chapter, or (2) where the transaction is not subject to the requirements of this chapter.

As used in this section "owners" shall also mean "tenant."

Commission of any act prohibited by this section is a misdemeanor and constitutes a cause for disciplinary action.

Added Stats 1969 ch 1583 § 3, as B & P C § 7026.9. Renumbered by Stats 1972 ch 1138 § 1.3. Amended Stats 1997 ch 812 § 7 (SB 857), ch 813 § 5 (SB 825).

§ 7158. [Section repealed 2021.]

Added Stats 1969 ch 1583 § 5 as § 7028.1. Amended and renumbered Stats 1972 ch 1138 § 1.4; Amended Stats 1994 ch 175 § 2 (SB 634), effective July 9, 1994; Stats 2020 ch 92 § 3 (AB 1869), effective September 18, 2020, repealed July 1, 2021.

—*See Penal Code Section 532e, Rebates, in Appendix.*

§ 7158. False completion certificates

(a) Any person who shall accept or receive a completion certificate or other evidence that performance of a contract for a work of improvement, including, but not limited to, a home improvement, is complete or satisfactorily concluded, with knowledge that the document is false and that the performance is not substantially completed, and who shall utter, offer, or use the document in connection with the making or accepting of any assignment or negotiation of the right to receive any payment from the owner, under or in connection with a contract, or for the purpose of obtaining or granting any credit or loan on the security of the right to receive any payment shall be guilty of a misdemeanor and subject to a fine of not less than five hundred dollars ($500) nor more than five thousand dollars ($5,000), or to imprisonment in the county jail for a term of not less than one month nor more than one year, or both.

(b) (1) Any person who violates this section as part of a plan or scheme to defraud an owner of a residential or nonresidential structure, including a mobilehome or manufactured home, in connection with the offer or performance of repairs to the structure for damage caused by a natural disaster, shall be ordered by the court to make full restitution to the victim based on the person's ability to pay, defined as the overall capability of the defendant to reimburse the costs, or a portion of the costs, including consideration of, but not limited to, all of the following:

(A) The defendant's present financial position.

(B) The defendant's reasonably discernible future financial position, provided that the court shall not consider a period of more than one year from the date of the hearing for purposes of determining the reasonably discernible future financial position of the defendant.

(C) The likelihood that the defendant will be able to obtain employment within one year from the date of the hearing.

(D) Any other factor that may bear upon the defendant's financial capability to reimburse the county for costs.

(2) In addition to full restitution, and imprisonment authorized by subdivision (a), the court may impose a fine of not less than five hundred dollars ($500) nor more than twenty-five thousand dollars ($25,000), based upon the defendant's ability to pay. This subdivision applies to natural disasters for which a state of emergency is proclaimed by the Governor pursuant to Section 8625 of the Government Code or for which an emergency or major disaster is declared by the President of the United States.

(c) This section shall become operative on July 1, 2021.

Added Stats 2020 ch 92 § 4 (AB 1869), effective September 18, 2020, operative July 1, 2021.

—*See Penal Code Section 532e, Rebates, in Appendix.*

§ 7159. Requirements for home improvement contracts

(a) (1) This section identifies the projects for which a home improvement contract is required, outlines the contract requirements, and lists the items that shall be included in the contract, or may be provided as an attachment.

(2) This section does not apply to service and repair contracts that are subject to Section 7159.10, if the contract for the applicable services complies with Sections 7159.10 to 7159.14, inclusive.

(3) This section does not apply to the sale, installation, and servicing of a fire alarm sold in conjunction with an alarm system, as defined in Section 7590.1, if all costs attributable to making the fire alarm system operable, including sale and installation costs, do not exceed five hundred dollars ($500), and the licensee complies with the requirements set forth in Section 7159.9.

(4) This section does not apply to any costs associated with monitoring a burglar or fire alarm system.

(5) Failure by the licensee, their agent or salesperson, or by a person subject to be licensed under this chapter, to provide the specified information, notices, and disclosures in the contract, or to otherwise fail to comply with any provision of this section, is cause for discipline.

(b) For purposes of this section, "home improvement contract" means an agreement, whether oral or written, or contained in one or more documents, between a contractor and an owner or between a contractor and a tenant, regardless of the number of residence or dwelling units contained in the building in which the tenant resides, if the work is to be performed in, to, or upon the residence or dwelling unit of the tenant, for the performance of a home improvement, as defined in Section 7151, and includes all labor, services, and materials to be furnished and performed thereunder, if the aggregate contract price specified in one or more improvement contracts, including all labor, services, and materials to be furnished by the contractor, exceeds five hundred dollars ($500). "Home improvement contract" also means an agreement, whether oral or written, or contained in one or more documents, between a salesperson, whether or not they are a home improvement salesperson, and an owner or a tenant, regardless of the number of residence or dwelling units contained in the building in which the tenant resides, which provides for the sale, installation, or furnishing of home improvement goods or services.

(c) In addition to the specific requirements listed under this section, every home improvement contract and any person subject to licensure under this chapter or their agent or salesperson shall comply with all of the following:

(1) The writing shall be legible.

(2) Any printed form shall be readable. Unless a larger typeface is specified in this article, text in any printed form shall be in at least 10-point typeface and the headings shall be in at least 10-point boldface type.

(3) (A) Before any work is started, the contractor shall give the buyer a copy of the contract signed and dated by both the contractor and the buyer. The buyer's receipt of the copy of the contract initiates the buyer's rights to cancel the contract pursuant to Sections 1689.5 to 1689.14, inclusive, of the Civil Code.

(B) The contract shall contain on the first page, in a typeface no smaller than that generally used in the body of the document, both of the following:

(i) The date the buyer signed the contract.

(ii) The name and address of the contractor to which the applicable "Notice of Cancellation" is to be mailed, immediately preceded by a statement advising the buyer that the "Notice of Cancellation" may be sent to the contractor at the address noted on the contract.

(4) The contract shall include a statement that, upon satisfactory payment being made for any portion of the work performed, the contractor, prior to any further payment being made, shall furnish to the person contracting for the home improvement or swimming pool work a full and unconditional release from any potential lien claimant claim or mechanics lien authorized pursuant to Sections 8400 and 8404 of the Civil Code for that portion of the work for which payment has been made.

(5) A change-order form for changes or extra work shall be incorporated into the contract and shall become part of the contract only if it is in writing and signed by the parties prior to the commencement of any work covered by a change order.

(6) The contract shall contain, in close proximity to the signatures of the owner and contractor, a notice stating that the owner or tenant

has the right to require the contractor to have a performance and payment bond.

(7) If the contract provides for a contractor to furnish joint control, the contractor shall not have any financial or other interest in the joint control.

(8) The provisions of this section are not exclusive and do not relieve the contractor from compliance with any other applicable provision of law.

(d) A home improvement contract and any changes to the contract shall be in writing and signed by the parties to the contract prior to the commencement of work covered by the contract or an applicable change order and, except as provided in paragraph (8) of subdivision (a) of Section 7159.5, shall include or comply with all of the following:

(1) The name, business address, and license number of the contractor.

(2) If applicable, the name and registration number of the home improvement salesperson that solicited or negotiated the contract.

(3) The following heading on the contract form that identifies the type of contract in at least 10-point boldface type: "Home Improvement."

(4) The following statement in at least 12-point boldface type: "You are entitled to a completely filled in copy of this agreement, signed by both you and the contractor, before any work may be started."

(5) The heading: "Contract Price," followed by the amount of the contract in dollars and cents.

(6) If a finance charge will be charged, the heading: "Finance Charge," followed by the amount in dollars and cents. The finance charge is to be set out separately from the contract amount.

(7) The heading: "Description of the Project and Description of the Significant Materials to be Used and Equipment to be Installed," followed by a description of the project and a description of the significant materials to be used and equipment to be installed. For swimming pools, the project description required under this paragraph also shall include a plan and scale drawing showing the shape, size, dimensions, and the construction and equipment specifications.

(8) If a downpayment will be charged, the details of the downpayment shall be expressed in substantially the following form, and shall include the text of the notice as specified in subparagraph (C):

(A) The heading: "Downpayment."

(B) A space where the actual downpayment appears.

(C) The following statement in at least 12-point boldface type:

"THE DOWNPAYMENT MAY NOT EXCEED $1,000 OR 10 PERCENT OF THE CONTRACT PRICE, WHICHEVER IS LESS."

(9) If payments, other than the downpayment, are to be made before the project is completed, the details of these payments, known as progress payments, shall be expressed in substantially the following

form, and shall include the text of the statement as specified in sub-paragraph (C):

(A) A schedule of progress payments shall be preceded by the heading: "Schedule of Progress Payments."

(B) Each progress payment shall be stated in dollars and cents and specifically reference the amount of work or services to be performed and materials and equipment to be supplied.

(C) The section of the contract reserved for the progress payments shall include the following statement in at least 12-point boldface type:

"The schedule of progress payments must specifically describe each phase of work, including the type and amount of work or services scheduled to be supplied in each phase, along with the amount of each proposed progress payment. IT IS AGAINST THE LAW FOR A CONTRACTOR TO COLLECT PAYMENT FOR WORK NOT YET COMPLETED, OR FOR MATERIALS NOT YET DELIVERED. HOWEVER, A CONTRACTOR MAY REQUIRE A DOWNPAY-MENT."

(10) The contract shall address the commencement of work to be performed in substantially the following form:

(A) A statement that describes what constitutes substantial commencement of work under the contract.

(B) The heading: "Approximate Start Date."

(C) The approximate date on which work will be commenced.

(11) The estimated completion date of the work shall be referenced in the contract in substantially the following form:

(A) The heading: "Approximate Completion Date."

(B) The approximate date of completion.

(12) If applicable, the heading: "List of Documents to be Incorporated into the Contract," followed by the list of documents incorporated into the contract.

(13) The heading: "Note About Extra Work and Change Orders," followed by the following statement:

"Extra Work and Change Orders become part of the contract once the order is prepared in writing and signed by the parties prior to the commencement of work covered by the new change order. The order must describe the scope of the extra work or change, the cost to be added or subtracted from the contract, and the effect the order will have on the schedule of progress payments."

(e) Except as provided in paragraph (8) of subdivision (a) of Section 7159.5, all of the following notices shall be provided to the owner as part of the contract form as specified or, if otherwise authorized under this subdivision, may be provided as an attachment to the contract:

(1) A notice concerning commercial general liability insurance. This notice may be provided as an attachment to the contract if the con-

Section VI

tract includes the following statement: "A notice concerning commercial general liability insurance is attached to this contract." The notice shall include the heading "Commercial General Liability Insurance (CGL)," followed by whichever of the following statements is both relevant and correct:

(A) "(The name on the license or 'This contractor') does not carry commercial general liability insurance."

(B) "(The name on the license or 'This contractor') carries commercial general liability insurance written by (the insurance company). You may call (the insurance company) at _____ to check the contractor's insurance coverage."

(C) "(The name on the license or 'This contractor') is self-insured."

(D) "(The name on the license or 'This contractor') is a limited liability company that carries liability insurance or maintains other security as required by law. You may call (the insurance company or trust company or bank) at _____ to check on the contractor's insurance coverage or security."

(2) A notice concerning workers' compensation insurance. This notice may be provided as an attachment to the contract if the contract includes the statement: "A notice concerning workers' compensation insurance is attached to this contract." The notice shall include the heading "Workers' Compensation Insurance" followed by whichever of the following statements is correct:

(A) "(The name on the license or 'This contractor') has no employees and is exempt from workers' compensation requirements."

(B) "(The name on the license or 'This contractor') carries workers' compensation insurance for all employees."

(3) A notice that provides the buyer with the following information about the performance of extra or change-order work:

(A) A statement that the buyer may not require a contractor to perform extra or change-order work without providing written authorization prior to the commencement of work covered by the new change order.

(B) A statement informing the buyer that extra work or a change order is not enforceable against a buyer unless the change order also identifies all of the following in writing prior to the commencement of work covered by the new change order:

(i) The scope of work encompassed by the order.

(ii) The amount to be added or subtracted from the contract.

(iii) The effect the order will make in the progress payments or the completion date.

(C) A statement informing the buyer that the contractor's failure to comply with the requirements of this paragraph does not preclude the recovery of compensation for work performed based upon legal or equitable remedies designed to prevent unjust enrichment.

(4) A notice with the heading "Mechanics Lien Warning" written as follows:

MECHANICS LIEN WARNING:

Anyone who helps improve your property, but who is not paid, may record what is called a mechanics lien on your property. A mechanics lien is a claim, like a mortgage or home equity loan, made against your property and recorded with the county recorder.

Even if you pay your contractor in full, unpaid subcontractors, suppliers, and laborers who helped to improve your property may record mechanics liens and sue you in court to foreclose the lien. If a court finds the lien is valid, you could be forced to pay twice or have a court officer sell your home to pay the lien. Liens can also affect your credit.

To preserve their right to record a lien, each subcontractor and material supplier must provide you with a document called a 'Preliminary Notice.' This notice is not a lien. The purpose of the notice is to let you know that the person who sends you the notice has the right to record a lien on your property if they are not paid.

BE CAREFUL. The Preliminary Notice can be sent up to 20 days after the subcontractor starts work or the supplier provides material. This can be a big problem if you pay your contractor before you have received the Preliminary Notices.

You will not get Preliminary Notices from your prime contractor or from laborers who work on your project. The law assumes that you already know they are improving your property.

PROTECT YOURSELF FROM LIENS. You can protect yourself from liens by getting a list from your contractor of all the subcontractors and material suppliers that work on your project. Find out from your contractor when these subcontractors started work and when these suppliers delivered goods or materials. Then wait 20 days, paying attention to the Preliminary Notices you receive.

PAY WITH JOINT CHECKS. One way to protect yourself is to pay with a joint check. When your contractor tells you it is time to pay for the work of a subcontractor or supplier who has provided you with a Preliminary Notice, write a joint check payable to both the contractor and the subcontractor or material supplier.

For other ways to prevent liens, visit CSLB's internet website at www.cslb.ca.gov or call CSLB at 800-321-CSLB (2752).

REMEMBER, IF YOU DO NOTHING, YOU RISK HAVING A LIEN PLACED ON YOUR HOME. This can mean that you may have to pay twice, or face the forced sale of your home to pay what you owe.

(5) The following notice shall be provided in at least 12-point typeface:

Information about the Contractors State License Board (CSLB): CSLB is the state consumer protection agency that licenses and regulates construction contractors.

Contact CSLB for information about the licensed contractor you are considering, including information about disclosable complaints, disciplinary actions, and civil judgments that are reported to CSLB.

Use only licensed contractors. If you file a complaint against a licensed contractor within the legal deadline (usually four years), CSLB has authority to investigate the complaint. If you use an unlicensed contractor, CSLB may not be able to help you resolve your complaint. Your only remedy may be in civil court, and you may be liable for damages arising out of any injuries to the unlicensed contractor or the unlicensed contractor's employees.

For more information:

Visit CSLB's internet website at www.cslb.ca.gov

Call CSLB at 800-321-CSLB (2752)

Write CSLB at P.O. Box 26000, Sacramento, CA 95826.

(6) (A) The notice set forth in subparagraph (B) and entitled "Three-Day Right to Cancel," or entitled "Five-Day Right to Cancel" for contracts with a senior citizen, shall be provided to the buyer unless the contract is:

(i) Negotiated at the contractor's place of business.

(ii) Subject to the "Seven-Day Right to Cancel," as set forth in paragraph (7).

(iii) Subject to licensure under the Alarm Company Act (Chapter 11.6 (commencing with Section 7590)), provided the alarm company licensee complies with Sections 1689.5, 1689.6, and 1689.7 of the Civil Code, as applicable.

(B) (i) Three-Day Right to Cancel

You, the buyer, have the right to cancel this contract within three business days. You may cancel by emailing, mailing, faxing, or delivering a written notice to the contractor at the contractor's place of business by midnight of the third business day after you received a signed and dated copy of the contract that includes this notice. Include your name, your address, and the date you received the signed copy of the contract and this notice.

If you cancel, the contractor must return to you anything you paid within 10 days of receiving the notice of cancellation. For your part, you must make available to the contractor at your residence, in substantially as good condition as you received them, goods delivered to you under this contract or sale. Or, you may, if you wish, comply with the contractor's instructions on how to return the goods at the contractor's expense and risk. If you do make the goods available to the contractor and the contractor does not pick them up within 20 days of the date of your notice of cancellation, you may keep them without any further obligation. If you fail to make the goods available to the contractor, or if you agree to return the goods to the contractor and fail to do so, then you remain liable for performance of all obligations under the contract.

(ii) References to "three" and "third" in the notice set forth in clause (i) shall be changed to "five" and "fifth," respectively, for a buyer who is a senior citizen.

(C) The notice required by this paragraph shall comply with all of the following:

(i) The text of the notice is at least 12-point boldface type.

(ii) The notice is in immediate proximity to a space reserved for the owner's signature.

(iii) The owner acknowledges receipt of the notice by signing and dating the notice form in the signature space.

(iv) The notice is written in the same language, e.g., Spanish, as that principally used in any oral sales presentation.

(v) The notice may be attached to the contract if the contract includes, in at least 12-point boldface type, a checkbox with one of the following statements, as applicable:

(I) For a contract with a senior citizen: "The law requires that the contractor give you a notice explaining your right to cancel. Initial the checkbox if the contractor has given you a 'Notice of the Five-Day Right to Cancel.'"

(II) For all other contracts: "The law requires that the contractor give you a notice explaining your right to cancel. Initial the checkbox if the contractor has given you a 'Notice of the Three-Day Right to Cancel.'"

(vi) (I) The notice shall be accompanied by a completed form in duplicate, captioned "Notice of Cancellation," which also shall be attached to the agreement or offer to purchase and be easily detachable, and which shall contain the following statement written in the same language, e.g., Spanish, as used in the contract:

"Notice of Cancellation"

_____
/enter date of transaction/
(Date)

You may cancel this transaction, without any penalty or obligation, within three business days from the above date.

If you cancel, any property traded in, any payments made by you under the contract or sale, and any negotiable instrument executed by you will be returned within 10 days following receipt by the seller of your cancellation notice, and any security interest arising out of the transaction will be canceled.

If you cancel, you must make available to the seller at your residence, in substantially as good condition as when received, any goods delivered to you under this contract or sale, or you may, if you wish, comply with the instructions of the seller regarding the return shipment of the goods at the seller's expense and risk.

If you do make the goods available to the seller and the seller does not pick them up within 20 days of the date of your notice of cancellation, you may retain or dispose of the goods without any further obligation. If you fail to make the goods available to the seller, or if you agree to return the goods to the seller and fail to do so, then you remain liable for performance of all obligations under the contract.

To cancel this transaction, mail or deliver a signed and dated copy of this cancellation notice, or any other written notice, or send a telegram to _____,

/name of seller/

at _____

/address of seller's place of business/

not later than midnight of _____.

(Date)

I hereby cancel this transaction. _____

(Date)

_____

(Buyer's signature)

(II) The reference to "three" in the statement set forth in subclause (I) shall be changed to "five" for a buyer who is a senior citizen.

(7)(A) The following notice entitled "Seven-Day Right to Cancel" shall be provided to the buyer for any contract that is written for the repair or restoration of residential premises damaged by any sudden or catastrophic event for which a state of emergency has been declared by the President of the United States or the Governor, or for which a local emergency has been declared by the executive officer or governing body of any city, county, or city and county:

Seven-Day Right to Cancel

You, the buyer, have the right to cancel this contract within seven business days. You may cancel by emailing, mailing, faxing, or delivering a written notice to the contractor at the contractor's place of business by midnight of the seventh business day after you received a signed and dated copy of the contract that includes this notice. Include your name, your address, and the date you received the signed copy of the contract and this notice.

If you cancel, the contractor must return to you anything you paid within 10 days of receiving the notice of cancellation. For your part, you must make available to the contractor at your residence, in substantially as good condition as you received them, goods delivered to you under this contract or sale. Or, you may, if you wish, comply with the contractor's instructions on how to return the goods at the contractor's expense and risk. If you do make the goods available to the contractor and the contractor does not pick them up within 20 days of the date of your notice of cancellation, you may keep them without any further obligation. If you fail to make the goods available to the contractor, or if you agree to return the goods to the contractor and fail to do so, then you remain liable for performance of all obligations under the contract.

(B) The "Seven-Day Right to Cancel" notice required by this subdivision shall comply with all of the following:

(i) The text of the notice is at least 12-point boldface type.

(ii) The notice is in immediate proximity to a space reserved for the owner's signature.

(iii) The owner acknowledges receipt of the notice by signing and dating the notice form in the signature space.

(iv) The notice is written in the same language, e.g., Spanish, as that principally used in any oral sales presentation.

(v) The notice may be attached to the contract if the contract includes, in at least 12-point boldface type, a checkbox with the following statement: "The law requires that the contractor give you a notice explaining your right to cancel. Initial the checkbox if the contractor has given you a 'Notice of the Seven-Day Right to Cancel.'"

(vi) The notice shall be accompanied by a completed form in duplicate, captioned "Notice of Cancellation," which shall also be attached to the agreement or offer to purchase and be easily detachable, and which shall contain the following statement written in the same language, e.g., Spanish, as used in the contract:

"Notice of Cancellation"

_____
/enter date of transaction/
(Date)

You may cancel this transaction, without any penalty or obligation, within seven business days from the above date.

If you cancel, any property traded in, any payments made by you under the contract or sale, and any negotiable instrument executed by you will be returned within 10 days following receipt by the seller of your cancellation notice, and any security interest arising out of the transaction will be canceled.

If you cancel, you must make available to the seller at your residence, in substantially as good condition as when received, any goods delivered to you under this contract or sale, or you may, if you wish, comply with the instructions of the seller regarding the return shipment of the goods at the seller's expense and risk.

If you do make the goods available to the seller and the seller does not pick them up within 20 days of the date of your notice of cancellation, you may retain or dispose of the goods without any further obligation. If you fail to make the goods available to the seller, or if you agree to return the goods to the seller and fail to do so, then you remain liable for performance of all obligations under the contract.

To cancel this transaction, mail or deliver a signed and dated copy of this cancellation notice, or any other written notice, or send a telegram to _____,

/name of seller/

at _____

/address of seller's place of business/

not later than midnight of _____.

(Date)

I hereby cancel this transaction. _____

(Date)

_____

(Buyer's signature)

(f) The five-day right to cancel added by the act that amended paragraph (6) of subdivision (e) shall apply to contracts entered into on or after January 1, 2021.

Added Stats 2005 ch 48 § 7 (SB 1113), effective July 18, 2005, operative January 1, 2006. Amended Stats 2005 ch 385 § 2 (AB 316), effective January 1, 2006; Stats 2006 ch 114 § 1 (AB 2073), effective January 1, 2007; Stats 2007 ch 130 § 30 (AB 299), effective January 1, 2008, Stats 2007 ch 230 § 1 (AB 244), effective January 1, 2008, (ch 230 prevails); Stats 2008 ch 179 § 18 (SB 1498), effective January 1, 2009; Stats 2009 ch 307 § 74 (SB 821), effective January 1, 2010; Stats 2010 ch 697 § 4 (SB 189), effective January 1, 2011, operative July 1, 2012, ch 698 § 39 (SB 392) (ch 698 prevails), effective January 1, 2011; Stats 2011 ch 44 § 1 (SB 190), effective January 1, 2012, operative July 1, 2012; Stats 2018 ch 406 § 3 (SB 904), effective January 1, 2019; Stats 2020 ch 158 § 2 (AB 2471), effective January 1, 2021; 2020 ch 312 § 73.5 (SB 1474), effective January 1, 2021 (ch 312 prevails).

§ 7159.1. Notice in sale of home improvement goods or services

(a) In any contract for the sale of home improvement goods or services offered by door-to-door sale that contains or is secured by a lien on real property, the contract shall be accompanied by the following notice in 18-point boldfaced type:

"WARNING TO BUYER: IF YOU SIGN THE CONTRACT WHICH ACCOMPANIES THIS NOTICE, YOU WILL BE PUTTING UP YOUR HOME AS SECURITY. THIS MEANS THAT YOUR HOME COULD BE SOLD WITHOUT YOUR PERMISSION AND WITHOUT ANY COURT ACTION IF YOU MISS ANY PAYMENT REQUIRED BY THIS CONTRACT."

This notice shall be written in the same language as the rest of the contract. It shall be on a separate piece of paper from the rest of the contract and shall be signed and dated by the buyer. The home improvement contractor or home improvement salesperson shall deliver to the buyer at the time of the buyer's signing and dating of the notice a legible copy of the signed and dated notice. A security interest created in any contract described in this section that does not provide the notice as required by this section shall be void and unenforceable.

(b) This section shall not apply to any of the following:

(1) Any contract that is subject to Chapter 1 (commencing with Section 1801) of Title 2 of Part 4 of Division 3 of the Civil Code.

(2) A mechanics lien established pursuant to Chapter 4 (commencing with Section 8400) of Title 2 of Part 6 of Division 4 of the Civil Code.

(3) Any contract that is subject to subdivision (a) of Section 7159.2.

Added Stats 1998 ch 571 § 1 (AB 2301). Amended Stats 2010 ch 697 § 5 (SB 189), effective January 1, 2011, operative July 1, 2012.

§ 7159.2. Security interest for home improvement goods or services

(a) No home improvement goods or services contract of a value of five thousand dollars ($5,000) or less shall provide for a security interest in real property, except for a mechanic's lien or other interest in property that arises by operation of law. Any lien in violation of this subdivision is void and unenforceable.

(b) When the proceeds of a loan secured by a mortgage on real property are used to fund goods or services pursuant to a home improvement goods or services contract of more than five thousand dollars ($5,000), the person or entity making the loan shall only pay a contractor under the home improvement goods or services contract from the proceeds of the loan by either of the following methods:

(1) By an instrument payable to the borrower or jointly to the borrower and the contractor.

(2) At the election of the borrower, through a third-party escrow agent pursuant to the terms of a written agreement signed by the borrower, the person or entity making the loan, and the contractor prior to the disbursement.

(c) Any person or entity who violates any provision of this section shall be liable for actual damages suffered by the borrower for damages that proximately result from the violation.

(d) Any person or entity who intentionally or as a pattern or practice violates any provision of this section shall be additionally liable for three times the contract price for the home improvement.

(e) Any person who is a senior citizen or disabled person, as defined in subdivisions (f) and (g) of Section 1761 of the Civil Code, as part of any action for a violation of this section, may seek and be awarded, in addition to the remedies provided in this section, up to five thousand dollars ($5,000) as provided in subdivision (b) of Section 1780 of the Civil Code.

Section VI

(f) The court shall award court costs and attorney's fees to a prevailing plaintiff in an action brought pursuant to this section. Reasonable attorney's fees may be awarded to a prevailing defendant upon a finding by the court that the plaintiff's prosecution of the action was not in good faith.

Added Stats 1998 ch 571 § 2 (AB 2301). Amended Stats 1999 ch 512 § 1 (SB 187).

§ 7159.5. [Section repealed 2021.]

Added Stats 2004 ch 566 § 8 (SB 30), operative July 1, 2005. Amended Stats 2005 ch 48 § 11 (SB 1113), effective July 18, 2005, operative January 1, 2006; Stats 2005 ch 385 § 5 (AB 316); Stats 2007 ch 230 § 2 (AB 244), effective January 1, 2008; Stats 2009 ch 307 § 75 (SB 821), effective January 1, 2010; Stats 2010 ch 697 § 6 (SB 189), effective January 1, 2011, operative July 1, 2012; Stats 2011 ch 44 § 2 (SB 190), effective January 1, 2012, operative July 1, 2012; Stats 2016 ch 634 § 5 (SB 1479), effective January 1, 2017; Stats 2020 ch 92 § 5 (AB 1869), effective September 18, 2020, repealed July 1, 2021.

§ 7159.5. Contract amount; Finance charges; Downpayment; Violations; Restitution and punishment

This section applies to all home improvement contracts, as defined in Section 7151.2, between an owner or tenant and a contractor, whether a general contractor or a specialty contractor, that is licensed or subject to be licensed pursuant to this chapter with regard to the transaction.

(a) Failure by the licensee or a person subject to be licensed under this chapter, or by their agent or salesperson, to comply with the following provisions is cause for discipline:

(1) The contract shall be in writing and shall include the agreed contract amount in dollars and cents. The contract amount shall include the entire cost of the contract, including profit, labor, and materials, but excluding finance charges.

(2) If there is a separate finance charge between the contractor and the person contracting for home improvement, the finance charge shall be set out separately from the contract amount.

(3) If a downpayment will be charged, the downpayment shall not exceed one thousand dollars ($1,000) or 10 percent of the contract amount, whichever amount is less.

(4) If, in addition to a downpayment, the contract provides for payments to be made prior to completion of the work, the contract shall include a schedule of payments in dollars and cents specifically referencing the amount of work or services to be performed and any materials and equipment to be supplied.

(5) Except for a downpayment, the contractor shall neither request nor accept payment that exceeds the value of the work performed or material delivered. The prohibition prescribed by this paragraph ex-

tends to advance payment in whole or in part from any lender or financier for the performance or sale of home improvement goods or services.

(6) Upon any payment by the person contracting for home improvement, and prior to any further payment being made, the contractor shall, if requested, obtain and furnish to the person a full and unconditional release from any potential lien claimant claim or mechanics lien authorized pursuant to Sections 8400 and 8404 of the Civil Code for any portion of the work for which payment has been made. The person contracting for home improvement may withhold all further payments until these releases are furnished.

(7) If the contract provides for a payment of a salesperson's commission out of the contract price, that payment shall be made on a pro rata basis in proportion to the schedule of payments made to the contractor by the disbursing party in accordance with paragraph (4).

(8) A contractor furnishing a performance and payment bond, lien and completion bond, or a bond equivalent or joint control approved by the registrar covering full performance and payment is exempt from paragraphs (3), (4), and (5), and need not include, as part of the contract, the statement regarding the downpayment specified in subparagraph (C) of paragraph (8) of subdivision (d) of Section 7159, the details and statement regarding progress payments specified in paragraph (9) of subdivision (d) of Section 7159, or the Mechanics Lien Warning specified in paragraph (4) of subdivision (e) of Section 7159. A contractor furnishing these bonds, bond equivalents, or a joint control approved by the registrar may accept payment prior to completion. If the contract provides for a contractor to furnish joint control, the contractor shall not have any financial or other interest in the joint control. Notwithstanding any other law, a licensee shall be licensed in this state in an active status for not less than two years prior to submitting an Application for Approval of Blanket Performance and Payment Bond as provided in Section 858.2 of Title 16 of the California Code of Regulations as it read on January 1, 2016.

(b) A violation of paragraph (1), (3), or (5) of subdivision (a) by a licensee or a person subject to be licensed under this chapter, or by their agent or salesperson, is a misdemeanor punishable by a fine of not less than one hundred dollars ($100) nor more than five thousand dollars ($5,000), or by imprisonment in a county jail not exceeding one year, or by both that fine and imprisonment.

(1) An indictment or information against a person who is not licensed but who is required to be licensed under this chapter shall be brought, or a criminal complaint filed, for a violation of this section, in accordance with paragraph (4) of subdivision (d) of Section 802 of the Penal Code, within four years from the date of the contract or, if the contract is not reduced to writing, from the date the buyer makes the first payment to the contractor.

(2) An indictment or information against a person who is licensed under this chapter shall be brought, or a criminal complaint filed, for a violation of this section, in accordance with paragraph (2) of subdivision (d) of Section 802 of the Penal Code, within two years from the date of the contract or, if the contract is not reduced to writing, from the date the buyer makes the first payment to the contractor.

(3) The limitations on actions in this subdivision shall not apply to any administrative action filed against a licensed contractor.

(c) (1) Any person who violates this section as part of a plan or scheme to defraud an owner or tenant of a residential or nonresidential structure, including a mobilehome or manufactured home, in connection with the offer or performance of repairs to the structure for damage caused by a natural disaster, shall be ordered by the court to make full restitution to the victim based on the person's ability to pay, defined as the overall capability of the defendant to reimburse the costs, or a portion of the costs, including consideration of, but not limited to, all of the following:

(A) The defendant's present financial position.

(B) The defendant's reasonably discernible future financial position, provided that the court shall not consider a period of more than one year from the date of the hearing for purposes of determining the reasonably discernible future financial position of the defendant.

(C) The likelihood that the defendant will be able to obtain employment within one year from the date of the hearing.

(D) Any other factor that may bear upon the defendant's financial capability to reimburse the county for costs.

(2) In addition to full restitution, and imprisonment authorized by this section, the court may impose a fine of not less than five hundred dollars ($500) nor more than twenty-five thousand dollars ($25,000), based upon the defendant's ability to pay. This subdivision applies to natural disasters for which a state of emergency is proclaimed by the Governor pursuant to Section 8625 of the Government Code, or for which an emergency or major disaster is declared by the President of the United States.

(d) This section shall become operative on July 1, 2021.

Added Stats 2020 ch 92 § 6 (AB 1869), effective September 18, 2020, operative July 1, 2021; Amended by Stat 2021 ch 249 § 4 (SB 757), effective January 1, 2022.

§ 7159.6. Work or change order

(a) An extra work or change order is not enforceable against a buyer unless the change order sets forth all of the following:

(1) The scope of work encompassed by the order.

(2) The amount to be added or subtracted from the contract.

(3) The effect the order will make in the progress payments or the completion date.

(b) The buyer may not require a contractor to perform extra or change-order work without providing written authorization.

(c) Failure to comply with the requirements of this section does not preclude the recovery of compensation for work performed based upon legal or equitable remedies designed to prevent unjust enrichment.

(d) This section shall become operative on January 1, 2006.

Added Stats 2004 ch 566 § 9 (SB 30), operative July 1, 2005. Amended Stats 2005 ch 48 § 12 (SB 1113), effective July 18, 2005, operative January 1, 2006.

§ 7159.9. Requirements for home improvement contracts, exemption for fire alarm system

(a) Section 7159 does not apply to the sale, installation, and servicing of a fire alarm sold in conjunction with an alarm system, as defined in Section 7590.1 of the Alarm Company Act (Chapter 11.6 (commencing with Section 7590)), provided the licensee does all of the following:

(1) Complies with the contract requirements set forth in Section 7599.54.

(2) Complies with Sections 1689.5, 1689.6, and 1689.7 of the Civil Code, as applicable.

(3) Executes the following certification statement in the contract or in a separate certification document signed by all parties to the contract:

"All costs attributable to making the fire alarm system operable for the residence identified by this document, including sale and installation costs, do not exceed five hundred dollars ($500)."

(4) Certifies to the following if the certification statement described in paragraph (3) is in a separate document:

"I certify that all statements and representations made by me in this document are true and accurate."

(b) The contract or separate certification document shall also include both of the following:

(1) The physical address of the residence for which the certification is applicable.

(2) The name, business address, and license number of the contractor as contained in the official records of the board.

(c) The licensee shall give an exact copy of all documents required pursuant to this section to the party who is contracting to have the alarm system installed.

(d) All documents required pursuant to this section shall be retained by the licensee for a period of five years in accordance with the provisions of Section 7111, and shall be made available to the board within 30 days of a written request.

Section VI

(e) Failure by the contractor to provide the board with the certification or contract within 30 days of a written request is cause for discipline.

(f) Failure by the licensee to provide the board with the certification or contract within 30 days of a written request creates a presumption that the licensee has violated the provisions of Section 7159, unless evidence to the contrary is presented within the timeframe specified by the board.

Added Stats 2006 ch 114 (AB 2073), effective January 1, 2007. Amended Stats 2007 ch 130 § 31 (AB 299), effective January 1, 2008; Stats 2018 ch 406 § 4 (SB 904), effective January 1, 2019.

§ 7159.10. Service and repair contract defined

(a)(1) "Service and repair contract" means an agreement between a contractor or salesperson for a contractor, whether a general contractor or a specialty contractor, who is licensed or subject to be licensed pursuant to this chapter with regard to the transaction, and a homeowner or a tenant, for the performance of a home improvement as defined in Section 7151, that conforms to the following requirements:

(A) The contract amount is seven hundred fifty dollars ($750) or less.

(B) The prospective buyer initiated contact with the contractor to request the work.

(C) The contractor does not sell the buyer goods or services beyond those reasonably necessary to take care of the particular problem that caused the buyer to contact the contractor.

(D) No payment is due, or accepted by the contractor, until the work is completed.

(2) As used in this subdivision, "the work is completed" means that all of the conditions that caused the buyer to contact the contractor for service and repairs have been fully corrected and, if applicable, the building department has accepted and approved the corrective work.

(b) For any contract written pursuant to subdivision (a) or otherwise presented to the buyer as a service and repair contract, unless all of the conforming requirements for service and repair contracts specified in subdivision (a) are met, the contract requirements for home improvements set forth in subdivisions (c), (d), and (e) of Section 7159 shall be applicable, including any rights to rescind the contract as set forth in Section 1689.6 or 1689.7 of the Civil Code, regardless of the aggregate contract price.

(c) If all of the requirements of subdivision (a) are met, only those notices and other requirements set forth in this section are applicable to the contract.

(d) Every service and repair contract described in subdivision (a) shall include, or otherwise comply with, all of the following:

(1) The contract, any changes to the contract, and any attachments shall be in writing and signed or acknowledged by the parties as set forth in this section, and shall be written in the same language (for example Spanish) as principally used in the oral sales presentation.

(2) The writing shall be legible.

(3) Any printed form shall be readable. Unless a larger typeface is specified in this article, the text shall be in at least 10-point typeface and the headings shall be in at least 10-point boldface type.

(4) Before any work is started, the contractor shall give the buyer a copy of the contract signed and dated by the buyer and by the contractor or the contractor's representative.

(5) The name, business address, and license number of the contractor.

(6) The date the contract was signed.

(7) A notice concerning commercial general liability insurance. This notice may be provided as an attachment to the contract if the contract includes the statement, "A notice concerning commercial general liability insurance is attached to this contract." The notice shall include the heading "Commercial General Liability Insurance (CGL)" followed by whichever of the following statements is both relevant and correct:

(A) "(The name on the license or 'This contractor') does not carry commercial general liability insurance."

(B) "(The name on the license or 'This contractor') carries commercial general liability insurance written by (the insurance company). You may call the (insurance company) at _____ to check the contractor's insurance coverage."

(C) "(The name on the license or 'This contractor') is self-insured."

(D) "(The name on the license or 'This contractor') is a limited liability company that carries liability insurance or maintains other security as required by law. You may call (the insurance company or trust company or bank) at _____
to check on the contractor's insurance coverage or security."

(8) A notice concerning workers' compensation insurance. This notice may be provided as an attachment to the contract if the contract includes the statement "A notice concerning workers' compensation insurance is attached to this contract." The notice shall include the heading "Workers' Compensation Insurance" followed by whichever of the following statements is both relevant and correct:

(A) "(The name on the license or 'This contractor') has no employees and is exempt from workers' compensation requirements."

(B) "(The name on the license or 'This contractor') carries workers' compensation insurance for all employees."

(e) Every service and repair contract described in subdivision (a) shall provide the following information, notices, and disclosures in the contract:

(1) Notice of the type of contract in at least 10-point boldface type: "Service and Repair."

(2) A notice in at least 12-point boldface type, signed and dated by the buyer: Notice to the Buyer: The law requires that service and repair contracts must meet all of the following requirements:

(A) The price must be no more than seven hundred and fifty dollars ($750).

(B) You, the buyer, must have initiated contact with the contractor to request the work.

(C) The contractor must not sell you goods or services beyond those reasonably necessary to take care of the particular problem that caused you to contact the contractor.

(D) No payment is due and the contractor may not accept any payment until the work is completed.

(3) The notice in at least 12-point boldface type: "Notice to the Buyer: You are entitled to a completely filled in and signed copy of this agreement before any work may be started."

(4) If applicable, the heading "List of Documents to be Incorporated into the Contract," followed by the list of documents to be incorporated into the contract.

(5) Where the contract is a fixed contract amount, the heading: "Contract Price" followed by the amount of the contract in dollars and cents.

(6) If a finance charge will be charged, the heading: "Finance Charge" followed by the amount in dollars and cents. The finance charge is to be set out separately from the contract amount.

(7) Where the contract is estimated by a time and materials formula, the heading "Estimated Contract Price" followed by the estimated contract amount in dollars and cents. The contract must disclose the set rate and the estimated cost of materials. The contract must also disclose how time will be computed, for example, in increments of quarter hours, half hours, or hours, and the statement: "The actual contract amount of a time and materials contract may not exceed the estimated contract amount without written authorization from the buyer."

(8) The heading: "Description of the Project and Materials to be Used and Equipment to be Installed" followed by a description of the project and materials to be used and equipment to be installed.

(9) The statement: "The law requires that the contractor offer you any parts that were replaced during the service call. If you do not want the parts, initial the checkbox labeled 'OK for contractor to take replaced parts.'"

(10) A checkbox labeled "OK for contractor to take replaced parts."

(11) If a service charge is charged, the heading "Amount of Service Charge" followed by the service charge, and the statement "You may be charged only one service charge, including any trip charge or inspection fee."

(12) (A) (i) The contract, or an attachment to the contract as specified under subparagraph (C) of this paragraph, must include, in immediate proximity to the space reserved for the buyer's signature, the following statement, in at least 12-point boldface type, which shall be dated and signed by the buyer:

YOUR RIGHTS TO CANCEL BEFORE WORK BEGINS

(A) You, the buyer, have the right to cancel this contract until:

1. You receive a copy of this contract signed and dated by you and the contractor; and

2. The contractor starts work.

(B) However, even if the work has begun you, the buyer, may still cancel the contract for any of the reasons specified in items 1 through 4 of this paragraph. If any of these reasons occur, you may cancel the contract within three business days of signing the contract for normal service and repairs, or within seven business days of signing a contract to repair or correct conditions resulting from any sudden or catastrophic event for which a state of emergency has been declared by the President of the United States or the Governor, or for which a local emergency has been declared by the executive officer or governing body of any city, county, or city and county:

1. You may cancel the contract if the price, including all labor and materials, is more than seven hundred fifty dollars ($750).

2. You may cancel the contract if you did not initiate the contact with the contractor to request the work.

3. You may cancel the contract if the contractor sold you goods or services beyond those reasonably necessary to take care of the particular problem that caused you to contact the contractor.

4. You may cancel the contract if the payment was due or the contractor accepted any money before the work was complete.

(C) If any of these reasons for canceling occurred, you may cancel the contract as specified under paragraph (B) above by e-mailing, mailing, faxing, or delivering a written notice to the contractor at the contractor's place of business within three business days or, if applicable, seven business days of the date you received a signed and dated copy of this contract. Include your name, your address, and the date you received a signed copy of the contract and this notice.

If you cancel, the contractor must return to you anything you paid within 10 days of receiving the notice of cancellation. For your part, you must make available to the contractor at your residence, in substantially as good condition as you received it, any goods delivered to you under this contract. Or, you may, if you wish, comply with the contractor's instructions on how to return the goods at the contractor's expense and risk. If you make the goods available to the contractor and the contractor does not pick them up within 20 days of the date of your notice of cancellation, you may keep them without any further obligation. If you fail to make the goods available to the contractor, or if you agree to return the goods to the contractor and fail to do so, then you remain liable for performance of all obligations under the contract.

(ii) References to "three" in the statement set forth in clause (i) shall be changed to "five" for a buyer who is a senior citizen.

(iii) The five-day right to cancel added by the act that added clause (ii) to this subparagraph shall apply to contracts entered into on or after January 1, 2021.

(B) This paragraph does not apply to home improvement contracts entered into by a person who holds an alarm company operator's license issued pursuant to Chapter 11.6 (commencing with Section 7590), provided the person complies with Sections 1689.5, 1689.6, and 1689.7 of the Civil Code, as applicable.

(C) The notice required in this paragraph may be incorporated as an attachment to the contract if the contract includes a checkbox and whichever statement is relevant in at least 12-point boldface type:

(i) "The law requires that the contractor give you a notice explaining your right to cancel. Initial the checkbox if the contractor has given you a 'Notice of Your Right to Cancel.'"

(ii) "The law requires that the contractor give you a notice explaining your right to cancel contracts for the repair or restoration of residential premises damaged by a disaster. Initial the checkbox if the contractor has given you a 'Notice of Your Right to Cancel.'"

(f) A bona fide service repairperson employed by a licensed contractor or subcontractor hired by a licensed contractor may enter into a service and repair contract on behalf of that contractor.

(g) The provisions of this section are not exclusive and do not relieve the contractor from compliance with any other applicable provision of law.

Added Stats 2004 ch 566 § 10 (SB 30), operative July 1, 2005. Amended Stats 2005 ch 48 § 13 (SB 1113), effective July 18, 2005, operative January 1, 2006, ch 385 § 6 (AB 316); Stats 2010 ch 698 § 40 (SB 392), effective January 1, 2011; Stats 2020 ch 158 § 3 (AB 2471), effective January 1, 2021.

§ 7159.11. Discipline for violation

A violation of any provision of Section 7159.10 by a licensee, or a person subject to be licensed under this chapter, or by his or her agent or salesperson, is cause for discipline.

Added Stats 2004 ch 566 § 11 (SB 30), operative July 1, 2005. Amended Stats 2005 ch 48 § 14 (SB 1113), effective July 18, 2005, operative January 1, 2006, ch 385 § 7 (AB 316).

§ 7159.14. [Section repealed 2021.]

Added Stats 2004 ch 566 § 14 (SB 30), operative July 1, 2005. Amended Stats 2005 ch 48 § 17 (SB 1113), effective July 18, 2005, operative January 1, 2006; Stats 2007 ch 230 § 3 (AB 244), effective January 1, 2008; Stats 2009 ch 307 § 76 (SB 821), effective January 1, 2010; Stats 2010 ch 697 § 7 (SB 189), effective January 1, 2011, operative July 1, 2012; Stats 2011 ch 44 § 3 (SB 190), effective January 1, 2012, operative July 1, 2012; Stats 2020 ch 92 § 7 (AB 1869), effective September 18, 2020, repealed July 1, 2021.

§ 7159.14. Further requirements; Statement of agreed amount; Payment due; Punishment for violations; Restitution

(a) This section applies to a service and repair contract as defined in Section 7159.10. A violation of this section by a licensee or a person subject to be licensed under this chapter, or by their agent or salesperson, is cause for discipline.

(1) The contract shall not exceed seven hundred fifty dollars ($750).

(2) The contract shall be in writing and shall state the agreed contract amount, which may be stated as either a fixed contract amount in dollars and cents or, if a time and materials formula is used, as an estimated contract amount in dollars and cents.

(3) The contract amount shall include the entire cost of the contract including profit, labor, and materials, but excluding finance charges.

(4) The actual contract amount of a time and materials contract may not exceed the estimated contract amount without written authorization from the buyer.

(5) The prospective buyer shall have initiated contact with the contractor to request work.

(6) The contractor shall not sell the buyer goods or services beyond those reasonably necessary to take care of the particular problem that caused the buyer to contact the contractor.

(7) Payment shall not be due before the project is completed.

(8) A service and repair contractor shall charge only one service charge. For purposes of this chapter, a service charge includes charges such as a service or trip charge, or an inspection fee.

(9) A service and repair contractor charging a service charge shall disclose in all advertisements that there is a service charge and, when the customer initiates the call for service, shall disclose the amount of the service charge.

(10) The service and repair contractor shall offer to the customer any parts that were replaced.

(11) Upon any payment by the buyer, the contractor shall, if requested, obtain and furnish to the buyer a full and unconditional re-

lease from any potential lien claimant claim or mechanics lien authorized pursuant to Sections 8400 and 8404 of the Civil Code for any portion of the work for which payment has been made.

(b) A violation of paragraph (1), (2), (3), (4), (5), (6), or (8) of subdivision (a) by a licensee or a person subject to be licensed under this chapter, or by their agent or salesperson, is a misdemeanor punishable by a fine of not less than one hundred dollars ($100) nor more than five thousand dollars ($5,000), or by imprisonment in a county jail not exceeding one year, or by both that fine and imprisonment.

(1) An indictment or information against a person who is not licensed but who is required to be licensed under this chapter shall be brought, or a criminal complaint filed, for a violation of this section, in accordance with paragraph (4) of subdivision (d) of Section 802 of the Penal Code, within four years from the date of the contract or, if the contract is not reduced to writing, from the date the buyer makes the first payment to the contractor.

(2) An indictment or information against a person who is licensed under this chapter shall be brought, or a criminal complaint filed, for a violation of this section, in accordance with paragraph (2) of subdivision (d) of Section 802 of the Penal Code, within two years from the date of the contract or, if the contract is not reduced to writing, from the date the buyer makes the first payment to the contractor.

(3) The limitations on actions in this subdivision do not apply to any administrative action filed against a licensed contractor.

(c) (1) Any person who violates this section as part of a plan or scheme to defraud an owner or tenant of a residential or nonresidential structure, including a mobilehome or manufactured home, in connection with the offer or performance of repairs to the structure for damage caused by a natural disaster, shall be ordered by the court to make full restitution to the victim based on the person's ability to pay, defined as the overall capability of the defendant to reimburse the costs, or a portion of the costs, including consideration of, but not limited to, all of the following:

(A) The defendant's present financial position.

(B) The defendant's reasonably discernible future financial position, provided that the court shall not consider a period of more than one year from the date of the hearing for purposes of determining the reasonably discernible future financial position of the defendant.

(C) The likelihood that the defendant will be able to obtain employment within one year from the date of the hearing.

(D) Any other factor that may bear upon the defendant's financial capability to reimburse the county for costs.

(2) In addition to full restitution, and imprisonment authorized by this section, the court may impose a fine of not less than five hundred dollars ($500) nor more than twenty-five thousand dollars ($25,000), based upon the defendant's ability to pay. This subdivision applies to

natural disasters for which a state of emergency is proclaimed by the Governor pursuant to Section 8625 of the Government Code, or for which an emergency or major disaster is declared by the President of the United States.

(d) This section shall become operative July 1, 2021.

Added Stats 2020 ch 92 § 8 (AB 1869), effective September 18, 2020, operative July 1, 2021.

§ 7160. Penalty for fraudulent misrepresentation

Any person who is induced to contract for a work of improvement, including but not limited to a home improvement, in reliance on false or fraudulent representations or false statements knowingly made, may sue and recover from such contractor or solicitor a penalty of five hundred dollars ($500), plus reasonable attorney's fees, in addition to any damages sustained by him by reason of such statements or representations made by the contractor or solicitor.

Added Stats 1969 ch 1583 § 6 as § 7028.2. Renumbered Stats 1972 ch 1138 § 1.5.

§ 7161. [Section repealed 2021.]

Added Stats 1969 ch 1583 § 9 as § 7116.2. Renumbered Stats 1972 ch 1138 § 4. Amended Stats 1994 ch 175 § 4 (SB 634), effective July 9, 1994; Stats 2006 ch 538 § 13 (SB 1852), effective January 1, 2007; Stats 2020 ch 92 § 9 (AB 1869), effective September 18, 2020, repealed July 1, 2021.

§ 7161. Specification of prohibited acts; Misdemeanor

It is a misdemeanor for any person to engage in any of the following acts, the commission of which is cause for disciplinary action against any licensee or applicant:

(a) Using false, misleading, or deceptive advertising as an inducement to enter into any contract for a work of improvement, including, but not limited to, any home improvement contract, whereby any member of the public may be misled or injured.

(b) Making any substantial misrepresentation in the procurement of a contract for a home improvement or other work of improvement or making any false promise of a character likely to influence, persuade, or induce any person to enter into the contract.

(c) Any fraud in the execution of, or in the material alteration of, any contract, trust deed, mortgage, promissory note, or other document incident to a home improvement transaction or other transaction involving a work of improvement.

(d) Preparing or accepting any trust deed, mortgage, promissory note, or other evidence of indebtedness upon the obligations of a home improvement transaction or other transaction for a work of improvement with knowledge that it specifies a greater monetary obligation than the consideration for the improvement work, which consideration may be a time sale price.

(e) Directly or indirectly publishing any advertisement relating to home improvements or other works of improvement that contains an assertion, representation, or statement of fact that is false, deceptive, or misleading, or by any means advertising or purporting to offer to the general public this improvement work with the intent not to accept contracts for the particular work or at the price that is advertised or offered to the public, except that any advertisement that is subject to and complies with the existing rules, regulations, or guides of the Federal Trade Commission shall not be deemed false, deceptive, or misleading.

(f) (1) Any person who violates subdivision (b), (c), (d), or (e) as part of a plan or scheme to defraud an owner of a residential or nonresidential structure, including a mobilehome or manufactured home, in connection with the offer or performance of repairs to the structure for damage caused by a natural disaster, shall be ordered by the court to make full restitution to the victim based on the person's ability to pay, defined as the overall capability of the defendant to reimburse the costs, or a portion of the costs, including consideration of, but not limited to, all of the following:

(A) The defendant's present financial position.

(B) The defendant's reasonably discernible future financial position, provided that the court shall not consider a period of more than one year from the date of the hearing for purposes of determining the reasonably discernible future financial position of the defendant.

(C) The likelihood that the defendant will be able to obtain employment within one year from the date of the hearing.

(D) Any other factor that may bear upon the defendant's financial capability to reimburse the county for costs.

(2) In addition to full restitution and imprisonment as authorized by this section, the court may impose a fine of not less than five hundred dollars ($500) nor more than twenty-five thousand dollars ($25,000), based upon the defendant's ability to pay. This subdivision applies to natural disasters for which a state of emergency is proclaimed by the Governor pursuant to Section 8625 of the Government Code or for which an emergency or major disaster is declared by the President of the United States.

(g) This section shall become operative on July 1, 2021.

Added Stats 2020 ch 92 § 10 (AB 1869), effective September 18, 2020, operative July 1, 2021.

§ 7162. Contents of contract; Representations as to goods and materials

(a) Notwithstanding any other provision of law, any representation by a person licensed pursuant to this chapter with respect to a trademark or brand name, quality, or size of any goods or materials, in reference to bathroom fixtures, a sink, stove, refrigerator, lighting, carpeting and other floor surfaces, burglar and smoke alarms, a solar energy system, paints, textured coatings, siding and other wall surfaces, insulation, roofing, air conditioning and heating systems, and appliances, to be provided by the person pursuant to a home improvement contract, as defined in Section 7151.2, shall set forth, in writing, in the contract or specifications and shall include a description of the goods or materials, including any brand name, model number, or similar designation.

(b) Failure to install the specific goods or materials as represented as required by this section constitutes a cause for disciplinary action under this chapter.

Added Stats 1981 ch 916 § 3; Amended Stats 2021 ch 249 § 5 (SB 757) effective January 1, 2022.

§ 7163. Enforceability of contract prior to buyer obtaining loan

(a) No contract for home improvement shall be enforceable against the buyer if the obtaining of a loan for all or a portion of the contract price is a condition precedent to the contract or if the contractor provides financing, or in any manner assists the buyer to obtain a loan or refers the buyer to any person who may loan or arrange a loan for all or a portion of the contract price unless all of the following requirements are satisfied:

(1) The third party, if any, agrees to make the loan.

(2) The buyer agrees to accept the loan or financing.

(3) The buyer does not rescind the loan or financing transaction, within the period prescribed for rescission, pursuant to the federal Truth in Lending Act (15 U.S.C. Sec. 1601 et seq.) or Regulation Z, if applicable.

(b) Until the requirements of paragraphs (1), (2), and (3) of subdivision (a) are satisfied, it shall be unlawful for the contractor to do any of the following:

(1) Deliver any property or perform any services other than obtaining building permits or other similar services preliminary to the commencement of the home improvement for which no mechanic's lien can be claimed.

(2) Represent in any manner that the contract is enforceable or that the buyer has any obligation thereunder.

Any violation of this subdivision shall render the contract unenforceable.

(c) If the contract is unenforceable pursuant to subdivision (a) or subdivision (b), the contractor shall immediately and without condition return all money, property, and other consideration given by the buyer. If the buyer gave any property as consideration and the contractor does not or cannot return it for whatever reason, the contractor shall immediately return the fair market value of the property or its value as designated in the contract, whichever is greater. Nothing herein shall prohibit a contractor from receiving a downpayment otherwise permitted by law provided the contractor returns the downpayment as herein required if the contract is unenforceable pursuant to subdivision (a) or (b).

(d)(1) Except as provided in paragraph (2), the buyer may retain without obligation in law or equity any services or property provided pursuant to a contract that is unenforceable pursuant to subdivision (a) or subdivision (b).

(2) If the contractor has delivered any property to the buyer pursuant to a contract which is unenforceable pursuant to subdivision (a) or subdivision (b), the buyer shall make the property available to the contractor for return provided that all of the following requirements are satisfied:

(A) The property can be practically returned to the contractor without causing any damage to the buyer.

(B) The contractor, at the contractor's expense, first returns to the buyer any money, property, and other consideration taken by the contractor provided that the property is returned in the condition that it was in immediately prior to its taking. If applicable, the contractor shall also, at its expense, reinstall any property taken in the manner in which the property had been installed prior to its taking.

(C) The contractor, at the contractor's expense, picks up the property within 60 days of the execution of the contract.

(e) For the purpose of this section, "home improvement" means "home improvement" as defined in Section 7151. Goods are included within the definition notwithstanding whether they are to be attached to real property or to be so affixed to real property as to become a part thereof whether or not severable therefrom.

(f) The rights and remedies provided the buyer under this section are nonexclusive and cumulative to all other rights and remedies under other laws.

(g) Any waiver of this section shall be deemed contrary to public policy and shall be void and unenforceable. However, the buyer may waive subdivisions (a) and (b) to the extent that the contract is executed in connection with the making of emergency repairs or services that are necessary for the immediate protection of persons or real or personal property. The buyer's waiver for emergency repairs or services shall be in a dated written statement that describes the emergency, states that the contractor has informed the buyer of subdivisions (a) and (b) and that the buyer waives those provisions, and is signed by each owner of the property. Waivers made on printed forms are void and unenforceable.

Added Stats 1985 ch 989 § 1. Amended Stats 1986 ch 1404 § 1, effective September 30, 1986; Stats 1991 ch 1160 § 46 (AB 2190); Stats 1993 ch 589 § 13 (AB 2211).

§ 7164. Contract and changes to be in writing; Requirements

(a) Notwithstanding Section 7044, every contract and any changes in a contract, between an owner and a contractor, for the construction of a single-family dwelling to be retained by the owner for at least one year shall be evidenced in writing signed by both parties.

(b) The writing shall contain the following:

(1) The name, address, and license number of the contractor.

(2) The approximate dates when the work will begin and be substantially completed.

(3) A legal description of the location where the work will be done.

(4) A statement with the heading "Mechanics Lien Warning" as follows:

"MECHANICS LIEN WARNING:

Anyone who helps improve your property, but who is not paid, may record what is called a mechanics lien on your property. A mechanics lien is a claim, like a mortgage or home equity loan, made against your property and recorded with the county recorder.

Even if you pay your contractor in full, unpaid subcontractors, suppliers, and laborers who helped to improve your property may record mechanics liens and sue you in court to foreclose the lien. If a court finds the lien is valid, you could be forced to pay twice or have a court officer sell your home to pay the lien. Liens can also affect your credit.

To preserve their right to record a lien, each subcontractor and material supplier must provide you with a document called a 'Preliminary Notice.' This notice is not a lien. The purpose of the notice is to let you know that the person who sends you the notice has the right to record a lien on your property if he or she is not paid.

BE CAREFUL. The Preliminary Notice can be sent up to 20 days after the subcontractor starts work or the supplier provides material. This can be a big problem if you pay your contractor before you have received the Preliminary Notices.

You will not get Preliminary Notices from your prime contractor or other persons you contract with directly or from laborers who work on your project. The law assumes that you already know they are improving your property.

PROTECT YOURSELF FROM LIENS. You can protect yourself from liens by getting a list from your contractor of all the subcontractors and material suppliers that work on your project. Find out from your contractor when these subcontractors started work and when these suppliers delivered goods or materials. Then wait 20 days, paying attention to the Preliminary Notices you receive.

PAY WITH JOINT CHECKS. One way to protect yourself is to pay with a joint check. When your contractor tells you it is time to pay for the work of a subcontractor or supplier who has provided you with a Preliminary Notice, write a joint check payable to both the contractor and the subcontractor or material supplier.

For other ways to prevent liens, visit CSLB's Web site at www.cslb.ca.gov or call CSLB at 800-321-CSLB (2752).

REMEMBER, IF YOU DO NOTHING, YOU RISK HAVING A LIEN PLACED ON YOUR HOME. This can mean that you may have to pay twice, or face the forced sale of your home to pay what you owe."

(5)(A) A statement prepared by the board through regulation that emphasizes the value of commercial general liability insurance and encourages the owner to verify the contractor's insurance coverage and status.

(B) A check box indicating whether or not the contractor carries commercial general liability insurance, and if that is the case, the name and the telephone number of the insurer.

(c) The writing may also contain other matters agreed to by the parties to the contract. The writing shall be legible and shall clearly describe any other document which is to be incorporated into the contract. Prior to commencement of any work, the owner shall be furnished a copy of the written agreement, signed by the contractor. The provisions of this section are not exclusive and do not relieve the contractor from compliance with all other applicable provisions of law.

(d) Every contract subject to the provisions of this section shall contain, in close proximity to the signatures of the owner and contractor, a notice in at least 10-point boldface type or in all capital letters, stating that the owner has the right to require the contractor to have a performance and payment bond and that the expense of the bond may be borne by the owner.

(e) The requirements in paragraph (5) of subdivision (b) shall become operative three months after the board adopts the regulations referenced in subparagraph (A) of paragraph (5) of subdivision (b).

(f) This section shall become operative on January 1, 2006.

Added Stats 2005 ch 48 § 19 (SB 1113), effective July 18, 2005, operative January 1, 2006. Amended Stats 2010 ch 697 § 8 (SB 189), effective January 1, 2011, operative July 1, 2012.

§ 7165. Conditions under which swimming pool contract financed by third-party lender is enforceable

The requirements of this section may be substituted for the requirements of paragraphs (1), (2), and (3) of subdivision (a) of Section 7163 if a swimming pool contract is to be financed by a third-party lender and if all the following conditions are met:

(a) The lender has agreed, in writing, to provide financing to the buyer for the maximum estimated construction cost of the swimming pool.

(b) The lender has provided the buyer a written copy of the terms and conditions of the loan for the maximum estimated construction cost of the swimming pool, including the following terms disclosed in the manner required by the federal Truth in Lending Act and Regulation Z: the annual percentage rate, the finance charge, the amount financed, the total number of payments, the payment schedule, and a description of the security interest to be taken by the lender.

(c) The lender has agreed in writing to the following:

(1) To offer to loan the maximum estimated construction cost on the terms and conditions disclosed pursuant to subdivision (b).

(2) If the construction cost of the swimming pool is determined after the completion of excavation to be less than the maximum estimated construction cost, to offer to loan the lesser amount needed to complete the construction of the swimming pool on the same security as, and at an annual percentage rate and monthly payment amount not to exceed, that disclosed in subdivision (b).

The lender's written agreement shall state the duration of the offer, which shall not be less than 15 days following the completion of the excavation of the swimming pool.

(d) The buyer acknowledges receipt of the writings required by subdivisions (a), (b), and (c) and, no sooner than three business days after receiving all of these writings, requests on the form prescribed in subdivision (e) that the contractor begin performance of the swimming pool contract prior to the expiration of any rescission period applicable to the loan.

(e) The request of a buyer, described in subdivision (d), shall be set forth on a document separate and apart from the swimming pool contract and shall contain the following notice in at least 10-point type unless otherwise stated:

"NOTICE

Under the law, this contract is not enforceable until:

(1) A third party agrees to make a loan to finance the construction cost of the swimming pool;

(2) You agree to accept the loan; and

(3) You do not cancel the loan within the period prescribed for cancellation under the federal Truth in Lending Act or Regulation Z (usually three business days after the loan is consummated).

Until the cancellation period is over, the contractor cannot deliver any materials or perform any services except preliminary services for which no mechanic's lien can be claimed.

However, as an alternative to the above, you can ask the contractor to start work and deliver materials before the cancellation period on the loan is over if all of the following have occurred:

(1) The lender has agreed, in writing, to provide you with financing for up to the maximum estimated construction cost of the swimming pool.

(2) The lender has provided you with a written copy of the terms and conditions of a loan for the maximum estimated cost, including the annual percentage rate, the finance charge, the amount financed, the total of payments, the payment schedule, and a description of the security interest to be taken by the lender.

(3) The lender has agreed in writing to offer these terms and conditions for a period not less than 15 days following completion of the excavation of the swimming pool.

(4) Three business days have passed since you received the writing mentioned in paragraphs (1), (2), and (3), and you then sign a copy of this form to request that the contractor begin construction of the swimming pool before the cancellation period on your loan is over.

The first day you can sign the request for the contractor to begin construction of the swimming pool is

---

(contractor to insert third business day after buyer receives writings described in subdivisions (a), (b), and (c))
If you sign this request, the contractor will be permitted to immediately begin performance of the contract, and if the contractor is not paid in accordance with the terms of the contract, he or she may file a lien against your property for the value of the labor and materials provided. [This paragraph shall be printed in 12-point type.]

REQUEST

I/we request that the contractor immediately start construction of the swimming pool.

_____
Date

Buyer(s)"

(f) The contractor shall provide the buyer a copy of the buyer's signed request at the time of signature.

(g) This section applies to each buyer who signs the swimming pool contract or the promissory note, other evidence of indebtedness, or security instrument incident to the loan for swimming pool construction.

(h) For the purpose of this section, "business day" has the meaning provided in Section 9 of the Civil Code.

Added Stats 1986 ch 1404 § 2, effective September 30, 1986, as § 7167.5. Renumbered by Stats 1991 ch 1160 § 51 (AB 2190).

—See Health and Safety Code Section 115920, Citations; 115921, Definitions; 115922, Safety Features; 115923, Enclosure; 115924, Consumer Notice; 15925, Inapplicability, in Appendix.

§ 7166. Application of article to contracts for construction of specified swimming pools

The provisions of Article 10 shall not apply to contracts for the construction of swimming pools to be built for the use and enjoyment of other than a single-family unit upon or contiguous to premises occupied only by a single-family unit, nor shall they apply to the construction of swimming pools built as part of an original building plan by the same contractor who builds a single-family dwelling unit on the premises.

Added Stats 1979 ch 747 § 2 as § 7170. Amended Stats 1980 ch 138 § 8, effective May 30, 1980. Amended and renumbered Stats 1991 ch 1160 § 54 (AB 2190).

§ 7167. Certain contracts for construction of swimming pool void; Recovery for work performed

(a) Any contract, the primary purpose of which is the construction of a swimming pool, that does not substantially comply with paragraph (4) or (5) of subdivision (c) or paragraph (7), (8), or (9) of subdivision (d) of Section 7159, shall be void and unenforceable by the contractor as contrary to public policy.

(b) Failure by the contractor to comply with paragraph (5) of subdivision (c) of Section 7159 as set forth in subdivision (a) of this section does not preclude the recovery of compensation for work performed based on quasi-contract, quantum meruit, restitution, or other similar legal or equitable remedies designed to prevent unjust enrichment.

Added Stats 2005 ch 48 § 21 (SB 1113), effective July 18, 2005, operative January 1, 2006. Amended Stats 2005 ch 385 § 10 (AB 316), effective January 1, 2006.

§ 7168. Reasonable attorney's fees

In any action between a person contracting for construction of a swimming pool and a swimming pool contractor arising out of a con-

Section VI

tract for swimming pool construction, the court shall award reasonable attorney's fees to the prevailing party.

Added Stats 1979 ch 747 § 2 as § 7169. Amended and renumbered Stats 1991 ch 1160 § 53 (AB 2190).

§ 7169. Development and availability of "solar energy system disclosure document"

(a) The board, in collaboration with the Public Utilities Commission, shall develop and make available a "solar energy system disclosure document" or documents that provide a consumer, at a minimum, accurate, clear, and concise information regarding the installation of a solar energy system, total costs of installation, anticipated savings, the assumptions and inputs used to estimate the savings, and the implications of various financing options.

(b) On or before July 1, 2018, the board, in collaboration with the Public Utilities Commission, shall develop, and make available on its internet website the disclosure document described in subdivision (a) that a solar energy system company shall provide to a consumer prior to completion of a sale, financing, or lease of a solar energy system. The "solar energy system disclosure document" shall be printed on the front page or cover page of every solar energy contract. The "solar energy system disclosure document" shall be printed in boldface 16-point type and include the following types of primary information:

(1) The total cost and payments for the system, including financing costs.

(2) Information on how and to whom customers may provide complaints.

(3) The consumer's right to the applicable cancellation period pursuant to Section 7159 of the Business and Professions Code.

(c) At the board's discretion, other types of supporting information the board and the commission deem appropriate or useful in furthering the directive described in subdivision (a) may be included in the solar energy disclosure document following the front page or cover page, including, but not limited to:

(1) The amounts and sources of financing obtained.

(2) The calculations used by the home improvement salesperson to determine how many panels the homeowner needs to install.

(3) The calculations used by the home improvement salesperson to determine how much energy the panels will generate.

(4) Any additional monthly fees the homeowner's electric company may bill, any turn-on charges, and any fees added for the use of an internet monitoring system of the panels or inverters.

(5) The terms and conditions of any guaranteed rebate.

(6) The final contract price, without the inclusion of possible rebates.

(7) The solar energy system company's contractor's license number.

(8) The impacts of solar energy system installations not performed to code.

(9) Types of solar energy system malfunctions.

(10) Information about the difference between a solar energy system lease and a solar energy system purchase.

(11) The impacts that the financing options, lease agreement terms, or contract terms will have on the sale of the consumer's home, including any balloon payments or solar energy system relocation that may be required if the contract is not assigned to the new owner of the home.

(12) A calculator that calculates performance of solar projects to provide solar customers the solar power system's projected output, which may include an expected performance-based buy-down calculator.

(d) A contract for sale, financing, or lease of a solar energy system and the solar energy system disclosure document shall be written in the same language as was principally used in the oral sales presentation made to the consumer or the print or digital marketing material given to the consumer.

(e) For solar energy systems utilizing Property Assessed Clean Energy (PACE) financing, the Financing Estimate and Disclosure form required by subdivision (b) of Section 5898.17 of the Streets and Highways Code shall satisfy the requirements of this section with respect to the financing contract only, but not, however, with respect to the underlying contract for installation of the solar energy system.

(f) The board shall post the PACE Financing Estimate and Disclosure form required by subdivision (b) of Section 5898.17 of the Streets and Highways Code on its internet website.

(g) For purposes of this section, "solar energy system" means a solar energy device to be installed on a residential building that has the primary purpose of providing for the collection and distribution of solar energy for the generation of electricity, that produces at least one kW, and not more than five MW, alternating current rated peak electricity, and that meets or exceeds the eligibility criteria established pursuant to Section 25782 of the Public Resources Code.

(h) This section does not apply to a solar energy system that is installed as a standard feature on new construction.

Added Stats 2017 ch 662 § 1 (AB 1070), effective January 1, 2018. Amended Stats 2019 ch 378 § 10 (SB 610), effective January 1, 2020; Stats 2021 ch 188 § 11 (SB 826), effective January 1, 2022.

Section VI

§ 7170. Complaints regarding solar energy systems companies and solar contractors

(a) The Contractors State License Board shall receive and review complaints and consumer questions regarding solar energy systems companies and solar contractors. The board shall also receive complaints received from state agencies regarding solar energy systems companies and solar contractors.

(b) Beginning on July 1, 2019, the board annually shall compile a report documenting consumer complaints relating to solar contractors. The report shall be made available publicly on the board's and the Public Utilities Commission's internet websites. The report shall contain all of the following:

(1) The number and types of complaints.

(2) The ZIP Code where the consumer complaint originated.

(3) The disposition of all complaints received against a solar contractor.

Added Stats 2017 ch 662 § 2 (AB 1070), effective January 1, 2018. Amended Stats 2020 ch 312 § 74 (SB 1474), effective January 1, 2021; Amended Stats 2021 ch 249 § 6 (SB 757) effective September 23, 2021.

Article 11
Asbestos Consultants

§ 7180. Requirement of certification

(a) No person shall, on or after July 1, 1992, engage in the practice of an asbestos consultant as defined in Section 7181, or as a site surveillance technician as defined in Section 7182, unless he or she is certified by the Division of Occupational Safety and Health pursuant to regulations required by subdivision (b) of Section 9021.5 of the Labor Code.

(b) Certification as an asbestos consultant or site surveillance technician shall not be required when a licensed contractor or registered asbestos abatement contractor takes no more than 12 bulk samples of suspected asbestos-containing material that is required to be removed, repaired, or disturbed as part of a construction project in a residential dwelling solely for any of the following purposes: (1) bid preparation for asbestos abatement; (2) evaluating exposure to its own employees during construction or asbestos abatement; or (3) determining for its own purposes or for the purpose of communicating whether or not a contract for asbestos abatement has been satisfactorily completed. Persons taking samples for the purposes described in this section shall be certified building inspectors under the Asbestos Hazard Emergency Response Act, as specified in Section 763 of Title

40 of the Code of Federal Regulations, appendix (c) to subpart (e). No licensed contractor or asbestos abatement contractor may provide professional health and safety services or perform any asbestos risk assessment. A bid for asbestos abatement may communicate the results and location of sampling for the presence of asbestos and how the asbestos will be abated. This section does not affect the requirement that asbestos abatement contractors be registered under Section 6501.5 of the Labor Code, nor does it permit a licensed contractor or asbestos abatement contractor to perform clearance air monitoring following asbestos abatement, unless otherwise permitted by law.

Added Stats 1990 ch 1255 § 1 (SB 732). Amended Stats 1996 ch 526 § 1 (SB 1486).

§ 7180.5. Requirement of certification for building owner or operator contracts

When a building owner or operator engages the services of a person to perform asbestos consulting or site surveillance technician activities as defined in Sections 7181 and 7182 after July 1, 1992, the building owner or operator shall contract with a person who is certified by the Division of Occupational Safety and Health pursuant to the regulations required by subdivision (b) of Section 9021.5 of the Labor Code.

Added Stats 1990 ch 1255 § 1 (SB 732).

§ 7181. "Asbestos consultant"

An "asbestos consultant," as used in this chapter, means any person who contracts to provide professional health and safety services relating to asbestos-containing material, as defined in subdivision (b) of Section 6501.8 of the Labor Code, including building inspections, abatement project design, contract administration, supervision of site surveillance technicians as defined in Section 7182, sample collections, preparation of asbestos management plans, and clearance air monitoring.

Added Stats 1990 ch 1255 § 1 (SB 732).

§ 7182. "Site surveillance technician"

A "site surveillance technician" means any person who acts as an independent onsite representative of an asbestos consultant who monitors the asbestos abatement activities of others, provides asbestos air monitoring services for area and personnel samples, and performs building surveys and contract administration at the direction of an asbestos consultant.

Added Stats 1990 ch 1255 § 1 (SB 732).

§ 7183. Notice of complete application; Issuance of certificate; Provisional certification card

(a) Within 15 days of receipt of an application for certification pursuant to this article, the division shall inform the applicant in writing either (1) that the application is complete and accepted, or (2) that it is deficient and that additional information, documentation, or examination, specified in the notification, is required to complete the application. Within 45 days of the date of filing of a completed application, the division shall issue to each person who qualifies for certification pursuant to this article, a certification card which shall identify the holder thereof and the type of certification for which he or she has qualified. If the division cannot comply with the notification deadlines specified in this section, the division shall issue a provisional certification card until all procedures specified in this section are completed.

(b) The certification required by this article shall satisfy all certification requirements of the division for asbestos consultants and site surveillance technicians.

Added Stats 1990 ch 1255 § 1 (SB 732).

§ 7183.5. Enforcement by division

The division shall enforce this article. In the event the division determines that a certified asbestos consultant or site surveillance technician obtained certification under false pretenses, or that a certified asbestos consultant or site surveillance technician acted in a grossly negligent or fraudulent manner, or engaged in repeated acts of negligence, the division shall revoke that person's certification. The division shall only revoke a certification after complying with all of the procedural requirements of Chapter 5 (commencing with Section 11500) of Division 3 of Part 1 of Title 2 of the Government Code.

Added Stats 1990 ch 1255 § 1 (SB 732).

§ 7184. Requirements for qualification as certified asbestos consultant

A person shall qualify as a certified asbestos consultant by meeting all of the following requirements:

(a) Having any one of the following:

(1) One year of asbestos-related experience, and a bachelor of science degree in engineering, architecture, industrial hygiene, construction management, or a related biological or physical science.

(2) Two years of asbestos-related experience, and a bachelor's degree.

(3) Three years of asbestos-related experience, and an associate of arts degree in engineering, architecture, industrial hygiene, construction management, or a related biological or physical science.

(4) Four years of asbestos-related experience and a high school diploma or its equivalent.

(b) Possession of a valid federal Asbestos Hazard Emergency Response Act (Subchapter II (commencing with Section 2641) of Chapter 53 of Title 15 of the United States Code) certificate for the type of work being performed, or its equivalent, as determined by the division.

(c) Demonstration of proficiency by achieving a passing score as determined by the division on an examination approved or administered by the division including, but not limited to, the following subjects:

(1) Physical characteristics of asbestos.

(2) Health effects of asbestos.

(3) Federal Occupational Safety and Health Administration, Division of Occupational Safety and Health, Environmental Protection Agency, air quality management districts, and State Department of Health Services regulatory requirements, including protective clothing, respiratory protection, exposure limits, personal hygiene, medical monitoring, disposal, and general industry safety hazards.

(4) State-of-the-art asbestos abatement and control work procedures. The division shall define and incorporate into the certification standards the term "state-of-the-art" for purposes of this article, in the regulations required by subdivision (b) of Section 9021.5 of the Labor Code.

(5) Federal Asbestos Hazard Emergency Response Act training information and procedures for inspectors, management planners, and supervisors, as provided for under Subchapter II (commencing with Section 2641) of Chapter 53 of Title 15 of the United States Code, or the equivalent, as determined by the division.

(6) Information concerning industrial hygiene sampling methodology, including asbestos sampling and analysis techniques and record-keeping.

Added Stats 1990 ch 1255 § 1 (SB 732).

§ 7185. Requirements for qualification as certified site surveillance technician

A person shall qualify as a certified site surveillance technician by meeting all of the following requirements:

(a) Having six months of asbestos-related experience under the supervision of an asbestos consultant.

(b) Possession of a high school diploma or equivalent.

(c) Possession of a valid federal Asbestos Hazard Emergency Response Act (Subchapter II (commencing with Section 2641) of Chapter

53 of Title 15 of the United States Code) certificate for the type of work being performed, or its equivalent, as determined by the division.

(d) Demonstration of proficiency by achieving a passing score, as determined by the division, on an examination approved or administered by the division covering the following subjects:

(1) Physical characteristics of asbestos.

(2) Health effects of asbestos.

(3) Federal Occupational Safety and Health Administration, Division of Occupational Safety and Health, Environmental Protection Agency, air quality management districts, and State Department of Health Services regulatory requirements, including protective clothing, respiratory protection, exposure limits, personal hygiene, medical monitoring, and general industry safety hazards.

(4) State-of-the-art asbestos abatement and control work procedures.

(5) Industrial hygiene sampling methodology, including sampling techniques and recordkeeping.

Added Stats 1990 ch 1255 § 1 (SB 732).

§ 7187. Financial conflict of interest; Legislative intent

When a building owner or operator contracts with an asbestos consultant or site surveillance technician for performance of the activities described in Sections 7181 and 7182, that asbestos consultant or site surveillance technician shall not have any financial or proprietary interest in an asbestos abatement contractor hired for the same project. However, this section shall not preclude the hiring of a consultant by a contractor for the purpose of providing health and safety services for the personnel of the contractor. This section shall not apply when a licensed contractor or registered asbestos abatement contractor takes no more than 12 bulk samples of suspected asbestos-containing material that is required to be removed, repaired, or disturbed as part of a construction project in a residential dwelling solely for any of the following purposes: (1) bid preparation for asbestos abatement; (2) evaluating exposure to its own employees during construction or asbestos abatement; or (3) determining for its own purposes or for the purpose of communicating whether or not a contract for asbestos abatement has been satisfactorily completed. Persons taking samples for the purposes described in this section shall be certified building inspectors under the Asbestos Hazard Emergency Response Act, as specified in Section 763 of Title 40 of the Code of Federal Regulations, appendix (c) to subpart (e). No licensed contractor or asbestos abatement contractor may provide professional health and safety services or perform any asbestos risk assessment. A licensed contractor or asbestos abatement contractor may seek compensation for bid preparation, including the cost of laboratory analysis of asbestos-containing material.

It is the intent of the Legislature in enacting this section to make certain that the asbestos-related work performed by a consultant, including, but not limited to, clearance air monitoring, project design, and contract administration, is performed in a manner which provides for independent professional judgment undertaken without consideration of the financial or beneficial interest of the contractor.

Added Stats 1990 ch 1255 § 1 (SB 732). Amended Stats 1996 ch 526 § 2 (SB 1486).

§ 7189. Penalties for violation

Any person who engages in the practices of an asbestos consultant or a site surveillance technician, who is not certified pursuant to this article, or who violates Section 7187, is subject to one of the following penalties:

(a) Conviction of a first offense is an infraction punishable by a fine of not less than one thousand dollars ($1,000) or more than three thousand dollars ($3,000).

(b) Conviction of a subsequent offense is a misdemeanor requiring revocation or suspension of any asbestos consultant's or site surveillance technician's certification, and a fine not not less than three thousand dollars ($3,000) or more than five thousand dollars ($5,000), or imprisonment in the county jail not exceeding one year, or both the fine and imprisonment.

The division shall only impose these penalties after complying with all of the procedural requirements of Chapter 5 (commencing with Section 11500) of Division 3 of Part 1 of Title 2 of the Government Code.

Added Stats 1990 ch 1255 § 1 (SB 732).

§ 7189.5. Application of article

This article shall apply to asbestos abatement projects within the meaning of asbestos-related work as defined in Section 6501.8 of the Labor Code, and which involves 100 square feet or more of surface area of asbestos containing material.

Added Stats 1990 ch 1255 § 1 (SB 732).

§ 7189.7. Construction of article

(a) Nothing in this article shall be construed to require agencies of the state to contract with asbestos consultants or site surveillance technicians who are not employees of the state as long as employees of the state who are assigned to perform the activities described in Sections 7181 and 7182 have been certified by the division pursuant to the regulations required by subdivision (b) of Section 9021.5 of the Labor Code. Where feasible, the state shall assign a state civil service classification of associate industrial hygienist or senior industrial hygienist to carry out asbestos consultation activities as described in Section 7181 for state-owned and leased buildings. The individuals in the classification assigned shall be certified as required in this article before performing these activities.

(b) Nothing in this article shall be construed to require attorneys who provide legal advice on asbestos-related matters to building owners or operators to be certified by the division pursuant to the regulations required by subdivision (b) of Section 9021.5 of the Labor Code.

Added Stats 1990 ch 1255 § 1 (SB 732).

Article 12
Prohibitions

§ 7190. Use of name or position of public official in advertisement or promotional material; Disclaimer

(a) The name or position of a public official may not be used in an advertisement or any promotional material by a person licensed under this chapter, without the written authorization of the public official. A printed advertisement or promotional material that uses the name or position of a public official with that public official's written authorization, shall also include a disclaimer in at least 10-point roman boldface type, that shall be in a color or print which contrasts with the background so as to be easily legible, and set apart from any other printed matter. The disclaimer shall consist of a statement that reads "The name of (specify name of public official) does not imply that (specify name of public official) endorses this product or service in (his or her) official capacity and does not imply an endorsement by any governmental entity." If the advertisement is broadcast, this statement shall be read in a clearly audible tone of voice.

(b) For purposes of this section, "public official" means a member, officer, employee, or consultant of a local government agency, as defined in Section 82041 of the Government Code, or state agency, as defined in Section 82049 of the Government Code.

Added Stats 1994 ch 1135 § 5 (AB 3302).

—*See Civil Code Section 1770, Unfair Practices, in Appendix.*

§ 7191. Title of provision for arbitration of disputes in contract for work on specified residential property

(a) If a contract for work on residential property with four or fewer units contains a provision for arbitration of a dispute between the principals in the transaction, the provision shall be clearly titled "ARBITRATION OF DISPUTES."

If a provision for arbitration is included in a printed contract, it shall be set out in at least 10-point roman boldface type or in contrasting red print in at least 8-point roman boldface type, and if the provision is included in a typed contract, it shall be set out in capital letters.

(b) Immediately before the line or space provided for the parties to indicate their assent or nonassent to the arbitration provision described in subdivision (a), and immediately following that arbitration provision, the following shall appear:

"NOTICE: BY INITIALING IN THE SPACE BELOW YOU ARE AGREEING TO HAVE ANY DISPUTE ARISING OUT OF THE MATTERS INCLUDED IN THE 'ARBITRATION OF DISPUTES' PROVISION DECIDED BY NEUTRAL ARBITRATION AS PROVIDED BY CALIFORNIA LAW AND YOU ARE GIVING UP ANY RIGHTS YOU MIGHT POSSESS TO HAVE THE DISPUTE LITIGATED IN A COURT OR JURY TRIAL. BY INITIALING IN THE SPACE BELOW YOU ARE GIVING UP YOUR JUDICIAL RIGHTS TO DISCOVERY AND APPEAL, UNLESS THOSE RIGHTS ARE SPECIFICALLY INCLUDED IN THE 'ARBITRATION OF DISPUTES' PROVISION. IF YOU REFUSE TO SUBMIT TO ARBITRATION AFTER AGREEING TO THIS PROVISION, YOU MAY BE COMPELLED TO ARBITRATE UNDER THE AUTHORITY OF THE BUSINESS AND PROFESSIONS CODE OR OTHER APPLICABLE LAWS. YOUR AGREEMENT TO THIS ARBITRATION PROVISION IS VOLUNTARY." "WE HAVE READ AND UNDERSTAND THE FOREGOING AND AGREE TO SUBMIT DISPUTES ARISING OUT OF THE MATTERS INCLUDED IN THE 'ARBITRATION OF DISPUTES' PROVISION TO NEUTRAL ARBITRATION."

If the above provision is included in a printed contract, it shall be set out either in at least 10-point roman boldface type or in contrasting red print in at least 8-point roman boldface type, and if the provision is included in a typed contract, it shall be set out in capital letters.

(c) A provision for arbitration of a dispute between a principal in a contract for work on a residential property with four or fewer units that does not comply with this section may not be enforceable against any person other than the licensee.

(d) This section does not limit the board's authority to investigate complaints or to discipline a licensee for violations of this code.

Added Stats 1994 ch 1135 § 5 (AB 3302).

Chapter 9.3

Home Inspectors

§ 7195. Definitions

For purposes of this chapter, the following definitions apply:

(a) (1) "Home inspection" is a noninvasive, physical examination, performed for a fee in connection with a transfer, as defined in subdivision (e), of real property, of the mechanical, electrical, or plumbing systems or the structural and essential components of a residential dwelling of one to four units designed to identify material defects in those systems, structures, and components. "Home inspection" includes any consultation regarding the property that is represented to be a home inspection or any confusingly similar term.

(2) In connection with a transfer, as defined in subdivision (e), of real property with a swimming pool or spa, a "home inspection" shall include a noninvasive physical examination of the pool or spa and dwelling for the purpose of identifying which, if any, of the seven drowning prevention safety features listed in subdivision (a) of Section 115922 of the Health and Safety Code the pool or spa is equipped.

(3) "Home inspection," if requested by the client, may include an inspection of energy efficiency. Energy efficiency items to be inspected may include the following:

(A) A noninvasive inspection of insulation R-values in attics, roofs, walls, floors, and ducts.

(B) The number of window glass panes and frame types.

(C) The heating and cooling equipment and water heating systems.

(D) The age and fuel type of major appliances.

(E) The exhaust and cooling fans.

(F) The type of thermostat and other systems.

(G) The general integrity and potential leakage areas of walls, window areas, doors, and duct systems.

(H) The solar control efficiency of existing windows.

(b) A "material defect" is a condition that significantly affects the value, desirability, habitability, or safety of the dwelling. Style or aesthetics shall not be considered in determining whether a system, structure, or component is defective.

(c) A "home inspection report" is a written report prepared for a fee and issued after a home inspection. The report clearly describes and identifies the inspected systems, structures, or components of the dwelling, any material defects identified, and any recommendations regarding the conditions observed or recommendations for evaluation by appropriate persons. In a dwelling with a pool or spa, the "home inspection report" shall identify which, if any, of the seven drowning prevention safety features listed in subdivision (a) of Section 115922 of the Health and Safety Code the pool or spa is equipped with and shall specifically state if the pool or spa has fewer than two of the listed drowning prevention safety features.

(d) A "home inspector" is any individual who performs a home inspection.

(e) "Transfer" is a transfer by sale, exchange, installment land sales contract, as defined in Section 2985 of the Civil Code, lease with an option to purchase, any other option to purchase, or ground lease coupled with improvements, of real property or residential stock cooperative, improved with or consisting of not less than one nor more than four dwelling units.

Added Stats 1996 ch 338 § 2 (SB 258). Amended Stats 2001 ch 773 § 2 (AB 1574); Stats 2017 ch 670 § 3 (SB 442), effective January 1, 2018.

§ 7195.5. Home inspection report for dwelling unit with in-ground landscape irrigation system

(a) For purposes of improving landscape water use and irrigation efficiency, a home inspection report on a dwelling unit prepared pursuant to this chapter on a parcel containing an in-ground landscape irrigation system, the operation of which is under the exclusive control of the owner or occupant of the dwelling, may include an irrigation system inspection report, prepared by either a home inspector or certified landscape irrigation auditor, that contains all of the following:

(1) Examination of the irrigation system controller, if present, noting observable defects in installation or operation, or both.

(2) Activation of each zone or circuit providing irrigation water to turf grass, noting malfunctions observed in the operation of each of the following:

(A) The irrigation valve.

(B) Visible irrigation supply piping.

(C) Sprinkler heads and stems.

(3) During activation of the system pursuant to paragraph (2), observation of any of the following during the period of operation, in minutes, specified in the report:

(A) Irrigation spray being directed to hardscape.

(B) Irrigation water leaving the irrigated area as surface runoff.

(C) Ponding of irrigation water on the surface of the irrigated area.

(4) Notation whether inspection is limited due to snow, ice, or other site conditions that impede an inspection.

(b) Notwithstanding any other law, a sanction or penalty regarding prohibited hours, days, or effects of operation of a landscape irrigation system shall not be levied upon either the home inspector, the landscape irrigation auditor, the occupant, or the owner of a property by any state or local agency or water purveyor as a consequence of the

Section VI

operation of a landscape irrigation system for the purpose of an irrigation system inspection carried out under this section.

(c) A home inspector is encouraged to provide information or access to information regarding water-efficient landscape irrigation systems within the home inspection report.

(d) To the extent funds are available, the Department of Water Resources, in consultation with the California Real Estate Inspection Association and the Department of Housing and Community Development, shall compile an estimate of the number of properties for which an irrigation system inspection report has been prepared each year, beginning with 2018, for inclusion in an update to the California Water Plan.

Added Stats 2018 ch 867 § 3 (AB 2371), effective January 1, 2019.

§ 7195.7. Opinion of valuation on property

A home inspector shall not give an opinion of valuation on a property.

Added Stats 2019 ch 267 § 1 (AB 1018), effective January 1, 2020.

§ 7196. Duties

It is the duty of a home inspector who is not licensed as a general contractor, structural pest control operator, or architect, or registered as a professional engineer to conduct a home inspection with the degree of care that a reasonably prudent home inspector would exercise.

Added Stats 1996 ch 338 § 2 (SB 258).

§ 7196.1. Application

(a) Nothing in this chapter shall be construed to allow home inspectors who are not registered engineers to perform any analysis of the systems, components, or structural integrity of a dwelling that would constitute the practice of civil, electrical, or mechanical engineering, or to exempt a home inspector from Chapter 3 (commencing with Section 5500), Chapter 7 (commencing with Section 6700), Chapter 9 (commencing with Section 7000), Chapter 14 (commencing with Section 8500) of Division 3, or Part 3 (commencing with Section 11300) of Division 4.

(b) This chapter does not apply to a registered engineer, licensed land surveyor, or licensed architect acting pursuant to their professional registration or license, nor does it affect the obligations of a real estate licensee or transferor under Article 1.5 (commencing with Section 1102) of Chapter 2 of Title 4 of Part 3 of Division 2 of, or Article 2 (commencing with Section 2079) of Chapter 3 of Title 6 of Part 4 of Division 3 of, the Civil Code.

(c) Except as required to comply with standards set forth in law or regulation, a real estate appraiser licensed under Part 3 (commencing with Section 11300) of Division 4, performing a real estate appraisal, shall not engage in the activity of a home inspector performing a home inspection.

Added Stats 1996 ch 338 § 2 (SB 258). Amended Stats 2019 ch 267 § 2 (AB 1018), effective January 1, 2020.

§ 7196.2. Yellow corrugated stainless steel; Home inspection report

(a) If a home inspector observes any shade of yellow corrugated stainless steel tubing during a home inspection, the home inspector shall include that observation, and the following notification, in the home inspection report:

"Manufacturers of yellow corrugated stainless steel tubing believe that yellow corrugated stainless steel tubing is safer if properly bonded and grounded as required by the manufacturer's installation instructions. Proper bonding and grounding of this product can only be determined by a licensed electrical contractor."

(b) For purposes of this section, "corrugated stainless steel tubing" means a flexible, stainless steel pipe used to supply natural gas and propane in residential, commercial, and industrial structures.

(c) The degree of care specified in Section 7196 shall be used in determining whether a home inspector has complied with the requirements of subdivision (a).

Added Stats 2018 ch 225 § 2 (SB 988), effective January 1, 2019.

§ 7197. Unfair practices

(a) It is an unfair business practice for a home inspector, a company that employs the inspector, or a company that is controlled by a company that also has a financial interest in a company employing a home inspector, to do any of the following:

(1) To perform or offer to perform, for an additional fee, any repairs to a structure on which the inspector, or the inspector's company, has prepared a home inspection report in the past 12 months.

(2) Inspect for a fee any property in which the inspector, or the inspector's company, has any financial interest or any interest in the transfer of the property.

(3) To offer or deliver any compensation, inducement, or reward to the owner of the inspected property, the broker, or agent, for the referral of any business to the inspector or the inspection company.

(4) Accept an engagement to make an inspection or to prepare a report in which the employment itself or the fee payable for the inspec-

Section VI

tion is contingent upon the conclusions in the report, preestablished findings, or the close of escrow.

(b) A home protection company that is affiliated with or that retains the home inspector does not violate this section if it performs repairs pursuant to claims made under the home protection contract.

(c) This section shall not affect the ability of a structural pest control operator to perform repairs pursuant to Section 8505 as a result of a structural pest control inspection.

(d) Paragraph (1) of subdivision (a) shall not affect the ability of a roofing contractor who holds a C-39 license, as defined in Section 832.39 of Title 16 of the California Code of Regulations, to perform repairs pursuant to the contractor's inspection of a roof for the specific purpose of providing a roof certification if all of the following conditions are met:

(1) Different employees perform the home inspection and the roof inspection.

(2) The roof inspection is ordered prior to, or at the same time as, the home inspection, or the roof inspection is completed before the commencement of the home inspection.

(3) The consumer is provided a consumer disclosure before the consumer authorizes the home inspection that includes all of the following:

(A) The same company that performs the roof inspection and roof repairs will perform the home inspection on the same property.

(B) Any repairs that are authorized by the consumer are for the repairs identified in the roofing contractor's roof inspection report and no repairs identified in the home inspection are authorized or allowed as specified in the roof inspection.

(C) The consumer has the right to seek a second opinion.

(4) For purposes of this subdivision, "roof certification" means a written statement by a licensed C-39 Roofing Contractor who has performed a roof inspection, made any necessary repairs, and warrants that the roof is free of leaks at the time that the certification is issued and should perform as designed for the specified term of the certification.

(e) Paragraph (1) of subdivision (a) shall not affect the ability of a plumbing contractor who holds a C-36 license, as defined in Section 832.36 of Title 16 of the California Code of Regulations, to perform repairs pursuant to the inspection of a sewer lateral pipe connecting a residence or business to a sewer system if the consumer is provided a consumer disclosure before the consumer authorizes the home inspection that includes all of the following notifications:

(1) The same company that performs the sewer lateral inspection and the sewer lateral repairs will perform the home inspection on the same property.

(2) Any repairs that are authorized by the consumer are for the repairs identified in the sewer lateral inspection report and no repairs identified in the home inspection report are authorized or allowed except as specified in the sewer lateral inspection report.

(3) The consumer has the right to seek a second opinion on the sewer lateral inspection.

Added Stats 1996 ch 338 § 2 (SB 258). Amended Stats 2004 ch 443 § 1 (AB 1725); Stats 2017 ch 508 § 1 (AB 1357), effective January 1, 2018; Stats 2021 ch 545 § 1 (SB 484), effective January 1, 2022.

§ 7198. Public policy

Contractual provisions that purport to waive the duty owed pursuant to Section 7196, or limit the liability of the home inspector to the cost of the home inspection report, are contrary to public policy and invalid.

Added Stats 1996 ch 338 § 2 (SB 258).

§ 7199. Statute of limitation

The time for commencement of a legal action for breach of duty arising from a home inspection report shall not exceed four years from the date of the inspection.

Added Stats 1996 ch 338 § 2 (SB 258).

Chapter 9.4

Home Energy Rating System (HERS) Home Inspections

§ 7199.5. HERS California home energy audit

(a) All home inspections, including those defined in paragraph (1) of subdivision (a) of Section 7195, may, if requested by the client, be accompanied by a Home Energy Rating System (HERS) California home energy audit pursuant to regulations adopted by the Energy Commission in compliance with Section 25942 of the Public Resources Code.

(b) If the client requests a HERS California home energy audit, the HERS California home inspection report accompanying any home inspection report defined in subdivision (c) of Section 7195 shall comply with the standards and requirements established by the Energy Commission for HERS California home energy audits as specified in Article 8 (commencing with Section 1670) of Chapter 4 of Division 2 of

Title 20 of the California Code of Regulations, implementing the California Home Energy Rating System Program.

Added Stats 2010 ch 453 § 1 (AB 1809), effective January 1, 2011.

§ 7199.7. Legislative intent

It is the intent of the Legislature that a Home Energy Rating System (HERS) California home energy audit may, at the request of the client, be performed by a home inspector who meets the requirements of Article 8 (commencing with Section 1670) of Chapter 4 of Division 2 of Title 20 of the California Code of Regulations.

Added Stats 2010 ch 453 § 1 (AB 1809), effective January 1, 2011.

Chapter 13.

Contractors State License Board
Rules and Regulations

Rules and regulations serve to interpret or make laws specific. The laws provide the authority for rules and regulations. Laws take precedence and are in effect, even if the affected rules and regulations have not been corrected to reflect any changes in the law.

If you have questions concerning a particular regulation, refer to the sections of the Business and Professions Code cited in the note after the particular regulation.

What follows is the statute text, history notes for current rules and regulations, and history notes for repealed rules and regulations. You can follow the progress of proposed regulatory actions on CSLB's website at *http://www.cslb.ca.gov/About_Us/Library/Laws/*.

LIST OF CURRENT BOARD RULES AND REGULATIONS

Section VI

CALIFORNIA CODE OF REGULATIONS

TITLE 16. DIVISION 8. CONTRACTORS STATE LICENSE BOARD

ARTICLE 1. DEFINITIONS

810. Definitions.

For the purposes of this chapter, "Board" means the Contractors State License Board and "Code," unless otherwise defined, means the Business and Professions Code.

(Authority cited: Section 7008, Business and Professions Code. Reference: Section 7008, Business and Professions Code.)

ARTICLE 1.5. REVENUE

811. Fees.

(a) The fee for:

(1) An application for an original license in a single classification is $300.

(2) An application for each additional classification is $75.

(3) An application to replace a responsible managing officer or employee is $75.

(4) Rescheduling an examination is $60.

(5) Scheduling or rescheduling an examination pursuant to Business and Professions Code Section 7137(c) is $60.

(6) Initial license of an active or inactive license is $180.

(7) Renewal of an active license is $450.

(8) Renewal of an inactive license is $225.

(9) Reactivation of an inactive license is the full amount of the renewal fee for an active license.

(10) An application for a home improvement salesperson registration is $75.

(11) Renewal of a home improvement salesperson registration is $95.

(12) An application for an asbestos certification examination is $75.

(13) An application for a hazardous substance removal or remedial action certification examination is $75.

(Authority cited: Section 7008, Business and Professions Code. Reference: Sections 7076.5 and 7137, Business and Professions Code.)

812. Dishonored Check Service Charge

The dishonored check service charge authorized by Section 6157 of the Government Code is $10.00 for each check.

(Authority cited: Section 7008, Business and Professions Code. Reference: Section 7008, Business and Professions Code; and Section 6157, Government Code.)

813. Abandonment of Application

(a) An application, other than a renewal application, shall be deemed abandoned whenever an applicant fails to return an application rejected for insufficiency or incompleteness within 90 days from date of original notice of rejection. This 90-day period may be extended by the Registrar for good cause.

(b) Any application so abandoned may not be reinstated; however, the applicant may file a new application accompanied by the required fee.

(Authority cited: Section 7008, Business and Professions Code. Reference: Section 7067, Business and Professions Code.)

ARTICLE 2. APPLICATION FOR LICENSE

816. Application Form for Original License

(a) The license application form prescribed by the Registrar shall seek from each member of the personnel of the applicant the following information:

(1) A record of the previous experience in the field of construction of the member of applicant's personnel who will qualify for the classification requested.

(2) Whether the applicant or a member of applicant's personnel or whether to his or her knowledge anyone with whom he/she has been associated in the contracting field has ever been licensed or had a professional or vocational license refused or revoked.

(b) The application shall be signed, under penalty of perjury, by each member of the personnel of the applicant.

(c) Nothing in this Rule shall be interpreted to limit the Registrar's authority to require an applicant to provide any other information necessary to determine the applicant's qualifications, or to exempt the applicant therefrom, or to enforce the provisions of the

Contractors License Law, except as otherwise required by law. The Registrar may exempt applicants who are eligible for waiver of examination, pursuant to Section 7065.1 of the Code, or who are not required to take the examination, pursuant to Section 7065 of the Code, from the requirement to submit information described in subsection (a)(1).

(Authority cited: Section 7008, Business and Professions Code. Reference: Sections 7066, 7067.6 and 7070, Business and Professions Code.)

819. Requirement of Corporations

A foreign or domestic corporation, applying for a license, shall complete a certification as prescribed by the Registrar, showing that it has fulfilled the filing requirements of the California Secretary of State as set out in Sections 200 and 2105 of the Corporations Code.

(Authority cited: Section 7008, Business and Professions Code. Reference: Section 7067, Business and Professions Code.)

824. Application Investigation Required

In addition to a review and verification of all applications for licensure, the Registrar shall conduct a comprehensive field investigation of a minimum of 3% of all such applications. Such investigation shall include those areas of experience claimed and such other areas as the Registrar deems appropriate for the protection of the public.

All claimed experience shall be supportable by documentation satisfactory to the Board. The Registrar shall provide to the Board, for its approval, acceptable forms of such documentation and shall inform the applicant in the application form that such documentation may be requested by the Board.

(Authority cited: Section 7008, Business and Professions Code. Reference: Section 7068, Business and Professions Code.)

825. Experience Requirement of Applicant

(a) Every applicant for a contractor's license must have had, within the last 10 years immediately preceding the filing of the application, not less than four years experience as a journeyman, foreman, supervising employee or contractor in the particular class within which the applicant intends to engage as a contractor. For purposes of this section, "journeyman" means an experienced worker in the trade who is fully qualified, as opposed to a trainee, and is able to perform the trade without supervision; or one who has completed an apprenticeship program.

(b) An applicant who was formerly a qualifier on a license in the same classification applied for may compute experience without regard to the ten-year limitation.

(c) An applicant shall not be jeopardized in computing time for service in the armed forces of the United States during a National Emergency and the length of service may be added to the 10 years mentioned above.

(d) Acceptable training in an accredited school or completion of an approved apprenticeship program in accordance with the California Labor Code (commencing with Section 3070 of the Labor Code, Chapter 4, of Division 3) or its equivalent, as approved by the Registrar, in the construction trade for which application is made will be counted as experience. In no case, however, will such training or completion of an approved apprenticeship program count for more than 3 years of the experience.

(e) The required experience shall be possessed by one member of the applicant entity or by a responsible managing employee therefore, and the member or responsible managing employee shall be required to take the examination.

(Authority cited: Section 7008, Business and Professions Code. Reference: Section 7068, Business and Professions Code.)

825.5. General Manufactured Housing Contractor Initial Installer Training Requirement

(a) Effective September 30, 2021, in addition to the experience requirements in California Code of Regulations, title 16, section 825 and other requirements for licensure in the Business and Professions Code, an applicant for a C–47 – general manufactured housing contractor license shall complete the initial installer training that is compliant with the training curriculum contained in section 3286.308(a) of the Code of Federal Regulations, title 24, subtitle B, chapter XX, subpart D.

(b) Applicants shall submit proof of compliance with subdivision (a) to the Board with their application for licensure. Proof of compliance shall be shown by the Certificate of Completion of Training identified in section 3286.303(c) of the Code of Federal Regulations, title 24, subtitle B, chapter XX, subpart D. An application submitted without the certificate prescribed by this subdivision is not complete within the meaning of section 7072 of the Business and Professions Code.

(c) The initial installer training shall be obtained through one or more qualified trainers, as confirmed by the United States Department of Housing and Urban Development under part 3286 of the Code of

Federal Regulations, title 24, subtitle B, chapter XX, subpart D, commencing with section 3286.301

(Authority cited: Sections 7008 and 7059, Business and Professions Code. Reference: Sections 7026.11, 7058, 7059, 7065 and 7068, Business and Professions Code; and part 3286 of the Code of Federal Regulations, title 24, subtitle B, chapter XX, subpart D, section 3286.301 et seq.)

826. Registrar to Pass on Experience

The Registrar may determine that an applicant who does not have the specific experience required in Section 825 has some comparable knowledge, training, and/or experience which is equivalent to the required experience.

827. Review of Application for Original License, Additional Classification, or Replacement of Qualifying Person

(a) Application Requiring Examination:

(1) The Board shall inform an applicant in writing within 60 days of receipt whether the application is complete and has been referred for examination or is deficient and what specific information is required. An application is "complete" when an acceptable application and fee have been filed by the applicant.

(2) When an application is returned which was previously rejected for deficiencies, the Board shall decide within 5 days of receipt whether the application is complete and accepted for filing.

(3) The Board shall decide within 115 days after a complete application has been referred for examination whether an applicant meets the requirements for licensure, provided that the examination has been successfully completed and the applicant has filed the bond(s), fee and other documents required by Division 3 of the Business and Professions Code.

(4) If an applicant has not successfully completed the examination as scheduled in subsection (3), or met the other requirements of that subsection (subject to the limitations of Business and Professions Code Section 7074), the Board shall decide within 45 days of the successful completion of a subsequently scheduled examination and the filing of acceptable bond(s), fee and other documents required by Division 3 of the Business and Professions Code, whether the applicant meets the requirements for licensure.

(5) The periods specified in subsection (3) and (4) shall be extended by a period of 60 days, if the application must be investigated.

(6) The minimum, median and maximum times for an application requiring examination for licensure as a contractor, for an additional classification, or for replacement of the qualifying person from the time of receipt of the application until the Board decided to issue the license, grant the additional classification or the replacement of the qualifying person, based on the Board's past two years performance, were:

(A) Application for Original License, with Examination:

Minimum......... 11 days

Median........... 253 days

Maximum ...... 726 days

(B) Application for Additional Classification, with Examination:

Minimum......... 20 days

Median............. 96 days

Maximum ...... 617 days

(C) Application for Replacement of the Qualifying Person, with Examination:

Minimum......... 20 days

Median............. 78 days

Maximum ...... 428 days

These periods include not only the Board's processing time, but also the time for which the applicant is responsible: e.g., the return of a rejected application, failure of and/or failure to appear at examinations, filing of the required bond(s) and fee.

(b) Applications Not Requiring Examination:

(1) The Board shall inform an applicant for licensure, without examination, as a contractor, for an additional classification, or for replacement of the qualifying person pursuant to Sections 7065 or 7065.1 of the Business and Professions Code within 50 days of receipt whether the application is complete and what the issuance or granting requirements are or that the application is deficient and what specific information is required.

(2) When an application is returned which was previously rejected for deficiencies, the Board shall decide within 5 days of receipt if the application is now complete and accepted for filing.

(3) Once the applicant has filed acceptable bond(s) and other documents required by Division 3 of the Business and Professions Code, the Board shall decide within 15 days whether the applicant meets the requirements for licensure.

(4) The period outlined in subsection (1) may be extended by 60 days if the application must be investigated.

(5) The minimum, median and maximum times for an application for licensure, without examination, as a contractor, for an additional classification, or for replacement of the qualifying person from the time of receipt of the application until the Board decided to issue the license, grant the additional classification or the replacement of the qualifying person, based on the Board's past two years performance were:

(A) Application for Original License, without Examination:

Minimum.............. 1 day

Median............. 48 days

Maximum ...... 349 days

(B) Application for Additional Classification, without Examination:

Minimum......... 24 days

Median.......... 58.5 days

Maximum ...... 358 days

(C) Application for Replacement of the Qualifying Person, without Examination:

Minimum.............. 1 day

Median............. 29 days

Maximum ...... 253 days

These periods include not only the Board's processing time, but also the time for which the applicant is responsible: e.g., return of a rejected application and filing of the required bond(s) and fee.

(Authority cited: Section 7008, Business and Professions Code; and Section 15376, Government Code. Reference: Section 15376, Government Code; and Sections 7065, 7065.1 and 7074, Business and Professions Code.)

828. Review of Application for Home Improvement Salesman Registration

(a) The Board shall inform, in writing, an applicant for registration as home improvement salesman within 30 days of receipt whether the application is deficient and what specific information is required or whether the registration has been issued.

(b) When an application is returned which was previously rejected for deficiencies, the Board shall decide whether the applicant meets the requirements for registration within 5 days after return of the completed application. A "completed application" means that an acceptable application form together with all required information, documentation and fee has been filed by the applicant.

(c) The time periods outlined in (a) and (b) may be extended by 5 weeks if the fee is in the form of a personal or company check, or by 60 days if an application requires investigation to determine if a statement of issues must be filed.

(d) The minimum, median and maximum processing times for an application for registration as a home improvement salesman from the time of receipt of the initial application until the Board makes a final decision on the application, based on the Board's past two years performance, are:

Minimum:............1 day

Median:..............8 days

Maximum:........53 days

(Authority cited: Section 7008, Business and Professions Code. Reference: Section 15376, Government Code; and Section 7153.1, Business and Professions Code.)

ARTICLE 3. CLASSIFICATION

830. Classification Policy

(a) All contractors to whom licenses are issued shall be classified by the Registrar as a specialty contractor, as defined in this article; a general engineering contractor (Class A), as defined in Section 7056 of the Code; or a general building contractor (Class B), as defined in Section 7057 of the Code.

(b) Contractors licensed in one classification shall be prohibited from contracting in the field of any other classification unless they are also licensed in that classification or are permitted to do so by Section 831.

(Authority cited: Section 7008, Business and Professions Code. Reference: Section 7059, Business and Professions Code.)

831. Incidental and Supplemental Defined

For purposes of Section 7059, work in other classifications is "incidental and supplemental" to the work for which a specialty contractor is licensed if that work is essential to accomplish the work in which the contractor is classified. A specialty contractor may use subcontractors to complete the incidental and supplemental work, or he may use his own employees to do so.

(Authority cited: Sections 7008 and 7059, Business and Professions Code. Reference: Section 7059, Business and Professions Code.)

832. Specialty Contractors Classified

Specialty contractors shall perform their trade using the art, experience, science and skill necessary to satisfactorily organize, administer, construct and complete projects under their classification, in accordance with the standards of their trade.

They are classified into the following subclassifications:

Asbestos Abatement	C-22
Boiler, Hot Water Heating and Steam Fitting	C-4
Building Moving/Demolition	C-21
Cabinet, Mill Work and Finish Carpentry	C-6
Concrete	C-8
Construction Zone Traffic Control	C-31
Drywall	C-9
Earthwork and Paving	C-12
Electrical	C-10
Elevator	C-11
Fencing	C-13
Fire Protection	C-16
Flooring and Floor Covering	C-15
Framing and Rough Carpentry	C-5
General Manufactured Housing	C-47
Glazing	C-17

Section VI

Welding C-60

Well Drilling (Water) C-57

(Authority cited: Sections 7008 and 7059, Business and Professions Code. Reference: Sections 7058 and 7059, Business and Professions Code.)

832.02. Class C-2—Insulation and Acoustical Contractor

An insulation and acoustical contractor installs any insulating media and preformed architectural acoustical materials for the purpose of temperature and/or sound control.

(Authority cited: Sections 7008 and 7059, Business and Professions Code. Reference: Sections 7058 and 7059, Business and Professions Code.)

832.04. Class C-4—Boiler, Hot-Water Heating and Steam Fitting Contractor

A boiler, hot-water heating and steam fitting contractor installs, services and repairs power boiler installations, hot-water heating systems and steam fitting, including fire-tube and water-tube steel power boilers and hot-water heating low pressure boilers, steam fitting and piping, fittings, valves, gauges, pumps, radiators, convectors, fuel oil tanks, fuel oil lines, chimneys, flues, heat insulation and all other equipment, including solar heating equipment, associated with these systems.

(Authority cited: Sections 7008 and 7059, Business and Professions Code. Reference: Sections 7058 and 7059, Business and Professions Code.)

832.05. Class C-5—Framing and Rough Carpentry Contractor

A framing and rough carpentry contractor performs any form work, framing or rough carpentry necessary to construct framed structures; installs or repairs individual components of framing systems and performs any rough carpentry or associated work, including but not limited to the construction or installation of: sub-flooring, siding, exterior staircases and railings, overhead doors, roof decking, truss members, and sheathing.

(Authority cited: Sections 7008 and 7059, Business and Professions Code. Reference: Sections 7058 and 7059, Business and Professions Code.)

832.06. Class C-6—Cabinet, Millwork and Finish Carpentry Contractor

A cabinet, millwork and finish carpentry contractor makes cabinets, cases, sashes, doors, trims, nonbearing partitions and other items of "finish carpentry" by cutting, surfacing, joining, gluing and fabricating wood or other products to provide a functional surface.

This contractor also places, erects, and finishes such cabinets and millwork in structures.

(Authority cited: Sections 7008 and 7059, Business and Professions Code. Reference: Sections 7058 and 7059, Business and Professions Code.)

832.07. Class C-7—Low Voltage Systems Contractor

A communication and low voltage contractor installs, services and maintains all types of communication and low voltage systems which are energy limited and do not exceed 91 volts. These systems include, but are not limited to telephone systems, sound systems, cable television systems, closed-circuit video systems, satellite dish antennas, instrumentation and temperature controls, and low voltage landscape lighting. Low voltage fire alarm systems are specifically not included in this section.

(Authority cited: Sections 7008 and 7059, Business and Professions Code. Reference: Sections 7058 and 7059, Business and Professions Code.)

832.08. Class C-8—Concrete Contractor

A concrete contractor forms, pours, places, finishes and installs specified mass, pavement, flat and other concrete work; and places and sets screeds for pavements or flatwork. This class shall not include contractors whose sole contracting business is the application of plaster coatings or the placing and erecting of steel or bars for the reinforcing of mass, pavement, flat and other concrete work.

(Authority cited: Sections 7008 and 7059, Business and Professions Code. Reference: Sections 7058 and 7059, Business and Professions Code.)

832.09. Class C-9—Drywall Contractor

A drywall contractor lays out and installs gypsum wall board and gypsum wallboard assemblies including nonstructural metal framing members, and performs the taping and texturing operations including the applications of compounds that adhere to wall board to produce a continuous smooth or textured surface.

(Authority cited: Sections 7008 and 7059, Business and Professions Code. Reference: Sections 7058 and 7059, Business and Professions Code.)

832.10. Class C-10—Electrical Contractor

An electrical contractor places, installs, erects or connects any electrical wires, fixtures, appliances, apparatus, raceways, conduits, solar photovoltaic cells or any part thereof, which generate, transmit, transform or utilize electrical energy in any form or for any purpose.

(Authority cited: Sections 7008 and 7059, Business and Professions Code. Reference: Sections 7058 and 7059, Business and Professions Code.)

832.11. Class C-11—Elevator Contractor

An elevator contractor fabricates, erects, installs and repairs elevators, including sheave beams, motors, sheaves, cable and wire rope, guides, cab, counterweights, doors (including sidewalk elevator doors), automatic and manual controls, signal systems, and all other devices and equipment associated with the safe and efficient installation and operation of electrical, hydraulic and manually operated elevators.

(Authority cited: Sections 7008 and 7059, Business and Professions Code. Reference: Sections 7058 and 7059, Business and Professions Code.)

832.12. Class C-12—Earthwork and Paving Contractors

An earthwork and paving contractor digs, moves, and places material forming the surface of the earth, other than water, in such a manner that a cut, fill, excavation, grade, trench, backfill, or tunnel (if incidental thereto) can be executed, including the use of explosives for these purposes. This classification includes the mixing, fabricating and placing of paving and any other surfacing materials.

(Authority cited: Sections 7008 and 7059, Business and Professions Code. Reference: Sections 7058 and 7059, Business and Professions Code.)

832.13. Class C-13—Fencing Contractor

A fencing contractor constructs, erects, alters, or repairs all types of fences, corrals, runs, railings, cribs, game court enclosures, guard rails and barriers, playground game equipment, backstops, posts, flagpoles, and gates, excluding masonry walls.

(Authority cited: Sections 7008 and 7059, Business and Professions Code. Reference: Sections 7058 and 7059, Business and Professions Code.)

832.15. Class C-15—Flooring and Floor Covering Contractors

A flooring and floor covering contractor prepares any surface for the installation of flooring and floor coverings, and installs carpet, resilient sheet goods, resilient tile, wood floors and flooring (including the finishing and repairing thereof), and any other materials established as flooring and floor covering material, except ceramic tile.

(Authority cited: Sections 7008 and 7059, Business and Professions Code. Reference: Sections 7058 and 7059, Business and Professions Code.)

832.16. Class C-16—Fire Protection Contractor

A fire protection contractor lays out, fabricates and installs all types of fire protection systems; including all the equipment associated with these systems, excluding electrical alarm systems.

(Authority cited: Section 7008 and 7059 of the Business and Professions Code. Reference: Sections 7058 and 7059, Business and Professions Code.)

832.17. Class C-17—Glazing Contractor

A glazing contractor selects, cuts, assembles and/or installs all makes and kinds of glass, glass work, mirrored glass, and glass substitute materials for glazing; executes the fabrication and glazing of frames, panels, sashes and doors; and/or installs these items in any structure.

(Authority cited: Sections 7008 and 7059, Business and Professions Code. Reference: Sections 7058 and 7059, Business and Professions Code.)

832.20. Class C-20—Warm-Air Heating, Ventilating and Air-Conditioning Contractor

A warm-air heating, ventilating and air-conditioning contractor fabricates, installs, maintains, services and repairs warm-air heating systems and water heating heat pumps, complete with warm-air appliances; ventilating systems complete with blowers and plenum chambers; air-conditioning systems complete with air-conditioning unit; and the ducts, registers, flues, humidity and thermostatic controls and air filters in connection with any of these systems. This classification shall include warm-air heating, ventilating and air-conditioning systems which utilize solar energy.

(Authority cited: Sections 7008 and 7059, Business and Professions Code. Reference: Sections 7026.1, 7058 and 7059, Business and Professions Code.)

832.21. Class C-21—Building Moving/Demolition Contractor

A building moving/demolition contractor raises, lowers, cribs, underpins, demolishes and moves or removes structures, including their foundations. This classification does not include the alterations, additions, repairs or rehabilitation of the permanently retained portions of such structures.

(Authority cited: Sections 7008 and 7059, Business and Professions Code. Reference: Sections 7058 and 7059, Business and Professions Code.)

832.22. Class C–22—Asbestos Abatement Contractor

(a) An asbestos abatement contractor performs abatement, including containment, encapsulation, or removal, and disposal of asbestos containing construction materials, as defined in Section 6501.8 of the Labor Code, in and on buildings and structures. All work performed and all documentation prepared by an asbestos abatement contractor shall be done in accordance with regulations and requirements of the Division of Occupational Safety and Health (DOSH) of the Department of Industrial Relations.

(b) The Board shall not issue an asbestos abatement contractor license unless the applicant or contractor is duly registered with DOSH pursuant to Section 6501.5 of the Labor Code or has an active

Section VI

application for registration in process with DOSH. All holders of the C-22—asbestos abatement contractor classification shall have completed DOSH registration training requirements, as contained in Title 8, California Code of Regulations, Section 1529.

(c) Within 90 days after the asbestos abatement contractor license is issued, the contractor shall submit to the Board proof that he or she is duly registered with DOSH pursuant to Section 6501.5 of the Labor Code.

No asbestos abatement work shall be performed nor documentation prepared until the contractor has submitted proof of his or her DOSH registration to the Board.

Failure of a licensee to provide proof of current registration with DOSH within 90 days after issuance shall result in the automatic suspension of the license or removal of the C-22—asbestos abatement contractor classification at the end of the 90 days.

(d) Every applicant for the C-22—asbestos abatement contractor classification must have had, within the last 10 years immediately preceding the filing of the application, not less than four years of experience performing asbestos abatement duties as a journeyman, foreman, supervising employee, or contractor working for or as any of the following:

(1) A licensed contractor who holds the C-22—asbestos abatement contractor classification or the asbestos certification, as defined in Section 7058.5 of the Code, and DOSH registration;

(2) A contractor who provides asbestos abatement services and is licensed in another state or federal jurisdiction;

(3) A utility company operating under the laws of a state or federal regulatory agency;

(4) A division of a state or the federal government; or

(5) The armed forces of the United States.

(e) The Board shall require as a condition precedent to the renewal of an asbestos abatement contractor license that the licensee have on file proof of current registration with DOSH pursuant to Section 6501.5 of the Labor Code.

(f) This classification does not include any addition to or alteration, repair, or rehabilitation of the permanently retained portions of such buildings and structures. Hazardous substance removal and remediation, as defined in Section 7058.7 of the Code, are specifically not included in this classification.

(Authority cited: Sections 7008 and 7059, Business and Professions Code. Reference: Sections 7058, 7058.5, 7058.7 and 7059, Business and Professions Code; and Sections 6501.5 and 6501.8, Labor Code.)

832.23. Class C-23—Ornamental Metal Contractor

An ornamental metals contractor assembles, casts, cuts, shapes, stamps, forges, welds, fabricates and installs, sheet, rolled and cast, brass, bronze, copper, cast iron, wrought iron, monel metal, stainless steel, steel, and/or any other metal for the architectural treatment and ornamental decoration of structures. This classification does not include the work of a sheet metal contractor.

(Authority cited: Sections 7008 and 7059, Business and Professions Code. Reference: Sections 7058 and 7059, Business and Professions Code.)

832.27. Class C-27—Landscaping Contractor

A landscape contractor constructs, maintains, repairs, installs, or subcontracts the development of landscape systems and facilities for public and private gardens and other areas which are designed to aesthetically, architecturally, horticulturally, or functionally improve the grounds within or surrounding a structure or a tract or plot of land. In connection therewith, a landscape contractor prepares and grades plots and areas of land for the installation of any architectural, horticultural and decorative treatment or arrangement.

(Authority cited: Sections 7008 and 7059, Business and Professions Code. Reference: Sections 7058 and 7059, Business and Professions Code.)

832.28. Class C-28—Lock and Security Equipment Contractor

A lock and security equipment contractor evaluates, sets up, installs, maintains and repairs all doors and door assemblies, gates, locks and locking devices, panic and fire rated exit devices, manual and automatic operated gate and door closures and releases, jail and prison locking devices and permanently installed or built in safes and vaults. This classification includes but is not limited to master key systems, metal window guards, security doors, card activated and electronic access control systems for control equipment, motion and other types of detectors and computer systems for control and audit of control systems and other associated equipment. Fire alarm systems are specifically not included in this section.

(Authority Cited: Sections 7008 and 7059, Business and Professions Code. Reference: Sections 7058 and 7059, Business and Professions Code.)

832.29. Class C-29—Masonry Contractor

A masonry contractor installs concrete units and baked clay products; concrete, glass and clay block; natural and manufactured stone; terra cotta; and fire brick or other material for refractory work. This classification includes the fabrication and installation of masonry component units for structural load bearing and non-load bearing walls for structures and fences installed with or without mortar; ceramic veneer (not tile) and thin brick that resembles full brick for facing; paving; and clear waterproofing, cleaning and caulking incidental to masonry construction.

(Authority cited: Sections 7008 and 7059, Business and Professions Code. Reference: Sections 7058 and 7059, Business and Professions Code.)

832.31. Class C-31—Construction Zone Traffic Control Contractor

A construction zone traffic control contractor prepares or removes lane closures, flagging or traffic diversions, utilizing portable devices, such as cones, delineators, barricades, sign stands, flashing beacons, flashing arrow trailers, and changeable message signs, on roadways, including, but not limited to, public streets, highways, or any public conveyance.

(Authority cited: Sections 7008 and 7059, Business and Professions Code. Reference: Sections 7058 and 7059, Business and Professions Code.)

832.32. Class C-32—Parking and Highway Improvement Contractor

A parking and highway improvement contractor applies and installs protective coatings, vehicle stops, guard rails and mechanical devices, directional lines, buttons, markers, signs and arrows on the horizontal surface of any game court, parking facility, airport, highway or roadway constructed of concrete, asphalt or similar material. This classification includes the surface preparatory work necessary for the application of protective coatings but does not include the re-paving of these surfaces.

(Authority cited: Sections 7008 and 7059, Business and Professions Code. Reference: Sections 7058 and 7059, Business and Professions Code.)

832.33. Class C-33—Painting and Decorating Contractors

A painting and decorating contractor prepares by scraping, sandblasting or other means and applies any of the following: paints, papers, textures, fabrics, pigments, oils, turpentines, japans, driers, thinners, varnishes, shellacs, stains, fillers, waxes, adhesives, water and any other vehicles, mediums and materials which adhere by evaporation and may be mixed, used and applied to the surfaces of structures and the appurtenances thereto for purposes of decorating, protecting, fireproofing and waterproofing.

(Authority cited: Sections 7008 and 7059, Business and Professions Code. Reference: Sections 7058 and 7059, Business and Professions Code.)

832.34. Class C-34—Pipeline Contractor

A pipeline contractor fabricates and installs pipelines for the conveyance of fluids, such as water, gas, or petroleum, or for the containment or protection of any other material, including the application of protective coatings or systems and the trenching, boring, shoring, backfilling, compacting, paving and surfacing necessary to complete the installation of such pipelines.

(Authority cited: Sections 7008 and 7059, Business and Professions Code. Reference: Sections 7058 and 7059, Business and Professions Code.)

832.35. Class C-35—Lathing and Plastering Contractor

(a) A lathing and plastering contractor coats surfaces with a mixture of sand, gypsum plaster, quick-lime or hydrated lime and water, or sand and cement and water, or a combination of such other materials that create a permanent surface coating, including coatings for the purpose of soundproofing and fireproofing. These coatings are applied with a plasterer's trowel or sprayed over any surface which offers a mechanical means for the support of such coating, and will adhere by suction. This contractor also installs lath (including metal studs) or any other material prepared or manufactured to provide a base or bond for such coating.

(b) A lathing and plastering contractor also applies and affixes wood and metal lath, or any other material prepared or manufactured to provide key or suction bases for the support of plaster coatings. This classification includes the channel work and metal studs for the support of metal or any other lathing material and for solid plaster partitions.

(Authority cited: Sections 7008 and 7059, Business and Professions Code. Reference: Sections 7058 and 7059, Business and Professions Code.)

832.36. Class C-36—Plumbing Contractor

A plumbing contractor provides a means for a supply of safe water, ample in volume and of suitable temperature for the purpose intended and the proper disposal of fluid waste from the premises in all structures and fixed works. This classification includes but is not limited to:

(a) Complete removal of waste from the premises or the construction and connection of on-site waste disposal systems;

(b) Piping, storage tanks and venting for a safe and adequate supply of gases and liquids for any purpose, including vacuum, compressed air and gases for medical, dental, commercial and industrial uses;

(c) All gas appliances, flues and gas connections for all systems including suspended space heating units. This does not include forced warm air units;

(d) Water and gas piping from the property owner's side of the utility meter to the structure or fixed works;

(e) Installation of any type of equipment to heat water, or fluids, to a temperature suitable for the purposes listed in this section, including the installation of solar equipment for this purpose; and

(f) The maintenance and replacement of all items described above and all health and safety devices such as, but not limited to, gas earthquake valves, gas control valves, back flow preventors, water conditioning equipment and regulating valves.

(Authority Cited: Sections 7008 and 7059, Business and Professions Code. Reference: Sections 7058 and 7059, Business and Professions Code.)

832.38. Class C-38—Refrigeration Contractor

A refrigeration contractor constructs, fabricates, erects, installs, maintains, services and repairs refrigerators, refrigerated rooms, and insulated refrigerated spaces, temperature insulation, air-conditioning units, ducts, blowers, registers, humidity and thermostatic controls for the control of air, liquid, and/or gas temperatures below fifty degrees Fahrenheit (50°), or ten degrees Celsius (10°).

(Authority cited: Sections 7008 and 7059, Business and Professions Code. Reference: Sections 7026.1, 7058 and 7059, Business and Professions Code.)

832.39. Class C-39—Roofing Contractor

A roofing contractor installs products and repairs surfaces that seal, waterproof and weatherproof structures. This work is performed to prevent water or its derivatives, compounds or solids from penetrating such protection and gaining access to material or space beyond. In the course of this work, the contractor examines and/or prepares surfaces and uses the following material: asphaltum, pitch, tar, felt, glass fabric, urethane foam, metal roofing systems, flax, shakes, shingles, roof tile, slate or any other roofing, waterproofing, weatherproofing or membrane material(s) or a combination thereof.

(Authority cited: Sections 7008 and 7059, Business and Professions Code. Reference: Sections 7058 and 7059, Business and Professions Code.)

832.42. Class C-42—Sanitation System Contractor

A sanitation system contractor fabricates and installs cesspools, septic tanks, storm drains, and other sewage disposal and drain structures. This classification includes the laying of cast-iron, steel, concrete, vitreous and non-vitreous pipe and any other hardware associated with these systems.

(Authority cited: Sections 7008 and 7059, Business and Professions Code. Reference: Sections 7058 and 7059, Business and Professions Code.)

832.43. Class C-43—Sheet Metal Contractor

A sheet metal contractor selects, cuts, shapes, fabricates and installs sheet metal such as cornices, flashings, gutters, leaders, pans, kitchen equipment, duct work (including insulation, patented chimneys, metal flues, metal roofing systems and any other installations requiring sheet metal).

(Authority cited: Sections 7008 and 7059, Business and Professions Code. Reference: Sections 7058 and 7059, Business and Professions Code.)

832.45. Class C-45—Sign Contractor

A sign contractor fabricates, installs, and erects electrical signs, including the wiring of such electrical signs, and non-electrical signs, including but not limited to: post or pole supported signs, signs attached to structures, painted wall signs, and modifications to existing signs.

(Authority cited: Sections 7008 and 7059, Business and Professions Code. Reference: Sections 7058 and 7059, Business and Professions Code.)

832.46. Class C-46—Solar Contractor

A solar contractor installs, modifies, maintains, and repairs thermal and photovoltaic solar energy systems.

A licensee classified in this section shall not undertake or perform building or construction trades, crafts, or skills, except when required to install a thermal or photovoltaic solar energy system.

(Authority cited: Sections 7008 and 7059, Business and Professions Code. Reference: Sections 7058 and 7059, Business and Professions Code.)

Note: Development of the examination is complete and in effect.

832.47. Class C-47—General Manufactured Housing Contractor

(a) A general manufactured housing contractor installs, alters, repairs, or prepares for moving any type of manufactured home as defined in Section 18007 of the Health and Safety Code, any; type of mobilehome as defined in Section 18008 of the Health and Safety Code, and any type of multifamily manufactured home as defined in Section 18008.7 of the Health and Safety Code, including the accessory buildings or structures, and the foundations. A manufactured home does not include any recreational vehicle, commercial coach, or factory-built housing as defined in Section 19971 of the Health and Safety Code.

(b) A general manufactured housing contractor may provide utility services on a single-family individual site placement. Utility services mean the connection of gas, water, sewer, and electrical utilities to the home.

(Authority cited: Sections 7008 and 7059, Business and Professions Code. Reference: Sections 7026.11, 7058 and 7059, Business and Professions Code.)

832.49. Class C-49—Tree and Palm Contractor

(a) A tree and palm contractor plants, maintains, and removes trees and palms. The duties include pruning, stump grinding, and tree, palm, or limb guying.

(b) Effective January 1, 2024, this regulation shall become operative.

(c) This regulation does not apply to, and a license shall not be required for, incidental pruning of trees or guying of planted trees and their limbs by a nurseryperson or incidental pruning of trees by a gardener as described in Section 7026.1 of the Code.

(Authority cited: Sections 7008 and 7059, Business and Professions Code. Reference: Sections 7026.1, 7058 and 7059, Business and Professions Code.)

832.50. Class C-50—Reinforcing Steel Contractor

A reinforcing steel contractor fabricates, places and ties steel mesh or steel reinforcing bars (rods), of any profile, perimeter, or cross-section, that are or may be used to reinforce concrete structures.

(Authority cited: Sections 7008 and 7059, Business and Professions Code. Reference: Sections 7058 and 7059, Business and Professions Code.)

832.51. Class C-51—Structural Steel Contractor

A structural steel contractor fabricates and erects structural steel shapes and plates, of any profile, perimeter or cross-section, that are or may be used as structural members for buildings and structures, including the riveting, welding, rigging, and metal roofing systems necessary to perform this work.

(Authority cited: Sections 7008 and 7059, Business and Professions Code. Reference: Sections 7058 and 7059, Business and Professions Code.)

832.53. Class C-53—Swimming Pool Contractor

A swimming pool contractor constructs swimming pools, spas or hot tubs, including installation of solar heating equipment using those trades or skills necessary for such construction.

(Authority cited: Sections 7008 and 7059, Business and Professions Code. Reference: Sections 7058 and 7059, Business and Professions Code.)

832.54. Class C-54—Tile Contractors (Ceramic and Mosaic)

A ceramic and mosaic tile contractor prepares surfaces as necessary and installs glazed wall, ceramic, mosaic, quarry, paver, faience, glass mosaic and stone tiles; thin tile that resembles full brick, natural or simulated stone slabs for bathtubs, showers and horizontal surfaces inside of buildings, or any tile units set in the traditional or innovative tile methods, excluding hollow or structural partition tile.

(Authority cited: Sections 7008 and 7059, Business and Professions Code. Reference: Sections 7058 and 7059, Business and Professions Code.)

832.55. Class C-55—Water Conditioning Contractor

A water conditioning contractor installs water conditioning equipment with the use of only such pipe and fittings as are necessary to connect the water conditioning equipment to the water supply system and to by-pass all those parts of the water supply system within the premises from which conditioned water is to be excluded.

(Authority cited: Sections 7008 and 7059, Business and Professions Code. Reference: Sections 7058 and 7059, Business and Professions Code.)

832.57. Class C-57—Well Drilling Contractor

A well drilling contractor installs and repairs water wells and pumps by boring, drilling, excavating, casing, cementing and cleaning to provide a supply of uncontaminated water.

(Authority cited: Sections 7008 and 7059, Business and Professions Code. Reference: Sections 7026.3, 7058 and 7059, Business and Professions Code.)

832.60. Class C-60—Welding Contractor

A welding contractor causes metals to become permanently attached, joined and fabricated by the use of gases and electrical energy, which creates temperatures of sufficient heat to perform this work.

(Authority cited: Sections 7008 and 7059, Business and Professions Code. Reference: Sections 7058 and 7059, Business and Professions Code.)

832.61. Classification C-61—Limited Specialty

(a) Limited specialty is a specialty contractor classification limited to a field and scope of operations of specialty contracting for which an applicant is qualified other than any of the specialty contractor classifications listed and defined in this article.

(b) An applicant classified and licensed in the classification Limited Specialty shall confine activities as a contractor to that field or fields and scope of operations set forth in the application and accepted by the Registrar or to that permitted by Section 831.

(c) Upon issuance of a C-61 license, the Registrar shall endorse upon the face of the original license certificate the field and scope of operations in which the licensee has demonstrated qualifications.

(d) A specialty contractor, other than a C-61 contractor, may perform work within the field and scope of the operations of Classification C-61, provided the work is consistent with established usage and procedure in the construction industry and is related to the specialty contractor's classification.

(Authority cited: Sections 7008 and 7059, Business and Professions Code. Reference: Sections 7058 and 7059, Business and Professions Code.)

832.62. Solar System Work Within Scope of Class A, Class B, and Class C-61 (Swimming Pool Maintenance)

(a) The phrase "in connection with fixed works requiring specialized engineering knowledge and skill" in Section 7056 of the Business and Professions Code shall include but not be limited to an active solar energy system.

(b) An active solar energy system constitutes use of more than two unrelated building trades or crafts within the meaning of Section 7057 of the Business and Professions Code.

(c) C-61 (Swimming Pool Maintenance Contractors) currently holding the SC-44 supplemental solar classification may continue to perform solar work authorized by Class SC-44 until one year after the implementation of the C-46 Solar Classification. Thereafter, classification C-61 (Swimming Pool Maintenance) is authorized to repair active solar heating systems for swimming pools.

(Authority cited: Sections 7008 and 7059, Business and Professions Code. Reference: Sections 7056, 7057 and 7058, Business and Professions Code.)

833. Asbestos Classification and Certification Limitations and Examination Requirement

(a) The C-22—asbestos abatement contractor classification shall operate as a stand-alone specialty contractor classification for asbestos abatement work, notwithstanding any other classification held by the licensed contractor.

(b) No general building contractor, as defined in Section 7057 of the Code, shall contract for any project that includes asbestos abatement work unless the general building contractor holds the C-22—asbestos abatement contractor classification or the asbestos certification, as defined in Section 7058.5 of the Code, and DOSH registration or unless the general building contractor subcontracts with an appropriately licensed contractor.

(c) The asbestos certification, as defined in Section 7058.5 of the Code, shall operate in conjunction with other classification(s) held by the licensed contractor. No licensed contractor who holds the asbestos certification shall contract for any project that includes asbestos abatement work in a trade for which the contractor is not licensed, unless the licensee also holds the C-22—asbestos abatement contractor classification.

(d) The Registrar may waive the trade examination, pursuant to Section 7065.3 of the Code, for the C-22—asbestos abatement contractor classification for a licensed contractor who holds the asbestos certification, as defined in Section 7058.5 of the Code, upon application and conclusive showing by the licensee that he or she possesses not less than four years journey-level experience in the C-22—asbestos abatement contractor classification within the last 10 years immediately preceding the filing of the application. The licensee shall have obtained the asbestos certification after having passed the written asbestos certification examination and shall have held the asbestos certification in active and good standing throughout the four-year experience period at a minimum.

(Authority cited: Sections 7008 and 7059, Business and Professions Code. Reference: Sections 7057, 7058, 7058.5, 7059 and 7065.3, Business and Professions Code.)

834. Limitation of Classification

(a) A licensee classified as a general engineering contractor shall operate only within those areas defined in Section 7056 of the Code.

(b) A licensee classified as a general building contractor, as defined in Section 7057 of the Code, shall take a prime contract or subcontract only as authorized by Section 7057.

(c) A licensee classified as a specialty contractor, as defined in Section 7058 of the Code, shall not act in the capacity of a contractor in any classification other than one in which he/she is classified except on work incidental or supplemental to the performance of a contract in a classification in which any contractor is licensed by the Board.

(Authority cited: Sections 7008 and 7059, Business and Professions Code. Reference: Sections 7056, 7057, 7058 and 7059, Business and Professions Code.)

Section VI

ARTICLE 4. EXAMINATIONS

840. Written Examinations Required of All Applicants

Except as provided in Section 7065.1 of the Code, an applicant, including an applicant for an additional classification or classifications, must pass the written examination prescribed by the Registrar. No oral examination shall be given to any applicant. The reading of the examination instructions or questions or the explanation of the wording or intent of any of the questions to an examinee by any Board personnel authorized to conduct examinations, or by any duly sworn translators, shall not be considered an oral examination.

(Authority cited: Section 7008, Business and Professions Code. Reference: Sections 7065 and 7068, Business and Professions Code.)

841. Elimination and Revision of Examination Questions

The Registrar shall, under the Board's direction, prepare and revise the written examinations for contractors' licenses.

The Registrar shall replace, eliminate or change any examination question or answer thereto brought to his/her attention if, in the Registrar's opinion, the question is misleading or unfair, or the approved answer is incorrect.

(Authority cited: Section 7008, Business and Professions Code. Reference: Sections 7011, 7065, 7065.05 and 7068, Business and Professions Code.)

ARTICLE 5. RENEWAL OF LICENSE

853. Renewal Application Form

(a) The Registrar shall mail to each licensee, prior to the expiration of the license, a renewal form with complete instructions for renewal of the license.

(b) A renewal application and fee must be postmarked or hand delivered to the Board's headquarters office on or before the expiration date of the license. Failure to comply with the requirements of this subsection shall result in the renewal application being deemed delinquent.

(c) An incomplete renewal application shall be returned to the licensee by the Registrar with an explanation of the reasons for its rejection. The licensee shall resubmit the completed renewal application to the Board, postmarked or hand delivered to the Board's headquarters office on or before the expiration date of the license.

Failure to comply with this subsection shall result in the expiration of the license as provided in Section 7140 of the Code.

(d) An expired license shall not be renewed until any accrued delinquency fee has been paid.

(Authority cited: Section 7008, Business and Professions Code. Reference: Sections 7137, 7140 and 7141, Business and Professions Code.)

ARTICLE 6. BONDS

856. Security in Lieu of Bond

(a) A certificate of deposit, submitted pursuant to Section 7071.12(a) of the code, shall:

(1) When filed in lieu of a contractor's bond

(A) by an applicant, show the name style as set out on page one of the application.

(B) by a licensee, show the name style as currently recorded in the official files of the Board.

(2) When filed in lieu of a bond of qualifying individual, show the name style as in (1) above and the name of the responsible managing individual.

(3) Be made payable to the Contractors State License Board. The word "trustee" shall not be included.

(4) Be issued for a period of not less than one year.

(5) Be automatically renewable at each maturity date.

(6) Provide that any interest earned shall be paid to the depositor.

(b) Assignment of a savings and loan association investment certificate or share account, or of a credit union certificate for funds or share account shall be upon a form prescribed and approved by the Registrar.

(1) The form shall show:

(A) The assignment of the account to the board.

(B) The name style as prescribed in subsection (a) above.

(C) The current address of the applicant or licensee.

(D) The name and address of the savings and loan association or credit union having custody of such funds.

Section VI

(E) A declaration signed by an officer of the savings and loan association or the credit union that it received written notice of the assignment. This declaration shall include the title of the officer signing it.

(F) A receipt for the assignment from the Board with direction to the savings and loan association or the credit union that the earnings on the assigned account or certificate shall be paid to the assignor.

(2) The assignment form shall be accompanied by the savings and loan association pass book or investment certificate, the credit union certificate for funds or share account pass book of the assignor which shall show the name of the depositor-investor, that of the licensee or applicant, and the responsible managing individual, if applicable, and the amount of the assignment required by law.

(c) Eligible bearer bonds submitted pursuant to Section 7071.12(c) of the code shall be delivered to a bank in Sacramento, California, which shall act as agent for the applicant, licensee or responsible managing employee. The bank shall deliver the bonds to the Treasurer of the State of California only on order of the Registrar or an employee designated by the Registrar.

(1) The Registrar shall prescribe and approve the forms for the deposit or withdrawal of bearer bonds.

(2) Interest coupons shall remain attached to bearer bonds deposited with the Treasurer until such bonds are permanently withdrawn from the depository, not be resubmitted for deposit.

(3) In order to insure that sufficient security is on deposit, the bid price of bearer bonds, as recorded in the bond securities listed on the Pacific Coast Stock Exchange or some other authoritative source on the first day of the month in which such bonds are submitted for deposit, shall be at least 25% in excess of the amount of the surety bond or cash deposit required to be submitted.

The Registrar shall prescribe such procedures and forms, and issue such orders as necessary to accept and process any cash deposit submitted pursuant to Section 7071.12(d) of the code. Personal checks shall not be accepted as cash.

(Authority cited: Section 7008, Business and Professions Code. Reference: Sections 7071.5, 7071.6, 7071.8, 7071.9, 7071.10 and 7071.12, Business and Professions Code.)

858. Blanket Performance and Payment Bond Defined

(a) The purpose of these sections is to establish requirements for contractors seeking to obtain approval from the Registrar for a blanket performance and payment bond (hereafter referred to as "blanket bond") as specified under the provisions of paragraph (a)(8) of Section 7159.5 of the Code.

(b) For the purposes of this Article, the term "blanket bond" means a single surety instrument, executed by an admitted surety that is conditioned for the payment in full of all claims that arise from the obligations created by a licensee under any contract that is subject to the provisions of Section 7159 of the Code (hereafter referred to as "home improvement contract") and as set forth in Section 858.1 of this Article.

(c) For the purposes of this Article, the term "obligation" has the same meaning as set forth under Section 1427 of the Civil Code: "An obligation is a legal duty, by which a person is bound to do or not to do a certain thing."

(Authority cited: Section 7008, Business and Professions Code. Reference: Sections 7151, 7159 and 7159.5, Business and Professions Code.)

858.1. Blanket Performance and Payment Bond Requirements

(a) A blanket bond that is filed on behalf of a licensee to satisfy the provisions of Section 858 shall be underwritten for a dollar amount that is sufficient to cover one-hundred percent (100%) of the home improvement contracts for which the licensee has an obligation.

(b) Upon written request by a licensee, the Registrar is authorized to approve a blanket bond that is capped according to the schedule listed under subsection (c) provided the following conditions are met:

(1) The licensee, or the parent company of the licensee, is required to submit annual reports (Form 10-K) to the United States Securities and Exchange Commission (U.S. SEC).

(2) Upon the filing of a request that the blanket bond be capped, a copy of the most recently filed Form 10-K shall be submitted to the Registrar. Thereafter, a copy of any Form 10-K report shall be submitted to the Registrar within 10 days of filing with the U.S. SEC.

(3) The net worth of the applicable firm shall, initially and annually thereafter, be not less than 10 times the sum of the blanket bond as determined by the Registrar. Each net worth calculation shall be applicable to the period for which the most recent Form 10-K report was submitted to the U.S. SEC.

(c) The blanket bonds for which a request has been submitted under subsection (b) shall comply with the following schedule:

(1) If a licensee, or the parent company of a licensee, is classified as a "large accelerated filer" by the U.S. SEC, the amount of the blanket bond shall be $10 million.

(2) If a licensee, or the parent company of a licensee, is classified as an "accelerated filer" by the U.S. SEC, the amount of the blanket bond shall be $5 million.

(3) If a licensee, or the parent company of a licensee, is classified as a "non-accelerated filer" by the U.S. SEC, the amount of the blanket bond shall be $1 million.

(d) A licensee who is granted approval of a blanket bond pursuant to subsections (b) and (c) is not subject to the biennial financial reporting requirement specified under Section 858.4(a)(2). However, the qualifier's certification statement must be submitted biennially as specified under that section.

(e) For the purpose of executing the qualifier's certification statement required under Section 858.2(a)(4), the provisions of subsections (a), (b), and (c) of Section 858.1 shall be referenced collectively as "the 100% rule."

On the date that this section becomes effective, any licensee that has a blanket bond on file with the Board that fails to comply with the 100% rule shall achieve compliance not later than 90 days after the effective date of the section. The Registrar is authorized to rescind the approval of the blanket bond in accordance with the provisions of Section 858.8 of this Article if the licensee fails to comply with any provision of this section.

(f) The form of the blanket bond specified under this section is subject to the approval of the Registrar and shall conform to the following with regard to content:

This bond shall be filed with the Registrar of Contractors
State of California
Contractors State License Board

                                        Surety Code: _____
                                        Bond No.: _____
                                        License No.: _____

BLANKET PERFORMANCE AND PAYMENT BOND
(Business and Professions Code Section 7159.5)

The term of this bond is _____ to _____.

KNOW ALL BY THESE PRESENTS: That _____

(Business Name as Shown on the License)

whose address for service is

_____

(Street Address)   (City)   (State)   (Zip Code)

as Principal, and _____

(Name of Surety)

a corporation organized under the laws of the State of _____ and authorized to transact a general surety business in the State of California, as Surety, are held and firmly bound unto each owner or tenant of a residence or dwelling unit as the beneficiaries with whom the Principal, as of the date of this bond and thereafter, enters into a home improvement contract as defined in Section 7151.2 of the Business and Professions Code for repairing, remodeling, altering, converting, or modernizing such building or structure; and the aggregate contract price specified in one or more improvement contracts including all labor services and materials to be furnished by the Principal as the contractor exceeds the dollar amount prescribed in subdivision (b) of Section 7759. of the Business and Professions Code in the just and full sum of the amount of each individual contract for which sum, well and truly to be paid, we bind ourselves, our heirs, executors, successors, and assigns, jointly and severally, firmly by these presents. blanket performance and payment bond is issued in the amount of

_____(\$_____).

(Bond Dollar Amount)

THE CONDITION OF THE OBLIGATION IS SUCH, That, WHEREAS, Sections 7159 and 7159.5 of the Business and Professions Code provide for bonding requirements for contractors entering into contracts covered by these provisions of law, AND, WHEREAS, the Principal desires to file a blanket guarantee to operate as security in accordance with Section 995.020 of the Code of Civil Procedure, to cover the performance and payment of all obligations resultant from such contracts in order to conduct business under the exemptions specified under paragraph (8) of subdivision (a) of Section 7159.5 of the Business and Professions Code.

NOW THEREFORE, if the Principal shall well and truly perform and fulfill all the understandings, covenants, terms, conditions, and agreements of said contracts, and shall also well and truly perform and fulfill all the undertakings, covenants, terms, conditions, and agreements of any and all duly authorized modifications of said contracts; and if the Principal shall promptly make payments to all persons, whether or not in direct contractual relationship with Principal, supplying labor or material or both for the prosecution of the work provided in said contracts, then this obligation is to be void; otherwise, it is to remain in full force and effect as though separate bonds in the full amount of the contract price had been written on the individual contracts.

PROVIDED, HOWEVER, this bond is issued subject to the following express conditions:

1. This bond may be cancelled by the Surety in accordance with the provisions of Sections 996.310 et seq. of the Code of Civil Procedure.

2. This bond shall be deemed continuous in form and shall remain in full force and effect and shall run concurrently with the license period for which the license is granted and shall continue beyond that period and every succeeding license period or periods for which said Principal may hold this license or until the effective date of rescission of the Registrar's approval of the bond, after which liability hereunder shall cease in accordance with provisions of Section 996.360 of the Code of Civil Procedure.

3. This bond to become effective _____
(Date)

4. Even though this bond may be in effect for more than one year, the Surety's aggregate liability for all contracts covered hereunder shall in no event exceed the amount set forth above.

5. The Surety signing this bond is jointly and severally liable on the obligations of the bond, the obligations of the statutes providing for this bond, and the applicable provisions of the Code of Civil Procedure regarding bonds.

_____

(Name of Surety)   (Address for Service)

I declare under penalty of perjury under the laws of the State of California that I have executed the foregoing bond under an unrevoked power of attorney. I further declare that I have relied upon the "Qualifier's Certification Statement" to determine that, as of the date of execution, the penal sum of this bond is a good faith valuation of the funds required to safeguard the financial interests of the beneficiaries relative to the obligations for which this bond is posted.

Executed in _____, _____ on _____,
(City and State)   (Date)

under the laws of the State of California.

Certificate of Authority # _____

Signature of Attorney-in-Fact _____

Printed or Typed Name of Attorney-in-Fact _____

Address of Attorney-in-Fact _____

Telephone Number of Attorney-in-Fact (__) _____

Signature of Principal (Qualifier for the License) _____

13B-39 rev. 07/2021

(Authority cited: Section 7008, Business and Professions Code. Reference: Sections 7151.2, 7159 and 7159.5, Business and Professions Code.)

858.2. Application for Approval of Blanket Performance and Payment Bond

(a) A licensee seeking approval of a blanket bond shall meet the applicable conditions specified under this Article and submit to the Board an Application for Approval of Blanket Performance and Payment Bond, form 13B-35 (rev. 9/2022), that includes the following information:

(1) The name and address of the licensee as listed on the license record and the license number.

(2) The name of every person listed on the license record of the applicant who, as specified under Section 7068 of the Code, is acting as a qualifier for the license.

(3) The reviewed year-end financial statements and a report prepared by a certified public accountant (CPA) duly licensed by the California Board of Accountancy or licensed by another state board of accountancy. The reviewed financial statements shall include supplemental information related to the liquidity ratios of the licensee's business and shall particularly include the current ratio and the quick ratio, the calculations for which are specified under subparagraphs (A) and (B) below. The review report, or a separate supplementary report, shall include an explanation that the information has been subject to the review of the CPA. The review report shall cover the two fiscal years immediately preceding application for approval of the blanket bond and should be prepared in accordance with the current Statements of Standards for Accounting and Review Services issued by the American Institute of Certified Public Accounts.

(A) Current ratio calculation: current assets; divided by current liabilities.

(B) Quick ratio calculation: current assets minus inventory; divided by current liabilities.

Section VI

(4) A certification statement, signed under penalty of perjury by the qualifier for the license, that shall conform to the following language:

QUALIFIER'S CERTIFICATION STATEMENT

(Unless otherwise noted, all section references are to the California Business and Professions Code.)

The undersigned declares that, in accordance with Sections 7068 and 7068.1 of the Code, they are a qualifier for the licensee identified below (hereafter referred to as "licensee") and are responsible for exercising the direct supervision and control of the licensee's operations as is necessary to secure full compliance with the laws and regulations that are under the jurisdiction of the Contractors State License Board. As a qualifier of the licensee, the undersigned has reviewed sufficient financial information to execute this certification as it pertains to the licensee's home improvement sales and services that are subject to the home improvement contract requirements specified under Section 7159 of the Code. As of close of business on (Date) _____, the blanket performance and payment bond (bond) number (Bond Number) _____ issued by (Name of Surety Company) _____ as Surety is, according to the qualifier's comprehension of the data derived from the licensee, in an aggregate amount that is sufficient to comply with the "100% rule" as specified in the provisions of Section 858.1 of Title 16, Division 8 of the California Code of Regulations.

The undersigned also certifies that they will monitor the relevant business activity of the licensee, exercise due diligence to secure ongoing compliance with the 100% rule, and notify the Registrar within 30 days of the licensee's refusal, failure, or inability to comply with the 100% rule.

The undersigned also certifies that, upon approval of the blanket bond by the Registrar, the contract forms that will be used by the licensee for all transactions that are subject to Section 7159 of the Code will contain a notice that informs the property owner that a blanket performance and payment bond is on file with the Registrar of Contractors, or in lieu thereof, a notice that clearly identifies the name and address of the Surety that has issued the blanket performance and payment bond.

As a qualifying individual for the licensee, the undersigned declares under penalty of perjury under the laws of the State of California that the foregoing is true and correct and that this declaration was executed on (Date) _____ at (City and State) _____, _____.

_____   _____

(Name of Licensee as it Appears on the License)   (License Number)

_____   _____
(Printed Name of Qualifier)   (Signature of Qualifier)

(b) A licensee shall be licensed in this state in an active status for not less than two years prior to submitting the application provided for by this section.

(c) Except as otherwise provided under this subsection, an application for approval of a blanket bond shall not be accepted for consideration if any member of the personnel of record of the licensee, or any home improvement salespersons registered to the licensee, was found to have been responsible for, participated in, or otherwise culpable relative to any legal action that is subject to disclosure under Section 7124.6(e)(2) or 7124.6(e)(3) of the Code, or is named on a license that is suspended pursuant to Section 7071.17 of the Code.

(1) Any person who, after the effective date of the most recent disciplinary order applicable to that individual, is listed on an active license for three consecutive years with no violations resulting in disciplinary action may make application as provided under this Article.

(d) The application shall be signed by the person qualifying on behalf of the licensee who has executed the qualifier's certification statement required under this section. In the case of a responsible managing employee qualifier, the application shall also be signed by the owner, partner, or current corporate officer.

(e) The application shall be accompanied by a blanket bond that complies with the provisions of Section 858.1 of this Article and is underwritten by a surety that has been admitted in the State of California.

(Authority cited: Section 7008, Business and Professions Code. Reference: Sections 7068, 7068.1, 7071.17, 7124.6, 7159 and 7159.5, Business and Professions Code.)

858.3. Minimum Standards for Blanket Performance and Payment Bond Approval—Cause for Denial

(a) For each of the year-end financial statements for which a report is required under Section 858.2, the following standards must be met in order to qualify for blanket bond approval:

(1) The quick ratio shall not be less than 1:1, or, in lieu thereof, the current ratio shall not be less than 2:1.

(b) In addition to any other cause for denial, the Registrar may deny or rescind approval of the blanket bond based on information in the reviewed report or the information contained in the supplemental information required under subparagraph (a)(3) of Section 858.2 if the information demonstrates the licensee will be unable to meet current liabilities.

(Authority cited: Section 7008, Business and Professions Code. Reference: Section 7159.5, Business and Professions Code.)

858.4. Blanket Performance and Payment Bond Biennial Certification and Financial Reporting Requirements

(a) Except as otherwise provided under this Article, a licensee that maintains a blanket bond under this Article shall comply with the following:

(1) A certification statement as specified in Section 858.2 of this Article, signed under penalty of perjury by the member of the personnel of record who is listed as the qualifier for the license in accordance with Section 7068 of the Code, shall be submitted biennially to the Registrar as specified under subsection (b).

(2) With each application to renew the license for which the blanket bond has been posted, reviewed year-end financial statements and a report prepared in accordance with the provisions of Section 858.2(a)(3) shall be submitted to the Registrar as follows:

(A) If it has been one calendar year or more since the Registrar's approval of the blanket bond, the licensee shall submit a copy of a review report and the accompanying financial statements covering the entire period that is subsequent to the approval, but not more than the two fiscal years immediately preceding the license renewal date.

(B) If it has been less than one calendar year since the Registrar's initial approval of the blanket bond, the reviewed report required by this subsection shall be submitted at next renewal period that is more than one calendar year subsequent to the initial approval of the blanket bond.

(b) The due date for the qualifier's certification statement and any reports required under this section shall coincide with the license renewal period of the license for which blanket bond approval has been granted. For each subsequent renewal cycle, the certification statement and reports of financial statements shall be submitted to the Registrar no later than the date the license is due to expire.

(c) The Registrar may rescind approval of the blanket bond based on information in the reviewed report or in the supplemental information that demonstrates the licensee's business may not be able to meet its current liabilities.

(d) If a licensee fails to submit the certification statement or comply with the financial reporting requirements as specified by this section, the Registrar may rescind approval of the blanket bond in accordance with the provisions of Section 858.8 of this Article.

(Authority cited: Section 7008, Business and Professions Code. Reference: Sections 7068, 7068.1 and 7159.5, Business and Professions Code.)

858.5. Blanket Performance and Payment Bond Audit Authorization and Procedures

(a) The Registrar may order an audit of a licensee that has an approved blanket bond on file if he or she deems an audit is necessary to ensure that the sum for which the blanket bond has been filed is sufficient to protect the public.

(1) The Registrar shall provide a licensee with not less than 30 days written notification that an audit is to be conducted pursuant to this section. The notice shall specify the period to be covered by the audit and set a date for the audit to begin. The audit period shall not exceed the period that is specified for the retention of licensee records under Section 7111 of the Code. Delivery of the notice shall be by certified mail to the current business address of record listed on the license record. Upon written request, the Registrar may grant the licensee an additional 30 days to prepare for the audit.

(2) For any audit conducted pursuant to this section, the licensee shall, pursuant to the receipt of the audit notice, provide access to the licensee's books, business records, and documents in accordance with the provisions of Section 7111 of the Code.

(b) Upon completion and review of the audit and all relevant information, the Registrar shall determine if the licensee is in compliance with the 100% rule specified under Section 858.1.

(Authority cited: Section 7008, Business and Professions Code. Reference: Sections 7111 and 7159.5, Business and Professions Code.)

858.6. Authorization and Procedures for Ordering the Amount of Blanket Performance and Payment Bond to Be Increased

(a) Pursuant to an audit conducted in accordance with Section 858.5 of this Article, the Registrar is authorized to order an increase in the dollar amount of the blanket bond to an amount that meets the requirements specified in Section 858.1 of this Article. The adjustment determination shall be based on the information contained in records of the licensee that are required to be made available for an audit as specified under this Article.

(b) An order to increase the sum of the blanket bond pursuant to this section shall be sent by certified and regular mail to the licensee's address of record. The order shall include a notice that failure to increase the dollar amount of the blanket bond within 30 days of the date of the order is cause for rescission of approval of the blanket bond.

(c) If a licensee fails to comply within 30 days of the date of an order that is issued pursuant to this section, the Registrar shall rescind approval of the blanket bond in accordance with the provisions of Section 858.8 of this Article.

(Authority cited: Section 7008, Business and Professions Code. Reference: Section 7159.5, Business and Professions Code.)

858.7. Maintenance of the Blanket Performance and Payment Bond

(a) In order for any licensee to maintain the Registrar's approval of a blanket bond in accordance with this Article, all provisions of this section are applicable:

(1) No member of the personnel of record of the licensee, nor home improvement salesperson registered to the licensee, shall have been found to have been responsible for, participated in, or otherwise culpable relative to any acts or omissions that resulted in any discipline that is subject to disclosure under Section 7124.6(e)(2) or 7124.6(e)(3) of the Code. The approval of the blanket bond posted by a licensee found to be in violation of this section is subject to rescission in accordance with the provisions of Section 858.8 of this Article. In determining whether or not to rescind approval of the blanket bond for violations of this section, the Registrar shall give due consideration to protection of the public as set forth in Section 7000.6 of the Code.

(2) No member of the personnel of record of the licensee, nor home improvement salespersons registered to the licensee, shall be named on a license that is suspended pursuant to Section 7071.17 of the Code. The approval of the blanket bond posted by a licensee found to be in violation of this section is subject to rescission in accordance with the provisions of Section 858.8 of this Article. In determining whether or not to rescind approval of the blanket bond for violations of this section, the Registrar shall give due consideration to protection of the public as set forth in Section 7000.6 of the Code.

(3) Whenever any qualifier who has executed and filed the qualifier's certification statement required under this Article disassociates from the licensee, a subsequent qualifier for the licensee shall complete, execute, and file the qualifier's certification statement contained in the application form specified under Section 858.2 of this Article. The qualifier's certification statement required by this paragraph must be filed within 90 days of the date that the former qualifier who executed the qualifier's certification statement disassociated from the license, as noted on the official license record of the Board.

(4) The failure to file an acceptable qualifier's certification statement within 90 days as specified under subdivision (3) of this subsection is cause for rescission of approval of the bond in accordance with the provisions of Section 858.8 of this Article. If a licensee files a written request prior to the date the qualifier's certification statement is due, the Registrar may grant an additional 30 days within which to file the certification statement. The licensee's request shall clearly state the reason(s) why additional time is needed to file the qualifier's certification statement.

(Authority cited: Section 7008, Business and Professions Code. Reference: Sections 7000.6, 7071.17, 7124.6 and 7159.5, Business and Professions Code.)

858.8. Rescission of Blanket Performance and Payment Bond Approval

(a) The Registrar may rescind the approval of any blanket bond (also referenced as "approval rescission" under this section) if any provision or condition specified under this Article is not satisfied.

(b) To rescind the approval of a blanket bond, the Registrar shall send written notice by certified and regular mail to the licensee's address of record that specifies the date of and the reasons for the Registrar's decision to rescind approval of the blanket bond. When appropriate, the notice shall also contain the conditions that must be met to prevent the rescission.

(c) The rescission shall, as of the date specified, extinguish the licensee's authorization to use the blanket bond in satisfaction of the provisions under subsection (a)(8) of Section 7159.5 of the Code.

(d) The licensee shall be given not less than 30 days notice prior to the effective date of the rescission of the blanket bond. Prior to the effective date of the rescission, the licensee may file a written appeal of the rescission of the blanket bond with the Registrar. A written appeal is considered timely if it is postmarked prior to the date the rescission would otherwise become effective. Where a rescission is not appealed timely, the blanket bond shall be rescinded on the effective date specified by the Registrar. If the rescission is appealed timely, the effective date of the rescission shall be delayed until a decision on the appeal is issued, and a notice regarding the appeal and the pending decision of the Registrar shall be posted as specified under subsection (b) of Section 858.9.

(e) Upon cancellation of the blanket bond, the Registrar's approval shall be automatically rescinded effective on the date of the cancellation.

(f) Upon the effective date of the Registrar's approval rescission, the licensee shall be subject to and comply with the provisions of subsections (a)(3), (4), and (5) of Section 7159.5 of the Code and shall, in addition to complying with all other requirements specified under Section 7159 of the Code, include the Mechanics' Lien Warning disclosure as part of all home improvement contracts that are subject to that section.

(Authority cited: Section 7008, Business and Professions Code. Reference: Sections 7159 and 7159.5, Business and Professions Code.)

858.9. Posting of Blanket Performance and Payment Bond Information to License Records

(a) Upon approval of a blanket bond by the Registrar, regardless of the effective date of the blanket bond, the following information shall be posted to the public license record of the licensee named as principal on the blanket bond:

(1) A statement indicating that the licensee has an approved blanket performance and payment bond on file with the Board.

(2) The date that the blanket bond was approved.

(3) The number of the blanket bond.

(4) The dollar amount for which the blanket bond has been filed.

(5) The name and address of the surety company on the blanket bond.

(b) Whenever a licensee is notified of a decision to rescind the approval of the licensee's blanket bond, the Registrar shall post a notice on the public license record indicating that the rescission is pending. The notice shall be posted to the license record no earlier than 5 calendar days and no later than 10 calendar days after the date that written notification of the rescission is sent to the licensee. If the rescission is appealed timely by the licensee, the Registrar shall also post a notice that an appeal has been filed and indicate that the decision to rescind the approval of the blanket bond is delayed pending the outcome of the licensee's appeal.

(c) Upon rescission of approval of a blanket bond or its cancellation, the statement specified in paragraph (1) of subsection (a) shall be changed to indicate the disposition of the blanket bond and the effective date thereof. The information in paragraphs (2), (3), (4), and (5) of subsection (a) shall remain on the license record for not less than five years after the date the blanket bond was rescinded or cancelled.

(Authority cited: Section 7008, Business and Professions Code. Reference: Section 7159.5, Business and Professions Code.)

ARTICLE 7. SPECIAL PROVISIONS

860. Penalty for Failure to Comply with Rules

Licensees and applicants for licenses shall comply with all rules and regulations of the Board and regulations issued by the Registrar. Violation of such rules and regulations shall constitute grounds for disciplinary action, or for the denial of a license.

(Authority cited: Section 7008, Business and Professions Code. Reference: Section 7008, Business and Professions Code.)

861. "Advertising" Defined

As used in Section 7030.5 of the Code, the term "advertising" includes but is not limited to the following: any card, contract proposal, sign, billboard, lettering on vehicles registered in this or any other state, brochure, pamphlet, circular, newspaper, magazine, airwave or any electronic transmission, and any form of directory under any listing denoting "Contractor" or any word or words of a similar import or meaning requesting any work for which a license is required by the Contractors License Law.

(Authority cited: Section 7008, Business and Professions Code. Reference: Section 7030.5, Business and Professions Code.)

861.5. Definition of "Structural Defect"

For the purpose of subdivision (b) of Section 7091 of the Code, "structural defect" is defined as meaning:

(1) A failure or condition that would probably result in a failure in the load bearing portions of a structure,

(2) which portions of the structure are not constructed in compliance with the codes in effect at the time for the location of the structure, provided that,

(3) such failure or condition results in the inability to reasonably use the affected portion of the structure for the purpose for which it was intended.

(Authority cited: Sections 7008, 7091, Business and Professions Code. Reference: Section 7091, Business and Professions Code.)

863. Public Access to Information

The Registrar shall establish a system whereby members of the public may obtain from board records information regarding complaints made against licensed contractors, their history of legal actions taken by the board, and license status, as hereafter specified. For purposes of this section, "complaint" means a written allegation which has been investigated and has been referred for legal action against the licensee. For purposes of this section, "legal action" means referral of the complaint for the issuance of a citation, accusation, statement of issues, or for the initiation of criminal action or injunctive proceedings.

(a) The Registrar shall maintain records showing the complaints received against licensees and, with respect to such complaints, shall make available to members of the public, upon request, the following information:

(1) The nature of all complaints on file against a licensee which have been investigated by a Deputy Registrar and referred for legal action against the licensee by the District Office. Information regarding complaints which are in the process of being screened, mediated, arbitrated or investigated shall not be disclosed.

(2) Such general cautionary statements as may be considered appropriate regarding the usefulness of complaint information to individual consumers in their selection of a contractor.

(3) Whenever complaint information is requested, the information disclosable under subsections (c) and (d) below shall also be released.

(b) If a complaint results in a legal action and is subsequently determined by the registrar, the Office of the Attorney General or a court of competent jurisdiction not to have merit, it shall be deleted from the complaint disclosure system.

(c) The Registrar shall maintain records showing a history of any legal actions taken by the board against all current license holders and shall make available to members of the public, upon request, all the following information:

(1) Whether any current license holder has ever been disciplined by the registrar and, if so, when and for what offense; and

(2) Whether any current licensee has ever been cited, and, if so, when and for what offense, and, whether such citation is on appeal or has been complied with;

(3) Whether any current license holder is named as a respondent in any currently pending disciplinary or legal action.

(d) The Registrar shall maintain records showing certain licensing and bonding information for all current license holders and shall make available to members of the public, upon request, all the following information regarding current license holders:

(1) The name of the licensee as it appears in the board's records; and

(2) The license number; and

(3) The classification(s) held; and

(4) The address of record; and

(5) The personnel of the licensee; and

(6) The date of original licensure; and

(7) Whether a bond or cash deposit is maintained and, if so, its amount; and

(8) If the licensee maintains a bond, the name and address of the bonding company and the bond's identification number, if any.

(e) Limitation of access to information. Further, the Registrar may set reasonable limits upon the number of requests for information responded per month from any one requestor.

(Authority cited: Section 7008, Business and Professions Code. Reference: Sections 7124.5 and 7124.6, Business and Professions Code.)

864. Continuance of License Under Section 7068.2

When a notice of disassociation of the responsible managing officer, responsible managing employee, responsible managing member, or responsible managing manager is given within the time and in the manner prescribed by Section 7068.2 of the code, the license shall remain in force for a period of 90 days from the date of such disassociation.

(Authority cited: Section 7008, Business and Professions Code. Reference: Section 7068.2, Business and Professions Code.)

865. Continuance of License Under Section 7076

(a) An application for the continuation of a business under an existing license may be submitted to the Registrar within 90 days of:

(1) the death of a person licensed as an individual,

(2) the death or the disassociation of a partner of a licensed partnership, or

(3) the death of an individual member or the disassociation of any entity of a licensed joint venture.

If the application is approved by the Registrar, the license shall remain in force for a period of up to one year from the date of death or disassociation.

(b) The Registrar may approve an extension to the one-year provision outlined in subsection (a) if additional time is necessary to complete projects contracted for or commenced before the disassociation or death.

(c) A license so extended is subject to all the provisions of the Contractors License Law including those relating to renewal and bond requirements.

(Authority cited: Section 7008, Business and Professions Code. Reference: Section 7076, Business and Professions Code.)

867. Procedure to Reactivate an Inactive License

(a) A reactivation of an inactive license shall be effective on the date on which an acceptable form is received by the Registrar, on the date on which the full renewal fee for an active license provided for in Section 7137 of the Code is paid, or on the date, if any, requested by the licensee, whichever last occurs.

(b) When an inactive license is reactivated, the Registrar shall issue to the licensee an active pocket license.

(c) The name, address, license number and classification of the reactivated licensee shall be posted publicly as prescribed by the Registrar.

(Authority cited: Section 7008, Business and Professions Code. Reference: Section 7076.5, Business and Professions Code.)

868. Criteria to Aid in Determining if Crimes, Professional Misconduct, or Acts Are Substantially Related to Qualifications, Functions, or Duties of a Licensee or Registrant.

(a) For the purposes of denial, suspension, or revocation of a license or registration pursuant to Section 141, Division 1.5 (commencing with Section 475), or Sections 7073 or 7123 of the Code, a crime, professional misconduct, or act shall be considered to be substantially related to the qualifications, functions, or duties of a licensee or registrant (under Division 3, Chapter 9 of the Code) if it evidences present or potential unfitness of an applicant, licensee, or registrant to perform the functions authorized by the license or registration in a manner consistent with the public health, safety, and welfare.

(b) In making the substantial relationship determination required under subdivision (a) for a crime, the Board or Registrar shall consider the following criteria:

(1) The nature and gravity of the offense,

(2) The number of years elapsed since the date of the offense, and

(3) The nature and duties of a contractor or home improvement salesperson.

(c) For purposes of subdivision (a), substantially-related crimes, professional misconduct, or acts shall include, but are not limited to, the following:

(1) Any violation of the provisions of Chapter 9 of Division 3 of the Code or other state or federal laws governing contractors or home improvement salespersons.

(2) Failure to comply with the provisions of the California Code of Regulations, Title 16, Division 8.

(3) Crimes, professional misconduct, or acts involving dishonesty, fraud, deceit, or theft with the intent to substantially benefit oneself or another or to substantially harm another.

(4) Crimes, professional misconduct, or acts involving physical violence against persons.

(5) Crimes, professional misconduct, or acts that indicate a substantial or repeated disregard for the health, safety, or welfare of the public.

(Authority cited: Section 7008, Business and Professions Code. Reference: Sections 141, 480, 481, 490, 493, 7066, 7069, 7073, 7090, 7123 and 7124, Business and Professions Code.)

868.1. Criteria to Aid in Determining if Financial Crimes Are Directly and Adversely Related to Fiduciary Qualifications, Functions, or Duties of a Licensee or Registrant for the Purpose of Considering Denials of Applications.

For the purpose of determining whether there are grounds to deny a license or registration to an applicant who has been convicted of a financial crime currently classified as a felony pursuant to Section

480 of the Code, the crime shall be considered to be directly and adversely related to the fiduciary qualifications, functions, or duties of a licensee or registrant if it involves dishonesty, fraud, deceit, or theft that resulted in: (i) direct financial benefit to the applicant or another person or entity, (ii) direct financial harm to another person or entity, or (iii) an attempt to obtain direct financial benefit or cause direct financial harm to another person or entity. The felony financial crimes shall include, but not be limited to, the following:

(a) Crimes involving the acquisition or provision of false, altered, forged, counterfeit, or fraudulent document(s), or the acquisition or provision of false or fraudulent statement(s).

(b) Crimes involving the use of personal identifying information for an unlawful purpose, including for the purpose of illegally obtaining money, credit, goods, services, real property, or medical information of another person (also known as identify theft).

(c) Crimes involving stolen property, embezzlement, grand theft, larceny, burglary, monetary transactions in property derived from a specified unlawful activity (also known as money laundering), or crimes related to obtaining money, labor, or property under false or fraudulent pretenses.

(d) Crimes involving an attempt or conspiracy to commit such crimes listed in subsections (a), (b), or (c).

(e) For the purposes of this section, "personal identifying information" has the meaning set forth in Penal Code section 530.55.

(Authority cited: Section 7008, Business and Professions Code. Reference: Sections 7.5, 480, 7069, 7073, 7090 and 7124, Business and Professions Code.)

869. Criteria for Rehabilitation

(a) When considering the denial, suspension, or revocation of a license or registration pursuant to Division 1.5 (commencing with Section 475) of the Code on the ground that the individual has been convicted of a crime, the Board or Registrar shall consider whether the applicant, licensee, or registrant made a showing of rehabilitation if the applicant, licensee, or registrant completed the criminal sentence at issue without a violation of parole or probation. In making this determination, the Board or Registrar shall consider the following criteria:

(1) The nature and gravity of the crime(s);

(2) The length(s) of the applicable parole or probation period(s);

(3) The extent to which the applicable parole or probation period was shortened or lengthened, and the reason(s) the period was modified;

(4) The terms or conditions of parole or probation, and the extent to which they bear on the applicant's rehabilitation; and

(5) The extent to which the terms or conditions of parole or probation were modified, and the reason(s) for modification.

(b) If subsection (a) is inapplicable, or the Board or Registrar determines that an applicant, licensee, or registrant did not make a showing of rehabilitation based on the criteria in subsection (a), the Board or Registrar shall apply the following criteria in evaluating an applicant's, licensee's, or registrant's rehabilitation:

(1) The Board or Registrar shall find that an applicant, licensee, or registrant made a showing of rehabilitation if, after considering the following criteria and the provisions of subsection (b)(2), the Board or Registrar finds that the individual is rehabilitated:

(A) Denial Based on Felony Convictions Within Seven Years of Application When considering the denial of a license or registration, the Board or Registrar may consider the applicant rehabilitated if the applicant was convicted of a felony within the preceding seven (7) years from the date of application that is substantially related to the qualifications, functions, or duties of a licensee or registration as defined in Section 868, and five (5) years have passed from the time of the applicant's release from incarceration or completion of probation if no incarceration was imposed, without the occurrence of additional substantially-related criminal activity, professional misconduct, acts, or omissions that also could be grounds for denial. This subsection does not apply to any crimes listed in subsection (b)(1)(B).

(B) Denial Based on Serious Felonies, Felonies Requiring Sex Offender Registration, or Felony Financial Crimes Directly and Adversely Related to the Qualifications, Functions, or Duties of a Licensee or Registrant When considering the denial of a license or registration on the ground that the applicant was convicted of a crime identified in Section 480(a)(1)(A) of the Code or a felony financial crime as defined in Section 868.1, the Board or Registrar may consider an applicant rehabilitated if seven (7) years have passed from the time of the applicant's release from incarceration or completion of probation if no incarceration was imposed, and the applicant committed no additional substantially-related criminal activity, professional misconduct, acts, or omissions that also could be grounds for denial.

(C) Discipline Based on Felony Convictions When considering the suspension or revocation of a license or registration, the Board or Registrar may consider a licensee or registrant rehabilitated if the licensee or registrant was convicted of a felony that is substantially related to the qualifications, functions, or duties of a licensee or registrant as defined in Section 868, and seven (7) years have passed from the time of release from incarceration or completion of probation if no incarceration was imposed, without the occurrence of additional substantially-related criminal activity, acts, or omissions that also could be grounds for suspension or revocation.

(D) Denial or Discipline Based on Misdemeanor Convictions When considering the denial, suspension, or revocation of a license or registration, the Board or Registrar may consider an applicant, licensee, or registrant rehabilitated if the applicant, licensee, or registrant was convicted of a misdemeanor that is substantially related to the qualifications, functions, or duties of a licensee or registrant as defined in Section 868, and three (3) years have passed from the time of release from incarceration or completion of probation if no incarceration was imposed, without the occurrence of additional substantially-related criminal activity, act(s), or omission(s) that also could be grounds for denial, suspension, or revocation.

(E) Denial or Discipline Based on Professional Misconduct, Acts, or Omissions For professional misconduct or acts that are substantially related to the qualifications, functions, or duties of a licensee or registrant as defined in Section 868, or for other acts or omissions that are grounds for denial, suspension, or revocation, the Board or Registrar may consider the applicant, licensee, or registrant rehabilitated if three (3) years have passed from the time of commission of the professional misconduct, act(s), or omission(s) without the occurrence of additional substantially-related criminal activity, professional misconduct, act(s), or omission(s) that also could be grounds for denial, suspension, or revocation.

(2) The amount of time needed to demonstrate rehabilitation under subsection (b)(1) may be increased or decreased by taking into account the following:

(A) The nature and gravity of the crime(s), professional misconduct, act(s), or omission(s) that are under consideration as, or that were, the grounds for denial, suspension, or revocation.

(B) Evidence of any crime(s), professional misconduct, act(s), or omission(s) committed subsequent to the crime(s), professional misconduct, act(s), or omission(s) that are under consideration as, or that were, the grounds for denial, suspension, or revocation, which also could be considered as grounds for denial, suspension, or revocation.

(C) The time that has elapsed since commission of the crime(s), professional misconduct, act(s), or omission(s) that are under consideration as, or that were, the grounds for denial, suspension, or revocation.

(D) The extent to which the applicant, licensee, or registrant has complied with any terms of parole, probation, restitution, or any other sanctions lawfully imposed against the applicant, licensee, or registrant.

(E) Consistent work history subsequent to the release from incarceration, or the completion of probation if no incarceration was imposed, or subsequent to the time of commission of the professional misconduct, act(s), or omission(s).

(F) Documents or testimony from credible individuals who have personal knowledge of the applicant's, licensee's, or registrant's life and activities subsequent to the time of commission of the crime(s), professional misconduct, act(s), or omission(s) who can attest to the applicant's, licensee's, or registrant's present fitness for licensure or registration.

(G) The acts underlying the conviction have been dismissed pursuant to Section 1203.4, 1203.4a, 1203.41, 1203.42, or 1203.425 of the Penal Code, or a comparable dismissal or expungement. An applicant who has a conviction that has been dismissed pursuant to Section 1203.4, 1203.4a, 1203.41, or 1203.42 of the Penal Code shall provide proof of the dismissal if it is not reflected on the report furnished by the Department of Justice.

(H) Other relevant evidence, if any, of rehabilitation submitted by the applicant, licensee, or registrant. For example, relevant evidence may include evidence of recovery from drug and/or alcohol addiction or abuse or completion of a drug and/or alcohol aversion or diversion program if the crime(s), professional misconduct, act(s), or omission(s) related to or involved drug and/or alcohol use; or evidence of completion of an anger management program if the crime(s), professional misconduct, act(s), or omission(s) demonstrated the applicant's, licensee's, or registrant's inability to control one's temper.

(c) When considering a petition for reinstatement of the license of a contractor or the registration of a home improvement salesperson, the Board shall evaluate evidence of rehabilitation submitted by the petitioner, considering those criteria specified in subsections (a) and (b) relating to licensees or registrants.

(Authority cited: Sections 481, 482 and 7008, Business and Professions Code. Reference: Sections 7.5, 141, 480, 481, 482, 488, 490, 493, 496, 7066, 7069, 7073, 7090, 7102, 7123 and 7124, Business and Professions Code.)

869.1. Applicant Defined

(a) All applicants for licensure shall furnish a full set of fingerprints for purposes of the board conducting a criminal history record check. The fingerprints will be used to allow the California Department of Justice and the Federal Bureau of Investigation to provide criminal history to the Board.

(b) For purposes of fingerprinting, "applicant" means any individual applying to be a member of the personnel of record.

(c) For purposes of fingerprinting, "applicant" means an individual applying for a home improvement salesperson registration.

(Authority cited: Section 7008, Business and Professions Code. Reference: Sections 7069 and 7153.1, Business and Professions Code.)

869.2. Exemptions

(a) Applicants for a joint venture license who hold a current active license in good standing are not subject to fingerprinting.

(b) Individuals already fingerprinted as required by Section 869.1 and for whom subsequent arrest information remains available at the Board need not submit fingerprints when submitting a subsequent application.

(Authority cited: Section 7008, Business and Professions Code. Reference: Sections 7069 and 7153.1, Business and Professions Code.)

869.3. Methods for Submitting Fingerprints

(a) Applicants residing inside the State of California shall submit their fingerprints through the electronic format certified by the California Department of Justice but, with approval of the Registrar, may submit their fingerprints on hard copy forms provided by the Registrar.

(b) Applicants residing outside the State of California may submit their fingerprints using the electronic format certified by the California Department of Justice but also may submit their fingerprints on hard copy forms provided by the Registrar.

(Authority cited: Section 7008, Business and Professions Code. Reference: Sections 7069 and 7153.1, Business and Professions Code.)

869.4. Subsequent Arrest History

(a) Once an applicant has been fingerprinted, the Board will maintain access to the applicant's subsequent arrest history until such time as the individual's license is cancelled, revoked or no longer renewable.

(b) Once the Board no longer receives subsequent arrest information, an individual seeking to apply for a license must be fingerprinted as required in Section 869.1.

(Authority cited: Section 7008, Business and Professions Code. Reference: Sections 7069 and 7153.1, Business and Professions Code.)

869.9. Criteria to Aid in Determining Earliest Date a Denied Applicant May Reapply for Licensure or Registration.

(a) For an applicant who is denied licensure or registration pursuant to subsection (a) of Section 480 of the Business and Professions Code, the date of reapplication shall be set by the Registrar at not less than one (1) year nor more than five (5) years after the denial. When computing the date for reapplication, the time shall commence from the effective date of the decision if an appeal is made or from the service of the notice of denial under Section 485(b) if a request for hearing is not made. The Registrar will consider the following criteria when setting the reapplication date of an individual who was denied a license or registration:

(1) For felony convictions listed in Section 869(b)(1)(B) that are substantially related to the qualifications, functions, or duties of a licensee as defined in Section 868, seven (7) years have passed from the time of release from incarceration or completion of probation if no incarceration was imposed, without the occurrence of additional substantially-related criminal activity, professional misconduct, act(s), or omission(s) that also could be grounds for denial.

(2) For felony convictions not listed in Section 869(b)(1)(B) that are substantially related to the qualifications, functions, or duties of a licensee as defined in Section 868, five (5) years have passed from the time of the applicant's release from incarceration or completion of probation if no incarceration was imposed, without the occurrence of additional substantially-related criminal activity, professional misconduct, act(s), or omission(s) that also could be grounds for denial.

(3) For misdemeanor convictions that are substantially related to the qualifications, functions, or duties of a licensee or registrant as defined in Section 868, three (3) years have passed from the time of release from incarceration or completion of probation if no incarceration was imposed, without the occurrence of additional

Section VI

substantially-related criminal activity, professional misconduct, act(s), or omission(s) that also could be grounds for denial.

(4) For professional misconduct that is substantially related to the qualifications, functions, or duties of a licensee or registrant as defined in Section 868, or for other acts or omissions that are grounds for denial, three (3) years have passed from the time of commission of the professional misconduct, act(s), or omission(s), without the occurrence of substantially-related criminal activity, professional misconduct, act(s), or omission(s) that also could be grounds for denial.

(5) The nature and gravity of the crime(s), professional misconduct, act(s), or omission(s) that were the grounds for denial.

(6) Evidence of any crime(s), professional misconduct, act(s), or omission(s) committed subsequent to the crime(s), professional misconduct, act(s), or omission(s) that were the grounds for denial, which also could be considered as grounds for denial.

(7) The time that has elapsed since commission of the crime(s), professional misconduct, act(s), or omission(s) that were the grounds for denial.

(8) The extent to which the applicant has complied with any terms of parole, probation, restitution, or any other sanctions lawfully imposed against the applicant in connection with the crime(s), professional misconduct, act(s), or omission(s) that were the grounds for denial.

(9) Consistent work history subsequent to the release from incarceration, or the completion of probation if no incarceration was imposed, or subsequent to the date of commission of the crime(s), professional misconduct, act(s), or omission(s) that were the grounds for denial.

(10) Documents or testimony from credible individuals who have personal knowledge of the applicant's life and activities subsequent to the date of commission of the crime(s), professional misconduct, act(s), or omission(s) that were the grounds for denial and who can attest to the applicant's present fitness for licensure or registration.

(11) Other relevant evidence, if any, of eligibility for reapplication submitted by the applicant. For example, relevant evidence may include evidence of recovery from drug and/or alcohol addiction or abuse or completion of a drug and/or alcohol aversion or diversion program if the crime(s), professional misconduct, act(s), or omission(s) that were the grounds for denial related to or involved drug and/or alcohol use; or evidence of completion of an anger management

program if the crime(s), professional misconduct, act(s), or omission(s) demonstrated the applicant's inability to control one's temper.

(b) Nothing in this section shall preclude the Registrar from denying the license or registration of an applicant who was previously denied a license or registration and who is eligible for reapplication in accordance with this section.

(Authority cited: Sections 481, 482 and 7008, Business and Professions Code. Reference: Sections 480, 482, 485, 486, 496, 7066, 7069, 7073 and 7124, Business and Professions Code.)

870. Factors to Apply in Determining Earliest Date a Revoked Licensee May Apply for Licensure

(1) The Registar shall have exclusive authority in setting the earliest date a revoked licensee may reapply for reissuance or reinstatement of a license.

(2) When extending the minimum one year period, the Registrar shall give due consideration to the gravity of the violation, the history of previous violations and criminal convictions and evaluate the application based on the following criteria:

Reapplication Dates:

5 years   License has been revoked:

(1) one or more times or

(2) for committing fraudulent acts or

(3) committing acts which have seriously endangered the public welfare and safety or

(4) for being convicted of a construction-related crime. (For the purposes of determining if a crime is construction-related, CCR Title 16, Chapter 8, Section 868 shall apply.)

4 years   License has been revoked:

(1) for committing violations on multiple construction projects; or

(2) for committing multiple violations of law for reasons other than fraud, danger to the public welfare and safety and for conviction of a construction-related crime.

3 years   License has been revoked and revoked licensee:

(1) has been issued more than one citation which has become final within one year immediately preceding the date of revocation or

(2) has been previously suspended by the Register as the result of a disciplinary action.

2 years   License has been revoked and revoked licensee has been issued a citation, which has become final within one year immediately preceding the date of revocation.

1 year   Licensee has been revoked for the first time and revoked licensee has no previous legal action history with the Board.

(Authority cited: Sections 7008 and 7059, Business and Professions Code. Reference: Sections 7058 and 7059, Business and Professions Code.)

871. Disciplinary Guidelines

In reaching a decision on a disciplinary action under the Administrative Procedure Act (Government Code Section 11400 et seq.), the board shall consider the disciplinary guidelines entitled "Disciplinary Guidelines" (rev. 12/11/96) which are hereby incorporated by reference. Deviation from these guidelines and orders, including the standard terms of probation, is appropriate where the board in its sole discretion determines that the facts of the particular case warrant such a deviation—for example, the presence of mitigating factors such as the age of the case; evidentiary problems.

(Authority cited: Section 7008, Business and Professions Code; and Sections 11400.20 and 11400.21, Government Code. Reference: Sections 7090 and 7095, Business and Professions Code; and Section 11425.50(e), Government Code.)

DISCIPLINARY GUIDELINES
(Rev. 12/11/96)

In assessing a disciplinary penalty against a person who has not had a previous citation, revocation, suspension nor denial of application, as the result of the filing of an accusation or a statement of issues, the Registrar shall give due consideration to the following guidelines. In addition to any penalties imposed, all persons that have had a license disciplined, whether or not the disciplinary action has been stayed, will be required to post a disciplinary bond pursuant to Section 7071.8. Unless otherwise specified, all references are to the Business and Professions Code.

Factors To Be Considered

In determining whether revocation, suspension or probation is to be imposed in a given case, factors such as the following should be considered:

1. Nature and severity of the act(s), offenses, or crime(s) under consideration.

2. Actual or potential harm to the public.

3. Performed work that was potentially hazardous to the health, safety, or general welfare of the public.

4. Prior disciplinary record.

5. Number and/or variety of current violations.

6. Mitigation evidence.

7. Rehabilitation evidence.

8. In case of a criminal conviction, compliance with terms of sentence and/or court-ordered probation.

Sections and Disciplinary Guidelines

125. Conspiracy with an Unlicensed Person

Minimum Penalty: Revocation, stayed, 3 years probation

Maximum Penalty: Revocation

If warranted:

1. Actual suspension of 5 days or more.

2. Standard terms and conditions in cases of probation. *(See page 566.)*

3. Submit copies of construction contracts to the Registrar upon demand during the probation period.

4. If not taken within the past 5 years, take and pass the CSLB law and business examination.

5. Take and pass a course in Contractors License Law or a course related to construction law at an accredited community college. All courses must be approved in advance by the Registrar.

6. Community Service time as determined by the Registrar; 5-21 days.

7. Pay CSLB investigation and enforcement costs.

Section VI

141. Disciplinary Action by Foreign Jurisdiction

Minimum Penalty: Revocation, stayed, 3 years probation

Maximum Penalty: Revocation

If warranted:

1. Actual suspension of 5 days or more.

2. Standard terms and conditions in cases of probation. *(See page 566.)*

3. Pay CSLB investigation and enforcement costs.

4. Community Service as determined by the Registrar; 5-21 days.

490. Conviction of a Crime—Substantial Relationship Required

Minimum Penalty: Revocation, stayed, 3 years probation

Maximum Penalty: Revocation

If warranted:

1. Absent compelling mitigating circumstances, conviction of a crime related to the functions of a contractor is a serious offense that warrants an outright revocation.

2. Actual suspension of at least 30 days.

3. Standard terms and conditions in cases of probation. *(See page 566.)*

4. Make restitution.

5. If not taken within the past 5 years, take and pass the CSLB law and business examination.

6. Prohibit receipt of down payments.

7. Community Service as determined by the Registrar; 5-21 days.

8. Pay CSLB investigation and enforcement costs.

496. Violation of Section 123—Subversion of Licensee Examinations

Minimum Penalty: Revocation

Maximum Penalty: Revocation

If warranted:

1. Pay CSLB investigation and enforcement costs.

498. Securing a License through Fraud, Deceit or Knowing Misrepresentation

Minimum Penalty: Revocation

Maximum Penalty: Revocation

If warranted:

1. Pay CSLB investigation and enforcement costs.

499. False Statement in Support of Application

Minimum Penalty: Revocation, stayed, 3 years probation

If warranted:

1. Absent compelling mitigating circumstances, making a false statement in support of an application of another person, is a serious offense that warrants an outright revocation.

2. Actual suspension of at least 30 days.

3. Standard terms and conditions in cases of probation. *(See page 566.)*

4. If not taken within the past 5 years, take and pass the CSLB law and business examination.

5. Take and pass a course in Contractors License Law or a course related to construction law at an accredited community college. All courses must be approved in advance by the Registrar.

6. Community Service as determined by CSLB; 5-21 days.

7. Pay CSLB investigation and enforcement costs.

860. (CCR) Penalty for Failure to Comply with Rules

Minimum Penalty: 5 day suspension, stayed, 1 year probation

Maximum Penalty: Revocation

If warranted:

1. Actual suspension of 5 days or more.

2. Standard terms and conditions in cases of probation. *(See page 566.)*

3. If not taken within the past 5 years, take and pass the CSLB law and business examination.

4. Take and pass a course in Contractors License Law or a course related to construction law at an accredited community college. All courses must be approved in advance by the Registrar.

5. Pay CSLB investigation and enforcement costs.

7018.5. Notice to Owner; Mechanics' Lien Law

Minimum Penalty: 5 day suspension, stayed, 1 year probation

Maximum Penalty: 60 day suspension, 1 year probation

If warranted:

1. Standard terms and conditions in cases of probation. *(See page 566.)*

2. Submit copies of construction contracts to the Registrar upon demand during the probation period.

3. If not taken within the past 5 years, take and pass the CSLB law and business examination.

4. Take and pass a course in Contractors License Law or a course related to construction law at an accredited community college. All courses must be approved in advance by the Registrar.

5. Pay CSLB investigation and enforcement costs.

7027.3. Fraudulent Use of a License Number

Minimum Penalty: Revocation

Maximum Penalty: Revocation

If warranted:

1. Pay CSLB investigation and enforcement costs.

7029.1. Contracting Jointly Without a Joint Venture License

Minimum Penalty: 5 day suspension, stayed, 1 year probation

Maximum Penalty: 60 day suspension, 1 year probation

If warranted:

1. Actual suspension of 5 days or more.

2. Standard terms and conditions in cases of probation. *(See page 566.)*

3. If not taken within the past 5 years, take and pass the CSLB law and business examination.

4. Take and pass a course in Contractors License Law or a course related to construction law at an accredited community college. All courses must be approved in advance by the Registrar.

5. Pay CSLB investigation and enforcement costs.

7029.5. Identification on Vehicle, Plumbing, Electrical Sign, and Well-drilling

Minimum Penalty: 5 day suspension, stayed, 1 year probation

Maximum Penalty: 60 suspension, 1 year probation

If warranted:

1. Standard terms and conditions in cases of probation. *(See page 566.)*

2. Pay CSLB investigation and enforcement costs.

7068.2. Failure to Notify; Disassociation of RMO/RME

Minimum Penalty: 60 day suspension, stayed, 1 year probation

Maximum Penalty: Revocation

If warranted:

1. Standard terms and conditions in cases of probation. *(See page 566.)*

2. If not taken within the past 5 years, take and pass the CSLB law and business examination.

3. Take and pass a course in Contractors License Law or a course related to construction law at an accredited community college. All courses must be approved in advance by the Registrar.

4. Pay CSLB investigation and enforcement costs.

7071.11. Judgment, Admitted Claim or Good Faith Payment on Bond

Minimum Penalty: 60 day suspension, stayed, 1 year probation

Maximum Penalty: Revocation

If warranted:

1. Actual suspension of 5 days or more.

2. Standard terms and conditions in cases of probation. *(See page 566.)*

3. Make restitution.

4. Pay CSLB investigation and enforcement costs.

7071.13. Reference in Advertising; Contractors Bond

Minimum Penalty: 5 day suspension, stayed, 1 year probation

Maximum Penalty: 60 day suspension, 1 year probation

If warranted:

1. Standard terms and conditions in cases of probation. *(See page 566.)*

2. Submit copies of advertisements relating to contracting business to the Registrar prior to their being displayed or published during the probation period.

3. If not taken within the past 5 years, take and pass the CSLB law and business examination.

4. Take and pass a course in Contractors License Law or a course related to construction law at an accredited community college. All courses must be approved in advance by the Registrar.

5. Pay CSLB investigation and enforcement costs.

7071.15. Failure to Maintain a Sufficient Bond

Minimum Penalty: 60 day suspension, stayed, 1 year probation

Maximum Penalty: Revocation

If warranted:

1. Actual suspension of 5 days or more.

2. Standard terms and conditions in cases of probation. *(See page 566.)*

3. If not taken within the past 5 years, take and pass the CSLB law and business examination.

4. Take and pass a course in Contractors License Law or a course related to construction law at an accredited community college. All courses must be approved in advance by the Registrar.

5. Pay CSLB investigation and enforcement costs.

7076. Failure to Notify; Death or Disassociation of Licensee Personnel

Minimum Penalty: 60 day suspension, stayed, 1 year probation

Maximum Penalty: Revocation

If warranted:

1. Standard terms and conditions in cases of probation. *(See page 566.)*

2. If not taken within the past 5 years, take and pass the CSLB law and business examination.

3. Take and pass a course in Contractors License Law or a course related to construction law at an accredited community college. All courses must be approved in advance by the Registrar.

4. Pay CSLB investigation and enforcement costs.

7083. Failure to Notify, Changes of Personnel, Business Name, Address, Bond Exemption, and Multiple License Exemption

Minimum Penalty: 60 day suspension, stayed, 1 year probation

Maximum Penalty: Revocation

If warranted:

1. Standard terms and conditions in cases of probation. *(See page 566.)*

2. If not taken within the past 5 years, take and pass the CSLB law and business examination.

3. Take and pass a course in Contractors License Law or a course related to construction law at an accredited community college. All courses must be approved in advance by the Registrar.

4. Pay CSLB investigation and enforcement costs.

7090. Failure to Obtain Building Permits

Minimum Penalty: 60 day suspension, stayed, 1 year probation

Maximum Penalty: Revocation

If warranted:

1. Actual suspension of 5 days or more.

2. Standard terms and conditions in cases of probation. *(See page 566.)*

3. Make restitution.

4. Submit copies of building permits to the Registrar upon demand for projects undertaken during the probation period.

Section VI

5. If not taken within the past 5 years, take and pass the CSLB trade examination.

6. Take and pass a course in Contractors License Law or a course related to construction law at an accredited community college. All courses must be approved in advance by the Registrar.

7. Pay CSLB investigation and enforcement costs.

7090.5. Fraud and Repeated Acts, Despite Corrections of Conditions

Minimum Penalty: Revocation, stayed, 3 years probation

Maximum Penalty: revocation

If warranted:

1. Actual suspension of 5 days or more.

2. Standard terms and conditions in cases of probation. *(See page 566.)*

3. Take and pass a course in accounting, bookkeeping and/or business management at an accredited community college. All courses must be approved in advance by the Registrar.

4. Submit copies of building permits to the Registrar upon demand for projects undertaken during the probation period.

5. Submit copies of construction contracts to the Registrar upon demand during the probation period.

6. Prohibit receipt of down payments.

7. Submit to the Registrar a detailed plan setting forth the procedure to be used to provide for direct supervising and control by the qualifying individual.

8. If not taken within the past 5 years, take and pass the CSLB law and business examination.

9. Take and pass a course in Contractors License Law or a course related to business law at an accredited community college. All courses must be approved in advance by the Registrar.

10. If not taken within the past 5 years, take and pass the CSLB trade examination.

11. Take and pass a vocational course(s) related to the trade(s) employed on the project. All courses must be approved in advance by the Registrar.

12. Pay CSLB investigation and enforcement costs.

7099.6. Failure to Comply with a Citation

Minimum Penalty: Revocation, stayed, 1 year probation

Maximum Penalty: Revocation

If warranted:

1. Actual suspension of 5 days or more.

2. Standard terms and conditions in cases of probation. *(See page 566.)*

3. Make restitution.

4. Take and pass a course in Contractors License Law or a course related to construction law at an accredited community college. All courses must be approved in advance by the Registrar.

5. Pay CSLB investigation and enforcement costs.

7103. Disciplinary Action by Another State

Minimum Penalty: Revocation, stayed, 3 years probation.

Maximum Penalty: Revocation

If warranted:

1. Actual suspension of 5 days or more.

2. Standard terms and conditions in cases of probation. *(See page 566.)*

3. Pay CSLB investigation and enforcement costs.

7107. Abandonment

Minimum Penalty: Revocation, stayed, 3 years probation

Maximum Penalty: Revocation

If warranted:

1. Absent compelling mitigating circumstances, abandonment of a project is a serious offense that warrants an actual period of suspension of at least 30 days.

2. Standard terms and conditions in cases of probation. *(See page 566.)*

3. Make restitution.

4. Submit copies of building permits to the Registrar upon demand for projects undertaken during the probation period.

5. Submit copies of construction contracts to the Registrar upon demand during the probation period.

6. Submit to the Registrar a detailed plan setting forth the procedure to be used to provide for direct supervision and control by the qualifying individual.

7. If not taken within the past 5 years, take and pass the CSLB law and business examination.

8. Take and pass a course in Contractors License Law or a course related to construction law at an accredited community college. All courses must be approved in advance by the Registrar.

9. If not taken within the past 5 years, take and pass the CSLB trade examination.

10. Take and pass a vocational course(s) related to the trade(s) employed on the project. All courses must be approved in advance by the Registrar.

11. During the period of probation, provide lien releases to project owners as soon as payment is received.

12. Pay CSLB investigation and enforcement costs.

7108. Misuse of Funds

Minimum Penalty: Revocation, stayed, 3 years probation

Maximum Penalty: Revocation

If warranted:

1. Absent compelling mitigating circumstances, misuse of funds is a serious offense that warrants an actual period of suspension of at least 30 days.

2. If diversion or misuse of funds is for personal use not related to construction work, outright revocation is appropriate.

3. Standard terms and conditions in cases of probation. *(See page 566.)*

4. Make restitution.

5. Take and pass a course in accounting, bookkeeping and/or business management at an accredited community college. All courses must be approved in advance by the Registrar.

6. Submit copies of construction contracts to the Registrar upon demand during the probation period.

7. If not taken within the past 5 years, take and pass the CSLB law and business examination.

8. Take and pass a course in Contractors License Law or course related to construction law at an accredited community college. All courses must be approved in advance by the Registrar.

9. Community Service as determined by CSLB; 5-21 days.

10. Pay CSLB investigation and enforcement costs.

7108.5. Prime Contractors and Subcontractors; Payment Required

Minimum Penalty: 60 day suspension, stayed, 1 year probation

Maximum Penalty: Revocation

If warranted:

1. Actual suspension of 5 days or more.

2. Standard terms and conditions in cases of probation. *(See page 566.)*

3. Make restitution.

4. Take and pass a course in accounting, bookkeeping and/or business management at an accredited community college. All courses must be approved in advance by the Registrar.

5. If not taken within the past 5 years, take and pass the CSLB law and business examination.

6. Take and pass a course in Contractors License Law or a course related to construction law at an accredited community college. All courses must be approved in advance by the Registrar.

7. Pay CSLB investigation and enforcement costs.

7109(a). Departure from Accepted Trade Standards for Workmanship

Minimum Penalty: Revocation, stayed, 2 years probation

Maximum Penalty: Revocation

If warranted:

1. Actual suspension of 5 days or more. If the departure from trade standards is substantial, actual suspension of at least 30 days.

Section VI

2. Standard terms and conditions in cases of probation. *(See page 566.)*

3. Make restitution.

4. Submit copies of building permits to the Registrar upon demand for projects undertaken during the probationary period.

5. Submit copies of construction contracts to the Registrar upon demand during the probation period.

6. Submit to the Registrar a detailed plan setting forth the procedure to be used to provide for direct supervising and control by the qualifying individual.

7. If not taken within the last 5 years, take and pass the CSLB law and business examination.

8. Take and pass a course in Contractors License Law or a course related to construction law at an accredited community college. All courses must be approved in advance by the Registrar.

9. If not taken within the past 5 years, take and pass the CSLB trade examination.

10. Take and pass a vocational course(s) related to the trade(s) employed on the project. All courses must be approved in advance by the Registrar.

11. Pay CSLB investigation and enforcement costs.

7109(b). Departure from Plans and/or Specifications

Minimum Penalty: Revocation, stayed, 2 years probation

Maximum Penalty: Revocation

If warranted:

1. Actual suspension of 5 days or more. If the departure from plans and/or specifications is substantial, actual suspension of at least 30 days.

2. Standard terms and conditions in cases of probation. *(See page 566.)*

3. Make restitution.

4. Submit copies of building permits to the Registrar upon demand for all projects undertaken during the probationary period.

5. Submit copies of construction contracts to the Registrar upon demand during the probation period.

6. Submit to the Registrar a detailed plan setting forth the procedure to be used to provide for direct supervising and control by the qualifying individual.

7. If not taken within the past 5 years, take and pass the CSLB law and business examination.

8. Take and pass a course in Contractors License Law or a course related to construction law at an accredited community college. All courses must be approved in advance by the Registrar.

9. If not taken within the past 5 years, take and pass the CSLB trade examination.

10. Take and pass a vocational course(s) related to the trade(s) employed on the project. All courses must be approved in advance by the Registrar.

11. Pay CSLB investigation and enforcement costs.

7109.5. Violation of Safety Orders

Minimum Penalty: Revocation, stayed, 2 years probation

Maximum Penalty: Revocation

If warranted:

1. Actual suspension of 5 days or more.

2. Standard terms and conditions in cases of probation. *(See page 566.)*

3. If not taken within the past 5 years, take and pass the CSLB law and business examination.

4. Take and pass a course in Contractors License Law or a course related to construction law at an accredited community college. All courses must be approved in advance by the Registrar.

5. Establish a safety program.

6. Pay CSLB investigation and enforcement costs.

7110. Violations of Other Laws; Disciplinary Action

Minimum Penalty: Revocation, stayed, 2 years probation

Maximum Penalty: Revocation

If warranted:

1. Actual suspension of 5 days or more.

Section VI

2. Standard terms and conditions in cases of probation. *(See page 566.)*

3. Make restitution.

4. Comply with orders or assessments of relevant agency.

5. If not taken within the past 5 years, take and pass the CSLB law and business examination.

6. Take and pass a course in Contractors License Law or a course related to construction law at an accredited community college. All courses must be approved in advance by the Registrar.

7. Submit copies of building permits to the Registrar upon demand for projects undertaken during the probation period.

8. Establish a safety program.

9. Pay CSLB investigation and enforcement costs.

7110.1. Violation of Labor Code Section 206.5; Requiring Release of Claim for Wages

Minimum Penalty: 60 day suspension, stayed, 1 year probation

Maximum Penalty: Revocation

If warranted:

1. Actual suspension of 5 days or more.

2. Standard terms and conditions in cases of probation. *(See page 566.)*

3. If not taken within the past 5 years, take and pass the CSLB law and business examination.

4. Take and pass a course in Contractors License Law or a course related to construction law at an accredited community college. All courses must be approved in advance by the Registrar.

5. Pay CSLB investigation and enforcement costs.

7110.5. Violation Pursuant to Section 98.9 of the Labor Code

Minimum Penalty: 60 day suspension, stayed, 1 year probation

Maximum Penalty: Revocation

If warranted:

1. Actual suspension of 5 days or more.

2. Standard terms and conditions in cases of probation. *(See page 566.)*

3. If not taken within the past 5 years, take and pass the CSLB law and business examination.

4. Take and pass a course in Contractors License Law or a course related to construction law at an accredited community college. All courses must be approved in advance by the Registrar.

5. Pay CSLB investigation and enforcement costs.

7111. Preservation of Records

Minimum Penalty: 60 day suspension, stayed, 1 year probation

Maximum Penalty: Revocation

If warranted:

1. Actual suspension of 5 days or more.

2. Standard terms and conditions in cases of probation. *(See page 566.)*

3. Take and pass a course in accounting, bookkeeping and/or business management at an accredited community college. All courses must be approved in advance by the Registrar.

4. If not taken within the past 5 years, take and pass the CSLB law and business examination.

5. Take and pass a course in Contractors License Law or a course related to construction law at an accredited community college. All courses must be approved in advance by the Registrar.

6. Pay CSLB investigation and enforcement costs.

7111.1. Failure of Licensee To Cooperate in an Investigation of a Complaint

Minimum Penalty: 60 day suspension, stayed, 1 year probation

Maximum Penalty: revocation

If warranted:

1. Actual suspension of 5 days or more.

2. Standard terms and conditions in cases of probation. *(See page 566.)*

3. If not taken within the past 5 years, take and pass CSLB law and business examination.

Section VI

4. Take and pass a course in Contractors License Law or a course related to construction law at an accredited community college. All courses must be approved in advance by the Registrar.

5. Pay CSLB investigation and enforcement costs.

7112. Misrepresentation on an Application

Minimum Penalty: Revocation, stayed, 3 years probation

Maximum Penalty: Revocation

If warranted:

1. Absent compelling mitigating circumstances, misrepresentation is a serious offense that warrants an outright revocation.

2. Actual suspension of at least 30 days.

3. Standard terms and conditions in cases of probation. *(See page 566.)*

4. Community Service as determined by CSLB; 5-21 days.

5. Pay CSLB investigation and enforcement costs.

7113. Failure to Complete Project for Contract Price

Minimum Penalty: Revocation, stayed, 2 years probation

Maximum Penalty: Revocation

If warranted:

1. Actual suspension of 5 days or more. If injury is substantial, actual suspension of at least 30 days.

2. Standard terms and conditions in cases of probation. *(See page 566.)*

3. Make restitution.

4. Complete an education course in estimating construction costs or a related course in the field of construction science. All courses must be approved in advance by the Registrar.

5. Prohibit receipt of down payments.

6. If not taken within the past 5 years, take and pass the CSLB law and business examination.

7. Take and pass a course in Contractors License Law or a course related to construction law at an accredited community college. All courses must be approved in advance by the Registrar.

8. Pay CSLB investigation and enforcement costs.

7113.5. Settlement of Lawful Obligations

Minimum Penalty: Revocation, stayed, 2 years probation

Maximum Penalty: Revocation

If warranted:

1. Actual suspension of 5 days or more.

2. Standard terms and conditions in cases of probation. *(See page 566.)*

3. Make restitution.

4. Take and pass a course in accounting, bookkeeping and/or business management at an accredited community college. All courses must be approved in advance by the Registrar.

5. Submit a list of all subcontractors used on construction projects to the Registrar upon demand during the probation period.

6. Submit a list of all material suppliers used on construction projects to the Registrar upon demand during the probation period.

7. Pay CSLB investigation and enforcement costs.

7114. Aiding and Abetting an Unlicensed Person

Minimum Penalty: Revocation, stayed, 2 years probation

Maximum Penalty: Revocation

If warranted:

1. Actual suspension of 5 days or more.

2. Standard terms and conditions in cases of probation. *(See page 566.)*

3. If not taken within the past 5 years, take and pass the CSLB law and business examination.

4. Take and pass a course in Contractors License Law or a course related to construction law at an accredited community college. All courses must be approved in advance by the Registrar.

5. Submit a list of all subcontractors used on construction projects to the Registrar upon demand during the probation period.

6. Pay CSLB investigation and enforcement costs.

Section VI

7114.1. Certifying to False Experience

Minimum Penalty: Revocation, stayed, 3 years probation

Maximum Penalty: Revocation

If warranted:

1. Absent compelling mitigating circumstances, certifying false experience is a serious offense that warrants an outright revocation.

2. Standard terms and conditions in cases of probation. *(See page 566.)*

3. Community Service as determined by CSLB; 5-21 days.

4. Pay CSLB investigation and enforcement costs.

7115. Violation of the Contractors License Law

Minimum Penalty: 5 day suspension, stayed, 1 year probation

Maximum Penalty: Revocation

If warranted:

1. Actual suspension of 5 days or more.

2. Standard terms and conditions in case of probation. *(See page 566.)*

3. Pay CSLB investigation and enforcement costs.

7116. Any Willful or Fraudulent Act

Minimum Penalty: Revocation, stayed, 3 years probation

Maximum Penalty: revocation

If warranted:

1. Absent compelling circumstances, fraud is a serious offense that warrants an actual suspension of at least 60 days.

2. If the injury is substantial, outright revocation is appropriate.

3. Standard terms and conditions in case of probation. *(See page 566.)*

4. Make restitution.

5. If not taken within the past 5 years, take and pass the CSLB law and business examination.

6. Take and pass a course in Contractors License Law or a course related to construction law at an accredited community college. All courses must be approved in advance by the Registrar.

7. Community Service as determined by CSLB; 5-21 days.

8. Pay CSLB investigation and enforcement costs.

7117. Variance from License as to Name or Personnel

Minimum Penalty: 5 day suspension, stayed, 1 year probation

Maximum Penalty: 364 day suspension, 2 years probation

If warranted:

1. Standard terms and conditions in case of probation. *(See page 566.)*

2. If not taken within the past 5 years, take and pass the CSLB law and business examination.

3. Take and pass a course in Contractors License Law or a course related to construction law at an accredited community college. All courses must be approved in advance by the Registrar.

4. Pay CSLB investigation and enforcement costs.

7117.5. Contracting with an Inactive, Suspended or Expired License

Minimum Penalty: Revocation, stayed, 2 years probation

Maximum Penalty: Revocation

If warranted:

1. Actual suspension of 5 days or more.

2. Standard terms and conditions in case of probation. *(See page 566.)*

3. If not taken within the past 5 years, take and pass the CSLB law and business examination.

4. Take and pass a course in Contractors License Law or a course related to construction law at an accredited community college. All courses must be approved in advance by the Registrar.

5. Pay CSLB investigation and enforcement costs.

7117.6. Contracting Out of Classification

Minimum Penalty: 60 day suspension, stayed, 1 year probation

Section VI

Maximum Penalty: Revocation

If warranted:

1. Actual suspension of 5 days or more.

2. Standard terms and conditions in case of probation. *(See page 566.)*

3. Submit copies of construction contracts to the Registrar upon demand during the probation period.

4. Submit copies of all advertisements relating to contracting business to the Registrar prior to their being displayed or published during the probation period.

5. Pay CSLB investigation and enforcement costs.

7118. Contracting with an Unlicensed Person

Minimum Penalty: Revocation, stayed, 2 years probation
Maximum Penalty: Revocation
If warranted:
1. Actual suspension of 5 days or more.

2. Standard terms and conditions in cases of probation. *(See page 566.)*

3. If not taken within the past 5 years, take and pass the CSLB law and business examination.

4. Take and pass a course in Contractors License Law or a course related to construction law at an accredited community college. All courses must be approved in advance by the Registrar.

5. Submit a list of all subcontractors used on construction projects to the Registrar upon demand during the probation period.

6. Community Service as determined by CSLB; 5-21 days.

7. Pay CSLB investigation and enforcement costs.

7118.4. Asbestos Related Inspection with Knowledge of Report being Required for Loan; Disclosure Required

Minimum Penalty: 60 day suspension, stayed, 1 year probation

Maximum Penalty: Revocation

If warranted:

1. Absent compelling mitigating circumstances, conducting an asbestos related inspection while maintaining a financial

relationship with an entity which performs corrective work without disclosing this fact is a serious offense that warrants an actual suspension of 60 days.

2. Standard terms and conditions in cases of probation. *(See page 566.)*

3. If not taken within the past 5 years, take and pass the CSLB law and business examination.

4. Take and pass a course in Contractors License Law or a course related to construction law at an accredited community college. All courses must be approved in advance by the Registrar.

5. Community Service as determined by CSLB; 5-21 days.

6. Pay CSLB investigation and enforcement costs.

7118.5. Asbestos-related Work; Contracting with Uncertified Contractor

Minimum Penalty: 60 day suspension, stayed, 1 year probation

Maximum Penalty: Revocation

If warranted:

1. Absent compelling mitigating circumstances, contracting with an uncertified asbestos contractor to perform asbestos related work is a serious offense that warrants an actual suspension of 60 days.

2. Standard terms and conditions in cases of probation. *(See page 566.)*

3. Submit a list of all subcontractors used on construction projects to the Registrar upon demand during the probation period.

4. Community Service as determined by CSLB; 5-21 days.

5. Pay CSLB investigation and enforcement costs.

7118.6. Asbestos-contracting with an Uncertified Person for Removal or Remedial Action

Minimum Penalty: 60 day suspension, stayed, 1 year probation

Maximum Penalty: Revocation

If warranted:

1. Absent compelling mitigating circumstances, contracting with an uncertified person for removal or remedial asbestos work is a serious offense that warrants an actual suspension of 60 days.

2. Standard terms and conditions in cases of probation. *(See page 566.)*

3. Submit a list of all subcontractors used on construction projects to the Registrar upon demand during the probation period.

4. Community Service as determined by CSLB; 5-21 days.

5. Pay CSLB investigation and enforcement costs.

7119. Lack of Reasonable Diligence

Minimum Penalty: 60 day suspension, stayed, 1 year probation

Maximum Penalty: Revocation

If warranted:

1. Actual suspension of 5 days or more.

2. Standard terms and conditions in cases of probation. *(See page 566.)*

3. Make restitution.

4. Prohibit receipt of down payments.

5. Pay CSLB investigation and enforcement costs.

7120. Failure to Pay Money

Minimum Penalty: 60 day suspension, stayed, 1 year probation

Maximum Penalty: Revocation

If warranted:

1. Actual suspension of 5 days or more.

2. Standard terms and conditions in cases of probation. *(See page 566.)*

3. Take and pass a course in accounting, bookkeeping and/or business management at an accredited community college. All courses must be approved in advance by the Registrar.

4. If not taken within the past 5 years, take and pass the CSLB law and business examination.

5. Take and pass a course in Contractors License Law or a course related to construction law at an accredited community college. All courses must be approved in advance by the Registrar.

6. Submit a list of all subcontractors used on construction projects to the Registrar upon demand during the probation period.

7. Submit a list of all material suppliers used on construction projects to the Registrar upon demand during the probation period.

8. Prohibit the receipt of down payments.

9. Provide lien releases to project owners on all future construction projects upon receipt of payments.

10. Pay CSLB investigation and enforcement costs.

7121. Prohibition against Association

Minimum Penalty: Revocation, stayed, 2 years probation

Maximum Penalty: Revocation

If warranted:

1. Actual suspension of 5 days or more.

2. Standard terms and conditions in cases of probation. *(See page 566.)*

3. Make restitution.

4. If not taken within the past 5 years, take and pass the CSLB law and business examination.

5. Take and pass a course in Contractors License Law or a course related to construction law at an accredited community college. All courses must be approved in advance by the Registrar.

6. Pay CSLB investigation and enforcement costs.

7123. Conviction of a Crime

Minimum Penalty: Revocation, stayed, 3 years probation

Maximum Penalty; Revocation

If warranted:

1. Absent compelling mitigating circumstances, conviction of a crime related to the functions of a contractor is a serious offense and warrants an outright revocation.

Section VI

2. Actual suspension of at least 30 days.

3. Standard terms and conditions in cases of probation. *(See page 566.)*

4. Make restitution.

5. If not taken within the past 5 years, take and pass the CSLB law and business examination.

6. Take and pass a course in Contractors License Law or a course related to construction law at an accredited community college. All courses must be approved in advance by the Registrar.

7. Prohibit the receipt of down payments.

8. Community Service as determined by CSLB; 5-21 days.

9. Pay CSLB investigation and enforcement costs.

7123.5. Violation of Prohibition against Overpricing Following an Emergency or Disaster (Penal Code Section 396)

Minimum Penalty: 6 month suspension, 3 years probation

Maximum Penalty: Revocation

If warranted:

1. Absent compelling mitigating circumstances, overpricing following an emergency or disaster is a serious offense and warrants an outright revocation.

2. Actual suspension of 6 months.

3. Standard terms and conditions in cases of probation. *(See page 566.)*

4. Make restitution.

5. If not taken within the past 5 years, take and pass the CSLB law and business examination.

6. Take and pass a course in Contractors License Law or a course related to construction law at an accredited community college. All courses must be approved in advance by the Registrar.

7. Prohibit the receipt of down payments.

8. Community Service as determined by CSLB; 5-21 days.

9. Pay CSLB investigation and enforcement costs.

7125(b). Filing False Workers' Compensation Exemption Reports

Minimum Penalty: Revocation, stayed, 2 years probation

Maximum Penalty: Revocation

If warranted:

1. Actual suspension of 5 days or more.

2. Standard terms and conditions in cases of probation. *(See page 566.)*

3. If not taken within the past 5 years, take and pass the CSLB law and business examination.

4. Take and pass a course in Contractors License Law or a course related to construction law at an accredited community college. All courses must be approved in advance by the Registrar.

5. Submit a list of persons employed on construction related projects to the Registrar upon demand during the probation period.

6. Make restitution.

7. Pay CSLB investigation and enforcement costs.

7154. Employment of a Nonregistered Home Improvement Salesperson

Minimum Penalty: 60 day suspension, stayed, 1 year probation

Maximum Penalty: Revocation

If warranted:

1. Actual suspension of 5 days or more.

2. Standard terms and conditions in cases of probation. *(See page 566.)*

3. If not taken within the past 5 years, take and pass the CSLB law and business examination.

4. Take and pass a course in Contractors License Law or a course related to construction law at an accredited community college. All courses must be approved in advance by the Registrar.

5. Pay CSLB investigation and enforcement costs.

7155. Violation of Contractors License Law by Home Improvement Salesperson

Minimum Penalty: 60 day suspension, stayed, 1 year probation

Maximum Penalty: Revocation

If warranted:

1. Actual suspension of 5 days or more.

2. Standard terms and conditions in cases of probation. *(See page 566.)*

3. Submit copies of construction contracts to the Registrar upon demand during the probation period.

4. If not taken within the past 5 years, take and pass the CSLB law and business examination.

5. Take and pass a course in Contractors License Law or a course related to construction law at an accredited community college. All courses must be approved in advance by the Registrar.

6. Pay CSLB investigation and enforcement costs.

7155.5. Liability of a Contractor for a Home Improvement Salesperson

Minimum Penalty: Suspension, stayed, 1 year probation

Maximum Penalty: Revocation

If warranted:

1. Actual suspension of 5 days or more.

2. Standard terms and conditions in cases of probation. *(See page 566.)*

3. If not taken within the past 5 years, take and pass the CSLB law and business examination.

4. Take and pass a course in Contractors License Law or a course related to construction law at an accredited community college. All courses must be approved in advance by the Registrar.

5. Submit copies of construction contracts to the Registrar upon demand during the probation period.

6. Prohibit the receipt of down payments.

7. Pay CSLB investigation and enforcement costs

7156. Registered Salespersons Violations

Minimum Penalty: 60 day suspension, stayed, 1 year probation

Maximum Penalty: Revocation

If warranted:

1. Actual suspension of 5 days or more.

2. Standard terms and conditions in cases of probation. *(See page 566.)*

3. Submit copies of construction contracts to the Registrar upon demand during the probation period.

4. Pay CSLB investigation and enforcement costs.

7157. Home Improvement Inducements

Minimum Penalty: 60 day suspension, stayed, 1 year probation

Maximum Penalty: Revocation

If warranted:

1. Actual suspension of at least 5 days.

2. Standard terms and conditions in cases of probation. *(See page 566.)*

3. If not taken within the past 5 years, take and pass the CSLB law and business examination.

4. Take and pass a course in Contractors License Law or a course related to construction law at an accredited community college. All courses must be approved in advance by the Registrar.

5. Submit copies of advertisements relating to contracting business to the Registrar prior to their being displayed or published during the probation period.

6. Prohibit the receipt of down payments.

7. Pay CSLB investigation and enforcement costs.

7158. False Completion Certificate

Minimum Penalty: Revocation, stayed, 3 years probation

Maximum Penalty: Revocation

Section VI

If warranted:

1. Absent compelling circumstances, knowingly using a false certificate is a serious offense that warrants an actual suspension of at least 30 days.

2. Standard terms and conditions in cases of probation. *(See page 566.)*

3. If not taken within the past 5 years, take and pass the CSLB law and business examination.

4. Take and pass a course in Contractors License Law or a course related to construction law at an accredited community college. All courses must be approved in advance by the Registrar.

5. Make restitution.

6. Submit copies of construction contracts to the Registrar upon demand during the probation period.

7. Prohibit receipt of down payments.

8. Community Service as determined by CSLB; 5-21 days.

9. Pay CSLB investigation and enforcement costs.

7159. Home Improvement Contract Requirements

Minimum Penalty: 60 day suspension, stayed, 1 year probation

Maximum Penalty: Revocation

If warranted:

1. If any injuries are involved, actual suspension of at least 30 days.

2. Standard terms and conditions in cases of probation. *(See page 566.)*

3. If not taken within the past 5 years, take and pass the CSLB law and business examination.

4. Take and pass a course in Contractors License Law or a course related to construction law at an accredited community college. All courses must be approved in advance by the Registrar.

5. Submit copies of construction contracts to the Registrar upon demand during the probation period.

6. Prohibit receipt of down payments.

7. Community Service as determined by CSLB; 5-21 days.

8. Pay CSLB investigation and enforcement costs.

7161. Misrepresentation; False Advertisement

Minimum Penalty: Revocation, stayed, 3 years probation

Maximum Penalty: Revocation

If warranted:

1. Absent compelling mitigating circumstances, misrepresentation and false or deceptive advertising are serious offenses that warrant an actual period of suspension of at least 30 days.

2. If injury is substantial, outright revocation is appropriate.

3. Standard terms and conditions in cases of probation. *(See page 566.)*

4. If not taken within the past 5 years, take and pass the CSLB law and business examination.

5. Take and pass a course in Contractors License Law or a course related to construction law at an accredited community college. All courses must be approved in advance by the Registrar.

6. Submit copies of construction contracts to the Registrar upon demand during the probation period.

7. Submit copies of advertisements relating to contracting business to the Registrar prior to their being displayed or published during the probation period.

8. Prohibit the receipt of down payments.

9. Community Service as determined by CSLB; 5-21 days.

10. Pay CSLB investigation and enforcement costs.

7162. Representation with Respect to Trademark or Brand Name; Quantity or Size

Minimum Penalty: Revocation, stayed, 2 years probation

Maximum Penalty: Revocation

If warranted:

1. Actual suspension of 5 days or more.

2. Standard terms and conditions in cases of probation. *(See page 566.)*

3. If not taken within the past 5 years, take and pass the CSLB law and business examination.

4. Take and pass a course in Contractors License Law or a course related to construction law at an accredited community college. All courses must be approved in advance by the Registrar.

5. Make restitution.

6. Submit copies of construction contracts to the Registrar upon demand during the probation period.

7. Submit copies of advertisements relating to contracting business to the Registrar prior to their being displayed or published during the probation period.

8. Prohibit the receipt of down payments.

9. Pay CSLB investigation and enforcement costs.

7164. Contract Form for Single Family Dwelling

Minimum Penalty: 60 day suspension, stayed, 1 year probation

Maximum Penalty: Revocation

If warranted:

1. Actual suspension of 5 days or more.

2. Standard terms and conditions in cases of probation. *(See page 566.)*

3. If not taken within the past 5 years, take and pass the CSLB law and business examination.

4. Take and pass a course in Contractors License Law or a course related to construction law at an accredited community college. All courses must be approved in advance by the Registrar.

5. Submit copies of construction contracts to the Registrar upon demand during the probation period.

6. Pay CSLB investigation and enforcement costs.

7165. Swimming Pool Construction Contract

Minimum Penalty: 60 day suspension, stayed, 1 year probation

Maximum Penalty: Revocation

If warranted:

1. Actual suspension of 5 days or more.

2. Standard terms and conditions in cases of probation. *(See page 566.)*

3. If not taken within the past 5 years, take and pass the CSLB law and business examination.

4. Take and pass a course in Contractors License Law or a course related to construction law at an accredited community college. All courses must be approved in advance by the Registrar.

5. Submit copies of construction contracts to the Registrar upon demand during the probation period.

6. Pay CSLB investigation and enforcement costs.

7183.5. Asbestos; Certification Obtained under False Pretenses

Minimum Penalty: Revocation, stayed, 3 years probation

Maximum Penalty: Revocation

If warranted:

1. Absent compelling mitigating circumstances, obtaining an asbestos certification under false pretenses is a serious offense and warrants an outright revocation.

2. Actual suspension of at least 30 days.

3. Standard terms and conditions in cases of probation. *(See page 566.)*

4. Community Service as determined by CSLB; 5-21 days.

5. Pay CSLB investigation and enforcement costs.

7189. Asbestos Certification; Conflicts of Interest

Minimum Penalty: 60 day suspension, stayed, 1 year probation

Maximum Penalty: Revocation

If warranted:

1. Absent compelling circumstances, a person defined as an "asbestos consultant" or a "site surveillance technician," having financial or proprietary interest in an asbestos contractor's company is a serious offense that warrants an actual suspension period of at least 30 days.

2. Standard terms and conditions in cases of probation. *(See page 566.)*

3. Submit copies of construction contracts to the Registrar upon demand during the probation period.

4. Prohibit the receipt of down payments.

5. Community Service as determined by CSLB; 5-21 days.

6. Pay CSLB investigation and enforcement costs.

All Other Violations

Minimum Penalty: 5 day suspension, stayed, 1 year probation

Maximum Penalty: Revocation

If warranted:

1. Actual suspension of 5 days or more.

2. Standard terms and conditions in cases of probation. *(See page 566.)*

3. If not taken within the past 5 years, take and pass the CSLB law and business examination.

4. Take and pass a course in Contractors License Law or a course related to construction law at an accredited community college. All courses must be approved in advance by the Registrar.

5. If not taken within the past 5 years, take and pass the CSLB trade examination.

6. Take and pass a vocational course(s) related to the trade(s) employed on the project. All courses must be approved in advance by the Registrar.

7. Submit copies of construction contracts to the Registrar upon demand during the probation period.

8. Make restitution

9. Pay CSLB investigation and enforcement costs.

Standard Terms and Conditions to Be Included in all Cases of Probation

1. Obey All Laws:

   Respondent shall comply with all federal, state and local laws governing the activities of a licensed contractor in California.

2. Interviews With Regional Deputy:

   Respondent and any of respondent's personnel of record shall appear in person for interviews with the Regional Deputy or designee upon request and reasonable notice.

3. Completion Of Probation:

Upon successful completion of probation, the contractor's license will be fully restored.

4. Violation Of Probation:

If respondent violates probation in any respect, the Registrar, after giving notice and opportunity to be heard, may revoke probation and impose the disciplinary order that was stayed. If the decision contains an order to make restitution, the Registrar may impose the disciplinary order without giving the respondent an opportunity to be heard should the respondent fail to comply with the restitution order.

5. Respondent shall submit copies of documents directly related to the person's construction operations to the Registrar upon demand during the probation period.

872. Disclosure of General Liability Insurance

(a) As used in this regulation, "home improvement contract" is defined in Code Section 7151.2 The following statement, must accompany every estimate (bid) intended to result in a home improvement contract and every home improvement contract. The heading shall be printed in at least 14-point type, the questions in at least 12-point type, and the comments in italics of at least 11-point type. The text should be bold where indicated. **This is 14-point type.** **This is 12-point type.** *This is 11-point type in italics.*

Information About Commercial General Liability Insurance Home Improvement

Pursuant to California Business & Professions Code § 7159.3 (SB 2029), home improvement contractors must provide this notice and disclose whether or not they carry commercial general liability insurance.

Did your contractor tell you whether he or she carries Commercial General Liability Insurance?

Home improvement contractors are required by law to tell you whether or not they carry Commercial General Liability Insurance. This written statement must accompany the bid, if there is one, and the contract.

What does this insurance cover?

Commercial General Liability Insurance can protect against third-party bodily injury and accidental property damage. It is not intended to cover the work the contractor performs.

Is this insurance required?

No. But the Contractors State License Board strongly recommends that all contractors carry it. The Board cautions you to evaluate the risk to your family and property when you hire a contractor who is not insured. Ask yourself, if something went wrong, would this contractor be able to cover losses ordinarily covered by insurance?

How can you make sure the contractor is insured?

If he or she is insured, your contractor is required to provide you with the name and telephone number of the insurance company. Check with the insurance company to verify that the contractor's insurance coverage will cover your project.

What about a contractor who is self-insured?

A self-insured contractor has made a business decision to be personally responsible for losses that would ordinarily be covered by insurance. Before contracting with a self-insured contractor, ask yourself, if something went wrong, would this contractor be able to cover losses ordinarily covered by insurance?

■ _____ does not carry Commercial General Liability
(CONTRACTOR'S NAME)
Insurance.

■ _____ carries Commercial General Liability
(CONTRACTOR'S NAME)
Insurance.

The insurance company is _____
(COMPANY NAME)

You may call the insurance company at _____
(TELEPHONE NUMBER)

to verify coverage.

For more information about Commercial General Liability Insurance, contact the Contractors State License Board at www.cslb.ca.gov or call 800-321-CSLB (2752).

(This form meets the requirements of Rule 872 and Sections 7159.3 and 7164, Business and Professions Code.)

(b) The following statement must accompany every contract described in Code Section 7164. The heading shall be printed in at least 14-point type, the questions in at least 12-point type, and the comments in italics of at least 11-point type. The text should be bold where indicated. **This is 14-point type. This is 12-point type.** *This is 11-point type in italics.*

Information About Commercial General Liability Insurance Single Family Home

Pursuant to California Business & Professions Code §7164 (SB 2029), contractors building single-family residences for owners who intend to occupy the home for at least a year must provide this notice and disclose whether or not they carry commercial general liability insurance.

Did your contractor tell you whether he or she carries Commercial General Liability Insurance?

Contractors building single-family residences for owners who intend to occupy the home for at least a year are required by law to tell you whether or not they carry Commercial General Liability Insurance. This written statement must accompany the contract.

What does this insurance cover?

Commercial General Liability Insurance can protect against third-party bodily injury and accidental property damage. It is not intended to cover the work the contractor performs.

Is this insurance required?

No. But the Contractors State License Board strongly recommends that all contractors carry it. The Board cautions you to evaluate the risk to your family and property when you

Section VI

hire a contractor who is not insured. Ask yourself, if something went wrong, would this contractor be able to cover losses ordinarily covered by insurance?

How can you make sure the contractor is insured?

If he or she is insured, your contractor is required to provide you with the name and telephone number of the insurance company. Check with the insurance company to verify that the contractor's insurance coverage will cover your project.

What about a contractor who is self-insured?

A self-insured contractor has made a business decision to be personally responsible for losses that would ordinarily be covered by insurance. Before contracting with a self-insured contractor, ask yourself, if something went wrong, would this contractor be able to cover losses ordinarily covered by insurance?

■ _____ does not carry Commercial General Liability
   (CONTRACTOR'S NAME)
Insurance.

■ _____ carries Commercial General Liability
   (CONTRACTOR'S NAME)
Insurance.

   The insurance company is _____
                                          (COMPANY NAME)
   You may call the insurance company at _____
                                                    (TELEPHONE NUMBER)
to verify coverage.

For more information about Commercial General Liability Insurance, contact the Contractors State License Board at *www.cslb.ca.gov* or call 800-321-CSLB (2752).

(This form meets the requirements of Rule 872 and Sections 7159.3 and 7164, Business and Professions Code.)

ARTICLE 8. CITATION

880. Order of Correction—Practical Feasibility

Before including an order of correction in a citation, due consideration shall be given to the practical feasibility of correction in accordance with, but not limited to, the following criteria:

(a) An order of correction is appropriate where it would not result in excessive destruction of or substantial waste of existing acceptable construction.

(b) An order of correction is appropriate where the owner of the construction project is willing to allow the cited licensee to correct.

(c) An order of correction is appropriate where it appears to the Registrar that the cited licensee has competence or ability to correct.

(Authority cited: Sections 7008 and 7099.1, Business and Professions Code. Reference: Sections 7099 and 7099.1, Business and Professions Code.)

881. Order of Correction—Alternative Compliance

A cited licensee may comply with an order of correction by having and paying for another licensee to do the corrective work. The cited licensee remains responsible, however, for any failure to fully comply with the order of correction.

An order of correction may, but need not, contain the alternative that the cited person may pay a specified sum to the owner of the construction project in lieu of correcting.

(Authority cited: Sections 7008 and 7099.1, Business and Professions Code. Reference: Sections 7099 and 7099.1, Business and Professions Code.)

882. Order of Correction—Time Required to Correct

Where an order of correction is included in a citation, due consideration shall be given to the time required to correct in accordance with, but not limited to, the following criteria:

(a) Accepted industry practice in that area relating to performance of such work under certain climate or weather conditions.

(b) A reasonable time in which to obtain necessary materials.

(c) The number of working days the construction project will be made accessible by the owner for corrections.

(Authority cited: Sections 7008 and 7099.1, Business and Professions Code. Reference: Sections 7099 and 7099.1, Business and Professions Code.)

883. Order of Correction—Extension of Time to Correct

If the cited person, after exercising substantial efforts and reasonable diligence, is unable to complete the correction within the time allowed because of conditions beyond his control, he may request an extension of time in which to correct. Such request must be made in writing, and must be made prior to the expiration of the time allowed in the order of correction. An extension may be granted upon showing of good cause which determination is within the discretion of the Registrar. If a request for extension of time is not made prior to the expiration of time allowed in the order of correction, failure to correct within the time allowed shall constitute a violation of the order of correction whether or not good cause for an extension of time existed.

(Authority cited: Sections 7008 and 7099.1, Business and Professions Code. Reference: Sections 7099 and 7099.1, Business and Professions Code.)

884. Assessments of Civil Penalties

(a) Civil penalties against persons who have been cited for violation of the Contractors State License Law shall be assessed in accordance with the following ranges of penalties.

Section Violated	Minimum Civil Penalty	Maximum Civil Penalty
7027.1	100	1,000
7028	200	8,000
7028.1	1,000	8,000
7028.5	200	8,000
7028.7	200	15,000
7029.1	200	2,500
7029.5	100	500
7029.6	100	500
7030	500	1,500
7030.1	1,000	8,000
7030.5	100	1,000
7031.5	100	500
7034	100	1,000
7058.7	500	8,000
7068.1	100	8,000
7068.2	100	1,000
7071.11	100	1,000
7071.13	100	500
7075	100	500

Section Violated	Minimum Civil Penalty	Maximum Civil Penalty
7076	100	1,000
7083	100	1,000
7083.1	100	1,000
7099.10	100	1,500
7099.11	100	1,500
7107	200	8,000
7108	200	8,000
7108.5	200	2,000
7108.6	200	2,000
7109	200	8,000
7109.5	500	8,000
7110	200	8,000
7110.1	100	1,000
7111	100	1,000
7111.1	100	1,500
7113	200	8,000
7114	500	30,000
7114.1	200	2,000
7115	100	8,000
7116	100	8,000
7117	100	1,000
7117.5	200	8,000
7117.6	200	8,000
7118	500	30,000
7118.4	3,000	8,000
7118.5	1,000	8,000
7118.6	1,000	8,000
7119	200	2,000
7120	200	2,000
7123	500	8,000
7125	100	500
7125.4	200	8,000
7154	100	1,000
7157	100	1,000
7158	500	8,000
7159	100	1,000
7159.5(a)(1), (a)(3),	100	8,000

Section Violated	Minimum Civil Penalty	Maximum Civil Penalty
and (a)(5),		
7159.5(a)(2), (a)(4), (a)(6), (a)(7), and (a)(8)	100	1,000
7159.10	100	500
7159.14	100	8,000
7161	100	8,000
7162	100	1,500
7164	100	1,000

(b) When determining the amount of assessed civil penalty, the Registrar shall take into consideration whether one or more of the following or similar circumstances apply:

1. the citation includes multiple violations;

2. the cited person has a history of violations of the same or similar sections of the Contractors State License Law;

3. in the judgment of the Registrar, a person has exhibited bad faith;

4. in the judgment of the Registrar, the violation is serious or harmful;

5. the citation involves a violation or violations perpetrated against a senior citizen or disabled person; and/or

6. the citation involves a violation or violations involving a construction project in connection with repairs for damages caused by a natural disaster as described in Section 7158 of the Code.

(c) Where a citation lists more than one violation and each of the violations relates to the same construction project, the total penalty assessment in each citation shall not exceed $8,000, except as provided for violations of Sections 7028.7, in which case the total penalty assessment in each citation shall not exceed $15,000, and for violations of Section 7114, 7118, or 7125.4, in which case the total penalty assessment in each citation shall not exceed $30,000.

(d) Where a citation lists more than one violation, the amount of assessed civil penalty shall be stated separately for each section violated.

(Authority cited: Sections 7008 and 7099.2, Business and Professions Code. Reference: Sections 7099, 7099.1 and 7115, Business and Professions Code.)

885. Appeal of Citation

Any person served with a citation pursuant to Section 7099 of the Business and Professions Code may contest the citation by appealing to the Registrar within 15 working days from the receipt of such citation. The 15 day period may be extended upon showing of good cause which determination is within the discretion of the Registrar.

The cited person may contest any or all of the following aspects of the citation:

1. The occurrence of a violation of the Contractors License Law;

2. The reasonableness of the order of correction, if an order of correction is included in the citation;

3. The period of time allowed for correction, if an order of correction is included in the citation;

4. The amount of the civil penalty, if a civil penalty is assessed in the citation.

(Authority cited: Section 7008, Business and Professions Code. Reference: Sections 7099.3, 7099.4 and 7099.5, Business and Professions Code.)

886. Service of Citation

Service of a citation shall be made in accordance with the provisions of Section 11505(c) of the Government Code, and, further, that a copy of the citation be sent by regular mail.

(Authority cited: Section 7008, Business and Professions Code. Reference: Sections 7099.3, 7099.4 and 7099.5, Business and Professions Code.)

887. Criteria to Evaluate the Gravity of a Violation of Business and Professions Code Section 7028.7

Before assessing a civil penalty under Section 7028.7 of the Business and Professions Code, the Registrar shall give due consideration to the gravity of the violation, including, but not limited to, a consideration of whether the cited person did one or more of the following:

1. Falsely represented that he/she was licensed.

2. Failed to perform work for which money was received.

3. Executed or used any false or misleading documents in order to induce a person to enter into a contract or to pay money.

4. Made false or misleading statements in order to induce a person to enter into a contract or pay money.

Section VI

5. Failed to apply funds which were received for the purpose of obtaining or paying for services, labor, materials, or equipment.

6. Performed work that was potentially hazardous to the health, safety, or general welfare of the public.

7. Performed work in violation of the building laws, safety laws, labor laws, compensation insurance laws, or unemployment insurance laws.

8. Performed work that did not meet acceptable trade standards for good and workmanlike construction.

9. Was convicted of a crime in connection with the violation.

10. Committed any act which would be cause for disciplinary action against a licensee.

11. Committed numerous or repeated violations.

(Authority cited: Sections 7008 and 7028.7, Business and Professions Code. Reference: Section 7028.7, Business and Professions Code.)

ARTICLE 9. ARBITRATION

890. Minimum Qualification Standards for Arbitrators

For the purposes of Section 7085.5 of the Code, regardless of the method of appointment or selection, arbitrators shall possess the following minimum qualifications:

(a) (1) Five (5) years of experience in the construction industry as a licensed contractor or a professional in a construction related field, such as an architect or engineer, or

(2) Five (5) years of experience as an attorney, judge, administrative law judge, arbitrator, or a combination thereof, handling a minimum of 8 construction related matters.

(b) Completion of an arbitrator's course on construction arbitration within the last 5 years including, but not limited to, training on the process, the ethics and the laws relating to arbitration. The training on the process of arbitration may include such topics as the role of the arbitrator, the use of effective questioning techniques, and the role of an expert in an arbitration proceeding.

(c) Completion of 8 hours of continuing education on construction arbitration every 5 years, including, but not limited to, the topics set forth in subsection (b).

(d) Completion of a training program related specifically to the Board's arbitration procedures, laws and policies.

(Authority cited: Sections 7008 and 7085.5(b)(3), Business and Professions Code. Reference: Section 7085 et seq., Business and Professions Code.)

HISTORY NOTES FOR
CURRENT BOARD RULES AND REGULATIONS

(History notes for repealed rules and regulations appear at the end of this section.)

810. DEFINITIONS

1. *Repealer of Article 1 (Sections 700 and 701) and new Article 1 (Section 700) filed 5-25-83; effective thirtieth day thereafter (Register 83, No. 22).*
2. *Section renumbered from 700 to 810, filed 2-27-84; effective upon filing pursuant to Government Code Section 11346.2(d) (Register 84, No. 9).*

811. FEES

1. *New section filed 12-31-2002 as an emergency; operative 1-1-2003 (Register 2003, No. 1). A Certificate of Compliance must be transmitted to OAL by 5-1-2003 or emergency language will be repealed by operation of law on the following day.*
2. *Certificate of Compliance as to 12-31-2002 order, including new subsection (e), subsection relettering and amendment of Note, transmitted to OAL 4-25-2003 and filed 6-5-2003 (Register 2003, No. 23).*
3. *Amendment of section and Note filed 11-18-2010; operative 12-18-2010 (Register 2010, No. 47).*
4. *Change without regulatory effect repealing subsections (a)-(a)(12) and subsection (b) designator and amending former subsection (b) and subsections (7)-(8) filed 8-7-2013 pursuant to section 100, title 1, California Code of Regulations (Register 2013, No. 32).*
5. *Redesignation of first paragraph and subsections (1)-(13) as subsections (a)-(a)(13) and amendment of newly designated subsections (a)(7), (a)(8) and (a)(11) filed 12-19-2019 as an emergency; operative 12-19-2019 (Register 2019, No. 51). A Certificate of Compliance must be transmitted to OAL by 6-16-2020 or emergency language will be repealed by operation of law on the following day.*
6. *Reinstatement of section as it existed prior to 12-19-2019 emergency amendment by operation of Government Code section 11346.1(f) (Register 2020, No. 44).*
7. *Redesignation of first paragraph and subsections (1)-(13) as subsections (a)-(a)(13) and amendment of newly designated subsections (a)(7), (a)(8) and (a)(11) refiled 11-10-2020 as an emergency; operative 11-10-2020. Emergency expiration extended 60 days (Executive Order N-40-20) plus an additional 60 days (Executive Order N-66-20) (Register 2020, No. 46). A Certificate of Compliance must be transmitted to OAL by 6-18-2021 or emergency language will be repealed by operation of law on the following day.*
8. *Certificate of Compliance as to 11-10-2020 order transmitted to OAL 4-8-2021 and filed 5-20-2021 (Register 2021, No. 21).*

812. DISHONORED CHECK SERVICE CHARGE

1. *New section filed 9-30-82; effective thirtieth day thereafter (Register 82, No. 40).*

2. *Section renumbered from 703 to 812, filed 2-27-84; effective upon filing pursuant to Government Code Section 11346.2(d) (Register 84, No. 9).*

813. ABANDONMENT OF APPLICATION

1. *New section filed 8-25-83; effective upon filing pursuant to Government Code Section 11346.2(d) (Register 83, No. 35).*

2. *Section renumbered from 705 to 813, filed 2-27-84; effective upon filing pursuant to Government Code Section 11346.2(d) (Register 84, No. 9).*

816. APPLICATION FORM FOR ORIGINAL LICENSE

1. *Amendment filed 9-8-77; effective thirtieth day thereafter (Register 77, No. 37).*

2. *Editorial correction of subsection (c) (Register 77, No. 52).*

3. *Amendment filed 8-25-83; effective upon filing pursuant to Government Code Section 11346.2(d) (Register 83, No. 35).*

4. *Section renumbered from 706 to 816, filed 2-27-84; effective upon filing pursuant to Government Code Section 11346.2(d) (Register 84, No. 9).*

5. *Amendment of subsections (a)(1) and (c) filed 6-6-86; effective thirtieth day thereafter (Register 86, No. 23).*

6. *Change without regulatory effect repealing subsection (a)(1), renumbering subsections and amending subsection (c) and Note filed 11-15-2016 pursuant to section 100, title 1, California Code of Regulations (Register 2016, No. 47).*

819. REQUIREMENT OF CORPORATIONS

1. *Amendment filed 7-19-74; effective thirtieth day thereafter (Register 74, No. 29).*

2. *Amendment filed 8-25-83; effective upon filing pursuant to Government Code Section 11346.2(d) (Register 83, No. 35).*

3. *Section renumbered from 714 to 819, filed 2-27-84; effective upon filing pursuant to Government Code Section 11346.2(d) (Register 84, No. 9).*

824. APPLICATION INVESTIGATION REQUIRED

1. *New section filed 1-24-80; effective thirtieth day thereafter (Register 80, No. 4).*

2. *Amendment filed 8-25-83; effective upon filing pursuant to Government Code Section 11346.2(d) (Register 83, No. 35).*

3. *Section renumbered from 723.1 to 824, filed 2-27-84; effective upon filing pursuant to Government Code Section 11346.2(d) (Register 84, No. 9).*

825. EXPERIENCE REQUIREMENT OF APPLICANT

1. *Amendment filed 9-8-77; effective thirtieth day thereafter (Register 77, No. 37). For prior history, see Register 74, No. 29.*

2. *Editorial correction (Register 77, No. 52).*

3. *Amendment filed 8-25-83; effective upon filing pursuant to Government Code Section 11346.2(d) (Register 83, No. 35).*

4. *Section renumbered from 724 to 825, filed 2-27-84; effective upon filing, pursuant to Government Code Section 11346.2(d) (Register 84, No. 9).*

5. *Amendment of subsection (a) filed 4-12-84; effective upon filing pursuant to Government Code Section 11346.2(d) Register 84, No. 15).*

825.5. GENERAL MANUFACTURED HOUSING CONTRACTOR INITIAL INSTALLER TRAINING REQUIREMENT

1. *New section filed 9-30-2021; operative 9-30-2021 pursuant to Government Code section 11343.4(b)(3) (Register 2021, No. 40). Filing deadline specified in Government Code section 11349.3(a) extended 60 calendar days pursuant to Executive Order N-40-20.*

826. REGISTRAR TO PASS ON EXPERIENCE

1. *Amendment filed 9-8-77; effective thirtieth day thereafter (Register 77, No. 37).*

2. *Amendment filed 8-25-83; effective upon filing pursuant to Government Code Section 11346.2(d) (Register 83, No. 35).*

3. *Section renumbered from 725 to 826, filed 2-27-84; effective upon filing pursuant to Government Code Section 11346.2(d) (Register 84, No. 9).*

827. REVIEW OF APPLICATION FOR ORIGINAL LICENSE, ADDITIONAL CLASSIFICATION, OR REPLACEMENT OF QUALIFYING PERSON

1. *New section filed 12-3-85; effective thirtieth day thereafter (Register 85, No. 49).*

828. REVIEW OF APPLICATION FOR HOME IMPROVEMENT SALESMAN REGISTRATION

1. *New section filed 10-26-84; effective thirtieth day thereafter (Register 84, No. 43).*

830. CLASSIFICATION POLICY

1. *Amendment filed 9-8-77; effective thirtieth day thereafter (Register 77, No. 37).*

2. *Amendment filed 8-19-83; effective thirtieth day thereafter (Register 83, No. 35).*

3. *Section renumbered from 730 to 830, filed 2-27-84; effective upon filing pursuant to Government Code Section 11346.2(d) (Register 84, No. 9).*

831. INCIDENTAL AND SUPPLEMENTAL DEFINED

1. *New section filed 8-19-83; effective thirtieth day thereafter (Register 83, No. 35).*

2. *Section renumbered from 730.1 to 831, filed 2-27-84; effective upon filing pursuant to Government Code Section 11346.2(d) (Register 84, No. 9).*

832. SPECIALTY CONTRACTORS CLASSIFIED

1. *Amendment filed 4-29-64; effective thirtieth day thereafter (Register 64, No. 9). For prior history see Register 55, No. 11 and Register 61, No. 19.*

2. *Amendment filed 7-18-68; designated effective 10-15-68 (Register 68, No. 27).*

3. *Amendment filed 5-8-73; effective thirtieth day thereafter (Register 73, No. 19).*

4. *Amendment filed 4-16-74 as procedural and organizational; designated effective 5-16-74 (Register 74, No. 16).*

5. *Amendment filed 8-19-83; effective thirtieth day thereafter (Register 83, No. 35).*

6. *Section renumbered from 732 to 832, filed 2-27-84; effective upon filing pursuant to Government Code Section 11346.2(d) (Register 84, No. 9).*

7. *Amendment filed 6-6-86; effective thirtieth day thereafter (Register 86, No. 23).*

8. *Amendment filed 10-22-86; effective thirtieth day thereafter (Register 86, No. 43).*

9. *Amendment filed 9-15-88; operative 10-15-88 Register 88, No. 39).*

10. *Amendment filed 11-9-95; effective thirtieth day thereafter (Register 95, No. 45).*

11. Change without regulatory effect amending section filed 11-15-2016 pursuant to section 100, title 1, California Code of Regulations (Register 2016, No. 47).

12. Amendment filed 3-30-2022; operative 1-1-2024 (Register 2022, No. 13)

832.02. CLASS C-2—INSULATION AND ACOUSTICAL CONTRACTOR

1. New section filed 9-18-47 as an emergency; effective upon filing (Register 9).

2. Amendment filed 4-12-61; effective 30th day thereafter (Register 61, No. 8).

3. Amendment filed 8-19-83; effective thirtieth day thereafter (Register 83, No. 35).

4. Section renumbered from 754.8 to 832.02, filed 2-27-84; effective upon filing pursuant to Government Code Section 11346.2(d) (Register 84, No. 9).

832.04. CLASS C-4—BOILER, HOT-WATER HEATING AND STEAM FITTING CONTRACTOR

1. New section filed 9-18-47 as an emergency; effective upon filing (Register 9).

2. Amendment filed 5-4-72; effective thirtieth day thereafter (Register 72, No. 19).

3. Amendment filed 4-28-82; effective thirtieth day thereafter (Register 82, No. 18).

4. Amendment filed 8-25-83; effective upon filing pursuant to Government Code Section 11346.2(d) (Register 83, No. 35).

5. Section renumbered from 754.1 to 832.04, filed 2-27-84; effective upon filing pursuant to Government Code Section 11346.2(d) (Register 84, No. 9).

832.05. CLASS C-5—FRAMING AND ROUGH CARPENTRY CONTRACTOR

1. New section filed 10-26-93; operative 11-25-93 (Register 93, No. 44).

2. Amendment filed 12-18-97; effective 01-01-98 (Register 97, No. 172)

3. Amendment of section heading, section and Note filed 5-24-2002; operative 1-1-2003 Register 2002, No.21).

4. Change without regulatory effect repealing second paragraph filed 8-7-2013 pursuant to section 100, title 1, California Code of Regulations (Register 2013, No. 32).

832.06. CLASS C-6—CABINET, MILLWORK AND FINISH CARPENTRY CONTRACTOR

1. New section filed 5-24-2002; operative 1-1-2003 (Register 2002, No. 21). For prior history, see Register 97, No. 51.

2. Change without regulatory effect repealing second paragraph filed 8-7-2013 pursuant to section 100, title 1, California Code of Regulations (Register 2013, No. 32).

832.07. CLASS C-7—LOW VOLTAGE SYSTEMS CONTRACTOR

1. New section filed 9-15-88; operative 10-15-88 (Register 88, No. 39).

2. Amendment filed 5-17-95; operative 6-16-95 (Register 95, No. 20).

832.08. CLASS C-8—CONCRETE CONTRACTOR

1. Amendment filed 10-12-72; effective thirtieth day thereafter (Register 72, No. 42).

2. Amendment filed 8-25-83; effective upon filing pursuant to Government Code Section 11346.2(d) (Register 83, No. 35).

3. Section renumbered from 739 to 832.08, filed 2-27-84; effective upon filing pursuant to Government Code Section 11346.2(d) (Register 84, No. 9).

832.09. CLASS C-9—DRYWALL CONTRACTOR

1. *New section filed 4-29-64; effective thirtieth day thereafter (Register 64, No. 9).*
2. *Amendment filed 10-14-65; effective thirtieth day thereafter (Register 65, No. 19).*
3. *Amendment filed 8-19-83; effective thirtieth day thereafter (Register 83, No. 34).*
4. *Section renumbered from 754.13 to 832.09, filed 2-27-84; effective upon filing pursuant to Government Code Section 11346.2(d) (Register 84, No. 9).*
5. *Amendment filed 5-8-2002; operative 6-7-2002 (Register 2002, No.19).*

832.10. CLASS C-10—ELECTRICAL CONTRACTOR

1. *Amendment filed 4-28-82; effective thirtieth day thereafter (Register 82, No. 18).*
2. *Amendment filed 8-19-83; effective thirtieth day thereafter (Register 83, No. 34).*
3. *Section renumbered from 733 to 832.10, filed 2-27-84, effective upon filing pursuant to Government Code Section 11346.2(d) (Register 84, No. 9).*

832.11. CLASS C-11—ELEVATOR CONTRACTOR

1. *New section filed 9-18-47 as an emergency; effective upon filing (Register 9).*
2. *Amendment filed 8-25-83; effective upon filing pursuant to Government Code Section 11346.2(d) (Register 83, No. 35).*
3. *Section renumbered from 754.3 to 832.11, filed 2-27-84; effective upon filing pursuant to Government Code Section 11346.2(d) (Register 84, No. 9).*

832.12. CLASS C-12—EARTHWORK AND PAVING CONTRACTORS

1. *Originally published 12-5-46 (Title 16).*
2. *Amendment filed 9-18-47 as an emergency; effective upon filing (Register 9).*
3. *Amendment filed 8-3-72; effective thirtieth day thereafter (Register 72, No. 32).*
4. *Amendment filed 8-25-83; effective upon filing pursuant to Government Code Section 11346.2(d) (Register 83, No. 35).*
5. *Section renumbered from 745 to 832.12, filed 2-27-84; effective upon filing pursuant to Government Code Section 11346.2(d) (Register 84, No. 9).*

832.13. CLASS C-13—FENCING CONTRACTOR

1. *New section filed 4-16-74; effective thirtieth day thereafter (Register 74, No. 16).*
2. *Amendment filed 8-25-83; effective upon filing pursuant to Government Code Section 11346.2(d) (Register 83, No. 35).*
3. *Section renumbered from 754.15 to 832.13, filed 2-27-84; effective upon filing pursuant to Government Code Section 11346.2(d) (Register 84, No. 9).*

832.14. CLASS C-14—METAL ROOFING CONTRACTOR

1. *New section filed 10-22-86; effective thirtieth day thereafter (Register 86, No. 43).*
2. *Repealer and new section filed 6-22-98; operative 7-1-98 pursuant to Government Code section 11343.4(d) (Register 98, No. 26).*

832.15. CLASS C-15—FLOORING AND FLOOR COVERING CONTRACTORS

1. *Originally published 12-5-46 (Title 16).*
2. *Amendment filed 9-18-47 as an emergency; effective upon filing (Register 9).*
3. *Amendment filed 8-3-72; effective thirtieth day thereafter (Register 72, No. 32).*
4. *Amendment filed 8-25-83; effective upon filing pursuant to Government Code Section 11346.2(d) (Register 83, No. 35).*
5. *Section renumbered from 741 to 832.15, filed 2-27-84; effective upon filing pursuant to Government Code Section 11346.2(d) (Register 84, No. 9).*

Section VI

832.16. CLASS C-16—FIRE PROTECTION CONTRACTOR

1. New section filed 4-27-49 (Register 16, No. 2).
2. Amendment filed 8-12-83; effective thirtieth day thereafter (Register 83, No. 33).
3. Section renumbered from 754.9 to 832.16, filed 2-27-84; effective upon filing pursuant to Government Code Section 11346.2(d) (Register 84, No. 9).
4. Amendment filed 8-21-90; operative 9-20-90 (Register 90, No. 41).
5. Change without regulatory effect amending section filed 11-15-2016 pursuant to section 100, title 1, California Code of Regulations (Register 2016, No. 47).

832.17. CLASS C-17—GLAZING CONTRACTOR

1. Amendment filed 10-29-69; effective thirtieth day thereafter (Register 69, No. 44).
2. Amendment filed 8-25-83; effective upon filing pursuant to Government Code Section 11346.2(d) (Register 83, No. 35).
3. Section renumbered from 750 to 832.17, filed 2-27-84; effective upon filing pursuant to Government Code Section 11346.2(d) (Register 84, No. 9).

832.20. CLASS C-20—WARM-AIR HEATING, VENTILATING AND AIR-CONDITIONING CONTRACTOR

1. Originally published 12-5-46 (Title 16).
2. Amendment filed 9-18-47 as an emergency; effective upon filing (Register 9).
3. Amendment filed 5-4-72; effective thirtieth day thereafter (Register 72, No. 19).
4. Amendment filed 4-28-82; effective thirtieth day thereafter (Register 82, No. 18).
5. Amendment filed 11-1-83; effective upon filing pursuant to Government Code Section 11346.2(d) (Register 83, No. 45).
6. Section renumbered from 746 to 832.20, filed 2-27-84; effective upon filing pursuant to Government Code Section 11346.2(d) (Register 84, No. 9).
7. Editorial correction filed 7-19-84 (Register 84, No. 29).

832.21. CLASS C-21–BUILDING MOVING/DEMOLITION CONTRACTOR

1. Amendment filed 1-31-72; effective thirtieth day thereafter (Register 72, No. 6). For prior history see Register 55, No. 11.
2. Amendment filed 8-3-72; effective thirtieth day thereafter (Register 72, No. 32).
3. Amendment filed 8-25-83; effective upon filing pursuant to Government Code Section 11346.2(d) (Register 83, No. 35).
4. Section renumbered from 752 to 832.21, filed 2-27-84; effective upon filing pursuant to Government Code Section 11346.2(d) (Register 84, No. 9).

832.22. CLASS C–22—ASBESTOS ABATEMENT CONTRACTOR

1. New section filed 12-30-2014; operative 1-1-2015 pursuant to Government Code section 11343.4(b)(3) (Register 2015, No. 1).

832.23. CLASS C-23—ORNAMENTAL METAL CONTRACTOR

1. Amendment filed 8-25-83; effective upon filing pursuant to Government Code Section 11346.2(d) (Register 83, No. 35).
2. Section renumbered from 749 to 832.23, filed 2-27-84; effective upon filing pursuant to Government Code Section 11346.2(d) (Register 84, No. 9).

832.27. CLASS C-27—LANDSCAPING CONTRACTOR

1. *Amendment filed 10-14-68; effective thirtieth day thereafter (Register 68, No. 39).*

2. *Amendment filed 8-19-83; effective thirtieth day thereafter (Register 83, No. 34).*

3. *Section renumbered from 747 to 832.27, filed 2-27-84; effective upon filing pursuant to Government Code Section 11346.2(d) (Register 84, No. 9).*

4. *Amendment filed 6-1-88; operative 7-1-88 (Register 88, No. 23).*

832.28. CLASS C-28—LOCK AND SECURITY EQUIPMENT CONTRACTOR

1. *New section filed 1-31-95; operative 3-1-95 (Register 95, No.6Z).*

832.29. CLASS C-29—MASONRY CONTRACTOR

1. *Amendment filed 8-25-83; effective upon filing pursuant to Government Code Section 11346.2(d) (Register 83, No. 35).*

2. *Section renumbered from 740 to 832.29, filed 2-27-84; effective upon filing pursuant to Government Code Section 11346.2(d) (Register 84, No. 9).*

832.31. CLASS C-31—CONSTRUCTION ZONE TRAFFIC CONTROL CONTRACTOR

1. *New section filed 9-18-2000; operative 9-18-2000 pursuant to Government Code Section 11343.4 (d) (Register 2000, No.38).*

832.32. CLASS C-32—PARKING AND HIGHWAY IMPROVEMENT CONTRACTOR

1. *New section filed 7-18-68; designated effective 10-15-68 (Register 68, No. 27).*

2. *Amendment filed 8-19-83; effective thirtieth day thereafter (Register 83, No. 34).*

3. *Section renumbered from 754.14 to 832.32, filed 2-27-84; effective upon filing pursuant to Government Code Section 11346.2(d) (Register 84, No. 9).*

832.33. CLASS C-33—PAINTING AND DECORATING CONTRACTORS

1. *Amendment filed 8-19-83; effective thirtieth day thereafter (Register 83, No. 34).*

2. *Section renumbered from 735 to 832.33, filed 2-27-84; effective upon filing pursuant to Government Code Section 11346.2(d) (Register 84, No. 9).*

832.34. CLASS C-34—PIPELINE CONTRACTOR

1. *New section filed 7-24-56; designated effective sixtieth day thereafter (Register 56, No. 14).*

2. *Amendment filed 8-19-83; effective thirtieth day thereafter (Register 83, No. 34).*

3. *Section renumbered from 754.11 to 832.34, filed 2-27-84; effective upon filing pursuant to Government Code Section 11346.2(d) (Register 84, No. 9).*

832.35. CLASS C-35—LATHING AND PLASTERING CONTRACTOR

1. *Amendment of section heading, new subsection (a) designator and new subsections (b) and (c) filed 12-18-97; operative 1-1-98 pursuant to Government Code section 11343.4(d) (Register 97, No. 51).*

2. *Change without regulatory effect repealing subsection (c) filed 8-7-2013 pursuant to section 100, title 1, California Code of Regulations (Register 2013, No. 32).*

832.36. CLASS C-36—PLUMBING CONTRACTOR

1. *Amendment filed 4-29-64; effective thirtieth day thereafter (Register 64, No. 9).*

2. *Amendment filed 4-28-82; effective thirtieth day thereafter (Register 82, No. 18).*

3. *Amendment filed 8-12-83; effective thirtieth day thereafter (Register 83, No. 33).*

4. *Section renumbered from 734 to 832.36, filed 2-27-84; effective upon filing pursuant to Government Code Section 11346.2(d) (Register 84, No. 9).*

5. *Amendment filed 5-25-89; operative 6-24-89 (Register 89, No. 22). 2. Editorial correction of printing error and restoration of History 1. (Register 92, No. 29).*

6. *Amendment filed 12-1-94; operative 12-31-94 (Register 94, No. 50Z).*

832.38. CLASS C-38—REFRIGERATION CONTRACTOR

1. *Amendment filed 5-4-72; effective thirtieth day thereafter (Register 72, No. 19).*

2. *Amendment filed 8-19-83; effective thirtieth day thereafter (Register 83, No. 34).*

3. *Section renumbered from 748 to 832.38, filed 2-27-84; effective upon filing pursuant to Government Code Section 11346.2(d) (Register 84, No. 9).*

832.39. CLASS C-39—ROOFING CONTRACTOR

1. *Amendment filed 8-25-83; effective upon filing pursuant to Government Code Section 11346.2(d) (Register 83, No. 35).*

2. *Section renumbered from 737 to 832.39, filed 2-27-84; effective upon filing pursuant to Government Code Section 11346.2(d) (Register 84, No. 9).*

3. *Amendment filed 6-22-98; operative 7-1-98 pursuant to Government Code section 11343.4 (d) (Register 98, No. 26).*

832.42. CLASS C-42—SANITATION SYSTEM CONTRACTOR

1. *New section filed 9-18-47 as an emergency; effective upon filing (Register 9).*

2. *Amendment filed 8-3-72; effective thirtieth day thereafter (Register 72, No. 32).*

3. *Amendment filed 8-19-83; effective thirtieth day thereafter (Register 83, No. 34).*

4. *Section renumbered from 754.4 to 832.42, filed 2-27-84; effective upon filing pursuant to Government Code Section 11346.2(d) (Register 84, No. 9).*

832.43. CLASS C-43—SHEET METAL CONTRACTOR

1. *Originally published 12-5-46 (Title 16).*

2. *Amendment filed 9-18-47 as an emergency; effective upon filing (Register 9).*

3. *Amendment filed 8-19-83; effective thirtieth day thereafter (Register 83, No. 34).*

4. *Section renumbered from 742 to 832.43, filed 2-27-84; effective upon filing pursuant to Government Code Section 11346.2(d) (Register 84, No. 9).*

5. *Amendment filed 6-22-98; operative 7-1-98 pursuant to Government Code section 11343.4 (d) (Register 98, No. 26).*

832.45. CLASS C-45—ELECTRICAL SIGN CONTRACTOR

1. *New section filed 9-18-47 as an emergency; effective upon filing (Register 9).*

2. *Amendment filed 8-25-83; effective upon filing pursuant to Government Code Section 11346.2(d) (Register 83, No. 35).*

3. *Section renumbered from 754.2 to 832.45, filed 2-27-84; effective upon filing pursuant to Government Code Section 11346.2(d) (Register 84, No. 9).*

4. *Amendment of section heading and section filed 11-30-2009; operative 12-30-2009 (Register 2009, No. 49).*

832.46. CLASS C-46—SOLAR CONTRACTOR

1. *New section filed 10-20-78; effective thirtieth day thereafter (Register 78, No. 42).*

2. *Amendment filed 4-28-82; effective thirtieth day thereafter (Register 82, No. 18).*

3. *Amendment filed 8-25-83; effective upon filing pursuant to Government Code Section 11346.2(d) (Register 83, No. 35).*

4. *Section renumbered from 754.16 to 832.46, filed 2-27-84; effective upon filing pursuant to Government Code Section 11346.2(d) (Register 84, No. 9).*

5. *Amendment filed 11-30-2009; operative 12-30-2009 (Register 2009, No. 49).*

832.47. CLASS C-47—GENERAL MANUFACTURED HOUSING CONTRACTOR

1. *New section filed 3-15-83; effective thirtieth day thereafter (Register 83, No. 12).*

2. *Section renumbered from 754.18 to 832.47, filed 2-27-84; effective upon filing pursuant to Government Code Section 11346.2(d) (Register 84, No. 9).*

3. *Amendment of section and Note filed 10-7-2008; operative 11-6-2008 (Register 2008, No. 41).*

832.49. CLASS C-49—TREE AND PALM CONTRACTOR

1. *New section filed 3-30-2022; operative 1-1-2024 (Register 2022, No. 13).*

832.50. CLASS C-50—REINFORCING STEEL CONTRACTOR

1. *New section filed 9-18-47 as an emergency; effective upon filing (Register 9).*

2. *Amendment filed 8-19-83; effective thirtieth day thereafter (Register 83, No. 34).*

3. *Section renumbered from 754.5 to 832.50, filed 2-27-84; effective upon filing pursuant to Government Code Section 11346.2(d) (Register 84, No. 9).*

4. *Amendment filed 6-1-88; operative 7-1-88 (Register 88, No. 23).*

832.51. CLASS C-51—STRUCTURAL STEEL CONTRACTOR

1. *New section filed 9-18-47 as an emergency; effective upon filing (Register 9).*

2. *Amendment filed 8-19-83; effective thirtieth day thereafter (Register 83, No. 34).*

3. *Section renumbered from 754.6 to 832.51, filed 2-27-84; effective upon filing pursuant to Government Code Section 11346.2(d) (Register 84, No. 9).*

4. *Amendment filed 11-30-98; effective thirtieth day thereafter (Register 98, No. 49).*

832.53. CLASS C-53—SWIMMING POOL CONTRACTOR

1. *New section filed 5-3-55; effective thirtieth day thereafter (Register 55, No. 7).*

2. *Amendment filed 4-28-82; effective thirtieth day thereafter (Register 82, No. 18).*

3. *Amendment filed 8-19-83; effective thirtieth day thereafter (Register 83, No. 34).*

4. *Section renumbered from 754.10 to 832.53, filed 2-27-84; effective upon filing pursuant to Government Code Section 11346.2(d) (Register 84, No. 9).*

832.54. CLASS C-54—TILE CONTRACTORS (CERAMIC AND MOSAIC)

1. *Originally published 12-5-46 (Title 16).*

2. *Amendment filed 9-18-47 as an emergency; effective upon filing (Register 9).*

3. *Amendment filed 8-25-83; effective upon filing pursuant to Government Code Section 11346.2(d) (Register 83, No. 35).*

4. *Section renumbered from 738 to 832.54, filed 2-27-84; effective upon filing pursuant to Government Code Section 11346.2(d) (Register 84, No. 9).*

5. *Amendment filed 5-16-2002; operative 5-16-2002 pursuant to Government Code section 11343.4 (Register 2002, No. 20).*

832.55. CLASS C-55—WATER CONDITIONING CONTRACTOR

1. *New section filed 5-24-61; designated effective 8-22-61 (Register 61, No. 10).*

2. *Amendment filed 8-19-83; effective thirtieth day thereafter (Register 83, No. 34).*

3. *Section renumbered from 754.12 to 832.55, filed 2-27-84; effective upon filing pursuant to Government Code Section 11346.2(d) (Register 84, No. 9).*

832.57. CLASS C-57—WELL DRILLING CONTRACTOR

1. *Originally published 12-5-46 (Title 16).*

2. *Amendment filed 10-19-48 as an emergency (Register 14, No. 3).*

3. *Amendment filed 8-25-83; effective upon filing pursuant to Government Code Section 11346.2(d) (Register 83, No. 35).*

4. *Section renumbered from 751 to 832.57, filed 2-27-84; effective upon filing pursuant to Government Code Section 11346.2(d) (Register 84, No. 9).*

832.60. CLASS C-60—WELDING CONTRACTOR

1. *New section filed 9-18-47 as an emergency; effective upon filing (Register 9).*

2. *Amendment filed 8-19-83; effective thirtieth day thereafter (Register 83, No. 34).*

3. *Section renumbered from 754.7 to 832.60, filed 2-27-84; effective upon filing pursuant to Government Code Section 11346.2(d) (Register 84, No. 9).*

832.61. CLASSIFICATION C-61, LIMITED SPECIALTY

1. *New section filed 9-5-61; effective thirtieth day thereafter (Register 61, No. 19).*

2. *Amendment filed 4-29-64; effective thirtieth day thereafter (Register 64, No. 9).*

3. *Amendment filed 9-8-77; effective thirtieth day thereafter (Register 77, No. 37).*

4. *Editorial correction (Register 77, No. 52).*

5. *Amendment filed 8-19-83; effective thirtieth day thereafter (Register 83, No. 34).*

6. *Section renumbered from 732.1 to 832.61, filed 2-27-84, effective upon filing pursuant to Government Code Section 11346.2(d) (Register 84, No. 9).*

832.62. SOLAR SYSTEM WORK WITHIN SCOPE OF CLASS A, CLASS B, AND CLASS C-61 (SWIMMING POOL MAINTENANCE)

1. *New section filed 4-28-82; effective thirtieth day thereafter (Register 82, No. 18).*

2. *Section renumbered from 754.17 to 832.62, filed 2-27-84, effective upon filing pursuant to Government Code Section 11346.2(d) (Register 84, No. 9).*

833. ASBESTOS CLASSIFICATION AND CERTIFICATION LIMITATIONS AND EXAMINATION REQUIREMENT

1. *New section filed 12-30-2014; operative 1-1-2015 pursuant to Government Code section 11343.4(b)(3) (Register 2015, No. 1). For prior history, see Register 86, No. 23.*

834. LIMITATION OF CLASSIFICATION

1. *New section filed 7-17-47 as an emergency (Register 9).*

2. *Amendment filed 4-29-64; effective thirtieth day thereafter (Register 64, No. 9).*

3. *Amendment filed 9-8-77; effective thirtieth day thereafter (Register 77, No. 37).*

4. *Editorial correction (Register 77, No. 52).*

5. *Amendment filed 11-1-83; effective upon filing pursuant to Government Code Section 11346.2(d) (Register 83, No. 45).*

6. *Section renumbered from 760 to 834, filed 2-27-84; effective upon filing pursuant to Government Code Section 11346.2(d) (Register 84, No. 9).*

7. *Editorial correction filed 7-19-84 (Register 84, No. 29).*

8. *Amendment of subsection (b) filed 8-10-99; effective thirtieth day thereafter (Register 99, No. 33).*

840. WRITTEN EXAMINATIONS REQUIRED OF ALL APPLICANTS

1. *Amendment filed 9-8-77; effective thirtieth day thereafter (Register 77, No. 37).*

2. *Editorial correction (Register 77, No. 52).*

3. *Amendment filed 5-6-83; effective thirtieth day thereafter (Register 83, No. 19).*

4. *Section renumbered from 765 to 840, filed 2-27-84; effective upon filing pursuant to Government Code Section 11346.2(d) (Register 84, No. 9).*

5. *Amendment filed 6-6-86; effective thirtieth day thereafter (Register 89, No. 23).*

841. ELIMINATION AND REVISION OF EXAMINATION QUESTIONS

1. *Amendment filed 9-8-77; effective thirtieth day thereafter (Register 77, No. 37).*

2. *Editorial correction (Register 77, No. 52).*

3. *Amendment filed 5-6-83; effective thirtieth day thereafter (Register 83, No. 19).*

4. *Section renumbered from 768 to 841, filed 2-27-84; effective upon filing pursuant to Government Code Section 11346.2(d) (Register 84, No. 9).*

853. RENEWAL APPLICATION FORM

1. *Amendment of subsections (b) and (c) and Note filed 2-9-2021; operative 4-1-2021 (Register 2021, No. 7).*

856. SECURITY IN LIEU OF BOND

1. *Amendment filed 11-23-71; effective thirtieth day thereafter (Register 71, No. 48). For prior history see Register 67, No. 17.*

2. *Amendment filed 1-28-77; effective thirtieth day thereafter (Register 77, No. 5).*

3. *Amendment filed 5-25-83; effective thirtieth day thereafter (Register 83, No. 22).*

4. *Section renumbered from 791 to 856, filed 2-27-84; effective upon filing pursuant to Government Code Section 11346.2(d) (Register 84, No. 9).*

5. *Amendment filed 11-9-95; effective thirtieth day thereafter (Register 95, No. 45).*

858. BLANKET PERFORMANCE AND PAYMENT BOND DEFINED

1. *New section filed 11-22-2011; operative 12-22-2011 (Register 2011, No. 47).*

858.1. BLANKET PERFORMANCE AND PAYMENT BOND REQUIREMENTS

1. *New section filed 11-22-2011; operative 12-22-2011 (Register 2011, No. 47).*

2. *Change without regulatory effect amending subsections (a) and (f) filed 11-10-2021 pursuant to section 100, title 1, California Code of Regulations (Register 2021, No. 46).*

858.2. APPLICATION FOR APPROVAL OF BLANKET PERFORMANCE AND PAYMENT BOND

1. *New section filed 11-22-2011; operative 12-22-2011 (Register 2011, No. 47).*

2. *Change without regulatory effect amending subsections (a)(3), (a)(4) and (b) and amending Note filed 11-10-2021 pursuant to section 100, title 1, California Code of Regulations (Register 2021, No. 46).*

3. Change without regulatory effect amending subsections (a) and (a)(4) filed 9-6-2022 pursuant to section 100, title 1, California Code of Regulations (Register 2022, No. 36).

858.3. MINIMUM STANDARDS FOR BLANKET PERFORMANCE AND PAYMENT BOND APPROVAL—CAUSE FOR DENIAL

1. New section filed 11-22-2011; operative 12-22-2011 (Register 2011, No. 47).

858.4. BLANKET PERFORMANCE AND PAYMENT BOND BIENNIAL CERTIFICATION AND FINANCIAL REPORTING REQUIREMENTS

1. New section filed 11-22-2011; operative 12-22-2011 (Register 2011, No. 47).

858.5. BLANKET PERFORMANCE AND PAYMENT BOND AUDIT AUTHORIZATION AND PROCEDURES

1. New section filed 11-22-2011; operative 12-22-2011 (Register 2011, No. 47).

858.6. AUTHORIZATION AND PROCEDURES FOR ORDERING THE AMOUNT OF BLANKET PERFORMANCE AND PAYMENT BOND TO BE INCREASED

1. New section filed 11-22-2011; operative 12-22-2011 (Register 2011, No. 47).

858.7. MAINTENANCE OF THE BLANKET PERFORMANCE AND PAYMENT BOND

1. New section filed 11-22-2011; operative 12-22-2011 (Register 2011, No. 47).

858.8. RESCISSION OF BLANKET PERFORMANCE AND PAYMENT BOND APPROVAL

1. New section filed 11-22-2011; operative 12-22-2011 (Register 2011, No. 47).

858.9. POSTING OF BLANKET PERFORMANCE AND PAYMENT BOND INFORMATION TO LICENSE RECORDS

1. New section filed 11-22-2011; operative 12-22-2011 (Register 2011, No. 47).

860. PENALTY FOR FAILURE TO COMPLY WITH RULES

1. Amendment filed 5-25-83; effective thirtieth day thereafter (Register 83, No. 22).

2. Section renumbered from 794 to 860, filed 2-27-84; effective upon filing pursuant to Government Code Section 11346.2(d) (Register 84, No. 9).

861. LICENSE NUMBER REQUIRED IN ADVERTISING

1. New section filed 10-20-78; effective thirtieth day thereafter (Register 78, No. 42).

2. Amendment filed 10-21-83; effective thirtieth day thereafter (Register 83, No. 43).

3. Section renumbered from 794.1 to 861, filed 2-27-84; effective upon filing pursuant to Government Code Section 11346.2(d) (Register 84, No. 9).

4. Editorial correction filed 7-19-84 (Register 84, No. 29).

5. Amendment of section heading and section filed 11-30-2009; operative 12-30-2009 (Register 2009, No. 49).

861.5 DEFINITION OF "STRUCTURAL DEFECT"

1. New section filed 08-28-96; effective thirtieth day thereafter (Register 96, No. 35).

863. PUBLIC ACCESS TO INFORMATION

1. *Repealer filed 8-1-62; effective thirtieth day thereafter (Register 62, No. 16).*

2. *New section filed 5-15-80; designated effective July 1, 1980 (Register 80, No. 20).*

3. *Amendment filed 10-24-83; effective thirtieth day thereafter (Register 83, No. 43).*

4. *Section renumbered from 722 to 863, filed 2-27-84; effective upon filing pursuant to Government Code Section 11346.2(d) (Register 84, No. 9).*

5. *Editorial correction filed 7-19-84 (Register 84, No. 29).*

6. *Amendment filed 4-10-92; operative 5-11-92 (Register 92, No. 18).*

864. CONTINUANCE OF LICENSE UNDER SECTION 7068.2

1. *Originally published 12-5-46 (Title 16).*

2. *Amendment filed 5-5-48 as an emergency (Register 12, No. 6).*

3. *Amendment filed 10-14-65; effective thirtieth day thereafter (Register 65, No. 19).*

4. *Amendment filed 5-25-83; effective thirtieth day thereafter (Register 83, No. 22).*

5. *Section renumbered from 796 to 864, filed 2-27-84; effective upon filing pursuant to Government Code Section 11346.2(d) (Register 84, No. 9).*

6. *Change without regulatory effect amending section filed 11-15-2016 pursuant to section 100, title 1, California Code of Regulations (Register 2016, No. 47).*

865. CONTINUANCE OF LICENSE UNDER SECTION 7076

1. *Amendment filed 10-14-68; effective thirtieth day thereafter (Register 68, No. 39). For prior history, see Section 65, No. 19.*

2. *Amendment filed 5-25-83; effective thirtieth day thereafter (Register 83, No. 22).*

3. *Section renumbered from 796.5 to 865, filed 2-27-84; effective upon filing pursuant to Government Code Section 11346.2(d) (Register 84, No. 9).*

4. *Amendment of subsections (a) and (b) filed 6-6-86; effective thirtieth day thereafter (Register 86, No. 23).*

5. *Change without regulatory effect separating second sentence of subsection (a)(3) into new paragraph filed 11-15-2016 pursuant to section 100, title 1, California Code of Regulations (Register 2016, No. 47).*

867. PROCEDURE TO REINSTATE INACTIVE LICENSE

1. *New section filed 8-1-62; designated effective 10-1-62 (Register 62, No. 16).*

2. *Amendment filed 5-25-83; effective thirtieth day thereafter (Register 83, No. 22).*

3. *Section renumbered from 799 to 867, filed 2-27-84; effective upon filing pursuant to Government Code Section 11346.2(d) (Register 84, No. 9).*

4. *Amendment filed 6-6-86; effective thirtieth day thereafter (Register 86, No. 23).*

5. *Change without regulatory effect amending subsection (a) filed 11-15-2016 pursuant to section 100, title 1, California Code of Regulations (Register 2016, No. 47).*

868. CRITERIA TO AID IN DETERMINING IF CRIMES, PROFESSIONAL MISCONDUCT, OR ACTS ARE SUBSTANTIALLY RELATED TO QUALIFICATIONS, FUNCTIONS, OR DUTIES OF A LICENSEE OR REGISTRANT.

1. *Amendment of section heading, section and Note filed 5-31-2006; operative 6-30-2006 (Register 2006, No. 22).*

Section VI

2. *Amendment of section heading, section and Note filed 5-3-2021; operative 5-3-2021 pursuant to Government Code section 11343.4(b)(3) (Register 2021, No. 19). Filing deadline specified in Government Code section 11349.3(a) extended 60 calendar days pursuant to Executive Order N-40-20 and an additional 60 calendar days pursuant to Executive Order N-71-20.868.1.*

868.1 CRITERIA TO AID IN DETERMINING IF FINANCIAL CRIMES ARE DIRECTLY AND ADVERSELY RELATED TO FIDUCIARY QUALIFICATIONS, FUNCTIONS, OR DUTIES OF A LICENSEE OR REGISTRANT FOR THE PURPOSE OF CONSIDERING DENIALS OF APPLICATIONS.

1. *New section filed 5-3-2021; operative 5-3-2021 pursuant to Government Code section 11343.4(b)(3) (Register 2021, No. 19). Filing deadline specified in Government Code section 11349.3(a) extended 60 calendar days pursuant to Executive Order N-40-20 and an additional 60 calendar days pursuant to Executive Order N-71-20.*

869. CRITERIA FOR REHABILITATION

1. *Amendment of section and Note filed 5-31-2006; operative 6-30-2006 (Register 2006, No. 22).*

2. *Amendment of section and Note filed 5-3-2021; operative 5-3-2021 pursuant to Government Code section 11343.4(b)(3) (Register 2021, No. 19). Filing deadline specified in Government Code section 11349.3(a) extended 60 calendar days pursuant to Executive Order N-40-20 and an additional 60 calendar days pursuant to Executive Order N-71-20.*

869.1. APPLICANT DEFINED

1. *New section filed 3-17-2005; operative 4-16-2005 (Register 2005, No. 11).*

2. *Change without regulatory effect amending subsection (c) filed 11-15-2016 pursuant to section 100, title 1, California Code of Regulations (Register 2016, No. 47).*

869.2. EXEMPTIONS

1. *New section filed 3-17-2005; operative 4-16-2005 (Register 2005, No. 11).*

869.3. METHODS FOR SUBMITTING FINGERPRINTS

1. *New section filed 3-17-2005; operative 4-16-2005 (Register 2005, No. 11).*

869.4. SUBSEQUENT ARREST HISTORY

1. *New section filed 3-17-2005; operative 4-16-2005 (Register 2005, No. 11).*

869.9. CRITERIA TO AID IN DETERMINING EARLIEST DATE A DENIED APPLICANT MAY REAPPLY FOR LICENSURE

1. *New section filed 5-31-2006; operative 6-30-2006 (Register 2006, No. 22).*

2. *Amendment of section heading, section and Note filed 5-3-2021; operative 5-3-2021 pursuant to Government Code section 11343.4(b)(3) (Register 2021, No. 19). Filing deadline specified in Government Code section 11349.3(a) extended 60 calendar days pursuant to Executive Order N-40-20 and an additional 60 calendar days pursuant to Executive Order N-71-20.*

870. FACTORS TO APPLY IN DETERMINING EARLIEST DATE A REVOKED LICENSEE MAY APPLY FOR LICENSURE

1. *New section filed 5-11-89; operative 6-10-89 (Register 89, No. 19).*

2. *Change without regulatory effect amending subsection (b) filed 11-15-2016 pursuant to section 100, title 1, California Code of Regulations (Register 2016, No. 47).*

871. DISCIPLINARY GUIDELINES

1. *New section filed 5-29-97; operative 5-29-97 pursuant to Government Code 11343.4(d) (Register 97, No. 22).*

872. DISCLOSURE OF GENERAL LIABILITY INSURANCE

1. *New section filed 11-28-2001; operative 2-26-2002 (Register 2001, No. 48).*

880. ORDER OF CORRECTION—PRACTICAL FEASIBILITY

1. *New Article 8 (Sections 803-806.1) filed 4-7-81; effective thirtieth day thereafter (Register 81, No. 15).*

2. *Section renumbered from 803 to 880, filed 2-27-84; effective upon filing pursuant to Government Code Section 11346.2(d) (Register 84, No. 9).*

881. ORDER OF CORRECTION—ALTERNATIVE COMPLIANCE

1. *New section filed 4-7-81; effective thirtieth day thereafter (Register 81, No. 15).*

2. *Section renumbered from 803.1 to 881, filed 2-27-84; effective upon filing pursuant to Government Code Section 11346.2(d) (Register 84, No. 9).*

882. ORDER OF CORRECTION—TIME REQUIRED TO CORRECT

1. *New section filed 4-7-81; effective thirtieth day thereafter (Register 81, No. 15).*

2. *Section renumbered from 804 to 882, filed 2-27-84; effective upon filing pursuant to Government Code Section 11346.2(d) (Register 84, No. 9).*

883. ORDER OF CORRECTION—EXTENSION OF TIME TO CORRECT

1. *New section filed 4-7-81; effective thirtieth day thereafter (Register 81, No. 15).*

2. *Section renumbered from 804.1 to 883, filed 2-27-84; effective upon filing pursuant to Government Code Section 11346.2(d) (Register 84, No. 9).*

3. *Editorial correction (Register 2017, No. 8).*

884. RECOMMENDED ASSESSMENTS OF CIVIL PENALTIES

1. *New section filed 4-7-81; effective thirtieth day thereafter (Register 81, No. 15).*

2. *Section renumbered from 805 to 884, filed 2-27-84; effective upon filing pursuant to Government Code Section 11346.2(d) (Register 84, No. 9).*

3. *Amendment filed 5-23-94; operative 6-22-94 (Register 94, No. 21).*

4. *Amendment of section and Note filed 1-31-2007; operative 3-2-2007 (Register 2007, No. 5).*

5. *Change without regulatory effect amending section and Note filed 11-10-2021 pursuant to section 100, title 1, California Code of Regulations; operative 1-1-2022 (Register 2021, No. 46).*

885. APPEAL OF CITATION

1. *New Section filed 4-7-81; effective thirtieth day thereafter (Register 81, No. 15).*

2. *Section renumbered from 806 to 885, filed 2-27-84; effective upon filing pursuant to Government Code Section 11346.2(d) (Register 84, No. 9).*

886. SERVICE OF CITATION

1. *New Section filed 4-7-81; effective thirtieth day thereafter (Register 81, No. 15).*

Section VI

2. *Section renumbered from 806.1 to 886, filed 2-27-84; effective upon filing pursuant to Government Code Section 11346.2(d) (Register 84, No. 9).*

887. CRITERIA TO EVALUATE THE GRAVITY OF A VIOLATION OF BUSINESS AND PROFESSIONS CODE SECTION 7028.7

1. *New section filed 5-13-82; effective thirtieth day thereafter (Register 82, No. 20).*
2. *Section renumbered from 807 to 887, filed 2-27-84; effective upon filing pursuant to Government Code Section 11346.2(d) (Register 84, No. 9).*

890. MINIMUM QUALIFICATION STANDARDS FOR ARBITRATORS

1. *New article 9 (section 890) and section filed 10-31-2001; operative 11-30-2001 (Register 2001, No. 44).*

HISTORY NOTES FOR REPEALED BOARD RULES AND REGULATIONS

701. PURPOSE OF LAW—PROTECTION, HEALTH AND SAFETY OF PUBLIC

1. *Repealer filed 5-25-83; effective thirtieth day thereafter (Register 83, No. 22).*

702. FEES

1. *New Article 1.5 (Section 702) filed 12-21-81; designated effective 2-1-82 (Register 81, No. 52).*
2. *Repealer filed 3-15-83; effective thirtieth day thereafter (Register 83, No. 12).*

707. ALL MEMBERS OF APPLICANT TO FURNISH INFORMATION

1. *Repealer filed 8-25-83; effective upon filing pursuant to Government Code Section 11346.2(d) (Register 83, No. 35).*

708. SIGNING AND VERIFICATION OF APPLICATION

1. *Amendment filed 7-19-74; effective thirtieth day thereafter (Register 74, No. 29).*
2. *Repealer filed 8-25-83; effective upon filing pursuant to Government Code Section 11346.2(d) (Register 83, No. 35).*

709. FURNISHING REFERENCES

1. *Repealer filed 3-3-53; effective thirtieth day thereafter (Register 53, No. 4).*

710. POWER OF REGISTRAR TO DENY INSUFFICIENT APPLICATIONS

1. *Amendment filed 9-8-77; effective thirtieth day thereafter (Register 77, No. 37).*
2. *Repealer filed 8-25-83; effective upon filing pursuant to Government Code Section 11346.2(d) (Register 83, No. 35).*

711.1. ABANDONMENT OF APPLICATION

1. *New section filed 1-22-76; effective thirtieth day thereafter (Register 76, No. 4).*
2. *Repealer filed 8-25-83; effective upon filing pursuant to Government Code Section 11346.2(d) (Register 83, No. 35).*

712. POWER OF REGISTRAR TO WAIVE FORMAL REQUIREMENTS

1. *Amendment filed 9-8-77; effective thirtieth day thereafter (Register 77, No. 37).*
2. *Repealer filed 8-25-83; effective upon filing pursuant to Government Code Section 11346.2(d) (Register 83, No. 35).*

713. TENDER OF FEE

1. Originally published 12-5-46 (Title 16).

2. Amendment filed 9-18-47 as an emergency (Register 9).

3. Repealer filed 1-23-50 (Register 19, No. 2).

716. POWER IN REGISTRAR TO WAIVE POSTING

1. Originally published 12-5-46 (Title 16).

2. Amendment filed 9-18-47 as an emergency (Register 9).

3. Repealer filed 1-27-71; effective thirtieth day thereafter (Register 71, No. 5).

719. BOND REQUIREMENT OF APPLICANTS

1. Repealer filed 8-1-62; effective thirtieth day thereafter (Register 62, No. 16).

720. POSTING OF BOND AS CONDITION OF REINSTATEMENT

1. Repealer filed 8-1-62; effective thirtieth day thereafter (Register 62, No. 16).

721. REGISTRAR MAY WAIVE BOND

1. Repealer filed 8-1-62; effective thirtieth day thereafter (Register 62, No. 16).

723. POLICY OF THE BOARD REGARDING EXPERIENCE

1. Amendment filed 9-8-77; effective thirtieth day thereafter (Register 77, No. 37).

2. Editorial correction (Register 77, No. 52).

3. Repealer filed 12-22-82; effective thirtieth day thereafter (Register 82, No. 52).

726. CREDIT FOR ADDITIONAL EXPERIENCE

1. Originally published 12-5-48 (Title 16).

2. Amendment filed 3-12-47 (Register 8).

3. Repealer filed 2-28-80; effective thirtieth day thereafter (Register 80, No. 9).

731. ALL CONTRACTORS TO BE CLASSIFIED

1. Repealer filed 12-22-82; effective thirtieth day thereafter (Register 82, No. 52).

753. CLASS C-22—STRUCTURAL PEST CONTROL CONTRACTOR

1. Repealer filed 10-18-55; effective thirtieth day thereafter (Register 55, No. 16).

754. CLASS C-56—WATERPROOFING, WEATHERPROOFING AND DAMP-PROOFING CONTRACTORS

1. Originally published 12-5-46 (Title 16).

2. Repealer filed 9-18-47 as an emergency; effective upon filing (Register 9).

755. PRIMARY AND SUPPLEMENTAL CLASSIFICATIONS

1. Amendment filed 9-8-77; effective thirtieth day thereafter (Register 77, No. 37).

2. Editorial correction (Register 77, No. 52).

3. Repealer filed 12-22-82; effective thirtieth day thereafter (Register 82, No. 52).

756. ASSIGNMENT OF PRIMARY CLASSIFICATION

1. Amendment filed 2-7-75; effective thirtieth day thereafter (Register 75, No. 6).

2. Amendment filed 9-8-77; effective thirtieth day thereafter (Register 77, No. 37).

3. Repealer filed 12-22-82; effective thirtieth day thereafter (Register 82, No. 52).

756.1. ASSIGNMENT OF SUPPLEMENTAL SOLAR CLASSIFICATION

1. *New section filed 10-20-78; effective thirtieth day thereafter (Register 78, No. 42).*
2. *Repealer filed 3-15-83; effective thirtieth day thereafter (Register 83, No. 12).*

756.2. QUALIFICATION FOR SUPPLEMENTAL SOLAR CLASSIFICATION

1. *New section filed 10-20-78; effective thirtieth day thereafter (Register 78, No. 42).*
2. *Repealer filed 4-28-82; effective thirtieth day thereafter (Register 82, No. 18).*

756.3. SOLAR PROJECT REPORTING REQUIREMENTS

1. *New section filed 10-20-78; effective thirtieth day thereafter (Register 78, No. 42).*
2. *Repealer filed 4-28-82; effective thirtieth day thereafter (Register 82, No. 18).*

756.4. EFFECTIVE DATE OF REGULATION

1. *New section filed 10-20-78; effective thirtieth day thereafter (Register 78, No. 42).*
2. *Repealer filed 4-28-82; effective thirtieth day thereafter (Register 82, No. 18).*

757. NO "SUPPLEMENTAL" CLASSIFICATION WHERE NO SPECIAL EXAMINATION

1. *Originally published 12-5-46 (Title 16).*
2. *Repealer filed 9-18-47 as an emergency; effective upon filing (Register 9).*

759. WAIVER OF RECLASSIFICATION EXAMINATIONS

1. *Amendment filed 9-8-77; effective thirtieth day thereafter (Register 77, No. 37).*
2. *Repealer filed 2-28-80; effective thirtieth day thereafter (Register 80, No. 9).*

764. POLICY OF THE BOARD REGARDING EXAMINATIONS

1. *Amendment filed 9-8-77; effective thirtieth day thereafter (Register 77, No. 37).*
2. *Editorial correction (Register 77, No. 52).*
3. *Repealer filed 12-22-82; effective thirtieth day thereafter (Register 82, No. 52).*

766. TYPES OF EXAMINATIONS

1. *Repealer filed 5-6-83; effective thirtieth day thereafter (Register 83, No. 19).*

767. "SPECIFIC" AND "BLANKET" EXAMINATIONS APPROVED

1. *Originally published 12-5-46 (Title 16).*
2. *Repealer filed 9-18-47 as an emergency; effective upon filing (Register 9).*

769. REGISTRAR TO REQUIRE EXAMINATION OF APPLICANTS

1. *Repealer filed 12-22-82; effective thirtieth day thereafter (Register 82, No. 52).*

770. REGISTRAR MAY CHANGE WRITTEN EXAMINATIONS

1. *Amendment filed 9-8-77; effective thirtieth day thereafter (Register 77, No. 37).*
2. *Repealer filed 5-6-83; effective thirtieth day thereafter (Register 83, No. 19).*

772. GRADING OF EXAMINATIONS

1. *Originally published 12-5-46 (Title 16).*
2. *Amendment filed 3-17-47 (Register 8).*
3. *Amendment filed 2-28-80; effective thirtieth day thereafter (Register 80, No. 9).*

4. *Repealer filed 4-15-83; effective upon filing pursuant to Government Code Section 11346.2(d) (Register 83, No. 16).*

773. REGISTRAR MAY MAKE RULES ON EXAMINATION PROCEDURE

1. *Amendment filed 9-8-77; effective thirtieth day thereafter (Register 77, No. 37).*
2. *Editorial correction (Register 77, No. 52).*
3. *Repealer filed 5-6-83; effective thirtieth day thereafter (Register 83, No. 19).*

774. NO EXAMINATION REQUIRED

1. *Sections 774 and 775 originally published 12-5-46 (Title 16).*
2. *Amendments to same filed 10-19-48 as emergencies (Register 14, No. 3).*
3. *Amendment filed 8-6-64; effective thirtieth day thereafter (Register 64, No. 17).*
4. *Repealer filed 8-25-83; effective upon filing pursuant to Government Code Section 11346.2(d) (Register 83, No. 35).*

817. OPERATING CAPITAL DEFINED

1. *New section filed 1-24-80; effective thirtieth day thereafter (Register 80, No. 4).*
2. *Amendment filed 8-25-83; effective upon filing pursuant to Government Code Section 11346.2(d) (Register 83, No. 35).*
3. *Section renumbered from 707.1 to 817, filed 2-27-84; effective upon filing pursuant to Government Code Section 11346.2(d) (Register 84, No. 9).*
4. *Change without regulatory effect repealing section filed 11-15-2016 pursuant to section 100, title 1, California Code of Regulations (Register 2016, No. 47).*

818. INSUFFICIENT OR INCOMPLETE APPLICATIONS—REJECTION

1. *Amendment filed 2-7-75; effective thirtieth day thereafter (Register 75, No. 6).*
2. *Amendment filed 8-25-83; effective upon filing pursuant to Government Code Section 11346.2(d) (Register 83, No. 35).*
3. *Section renumbered from 711 to 818, filed 2-27-84; effective upon filing pursuant to Government Code Section 11346.2(d) (Register 84, No. 9).*
4. *Repealer filed 11-9-95; effective thirtieth day thereafter (Register 95, No. 45).*

820. POSTING OF NAMES OF APPLICANTS

1. *Originally published 12-5-46 (Title 16).*
2. *Amendment filed 7-31-50 as a procedural rule; effective upon filing (Register 21, No. 4).*
3. *Amendment filed 1-27-71; effective thirtieth day thereafter (Register 71, No. 5).*
4. *Amendment filed 2-7-75; effective thirtieth day thereafter (Register 75, No. 6).*
5. *Amendment filed 8-25-83; effective upon filing pursuant to Government Code Section 11346.2(d) (Register 83, No. 35).*
6. *Section renumbered from 715 to 820, filed 2-27-84; effective upon filing pursuant to Government Code Section 11346.2(d) (Register 84, No. 9).*
7. *Repealer filed 11-9-95; effective thirtieth day thereafter (Register 95, No.45).*

821. JOINT VENTURE LICENSE DEFINED

1. *Originally published 12-5-46 (Title 16).*
2. *Amendment filed 10-18-49 as an emergency (Register 18, No. 3).*
3. *Amendment filed 12-16-63; effective thirtieth day thereafter (Register 63, No. 25).*

4. *Amendment filed 8-25-83; effective upon filing pursuant to Government Code Section 11346.2(d) (Register 83, No. 35).*

5. *Section renumbered from 717 to 821, filed 2-27-84; effective upon filing pursuant to Government Code Section 11346.2(d) (Register 84, No. 9).*

6. *Repealer filed 11-9-95; effective thirtieth day thereafter (Register 95, No.45).*

822. LICENSING REQUIREMENTS FOR JOINT VENTURE LICENSE

1. *Amendment filed 9-8-77; effective thirtieth day thereafter (Register 77, No. 37). For prior history, see Register 71, No. 5.*

2. *Amendment filed 8-25-83; effective upon filing pursuant to Government Code Section 11346.2(d) (Register 83, No. 35).*

3. *Section renumbered from 718 to 822, filed 2-27-84; effective upon filing pursuant to Government Code Section 11346.2(d) (Register 84, No. 9).*

4. *Repealer filed 11-9-95; effective thirtieth day thereafter (Register 95, No.45).*

823. DEFINITIONS: BONA FIDE EMPLOYEE; DIRECT SUPERVISION AND CONTROL

1. *Editorial correction filed 7-19-84 (Register 84, No. 29).*

2. *Change without regulatory effect repealing section filed 6-2-2022 pursuant to section 100, title 1, California Code of Regulations (Register 2022, No. 22).*

829. CREDIT FOR EXPERIENCE

1. *New section filed 5-30-90; operative 6-29-90 (Register 90, No. 29).*

2. *Repealer filed 8-10-2006; operative 9-9-2006 (Register 2006, No. 32).*

832.06. CLASS C-6—CABINET AND MILLWORK CONTRACTORS

1. *Amendment filed 8-25-83; effective upon filing pursuant to Government Code Section 11346.2(d) (Register 83, No. 35).*

2. *Section renumbered from 744 to 832.06, filed 2-27-84; effective upon filing pursuant to Government Code Section 11346.2(d) (Register 84, No. 9).*

3. *Repealer filed 12-18-97; effective 01-01-98 (Register 97, No.172).*

832.14. CLASS C-14—METAL ROOFING CONTRACTOR

1. *New section filed 10-22-86; effective thirtieth day thereafter (Register 86, No. 43).*

2. *Repealer and new section filed 6-22-98; operative 7-1-98 pursuant to Government Code section 11343.4(d) (Register 98, No. 26).*

3. *Change without regulatory effect repealing section filed 8-7-2013 pursuant to section 100, title 1, California Code of Regulations (Register 2013, No. 32).*

832.26. CLASS C-26—LATHING CONTRACTORS

1. *Amendment filed 9-23-83; effective upon filing pursuant to Government Code Section 11346.2(d) (Register 83, No. 39).*

2. *Section renumbered from 743 to 832.26, filed 2-27-84; effective upon filing pursuant to Government Code Section 11346.2(d) (Register 84, No. 9).*

3. *Repealer filed 12-18-97; effective 01-01-98 (Register 97, No.172).*

833. ADDITIONAL CLASSIFICATIONS

1. *Sections 758 and 759 originally published 12-5-46 (Title 16).*

2. *Amendments to same filed 10-19-48 as emergencies (Register 14, No. 3).*

3. *Amendment filed 9-8-77; effective thirtieth day thereafter (Register 77, No. 37).*

4. *Amendment filed 8-19-83; effective thirtieth day thereafter (Register 83, No. 35).*

5. *Section renumbered from 758 to 833, filed 2-27-84; effective upon filing pursuant to Government Code Section 11346.2(d) (Register 84, No. 9).*

6. *Repealer filed 6-6-86; effective thirtieth day thereafter (Register 86, No. 23).*

842. APPLICANTS MAY BE RE-EXAMINED

1. *Amendment filed 7-19-66; effective thirtieth day thereafter (Register 66, No. 23).*

2. *Amendment filed 9-8-77; effective thirtieth day thereafter (Register 77, No. 37).*

3. *Amendment filed 5-6-83; effective thirtieth day thereafter (Register 83, No. 19).*

4. *Section renumbered from 771 to 842, filed 2-27-84; effective upon filing pursuant to Government Code Section 11346.2(d) (Register 84, No. 9).*

5. *Amendment filed 6-6-86; effective thirtieth day thereafter (Register 86, No. 23).*

6. *Repealer filed 11-30-2009; operative 12-30-2009 (Register 2009, No. 49).*

843. WAIVER OF EXAMINATION

1. *New section filed 7-2-81; effective thirtieth day thereafter (Register 81, No. 27). For history of former section, see Registers 80, No. 9; 77, No. 52; 77, No. 37; 62, No. 1 and 57, No. 6.*

2. *Section renumbered from 775 to 843, filed 2-27-84; effective upon filing pursuant to Government Code Section 11346.2(d) (Register 84, No. 9).*

3. *Repealer filed 6-6-86; effective thirtieth day thereafter (Register 86, No. 23).*

844. FAILURE TO APPEAR FOR EXAMINATION

1. *Originally filed 12-5-46 (Title 16).*

2. *Amendment filed 4-30-47 (Register 8).*

3. *Amendment filed 9-8-77; effective thirtieth day thereafter (Register 77, No. 37).*

4. *Amendment filed 8-25-83; effective upon filing pursuant to Government Code Section 11346.2(d) (Register 83, No. 35).*

5. *Section renumbered from 776 to 844, filed 2-27-84; effective upon filing pursuant to Government Code Section 11346.2(d) (Register 84, No. 9).*

6. *Repealer filed 6-6-86; effective thirtieth day thereafter (Register 86, No. 23).*

852. RENEWAL OF LICENSES

1. *New section filed 6-22-78; effective thirtieth day thereafter (Register 78, No. 25). For history of prior section 780, see Register 66, No. 23.*

2. *Amendment filed 5-25-83; effective thirtieth day thereafter (Register 83, No. 22).*

3. *Section renumbered from 780 to 852, filed 2-27-84; effective upon filing pursuant to Government Code Section 11346.2(d) (Register 84, No. 9).*

4. *Change without regulatory effect repealing section filed 11-9-95 pursuant to section 100, title 1, California Code of Regulations (Register 95, No. 45).*

854. RENEWAL FEE AND REACTIVATION CREDIT

1. *New section filed 6-3-97; operative 6-3-97 pursuant to Government Code section 11343.4(d) (Register 97, No. 23).*

2. *Change without regulatory effect repealing section filed 8-7-2013 pursuant to section 100, title 1, California Code of Regulations (Register 2013, No. 32).*

862. NOTICE TO OWNER

1. *New section filed 6-5-80; effective thirtieth day thereafter (Register 80, No. 23).*

2. *Amendment filed 3-26-82; effective thirtieth day thereafter (Register 82, No. 13).*

3. *Section renumbered from 794.2 to 862, filed 2-27-84; effective upon filing pursuant to Government Code Section 11346.2(d) (Register 84, No. 9).*

4. *Amendment filed 3-6-84; effective upon filing pursuant to Government Code Section 11346.2(d) (Register 84, No. 9).*

5. *Change without regulatory effect repealing section filed 11-9-95 pursuant to section 100, title 1, California Code of Regulations (Register 95, No. 45).*

866. PROCEDURE TO INACTIVATE LICENSE

1. *New section filed 8-1-62; designated effective 10-1-62 (Register 62, No. 16).*

2. *Amendment filed 5-25-83; effective thirtieth day thereafter (Register 83, No. 22).*

3. *Section renumbered from 798 to 866, filed 2-27-84; effective upon filing pursuant to Government Code Section 11346.2(d) (Register 84, No. 9).*

4. *Repealer filed 6-6-86; effective thirtieth day thereafter (Register 86, No. 23).*

869.5. INQUIRY INTO CRIMINAL CONVICTIONS

1. *New section filed 3-17-2005; operative 4-16-2005 (Register 2005, No. 11).*

2. *Change without regulatory effect amending section filed 11-15-2016 pursuant to section 100, title 1, California Code of Regulations (Register 2016, No. 47).*

3. *Repealer filed 5-3-2021; operative 5-3-2021 pursuant to Government Code section 11343.4(b)(3) (Register 2021, No. 19). Filing deadline specified in Government Code section 11349.3(a) extended 60 calendar days pursuant to Executive Order N-40-20 and an additional 60 calendar days pursuant to Executive Order N-71-20.*

872.1. CHECKLIST FOR HOMEOWNERS

1. *New section filed 11-28-2001; operative 2-26-2002 (Register 2001, No. 48).*

2. *Change without regulatory effect amending subsections (b) and (c) and Note filed 11-22-2021 pursuant to section 100, title 1, California Code of Regulations (Register 2021, No. 48)*

APPENDIX

Extracts from Laws Related to
CSLB Laws & Regulations

CALIFORNIA CONSTITUTION

Article XIV

LABOR RELATIONS

§ 3. Mechanics liens

Mechanics, persons furnishing materials, artisans, and laborers of every class, shall have a lien upon the property upon which they have bestowed labor or furnished material for the value of such labor done and material furnished; and the Legislature shall provide, by law, for the speedy and efficient enforcement of such liens.

Adopted June 8, 1976.

BUSINESS AND PROFESSIONS CODE

DIVISION 3

PROFESSIONS AND VOCATIONS GENERALLY

Chapter 3

Architecture

Article 3

Application of Chapter

§ 5537. When plans and drawings by uncertificated persons permitted

(a) This chapter does not prohibit any person from preparing plans, drawings, or specifications for any of the following:

(1) Single–family dwellings of woodframe construction not more than two stories and basement in height.

(2) Multiple dwellings containing no more than four dwelling units of woodframe construction not more than two stories and basement in height. However, this paragraph shall not be construed as allowing an unlicensed person to design multiple clusters of up to four dwelling units each to form apartment or condominium complexes where the total exceeds four units on any lawfully divided lot.

(3) Garages or other structures appurtenant to buildings described under subdivision (a), of woodframe construction not more than two stories and basement in height.

(4) Agricultural and ranch buildings of woodframe construction, unless the building official having jurisdiction deems that an undue risk to the public health, safety, or welfare is involved.

(b) If any portion of any structure exempted by this section deviates from substantial compliance with conventional framing requirements for woodframe construction found in the most recent edition of Title 24 of the California Code of Regulations or tables of limitation for woodframe construction, as defined by the applicable building code duly adopted by the local jurisdiction or the state, the building official having jurisdiction shall require the preparation of plans, drawings, specifications, or calculations for that portion by, or under the responsible control of, a licensed architect or registered engineer. The documents for that portion shall bear the stamp and signature of the licensee who is responsible for their preparation. Substantial compliance for purposes of this section is not intended to restrict the ability of the building officials to approve plans pursuant to existing law and is only intended to clarify the intent of Chapter 405 of the Statutes of 1985.

Added Stats 1939 ch 33 § 1. Amended Stats 1963 ch 2133 § 17; Stats 1984 ch 1405 § 6; Stats 1985 ch 1327 § 4.5; Stats 1986 ch 204 § 1; Stats 1987 ch 589 § 2; Stats 1990 ch 94 § 5 (AB 1005); Stats 1996 ch 184 § 8 (SB 1607).

§ 5537.2. Application of chapter to contractors

This chapter shall not be construed as authorizing a licensed contractor to perform design services beyond those described in Section 5537 or in Chapter 9 (commencing with Section 7000), unless those services are performed by or under the direct supervision of a person licensed to practice architecture under this chapter, or a professional or civil engineer licensed pursuant to Chapter 7 (commencing with Section 6700) of Division 3, insofar as the professional or civil engineer practices the profession for which he or she is registered under that chapter.

However, this section does not prohibit a licensed contractor from performing any of the services permitted by Chapter 9 (commencing with Section 7000) of Division 3 within the classification for which the license is issued. Those services may include the preparation of shop and field drawings for work which he or she has contracted or offered to perform, and designing systems and facilities which are necessary to the completion of contracting services which he or she has contracted or offered to perform.

However, a licensed contractor may not use the title "architect," unless he or she holds a license as required in this chapter.

Added Stats 1963 ch 2133 § 19. Amended Stats 1984 ch 1405 § 7; Stats 1985 ch 1327 § 6.

Chapter 3.5

Landscape Architecture

Article 3

Application of Chapter

§ 5641.4. Licensed landscape contractor exempt; Title

A landscape contractor licensed under the statutes of this state, insofar as he or she works within the classification for which the license is issued, may design systems and facilities for work to be performed and supervised by that landscape contractor and is exempt from the provisions of this chapter, except that a landscape contractor may not use the title "landscape architect" unless he or she holds a license as required under this chapter.

Added Stats 2004 ch 691 § 16 (SB 1549). Amended Stats 2005 ch 48 § 1 (SB 1113), effective July 18, 2005.

Chapter 7

Professional Engineers

Article 3

Application of Chapter

§ 6737.3. Exemption of contractors

A contractor licensed under Chapter 9 (commencing with Section 7000) of Division 3 is exempt from the provisions of this chapter relating to the practice of electrical or mechanical engineering so long as the services he or she holds himself or herself out as able to perform or does perform, which services are subject to the provisions of this chapter, are performed by, or under the responsible charge of a registered electrical or mechanical engineer insofar as the electrical or mechanical engineer practices the branch of engineering for which he or she is registered.

This section shall not prohibit a licensed contractor, while engaged in the business of contracting for the installation of electrical or mechanical systems or facilities, from designing those systems or facilities in accordance with applicable construction codes and standards for work to be performed and supervised by that contractor within the classification for which his or her license is issued, or from preparing electrical or mechanical shop or field drawings for work which he or she has contracted to perform. Nothing in this section is intended to imply that a licensed contractor may design work which is to be installed by another person.

Added Stats 1967 ch 1463 § 10. Amended Stats 1994 ch 26 § 201 (AB 1807), effective March 30, 1994; Stats 2003 ch 607 § 28 (SB 1077).

Chapter 11.6

Alarm Companies

Article 1

General Provisions

§ 7590.1. Definitions

The following terms as used in this chapter have the meaning expressed in this article:

(a) (1) "Advertisement" means:

(A) Any written or printed communication for the purpose of soliciting, describing, or promoting the licensed business of the licensee, including a brochure, letter, pamphlet, newspaper, periodical, publication, or other writing.

(B) A directory listing caused or permitted by the licensee which indicates their licensed activity.

(C) A radio, television, or similar airwave transmission that solicits or promotes the licensed business of the licensee.

(2) "Advertisement" does not include any of the following:

(A) Any printing or writing used on buildings, vehicles, uniforms, badges, or other property where the purpose of the printing or writing is identification.

(B) Any printing or writing on communications, memoranda, or any other writings used in the ordinary course of business where the sole purpose of the writing is other than the solicitation or promotion of business.

(C) Any printing or writing on novelty objects used in the promotion of the licensee's business where the printing of the information required by this chapter would be impractical due to the available area or surface.

(b) "Alarm agent" means a person employed by an alarm company operator whose duties, being physically conducted within the state, include selling on premises, altering, installing, maintaining, moving, repairing, replacing, servicing, responding, or monitoring an alarm system, and those ancillary devices connected to and controlled by the alarm system, including person employed by an alarm company to perform any of the duties described in this subdivision or any person in training for any of the duties described in this subdivision.

(c) (1) "Alarm system" means an assembly of equipment and devices arranged to detect a hazard or signal the presence of an off-normal situation.

(2) "Alarm system" does not include a fire protection system, as defined in the California Fire Code.

(d) "Branch office" means any location, other than the principal place of business of the licensee, which is licensed as set forth in Article 11 (commencing with Section 7599.20).

(e) "Branch office manager" means an individual designated by the qualified manager to manage the licensee's branch office and who has met the requirements as set forth in Article 11 (commencing with Section 7599.20).

(f) "Bureau" means the Bureau of Security and Investigative Services.

(g) "Chief" means the Chief of the Bureau of Security and Investigative Services.

(h) "Deadly weapon" means and includes any instrument or weapon of the kind commonly known as a blackjack, slungshot, billy, sandclub, sandbag, or metal knuckles; any dirk, dagger, pistol, revolver, or any other firearm; any knife having a blade longer than five inches; any razor with an unguarded blade; or any metal pipe or bar used or intended to be used as a club.

(i) "Department" means the Department of Consumer Affairs.

(j) "Director" means the Director of Consumer Affairs.

(k) "Employee" means an individual who works for an employer, is listed on the employer's payroll records, and is under the employer's direction and control.

(l) "Employer" means a person who employs an individual for wages or salary, lists the individual on the employer's payroll records, and withholds all legally required deductions and contributions.

(m) "Employer-employee relationship" means an individual who works for another and where the individual's name appears on the payroll records of the employer.

Appendix

(n) "Firearm permit" means and includes "firearms permit," "firearms qualification card," "firearms qualification," and "firearms qualification permit."

(o) "Firearms permit" means a permit issued by the bureau, pursuant to Article 6 (commencing with Section 7596), to a licensee, a qualified manager, or an alarm agent, to carry an exposed firearm while on duty.

(p) "Licensee" means a business entity, whether an individual, partnership, limited liability company, or corporation licensed under this chapter.

(q) "Manager" means an individual designated under an operating agreement of a manager-managed limited liability company who is responsible for performing the management functions for the limited liability company specified in subdivision (c) of Section 17704.07 of the Corporations Code.

(r) "Member" means an individual who is a member of a limited liability company as defined in subdivision (p) of Section 17701.02 of the Corporations Code.

(s) "Person" means any individual, firm, company, association, organization, partnership, limited liability company, or corporation.

(t) "Qualified manager" means an individual who is in active control, management, and direction of the licensee's business, and who is in possession of a current and valid qualified manager's certificate pursuant to this chapter.

(u) "Registrant" means any person registered or who has applied for registration under this chapter.

(v) "Residential sales agreement" means and includes an agreement between an alarm company operator and an owner or tenant for the purchase of an alarm system to be utilized in the personal residence of the owner or tenant.

Added Stats 1982 ch 1210 § 12. Amended Stats 1986 ch 1168 § 1; Stats 1989 ch 1104 § 32; Stats 1993 ch 1263 § 12 (AB 936); Stats 1994 ch 1010 § 13 (SB 2053); Stats 2012 ch 291 § 2 (SB 1077), effective January 1, 2013, repealed January 1, 2016; Stats 2015 ch 140 § 1 (SB 177), effective January 1, 2016, repealed January 1, 2019. Amended Stats 2017 ch 573 § 37 (SB 800), effective January 1, 2018, repealed January 1, 2019. Stats 2018 ch 406 § 5 (SB 904), effective January 1, 2019; Stats 2021 ch 376 § 19 (AB 830), effective January 1, 2022.

Chapter 14

Structural Pest Control Operators

Article 1

General Provisions

§ 8513. Mechanics lien; Notice to owner; Release

(a) The board shall prescribe a form entitled "Notice to Owner" that shall describe; in nontechnical language and in a clear and coherent manner using words with common and everyday meaning, the pertinent provisions of this state's mechanics lien laws and the rights and responsibilities of an owner of property and a registered pest control company thereunder. Each company registered under this chapter, prior to entering into a contract with an owner for work for which a company registration is required, shall give a copy of this "Notice to Owner" to the owner, his or her agent, or the payer.

(b) No company that is required to be registered under this chapter shall require or request a waiver of lien rights from any subcontractor, employee, or supplier.

(c) Each company registered under this chapter that acts as a subcontractor for another company registered under this chapter shall, within 20 days of commencement of any work for which a company registration is required, give the preliminary notice in accordance with Chapter 2 (commencing with Section 8200) of Title 2 of Part 6 of Division 4 of the Civil Code, to the owner, his or her agent, or the payer.

(d) Each company registered under this chapter that acts as a prime contractor for work for which a company registration is required shall, prior to accepting payment for the work, furnish to the owner, his or her agent, or the payer a full and unconditional release from any claim of mechanics lien by any subcontractor entitled to enforce a mechanics lien pursuant to Section 8410 of the Civil Code.

(e) Each company registered under this chapter that subcontracts to another company registered under this chapter work for which a company registration is required shall furnish to the subcontractor the name of the owner, his or her agent, or the payer.

(f) A violation of the provisions of this section is a ground for disciplinary action.

Added Stats 1982 ch 770 § 1. Amended Stats 1985 ch 1348 § 18, operative January 1, 1987; Stats 1994 ch 844 § 8 (SB 2070); Stats 2001 ch 306 § 12 (AB 446); Stats 2010 ch 697 § 9 (SB 189), effective January 1, 2011, operative July 1, 2012; Stats 2011 ch 44 § 4 (SB 190), effective January 1, 2012, operative July 1, 2012; Stats 2015 ch 430 § 34 (AB 181), effective January 1, 2016.

Appendix

Article 3

Application of the Chapter

§ 8556. Removal and replacement of damaged areas; Application of wood preservative; Contracting for performance of soil treatment pest control work

(a) Licensed contractors acting in their capacity as such, may remove and replace any structure or portions of a structure damaged by wood destroying pests or organisms if that work is incidental to other work being performed on the structure involved or if that work has been identified by a structural pest control inspection report. Licensed contractors acting in their capacity as such may apply wood preservatives directly to end cuts and drill holes of pressure treated wood, and to foundation wood as required by building codes, as well as to fencing and decking, by brush, dip, or spray method and need not obtain a license under this chapter for performance of that work, provided a disclosure in the following form is submitted to the customer in writing: "The application of a wood preservative is intended to prevent the establishment and flourishing of organisms which can deteriorate wood. If you suspect pest infestation or infection, contact a registered structural pest control company prior to the application of a wood preservative."

These exemptions do not authorize the performance of any other acts defined in Section 8505.

(b) A licensed contractor may contract for the performance of any soil treatment pest control work to eliminate, exterminate, control, or prevent infestations or infections of pests or organisms in the ground beneath or adjacent to any existing building or structure or in or upon any site upon which any building or structure is to be constructed, but the actual performance of any such work must be done by a registered structural pest control company.

Added Stats 1941 ch 1163 § 1. Amended Stats 1953 ch 1163 § 1; Stats 1957 ch 1686 § 2; Stats 1968 ch 804 § 1; Stats 1979 ch 687 § 2; Stats 1985 ch 1348 § 33, operative January 1, 1987; Stats 1989 ch 1401 § 3; Stats 1998 ch 970 § 94 (AB 2802); Stats 1999 ch 983 § 10.4 (SB 1307).

DIVISION 4

REAL ESTATE

PART 1

LICENSING OF PERSONS

Chapter 3

Estate Regulations

Article 1

Scope of Regulation

§ 10133.1. Inapplicability of certain provisions to designated persons and organizations

(a) Subdivisions (d) and (e) of Section 10131, Section 10131.1, Article 5 (commencing with Section 10230), and Article 7 (commencing with Section 10240) of this code and Section 1695.13 of the Civil Code do not apply to any of the following:

(1) Any person or employee thereof doing business under any law of this state, any other state, or the United States relating to banks, trust companies, savings and loan associations, industrial loan companies, pension trusts, credit unions, or insurance companies.

(2) Any nonprofit cooperative association organized under Chapter 1 (commencing with Section 54001) of Division 20 of the Food and Agricultural Code, in loaning or advancing money in connection with any activity mentioned therein.

(3) Any corporation, association, syndicate, joint stock company, or partnership engaged exclusively in the business of marketing agricultural, horticultural, viticultural, dairy, livestock, poultry, or bee products on a cooperative nonprofit basis, in loaning or advancing money to the members thereof or in connection with any business of that type.

(4) Any corporation securing money or credit from any federal intermediate credit bank organized and existing pursuant to the provisions of an act of Congress entitled the "Agricultural Credits Act of 1923," in loaning or advancing money or credit so secured.

(5) Any person licensed to practice law in this state, not actively and principally engaged in the business of negotiating loans secured

by real property, when that person renders services in the course of his or her practice as an attorney at law, and the disbursements of that person, whether paid by the borrower or other person, are not charges or costs and expenses regulated by or subject to the limitations of Article 7 (commencing with Section 10240), and the fees and disbursements are not shared, directly or indirectly, with the person negotiating the loan or the lender.

(6) Any person licensed as a finance lender when acting under the authority of that license.

(7) Any cemetery authority as defined by Section 7018 of the Health and Safety Code, that is authorized to do business in this state or its authorized agent.

(8) Any person authorized in writing by a savings institution to act as an agent of that institution, as authorized by Section 6520 of the Financial Code or comparable authority of the Office of the Comptroller of the Currency of the United States Department of the Treasury by its regulations, when acting under the authority of that written authorization.

(9) Any person who is licensed as a securities broker or securities dealer under any law of this state, or of the United States, or any employee, officer, or agent of that person, if that person, employee, officer, or agent is acting within the scope of authority granted by that license in connection with a transaction involving the offer, sale, purchase, or exchange of a security representing an ownership interest in a pool of promissory notes secured directly or indirectly by liens on real property, which transaction is subject to any law of this state or the United States regulating the offer or sale of securities.

(10) Any person licensed as a residential mortgage lender or servicer when acting under the authority of that license.

(11) Any organization that has been approved by the United States Department of Housing and Urban Development pursuant to Section 106(a)(1)(iii) of the federal Housing and Urban Development Act of 1968 (12 U.S.C. Sec. 1701x), to provide counseling services, or an employee of such an organization, when those services are provided at no cost to the borrower and are in connection with the modification of the terms of a loan secured directly or collaterally by a lien on residential real property containing four or fewer dwelling units.

(12) Any person licensed as a PACE program administrator when acting under the authority of that license.

(13) A PACE solicitor, when enrolled by a person licensed as a program administrator and acting pursuant to an agreement with that program administrator licensee.

(14) A PACE solicitor agent, when enrolled by a person licensed as a program administrator and acting pursuant to an agreement between a PACE solicitor and that program administrator licensee.

(b) Persons described in paragraph (1), (2), or (3), as follows, are exempt from the provisions of subdivisions (d) and (e) of Section 10131 or Section 10131.1 with respect to the collection of payments or performance of services for lenders or on notes of owners in connection with loans secured directly or collaterally by liens on real property:

(1) The person makes collections on 10 or less of those loans, or in amounts of forty thousand dollars ($40,000) or less, in any calendar year.

(2) The person is a corporation licensed as an escrow agent under Division 6 (commencing with Section 17000) of the Financial Code and the payments are deposited and maintained in the escrow agent's trust account.

(3) An employee of a real estate broker who is acting as the agent of a person described in paragraph (4) of subdivision (b) of Section 10232.4.

For purposes of this subdivision, performance of services does not include soliciting borrowers, lenders, or purchasers for, or negotiating, loans secured directly or collaterally by a lien on real property.

(c) (1) Subdivision (d) of Section 10131 does not apply to an employee of a real estate broker who, on behalf of the broker, assists the broker in meeting the broker's obligations to its customers in residential mortgage loan transactions, as defined in Section 50003 of the Financial Code, where the lender is an institutional lender, as defined in Section 50003 of the Financial Code, provided the employee does not participate in any negotiations occurring between the principals.

(2) A broker shall exercise reasonable supervision and control over the activities of nonlicensed employees acting under this subdivision, and shall comply with Section 10163 for each location where the nonlicensed persons are employed.

(d) This section does not restrict the ability of the commissioner to discipline a broker or corporate broker licensee or its designated officer, or both the corporate broker licensee and its designated officer, for misconduct of a nonlicensed employee acting under this subdivision, or, pursuant to Section 10080, to adopt, amend, or repeal rules or regulations governing the employment or supervision of an employee who is a nonlicensed person as described in this subdivision.

(e) This section shall become operative on January 1, 2019.

Added Stats 2017 ch 475 § 2 (AB 1284), effective October 4, 2017, operative January 1, 2019. Amended Stats 2018 ch 285 § 29 (AB 2884), effective January 1, 2019.

Appendix

PART 3

LICENSING AND CERTIFICATION OF REAL ESTATE APPRAISERS

Chapter 4

Licenses and Certification Application

§ 11345.2. Acting as controlling person for a registrant; Reporting specified acts

(a) An individual shall not act as a controlling person for a registrant if any of the following apply:

(1) The individual has entered a plea of guilty or no contest to, or been convicted of, a felony. If the individual's felony conviction has been dismissed pursuant to Section 1203.4, 1203.4a, 1203.41, 1203.42, or 1203.425 of the Penal Code, the bureau may allow the individual to act as a controlling person.

(2) The individual has had a license or certificate to act as an appraiser or to engage in activities related to the transfer of real property refused, denied, canceled, or revoked in this state or any other state.

(b) Any individual who acts as a controlling person of an appraisal management company and who enters a plea of guilty or no contest to, or is convicted of, a felony, or who has a license or certificate as an appraiser refused, denied, canceled, or revoked in any other state shall report that fact or cause that fact to be reported to the bureau, in writing, within 10 days of the date the individual has knowledge of that fact.

(c) This section shall become operative on July 1, 2020.

Added Stats 2018 ch 995 § 15 (AB 2138), effective January 1, 2019, operative July 1, 2020. Amended Stats 2019 ch 578 § 5 (AB 1076), effective January 1, 2020, operative July 1, 2020; Stats 2021 ch 431 § 50 (SB 800), effective January 1, 2022.

DIVISION 7

GENERAL BUSINESS REGULATIONS

PART 3

REPRESENTATIONS TO THE PUBLIC

Chapter 1

Advertising

Article 6

Water Treatment Devices

§ 17577.3. Contracts

(a) A contract or offer which is subject to approval, for the sale, lease, or rental of a water treatment device shall be deemed a home solicitation contract or offer, as defined in subdivision (a) of Section 1689.5 of the Civil Code regardless of where the contract or offer was made, and shall be subject to the provisions of Sections 1689.5 to 1689.13, inclusive, of the Civil Code if the contract or offer arises out of a scheduled presentation to promote the sale, lease, or rental of a water treatment device to a person invited to attend the presentation at a location other than a private residence.

(b) A water treatment device or any other materials that are the subject of a contract offer described in subdivision (a) may be delivered and installed during the rescission period provided in Sections 1689.5 to 1689.13, inclusive, of the Civil Code. Notwithstanding any other law, if a buyer exercises his or her right to rescind the contract in accordance with those rescission provisions, the seller shall be responsible for all costs in removing the installed water treatment device or any other materials and shall remove that device or any other materials within 20 days of the rescission. If the seller's services result in the alteration of property of the buyer, the seller shall restore the property to substantially as good condition as it was at the time the services were rendered.

(c) A water treatment device or any other materials that are the subject of a contract offer described in subdivision (a) shall be delivered and installed in accordance with Section 7163 and the federal Truth in Lending Act (15 U.S.C. Sec. 1601 et seq.), as applicable.

Added Stats 1988 ch 1053 § 7. Amended Stats 2018 ch 932 § 1 (SB 981), effective January 1, 2019.

CIVIL CODE

DIVISION 1

PERSONS

PART 2

PERSONAL RIGHTS

§ 43.99. Liability of person or entity under contract with residential building permit applicant for quality review of compliance with State Housing Law

(a) There shall be no monetary liability on the part of, and no cause of action for damages shall arise against, any person or other legal entity that is under contract with an applicant for a residential building permit to provide independent quality review of the plans and specifications provided with the application in order to determine compliance with all applicable requirements imposed pursuant to the State Housing Law (Part 1.5 (commencing with Section 17910) of Division 13 of the Health and Safety Code), or any rules or regulations adopted pursuant to that law, or under contract with that applicant to provide independent quality review of the work of improvement to determine compliance with these plans and specifications, if the person or other legal entity meets the requirements of this section and one of the following applies:

(1) The person, or a person employed by any other legal entity, performing the work as described in this subdivision, has completed not less than five years of verifiable experience in the appropriate field and has obtained certification as a building inspector, combination inspector, or combination dwelling inspector from the International Conference of Building Officials (ICBO) and has successfully passed the technical written examination promulgated by ICBO for those certification categories.

(2) The person, or a person employed by any other legal entity, performing the work as described in this subdivision, has completed not less than five years of verifiable experience in the appropriate field and is a registered professional engineer, licensed general contractor, or a licensed architect rendering independent quality review of the

work of improvement or plan examination services within the scope of his or her registration or licensure.

(3) The immunity provided under this section does not apply to any action initiated by the applicant who retained the qualified person.

(4) A "qualified person" for purposes of this section means a person holding a valid certification as one of those inspectors.

(b) Except for qualified persons, this section shall not relieve from, excuse, or lessen in any manner, the responsibility or liability of any person, company, contractor, builder, developer, architect, engineer, designer, or other individual or entity who develops, improves, owns, operates, or manages any residential building for any damages to persons or property caused by construction or design defects. The fact that an inspection by a qualified person has taken place may not be introduced as evidence in a construction defect action, including any reports or other items generated by the qualified person. This subdivision shall not apply in any action initiated by the applicant who retained the qualified person.

(c) Nothing in this section, as it relates to construction inspectors or plans examiners, shall be construed to alter the requirements for licensure, or the jurisdiction, authority, or scope of practice, of architects pursuant to Chapter 3 (commencing with Section 5500) of Division 3 of the Business and Professions Code, professional engineers pursuant to Chapter 7 (commencing with Section 6700) of Division 3 of the Business and Professions Code, or general contractors pursuant to Chapter 9 (commencing with Section 7000) of Division 3 of the Business and Professions Code.

(d) Nothing in this section shall be construed to alter the immunity of employees of the Department of Housing and Community Development under the Government Claims Act (Division 3.6 (commencing with Section 810) of Title 1 of the Government Code) when acting pursuant to Section 17965 of the Health and Safety Code.

(e) The qualifying person shall engage in no other construction, design, planning, supervision, or activities of any kind on the work of improvement, nor provide quality review services for any other party on the work of improvement.

(f) The qualifying person, or other legal entity, shall maintain professional errors and omissions insurance coverage in an amount not less than two million dollars ($2,000,000).

(g) The immunity provided by subdivision (a) does not inure to the benefit of the qualified person for damages caused to the applicant solely by the negligence or willful misconduct of the qualified person resulting from the provision of services under the contract with the applicant.

Added Stats 2002 ch 722 § 2 (SB 800). Amended Stats 2012 ch 759 § 1 (AB 2690), effective January 1, 2013.

DIVISION 2

PROPERTY

PART 2

REAL OR IMMOVABLE PROPERTY

TITLE 7

Requirements for Actions for Construction Defects

Chapter 1

Definitions

§ 895. Definitions

(a) "Structure" means any residential dwelling, other building, or improvement located upon a lot or within a common area.

(b) "Designed moisture barrier" means an installed moisture barrier specified in the plans and specifications, contract documents, or manufacturer's recommendations.

(c) "Actual moisture barrier" means any component or material, actually installed, that serves to any degree as a barrier against moisture, whether or not intended as a barrier against moisture.

(d) "Unintended water" means water that passes beyond, around, or through a component or the material that is designed to prevent that passage.

(e) "Close of escrow" means the date of the close of escrow between the builder and the original homeowner. With respect to claims by an association, as defined in Section 4080, "close of escrow" means the date of substantial completion, as defined in Section 337.15 of the Code of Civil Procedure, or the date the builder relinquishes control over the association's ability to decide whether to initiate a claim under this title, whichever is later.

(f) "Claimant" or "homeowner" includes the individual owners of single-family homes, individual unit owners of attached dwellings and, in the case of a common interest development, any association as defined in Section 4080.

Added Stats 2002 ch 722 § 3 (SB 800). Amended Stats 2012 ch 181 § 29 (AB 806), effective January 1, 2013, operative January 1, 2014.

Chapter 2

Actionable Defects

§ 896. Standards for residential construction

In any action seeking recovery of damages arising out of, or related to deficiencies in, the residential construction, design, specifications, surveying, planning, supervision, testing, or observation of construction, a builder, and to the extent set forth in Chapter 4 (commencing with Section 910), a general contractor, subcontractor, material supplier, individual product manufacturer, or design professional, shall, except as specifically set forth in this title, be liable for, and the claimant's claims or causes of action shall be limited to violation of, the following standards, except as specifically set forth in this title. This title applies to original construction intended to be sold as an individual dwelling unit. As to condominium conversions, this title does not apply to or does not supersede any other statutory or common law.

(a) With respect to water issues:

(1) A door shall not allow unintended water to pass beyond, around, or through the door or its designed or actual moisture barriers, if any.

(2) Windows, patio doors, deck doors, and their systems shall not allow water to pass beyond, around, or through the window, patio door, or deck door or its designed or actual moisture barriers, including, without limitation, internal barriers within the systems themselves. For purposes of this paragraph, "systems" include, without limitation, windows, window assemblies, framing, substrate, flashings, and trim, if any.

(3) Windows, patio doors, deck doors, and their systems shall not allow excessive condensation to enter the structure and cause damage to another component. For purposes of this paragraph, "systems" include, without limitation, windows, window assemblies, framing, substrate, flashings, and trim, if any.

(4) Roofs, roofing systems, chimney caps, and ventilation components shall not allow water to enter the structure or to pass beyond, around, or through the designed or actual moisture barriers, including, without limitation, internal barriers located within the systems themselves. For purposes of this paragraph, "systems" include, without limitation, framing, substrate, and sheathing, if any.

(5) Decks, deck systems, balconies, balcony systems, exterior stairs, and stair systems shall not allow water to pass into the adjacent structure. For purposes of this paragraph, "systems" include, without limitation, framing, substrate, flashing, and sheathing, if any.

(6) Decks, deck systems, balconies, balcony systems, exterior stairs, and stair systems shall not allow unintended water to pass within the systems themselves and cause damage to the systems. For purposes of this paragraph, "systems" include, without limitation, framing, substrate, flashing, and sheathing, if any.

(7) Foundation systems and slabs shall not allow water or vapor to enter into the structure so as to cause damage to another building component.

(8) Foundation systems and slabs shall not allow water or vapor to enter into the structure so as to limit the installation of the type of flooring materials typically used for the particular application.

(9) Hardscape, including paths and patios, irrigation systems, landscaping systems, and drainage systems, that are installed as part of the original construction, shall not be installed in such a way as to cause water or soil erosion to enter into or come in contact with the structure so as to cause damage to another building component.

(10) Stucco, exterior siding, exterior walls, including, without limitation, exterior framing, and other exterior wall finishes and fixtures and the systems of those components and fixtures, including, but not limited to, pot shelves, horizontal surfaces, columns, and plant-ons, shall be installed in such a way so as not to allow unintended water to pass into the structure or to pass beyond, around, or through the designed or actual moisture barriers of the system, including any internal barriers located within the system itself. For purposes of this paragraph, "systems" include, without limitation, framing, substrate, flashings, trim, wall assemblies, and internal wall cavities, if any.

(11) Stucco, exterior siding, and exterior walls shall not allow excessive condensation to enter the structure and cause damage to another component. For purposes of this paragraph, "systems" include, without limitation, framing, substrate, flashings, trim, wall assemblies, and internal wall cavities, if any.

(12) Retaining and site walls and their associated drainage systems shall not allow unintended water to pass beyond, around, or through its designed or actual moisture barriers including, without limitation, any internal barriers, so as to cause damage. This standard does not apply to those portions of any wall or drainage system that are designed to have water flow beyond, around, or through them.

(13) Retaining walls and site walls, and their associated drainage systems, shall only allow water to flow beyond, around, or through the areas designated by design.

(14) The lines and components of the plumbing system, sewer system, and utility systems shall not leak.

(15) Plumbing lines, sewer lines, and utility lines shall not corrode so as to impede the useful life of the systems.

(16) Sewer systems shall be installed in such a way as to allow the designated amount of sewage to flow through the system.

(17) Showers, baths, and related waterproofing systems shall not leak water into the interior of walls, flooring systems, or the interior of other components.

(18) The waterproofing system behind or under ceramic tile and tile countertops shall not allow water into the interior of walls, flooring systems, or other components so as to cause damage. Ceramic tile systems shall be designed and installed so as to deflect intended water to the waterproofing system.

(b) With respect to structural issues:

(1) Foundations, load bearing components, and slabs, shall not contain significant cracks or significant vertical displacement.

(2) Foundations, load bearing components, and slabs shall not cause the structure, in whole or in part, to be structurally unsafe.

(3) Foundations, load bearing components, and slabs, and underlying soils shall be constructed so as to materially comply with the design criteria set by applicable government building codes, regulations, and ordinances for chemical deterioration or corrosion resistance in effect at the time of original construction.

(4) A structure shall be constructed so as to materially comply with the design criteria for earthquake and wind load resistance, as set forth in the applicable government building codes, regulations, and ordinances in effect at the time of original construction.

(c) With respect to soil issues:

(1) Soils and engineered retaining walls shall not cause, in whole or in part, damage to the structure built upon the soil or engineered retaining wall.

(2) Soils and engineered retaining walls shall not cause, in whole or in part, the structure to be structurally unsafe.

(3) Soils shall not cause, in whole or in part, the land upon which no structure is built to become unusable for the purpose represented at the time of original sale by the builder or for the purpose for which that land is commonly used.

(d) With respect to fire protection issues:

(1) A structure shall be constructed so as to materially comply with the design criteria of the applicable government building codes, regulations, and ordinances for fire protection of the occupants in effect at the time of the original construction.

(2) Fireplaces, chimneys, chimney structures, and chimney termination caps shall be constructed and installed in such a way so as not to cause an unreasonable risk of fire outside the fireplace enclosure or chimney.

(3) Electrical and mechanical systems shall be constructed and installed in such a way so as not to cause an unreasonable risk of fire.

(e) With respect to plumbing and sewer issues:

Plumbing and sewer systems shall be installed to operate properly and shall not materially impair the use of the structure by its inhabitants. However, no action may be brought for a violation of this subdivision more than four years after close of escrow.

(f) With respect to electrical system issues:

Electrical systems shall operate properly and shall not materially impair the use of the structure by its inhabitants. However, no action shall be brought pursuant to this subdivision more than four years from close of escrow.

(g) With respect to issues regarding other areas of construction:

(1) Exterior pathways, driveways, hardscape, sidewalls, sidewalks, and patios installed by the original builder shall not contain cracks that display significant vertical displacement or that are excessive. However, no action shall be brought upon a violation of this paragraph more than four years from close of escrow.

(2) Stucco, exterior siding, and other exterior wall finishes and fixtures, including, but not limited to, pot shelves, horizontal surfaces, columns, and plant-ons, shall not contain significant cracks or separations.

(3) (A) To the extent not otherwise covered by these standards, manufactured products, including, but not limited to, windows, doors, roofs, plumbing products and fixtures, fireplaces, electrical fixtures, HVAC units, countertops, cabinets, paint, and appliances shall be installed so as not to interfere with the products' useful life, if any.

(B) For purposes of this paragraph, "useful life" means a representation of how long a product is warranted or represented, through its limited warranty or any written representations, to last by its manufacturer, including recommended or required maintenance. If there is no representation by a manufacturer, a builder shall install manufactured products so as not to interfere with the product's utility.

(C) For purposes of this paragraph, "manufactured product" means a product that is completely manufactured offsite.

(D) If no useful life representation is made, or if the representation is less than one year, the period shall be no less than one year. If a manufactured product is damaged as a result of a violation of these standards, damage to the product is a recoverable element of damages. This subparagraph does not limit recovery if there has been damage to another building component caused by a manufactured product during the manufactured product's useful life.

(E) This title does not apply in any action seeking recovery solely for a defect in a manufactured product located within or adjacent to a structure.

(4) Heating shall be installed so as to be capable of maintaining a room temperature of 70 degrees Fahrenheit at a point three feet above the floor in any living space if the heating was installed pursuant to a building permit application submitted prior to January 1, 2008, or capable of maintaining a room temperature of 68 degrees Fahrenheit at a point three feet above the floor and two feet from ex-

terior walls in all habitable rooms at the design temperature if the heating was installed pursuant to a building permit application submitted on or before January 1, 2008.

(5) Living space air-conditioning, if any, shall be provided in a manner consistent with the size and efficiency design criteria specified in Title 24 of the California Code of Regulations or its successor.

(6) Attached structures shall be constructed to comply with interunit noise transmission standards set by the applicable government building codes, ordinances, or regulations in effect at the time of the original construction. If there is no applicable code, ordinance, or regulation, this paragraph does not apply. However, no action shall be brought pursuant to this paragraph more than one year from the original occupancy of the adjacent unit.

(7) Irrigation systems and drainage shall operate properly so as not to damage landscaping or other external improvements. However, no action shall be brought pursuant to this paragraph more than one year from close of escrow.

(8) Untreated wood posts shall not be installed in contact with soil so as to cause unreasonable decay to the wood based upon the finish grade at the time of original construction. However, no action shall be brought pursuant to this paragraph more than two years from close of escrow.

(9) Untreated steel fences and adjacent components shall be installed so as to prevent unreasonable corrosion. However, no action shall be brought pursuant to this paragraph more than four years from close of escrow.

(10) Paint and stains shall be applied in such a manner so as not to cause deterioration of the building surfaces for the length of time specified by the paint or stain manufacturers' representations, if any. However, no action shall be brought pursuant to this paragraph more than five years from close of escrow.

(11) Roofing materials shall be installed so as to avoid materials falling from the roof.

(12) The landscaping systems shall be installed in such a manner so as to survive for not less than one year. However, no action shall be brought pursuant to this paragraph more than two years from close of escrow.

(13) Ceramic tile and tile backing shall be installed in such a manner that the tile does not detach.

(14) Dryer ducts shall be installed and terminated pursuant to manufacturer installation requirements. However, no action shall be brought pursuant to this paragraph more than two years from close of escrow.

(15) Structures shall be constructed in such a manner so as not to impair the occupants' safety because they contain public health hazards as determined by a duly authorized public health official, health

agency, or governmental entity having jurisdiction. This paragraph does not limit recovery for any damages caused by a violation of any other paragraph of this section on the grounds that the damages do not constitute a health hazard.

Added Stats 2002 ch 722 § 3 (SB 800). Amended Stats 2003 ch 762 § 1 (AB 903); Stats 2006 ch 567 § 2 (AB 2303), effective January 1, 2007; Stats 2012 ch 770 § 2 (AB 2697), effective January 1, 2013.

§ 897. Intent of standards

The standards set forth in this chapter are intended to address every function or component of a structure. To the extent that a function or component of a structure is not addressed by these standards, it shall be actionable if it causes damage.

Added Stats 2002 ch 722 § 3 (SB 800).

Chapter 3

Obligations

§ 900. Warranty covering fit and finish items

As to fit and finish items, a builder shall provide a homebuyer with a minimum one–year express written limited warranty covering the fit and finish of the following building components. Except as otherwise provided by the standards specified in Chapter 2 (commencing with Section 896), this warranty shall cover the fit and finish of cabinets, mirrors, flooring, interior and exterior walls, countertops, paint finishes, and trim, but shall not apply to damage to those components caused by defects in other components governed by the other provisions of this title. Any fit and finish matters covered by this warranty are not subject to the provisions of this title. If a builder fails to provide the express warranty required by this section, the warranty for these items shall be for a period of one year.

Added Stats 2002 ch 722 § 3 (SB 800).

§ 901. Enhanced protection agreement

A builder may, but is not required to, offer greater protection or protection for longer time periods in its express contract with the homeowner than that set forth in Chapter 2 (commencing with Section 896). A builder may not limit the application of Chapter 2 (commencing with Section 896) or lower its protection through the express contract with the homeowner. This type of express contract constitutes an "enhanced protection agreement."

Added Stats 2002 ch 722 § 3 (SB 800).

§ 902. Effect of enhanced protection agreement

If a builder offers an enhanced protection agreement, the builder may choose to be subject to its own express contractual provisions in place of the provisions set forth in Chapter 2 (commencing with Section 896). If an enhanced protection agreement is in place, Chapter 2 (commencing with Section 896) no longer applies other than to set forth minimum provisions by which to judge the enforceability of the particular provisions of the enhanced protection agreement.

Added Stats 2002 ch 722 § 3 (SB 800).

§ 903. Written copy of enhanced protection agreement

If a builder offers an enhanced protection agreement in place of the provisions set forth in Chapter 2 (commencing with Section 896), the election to do so shall be made in writing with the homeowner no later than the close of escrow. The builder shall provide the homeowner with a complete copy of Chapter 2 (commencing with Section 896) and advise the homeowner that the builder has elected not to be subject to its provisions. If any provision of an enhanced protection agreement is later found to be unenforceable as not meeting the minimum standards of Chapter 2 (commencing with Section 896), a builder may use this chapter in lieu of those provisions found to be unenforceable.

Added Stats 2002 ch 722 § 3 (SB 800).

§ 904. Enforcement of construction standards in lieu of particular enhanced protection agreement provision

If a builder has elected to use an enhanced protection agreement, and a homeowner disputes that the particular provision or time periods of the enhanced protection agreement are not greater than, or equal to, the provisions of Chapter 2 (commencing with Section 896) as they apply to the particular deficiency alleged by the homeowner, the homeowner may seek to enforce the application of the standards set forth in this chapter as to those claimed deficiencies. If a homeowner seeks to enforce a particular standard in lieu of a provision of the enhanced protection agreement, the homeowner shall give the builder written notice of that intent at the time the homeowner files a notice of claim pursuant to Chapter 4 (commencing with Section 910).

Added Stats 2002 ch 722 § 3 (SB 800).

Appendix

§ 905. Responsive pleading in action to enforce construction standards of this chapter in lieu of enhanced protection agreement

If a homeowner seeks to enforce Chapter 2 (commencing with Section 896), in lieu of the enhanced protection agreement in a subsequent litigation or other legal action, the builder shall have the right to have the matter bifurcated, and to have an immediately binding determination of his or her responsive pleading within 60 days after the filing of that pleading, but in no event after the commencement of discovery, as to the application of either Chapter 2 (commencing with Section 896) or the enhanced protection agreement as to the deficiencies claimed by the homeowner. If the builder fails to seek that determination in the timeframe specified, the builder waives the right to do so and the standards set forth in this title shall apply. As to any nonoriginal homeowner, that homeowner shall be deemed in privity for purposes of an enhanced protection agreement only to the extent that the builder has recorded the enhanced protection agreement on title or provided actual notice to the nonoriginal homeowner of the enhanced protection agreement. If the enhanced protection agreement is not recorded on title or no actual notice has been provided, the standards set forth in this title apply to any nonoriginal homeowners' claims.

Added Stats 2002 ch 722 § 3 (SB 800).

§ 906. Effect of election of enhanced protection agreement on provisions of prelitigation procedures

A builder's election to use an enhanced protection agreement addresses only the issues set forth in Chapter 2 (commencing with Section 896) and does not constitute an election to use or not use the provisions of Chapter 4 (commencing with Section 910). The decision to use or not use Chapter 4 (commencing with Section 910) is governed by the provisions of that chapter.

Added Stats 2002 ch 722 § 3 (SB 800).

§ 907. Obligation of homeowner to follow reasonable maintenance obligations

A homeowner is obligated to follow all reasonable maintenance obligations and schedules communicated in writing to the homeowner by the builder and product manufacturers, as well as commonly accepted maintenance practices. A failure by a homeowner to follow these obligations, schedules, and practices may subject the homeowner to the affirmative defenses contained in Section 944.

Added Stats 2002 ch 722 § 3 (SB 800).

Chapter 4

Prelitigation Procedure

§ 910. Procedures required prior to filing action for violation of construction standards

Prior to filing an action against any party alleged to have contributed to a violation of the standards set forth in Chapter 2 (commencing with Section 896), the claimant shall initiate the following prelitigation procedures:

(a) The claimant or his or her legal representative shall provide written notice via certified mail, overnight mail, or personal delivery to the builder, in the manner prescribed in this section, of the claimant's claim that the construction of his or her residence violates any of the standards set forth in Chapter 2 (commencing with Section 896). That notice shall provide the claimant's name, address, and preferred method of contact, and shall state that the claimant alleges a violation pursuant to this part against the builder, and shall describe the claim in reasonable detail sufficient to determine the nature and location, to the extent known, of the claimed violation. In the case of a group of homeowners or an association, the notice may identify the claimants solely by address or other description sufficient to apprise the builder of the locations of the subject residences. That document shall have the same force and effect as a notice of commencement of a legal proceeding.

(b) The notice requirements of this section do not preclude a homeowner from seeking redress through any applicable normal customer service procedure as set forth in any contractual, warranty, or other builder–generated document; and, if a homeowner seeks to do so, that request shall not satisfy the notice requirements of this section.

Added Stats 2002 ch 722 § 3 (SB 800).

§ 911. "Builder" defined

(a) For purposes of this title, except as provided in subdivision (b), "builder" means any entity or individual, including, but not limited to a builder, developer, general contractor, contractor, or original seller, who, at the time of sale, was also in the business of selling residential units to the public for the property that is the subject of the homeowner's claim or was in the business of building, developing, or constructing residential units for public purchase for the property that is the subject of the homeowner's claim.

(b) For the purposes of this title, "builder" does not include any entity or individual whose involvement with a residential unit that is

Appendix

the subject of the homeowner's claim is limited to his or her capacity as general contractor or contractor and who is not a partner, member of, subsidiary of, or otherwise similarly affiliated with the builder. For purposes of this title, these nonaffiliated general contractors and nonaffiliated contractors shall be treated the same as subcontractors, material suppliers, individual product manufacturers, and design professionals.

Added Stats 2002 ch 722 § 3 (SB 800). Amended Stats 2003 ch 762 § 2 (AB 903).

§ 912. Builder's duties

A builder shall do all of the following:

(a) Within 30 days of a written request by a homeowner or his or her legal representative, the builder shall provide copies of all relevant plans, specifications, mass or rough grading plans, final soils reports, Bureau of Real Estate public reports, and available engineering calculations, that pertain to a homeowner's residence specifically or as part of a larger development tract. The request shall be honored if it states that it is made relative to structural, fire safety, or soils provisions of this title. However, a builder is not obligated to provide a copying service, and reasonable copying costs shall be borne by the requesting party. A builder may require that the documents be copied onsite by the requesting party, except that the homeowner may, at his or her option, use his or her own copying service, which may include an offsite copy facility that is bonded and insured. If a builder can show that the builder maintained the documents, but that they later became unavailable due to loss or destruction that was not the fault of the builder, the builder may be excused from the requirements of this subdivision, in which case the builder shall act with reasonable diligence to assist the homeowner in obtaining those documents from any applicable government authority or from the source that generated the document. However, in that case, the time limits specified by this section do not apply.

(b) At the expense of the homeowner, who may opt to use an offsite copy facility that is bonded and insured, the builder shall provide to the homeowner or his or her legal representative copies of all maintenance and preventative maintenance recommendations that pertain to his or her residence within 30 days of service of a written request for those documents. Those documents shall also be provided to the homeowner in conjunction with the initial sale of the residence.

(c) At the expense of the homeowner, who may opt to use an offsite copy facility that is bonded and insured, a builder shall provide to the homeowner or his or her legal representative copies of all manufactured products maintenance, preventive maintenance, and limited warranty information within 30 days of a written request for those documents. These documents shall also be provided to the homeowner in conjunction with the initial sale of the residence.

(d) At the expense of the homeowner, who may opt to use an offsite copy facility that is bonded and insured, a builder shall provide to the homeowner or his or her legal representative copies of all of the builder's limited contractual warranties in accordance with this part in effect at the time of the original sale of the residence within 30 days of a written request for those documents. Those documents shall also be provided to the homeowner in conjunction with the initial sale of the residence.

(e) A builder shall maintain the name and address of an agent for notice pursuant to this chapter with the Secretary of State or, alternatively, elect to use a third party for that notice if the builder has notified the homeowner in writing of the third party's name and address, to whom claims and requests for information under this section may be mailed. The name and address of the agent for notice or third party shall be included with the original sales documentation and shall be initialed and acknowledged by the purchaser and the builder's sales representative.

This subdivision applies to instances in which a builder contracts with a third party to accept claims and act on the builder's behalf. A builder shall give actual notice to the homeowner that the builder has made such an election, and shall include the name and address of the third party.

(f) A builder shall record on title a notice of the existence of these procedures and a notice that these procedures impact the legal rights of the homeowner. This information shall also be included with the original sales documentation and shall be initialed and acknowledged by the purchaser and the builder's sales representative.

(g) A builder shall provide, with the original sales documentation, a written copy of this title, which shall be initialed and acknowledged by the purchaser and the builder's sales representative.

(h) As to any documents provided in conjunction with the original sale, the builder shall instruct the original purchaser to provide those documents to any subsequent purchaser.

(i) Any builder who fails to comply with any of these requirements within the time specified is not entitled to the protection of this chapter, and the homeowner is released from the requirements of this chapter and may proceed with the filing of an action, in which case the remaining chapters of this part shall continue to apply to the action.

Added Stats 2002 ch 722 § 3 (SB 800). Amended Stats 2003 ch 762 § 3 (AB 903); Stats 2013 ch 352 § 50 (AB 1317), effective September 26, 2013, operative July 1, 2013.

Appendix

§ 913. Acknowledgement of receipt of notice

A builder or his or her representative shall acknowledge, in writing, receipt of the notice of the claim within 14 days after receipt of the notice of the claim. If the notice of the claim is served by the claimant's legal representative, or if the builder receives a written representation letter from a homeowner's attorney, the builder shall include the attorney in all subsequent substantive communications, including, without limitation, all written communications occurring pursuant to this chapter, and all substantive and procedural communications, including all written communications, following the commencement of any subsequent complaint or other legal action, except that if the builder has retained or involved legal counsel to assist the builder in this process, all communications by the builder's counsel shall only be with the claimant's legal representative, if any.

Added Stats 2002 ch 722 § 3 (SB 800).

§ 914. Nonadversarial procedure established

(a) This chapter establishes a nonadversarial procedure, including the remedies available under this chapter which, if the procedure does not resolve the dispute between the parties, may result in a subsequent action to enforce the other chapters of this title. A builder may attempt to commence nonadversarial contractual provisions other than the nonadversarial procedures and remedies set forth in this chapter, but may not, in addition to its own nonadversarial contractual provisions, require adherence to the nonadversarial procedures and remedies set forth in this chapter, regardless of whether the builder's own alternative nonadversarial contractual provisions are successful in resolving the dispute or ultimately deemed enforceable.

At the time the sales agreement is executed, the builder shall notify the homeowner whether the builder intends to engage in the nonadversarial procedure of this section or attempt to enforce alternative nonadversarial contractual provisions. If the builder elects to use alternative nonadversarial contractual provisions in lieu of this chapter, the election is binding, regardless of whether the builder's alternative nonadversarial contractual provisions are successful in resolving the ultimate dispute or are ultimately deemed enforceable.

(b) Nothing in this title is intended to affect existing statutory or decisional law pertaining to the applicability, viability, or enforceability of alternative dispute resolution methods, alternative remedies, or contractual arbitration, judicial reference, or similar procedures requiring a binding resolution to enforce the other chapters of this title or any other disputes between homeowners and builders. Nothing in this title is intended to affect the applicability, viability, or enforceability, if any, of contractual arbitration or judicial reference after a nonadversarial procedure or provision has been completed.

Added Stats 2002 ch 722 § 3 (SB 800).

§ 915. Actions resulting in nonapplication of chapter

If a builder fails to acknowledge receipt of the notice of a claim within the time specified, elects not to go through the process set forth in this chapter, or fails to request an inspection within the time specified, or at the conclusion or cessation of an alternative nonadversarial proceeding, this chapter does not apply and the homeowner is released from the requirements of this chapter and may proceed with the filing of an action. However, the standards set forth in the other chapters of this title shall continue to apply to the action.

Added Stats 2002 ch 722 § 3 (SB 800).

§ 916. Inspection of claimed unmet standards by builder

(a) If a builder elects to inspect the claimed unmet standards, the builder shall complete the initial inspection and testing within 14 days after acknowledgment of receipt of the notice of the claim, at a mutually convenient date and time. If the homeowner has retained legal representation, the inspection shall be scheduled with the legal representative's office at a mutually convenient date and time, unless the legal representative is unavailable during the relevant time periods. All costs of builder inspection and testing, including any damage caused by the builder inspection, shall be borne by the builder. The builder shall also provide written proof that the builder has liability insurance to cover any damages or injuries occurring during inspection and testing. The builder shall restore the property to its pretesting condition within 48 hours of the testing. The builder shall, upon request, allow the inspections to be observed and electronically recorded, video recorded, or photographed by the claimant or his or her legal representative.

(b) Nothing that occurs during a builder's or claimant's inspection or testing may be used or introduced as evidence to support a spoliation defense by any potential party in any subsequent litigation.

(c) If a builder deems a second inspection or testing reasonably necessary, and specifies the reasons therefor in writing within three days following the initial inspection, the builder may conduct a second inspection or testing. A second inspection or testing shall be completed within 40 days of the initial inspection or testing. All requirements concerning the initial inspection or testing shall also apply to the second inspection or testing.

(d) If the builder fails to inspect or test the property within the time specified, the claimant is released from the requirements of this section and may proceed with the filing of an action. However, the standards set forth in the other chapters of this title shall continue to apply to the action.

(e) If a builder intends to hold a subcontractor, design professional, individual product manufacturer, or material supplier, including an insurance carrier, warranty company, or service company, responsible for its contribution to the unmet standard, the builder shall provide notice to that person or entity sufficiently in advance to allow them to attend the initial, or if requested, second inspection of any alleged unmet standard and to participate in the repair process. The claimant and his or her legal representative, if any, shall be advised in a reasonable time prior to the inspection as to the identity of all persons or entities invited to attend. This subdivision does not apply to the builder's insurance company. Except with respect to any claims involving a repair actually conducted under this chapter, nothing in this subdivision shall be construed to relieve a subcontractor, design professional, individual product manufacturer, or material supplier of any liability under an action brought by a claimant.

Added Stats 2002 ch 722 § 3 (SB 800). Amended Stats 2003 ch 762 § 4 (AB 903); Stats. 2009, Ch. 140 (AB 176).

§ 917. Offer to repair

Within 30 days of the initial or, if requested, second inspection or testing, the builder may offer in writing to repair the violation. The offer to repair shall also compensate the homeowner for all applicable damages recoverable under Section 944, within the timeframe for the repair set forth in this chapter. Any such offer shall be accompanied by a detailed, specific, step–by–step statement identifying the particular violation that is being repaired, explaining the nature, scope, and location of the repair, and setting a reasonable completion date for the repair. The offer shall also include the names, addresses, telephone numbers, and license numbers of the contractors whom the builder intends to have perform the repair. Those contractors shall be fully insured for, and shall be responsible for, all damages or injuries that they may cause to occur during the repair, and evidence of that insurance shall be provided to the homeowner upon request. Upon written request by the homeowner or his or her legal representative, and within the timeframes set forth in this chapter, the builder shall also provide any available technical documentation, including, without limitation, plans and specifications, pertaining to the claimed violation within the particular home or development tract. The offer shall also advise the homeowner in writing of his or her right to request up to three additional contractors from which to select to do the repair pursuant to this chapter.

Added Stats 2002 ch 722 § 3 (SB 800).

§ 918. Authorization to proceed with repair

Upon receipt of the offer to repair, the homeowner shall have 30 days to authorize the builder to proceed with the repair. The homeowner may alternatively request, at the homeowner's sole option and discretion, that the builder provide the names, addresses, telephone numbers, and license numbers for up to three alternative contractors who are not owned or financially controlled by the builder and who regularly conduct business in the county where the structure is located. If the homeowner so elects, the builder is entitled to an additional noninvasive inspection, to occur at a mutually convenient date and time within 20 days of the election, so as to permit the other proposed contractors to review the proposed site of the repair. Within 35 days after the request of the homeowner for alternative contractors, the builder shall present the homeowner with a choice of contractors. Within 20 days after that presentation, the homeowner shall authorize the builder or one of the alternative contractors to perform the repair.

Added Stats 2002 ch 722 § 3 (SB 800).

§ 919. Offer to mediate dispute

The offer to repair shall also be accompanied by an offer to mediate the dispute if the homeowner so chooses. The mediation shall be limited to a four–hour mediation, except as otherwise mutually agreed before a nonaffiliated mediator selected and paid for by the builder. At the homeowner's sole option, the homeowner may agree to split the cost of the mediator, and if he or she does so, the mediator shall be selected jointly. The mediator shall have sufficient availability such that the mediation occurs within 15 days after the request to mediate is received and occurs at a mutually convenient location within the county where the action is pending. If a builder has made an offer to repair a violation, and the mediation has failed to resolve the dispute, the homeowner shall allow the repair to be performed either by the builder, its contractor, or the selected contractor.

Added Stats 2002 ch 722 § 3 (SB 800).

§ 920. Actions resulting in filing of an action by homeowner; Applicable standards

If the builder fails to make an offer to repair or otherwise strictly comply with this chapter within the times specified, the claimant is released from the requirements of this chapter and may proceed with the filing of an action. If the contractor performing the repair does not complete the repair in the time or manner specified, the claimant may file an action. If this occurs, the standards set forth in the other chapters of this part shall continue to apply to the action.

Added Stats 2002 ch 722 § 3 (SB 800).

§ 921. Procedure when resolution involves repair by builder

(a) In the event that a resolution under this chapter involves a repair by the builder, the builder shall make an appointment with the claimant, make all appropriate arrangements to effectuate a repair of the claimed unmet standards, and compensate the homeowner for all damages resulting therefrom free of charge to the claimant. The repair shall be scheduled through the claimant's legal representative, if any, unless he or she is unavailable during the relevant time periods. The repair shall be commenced on a mutually convenient date within 14 days of acceptance or, if an alternative contractor is selected by the homeowner, within 14 days of the selection, or, if a mediation occurs, within seven days of the mediation, or within five days after a permit is obtained if one is required. The builder shall act with reasonable diligence in obtaining any such permit.

(b) The builder shall ensure that work done on the repairs is done with the utmost diligence, and that the repairs are completed as soon as reasonably possible, subject to the nature of the repair or some unforeseen event not caused by the builder or the contractor performing the repair. Every effort shall be made to complete the repair within 120 days.

Added Stats 2002 ch 722 § 3 (SB 800).

§ 922. Observation and electronic recording, videotaping, or photographing of repair allowed

The builder shall, upon request, allow the repair to be observed and electronically recorded, video recorded, or photographed by the claimant or his or her legal representative. Nothing that occurs during the repair process may be used or introduced as evidence to support a spoliation defense by any potential party in any subsequent litigation.

Added Stats 2002 ch 722 § 3 (SB 800). Amended Stats. 2009, Ch. 88 (AB 176).

§ 923. Availability to homeowner of correspondence, photographs and other material pertaining to repairs

The builder shall provide the homeowner or his or her legal representative, upon request, with copies of all correspondence, photographs, and other materials pertaining or relating in any manner to the repairs.

Added Stats 2002 ch 722 § 3 (SB 800).

§ 924. Offer to repair some, but not all, of claimed unmet standards

If the builder elects to repair some, but not all of, the claimed unmet standards, the builder shall, at the same time it makes its offer, set forth with particularity in writing the reasons, and the support for those reasons, for not repairing all claimed unmet standards.

Added Stats 2002 ch 722 § 3 (SB 800).

§ 925. Failure to timely complete repairs

If the builder fails to complete the repair within the time specified in the repair plan, the claimant is released from the requirements of this chapter and may proceed with the filing of an action. If this occurs, the standards set forth in the other chapters of this title shall continue to apply to the action.

Added Stats 2002 ch 722 § 3 (SB 800).

§ 926. Release or waiver in exchange for repair work prohibited

The builder may not obtain a release or waiver of any kind in exchange for the repair work mandated by this chapter. At the conclusion of the repair, the claimant may proceed with filing an action for violation of the applicable standard or for a claim of inadequate repair, or both, including all applicable damages available under Section 944.

Added Stats 2002 ch 722 § 3 (SB 800).

§ 927. Statute of limitations

If the applicable statute of limitations has otherwise run during this process, the time period for filing a complaint or other legal remedies for violation of any provision of this title, or for a claim of inadequate repair, is extended from the time of the original claim by the claimant to 100 days after the repair is completed, whether or not the particular violation is the one being repaired. If the builder fails to acknowledge the claim within the time specified, elects not to go through this statutory process, or fails to request an inspection within the time specified, the time period for filing a complaint or other legal remedies for violation of any provision of this title is extended from the time of the original claim by the claimant to 45 days after the time for responding to the notice of claim has expired. If the builder elects to attempt to enforce its own nonadversarial procedure in lieu of the procedure set forth in this chapter, the time period for filing a complaint or other legal remedies for violation of any provision of this

part is extended from the time of the original claim by the claimant to
100 days after either the completion of the builder's alternative nonadversarial procedure, or 100 days after the builder's alternative
nonadversarial procedure is deemed unenforceable, whichever is later.

Added Stats 2002 ch 722 § 3 (SB 800).

§ 928. Mediation procedure

If the builder has invoked this chapter and completed a repair, pri-
or to filing an action, if there has been no previous mediation between
the parties, the homeowner or his or her legal representative shall
request mediation in writing. The mediation shall be limited to four
hours, except as otherwise mutually agreed before a nonaffiliated
mediator selected and paid for by the builder. At the homeowner's
sole option, the homeowner may agree to split the cost of the mediator
and if he or she does so, the mediator shall be selected jointly. The
mediator shall have sufficient availability such that the mediation
will occur within 15 days after the request for mediation is received
and shall occur at a mutually convenient location within the county
where the action is pending. In the event that a mediation is used at
this point, any applicable statutes of limitations shall be tolled from
the date of the request to mediate until the next court day after the
mediation is completed, or the 100–day period, whichever is later.

Added Stats 2002 ch 722 § 3 (SB 800).

§ 929. Cash offer in lieu of repair

(a) Nothing in this chapter prohibits the builder from making only a
cash offer and no repair. In this situation, the homeowner is free to
accept the offer, or he or she may reject the offer and proceed with the
filing of an action. If the latter occurs, the standards of the other
chapters of this title shall continue to apply to the action.

(b) The builder may obtain a reasonable release in exchange for the
cash payment. The builder may negotiate the terms and conditions of
any reasonable release in terms of scope and consideration in conjunction with a cash payment under this chapter.

Added Stats 2002 ch 722 § 3 (SB 800).

§ 930. Strict construction of requirements; Failure of claimant to conform

(a) The time periods and all other requirements in this chapter are
to be strictly construed, and, unless extended by the mutual agreement of the parties in accordance with this chapter, shall govern the
rights and obligations under this title. If a builder fails to act in accordance with this section within the timeframes mandated, unless

extended by the mutual agreement of the parties as evidenced by a postclaim written confirmation by the affected homeowner demonstrating that he or she has knowingly and voluntarily extended the statutory timeframe, the claimant may proceed with filing an action. If this occurs, the standards of the other chapters of this title shall continue to apply to the action.

(b) If the claimant does not conform with the requirements of this chapter, the builder may bring a motion to stay any subsequent court action or other proceeding until the requirements of this chapter have been satisfied. The court, in its discretion, may award the prevailing party on such a motion, his or her attorney's fees and costs in bringing or opposing the motion.

Added Stats 2002 ch 722 § 3 (SB 800).

§ 931. Claim combined with other causes of action

If a claim combines causes of action or damages not covered by this part, including, without limitation, personal injuries, class actions, other statutory remedies, or fraud–based claims, the claimed unmet standards shall be administered according to this part, although evidence of the property in its unrepaired condition may be introduced to support the respective elements of any such cause of action. As to any fraud–based claim, if the fact that the property has been repaired under this chapter is deemed admissible, the trier of fact shall be informed that the repair was not voluntarily accepted by the homeowner. As to any class action claims that address solely the incorporation of a defective component into a residence, the named and unnamed class members need not comply with this chapter.

Added Stats 2002 ch 722 § 3 (SB 800).

§ 932. Subsequent discovered claims of unmet standards

Subsequently discovered claims of unmet standards shall be administered separately under this chapter, unless otherwise agreed to by the parties. However, in the case of a detached single family residence, in the same home, if the subsequently discovered claim is for a violation of the same standard as that which has already been initiated by the same claimant and the subject of a currently pending action, the claimant need not reinitiate the process as to the same standard. In the case of an attached project, if the subsequently discovered claim is for a violation of the same standard for a connected component system in the same building as has already been initiated by the same claimant, and the subject of a currently pending action, the claimant need not reinitiate this process as to that standard.

Added Stats 2002 ch 722 § 3 (SB 800).

Appendix

§ 933. Evidence of repair work

If any enforcement of these standards is commenced, the fact that a repair effort was made may be introduced to the trier of fact. However, the claimant may use the condition of the property prior to the repair as the basis for contending that the repair work was inappropriate, inadequate, or incomplete, or that the violation still exists. The claimant need not show that the repair work resulted in further damage nor that damage has continued to occur as a result of the violation.

Added Stats 2002 ch 722 § 3 (SB 800).

§ 934. Evidence of parties' conduct

Evidence of both parties' conduct during this process may be introduced during a subsequent enforcement action, if any, with the exception of any mediation. Any repair efforts undertaken by the builder, shall not be considered settlement communications or offers of settlement and are not inadmissible in evidence on such a basis.

Added Stats 2002 ch 722 § 3 (SB 800).

§ 935. Similar requirements of Civil Code Section 6000

To the extent that provisions of this chapter are enforced and those provisions are substantially similar to provisions in Section 6000, but an action is subsequently commenced under Section 6000, the parties are excused from performing the substantially similar requirements under Section 6000.

Added Stats 2002 ch 722 § 3 (SB 800). Amended Stats 2012 ch 181 § 30 (AB 806), effective January 1, 2013, operative January 1, 2014.

§ 936. Applicability of title to other entities involved in construction process

Each and every provision of the other chapters of this title apply to general contractors, subcontractors, material suppliers, individual product manufacturers, and design professionals to the extent that the general contractors, subcontractors, material suppliers, individual product manufacturers, and design professionals caused, in whole or in part, a violation of a particular standard as the result of a negligent act or omission or a breach of contract. In addition to the affirmative defenses set forth in Section 945.5, a general contractor, subcontractor, material supplier, design professional, individual product manufacturer, or other entity may also offer common law and contractual defenses as applicable to any claimed violation of a standard. All actions by a claimant or builder to enforce an express contract, or any provision thereof, against a general contractor, subcontractor,

material supplier, individual product manufacturer, or design professional is preserved. Nothing in this title modifies the law pertaining
to joint and several liability for builders, general contractors, subcontractors, material suppliers, individual product manufacturer, and
design professionals that contribute to any specific violation of this
title. However, the negligence standard in this section does not apply
to any general contractor, subcontractor, material supplier, individual
product manufacturer, or design professional with respect to claims
for which strict liability would apply.

Added Stats 2002 ch 722 § 3 (SB 800). Amended Stats 2003 ch 762 § 5 (AB 903).

§ 937. Claims and damages not covered by this title

Nothing in this title shall be interpreted to eliminate or abrogate
the requirement to comply with Section 411.35 of the Code of Civil
Procedure or to affect the liability of design professionals, including
architects and architectural firms, for claims and damages not covered by this title.

Added Stats 2002 ch 722 § 3 (SB 800).

§ 938. Date of sale for applicability of title

This title applies only to new residential units where the purchase
agreement with the buyer was signed by the seller on or after January 1, 2003.

Added Stats 2002 ch 722 § 3 (SB 800). Amended Stats 2003 ch 762 § 6 (AB 903).

Chapter 5

Procedure

§ 941. Time limit for bringing action

(a) Except as specifically set forth in this title, no action may be
brought to recover under this title more than 10 years after substantial completion of the improvement but not later than the date of recordation of a valid notice of completion.

(b) As used in this section, "action" includes an action for indemnity
brought against a person arising out of that person's performance or
furnishing of services or materials referred to in this title, except that
a cross–complaint for indemnity may be filed pursuant to subdivision
(b) of Section 428.10 of the Code of Civil Procedure in an action
which has been brought within the time period set forth in subdivision (a).

(c) The limitation prescribed by this section may not be asserted by
way of defense by any person in actual possession or the control, as

owner, tenant or otherwise, of such an improvement, at the time any deficiency in the improvement constitutes the proximate cause for which it is proposed to make a claim or bring an action.

(d) Sections 337.15 and 337.1 of the Code of Civil Procedure do not apply to actions under this title.

(e) Existing statutory and decisional law regarding tolling of the statute of limitations shall apply to the time periods for filing an action or making a claim under this title, except that repairs made pursuant to Chapter 4 (commencing with Section 910), with the exception of the tolling provision contained in Section 927, do not extend the period for filing an action, or restart the time limitations contained in subdivision (a) or (b) of Section 7091 of the Business and Professions Code. If a builder arranges for a contractor to perform a repair pursuant to Chapter 4 (commencing with Section 910), as to the builder the time period for calculating the statute of limitation in subdivision (a) or (b) of Section 7091 of the Business and Professions Code shall pertain to the substantial completion of the original construction and not to the date of repairs under this title. The time limitations established by this title do not apply to any action by a claimant for a contract or express contractual provision. Causes of action and damages to which this chapter does not apply are not limited by this section.

Added Stats 2002 ch 722 § 3 (SB 800). Amended Stats 2003 ch 62 § 12 (SB 600), ch 762 § 7 (AB 903) (ch 762 prevails).

§ 942. Showing required for claim

In order to make a claim for violation of the standards set forth in Chapter 2 (commencing with Section 896), a homeowner need only demonstrate, in accordance with the applicable evidentiary standard, that the home does not meet the applicable standard, subject to the affirmative defenses set forth in Section 945.5. No further showing of causation or damages is required to meet the burden of proof regarding a violation of a standard set forth in Chapter 2 (commencing with Section 896), provided that the violation arises out of, pertains to, or is related to, the original construction.

Added Stats 2003 ch 762 § 9 (AB 903).

§ 943. Other causes of action; Claims involving detached single–family home

(a) Except as provided in this title, no other cause of action for a claim covered by this title or for damages recoverable under Section 944 is allowed. In addition to the rights under this title, this title does not apply to any action by a claimant to enforce a contract or express contractual provision, or any action for fraud, personal injury, or violation of a statute. Damages awarded for the items set forth in Section 944 in such other cause of action shall be reduced by the amounts recovered pursuant to Section 944 for violation of the standards set forth in this title.

(b) As to any claims involving a detached single–family home, the homeowner's right to the reasonable value of repairing any nonconformity is limited to the repair costs, or the diminution in current value of the home caused by the nonconformity, whichever is less, subject to the personal use exception as developed under common law.

Added Stats 2002 ch 722 § 3 (SB 800), as CC § 942. Renumbered by Stats 2003 ch 762 § 8 (AB 903).

§ 944. Damages

If a claim for damages is made under this title, the homeowner is only entitled to damages for the reasonable value of repairing any violation of the standards set forth in this title, the reasonable cost of repairing any damages caused by the repair efforts, the reasonable cost of repairing and rectifying any damages resulting from the failure of the home to meet the standards, the reasonable cost of removing and replacing any improper repair by the builder, reasonable relocation and storage expenses, lost business income if the home was used as a principal place of a business licensed to be operated from the home, reasonable investigative costs for each established violation, and all other costs or fees recoverable by contract or statute.

Added Stats 2002 ch 722 § 3 (SB 800).

§ 945. Original purchasers and successors-in-interest

The provisions, standards, rights, and obligations set forth in this title are binding upon all original purchasers and their successors-in-interest. For purposes of this title, associations and others having the rights set forth in Sections 5980 and 5985 shall be considered to be original purchasers and shall have standing to enforce the provisions, standards, rights, and obligations set forth in this title.

Added Stats 2002 ch 722 § 3 (SB 800). Amended Stats 2005 ch 37 § 1 (SB 853), effective January 1, 2006; Stats 2012 ch 181 § 31 (AB 806), effective January 1, 2013, operative January 1, 2014; Stats 2018 ch 92 § 34 (SB 1289), effective January 1, 2019.

§ 945.5. Affirmative defenses

A builder, general contractor, subcontractor, material supplier, individual product manufacturer, or design professional, under the principles of comparative fault pertaining to affirmative defenses, may be excused, in whole or in part, from any obligation, damage, loss, or liability if the builder, general contractor, subcontractor, material supplier, individual product manufacturer, or design professional, can demonstrate any of the following affirmative defenses in response to a claimed violation:

(a) To the extent it is caused by an unforeseen act of nature which caused the structure not to meet the standard. For purposes of this section an "unforeseen act of nature" means a weather condition, earthquake, or manmade event such as war, terrorism, or vandalism, in excess of the design criteria expressed by the applicable building codes, regulations, and ordinances in effect at the time of original construction.

(b) To the extent it is caused by a homeowner's unreasonable failure to minimize or prevent those damages in a timely manner, including the failure of the homeowner to allow reasonable and timely access for inspections and repairs under this title. This includes the failure to give timely notice to the builder after discovery of a violation, but does not include damages due to the untimely or inadequate response of a builder to the homeowner's claim.

(c) To the extent it is caused by the homeowner or his or her agent, employee, general contractor, subcontractor, independent contractor, or consultant by virtue of their failure to follow the builder's or manufacturer's recommendations, or commonly accepted homeowner maintenance obligations. In order to rely upon this defense as it relates to a builder's recommended maintenance schedule, the builder shall show that the homeowner had written notice of these schedules and recommendations and that the recommendations and schedules were reasonable at the time they were issued.

(d) To the extent it is caused by the homeowner or his or her agent's or an independent third party's alterations, ordinary wear and tear, misuse, abuse, or neglect, or by the structure's use for something other than its intended purpose.

(e) To the extent that the time period for filing actions bars the claimed violation.

(f) As to a particular violation for which the builder has obtained a valid release.

(g) To the extent that the builder's repair was successful in correcting the particular violation of the applicable standard.

(h) As to any causes of action to which this statute does not apply, all applicable affirmative defenses are preserved.

Added Stats 2002 ch 722 § 3 (SB 800). Amended Stats 2003 ch 762 § 10 (AB 903).

TITLE 8

Reconstruction of Homes Lost in Cedar Fire, October 2003

§ 945.6. [Section repealed 2008.]

Added Stats 2005 ch 40 § 2 (AB 662), effective July 11, 2005, repealed January 1, 2008. Repealed, operative January 1, 2008, by its own terms.

PART 4

ACQUISITION OF PROPERTY

TITLE 4
Transfer

Chapter 2

Transfer of Real Property

Article 1.4

Installation of Water Use Efficiency Improvements

§ 1101.1. Legislative findings and declarations

The Legislature finds and declares all of the following:

(a) Adequate water supply reliability for all uses is essential to the future economic and environmental health of California.

(b) Environmentally sound strategies to meet future water supply and wastewater treatment needs are key to protecting and restoring aquatic resources in California.

(c) There is a pressing need to address water supply reliability issues raised by growing urban areas.

(d) Economic analysis by urban water agencies has identified urban water conservation as a cost-effective approach to addressing water supply needs.

(e) There are many water conservation practices that produce significant energy and other resource savings that should be encouraged as a matter of state policy.

(f) Since the 1991 signing of the "Memorandum of Understanding Regarding Urban Water Conservation in California," many urban water and wastewater treatment agencies have gained valuable experience that can be applied to produce significant statewide savings of water, energy, and associated infrastructure costs. This experience indicates a need to regularly revise and update water conservation methodologies and practices.

(g) To address these concerns, it is the intent of the Legislature to require that residential and commercial real property built and available for use or occupancy on or before January 1, 1994, be equipped with water-conserving plumbing fixtures.

(h) It is further the intent of the Legislature that retail water suppliers are encouraged to provide incentives, financing mechanisms, and funding to assist property owners with these retrofit obligations.

Added Stats 2009 ch 587 § 1 (SB 407), effective January 1, 2010.

§ 1101.2. Applicability of article

Except as provided in Section 1101.7, this article shall apply to residential and commercial real property built and available for use on or before January 1, 1994.

Added Stats 2009 ch 587 § 1 (SB 407), effective January 1, 2010.

§ 1101.3. Definitions

For the purposes of this article:

(a) "Commercial real property" means any real property that is improved with, or consisting of, a building that is intended for commercial use, including hotels and motels, that is not a single-family residential real property or a multifamily residential real property.

(b) "Multifamily residential real property" means any real property that is improved with, or consisting of, a building containing more than one unit that is intended for human habitation, or any mixed residential-commercial buildings or portions thereof that are intended for human habitation. Multifamily residential real property includes residential hotels but does not include hotels and motels that are not residential hotels.

(c) "Noncompliant plumbing fixture" means any of the following:

(1) Any toilet manufactured to use more than 1.6 gallons of water per flush.

(2) Any urinal manufactured to use more than one gallon of water per flush.

(3) Any showerhead manufactured to have a flow capacity of more than 2.5 gallons of water per minute.

(4) Any interior faucet that emits more than 2.2 gallons of water per minute.

(d) "Single-family residential real property" means any real property that is improved with, or consisting of, a building containing not more than one unit that is intended for human habitation.

(e) "Water-conserving plumbing fixture" means any fixture that is in compliance with current building standards applicable to a newly constructed real property of the same type.

(f) "Sale or transfer" means the sale or transfer of an entire real property estate or the fee interest in that real property estate and does not include the sale or transfer of a partial interest, including a leasehold.

Added Stats 2009 ch 587 § 1 (SB 407), effective January 1, 2010.

§ 1101.4. Single-family residential real property; Compliance

(a) For all building alterations or improvements to single-family residential real property, as a condition for issuance of a certificate of final completion and occupancy or final permit approval by the local building department, the permit applicant shall replace all noncompliant plumbing fixtures with water-conserving plumbing fixtures.

(b) On or before January 1, 2017, noncompliant plumbing fixtures in any single-family residential real property shall be replaced by the property owner with water-conserving plumbing fixtures.

(c) A seller or transferor of single-family residential real property shall disclose in writing to the prospective purchaser or transferee the requirements of subdivision (b) and whether the real property includes any noncompliant plumbing fixtures.

Added Stats 2009 ch 587 § 1 (SB 407), effective January 1, 2010. Amended Stats 2019 § 2 (AB 892), effective January 1, 2020.

§ 1101.5. Water-conserving plumbing fixtures; Replacement of noncompliant plumbing fixtures

(a) On or before January 1, 2019, all noncompliant plumbing fixtures in any multifamily residential real property and in any commercial real property shall be replaced with water-conserving plumbing fixtures.

(b) An owner or the owner's agent may enter the owner's property for the purpose of installing, repairing, testing, and maintaining water-conserving plumbing fixtures required by this section, consistent with notice requirements of Section 1954.

(c) On and after January 1, 2019, the water-conserving plumbing fixtures required by this section shall be operating at the manufacturer's rated water consumption at the time that the tenant takes possession. A tenant shall be responsible for notifying the owner or owner's agent if the tenant becomes aware that a water-conserving plumbing fixture within his or her unit is not operating at the manufacturer's rated water consumption. The owner or owner's agent shall correct an inoperability in a water-conserving plumbing fixture upon notice by the tenant or if detected by the owner or the owner's agent.

(d) (1) On and after January 1, 2014, all noncompliant plumbing fixtures in any multifamily residential real property and any commercial real property shall be replaced with water-conserving plumbing fixtures in the following circumstances:

(A) For building additions in which the sum of concurrent building permits by the same permit applicant would increase the floor area of the space in a building by more than 10 percent, the building permit applicant shall replace all noncompliant plumbing fixtures in the building.

(B) For building alterations or improvements in which the total construction cost estimated in the building permit is greater than one hundred fifty thousand dollars ($150,000), the building permit applicant shall replace all noncompliant plumbing fixtures that service the specific area of the improvement.

(C) Notwithstanding subparagraph (A) or (B), for any alterations or improvements to a room in a building that require a building permit and that room contains any noncompliant plumbing fixtures, the building permit applicant shall replace all noncompliant plumbing fixtures in that room.

(2) Replacement of all noncompliant plumbing fixtures with water-conserving plumbing fixtures, as described in paragraph (1), shall be a condition for issuance of a certificate of final completion and occupancy or final permit approval by the local building department.

(e) On and after January 1, 2019, a seller or transferor of multifamily residential real property or of commercial real property shall disclose to the prospective purchaser or transferee, in writing, the requirements of subdivision (a) and whether the property includes any noncompliant plumbing fixtures. This disclosure may be included in other transactional documents.

Added Stats 2009 ch 587 § 1 (SB 407), effective January 1, 2010. Amended Stats 2013 ch 183 § 1 (SB 745), effective January 1, 2014.

§ 1101.6. Requirements of article postponed with respect to building for which demolition permit has been issued

The duty of an owner or building permit applicant to comply with the requirements of this article shall be postponed for one year from the date of issuance of a demolition permit for the building. If the building is demolished within the one-year postponement, the requirements of this article shall not apply. If the building is not demolished after the expiration of one year, the provisions of this article shall apply, subject to appeal to the local building department, even though the demolition permit is still in effect or a new demolition permit has been issued.

Added Stats 2009 ch 587 § 1 (SB 407), effective January 1, 2010.

§ 1101.7. Applicability of article

This article shall not apply to any of the following:

(a) Registered historical sites.

(b) Real property for which a licensed plumber certifies that, due to the age or configuration of the property or its plumbing, installation of water-conserving plumbing fixtures is not technically feasible.

(c) A building for which water service is permanently disconnected.

Added Stats 2009 ch 587 § 1 (SB 407), effective January 1, 2010.

§ 1101.8. Enactment of local ordinances; Establishment of policies

A city, county, or city and county, or a retail water supplier may do either of the following:

(a) Enact local ordinances or establish policies that promote compliance with this article.

(b) Enact local ordinances or establish policies that will result in a greater amount of water savings than those provided for in this article.

Added Stats 2009 ch 587 § 1 (SB 407), effective January 1, 2010.

§ 1101.9. City, county, or city and county exempted from requirements of article; Conditions

Any city, county, or city and county that has adopted an ordinance requiring retrofit of noncompliant plumbing fixtures prior to July 1, 2009, shall be exempt from the requirements of this article so long as the ordinance remains in effect.

Added Stats 2009 ch 587 § 1 (SB 407), effective January 1, 2010.

Article 1.5

Disclosures Upon Transfer of Residential Property

§ 1102.155. Disclosures relating to water-conserving plumbing fixtures

(a) (1) The seller of single-family residential real property subject to this article shall disclose, in writing, that Section 1101.4requires that California single-family residences be equipped with water-conserving plumbing fixtures on or after January 1, 2017, and shall disclose whether the property includes any noncompliant plumbing fixtures as defined in subdivision (c) of Section 1101.3.

(2) The seller shall affirm that this representation is that of the seller and not a representation of any agent, and that this disclosure is not intended to be part of any contract between the buyer and the seller. The seller shall further affirm that this disclosure is not a warranty of any kind by the seller or any agent representing any principal in the transaction and is not a substitute for any inspections or warranties that any principal may wish to obtain.

(b) This section shall become operative on January 1, 2017.

Added Stats 2009 ch 587 § 2 (SB 407), effective January 1, 2010, operative January 1, 2017. Amended Stats 2018 ch 907 § 18 (AB 1289), effective January 1, 2019.

§ 1102.4. Liability for errors or omissions

(a) Neither the seller nor any seller's agent or buyer's agent shall be liable for any error, inaccuracy, or omission of any information delivered pursuant to this article if the error, inaccuracy, or omission was not within the personal knowledge of the seller or that listing or buyer's agent, was based on information timely provided by public agencies or by other persons providing information as specified in subdivision (c) that is required to be disclosed pursuant to this article, and ordinary care was exercised in obtaining and transmitting it.

(b) The delivery of any information required to be disclosed by this article to a prospective buyer by a public agency or other person providing information required to be disclosed pursuant to this article shall be deemed to comply with the requirements of this article and shall relieve the seller or any listing or buyer's agent of any further duty under this article with respect to that item of information.

(c) The delivery of a report or opinion prepared by a licensed engineer, land surveyor, geologist, structural pest control operator, contractor, a C-39 roofing contractor conducting a roof inspection pursuant to subdivision (d) of Section 7197 of the Business and Professions Code, or other expert, dealing with matters within the scope of the professional's license or expertise, shall be sufficient compliance for application of the exemption provided by subdivision (a) if the information is provided to the prospective buyer pursuant to a request therefor, whether written or oral. In responding to such a request, an expert may indicate, in writing, an understanding that the information provided will be used in fulfilling the requirements of Section 1102.6 and, if so, shall indicate the required disclosures, or parts thereof, to which the information being furnished is applicable. Where such a statement is furnished, the expert shall not be responsible for any items of information or parts thereof, other than those expressly set forth in the statement.

Added Stats 1985 ch 1574 § 2, operative January 1, 1987. Amended Stats 1986 ch 460 § 4; Stats 2017 ch 508 § 2 (AB 1357), effective January 1, 2018. Stats 2018 ch 907 § 11 (AB 1289), effective January 1, 2019.

DIVISION 3

OBLIGATIONS

PART 2

CONTRACTS

TITLE 5

Extinction of Contracts

Chapter 2

Rescission

§ 1689.5. Definitions

As used in Sections 1689.6 to 1689.11, inclusive, and in Section 1689.14:

(a) "Home solicitation contract or offer" means any contract, whether single or multiple, or any offer which is subject to approval, for the sale, lease, or rental of goods or services or both, made at other than appropriate trade premises in an amount of twenty-five dollars ($25) or more, including any interest or service charges. "Home solicitation contract" does not include any contract under which the buyer has the right to rescind pursuant to Title 1, Chapter 2, Section 125 of the Federal Consumer Credit Protection Act (P.L. 90-321) and the regulations promulgated pursuant thereto.

(b) "Appropriate trade premises," means premises where either the owner or seller normally carries on a business, or where goods are normally offered or exposed for sale in the course of a business carried on at those premises.

(c) "Goods" means tangible chattels bought for use primarily for personal, family, or household purposes, including certificates or coupons exchangeable for these goods, and including goods that, at the time of the sale or subsequently, are to be so affixed to real property as to become a part of the real property whether or not severable therefrom, but does not include any vehicle required to be registered under the Vehicle Code, nor any goods sold with this vehicle if sold under a contract governed by Section 2982, and does not include any mobilehome, as defined in Section 18008 of the Health and Safety Code, nor any goods sold with this mobilehome if either are sold under a contract subject to Section 18036.5 of the Health and Safety Code.

(d) "Services" means work, labor and services, including, but not limited to, services furnished in connection with the repair, restoration, alteration, or improvement of residential premises, or services furnished in connection with the sale or repair of goods as defined in Section 1802.1, and courses of instruction, regardless of the purpose for which they are taken, but does not include the services of attorneys, real estate brokers and salesmen, securities dealers or investment counselors, physicians, optometrists, or dentists, nor financial services offered by banks, savings institutions, credit unions, industrial loan companies, personal property brokers, consumer finance lenders, or commercial finance lenders, organized pursuant to state or federal law, that are not connected with the sale of goods or services, as defined herein, nor the sale of insurance that is not connected with the sale of goods or services as defined herein, nor services in connection with the sale or installation of mobilehomes or of goods sold with a mobilehome if either are sold or installed under a contract subject to Section 18036.5 of the Health and Safety Code, nor services for which the tariffs, rates, charges, costs, or expenses, including in each instance the time sale price, is required by law to be filed with and approved by the federal government or any official, department, division, commission, or agency of the United States or of the state.

(e) "Business day" means any calendar day except Sunday, or the following business holidays: New Year's Day, Washington's Birthday, Memorial Day, Independence Day, Labor Day, Columbus Day, Veterans' Day, Thanksgiving Day, and Christmas Day.

(f) This section shall become operative on January 1, 2006.

Added Stats 2005 ch 48 § 23 (SB 1113), effective July 18, 2005, operative January 1, 2006.

§ 1689.6. Right to cancel home solicitation contract or offer

(a) (1) Except for a contract written pursuant to Section 7151.2 or 7159.10 of the Business and Professions Code, in addition to any other right to revoke an offer, the buyer has the right to cancel a home solicitation contract or offer until midnight of the third business day, or until midnight of the fifth business day if the buyer is a senior citizen, after the day on which the buyer signs an agreement or offer to purchase which complies with Section 1689.7.

(2) In addition to any other right to revoke an offer, the buyer has the right to cancel a home solicitation contract written pursuant to Section 7151.2 of the Business and Professions Code until midnight of the third business day, or until midnight of the fifth business day if

the buyer is a senior citizen, after the buyer receives a signed and dated copy of the contract or offer to purchase that complies with Section 1689.7 of this code.

(3) (A) In addition to any other right to revoke an offer, the buyer has the right to cancel a home solicitation contract or offer to purchase written pursuant to Section 7159.10 of the Business and Professions Code, until the buyer receives a signed and dated copy of a service and repair contract that complies with the contract requirements specified in Section 7159.10 of the Business and Professions Code and the work commences.

(B) For any contract written pursuant to Section 7159.10 of the Business and Professions Code, or otherwise presented to the buyer as a service and repair contract, unless all of the conforming requirements listed under subdivision (a) of that section are met, the requirements set forth under Section 7159 of the Business and Professions Code shall be applicable, regardless of the aggregate contract price, including the right to cancel as set forth under this section.

(4) The five-day right to cancel added by the act that amended paragraphs (1) and (2) shall apply to contracts entered into, or offers to purchase conveyed, on or after January 1, 2021.

(b) In addition to any other right to revoke an offer, any buyer has the right to cancel a home solicitation contract or offer for the purchase of a personal emergency response unit until midnight of the seventh business day after the day on which the buyer signs an agreement or offer to purchase which complies with Section 1689.7. This subdivision shall not apply to a personal emergency response unit installed with, and as part of, a home security alarm system subject to the Alarm Company Act (Chapter 11.6 (commencing with Section 7590) of Division 3 of the Business and Professions Code) which has two or more stationary protective devices used to enunciate an intrusion or fire and is installed by an alarm company operator operating under a current license issued pursuant to the Alarm Company Act, which shall instead be subject to subdivision (a).

(c) In addition to any other right to revoke an offer, a buyer has the right to cancel a home solicitation contract or offer for the repair or restoration of residential premises damaged by a disaster that was not void pursuant to Section 1689.14, until midnight of the seventh business day after the buyer signs and dates the contract unless the provisions of Section 1689.15 are applicable.

(d) Cancellation occurs when the buyer gives written notice of cancellation to the seller at the address specified in the agreement or offer.

(e) Notice of cancellation, if given by mail, is effective when deposited in the mail properly addressed with postage prepaid.

(f) Notice of cancellation given by the buyer need not take the particular form as provided with the contract or offer to purchase and, however expressed, is effective if it indicates the intention of the buyer not to be bound by the home solicitation contract or offer.

(g) "Personal emergency response unit," for purposes of this section, means an in-home radio transmitter device or two-way radio device generally, but not exclusively, worn on a neckchain, wrist strap, or clipped to clothing, and connected to a telephone line through which a monitoring station is alerted of an emergency and emergency assistance is summoned.

Added Stats 2005 ch 48 § 25 (SB 1113), effective July 18, 2005, operative January 1, 2006. Amended Stats 2005 ch 385 § 11 (AB 316); Stats 2020 ch 158 § 5 (AB 2471), effective January 1, 2021.

§ 1689.7. Form of home solicitation contract or offer; Notice of cancellation

(a) (1) Except for contracts written pursuant to Sections 7151.2 and 7159.10 of the Business and Professions Code, in a home solicitation contract or offer, the buyer's agreement or offer to purchase shall be written in the same language, e.g., Spanish, as principally used in the oral sales presentation, shall be dated, shall be signed by the buyer, and except as provided in paragraph (2), shall contain in immediate proximity to the space reserved for the buyer's signature, a conspicuous statement in a size equal to at least 10-point boldface type, as follows:

(A) For a buyer who is a senior citizen: "You, the buyer, may cancel this transaction at any time prior to midnight of the fifth business day after the date of this transaction. See the attached notice of cancellation form for an explanation of this right."

(B) For all other buyers: "You, the buyer, may cancel this transaction at any time prior to midnight of the third business day after the date of this transaction. See the attached notice of cancellation form for an explanation of this right."

(2) The statement required pursuant to this subdivision for a home solicitation contract or offer for the purchase of a personal emergency response unit, as defined in Section 1689.6, that is not installed with and as part of a home security alarm system subject to the Alarm Company Act (Chapter 11.6 (commencing with Section 7590) of Division 3 of the Business and Professions Code) that has two or more stationary protective devices used to enunciate an intrusion or fire and is installed by an alarm company operator operating under a current license issued pursuant to the Alarm Company Act, is as follows: "You, the buyer, may cancel this transaction at any time prior to midnight of the seventh business day after the date of this transaction. See the attached notice of cancellation form for an explanation of this right."

(3) Except for contracts written pursuant to Sections 7151.2 and 7159.10 of the Business and Professions Code, the statement required pursuant to this subdivision for the repair or restoration of residential premises damaged by a disaster pursuant to subdivision (c) of Section 1689.6 is as follows: "You, the buyer, may cancel this transaction at any time prior to midnight of the seventh business day after the date of this transaction. See the attached notice of cancellation form for an explanation of this right."

(4) (A) A home solicitation contract written pursuant to Section 7151.2 of the Business and Professions Code shall be written in the same language, e.g., Spanish, as principally used in the oral sales presentation. The contract, or an attachment to the contract that is subject to Section 7159 of the Business and Professions Code shall include in immediate proximity to the space reserved for the buyer's signature, the following statement in a size equal to at least 12-point boldface type, which shall be dated and signed by the buyer:

"Three-Day Right to Cancel

You, the buyer, have the right to cancel this contract within three business days. You may cancel by e-mailing, mailing, faxing, or delivering a written notice to the contractor at the contractor's place of business by midnight of the third business day after you received a signed and dated copy of the contract that includes this notice. Include your name, your address, and the date you received the signed copy of the contract and this notice.

If you cancel, the contractor must return to you anything you paid within 10 days of receiving the notice of cancellation. For your part, you must make available to the contractor at your residence, in substantially as good condition as you received it, any goods delivered to you under this contract or sale. Or, you may, if you wish, comply with the contractor's instructions on how to return the goods at the contractor's expense and risk. If you do make the goods available to the contractor and the contractor does not pick them up within 20 days of the date of your notice of cancellation, you may keep them without any further obligation. If you fail to make the goods available to the contractor, or if you agree to return the goods to the contractor and fail to do so, then you remain liable for performance of all obligations under the contract."

(B) References to "three" and "third" in the statement set forth in subparagraph (A) shall be changed to "five" and "fifth," respectively, for a buyer who is a senior citizen.

(b) The agreement or offer to purchase shall contain on the first page, in a type size no smaller than that generally used in the body of the document, the following: (1) the name and address of the seller to which the notice is to be mailed, and (2) the date the buyer signed the agreement or offer to purchase.

(c) (1) Except for contracts written pursuant to Sections 7151.2 and 7159.10 of the Business and Professions Code, or except as provided in subdivision (d), the agreement or offer to purchase shall be accompanied by a completed form in duplicate, captioned "Notice of Cancellation" which shall be attached to the agreement or offer to purchase and be easily detachable, and which shall contain in type of at least 10-point the following statement written in the same language, e.g., Spanish, as used in the contract:

"Notice of Cancellation"

_____/enter date of transaction/_____
(Date)

"You may cancel this transaction, without any penalty or obligation, within three business days from the above date.

If you cancel, any property traded in, any payments made by you under the contract or sale, and any negotiable instrument executed by you will be returned within 10 days following receipt by the seller of your cancellation notice, and any security interest arising out of the transaction will be canceled.

If you cancel, you must make available to the seller at your residence, in substantially as good condition as when received, any goods delivered to you under this contract or sale, or you may, if you wish, comply with the instructions of the seller regarding the return shipment of the goods at the seller's expense and risk.

If you do make the goods available to the seller and the seller does not pick them up within 20 days of the date of your notice of cancellation, you may retain or dispose of the goods without any further obligation. If you fail to make the goods available to the seller, or if you agree to return the goods to the seller and fail to do so, then you remain liable for performance of all obligations under the contract."

To cancel this transaction, mail or deliver a signed and dated copy of this cancellation notice, or any other written notice, or send a telegram to _____ ,

/name of seller/

at_____

/address of seller's place of business/

not later than midnight of _____

(Date)

I hereby cancel this transaction._____

(Date)

_____

(Buyer's signature)

(2) The reference to "three" in the statement set forth in paragraph (1) shall be changed to "five" for a buyer who is a senior citizen.

(d) Any agreement or offer to purchase a personal emergency response unit, as defined in Section 1689.6, which is not installed with and as part of a home security alarm system subject to the Alarm Company Act which has two or more stationary protective devices used to enunciate an intrusion or fire and is installed by an alarm company operator operating under a current license issued pursuant to the Alarm Company Act, shall be subject to the requirements of subdivision (c), and shall be accompanied by the "Notice of Cancellation" required by subdivision (c), except that the first paragraph of that notice shall be deleted and replaced with the following paragraph:

You may cancel this transaction, without any penalty or obligation, within seven business days from the above date.

(e) A home solicitation contract written pursuant to Section 7151.2 of the Business and Professions Code for the repair or restoration of residential premises damaged by a disaster that is subject to subdivision (c) of Section 1689.6, shall be written in the same language, e.g., Spanish, as principally used in the oral sales presentation. The contract, or an attachment to the contract that is subject to Section 7159 of the Business and Professions Code shall include, in immediate proximity to the space reserved for the buyer's signature, the following statement in a size equal to at least 12-point boldface type, which shall be signed and dated by the buyer:

"Seven-Day Right to Cancel

You, the buyer, have the right to cancel this contract within seven business days. You may cancel by e-mailing, mailing, faxing, or delivering a written notice to the contractor at the contractor's place of business by midnight of the seventh business day after you received a signed and dated copy of the contract that includes this notice. Include your name, your address, and the date you received the signed copy of the contract and this notice.

If you cancel, the contractor must return to you anything you paid within 10 days of receiving the notice of cancellation. For your part, you must make available to the contractor at your residence, in substantially as good condition as you received it, any goods delivered to you under this contract or sale. Or, you may, if you wish, comply with the contractor's instructions on how to return the goods at the contractor's expense and risk. If you do make the goods available to the contractor and the contractor does not pick them up within 20 days of the date of your notice of cancellation, you may keep them without any further obligation. If you fail to make the goods available to the contractor, or if you agree to return the goods to the contractor and fail to do so, then you remain liable for performance of all obligations under the contract."

(f) The seller shall provide the buyer with a copy of the contract or offer to purchase and the attached notice of cancellation, and shall inform the buyer orally of the buyer's right to cancel and the requirement that cancellation be in writing, at the time the home solicitation contract or offer is executed.

(g) Until the seller has complied with this section the buyer may cancel the home solicitation contract or offer.

(h) "Contract or sale" as used in subdivision (c) means "home solicitation contract or offer" as defined by Section 1689.5.

(i) The five-day right to cancel added by the act that added subparagraph (A) to paragraph (1) and subparagraph (B) to paragraph (4) of subdivision (a), and paragraph (2) to subdivision (c) applies to contracts, or offers to purchase conveyed, entered into, on or after January 1, 2021.

Added Stats 2005 ch 48 § 27 (SB 1113), effective July 18, 2005, operative January 1, 2006. Amended Stats 2005 ch 385 § 12 (AB 316), effective January 1, 2006; Stats 2020 ch 158 § 6 (AB 2471), effective January 1, 2021; Stats 2021 ch 124 § 4 (AB 938), effective January 1, 2022.

§ 1689.8. Home solicitation contract or offer for home improvements which provides for lien on real property

(a) Every home solicitation contract or offer for home improvement goods or services which provides for a lien on real property is subject to the provisions of Chapter 1 (commencing with Section 1801) of Title 2 of Part 4 of Division 3.

(b) For purposes of this section, "home improvement goods or services" means goods and services, as defined in Section 1689.5, which are bought in connection with the improvement of real property. Such home improvement goods and services include, but are not limited to, burglar alarms, carpeting, texture coating, fencing, air conditioning or heating equipment, and termite extermination. Home improvement goods include goods which, at the time of sale or subsequently, are to be so affixed to real property as to become a part of real property whether or not severable therefrom.

Added Stats 1979 ch 1012 § 6.

§ 1689.9. Absence of buyer's right to cancel home solicitation contract or offer if goods affixed to sold or encumbered real property

Where the goods sold under any home solicitation contract are so affixed to real property as to become a part thereof, whether or not severable therefrom, the buyer shall not have the right to cancel as provided in Section 1689.6 or Section 1689.7 if, subsequent to his signing such contract, he has sold or encumbered such real property to a bona fide purchaser or encumbrancer who was not a party to such sale of goods or to any loan agreement in connection therewith.

Added Stats 1971 ch 375 § 5.

§ 1689.10. Tender of payments to buyer upon cancellation of home solicitation contract or offer

(a) Except as provided in Sections 1689.6 to 1689.11, inclusive, within 10 days after a home solicitation contract or offer has been canceled, the seller must tender to the buyer any payments made by the buyer and any note or other evidence of indebtedness.

(b) If the downpayment includes goods traded in, the goods must be tendered in substantially as good condition as when received.

(c) Until the seller has complied with the obligations imposed by Sections 1689.7 to 1689.11, inclusive, the buyer may retain possession of goods delivered to him by the seller and has a lien on the goods for any recovery to which he is entitled.

Added Stats 1971 ch 375 § 6. Amended Stats 1973 ch 554 § 5.

§ 1689.11. Tender of goods by buyer upon cancellation of home solicitation contract or offer

(a) Except as provided in subdivision (c) of Section 1689.10, within 20 days after a home solicitation contract or offer has been canceled, the buyer, upon demand, must tender to the seller any goods delivered by the seller pursuant to the sale or offer, but he is not obligated to tender at any place other than his own address. If the seller fails to demand possession of goods within 20 days after cancellation, the goods become the property of the buyer without obligation to pay for them.

(b) The buyer has a duty to take reasonable care of the goods in his possession both prior to cancellation and during the 20–day period following. During the 20–day period after cancellation, except for the buyer's duty of care, the goods are at the seller's risk.

(c) If the seller has performed any services pursuant to a home solicitation contract or offer prior to its cancellation, the seller is entitled to no compensation. If the seller's services result in the alteration of property of the buyer, the seller shall restore the property to substantially as good condition as it was at the time the services were rendered.

Added Stats 1971 ch 375 § 7. Amended Stats 1973 ch 554 § 6.

§ 1689.12. Waiver or confession of judgment invalid

Any waiver or confession of judgment of the provisions of Sections 1689.5 to 1689.11, inclusive, shall be deemed contrary to public policy and shall be void and unenforceable.

Added Stats 1971 ch 375 § 8. Amended Stats 1973 ch 554 § 7.

§ 1689.13. Applicability to emergency repairs or services

Sections 1689.5, 1689.6, 1689.7, 1689.10, 1689.12, and 1689.14 do not apply to a contract that meets all of the following requirements:

(a) The contract is initiated by the buyer or the buyer's agent or insurance representative.

(b) The contract is executed in connection with making of emergency or immediately necessary repairs that are necessary for the immediate protection of persons or real or personal property.

(c) (1) The buyer gives the seller a separate statement that is dated and signed that describes the situation that requires immediate remedy, and expressly acknowledges and waives the right to cancel the sale within three, five, or seven business days, whichever applies.

(2) The waiver of the five-day right to cancel added by the act that amended paragraph (1) shall apply to contracts entered into, or offers to purchase conveyed, on or after January 1, 2021.

Added Stats 2005 ch 48 § 29 (SB 1113), effective July 18, 2005, operative January 1, 2006. Amended Stats 2020 ch 158 § 7 (AB 2471), effective January 1, 2021.

§ 1689.14. Home solicitation contract or offer for repair signed following disaster; Void as specified

(a) Any home solicitation contract or offer for the repair or restoration of residential premises signed by the buyer on or after the date on which a disaster causes damage to the residential premises, but not later than midnight of the seventh business day after this date, shall be void, unless the buyer or his or her agent or insurance representative solicited the contract or offer at the appropriate trade premises of the seller. Any contract covered by this subdivision shall not be void if solicited by the buyer or his or her agent or insurance representative regardless of where the contract is made. For purposes of this section, buyer solicitation includes a telephone call from the buyer to the appropriate trade premises of the seller whether or not the call is in response to a prior home solicitation.

(b) As used in this section and Section 1689.6, "disaster" means an earthquake, flood, fire, hurricane, riot, storm, tidal wave, or other similar sudden or catastrophic occurrence for which a state of emergency has been declared by the President of the United States or the Governor or for which a local emergency has been declared by the executive officer or governing body of any city, county, or city and county.

Added Stats 1st Ex Sess 1993–94 ch 51 § 5 (AB 57 X). Amended Stats 1995 ch 123 § 1 (AB 1610), effective July 18, 1995.

§ 1689.15. Commencment of work; Right of cancellation

Notwithstanding any other provision of law, a contractor who is duly licensed pursuant to Chapter 9 (commencing with Section 7000) of Division 3 of the Business and Professions Code may commence work on a service and repair project as soon as the buyer receives a signed and dated copy of a service and repair contract that meets all of the contract requirements specified in Section 7159.10 of the Business and Professions Code. The buyer retains any right of cancellation applicable to home solicitations under Sections 1689.5 to 1689.14, inclusive, until such time as the buyer receives a signed and dated copy of a service and repair contract that meets all of the contract requirements specified in Section 7159.10 of the Business and Professions Code and the licensee in fact commences that project, at which time any cancellation rights provided in Sections 1689.5 to 1689.14, inclusive, are extinguished by operation of law.

Added Stats 2004 ch 566 § 20 (SB 30), operative July 1, 2005. Amended Stats 2005 ch 48 § 30 (SB 1113), effective July 18, 2005, operative January 1, 2006, ch 385 § 13 (AB 316).

Appendix

PART 4

OBLIGATIONS ARISING FROM PARTICULAR
TRANSACTIONS

TITLE 1.5
Consumers Legal Remedies Act

Chapter 3
Deceptive Practices

§ 1770. Unlawful acts and practices

(a) The unfair methods of competition and unfair or deceptive acts or practices listed in this subdivision undertaken by any person in a transaction intended to result or that results in the sale or lease of goods or services to any consumer are unlawful:

(1) Passing off goods or services as those of another.

(2) Misrepresenting the source, sponsorship, approval, or certification of goods or services.

(3) Misrepresenting the affiliation, connection, or association with, or certification by, another.

(4) Using deceptive representations or designations of geographic origin in connection with goods or services.

(5) Representing that goods or services have sponsorship, approval, characteristics, ingredients, uses, benefits, or quantities that they do not have or that a person has a sponsorship, approval, status, affiliation, or connection that the person does not have.

(6) Representing that goods are original or new if they have deteriorated unreasonably or are altered, reconditioned, reclaimed, used, or secondhand.

(7) Representing that goods or services are of a particular standard, quality, or grade, or that goods are of a particular style or model, if they are of another.

(8) Disparaging the goods, services, or business of another by false or misleading representation of fact.

(9) Advertising goods or services with intent not to sell them as advertised.

(10) Advertising goods or services with intent not to supply reasonably expectable demand, unless the advertisement discloses a limitation of quantity.

(11) Advertising furniture without clearly indicating that it is unassembled if that is the case.

(12) Advertising the price of unassembled furniture without clearly indicating the assembled price of that furniture if the same furniture is available assembled from the seller.

(13) Making false or misleading statements of fact concerning reasons for, existence of, or amounts of, price reductions.

(14) Representing that a transaction confers or involves rights, remedies, or obligations that it does not have or involve, or that are prohibited by law.

(15) Representing that a part, replacement, or repair service is needed when it is not.

(16) Representing that the subject of a transaction has been supplied in accordance with a previous representation when it has not.

(17) Representing that the consumer will receive a rebate, discount, or other economic benefit, if the earning of the benefit is contingent on an event to occur subsequent to the consummation of the transaction.

(18) Misrepresenting the authority of a salesperson, representative, or agent to negotiate the final terms of a transaction with a consumer.

(19) Inserting an unconscionable provision in the contract.

(20) Advertising that a product is being offered at a specific price plus a specific percentage of that price unless (A) the total price is set forth in the advertisement, which may include, but is not limited to, shelf tags, displays, and media advertising, in a size larger than any other price in that advertisement, and (B) the specific price plus a specific percentage of that

price represents a markup from the seller's costs or from the wholesale price of the product. This subdivision shall not apply to in-store advertising by businesses that are open only to members or cooperative organizations organized pursuant to Division 3 (commencing with Section 12000) of Title 1 of the Corporations Code if more than 50 percent of purchases are made at the specific price set forth in the advertisement.

(21) Selling or leasing goods in violation of Chapter 4 (commencing with Section 1797.8) of Title 1.7.

(22) (A) Disseminating an unsolicited prerecorded message by telephone without an unrecorded, natural voice first informing the person answering the telephone of the name of the caller or the organization being represented, and either the address or the telephone number of the caller, and without obtaining the consent of that person to listen to the prerecorded message.

(B) This subdivision does not apply to a message disseminated to a business associate, customer, or other person having an established relationship with the person or organization making the call, to a call for the purpose of collecting an existing obligation, or to any call generated at the request of the recipient.

(23) (A) The home solicitation, as defined in subdivision (h) of Section 1761, of a consumer who is a senior citizen where a loan or assessment is made encumbering the primary residence of that consumer for purposes of

paying for home improvements and where the transaction is part of a pattern or practice in violation any of the following:

(i) Subsection (h) or (i) of Section 1639 of Title 15 of the United States Code.

(ii) Paragraph (1), (2), or (4) of subdivision (a) of Section 226.34 of Title 12 of the Code of Federal Regulations.

(iii) Section 22684, 22685, 22686, or 22687 of the Financial Code.

(iv) Section 5898.16, 5898.17, 5913, 5922, 5923, 5924, 5925, 5926, or 5940 of the Streets and Highways Code.

(B) A third party shall not be liable under this subdivision unless (i) there was an agency relationship between the party who engaged in home solicitation and the third party, or (ii) the third party had actual knowledge of, or participated in, the unfair or deceptive transaction. A third party who is a holder in due course under a home solicitation transaction shall not be liable under this subdivision.

(24) (A) Charging or receiving an unreasonable fee to prepare, aid, or advise any prospective applicant, applicant, or recipient in the procurement, maintenance, or securing of public social services.

(B) For purposes of this paragraph:

(i) "Public social services" means those activities and functions of state and local government administered or supervised by the State Department of Health Care Services, the State Department of Public Health, or the State Department of Social Services, and involved in providing aid or services, or both, including health care services, and medical assistance, to those persons who, because of their economic circumstances or social condition, are in need of that aid or those services and may benefit from them.

(ii) "Public social services" also includes activities and functions administered or supervised by the United States Department of Veterans Affairs or the California Department of Veterans Affairs involved in providing aid or services, or both, to veterans, including pension benefits.

(iii) "Unreasonable fee" means a fee that is exorbitant and disproportionate to the services performed. Factors to be considered, if appropriate, in determining the reasonableness of a fee, are based on the circumstances existing at the time of the service and shall include, but not be limited to, all of the following:

(I) The time and effort required.

(II) The novelty and difficulty of the services.

(III) The skill required to perform the services.

(IV) The nature and length of the professional relationship.

(V) The experience, reputation, and ability of the person providing the services.

(C) This paragraph shall not apply to attorneys licensed to practice law in California, who are subject to the California Rules of Professional Conduct and to the mandatory fee arbitration provisions of Article 13 (commencing with Section 6200) of Chapter 4 of Division 3 of the Business and Professions Code, when the fees charged or received are for providing representation in administrative agency appeal proceedings or court proceedings for purposes of procuring, maintaining, or securing public social services on behalf of a person or group of persons.

(25) (A) Advertising or promoting any event, presentation, seminar, workshop, or other public gathering regarding veterans' benefits or entitlements that does not include the following statement in the same type size and font as the term "veteran" or any variation of that term:

(i) "I am not authorized to file an initial application for Veterans' Aid and Attendance benefits on your behalf, or to represent you before the Board of Veterans' Appeals within the United States Department of Veterans Affairs in any proceeding on any matter, including an application for those benefits. It would be illegal for me to accept a fee for preparing that application on your behalf." The requirements of this clause do not apply to a person licensed to act as an agent or attorney in proceedings before the Agency of Original Jurisdiction and the Board of Veterans' Appeals within the United States Department of Veterans Affairs when that person is offering those services at the advertised event.

(ii) The statement in clause (i) shall also be disseminated, both orally and in writing, at the beginning of any event, presentation, seminar, workshop, or public gathering regarding veterans' benefits or entitlements.

(B) Advertising or promoting any event, presentation, seminar, workshop, or other public gathering regarding veterans' benefits or entitlements that is not sponsored by, or affiliated with, the United States Department of Veterans Affairs, the California Department of Veterans Affairs, or any other congressionally chartered or recognized organization of honorably discharged members of the Armed Forces of the United States, or any of their auxiliaries that does not include the following statement, in the same type size and font as the term "veteran" or the variation of that term:

"This event is not sponsored by, or affiliated with, the United States Department of Veterans Affairs, the California Department of Veterans Affairs, or any other congressionally chartered or recognized organization of honorably discharged members of the Armed Forces of the United States, or any of their auxiliaries. None of the insurance products promoted at this sales event are endorsed by those organizations, all of which offer free advice to veterans about how to qualify and apply for benefits."

(i) The statement in this subparagraph shall be disseminated, both orally and in writing, at the beginning of any event, presentation, seminar, workshop, or public gathering regarding veterans' benefits or entitlements.

(ii) The requirements of this subparagraph shall not apply in a case where the United States Department of Veterans Affairs, the California Department of Veterans Affairs, or other congressionally chartered or recognized organization of honorably discharged members of the Armed Forces of the United States, or any of their auxiliaries have granted written permission to the advertiser or promoter for the use of its name, symbol, or insignia to advertise or promote the event, presentation, seminar, workshop, or other public gathering.

(26) Advertising, offering for sale, or selling a financial product that is illegal under state or federal law, including any cash payment for the assignment to a third party of the consumer's right to receive future pension or veteran's benefits.

(27) Representing that a product is made in California by using a Made in California label created pursuant to Section 12098.10 of the Government Code, unless the product complies with Section 12098.10 of the Government Code.

(28) (A) Failing to include either of the following in a solicitation by a covered person, or an entity acting on behalf of a covered person, to a consumer for a consumer financial product or service:

(i) The name of the covered person, and, if applicable, the entity acting on behalf of the covered person, and relevant contact information, including a mailing address and telephone number.

(ii) The following disclosure statement in at least 18-point bold type and in the language in which the solicitation is drafted: "THIS IS AN ADVERTISEMENT. YOU ARE NOT REQUIRED TO MAKE ANY PAYMENT OR TAKE ANY OTHER ACTION IN RESPONSE TO THIS OFFER."

(B) For purposes of this paragraph:

(i) "Consumer financial product or service" has the same meaning as defined in Section 90005 of the Financial Code.

(ii) (I) "Covered person" has the same meaning as defined in Section 90005 of the Financial Code.

(II) "Covered person" does not mean an entity exempt from Division 24 (commencing with Section 90000) of the Financial Code pursuant to Section 90002 of the Financial Code.

(iii) "Solicitation" means an advertisement or marketing communication through writing or graphics that is directed to, or likely to give the impression of being directed to, an individually identified person, residence, or business location. "Solicitation" does not include any of the following:

(I) Communication through a mass advertisement, including in a catalog, on a radio or television broadcast, or on a publicly accessible internet website, if that communication is not directed to, or is not likely to give the impression of being directed to, an individually identified person, residence, or business location.

(II) Communication via a telephone, mail, or electronic communication that was initiated by a consumer.

(III) A written credit or insurance solicitation that is subject to the disclosure requirements of subsection (d) of Section 1681m of Title 15 of the United States Code.

(b) (1) It is an unfair or deceptive act or practice for a mortgage broker or lender, directly or indirectly, to use a home improvement contractor to negotiate the terms of any loan that is secured, whether in whole or in part, by the residence of the borrower and that is used to finance a home improvement contract or any portion of a home improvement contract. For purposes of this subdivision, "mortgage broker or lender" includes a finance lender licensed pursuant to the California Financing Law (Division 9 (commencing with Section 22000) of the Financial Code), a residential mortgage lender licensed pursuant to the California Residential Mortgage Lending Act (Division 20 (commencing with Section 50000) of the Financial Code), or a real estate broker licensed under the Real Estate Law (Division 4 (commencing with Section 10000) of the Business and Professions Code).

(2) This section shall not be construed to either authorize or prohibit a home improvement contractor from referring a consumer to a mortgage broker or lender by this subdivision. However, a home improvement contractor may refer a consumer to a mortgage lender or broker if that referral does not violate Section 7157 of the Business and Professions Code or any other law. A mortgage lender or broker may purchase an executed home improvement contract if that purchase does not violate Section 7157 of the Business and Professions Code or any other law. Nothing in this paragraph shall have any effect on the application of Chapter 1 (commencing with Section 1801) of Title 2 to a home improvement transaction or the financing of a home improvement transaction.

Added Stats 1970 ch 1550 § 1. Amended Stats 1975 ch 379 § 1; Stats 1979 ch 819 § 4, effective September 19, 1979; Stats 1984 ch 1171 § 1; Stats 1986 ch 1497 § 1; Stats 1990 ch 1641 § 1 (AB 4084); Stats 1995 ch 255 § 2 (SB 320); Stats 1996 ch 684 § 1 (SB 2045); Stats 2008 ch 479 § 1 (SB 1136), effective January 1, 2009; Stats 2009 ch 140 § 26 (AB 1164), effective January 1, 2010; Stats 2011 ch 79 § 1 (SB 180), effective January 1, 2012; Stats 2012 ch 653 § 1 (SB 1170), effective January 1, 2013; Stats 2013 ch 541 § 1 (SB 12), effective January 1, 2014; Stats 2015 ch 246 § 1 (SB 386), effective January 1, 2016; Stats 2016 ch 86 § 19 (SB 1171), effective January 1, 2017; Stats 2019 ch 143 § 14 (SB 251), effective January 1, 2020; Stats 2021 ch 589 § 1 (AB 790), effective January 1, 2022; Stat 2022 ch 324 § 1 (AB 1904), effective January 1, 2023.

TITLE 1.7

Consumer Warranties

Chapter 5

Home Roof Warranties

§ 1797.90. Application of chapter

This chapter shall apply to all contracts and warranties for roofing materials used on a residential structure, including, but not limited to, a manufactured home or mobilehome, and to all contracts and warranties for the installation, repair, or replacement of all or any portion of the roof of a residential structure, including, but not limited to, a manufactured home or mobilehome.

Added Stats 1993 ch 835 § 1 (SB 409).

§ 1797.91. Necessity for written contract

Any contract for roofing materials, or for the installation, repair, or replacement of all or any portion of the roof of a residential structure, including, but not limited to, a manufactured home or mobilehome, shall be in writing if the contract includes any warranty of the materials or workmanship that extends for any period of time beyond completion of the work.

Added Stats 1993 ch 835 § 1 (SB 409).

§ 1797.92. Beneficiaries of warranty

For any contract subject to this chapter that is entered into on or after January 1, 1994, the warranty obligations shall inure to the benefit of, and shall be directly enforceable by, all subsequent purchasers and transferees of the residential structure, without limitation, unless the contract contains a clear and conspicuous provision limiting transferability of the warranty.

Added Stats 1993 ch 835 § 1 (SB 409).

§ 1797.93. Lifetime warranties

If any warranty subject to this chapter, uses the term "lifetime," "life," or a similar representation to describe the duration of the warranty, then the warranty shall disclose with such clarity and prominence as will be noticed and understood by prospective purchasers, the life to which the representation refers.

Added Stats 1993 ch 835 § 1 (SB 409).

TITLE 2
Credit Sales

Chapter 1
Retail Installment Sales

Article 4

Restrictions on Retail Installment Contracts

§ 1804.3. Security interests

(a) No contract other than one for services shall provide for a security interest in any goods theretofore fully paid for or which have not been sold by the seller.

(b) Any contract for goods which provides for a security interest in real property where the primary goods sold are not to be attached to the real property shall be a violation of this chapter and subject to the penalties set forth in Article 12.2 (commencing with Section 1812.6).

(c) This section shall become operative October 1, 1982.

Added Stats 1980 ch 1380 § 11, effective October 1, 1980, operative July 1, 1981. Amended Stats 1981 ch 107 § 4, effective June 29, 1981, operative April 1, 1982; Stats 1982 ch 129 § 4, effective March 25, 1982, operative October 1, 1982.

Article 5

Finance Charge Limitation

§ 1805.6. Undelivered goods; Home improvement contract

(a) Notwithstanding the provisions of any contract to the contrary, except as provided in subdivision (b) or (c), no retail seller shall assess any finance charge for goods purchased under a retail installment contract until the goods are in the buyer's possession.

(b) A finance charge may be assessed for such undelivered goods, as follows:

(1) From the date when such goods are available for pickup by the buyer and the buyer is notified of their availability, or

(2) From the date of purchase, when such goods are delivered or available for pickup by the buyer within 10 days of the date of purchase.

(c) In the case of a home improvement contract as defined in Section 7151.2 of the Business and Professions Code, a finance charge may be assessed from the approximate date of commencement of the work as set forth in the home improvement contract.

Added Stats 1975 ch 1041 § 1. Amended Stats 1976 ch 1271 § 3, effective September 28, 1976; Stats 1977 ch 868 § 3; Stats 1979 ch 1000 § 4; Stats 1980 ch 1380 § 15, effective October 1, 1980; Stats 1981 ch 1075 § 8, operative October 1, 1982.

Article 10

Retail Installment Accounts

§ 1810.10. Charge for undelivered goods

(a) Notwithstanding the provision of any contract to the contrary, except as provided in subdivision (b) or (c), no retail seller shall assess any finance charge against the outstanding balance for goods purchased under a retail installment account until the goods are in the buyer's possession.

(b) A finance charge may be assessed against the outstanding balance for such undelivered goods, as follows:

(1) From the date when such goods are available for pickup by the buyer and the buyer is notified of their availability, or

(2) From the date of purchase, when such goods are delivered or available for pickup by the buyer within 10 days of the date of purchase.

(c) In the case of a home improvement contract as defined in Section 7151.2 of the Business and Professions Code, a finance charge may be assessed against the amount financed from the approximate date of commencement of the work as set forth in the home improvement contract.

Added Stats 1975 ch 1041 § 2. Amended Stats 1976 ch 1271 § 5, effective September 28, 1976; Stats 1977 ch 868 § 5; Stats 1979 ch 1000 § 6.

TITLE 5
Hiring

Chapter 2
Hiring of Real Property

§ 1954. Landlord's right of access to dwelling unit; Notice of entry

(a) A landlord may enter the dwelling unit only in the following cases:

(1) In case of emergency.

(2) To make necessary or agreed repairs, decorations, alterations or improvements, supply necessary or agreed services, or exhibit the

dwelling unit to prospective or actual purchasers, mortgagees, tenants, workers, or contractors or to make an inspection pursuant to subdivision (f) of Section 1950.5.

(3) When the tenant has abandoned or surrendered the premises.

(4) Pursuant to court order.

(5) For the purposes set forth in Chapter 2.5 (commencing with Section 1954.201).

(6) To comply with the provisions of Article 2.2 (commencing with Section 17973) of Chapter 5 of Part 1.5 of Division 13 of the Health and Safety Code.

(b) Except in cases of emergency or when the tenant has abandoned or surrendered the premises, entry may not be made during other than normal business hours unless the tenant consents to an entry during other than normal business hours at the time of entry.

(c) The landlord may not abuse the right of access or use it to harass the tenant.

(d) (1) Except as provided in subdivision (e), or as provided in paragraph (2) or (3), the landlord shall give the tenant reasonable notice in writing of his or her intent to enter and enter only during normal business hours. The notice shall include the date, approximate time, and purpose of the entry. The notice may be personally delivered to the tenant, left with someone of a suitable age and discretion at the premises, or, left on, near, or under the usual entry door of the premises in a manner in which a reasonable person would discover the notice. Twenty-four hours shall be presumed to be reasonable notice in absence of evidence to the contrary. The notice may be mailed to the tenant. Mailing of the notice at least six days prior to an intended entry is presumed reasonable notice in the absence of evidence to the contrary.

(2) If the purpose of the entry is to exhibit the dwelling unit to prospective or actual purchasers, the notice may be given orally, in person or by telephone, if the landlord or his or her agent has notified the tenant in writing within 120 days of the oral notice that the property is for sale and that the landlord or agent may contact the tenant orally for the purpose described above. Twenty-four hours is presumed reasonable notice in the absence of evidence to the contrary. The notice shall include the date, approximate time, and purpose of the entry. At the time of entry, the landlord or agent shall leave written evidence of the entry inside the unit.

(3) The tenant and the landlord may agree orally to an entry to make agreed repairs or supply agreed services. The agreement shall include the date and approximate time of the entry, which shall be within one week of the agreement. In this case, the landlord is not required to provide the tenant a written notice.

(e) No notice of entry is required under this section:

(1) To respond to an emergency.

(2) If the tenant is present and consents to the entry at the time of entry.

Appendix

(3) After the tenant has abandoned or surrendered the unit.

Added Stats 1975 ch 302 § 2. Amended Stats 2002 ch 301 § 3 (SB 1403), ch 1061 § 2.5 (AB 2330); Stats 2003 ch 62 § 18 (SB 600), ch 787 § 1 (SB 345) (ch 787 prevails); Stats 2016 ch 623 § 1 (SB 7), effective January 1, 2017. Stats 2018 ch 445 § 1 (SB 721), effective January 1, 2019.

TITLE 12
Indemnity

§ 2782. Construction contracts; Agreements indemnifying promisee or relieving public agency from liability as void; Subcontractor's defense or indemnity obligation; Builder's or general contractor's rights to damages; Equitable indemnity

(a) Except as provided in Sections 2782.1, 2782.2, 2782.5, and 2782.6, provisions, clauses, covenants, or agreements contained in, collateral to, or affecting any construction contract and that purport to indemnify the promisee against liability for damages for death or bodily injury to persons, injury to property, or any other loss, damage or expense arising from the sole negligence or willful misconduct of the promisee or the promisee's agents, servants, or independent contractors who are directly responsible to the promisee, or for defects in design furnished by those persons, are against public policy and are void and unenforceable; provided, however, that this section shall not affect the validity of any insurance contract, workers' compensation, or agreement issued by an admitted insurer as defined by the Insurance Code.

(b) (1) Except as provided in Sections 2782.1, 2782.2, and 2782.5, provisions, clauses, covenants, or agreements contained in, collateral to, or affecting any construction contract with a public agency entered into before January 1, 2013, that purport to impose on the contractor, or relieve the public agency from, liability for the active negligence of the public agency are void and unenforceable.

(2) Except as provided in Sections 2782.1, 2782.2, and 2782.5, provisions, clauses, covenants, or agreements contained in, collateral to, or affecting any construction contract with a public agency entered into on or after January 1, 2013, that purport to impose on any contractor, subcontractor, or supplier of goods or services, or relieve the public agency from, liability for the active negligence of the public agency are void and unenforceable.

(c) (1) Except as provided in subdivision (d) and Sections 2782.1, 2782.2, and 2782.5, provisions, clauses, covenants, or agreements contained in, collateral to, or affecting any construction contract entered into on or after January 1, 2013, with the owner of privately owned real property to be improved and as to which the owner is not acting as a contractor or supplier of materials or equipment to the work, that purport to impose on any contractor, subcontractor, or supplier of goods or services, or relieve the owner from, liability are unenforceable to the extent of the active negligence of the owner, including that of its employees.

(2) For purposes of this subdivision, an owner of privately owned real property to be improved includes the owner of any interest therein, other than a mortgage or other interest that is held solely as security for performance of an obligation.

(3) This subdivision shall not apply to a homeowner performing a home improvement project on his or her own single family dwelling.

(d) For all construction contracts, and amendments thereto, entered into after January 1, 2009, for residential construction, as used in Title 7 (commencing with Section 895) of Part 2 of Division 2, all provisions, clauses, covenants, and agreements contained in, collateral to, or affecting any construction contract, and amendments thereto, that purport to insure or indemnify, including the cost to defend, the builder, as defined in Section 911, or the general contractor or contractor not affiliated with the builder, as described in subdivision (b) of Section 911, by a subcontractor against liability for claims of construction defects are unenforceable to the extent the claims arise out of, pertain to, or relate to the negligence of the builder or contractor or the builder's or contractor's other agents, other servants, or other independent contractors who are directly responsible to the builder, or for defects in design furnished by those persons, or to the extent the claims do not arise out of, pertain to, or relate to the scope of work in the written agreement between the parties. This section shall not be waived or modified by contractual agreement, act, or omission of the parties. Contractual provisions, clauses, covenants, or agreements not expressly prohibited herein are reserved to the agreement of the parties. Nothing in this subdivision shall prevent any party from exercising its rights under subdivision (a) of Section 910. This subdivision shall not affect the obligations of an insurance carrier under the holding of Presley Homes, Inc. v. American States Insurance Company (2001) 90 Cal.App.4th 571. Nor shall this subdivision affect the obligations of a builder or subcontractor pursuant to Title 7 (commencing with Section 895) of Part 2 of Division 2.

(e) Subdivision (d) does not prohibit a subcontractor and builder or general contractor from mutually agreeing to the timing or immediacy of the defense and provisions for reimbursement of defense fees and costs, so long as that agreement does not waive or modify the provisions of subdivision (d) subject, however, to paragraphs (1) and (2). A subcontractor shall owe no defense or indemnity obligation to a builder or general contractor for a construction defect claim unless and until the builder or general contractor provides a written tender of the claim, or portion thereof, to the subcontractor which includes all of the information provided to the builder or general contractor by the claimant or claimants, including, but not limited to, information provided pursuant to subdivision (a) of Section 910, relating to claims caused by that subcontractor's scope of work. This written tender shall have the same force and effect as a notice of commencement of a legal proceeding. If a builder or general contractor tenders a claim for construction defects, or a portion thereof, to a subcontractor in the manner specified by this provision, the subcontractor shall elect to perform either of the following, the performance of which shall be deemed to satisfy the subcontractor's defense obligation to the builder or general contractor:

(1) Defend the claim with counsel of its choice, and the subcontractor shall maintain control of the defense for any claim or portion of claim to which the defense obligation applies. If a subcontractor elects to defend under this paragraph, the subcontractor shall provide written notice of the election to the builder or general contractor within a reasonable time period following receipt of the written tender, and in no event later than 90 days following that receipt. Consistent with subdivision (d), the defense by the subcontractor shall be a complete defense of the builder or general contractor of all claims or portions thereof to the extent alleged to be caused by the subcontractor, including any vicarious liability claims against the builder or general contractor resulting from the subcontractor's scope of work, but not including claims resulting from the scope of work, actions, or omissions of the builder, general contractor, or any other party. Any vicarious liability imposed upon a builder or general contractor for claims caused by the subcontractor electing to defend under this paragraph shall be directly enforceable against the subcontractor by the builder, general contractor, or claimant.

(2) Pay, within 30 days of receipt of an invoice from the builder or general contractor, no more than a reasonable allocated share of the builder's or general contractor's defense fees and costs, on an ongoing basis during the pendency of the claim, subject to reallocation consistent with subdivision (d), and including any amounts reallocated upon final resolution of the claim, either by settlement or judgment. The builder or general contractor shall allocate a share to itself to the extent a claim or claims are alleged to be caused by its work, actions, or omissions, and a share to each subcontractor to the extent a claim or claims are alleged to be caused by the subcontractor's work, actions, or omissions, regardless of whether the builder or general contractor actually tenders the claim to any particular subcontractor, and regardless of whether that subcontractor is participating in the defense. Any amounts not collected from any particular subcontractor may not be collected from any other subcontractor.

(f) Notwithstanding any other provision of law, if a subcontractor fails to timely and adequately perform its obligations under paragraph (1) of subdivision (e), the builder or general contractor shall have the right to pursue a claim against the subcontractor for any resulting compensatory damages, consequential damages, and reasonable attorney's fees. If a subcontractor fails to timely perform its obligations under paragraph (2) of subdivision (e), the builder or general contractor shall have the right to pursue a claim against the subcontractor for any resulting compensatory and consequential damages, as well as for interest on defense and indemnity costs, from the date incurred, at the rate set forth in subdivision (g) of Section 3260, and for the builder's or general contractor's reasonable attorney's fees incurred to recover these amounts. The builder or general contractor shall bear the burden of proof to establish both the subcontractor's failure to perform under either paragraph (1) or (2) of subdivision (e) and any resulting damages. If, upon request by a subcontractor, a builder or general contractor does not reallocate defense fees to subcontractors within 30 days following final resolution of the claim as described above, the subcontractor shall have the right to pursue a claim against the builder or general contractor for any resulting compensatory and consequential damages, as well as for interest on the fees, from the date of final resolution of the claim, at the rate set forth in subdivision (g) of Section 3260, and the subcontractor's reasonable attorney's fees incurred in connection therewith. The subcontractor shall bear the burden of proof to establish both the failure to reallocate the fees and any resulting damages. Nothing in this section shall prohibit the parties from mutually agreeing to reasonable contractual provisions for damages if any party fails to elect for or perform its obligations as stated in this section.

(g) A builder, general contractor, or subcontractor shall have the right to seek equitable indemnity for any claim governed by this section.

(h) Nothing in this section limits, restricts, or prohibits the right of a builder, general contractor, or subcontractor to seek equitable indemnity against any supplier, design professional, or product manufacturer.

(i) As used in this section, "construction defect" means a violation of the standards set forth in Sections 896 and 897.

(h) Nothing in this section limits, restricts, or prohibits the right of a builder, general contractor, or subcontractor to seek equitable indemnity against any supplier, design professional, or product manufacturer.

(i) As used in this section, "construction defect" means a violation of the standards set forth in Sections 896 and 897.

Appendix

Added Stats 1967 ch 1327 § 1. Amended Stats 1980 ch 211 § 1; Stats 1982 ch 386 § 1; Stats 1985 ch 567 § 1; Stats 1990 ch 814 § 1 (SB 1922); Stats 2005 ch 394 § 1 (AB 758), effective January 1, 2006; Stats 2007 ch 32 § 1 (SB 138), effective January 1, 2008; Stats 2008 ch 467 § 1 (AB 2738), effective January 1, 2009; Stats 2011 ch 707 § 2 (SB 474), effective January 1, 2012.

§ 2782.6. Exception for professional engineer or geologist; "Hazardous materials" [Effective until January 1, 2024; Operative until January 1, 2024]

(a) Nothing in subdivision (a) of Section 2782 prevents an agreement to indemnify a professional engineer or geologist or the agents, servants, independent contractors, subsidiaries, or employees of that engineer or geologist from liability as described in Section 2782 in providing hazardous materials identification, evaluation, preliminary assessment, design, remediation services, or other services of the types described in Sections 25322 and 25323 of the Health and Safety Code or the federal National Oil and Hazardous Substances Pollution Contingency Plan (40 C.F.R. Sec. 300.1 et seq.), if all of the following criteria are satisfied:

(1) The services in whole or in part address subterranean contamination or other concealed conditions caused by the hazardous materials.

(2) The promisor is responsible, or potentially responsible, for all or part of the contamination.

(b) The indemnification described in this section is valid only for damages arising from, or related to, subterranean contamination or concealed conditions, and is not applicable to the first two hundred fifty thousand dollars ($250,000) of liability or a greater amount as is agreed to by the parties.

(c) This section does not authorize contracts for indemnification, by promisors specified in paragraph (2) of subdivision (a), of any liability of a promisee arising from the gross negligence or willful misconduct of the promisee.

(d) "Hazardous materials," as used in this section, means any hazardous or toxic substance, material, or waste that is or becomes subject to regulation by any agency of the state, any municipality or political subdivision of the state, or the United States. "Hazardous materials" includes, but is not limited to, any material or substance that is any of the following:

(1) A hazardous substance, as defined in Section 25316 of the Health and Safety Code.

(2) Hazardous material, as defined in subdivision (n) of Section 25501 of the Health and Safety Code.

(3) A regulated substance, as defined in subdivision (i) of Section 25532 of the Health and Safety Code.

(4) Hazardous waste, as defined in Section 25117 of the Health and Safety Code.

(5) Extremely hazardous waste, as defined in Section 25115 of the Health and Safety Code.

(6) Petroleum.

(7) Asbestos.

(8) Designated as a hazardous substance for purposes of Section 311 of the Federal Water Pollution Control Act, as amended (33 U.S.C. Sec. 1321).

(9) Hazardous waste, as defined by subsection (5) of Section 1004 of the federal Resource Conservation and Recovery Act of 1976, as amended (42 U.S.C. Sec. 6903).

(10) A hazardous substance, as defined by subsection (14) of Section 101 of the federal Comprehensive Environmental Response, Compensation, and Liability Act of 1980, as amended (42 U.S.C. Sec. 9601).

(11) A regulated substance, as defined by subsection (7) of Section 9001 of the federal Solid Waste Disposal Act, as amended (42 U.S.C. Sec. 6991).

(e) Nothing in this section shall be construed to alter, modify, or otherwise affect the liability of the promisor or promisee, under an indemnity agreement meeting the criteria of this section, to third parties for damages for death or bodily injury to persons, injury to property, or any other loss, damage, or expense.

(f) This section does not apply to public entities, as defined by Section 811.2 of the Government Code.

Added Stats 1990 ch 814 § 2 (SB 1922). Amended Stats 2018 ch 59 § 1 (SB 1502), effective January 1, 2019; Stats 2021 ch 115 § 1 (AB 148), effective July 22, 2021.

§ 2782.6. Exception for professional engineer or geologist; "Hazardous materials" [Effective January 1, 2023; Operative January 1, 2024]

(a) Nothing in subdivision (a) of Section 2782 prevents an agreement to indemnify a professional engineer or geologist or the agents, servants, independent contractors, subsidiaries, or employees of that engineer or geologist from liability as described in Section 2782 in providing hazardous materials identification, evaluation, preliminary assessment, design, remediation services, or other services of the types described in Sections 78125 and 78135 of the Health and Safety Code or the federal National Oil and Hazardous Substances Pollution Contingency Plan (40 C.F.R. Sec. 300.1 et seq.), if all of the following criteria are satisfied:

(1) The services in whole or in part address subterranean contamination or other concealed conditions caused by the hazardous materials.

(2) The promisor is responsible, or potentially responsible, for all or part of the contamination.

(b) The indemnification described in this section is valid only for damages arising from, or related to, subterranean contamination or concealed conditions, and is not applicable to the first two hundred fifty thousand dollars ($250,000) of liability or a greater amount as is agreed to by the parties.

(c) This section does not authorize contracts for indemnification, by promisors specified in paragraph (2) of subdivision (a), of any liability of a promisee arising from the gross negligence or willful misconduct of the promisee.

(d) "Hazardous materials," as used in this section, means any hazardous or toxic substance, material, or waste that is or becomes subject to regulation by any agency of the state, any municipality or political subdivision of the state, or the United States. "Hazardous materials" includes, but is not limited to, any material or substance that is any of the following:

(1) A hazardous substance, as defined in subdivision (a) of Section 78075 of the Health and Safety Code.

(2) Hazardous material, as defined in subdivision (n) of Section 25501 of the Health and Safety Code.

(3) A regulated substance, as defined in subdivision (i) of Section 25532 of the Health and Safety Code.

(4) Hazardous waste, as defined in Section 25117 of the Health and Safety Code.

(5) Extremely hazardous waste, as defined in Section 25115 of the Health and Safety Code.

(6) Petroleum.

(7) Asbestos.

(8) Designated as a hazardous substance for purposes of Section 311 of the Federal Water Pollution Control Act, as amended (33 U.S.C. Sec. 1321).

(9) Hazardous waste, as defined by subsection (5) of Section 1004 of the federal Resource Conservation and Recovery Act of 1976, as amended (42 U.S.C. Sec. 6903).

(10) A hazardous substance, as defined by subsection (14) of Section 101 of the federal Comprehensive Environmental Response, Compensation, and Liability Act of 1980, as amended (42 U.S.C. Sec. 9601).

(11) A regulated substance, as defined by subsection (7) of Section 9001 of the federal Solid Waste Disposal Act, as amended (42 U.S.C. Sec. 6991).

(e) Nothing in this section shall be construed to alter, modify, or otherwise affect the liability of the promisor or promisee, under an indemnity agreement meeting the criteria of this section, to third parties for damages for death or bodily injury to persons, injury to property, or any other loss, damage, or expense.

(f) This section does not apply to public entities, as defined by Section 811.2 of the Government Code.

Added Stats 1990 ch 814 § 2 (SB 1922). Amended Stats 2018 ch 59 § 1 (SB 1502), effective January 1, 2019; Stats 2021 ch 115 § 1 (AB 148), effective July 22, 2021; Stat 2022 ch 258 § 6 (AB 2327), effective January 1, 2023, operative January 1, 2024.

§ 2782.8. Contracts for design professional services; Limitations on indemnity; Applicability

(a) For all contracts, and amendments thereto, entered into on or after January 1, 2018, for design professional services, all provisions, clauses, covenants, and agreements contained in, collateral to, or affecting any such contract, and amendments thereto, that purport to indemnify, including the duty and the cost to defend, the indemnitee by a design professional against liability for claims against the indemnitee, are unenforceable, except to the extent that the claims against the indemnitee arise out of, pertain to, or relate to the negligence, recklessness, or willful misconduct of the design professional. In no event shall the cost to defend charged to the design professional exceed the design professional's proportionate percentage of fault. However, notwithstanding the previous sentence, in the event one or more defendants is unable to pay its share of defense costs due to bankruptcy or dissolution of the business, the design professional shall meet and confer with other parties regarding unpaid defense costs. The duty to indemnify, including the duty and the cost to defend, is limited as provided in this section. This section shall not be waived or modified by contractual agreement, act, or omission of the parties. Contractual provisions, clauses, covenants, or agreements not expressly prohibited herein are reserved to the agreement of the parties.

(b) All contracts and all solicitation documents, including requests for proposal, invitations for bid, and other solicitation for design professional services are deemed to incorporate by reference the provisions of this section.

(c) For purposes of this section, "design professional" includes all of the following:

(1) An individual licensed as an architect pursuant to Chapter 3 (commencing with Section 5500) of Division 3 of the Business and Professions Code, and a business entity offering architectural services in accordance with that chapter.

(2) An individual licensed as a landscape architect pursuant to Chapter 3.5 (commencing with Section 5615) of Division 3 of the Business and Professions Code, and a business entity offering landscape architectural services in accordance with that chapter.

(3) An individual registered as a professional engineer pursuant to Chapter 7 (commencing with Section 6700) of Division 3 of the Busi-

Appendix

ness and Professions Code, and a business entity offering professional engineering services in accordance with that chapter.

(4) An individual licensed as a professional land surveyor pursuant to Chapter 15 (commencing with Section 8700) of Division 3 of the Business and Professions Code, and a business entity offering professional land surveying services in accordance with that chapter.

(d) This section shall apply only to a professional service contract, or any amendment thereto, entered into on or after January 1, 2018.

(e) The provisions of this section pertaining to the duty and cost to defend shall not apply to either of the following:

(1) Any contract for design professional services, or amendments thereto, where a project-specific general liability policy insures all project participants for general liability exposures on a primary basis and also covers all design professionals for their legal liability arising out of their professional services on a primary basis.

(2) A design professional who is a party to a written design-build joint venture agreement.

(f) Nothing in this section shall abrogate the provisions of Section 1104 of the Public Contract Code.

(g) Indemnitee, for purposes of this section, does not include any agency of the state.

Added Stats 2006 ch 455 § 1 (AB 573), effective January 1, 2007. Amended Stats 2010 ch 510 § 1 (SB 972), effective January 1, 2011; Stats 2017 ch 8 § 1 (SB 496), effective January 1, 2018.

§ 2782.9. Construction contracts on which wrap-up insurance policy applicable; Agreements indemnifying another from liability void; Equitable indemnity; Waiver or modification

(a) All contracts, provisions, clauses, amendments, or agreements contained therein entered into after January 1, 2009, for a residential construction project on which a wrap-up insurance policy, as defined in subdivision (b) of Section 11751.82 of the Insurance Code, or other consolidated insurance program, is applicable, that require an enrolled and participating subcontractor or other participant to indemnify, hold harmless, or defend another for any claim or action covered by that program, arising out of that project are unenforceable.

(b) To the extent any contractual provision is deemed unenforceable pursuant to this section, any party may pursue an equitable indemnity claim against another party for a claim or action unless there is coverage for the claim or action under the wrap-up policy or policies. Nothing in this section shall prohibit a builder or general contractor from requiring a reasonably allocated contribution from a subcontractor or other participant to the self-insured retention or deductible required under the wrap-up policy or other consolidated insurance program, if the maximum amount and method of collection of the participant's contribution is disclosed in the contract with the participant and the contribution is reasonably limited so that each participant may have some financial obligation in the event of a claim alleged to be caused by that participant's scope of work. The contribution shall only be collected when and as any such self-insured retention or deductible is incurred by the builder or general contractor and in an amount that bears a reasonable and proportionate relationship to the alleged liability arising from the claim or claims alleged to be caused by the participant's scope of work, when viewed in the context of the entirety of the alleged claim or claims. Any contribution shall only be collected from a participant after written notice to the participant of the amount of and basis for the contribution. In no event shall the total amount of contributions collected from participants exceed the amount of any self-insured retention or deductible due and payable by the builder or general contractor for the claim or claims. However, this requirement does not prohibit any legally permissible recovery of costs and legal fees to collect a participant's contribution if the contribution satisfies the requirements of this subdivision and is not paid by the participant when due.

(c) This section shall not be waived or modified by contractual agreement, act, or omission of the parties.

Added Stats 2008 ch 467 § 2 (AB 2738), effective January 1, 2009.

§ 2782.95. Provisions governing construction where wrap-up insurance policy covers private residential improvement; Disclosure; Bidding

For any wrap-up insurance policy or other consolidated insurance program that insures a private residential (as that term is used in Title 7 (commencing with Section 895) of Part 2 of Division 2) work of improvement that first commences construction after January 1, 2009, the following shall apply:

(a) The owner, builder, or general contractor obtaining the wrap-up insurance policy or other consolidated insurance program shall disclose the total amount or method of calculation of any credit or compensation for premium required from a subcontractor or other participant for that wrap-up policy in the contract documents.

(b) The contract documents shall disclose, if and to the extent known:

(1) The policy limits.

(2) The scope of policy coverage.

(3) The policy term.

(4) The basis upon which the deductible or occurrence is triggered by the insurance carrier.

Appendix

(5) If the policy covers more than one work of improvement, the number of units, if any, indicated on the application for the insurance policy.

(6) A good faith estimate of the amount of available limits remaining under the policy as of a date indicated in the disclosure obtained from the insurer.

(7) Disclosures made pursuant to paragraphs (5) and (6) are recognized to be based upon information at a given moment in time and may not accurately reflect the actual number of units covered by the policy nor the amount of insurance available, if any, when a later claim is made. These disclosures are presumptively made in good faith if the disclosure pursuant to paragraph (5) is the same as that contained in the application to the wrap-up insurer and the disclosure pursuant to paragraph (6) was obtained from the wrap-up insurer or broker. The presumptions stated above shall be overcome only by a showing that the insurer, broker, builder, or general contractor intentionally misrepresented the facts identified in paragraphs (5) or (6).

(c) Upon the written request of any participant, a copy of the insurance policy shall be provided, if available, that shows the coverage terms and items in paragraphs (1) to (4), inclusive, of subdivision (b) above. If the policy is not available at the time of the request, a copy of the insurance binder or declaration of coverage may be provided in lieu of the actual policy. Paragraphs (1) to (4), inclusive, of subdivision (b) may be satisfied by providing the participant with a copy of the binder or declaration. Any party receiving a copy of the policy, binder, or declaration shall not disclose it to third parties other than the participant's insurance broker or attorney unless required to do so by law. The participant's insurance broker or attorney may not disclose the policy, binder, or declaration to any third party unless required to do so by law.

(d) If the owner, builder, or general contractor obtaining the wrap-up insurance policy or other consolidated insurance program does not disclose the total amount or method of calculation of the premium credit or compensation to be charged to the participant prior to the time the participant submits its bid, the participant shall not be legally bound by the bid unless that participant has the right to increase the bid up to the amount equal to the difference between the amount the participant included, if any, for insurance in the original bid and the amount of the actual bid credit required by the owner, builder, or general contractor obtaining the wrap-up insurance policy or other consolidated insurance program. This subdivision shall not apply if the owner, builder, or general contractor obtaining the wrap-up insurance policy or other consolidated insurance program did not require the subcontractor to offset the original bid amount with a deduction for the wrap-up insurance policy or program.

Added Stats 2008 ch 467 § 3 (AB 2738), effective January 1, 2009.

§ 2782.96. Provisions governing construction where wrap-up insurance policy covers public work; Calculations to be clearly delineated in bid document; Disclosure

If an owner, builder, or general contractor obtains a wrap-up insurance policy or other consolidated insurance program for a public work as defined in Section 1720 of the Labor Code or any other project other than residential construction, as that term is used in Title 7 (commencing with Section 895) of Part 2 of Division 2, that is put out for bid after January 1, 2009, the following shall apply:

(a) The total amount or method of calculation of any credit or compensation for premium required from a subcontractor or other participant for that policy shall be clearly delineated in the bid documents.

(b) The named insured, to the extent known, shall disclose to the subcontractor or other participant in the contract documents the policy limits, known exclusions, and the length of time the policy is intended to remain in effect. In addition, upon written request, once available, the named insured shall provide copies of insurance policies to all those who are covered by the policy. Until such time as the policies are available, the named insured may also satisfy the disclosure requirements of this subdivision by providing the subcontractor or other participant with a copy of the insurance binder or declaration of coverage. Any party receiving a copy of the policy, binder, or declaration shall not disclose it to third parties other than the participant's insurance broker or attorney unless required to do so by law. The participant's insurance broker or attorney may not disclose the policy, binder, or declaration to any third party unless required to do so by law.

(c) The disclosure requirements in subdivisions (a) and (b) do not apply to an insurance policy purchased by an owner, builder, or general contractor that provides additional coverage beyond what was contained in the original wrap-up policy or other consolidated insurance program if no credit or compensation for premium is required of the subcontractor for the additional insurance policy.

Added Stats 2008 ch 467 § 4 (AB 2738), effective January 1, 2009. Amended Stats. 2009, Ch. 140 (AB 1164).

Appendix

PART 6

WORKS OF IMPROVEMENT

TITLE 1

Works of Improvement Generally

Chapter 1

General Provisions

Article 1

Definitions

§ 8000. Definitions as governing construction of part

Unless the provision or context otherwise requires, the definitions in this article govern the construction of this part.

Added Stats 2010 ch 697 § 20 (SB 189), effective January 1, 2011, operative July 1, 2012.

Law Revision Commission Comments:

2010—Section 8000 continues former Section 3082 without substantive change.

§ 8002. "Admitted surety insurer"

"Admitted surety insurer" has the meaning provided in Section 995.120 of the Code of Civil Procedure.

Added Stats 2010 ch 697 § 20 (SB 189), effective January 1, 2011, operative July 1, 2012.

Law Revision Commission Comments:

2010—Section 8002 is new. It is included for drafting convenience. "Admitted surety insurer" replaces references in former law to a corporate surety authorized to write or issue surety bonds in the State of California.

See Sections 8424 (lien claim release bond), 8510 (stop payment notice release bond), 8534 (construction lender objection to bonded stop payment notice), 8604 (lending institution objection to surety on payment bond), 8606 (payment bond).

§ 8004. "Claimant"

"Claimant" means a person that has a right under this part to record a claim of lien, give a stop payment notice, or assert a claim against a payment bond, or do any combination of the foregoing.

Added Stats 2010 ch 697 § 20 (SB 189), effective January 1, 2011, operative July 1, 2012.

Law Revision Commission Comments:

2010—Section 8004 restates former Section 3085 without substantive change.

See also Sections 8026 ("lien"), 8030 ("payment bond"), 8032 ("person"), 8044 ("stop payment notice").

§ 8006.   "Construction lender"

"Construction lender" means either of the following:

(a) A mortgagee or beneficiary under a deed of trust lending funds with which the cost of all or part of a work of improvement is to be paid, or the assignee or successor in interest of the mortgagee or beneficiary.

(b) An escrow holder or other person holding funds provided by an owner, lender, or another person as a fund for with which the cost of all or part of a work of improvement is to be paid.

Added Stats 2010 ch 697 § 20 (SB 189), effective January 1, 2011, operative July 1, 2012.

Law Revision Commission Comments:

2010—Section 8006 restates former Section 3087 without substantive change.

See also Section 14 (present includes future).

See also Sections 8032 ("person"), 8050 ("work of improvement").

§ 8008.   "Contract"

"Contract" means an agreement that provides for all or part of a work of improvement.

Added Stats 2010 ch 697 § 20 (SB 189), effective January 1, 2011, operative July 1, 2012.

Law Revision Commission Comments:

2010—Section 8008 broadens the definition of "contract" in former Section 3088. There are instances in this part where the term is not used in its defined sense. See, e.g., Section 8444(d)(2). See also Section 8000 (application of definitions).

An agreement between an owner and a direct contractor that provides for all or part of a work of improvement is a "direct contract." See Section 8016.

See also Section 8050 ("work of improvement").

§ 8010.   "Contract price"

"Contract price" means the price agreed to in a direct contract for a work of improvement.

Added Stats 2010 ch 697 § 20 (SB 189), effective January 1, 2011, operative July 1, 2012.

Law Revision Commission Comments:

2010—Section 8010 is new. It is included for drafting convenience.
See also Sections 8016 ("direct contract"), 8050 ("work of improvement").

§ 8012. "Contractor"

"Contractor" includes a direct contractor, subcontractor, or both. This section does not apply to Sections 8018 and 8046.

Added Stats 2010 ch 697 § 20 (SB 189), effective January 1, 2011, operative July 1, 2012.

Law Revision Commission Comments:

2010—Section 8012 is new. It is included for drafting convenience.
See also Sections 8018 ("direct contractor"), 8046 ("subcontractor").

§ 8014. "Design professional"

"Design professional" means a person licensed as an architect pursuant to Chapter 3 (commencing with Section 5500) of Division 3 of the Business and Professions Code, licensed as a landscape architect pursuant to Chapter 3.5 (commencing with Section 5615) of Division 3 of the Business and Professions Code, registered as a professional engineer pursuant to Chapter 7 (commencing with Section 6700) of Division 3 of the Business and Professions Code, or licensed as a land surveyor pursuant to Chapter 15 (commencing with Section 8700) of Division 3 of the Business and Professions Code.

Added Stats 2010 ch 697 § 20 (SB 189), effective January 1, 2011, operative July 1, 2012.

Law Revision Commission Comments:

2010—Section 8014 generalizes the first paragraph of former Section 3081.1, and adds a licensed landscape architect to the persons included within the definition of "design professional."
See also Sections 8032 ("person"), 8050 ("work of improvement").

§ 8016. "Direct contract"

"Direct contract" means a contract between an owner and a direct contractor that provides for all or part of a work of improvement.

Added Stats 2010 ch 697 § 20 (SB 189), effective January 1, 2011, operative July 1, 2012.

Law Revision Commission Comments:

2010—Section 8016 restates former Section 3088 without substantive change.
See also Sections 8008 ("contract"), 8018 ("direct contractor"), 8050 ("work of improvement").

§ 8018. "Direct contractor"

"Direct contractor" means a contractor that has a direct contractual relationship with an owner. A reference in another statute to a "prime contractor" in connection with the provisions in this part means a "direct contractor."

Added Stats 2010 ch 697 § 20 (SB 189), effective January 1, 2011, operative July 1, 2012.

Law Revision Commission Comments:

2010—Section 8018 supersedes former Section 3095 ("original contractor"). A direct contractor within the meaning of this section is one that contracts directly with the owner, as opposed to one that contracts with another contractor (i.e., a subcontractor).

A direct contractor is at times referred to in other code sections as a "prime contractor." See e.g., Pub. Cont. Code § 4113.

§ 8020. "Funds"

For the purposes of Title 3 (commencing with Section 9000), "funds" means warrant, check, money, or bonds (if bonds are to be issued in payment of the public works contract).

Added Stats 2010 ch 697 § 20 (SB 189), effective January 1, 2011, operative July 1, 2012.

Law Revision Commission Comments:

2010—Section 8020 is new. It is included for drafting convenience. It generalizes provisions of former Sections 3186, 3187, and 3196.

See also Section 8038 ("public works contract").

§ 8022. "Labor, service, equipment, or material"

"Labor, service, equipment, or material" includes, but is not limited to, labor, skills, services, material, supplies, equipment, appliances, power, and surveying, provided for a work of improvement.

Added Stats 2010 ch 697 § 20 (SB 189), effective January 1, 2011, operative July 1, 2012.

Law Revision Commission Comments:

2010—Section 8022 is new. It is included for drafting convenience. The phrase is intended to replace various phrases used throughout the former law, including "labor or material," "labor, services, equipment, or materials," "appliances, teams, or power," and the like, and is not intended to effect any change in the law. The definition applies to variant grammatical forms of the phrase used in this part, such as "labor, service, equipment, and material."

See also Section 8050 ("work of improvement").

Appendix

§ 8024. "Laborer"; Standing to enforce rights or claims of laborer; Public policy

(a) "Laborer" means a person who, acting as an employee, performs labor upon, or bestows skill or other necessary services on, a work of improvement.

(b) "Laborer" includes a person or entity to which a portion of a laborer's compensation for a work of improvement, including, but not limited to, employer payments described in Section 1773.1 of the Labor Code and implementing regulations, is paid by agreement with that laborer or the collective bargaining agent of that laborer.

(c) A person or entity described in subdivision (b) that has standing under applicable law to maintain a direct legal action, in its own name or as an assignee, to collect any portion of compensation owed for a laborer for a work of improvement, shall have standing to enforce any rights or claims of the laborer under this part, to the extent of the compensation agreed to be paid to the person or entity for labor on that improvement. This subdivision is intended to give effect to the longstanding public policy of this state to protect the entire compensation of a laborer on a work of improvement, regardless of the form in which that compensation is to be paid.

Added Stats 2010 ch 697 § 20 (SB 189), effective January 1, 2011, operative July 1, 2012.

Law Revision Commission Comments:

2010—Subdivision (a) of Section 8024 continues former Section 3089(a) without substantive change.

Subdivision (b) restates the first sentence of former Section 3089(b) and a part of former Section 3111 without substantive change.

Subdivision (c) restates the second and third sentences of former Section 3089(b) and a part of former Section 3111 without substantive change.

See also Sections 8032 ("person"), 8050 ("work of improvement").

§ 8026. "Lien"

"Lien" means a lien under Title 2 (commencing with Section 8160) and includes a lien of a design professional under Section 8302, a lien for a work of improvement under Section 8400, and a lien for a site improvement under Section 8402.

Added Stats 2010 ch 697 § 20 (SB 189), effective January 1, 2011, operative July 1, 2012.

Law Revision Commission Comments:

2010—Section 8026 is new. It is included for drafting convenience. There are instances in this part where the term is not used in its defined sense. See Section 8000 (application of definitions).

Note that the application of this part to a design professionals lien is limited. See Section 8308 (application of part).

See also Sections 8014 ("design professional"), 8042 ("site improvement"), 8050 ("work of improvement").

§ 8028. "Material supplier"

"Material supplier" means a person that provides material or supplies to be used or consumed in a work of improvement.

Added Stats 2010 ch 697 § 20 (SB 189), effective January 1, 2011, operative July 1, 2012.

Law Revision Commission Comments:

2010—Section 8028 continues former Section 3090 without substantive change. It replaces the term "materialman" with the term "material supplier" to conform to contemporary usage under this part.

See also Sections 8032 ("person"), 8050 ("work of improvement").

§ 8030. "Payment bond"

(a) For the purposes of Title 2 (commencing with Section 8160), "payment bond" means a bond given under Section 8600.

(b) For the purposes of Title 3 (commencing with Section 9000), "payment bond" means a bond required by Section 9550.

Added Stats 2010 ch 697 § 20 (SB 189), effective January 1, 2011, operative July 1, 2012.

Law Revision Commission Comments:

2010—Section 8030 supersedes former Section 3096. There are instances in this part where the term is not used in its defined sense. See, e.g., Sections 8452 (payment bond obtained by holder of mortgage or deed of trust), 8720-8722 (payment bond as security for large project).

See also Section 8000 (application of definitions).

§ 8032. "Person"

"Person" means an individual, corporation, public entity, business trust, estate, trust, partnership, limited liability company, association, or other entity.

Added Stats 2010 ch 697 § 20 (SB 189), effective January 1, 2011, operative July 1, 2012.

Law Revision Commission Comments:

2010—Section 8032 is a new definition. It is included for drafting convenience. It supplements Section 14 ("person" includes corporation as well as natural person).

See also Section 8036 ("public entity").

Appendix

§ 8034. "Preliminary notice"

(a) For the purposes of Title 2 (commencing with Section 8160), "preliminary notice" means the notice provided for in Chapter 2 (commencing with Section 8200) of Title 2.

(b) For the purposes of Title 3 (commencing with Section 9000), "preliminary notice" means the notice provided for in Chapter 3 (commencing with Section 9300) of Title 3.

Added Stats 2010 ch 697 § 20 (SB 189), effective January 1, 2011, operative July 1, 2012.

Law Revision Commission Comments:

2010—Section 8034 supersedes parts of former Sections 3097 and 3098. The substantive requirements for preliminary notice on a private work are relocated to Section 8200 et seq. The substantive requirements for preliminary notice on a public work are relocated to Section 9300 *et seq.*

§ 8036. "Public entity"

"Public entity" means the state, Regents of the University of California, a county, city, district, public authority, public agency, and any other political subdivision or public corporation in the state.

Added Stats 2010 ch 697 § 20 (SB 189), effective January 1, 2011, operative July 1, 2012.

Law Revision Commission Comments:

2010—Section 8036 continues former Section 3099 without change.
See also Section 14 ("county" includes city and county).

§ 8038. "Public works contract"

"Public works contract" has the meaning provided in Section 1101 of the Public Contract Code.

Added Stats 2010 ch 697 § 20 (SB 189), effective January 1, 2011, operative July 1, 2012.

Law Revision Commission Comments:

2010—Section 8038 supersedes former Section 3100 ("public work"). Under Public Contract Code Section 1101, "public works contract" means an agreement for the erection, construction, alteration, repair, or improvement of any public structure, building, road, or other public improvement of any kind.

§ 8040. "Site"

"Site" means the real property on which a work of improvement is situated or planned.

Added Stats 2010 ch 697 § 20 (SB 189), effective January 1, 2011, operative July 1, 2012.

Law Revision Commission Comments:

2010—Section 8040 continues former Section 3101 without substantive change, except to add a reference to a planned work of improvement. See Section 8302 (design professionals lien).

See also Section 8050 ("work of improvement").

§ 8042. "Site improvement"

"Site improvement" means any of the following work on real property:

(a) Demolition or removal of improvements, trees, or other vegetation.

(b) Drilling test holes.

(c) Grading, filling, or otherwise improving the real property or a street, highway, or sidewalk in front of or adjoining the real property.

(d) Construction or installation of sewers or other public utilities.

(e) Construction of areas, vaults, cellars, or rooms under sidewalks.

(f) Any other work or improvements in preparation of the site for a work of improvement.

Added Stats 2010 ch 697 § 20 (SB 189), effective January 1, 2011, operative July 1, 2012.

Law Revision Commission Comments:

2010—Section 8042 continues former Section 3102 without substantive change, except that subdivision (f) makes clear that the reference in former law to "making any improvements" means preparatory work, and does not include construction of a structure.

See also Sections 8040 ("site"), 8048 ("work"), 8050 ("work of improvement").

§ 8044. "Stop payment notice"; "Bonded stop payment notice"; "Stop notice"

(a)(1) For the purposes of Title 2 (commencing with Section 8160), "stop payment notice" means the notice given by a claimant under Chapter 5 (commencing with Section 8500) of Title 2.

(2) A stop payment notice given under Title 2 (commencing with Section 8160) may be bonded or unbonded. A "bonded stop payment notice" is a notice given with a bond under Section 8532. An "unbonded stop payment notice" is a notice not given with a bond under Section 8532.

(3) Except to the extent Title 2 (commencing with Section 8160) distinguishes between a bonded and an unbonded stop payment notice, a reference in that title to a stop payment notice includes both a bonded and an unbonded notice.

(b) For the purposes of Title 3 (commencing with Section 9000), "stop payment notice" means the notice given by a claimant under Chapter 4 (commencing with Section 9350) of Title 3.

(c) A reference in another statute to a "stop notice" in connection with the remedies provided in this part means a stop payment notice.

Added Stats 2010 ch 697 § 20 (SB 189), effective January 1, 2011, operative July 1, 2012.

Law Revision Commission Comments:

2010—Section 8044 supersedes former Section 3103. The term "stop payment notice" replaces the term "stop notice" used in former law.
See also Section 8004 ("claimant").

§ 8046. "Subcontractor"

"Subcontractor" means a contractor that does not have a direct contractual relationship with an owner. The term includes a contractor that has a contractual relationship with a direct contractor or with another subcontractor.

Added Stats 2010 ch 697 § 20 (SB 189), effective January 1, 2011, operative July 1, 2012.

Law Revision Commission Comments:

2010—The first sentence of Section 8046 continues former Section 3104 without substantive change. The second sentence is new; it makes clear that the term "subcontractor" includes a subcontractor of a subcontractor.
See also Section 8018 ("direct contractor").

§ 8048. "Work"

"Work" means labor, service, equipment, or material provided to a work of improvement.

Added Stats 2010 ch 697 § 20 (SB 189), effective January 1, 2011, operative July 1, 2012.

Law Revision Commission Comments:

2010—Section 8048 is new. It is included for drafting convenience.
See also Sections 8022 ("labor, service, equipment, or material"), 8050 ("work of improvement").

§ 8050. "Work of improvement"

(a) "Work of improvement" includes, but is not limited to:
(1) Construction, alteration, repair, demolition, or removal, in whole or in part, of, or addition to, a building, wharf, bridge, ditch, flume, aqueduct, well, tunnel, fence, machinery, railroad, or road.
(2) Seeding, sodding, or planting of real property for landscaping purposes.
(3) Filling, leveling, or grading of real property.

(b) Except as otherwise provided in this part, "work of improvement" means the entire structure or scheme of improvement as a whole, and includes site improvement.

Added Stats 2010 ch 697 § 20 (SB 189), effective January 1, 2011, operative July 1, 2012.

Law Revision Commission Comments:

2010—Section 8050 restates former Section 3106. The section is revised to reorganize and tabulate the different types of work falling within the definition, to expand the coverage of the definition, and to make various technical, nonsubstantive revisions. The term "real property" replaces "lot or tract of land."

A site improvement is treated under this part in the same manner as a work of improvement, except as specifically provided in this part. See e.g., Sections 8450 (priority of lien), 8458 (priority of site improvement lien).

See also Section 8042 ("site improvement").

Article 2

Miscellaneous Provisions

§ 8052. Operative date; Effectiveness of notice on work of improvement; Provisions construed as restatements and continuations

(a) This part is operative on July 1, 2012.

(b) Notwithstanding subdivision (a), the effectiveness of a notice given or other action taken on a work of improvement before July 1, 2012, is governed by the applicable law in effect before July 1, 2012, and not by this part.

(c) A provision of this part, insofar as it is substantially the same as a previously existing provision relating to the same subject matter, shall be construed as a restatement and continuation thereof and not as a new enactment.

Added Stats 2010 ch 697 § 20 (SB 189), effective January 1, 2011, operative July 1, 2012.

Law Revision Commission Comments:

2010—Section 8052 is new. Although this part applies generally to all works of improvement on or after July 1, 2012, it does not govern notices given or actions taken prior to July 1, 2012, on a work of improvement. Such notices or actions are governed by former law.

Subdivision (c) states the relationship between a provision of this part and a provision of former law that the provision of this part continues or restates. See also Section 107 of Chapter 697 of the Statutes of 2010.

See also Section 8050 ("work of improvement").

Appendix

§ 8054. Applicability of part

(a) This part does not apply to a transaction governed by the Oil and Gas Lien Act (Chapter 2.5 (commencing with Section 1203.50) of Title 4 of Part 3 of the Code of Civil Procedure).

(b) This part does not apply to or change improvement security under the Subdivision Map Act (Division 2 (commencing with Section 66410) of Title 7 of the Government Code).

(c) This part does not apply to a transaction governed by Sections 20457 to 20464, inclusive, of the Public Contract Code.

Added Stats 2010 ch 697 § 20 (SB 189), effective January 1, 2011, operative July 1, 2012.

Law Revision Commission Comments:

2010—Subdivision (a) of Section 8054 restates former Section 3266(a).

Subdivision (b) is new. It clarifies the interrelation between this part and the Subdivision Map Act. For relevant provisions of that act, see Government Code Sections 66499-66499.10 (improvement security).

Subdivision (c) restates former Section 3266(b). This provision updates the former cross-reference to Streets and Highways Code Sections 5290-5297, which were repealed in 1982 when the Public Contract Code was created. See 1982 Cal. Stat. ch. 465, § 56. The repealed sections were superseded by Public Contract Code Sections 20457-20464. See 1982 Cal. Stat. ch. 465, § 11. The new sections apply to bonds in "street work" projects under Division 2 (commencing with Section 1600) of the Public Contract Code. See Pub. Cont. Code § 20457.

§ 8056. Applicable Code of Civil Procedure provisions

Except as otherwise provided in this part, Part 2 (commencing with Section 307) of the Code of Civil Procedure provides the rules of practice in proceedings under this part.

Added Stats 2010 ch 697 § 20 (SB 189), effective January 1, 2011, operative July 1, 2012.

Law Revision Commission Comments:

2010—Section 8056 continues the first sentence of former Section 3259 without substantive change. The second sentence of former Section 3259 is not continued; this part does not include special provisions relating to new trials or appeals.

Section 8056 makes former Section 3149, relating to joinder and consolidation of actions, unnecessary. Part 2 of the Code of Civil Procedure enables persons claiming liens on the same property to join in the same action to enforce their liens. See Code Civ. Proc. § 378 (permissive joinder). If separate actions are commenced, the court may consolidate them. See Code Civ. Proc. § 1048 (consolidation of actions).

§ 8058. "Day"

For purposes of this part, "day" means a calendar day.

Added Stats 2010 ch 697 § 20 (SB 189), effective January 1, 2011, operative July 1, 2012.

Law Revision Commission Comments:

2010—Section 8058 is new. A reference to the term "day" in a statute typically means a calendar day, unless otherwise specifically indicated. Iverson v. Superior Court, 167 Cal. App. 3d 544, 548, 213 Cal. Rptr. 399 (1985).)

See also Sections 10 (computing time), 11 (holidays).

§ 8060. Filing documents with county recorder; Duties of county recorder

(a) If this part provides for filing a contract, plan, or other paper with the county recorder, the provision is satisfied by filing the paper in the office of the county recorder of the county in which the work of improvement or part of it is situated.

(b) If this part provides for recording a notice, claim of lien, release of lien, payment bond, or other paper, the provision is satisfied by filing the paper for record in the office of the county recorder of the county in which the work of improvement or part of it is situated.

(c) The county recorder shall number, index, and preserve a contract, plan, or other paper presented for filing under this part, and shall number, index, and transcribe into the official records, in the same manner as a conveyance of real property, a notice, claim of lien, payment bond, or other paper recorded under this part.

(d) The county recorder shall charge and collect the fees provided in Article 5 (commencing with Section 27360) of Chapter 6 of Part 3 of Division 2 of Title 3 of the Government Code for performing duties under this section.

Added Stats 2010 ch 697 § 20 (SB 189), effective January 1, 2011, operative July 1, 2012.

Law Revision Commission Comments:

2010—Subdivisions (a) and (b) of Section 8060 are new. They generalize a number of provisions of former law. See also Section 1170 (recordation), Gov't Code §§ 27280, 27287 (recordation of documents).

Subdivisions (c) and (d) continue former Section 3258 without substantive change.

See also Sections 8008 ("contract"), 8024 ("lien"), 8030 ("payment bond"), 8050 ("work of improvement").

§ 8062. Construction of acts of owner; Exoneration of surety on performance or payment bond

No act of an owner in good faith and in compliance with a provision of this part shall be construed to prevent a direct contractor's performance of the contract, or exonerate a surety on a performance or payment bond.

Added Stats 2010 ch 697 § 20 (SB 189), effective January 1, 2011, operative July 1, 2012.

Law Revision Commission Comments:

2010—Section 8062 restates former Section 3263 without substantive change.
See also Section 8152 (no release of surety from liability).
See also Sections 8008 ("contract"), 8018 ("direct contractor"), 8030 ("payment bond").

§ 8064. Acts on behalf of co-owner; Requirements

An owner may give a notice or execute or file a document under this part on behalf of a co-owner if the owner acts on the co-owner's behalf and includes in the notice or document the name and address of the co-owner on whose behalf the owner acts.

Added Stats 2010 ch 697 § 20 (SB 189), effective January 1, 2011, operative July 1, 2012.

Law Revision Commission Comments:

2010—Section 8064 is new. It generalizes provisions found in former Sections 3092 (notice of cessation) and 3093 (notice of completion).

§ 8066. Acts within scope of agent's authority

An act that may be done by or to a person under this part may be done by or to the person's agent to the extent the act is within the scope of the agent's authority.

Added Stats 2010 ch 697 § 20 (SB 189), effective January 1, 2011, operative July 1, 2012.

Law Revision Commission Comments:

2010—Section 8066 is a specific application of Section 2305. This section makes clear that an agent's authority is limited to the scope of the agency. Thus, to the extent a direct contractor is deemed to be the agent of an owner for the purpose of engaging a subcontractor, the scope of the agency does not include other acts, such as compromise of litigation.
For provisions relating to the agency authority of co-owners, see Section 8064 (co-owners).
See also Section 8032 ("person").

Chapter 2

Notice

§ 8100. Form of notice; "Writings"

Notice under this part shall be in writing. Writing includes printing and typewriting.

Added Stats 2010 ch 697 § 20 (SB 189), effective January 1, 2011, operative July 1, 2012.

Law Revision Commission Comments:

2010—Section 8100 generalizes various provisions of former law. See, e.g., former Sections 3092 (notice of cessation), 3093 (notice of completion), 3094 (notice of nonresponsibility), 3097 (preliminary notice (private work)), 3103 (stop notice).

See also Evid. Code § 250 ("writing").

§ 8102. Contents of notice; Sufficiency

(a) Notice under this part shall, in addition to any other information required by statute for that type of notice, include all of the following information to the extent known to the person giving the notice:

(1) The name and address of the owner or reputed owner.

(2) The name and address of the direct contractor.

(3) The name and address of the construction lender, if any.

(4) A description of the site sufficient for identification, including the street address of the site, if any. If a sufficient legal description of the site is given, the effectiveness of the notice is not affected by the fact that the street address is erroneous or is omitted.

(5) The name, address, and relationship to the parties of the person giving the notice.

(6) If the person giving the notice is a claimant:

(A) A general statement of the work provided.

(B) The name of the person to or for whom the work is provided.

(C) A statement or estimate of the claimant's demand, if any, after deducting all just credits and offsets.

(b) Notice is not invalid by reason of any variance from the requirements of this section if the notice is sufficient to substantially inform the person given notice of the information required by this section and other information required in the notice.

Added Stats 2010 ch 697 § 20 (SB 189), effective January 1, 2011, operative July 1, 2012.

Law Revision Commission Comments:

2010—Section 8102 is new. It generalizes and standardizes provisions found throughout former law. See, e.g., former Sections 3092 (notice of cessation), 3093 (notice of completion), 3097 (preliminary notice), 3103 (stop notice).

See also Sections 8004 ("claimant"), 8006 ("construction lender"), 8018 ("direct contractor"), 8032 ("person"), 8040 ("site"), 8048 ("work").

§ 8104. Failure to pay full compensation to laborer; Notice required; Contents; Grounds for disciplinary action

(a) A direct contractor or subcontractor on a work of improvement governed by this part that employs a laborer and fails to pay the full compensation due the laborer, including any employer payments described in Section 1773.1 of the Labor Code and implementing regulations, shall not later than the date the compensation became delinquent, give the laborer, the laborer's bargaining representative, if any, the construction lender or reputed construction lender, if any, and the owner or reputed owner, notice that includes all of the following information, in addition to the information required by Section 8102:

(1) The name and address of the laborer, and of any person or entity described in subdivision (b) of Section 8024 to which employer payments are due.

(2) The total number of straight time and overtime hours worked by the laborer on each job.

(3) The amount then past due and owing.

(b) Failure to give the notice required by subdivision (a) constitutes grounds for disciplinary action under the Contractors' State License Law, Chapter 9 (commencing with Section 7000) of Division 3 of the Business and Professions Code.

Added Stats 2010 ch 697 § 20 (SB 189), effective January 1, 2011, operative July 1, 2012.

Law Revision Commission Comments:

2010—Section 8104 restates former Section 3097(k), with the additional requirement that the information provided be given to the owner or reputed owner, and include the name and address of the unpaid laborer. See also Sections 8100-8118 (notice).

The reference to the Registrar of Contractors in the final sentence of former Section 3097(k) is revised to refer to the Contractors' State License Law. This is a technical, nonsubstantive change.

The information required in this notice is in addition to the information required by Section 8102 (contents of notice).

Compliance with this section does not excuse compliance with Section 8202(b), if applicable. See Section 8202 (contents of preliminary notice).

See also Sections 8006 ("construction lender"), 8018 ("direct contractor"), 8024 ("laborer"), 8032 ("person"), 8046 ("subcontractor"), 8050 ("work of improvement").

§ 8106. Manner of giving notice

Except as otherwise provided by statute, notice under this part shall be given by any of the following means:

(a) Personal delivery.

(b) Mail in the manner provided in Section 8110.

(c) Leaving the notice and mailing a copy in the manner provided in Section 415.20 of the Code of Civil Procedure for service of summons and complaint in a civil action.

Added Stats 2010 ch 697 § 20 (SB 189), effective January 1, 2011, operative July 1, 2012.

Law Revision Commission Comments:

2010—Section 8106 is new. It generalizes and standardizes provisions found throughout former law. See, e.g., former Sections 3097 (preliminary notice), 3103 (stop notice), 3144.5 (notice of release bond), 3227 (notice to principal and surety), 3259.5 (notice of recordation of notice of completion), 3260.2 (stop work notice).

Under subdivision (c), when notice is given in the manner provided in Code of Civil Procedure Section 415.20 for service of summons and complaint, the notice is complete five days after mailing the notice. See Section 8116 (when notice complete). The 10 day delay provided in the Code of Civil Procedure for completion of service under that code is inapplicable.

This part may prescribe a different or more limited manner of giving a particular notice. See, e.g., Section 8486 (service of petition for order releasing lien).

§ 8108. Person to be notified at person's residence, place of business, or specified addresses

Except as otherwise provided by this part, notice under this part shall be given to the person to be notified at the person's residence, the person's place of business, or at any of the following addresses:

(a) If the person to be notified is an owner other than a public entity, the owner's address shown on the direct contract, the building permit, or a construction trust deed.

(b) If the person to be notified is a public entity, the office of the public entity or another address specified by the public entity in the contract or elsewhere for service of notices, papers, and other documents.

(c) If the person to be notified is a construction lender, the construction lender's address shown on the construction loan agreement or construction trust deed.

(d) If the person to be notified is a direct contractor or a subcontractor, the contractor's address shown on the building permit, on the contractor's contract, or on the records of the Contractors' State License Board.

(e) If the person to be notified is a claimant, the claimant's address shown on the claimant's contract, preliminary notice, claim of lien, stop payment notice, or claim against a payment bond, or on the records of the Contractors' State License Board.

(f) If the person to be notified is a surety on a bond, the surety's address shown on the bond for service of notices, papers, and other documents, or on the records of the Department of Insurance.

Added Stats 2010 ch 697 § 20 (SB 189), effective January 1, 2011, operative July 1, 2012.

Law Revision Commission Comments:

2010—Section 8108 is new. It generalizes and standardizes provisions found throughout former law. For an example of a more particularized notice provision, see Section 8506.

Subdivision (f) does not continue the unique provisions found in former Section 3227 for notice to alternate persons in the case of a personal surety or admitted surety insurer. The bond and undertaking law requires every bond to include the address at which the principal and sureties may be served with notices, papers, and other documents. See Code Civ. Proc. § 995.320.

See also Sections 8004 ("claimant"), 8006 ("construction lender"), 8008 ("contract"), 8012 ("contractor"), 8016 ("direct contract"), 8018 ("direct contractor"), 8026 ("lien"), 8030 ("payment bond"), 8032 ("person"), 8034 ("preliminary notice"), 8036 ("public entity"), 8044 ("stop payment notice"), 8046 ("subcontractor").

§ 8110. Registered or certified mail, express mail, or overnight delivery by express service carrier

Except as otherwise provided by this part, notice by mail under this part shall be given by registered or certified mail, express mail, or overnight delivery by an express service carrier.

Added Stats 2010 ch 697 § 20 (SB 189), effective January 1, 2011, operative July 1, 2012.

Law Revision Commission Comments:

2010—Section 8110 is a new provision included for drafting convenience. It generalizes a number of provisions of former law, and expands the methods of giving notice to include delivery by express service carrier.

For an example of a more particularized notice provision, see Section 8486.

§ 8114. Posting of notice

A notice required by this part to be posted shall be displayed in a conspicuous location at the site.

Added Stats 2010 ch 697 § 20 (SB 189), effective January 1, 2011, operative July 1, 2012.

Law Revision Commission Comments:

2010—Section 8114 is new. It generalizes provisions found in former law. See, e.g., former Sections 3094 (notice of nonresponsibility), 3260.2 (stop work notice).

See also Section 8040 ("site").

§ 8116. When notice is complete and deemed to have been given at specified times

Notice under this part is complete and deemed to have been given at the following times:

(a) If given by personal delivery, when delivered.

(b) If given by mail, when deposited in the mail or with an express service carrier in the manner provided in Section 1013 of the Code of Civil Procedure.

(c) If given by leaving the notice and mailing a copy in the manner provided in Section 415.20 of the Code of Civil Procedure for service of summons in a civil action, five days after mailing.

(d) If given by posting, when displayed.

(e) If given by recording, when recorded in the office of the county recorder.

Added Stats 2010 ch 697 § 20 (SB 189), effective January 1, 2011, operative July 1, 2012.

Law Revision Commission Comments:

2010—Section 8116 is new. It generalizes and standardizes provisions found in former law. See, e.g., former Section 3097(f)(3) (service of preliminary notice).

Under subdivision (b), when notice is given in the manner provided in Code of Civil Procedure Section 1013, the notice is complete when deposited in the mail or with an express service carrier. The 10 and 20 day delays provided in the Code of Civil Procedure for completion of service under that code are inapplicable. For an exception to this rule, see Section 8486 (notice of hearing on lien release petition).

Under subdivision (c), when notice is given in the manner provided in Code of Civil Procedure Section 415.20 for service of summons and complaint, the notice is complete five days after mailing of the notice. The 10 day delay provided in the Code of Civil Procedure for completion of service under that code is inapplicable.

See also Sections 1170 (recordation), 8058 (calculation of time), 8060 (filing and recordation of papers), 8110 (mailed notice), 8114 (posting of notice).

§ 8118. Proof that notice was given; Proof of notice declaration; Contents

(a) Proof that notice was given to a person in the manner required by this part shall be made by a proof of notice declaration that states all of the following:

(1) The type or description of the notice given.

(2) The date, place, and manner of notice, and facts showing that notice was given in the manner required by statute.

(3) The name and address of the person to which notice was given, and, if appropriate, the title or capacity in which the person was given notice.

(b) If the notice is given by mail, the declaration shall be accompanied by one of the following:

(1) Documentation provided by the United States Postal Service showing that payment was made to mail the notice using registered or certified mail, or express mail.

(2) Documentation provided by an express service carrier showing that payment was made to send the notice using an overnight delivery service.

(3) A return receipt, delivery confirmation, signature confirmation, tracking record, or other proof of delivery or attempted delivery provided by the United States Postal Service, or a photocopy of the record of delivery and receipt maintained by the United States Postal Service, showing the date of delivery and to whom delivered, or in the event of nondelivery, by the returned envelope itself.

(4) A tracking record or other documentation provided by an express service carrier showing delivery or attempted delivery of the notice.

Appendix

Added Stats 2010 ch 697 § 20 (SB 189), effective January 1, 2011, operative July 1, 2012.

Law Revision Commission Comments:

2010—Section 8118 is new. It generalizes and standardizes provisions found throughout former law, and expands the methods of proof to include documentation of the mailing provided by the United States Postal Service or an express service carrier. See, e.g., former Sections 3097 (preliminary notice), 3260.2 (stop work notice). Subdivision (b) specifies the documentation that must be attached to a proof of notice declaration when notice is given by mail. Documentation establishing proof of delivery or attempted delivery of the notice as specified in subdivision (b)(3)-(4) is sufficient, but not necessary, to satisfy the requirement of the subdivision. Proof that payment was made to the United States Postal Service or an express service carrier for an approved method of delivery is also sufficient. See subdivision (b)(1)-(2).See also Section 8110 (mailed notice).See also Section 8032 ("person").

§ 8119. Delivery of notices and claims for work on common area within common interest development

(a) With respect to a work of improvement on a common area within a common interest development: (1) The association is deemed to be an agent of the owners of separate interests in the common interest development for all notices and claims required by this part. (2) If any provision of this part requires the delivery or service of a notice or claim to or on the owner of common area property, the notice or claim may be delivered to or served on the association.

(b) For the purposes of this section, the terms "association," "common area," "common interest development," and "separate interest" have the meanings provided in Article 2 (commencing with Section 4075) of Chapter 1 of Part 5 and Article 2 (commencing with Section 6526) of Chapter 1 of Part 5.3.

Added Stats 2017 ch 44 § 5 (AB 534), effective January 1, 2018.

Chapter 3

Waiver and Release

§ 8120. Applicability of chapter

The provisions of this chapter apply to a work of improvement governed by this part.

Added Stats 2010 ch 697 § 20 (SB 189), effective January 1, 2011, operative July 1, 2012.

Law Revision Commission Comments:

2010—Section 8120 is new. It provides the scope of applicability of the provisions of Chapter 3 of Title 1.See also Section 8050 ("work of improvement").

§ 8122. Affecting claimant's rights; Exception

An owner, direct contractor, or subcontractor may not, by contract or otherwise, waive, affect, or impair any other claimant's rights under this part, whether with or without notice, and any term of a contract that purports to do so is void and unenforceable unless and until the claimant executes and delivers a waiver and release under this article.

Added Stats 2010 ch 697 § 20 (SB 189), effective January 1, 2011, operative July 1, 2012.

Law Revision Commission Comments:

2010—Section 8122 continues the first and second sentences of former Section 3262(a) without substantive change, except to add a reference to a subcontractor. See also Sections 8004 ("claimant"), 8008 ("contract"), 8018 ("direct contractor"), 8046 ("subcontractor").

§ 8124. Effect of claimant's waiver and release on payment bond from lien or claim; Conditions

A claimant's waiver and release does not release the owner, construction lender, or surety on a payment bond from a lien or claim unless both of the following conditions are satisfied:

(a) The waiver and release is in substantially the form provided in this article and is signed by the claimant.

(b) If the release is a conditional release, there is evidence of payment to the claimant. Evidence of payment may be either of the following:

(1) The claimant's endorsement on a single or joint payee check that has been paid by the financial institution on which it was drawn.

(2) Written acknowledgment of payment by the claimant.

Added Stats 2010 ch 697 § 20 (SB 189), effective January 1, 2011, operative July 1, 2012.

Law Revision Commission Comments:

2010—Section 8124 continues the third and fourth sentences of former Section 3262(a) without substantive change. The term "financial institution" replaces "bank" in subdivision (b) and in the forms provided in this article.

The waiver and release may be signed by the claimant's agent. See Section 8066 (agency).

See also Sections 8004 ("claimant"), 8006 ("construction lender"), 8026 ("lien"), 8030 ("payment bond").

§ 8126. Validity and enforceability of oral or written statement

An oral or written statement purporting to waive, release, impair or otherwise adversely affect a lien or claim is void and unenforceable and does not create an estoppel or impairment of the lien or claim unless either of the following conditions is satisfied:

(a) The statement is pursuant to a waiver and release under this article.

(b) The claimant has actually received payment in full for the claim.

Added Stats 2010 ch 697 § 20 (SB 189), effective January 1, 2011, operative July 1, 2012.

Law Revision Commission Comments:

2010—Section 8126 continues former Section 3262(b)(1) without substantive change. See also Section 8004 ("claimant"), 8026 ("lien").

§ 8128.   Reduction or release of stop payment notice; Writing; Effect

(a) A claimant may reduce the amount of, or release in its entirety, a stop payment notice. The reduction or release shall be in writing and may be given in a form other than a waiver and release form provided in this article.

(b) The writing shall identify whether it is a reduction of the amount of the stop payment notice, or a release of the notice in its entirety. If the writing is a reduction, it shall state the amount of the reduction, and the amount to remain withheld after the reduction.

(c) A claimant's reduction or release of a stop payment notice has the following effect:

(1) The reduction or release releases the claimant's right to enforce payment of the claim stated in the notice to the extent of the reduction or release.

(2) The reduction or release releases the person given the notice from the obligation to withhold funds pursuant to the notice to the extent of the reduction or release.

(3) The reduction or release does not preclude the claimant from giving a subsequent stop payment notice that is timely and proper.

(4) The reduction or release does not release any right of the claimant other than the right to enforce payment of the claim stated in the stop payment notice to the extent of the reduction or release.

Added Stats 2010 ch 697 § 20 (SB 189), effective January 1, 2011, operative July 1, 2012.

Law Revision Commission Comments:

2010—Subdivisions (a) and (c) of Section 8128 generalize former Section 3262(b)(2), so as to apply to a stop payment notice given to a construction lender as well as to a stop payment notice given to an owner.

Subdivision (b) is new.

See also Sections 8004 ("claimant"), 8032 ("person"), 8044 ("stop payment notice").

§ 8130. Enforceability of accord and satisfaction or agreement and settlement; Effect of article

This article does not affect the enforceability of either an accord and satisfaction concerning a good faith dispute or an agreement made in settlement of an action pending in court if the accord and satisfaction or agreement and settlement make specific reference to the lien or claim.

Added Stats 2010 ch 697 § 20 (SB 189), effective January 1, 2011, operative July 1, 2012.

Law Revision Commission Comments:

2010—Section 8130 continues former Section 3262(c) without substantive change. See also Section 8026 ("lien").

§ 8132. Conditional waiver and release in exchange for progress payment; Form

If a claimant is required to execute a waiver and release in exchange for, or in order to induce payment of, a progress payment and the claimant is not, in fact, paid in exchange for the waiver and release or a single payee check or joint payee check is given in exchange for the waiver and release, the waiver and release shall be null, void, and unenforceable unless it is in substantially the following form:

CONDITIONAL WAIVER AND RELEASE ON PROGRESS

PAYMENT NOTICE: THIS DOCUMENT WAIVES THE CLAIM-ANT'S LIEN, STOP PAYMENT NOTICE, AND PAYMENT BOND RIGHTS EFFECTIVE ON RECEIPT OF PAYMENT. A PERSON SHOULD NOT RELY ON THIS DOCUMENT UNLESS SATISFIED THAT THE CLAIMANT HAS RECEIVED PAYMENT.

Identifying Information
Name of Claimant: _____
Name of Customer: _____
Job Location: _____
Owner: _____
Through Date: _____
Conditional Waiver and Release

This document waives and releases lien, stop payment notice, and payment bond rights the claimant has for labor and service provided, and equipment and material delivered, to the customer on this job through the Through Date of this document. Rights based upon labor or service provided, or equipment or material delivered, pursuant to a written change order that has been fully executed by the parties prior to the date that this document is signed by the claimant, are waived and released by this document, unless listed as an Exception below.

This document is effective only on the claimant's receipt of payment from the financial institution on which the following check is drawn:

Maker of Check: _____

Amount of Check: $ _____

Check Payable to: _____

Exceptions

This document does not affect any of the following:

(1) Retentions.

(2) Extras for which the claimant has not received payment.

(3) The following progress payments for which the claimant has previously given a conditional waiver and release but has not received payment:

Date(s) of waiver and release: _____

Amount(s) of unpaid progress payment(s): $ _____

(4) Contract rights, including (A) a right based on rescission, abandonment, or breach of contract, and (B) the right to recover compensation for work not compensated by the payment.

Signature

Claimant's Signature: _____

Claimant's Title: _____

Date of Signature:_____

Added Stats 2010 ch 697 § 20 (SB 189), effective January 1, 2011, operative July 1, 2012.

Law Revision Commission Comments:

2010—Section 8132 restates former Section 3262(d)(1) without substantive change, except to add language relating to progress payments covered by previous releases that have not been paid. The statutory form is recast for clarity.See also Sections 8004 ("claimant"), 8008 ("contract"), 8026 ("lien"), 8030 ("payment bond"), 8032 ("person"), 8044 ("stop payment notice"), 8048 ("work").

§ 8134. Unconditional waiver and release in exchange for progress payment; Form

If the claimant is required to execute a waiver and release in exchange for, or in order to induce payment of, a progress payment and the claimant asserts in the waiver that the claimant has, in fact, been paid the progress payment, the waiver and release shall be null, void, and unenforceable unless it is in substantially the following form, with the text of the "Notice to Claimant" in at least as large a type as the largest type otherwise in the form:

UNCONDITIONAL WAIVER AND RELEASE ON PROGRESS

PAYMENT NOTICE TO CLAIMANT: THIS DOCUMENT WAIVES AND RELEASES LIEN, STOP PAYMENT NOTICE, AND PAYMENT BOND RIGHTS UNCONDITIONALLY AND STATES THAT YOU HAVE BEEN PAID FOR GIVING UP THOSE RIGHTS. THIS

DOCUMENT IS ENFORCEABLE AGAINST YOU IF YOU SIGN IT, EVEN IF YOU HAVE NOT BEEN PAID. IF YOU HAVE NOT BEEN PAID, USE A CONDITIONAL WAIVER AND RELEASE FORM.

Identifying Information

Name of Claimant: _____

Name of Customer: _____

Job Location: _____

Owner: _____

Through Date: _____

Unconditional Waiver and Release

This document waives and releases lien, stop payment notice, and payment bond rights the claimant has for labor and service provided, and equipment and material delivered, to the customer on this job through the Through Date of this document. Rights based upon labor or service provided, or equipment or material delivered, pursuant to a written change order that has been fully executed by the parties prior to the date that this document is signed by the claimant, are waived and released by this document, unless listed as an Exception below. The claimant has received the following progress payment:

$ _____

Exceptions

This document does not affect any of the following:

(1) Retentions.

(2) Extras for which the claimant has not received payment.

(3) Contract rights, including (A) a right based on rescission, abandonment, or breach of contract, and (B) the right to recover compensation for work not compensated by the payment.

Signature

Claimant's Signature: _____

Claimant's Title: _____

Date of Signature:_____

Added Stats 2010 ch 697 § 20 (SB 189), effective January 1, 2011, operative July 1, 2012.

Law Revision Commission Comments:

2010—Section 8134 restates former Section 3262(d)(2) without substantive change. The statutory form is recast for clarity.See also Sections 8004 ("claimant"), 8008 ("contract"), 8026 ("lien"), 8030 ("payment bond"), 8044 ("stop payment notice"), 8048 ("work").

§ 8136. Conditional waiver and release in exchange for final payment; Form

If the claimant is required to execute a waiver and release in exchange for, or in order to induce payment of, a final payment and the claimant is not, in fact, paid in exchange for the waiver and release or a single payee check or joint payee check is given in exchange for the waiver and release, the waiver and release shall be null, void, and unenforceable unless it is in substantially the following form:

CONDITIONAL WAIVER AND RELEASE ON FINAL PAYMENT

NOTICE: THIS DOCUMENT WAIVES THE CLAIMANT'S LIEN, STOP PAYMENT NOTICE, AND PAYMENT BOND RIGHTS EFFECTIVE ON RECEIPT OF PAYMENT. A PERSON SHOULD NOT RELY ON THIS DOCUMENT UNLESS SATISFIED THAT THE CLAIMANT HAS RECEIVED PAYMENT.

Identifying Information

Name of Claimant: _____

Name of Customer: _____

Job Location: _____

Owner: _____

Conditional Waiver and Release

This document waives and releases lien, stop payment notice, and payment bond rights the claimant has for labor and service provided, and equipment and material delivered, to the customer on this job. Rights based upon labor or service provided, or equipment or material delivered, pursuant to a written change order that has been fully executed by the parties prior to the date that this document is signed by the claimant, are waived and released by this document, unless listed as an Exception below. This document is effective only on the claimant's receipt of payment from the financial institution on which the following check is drawn:

Maker of Check: _____

Amount of Check: $ _____

Check Payable to: _____

Exceptions

This document does not affect any of the following:

Disputed claims for extras in the amount of: $ _____

Signature

Claimant's Signature: _____

Claimant's Title: _____

Date of Signature:_____

Added Stats 2010 ch 697 § 20 (SB 189), effective January 1, 2011, operative July 1, 2012.

Law Revision Commission Comments:

2010—Section 8136 restates former Section 3262(d)(3) without substantive change, except to add a line for identification of the waivant's customer. The statutory form is recast for clarity.

See also Sections 8004 ("claimant"), 8026 ("lien"), 8030 ("payment bond"), 8032 ("person"), 8044 ("stop payment notice").

§ 8138. Unconditional waiver and release in exchange for final payment; Form

If the claimant is required to execute a waiver and release in exchange for, or in order to induce payment of, a final payment and the claimant asserts in the waiver that the claimant has, in fact, been paid the final payment, the waiver and release shall be null, void, and unenforceable unless it is in substantially the following form, with the text of the "Notice to Claimant" in at least as large a type as the largest type otherwise in the form:

UNCONDITIONAL WAIVER AND RELEASE ON FINAL PAYMENT

NOTICE TO CLAIMANT: THIS DOCUMENT WAIVES AND RELEASES LIEN, STOP PAYMENT NOTICE, AND PAYMENT BOND RIGHTS UNCONDITIONALLY AND STATES THAT YOU HAVE BEEN PAID FOR GIVING UP THOSE RIGHTS. THIS DOCUMENT IS ENFORCEABLE AGAINST YOU IF YOU SIGN IT, EVEN IF YOU HAVE NOT BEEN PAID. IF YOU HAVE NOT BEEN PAID, USE A CONDITIONAL WAIVER AND RELEASE FORM.

Identifying Information
Name of Claimant: _____
Name of Customer: _____
Job Location: _____
Owner: _____
Unconditional Waiver and Release
This document waives and releases lien, stop payment notice, and payment bond rights the claimant has for all labor and service provided, and equipment and material delivered, to the customer on this job. Rights based upon labor or service provided, or equipment or material delivered, pursuant to a written change order that has been fully executed by the parties prior to the date that this document is signed by the claimant, are waived and released by this document, unless listed as an Exception below. The claimant has been paid in full.

Exceptions
This document does not affect the following:
Disputed claims for extras in the amount of: $ _____
Signature
Claimant's Signature: _____
Claimant's Title: _____
Date of Signature:_____

Added Stats 2010 ch 697 § 20 (SB 189), effective January 1, 2011, operative July 1, 2012.

Law Revision Commission Comments:

2010—Section 8138 restates former Section 3262(d)(4) without substantive change. The statutory form is recast for clarity.

See also Sections 8004 ("claimant"), 8026 ("lien"), 8030 ("payment bond"), 8044 ("stop payment notice").

TITLE 2

Private Works of Improvement

Chapter 4

Mechanics Lien

Article 2

Conditions to Enforcing a Lien

§ 8416. Claim of mechanics lien; Form; Contents; Service; Failure to serve

(a) A claim of mechanics lien shall be a written statement, signed and verified by the claimant, containing all of the following:

(1) A statement of the claimant's demand after deducting all just credits and offsets.

(2) The name of the owner or reputed owner, if known.

(3) A general statement of the kind of work furnished by the claimant.

(4) The name of the person by whom the claimant was employed or to whom the claimant furnished work.

(5) A description of the site sufficient for identification.

(6) The claimant's address.

(7) A proof of service affidavit completed and signed by the person serving a copy of the claim of mechanics lien pursuant to subdivision (c). The affidavit shall show the date, place, and manner of service, and facts showing that the service was made in accordance with this section. The affidavit shall show the name and address of the owner or reputed owner upon whom the copy of the claim of mechanics lien was served pursuant to paragraphs (1) or (2) of subdivision (c), and the title or capacity in which the person or entity was served.

(8) The following statement, printed in at least 10-point boldface type. The letters of the last sentence shall be printed in uppercase type, excepting the Internet Web site address of the Contractors' State License Board, which shall be printed in lowercase type:

"NOTICE OF MECHANICS LIEN
ATTENTION!

Upon the recording of the enclosed MECHANICS LIEN with the county recorder's office of the county where the property is located, your property is subject to the filing of a legal action seeking a court-ordered foreclosure sale of the real property on which the lien has been recorded. That legal action must be filed with the court no later than 90 days after the date the mechanics lien is recorded.

The party identified in the enclosedmechanics lien may have provided labor or materials for improvements to your property and may not have been paid for these items. You are receiving this notice because it is a required step in filing a mechanics lien foreclosure action against your property. The foreclosure action will seek a sale of your property in order to pay for unpaid labor, materials, or improvements provided to your property. This may affect your ability to borrow against, refinance, or sell the property until the mechanics lien is released.

BECAUSE THE LIEN AFFECTS YOUR PROPERTY, YOU MAY WISH TOSPEAK WITH YOUR CONTRACTOR IMMEDIATELY, OR CONTACT AN ATTORNEY, OR FOR MORE INFORMATION ON MECHANICS LIENS GO TO THE CONTRACTORS' STATE LICENSE BOARD WEB SITE AT www.cslb.ca.gov."

(b) A claim of mechanics lien in otherwise proper form, verified and containing the information required in subdivision (a), shall be accepted by the recorder for recording and shall be deemed duly recorded without acknowledgment.

(c) A copy of the claim of mechanics lien, which includes the Notice of Mechanics Lien required by paragraph (8) of subdivision (a), shall be served on the owner or reputed owner. Service shall be made as follows:

(1) For an owner or reputed owner to be notified who resides in or outside this state, by registered mail, certified mail, or first-class mail, evidenced by a certificate of mailing, postage prepaid, addressed to the owner or reputed owner at the owner's or reputed owner's residence or place of business address or at the address shown by the building permit on file with the authority issuing a building permit for the work, or as otherwise provided in Section 8174.

(2) If the owner or reputed owner cannot be served by this method, then the copy of the claim of mechanics lien may be given by registered mail, certified mail, or first-class mail, evidenced by a certificate of mailing, postage prepaid, addressed to the construction lender or to the original contractor.

(d) Service of the copy of the claim of mechanics lien by registered mail, certified mail, or first-class mail, evidenced by a certificate of mailing, postage prepaid, is complete at the time of the deposit of that first-class, certified, or registered mail.

(e) Failure to serve the copy of the claim of mechanics lien as prescribed by this section, including the Notice of Mechanics Lien required by paragraph (8) of subdivision (a), shall cause the claim of mechanics lien to be unenforceable as a matter of law.

Added Stats 2010 ch 697 § 20 (SB 189), effective January 1, 2011, operative July 1, 2012. Amended Stats 2011 ch 673 § 2 (AB 456), effective January 1, 2012.

§ 8422. Effect of erroneous information

(a) Except as provided in subdivisions (b) and (c), erroneous information contained in a claim of lien relating to the claimant's demand, credits and offsets deducted, the work provided, or the description of the site, does not invalidate the claim of lien.

(b) Erroneous information contained in a claim of lien relating to the claimant's demand, credits and offsets deducted, or the work provided, invalidates the claim of lien if the court determines either of the following:

(1) The claim of lien was made with intent to defraud.

(2) An innocent third party, without notice, actual or constructive, became the bona fide owner of the property after recordation of the claim of lien, and the claim of lien was so deficient that it did not put the party on further inquiry in any manner.

(c) Any person who shall willfully include in a claim of lien labor, services, equipment, or materials not furnished for the property described in the claim, shall thereby forfeit the person's lien.

Added Stats 2010 ch 697 § 20 (SB 189), effective January 1, 2011, operative July 1, 2012. Amended Stats 2011 ch 44 § 5 (SB 190), effective January 1, 2012, operative July 1, 2012.

Chapter 5

Stop Payment Notice

Article 1

General Provisions

§ 8504. False stop payment notice or information; Forfeiture of rights to participate in distribution of funds

A claimant that willfully gives a false stop payment notice or that willfully includes in the notice a demand to withhold for work that has not been provided forfeits all right to participate in the distribution of the funds withheld and all right to a lien under Chapter 4 (commencing with Section 8400).

Added Stats 2010 ch 697 § 20 (SB 189), effective January 1, 2011, operative July 1, 2012.

Law Revision Commission Comments:

2010— Section 8504 restates former Section 3168 without substantive change.

See also Sections 8004 ("claimant"), 8026 ("lien"), 8044 ("stop payment notice"), 8048 ("work").

CODE OF CIVIL PROCEDURE

PART 1

COURTS OF JUSTICE

TITLE 1

Organization and Jurisdiction

Chapter 5.5

Small Claims Court

Article 2

Small Claims Court

§ 116.220. Jurisdiction

(a) The small claims court has jurisdiction in the following actions:

(1) Except as provided in subdivisions (c), (e), and (f), for recovery of money, if the amount of the demand does not exceed five thousand dollars ($5,000).

(2) Except as provided in subdivisions (c), (e), and (f), to enforce payment of delinquent unsecured personal property taxes in an amount not to exceed five thousand dollars ($5,000), if the legality of the tax is not contested by the defendant.

(3) To issue the writ of possession authorized by Sections 1861.5 and 1861.10 of the Civil Code if the amount of the demand does not exceed five thousand dollars ($5,000).

(4) To confirm, correct, or vacate a fee arbitration award not exceeding five thousand dollars ($5,000) between an attorney and client that is binding or has become binding, or to conduct a hearing de novo between an attorney and client after nonbinding arbitration of a fee dispute involving no more than five thousand dollars ($5,000) in controversy, pursuant to Article 13 (commencing with Section 6200) of Chapter 4 of Division 3 of the Business and Professions Code.

(5) For an injunction or other equitable relief only when a statute expressly authorizes a small claims court to award that relief.

(b) In any action seeking relief authorized by paragraphs (1) to (4), inclusive, of subdivision (a), the court may grant equitable relief in the form of rescission, restitution, reformation, and specific performance, in lieu of, or in addition to, money damages. The court may issue a conditional judgment. The court shall retain jurisdiction until full payment and performance of any judgment or order.

(c) Notwithstanding subdivision (a), the small claims court has jurisdiction over a defendant guarantor as follows:

(1) For any action brought by a natural person against the Registrar of the Contractors' State License Board as the defendant guarantor, the small claims jurisdictional limit stated in Section 116.221 shall apply.

(2) For any action against a defendant guarantor that does not charge a fee for its guarantor or surety services, if the amount of the demand does not exceed two thousand five hundred dollars ($2,500).

(3) For any action brought by a natural person against a defendant guarantor that charges a fee for its guarantor or surety services, if the amount of the demand does not exceed six thousand five hundred dollars ($6,500).

(4) For any action brought by an entity other than a natural person against a defendant guarantor that charges a fee for its guarantor or surety services or against the Registrar of the Contractors' State License Board as the defendant guarantor, if the amount of the demand does not exceed four thousand dollars ($4,000).

(d) In any case in which the lack of jurisdiction is due solely to an excess in the amount of the demand, the excess may be waived, but any waiver is not operative until judgment.

(e) Notwithstanding subdivision (a), in any action filed by a plaintiff incarcerated in a Department of Corrections and Rehabilitation facility, the small claims court has jurisdiction over a defendant only if the plaintiff has alleged in the complaint that he or she has exhausted his or her administrative remedies against that department, including compliance with Sections 905.2 and 905.4 of the Government Code. The final administrative adjudication or determination of the plaintiff's administrative claim by the department may be attached to the complaint at the time of filing in lieu of that allegation.

(f) In any action governed by subdivision (e), if the plaintiff fails to provide proof of compliance with the requirements of subdivision (e) at the time of trial, the judicial officer shall, at his or her discretion, either dismiss the action or continue the action to give the plaintiff an opportunity to provide that proof.

(g) For purposes of this section, "department" includes an employee of a department against whom a claim has been filed under this chapter arising out of his or her duties as an employee of that department.

Added Stats 1990 ch 1305 § 3 (SB 2627). Amended Stats 1990 ch 1683 § 3 (AB 3916); Stats 1991 ch 133 § 1 (AB 1827), ch 915 § 3 (SB 771); Stats 1992 ch 8 § 1 (AB 1551), effective February 19, 1992, ch 142 § 2 (SB 1376); Stats 1993 ch 1262 § 5 (AB 1272), ch 1264 § 95 (SB 574); Stats 1994 ch 479 § 10 (AB 3219); Stats 1995 ch 366 § 1 (AB 725); Stats 1998 ch 240 § 2 (AB 771); Stats 1999 ch 982 § 6 (AB 1678); Stats 2006

Appendix

ch 150 § 1 (AB 2455), effective January 1, 2007; Stats 2008 ch 157 § 4 (SB 1432), effective January 1, 2009; Stats. 2009, Ch. 468 (AB 712).

§ 116.221. Additional jurisdiction

In addition to the jurisdiction conferred by Section 116.220, the small claims court has jurisdiction in an action brought by a natural person, if the amount of the demand does not exceed ten thousand dollars ($10,000), except as otherwise prohibited by subdivision (c) of Section 116.220 or subdivision (a) of Section 116.231.

Added Stats 2005 ch 600 § 2 (SB 422), effective January 1, 2006. Amended Stats 2011 ch 64 § 1 (SB 221), effective January 1, 2012; Stats 2018 ch 92 § 41 (SB 1289), effective January 1, 2019.

PART 2

CIVIL ACTIONS

TITLE 14
Miscellaneous Provisions

Chapter 2
Bonds and Undertakings

Article 1
Preliminary Provisions and Definitions

§ 995.010. Short title

This chapter shall be known and may be cited as the Bond and Undertaking Law.

Added Stats 1982 ch 998 § 1.

§ 995.020. Application of chapter

(a) The provisions of this chapter apply to a bond or undertaking executed, filed, posted, furnished, or otherwise given as security pursuant to any statute of this state, except to the extent the statute prescribes a different rule or is inconsistent.

(b) The provisions of this chapter apply to a bond or undertaking given at any of the following times:

(1) On or after January 1, 1983.

(2) Before January 1, 1983, to the extent another surety is substituted for the original surety on or after January 1, 1983, or to the extent the principal gives a new, additional, or supplemental bond or undertaking on or after January 1, 1983.

Except to the extent provided in this section, the law governing a bond or undertaking given before January 1, 1983, is the law applicable to the bond or undertaking immediately before January 1, 1983, pursuant to Section 414 of Chapter 517 of the Statutes of 1982.

(c) The provisions of this chapter do not apply to a bail bond or an undertaking of bail.

Added Stats 1982 ch 998 § 1. Amended Stats 1983 ch 18 § 18.2, effective April 21, 1983.

§ 995.030. Manner of service

If service of a notice, paper, or other document is required under this chapter, service shall be made in the same manner as service of process in civil actions generally.

Added Stats 1982 ch 998 § 1.

§ 995.040. Affidavits

An affidavit made under this chapter shall conform to the standards prescribed for an affidavit made pursuant to Section 437c.

Added Stats 1982 ch 998 § 1.

§ 995.050. Extensions of time

The times provided in this chapter, or in any other statute relating to a bond given in an action or proceeding, may be extended pursuant to Sections 1054 and 1054.1.

Added Stats 1982 ch 998 § 1.

§ 995.110. Application of definitions

Unless the provision or context otherwise requires, the definitions in this article govern the construction of this chapter.

Added Stats 1982 ch 998 § 1.

§ 995.120. "Admitted surety insurer"

(a) "Admitted surety insurer" means a corporate insurer or a reciprocal or interinsurance exchange to which the Insurance Commissioner has issued a certificate of authority to transact surety insurance in this state, as defined in Section 105 of the Insurance Code.

(b) For the purpose of application of this chapter to a bond given pursuant to any statute of this state, the phrases "admitted surety insurer," "authorized surety company," "bonding company," "corporate surety," and comparable phrases used in the statute mean "admitted surety insurer" as defined in this section.

Added Stats 1982 ch 998 § 1.

§ 995.130. "Beneficiary"

(a) "Beneficiary" means the person for whose benefit a bond is given, whether executed to, in favor of, in the name of, or payable to the person as an obligee.

(b) If a bond is given for the benefit of the State of California or the people of the state, "beneficiary" means the court, officer, or other person required to determine the sufficiency of the sureties or to approve the bond.

(c) For the purpose of application of this chapter to a bond given pursuant to any statute of this state, the terms "beneficiary," "obligee," and comparable terms used in the statute mean "beneficiary" as defined in this section.

Added Stats 1982 ch 998 § 1.

§ 995.140. "Bond"

(a) "Bond" includes both of the following:

(1) A surety, indemnity, fiduciary, or like bond executed by both the principal and sureties.

(2) A surety, indemnity, fiduciary, or like undertaking executed by the sureties alone.

(b) A bond provided for or given "in an action or proceeding" does not include a bond provided for, or given as, a condition of a license or permit.

Added Stats 1982 ch 998 § 1.

§ 995.150. "Court"

"Court" means, if a bond is given in an action or proceeding, the court in which the action or proceeding is pending.

Added Stats 1982 ch 998 § 1.

§ 995.160. "Officer"

"Officer" means the sheriff, marshal, clerk of court, judge or magistrate (if there is no clerk), board, commission, department, or other public official or entity to whom the bond is given or with whom a copy of the bond is filed or who is required to determine the sufficiency of the sureties or to approve the bond.

Added Stats 1982 ch 998 § 1. Amended Stats 1996 ch 872 § 19 (AB 3472).

§ 995.170. "Principal"

(a) "Principal" means the person who gives a bond.

(b) For the purpose of application of this chapter to a bond given pursuant to any statute of this state, the terms "obligor," "principal," and comparable terms used in the statute mean "principal" as defined in this section.

Added Stats 1982 ch 998 § 1.

§ 995.180. "Statute"

"Statute" includes administrative regulation promulgated pursuant to statute.

Added Stats 1982 ch 998 § 1.

§ 995.185. "Surety"

(a) "Surety" has the meaning provided in Section 2787 of the Civil Code and includes personal surety and admitted surety insurer.

(b) For the purpose of application of this chapter to a bond given pursuant to any statute of this state, the terms "bail," "guarantor," "bondsman," "surety," and comparable terms used in the statute mean "surety" as defined in this section.

Added Stats 1982 ch 998 § 1.

§ 995.190. "Undertaking"

"Undertaking" means a surety, indemnity, fiduciary, or like undertaking executed by the sureties alone.

Added Stats 1982 ch 998 § 1.

Article 2

General Provisions

Appendix

§ 995.210. Bonds and undertakings interchangeable

Unless the provision or context otherwise requires:

(a) If a statute provides for a bond, an undertaking that otherwise satisfies the requirements for the bond may be given in its place with the same effect as if a bond were given, and references in the statute to the bond shall be deemed to be references to the undertaking.

(b) If a statute provides for an undertaking, a bond that otherwise satisfies the requirements for the undertaking may be given in its place with the same effect as if an undertaking were given, and references in the statute to the undertaking shall be deemed to be references to the bond.

Added Stats 1982 ch 998 § 1.

§ 995.220. Bond not required of public entity or officer

Notwithstanding any other statute, if a statute provides for a bond in an action or proceeding, including but not limited to a bond for issuance of a restraining order or injunction, appointment of a receiver, or stay of enforcement of a judgment on appeal, the following public entities and officers are not required to give the bond and shall have the same rights, remedies, and benefits as if the bond were given:

(a) The State of California or the people of the state, a state agency, department, division, commission, board, or other entity of the state, or a state officer in an official capacity or on behalf of the state.

(b) A county, city, or district, or public authority, public agency, or other political subdivision in the state, or an officer of the local public entity in an official capacity or on behalf of the local public entity.

(c) The United States or an instrumentality or agency of the United States, or a federal officer in an official capacity or on behalf of the United States or instrumentality or agency.

Added Stats 1982 ch 998 § 1.

§ 995.230. Reduction or waiver by beneficiary

The beneficiary of a bond given in an action or proceeding may in writing consent to the bond in an amount less than the amount required by statute or may waive the bond.

Added Stats 1982 ch 998 § 1.

§ 995.240. Waiver in case of indigency

The court may, in its discretion, waive a provision for a bond in an action or proceeding and make such orders as may be appropriate as if the bond were given, if the court determines that the principal is unable to give the bond because the principal is indigent and is unable to obtain sufficient sureties, whether personal or admitted surety insurers. In exercising its discretion the court shall take into consideration all factors it deems relevant, including but not limited to the character of the action or proceeding, the nature of the beneficiary, whether public or private, and the potential harm to the beneficiary if the provision for the bond is waived.

Added Stats 1982 ch 998 § 1.

§ 995.250. Cost of bond recoverable

If a statute allows costs to a party in an action or proceeding, the costs shall include all of the following:

(a) The premium on a bond reasonably paid by the party pursuant to a statute that provides for the bond in the action or proceeding.

(b) The premium on a bond reasonably paid by the party in connection with the action or proceeding, unless the court determines that the bond was unnecessary.

Added Stats 1982 ch 998 § 1.

§ 995.260. Evidence of bond

If a bond is recorded pursuant to statute, a certified copy of the record of the bond with all affidavits, acknowledgments, endorsements, and attachments may be admitted in evidence in an action or proceeding with the same effect as the original, without further proof.

Added Stats 1982 ch 998 § 1.

Article 3

Execution and Filing

§ 995.310. Sureties on bond

Unless the statute providing for the bond requires execution by an admitted surety insurer, a bond shall be executed by two or more sufficient personal sureties or by one sufficient admitted surety insurer or by any combination of sufficient personal sureties and admitted surety insurers.

Added Stats 1982 ch 998 § 1.

§ 995.311. Sureties on bond on public works contract; Status verification procedures

(a) Notwithstanding any other provision of law, any bond required on a public works contract, as defined in Section 1101 of the Public Contract Code, shall be executed by an admitted surety insurer. A public agency approving the bond on a public works contract shall have a duty to verify that the bond is being executed by an admitted surety insurer.

(b) A public agency may fulfill its duty under subdivision (a) by verifying the status of the party executing the bond in one of the following ways:

Appendix

(1) Printing out information from the website of the Department of Insurance confirming the surety is an admitted surety insurer and attaching it to the bond.

(2) Obtaining a certificate from the county clerk that confirms the surety is an admitted insurer and attaching it to the bond.

Added Stats 2001 ch 181 § 1 (AB 263).

§ 995.320. Contents of bond

(a) A bond shall be in writing signed by the sureties under oath and shall include all of the following:

(1) A statement that the sureties are jointly and severally liable on the obligations of the statute providing for the bond.

(2) The address at which the principal and sureties may be served with notices, papers, and other documents under this chapter.

(3) If the amount of the bond is based upon the value of property or an interest in property, a description of the property or interest, and the principal's estimate of the value of the property or interest, or if given pursuant to the estimate of the beneficiary or court, the value as so estimated.

(b) The sureties signing the bond are jointly and severally liable on the obligations of the bond, the provisions of this chapter, and the statute providing for the bond.

Added Stats 1982 ch 998 § 1.

§ 995.330. Form of bond

A bond or undertaking given in an action or proceeding may be in the following form:

"(Title of court. Title of cause.)

Whereas the ... desires to give (a bond) (an undertaking) for (state what) as provided by (state sections of code requiring bond or under-taking); now, therefore, the undersigned (principal and) (sureties) (surety) hereby (obligate ourselves, jointly and severally) (obligates itself) to (name who) under the statutory obligations, in the amount of ... dollars."

Added Stats 1982 ch 998 § 1.

§ 995.340. Filing required

If a bond is given in an action or proceeding:

(a) The bond shall be filed with the court unless the statute providing for the bond requires that the bond be given to another person.

(b) If the statute providing for the bond requires that the bond be given to an officer, the officer shall file the bond with the court unless the statute providing for the bond otherwise provides.

(c) A bond filed with the court shall be preserved in the office of the clerk of the court.

Added Stats 1982 ch 998 § 1.

§ 995.350. Entry in register of actions

(a) Upon the filing of a bond with the court in an action or proceeding, the clerk shall enter in the register of actions the following information:

(1) The date and amount of the bond.

(2) The names of the sureties on the bond.

(b) In the event of the loss of the bond, the entries in the register of actions are prima facie evidence of the giving of the bond in the manner required by statute.

Added Stats 1982 ch 998 § 1.

§ 995.360. Return of bond

A bond given in an action or proceeding may be withdrawn from the file and returned to the principal on order of the court only if one of the following conditions is satisfied:

(a) The beneficiary so stipulates.

(b) The bond is no longer in force and effect and the time during which the liability on the bond may be enforced has expired.

Added Stats 1982 ch 998 § 1.

§ 995.370. Service of copy of bond

At the time a bond is given, the principal shall serve a copy of the bond on the beneficiary. An affidavit of service shall be given and filed with the bond.

Added Stats 1982 ch 998 § 1.

§ 995.380. Defect in bond

(a) If a bond does not contain the substantial matter or conditions required by this chapter or by the statute providing for the bond, or if there are any defects in the giving or filing of the bond, the bond is not void so as to release the principal and sureties from liability.

(b) The beneficiary may, in proceedings to enforce the liability on the bond, suggest the defect in the bond, or its giving or filing, and enforce the liability against the principal and the persons who intended to become and were included as sureties on the bond.

Added Stats 1982 ch 998 § 1.

Article 4

Approval and Effect

§ 995.410. Approval of bond

(a) A bond becomes effective without approval unless the statute providing for the bond requires that the bond be approved by the court or officer.

(b) If the statute providing for a bond requires that the bond be approved, the court or officer may approve or disapprove the bond on the basis of the affidavit or certificate of the sureties or may require the attendance of witnesses and the production of evidence and may examine the sureties under oath touching their qualifications.

(c) Nothing shall be construed to preclude approval of a bond in an amount greater than that required by statute.

Added Stats 1982 ch 998 § 1.

§ 995.420. Time bond becomes effective

(a) Unless the statute providing for a bond provides that the bond becomes effective at a different time, a bond is effective at the time it is given or, if the statute requires that the bond be approved, at the time it is approved.

(b) If the statute providing for a bond provides that the bond becomes effective at a time other than the time it is given or approved, the bond is effective at the time provided unless an objection is made to the bond before that time. If an objection is made to a bond before the time provided, the bond becomes effective when the court makes an order determining the sufficiency of the bond.

Added Stats 1982 ch 998 § 1.

§ 995.430. Term of bond

A bond remains in force and effect until the earliest of the following events:

(a) The sureties withdraw from or cancel the bond or a new bond is given in place of the original bond.

(b) The purpose for which the bond was given is satisfied or the purpose is abandoned without any liability having been incurred.

(c) A judgment of liability on the bond that exhausts the amount of the bond is satisfied.

(d) The term of the bond expires. Unless the statute providing for the bond prescribes a fixed term, the bond is continuous.

Added Stats 1982 ch 998 § 1.

§ 995.440. Term of license or permit bond

A bond given as a condition of a license or permit shall be continuous in form, remain in full force and effect, and run concurrently with the license or permit period and any and all renewals, or until cancellation or withdrawal of the surety from the bond.

Added Stats 1982 ch 998 § 1.

Article 5

Personal Sureties

§ 995.510. Qualifications of surety

(a) A personal surety on a bond is sufficient if all of the following conditions are satisfied:

(1) The surety is a person other than the principal. No officer of the court or member of the State Bar shall act as a surety.

(2) The surety is a resident, and either an owner of real property or householder, within the state.

(3) The surety is worth the amount of the bond in real or personal property, or both, situated in this state, over and above all debts and liabilities, exclusive of property exempt from enforcement of a money judgment.

(b) If the amount of a bond exceeds ten thousand dollars ($10,000) and is executed by more than two personal sureties, the worth of a personal surety may be less than the amount of the bond, so long as the aggregate worth of all sureties executing the bond is twice the amount of the bond.

Added Stats 1982 ch 998 § 1.

§ 995.520. Affidavit of surety

(a) A bond executed by personal sureties shall be accompanied by an affidavit of qualifications of each surety.

(b) The affidavit shall contain all of the following information:

(1) The name, occupation, residence address, and business address (if any) of the surety.

(2) A statement that the surety is a resident, and either an owner of real property or householder, within the state.

(3) A statement that the surety is worth the amount of the bond in real or personal property, or both, situated in this state, over and above all debts and liabilities, exclusive of property exempt from enforcement of a money judgment.

(c) If the amount of the bond exceeds five thousand dollars ($5,000), the affidavit shall contain, in addition to the information required by subdivision (b), all of the following information:

(1) A description sufficient for identification of real and personal property of the surety situated in this state and the nature of the surety's interest therein that qualifies the surety on the bond.

(2) The surety's best estimate of the fair market value of each item of property.

(3) A statement of any charge or lien and its amount, known to the surety, whether of public record or not, against any item of property.

(4) Any other impediment or cloud known to the surety on the free right of possession, use, benefit, or enjoyment of the property.

(d) If the amount of the bond exceeds ten thousand dollars ($10,000) and is executed by more than two sureties, the affidavit may state that the surety is worth less than the amount of the bond and the bond may stipulate that the liability of the surety is limited to the worth of the surety stated in the affidavit, so long as the aggregate worth of all sureties executing the bond is twice the amount of the bond.

Added Stats 1982 ch 998 § 1.

Article 6

Admitted Surety Insurers

§ 995.610. Admitted surety insurer in lieu of personal sureties

(a) If a statute provides for a bond with any number of sureties, one sufficient admitted surety insurer may become and shall be accepted as sole surety on the bond.

(b) The admitted surety insurer is subject to all the liabilities and entitled to all the rights of personal sureties.

Added Stats 1982 ch 998 § 1.

§ 995.620. More than one surety

Two or more admitted surety insurers may be sureties on a bond by executing the same or separate bonds for amounts aggregating the required amount of the bond. Each admitted surety insurer is jointly and severally liable to the extent of the amount of the liability assumed by it.

Added Stats 1982 ch 998 § 1.

§ 995.630.   Authentication of bond

An admitted surety insurer shall be accepted or approved by the court or officer as surety on a bond without further acknowledgment if the bond is executed in the name of the surety insurer under penalty of perjury or the fact of execution of the bond is duly acknowledged before an officer authorized to take and certify acknowledgments, and either one of the following conditions, at the option of the surety insurer, is satisfied:

(a) A copy of the transcript or record of the unrevoked appointment, power of attorney, bylaws, or other instrument, duly certified by the proper authority and attested by the seal of the insurer entitling or authorizing the person who executed the bond to do so for and in behalf of the insurer, is filed in the office of the clerk of the county in which the court or officer is located.

(b) A copy of a power of attorney is attached to the bond.

Added Stats 1982 ch 998 § 1. Amended Stats 1992 ch 380 § 1 (SB 1521).

§ 995.640.   Certificate of authority

Upon review of the Internet Web site of the Department of Insurance, the county clerk of any county shall, upon request of any person, do any of the following:

(a) Issue a certificate stating whether a surety is admitted or if the certificate of authority of an admitted surety insurer issued by the Insurance Commissioner authorizing the insurer to transact surety insurance has been surrendered, revoked, canceled, annulled, or suspended, and, in the event that it has, whether renewed authority has been granted. The county clerk in issuing the certificate shall rely solely upon the information furnished by the Insurance Commissioner pursuant to Article 2 (commencing with Section 12070) of Chapter 1 of Part 4 of Division 2 of the Insurance Code.

(b) Issue a certificate stating whether a copy of the transcript or record of the unrevoked appointment, power of attorney, bylaws, or other instrument, duly certified by the proper authority and attested by the seal of an admitted surety insurer entitling or authorizing the person who executed a bond to do so for and on behalf of the insurer, is filed in the office of the clerk.

Added Stats 1982 ch 998 § 1. Amended Stats 2004 ch 183 § 44 (AB 3082); Stats 2005 ch 22 § 19 (SB 1108), effective January 1, 2006; Stats 2008 ch 351 § 1 (SB 1279), effective January 1, 2009.

§ 995.650.   Objection to sufficiency of surety

If an objection is made to the sufficiency of an admitted surety insurer, the person making the objection shall attach to and incorporate in the objection one or both of the following:

Appendix

(a) The certificate of the county clerk of the county in which the court is located stating that the insurer is not listed as an admitted surety insurer on the department's Internet Web site or that the certificate of authority of the insurer has been surrendered, revoked, canceled, annulled, or suspended and has not been renewed.

(b) An affidavit stating facts that establish the insufficiency of the insurer.

Added Stats 1982 ch 998 § 1. Amended Stats 2008 ch 351 § 2 (SB 1279), effective January 1, 2009.

§ 995.660. Determination of sufficiency of surety

(a) If an objection is made to the sufficiency of an admitted surety insurer on a bond or if the bond is required to be approved, the insurer shall submit to the court or officer the following documents:

(1) The original, or a certified copy, of the unrevoked appointment, power of attorney, bylaws, or other instrument entitling or authorizing the person who executed the bond to do so, within 10 calendar days of the insurer's receipt of a request to submit the instrument.

(2) A certified copy of the certificate of authority of the insurer issued by the Insurance Commissioner, within 10 calendar days of the insurer's receipt of a request to submit the copy.

(3) A certificate from the clerk of the county in which the court or officer is located that the certificate of authority of the insurer has not been surrendered, revoked, canceled, annulled, or suspended or, in the event that it has, that renewed authority has been granted, within 10 calendar days of the insurer's receipt of the certificate.

(4) Copies of the insurer's most recent annual statement and quarterly statement filed with the Department of Insurance pursuant to Article 10 (commencing with Section 900) of Chapter 1 of Part 2 of Division 1 of the Insurance Code, within 10 calendar days of the insurer's receipt of a request to submit the statements.

(b) If the admitted surety insurer complies with subdivision (a), and if it appears that the bond was duly executed, that the insurer is authorized to transact surety insurance in the state, and that its assets exceed its liabilities in an amount equal to or in excess of the amount of the bond, the insurer is sufficient and shall be accepted or approved as surety on the bond, subject to Section 12090 of the Insurance Code.

Added Stats 1982 ch 998 § 1. Amended Stats 1992 ch 379 § 1 (SB 1502); Stats 1994 ch 487 § 1 (AB 3493).

§ 995.670. Admitted surety to comply only with specified requirements relating to objections to surety's sufficiency

(a) This section applies to a bond executed, filed, posted, furnished, or otherwise given as security pursuant to any statute of this state or any law or ordinance of a public agency.

No public agency shall require an admitted surety insurer to comply with any requirements other than those in Section 995.660 whenever an objection is made to the sufficiency of the admitted surety insurer on the bond or if the bond is required to be approved.

(b) For the purposes of this section, "public agency" means the state, any agency or authority, any city, county, city and county, district, municipal or public corporation, or any instrumentality thereof.

Added Stats 1992 ch 997 § 1 (AB 2872). Amended Stats 1994 ch 487 § 2 (AB 3493).

§ 995.675. Listing surety insurer

Notwithstanding Sections 995.660 and 995.670, the California Integrated Waste Management Board, the State Water Resources Control Board, and the Department of Toxic Substances Control may require, in order to comply with Subtitle C or Subtitle D of the federal Resource Conservation and Recovery Act of 1976, as amended (42 U.S.C. Sec. 6901 et seq.), an admitted surety insurer to be listed in Circular 570 issued by the United States Treasury.

Added Stats 1998 ch 477 § 1 (AB 2353).

Article 7

Deposit in Lieu of Bond

§ 995.710. Deposit of money, certificates, accounts, bonds, or notes

(a) Except as provided in subdivision (e) or to the extent the statute providing for a bond precludes a deposit in lieu of bond or limits the form of deposit, the principal may, without prior court approval, instead of giving a bond, deposit with the officer any of the following:

(1) Lawful money of the United States or a cashier's check, made payable to the officer, issued by a bank, savings association, or credit union authorized to do business in this state. The money shall be held in trust by the officer in interest-bearing deposit or share accounts.

(2) Bonds or notes, including bearer bonds and bearer notes, of the United States or the State of California. The deposit of a bond or note pursuant to this section shall be accomplished by filing with the court, and serving upon all parties and the appropriate officer of the bank holding the bond or note, instructions executed by the person or

entity holding title to the bond or note that the treasurer of the county where the judgment was entered is the custodian of that account for the purpose of staying enforcement of the judgment, and that the title holder assigns to the treasurer the right to collect, sell, or otherwise apply the bond or note to enforce the judgment debtor's liability pursuant to Section 995.760.

(3) Certificates of deposit payable to the officer, not exceeding the federally insured amount, issued by banks or savings associations authorized to do business in this state and insured by the Federal Deposit Insurance Corporation.

(4) Savings accounts assigned to the officer, not exceeding the federally insured amount, together with evidence of the deposit in the savings accounts with banks authorized to do business in this state and insured by the Federal Deposit Insurance Corporation.

(5) Investment certificates or share accounts assigned to the officer, not exceeding the federally insured amount, issued by savings associations authorized to do business in this state and insured by the Federal Deposit Insurance Corporation.

(6) Share certificates payable to the officer, not exceeding the guaranteed or insured amount, issued by a credit union, as defined in Section 14002 of the Financial Code, whose share accounts are insured by the National Credit Union Administration or guaranteed or insured by any other agency that the Commissioner of Financial Protection and Innovation has not deemed to be unsatisfactory.

(b) The deposit shall be in an amount or have a face value, or, in the case of bonds or notes, have a market value, equal to or in excess of the amount that would be required to be secured by the bond if the bond were given by an admitted surety insurer. Notwithstanding any other provision of this chapter, in the case of a deposit of bonds or notes other than in an action or proceeding, the officer may, in the officer's discretion, require that the amount of the deposit be determined not by the market value of the bonds or notes but by a formula based on the principal amount of the bonds or notes.

(c) The deposit shall be accompanied by an agreement executed by the principal authorizing the officer to collect, sell, or otherwise apply the deposit to enforce the liability of the principal on the deposit. The agreement shall include the address at which the principal may be served with notices, papers, and other documents under this chapter.

(d) The officer may prescribe terms and conditions to implement this section.

(e) This section does not apply to deposits with the Secretary of State.

Added Stats 1982 ch 998 § 1. Amended Stats 1983 ch 18 § 18.5, effective April 21, 1983; Stats 1996 ch 1064 § 6 (AB 3351), operative July 1, 1997; Stats 1998 ch 829 § 16 (SB 1652); Stats 1999 ch 892 § 11 (AB 1672); Stats 2014 ch 305 § 1 (AB 1856), effective January 1, 2015; Stat 2022 ch 452 § 41 (SB 1498), effective January 1, 2023.

§ 995.720. Valuation of bonds or notes

(a) The market value of bonds or notes, including bearer bonds and bearer notes, shall be agreed upon by stipulation of the principal and beneficiary or, if the bonds or notes are given in an action or proceeding and the principal and beneficiary are unable to agree, the market value shall be determined by court order in the manner prescribed in this section. A certified copy of the stipulation or court order shall be delivered to the officer at the time of the deposit of the bonds or notes.

(b) If the bonds or notes are given in an action or proceeding, the principal may file a written application with the court to determine the market value of the bonds or notes. The application shall be served upon the beneficiary and proof of service shall be filed with the application. The application shall contain all of the following:

(1) A specific description of the bonds or notes.

(2) A statement of the current market value of the bonds or notes as of the date of the filing of the application.

(3) A statement of the amount of the bonds or notes that the principal believes would be equal to the required amount of the deposit.

(c) The application pursuant to subdivision (b) shall be heard by the court not less than five days or more than 10 days after service of the application. If at the time of the hearing no objection is made to the current market value of the bonds or notes alleged in the application, the court shall fix the amount of the bonds or notes on the basis of the market value alleged in the application. If the beneficiary contends that the current market value of the bonds or notes is less than alleged in the application, the principal shall offer evidence in support of the application, and the beneficiary may offer evidence in opposition. At the conclusion of the hearing, the court shall make an order determining the market value of the bonds or notes and shall fix and determine the amount of the bonds or notes to be deposited by the principal.

Added Stats 1982 ch 998 § 1. Amended Stats 2014 ch 305 § 2 (AB 1856), effective January 1, 2015.

§ 995.730. Effect of deposit

A deposit given instead of a bond has the same force and effect, is treated the same, and is subject to the same conditions, liability, and statutory provisions, including provisions for increase and decrease of amount, as the bond.

Added Stats 1982 ch 998 § 1.

§ 995.740. Interest on deposit

If no proceedings are pending to enforce the liability of the principal on the deposit, the officer shall:

(a) Pay quarterly, on demand, any interest on the deposit, when earned in accordance with the terms of the account or certificate, to the principal.

(b) Deliver to the principal, on demand, any interest coupons attached to bonds or notes, including bearer bonds and bearer notes, as the interest coupons become due and payable, or pay annually any interest payable on the bonds or notes.

Added Stats 1982 ch 998 § 1. Amended Stats 2014 ch 305 § 3 (AB 1856), effective January 1, 2015.

§ 995.750. Obligation of principal

(a) The principal shall pay the amount of the liability on the deposit within 30 days after the date on which the judgment of liability becomes final.

(b) If the deposit was given to stay enforcement of a judgment on appeal, the principal shall pay the amount of the liability on the deposit, including damages and costs awarded against the principal on appeal, within 30 days after the filing of the remittitur from the appellate court in the court from which the appeal is taken.

Added Stats 1982 ch 998 § 1.

§ 995.760. Enforcement against deposit

(a) If the principal does not pay the amount of the liability on the deposit within the time prescribed in Section 995.750, the deposit shall be collected, sold, or otherwise applied to the liability upon order of the court that entered the judgment of liability, made upon five days' notice to the parties.

(b) Bonds or notes, including bearer bonds and bearer notes, without a prevailing market price shall be sold at public auction. Notice of sale shall be served on the principal. Bonds or notes having a prevailing market price may be sold at private sale at a price not lower than the prevailing market price.

(c) The deposit shall be distributed in the following order:

(1) First, to pay the cost of collection, sale, or other application of the deposit.

(2) Second, to pay the judgment of liability of the principal on the deposit.

(3) Third, the remainder, if any, shall be returned to the principal.

Added Stats 1982 ch 998 § 1. Amended Stats 2014 ch 305 § 4 (AB 1856), effective January 1, 2015.

§ 995.770. Return of deposit

A deposit given pursuant to this article shall be returned to the principal at the earliest of the following times:

(a) Upon substitution of a sufficient bond for the deposit. The bond shall be in full force and effect for all liabilities incurred, and for acts, omissions, or causes existing or which arose, during the period the deposit was in effect.

(b) The time provided by Section 995.360 for return of a bond.

(c) The time provided by statute for return of the deposit.

Added Stats 1982 ch 998 § 1.

Article 8

Bonds to the State of California

§ 995.810. Application of article

The provisions of this article apply to a bond executed to, in favor of, in the name of, or payable to the State of California or the people of the state, including but not limited to an official bond.

Added Stats 1982 ch 998 § 1.

§ 995.820. Bond by officer of court

Except as otherwise provided by statute, a bond given by an officer of the court for the faithful discharge of the officer's duties and obedience to the orders of the court shall be to the State of California.

Added Stats 1982 ch 998 § 1.

§ 995.830. Bond where no beneficiary provided

If a statute or court order pursuant thereto providing for a bond does not specify the beneficiary of the bond, the bond shall be to the State of California.

Added Stats 1982 ch 998 § 1.

§ 995.840. Court approval of bond

If a bond under this article is given in an action or proceeding:

(a) The bond shall be approved by the court.

(b) Any party for whose benefit the bond is given may object to the bond.

Added Stats 1982 ch 998 § 1.

Appendix

§ 995.850. Enforcement by or for benefit of persons damaged

(a) The liability on a bond under this article may be enforced by or for the benefit of, and in the name of, any and all persons for whose benefit the bond is given who are damaged by breach of the condition of the bond.

(b) A person described in subdivision (a) may, in addition to any other remedy the person has, enforce the liability on the bond in the person's own name, without assignment of the bond.

Added Stats 1982 ch 998 § 1.

Article 9

Objections to Bonds

§ 995.910. Article limited to actions and proceedings

This article governs objections to a bond given in an action or proceeding.

Added Stats 1982 ch 998 § 1.

§ 995.920. Grounds for objection

The beneficiary may object to a bond on any of the following grounds:

(a) The sureties are insufficient.

(b) The amount of the bond is insufficient.

(c) The bond, from any other cause, is insufficient.

Added Stats 1982 ch 998 § 1.

§ 995.930. Manner of making objection

(a) An objection shall be in writing and shall be made by noticed motion. The notice of motion shall specify the precise grounds for the objection. If a ground for the objection is that the amount of the bond is insufficient, the notice of motion shall state the reason for the insufficiency and shall include an estimate of the amount that would be sufficient.

(b) The objection shall be made within 10 days after service of a copy of the bond on the beneficiary or such other time as is required by the statute providing for the bond.

(c) If no objection is made within the time required by statute, the beneficiary is deemed to have waived all objections except upon a showing of good cause for failure to make the objection within the time required by statute or of changed circumstances.

Added Stats 1982 ch 998 § 1. Amended Stats 1984 ch 538 § 33.

§ 995.940. Objection to sufficiency of bond based on market value

If a ground for the objection is that the value of property or an interest in property on which the amount of the bond is based exceeds the value estimated in the bond:

(a) The objection shall state the beneficiary's estimate of the market value of the property or interest in property.

(b) The principal may accept the beneficiary's estimate of the market value of the property or interest in property and immediately file an increased bond based on the estimate. In such case, no hearing shall be held on that ground for the objection, and the beneficiary is bound by the estimate of the market value of the property or interest in property.

Added Stats 1982 ch 998 § 1.

§ 995.950. Hearing on objection

(a) Unless the parties otherwise agree, the hearing on an objection shall be held not less than two or more than five days after service of the notice of motion.

(b) The hearing shall be conducted in such manner as the court determines is proper. The court may permit witnesses to attend and testify and evidence to be procured and introduced in the same manner as in the trial of a civil case.

(c) If the value of property or an interest in property is a ground for the objection, the court shall estimate its value. The court may appoint one or more disinterested persons to appraise property or an interest in property for the purpose of estimating its value.

Added Stats 1982 ch 998 § 1.

§ 995.960. Determination of sufficiency of bond

(a) Upon the hearing, the court shall make an order determining the sufficiency or insufficiency of the bond.

(b) If the court determines that the bond is insufficient:

(1) The court shall specify in what respect the bond is insufficient and shall order that a bond with sufficient sureties and in a sufficient amount be given within five days. If a sufficient bond is not given within the time required by the court order, all rights obtained by giving the bond immediately cease and the court shall upon ex parte motion so order.

(2) If a bond is in effect, the bond remains in effect until a bond with sufficient sureties and in a sufficient amount is given in its place, or the time in which to give the bond has expired, whichever first occurs. If the time in which to give a sufficient bond expires, the original

bond remains in full force and effect for all liabilities incurred before, and for acts, omissions, or causes existing or which arose before, expiration.

(c) If the court determines that a bond is sufficient, no future objection to the bond may be made except upon a showing of changed circumstances.

Added Stats 1982 ch 998 § 1.

Article 10

Insufficient and Excessive Bonds

§ 996.010. Bond in action or proceeding

(a) If a bond is given in an action or proceeding, the court may determine that the bond is or has from any cause become insufficient because the sureties are insufficient or because the amount of the bond is insufficient.

(b) The court determination shall be upon motion supported by affidavit or upon the court's own motion. The motion shall be deemed to be an objection to the bond. The motion shall be heard and notice of motion shall be given in the same manner as an objection to the bond.

(c) Upon the determination the court shall order that a sufficient new, additional, or supplemental bond be given within a reasonable time not less than five days. The court order is subject to any limitations in the statute providing for the bond.

(d) If a sufficient bond is not given within the time required by the court order, all rights obtained by giving the original bond immediately cease and the court shall upon ex parte motion so order.

Added Stats 1982 ch 998 § 1.

§ 996.020. Bond other than in action or proceeding

(a) If a bond is given other than in an action or proceeding and it is shown by affidavit of a credible witness or it otherwise comes to the attention of the officer that the bond is or has from any cause become insufficient because the sureties are insufficient or because the amount of the bond is insufficient, the officer may serve an order on the principal to appear and show cause why the officer should not make a determination that the bond is insufficient. The order shall name a day not less than three or more than 10 days after service.

(b) If the principal fails to appear or show good cause on the day named why a determination that the bond is insufficient should not be made, the officer may determine that the bond is insufficient and order a sufficient new, additional, or supplemental bond to be given.

(c) If a sufficient bond is not given within 10 days after the order, the officer shall make an order vacating the rights obtained by giving the original bond, including declaring vacant any office and suspending or revoking any license or certificate for which the bond was given. Any office vacated, license suspended or revoked, or any other rights lost, for failure to give a new, additional, or supplemental bond, shall not be reinstated until a new, additional, or supplemental bond is given.

Added Stats 1982 ch 998 § 1.

§ 996.030. Reduced bond

(a) The court if a bond is given or ordered in an action or proceeding, or the officer if a bond is given or ordered other than in an action or proceeding, may determine that the amount of the bond is excessive and order the amount reduced to an amount that in the discretion of the court or officer appears proper under the circumstances. The order is subject to any limitations in the statute providing for the bond.

(b) The determination shall be made upon motion or affidavit of the principal in the same manner as a motion or affidavit for a determination under this article that a bond is insufficient. The notice of motion or the order to show cause made pursuant to affidavit shall be served on the beneficiary. The determination shall be made in the same manner and pursuant to the same procedures as a determination under this article that the bond is insufficient.

(c) The principal may give a new bond for the reduced amount. The sureties may be the same sureties as on the original bond.

Added Stats 1982 ch 998 § 1. Amended Stats 1988 ch 309 § 1.

Article 11

Release or Substitution of Sureties on Bond Given in Action or Proceeding

§ 996.110. Application for substitution and release

(a) A surety on a bond given in an action or proceeding may at any time apply to the court for an order that the surety be released from liability on the bond.

(b) The principal on a bond may, if a surety applies for release from liability on a bond, apply to the court for an order that another surety be substituted for the original surety.

(c) The applicant shall serve on the principal or surety (other than the applicant) and on the beneficiary a copy of the application and a notice of hearing on the application. Service shall be made not less than 15 days before the date set for hearing.

Added Stats 1982 ch 998 § 1.

§ 996.120. Hearing

Upon the hearing of the application, the court shall determine whether injury to the beneficiary would result from substitution or release of the surety. If the court determines that release would not reduce the amount of the bond or the number of sureties below the minimum required by the statute providing for the bond, substitution of a sufficient surety is not necessary and the court shall order the release of the surety. If the court determines that no injury would result from substitution of the surety, the court shall order the substitution of a sufficient surety within such time as appears reasonable.

Added Stats 1982 ch 998 § 1.

§ 996.130. Substitution and release

(a) If a substitute surety is given, the substitute surety is subject to all the provisions of this chapter, including but not limited to the provisions governing insufficient and excessive bonds.

(b) Upon the substitution of a sufficient surety, the court shall order the release of the original surety from liability on the bond.

Added Stats 1982 ch 998 § 1.

§ 996.140. Failure to give substitute surety

If the principal does not give a sufficient substitute surety within the time ordered by the court or such longer time as the surety consents to, all rights obtained by giving the original bond immediately cease and the court shall upon ex parte motion so order.

Added Stats 1982 ch 998 § 1.

§ 996.150. Liability of released surety

If a surety is ordered released from liability on a bond:

(a) The bond remains in full force and effect for all liabilities incurred before, and for acts, omissions, or causes existing or which arose before, the release. Legal proceedings may be had therefor in all respects as though there had been no release.

(b) The surety is not liable for any act, default, or misconduct of the principal or other breach of the condition of the bond that occurs after, or for any liabilities on the bond that arise after, the release.

(c) The release does not affect the bond as to the remaining sureties, or alter or change their liability in any respect.

Added Stats 1982 ch 998 § 1.

Article 12

New, Additional, and Supplemental Bonds

§ 996.210. When bond given

(a) The principal shall give a new, additional, or supplemental bond if the court or officer orders that a new, additional, or supplemental bond be given.

(b) The principal may give a new bond if a surety withdraws from or cancels the original bond or to obtain the release of sureties from liability on the original bond.

Added Stats 1982 ch 998 § 1.

§ 996.220. Contents of bond

(a) A new, additional, or supplemental bond shall be in the same form and have the same obligation as the original bond and shall be in all other respects the same as the original bond, and shall be in such amount as is necessary for the purpose for which the new, additional, or supplemental bond is given.

(b) A supplemental bond shall, in addition to any other requirements, recite the names of the remaining original sureties, the name of the new surety, and the amount for which the new surety is liable. The supplemental bond shall be for the amount for which the original surety was liable on the original bond.

Added Stats 1982 ch 998 § 1.

§ 996.230. Provisions applicable to bond

A new, additional, or supplemental bond is subject to all the provisions applicable to the original bond and to the provisions of this chapter, including but not limited to the provisions governing giving and objecting to a bond and liabilities and enforcement procedures.

Added Stats 1982 ch 998 § 1.

§ 996.240. Effect of new bond

If a new bond is given in place of the original bond:

(a) The original bond remains in full force and effect for all liabilities incurred before, and for acts, omissions, or causes existing or which arose before, the new bond became effective.

(b) The sureties on the original bond are not liable for any act, default, or misconduct of the principal or other breach of the condition

Appendix

of the bond that occurs after or for any liabilities on the bond that arise after, the new bond becomes effective.

Added Stats 1982 ch 998 § 1.

§ 996.250. Effect of additional or supplemental bond

(a) An additional or supplemental bond does not discharge or affect the original bond. The original bond remains in full force and effect as if the additional or supplemental bond had not been given.

(b) After an additional or supplemental bond is given, the principal and sureties are liable upon either or both bonds for injury caused by breach of any condition of the bonds. Subject to subdivision (c), the beneficiary may enforce the liability on either bond, or may enforce the liability separately on both bonds and recover separate judgments of liability on both.

(c) If the beneficiary recovers separate judgments of liability on both bonds for the same cause of action, the beneficiary may enforce both judgments. The beneficiary may collect, by execution or otherwise, the costs of both proceedings to enforce the liability and the amount actually awarded to the beneficiary on the same cause of action in only one of the proceedings, and no double recovery shall be allowed.

(d) If the sureties on either bond have been compelled to pay any sum of money on account of the principal, they are entitled to recover from the sureties on the remaining bond a distributive part of the sum paid, in the proportion the amounts of the bonds bear one to the other and to the sums paid.

Added Stats 1982 ch 998 § 1.

Article 13

Cancellation of Bond or Withdrawal of Sureties

§ 996.310. Application of article

This article governs cancellation of or withdrawal of a surety from a bond given other than in an action or proceeding.

Added Stats 1982 ch 998 § 1.

§ 996.320. Notice of cancellation or withdrawal

A surety may cancel or withdraw from a bond by giving a notice of cancellation or withdrawal to the officer to whom the bond was given in the same manner the bond was given, notwithstanding Section

995.030. The surety shall at the same time mail or deliver a copy of the notice of cancellation or withdrawal to the principal.

Added Stats 1982 ch 998 § 1.

§ 996.330. Effective date of cancellation or withdrawal

Cancellation or withdrawal of a surety is effective at the earliest of the following times:

(a) Thirty days after notice of cancellation or withdrawal is given.

(b) If a new surety is substituted for the original surety, the date the substitution becomes effective.

(c) If a new bond is given, the date the new bond becomes effective.

Added Stats 1982 ch 998 § 1.

§ 996.340. Effect of cancellation or withdrawal

(a) If the principal does not give a new bond within 30 days after notice of cancellation or withdrawal is given, all rights obtained by giving the original bond immediately cease, any office for which the bond is given is vacant, any commission for which the bond is given is revoked, and any license or registration for which the bond is given is suspended.

(b) A person whose license or registration is suspended shall not operate or carry on business pursuant to the license or registration during the period of suspension. A license or registration that is suspended may be revived only by the giving of a new bond during the license or registration period in which the cancellation or withdrawal occurred.

Added Stats 1982 ch 998 § 1. Amended Stats 1983 ch 18 § 19, effective April 21, 1983.

§ 996.350. New bond not required

If the withdrawal of a surety does not reduce the amount of the bond or the number of sureties below the minimum required by the statute providing for the bond, no new bond is required or necessary to maintain the original bond in effect.

Added Stats 1982 ch 998 § 1.

§ 996.360. Liability of surety

If a surety cancels or withdraws from a bond:

(a) The bond remains in full force and effect for all liabilities incurred before, and for acts, omissions, or causes existing or which arose before, the cancellation or withdrawal. Legal proceedings may be had therefor in all respects as though there had been no cancellation or withdrawal.

(b) The surety is not liable for any act, default, or misconduct of the principal or other breach of the condition of the bond that occurs after, or for any liabilities on the bond that arise after, the cancellation or withdrawal.

(c) The cancellation or withdrawal does not affect the bond as to the remaining sureties, or alter or change their liability in any respect.

Added Stats 1982 ch 998 § 1.

Article 14

Liability of Principal and Sureties

§ 996.410. Enforcement of liability on bond

(a) The beneficiary may enforce the liability on a bond against both the principal and sureties.

(b) If the beneficiary is a class of persons, any person in the class may enforce the liability on a bond in the person's own name, without assignment of the bond.

Added Stats 1982 ch 998 § 1.

§ 996.420. Surety subject to jurisdiction of court

(a) A surety on a bond given in an action or proceeding submits itself to the jurisdiction of the court in all matters affecting its liability on the bond.

(b) This section does not apply to a bond of a public officer or fiduciary.

Added Stats 1982 ch 998 § 1.

§ 996.430. Action to enforce liability

(a) The liability on a bond may be enforced by civil action. Both the principal and the sureties shall be joined as parties to the action.

(b) If the bond was given in an action or proceeding, the action shall be commenced in the court in which the action or proceeding was pending. If the bond was given other than in an action or proceeding, the action shall be commenced in any court of competent jurisdiction, and the amount of damage claimed in the action, not the amount of the bond, determines the jurisdictional classification of the case.

(c) A cause of action on a bond may be transferred and assigned as other causes of action.

Added Stats 1982 ch 998 § 1. Amended Stats 1998 ch 931 § 105 (SB 2139), effective September 28, 1998.

§ 996.440. Motion to enforce liability

(a) If a bond is given in an action or proceeding, the liability on the bond may be enforced on motion made in the court without the necessity of an independent action.

(b) The motion shall not be made until after entry of the final judgment in the action or proceeding in which the bond is given and the time for appeal has expired or, if an appeal is taken, until the appeal is finally determined. The motion shall not be made or notice of motion served more than one year after the later of the preceding dates.

(c) Notice of motion shall be served on the principal and sureties at least 30 days before the time set for hearing of the motion. The notice shall state the amount of the claim and shall be supported by affidavits setting forth the facts on which the claim is based. The notice and affidavits shall be served in accordance with any procedure authorized by Chapter 5 (commencing with Section 1010).

(d) Judgment shall be entered against the principal and sureties in accordance with the motion unless the principal or sureties serve and file affidavits in opposition to the motion showing such facts as may be deemed by the judge hearing the motion sufficient to present a triable issue of fact. If such a showing is made, the issues to be tried shall be specified by the court. Trial shall be by the court and shall be set for the earliest date convenient to the court, allowing sufficient time for such discovery proceedings as may be requested.

(e) The principal and sureties shall not obtain a stay of the proceedings pending determination of any conflicting claims among beneficiaries.

Added Stats 1982 ch 998 § 1.

§ 996.450. Statute of limitations

No provision in a bond is valid that attempts by contract to shorten the period prescribed by Section 337 or other statute for the commencement of an action on the bond or the period prescribed by Section 996.440 for a motion to enforce a bond. This section does not apply if the principal, beneficiary, and surety accept a provision for a shorter period in a bond.

Added Stats 1982 ch 998 § 1.

§ 996.460. Judgment of liability

(a) Notwithstanding Section 2845 of the Civil Code, a judgment of liability on a bond shall be in favor of the beneficiary and against the principal and sureties and shall obligate each of them jointly and severally.

(b) The judgment shall be in an amount determined by the court.

(c) A judgment that does not exhaust the full amount of the bond decreases the amount of the bond but does not discharge the bond. The liability on the bond may be enforced thereafter from time to time until the amount of the bond is exhausted.

(d) The judgment may be enforced by the beneficiary directly against the sureties. Nothing in this section affects any right of subrogation of a surety against the principal or any right of a surety to compel the principal to satisfy the judgment.

Added Stats 1982 ch 998 § 1.

§ 996.470. Limitation on liability of surety

(a) Notwithstanding any other statute other than Section 996.480, the aggregate liability of a surety to all persons for all breaches of the condition of a bond is limited to the amount of the bond. Except as otherwise provided by statute, the liability of the principal is not limited to the amount of the bond.

(b) If a bond is given in an amount greater than the amount required by statute or by order of the court or officer pursuant to statute, the liability of the surety on the bond is limited to the amount required by statute or by order of the court or officer, unless the amount of the bond has been increased voluntarily or by agreement of the parties to satisfy an objection to the bond made in an action or proceeding.

(c) The liability of a surety is limited to the amount stipulated in any of the following circumstances:

(1) The bond contains a stipulation pursuant to Section 995.520 that the liability of a personal surety is limited to the worth of the surety.

(2) The bond contains a stipulation that the liability of a surety is an amount less than the amount of the bond pursuant to a statute that provides that the liability of sureties in the aggregate need not exceed the amount of the bond.

Added Stats 1982 ch 998 § 1. Amended Stats 1993 ch 527 § 2 (AB 908).

§ 996.475. Liability of surety pursuant to other statute

Nothing in this chapter is intended to limit the liability of a surety pursuant to any other statute. This section is declaratory of, and not a change in, existing law.

Added Stats 1984 ch 538 § 33.3.

§ 996.480. Voluntary payment by surety

(a) If the nature and extent of the liability of the principal is established by final judgment of a court and the time for appeal has expired or, if an appeal is taken, the appeal is finally determined and the judgment is affirmed:

(1) A surety may make payment on a bond without awaiting enforcement of the bond. The amount of the bond is reduced to the extent of any payment made by the surety in good faith.

(2) If the beneficiary makes a claim for payment on a bond given in an action or proceeding after the liability of the principal is so established and the surety fails to make payment, the surety is liable for costs incurred in obtaining a judgment against the surety, including a reasonable attorney's fee, and interest on the judgment from the date of the claim, notwithstanding Section 996.470.

(b) Partial payment of a claim by a surety shall not be considered satisfaction of the claim and the beneficiary may enforce the liability on the bond. If a right is affected or a license is suspended or revoked until payment of a claim, the right continues to be affected and the license continues to be suspended or revoked until the claim is satisfied in full.

Added Stats 1982 ch 998 § 1.

§ 996.490. Effect of payment by surety

(a) Payment by a surety of the amount of a bond constitutes a full discharge of all the liability of the surety on the bond.

(b) Each surety is liable to contribution to cosureties who have made payment in proportion to the amount for which each surety is liable.

Added Stats 1982 ch 998 § 1.

§ 996.495. Enforcement of judgment

A judgment of liability on a bond may be enforced in the same manner and to the same extent as other money judgments.

Added Stats 1982 ch 998 § 1.

Article 15

Enforcement Lien

§ 996.510. Application of article

This article applies to proceedings for the benefit of the state to enforce the liability on a bond executed to, in favor of, or payable to the state or the people of the state, including but not limited to an official bond.

Added Stats 1982 ch 998 § 1.

§ 996.520. Affidavit

The person enforcing the liability may file with the court in the proceedings an affidavit stating the following:

(a) The bond was executed by the defendant or one or more of the defendants (designating whom).

(b) The bond is one to which this article applies.

(c) The defendant or defendants have real property or an interest in real property (designating the county or counties in which the real property is situated).

(d) The liability is being enforced for the benefit of the state.

Added Stats 1982 ch 998 § 1.

§ 996.530. Certification by clerk

The clerk receiving the affidavit shall certify to the recorder of the county in which the real property is situated all of the following:

(a) The names of the parties.

(b) The court in which the proceedings are pending.

(c) The amount claimed.

(d) The date of commencement of the proceedings.

Added Stats 1982 ch 998 § 1.

§ 996.540. Recordation of certificate

(a) Upon receiving the certificate the county recorder shall endorse upon it the time of its receipt.

(b) The certificate shall be filed and recorded in the same manner as notice of the pendency of an action affecting real property.

Added Stats 1982 ch 998 § 1.

§ 996.550. Lien of judgment

(a) Any judgment recovered is a lien upon all real property belonging to the defendant situated in any county in which the certificate is filed, from the filing of the certificate.

(b) The lien is for the amount for which the owner of the real property is liable upon the judgment.

Added Stats 1982 ch 998 § 1.

§ 996.560. Specific performance of agreement to sell property

If an agreement to sell real property affected by the lien created by the filing of a certificate was made before the filing of the certificate and the purchase price under the agreement was not due until after the filing of the certificate, and the purchaser is otherwise entitled to specific performance of the agreement:

(a) The court in an action to compel specific performance of the agreement shall order the purchaser to pay the purchase price, or so much of the purchase price as may be due, to the State Treasurer, and to take the State Treasurer's receipt for payment.

(b) Upon payment, the purchaser is entitled to enforcement of specific performance of the agreement. The purchaser takes the real property free from the lien created by the filing of the certificate.

(c) The State Treasurer shall hold the payment pending the proceedings referred to in the certificate. The payment is subject to the lien created by the filing of the certificate.

Added Stats 1982 ch 998 § 1.

Appendix

FAMILY CODE

DIVISION 17
SUPPORT SERVICES

Chapter 2
Child Support Enforcement

Article 2

Collections and Enforcement

§ 17520. Consolidated lists of persons; License renewals; Review procedures; Report to Legislature; Rules and regulations; Forms; Use of information; Suspension or revocation of driver's license; Severability

(a) As used in this section:

(1) "Applicant" means a person applying for issuance or renewal of a license.

(2) "Board" means an entity specified in Section 101 of the Business and Professions Code, the entities referred to in Sections 1000 and 3600 of the Business and Professions Code, the State Bar of California, the Department of Real Estate, the Department of Motor Vehicles, the Secretary of State, the Department of Fish and Wildlife, and any other state commission, department, committee, examiner, or agency that issues a license, certificate, credential, permit, registration, or any other authorization to engage in a business, occupation, or profession, or to the extent required by federal law or regulations, for recreational purposes. This term includes all boards, commissions, departments, committees, examiners, entities, and agencies that issue a license, certificate, credential, permit, registration, or any other authorization to engage in a business, occupation, or profession. The failure to specifically name a particular board, commission, department, committee, examiner, entity, or agency that issues a license, certificate, credential, permit, registration, or any other authorization to engage in a business, occupation, or profession does not exclude that board, commission, department, committee, examiner, entity, or agency from this term.

(3) "Certified list" means a list provided by the local child support agency to the Department of Child Support Services in which the local child support agency verifies, under penalty of perjury, that the

names contained therein are support obligors found to be out of compliance with a judgment or order for support in a case being enforced under Title IV-D of the federal Social Security Act.

(4) "Compliance with a judgment or order for support" means that, as set forth in a judgment or order for child or family support, the obligor is no more than 30 calendar days in arrears in making payments in full for current support, in making periodic payments in full, whether court ordered or by agreement with the local child support agency, on a support arrearage, or in making periodic payments in full, whether court ordered or by agreement with the local child support agency, on a judgment for reimbursement for public assistance, or has obtained a judicial finding that equitable estoppel as provided in statute or case law precludes enforcement of the order. The local child support agency is authorized to use this section to enforce orders for spousal support only when the local child support agency is also enforcing a related child support obligation owed to the obligee parent by the same obligor, pursuant to Sections 17400 and 17604.

(5) "License" includes membership in the State Bar of California, and a certificate, credential, permit, registration, or any other authorization issued by a board that allows a person to engage in a business, occupation, or profession, or to operate a commercial motor vehicle, including appointment and commission by the Secretary of State as a notary public. "License" also includes any driver's license issued by the Department of Motor Vehicles, any commercial fishing license issued by the Department of Fish and Wildlife, and to the extent required by federal law or regulations, any license used for recreational purposes. This term includes all licenses, certificates, credentials, permits, registrations, or any other authorization issued by a board that allows a person to engage in a business, occupation, or profession. The failure to specifically name a particular type of license, certificate, credential, permit, registration, or other authorization issued by a board that allows a person to engage in a business, occupation, or profession, does not exclude that license, certificate, credential, permit, registration, or other authorization from this term.

(6) "Licensee" means a person holding a license, certificate, credential, permit, registration, or other authorization issued by a board, to engage in a business, occupation, or profession, or a commercial driver's license as defined in Section 15210 of the Vehicle Code, including an appointment and commission by the Secretary of State as a notary public. "Licensee" also means a person holding a driver's license issued by the Department of Motor Vehicles, a person holding a commercial fishing license issued by the Department of Fish and Wildlife, and to the extent required by federal law or regulations, a person holding a license used for recreational purposes. This term includes all persons holding a license, certificate, credential, permit, registration, or any other authorization to engage in a business, occupation, or profession, and the failure to specifically name a particular type of

license, certificate, credential, permit, registration, or other authorization issued by a board does not exclude that person from this term. For licenses issued to an entity that is not an individual person, "licensee" includes an individual who is either listed on the license or who qualifies for the license.

(b) The local child support agency shall maintain a list of those persons included in a case being enforced under Title IV-D of the federal Social Security Act against whom a support order or judgment has been rendered by, or registered in, a court of this state, and who are not in compliance with that order or judgment. The local child support agency shall submit a certified list with the names, social security numbers, individual taxpayer identification numbers, or other uniform identification numbers, and last known addresses of these persons and the name, address, and telephone number of the local child support agency who certified the list to the department. The local child support agency shall verify, under penalty of perjury, that the persons listed are subject to an order or judgment for the payment of support and that these persons are not in compliance with the order or judgment. The local child support agency shall submit to the department an updated certified list on a monthly basis.

(c) The department shall consolidate the certified lists received from the local child support agencies and, within 30 calendar days of receipt, shall provide a copy of the consolidated list to each board that is responsible for the regulation of licenses, as specified in this section.

(d) On or before November 1, 1992, or as soon thereafter as economically feasible, as determined by the department, all boards subject to this section shall implement procedures to accept and process the list provided by the department, in accordance with this section. Notwithstanding any other law, all boards shall collect social security numbers or individual taxpayer identification numbers from all applicants for the purposes of matching the names of the certified list provided by the department to applicants and licensees and of responding to requests for this information made by child support agencies.

(e) (1) Promptly after receiving the certified consolidated list from the department, and prior to the issuance or renewal of a license, each board shall determine whether the applicant is on the most recent certified consolidated list provided by the department. The board shall have the authority to withhold issuance or renewal of the license of an applicant on the list.

(2) If an applicant is on the list, the board shall immediately serve notice as specified in subdivision (f) on the applicant of the board's intent to withhold issuance or renewal of the license. The notice shall be made personally or by mail to the applicant's last known mailing address on file with the board. Service by mail shall be complete in accordance with Section 1013 of the Code of Civil Procedure.

(A) The board shall issue a temporary license valid for a period of 150 days to any applicant whose name is on the certified list if the applicant is otherwise eligible for a license.

(B) Except as provided in subparagraph (D), the 150-day time period for a temporary license shall not be extended. Except as provided in subparagraph (D), only one temporary license shall be issued during a regular license term and it shall coincide with the first 150 days of that license term. As this paragraph applies to commercial driver's licenses, "license term" shall be deemed to be 12 months from the date the application fee is received by the Department of Motor Vehicles. A license for the full or remainder of the license term shall be issued or renewed only upon compliance with this section.

(C) In the event that a license or application for a license or the renewal of a license is denied pursuant to this section, any funds paid by the applicant or licensee shall not be refunded by the board.

(D) This paragraph shall apply only in the case of a driver's license, other than a commercial driver's license. Upon the request of the local child support agency or by order of the court upon a showing of good cause, the board shall extend a 150-day temporary license for a period not to exceed 150 extra days.

(3) (A) The department may, when it is economically feasible for the department and the boards to do so as determined by the department, in cases where the department is aware that certain child support obligors listed on the certified lists have been out of compliance with a judgment or order for support for more than four months, provide a supplemental list of these obligors to each board with which the department has an interagency agreement to implement this paragraph. Upon request by the department, the licenses of these obligors shall be subject to suspension, provided that the licenses would not otherwise be eligible for renewal within six months from the date of the request by the department. The board shall have the authority to suspend the license of any licensee on this supplemental list.

(B) If a licensee is on a supplemental list, the board shall immediately serve notice as specified in subdivision (f) on the licensee that the license will be automatically suspended 150 days after notice is served, unless compliance with this section is achieved. The notice shall be made personally or by mail to the licensee's last known mailing address on file with the board. Service by mail shall be complete in accordance with Section 1013 of the Code of Civil Procedure.

(C) The 150-day notice period shall not be extended.

(D) In the event that any license is suspended pursuant to this section, any funds paid by the licensee shall not be refunded by the board.

(E) This paragraph shall not apply to licenses subject to annual renewal or annual fee.

(f) Notices shall be developed by each board in accordance with guidelines provided by the department and subject to approval by the department. The notice shall include the address and telephone number of the local child support agency that submitted the name on the certified list, and shall emphasize the necessity of obtaining a release from that local child support agency as a condition for the issuance, renewal, or continued valid status of a license or licenses.

(1) In the case of applicants not subject to paragraph (3) of subdivision (e), the notice shall inform the applicant that the board shall issue a temporary license, as provided in subparagraph (A) of paragraph (2) of subdivision (e), for 150 calendar days if the applicant is otherwise eligible and that upon expiration of that time period the license will be denied unless the board has received a release from the local child support agency that submitted the name on the certified list.

(2) In the case of licensees named on a supplemental list, the notice shall inform the licensee that the license will continue in its existing status for no more than 150 calendar days from the date of mailing or service of the notice and thereafter will be suspended indefinitely unless, during the 150-day notice period, the board has received a release from the local child support agency that submitted the name on the certified list. Additionally, the notice shall inform the licensee that any license suspended under this section will remain so until the expiration of the remaining license term, unless the board receives a release along with applications and fees, if applicable, to reinstate the license during the license term.

(3) The notice shall also inform the applicant or licensee that if an application is denied or a license is suspended pursuant to this section, any funds paid by the applicant or licensee shall not be refunded by the board. The Department of Child Support Services shall also develop a form that the applicant shall use to request a review by the local child support agency. A copy of this form shall be included with every notice sent pursuant to this subdivision.

(g) (1) Each local child support agency shall maintain review procedures consistent with this section to allow an applicant to have the underlying arrearage and any relevant defenses investigated, to provide an applicant information on the process of obtaining a modification of a support order, or to provide an applicant assistance in the establishment of a payment schedule on arrearages if the circumstances so warrant.

(2) It is the intent of the Legislature that a court or local child support agency, when determining an appropriate payment schedule for arrearages, base its decision on the facts of the particular case and the priority of payment of child support over other debts. The payment schedule shall also recognize that certain expenses may be essential to enable an obligor to be employed. Therefore, in reaching its decision, the court or the local child support agency shall consider both of these goals in setting a payment schedule for arrearages.

(h) If the applicant wishes to challenge the submission of their name on the certified list, the applicant shall make a timely written request for review to the local child support agency who certified the applicant's name. A request for review pursuant to this section shall be resolved in the same manner and timeframe provided for resolution of a complaint pursuant to Section 17800. The local child support agency shall immediately send a release to the appropriate board and the applicant, if any of the following conditions are met:

(1) The applicant is found to be in compliance or negotiates an agreement with the local child support agency for a payment schedule on arrearages or reimbursement.

(2) The applicant has submitted a request for review, but the local child support agency will be unable to complete the review and send notice of its findings to the applicant within the time specified in Section 17800.

(3) The applicant has filed and served a request for judicial review pursuant to this section, but a resolution of that review will not be made within 150 days of the date of service of notice pursuant to subdivision (f). This paragraph applies only if the delay in completing the judicial review process is not the result of the applicant's failure to act in a reasonable, timely, and diligent manner upon receiving the local child support agency's notice of findings.

(4) The applicant has obtained a judicial finding of compliance as defined in this section.

(i) An applicant is required to act with diligence in responding to notices from the board and the local child support agency with the recognition that the temporary license will lapse or the license suspension will go into effect after 150 days and that the local child support agency and, where appropriate, the court must have time to act within that period. An applicant's delay in acting, without good cause, which directly results in the inability of the local child support agency to complete a review of the applicant's request or the court to hear the request for judicial review within the 150-day period shall not constitute the diligence required under this section which would justify the issuance of a release.

(j) Except as otherwise provided in this section, the local child support agency shall not issue a release if the applicant is not in compliance with the judgment or order for support. The local child support agency shall notify the applicant, in writing, that the applicant may, by filing an order to show cause or notice of motion, request any or all of the following:

(1) Judicial review of the local child support agency's decision not to issue a release.

(2) A judicial determination of compliance.

(3) A modification of the support judgment or order.

The notice shall also contain the name and address of the court in which the applicant shall file the order to show cause or notice of motion and inform the applicant that their name shall remain on the certified list if the applicant does not timely request judicial review. The applicant shall comply with all statutes and rules of court regarding orders to show cause and notices of motion.

This section does not limit an applicant from filing an order to show cause or notice of motion to modify a support judgment or order or to fix a payment schedule on arrearages accruing under a support judgment or order or to obtain a court finding of compliance with a judgment or order for support.

(k) The request for judicial review of the local child support agency's decision shall state the grounds for which review is requested and judicial review shall be limited to those stated grounds. The court shall hold an evidentiary hearing within 20 calendar days of the filing of the request for review. Judicial review of the local child support agency's decision shall be limited to a determination of each of the following issues:

(1) Whether there is a support judgment, order, or payment schedule on arrearages or reimbursement.

(2) Whether the petitioner is the obligor covered by the support judgment or order.

(3) Whether the support obligor is or is not in compliance with the judgment or order of support.

(4) (A) The extent to which the needs of the obligor, taking into account the obligor's payment history and the current circumstances of both the obligor and the obligee, warrant a conditional release as described in this subdivision.

(B) The request for judicial review shall be served by the applicant upon the local child support agency that submitted the applicant's name on the certified list within seven calendar days of the filing of the petition. The court has the authority to uphold the action, unconditionally release the license, or conditionally release the license.

(C) If the judicial review results in a finding by the court that the obligor is in compliance with the judgment or order for support, the local child support agency shall immediately send a release in accordance with subdivision (*l*) to the appropriate board and the applicant. If the judicial review results in a finding by the court that the needs of the obligor warrant a conditional release, the court shall make findings of fact stating the basis for the release and the payment necessary to satisfy the unrestricted issuance or renewal of the license without prejudice to a later judicial determination of the amount of support arrearages, including interest, and shall specify payment terms, compliance with which are necessary to allow the release to remain in effect.

(*l*) (1) The department shall prescribe release forms for use by local child support agencies. When the obligor is in compliance, the local child support agency shall mail to the applicant and the appropriate board a release stating that the applicant is in compliance. The receipt of a release shall serve to notify the applicant and the board that, for the purposes of this section, the applicant is in compliance with the judgment or order for support. A board that has received a release from the local child support agency pursuant to this subdivision shall process the release within five business days of its receipt.

(2) When the local child support agency determines, subsequent to the issuance of a release, that the applicant is once again not in compliance with a judgment or order for support, or with the terms of repayment as described in this subdivision, the local child support agency may notify the board, the obligor, and the department in a format prescribed by the department that the obligor is not in compliance.

(3) The department may, when it is economically feasible for the department and the boards to develop an automated process for complying with this subdivision, notify the boards in a manner prescribed by the department, that the obligor is once again not in compliance. Upon receipt of this notice, the board shall immediately notify the obligor on a form prescribed by the department that the obligor's license will be suspended on a specific date, and this date shall be no longer than 30 days from the date the form is mailed. The obligor shall be further notified that the license will remain suspended until a new release is issued in accordance with subdivision (h). This section does not limit the obligor from seeking judicial review of suspension pursuant to the procedures described in subdivision (k).

(m) The department may enter into interagency agreements with the state agencies that have responsibility for the administration of boards necessary to implement this section, to the extent that it is cost effective to implement this section. These agreements shall provide for the receipt by the other state agencies and boards of federal funds to cover that portion of costs allowable in federal law and regulation and incurred by the state agencies and boards in implementing this section. Notwithstanding any other law, revenue generated by a board or state agency shall be used to fund the nonfederal share of costs incurred pursuant to this section. These agreements shall provide that boards shall reimburse the department for the nonfederal share of costs incurred by the department in implementing this section. The boards shall reimburse the department for the nonfederal share of costs incurred pursuant to this section from moneys collected from applicants and licensees.

(n) Notwithstanding any other law, in order for the boards subject to this section to be reimbursed for the costs incurred in administering its provisions, the boards may, with the approval of the appropriate department director, levy on all licensees and applicants a surcharge on any fee or fees collected pursuant to law, or, alternatively, with the approval of the appropriate department director, levy on the applicants or licensees named on a certified list or supplemental list, a special fee.

Appendix

(o) The process described in subdivision (h) shall constitute the sole administrative remedy for contesting the issuance of a temporary license or the denial or suspension of a license under this section. The procedures specified in the administrative adjudication provisions of the Administrative Procedure Act (Chapter 4.5 (commencing with Section 11400) and Chapter 5 (commencing with Section 11500) of Part 1 of Division 3 of Title 2 of the Government Code) shall not apply to the denial, suspension, or failure to issue or renew a license or the issuance of a temporary license pursuant to this section.

(p) In furtherance of the public policy of increasing child support enforcement and collections, on or before November 1, 1995, the State Department of Social Services shall make a report to the Legislature and the Governor based on data collected by the boards and the district attorneys in a format prescribed by the State Department of Social Services. The report shall contain all of the following:

(1) The number of delinquent obligors certified by district attorneys under this section.

(2) The number of support obligors who also were applicants or licensees subject to this section.

(3) The number of new licenses and renewals that were delayed, temporary licenses issued, and licenses suspended subject to this section and the number of new licenses and renewals granted and licenses reinstated following board receipt of releases as provided by subdivision (h) by May 1, 1995.

(4) The costs incurred in the implementation and enforcement of this section.

(q) A board receiving an inquiry as to the licensed status of an applicant or licensee who has had a license denied or suspended under this section or has been granted a temporary license under this section shall respond only that the license was denied or suspended or the temporary license was issued pursuant to this section. Information collected pursuant to this section by a state agency, board, or department shall be subject to the Information Practices Act of 1977 (Chapter 1 (commencing with Section 1798) of Title 1.8 of Part 4 of Division 3 of the Civil Code).

(r) Any rules and regulations issued pursuant to this section by a state agency, board, or department may be adopted as emergency regulations in accordance with the rulemaking provisions of the Administrative Procedure Act (Chapter 3.5 (commencing with Section 11340) of Part 1 of Division 3 of Title 2 of the Government Code). The adoption of these regulations shall be deemed an emergency and necessary for the immediate preservation of the public peace, health, and safety, or general welfare. The regulations shall become effective immediately upon filing with the Secretary of State.

(s) The department and boards, as appropriate, shall adopt regulations necessary to implement this section.

(t) The Judicial Council shall develop the forms necessary to implement this section, except as provided in subdivisions (f) and (*l*).

(u) The release or other use of information received by a board pursuant to this section, except as authorized by this section, is punishable as a misdemeanor.

(v) The State Board of Equalization shall enter into interagency agreements with the department and the Franchise Tax Board that will require the department and the Franchise Tax Board to maximize the use of information collected by the State Board of Equalization, for child support enforcement purposes, to the extent it is cost effective and permitted by the Revenue and Taxation Code.

(w) (1) The suspension or revocation of a driver's license, including a commercial driver's license, under this section shall not subject the licensee to vehicle impoundment pursuant to Section 14602.6 of the Vehicle Code.

(2) Notwithstanding any other law, the suspension or revocation of a driver's license, including a commercial driver's license, under this section shall not subject the licensee to increased costs for vehicle liability insurance.

(x) If any provision of this section or the application thereof to any person or circumstance is held invalid, that invalidity shall not affect other provisions or applications of this section which can be given effect without the invalid provision or application, and to this end the provisions of this section are severable.

(y) All rights to administrative and judicial review afforded by this section to an applicant shall also be afforded to a licensee.

Added Stats 1999 ch 654 § 3.5 (AB 370). Amended Stats 2001 ch 755 § 14 (SB 943), effective October 12, 2001; Stats 2013 ch 352 § 79 (AB 1317), effective September 26, 2013, operative July 1, 2013; Stats 2014 ch 752 § 10 (SB 1159), effective January 1, 2015; Stats 2018 ch 838 § 7 (SB 695), effective January 1, 2019; Stats 2019 ch 115 § 156 (AB 1817), effective January 1, 2020.

Appendix

FINANCIAL CODE

DIVISION 9

CALIFORNIA FINANCING LAW

Chapter 3.5

Program Administrators

§ 22680. Process for enrolling PACE solicitors

(a) A person shall not engage in the business of a PACE solicitor unless that person is enrolled with a program administrator pursuant to the requirements of this section.

(b) A program administrator shall establish and maintain a process for enrolling PACE solicitors that is acceptable to the commissioner. That process shall include both of the following:

(1) A written agreement between the program administrator and the PACE solicitor that shall set forth the obligations of the PACE solicitor and its PACE solicitor agents.

(2) A review of readily and publicly available information regarding each PACE solicitor.

(c) A program administrator shall establish and maintain a process for enrolling PACE solicitor agents that is acceptable to the commissioner. That process shall include a background check of each PACE solicitor agent. A program administrator may rely on a background check conducted by the Contractors' State License Board to comply with this requirement.

(d) A program administrator shall not enroll a PACE solicitor or a PACE solicitor agent that does not satisfy at least one of the following criteria:

(1) Maintain in good standing a license from the Contractors' State License Board.

(2) Maintain a registration in good standing with the Contractors' State License Board as a home improvement salesperson.

(3) Be exempt from, or not subject to, licensure or registration under the Contractors' State License Law (Chapter 9 (commencing with Section 7000) of Division 3 of the Business and Professions Code).

(e) A program administrator shall not enroll a PACE solicitor if, as a result of the review conducted as part of the program administrator's enrollment process, the program administrator finds any of the following:

(1) A clear pattern of consumer complaints about the PACE solicitor regarding dishonesty, misrepresentations, or omissions.

(2) A high likelihood that the PACE solicitor will solicit assessment contracts in a manner that does not comply with applicable law.

(3) A clear pattern on the part of the PACE solicitor of failing to timely receive and respond to property owner complaints regarding the PACE solicitor.

(f) A program administrator shall establish and maintain a process to promote and evaluate the compliance of PACE solicitors and PACE solicitor agents with the requirements of applicable law that is acceptable to the commissioner. That process shall include all of the following, at a minimum:

(1) A risk-based, commercially reasonable procedure to monitor and test the compliance of PACE solicitors and PACE solicitor agents with the requirements of subdivision (a) of Section 22689

(2) A procedure to regularly monitor the license or registration status of PACE solicitors and PACE solicitor agents.

(3) A periodic review of the solicitation activities of PACE solicitors enrolled with the program administrator, to be conducted at least once every two years.

(g) A program administrator shall establish and implement a process, which is acceptable to the commissioner, for canceling the enrollment of PACE solicitors and PACE solicitor agents who fail to maintain the minimum qualifications required by this section, or who violate any provision of this division.

Added Stats 2017 ch 475 § 71 (AB 1284), effective October 4, 2017, operative January 1, 2019. Stats 2018 ch 798 § 2 (AB 2063), effective January 1, 2019; Stats 2018 ch 813 § 5 (AB 2063), effective January 1, 2019 (ch 813 prevails).

Appendix

GOVERNMENT CODE

TITLE 1
General

DIVISION 4

PUBLIC OFFICERS AND EMPLOYEES

Chapter 4

Resignations and Vacancies

Article 2

Vacancies

§ 1774. Filling vacancies; Interim appointments; When office deemed vacant

(a) When an office, the appointment to which is vested in the Governor and Senate, either becomes vacant or the term of the incumbent thereof expires, the Governor may appoint a person to the office or reappoint the incumbent after the expiration of the term. Until Senate confirmation of the person appointed or reappointed, that person serves at the pleasure of the Governor. If the term of office of an incumbent subject to this section expires, the Governor shall have 60 days after the expiration date to reappoint the incumbent. If the incumbent is not reappointed within the 60–day period, the office shall be deemed to be vacant as of the first day following the end of the 60–day period.

(b) With respect to the appointment or reappointment by the Governor of a person to an office subject to confirmation by the Senate, the Governor shall submit the name of the person appointed, or the name of the incumbent reappointed, and the effective date of the appointment or reappointment to the Senate or, if the Senate is in recess or has adjourned, to the Secretary of the Senate, within 60 days after the person first began performing the duties of the office, or, as to the reappointment of an incumbent, within 90 days after the expiration date of the term. If the Governor does not provide the required notification within 60 days after the person first began performing the duties of the office, or, as to the reappointment of an incumbent to an office after the expiration date of the term, within 90 days after the expiration of the term, the office shall be deemed to be vacant as of the first day immediately following the end of the applicable period.

(c) If the Senate either refuses to confirm, or fails to confirm within 365 days after the day the person first began performing the duties of the office, or, with respect to an incumbent whose appointment to that office previously had been confirmed by the Senate and who is reappointed to that office, within 365 days after the expiration date of the term, the following shall apply:

(1) If the Senate refuses to confirm, the person may continue to serve in that office until 60 days have elapsed since the refusal to confirm or until 365 days have elapsed since the person first began performing the duties of the office, whichever occurs first, or with respect to an incumbent whose appointment to that office previously had been confirmed by the Senate and who is reappointed to that office, until 60 days have elapsed since refusal or until 365 days after the expiration date of the prior term, and the office for which the appointment was made shall be deemed to be vacant as of the first day immediately following the end of the applicable period.

(2) If the Senate fails to confirm within the applicable 365–day period, the person may not continue to serve in that office, and the office for which the appointment was made shall be deemed to be vacant as of the first day immediately following the end of the 365–day period.

Enacted Stats 1943 ch 134. Amended Stats 1955 ch 1881 § 1; Stats 1973 ch 603 § 1, effective September 18, 1973; Stats 1980 ch 1338 § 1; Stats 1982 ch 801 § 1.

DIVISION 5

PUBLIC WORK AND PUBLIC PURCHASES

Chapter 3.1

Protection of Underground Infrastructure

Article 2

Regional Notification Center System

§ 4216. Definitions

As used in this article, the following definitions apply:

(a) "Active subsurface installation" means a subsurface installation currently in use or currently carrying service.

(b) "Board" means the California Underground Facilities Safe Excavation Board, also known as the "Dig Safe Board."

(c) "Area of continual excavation" means a location where excavation is part of the normal business activities of agricultural operations and flood control facilities.

(d) "Delineate" means to mark in white the location or path of the proposed excavation using the guidelines in Appendix B of the "Guidelines for Excavation Delineation" published in the most recent version of the Best Practices guide of the Common Ground Alliance. If there is a conflict between the marking practices in those guidelines and other provisions of this article, this article shall control. "Delineation" also includes physical identification of the area to be excavated using alternative marking methods, including, but not limited to, flags, stakes, whiskers, or a combination of these methods, if an excavator makes a determination that standard delineation may be misleading to those persons using affected streets and highways, or be misinterpreted as a traffic or pedestrian control, and the excavator has contacted the regional notification center to advise the operators that the excavator will physically identify the area to be excavated using alternative marking methods.

(e) "Electronic positive response" means an electronic response from an operator to the regional notification center providing the status of an operator's statutorily required response to a ticket.

(f) (1) "Emergency" means a sudden, unexpected occurrence, involving a clear and imminent danger, demanding immediate action to prevent or mitigate loss of, or damage to, life, health, property, or essential public services.

(2) "Unexpected occurrence" includes, but is not limited to, a fire, flood, earthquake or other soil or geologic movement, riot, accident, damage to a subsurface installation requiring immediate repair, or sabotage.

(g) "Excavation" means any operation in which earth, rock, or other material in the ground is moved, removed, or otherwise displaced by means of tools, equipment, or explosives in any of the following ways: grading, trenching, digging, ditching, drilling, augering, tunneling, scraping, cable or pipe plowing and driving, or any other way.

(h) Except as provided in Section 4216.8, "excavator" means any person, firm, contractor or subcontractor, owner, operator, utility, association, corporation, partnership, business trust, public agency, or other entity that, with their own employees or equipment, performs any excavation.

(i) "Hand tool" means a piece of equipment used for excavating that uses human power and is not powered by any motor, engine, hydraulic, or pneumatic device.

(j) "High priority subsurface installation" means high-pressure natural gas pipelines with normal operating pressures greater than

415kPA gauge (60psig), petroleum pipelines, pressurized sewage pipelines, high-voltage electric supply lines, conductors, or cables that have a potential to ground of greater than or equal to 60kv, or hazardous materials pipelines that are potentially hazardous to workers or the public if damaged.

(k) "Inactive subsurface installation" means either of the following:

(1) The portion of an underground subsurface installation that is not active but is still connected to the subsurface installation, or to any other subsurface installation, that is active or still carries service.

(2) A new underground subsurface installation that has not been connected to any portion of an existing subsurface installation.

(l) "Legal excavation start date and time" means two working days, not including the date of notification, unless the excavator specifies a later date and time, which shall not be more than 14 calendar days from the date of notification. For excavation in an area of continual excavation, "legal excavation start date and time" means two working days, not including the date of notification, unless the excavator specifies a later date and time, which shall not be more than six months from the date of notification.

(m) "Local agency" means a city, county, city and county, school district, or special district.

(n) (1) "Locate and field mark" means to indicate the existence of any owned or maintained subsurface installations by using the guidelines in Appendix B of the "Guidelines for Operator Facility Field Delineation" published in the most recent version of the Best Practices guide of the Common Ground Alliance and in conformance with the uniform color code of the American Public Works Association. If there is a conflict between the marking practices in the guidelines and this article, this article shall control.

(2) "Locate and field mark" does not require an indication of the depth.

(o) "Operator" means any person, corporation, partnership, business trust, public agency, or other entity that owns, operates, or maintains a subsurface installation. For purposes of Section 4216.1, an "operator" does not include an owner of real property where subsurface installations are exclusively located if they are used exclusively to furnish services on that property and the subsurface facilities are under the operation and control of that owner.

(p) "Qualified person" means a person who completes a training program in accordance with the requirements of Section 1509 of Title 8 of the California Code of Regulations Injury and Illness Prevention Program, that meets the minimum locators training guidelines and practices published in the most recent version of the Best Practices guide of the Common Ground Alliance.

(q) "Regional notification center" means a nonprofit association or other organization of operators of subsurface installations that provides advance warning of excavations or other work close to existing subsurface installations, for the purpose of protecting those installations from damage, removal, relocation, or repair.

(r) "State agency" means every state agency, department, division, bureau, board, or commission.

(s) "Subsurface installation" means any underground pipeline, conduit, duct, wire, or other structure, except nonpressurized sewerlines, nonpressurized storm drains, or other nonpressurized drain lines.

(t) "Ticket" means an excavation location request issued a number by the regional notification center.

(u) "Tolerance zone" means 24 inches on each side of the field marking placed by the operator in one of the following ways:

(1) Twenty-four inches from each side of a single marking, assumed to be the centerline of the subsurface installation.

(2) Twenty-four inches plus one-half the specified size on each side of a single marking with the size of installation specified.

(3) Twenty-four inches from each outside marking that graphically shows the width of the outside surface of the subsurface installation on a horizontal plane.

(v) "Working day" for the purposes of determining excavation start date and time means a weekday Monday through Friday, from 7:00 a.m. to 5:00 p.m., except for federal holidays and state holidays, as defined in Section 19853, or as otherwise posted on the internet website of the regional notification center.

Added Stats 1989 ch 928 § 4. Amended Stats 2004 ch 77 § 1 (AB 1264); Stats 2006 ch 651 § 1 (SB 1359), effective January 1, 2007; Stats 2007 ch 343 § 5 (SB 144), effective January 1, 2008; Stats 2016 ch 809 § 2 (SB 661), effective January 1, 2017; Stats 2017 ch 26 § 45 (SB 92), effective June 27, 2017; Stats 2020 ch 307 § 1 (SB 865), effective January 1, 2021.

§ 4216.1. Participation in center by operators of subsurface installations; Fees

Every operator of a subsurface installation, except the Department of Transportation, shall become a member of, participate in, and share in the costs of, a regional notification center. Operators of subsurface installations who are members of, participate in, and share in, the costs of a regional notification center, including, but not limited to, the Underground Service Alert—Northern California or the Underground Service Alert—Southern California are in compliance with this section and Section 4216.9. A regional notification center shall not charge a fee to a person for notifying the regional notification center to obtain a ticket or to renew a ticket.

Added Stats 1989 ch 928 § 4. Amended Stats 2016 ch 809 § 3 (SB 661), effective January 1, 2017; Stats 2020 ch 307 § 2 (SB 865), effective January 1, 2021.

§ 4216.2. Delineation of area; Required notification and response; Ticket prerequisites, period of validity, and expiration; Records; Special access sites

(a) Before notifying the appropriate regional notification center, an excavator planning to conduct an excavation shall delineate the area to be excavated. If the area is not delineated, an operator may, at the operator's discretion, choose not to locate and field mark until the area to be excavated has been delineated.

(b) Except in an emergency, an excavator planning to conduct an excavation shall notify the appropriate regional notification center of the excavator's intent to excavate at least two working days, and not more than 14 calendar days, before beginning that excavation. The date of the notification shall not count as part of the two-working-day notice. If an excavator gives less notice than the legal excavation start date and time and the excavation is not an emergency, the regional notification center will take the information and provide a ticket, but an operator has until the legal excavation start date and time to respond. However, an excavator and an operator may mutually agree to a different notice and start date. The contact information for operators notified shall be available to the excavator.

(c) When the excavation is proposed within 10 feet of a high priority subsurface installation, the operator of the high priority subsurface installation shall notify the excavator of the existence of the high priority subsurface installation to set up an onsite meeting prior to the legal excavation start date and time or at a mutually agreed upon time to determine actions or activities required to verify the location and prevent damage to the high priority subsurface installation. As part of the meeting, the excavator shall discuss with the operator the method and tools that will be used during the excavation and the information the operator will provide to assist in verifying the location of the subsurface installation. The excavator shall not begin excavating until after the completion of the onsite meeting.

(d) Except in an emergency, every excavator covered by Section 4216.8 planning to conduct an excavation on private property that does not require an excavation permit may contact the appropriate regional notification center if the private property is known, or reasonably should be known, to contain a subsurface installation other than the underground facility owned or operated by the excavator. Before notifying the appropriate regional notification center, an excavator shall delineate the area to be excavated. Any temporary marking placed at the planned excavation location shall be clearly seen, functional, and considerate to surface aesthetics and the local community. An excavator shall check if any local ordinances apply to the placement of temporary markings.

(e) The regional notification center shall provide a ticket to the person who contacts the center pursuant to this section and shall notify any member, if known, who has a subsurface installation in the area of the proposed excavation. A ticket shall be valid for 28 days from the date of issuance. If work continues beyond 28 days, the excavator shall renew the ticket either by accessing the center's internet website or by calling "811" by the end of the 28th day.

(f) A record of all notifications by an excavator or operator to the regional notification center shall be maintained for a period of not less than three years. The record shall be available for inspection by the excavator and any member, or their representative, during normal working hours and according to guidelines for inspection as may be established by the regional notification centers. A regional notification center shall provide notification records to the board quarterly and shall provide notifications of damage to the board within five business days of receipt at the regional notification center.

(g) Unless an emergency exists, an excavator shall not begin excavation until the excavator receives a response from all known operators of subsurface installations within the delineated boundaries of the proposed area of excavation pursuant to subdivision (a) of Section 4216.3 and until the completion of any onsite meeting, if required by subdivision (c).

(h) If a site requires special access, an excavator shall request an operator to contact the excavator regarding that special access or give special instructions on the location request.

(i) If a ticket obtained by an excavator expires but work is ongoing, the excavator shall contact the regional notification center and get a new ticket and wait a minimum of two working days, not including the date of the contact, before restarting excavation. All excavation shall cease during the waiting period.

Added Stats 1989 ch 928 § 4. Amended Stats 2004 ch 77 § 2 (AB 1264); Stats 2006 ch 651 § 2 (SB 1359), effective January 1, 2007; Stats 2016 ch 809 § 4 (SB 661), effective January 1, 2017; Stats 2017 ch 26 § 46 (SB 92), effective June 27, 2017; Stats 2020 ch 307 § 3 (SB 865), effective January 1, 2021.

§ 4216.3. Location and field marking of subsurface installations; Records; Relocation and remarking; Operator response; Notification of failure to comply

(a) (1) (A) Unless the excavator and operator mutually agree to a later start date and time, or otherwise agree to the sequence and timeframe in which the operator will locate and field mark, an operator shall do one of the following before the legal excavation start date and time:

(i) Locate and field mark within the area delineated for excavation and, where multiple subsurface installations of the same type are known to exist together, mark the number of subsurface installations.

(ii) To the extent and degree of accuracy that the information is available, provide information to an excavator where the operator's active or inactive subsurface installations are located.

(iii) Advise the excavator it operates no subsurface installations in the area delineated for excavation.

(B) An operator shall mark newly installed subsurface installations in areas with continuing excavation activity.

(C) An operator shall indicate with an "A" inside a circle the presence of any abandoned subsurface installations, if known, within the delineated area. The markings are to make an excavator aware that there are abandoned subsurface installations within that delineated work area.

(2) Only a qualified person shall perform subsurface installation locating activities.

(3) A qualified person performing subsurface installation locating activities on behalf of an operator shall use a minimum of a single-frequency utility locating device and shall have access to alternative sources for verification, if necessary.

(4) An operator shall amend, update, maintain, and preserve all plans and records for its subsurface installations as that information becomes known. If there is a change in ownership of a subsurface installation, the records shall be turned over to the new operator. Commencing January 1, 2017, records on abandoned subsurface installations, to the extent that those records exist, shall be retained.

(5) Commencing January 1, 2023, all new subsurface installations shall be mapped using a geographic information system and maintained as permanent records of the operator. This paragraph shall not apply to oil and gas flowlines three inches or less in diameter that are located within the administrative boundaries of an oil field as designated by the Geologic Energy Management Division. For purposes of this paragraph, the following terms have the following meanings:

(A) "Flowline" means any pipeline that connects an oil, gas, or natural gas liquids well with a gathering line or header.

(B) "Gathering line" means a pipeline that transports liquid hydrocarbons between any of the following: multiple wells, a testing facility, a treating and production facility, a storage facility, or a custody transfer facility.

(C) "Header" means a chamber from which liquid or gas is distributed to or from smaller pipelines.

(6) Nothing in this section shall be interpreted to preempt the Professional Land Surveyors' Act, as described in Chapter 15 (commencing with Section 8700) of Division 3 of the Business and Professions Code.

(b) If the field marks are no longer reasonably visible, an excavator shall renotify the regional notification center with a request for remarks that can be for all or a portion of the excavation. Excavation shall cease in the area to be remarked. If the delineation markings are no longer reasonably visible, the excavator shall redelineate the area to be remarked. If remarks are requested, the operator shall have two working days, not including the date of request, to remark the subsurface installation. If the area to be remarked is not the full extent of the original excavation, the excavator shall delineate the portion to be remarked and provide a description of the area requested to be remarked on the ticket. The excavator shall provide a description for the area to be remarked that falls within the area of the original location request.

(c) (1) (A) On and after January 1, 2021, every operator shall supply an electronic positive response through the regional notification center before the legal excavation start date and time. Upon a showing of good cause by an operator, the board may extend the time by which the operator is required to comply with this requirement. The board shall not grant an extension beyond December 31, 2021. The board shall determine which facts or circumstances constitute good cause.

(B) The regional notification center shall make the responses required by subparagraph (A) available to the excavator.

(2) The regional notification centers shall annually report to the board regarding their continual technological development in their roles of facilitating communication between excavators and operators in a manner that enhances safety, accountability, and efficiency.

(d) (1) On or before January 1, 2021, the board shall adopt regulations to implement subparagraph (A) of paragraph (1) of subdivision (c). The initial adoption, amendment, or repeal of a regulation authorized by this section is deemed to address an emergency, for purposes of Sections 11346.1 and 11349.6, and the board is hereby exempted for that purpose from the requirements of subdivision (b) of Section 11346.1. After the initial adoption, amendment, or repeal of an emergency regulation pursuant to this section, the board shall not request approval from the Office of Administrative Law to readopt the regulation as an emergency regulation pursuant to Section 11346.1.

(2) It is the intent of the Legislature, in authorizing the deviations in this section from the requirements and procedures of Chapter 3.5 (commencing with Section 11340) of Part 1 of Division 3 of Title 2, to authorize the board to expedite the exercise of its power to implement regulations as its unique operational circumstances require.

(e) The excavator shall notify the appropriate regional notification center of the failure of an operator to identify subsurface installations pursuant to subparagraph (A) or (B) of paragraph (1) of subdivision (a), or subdivision (b). The notification shall include the ticket issued by the regional notification center. The regional notification center shall maintain a record of all notifications received pursuant to this subdivision for a period of not less than three years. The record shall be available for inspection pursuant to subdivision (f) of Section 4216.2.

(f) If an operator or local agency knows that it has a subsurface installation embedded or partially embedded in the pavement that is not visible from the surface, the operator or local agency shall contact the excavator before pavement removal to communicate and determine a plan of action to protect that subsurface installation and excavator.

Added Stats 1989 ch 928 § 4. Amended Stats 2005 ch 114 § 1 (SB 140), effective January 1, 2006; Stats 2006 ch 651 § 3 (SB 1359), effective January 1, 2007; Stats 2016 ch 809 § 5 (SB 661), effective January 1, 2017; Stats 2019 ch 453 § 1 (AB 1166), effective January 1, 2020; Stats 2020 ch 307 § 4 (SB 865), effective January 1, 2021.

§ 4216.4. Manual location of subsurface installations in conflict with excavation; Use of vacuum excavation devices; Use of power operated or boring equipment; Duty of care; Notification of damage; Required communication between parties

(a) (1) Except as provided in paragraph (2), if an excavation is within the tolerance zone of a subsurface installation, the excavator shall determine the exact location of the subsurface installations in conflict with the excavation using hand tools before using any power-driven excavation or boring equipment within the tolerance zone of the subsurface installations. In all cases the excavator shall use reasonable care to prevent damaging subsurface installations.

(2) (A) An excavator may use a vacuum excavation device to expose subsurface installations within the tolerance zone if the operator has marked the subsurface installation, the excavator has contacted any operator whose subsurface installations may be in conflict with the excavation, and the operator has agreed to the use of a vacuum excavation device. An excavator shall inform the regional notification center of their intent to use a vacuum excavation device when obtaining a ticket.

(B) An excavator may use power-operated or boring equipment for the removal of any existing pavement only if there is no known subsurface installation contained in the pavement.

(C) Beginning July 1, 2020, an excavator may use power-operated or boring equipment, as determined by the board, prior to determining the exact location of subsurface installations. The board shall adopt regulations to implement this paragraph on or before July 1, 2020.

Appendix

(3) An excavator shall presume all subsurface installations to be active, and shall use the same care around subsurface installations that may be inactive as the excavator would use around active subsurface installations.

(b) If the exact location of the subsurface installation cannot be determined by hand excavating in accordance with subdivision (a), the excavator shall request the operator to provide additional information to the excavator, to the extent that information is available to the operator, to enable the excavator to determine the exact location of the installation. If the excavator has questions about the markings that an operator has placed, the excavator may contact the notification center to send a request to have the operator contact the excavator directly. The regional notification center shall provide the excavator with the contact telephone number of the subsurface installation operator.

(c) (1) An excavator discovering or causing damage to a subsurface installation, including all breaks, leaks, nicks, dents, gouges, grooves, or other damage to subsurface installation lines, conduits, coatings, or cathodic protection, shall immediately notify the subsurface installation operator. The excavator may contact the regional notification center to obtain the contact information of the subsurface installation operator. If the operator is unknown and the damage or discovery of damage occurs outside the working hours of the regional notification center, the excavator may follow the instructions provided by the regional notification center through its internet website or the telephone line recorded message.

(2) An excavator shall call 911 emergency services upon discovering or causing damage to either of the following:

(A) A gas or hazardous liquid pipeline subsurface installation in which the damage results in the escape of any flammable, toxic, or corrosive gas or liquid.

(B) A high priority subsurface installation of any kind.

(3) An excavator discovering or causing damage shall notify the regional notification center within 48 hours of discovering or causing the damage.

(4) Nothing in this section preempts or impedes the board's authority to impose more restrictive notification windows.

(d) Each excavator, operator, or locator shall communicate with each other and respect the appropriate safety requirements and ongoing activities of the other parties, if known, at an excavation site.

Added Stats 1989 ch 928 § 4. Amended Stats 2005 ch 114 § 2 (SB 140), effective January 1, 2006; Stats 2006 ch 263 § 1 (AB 463), effective September 14, 2006, ch 651 § 4 (SB 1359), effective January 1, 2007; Stats 2016 ch 809 § 6 (SB 661), effective January 1, 2017; Stats 2018 ch 708 § 1 (AB 1914), effective January 1, 2019; Stats 2020 ch 307 § 5 (SB 865), effective January 1, 2021.

§ 4216.6. Penalties for violation; Enforcement; Annual report of statewide information regarding incident events

(a) (1) Any operator or excavator who negligently violates this article is subject to a civil penalty in an amount not to exceed ten thousand dollars ($10,000).

(2) Any operator or excavator who knowingly and willfully violates any of the provisions of this article is subject to a civil penalty in an amount not to exceed fifty thousand dollars ($50,000).

(3) Any operator or excavator who knowingly and willfully violates any of the provisions of this article in a way that results in damage to a gas or hazardous liquid pipeline subsurface installation and that results in the escape of any flammable, toxic, or corrosive gas or liquid is subject to a civil penalty in an amount not to exceed one hundred thousand dollars ($100,000).

(4) Except as otherwise specifically provided in this article, this section is not intended to affect any civil remedies otherwise provided by law for personal injury or for property damage, including any damage to subsurface installations, nor is this section intended to create any new civil remedies for those injuries or that damage.

(5) This article shall not be construed to limit any other provision of law granting governmental immunity to state or local agencies or to impose any liability or duty of care not otherwise imposed by law upon any state or local agency.

(b) An action may be brought by the Attorney General, the district attorney, or the local or state agency that issued the permit to excavate, for the enforcement of the civil penalty pursuant to this section in a civil action brought in the name of the people of the State of California. If penalties are collected as a result of a civil suit brought by a state or local agency for collection of those civil penalties, the penalties imposed shall be paid to the general fund of the agency. If more than one agency is involved in enforcement, the penalties imposed shall be apportioned among them by the court in a manner that will fairly offset the relative costs incurred by the state or local agencies, or both, in collecting these fees.

(c) This article may also be enforced by the following agencies, either following a recommendation of the Dig Safe Board that the agency shall act to accept, amend, or reject, or through the agency's own investigations, as follows:

(1) The Registrar of Contractors of the Contractors State License Board shall enforce this article on contractors, as defined in Article 2 (commencing with Section 7025) of Chapter 9 of Division 3 of the Business and Professions Code, and telephone corporations, as defined in Section 234 of the Public Utilities Code, when acting as a contractor, as defined in Article 2 (commencing with Section 7025) of Chapter 9 of Division 3 of the Business and Professions Code. Noth-

ing in this section affects the Public Utilities Commission's existing authority over a public utility.

(2) The Public Utilities Commission shall enforce this article on gas corporations, as defined in Section 222 of the Public Utilities Code, and electrical corporations, as defined in Section 218 of the Public Utilities Code, and water corporations, as defined in Section 241 of the Public Utilities Code.

(3) The Office of the State Fire Marshal shall enforce this article on operators of hazardous liquid pipeline facilities, as defined in Section 60101 of Chapter 601 of Subtitle VIII of Title 49 of the United States Code.

(d) A local governing board may enforce this article on local agencies under the governing board's jurisdiction.

(e) Commencing July 1, 2020, the Dig Safe Board shall enforce this article on persons other than those listed in subdivisions (c) and (d). The board shall not initiate an enforcement action pursuant to this subdivision for a violation that occurred prior to July 1, 2020. As the enforcing body for persons other than those listed in subdivisions (c) and (d), the board may collect any monetary penalties imposed upon those persons.

(f) Moneys collected as a result of penalties imposed pursuant to subdivisions (c) and (e) shall be deposited into the Safe Energy Infrastructure and Excavation Fund.

(g) Statewide information provided by operators and excavators regarding incident events shall be compiled and made available in an annual report by regional notification centers and posted on the internet websites of the regional notification centers and shall be made available to the board upon request.

(h) For purposes of subdivision (g), the following terms have the following meanings:

(1) "Incident event" means the occurrence of excavator downtime, damages, near misses, and violations.

(2) "Statewide information" means information submitted by operators and excavators using the California Regional Common Ground Alliance's Virtual Private Damage Information Reporting Tool. Supplied data shall comply with the Damage Information Reporting Tool's minimum essential information as listed in the most recent version of the Best Practices guide of the Common Ground Alliance.

Added Stats 1989 ch 928 § 4. Amended Stats 2013 ch 250 § 1 (AB 811), effective January 1, 2014; Stats 2016 ch 809 § 7 (SB 661), effective January 1, 2017; Stats 2017 ch 26 § 47 (SB 92), effective June 27, 2017; Stats 2018 ch 51 § 7 (SB 854), effective June 27, 2018; Stats 2020 ch 307 § 6 (SB 865), effective January 1, 2021; Stats 2021 ch 726 § 1 (SB 297), effective January 1, 2022.

§ 4216.7. Liability of excavator; Liability of operator of subsurface installation; Savings provisions

(a) If a subsurface installation is damaged by an excavator as a result of failing to comply with Section 4216.2, 4216.4, or 4216.10 or subdivision (b) of Section 4216.3, or as a result of failing to comply with the operator's requests to protect the subsurface installation as specified by the operator before the start of excavation, the excavator shall be liable to the operator of the subsurface installation for resulting damages, costs, and expenses to the extent the damages, costs, and expenses were proximately caused by the excavator's failure to comply.

(b) If an operator has failed to become a member of, participate in, or share in the costs of, a regional notification center, that operator shall forfeit the operator's claim for damages to the operator's subsurface installation arising from an excavation against an excavator who has complied with this article to the extent damages were proximately caused by the operator's failure to comply with this article.

(c) If an operator of a subsurface installation without a reasonable basis, as determined by a court of competent jurisdiction, has failed to comply with the provisions of Section 4216.3, including, but not limited to, the requirement to field mark the appropriate location of subsurface installations within two working days of notification, as defined by subdivision (v) of Section 4216 and subdivision (b) of Section 4216.2, has failed to comply with subdivision (c) of Section 4216.2, or has failed to comply with subdivision (b) of Section 4216.4, the operator shall be liable for damages to the excavator who has complied with Section 4216.2, subdivisions (b) and (e) of Section 4216.3, and Section 4216.4, including liquidated damages, liability, losses, costs, and expenses, actually incurred by the excavator, resulting from the operator's failure to comply with these specified requirements to the extent the damages, costs, and expenses were proximately caused by the operator's failure to comply.

(d) (1) An excavator who damages a subsurface installation due to an inaccurate field mark by an operator, or by a third party under contract to perform field marking for the operator, shall not be liable for damages, replacement costs, or other expenses arising from damages to the subsurface installation if the excavator complied with Section 4216.10 or Sections 4216.2 and 4216.4.

(2) This section is not intended to create any presumption or to affect the burden of proof in any action for personal injuries or property damage, other than damage to the subsurface installation, nor is this section intended to affect, create, or eliminate any remedy for personal injury or property damage, other than damage to the subsurface installation.

(e) For the purposes of this section, "inaccurate field mark" means a mark, or set of markings, made pursuant to Section 4216.3 or 4216.10, that did not correctly indicate the approximate location of a subsurface installation affected by an excavation and includes the actual physical location of a subsurface installation affected by an excavation that should have been marked pursuant to Section 4216.3 but was not.

(f) Nothing in this section shall be construed to do any of the following:

(1) Affect claims, including, but not limited to, third-party claims brought against the excavator or operator by other parties for damages arising from the excavation.

(2) Exempt the excavator or operator from the excavator's or the operator's duty to mitigate any damages as required by common or other applicable law.

(3) Exempt the excavator or operator from liability to each other or third parties based on equitable indemnity or comparative or contributory negligence.

(g) A court or arbitrator shall award reasonable attorney's costs and fees, including expert witness fees, to an excavator if either of the following apply:

(1) The court or arbitrator determines that an excavator is not liable for damages to a subsurface installation for a reason described in subdivision (d).

(2) The excavator makes an offer to settle the matter that is not accepted and the plaintiff fails to obtain a more favorable judgment or award.

Added Stats 2017 ch 26 § 49 (SB 92), effective June 27, 2017, operative July 1, 2020; Amended Stats 2021 ch 173 § 1 (AB 930), effective January 1, 2022.

§ 4216.9. Initial ticket required for valid permit

(a) A permit to excavate issued by any local agency, as defined in Section 4216, or any state agency, shall not be valid unless the applicant has been provided an initial ticket by a regional notification center pursuant to Section 4216.2. For purposes of this section, "state agency" means every state agency, department, division, bureau, board, or commission, including the Department of Transportation.

(b) This article does not exempt any person or corporation from Sections 7951, 7952, and 7953 of the Public Utilities Code.

Added Stats 1989 ch 928 § 4. Amended Stats 2016 ch 809 § 9 (SB 661), effective January 1, 2017.

§ 4216.10. Continual excavation ticket in lieu of notification and locate and field marking; Operator response; Notification

and onsite meeting for area including or near high priority subsurface installation; Period of validity; Renewal

(a) In lieu of the notification and locate and field mark requirements of Sections 4216.2 and 4216.3, an excavator may contact a regional notification center to request a continual excavation ticket for an area of continual excavation. The regional notification center shall provide a ticket to the person who contacts the center pursuant to this section and shall notify any member, if known, who has a subsurface installation in the area of continual excavation. The ticket provided to the excavator shall include the contact information for notified operators.

(b) An operator shall provide a response to the excavator pursuant to subdivision (a) of Section 4216.3.

(c) (1) When the area of continual excavation includes, or is within 10 feet of, a high priority subsurface installation, the operator of the high priority subsurface installation shall notify the excavator of the existence of the high priority subsurface installation to set up an onsite meeting prior to the legal excavation start date and time or at a mutually agreed upon time to determine actions or activities required to verify the location and to prevent damage to the high priority subsurface installation during the continual excavation time period. The onsite meeting shall be used to develop a mutually agreed upon plan for excavation activities that may be conducted within 25 feet of each side of the subsurface installation. Additional onsite meetings should also be held following unexpected occurrences or prior to excavation activities that may create conflicts with subsurface installations. As part of the meeting, the excavator shall discuss with the operator the method and tools that will be used during the excavation and the information the operator will provide to assist in verifying the location of the subsurface installation. The excavator shall not begin excavating until after the completion of the onsite meeting and information has been provided describing the activities that can be safely conducted to prevent damage to the high priority subsurface installation.

(2) When the area of continual excavation includes a subsurface installation but does not include, or is not within 10 feet of, a high priority subsurface installation, the excavator or the operator may request an onsite meeting at a mutually agreed upon time to determine actions or activities required to verify the location and to prevent damage to the subsurface installation during the continual excavation time period. The onsite meeting may be used to develop a plan for excavation activities that may be conducted within five feet of each side of the subsurface installation. The operator and excavator may mutually agree to conduct additional onsite meetings following unexpected occurrences or prior to excavation activities that may cre-

ate conflicts with subsurface installations. As part of the meeting, the excavator may discuss with the operator the method and tools that will be used during the excavation and the information the operator will provide to assist in verifying the location of the subsurface installation. If an onsite meeting is requested prior to the legal excavation start date and time, the excavator shall not begin excavating until after the completion of the onsite meeting and information has been provided describing the activities that can be safely conducted to prevent damage to the subsurface installation.

(3) The excavator and operator shall maintain records regarding the plan of excavation, any locate and field mark and standby activities, and any other information deemed necessary by the excavator and operator. Excavation activities outside the scope of the plan shall be undertaken subsequent to notification pursuant to Section 4216.2.

(d) A ticket for an area of continual excavation shall be valid for one year from the date of issuance. The excavator may renew the ticket within two working days either by accessing the regional notification center's Internet Web site or by calling "811."

(e) The board shall, in consultation with the regional notification centers, develop through regulation a process by which the renewal requirement for a continual excavation ticket may be modified or eliminated for areas of continual excavation in which no subsurface installations are present.

(f) This section shall become operative on July 1, 2020.

Added Stats 2016 ch 809 § 10 (SB 661), effective January 1, 2017, operative November 1, 2017. Amended Stats 2017 ch 26 § 50 (SB 92), effective June 27, 2017, operative July 1, 2020.

§ 4216.11. Adoption of regulations establishing onsite meeting and mutually agreed-upon plan minimum elements

On or before January 1, 2020, the board shall adopt regulations to establish minimum elements for the onsite meeting and minimum elements for the mutually agreed-upon plan described in paragraph (1) of subdivision (c) of Section 4616.10 for managing an area of continual excavation.

Added Stats 2017 ch 26 § 51 (SB 92), effective June 27, 2017.

§ 4216.12. California Underground Facilities Safe Excavation Board; Duties; Review

(a) The Dig Safe Board is hereby created under, and shall be assisted by the staff of, the Office of the State Fire Marshal until January 1, 2022. On and after January 1, 2022, the board shall be within the Office of Energy Infrastructure Safety within the Natural Resources

Agency pursuant to Part 7.3 (commencing with Section 15470) of Division 3 of Title 2.

(b) The board shall perform the following tasks:

(1) Coordinate education and outreach activities that encourage safe excavation practices, as described in Section 4216.17.

(2) Develop standards, as described in Section 4216.18.

(3) Investigate possible violations of this article, as described in Section 4216.19.

(4) Enforce this article to the extent authorized by subdivision (e) of Section 4216.6.

(c) Notwithstanding any other law, on and after January 1, 2020, the board shall be subject to review by the appropriate policy committees of the Legislature at least once every three years.

Added Stats 2016 ch 809 § 11 (SB 661), effective January 1, 2017. Amended Stats 2017 ch 26 § 52 (SB 92), effective June 27, 2017; Stats 2020 ch 307 § 7 (SB 865), effective January 1, 2021.

§ 4216.13. Members of California Underground Facilities Safe Excavation Board; Appointment and qualifications; Ex officio members

(a) The board shall be composed of nine members, of which seven shall be appointed by the Governor, one shall be appointed by the Speaker of the Assembly, and one shall be appointed by the Senate Committee on Rules.

(b) The seven members appointed by the Governor shall be appointed, as follows:

(1) Three members shall have knowledge and expertise in the operation of subsurface installations. Of those three members, one shall have knowledge and expertise in the operation of the subsurface installations of a municipal utility. At least one of the three members shall have knowledge and experience in the operation of high priority subsurface installations.

(2) Three members shall have knowledge and experience in contract excavation for employers who are not operators of subsurface installations. Of the three members, one member shall be a general engineering contractor, one member shall be a general building contractor, and one member shall be a specialty contractor. For the purposes of this section, the terms "general engineering contractor," "general building contractor," and "specialty contractor" shall have the meanings given in Article 4 (commencing with Section 7055) of Chapter 9 of Division 3 of the Business and Professions Code.

(3) One member shall have knowledge and expertise in performing or managing agricultural operations in the vicinity of subsurface installations.

Appendix

(c) The member appointed by the Speaker of the Assembly shall have knowledge and expertise in representing in safety matters the workers employed by contract excavators.

(d) The member appointed by the Senate Committee on Rules shall have knowledge and expertise in subsurface installation location and marking and shall not be under the direct employment of an operator.

(e) The board may invite two directors of operations or other appropriate representatives of regional notification centers to be nonvoting ex officio members of the board.

Added Stats 2016 ch 809 § 12 (SB 661), effective January 1, 2017. Amended Stats 2017 ch 26 § 53 (SB 92), effective June 27, 2017.

§ 4216.14. Terms of members of California Underground Facilities Safe Excavation Board; Vacancy; Removal; Chairperson

(a) The term of a member of the board is four years. Of the first members of the board, four members, determined by lot, shall serve for two years so that the terms of the members shall be staggered.

(b) A member shall not be appointed for more than two consecutive full terms.

(c) To the extent possible, the appointing power shall fill any vacancy in the membership of the board within 60 days after the vacancy occurs.

(d) Upon the recommendation of the board, the Governor may remove a member appointed by the Governor for incompetence or misconduct.

(e) The board shall select a chairperson from among its members at the first meeting of each calendar year or when a vacancy in the chair exists.

(f) Subject to subdivision (g), the manner in which the chairperson is selected and the chairperson's term of office shall be determined by the board.

(g) A member of the board shall not serve more than two consecutive years as the chairperson of the board.

Added Stats 2016 ch 809 § 13 (SB 661), effective January 1, 2017.

§ 4216.15. Meetings of California Underground Facilities Safe Excavation Board

The board shall meet at least once every three months. The board shall hold meetings in Sacramento and Los Angeles, and in other locations in the state it deems necessary.

Added Stats 2016 ch 809 § 14 (SB 661), effective January 1, 2017.

§ 4216.16. California Underground Facilities Safe Excavation Board; Funding for operational expenses

The board may obtain funding for its operational expenses from:

(a) A federal grant.

(b) A fee charged to members of the regional notification centers not to exceed the reasonable regulatory cost incident to enforcement of this article. The board shall apportion the fee in a manner consistent with formulas used by the regional notification centers. Revenues derived from the imposition of this fee shall be deposited in the Safe Energy Infrastructure and Excavation Fund.

(c) Any other source.

(d) The board shall not charge a fee to a person for notifying the regional notification center to obtain a ticket or to renew a ticket.

Added Stats 2016 ch 809 § 15 (SB 661), effective January 1, 2017.

§ 4216.17. California Underground Facilities Safe Excavation Board; Annual meeting; Grants for use of moneys in Safe Energy Infrastructure and Excavation Fund

(a) The board shall annually convene a meeting for the following purposes:

(1) To understand the existing needs for education and outreach, including to those groups with the highest awareness and education needs, including, but not limited to, homeowners.

(2) To facilitate discussion on how to coordinate existing education and outreach efforts with state and local government agencies, California operators, regional notification centers, and trade associations that fund outreach and education programs that encourage safe excavation practices.

(b) In addition to state and local government agencies, California operators, regional notification centers, and trade associations that fund outreach and education programs that encourage safe excavation practices, the meeting pursuant to subdivision (a) shall include representatives of groups that may be the target of those outreach and education efforts.

(c) For violations that are neither egregious nor persistent, the board shall offer violators the option of completing an educational course in lieu of paying a fine. To develop the programming for the educational option, the board may contract with a third party or create the curriculum itself.

(d) Upon appropriation by the Legislature, moneys in the Safe Energy Infrastructure and Excavation Fund shall be available to the board to fund the educational course developed pursuant to subdivision (c).

Appendix

Added Stats 2016 ch 809 § 16 (SB 661), effective January 1, 2017. Amended Stats 2020 ch 307 § 8 (SB 865), effective January 1, 2021.

§ 4216.18. Development of standards for safety practices in excavating around subsurface installations

The board shall develop a standard or set of standards relevant to safety practices in excavating around subsurface installations and procedures and guidance in encouraging those practices. When possible, standards should be informed by publicly available data, including, but not limited to, that collected by state and federal agencies and by the regional notification centers pursuant to subdivision (g) of Section 4216.6, and the board should refrain from using data about facility events not provided either to a state or federal agency or as statewide information, as defined in paragraph (2) of subdivision (h) of Section 4216.6. The standard or set of standards are not intended to replace other relevant standards, including the Best Practices of the Common Ground Alliance, but are to inform areas currently without established standards. The standard or set of standards shall address all of the following:

(a) Evidence necessary for excavators and operators to demonstrate compliance with Sections 4216.2, 4216.3, 4216.4, and 4216.10.

(b) What constitutes reasonable care, as required by paragraph (1) of subdivision (a) of Section 4216.4, in using hand tools around subsurface installations within the tolerance zone, considering the need to balance worker safety in trenches with the protection of subsurface installations. As part of determining reasonable care, the board shall consider the appropriate additional excavating depth an excavator should make if either of the following occur:

(1) The subsurface installation is delineated within the tolerance zone but it is not in conflict with the excavation.

(2) The location of a subsurface installation is determined, but additional subsurface installations may exist immediately below the located subsurface installation.

(c) What constitutes reasonable care, as required by paragraph (1) of subdivision (a) of Section 4216.4, in grading activities on road shoulders and dirt roads which may include standards for potholing.

Added Stats 2016 ch 809 § 17 (SB 661), effective January 1, 2017. Amended Stats 2017 ch 26 § 54 (SB 92), effective June 27, 2017.

§ 4216.19. Investigation of violations and reported incident events; Transmission of investigation results; Sanctions (Operative July 1, 2020)

(a) The board shall investigate possible violations of this article.

(b) The board may investigate reports of incident events, as defined in paragraph (1) of subdivision (h) of Section 4216.6 and complaints from affected parties and members of the public.

(c) In determining whether to pursue an investigation, the board shall consider whether the parties have settled the matter and whether further enforcement is necessary as a deterrent to maintain the integrity of subsurface installations and to protect the safety of excavators and the public.

(d) If the board, upon the completion of an investigation, finds a probable violation of the article, the board shall transmit the investigation results and any recommended penalty to the state or local agency pursuant to subdivision (c) or (d) of Section 4216.6.

(e) Sanctions shall be graduated and may include notification and information letters, direction to attend relevant education, and financial penalties. When considering the issuance of citations and assessment of penalties, the board shall consider all of the following:

(1) The type of violation and its gravity.

(2) The degree of culpability.

(3) The operator's or excavator's history of violations.

(4) The operator's or excavator's history of work conducted without violations.

(5) The efforts taken by the violator to prevent violation and, once the violation occurred, the efforts taken to mitigate the safety consequences of the violation.

(f) This section shall become operative on July 1, 2020.

Added Stats 2016 ch 809 § 18 (SB 661), effective January 1, 2017. Amended Stats 2017 ch 26 § 55 (SB 92), effective June 27, 2017, operative July 1, 2020; Stats 2018 ch 51 § 8 (SB 854), effective June 27, 2018.

§ 4216.21. Timing of filing court action for damages to subsurface installation based on specified violations under investigation by board; Notification of board when certain actions filed (First of two; Inoperative July 1, 2020; Repealed January 1, 2021)

(a) For an investigation that the board undertakes as a result of a complaint of a violation of Section 4216.2, 4216.3, or 4216.4, the complainant shall not file an action in court for damages based on those violations until the investigation is complete, or for 6 months after the investigation begins, whichever comes first, during which time, applicable statutes of limitation shall be tolled.

(b) If a complainant files an action in court against a person for damages based upon violations of Section 4216.2, 4216.3, or 4216.4, after the completion of a board investigation in which the person was found not to have violated the article, the complainant shall also notify the board when the action is filed.,

(c) This section only applies to a claim for damages to a subsurface installation.

(d) This section shall become inoperative on July 1, 2020, and shall be repealed on January 1, 2021.

Added Stats 2016 ch 809 § 19 (SB 661), effective January 1, 2017. Amended Stats 2017 ch 26 § 56 (SB 92), effective June 27, 2017, operative July 1, 2020, repealed January 1, 2021.

§ 4216.21. Timing of filing court action for damages to subsurface installation based on specified violations under investigation by board; Notification of board when certain actions filed (Second of two; Operative July 1, 2020)

(a) For an investigation that the board undertakes as a result of a complaint of a violation of Section 4216.2, 4216.3, 4216.4, or 4216.10, the complainant shall not file an action in court for damages based on those violations until the investigation is complete, or for 6 months after the investigation begins, whichever comes first, during which time, applicable statutes of limitation shall be tolled.

(b) If a complainant files an action in court against a person for damages based upon violations of Section 4216.2, 4216.3, 4216.4, or 4216.10, after the completion of a board investigation in which the person was found not to have violated the article, the complainant shall also notify the board when the action is filed.

(c) This section only applies to a claim for damages to a subsurface installation.

(d) This section shall become operative on July 1, 2020.

Added Stats 2017 ch 26 § 57 (SB 92), effective June 27, 2017, operative July 1, 2020.

§ 4216.22. Prescription of rules and regulations

Consistent with all laws of this state, the board may prescribe rules and regulations as may be necessary or proper to carry out the purposes and intent of this act and to exercise the powers and duties conferred upon it by this act.

Added Stats 2016 ch 809 § 20 (SB 661), effective January 1, 2017.

§ 4216.23. Yearly report to Governor and Legislature

(a) Notwithstanding Section 10231.5, the board shall report to the Governor and the Legislature on or before February 1, 2018, and each year thereafter, on the activities of the board and any recommendations of the board.

(b) A report to be submitted pursuant to subdivision (a) shall be submitted in compliance with Section 9795.

Added Stats 2016 ch 809 § 21 (SB 661), effective January 1, 2017.

§ 4216.24. Safe Energy Infrastructure and Excavation Fund; Use of funds

The Safe Energy Infrastructure and Excavation Fund is hereby established in the State Treasury. Moneys deposited into the fund shall be used, upon appropriation by the Legislature, to cover the operational expenses of the board and for the purposes specified in subdivision (c) of Section 4216.17, except that revenues derived from penalties imposed pursuant to Section 4216.6 shall not be used for operational expenses.

Added Stats 2016 ch 809 § 22 (SB 661), effective January 1, 2017. Amended Stats 2017 ch 561 § 67 (AB 1516), effective January 1, 2018.

DIVISION 6

PUBLIC BONDS AND OBLIGATIONS

Chapter 14

Infrastructure Financing

§ 5956.6. Contents of agreements between agency and private entity

(a) For purposes of facilitating projects, the agreements specified in Section 5956.4 may include provisions for the lease of rights-of-way in, and airspace over, property owned by a governmental agency, for the granting of necessary easements, and for the issuance of permits or other authorizations to enable the private entity to construct infrastructure facilities supplemental to existing government-owned facilities. Infrastructure constructed by a private entity pursuant to this chapter shall, at all times, be owned by a governmental agency, unless the governmental agency, in its discretion, elects to provide for ownership of the facility by the private entity during the term of the agreement. The agreement shall provide for the lease of those facilities to, or ownership by, the private entity for up to 35 years. In consideration therefor, the agreement shall provide for complete reversion of the privately constructed facility to the governmental agency at the expiration of the lease at no charge to the governmental agency. Subsequent to the expiration of the lease or ownership period, the governmental agency may continue to charge fees for use of the infrastructure facility. If, after the expiration of the lease or ownership period, the governmental agency continues to lease airspace rights to the private entity, it shall do so at fair market value.

(b) The agreement between the governmental agency and the private entity shall include, but need not be limited to, provisions to ensure the following:

(1) Compliance with the California Environmental Quality Act (Division 13 (commencing with Section 21000) of the Public Resources Code). Neither the act of selecting a proposed project or a private entity, nor the execution of an agreement with a private entity, shall require prior compliance with the act. However, appropriate compliance with the act shall thereafter occur before project development commences.

(2) Performance bonds as security to ensure completion of the construction of the facility and contractual provisions that are necessary to protect the revenue streams of the project.

(3) Adequate financial resources of the private entity to design, build, and operate the facility, after the date of the agreement.

(4) Authority for the governmental agency to impose user fees for use of the facility in an amount sufficient to protect the revenue streams necessary for projects or facilities undertaken pursuant to this chapter. User fee revenues shall be dedicated exclusively to payment of the private entity's direct and indirect capital outlay costs for the project, direct and indirect costs associated with operations, direct and indirect user fee collection costs, direct and indirect costs of administration of the facility, reimbursement for the direct and indirect costs of maintenance, and a negotiated reasonable return on investment to the private entity.

(5) As a precondition to the imposition or increase of a user fee, the governmental agency shall conduct at least one public hearing at which public testimony will be received regarding a proposed user fee revenue or increase in user fee revenues. The public hearing shall precede the action by the governmental agency to actually impose a user fee or to increase an existing user fee. The governmental agency shall consider the public testimony prior to imposing a new or increased user fee. The governmental agency shall provide the following notices and utilize the following procedures:

(A) Notice of the date, time, and place of the meeting, including a general explanation of the matter to be considered, shall be mailed at least 14 days prior to the meeting to any interested party who files a written request with the governmental agency for mailed notice of the meeting on new or increased fees or service charges. Any written request for mailed notices shall be valid for one year from the date on which it is filed unless a renewal request is filed prior to the expiration of the one-year period for which the written request was filed. The legislative body may establish a reasonable annual charge for sending notices based on the estimated cost of providing the service.

(B) At least 10 days prior to the meeting, the governmental agency shall make available to the public data that supports the amount of the fee or the increase in the fee.

(C) (i) At least 10 days prior to the meeting, the governmental agency shall publish a notice in a newspaper of general circulation in that agency's jurisdiction stating the date, time, and place of the meeting, including a general explanation of the matter to be considered.

(ii) Any costs incurred by the governmental agency in conducting the meeting or meetings required by this section may be recovered from fees charged for the services that are the subject of the fee.

(iii) For transportation projects specifically authorized by this chapter, at least 10 days prior to the meeting, the governmental agency shall publish for four consecutive times, a notice in the newspaper of general circulation in the affected area stating in no smaller that 10-point type a notice specifying the subject of the hearing, the date, time, and place of the meeting, and, in at least 8-point type, a general explanation of the matter to be considered.

(D) No local agency shall levy a new fee or service charge or increase an existing fee or service charge to an amount that exceeds the estimated amount required to provide the service for which the fee or service charge is levied and a reasonable rate of return on investment, pursuant to paragraph (4). Any action by a local agency to levy a new fee or service charge or to approve an increase in an existing fee or service charge pursuant to this chapter shall be taken only by ordinance or resolution. The legislative body of a local agency shall not delegate the authority to adopt a new fee or service charge, or to increase a fee or service charge.

(6) Require that if the legislative body of the governmental agency determines that fees or service charges create revenues in excess of the actual cost for which the user fee revenues are dedicated and a reasonable rate of return on investment, pursuant to paragraph (4), those revenues shall either be applied to any indebtedness incurred by the private entity with respect to the project, be paid into a reserve account in order to offset future operation costs, be paid into the appropriate government account, be used to reduce the user fee or service charge creating the excess, or a combination of these sources.

(7) Require the private entity to maintain the facility in good operating condition at all times, including the time the facility reverts to the governmental agency.

(8) Preparation by the private entity of an annual audited report accounting for the income received and expenses to operate the facility. The private entity shall make that report available to any member of the public for a cost not to exceed the cost of reproduction of the report.

Appendix

(9) Provision for a buyout of the private entity by the governmental entity in the event of termination or default before the end of the lease term.

(10) Provision for appropriate indemnity promises between the governmental agency and the private entity.

(11) Provision requiring the private entity to maintain insurance with those coverages and in those amounts that the governmental agency deems appropriate.

(12) In the event of a dispute between the governmental agency and the private entity, both parties shall be entitled to all available legal or equitable remedies.

(13) Payment bonds to secure the payment of claims of laborers, mechanics, and materials suppliers employed on the work under the contract. Payment bonds required under this subdivision shall conform to the requirements of Sections 9550 to 9566, inclusive, of the Civil Code.

Added Stats 1996 ch 1040 § 1 (AB 2660). Amended Stats 2013 ch 94 § 1 (AB 164), effective January 1, 2014.

TITLE 2

Government of the State of California

DIVISION 3

EXECUTIVE DEPARTMENT

PART 1

STATE DEPARTMENTS AND AGENCIES

Chapter 1

State Agencies

Article 1

General

§ 11009.5. Reduction or waiver of business licensing fees due to declared emergency

(a) For purposes of this section:

(1) "Displaced" means a condition in which the person or business is unable to return to the address of record or other address associated with the license before experiencing economic hardship.

(2) "Economic hardship" means the inability to pay living or business expenses, unless otherwise defined by a state agency pursuant to subdivision (c).

(3) "Emergency" means an emergency as defined in Section 8558 or a declared federal emergency.

(4) "License" includes, but is not limited to, a certificate, registration, or other required document to engage in business.

(b) Notwithstanding any other law, a state agency that issues any business license may establish a process for a person or business that has been displaced or is experiencing economic hardship as a result of an emergency to submit an application, that the agency may grant, for a reduction or waiver of any fees required by the agency to obtain a license, renew or activate a license, or replace a physical license for display.

(c) A fee or waiver process established pursuant to subdivision (b) shall specify, at a minimum, all of the following:

(1) The methodology used by the agency for determining whether a person, as a result of an emergency, has been displaced or is experiencing economic hardship.

(2) The procedure for applying for a reduction or fee waiver.

(3) That the application shall be made within one year of the date on which the emergency was proclaimed or declared.

Added Stats 2019 ch 854 § 1 (SB 601), effective January 1, 2020.

Chapter 2

State Departments

Article 2

Investigations and Hearings

§ 11181. Acts authorized in connection with investigations and actions

In connection with any investigation or action authorized by this article, the department head may do any of the following:

(a) Inspect and copy books, records, and other items described in subdivision (e).

(b) Hear complaints.

(c) Administer oaths.

(d) Certify to all official acts.

(e) Issue subpoenas for the attendance of witnesses and the production of papers, books, accounts, documents, any writing as defined by Section 250 of the Evidence Code, tangible things, and testimony pertinent or material to any inquiry, investigation, hearing, proceeding, or action conducted in any part of the state.

(f) Promulgate interrogatories pertinent or material to any inquiry, investigation, hearing, proceeding, or action.

(g) Divulge information or evidence related to the investigation of unlawful activity discovered from interrogatory answers, papers, books, accounts, documents, and any other item described in subdivision (e), or testimony, to the Attorney General or to any prosecuting attorney of this state, any other state, or the United States who has a responsibility for investigating the unlawful activity investigated or discovered, or to any governmental agency responsible for enforcing laws related to the unlawful activity investigated or discovered, if the Attorney General, prosecuting attorney, or agency to which the information or evidence is divulged agrees to maintain the confidentiality of the information received to the extent required by this article.

(h) Present information or evidence obtained or developed from the investigation of unlawful activity to a court or at an administrative hearing in connection with any action or proceeding.

Added Stats 1945 ch 111 § 3. Amended Stats 1981 ch 778 § 1; Stats 1987 ch 1453 § 8; Stats 2001 ch 74 § 2 (AB 260); Stats 2003 ch 876 § 6 (SB 434).

§ 11183. Divulging information; Offense; Disqualification

Except in a report to the head of the department or when called upon to testify in any court or proceeding at law or as provided in Section 11180.5 or subdivisions (g) and (h) of Section 11181, an officer shall not divulge any information or evidence acquired by the officer from the interrogatory answers or subpoenaed private books, documents, papers, or other items described in subdivision (e) of Section 11181 of any person while acting or claiming to act under any authorization pursuant to this article, in respect to the confidential or private transactions, property or business of any person. An officer who divulges information or evidence in violation of this section is guilty of a misdemeanor and disqualified from acting in any official capacity in the department.

Added Stats 1945 ch 111 § 3. Amended Stats 1981 ch 778 § 2; Stats 2003 ch 876 § 7 (SB 434).

Chapter 3.5

Administrative Regulations and Rulemaking

Article 3

Filing and Publication

§ 11343. Procedure

Every state agency shall:

(a) Transmit to the office for filing with the Secretary of State a certified copy of every regulation adopted or amended by it except one that is a building standard.

(b) Transmit to the office for filing with the Secretary of State a certified copy of every order of repeal of a regulation required to be filed under subdivision (a).

(c) (1) Within 15 days of the office filing a state agency's regulation with the Secretary of State, post the regulation on its internet website in an easily marked and identifiable location. The state agency shall keep the regulation on its internet website for at least six months from the date the regulation is filed with the Secretary of State.

(2) Within five days of posting, the state agency shall send to the office the internet website link of each regulation that the agency posts on its internet website pursuant to paragraph (1).

(3) This subdivision shall not apply to a state agency that does not maintain an internet website.

(d) Deliver to the office, at the time of transmittal for filing a regulation or order of repeal, a citation of the authority pursuant to which it or any part thereof was adopted.

(e) Deliver to the office a copy of the notice of proposed action required by Section 11346.4.

(f) Transmit to the California Building Standards Commission for approval a certified copy of every regulation, or order of repeal of a regulation, that is a building standard, together with a citation of authority pursuant to which it or any part thereof was adopted, a copy of the notice of proposed action required by Section 11346.4, and any other records prescribed by the California Building Standards Law (Part 2.5 (commencing with Section 18901) of Division 13 of the Health and Safety Code).

(g) Whenever a certification is required by this section, it shall be made by the head of the state agency that is adopting, amending, or repealing the regulation, or by a designee of the agency head, and the certification and delegation shall be in writing.

Appendix

Added Stats 1979 ch 567 § 1. Amended Stats 1979 ch 1152 § 12.2, operative July 1, 1980; Stats 1980 ch 204 § 1, effective June 20, 1980; Stats 1981 ch 865 § 5; Stats 1982 ch 749 § 1, effective September 8, 1982; Stats 1983 ch 291 § 1; Stats 1987 ch 1375 § 3; Stats 1988 ch 1194 sec 1.2, operative January 1, 1989; Stats 2000 ch 1060 § 9 (AB 1822); Stats 2002 ch 389 § 3 (AB 1857); Stats 2012 ch 295 § 1 (SB 1099), effective January 1, 2013; Stat 2022, ch 48 § 22 (SB 189), effective June 30, 2022.

§ 11343.4. Effective date of regulation or order of repeal; Applicability

(a) Except as otherwise provided in subdivision (b), a regulation or an order of repeal required to be filed with the Secretary of State shall become effective on a quarterly basis as follows:

(1) January 1 if the regulation or order of repeal is filed on September 1 to November 30, inclusive.

(2) April 1 if the regulation or order of repeal is filed on December 1 to February 29, inclusive.

(3) July 1 if the regulation or order of repeal is filed on March 1 to May 31, inclusive.

(4) October 1 if the regulation or order of repeal is filed on June 1 to August 31, inclusive.

(b) The effective dates in subdivision (a) shall not apply in all of the following:

(1) The effective date is specifically provided by the statute pursuant to which the regulation or order of repeal was adopted, in which event it becomes effective on the day prescribed by the statute.

(2) A later date is prescribed by the state agency in a written instrument filed with, or as part of, the regulation or order of repeal.

(3) The agency makes a written request to the office demonstrating good cause for an earlier effective date, in which case the office may prescribe an earlier date.

(4) (A) A regulation adopted by the Fish and Game Commission that is governed by Article 2 (commencing with Section 250) of Chapter 2 of Division 1 of the Fish and Game Code.

(B) A regulation adopted by the Fish and Game Commission that requires a different effective date in order to conform to a federal regulation.

Added Stats 1994 ch 1039 § 16 (AB 2531). Amended Stats 2000 ch 1060 § 10 (AB 1822); Stats 2012 ch 295 § 2 (SB 1099), effective January 1, 2013; Stats 2016 ch 546 § 26 (SB 1473), effective January 1, 2017.

Article 4

The California Code of Regulations, the California Code of Regulations Supplement, and the California Regulatory Notice Register

§ 11344. Publication of Code of Regulations and Code of Regulations Supplement; Availability of regulations on internet

The office shall do all of the following:

(a) Provide for the official compilation, printing, and publication of adoption, amendment, or repeal of regulations, which shall be known as the California Code of Regulations. On and after July 1, 1998, the office shall make available on the Internet, free of charge, the full text of the California Code of Regulations, and may contract with another state agency or a private entity in order to provide this service.

(b) Make available on its Internet Web site a list of, and a link to the full text of, each regulation filed with the Secretary of State that is pending effectiveness pursuant to Section 11343.4.

(c) Provide for the compilation, printing, and publication of weekly updates of the California Code of Regulations. This publication shall be known as the California Code of Regulations Supplement and shall contain amendments to the code.

(d) Provide for the publication dates and manner and form in which regulations shall be printed and distributed and ensure that regulations are available in printed form at the earliest practicable date after filing with the Secretary of State.

(e) Ensure that each regulation is printed together with a reference to the statutory authority pursuant to which it was enacted and the specific statute or other provision of law which the regulation is implementing, interpreting, or making specific.

Added Stats 1983 ch 797 § 7. Amended Stats 1987 ch 1375 § 3.5; Stats 1994 ch 1039 § 17 (AB 2531); Stats 1996 ch 501 § 2 (SB 1910); Stats 2000 ch 1060 § 13 (AB 1822); Stats 2012 ch 295 § 3 (SB 1099), effective January 1, 2013.

Chapter 5.6

Department of Technology

§ 11545. Department of Technology; Appointment and duties of Director of Technology

(a) (1) There is in state government the Department of Technology within the Government Operations Agency. The Director of Technology shall be appointed by, and serve at the pleasure of, the Governor, subject to Senate confirmation. The Director of Technology shall supervise the Department of Technology and report directly to the Governor on issues relating to information technology.

(2) Unless the context clearly requires otherwise, whenever the term "office of the State Chief Information Officer" or "California Technology Agency" appears in any statute, regulation, or contract, or any other code, it shall be construed to refer to the Department of Technology, and whenever the term "State Chief Information Officer" or "Secretary of California Technology" appears in any statute, regulation, or contract, or any other code, it shall be construed to refer to the Director of Technology.

(3) The Director of Technology shall be the State Chief Information Officer.

(b) The duties of the Director of Technology shall include, but are not limited to, all of the following:

(1) Advising the Governor on the strategic management and direction of the state's information technology resources.

(2) Establishing and enforcing state information technology strategic plans, policies, standards, and enterprise architecture. This shall include the periodic review and maintenance of the information technology sections of the State Administrative Manual and procurement procedures related to information technology projects, except for sections on information technology fiscal policy. The Director of Technology shall consult with the Director of General Services, the Director of Finance, and other relevant agencies concerning policies and standards these agencies are responsible to issue that relate to information technology.

(3) Minimizing overlap, redundancy, and cost in state information technology operations by promoting the efficient and effective use of information technology.

(4) Providing technology direction to agency and department chief information officers to ensure the integration of statewide technology initiatives, compliance with information technology policies and standards, and the promotion of the alignment and effective management of information technology services. This paragraph does not limit the authority of a constitutional officer, cabinet agency secretary, or department director to establish programmatic priorities and business direction to the respective agency or department chief information officer.

(5) Working to improve organizational maturity and capacity in the effective management of information technology.

(6) Establishing performance management and improvement processes to ensure state information technology systems and services are efficient and effective.

(7) Approving, suspending, terminating, and reinstating information technology projects.

(8) Performing enterprise information technology functions and services, including, but not limited to, implementing Geographic Information Systems (GIS), shared services, applications, and program and project management activities in partnership with the owning agency or department.

(c) (1) The department may provide GIS data to a regional notification center, as defined in subdivision (q) of Section 4216, as provided to a state agency in accordance with this chapter, for the purposes of a regional notification center carrying out its duties pursuant to Article 2 (commencing with Section 4216) of Chapter 3.1 of Division 5 of Title 1.

(2) The department shall collect payment from a regional notification center to cover its reasonable costs for providing GIS data pursuant to this subdivision. Funds collected pursuant to this subdivision shall be deposited into the Technology Services Revolving Fund created pursuant to Section 11544.

(3) A state agency shall not be liable to a regional notification center or other third party for providing GIS data pursuant to this subdivision.

(d) The Director of Technology shall produce an annual information technology strategic plan that shall guide the acquisition, management, and use of information technology. State agencies shall cooperate with the department in the development of this plan, as required by the Director of Technology.

(1) Upon establishment of the information technology strategic plan, the Director of Technology shall take all appropriate and necessary steps to implement the plan, subject to any modifications and adjustments deemed necessary and reasonable.

(2) The information technology strategic plan shall be submitted to the Joint Legislative Budget Committee by January 15 of every year.

(e) The Director of Technology shall produce an annual information technology performance report that shall assess and measure the state's progress toward enhancing its information technology program for human capital management; reducing and avoiding costs and risks associated with the acquisition, development, implementation, management, and operation of information technology assets, infrastructure, and systems; improving energy efficiency in the use of information technology assets; enhancing the security, reliability, and quality of information technology networks, services, and systems; and improving the information technology procurement process. This report shall also include cost savings and avoidances achieved through improvements to the way the state acquires, develops, implements, manages, and operates state technology assets, infrastructure, and systems. The department shall establish those policies and procedures required to improve the performance of the state's information technology program.

Appendix

(1) The department shall maintain an information technology performance management framework that includes the performance measures and targets that the department will utilize to assess the performance of, and measure the costs and risks avoided by, the state's information technology program.

(2) State agencies shall take all necessary steps to achieve the targets set forth by the department and shall report their progress to the department on a quarterly basis.

(3) Notwithstanding Section 10231.5, the information technology performance report shall be submitted to the Joint Legislative Budget Committee, including any changes, by January 15 of every year. To enhance transparency, the department shall post performance targets and progress toward these targets on its public internet website.

(f) If the Governor's Reorganization Plan No. 2 of 2012 becomes effective, this section shall prevail over Section 186 of the Governor's Reorganization Plan No. 2 of 2012, regardless of the dates on which this section and that plan take effect, and this section shall become operative on July 1, 2013.

Added Stats 2012 ch 139 § 2 (AB 1498), effective January 1, 2012, operative July 1, 2013. Amended Stats 2014 ch 28 § 8 (SB 854), effective June 20, 2014 (repealer repealed); Stats 2017 ch 193 § 1 (AB 475), effective January 1, 2018; Stats 2019 ch 494 § 1 (AB 754), effective January 1, 2020.

PART 2.8

DEPARTMENT OF FAIR EMPLOYMENT AND HOUSING

Chapter 6

Discrimination Prohibited

Article 1

Unlawful Practices, Generally

§ 12944. Discrimination by licensing board

(a) It shall be unlawful for a licensing board to require any examination or establish any other qualification for licensing that has an adverse impact on any class by virtue of its race, creed, color, national origin or ancestry, sex, gender, gender identity, gender expression, age, medical condition, genetic information, physical disability, mental disability, reproductive health decisionmaking, or sexual orientation, unless the practice can be demonstrated to be job related.

Where the council, after hearing, determines that an examination is unlawful under this subdivision, the licensing board may continue to use and rely on the examination until such time as judicial review by the superior court of the determination is exhausted.

If an examination or other qualification for licensing is determined to be unlawful under this section, that determination shall not void, limit, repeal, or otherwise affect any right, privilege, status, or responsibility previously conferred upon any person by the examination or by a license issued in reliance on the examination or qualification.

(b) It shall be unlawful for a licensing board to fail or refuse to make reasonable accommodation to an individual's mental or physical disability or medical condition.

(c) It shall be unlawful for any licensing board, unless specifically acting in accordance with federal equal employment opportunity guidelines or regulations approved by the council, to print or circulate or cause to be printed or circulated any publication, or to make any non-job-related inquiry, either verbal or through use of an application form, which expresses, directly or indirectly, any limitation, specification, or discrimination as to race, religious creed, color, national origin, ancestry, physical disability, mental disability, medical condition, genetic information, sex, gender, gender identity, gender expression, age, reproductive health decisionmaking, or sexual orientation or any intent to make any such limitation, specification, or discrimination. Nothing in this subdivision shall prohibit any licensing board from making, in connection with prospective licensure or certification, an inquiry as to, or a request for information regarding, the physical fitness of applicants if that inquiry or request for information is directly related and pertinent to the license or the licensed position the applicant is applying for. Nothing in this subdivision shall prohibit any licensing board, in connection with prospective examinations, licensure, or certification, from inviting individuals with physical or mental disabilities to request reasonable accommodations or from making inquiries related to reasonable accommodations.

(d) It is unlawful for a licensing board to discriminate against any person because the person has filed a complaint, testified, or assisted in any proceeding under this part.

(e) It is unlawful for any licensing board to fail to keep records of applications for licensing or certification for a period of two years following the date of receipt of the applications.

(f) As used in this section, "licensing board" means any state board, agency, or authority in the Business, Consumer Services, and Housing Agency that has the authority to grant licenses or certificates which are prerequisites to employment eligibility or professional status.

Added Stats 1980 ch 992 § 4. Amended Stats 1992 ch 912 § 6 (AB 1286), ch 913 § 24 (AB 1077); Stats 1999 ch 592 § 8 (AB 1001); Stats 2011 ch 261 § 15 (SB 559), effective January 1, 2012, ch 719 § 19.5 (AB 887), effective January 1, 2012; Stats 2012 ch 46 § 37 (SB 1038), effective June 27, 2012, operative January 1, 2013. See this section as

Appendix

modified in Governor's Reorganization Plan No. 2 § 210 of 2012. Amended Stats 2012 ch 147 § 17 (SB 1039), effective January 1, 2013, operative July 1, 2013 (ch 147 prevails); Stat 2022 ch 48 § 38 (SB 189), effective June 30, 2022; Stats 2022 ch 630 § 8 (SB 523), effective January 1, 2023.

PART 12.3

UNDERGROUND ECONOMIC ACTIVITIES

§ 15925. Agency request for information in case involving tax or fee administration associated with underground economic activities

(a) For a case, including, but not limited to, a Joint Enforcement Strike Force on the Underground Economy case, that involves tax or fee administration associated with underground economic activities, including known or suspected felony violations involving tax-related or fee-related crimes, an agency listed in subdivision (a) of Section 329 of the Unemployment Insurance Code may request information pursuant to subdivision (b) from the Employment Development Department, the California Department of Tax and Fee Administration, and the Franchise Tax Board.

(b) Upon request of an agency listed in subdivision (a) of Section 329 of the Unemployment Insurance Code, the Employment Development Department, the California Department of Tax and Fee Administration, and the Franchise Tax Board shall fully and timely provide the requesting agency with intelligence, data, including confidential tax and fee information, documents, information, complaints, reports, analysis, findings, or lead referrals for the following purposes:

(1) To assess leads or referrals in order to determine if an investigation is warranted.

(2) To conduct investigations.

(3) To determine restitution owed to the state.

(4) To prosecute violations.

(5) To conduct data analytics associated with assessing a lead or referral or conducting an investigation pursuant to the Joint Enforcement Strike Force on the Underground Economy.

(c) (1) Any person from an agency listed in subdivision (a) of Section 329 of the Unemployment Insurance Code who received confidential information obtained pursuant to this section shall not divulge, or make known in any manner not provided by law, any of the confidential information received by or reported to the agency. Confidential information authorized to be provided pursuant to this section shall retain its confidential status and shall otherwise remain subject to the confidentiality provisions contained in, but not limited to, all of the following provisions:

(A) Section 11183 as that section pertains to the Department of Justice.

(B) Sections 1094, 1095, and 2111 of the Unemployment Insurance Code as those sections pertain to the Employment Development Department. Part 603 of Title 20 of the Code of Federal Regulations as those provisions pertain to the disclosure of confidential unemployment compensation information.

(C) Sections 19542, 19542.1, and 19542.3 of the Revenue and Taxation Code as those sections pertain to the Franchise Tax Board.

(D) Section 15619 of this code, Section 42464.8 of the Public Resources Code, and Sections 7056, 7056.5, 8255, 9255, 9255.1, 30455, 32455, 32457, 38705, 38706, 43651, 45981, 45982, 45983, 45984, 46751, 50159, 50160, 50161, 55381, 60608, and 60609 of the Revenue and Taxation Code, as those sections pertain to the California Department of Tax and Fee Administration.

(E) Any other information confidentiality provisions in federal and state law.

(2) Except for restrictions imposed by federal law, nothing in this subdivision shall be construed to prohibit the sharing of confidential information authorized pursuant to subdivision (b).

(d) Information requested pursuant to this section shall not include federal tax data without authorization from the Internal Revenue Service.

Added Stats 2019 ch 626 § 1 (AB 1296), effective January 1, 2020.

§ 15926. Collaboration of investigative teams for recovery of lost revenues

(a) The Department of Justice, at a minimum, shall maintain the two multiagency Tax Recovery in the Underground Economy Criminal Enforcement Program investigative teams, formerly known as the Tax Recovery and Criminal Enforcement Task Force, in Sacramento and Los Angeles. These investigative teams, including the Department of Justice, the Employment Development Department, the California Department of Tax and Fee Administration, and the Franchise Tax Board shall continue their collaboration for the recovery of lost revenues to the state by investigating and prosecuting criminal offenses in the state's underground economy, including, but not limited to, tax-related and fee-related crimes such as tax evasion or tax fraud.

(b) For the purpose of this section, "collaboration" means the following:

(1) Each agency works with the investigative teams to assess leads.

(2) When a case may involve the jurisdiction of an agency, the agency assists the investigative team with the investigation and prosecution of the case.

Added Stats 2019 ch 626 § 1 (AB 1296), effective January 1, 2020.

TITLE 4
Government of Cities

DIVISION 3
OFFICERS

PART 2
LEGISLATIVE BODY

Chapter 3
General Powers

§ 37101.7. Tax; Contractors licensed by state

(a) In accordance with the provisions of subdivision (b), the legislative body may license for revenue, and fix the license tax upon, persons who transact in the city the business of a contractor licensed pursuant to Chapter 9 (commencing with Section 7000) of Division 3 of the Business and Professions Code.

(b) The ordinance which adopts the license and license tax shall not impose a greater license tax upon those persons subject to it who, as contractors, have no fixed place of business within the city, than upon those contractors who have a fixed place of business within the city; provided, however, that such ordinance may impose a license tax graduated according to gross receipts attributable to contracting work done within a city, regardless of whether or not the contractor has a fixed place of business within the city.

Added Stats 1965 ch 1043 § 1.

TITLE 7
Planning and Land Use

DIVISION 1
PLANNING AND ZONING

Chapter 4
Zoning Regulations

Article 2

Adoption of Regulations

§ 65850.5. Solar energy a statewide concern; Adoption of local ordinances for expedited, streamlined permit process for small, residential rooftop solar energy systems; Definitions

(a) The implementation of consistent statewide standards to achieve the timely and cost-effective installation of solar energy systems is not a municipal affair, as that term is used in Section 5 of Article XI of the California Constitution, but is instead a matter of statewide concern. It is the intent of the Legislature that local agencies not adopt ordinances that create unreasonable barriers to the installation of solar energy systems, including, but not limited to, design review for aesthetic purposes, and not unreasonably restrict the ability of homeowners and agricultural and business concerns to install solar energy systems. It is the policy of the state to promote and encourage the use of solar energy systems and to limit obstacles to their use. It is the intent of the Legislature that local agencies comply not only with the language of this section, but also the legislative intent to encourage the installation of solar energy systems by removing obstacles to, and minimizing costs of, permitting for such systems.

(b) A city or county shall administratively approve applications to install solar energy systems through the issuance of a building permit or similar nondiscretionary permit. Review of the application to install a solar energy system shall be limited to the building official's review of whether it meets all health and safety requirements of local, state, and federal law. The requirements of local law shall be limited to those standards and regulations necessary to ensure that the solar energy system will not have a specific, adverse impact upon the public health or safety. However, if the building official of the city or county makes a finding, based on substantial evidence, that the solar energy system could have a specific, adverse impact upon the public health and safety, the city or county may require the applicant to apply for a use permit.

(c) A city, county, or city and county may not deny an application for a use permit to install a solar energy system unless it makes written findings based upon substantial evidence in the record that the proposed installation would have a specific, adverse impact upon the public health or safety, and there is no feasible method to satisfactorily mitigate or avoid the specific, adverse impact. The findings shall include the basis for the rejection of potential feasible alternatives of preventing the adverse impact.

(d) The decision of the building official pursuant to subdivisions (b) and (c) may be appealed to the planning commission of the city, county, or city and county.

(e) Any conditions imposed on an application to install a solar energy system shall be designed to mitigate the specific, adverse impact upon the public health and safety at the lowest cost possible.

(f) (1) A solar energy system shall meet applicable health and safety standards and requirements imposed by state and local permitting authorities.

(2) Solar energy systems for heating water in single family residences and solar collectors used for heating water in commercial or swimming pool applications shall be certified by an accredited listing agency as defined in the California Plumbing and Mechanical Codes.

(3) A solar energy system for producing electricity shall meet all applicable safety and performance standards established by the California Electrical Code, the Institute of Electrical and Electronics Engineers, and accredited testing laboratories such as Underwriters Laboratories and, where applicable, rules of the Public Utilities Commission regarding safety and reliability.

(4) No later than January 1, 2021, an application to install a solar energy system shall include a reference to the requirement to notify the appropriate regional notification center of an excavator's intent to excavate, pursuant to Article 2 (commencing with Section 4216) of Chapter 3.1 of Division 5 of Title 1, before conducting an excavation, including, but not limited to, installing a grounding rod.

(5) No later than January 1, 2021, the Office of Planning and Research shall add a reference to the California Solar Permitting Guidebook regarding the requirement to notify the appropriate regional notification center of an excavator's intent to excavate pursuant to Article 2 (commencing with Section 4216) of Chapter 3.1 of Division 5 of Title 1, before conducting an excavation, including, but not limited to, installing a grounding rod.

(6) A city, county, or city and county shall not be liable for any damages associated with the failure of a person required to obtain a

solar energy system permit to notify the appropriate regional notification center of an intended excavation.

(g) (1) On or before September 30, 2015, every city, county, or city and county, in consultation with the local fire department or district and the utility director, if the city, county, or city and county operates a utility, shall adopt an ordinance, consistent with the goals and intent of subdivision (a), that creates an expedited, streamlined permitting process for small residential rooftop solar energy systems. In developing an expedited permitting process, the city, county, or city and county shall adopt a checklist of all requirements with which small rooftop solar energy systems shall comply to be eligible for expedited review. An application that satisfies the information requirements in the checklist, as determined by the city, county, and city and county, shall be deemed complete. Upon confirmation by the city, county, or city and county of the application and supporting documents being complete and meeting the requirements of the checklist, and consistent with the ordinance, a city, county, or city and county shall, consistent with subdivision (b), approve the application and issue all required permits or authorizations. Upon receipt of an incomplete application, a city, county, or city and county shall issue a written correction notice detailing all deficiencies in the application and any additional information required to be eligible for expedited permit issuance.

(2) The checklist and required permitting documentation shall be published on a publically accessible internet website if the city, county, or city and county has an internet website and the city, county, or city and county shall allow for electronic submittal of a permit application and associated documentation, and shall authorize the electronic signature on all forms, applications, and other documentation in lieu of a wet signature by an applicant. In developing the ordinance, the city, county, or city and county shall substantially conform its expedited, streamlined permitting process with the recommendations for expedited permitting, including the checklists and standard plans contained in the most current version of the California Solar Permitting Guidebook and adopted by the Governor's Office of Planning and Research. A city, county, or city and county may adopt an ordinance that modifies the checklists and standards found in the guidebook due to unique climactic, geological, seismological, or topographical conditions. If a city, county, or city and county determines that it is unable to authorize the acceptance of an electronic signature on all forms, applications, and other documents in lieu of a wet signature by an applicant, the city, county, or city and county shall state, in the ordinance required under this subdivision, the reasons for its inability to accept electronic signatures and acceptance of an electronic signature shall not be required.

(h) For a small residential rooftop solar energy system eligible for expedited review, only one inspection shall be required, which shall be done in a timely manner and may include a consolidated inspection, except that a separate fire safety inspection may be performed in a city, county, or city and county that does not have an agreement with a local fire authority to conduct a fire safety inspection on behalf of the fire authority. If a small residential rooftop solar energy system fails inspection, a subsequent inspection is authorized, however the subsequent inspection need not conform to the requirements of this subdivision.

(i) A city, county, or city and county shall not condition approval for any solar energy system permit on the approval of a solar energy system by an association, as that term is defined in Section 4080 of the Civil Code.

(j) The following definitions apply to this section:

(1) "A feasible method to satisfactorily mitigate or avoid the specific, adverse impact" includes, but is not limited to, any cost-effective method, condition, or mitigation imposed by a city, county, or city and county on another similarly situated application in a prior successful application for a permit. A city, county, or city and county shall use its best efforts to ensure that the selected method, condition, or mitigation meets the conditions of subparagraphs (A) and (B) of paragraph (1) of subdivision (d) of Section 714 of the Civil Code.

(2) "Electronic submittal" means the utilization of one or more of the following:

(A) Email.

(B) The Internet.

(C) Facsimile.

(3) "Small residential rooftop solar energy system" means all of the following:

(A) A solar energy system that is no larger than 10 kilowatts alternating current nameplate rating or 30 kilowatts thermal.

(B) A solar energy system that conforms to all applicable state fire, structural, electrical, and other building codes as adopted or amended by the city, county, or city and county and paragraph (3) of subdivision (c) of Section 714 of the Civil Code.

(C) A solar energy system that is installed on a single or duplex family dwelling.

(D) A solar panel or module array that does not exceed the maximum legal building height as defined by the authority having jurisdiction.

(4) "Solar energy system" has the same meaning set forth in paragraphs (1) and (2) of subdivision (a) of Section 801.5 of the Civil Code.

(5) "Specific, adverse impact" means a significant, quantifiable, direct, and unavoidable impact, based on objective, identified, and writ-

ten public health or safety standards, policies, or conditions as they existed on the date the application was deemed complete.

Added Stats 2004 ch 789 § 4 (AB 2473). Amended Stats 2014 ch 521 § 3 (AB 2188), effective January 1, 2015; Stats 2019 ch 494 § 2 (AB 754), effective January 1, 2020.

DIVISION 2

SUBDIVISIONS

Chapter 5

Improvement Security

§ 66499.7. Release of security; Notice of completion

The security furnished by the subdivider shall be released in whole or in part in the following manner:

(a) Security given for faithful performance of any act or agreement shall be released upon the performance of the act or final completion and acceptance of the required work. The legislative body may provide for the partial release of the security upon the partial performance of the act or the acceptance of the work as it progresses, consistent with the provisions of this section. The security may be a surety bond, a cash deposit, a letter of credit, escrow account, or other form of performance guarantee required as security by the legislative body that meets the requirements as acceptable security pursuant to law. If the security furnished by the subdivider is a documentary evidence of security such as a surety bond or a letter of credit, the legislative body shall release the documentary evidence and return the original to the issuer upon performance of the act or final completion and acceptance of the required work. In the event that the legislative body is unable to return the original documentary evidence to the issuer, the security shall be released by written notice sent by certified mail to the subdivider and issuer of the documentary evidence within 30 days of the acceptance of the work. The written notice shall contain a statement that the work for which the security was furnished has been performed or completed and accepted by the legislative body, a description of the project subject to the documentary evidence and the notarized signature of the authorized representative of the legislative body.

(b) At the time that the subdivider believes that the obligation to perform the work for which security was required is complete, the subdivider may notify the local agency in writing of the completed work, including a list of work completed. Upon receipt of the written notice, the local agency shall have 45 days to review and comment or approve the completion of the required work. If the local agency does not agree that all work has been completed in accordance with the plans and specifications for the improvements, it shall supply a list of all remaining work to be completed.

(c) Within 45 days of receipt of the list of remaining work from the local agency, the subdivider may then provide cost estimates for all remaining work for review and approval by the local agency. Upon receipt of the cost estimates, the local agency shall then have 45 days to review, comment, and approve, modify, or disapprove those cost estimates. No local agency shall be required to engage in this process of partial release more than once between the start of work and completion and acceptance of all work; however, nothing in this section prohibits a local agency from allowing for a partial release as it otherwise deems appropriate.

(d) If the local agency approves the cost estimate, the local agency shall release all performance security except for security in an amount up to 200 percent of the cost estimate of the remaining work. The process allowing for a partial release of performance security shall occur when the cost estimate of the remaining work does not exceed 20 percent of the total original performance security unless the local agency allows for a release at an earlier time. Substitute bonds or other security may be used as a replacement for the performance security, subject to the approval of the local agency. If substitute bonds or other security is used as a replacement for the performance security released, the release shall not be effective unless and until the local agency receives and approves that form of replacement security. A reduction in the performance security, authorized under this section, is not, and shall not be deemed to be, an acceptance by the local agency of the completed improvements, and the risk of loss or damage to the improvements and the obligation to maintain the improvements shall remain the sole responsibility of the subdivider until all required public improvements have been accepted by the local agency and all other required improvements have been fully completed in accordance with the plans and specifications for the improvements.

(e) The subdivider shall complete the works of improvement until all remaining items are accepted by the local agency.

(f) Upon the completion of the improvements, the subdivider, or his or her assigns, shall be notified in writing by the local agency within 45 days.

(g) Within 45 days of the issuance of the notification by the local agency, the release of any remaining performance security shall be placed upon the agenda of the legislative body of the local agency for approval of the release of any remaining performance security. If the local agency delegates authority for the release of performance security to a public official or other employee, any remaining performance security shall be released within 60 days of the issuance of the written statement of completion.

(h) Security securing the payment to the contractor, his or her subcontractors, and to persons furnishing labor, materials, or equipment shall, after passage of the time within which claims of lien are required to be recorded pursuant to Article 2 (commencing with Section 8410) of Chapter 4 of Title 2 of Part 6 of Division 4 of the Civil Code and after acceptance of the work, be reduced to an amount equal to the total claimed by all claimants for whom claims of lien have been recorded and notice thereof given in writing to the legislative body, and if no claims have been recorded, the security shall be released in full.

(i) The release shall not apply to any required guarantee and warranty period required by Section 66499.9 for the guarantee or warranty nor to the amount of the security deemed necessary by the local agency for the guarantee and warranty period nor to costs and reasonable expenses and fees, including reasonable attorney's fees.

(j) The legislative body may authorize any of its public officers or employees to authorize release or reduction of the security in accordance with the conditions hereinabove set forth and in accordance with any rules that it may prescribe.

Added Stats 1974 ch 1536 § 4, operative March 1, 1975. Amended Stats 1982 ch 87 § 24, effective March 1, 1982; Stats 1983 ch 1195 § 2; Stats 1988 ch 1308 § 5; Stats 1997 ch 124 § 1 (SB 562); Stats 2005 ch 411 § 1 (AB 1460), effective January 1, 2006, repealed January 1, 2011; Stats 2006 ch 643 § 22 (SB 1196), effective January 1, 2007; Stats 2010 ch 697 § 36 (SB 189), ch 174 § 1 (SB 1019) (ch 174 prevails), effective January 1, 2011, repealed January 1, 2016; Stats 2011 ch 44 § 6 (SB 189), ch 174 § 1 (SB 190), effective January 1, 2012, operative July 1, 2012, repealed January 1, 2016. The repealed section related to Release of security; Notice of completion; Stats 2015 ch 269 § 17 (SB 184), effective January 1, 2016.

Appendix

HEALTH AND SAFETY CODE

DIVISION 12
FIRES AND FIRE PROTECTION

PART 2
FIRE PROTECTION

Chapter 1
State Fire Marshal

Article 1

General

§ 13110. Authority of State Fire Marshal to propose, adopt and administer regulations and establish and collect fees

(a) Notwithstanding any other provision of this part, the State Fire Marshal may propose, adopt, and administer the regulations that he or she deems necessary in order to ensure fire safety in buildings and structures within this state including regulations related to construction, modification, installation, testing, inspection, labeling, listing, certification, registration, licensing, reporting, operation, and maintenance. Regulations that are building standards shall be submitted to the State Building Standards Commission for approval pursuant to Chapter 4 (commencing with Section 18935) of Part 2.5 of Division 13.

(b) The Office of the State Fire Marshal may establish and collect reasonable fees necessary to implement this section, consistent with Section 3 of Article XIII A of the California Constitution.

Added Stats 2013 ch 377 § 4 (AB 433), effective January 1, 2014.

DIVISION 13
HOUSING

PART 1.5

REGULATION OF BUILDINGS USED FOR HUMAN HABITATION

Chapter 2

Rules and Regulations

§ 17926. Carbon monoxide devices required; Number and placement; Violation; Local ordinance; Standards for installation of carbon monoxide detectors in hotel and motel dwelling units

(a) An owner of a dwelling unit intended for human occupancy shall install a carbon monoxide device, approved and listed by the State Fire Marshal pursuant to Section 13263, in each existing dwelling unit having a fossil fuel burning heater or appliance, fireplace, or an attached garage, within the earliest applicable time period as follows:

(1) For all existing single-family dwelling units intended for human occupancy on or before July 1, 2011.

(2) For all existing hotel and motel dwelling units intended for human occupancy on or before January 1, 2017.

(3) For all other existing dwelling units intended for human occupancy on or before January 1, 2013.

(b) With respect to the number and placement of carbon monoxide devices, an owner shall install the devices in a manner consistent with building standards applicable to new construction for the relevant type of occupancy or with the manufacturer's instructions, if it is technically feasible to do so.

(c) (1) Notwithstanding Section 17995, and except as provided in paragraph (2), a violation of this section is an infraction punishable by a maximum fine of two hundred dollars ($200) for each offense.

(2) Notwithstanding paragraph (1), a property owner shall receive a 30-day notice to correct. If an owner receiving notice fails to correct within that time period, the owner may be assessed the fine pursuant to paragraph (2).

(d) No transfer of title shall be invalidated on the basis of a failure to comply with this section, and the exclusive remedy for the failure to comply with this section is an award of actual damages not to exceed one hundred dollars ($100), exclusive of any court costs and attorney's fees. This subdivision is not intended to affect any duties, rights, or remedies otherwise available at law.

(e) A local ordinance requiring carbon monoxide devices may be enacted or amended if the ordinance is consistent with this chapter.

(f) On or before July 1, 2015, the department shall submit for adoption and approval pursuant to Chapter 4 (commencing with Section 18935) of Part 2.5, building standards for the installation of carbon monoxide detectors in hotel and motel dwelling units intended for human occupancy. In developing these standards, the department shall do both of the following:

(1) Convene and consult a stakeholder group that includes members with expertise in multifamily dwellings, lodging, maintenance, and construction.

(2) Review and consider the most current national codes and standards available related to the installation of carbon monoxide detection.

(g) For purposes of this section and Section 17926.1, "dwelling unit intended for human occupancy" has the same meaning as that term is defined in Section 13262.

Added Stats 2010 ch 19 § 4 (SB 183), effective January 1, 2011; Amended Stats 2012 ch 420 § 4 (SB 1394), effective January 1, 2013; Stats 2014 ch 298 § 4 (AB 2753), effective January 1, 2015.

§ 17926.2. Temporary suspension of enforcement of carbon monoxide device regulations; Effect of change in building standards

(a) If the department, in consultation with the State Fire Marshal, determines that a sufficient amount of tested and approved carbon monoxide devices are not available to property owners to meet the requirements of the Carbon Monoxide Poisoning Prevention Act of 2009 and Sections 17926 and 17926.1, the department may suspend enforcement of the requirements of Sections 17926 and 17926.1 for up to six months. If the department elects to suspend enforcement of these requirements, the department shall notify the Secretary of State of its decision and shall post a public notice that describes its findings and decision on the departmental Internet Web site.

(b) If the California Building Standards Commission adopts or updates building standards relating to carbon monoxide devices, the owner or owner's agent, who has installed a carbon monoxide device as required by Section 17926 or 17926.1, shall not be required to install a new device meeting the requirements of those building standards within an individual dwelling unit until the owner makes application for a permit for alterations, repairs, or additions to that dwelling unit, the cost of which will exceed one thousand dollars ($1,000).

Added Stats 2010 ch 19 § 6 (SB 183), effective January 1, 2011.

Chapter 5

Administration and Enforcement

Article 2.2

Exterior Elevated Elements; Inspections

§ 17973. Inspection requirements

(a) Exterior elevated elements that include load-bearing components in all buildings containing three or more multifamily dwelling units shall be inspected. The inspection shall be performed by a licensed architect; licensed civil or structural engineer; a building contractor holding any or all of the "A," "B," or "C-5" license classifications issued by the Contractors State License Board, with a minimum of five years' experience, as a holder of the aforementioned classifications or licenses, in constructing multistory wood frame buildings; or an individual certified as a building inspector or building official from a recognized state, national, or international association, as determined by the local jurisdiction. These individuals shall not be employed by the local jurisdiction while performing these inspections. The purpose of the inspection is to determine that exterior elevated elements and their associated waterproofing elements are in a generally safe condition, adequate working order, and free from any hazardous condition caused by fungus, deterioration, decay, or improper alteration to the extent that the life, limb, health, property, safety, or welfare of the public or the occupants is not endangered. The person or business performing the inspection shall be hired by the owner of the building.

(b) For purposes of this section, the following terms have the following definitions:

(1) "Associated waterproofing elements" include flashings, membranes, coatings, and sealants that protect the load-bearing components of exterior elevated elements from exposure to water and the elements.

(2) "Exterior elevated element" means the following types of structures, including their supports and railings: balconies, decks, porches, stairways, walkways, and entry structures that extend beyond exterior walls of the building and which have a walking surface that is elevated more than six feet above ground level, are designed for human occupancy or use, and rely in whole or in substantial part on wood or wood-based products for structural support or stability of the exterior elevated element.

(3) "Load-bearing components" are those components that extend beyond the exterior walls of the building to deliver structural loads from the exterior elevated element to the building.

(c) The inspection required by this section shall at a minimum include:

(1) Identification of each type of exterior elevated element that, if found to be defective, decayed, or deteriorated to the extent that it does not meet its load requirements, would, in the opinion of the inspector, constitute a threat to the health or safety of the occupants.

(2) Assessment of the load-bearing components and associated waterproofing elements of the exterior elevated elements identified in paragraph (1) using methods allowing for evaluation of their performance by direct visual examination or comparable means of evaluating their performance. For purposes of this section, a sample of at least 15 percent of each type of exterior elevated element shall be inspected.

(3) The evaluation and assessment shall address each of the following as of the date of the evaluation:

(A) The current condition of the exterior elevated elements.

(B) Expectations of future performance and projected service life.

(C) Recommendations of any further inspection necessary.

(4) A written report of the evaluation stamped or signed by the inspector presented to the owner of the building or the owner's designated agent within 45 days of completion of the inspection. The report shall include photographs, any test results, and narrative sufficient to establish a baseline of the condition of the components inspected that can be compared to the results of subsequent inspections. In addition to the evaluation required by this section, the report shall advise which, if any, exterior elevated element poses an immediate threat to the safety of the occupants, and whether preventing occupant access or conducting emergency repairs, including shoring, are necessary.

(d) The inspection shall be completed by January 1, 2025, and by January 1 every six years thereafter. The inspector conducting the inspection shall produce an initial report pursuant to paragraph (4) of subdivision (c) and, if requested by the owner, a final report indicating that any required repairs have been completed. A copy of any report that recommends immediate repairs, advises that any building assembly poses an immediate threat to the safety of the occupants, or that preventing occupant access or emergency repairs, including shoring, are necessary, shall be provided by the inspector to the owner of the building and to the local enforcement agency within 15 days of completion of the report. Subsequent inspection reports shall incorporate copies of prior inspection reports, including the locations of the exterior elevated elements inspected. Local enforcement agencies may determine whether any additional information is to be provided in the report and may require a copy of the initial or final reports, or both, be submitted to the local jurisdiction. Copies of all inspection reports shall be maintained in the building owner's permanent records for not less than two inspection cycles, and shall be disclosed and delivered to the buyer at the time of any subsequent sale of the building.

(e) The inspection of buildings for which a building permit application has been submitted on or after January 1, 2019, shall occur no later than six years following issuance of a certificate of occupancy from the local jurisdiction and shall otherwise comply with the provisions of this section.

(f) If the property was inspected within three years prior to January 1, 2019, by an inspector as described in subdivision (a) and a report of that inspector was issued stating that the exterior elevated elements and associated waterproofing elements are in proper working condition and do not pose a threat to the health and safety of the public, no new inspection pursuant to this section shall be required until January 1, 2025.

(g) An exterior elevated element found by the inspector that is in need of repair or replacement shall be corrected by the owner of the building. All necessary permits for repair or replacement shall be obtained from the local jurisdiction. All repair and replacement work shall be performed by a qualified and licensed contractor in compliance with all of the following:

(1) The recommendations of a licensed professional described in subdivision (a).

(2) Any applicable manufacturer's specifications.

(3) The California Building Standards Code, consistent with subdivision (d) of Section 17922 of the Health and Safety Code.

(4) All local jurisdictional requirements.

(h) (1) An exterior elevated element that the inspector advises poses an immediate threat to the safety of the occupants, or finds preventing occupant access or emergency repairs, including shoring, or both, are necessary, shall be considered an emergency condition and the owner of the building shall perform required preventive measures immediately. Immediately preventing occupant access to the exterior elevated element until emergency repairs can be completed constitutes compliance with this paragraph. Repairs of emergency conditions shall comply with the requirements of subdivision (g), be inspected by the inspector, and reported to the local enforcement agency.

(2) The owner of the building requiring corrective work to an exterior elevated element that, in the opinion of the inspector, does not pose an immediate threat to the safety of the occupants, shall apply for a permit within 120 days of receipt of the inspection report. Once the permit is approved, the owner of the building shall have 120 days to make the repairs unless an extension of time is granted by the local enforcement agency.

Appendix

(i) (1) The owner of the building shall be responsible for complying with the requirements of this section.

(2) If the owner of the building does not comply with the repair requirements within 180 days, the inspector shall notify the local enforcement agency and the owner of the building. If within 30 days of the date of the notice the repairs are not completed, the owner of the building shall be assessed a civil penalty based on the fee schedule set by the local authority of not less than one hundred dollars ($100) nor more than five hundred dollars ($500) per day until the repairs are completed, unless an extension of time is granted by the local enforcement agency.

(3) In the event that a civil penalty is assessed pursuant to this section, a building safety lien may be recorded in the county recorder's office by the local jurisdiction in the county in which the parcel of land is located and from the date of recording shall have the force, effect, and priority of a judgment lien.

(j) (1) A building safety lien authorized by this section shall specify the amount of the lien, the name of the agency on whose behalf the lien is imposed, the street address, the legal description and assessor's parcel number of the parcel on which the lien is imposed, and the name and address of the recorded owner of the building.

(2) In the event that the lien is discharged, released, or satisfied, either through payment or foreclosure, notice of the discharge containing the information specified in paragraph (1) shall be recorded by the governmental agency. A safety lien and the release of the lien shall be indexed in the grantor-grantee index.

(3) A building safety lien may be foreclosed by an action brought by the appropriate local jurisdiction for a money judgment.

(4) Notwithstanding any other law, the county recorder may impose a fee on the city to reimburse the costs of processing and recording the lien and providing notice to the owner of the building. A city may recover from the owner of the building any costs incurred regarding the processing and recording of the lien and providing notice to the owner of the building as part of its foreclosure action to enforce the lien.

(k) The continued and ongoing maintenance of exterior elevated elements in a safe and functional condition in compliance with these provisions shall be the responsibility of the owner of the building.

(l) Local enforcement agencies shall have the ability to recover enforcement costs associated with the requirements of this section.

(m) For any building subject to the provisions of this section that is proposed for conversion to condominiums to be sold to the public after January 1, 2019, the inspection required by this section shall be conducted prior to the first close of escrow of a separate interest in the project and shall include the inspector's recommendations for repair or replacement of any exterior elevated element found to be defective, decayed, or deteriorated to the extent that it does not meet its load requirements, and would, in the opinion of the inspector, constitute a threat to the health or safety of the occupants. The inspection report and written confirmation by the inspector that any repairs or replacements recommended by the inspector have been completed shall be submitted to the Department of Real Estate by the proponent of the conversion and shall be a condition to the issuance of the final public report. A complete copy of the inspection report and written confirmation by the inspector that any repairs or replacements recommended by the inspector have been completed shall be included with the written statement of defects required by Section 1134 of the Civil Code, and provided to the local jurisdiction in which the project is located. The inspection, report, and confirmation of completed repairs shall be a condition of the issuance of a final inspection or certificate of occupancy by the local jurisdiction.

(n) This section shall not apply to a common interest development, as defined in Section 4100 of the Civil Code.

(o) The governing body of any city, county, or city and county, may enact ordinances or laws imposing requirements greater than those imposed by this section.

Added Stats 2018 ch 445 § 2 (SB 721), effective January 1, 2019; Amended Stats 2021 ch 367 § 34 (SB 607), effective January 1, 2022.

PART 3

MISCELLANEOUS

Chapter 9

Local Building Permits

Article 1

Contents

§ 19825. Building permit application; Form; Owner-Builder Declaration; Documentation and verification

(a) Every city, county, or city and county, whether general law or chartered, that requires the issuance of a permit as a condition precedent to the construction, alteration, improvement, demolition, or repair of any building or structure, shall require the execution of a permit application, in substantially the same form set forth under this subdivision, and require any individual who executes the Owner-Builder Declaration to present documentation sufficient to identify the property owner and, as necessary, verify the signature of the property owner. A city, county, or city and county may require additional information on the permit application.

PERMIT APPLICATION
BUILDING PROJECT IDENTIFICATION

Applicant's Mailing Address   _____

Property Location or Address   _____

Property Owner's Name   _____
Property Owner's Telephone No.   _____

Licensed Design Professional (Architect   _____
or Engineer) in charge of the project   _____

Mailing Address of Licensed Design   _____
Professional   _____

License No. _____

LICENSED CONTRACTOR'S DECLARATION

I hereby affirm under penalty of perjury that I am licensed under provisions of Chapter 9 (commencing with Section 7000) of Division 3 of the Business and Professions Code, and my license is in full force and effect.

License Class _____ License No. _____
Date _____ Contractor Signature _____

OWNER-BUILDER DECLARATION

I hereby affirm under penalty of perjury that I am exempt from the Contractors' State License Law for the reason(s) indicated below by the checkmark(s) I have placed next to the applicable item(s) (Section 7031.5, Business and Professions Code: Any city or county that requires a permit to construct, alter, improve, demolish, or repair any structure, prior to its issuance, also requires the applicant for the permit to file a signed statement that he or she is licensed pursuant to the provisions of the Contractors' State License Law (Chapter 9 (commencing with Section 7000) of Division 3 of the Business and Professions Code) or that he or she is exempt from licensure and the basis for the alleged exemption. Any violation of Section 7031.5 by any applicant for a permit subjects the applicant to a civil penalty of not more than five hundred dollars ($500).):

(_) I, as owner of the property, or my employees with wages as their sole compensation, will do (_) all of or (_) portions of the work, and the structure is not intended or offered for sale (Section 7044, Business and Professions Code: The Contractors' State License Law does not apply to an owner of property who, through employees' or personal effort, builds or improves the property, provided that the improvements are not intended or offered for sale. If, however, the building or improvement is sold within one year of completion, the Owner-Builder will have the burden of proving that it was not built or improved for the purpose of sale.).

(_) I, as owner of the property, am exclusively contracting with licensed Contractors to construct the project (Section 7044, Business and Professions Code: The Contractors' State License Law does not apply to an owner of property who builds or improves thereon, and who contracts for the projects with a licensed Contractor pursuant to the Contractors' State License Law.).

(_) I am exempt from licensure under the Contractors' State License Law for the following reason:

_____

By my signature below I acknowledge that, except for my personal residence in which I must have resided for at least one year prior to completion of the improvements covered by this permit, I cannot legally sell a structure that I have built as an owner-builder if it has not been constructed in its entirety by licensed contractors. I understand that a copy of the applicable law, Section 7044 of the Business and Professions Code, is available upon request when this application is submitted or at the following Web site: http://www.leginfo.ca.gov/calaw.html.

Date _____

Signature of Property Owner or Authorized Agent _____

WORKERS' COMPENSATION DECLARATION

WARNING: FAILURE TO SECURE WORKERS' COMPENSATION COVERAGE IS UNLAWFUL, AND SHALL SUBJECT AN EMPLOYER TO CRIMINAL PENALTIES AND CIVIL FINES UP TO ONE HUNDRED THOUSAND DOLLARS ($100,000), IN ADDITION TO THE COST OF COMPENSATION, DAMAGES AS PROVIDED FOR IN SECTION 3706 OF THE LABOR CODE, INTEREST, AND ATTORNEY'S FEES.

I hereby affirm under penalty of perjury one of the following declarations:

_____ I have and will maintain a certificate of consent to self-insure for workers' compensation, issued by the Director of Industrial Relations as provided for by Section 3700 of the Labor Code, for the performance of the work for which this permit is issued.

Policy No. _____

_____ I have and will maintain workers' compensation insurance, as required by Section 3700 of the Labor Code, for the performance of the work for

Appendix

which this permit is issued. My workers' compensation insurance carrier and policy number are:

Carrier _____ Policy Number _____ Expiration Date _____

Name of Agent _____ Phone #_____

_____ I certify that, in the performance of the work for which this permit is issued, I shall not employ any person in any manner so as to become subject to the workers' compensation laws of California, and agree that, if I should become subject to the workers' compensation provisions of Section 3700 of the Labor Code, I shall forthwith comply with those provisions.

_____   _____
Signature of Applicant   Date

DECLARATION REGARDING CONSTRUCTION LENDING AGENCY

I hereby affirm under penalty of perjury that there is a construction lending agency for the performance of the work for which this permit is issued (Section 8172, Civil Code).

Lender's Name _____

Branch Designation _____

Lender's Address _____

By my signature below, I certify to each of the following:
I am the property owner or authorized to act on the property owner's behalf.
I have read this application and the information I have provided is correct.
I agree to comply with all applicable city and county ordinances and state laws relating to building construction.
I authorize representatives of this city or county to enter the above-identified property for inspection purposes.

Signature of Property Owner or Authorized Agent _____

Date _____

(b) When the Permit Application and the Owner-Builder Declaration have been executed by a person other than the property owner, prior to issuing the permit, the following shall be completed by the property owner and returned to the agency responsible for issuing the permit:

AUTHORIZATION OF AGENT TO ACT ON PROPERTY OWNER'S BEHALF

Excluding the Notice to Property Owner, the execution of which I understand is my personal responsibility, I hereby authorize the following person(s) to act as my agent(s) to apply for, sign, and file the documents necessary to obtain an Owner-Builder Permit for my project.

Scope of Construction Project (or Description of Work):

_____

Project Location or Address: _____

Name of Authorized Agent: _____

Address of Authorized Agent: _____

Phone Number of Authorized Agent: _____

I declare under penalty of perjury that I am the property owner for the address listed above and I personally filled out the above information and certify its accuracy.

Property Owner's Signature: _____ Date: _____

Note: A copy of the owner's driver's license, form notarization, or other verification acceptable to the agency is required to be presented when the permit is issued to verify the property owner's signature.

(c) When the Owner-Builder Declaration required under subdivision (a) is executed, a Notice to Property Owner also shall be executed by the property owner in substantially the same form set forth under this section. The Notice to Property Owner shall appear on the official letterhead of the issuer and shall be provided to the applicant by one of the following methods chosen by the permitting authority: regular mail, electronic format, or given directly to the applicant at the time the application for the permit is made. Except as otherwise provided, the Notice to Property Owner pursuant to this section shall be completed and signed by the property owner and returned prior to issuance of the permit. An agent of the owner shall not execute this notice unless the property owner obtains the prior approval of the permitting authority. A permit shall not be issued unless the property owner complies with this section.

NOTICE TO PROPERTY OWNER

Dear Property Owner:

An application for a building permit has been submitted in your name listing yourself as the builder of the property improvements specified at

_____.

We are providing you with an Owner-Builder Acknowledgment and Information Verification Form to make you aware of your responsibilities and possible risk you may incur by having this permit issued in your name as the Owner-Builder.

We will not issue a building permit until you have read, initialed your understanding of each provision, signed, and returned this form to us at our official address indicated. An agent of the owner cannot execute this notice unless you, the property owner, obtain the prior approval of the permitting authority.

OWNER'S ACKNOWLEDGMENT AND VERIFICATION OF INFORMATION

DIRECTIONS: Read and initial each statement below to signify you understand or verify this information.

_____ 1. I understand a frequent practice of unlicensed persons is to have the property owner obtain an "Owner-Builder" building permit that erroneously implies that the property owner is providing his or her own labor and material personally. I, as an Owner-Builder, may be held liable and subject to serious financial risk for any injuries sustained by an unlicensed person and his or her employees while working on my property. My homeowner's insurance may not provide coverage for those injuries. I am willfully acting as an Owner-Builder and am aware of the limits of my insurance coverage for injuries to workers on my property.

_____ 2. I understand building permits are not required to be signed by property owners unless they are responsible for the construction and are not hiring a licensed Contractor to assume this responsibility.

_____ 3. I understand as an "Owner-Builder" I am the responsible party of record on the permit. I understand that I may protect myself from potential financial risk by hiring a licensed Contractor and having the permit filed in his or her name instead of my own.

_____ 4. I understand Contractors are required by law to be licensed and bonded in California and to list their license numbers on permits and contracts.

_____ 5. I understand if I employ or otherwise engage any persons, other than California licensed Contractors, and the total value of my construction is at least five hundred dollars ($500), including labor and materials, I may be considered an "employer" under state and federal law.

_____ 6. I understand if I am considered an "employer" under state and federal law, I must register with the state and federal government, withhold payroll taxes, provide workers' compensation disability insurance, and contribute to unemployment compensation for each "employee." I also understand my failure to abide by these laws may subject me to serious financial risk.

_____ 7. I understand under California Contractors' State License Law, an Owner-Builder who builds single-family residential structures cannot legally build them with the intent to offer them for sale, unless all work is performed by licensed subcontractors and the number of structures does not exceed four within any calendar year, or all of the work is performed under contract with a licensed general building Contractor.

_____ 8. I understand as an Owner-Builder if I sell the property for which this permit is issued, I may be held liable for any financial or personal injuries sustained by any subsequent owner(s) that result from any latent construction defects in the workmanship or materials.

_____ 9. I understand I may obtain more information regarding my obligations as an "employer" from the Internal Revenue Service, the United States Small Business Administration, the California Department of Benefit Payments, and the California Division of Industrial Accidents. I also understand I may contact the California Contractors' State License Board (CSLB) at 1-800- 321-CSLB (2752) or www.cslb.ca.gov for more information about licensed contractors.

_____ 10. I am aware of and consent to an Owner-Builder building permit applied for in my name, and understand that I am the party legally and financially responsible for proposed construction activity at the following address:

_____

_____ 11. I agree that, as the party legally and financially responsible for this proposed construction activity, I will abide by all applicable laws and requirements that govern Owner- Builders as well as employers.

_____ 12. I agree to notify the issuer of this form immediately of any additions, deletions, or changes to any of the information I have provided on this form.

Licensed contractors are regulated by laws designed to protect the public. If you contract with someone who does not have a license, the Contractors' State License Board may be unable to assist you with any financial loss you may sustain as a result of a complaint. Your only remedy against unlicensed Contractors may be in civil court. It is also important for you to understand that if an unlicensed Contractor or employee of that individual or firm is injured while working on your property, you may be held liable for damages. If you obtain a permit as Owner-Builder and wish to hire Contractors, you will be responsible for verifying whether or not those Contractors are properly licensed and the status of their workers' compensation insurance coverage.

Before a building permit can be issued, this form must be completed and signed by the property owner and returned to the agency responsible for issuing the permit.

Note: A copy of the property owner's driver's license, form notarization, or other verification acceptable to the agency is required to be presented when the permit is issued to verify the property owner's signature.

Appendix

Signature of property owner _____   Date: _____

Added Stats 2008 ch 66 § 2 (AB 2335), effective January 1, 2009. Amended Stats 2010
ch 697 § 39 (SB 189), effective January 1, 2011, operative July 1, 2012.

DIVISION 20

MISCELLANEOUS HEALTH AND SAFETY PROVISIONS

Chapter 6.7

Underground Storage of Hazardous Substances

§ 25281. Definitions [Effective until January 1, 2024; Operative until January 1, 2024]

For purposes of this chapter and unless otherwise expressly pro-vided, the following definitions apply:

(a) "Automatic line leak detector" means any method of leak detec-tion, as determined in regulations adopted by the board, that alerts the owner or operator of an underground storage tank to the presence of a leak. "Automatic line leak detector" includes, but is not lim-ited to, any device or mechanism that alerts the owner or operator of an underground storage tank to the pres-ence of a leak by restricting or shutting off the flow of a hazardous substance through piping, or by triggering an audible or visual alarm, and that detects leaks of three gallons or more per hour at 10 pounds per square inch line pressure within one hour.

(b) "Board" means the State Water Resources Control Board. "Re-gional board" means a California regional water quality control board.

(c) "Compatible" means the ability of two or more substances to maintain their respective physical and chemical properties upon con-tact with one another for the design life of the tank system under conditions like-ly to be encountered in the tank system.

(d)
(1) "Certified Unified Program Agency" or "CUPA" means the agen-cy certified by the Secretary for Envi-ronmental Protection to imple-ment the unified pro-gram specified in Chapter 6.11 (commencing with Section 25404) within a jurisdiction.

(2) "Participating Agency" or "PA" means an agency that has a writ-ten agreement with the CUPA pursuant to subdivision (d) of Section 25404.3, and is approved by the secretary to implement or enforce the

unified pro-gram element specified in paragraph (3) of subdivision (c) of Section 25404, in accordance with Sections 25404.1 and 25404.2.

(3) "Unified Program Agency" or "UPA" means the CUPA, or its participating agencies to the extent each PA has been designated by the CUPA, pursuant to a written agreement, to implement or enforce the unified program element specified in paragraph (3) of subdivi-sion (c) of Section 25404. For purposes of this chapter, a UPA has the re-sponsibility and authority, to the extent provided by this chapter and Sections 25404.1 to 25404.2, inclusive, to implement and en-force only those requirements of this chapter listed in paragraph (3) of subdivi-sion (c) of Section 25404 and the regulations adopted to implement those requirements. Except as provided in Section 25296.09, after a CUPA has been certified by the secretary, the UPA shall be the only local agency authorized to enforce the require-ments of this chapter listed in paragraph (3) of subdivi-sion (c) of Section 25404 within the jurisdiction of the CUPA. This paragraph shall not be construed to limit the authority or responsibility granted to the board and the re-gional boards by this chapter to implement and enforce this chapter and the regulations adopted pur-suant to this chapter.

(e) "Department" means the Department of Toxic Substances Con-trol.

(f) "Facility" means any one, or combination of, under-ground stor-age tanks used by a single business entity at a single location or site.

(g) "Federal act" means Subchapter IX (commencing with Section 6991) of Chapter 82 of Title 42 of the Unit-ed States Code, as added by the Hazardous and Solid Waste Amendments of 1984 (Public Law 98-616), or as it may subsequently be amended or supplemented.

(h) "Hazardous substance" means either of the follow-ing:

(1) All of the following liquid and solid substances, un-less the de-partment, in consultation with the board, de-termines that the sub-stance could not adversely affect the quality of the waters of the state:

(A) Substances on the list prepared by the Director of Industrial Re-lations pursuant to Section 6382 of the Labor Code.

(B) Hazardous substances, as defined in Section 25316.

(C) Any substance or material that is classified by the National Fire Protection Association (NFPA) as a flam-mable liquid, a class II com-bustible liquid, or a class III-A combustible liquid.

(2) Any regulated substance, as defined in subsection (7) of Section 6991 of Title 42 of the United States Code, as that section reads on January 1, 2012, or as it may subsequently be amended or supple-mented.

(i) "Local agency" means one of the following, as speci-fied in subdi-vision (b) of Section 25283:

(1) The unified program agency.

(2) Before July 1, 2013, a city or county.

(3) On and after July 1, 2013, a city or county certified by the board to implement the local oversight program pursuant to Section 25297.01.

(j) "Operator" means any person in control of, or hav-ing daily responsibility for, the daily operation of an un-derground storage tank system.

(k) "Owner" means the owner of an underground storage tank.

(l) "Person" means an individual, trust, firm, joint stock company, corporation, including a government corporation, partnership, limited liability company, or association. "Person" also includes any city, county, dis-trict, the state, another state of the United States, any department or agency of this state or another state, or the United States to the extent authorized by federal law.

(m) "Pipe" means any pipeline or system of pipelines that is used in connection with the storage of hazardous substances and that is not intended to transport haz-ardous substances in interstate or intrastate commerce or to transfer hazardous materials in bulk to or from a marine vessel.

(n) "Primary containment" means the first level of containment, such as the portion of a tank that comes into immediate contact on its inner surface with the hazardous substance being contained.

(o) "Product tight" means impervious to the sub-stance that is contained, or is to be contained, so as to prevent the seepage of the substance from the con-tainment.

(p) "Release" means any spilling, leaking, emitting, discharging, escaping, leaching, or disposing from an underground storage tank into or on the waters of the state, the land, or the subsurface soils.

(q) "Secondary containment" means the level of con-tainment external to, and separate from, the primary containment.

(r) "Single walled" means construction with walls made of only one thickness of material. For the purpos-es of this chapter, laminated, coated, or clad materials are considered single walled.

(s) "Special inspector" means a professional engineer, registered pursuant to Chapter 7 (commencing with Section 6700) of Division 3 of the Business and Professions Code, who is qualified to attest, at a mini-mum, to structural soundness, seismic safety, the com-patibility of construction materials with contents, ca-thodic protection, and the mechanical compatibility of the structural elements of underground storage tanks.

(t)(1) "Storage" or "store" means the containment, han-dling, or treatment of hazardous substances, either on a temporary basis or for a period of years.

(2) "Storage" or "store" does not include the storage of hazardous wastes in an underground storage tank if the person operating the tank has been issued a hazard-ous waste facilities permit by the de-

partment pursuant to Section 25200 or 25201.6 or granted interim status under Section 25200.5.

(3) "Storage" or "store" does not include the storage of hazardous wastes in an underground storage tank if all of the following apply:

(A) The facility has been issued a unified program fa-cility permit pursuant to Section 25404.2 for genera-tion, treatment, accumulation, or storage of hazardous waste in a tank.

(B) The tank is located in an underground area, as de-fined in Section 280.12 of Title 40 of the Code of Federal Regulations.

(C) The tank is subject to Chapter 6.67 (commencing with Section 25270).

(D) The tank complies with the hazardous waste tank standards pursuant to Article 10 (commencing with Section 66265.190) of Chapter 15 of Title 22 of the Cali-fornia Code of Regulations.

(4) "Storage" or "store" does not include the storage of hazardous wastes in an underground storage tank if all of the following apply:

(A) The facility has been issued a unified program fa-cility permit pursuant to Section 25404.2 for genera-tion, treatment, accumulation, or storage of hazardous waste in a tank.

(B) The tank is located in a structure that is at least 10 percent below the ground surface, including, but not limited to, a basement, cellar, shaft, pit, or vault.

(C) The structure in which the tank is located, at a min-imum, provides for secondary containment of the con-tents of the tank, piping, and ancillary equipment, until cleanup occurs.

(D) The tank complies with the hazardous waste tank standards pursuant to Article 10 (commencing with Section 66265.190) of Chapter 15 of Title 22 of the Cali-fornia Code of Regulations.

(u) "Tank" means a stationary device designed to con-tain an accumulation of hazardous substances which is constructed primarily of nonearthen materials, includ-ing, but not limited to, wood, concrete, steel, or plastic that provides structural support.

(v) "Tank integrity test" means a test method capable of detecting an unauthorized release from an under-ground storage tank consistent with the minimum standards adopted by the board.

(w) "Tank tester" means an individual who performs tank integrity tests on underground storage tanks.

(x) "Unauthorized release" means any release of any hazardous substance that does not conform to this chapter, including an unau-thorized release specified in Section 25295.5.

(y)(1) "Underground storage tank" means any one or combination of tanks, including pipes connected there-to, that is used for the storage of hazardous substances and that is substantially or totally beneath the surface of the ground. "Underground storage tank" does not in-clude any of the following:

(A) A tank with a capacity of 1,100 gallons or less that is located on a farm and that stores motor vehicle fuel used primarily for agricultural purposes and not for re-sale.

(B) A tank that is located on a farm or at the residence of a person, that has a capacity of 1,100 gallons or less, and that stores home heating oil for consumptive use on the premises where stored.

(C) Structures, such as sumps, separators, storm drains, catch basins, oil field gathering lines, refinery pipelines, lagoons, evaporation ponds, well cellars, sep-aration sumps, and lined and un-lined pits, sumps, and lagoons. A sump that is a part of a monitoring system required under Section 25290.1, 25290.2, 25291, or 25292 and sumps or other structures defined as un-derground storage tanks un-der the federal act are not exempted by this subparagraph.

(D) A tank holding hydraulic fluid for a closed loop mechanical system that uses compressed air or hydrau-lic fluid to operate lifts, elevators, and other similar de-vices.

(E) A tank in an underground area, as defined in Section 25270.2, and associated piping, that is sub-ject to Chapter 6.67 (commencing with Section 25270).

(2) Structures identified in subparagraphs (C) and (D) of paragraph (1) may be regulated by the board and any regional board pursuant to the Porter-Cologne Water Quality Control Act (Division 7 (commencing with Section 13000) of the Water Code) to ensure that they do not pose a threat to water quality.

(z) "Underground tank system" or "tank system" means an underground storage tank, connected piping, ancillary equipment, and containment system, if any.

(aa)

(1) "Unified program facility" means all contiguous land and structures, other appurtenances, and im-provements on the land that are subject to the require-ments of paragraph (3) of subdivision (c) of Section 25404.

(2) "Unified program facility permit" means a permit issued pursuant to Chapter 6.11 (commencing with Section 25404), and that encompasses the permit-ting requirements of Section 25284.

(3) "Permit" means a permit issued pursuant to Section 25284 or a unified program facility permit as defined in paragraph (2).

Added Stats 1983 ch 1046 § 3. Amended and renumbered by Stats 1984 ch 1038 § 2. Amended Stats 1986 ch 935 § 1, ch 1390 § 1, effective September 30, 1986, operative until January 1, 1987, ch 1390 § 2, effective September 30, 1986, operative January 1, 1987; Stats 1987 ch 1372 § 1; Stats 1989 ch 1397 § 3; 1991 Governor's Reorganization Plan No. 1 § 10, effective July 17, 1991; Stats 1991 ch 1138 § 1 (AB 1954); Stats 1992 ch 654 § 2 (AB 3089), effective September 12, 1992; Stats 1993 ch 432 § 2 (AB 1061), effective September 24, 1993; Stats 1994 ch 1200 § 35 (SB 469), effective September 30, 1994; Stats 1995 ch 639 § 52 (SB 1191); Stats 1999 ch 328 § 1 (SB 665); Stats 2002 ch 999 § 11 (AB 2481); Stats 2003 ch 42 § 4 (AB 1702), effective July 7, 2003, ch 341 § 1

(SB 1002), effective September 8, 2003; Stats 2012 ch 532 § 7 (AB 1566), effective January 1, 2013, ch 536 § 1.5 (AB 1701), effective January 1, 2013; Stats 2015 ch 452 § 9 (SB 612), effective January 1, 2016.

§ 25281. Definitions [Effective January 1, 2023; Operative January 1, 2024]

For purposes of this chapter and unless otherwise expressly provided, the following definitions apply:

(a) "Automatic line leak detector" means any method of leak detection, as determined in regulations adopted by the board, that alerts the owner or operator of an underground storage tank to the presence of a leak. "Automatic line leak detector" includes, but is not limited to, any device or mechanism that alerts the owner or operator of an underground storage tank to the presence of a leak by restricting or shutting off the flow of a hazardous substance through piping, or by triggering an audible or visual alarm, and that detects leaks of three gallons or more per hour at 10 pounds per square inch line pressure within one hour.

(b) "Board" means the State Water Resources Control Board. "Regional board" means a California regional water quality control board.

(c) "Compatible" means the ability of two or more substances to maintain their respective physical and chemical properties upon contact with one another for the design life of the tank system under conditions likely to be encountered in the tank system.

(d) (1) "Certified Unified Program Agency" or "CUPA" means the agency certified by the Secretary for Environmental Protection to implement the unified program specified in Chapter 6.11 (commencing with Section 25404) within a jurisdiction.

(2) "Participating Agency" or "PA" means an agency that has a written agreement with the CUPA pursuant to subdivision (d) of Section 25404.3, and is approved by the secretary to implement or enforce the unified program element specified in paragraph (3) of subdivision (c) of Section 25404, in accordance with Sections 25404.1 and 25404.2.

(3) "Unified Program Agency" or "UPA" means the CUPA, or its participating agencies to the extent each PA has been designated by the CUPA, pursuant to a written agreement, to implement or enforce the unified program element specified in paragraph (3) of subdivision (c) of Section 25404. For purposes of this chapter, a UPA has the responsibility and authority, to the extent provided by this chapter and Sections 25404.1 to 25404.2, inclusive, to implement and enforce only those requirements of this chapter listed in paragraph (3) of subdivision (c) of Section 25404 and the regulations adopted to implement those requirements. Except as provided in Section 25296.09, after a CUPA has been certified by the secretary, the UPA shall be the only

local agency authorized to enforce the requirements of this chapter listed in paragraph (3) of subdivision (c) of Section 25404 within the jurisdiction of the CUPA. This paragraph shall not be construed to limit the authority or responsibility granted to the board and the regional boards by this chapter to implement and enforce this chapter and the regulations adopted pursuant to this chapter.

(e) "Department" means the Department of Toxic Substances Control.

(f) "Facility" means any one, or combination of, underground storage tanks used by a single business entity at a single location or site.

(g) "Federal act" means Subchapter IX (commencing with Section 6991) of Chapter 82 of Title 42 of the United States Code, as added by the Hazardous and Solid Waste Amendments of 1984 (Public Law 98-616), or as it may subsequently be amended or supplemented.

(h) "Hazardous substance" means either of the following:

(1) All of the following liquid and solid substances, unless the department, in consultation with the board, determines that the substance could not adversely affect the quality of the waters of the state:

(A) Substances on the list prepared by the Director of Industrial Relations pursuant to Section 6382 of the Labor Code.

(B) Hazardous substances, as defined in subdivision (a) of Section 78075.

(C) Any substance or material that is classified by the National Fire Protection Association (NFPA) as a flammable liquid, a class II combustible liquid, or a class III-A combustible liquid.

(2) Any regulated substance, as defined in subsection (7) of Section 6991 of Title 42 of the United States Code, as that section reads on January 1, 2012, or as it may subsequently be amended or supplemented.

(i) "Local agency" means one of the following, as specified in subdivision (b) of Section 25283:

(1) The unified program agency.

(2) Before July 1, 2013, a city or county.

(3) On and after July 1, 2013, a city or county certified by the board to implement the local oversight program pursuant to Section 25297.01.

(j) "Operator" means any person in control of, or having daily responsibility for, the daily operation of an underground storage tank system.

(k) "Owner" means the owner of an underground storage tank.

(l) "Person" means an individual, trust, firm, joint stock company, corporation, including a government corporation, partnership, limited liability company, or association. "Person" also includes any city, county, district, the state, another state of the United States, any department or agency of this state or another state, or the United States to the extent authorized by federal law.

(m) "Pipe" means any pipeline or system of pipelines that is used in connection with the storage of hazardous substances and that is not intended to transport hazardous substances in interstate or intrastate commerce or to transfer hazardous materials in bulk to or from a marine vessel.

(n) "Primary containment" means the first level of containment, such as the portion of a tank that comes into immediate contact on its inner surface with the hazardous substance being contained.

(o) "Product tight" means impervious to the substance that is contained, or is to be contained, so as to prevent the seepage of the substance from the containment.

(p) "Release" means any spilling, leaking, emitting, discharging, escaping, leaching, or disposing from an underground storage tank into or on the waters of the state, the land, or the subsurface soils.

(q) "Secondary containment" means the level of containment external to, and separate from, the primary containment.

(r) "Single walled" means construction with walls made of only one thickness of material. For purposes of this chapter, laminated, coated, or clad materials are considered single walled.

(s) "Special inspector" means a professional engineer, registered pursuant to Chapter 7 (commencing with Section 6700) of Division 3 of the Business and Professions Code, who is qualified to attest, at a minimum, to structural soundness, seismic safety, the compatibility of construction materials with contents, cathodic protection, and the mechanical compatibility of the structural elements of underground storage tanks.

(t) (1) "Storage" or "store" means the containment, handling, or treatment of hazardous substances, either on a temporary basis or for a period of years.

(2) "Storage" or "store" does not include the storage of hazardous wastes in an underground storage tank if the person operating the tank has been issued a hazardous waste facilities permit by the department pursuant to Section 25200 or 25201.6 or granted interim status under Section 25200.5.

(3) "Storage" or "store" does not include the storage of hazardous wastes in an underground storage tank if all of the following apply:

(A) The facility has been issued a unified program facility permit pursuant to Section 25404.2 for generation, treatment, accumulation, or storage of hazardous waste in a tank.

(B) The tank is located in an underground area, as defined in Section 280.12 of Title 40 of the Code of Federal Regulations.

(C) The tank is subject to Chapter 6.67 (commencing with Section 25270).

(D) The tank complies with the hazardous waste tank standards pursuant to Article 10 (commencing with Section 66265.190) of Chapter 15 of Title 22 of the California Code of Regulations.

(4) "Storage" or "store" does not include the storage of hazardous wastes in an underground storage tank if all of the following apply:

(A) The facility has been issued a unified program facility permit pursuant to Section 25404.2 for generation, treatment, accumulation, or storage of hazardous waste in a tank.

(B) The tank is located in a structure that is at least 10 percent below the ground surface, including, but not limited to, a basement, cellar, shaft, pit, or vault.

(C) The structure in which the tank is located, at a minimum, provides for secondary containment of the contents of the tank, piping, and ancillary equipment, until cleanup occurs.

(D) The tank complies with the hazardous waste tank standards pursuant to Article 10 (commencing with Section 66265.190) of Chapter 15 of Title 22 of the California Code of Regulations.

(u) "Tank" means a stationary device designed to contain an accumulation of hazardous substances which is constructed primarily of nonearthen materials, including, but not limited to, wood, concrete, steel, or plastic that provides structural support.

(v) "Tank integrity test" means a test method capable of detecting an unauthorized release from an underground storage tank consistent with the minimum standards adopted by the board.

(w) "Tank tester" means an individual who performs tank integrity tests on underground storage tanks.

(x) "Unauthorized release" means any release of any hazardous substance that does not conform to this chapter, including an unauthorized release specified in Section 25295.5.

(y) (1) "Underground storage tank" means any one or combination of tanks, including pipes connected thereto, that is used for the storage of hazardous substances and that is substantially or totally beneath the surface of the ground. "Underground storage tank" does not include any of the following:

(A) A tank with a capacity of 1,100 gallons or less that is located on a farm and that stores motor vehicle fuel used primarily for agricultural purposes and not for resale.

(B) A tank that is located on a farm or at the residence of a person, that has a capacity of 1,100 gallons or less, and that stores home heating oil for consumptive use on the premises where stored.

(C) Structures, such as sumps, separators, storm drains, catch basins, oil field gathering lines, refinery pipelines, lagoons, evaporation ponds, well cellars, separation sumps, and lined and unlined pits, sumps, and lagoons. A sump that is a part of a monitoring system required under Section 25290.1, 25290.2, 25291, or 25292 and sumps or other structures defined as underground storage tanks under the federal act are not exempted by this subparagraph.

(D) A tank holding hydraulic fluid for a closed loop mechanical system that uses compressed air or hydraulic fluid to operate lifts, elevators, and other similar devices.

(E) A tank in an underground area, as defined in Section 25270.2, and associated piping, that is subject to Chapter 6.67 (commencing with Section 25270).

(2) Structures identified in subparagraphs (C) and (D) of paragraph (1) may be regulated by the board and any regional board pursuant to the Porter-Cologne Water Quality Control Act (Division 7 (commencing with Section 13000) of the Water Code) to ensure that they do not pose a threat to water quality.

(z) "Underground tank system" or "tank system" means an underground storage tank, connected piping, ancillary equipment, and containment system, if any.

(aa) (1) "Unified program facility" means all contiguous land and structures, other appurtenances, and improvements on the land that are subject to the requirements of paragraph (3) of subdivision (c) of Section 25404.

(2) "Unified program facility permit" means a permit issued pursuant to Chapter 6.11 (commencing with Section 25404), and that encompasses the permitting requirements of Section 25284.

(3) "Permit" means a permit issued pursuant to Section 25284 or a unified program facility permit as defined in paragraph (2).

Added Stats 1983 ch 1046 § 3. Amended and renumbered by Stats 1984 ch 1038 § 2. Amended Stats 1986 ch 935 § 1, ch 1390 § 1, effective September 30, 1986, operative until January 1, 1987, ch 1390 § 2, effective September 30, 1986, operative January 1, 1987; Stats 1987 ch 1372 § 1; Stats 1989 ch 1397 § 3; 1991 Governor's Reorganization Plan No. 1 § 10, effective July 17, 1991; Stats 1991 ch 1138 § 1 (AB 1954); Stats 1992 ch 654 § 2 (AB 3089), effective September 12, 1992; Stats 1993 ch 432 § 2 (AB 1061), effective September 24, 1993; Stats 1994 ch 1200 § 35 (SB 469), effective September 30, 1994; Stats 1995 ch 639 § 52 (SB 1191); Stats 1999 ch 328 § 1 (SB 665); Stats 2002 ch 999 § 11 (AB 2481); Stats 2003 ch 42 § 4 (AB 1702), effective July 7, 2003, ch 341 § 1 (SB 1002), effective September 8, 2003; Stats 2012 ch 532 § 7 (AB 1566), effective January 1, 2013, ch 536 § 1.5 (AB 1701), effective January 1, 2013; Stats 2015 ch 452 § 9 (SB 612), effective January 1, 2016; Stat 2022 ch 258 § 72 (AB 2327), effective January 1, 2023, operative January 1, 2024.

Appendix

Chapter 6.95

Hazardous Materials Release Response Plans and Inventory

Article 2

Hazardous Materials Management

§ 25536.7. Skilled and trained workforce required; Instruction and training; Apprenticeships; Applicability

(a) (1) An owner or operator of a stationary source that is engaged in activities described in Code 324110 or 325110 of the North American Industry Classification System (NAICS), as that code read on January 1, 2014, and with one or more covered processes that is required to prepare and submit an RMP pursuant to this article, when contracting for the performance of construction, alteration, demolition, installation, repair, or maintenance work at the stationary source, shall require that its contractors and any subcontractors use a skilled and trained workforce to perform all onsite work within an apprenticeable occupation in the building and construction trades. This section shall not apply to oil and gas extraction operations.

(2) The Chief of the Division of Apprenticeship Standards of the Department of Industrial Relations may approve a curriculum of in-person classroom and laboratory instruction for approved advanced safety training for workers at high hazard facilities. That safety training may be provided by an apprenticeship program approved by the chief or by instruction provided by the Chancellor of the California Community Colleges. The chief shall approve a curriculum in accordance with this paragraph by January 1, 2016, and shall periodically revise the curriculum to reflect current best practices. Upon receipt of certification from the apprenticeship program or community college, the chief shall issue a certificate to a worker who completes the approved curriculum.

(3) For purposes of paragraph (2) of subdivision (b) of Section 3075 of the Labor Code, a stationary source covered by this section shall be considered in determining whether existing apprenticeship programs do not have the capacity, or have neglected or refused, to dispatch sufficient apprentices to qualified employers who are willing to abide by the applicable apprenticeship standards.

(4) This section does not apply to contracts awarded before January 1, 2014, unless the contract is extended or renewed after that date.

(5) (A) This section does not apply to the employees of the owner or operator of the stationary source or prevent the owner or operator of the stationary source from using its own employees to perform any

work that has not been assigned to contractors while the employees of the contractor are present and working.

(B) An apprenticeship program approved by the chief may enroll, with advanced standing, applicants with relevant prior work experience at a stationary source that is subject to this section, in accordance with the approved apprenticeship standards of the program.

(6) The criteria of subparagraph (A) of paragraph (10) of subdivision (b), subparagraph (C) of paragraph (10) of subdivision (b), and subparagraph (B) of paragraph (11) of subdivision (b) shall not apply to either of the following:

(A) To the extent that the contractor has requested qualified workers from the local hiring halls that dispatch workers in the apprenticeable occupation and, due to workforce shortages, the contractor is unable to obtain sufficient qualified workers within 48 hours of the request, Saturdays, Sundays, and holidays excepted. This section does not prevent contractors from obtaining workers from any source.

(B) To the extent that compliance is impracticable because an emergency requires immediate action to prevent harm to public health or safety or to the environment, but the criteria applies as soon as the emergency is over or it becomes practicable for contractors to obtain a qualified workforce.

(7) The requirement specified in paragraph (1) for a skilled and trained workforce, as defined in paragraph (11) of subdivision (b), apply to each individual contractor's and subcontractor's onsite workforce.

(8) This section does not make the construction, alteration, demolition, installation, repair, or maintenance work at a stationary source that is subject to this section a public work, within the meaning of Chapter 1 (commencing with Section 1720) of Part 7 of Division 2 of the Labor Code. This section does not preclude the use of an alternative workweek schedule adopted pursuant to Section 511 or 514 of the Labor Code.

(b) As used in this section:

(1) "Apprenticeable occupation" means an occupation for which the chief has approved an apprenticeship program pursuant to Section 3075 of the Labor Code.

(2) "Approved advanced safety training for workers at high hazard facilities" means a curriculum approved by the chief pursuant to paragraph (2) of subdivision (a).

(3) "Building and construction trades" has the same meaning as in Section 3075.5 of the Labor Code.

(4) "Chief" means the Chief of the Division of Apprenticeship Standards of the Department of Industrial Relations.

(5) "Construction," "alteration," "demolition," "installation," "repair," and "maintenance" have the same meanings as in Sections 1720 and 1771 of the Labor Code.

(6) "Graduate of an apprenticeship program" means either of the following:

(A) An individual that has been issued a certificate of completion under the authority of the California Apprenticeship Council or the chief for completing an apprenticeship program approved by the chief pursuant to Section 3075 of the Labor Code.

(B) An individual that has completed an apprenticeship program located outside California and approved for federal purposes pursuant to the apprenticeship regulations adopted by the federal Secretary of Labor.

(7) "Onsite work" shall not include catalyst handling and loading, chemical cleaning, or inspection and testing that was not within the scope of a prevailing wage determination issued by the Director of Industrial Relations as of January 1, 2013.

(8) "Prevailing hourly wage rate" means the general prevailing rate of per diem wages, as determined by the Director of Industrial Relations pursuant to Sections 1773 and 1773.9 of the Labor Code, but does not include shift differentials, travel and subsistence, or holiday pay. Notwithstanding subdivision (c) of Section 1773.1 of the Labor Code, the requirement that employer payments not reduce the obligation to pay the hourly straight time or overtime wages found to be prevailing does not apply if otherwise provided in a bona fide collective bargaining agreement covering the worker.

(9) "Registered apprentice" means an apprentice registered in an apprenticeship program approved by the chief pursuant to Section 3075 of the Labor Code who is performing work covered by the standards of that apprenticeship program and receiving the supervision required by the standards of that apprenticeship program.

(10) "Skilled journeyperson" means a worker who meets all of the following criteria:

(A) The worker either graduated from an apprenticeship program for the applicable occupation that was approved by the chief, or has at least as many hours of on-the-job experience in the applicable occupation that would be required to graduate from an apprenticeship program for the applicable occupation that is approved by the chief.

(B) The worker is being paid at least a rate equivalent to the prevailing hourly wage rate for a journeyperson in the applicable occupation and geographic area.

(C) The worker has completed within the prior three calendar years at least 20 hours of approved advanced safety training for workers at high hazard facilities. This requirement applies only to work performed on or after July 1, 2018.

(11) "Skilled and trained workforce" means a workforce that meets both of the following criteria:

(A) All the workers are either registered apprentices or skilled journeypersons.

(B) (i) As of January 1, 2014, at least 30 percent of the skilled journeypersons are graduates of an apprenticeship program for the applicable occupation.

(ii) As of January 1, 2015, at least 45 percent of the skilled journeypersons are graduates of an apprenticeship program for the applicable occupation.

(iii) As of January 1, 2016, at least 60 percent of the skilled journeypersons are graduates of an apprenticeship program for the applicable occupation.

Added Stats 2013 ch 795 § 2 (SB 54), effective January 1, 2014. Amended Stats 2016 ch 774 § 3 (SB 693), effective January 1, 2017. Stats 2017 ch 608 § 1 (AB 55), effective January 1, 2018. Stats 2018 ch 704 § 16 (AB 235), effective September 22, 2018; Stats 2019 § 165 (AB 991), effective January 1, 2020.

§ 25536.9. Filing requirement for owner or operator claiming exemption

On or before February 1, 2018, an owner or operator of a stationary source that claims that it is exempt from the requirement in paragraph (1) of subdivision (a) of Section 25536.7 pursuant to the exception in paragraph (4) of subdivision (a) of Section 25536.7 shall file with the unified program agency a complete copy of the contract described in paragraph (4) of subdivision (a) of Section 25536.7 and a second copy of that contract that has been redacted only to the extent necessary to protect sensitive information and that shall include the identity of the contractor, the scope of the work covered by the contract, the date of execution of the contract, and the term of the contract. The complete copy of the contract that is not redacted is not a public record and shall be kept confidential by the unified program agency. The redacted copy of the contract shall be a public record available for inspection from the unified program agency.

Added Stats 2017 ch 608 § 2 (AB 55), effective January 1, 2018; Amended stats 2021 ch 115 § 48 (AB 148), effective July 22, 2021.

Chapter 10.35

Asbestos and Hazardous Substance Removal Contracts

§ 25914. Legislative findings and declarations

The Legislature hereby finds and declares that it is the public policy of the state to ensure that work performed on behalf of the public or private entity or person be done properly to safeguard the public health and safety when removing asbestos and hazardous substances.

Added Stats 1991 ch 789 § 1 (AB 1639).

§ 25914.1. Definitions

For purposes of this chapter, the following definitions shall apply:

(a) "Asbestos" has the same meaning as defined in Section 6501.7 of the Labor Code.

(b) "Asbestos–related work," is defined in Chapter 6 (commencing with Section 6500) of Part 1 of Division 5 of the Labor Code, including Section 6501.8 of the Labor Code, and involves 100–square feet or more of surface area of asbestos–containing material and is such that it requires that the contractor who performs the work must be certified in accordance with subdivision (a) of Section 7058.5 of the Business and Professions Code.

(c) "Hazardous substance removal" has the same meaning as used in Section 7058.7 of the Business and Professions Code.

Added Stats 1991 ch 789 § 1 (AB 1639).

§ 25914.2. Separate contract for undisclosed presence; Continuance of work in unaffected areas; Emergency condition

(a) All asbestos–related work and hazardous substance removal shall be performed pursuant to a contract separate from any other work to be performed, when the presence of asbestos or hazardous substances is not disclosed in the bid or contract documents.

(b) All asbestos–related and hazardous substance removal work which is disclosed in the bid or contract documents shall not require a separate contract from any other work to be performed.

(c) In the event the contractor encounters on the site materials he or she reasonably believes to be asbestos or a hazardous substance, and the asbestos or hazardous substance has not been rendered harmless, the contractor may continue work in unaffected areas reasonably believed safe, and shall immediately cease work on the area affected and report the condition to the owner, or the owner's representative, or architect in writing.

(d) With regard to a public entity, if an emergency condition arises, as defined in Section 10122 or 22035 of the Public Contract Code, then all asbestos–related and hazardous substance removal shall be contracted and performed pursuant to Section 10122 or 22035 of the Public Contract Code, respectively. Contractors performing the work shall have all registration and certificates required pursuant to the Labor Code and the Business and Professions Code.

Added Stats 1991 ch 789 § 1 (AB 1639).

§ 25914.3. Uncertified contractor

Notwithstanding any other provision of law, a contractor who is not certified pursuant to Section 7058.6 of the Business and Professions Code may bid on a project involving asbestos related work so long as the asbestos–related work is performed by a contractor who is registered pursuant to Section 6501.5 of the Labor Code and certified pursuant to Section 7058.6 of the Business and Professions Code.

Added Stats 1991 ch 789 § 1 (AB 1639).

Division 103 Disease Prevention and Health Promotion

PART 5

ENVIRONMENTAL AND OCCUPATIONAL EPIDEMIOLOGY

Chapter 4

Residential Lead-Based Paint Hazard Reduction

§ 105250.5. Review and amendment of regulations governing lead-related construction work; Certifications or accreditation fees

(a) The department shall review and amend its regulations governing lead-related construction work, including training and certification for workers and accreditation for trainers in lead-safe work practices to comply with regulations adopted pursuant to Sections 105250 and 124160 and the United States Environmental Protection Agency's Lead Renovation, Repair and Painting Rule (40 C.F.R. 745).

(b) The amended regulations adopted pursuant to subdivision (a) shall include, but not be limited to, requiring a copy of the worker and firm certification to be provided before the start of the job to the prime contractor or other employers on the site and to be posted on the job site beside the Division of Occupational Safety and Health Lead-Work Pre-Job Notification required by subdivision (p) of Section 1532.1 of Title 8 of the California Code of Regulations.

(c) Consistent with Section 105250, the department shall also adopt regulations establishing fees for the certifications or accreditations established pursuant to this section. The fees imposed under this section shall be established at levels not exceeding an amount sufficient to cover the costs of developing, administering, and enforcing the standards and regulations adopted under this section. The fees estab-

Appendix

lished pursuant to this section shall be deposited into the Lead-Related Construction Fund, established pursuant to Section 105250.

(d)(1) Notwithstanding the rulemaking provisions of the Administrative Procedure Act (Chapter 3.5 (commencing with Section 11340) of Part 1 of Division 3 of Title 2 of the Government Code), the department may implement and administer this section through all-county letters or similar instructions from the department until regulations are adopted. The department shall adopt emergency regulations implementing these provisions. The department may readopt any emergency regulation authorized by this section that is the same as, or substantially equivalent to, an emergency regulation previously adopted under this section.

(2) The initial adoption of emergency regulations pursuant to this section and two readoptions of emergency regulations shall be deemed an emergency and necessary for the immediate preservation of the public peace, health, safety, or general welfare. Initial emergency regulations and the two readoptions of emergency regulations authorized by this section shall be exempt from review by the Office of Administrative Law. The initial emergency regulations and the two readoptions of emergency regulations authorized by this section shall be submitted to the Office of Administrative Law for filing with the Secretary of State, and each shall remain in effect for no more than 180 days, by which time final regulations may be adopted.

Added Stats 2022 ch 507 § 1 (SB 1076), effective January 1, 2023.

§ 105254. Types of lead construction work requiring certification

(a) The following persons engaged in the following types of lead construction work shall have a certificate:

(1) Persons who receive pay for doing lead hazard evaluations, including, but not limited to, lead inspections, lead risk assessments, or lead clearance inspections, in residential or public buildings.

(2) Persons preparing or designing plans for the abatement of lead-based paint or lead hazards from residential or public buildings.

(3) Persons doing work designed to reduce or eliminate lead hazards on a permanent basis (to last 20 years or more) from residential or public buildings.

(4) Persons inspecting for lead or doing lead abatement activities in a public elementary school, preschool, or day care center.

(5) Persons doing lead-related construction work in a residential or public building that will expose a person to airborne lead at or above the eight-hour permissible exposure limit of 50 micrograms per cubic meter.

(b) On and after January 1, 2024, the following shall also have a certificate: a firm, as defined by Section 745.83 of Title 40 of the Code of Federal Regulations, and at least one person onsite and employed by a firm, doing renovation, repair, or painting work for compensation in a residential or public building that will disturb lead-based paint, as defined in Section 35033 of Title 17 of the California Code of Regulations, or presumed lead-based paint, as defined in Section 35043 of Title 17 of the California Code of Regulations, which regulations were adopted by the State Department of Public Health pursuant to Sections 105250 and 124160.

(c) Persons performing routine maintenance and repairs in housing are not required to have a certificate if they are not performing any of the activities listed under subdivisions (a) and (b).

(d) The department may adopt regulations to modify certification requirements for persons engaged in lead construction work based on changes to state or federal law, or programmatic need.

(e) The department or any local enforcement agency may, consistent with Section 17972, enter, inspect, and photograph any premises where abatement, a lead hazard evaluation, or renovation, repair, or painting is being conducted or has been ordered, enter the place of business of any person who conducts abatement, lead hazard evaluations, or renovation, repair, or painting, and inspect and copy any business record of any person who conducts abatement, lead hazard evaluation, or renovation, repair, or painting to determine whether the person is complying with this section.

(f) (1) A violation of subdivision (a) shall be punishable by a civil penalty of no less than five thousand dollars ($5,000) per violation per day.

(2) A violation of subdivision (b) shall be punishable by a civil penalty of no less than ten thousand dollars ($10,000) per violation per day.

(3) Each subsequent violation of this section may be subject to imposition of a civil penalty of no more than thirty-seven thousand five hundred dollars ($37,500) per violation per day or punishable by imprisonment for no more than six months in the county jail, a fine of no more than one thousand dollars ($1,000), or by both that imprisonment and fine. In assessing the amount of the criminal or civil penalty, any one or more of the relevant circumstances shall be considered: the nature and seriousness of the misconduct, the number of violations, the persistence of the misconduct, the length of time over which the misconduct occurred, the willfulness of the misconduct, and the violator's assets, liabilities, net worth, and other relevant factors.

(g) (1) The State Department of Public Health shall develop and implement an education and outreach program for every person and firm that is required to have a certificate pursuant to subdivisions (a) and (b). The program shall include information on who is required to have a certificate and the requirements and process to obtain a certificate. The program shall be implemented on or before July 1, 2023.

Appendix

(2)   The   department   shall   provide   educational   and   outreach materials to the Contractors State License Board for the board
to make the materials available to contractors and consumers on its
internet website.

Added Stats 2002 ch 931 § 7 (SB 460). Amended Stats 2022 ch 507 § 2 (SB 1076),
effective January 1, 2023.

DIVISION 104

ENVIRONMENTAL HEALTH

PART 10

RECREATIONAL SAFETY

Chapter 5

Safe Recreational Water Use

Article 2.5

The Swimming Pool Safety Act

§ 115920. Citation

This act shall be known and may be cited as the Swimming Pool
Safety Act.

Added Stats 1996 ch 925 [§ 3] (AB 3305).

§ 115921. Definitions

As used in this article the following terms have the following meanings:

(a) "Swimming pool" or "pool" means any structure intended for
swimming or recreational bathing that contains water over 18 inches
deep. "Swimming pool" includes in-ground and aboveground structures and includes, but is not limited to, hot tubs, spas, portable spas,
and nonportable wading pools.

(b) "Public swimming pool" means a swimming pool operated for the
use of the general public with or without charge, or for the use of the
members and guests of a private club. Public swimming pool does not
include a swimming pool located on the grounds of a private single-
family home.

(c) "Enclosure" means a fence, wall, or other barrier that isolates a
swimming pool from access to the home.

(d) "Approved safety pool cover" means a manually or power-operated safety pool cover that meets all of the performance standards of the American Society for Testing and Materials (ASTM), in compliance with standard F1346–91.

(e) "Exit alarms" means devices that make audible, continuous alarm sounds when any door or window, that permits access from the residence to the pool area that is without any intervening enclosure, is opened or is left ajar. Exit alarms may be battery operated or may be connected to the electrical wiring of the building.

(f) "ANSI/APSP performance standard" means a standard that is accredited by the American National Standards Institute (ANSI) and published by the Association of Pool and Spa Professionals (APSP).

(g) "Suction outlet" means a fitting or fixture typically located at the bottom or on the sides of a swimming pool that conducts water to a recirculating pump.

Added Stats 1996 ch 925 § 3.5 (AB 3305). Amended Stats 2012 ch 679 § 1 (AB 2114), effective January 1, 2013.

§ 115922. Safety features; inspection

(a) Commencing January 1, 2007, except as provided in Section 115925, whenever a building permit is issued for construction of a new swimming pool or spa, or any building permit is issued for remodeling of an existing pool or spa, at a private, single-family home, it shall be equipped with at least one of the following seven drowning prevention safety features:

(1) The pool shall be isolated from access to a home by an enclosure that meets the requirements of Section 115923.

(2) The pool shall incorporate removable mesh pool fencing that meets American Society for Testing and Materials (ASTM) Specifications F 2286 standards in conjunction with a gate that is self-closing and self-latching and can accommodate a key lockable device.

(3) The pool shall be equipped with an approved safety pool cover that meets all requirements of the ASTM Specifications F 1346.

(4) The residence shall be equipped with exit alarms on those doors providing direct access to the pool.

(5) All doors providing direct access from the home to the swimming pool shall be equipped with a self-closing, self-latching device with a release mechanism placed no lower than 54 inches above the floor.

(6) Swimming pool alarms that, when placed in pools, will sound upon detection of accidental or unauthorized entrance into the water. These pool alarms shall meet and be independently certified to the ASTM Standard F 2208 "Standards Specification for Pool Alarms" which includes surface motion, pressure, sonar, laser, and infrared type alarms. For purposes of this article, "swimming pool alarms" shall not include swimming protection alarm devices designed for in-

Appendix

dividual use, such as an alarm attached to a child that sounds when the child exceeds a certain distance or becomes submerged in water.

(7) Other means of protection, if the degree of protection afforded is equal to or greater than that afforded by any of the devices set forth above, and have been independently verified by an approved testing laboratory as meeting standards for those devices established by the ASTM or the American Society of Mechanical Engineers (ASME).

(b) Prior to the issuance of any final approval for the completion of permitted construction or remodeling work, the local building code official shall inspect the drowning safety prevention devices required by this act and if no violations are found, shall give final approval.

Added Stats 1996 ch 925 [§ 3] (AB 3305). Amended Stats 2006 ch 478 § 2 (AB 2977), effective January 1, 2007.

§ 115923. Enclosure

An enclosure shall have all of the following characteristics:

(a) Any access gates through the enclosure open away from the swimming pool, and are self–closing with a self–latching device placed no lower than 60 inches above the ground.

(b) A minimum height of 60 inches.

(c) A maximum vertical clearance from the ground to the bottom of the enclosure of two inches.

(d) Gaps or voids, if any, do not allow passage of a sphere equal to or greater than four inches in diameter.

(e) An outside surface free of protrusions, cavities, or other physical characteristics that would serve as handholds or footholds that could enable a child below the age of five years to climb over.

Added Stats 1996 ch 925 [§ 3] (AB 3305).

§ 115924. Consumer notice; Availability of information on Web site

(a) Any person entering into an agreement to build a swimming pool or spa, or to engage in permitted work on a pool or spa covered by this article, shall give the consumer notice of the requirements of this article.

(b) Pursuant to existing law, the Department of Health Services shall have available on the department's Web site, commencing January 1, 2007, approved pool safety information available for consumers to download. Pool contractors are encouraged to share this information with consumers regarding the potential dangers a pool or spa poses to toddlers. Additionally, pool contractors may provide the consumer with swimming pool safety materials produced from organizations such as the United States Consumer Product Safety Commission, Drowning Prevention Foundation, California Coalition for Children's Safety & Health, Safe Kids Worldwide, Association of Pool and Spa Professionals, or the American Academy of Pediatrics.

Added Stats 1996 ch 925 [§ 3] (AB 3305). Amended Stats 2006 ch 478 § 3 (AB 2977), effective January 1, 2007.

§ 115925. Inapplicability

The requirements of this article shall not apply to any of the following:
(a) Public swimming pools.
(b) Hot tubs or spas with locking safety covers that comply with the American Society for Testing Materials–Emergency Performance Specification (ASTM–ES 13–89).
(c) Any pool within the jurisdiction of any political subdivision that adopts an ordinance for swimming pool safety that includes requirements that are at least as stringent as this article.
(d) An apartment complex, or any residential setting other than a single–family home.

Added Stats 1996 ch 925 [§ 3] (AB 3305).

§ 115926. State social services

This article does not apply to any facility regulated by the State Department of Social Services even if the facility is also used as the private residence of the operator. Pool safety in those facilities shall be regulated pursuant to regulations adopted therefor by the State Department of Social Services.

Added Stats 1996 ch 925 [§ 3] (AB 3305).

§ 115927. Interpretation

Notwithstanding any other provision of law, this article shall not be subject to further modification or interpretation by any regulatory agency of the state, this authority being reserved exclusively to local jurisdictions, as provided for in subdivision (e) of Section 115922 and subdivision (c) of Section 115924.

Added Stats 1996 ch 925 [§ 3] (AB 3305).

Appendix

§ 115928. New swimming pool or spa construction standards

Whenever a building permit is issued for the construction of a new swimming pool or spa, the pool or spa shall meet all of the following requirements:
(a) (1) The suction outlets of the pool or spa for which the permit is issued shall be equipped to provide circulation throughout the pool or spa as prescribed in paragraphs (2) and (3).
(2) The swimming pool or spa shall either have at least two circulation suction outlets per pump that shall be hydraulically balanced and symmetrically plumbed through one or more "T" fittings, and

that are separated by a distance of at least three feet in any dimension between the suction outlets, or be designed to use alternatives to suction outlets, including, but not limited to, skimmers or perimeter overflow systems to conduct water to the recirculation pump.

(3) The circulation system shall have the capacity to provide a complete turnover of pool water, as specified in Section 3124B of Chapter 31B of the California Building Standards Code (Title 24 of the California Code of Regulations).

(b) Suction outlets shall be covered with antientrapment grates, as specified in the ANSI/APSP-16 performance standard or successor standard designated by the federal Consumer Product Safety Commission, that cannot be removed except with the use of tools. Slots or openings in the grates or similar protective devices shall be of a shape, area, and arrangement that would prevent physical entrapment and would not pose any suction hazard to bathers.

(c) Any backup safety system that an owner of a new swimming pool or spa may choose to install in addition to the requirements set forth in subdivisions (a) and (b) shall meet the standards as published in the document, "Guidelines for Entrapment Hazards: Making Pools and Spas Safer," Publication Number 363, March 2005, United States Consumer Product Safety Commission.

Added Stats 2002 ch 679 § 1 (SB 1726). Amended Stats 2003 ch 62 § 194 (SB 600); Stats 2006 ch 478 § 4 (AB 2977), effective January 1, 2007; Stats 2007 ch 596 § 19 (AB 382), effective January 1, 2008; Stats 2012 ch 679 § 2 (AB 2114), effective January 1, 2013.

§ 115928.5. Issuance of building permit for remodeling or modification of an existing swimming pool, toddler pool, or spa

Whenever a building permit is issued for the remodel or modification of an existing swimming pool, toddler pool, or spa, the permit shall require that the suction outlet or suction outlets of the existing swimming pool, toddler pool, or spa be upgraded so as to be equipped with antientrapment grates, as specified in the ANSI/APSP-16 performance standard or a successor standard designated by the federal Consumer Product Safety Commission.

Added Stats 2007 ch 596 § 20 (AB 382), effective January 1, 2008. Amended Stats 2012 ch 679 § 3 (AB 2114), effective January 1, 2013.

Article 5

Swimming Pool Sanitation

§ 116064. Public wading pool safety devices

(a) As used in this section the following words have the following meanings:

(1) (A) "Public wading pool" means a pool that meets all of the following criteria:

(i) It has a maximum water depth not exceeding 18 inches.

(ii) It is a pool other than a pool that is located on the premises of a one-unit or two-unit residence, intended solely for the use of the residents or guests.

(B) "Public wading pool" includes, but is not limited to, a pool owned or operated by private persons or agencies, or by state or local governmental agencies.

(C) "Public wading pool" includes, but is not limited to, a pool located in an apartment house, hotel, or similar setting, that is intended for the use of residents or guests.

(2) "Alteration" means any of the following:

(A) To change, modify, or rearrange the structural parts or the design.

(B) To enlarge.

(C) To move the location of.

(D) To install a new water circulation system.

(E) To make any repairs costing fifty dollars ($50) or more to an existing circulation system.

(3) "ANSI/APSP performance standard" means a standard that is accredited by the American National Standards Institute (ANSI) and published by the Association of Pool and Spa Professionals (APSP).

(4) "Suction outlet" means a fitting or fixture typically located at the bottom or on the sides of a swimming pool that conducts water to a recirculating pump.

(b) A public wading pool shall have at least two circulation suction outlets per pump that are hydraulically balanced and symmetrically plumbed through one or more "T" fittings, and are separated by a distance of at least three feet in any dimension between the suction outlets.

(c) All public wading pool suction outlets shall be covered with antivortex grates or similar protective devices. All suction outlets shall be covered with grates or antivortex plates that cannot be removed except with the use of tools. Slots or openings in the grates or similar protective devices shall be of a shape, area, and arrangement that would prevent physical entrapment and would not pose any suction hazard to bathers.

Appendix

(d) (1) The State Department of Health Services may adopt regulations pursuant to this section.

(2) The regulations may include, but not be limited to, standards permitting the use of alternative devices or safeguards, or incorporating new technologies, that produce, at a minimum, equivalent protection against entrapment and suction hazard, whenever these devices, safeguards, or technologies become available to the public.

(3) Regulations adopted pursuant to this section constitute building standards and shall be forwarded pursuant to Section 11343 of the Government Code to the California Building Standards Commission for approval as set forth in Section 18907 of the Health and Safety Code.

(e) The California Building Standards Commission shall approve the building standards as set forth in this section and publish them in the California Building Standards Code by November 1, 1999. The commission shall publish the text of this section in Title 24 of the California Code of Regulations, Part 2, Chapter 31B, requirements for public swimming pools, with the following note: "NOTE: These building standards are in statute but have not been adopted through the regulatory process." Enforcement of the standards set forth in this section does not depend upon adoption of regulations, therefore, enforcement agencies shall enforce the standards pursuant to the timeline set forth in this section prior to adoption of related regulations.

(f) The maximum velocity in the pump suction hydraulic system shall not exceed six feet per second when 100 percent of the pump's flow comes from the circulation system and any suction outlet in the system is completely blocked.

(g) On and after January 1, 1998, all newly constructed public wading pools shall be constructed in compliance with this section.

(h) Commencing January 1, 1998, whenever a construction permit is issued for alteration of an existing public wading pool, it shall be retrofitted so as to be in compliance with this section.

(i) By January 1, 2000, every public wading pool, regardless of the date of original construction, shall be retrofitted to comply with this section.

Added Stats 1997 ch 913 § 2 (SB 873). Amended Stats 2012 ch 295 § 4 (SB 1099), effective January 1, 2013, ch 679 § 4.5 (AB 2114), effective January 1, 2013.

§ 116064.1. [Section repealed 2012.]

Added Stats 2009 ch 267 § 2 (AB 1020), effective January 1, 2010. Repealed Stats 2012 ch 23 § 30 (AB 1467), effective June 27, 2012. The repealed section related to Legislative findings and declarations.

§ 116064.2. Anti-entrapment devices or systems as applicable standard; Deadline for installation; Alternative devices or systems; New construction; Retrofitting; Compliance and documentation; Enforcement

(a) As used in this section, the following words have the following meanings:

(1) "ANSI/APSP performance standard" means a standard that is accredited by the American National Standards Institute (ANSI) and published by the Association of Pool and Spa Professionals (APSP).

(2) "ASME/ANSI performance standard" means a standard that is accredited by the American National Standards Institute and published by the American Society of Mechanical Engineers.

(3) "ASTM performance standard" means a standard that is developed and published by ASTM International.

(4) "Public swimming pool" means an outdoor or indoor structure, whether in-ground or above-ground, intended for swimming or recreational bathing, including a swimming pool, hot tub, spa, or nonportable wading pool, that is any of the following:

(A) Open to the public generally, whether for a fee or free of charge.

(B) Open exclusively to members of an organization and their guests, residents of a multiunit apartment building, apartment complex, residential real estate development, or other multifamily residential area, or patrons of a hotel or other public accommodations facility.

(C) Located on the premises of an athletic club, or public or private school.

(5) "Qualified individual" means a contractor who holds a current valid license issued by the State of California or a professional engineer licensed in the State of California who has experience working on public swimming pools.

(6) "Safety vacuum release system" means a vacuum release system that ceases operation of the pump, reverses the circulation flow, or otherwise provides a vacuum release at a suction outlet when a blockage is detected.

(7) "Skimmer equalizer line" means a suction outlet located below the waterline, typically on the side of the pool, and connected to the body of a skimmer that prevents air from being drawn into the pump if the water level drops below the skimmer weir. However, a skimmer equalizer line is not a suction outlet for purposes of subdivisions (c) and (d).

(8) "Suction outlet" means a fitting or fixture of a swimming pool that conducts water to a recirculating pump.

(9) "Unblockable suction outlet" means a suction outlet, including the sump, that has a perforated (open) area that cannot be shadowed by the area of the 18 inch by 23 inch Body Blocking Element of the

Appendix

ANSI/APSP-16 performance standard, and that the rated flow through any portion of the remaining open area cannot create a suction force in excess of the removal force values in Table 1 of that standard.

(b) (1) Subject to subdivision (e), every public swimming pool shall be equipped with antientrapment devices or systems that comply with the ANSI/APSP-16 performance standard or successor standard designated by the federal Consumer Product Safety Commission.

(2) A public swimming pool that has a suction outlet in any location other than on the bottom of the pool shall be designed so that the recirculation system shall have the capacity to provide a complete turnover of pool water within the following time:

(A) One-half hour or less for a spa pool.

(B) One-half hour or less for a spray ground.

(C) One hour or less for a wading pool.

(D) Two hours or less for a medical pool.

(E) Six hours or less for all other types of public pools.

(c) Subject to subdivisions (d) and (e), every public swimming pool with a single suction outlet that is not an unblockable suction outlet shall be equipped with at least one or more of the following devices or systems that are designed to prevent physical entrapment by pool drains:

(1) A safety vacuum release system that has been tested by a nationally recognized testing laboratory and found to conform to ASME/ANSI performance standard A112.19.17, as in effect on December 31, 2009, or ASTM performance standard F2387, as in effect on December 31, 2009.

(2) A suction-limiting vent system with a tamper-resistant atmospheric opening, provided that it conforms to any applicable ASME/ANSI or ASTM performance standard.

(3) A gravity drainage system that utilizes a collector tank, provided that it conforms to any applicable ASME/ANSI or ASTM performance standard.

(4) An automatic pump shutoff system tested by a department-approved independent third party and found to conform to any applicable ASME/ANSI or ASTM performance standard.

(5) Any other system that is deemed, in accordance with federal law, to be equally effective as, or more effective than, the systems described in paragraph (1) at preventing or eliminating the risk of injury or death associated with the circulation system of the pool and suction outlets.

(d) Every public swimming pool constructed on or after January 1, 2010, shall have at least two suction outlets per pump that are hydraulically balanced and symmetrically plumbed through one or more "T" fittings, and that are separated by a distance of at least three feet in any dimension between the suction outlets. A public swimming pool constructed on or after January 1, 2010, that meets the requirements of this subdivision, shall be exempt from the requirements of subdivision (c).

(e) A public swimming pool constructed prior to January 1, 2010, shall be retrofitted to comply with subdivisions (b) and (c) by no later than July 1, 2010, except that no further retrofitting is required for a public swimming pool that completed a retrofit between December 19, 2007, and January 1, 2010, that complied with the Virginia Graeme Baker Pool and Spa Safety Act (15 U.S.C. Sec. 8001 et seq.) as in effect on the date of issue of the construction permit, or for a nonportable wading pool that completed a retrofit prior to January 1, 2010, that complied with state law on the date of issue of the construction permit. A public swimming pool owner who meets the exception described in this subdivision shall do one of the following prior to September 30, 2010:

(1) File the form issued by the department pursuant to subdivision (f), as otherwise provided in subdivision (h).

(2) (A) File a signed statement attesting that the required work has been completed.

(B) Provide a document containing the name and license number of the qualified individual who completed the required work.

(C) Provide either a copy of the final building permit, if required by the local agency, or a copy of one of the following documents if no permit was required:

(i) A document that describes the modification in a manner that provides sufficient information to document the work that was done to comply with federal law.

(ii) A copy of the final paid invoice. The amount paid for the services may be omitted or redacted from the final invoice prior to submission.

(f) Prior to March 31, 2010, the department shall issue a form for use by an owner of a public swimming pool to indicate compliance with this section. The department shall consult with county health officers and directors of departments of environmental health in developing the form and shall post the form on the department's Internet Web site. The form shall be completed by the owner of a public swimming pool prior to filing the form with the appropriate city, county, or city and county department of environmental health. The form shall include, but not be limited to, the following information:

(1) A statement of whether the pool operates with a single suction outlet or multiple suction outlets that comply with subdivision (d).

(2) Identification of the type of antientrapment devices or systems that have been installed pursuant to subdivision (b) and the date or dates of installation.

(3) Identification of the type of devices or systems designed to prevent physical entrapment that have been installed pursuant to subdivision (c) in a public swimming pool with a single suction outlet that

is not an unblockable suction outlet and the date or dates of installation or the reason why the requirement is not applicable.

(4) A signature and license number of a qualified individual who certifies that the factual information provided on the form in response to paragraphs (1) to (3), inclusive, is true to the best of his or her knowledge.

(g) A qualified individual who improperly certifies information pursuant to paragraph (4) of subdivision (f) shall be subject to potential disciplinary action at the discretion of the licensing authority.

(h) Except as provided in subdivision (e), each public swimming pool owner shall file a completed copy of the form issued by the department pursuant to this section with the city, county, or city and county department of environmental health in the city, county, or city and county in which the swimming pool is located. The form shall be filed within 30 days following the completion of the swimming pool construction or installation required pursuant to this section or, if the construction or installation is completed prior to the date that the department issues the form pursuant to this section, within 30 days of the date that the department issues the form. The public swimming pool owner or operator shall not make a false statement, representation, certification, record, report, or otherwise falsify information that he or she is required to file or maintain pursuant to this section.

(i) In enforcing this section, health officers and directors of city, county, or city and county departments of environmental health shall consider documentation filed on or with the form issued pursuant to this section by the owner of a public swimming pool as evidence of compliance with this section. A city, county, or city and county department of environmental health may verify the accuracy of the information filed on or with the form.

(j) To the extent that the requirements for public wading pools imposed by Section 116064 conflict with this section, the requirements of this section shall prevail.

(k) The department shall have no authority to take any enforcement action against any person for violation of this section and has no responsibility to administer or enforce the provisions of this section.

Added Stats 2009 ch 267 § 3 (AB 1020), effective January 1, 2010. Amended Stats 2010 ch 328 § 135 (SB 1330), effective January 1, 2011; Stats 2012 ch 23 § 31 (AB 1467), effective June 27, 2012; ch 679 § 5 (AB 2114), effective January 1, 2013.

INSURANCE CODE

PART 3

LIABILITY, WORKERS' COMPENSATION, AND COMMON CARRIER LIABILITY INSURANCE

Chapter 2

Workers' Compensation Policies

Article 2

Policy Provisions

§ 11665. Insurance policy for contractor holding C-39 license

(a) An insurer who issues a workers' compensation insurance policy to a roofing contractor holding a C-39 license from the Contractors' State License Board shall perform an annual payroll audit for the contractor. This audit shall include an in-person visit to the place of business of the roofing contractor to verify whether the number of employees reported by the contractor is accurate. The insurer may impose a surcharge on each policyholder audited under this subdivision in an amount necessary to recoup the reasonable costs of conducting the annual payroll audits.

(b) The commissioner shall direct the rating organization designated as his or her statistical agent to compile pertinent statistical data on those holding C-39 licenses, as reported by the appropriate state entity, on an annual basis and provide a report to him or her each year. The data shall track the total annual payroll and loss data reported on those holding C-39 licenses in accordance with the standard workers' compensation insurance classifications applicable to roofing operations. The data shall include the number of employers, total payroll, total losses, and the losses per one hundred dollars ($100) of payroll by the employers' annual payroll intervals as follows:

1 to 4,999
5,000 to 9,999
10,000 to 14,999
15,000 to 19,999
20,000 to 24,999
25,000 to 29,999

Appendix

30,000 to 39,999
40,000 to 49,999
50,000 to 74,999
75,000 to 99,999
100,000 to 199,999
200,000 to 299,999
300,000 to 399,999
400,000 to 499,999
500,000 to 599,999
600,000 to 699,999
700,000 to 799,999
800,000 to 899,999
900,000 to 999,999
1,000,000 to 1,099,999
1,100,000 to 1,199,999
1,200,000 to 1,299,999
1,300,000 to 1,399,999
1,400,000 to 1,499,999
1,500,000 or more

The report shall also be provided to the Legislature by the commissioner, in compliance with Section 9795 of the Government Code.

Added Stats 2006 ch 38 § 3 (AB 881), effective January 1, 2007, repealed January 1, 2011. Amended Stats 2010 ch 423 § 3 (AB 2305), effective January 1, 2011, repealed January 1, 2013; Stats 2012 ch 389 § 3 (AB 2219), effective January 1, 2013; Stats 2013 ch 76 § 140 (AB 383), effective January 1, 2014.

Chapter 3

Regulation of Business of Workers' Compensation Insurance

Article 4

Penalties for Misrepresentation

§ 11760.1. Audit of employer; Failure to provide access to records; Costs

(a) If an employer fails to provide for access by the insurer or its authorized representative to its records, to enable the insurer to perform an audit to determine the remuneration earned by the employer's employees and by any of its uninsured subcontractors and the employees of any of its uninsured subcontractors during the policy period, the employer shall be liable to pay to the insurer a total premium for the policy equal to three times the insurer's then-current estimate of the annual premium on the expiration date of the policy. The employer shall also be liable, in addition to the premium, for costs incurred by the insurer in its attempts to perform an audit, after the insured has failed upon the insurer's third request during at least a 90-day period to provide access, and the insured has provided no compelling business reason for the failure. This section shall only apply if the insurer elects to comply with the conditions set forth in subdivision (d).

(b) "Access" shall mean access at any time during regular business hours during the policy period and within three years after the policy period ends. "Access" may also include any other time mutually agreed upon by the employer and insurer.

(c) The insurer shall have and follow regular and reasonable rules and procedures to notify employers of their duty to provide for access to records, and to contact employers to make appointments during regular business hours for that purpose.

(d) Upon the employer's failure to provide access after the insurer's third request during at least a 90-day period, the insurer may notify the employer through its mailing of a certified, return-receipt, document of the increased premium and the total amount of the costs incurred by the insurer for its attempts to perform an audit as described under subdivision (a). Upon the expiration of 30 days after the delivery of the notice, collection by the insurer of the amount of premium and costs described under subdivision (a), less all premiums previously paid by the employer for the policy, shall be fully enforceable and executable.

(e) If the employer provides for access to its records after having received the notice described in subdivision (d), and if the insurer then succeeds in performing the audit to its satisfaction, the insurer shall revise the total premium and costs payable for the policy by the employer to reflect the results of its audit.

Added Stats 2007 ch 615 § 1 (AB 812), effective January 1, 2008.

Appendix

LABOR CODE

DIVISION 1
DEPARTMENT OF INDUSTRIAL RELATIONS

Chapter 1
General Powers and Duties

§ 62.5. Workers' Compensation Administration Revolving Fund; Uninsured Employers Benefits Trust Fund; Subsequent Injuries Benefits Trust Fund; Occupational Safety and Health Fund; Labor Enforcement and Compliance Fund; Surcharges on employers

(a) (1) The Workers' Compensation Administration Revolving Fund is hereby created as a special account in the State Treasury. Money in the fund may be expended by the department, upon appropriation by the Legislature, for all of the following purposes, and may not be used or borrowed for any other purpose:

(A) For the administration of the workers' compensation program set forth in this division and Division 4 (commencing with Section 3200), other than the activities financed pursuant to paragraph (2) of subdivision (a) of Section 3702.5.

(B) For the Return-to-Work Program set forth in Section 139.48.

(C) For the enforcement of the insurance coverage program established and maintained by the Labor Commissioner pursuant to Section 90.3.

(2) The fund shall consist of surcharges made pursuant to paragraph (1) of subdivision (f).

(b) (1) The Uninsured Employers Benefits Trust Fund is hereby created as a special trust fund account in the State Treasury, of which the director is trustee, and its sources of funds are as provided in paragraph (1) of subdivision (f). Notwithstanding Section 13340 of the Government Code, the fund is continuously appropriated for the payment of nonadministrative expenses of the workers' compensation program for workers injured while employed by uninsured employers in accordance with Article 2 (commencing with Section 3710) of Chapter 4 of Part 1 of Division 4, and shall not be used for any other purpose. All moneys collected shall be retained in the trust fund until paid as benefits to workers injured while employed by uninsured employers. Nonadministrative expenses include audits and reports of services prepared pursuant to subdivision (b) of Section 3716.1. The surcharge amount for this fund shall be stated separately.

(2) Notwithstanding any other provision of law, all references to the Uninsured Employers Fund shall mean the Uninsured Employers Benefits Trust Fund.

(3) Notwithstanding paragraph (1), in the event that budgetary restrictions or impasse prevent the timely payment of administrative expenses from the Workers' Compensation Administration Revolving Fund, those expenses shall be advanced from the Uninsured Employers Benefits Trust Fund. Expense advances made pursuant to this paragraph shall be reimbursed in full to the Uninsured Employers Benefits Trust Fund upon enactment of the annual Budget Act.

(4) Any moneys from penalties collected pursuant to Section 3722 as a result of the insurance coverage program established under Section 90.3 shall be deposited in the State Treasury to the credit of the Workers' Compensation Administration Revolving Fund created under this section, to cover expenses incurred by the director under the insurance coverage program. The amount of any penalties in excess of payment of administrative expenses incurred by the director for the insurance coverage program established under Section 90.3 shall be deposited in the State Treasury to the credit of the Uninsured Employers Benefits Trust Fund for nonadministrative expenses, as prescribed in paragraph (1), and notwithstanding paragraph (1), shall only be available upon appropriation by the Legislature.

(c) (1) The Subsequent Injuries Benefits Trust Fund is hereby created as a special trust fund account in the State Treasury, of which the director is trustee, and its sources of funds are as provided in paragraph (1) of subdivision (f). Notwithstanding Section 13340 of the Government Code, the fund is continuously appropriated for the nonadministrative expenses of the workers' compensation program for workers who have suffered serious injury and who are suffering from previous and serious permanent disabilities or physical impairments, in accordance with Article 5 (commencing with Section 4751) of Chapter 2 of Part 2 of Division 4, and Section 4 of Article XIV of the California Constitution, and shall not be used for any other purpose. All moneys collected shall be retained in the trust fund until paid as benefits to workers who have suffered serious injury and who are suffering from previous and serious permanent disabilities or physical impairments. Nonadministrative expenses include audits and reports of services pursuant to subdivision (c) of Section 4755. The surcharge amount for this fund shall be stated separately.

(2) Notwithstanding any other law, all references to the Subsequent Injuries Fund shall mean the Subsequent Injuries Benefits Trust Fund.

(3) Notwithstanding paragraph (1), in the event that budgetary restrictions or impasse prevent the timely payment of administrative expenses from the Workers' Compensation Administration Revolving Fund, those expenses shall be advanced from the Subsequent Injuries

Benefits Trust Fund. Expense advances made pursuant to this paragraph shall be reimbursed in full to the Subsequent Injuries Benefits Trust Fund upon enactment of the annual Budget Act.

(d) (1) The Occupational Safety and Health Fund is hereby created as a special account in the State Treasury. Moneys in the account may be expended by the department, upon appropriation by the Legislature, for support of the Division of Occupational Safety and Health, the Occupational Safety and Health Standards Board, and the Occupational Safety and Health Appeals Board, and the activities these entities perform as set forth in this division, and Division 5 (commencing with Section 6300).

(2) On and after the effective date of the act amending this section to add this paragraph in the 2013-14 Regular Session of the Legislature, any moneys in the Cal-OSHA Targeted Inspection and Consultation Fund and any assets, liabilities, revenues, expenditures, and encumbrances of that fund, less five million dollars ($5,000,000), shall be transferred to the Occupational Safety and Health Fund. On June 30, 2014, the remaining five million dollars ($5,000,000) in the Cal-OSHA Targeted Inspection and Consultation Fund, or any remaining balance in that fund, shall be transferred to, and become part of, the Occupational Safety and Health Fund.

(e) The Labor Enforcement and Compliance Fund is hereby created as a special account in the State Treasury. Moneys in the fund may be expended by the department, upon appropriation by the Legislature, for the support of the activities that the Division of Labor Standards Enforcement performs pursuant to this division and Division 2 (commencing with Section 200), Division 3 (commencing with Section 2700), and Division 4 (commencing with Section 3200). The fund shall consist of surcharges imposed pursuant to paragraph (3) of subdivision (f).

(f) (1) Separate surcharges shall be levied by the director upon all employers, as defined in Section 3300, for purposes of deposit in the Workers' Compensation Administration Revolving Fund, the Uninsured Employers Benefits Trust Fund, the Subsequent Injuries Benefits Trust Fund, and the Occupational Safety and Health Fund. The total amount of the surcharges shall be allocated between self-insured employers and insured employers in proportion to payroll respectively paid in the most recent year for which payroll information is available. The director shall adopt reasonable regulations governing the manner of collection of the surcharges. The regulations shall require the surcharges to be paid by self-insurers to be expressed as a percentage of indemnity paid during the most recent year for which information is available, and the surcharges to be paid by insured employers to be expressed as a percentage of premium. In no event shall the surcharges paid by insured employers be considered a premium for computation of a gross premium tax or agents' commission. In no event shall the total amount of the surcharges paid by insured and self-insured employers exceed the amounts reasonably necessary to carry out the purposes of this section.

(2) The surcharge levied by the director for the Occupational Safety and Health Fund, pursuant to paragraph (1), shall not generate revenues in excess of fifty-seven million dollars ($57,000,000) on and after the 2013–14 fiscal year, adjusted for each fiscal year as appropriate to fund any increases in the appropriation as approved by the Legislature, and to reconcile any over/under assessments from previous fiscal years pursuant to Sections 15606 and 15609 of Title 8 of the California Code of Regulations. For the 2013-14 fiscal yearonly, the revenue cap established in this paragraph shall be reduced by an amount equivalent to the balance transferred from the Cal-OSHA Targeted Inspection and Consultation Fund established in Section 62.7, less any amount of that balance loaned to the State Public Works Enforcement Fund, to the Occupational Safety and Health Fund pursuant to subdivision (d).

(3) A separate surcharge shall be levied by the director upon all employers, as defined in Section 3300, for purposes of deposit in the Labor Enforcement and Compliance Fund. The total amount of the surcharges shall be allocated between employers in proportion to payroll respectively paid in the most recent year for which payroll information is available. The director shall adopt reasonable regulations governing the manner of collection of the surcharges. In no event shall the total amount of the surcharges paid by employers exceed the amounts reasonably necessary to carry out the purposes of this section.

(4) The surcharge levied by the director for the Labor Enforcement and Compliance Fund shall not exceed forty-six million dollars ($46,000,000) in the 2013–14 fiscal year, adjusted as appropriate to fund any increases in the appropriation as approved by the Legislature, and to reconcile any over/under assessments from previous fiscal years pursuant to Sections 15606 and 15609 of Title 8 of the California Code of Regulations.

(5) The regulations adopted pursuant to paragraph (1) to (4), inclusive, shall be exempt from the rulemaking provisions of the Administrative Procedure Act (Chapter 3.5 (commencing with Section 11340) of Part 1 of Division 3 of Title 2 of the Government Code).

Added Stats 2009 ch 341 § 12 (SB 73), effective January 1, 2010. Amended Stats 2012 ch 363 § 4 (SB 863), effective January 1, 2013; Stats 2013 ch 28 § 33 (SB 71), effective June 27, 2013.

Appendix

Chapter 4

Division of Labor Standards Enforcement

§ 98.6. Discrimination, discharge, or refusal to hire for exercise of employee rights; Reinstatement and reimbursement; Refusal to reinstate as misdemeanor; Applicability; Employer prohibited from retaliation

(a) A person shall not discharge an employee or in any manner discriminate, retaliate, or take any adverse action against any employee or applicant for employment because the employee or applicant engaged in any conduct delineated in this chapter, including the conduct described in subdivision (k) of Section 96, and Chapter 5 (commencing with Section 1101) of Part 3 of Division 2, or because the employee or applicant for employment has filed a bona fide complaint or claim or instituted or caused to be instituted any proceeding under or relating to his or her rights that are under the jurisdiction of the Labor Commissioner, made a written or oral complaint that he or she is owed unpaid wages, or because the employee has initiated any action or notice pursuant to Section 2699, or has testified or is about to testify in a proceeding pursuant to that section, or because of the exercise by the employee or applicant for employment on behalf of himself, herself, or others of any rights afforded him or her.

(b) (1) Any employee who is discharged, threatened with discharge, demoted, suspended, retaliated against, subjected to an adverse action, or in any other manner discriminated against in the terms and conditions of his or her employment because the employee engaged in any conduct delineated in this chapter, including the conduct described in subdivision (k) of Section 96, and Chapter 5 (commencing with Section 1101) of Part 3 of Division 2, or because the employee has made a bona fide complaint or claim to the division pursuant to this part, or because the employee has initiated any action or notice pursuant to Section 2699 shall be entitled to reinstatement and reimbursement for lost wages and work benefits caused by those acts of the employer.

(2) An employer who willfully refuses to hire, promote, or otherwise restore an employee or former employee who has been determined to be eligible for rehiring or promotion by a grievance procedure, arbitration, or hearing authorized by law, is guilty of a misdemeanor.

(3) In addition to other remedies available, an employer who violates this section is liable for a civil penalty not exceeding ten thousand dollars ($10,000) per employee for each violation of this section, to be awarded to the employee or employees who suffered the violation.

(c) (1) Any applicant for employment who is refused employment, who is not selected for a training program leading to employment, or who in any other manner is discriminated against in the terms and conditions of any offer of employment because the applicant engaged in any conduct delineated in this chapter, including the conduct described in subdivision (k) of Section 96, and Chapter 5 (commencing with Section 1101) of Part 3 of Division 2, or because the applicant has made a bona fide complaint or claim to the division pursuant to this part, or because the employee has initiated any action or notice pursuant to Section 2699 shall be entitled to employment and reimbursement for lost wages and work benefits caused by the acts of the prospective employer.

(2) This subdivision shall not be construed to invalidate any collective bargaining agreement that requires an applicant for a position that is subject to the collective bargaining agreement to sign a contract that protects either or both of the following as specified in subparagraphs (A) and (B), nor shall this subdivision be construed to invalidate any employer requirement of an applicant for a position that is not subject to a collective bargaining agreement to sign an employment contract that protects either or both of the following:

(A) An employer against any conduct that is actually in direct conflict with the essential enterprise-related interests of the employer and where breach of that contract would actually constitute a material and substantial disruption of the employer's operation.

(B) A firefighter against any disease that is presumed to arise in the course and scope of employment, by limiting his or her consumption of tobacco products on and off the job.

(d) The provisions of this section creating new actions or remedies that are effective on January 1, 2002, to employees or applicants for employment do not apply to any state or local law enforcement agency, any religious association or corporation specified in subdivision (d) of Section 12926 of the Government Code, except as provided in Section 12926.2 of the Government Code, or any person described in Section 1070 of the Evidence Code.

(e) An employer, or a person acting on behalf of the employer, shall not retaliate against an employee because the employee is a family member of a person who has, or is perceived to have, engaged in any conduct delineated in this chapter.

(f) For purposes of this section, "employer" or "a person acting on behalf of the employer" includes, but is not limited to, a client employer as defined in paragraph (1) of subdivision (a) of Section 2810.3 and an employer listed in subdivision (b) of Section 6400.

(g) Subdivisions (e) and (f) shall not apply to claims arising under subdivision (k) of Section 96 unless the lawful conduct occurring during nonwork hours away from the employer's premises involves the exercise of employee rights otherwise covered under subdivision (a).

Added Stats 1978 ch 1250 § 1. Amended Stats 2001 ch 820 § 2 (AB 1015); Stats 2004 ch 221 § 1 (SB 1809), effective August 11, 2004; Stats 2005 ch 22 § 140 (SB 1108), effective January 1, 2006; Stats 2013 ch 577 § 3 (SB 666), effective January 1, 2014, ch 732

§ 2 (AB 263), effective January 1, 2014; Stats 2014 ch 79 § 1 (AB 2751), effective January 1, 2015; Stats 2015 ch 792 § 1 (AB 1509), effective January 1, 2016.

§ 98.7. Investigation of employee complaint; Judicial relief

(a) (1) Any person who believes that they have been discharged or otherwise discriminated against in violation of any law under the jurisdiction of the Labor Commissioner may file a complaint with the division within one year after the occurrence of the violation. The one-year period may be extended for good cause. The complaint shall be investigated by a discrimination complaint investigator in accordance with this section. The Labor Commissioner shall establish procedures for the investigation of discrimination complaints, including, but not limited to, relief pursuant to paragraph (2) of subdivision (b). A summary of the procedures shall be provided to each complainant and respondent at the time of initial contact. The Labor Commissioner shall inform complainants charging a violation of Section 6310 or 6311, at the time of initial contact, of the complainant's right to file a separate, concurrent complaint with the United States Department of Labor within 30 days after the occurrence of the violation.

(2) The division may, with or without receiving a complaint, commence investigating an employer, in accordance with this section, that it suspects to have discharged or otherwise discriminated against an individual in violation of any law under the jurisdiction of the Labor Commissioner. The division may proceed without a complaint in those instances where suspected retaliation has occurred during the course of adjudicating a wage claim pursuant to Section 98, or during a field inspection pursuant to Section 90.5, in accordance with this section, or in instances of suspected immigration-related threats in violation of Section 244, 1019, or 1019.1.

(b) (1) Each complaint of unlawful discharge or discrimination shall be assigned to a discrimination complaint investigator who shall prepare and submit a report to the Labor Commissioner based on an investigation of the complaint. The Labor Commissioner or the commissioner's designee shall receive and review the reports. The investigation shall include, where appropriate, interviews with the complainant, respondent, and any witnesses who may have information concerning the alleged violation, and a review of any documents that may be relevant to the disposition of the complaint. The identity of a witness shall remain confidential unless the identification of the witness becomes necessary to proceed with the investigation or to prosecute an action to enforce a determination. The investigation report submitted to the Labor Commissioner or designee shall include the statements and documents obtained in the investigation, and the findings of the investigator concerning whether a violation occurred. The Labor Commissioner may hold an investigative hearing whenever the Labor Commissioner determines that a hearing is necessary to fully establish the facts. In the hearing the complainant and respondent shall have the opportunity to present evidence. The Labor Commissioner shall issue, serve, and enforce any necessary subpoenas. If a complainant files an action in court against an employer based on the same or similar facts as a complaint made under this section, the Labor Commissioner may, at the commissioner's discretion, close the investigation. If a complainant has already challenged the complainant's discipline or discharge through the State Personnel Board, or other internal governmental procedure, or through a collective bargaining agreement grievance procedure that incorporates antiretaliation provisions under this code, the Labor Commissioner may reject the complaint.

(2) (A) The Labor Commissioner, during the course of an investigation pursuant to this section, upon finding reasonable cause to believe that any person has engaged in or is engaging in a violation, may petition the superior court in any county in which the violation in question is alleged to have occurred or in which the person resides or transacts business, for appropriate temporary or preliminary injunctive relief, or both temporary and preliminary injunctive relief.

(B) Upon filing of a petition pursuant to this paragraph, the Labor Commissioner shall cause notice of the petition to be served on the person, and the court shall have jurisdiction to grant temporary injunctive relief as the court determines to be just and proper.

(C) In addition to any harm resulting directly to an individual from a violation of any law under the jurisdiction of the Labor Commissioner, the court shall consider the chilling effect on other employees asserting their rights under those laws in determining if temporary injunctive relief is just and proper.

(D) If an employee has been discharged or faced adverse action for raising a claim of retaliation for asserting rights under any law under the jurisdiction of the Labor Commissioner, a court shall order appropriate injunctive relief on a showing that reasonable cause exists to believe that an employee has been discharged or subjected to adverse action for raising a claim of retaliation or asserting rights under any law under the jurisdiction of the Labor Commissioner.

(E) The temporary injunctive relief shall remain in effect until the Labor Commissioner issues a determination or citations, or until the completion of review pursuant to subdivision (b) of Section 98.74, whichever period is longer, or at a time certain set by the court. Afterwards, the court may issue a preliminary or permanent injunction if it is shown to be just and proper. Any temporary injunctive relief shall not prohibit an employer from disciplining or terminating an employee for conduct that is unrelated to the claim of the retaliation.

(F) Notwithstanding Section 916 of the Code of Civil Procedure, injunctive relief granted pursuant to this section shall not be stayed pending appeal.

(c) (1) If the Labor Commissioner determines a violation has occurred, the Labor Commissioner may issue a determination in accordance with this section or issue a citation in accordance with Section 98.74. If the Labor Commissioner issues a determination, the commissioner shall notify the complainant and respondent and direct the respondent to cease and desist from any violation and take any action deemed necessary to remedy the violation, including, where appropriate, rehiring or reinstatement, reimbursement of lost wages and interest thereon, payment of penalties, payment of reasonable attorney's fees associated with any hearing held by the Labor Commissioner in investigating the complaint, and the posting of notices to employees. If the respondent does not comply with the order within 30 days following notification of the Labor Commissioner's determination, the Labor Commissioner shall bring an action promptly in an appropriate court against the respondent. An action by the Labor Commissioner seeking injunctive relief, reimbursement of lost wages and interest thereon, payment of penalties, and any other appropriate relief, shall not accrue until a respondent fails to comply with the order for more than 30 days following notification of the commissioner's determination. The Labor Commissioner shall commence an action within three years of its accrual, regardless of whether the commissioner seeks penalties in the action. If the Labor Commissioner fails to bring an action in court promptly, the complainant may bring an action against the Labor Commissioner in any appropriate court for a writ of mandate to compel the Labor Commissioner to bring an action in court against the respondent. If the complainant prevails in their action for a writ, the court shall award the complainant court costs and reasonable attorney's fees, notwithstanding any other law. Regardless of any delay in bringing an action in court, the Labor Commissioner shall not be divested of jurisdiction. In any action, the court may permit the claimant to intervene as a party plaintiff to the action and shall have jurisdiction, for cause shown, to restrain the violation and to order all appropriate relief. Appropriate relief includes, but is not limited to, rehiring or reinstatement of the complainant, reimbursement of lost wages and interest thereon, and any other compensation or equitable relief as is appropriate under the circumstances of the case. The Labor Commissioner shall petition the court for appropriate temporary relief or a restraining order unless the commissioner determines good cause exists for not doing so.

(2) If the Labor Commissioner is a prevailing party in an enforcement action pursuant to this section, the court shall determine the reasonable attorney's fees incurred by the Labor Commissioner in prosecuting the enforcement action and assess that amount as a cost upon the employer.

(3) An employer who willfully refuses to comply with an order of a court pursuant to this section to hire, promote, or otherwise restore an employee or former employee who has been determined to be eligible for such relief, or who refuses to comply with an order to post a notice to employees or otherwise cease and desist from the violation shall, in addition to any other penalties available, be subject to a penalty of one hundred dollars ($100) per day for each day the employer continues to be in noncompliance with the court order, up to a maxi-

mum of twenty thousand dollars ($20,000). Any penalty pursuant to this section shall be paid to the affected employee.

(d) (1) If the Labor Commissioner determines no violation has occurred, the commissioner shall notify the complainant and respondent and shall dismiss the complaint. The Labor Commissioner may direct the complainant to pay reasonable attorney's fees associated with any hearing held by the Labor Commissioner if the Labor Commissioner finds the complaint was frivolous, unreasonable, groundless, and was brought in bad faith. The complainant may, after notification of the Labor Commissioner's determination to dismiss a complaint, bring an action in an appropriate court, which shall have jurisdiction to determine whether a violation occurred, and if so, to restrain the violation and order all appropriate relief to remedy the violation. Appropriate relief includes, but is not limited to, rehiring or reinstatement of the complainant, reimbursement of lost wages and interest thereon, and other compensation or equitable relief as is appropriate under the circumstances of the case. When dismissing a complaint, the Labor Commissioner shall advise the complainant of their right to bring an action in an appropriate court if the complainant disagrees with the determination of the Labor Commissioner, and in the case of an alleged violation of Section 6310 or 6311, to file a complaint against the state program with the United States Department of Labor. Any time limitation for a complainant to bring an action in court shall be tolled from the time of filing the complaint with the division until the issuance of the Labor Commissioner's determination.

(2) The filing of a timely complaint against the state program with the United States Department of Labor shall stay the Labor Commissioner's dismissal of the division complaint until the United States Secretary of Labor makes a determination regarding the alleged violation. Within 15 days of receipt of that determination, the Labor Commissioner shall notify the parties whether the commissioner will reopen the complaint filed with the division or whether the dismissal will be reaffirmed.

(e) The Labor Commissioner shall notify the complainant and respondent of the commissioner's determination under subdivision (c) or paragraph (1) of subdivision (d), not later than one year after the filing of the complaint. Determinations by the Labor Commissioner under subdivision (c) or (d) shall be final and not subject to administrative appeal except for cases arising under Sections 6310 and 6311, which may be appealed by the complainant to the Director of Industrial Relations pursuant to an appeal process, including time limitations, that is consistent with the mandates of the United States Department of Labor. The appeal from a determination for cases arising under Sections 6310 and 6311 shall set forth specifically and in full detail the grounds upon which the complainant considers the Labor Commissioner's determination to be unjust or unlawful, and every issue to be considered by the director. The director may consider any issue relating to the initial determination and may modify, affirm, or reverse the Labor Commissioner's determination. The director's determination shall be the determination of the Labor Commissioner for cases arising under Sections 6310 and 6311 that are appealed to the director. The director shall notify the complainant and respondent of the director's determination within 10 days of receipt of the appeal.

(f) The rights and remedies provided by this section do not preclude an employee from pursuing any other rights and remedies under any other law.

(g) In the enforcement of this section, there is no requirement that an individual exhaust administrative remedies or procedures.

Added Stats 1985 ch 1479 § 2. Amended Stats 1999 ch 615 § 1 (AB 1127); Stats 2001 ch 134 § 1 (AB 1069); Stats 2002 ch 664 § 158 (AB 3034); Stats 2013 ch 732 § 3 (AB 263), effective January 1, 2014; Stats 2017 ch 28 § 9 (SB 96), effective June 27, 2017; Stats 2017 ch 460 § 1 (SB 306), effective January 1, 2018; Stats 2020 ch 344 § 1 (AB 1947), effective January 1, 2021.

§ 106. Authorization to issue citations and serve penalty assessment orders

(a) The Labor Commissioner may authorize an employee of any of the agencies that participate in the Joint Enforcement Strike Force on the Underground Economy, as defined in Section 329 of the Unemployment Insurance Code, to issue citations pursuant to Sections 226.4 and 1022 and issue and serve a penalty assessment order pursuant to subdivision (a) of Section 3722.

(b) No employees shall issue citations or penalty assessment orders pursuant to this section unless they have been specifically designated, authorized, and trained by the Labor Commissioner for this purpose. Appeals of all citations or penalty assessment orders shall follow the procedures prescribed in Section 226.5, 1023, or 3725, whichever is applicable.

Added Stats 1994 ch 1117 § 1 (SB 1490). Amended Stats 1999 ch 306 § 1 (SB 319); Stats 2004 ch 685 § 1 (AB 3020).

Chapter 4.5

Electrician Certification

§ 108.2. Certification of electricians

(a) Persons who perform work as electricians shall become certified pursuant to Section 108. Uncertified persons shall not perform electrical work for which certification is required.

(b) (1) Certification is required only for those persons who perform work as electricians for contractors licensed as class C-10 electrical contractors under the Contractors' State License Board Rules and Regulations.

(2) Certification is not required for persons performing work for contractors licensed as class C-7 low voltage systems or class C-45 electric sign contractors as long as the work performed is within the scope of the class C-7 or class C-45 license, including incidental and supplemental work as defined in Section 7059 of the Business and Professions Code, and regardless of whether the same contractor is also licensed as a class C-10 contractor.

(3) Certification is not required for work performed by a worker on a high-voltage electrical transmission or distribution system owned by a local publicly owned electric utility, as defined in Section 224.3 of the Public Utilities Code; an electrical corporation, as defined in Section 218 of the Public Utilities Code; a person, as defined in Section 205 of the Public Utilities Code; or a corporation, as defined in Section 204 of the Public Utilities Code; when the worker is employed by the utility or a licensed contractor principally engaged in installing or maintaining transmission or distribution systems.

(4) Individuals desiring to be certified shall submit an application for certification and examination that includes an employment history report from the Social Security Administration. The individual may redact his or her social security number from the employment history report before it is submitted.

(c) The division shall maintain separate certifications for general electrician, fire/life safety technician, residential electrician, voice data video technician, and nonresidential lighting technician.

(d) Notwithstanding subdivision (a), certification is not required for registered apprentices performing electrical work as part of an apprenticeship program approved under Chapter 4 of Division 3 (commencing with Section 3070), a federal Office of Apprenticeship program, or a state apprenticeship program authorized by the federal Office of Apprenticeship. An apprentice who is within one year of completion of his or her term of apprenticeship shall be permitted to take the certification examination and, upon passing the examination, shall be certified immediately upon completion of the term of apprenticeship.

(e) Notwithstanding subdivision (a), certification is not required for any person employed pursuant to Section 108.4.

(f) Notwithstanding subdivision (a), certification is not required for a nonresidential lighting trainee (1) who is enrolled in an on-the-job instructional training program approved by the Chief of the Division of Apprenticeship Standards pursuant to Section 3090, and (2) who is under the onsite supervision of a nonresidential lighting technician certified pursuant to Section 108.

(g) Notwithstanding subdivision (a), the qualifying person for a class C-10 electrical contractor license issued by the Contractors' State License Board need not also be certified pursuant to Section 108 to perform electrical work for that licensed contractor or to supervise an uncertified person employed by that licensed contractor pursuant to Section 108.4.

(h) The following shall constitute additional grounds for disciplinary proceedings, including suspension or revocation of the license of a class C-10 electrical contractor pursuant to Article 7 (commencing with Section 7090) of Chapter 9 of Division 3 of the Business and Professions Code:

(1) The contractor willfully employs one or more uncertified persons to perform work as electricians in violation of this section.

(2) The contractor willfully fails to provide the adequate supervision of uncertified workers required by paragraph (3) of subdivision (a) of Section 108.4.

(3) The contractor willfully fails to provide adequate supervision of apprentices performing work pursuant to subdivision (d).

(i) The Labor Commissioner shall maintain a process for referring cases to the Contractors' State License Board when it has been determined that a violation of this section has likely occurred. The Labor Commissioner shall have a memorandum of understanding with the Registrar of Contractors in furtherance of this section.

(j) Upon receipt of a referral by the Labor Commissioner alleging a violation under this section, the Registrar of Contractors shall open an investigation. Any disciplinary action against the licensee shall be initiated within 60 days of the receipt of the referral. The Registrar of Contractors may initiate disciplinary action against any licensee upon his or her own investigation, the filing of any complaint, or any finding that results from a referral from the Labor Commissioner alleging a violation under this section. Failure of the employer or employee to provide evidence of certification or trainee status shall create a rebuttable presumption of violation of this provision.

(k) For the purposes of this section, "electricians" has the same meaning as the definition set forth in Section 108.

Added Stats 2012 ch 46 § 79 (SB 1038), effective June 27, 2012.

§ 108.3. Division of Labor Standards Enforcement; Certifications tests in non-English languages; Apprenticeship programs

The Division of Labor Standards Enforcement shall do all of the following:

(a) Make information about electrician certification available in non-English languages spoken by a substantial number of construction workers, as defined in Section 7296.2 of the Government Code.

(b) Provide for the administration of certification tests in Spanish and, to the extent practicable, other non-English languages spoken by a substantial number of applicants, as defined in Section 7296.2 of the Government Code, except insofar as the ability to understand warning signs, instructions, and certain other information in English is necessary for safety reasons.

(c) Ensure, in conjunction with the California Apprenticeship Council, that all electrician apprenticeship programs approved under Chapter 4 (commencing with Section 3070) of Division 3 that impose minimum formal education requirements as a condition of entry provide for reasonable alternative means of satisfying those requirements.

(d) Ensure, in conjunction with the California Apprenticeship Council, that all electrician apprenticeship programs approved under Chapter 4 (commencing with Section 3070) of Division 3 have adopted reasonable procedures for granting credit toward a term of apprenticeship for other vocational training and on-the-job training experience.

Added Stats 2012 ch 46 § 79 (SB 1038), effective June 27, 2012.

Chapter 5

Division of Workers' Compensation

§ 139.2. Qualified medical evaluators; Requirements; Appointment and reappointment; Termination; Panels; Review; Regulations; Fee

(a) The administrative director shall appoint qualified medical evaluators in each of the respective specialties as required for the evaluation of medical-legal issues. The appointments shall be for two-year terms.

(b) The administrative director shall appoint or reappoint as a qualified medical evaluator a physician, as defined in Section 3209.3, who is licensed to practice in this state and who demonstrates that he or she meets the requirements in paragraphs (1), (2), (6), and (7), and, if the physician is a medical doctor, doctor of osteopathy, doctor of chiropractic, or a psychologist, that he or she also meets the applicable requirements in paragraph (3), (4), or (5).

(1) Prior to his or her appointment as a qualified medical evaluator, passes an examination written and administered by the administrative director for the purpose of demonstrating competence in evaluating medical-legal issues in the workers' compensation system. Physicians shall not be required to pass an additional examination as a condition of reappointment. A physician seeking appointment as a qualified medical evaluator on or after January 1, 2001, shall also complete prior to appointment, a course on disability evaluation report writing approved by the administrative director. The administrative director shall specify the curriculum to be covered by disability evaluation report writing courses, which shall include, but is not limited to, 12 or more hours of instruction.

(2) Devotes at least one-third of total practice time to providing direct medical treatment, or has served as an agreed medical evaluator on eight or more occasions in the 12 months prior to applying to be appointed as a qualified medical evaluator.

(3) Is a medical doctor or doctor of osteopathy and meets one of the following requirements:

(A) Is board certified in a specialty by a board recognized by the administrative director and either the Medical Board of California or the Osteopathic Medical Board of California.

(B) Has successfully completed a residency training program accredited by the Accreditation Council for Graduate Medical Education or the osteopathic equivalent.

(C) Was an active qualified medical evaluator on June 30, 2000.

(D) Has qualifications that the administrative director and either the Medical Board of California or the Osteopathic Medical Board of California, as appropriate, both deem to be equivalent to board certification in a specialty.

(4) Is a doctor of chiropractic and has been certified in California workers' compensation evaluation by a provider recognized by the administrative director. The certification program shall include instruction on disability evaluation report writing that meets the standards set forth in paragraph (1).

(5) Is a psychologist and meets one of the following requirements:

(A) Is board certified in clinical psychology by a board recognized by the administrative director.

(B) Holds a doctoral degree in psychology, or a doctoral degree deemed equivalent for licensure by the Board of Psychology pursuant to Section 2914 of the Business and Professions Code, from a university or professional school recognized by the administrative director and has not less than five years' postdoctoral experience in the diagnosis and treatment of emotional and mental disorders.

(C) Has not less than five years' postdoctoral experience in the diagnosis and treatment of emotional and mental disorders, and has served as an agreed medical evaluator on eight or more occasions prior to January 1, 1990.

(6) Does not have a conflict of interest as determined under the regulations adopted by the administrative director pursuant to subdivision (o).

(7) Meets any additional medical or professional standards adopted pursuant to paragraph (6) of subdivision (j).

(c) The administrative director shall adopt standards for appointment of physicians who are retired or who hold teaching positions who are exceptionally well qualified to serve as a qualified medical evaluator even though they do not otherwise qualify under paragraph (2) of subdivision (b). A physician whose full-time practice is limited to the forensic evaluation of disability shall not be appointed as a qualified medical evaluator under this subdivision.

(d) The qualified medical evaluator, upon request, shall be reappointed if he or she meets the qualifications of subdivision (b) and meets all of the following criteria:

(1) Is in compliance with all applicable regulations and evaluation guidelines adopted by the administrative director.

(2) Has not had more than five of his or her evaluations that were considered by a workers' compensation administrative law judge at a contested hearing rejected by the workers' compensation administrative law judge or the appeals board pursuant to this section during the most recent two-year period during which the physician served as a qualified medical evaluator. If the workers' compensation administrative law judge or the appeals board rejects the qualified medical evaluator's report on the basis that it fails to meet the minimum standards for those reports established by the administrative director or the appeals board, the workers' compensation administrative law judge or the appeals board, as the case may be, shall make a specific finding to that effect, and shall give notice to the medical evaluator and to the administrative director. Any rejection shall not be counted as one of the five qualifying rejections until the specific finding has become final and time for appeal has expired.

(3) Has completed within the previous 24 months at least 12 hours of continuing education in impairment evaluation or workers' compensation-related medical dispute evaluation approved by the administrative director.

(4) Has not been terminated, suspended, placed on probation, or otherwise disciplined by the administrative director during his or her most recent term as a qualified medical evaluator.

If the evaluator does not meet any one of these criteria, the administrative director may, in his or her discretion, reappoint or deny reappointment according to regulations adopted by the administrative director. A physician who does not currently meet the requirements for initial appointment or who has been terminated under subdivision (e) because his or her license has been revoked or terminated by the licensing authority shall not be reappointed.

(e) The administrative director may, in his or her discretion, suspend or terminate a qualified medical evaluator during his or her term of appointment without a hearing as provided under subdivision (k) or (l) whenever either of the following conditions occurs:

(1) The evaluator's license to practice in California has been suspended by the relevant licensing authority so as to preclude practice, or has been revoked or terminated by the licensing authority.

(2) The evaluator has failed to timely pay the fee required by the administrative director pursuant to subdivision (n).

(f) The administrative director shall furnish a physician, upon request, with a written statement of its reasons for termination of, or for denying appointment or reappointment as, a qualified medical evaluator. Upon receipt of a specific response to the statement of reasons, the administrative director shall review his or her decision not to appoint or reappoint the physician or to terminate the physician and shall notify the physician of its final decision within 60 days after receipt of the physician's response.

(g) The administrative director shall establish agreements with qualified medical evaluators to ensure the expeditious evaluation of cases assigned to them for comprehensive medical evaluations.

(h) (1) When requested by an employee or employer pursuant to Section 4062.1, the medical director appointed pursuant to Section 122 shall assign three-member panels of qualified medical evaluators within five working days after receiving a request for a panel. Preference in assigning panels shall be given to cases in which the employee is not represented. If a panel is not assigned within 20 working days, the employee shall have the right to obtain a medical evaluation from any qualified medical evaluator of his or her choice within a reasonable geographic area. The medical director shall use a random selection method for assigning panels of qualified medical evaluators. The medical director shall select evaluators who are specialists of the type requested by the employee. The medical director shall advise the employee that he or she should consult with his or her treating physician prior to deciding which type of specialist to request.

(2) The administrative director shall promulgate a form that shall notify the employee of the physicians selected for his or her panel after a request has been made pursuant to Section 4062.1 or 4062.2. The form shall include, for each physician on the panel, the physician's name, address, telephone number, specialty, number of years in practice, and a brief description of his or her education and training, and shall advise the employee that he or she is entitled to receive transportation expenses and temporary disability for each day necessary for the examination. The form shall also state in a clear and conspicuous location and type: "You have the right to consult with an information and assistance officer at no cost to you prior to selecting the doctor to prepare your evaluation, or you may consult with an attorney. If your claim eventually goes to court, the workers' compensation administrative law judge will consider the evaluation prepared by the doctor you select to decide your claim."

(3) When compiling the list of evaluators from which to select randomly, the medical director shall include all qualified medical evaluators who meet all of the following criteria:

(A) He or she does not have a conflict of interest in the case, as defined by regulations adopted pursuant to subdivision (o).

(B) He or she is certified by the administrative director to evaluate in an appropriate specialty and at locations within the general geographic area of the employee's residence. An evaluator shall not conduct qualified medical evaluations at more than 10 locations.

(C) He or she has not been suspended or terminated as a qualified medical evaluator for failure to pay the fee required by the administrative director pursuant to subdivision (n) or for any other reason.

(4) When the medical director determines that an employee has requested an evaluation by a type of specialist that is appropriate for the employee's injury, but there are not enough qualified medical evaluators of that type within the general geographic area of the employee's residence to establish a three-member panel, the medical director shall include sufficient qualified medical evaluators from other geographic areas and the employer shall pay all necessary travel costs incurred in the event the employee selects an evaluator from another geographic area.

(i) The medical director appointed pursuant to Section 122 shall continuously review the quality of comprehensive medical evaluations and reports prepared by agreed and qualified medical evaluators and the timeliness with which evaluation reports are prepared and submitted. The review shall include, but not be limited to, a review of a random sample of reports submitted to the division, and a review of all reports alleged to be inaccurate or incomplete by a party to a case for which the evaluation was prepared. The medical director shall submit to the administrative director an annual report summarizing the results of the continuous review of medical evaluations and reports prepared by agreed and qualified medical evaluators and make recommendations for the improvement of the system of medical evaluations and determinations.

(j) After public hearing pursuant to Section 5307.3, the administrative director shall adopt regulations concerning the following issues:

(1) (A) Standards governing the timeframes within which medical evaluations shall be prepared and submitted by agreed and qualified medical evaluators. Except as provided in this subdivision, the timeframe for initial medical evaluations to be prepared and submitted shall be no more than 30 days after the evaluator has seen the employee or otherwise commenced the medical evaluation procedure. The administrative director shall develop regulations governing the provision of extensions of the 30-day period in both of the following cases:

(i) When the evaluator has not received test results or consulting physician's evaluations in time to meet the 30-day deadline.

(ii) To extend the 30-day period by not more than 15 days when the failure to meet the 30-day deadline was for good cause.

(B) For purposes of subparagraph (A), "good cause" means any of the following:

(i) Medical emergencies of the evaluator or evaluator's family.

(ii) Death in the evaluator's family.

(iii) Natural disasters or other community catastrophes that interrupt the operation of the evaluator's business.

(C) The administrative director shall develop timeframes governing availability of qualified medical evaluators for unrepresented employees under Section 4062.1. These timeframes shall give the employee the right to the addition of a new evaluator to his or her panel, selected at random, for each evaluator not available to see the employee within a specified period of time, but shall also permit the employee to waive this right for a specified period of time thereafter.

(2) Procedures to be followed by all physicians in evaluating the existence and extent of permanent impairment and limitations resulting from an injury in a manner consistent with Sections 4660 and 4660.1.

(3) Procedures governing the determination of any disputed medical treatment issues in a manner consistent with Section 5307.27.

(4) Procedures to be used in determining the compensability of psychiatric injury. The procedures shall be in accordance with Section 3208.3 and shall require that the diagnosis of a mental disorder be expressed using the terminology and criteria of the American Psychiatric Association's Diagnostic and Statistical Manual of Mental Disorders, Third Edition-Revised, or the terminology and diagnostic criteria of other psychiatric diagnostic manuals generally approved and accepted nationally by practitioners in the field of psychiatric medicine.

(5) Guidelines for the range of time normally required to perform the following:

(A) A medical-legal evaluation that has not been defined and valued pursuant to Section 5307.6. The guidelines shall establish minimum times for patient contact in the conduct of the evaluations, and shall be consistent with regulations adopted pursuant to Section 5307.6.

(B) Any treatment procedures that have not been defined and valued pursuant to Section 5307.1.

(C) Any other evaluation procedure requested by the Insurance Commissioner, or deemed appropriate by the administrative director.

(6) Any additional medical or professional standards that a medical evaluator shall meet as a condition of appointment, reappointment, or maintenance in the status of a medical evaluator.

(k) Except as provided in this subdivision, the administrative director may, in his or her discretion, suspend or terminate the privilege of a physician to serve as a qualified medical evaluator if the administrative director, after hearing pursuant to subdivision (l) determines, based on substantial evidence, that a qualified medical evaluator:

(1) Has violated any material statutory or administrative duty.

(2) Has failed to follow the medical procedures or qualifications established pursuant to paragraph (2), (3), (4), or (5) of subdivision (j).

(3) Has failed to comply with the timeframe standards established pursuant to subdivision (j).

(4) Has failed to meet the requirements of subdivision (b) or (c).

(5) Has prepared medical-legal evaluations that fail to meet the minimum standards for those reports established by the administrative director or the appeals board.

(6) Has made material misrepresentations or false statements in an application for appointment or reappointment as a qualified medical evaluator.

A hearing shall not be required prior to the suspension or termination of a physician's privilege to serve as a qualified medical evaluator when the physician has done either of the following:

(A) Failed to timely pay the fee required pursuant to subdivision (n).

(B) Had his or her license to practice in California suspended by the relevant licensing authority so as to preclude practice, or had the license revoked or terminated by the licensing authority.

(*l*) The administrative director shall cite the qualified medical evaluator for a violation listed in subdivision (k) and shall set a hearing on the alleged violation within 30 days of service of the citation on the qualified medical evaluator. In addition to the authority to terminate or suspend the qualified medical evaluator upon finding a violation listed in subdivision (k), the administrative director may, in his or her discretion, place a qualified medical evaluator on probation subject to appropriate conditions, including ordering continuing education or training. The administrative director shall report to the appropriate licensing board the name of any qualified medical evaluator who is disciplined pursuant to this subdivision.

(m) The administrative director shall terminate from the list of medical evaluators any physician where licensure has been terminated by the relevant licensing board, or who has been convicted of a misdemeanor or felony related to the conduct of his or her medical practice, or of a crime of moral turpitude. The administrative director shall suspend or terminate as a medical evaluator any physician who has been suspended or placed on probation by the relevant licensing board. If a physician is suspended or terminated as a qualified medical evaluator under this subdivision, a report prepared by the physician that is not complete, signed, and furnished to one or more of the parties prior to the date of conviction or action of the licensing board, whichever is earlier, shall not be admissible in any proceeding before the appeals board nor shall there be any liability for payment for the report and any expense incurred by the physician in connection with the report.

Appendix

(n) A qualified medical evaluator shall pay a fee, as determined by the administrative director, for appointment or reappointment. These fees shall be based on a sliding scale as established by the administrative director. All revenues from fees paid under this subdivision shall be deposited into the Workers' Compensation Administration Revolving Fund and are available for expenditure upon appropriation by the Legislature, and shall not be used by any other department or agency or for any purpose other than administration of the programs of the Division of Workers' Compensation related to the provision of medical treatment to injured employees.

(o) An evaluator shall not request or accept any compensation or other thing of value from any source that does or could create a conflict with his or her duties as an evaluator under this code. The administrative director, after consultation with the Commission on Health and Safety and Workers' Compensation, shall adopt regulations to implement this subdivision.

Added Stats 1989 ch 892 § 23. Amended Stats 1990 ch 1550 § 16 (AB 2910). Amended Stats 1992 ch 1352 § 4.5 (AB 3660), effective September 30, 1992; Stats 1993 ch 4 § 1 (SB 31), effective April 3, 1993, ch 121 § 18 (AB 110), effective July 16, 1993, ch 1242 § 18 (SB 223); Stats 1994 ch 301 § 2 (SB 1004), effective July 20, 1994, ch 1118 § 2 (SB 1768); Stats 1995 ch 319 § 1 (AB 1968); Stats 2000 ch 54 § 1 (AB 776); Stats 2003 ch 228 § 27 (AB 1756), effective August 11, 2003, ch 639 § 10 (SB 228); Stats 2004 ch 34 § 2 (SB 899), effective April 19, 2004; Stats 2012 ch 363 § 5 (SB 863), effective January 1, 2013; Stats 2013 ch 287 § 2 (SB 375), effective January 1, 2014; Stats 2014 ch 71 § 106 (SB 1304), effective January 1, 2015; Stats 2016 ch 86 § 214 (SB 1171), effective January 1, 2017.

§ 139.32. Restrictions on interested parties with financial interests in any entity providing services; Violation

(a) For the purpose of this section, the following definitions apply:

(1) "Financial interest in another entity" means, subject to subdivision (h), either of the following:

(A) Any type of ownership, interest, debt, loan, lease, compensation, remuneration, discount, rebate, refund, dividend, distribution, subsidy, or other form of direct or indirect payment, whether in money or otherwise, between the interested party and the other entity to which the employee is referred for services.

(B) An agreement, debt instrument, or lease or rental agreement between the interested party and the other entity that provides compensation based upon, in whole or in part, the volume or value of the services provided as a result of referrals.

(2) "Interested party" means any of the following:

(A) An injured employee.

(B) The employer of an injured employee, and, if the employer is insured, its insurer.

(C) A claims administrator, which includes, but is not limited to, a self-administered workers' compensation insurer, a self-administered self-insured employer, a self-administered joint powers authority, a self-administered legally uninsured employer, a third-party claims administrator for an insurer, a self-insured employer, a joint powers authority, or a legally uninsured employer or a subsidiary of a claims administrator.

(D) An attorney-at-law or law firm that is representing or advising an employee regarding a claim for compensation under Division 4 (commencing with Section 3200).

(E) A representative or agent of an interested party, including either of the following:

(i) An employee of an interested party.

(ii) Any individual acting on behalf of an interested party, including the immediate family of the interested party or of an employee of the interested party. For purposes of this clause, immediate family includes spouses, children, parents, and spouses of children.

(F) A provider of any medical services or products.

(3) "Services" means, but is not limited to, any of the following:

(A) A determination regarding an employee's eligibility for compensation under Division 4 (commencing with Section 3200), that includes both of the following:

(i) A determination of a permanent disability rating under Section 4660.

(ii) An evaluation of an employee's future earnings capacity resulting from an occupational injury or illness.

(B) Services to review the itemization of medical services set forth on a medical bill submitted under Section 4603.2.

(C) Copy and document reproduction services.

(D) Interpreter services.

(E) Medical services, including the provision of any medical products such as surgical hardware or durable medical equipment.

(F) Transportation services.

(G) Services in connection with utilization review pursuant to Section 4610.

(b) All interested parties shall disclose any financial interest in any entity providing services.

(c) Except as otherwise permitted by law, it is unlawful for an interested party other than a claims administrator or a network service provider to refer a person for services provided by another entity, or to use services provided by another entity, if the other entity will be paid for those services pursuant to Division 4 (commencing with Section 3200) and the interested party has a financial interest in the other entity.

(d) (1) It is unlawful for an interested party to enter into an arrangement or scheme, such as a cross-referral arrangement, that the

Appendix

interested party knows, or should know, has a purpose of ensuring referrals by the interested party to a particular entity that, if the interested party directly made referrals to that other entity, would be in violation of this section.

(2) It is unlawful for an interested party to offer, deliver, receive, or accept any rebate, refund, commission, preference, patronage, dividend, discount, or other consideration, whether in the form of money or otherwise, as compensation or inducement to refer a person for services.

(e) A claim for payment shall not be presented by an entity to any interested party, individual, third-party payer, or other entity for any services furnished pursuant to a referral prohibited under this section.

(f) An insurer, self-insurer, or other payer shall not knowingly pay a charge or lien for any services resulting from a referral for services or use of services in violation of this section.

(g) (1) A violation of this section shall be misdemeanor. If an interested party is a corporation, any director or officer of the corporation who knowingly concurs in a violation of this section shall be guilty of a misdemeanor. The appropriate licensing authority for any person subject to this section shall review the facts and circumstances of any conviction pursuant to this section and take appropriate disciplinary action if the licensee has committed unprofessional conduct, provided that the appropriate licensing authority may act on its own discretion independent of the initiation or completion of a criminal prosecution. Violations of this section are also subject to civil penalties of up to fifteen thousand dollars ($15,000) for each offense, which may be enforced by the Insurance Commissioner, Attorney General, or a district attorney.

(2) For an interested party, a practice of violating this section shall constitute a general business practice that discharges or administers compensation obligations in a dishonest manner, which shall be subject to a civil penalty under subdivision (e) of Section 129.5.

(3) For an interested party who is an attorney, a violation of subdivision (b) or (c) shall be referred to the Board of Governors of the State Bar of California, which shall review the facts and circumstances of any violation pursuant to subdivision (b) or (c) and take appropriate disciplinary action if the licensee has committed unprofessional conduct.

(4) Any determination regarding an employee's eligibility for compensation shall be void if that service was provided in violation of this section.

(h) The following arrangements between an interested party and another entity do not constitute a "financial interest in another entity" for purposes of this section:

(1) A loan between an interested party and another entity, if the loan has commercially reasonable terms, bears interest at the prime rate or a higher rate that does not constitute usury, and is adequately secured, and the loan terms are not affected by either the interested party's referral of any employee or the volume of services provided by the entity that receives the referral.

(2) A lease of space or equipment between an interested party and another entity, if the lease is written, has commercially reasonable terms, has a fixed periodic rent payment, has a term of one year or more, and the lease payments are not affected by either the interested party's referral of any person or the volume of services provided by the entity that receives the referral.

(3) An interested party's ownership of the corporate investment securities of another entity, including shares, bonds, or other debt instruments that were purchased on terms that are available to the general public through a licensed securities exchange or NASDAQ.

(i) The prohibitions described in this section do not apply to any of the following:

(1) Services performed by, or determinations of compensation issues made by, employees of an interested party in the course of that employment.

(2) A referral for legal services if that referral is not prohibited by the Rules of Professional Conduct of the State Bar.

(3) A physician's referral that is exempted by Section 139.31 from the prohibitions prescribed by Section 139.3.

Added Stats 2012 ch 363 § 6 (SB 863), effective January 1, 2013.

§ 139.48. Return-to-work program; Funding; Purpose; Applicability of section

(a) There is in the department a return-to-work program administered by the director, funded by one hundred twenty million dollars ($120,000,000) annually derived from non-General Funds of the Workers' Compensation Administration Revolving Fund, for the purpose of making supplemental payments to workers whose permanent disability benefits are disproportionately low in comparison to their earnings loss. Moneys shall remain available for use by the return-to-work program without respect to the fiscal year.

(b) Eligibility for payments and the amount of payments shall be determined by regulations adopted by the director, based on findings from studies conducted by the director in consultation with the Commission on Health and Safety and Workers' Compensation. Determinations of the director shall be subject to review at the trial level of the appeals board upon the same grounds as prescribed for petitions for reconsideration.

Appendix

(c) This section shall apply only to injuries sustained on or after January 1, 2013.

Added Stats 2012 ch 363 § 6.5 (SB 863), effective January 1, 2013. Amended Stats 2013 ch 28 § 37 (SB 71), effective June 27, 2013.

§ 139.5. Independent review program; Requirements; Liability

(a) (1) The administrative director shall contract with one or more independent medical review organizations and one or more independent bill review organizations to conduct reviews pursuant to Article 2 (commencing with Section 4600) of Chapter 2 of Part 2 of Division 4. The independent review organizations shall be independent of any workers' compensation insurer or workers' compensation claims administrator doing business in this state. The administrative director may establish additional requirements, including conflict-of-interest standards, consistent with the purposes of Article 2 (commencing with Section 4600) of Chapter 2 of Part 2 of Division 4, that an organization shall be required to meet in order to qualify as an independent review organization and to assist the division in carrying out its responsibilities.

(2) To enable the independent review program to go into effect for injuries occurring on or after January 1, 2013, and until the administrative director establishes contracts as otherwise specified by this section, independent review organizations under contract with the Department of Managed Health Care pursuant to Section 1374.32 of the Health and Safety Code may be designated by the administrative director to conduct reviews pursuant to Article 2 (commencing with Section 4600) of Chapter 2 of Part 2 of Division 4. The administrative director may use an interagency agreement to implement the independent review process beginning January 1, 2013. The administrative director may initially contract directly with the same organizations that are under contract with the Department of Managed Health Care on substantially the same terms without competitive bidding until January 1, 2015.

(b) (1) The independent medical review organizations and the medical professionals retained to conduct reviews shall be deemed to be consultants for purposes of this section.

(2) There shall be no monetary liability on the part of, and no cause of action shall arise against, any consultant on account of any communication by that consultant to the administrative director or any other officer, employee, agent, contractor, or consultant of the Division of Workers' Compensation, or on account of any communication by that consultant to any person when that communication is required by the terms of a contract with the administrative director pursuant to this section and the consultant does all of the following:

(A) Acts without malice.

(B) Makes a reasonable effort to determine the facts of the matter communicated.

(C) Acts with a reasonable belief that the communication is warranted by the facts actually known to the consultant after a reasonable effort to determine the facts.

(3) The immunities afforded by this section shall not affect the availability of any other privilege or immunity which may be afforded by law. This section shall not be construed to alter the laws regarding the confidentiality of medical records.

(c) (1) An organization contracted to perform independent medical review or independent bill review shall be required to employ a medical director who shall be responsible for advising the contractor on clinical issues. The medical director shall be a physician and surgeon licensed by the Medical Board of California or the Osteopathic Medical Board of California.

(2) The independent review organization, any experts it designates to conduct a review, or any officer, director, or employee of the independent review organization shall not have any material professional, familial, or financial affiliation, as determined by the administrative director, with any of the following:

(A) The employer, insurer or claims administrator, or utilization review organization.

(B) Any officer, director, employee of the employer, or insurer or claims administrator.

(C) A physician, the physician's medical group, the physician's independent practice association, or other provider involved in the medical treatment in dispute.

(D) The facility or institution at which either the proposed health care service, or the alternative service, if any, recommended by the employer, would be provided.

(E) The development or manufacture of the principal drug, device, procedure, or other therapy proposed by the employee whose treatment is under review, or the alternative therapy, if any, recommended by the employer.

(F) The employee or the employee's immediate family, or the employee's attorney.

(d) The independent review organizations shall meet all of the following requirements:

(1) The organization shall not be an affiliate or a subsidiary of, nor in any way be owned or controlled by, a workers' compensation insurer, claims administrator, or a trade association of workers' compensation insurers or claims administrators. A board member, director, officer, or employee of the independent review organization shall not serve as a board member, director, or employee of a workers' compensation insurer or claims administrator. A board member, director, or

officer of a workers' compensation insurer or claims administrator or a trade association of workers' compensation insurers or claims administrators shall not serve as a board member, director, officer, or employee of an independent review organization.

(2) The organization shall submit to the division the following information upon initial application to contract under this section and, except as otherwise provided, annually thereafter upon any change to any of the following information:

(A) The names of all stockholders and owners of more than 5 percent of any stock or options, if a publicly held organization.

(B) The names of all holders of bonds or notes in excess of one hundred thousand dollars ($100,000), if any.

(C) The names of all corporations and organizations that the independent review organization controls or is affiliated with, and the nature and extent of any ownership or control, including the affiliated organization's type of business.

(D) The names and biographical sketches of all directors, officers, and executives of the independent review organization, as well as a statement regarding any past or present relationships the directors, officers, and executives may have with any employer, workers' compensation insurer, claims administrator, medical provider network, managed care organization, provider group, or board or committee of an employer, workers' compensation insurer, claims administrator, medical provider network, managed care organization, or provider group.

(E) (i) The percentage of revenue the independent review organization receives from expert reviews, including, but not limited to, external medical reviews, quality assurance reviews, utilization reviews, and bill reviews.

(ii) The names of any workers' compensation insurer, claims administrator, or provider group for which the independent review organization provides review services, including, but not limited to, utilization review, bill review, quality assurance review, and external medical review. Any change in this information shall be reported to the department within five business days of the change.

(F) A description of the review process, including, but not limited to, the method of selecting expert reviewers and matching the expert reviewers to specific cases.

(G) A description of the system the independent medical review organization uses to identify and recruit medical professionals to review treatment and treatment recommendation decisions, the number of medical professionals credentialed, and the types of cases and areas of expertise that the medical professionals are credentialed to review.

(H) A description of how the independent review organization ensures compliance with the conflict-of-interest requirements of this section.

(3) The organization shall demonstrate that it has a quality assurance mechanism in place that does all of the following:

(A) Ensures that any medical professionals retained are appropriately credentialed and privileged.

(B) Ensures that the reviews provided by the medical professionals or bill reviewers are timely, clear, and credible, and that reviews are monitored for quality on an ongoing basis.

(C) Ensures that the method of selecting medical professionals for individual cases achieves a fair and impartial panel of medical professionals who are qualified to render recommendations regarding the clinical conditions and the medical necessity of treatments or therapies in question.

(D) Ensures the confidentiality of medical records and the review materials, consistent with the requirements of this section and applicable state and federal law.

(E) Ensures the independence of the medical professionals or bill reviewers retained to perform the reviews through conflict-of-interest policies and prohibitions, and ensures adequate screening for conflicts of interest, pursuant to paragraph (5).

(4) Medical professionals selected by independent medical review organizations to review medical treatment decisions shall be licensed physicians, as defined by Section 3209.3, in good standing, who meet the following minimum requirements:

(A) The physician shall be a clinician knowledgeable in the treatment of the employee's medical condition, knowledgeable about the proposed treatment, and familiar with guidelines and protocols in the area of treatment under review.

(B) Notwithstanding any other law, the physician shall hold a nonrestricted license in any state of the United States, and for physicians and surgeons holding an M.D. or D.O. degree, a current certification by a recognized American medical specialty board in the area or areas appropriate to the condition or treatment under review. The independent medical review organization shall give preference to the use of a physician licensed in California as the reviewer.

(C) The physician shall have no history of disciplinary action or sanctions, including, but not limited to, loss of staff privileges or participation restrictions, taken or pending by any hospital, government, or regulatory body.

(D) Commencing January 1, 2014, the physician shall not hold an appointment as a qualified medical evaluator pursuant to Section 139.2.

(5) Neither the expert reviewer, nor the independent review organization, shall have any material professional, material familial, or material financial affiliation with any of the following:

(A) The employer, workers' compensation insurer or claims administrator, or a medical provider network of the insurer or claims administrator, except that an academic medical center under contract to the insurer or claims administrator to provide services to employees may qualify as an independent medical review organization provided it will not provide the service and provided the center is not the developer or manufacturer of the proposed treatment.

(B) Any officer, director, or management employee of the employer or workers' compensation insurer or claims administrator.

(C) The physician, the physician's medical group, or the independent practice association proposing the treatment.

(D) The institution at which the treatment would be provided.

(E) The development or manufacture of the treatment proposed for the employee whose condition is under review.

(F) The employee or the employee's immediate family.

(6) For purposes of this subdivision, the following terms shall have the following meanings:

(A) "Material familial affiliation" means any relationship as a spouse, child, parent, sibling, spouse's parent, or child's spouse.

(B) "Material financial affiliation" means any financial interest of more than 5 percent of total annual revenue or total annual income of an independent review organization or individual to which this subdivision applies. "Material financial affiliation" does not include payment by the employer to the independent review organization for the services required by the administrative director's contract with the independent review organization, nor does "material financial affiliation" include an expert's participation as a contracting medical provider where the expert is affiliated with an academic medical center or a National Cancer Institute-designated clinical cancer research center.

(C) "Material professional affiliation" means any physician-patient relationship, any partnership or employment relationship, a shareholder or similar ownership interest in a professional corporation, or any independent contractor arrangement that constitutes a material financial affiliation with any expert or any officer or director of the independent review organization. "Material professional affiliation" does not include affiliations that are limited to staff privileges at a health facility.

(e) The division shall provide, upon the request of any interested person, a copy of all nonproprietary information, as determined by the administrative director, filed with it by an independent review organization under contract pursuant to this section. The division may charge a fee to the interested person for copying the requested information.

(f) The Legislature finds and declares that the services described in this section are of such a special and unique nature that they must be contracted out pursuant to paragraph (3) of subdivision (b) of Section 19130 of the Government Code. The Legislature further finds and declares that the services described in this section are a new state function pursuant to paragraph (2) of subdivision (b) of Section 19130 of the Government Code.

Added Stats 2012 ch 363 § 7 (SB 863), effective January 1, 2013. Amended Stats 2013 ch 287 § 3 (SB 375), effective January 1, 2014; Stats 2014 ch 71 § 107 (SB 1304), effective January 1, 2015.

DIVISION 2

EMPLOYMENT REGULATION AND SUPERVISION

PART 1

COMPENSATION

Chapter 1

Payment of Wages

Article 1

General Occupations

§ 206.5. Prohibition against, and invalidity of, release of claim for wages; Violation as misdemeanor

(a) An employer shall not require the execution of a release of a claim or right on account of wages due, or to become due, or made as an advance on wages to be earned, unless payment of those wages has been made. A release required or executed in violation of the provisions of this section shall be null and void as between the employer and the employee. Violation of this section by the employer is a misdemeanor.

(b) For purposes of this section, "execution of a release" includes requiring an employee, as a condition of being paid, to execute a statement of the hours he or she worked during a pay period which the employer knows to be false.

Added Stats 1959 ch 1066 § 1. Amended Stats 2008 ch 224 § 1 (AB 2075), effective January 1, 2009.

§ 226.8. Unlawful activities; Penalties; Disciplinary action; Information to be posted on Internet Web site; Enforcement

(a) It is unlawful for any person or employer to engage in any of the following activities:

(1) Willful misclassification of an individual as an independent contractor.

(2) Charging an individual who has been willfully misclassified as an independent contractor a fee, or making any deductions from compensation, for any purpose, including for goods, materials, space rental, services, government licenses, repairs, equipment maintenance, or fines arising from the individual's employment where any of the acts described in this paragraph would have violated the law if the individual had not been misclassified.

(b) If the Labor and Workforce Development Agency or a court issues a determination that a person or employer has engaged in any of the enumerated violations of subdivision (a), the person or employer shall be subject to a civil penalty of not less than five thousand dollars ($5,000) and not more than fifteen thousand dollars ($15,000) for each violation, in addition to any other penalties or fines permitted by law.

(c) If the Labor and Workforce Development Agency or a court issues a determination that a person or employer has engaged in any of the enumerated violations of subdivision (a) and the person or employer has engaged in or is engaging in a pattern or practice of these violations, the person or employer shall be subject to a civil penalty of not less than ten thousand dollars ($10,000) and not more than twenty-five thousand dollars ($25,000) for each violation, in addition to any other penalties or fines permitted by law.

(d) (1) If the Labor and Workforce Development Agency or a court issues a determination that a person or employer that is a licensed contractor pursuant to the Contractors' State License Law has violated subdivision (a), the agency, in addition to any other remedy that has been ordered, shall transmit a certified copy of the order to the Contractors' State License Board.

(2) The registrar of the Contractors' State License Board shall initiate disciplinary action against a licensee within 30 days of receiving a certified copy of an agency or court order that resulted in disbarment pursuant to paragraph (1).

(e) If the Labor and Workforce Development Agency or a court issues a determination that a person or employer has violated subdivision (a), the agency or court, in addition to any other remedy that has been ordered, shall order the person or employer to display prominently on its Internet Web site, in an area which is accessible to all employees and the general public, or, if the person or employer does not have an Internet Web site, to display prominently in an area that is accessible to all employees and the general public at each location where a violation of subdivision (a) occurred, a notice that sets forth all of the following:

(1) That the Labor and Workforce Development Agency or a court, as applicable, has found that the person or employer has committed a

serious violation of the law by engaging in the willful misclassification of employees.

(2) That the person or employer has changed its business practices in order to avoid committing further violations of this section.

(3) That any employee who believes that he or she is being misclassified as an independent contractor may contact the Labor and Workforce Development Agency. The notice shall include the mailing address, email address, and telephone number of the agency.

(4) That the notice is being posted pursuant to a state order.

(f) In addition to including the information specified in subdivision (e), a person or employer also shall satisfy the following requirements in preparing the notice:

(1) An officer shall sign the notice.

(2) It shall post the notice for one year commencing with the date of the final decision and order.

(g) (1) In accordance with the procedures specified in Sections 98 to 98.2, inclusive, the Labor Commissioner may issue a determination that a person or employer has violated subdivision (a).

(2) If, upon inspection or investigation, the Labor Commissioner determines that a person or employer has violated subdivision (a), the Labor Commissioner may issue a citation to assess penalties set forth in subdivisions (b) and (c) in addition to any other penalties or damages that are otherwise available at law. The procedures for issuing, contesting, and enforcing judgments shall be the same as those set forth in Section 1197.1.

(3) The Labor Commissioner may enforce this section pursuant to Section 98 or in a civil suit.

(h) Any administrative or civil penalty pursuant to subdivision (b) or (c) or disciplinary action pursuant to subdivision (d) or (e) shall remain in effect against any successor corporation, owner, or business entity that satisfies both of the following:

(1) Has one or more of the same principals or officers as the person or employer subject to the penalty or action.

(2) Is engaged in the same or a similar business as the person or employer subject to the penalty or action.

(i) For purposes of this section, the following definitions apply:

(1) "Determination" means an order, decision, award, or citation issued by an agency or a court of competent jurisdiction for which the time to appeal has expired and for which no appeal is pending.

(2) "Labor and Workforce Development Agency" means the Labor and Workforce Development Agency or any of its departments, divisions, commissions, boards, or agencies.

(3) "Officer" means the chief executive officer, president, any vice president in charge of a principal business unit, division, or function, or any other officer of the corporation who performs a policymaking

Appendix

function. If the employer is a partnership, "officer" means a partner. If the employer is a sole proprietor, "officer" means the owner.

(4) "Willful misclassification" means avoiding employee status for an individual by voluntarily and knowingly misclassifying that individual as an independent contractor.

(j) Nothing in this section is intended to limit any rights or remedies otherwise available at law.

Added Stats 2011 ch 706 § 1 (SB 459), effective January 1, 2012. Amended Stats 2012 ch 162 § 116 (SB 1171), effective January 1, 2013.

PART 3

PRIVILEGES AND IMMUNITIES

Chapter 3.1

Unfair Immigration-Related Practices

§ 1019. Retaliatory use of immigration-related practices

(a) It is unlawful for an employer or any other person or entity to engage in, or to direct another person or entity to engage in, unfair immigration-related practices against any person for the purpose of, or with the intent of, retaliating against any person for exercising any right protected under this code or by any local ordinance applicable to employees. Exercising a right protected by this code or local ordinance includes the following:

(1) Filing a complaint or informing any person of an employer's or other party's alleged violation of this code or local ordinance, so long as the complaint or disclosure is made in good faith.

(2) Seeking information regarding whether an employer or other party is in compliance with this code or local ordinance.

(3) Informing a person of his or her potential rights and remedies under this code or local ordinance, and assisting him or her in asserting those rights.

(b) (1) As used in this chapter, "unfair immigration-related practice" means any of the following practices, when undertaken for the retaliatory purposes prohibited by subdivision (a):

(A) Requesting more or different documents than are required under Section 1324a(b) of Title 8 of the United States Code, or a refusal to honor documents tendered pursuant to that section that on their face reasonably appear to be genuine.

(B) Using the federal E-Verify system to check the employment authorization status of a person at a time or in a manner not required under Section 1324a(b) of Title 8 of the United States Code, or not authorized under any memorandum of understanding governing the use of the federal E-Verify system.

(C) Threatening to file or the filing of a false police report, or a false report or complaint with any state or federal agency.

(D) Threatening to contact or contacting immigration authorities.

(2) "Unfair immigration-related practice" does not include conduct undertaken at the express and specific direction or request of the federal government.

(c) Engaging in an unfair immigration-related practice against a person within 90 days of the person's exercise of rights protected under this code or local ordinance applicable to employees shall raise a rebuttable presumption of having done so in retaliation for the exercise of those rights.

(d) (1) An employee or other person who is the subject of an unfair immigration-related practice prohibited by this section, or a representative of that employee or person, may bring a civil action for equitable relief and any applicable damages or penalties.

(2) Upon a finding by a court of applicable jurisdiction of a violation of this section, upon application by a party or on its own motion, a court may do the following:

(A) For a first violation, order the appropriate government agencies to suspend all licenses that are held by the violating party for a period of up to 14 days. On receipt of the court's order and notwithstanding any other law, the appropriate agencies shall suspend the licenses according to the court's order.

(B) For a second violation, order the appropriate government agencies to suspend all licenses that are held by the violating party for a period of up to 30 days. On receipt of the court's order and notwithstanding any other law, the appropriate agencies shall immediately suspend the licenses.

(C) For a third or subsequent violation, order the appropriate government agencies to suspend for a period of up to 90 days all licenses that are held by the violating party. On receipt of the court's order and notwithstanding any other law, the appropriate agencies shall immediately suspend the licenses.

(3) In determining whether a suspension of all licenses is appropriate under this subdivision, the court shall consider whether the employer knowingly committed an unfair immigration-related practice, the good faith efforts of the employer to resolve any alleged unfair immigration-related practice after receiving notice of the violations, as well as the harm other employees of the employer, or employees of other employers on a multiemployer job site, will suffer as a result of the suspension of all licenses.

(4) An employee or other person who is the subject of an unfair immigration-related practice prohibited by this section, and who prevails in an action authorized by this section, shall recover his or her

Appendix

reasonable attorney's fees and costs, including any expert witness costs.

(e) As used in this chapter:

(1) "License" means any agency permit, certificate, approval, registration, or charter that is required by law and that is issued by any agency for the purposes of operating a business in this state and that is specific to the business location or locations where the unfair immigration-related practice occurred. "License" does not include a professional license.

(2) "Violation" means each incident when an unfair immigration-related practice was committed, without reference to the number of employees involved in the incident.

Added Stats 2013 ch 732 § 4 (AB 263), effective January 1, 2014. Amended Stats 2014 ch 79 § 2 (AB 2751), effective January 1, 2015; Stats 2015 ch 303 § 375 (AB 731), effective January 1, 2016.

§ 1019.1. Unlawful practices by employer

(a) It is unlawful for an employer, in the course of satisfying the requirements of Section 1324a(b) of Title 8 of the United States Code, to do any of the following:

(1) Request more or different documents than are required under Section 1324a(b) of Title 8 of the United States Code.

(2) Refuse to honor documents tendered that on their face reasonably appear to be genuine.

(3) Refuse to honor documents or work authorization based upon the specific status or term of status that accompanies the authorization to work.

(4) Attempt to reinvestigate or reverify an incumbent employee's authorization to work using an unfair immigration-related practice.

(b) (1) Any person who violates this section shall be subject to a penalty imposed by the Labor Commissioner and liability for equitable relief.

(2) An applicant for employment or an employee who is subject to an unlawful act that is prohibited by this section, or a representative of that applicant for employment or employee, may file a complaint with the Division of Labor Standards Enforcement pursuant to Section 98.7.

(3) The penalty recoverable by the applicant or employee, or by the Labor Commissioner, for a violation of this section shall not exceed ten thousand dollars ($10,000) per violation.

Added Stats 2016 ch 782 § 1 (SB 1001), effective January 1, 2017.

§ 1019.2. Prohibition against employer reverifying employment eligibility of current employee at time or in manner not required by specified federal law; Penalty; Effect on compliance with MOU governing use of federal E-Verify system

(a) Except as otherwise required by federal law, a public or private employer, or a person acting on behalf of a public or private employer, shall not reverify the employment eligibility of a current employee at a time or in a manner not required by Section 1324a(b) of Title 8 of the United States Code.

(b) (1) Except as provided in paragraph (2), an employer who violates subdivision (a) shall be subject to a civil penalty of up to ten thousand dollars ($10,000). The penalty shall be recoverable by the Labor Commissioner.

(2) The actions of an employer that violate subdivision (a) and result in a civil penalty under paragraph (1) shall not also form the basis for liability or penalty under Section 1019.1.

(c) Subdivision (a) shall be interpreted and applied consistent with federal law and regulations. This section does not prohibit an employer from doing any of the following:

(1) Reverifying an employees' employment authorization in a time and manner consistent with Section 274a.2(b)(1)(vii) of Title 8 of the Code of Federal Regulations.

(2) Taking any lawful action to review the employment authorization of an employee upon knowing that the employee is, or has become, unauthorized to be employed in the United States, consistent with Section 1324a(a)(2) of Title 8 of the United States Code, including in response to specific and detailed information from any agency within the United States Department of Homeland Security indicating that an employee is not authorized to be employed in the United States.

(3) Reminding an employee, at least 90 days before the date reverification is required, that the employee will be required to present a document identified in List A or a combination of one document from List B and one document from List C, as required by the I-9 Employment Eligibility Verification Form, showing continued employment authorization on the date that their current employment authorization will expire or on the date that their current documentation will expire, whichever date is sooner.

(4) Taking any lawful action to correct errors or omissions in a missing or incomplete I-9 Employment Eligibility Verification Form.

(d) In accordance with state and federal law, nothing in this chapter shall be interpreted, construed, or applied to restrict or limit an employer's compliance with a memorandum of understanding governing the use of the federal E-Verify system.

(e) For purposes of this section, the term "knowing" is defined as set forth in Section 274a.1(*l*) of Title 8 of the Code of Federal Regulations and as interpreted by applicable federal rules, regulations, and controlling federal case law. The term "knowing" includes not only actual knowledge, but also knowledge that may fairly be inferred through notice of certain facts and circumstances that would lead a person, through the exercise of reasonable care, to know about a certain condition. Constructive knowledge may be found under the circumstances described in Section 274a.1(*l*)(2) of Title 8 of the Code of Federal Regulations and may not be inferred from an employee's foreign appearance or accent.

Added Stats 2017 ch 492 § 5 (AB 450), effective January 1, 2018. Amended Stats 2019 ch 364 § 10 (SB 112), effective September 27, 2019.

Chapter 3.6

Employer Use of Consumer Credit Reports

§ 1024.6. Update of personal information by employee

An employer may not discharge an employee or in any manner discriminate, retaliate, or take any adverse action against an employee because the employee updates or attempts to update his or her personal informationbased on a lawful change of name, social security number, or federal employment authorization document. An employer's compliance with this section shall not serve as the basis for a claim of discrimination, including any disparate treatment claim.

Added Stats 2013 ch 732 § 5 (AB 263), effective January 1, 2014. Amended Stats 2014 ch 79 § 3 (AB 2751), effective January 1, 2015.

Chapter 5

Political Affiliations

§ 1102.5. Employee's right to disclose information to government or law enforcement agency; Employer prohibited from retaliation; Civil penalty; Confidential communications

(a) An employer, or any person acting on behalf of the employer, shall not make, adopt, or enforce any rule, regulation, or policy preventing an employee from disclosing information to a government or law enforcement agency, to a person with authority over the employee, or to another employee who has authority to investigate, discover, or correct the violation or noncompliance, or from providing information to, or testifying before, any public body conducting an investigation, hearing, or inquiry, if the employee has reasonable cause to believe that the information discloses a violation of state or federal statute, or a violation of or noncompliance with a local, state, or federal rule or regulation, regardless of whether disclosing the information is part of the employee's job duties.

(b) An employer, or any person acting on behalf of the employer, shall not retaliate against an employee for disclosing information, or because the employer believes that the employee disclosed or may disclose information, to a government or law enforcement agency, to a person with authority over the employee or another employee who has the authority to investigate, discover, or correct the violation or noncompliance, or for providing information to, or testifying before, any public body conducting an investigation, hearing, or inquiry, if the employee has reasonable cause to believe that the information discloses a violation of state or federal statute, or a violation of or noncompliance with a local, state, or federal rule or regulation, regardless of whether disclosing the information is part of the employee's job duties.

(c) An employer, or any person acting on behalf of the employer, shall not retaliate against an employee for refusing to participate in an activity that would result in a violation of state or federal statute, or a violation of or noncompliance with a local, state, or federal rule or regulation.

(d) An employer, or any person acting on behalf of the employer, shall not retaliate against an employee for having exercised their rights under subdivision (a), (b), or (c) in any former employment.

(e) A report made by an employee of a government agency to their employer is a disclosure of information to a government or law enforcement agency pursuant to subdivisions (a) and (b).

(f) In addition to other penalties, an employer that is a corporation or limited liability company is liable for a civil penalty not exceeding ten thousand dollars ($10,000) for each violation of this section.

(g) This section does not apply to rules, regulations, or policies that implement, or to actions by employers against employees who violate, the confidentiality of the lawyer-client privilege of Article 3 (commencing with Section 950) of, or the physician-patient privilege of Article 6 (commencing with Section 990) of, Chapter 4 of Division 8 of the Evidence Code, or trade secret information.

(h) An employer, or a person acting on behalf of the employer, shall not retaliate against an employee because the employee is a family member of a person who has, or is perceived to have, engaged in any acts protected by this section.

(i) For purposes of this section, "employer" or "a person acting on behalf of the employer" includes, but is not limited to, a client em-

Appendix

ployer as defined in paragraph (1) of subdivision (a) of Section 2810.3 and an employer listed in subdivision (b) of Section 6400.

(j) The court is authorized to award reasonable attorney's fees to a plaintiff who brings a successful action for a violation of these provisions.

Added Stats 1984 ch 1083 § 1. Amended Stats 2003 ch 484 § 2 (SB 777); Stats 2013 ch 577 § 5 (SB 666), effective January 1, 2014; Stats 2013 ch 732 § 6 (AB 263), effective January 1, 2014; Stats 2013 ch 781 § 4.1 (AB 496), effective January 1, 2014 (ch 781 prevails); Stats 2015 ch 792 § 2 (AB 1509), effective January 1, 2016; Stats 2020 ch 344 § 2 (AB 1947), effective January 1, 2021.

§ 1103. Violation of chapter as misdemeanor; Punishment

An employer or any other person or entity that violates this chapter is guilty of a misdemeanor punishable, in the case of an individual, by imprisonment in the county jail not to exceed one year or a fine not to exceed one thousand dollars ($1,000) or both that fine and imprisonment, or, in the case of a corporation, by a fine not to exceed five thousand dollars ($5,000).

Enacted 1937. Amended Stats 2013 ch 732 § 7 (AB 263), effective January 1, 2014.

PART 7

PUBLIC WORKS AND PUBLIC AGENCIES

Chapter 1

Public Works

Article 1

Scope and Operation

§ 1720. "Public works"; "Paid for in whole or in part out of public funds"; Exclusions

(a) As used in this chapter, "public works" means all of the following:

(1) Construction, alteration, demolition, installation, or repair work done under contract and paid for in whole or in part out of public funds, except work done directly by a public utility company pursuant to order of the Public Utilities Commission or other public authority. For purposes of this paragraph, "construction" includes work performed during the design, site assessment, feasibility study, and other preconstruction phases of construction, including, but not limited to, inspection and land surveying work, regardless of whether any

further construction work is conducted, and work performed during the postconstruction phases of construction, including, but not limited to, all cleanup work at the jobsite. For purposes of this paragraph, "installation" includes, but is not limited to, the assembly and disassembly of freestanding and affixed modular office systems.

(2) Work done for irrigation, utility, reclamation, and improvement districts, and other districts of this type. "Public works" does not include the operation of the irrigation or drainage system of an irrigation or reclamation district, except as used in Section 1778 relating to retaining wages.

(3) Street, sewer, or other improvement work done under the direction and supervision or by the authority of an officer or public body of the state, or of a political subdivision or district thereof, whether the political subdivision or district operates under a freeholder's charter or not.

(4) The laying of carpet done under a building lease-maintenance contract and paid for out of public funds.

(5) The laying of carpet in a public building done under contract and paid for in whole or in part out of public funds.

(6) Public transportation demonstration projects authorized pursuant to Section 143 of the Streets and Highways Code.

(7) (A) Infrastructure project grants from the California Advanced Services Fund pursuant to Section 281 of the Public Utilities Code.

(B) For purposes of this paragraph, the Public Utilities Commission is not the awarding body or the body awarding the contract, as defined in Section 1722.

(8) Tree removal work done in the execution of a project under paragraph (1).

(b) For purposes of this section, "paid for in whole or in part out of public funds" means all of the following:

(1) The payment of money or the equivalent of money by the state or political subdivision directly to or on behalf of the public works contractor, subcontractor, or developer.

(2) Performance of construction work by the state or political subdivision in execution of the project.

(3) Transfer by the state or political subdivision of an asset of value for less than fair market price.

(4) Fees, costs, rents, insurance or bond premiums, loans, interest rates, or other obligations that would normally be required in the execution of the contract, that are paid, reduced, charged at less than fair market value, waived, or forgiven by the state or political subdivision.

(5) Money loaned by the state or political subdivision that is to be repaid on a contingent basis.

(6) Credits that are applied by the state or political subdivision against repayment obligations to the state or political subdivision.

Appendix

(c) Notwithstanding subdivision (b), all of the following apply:

(1) Private residential projects built on private property are not subject to this chapter unless the projects are built pursuant to an agreement with a state agency, a redevelopment agency, a successor agency to a redevelopment agency when acting in that capacity, or a local public housing authority.

(2) If the state or a political subdivision requires a private developer to perform construction, alteration, demolition, installation, or repair work on a public work of improvement as a condition of regulatory approval of an otherwise private development project, and the state or political subdivision contributes no more money, or the equivalent of money, to the overall project than is required to perform this public improvement work, and the state or political subdivision maintains no proprietary interest in the overall project, then only the public improvement work shall thereby become subject to this chapter.

(3) (A) If the state or a political subdivision reimburses a private developer for costs that would normally be borne by the public, or provides directly or indirectly a public subsidy to a private development project that is de minimis in the context of the project, an otherwise private development project shall not thereby become subject to this chapter.

(B) (i) For purposes of subparagraph (A), a public subsidy is de minimis if it is both less than six hundred thousand dollars ($600,000) and less than 2 percent of the total project cost.

(ii) Notwithstanding clause (i), for purposes of subparagraph (A), a public subsidy for a project that consists entirely of single-family dwellings is de minimis if it is less than 2 percent of the total project cost.

(iii) This subparagraph shall not apply to a project that was advertised for bid, or a contract that was awarded, before July 1, 2021.

(4) The construction or rehabilitation of affordable housing units for low- or moderate-income persons pursuant to paragraph (5) or (7) of subdivision (e) of Section 33334.2 of the Health and Safety Code that are paid for solely with moneys from the Low and Moderate Income Housing Fund established pursuant to Section 33334.3 of the Health and Safety Code or that are paid for by a combination of private funds and funds available pursuant to Section 33334.2 or 33334.3 of the Health and Safety Code do not constitute a project that is paid for in whole or in part out of public funds.

(5) Unless otherwise required by a public funding program, the construction or rehabilitation of privately owned residential projects is not subject to this chapter if one or more of the following conditions are met:

(A) The project is a self-help housing project in which no fewer than 500 hours of construction work associated with the homes are to be performed by the home buyers.

(B) The project consists of rehabilitation or expansion work associated with a facility operated on a not-for-profit basis as temporary or transitional housing for homeless persons with a total project cost of less than twenty-five thousand dollars ($25,000).

(C) Assistance is provided to a household as either mortgage assistance, downpayment assistance, or for the rehabilitation of a single-family home.

(D) The project consists of new construction, expansion, or rehabilitation work associated with a facility developed by a nonprofit organization to be operated on a not-for-profit basis to provide emergency or transitional shelter and ancillary services and assistance to homeless adults and children. The nonprofit organization operating the project shall provide, at no profit, not less than 50 percent of the total project cost from nonpublic sources, excluding real property that is transferred or leased. Total project cost includes the value of donated labor, materials, and architectural and engineering services.

(E) The public participation in the project that would otherwise meet the criteria of subdivision (b) is public funding in the form of below-market interest rate loans for a project in which occupancy of at least 40 percent of the units is restricted for at least 20 years, by deed or regulatory agreement, to individuals or families earning no more than 80 percent of the area median income.

(d) Notwithstanding any provision of this section to the contrary, the following projects are not, solely by reason of this section, subject to this chapter:

(1) Qualified residential rental projects, as defined by Section 142(d) of the Internal Revenue Code, financed in whole or in part through the issuance of bonds that receive allocation of a portion of the state ceiling pursuant to Chapter 11.8 (commencing with Section 8869.80) of Division 1 of Title 2 of the Government Code on or before December 31, 2003.

(2) Single-family residential projects financed in whole or in part through the issuance of qualified mortgage revenue bonds or qualified veterans' mortgage bonds, as defined by Section 143 of the Internal Revenue Code, or with mortgage credit certificates under a Qualified Mortgage Credit Certificate Program, as defined by Section 25 of the Internal Revenue Code, that receive allocation of a portion of the state ceiling pursuant to Chapter 11.8 (commencing with Section 8869.80) of Division 1 of Title 2 of the Government Code on or before December 31, 2003.

(3) Low-income housing projects that are allocated federal or state low-income housing tax credits pursuant to Section 42 of the Internal Revenue Code, Chapter 3.6 (commencing with Section 50199.4) of Part 1 of Division 31 of the Health and Safety Code, or Section 12206, 17058, or 23610.5 of the Revenue and Taxation Code, on or before December 31, 2003.

(e) Notwithstanding paragraph (1) of subdivision (a), construction, alteration, demolition, installation, or repair work on the electric transmission system located in California constitutes a public works project for the purposes of this chapter.

(f) If a statute, other than this section, or a regulation, other than a regulation adopted pursuant to this section, or an ordinance or a contract applies this chapter to a project, the exclusions set forth in subdivision (d) do not apply to that project.

(g) For purposes of this section, references to the Internal Revenue Code mean the Internal Revenue Code of 1986, as amended, and include the corresponding predecessor sections of the Internal Revenue Code of 1954, as amended.

(h) The amendments made to this section by either Chapter 938 of the Statutes of 2001 or the act adding this subdivision shall not be construed to preempt local ordinances requiring the payment of prevailing wages on housing projects.

Enacted 1937. Amended Stats 1953 ch 1706 § 1; Stats 1972 ch 717 § 1; Stats 1973 ch 77 § 19; Stats 1989 ch 278 § 1; Stats 2000 ch 881 § 1 (SB 1999); Stats 2001 ch 938 § 2 (SB 975); Stats 2002 ch 1048 § 1 (SB 972); Stats 2012 ch 810 § 1 (AB 1598), effective January 1, 2013; Stats 2014 ch 864 § 1 (AB 26), effective January 1, 2015, Stats 2014 ch 900 § 1.5 (AB 2272), effective January 1, 2015; Stats 2015 ch 547 § 4 (SB 350), effective January 1, 2016; Stats 2016 ch 86 § 215 (SB 1171), effective January 1, 2017. Stats 2017 ch 610 § 1 (AB 199), effective January 1, 2018. Stats 2017 ch 616 § 2 (AB 1066), effective January 1, 2018 (ch 616 prevails); Stats 2018 ch 92 § 160 (SB 1289), effective January 1, 2019; Stats 2019 ch 719 § 1 (AB 1768), effective January 1, 2020.

§ 1720.9. "Public works" as including hauling and delivery of ready-mixed concrete; Applicable prevailing wage rate; Written subcontract agreement; Submission of certified copy of payroll records; Applicability

(a) For the limited purposes of Article 2 (commencing with Section 1770), "public works" also means the hauling and delivery of ready-mixed concrete to carry out a public works contract, with respect to contracts involving any state agency, including the California State University and the University of California, or any political subdivision of the state.

(b) For purposes of this section, "ready-mixed concrete" means concrete that is manufactured in a factory or a batching plant, according to a set recipe, and then delivered in a liquefied state by mixer truck for immediate incorporation into a project.

(c) For purposes of this section, the "hauling and delivery of ready-mixed concrete to carry out a public works contract" means the job duties for a ready mixer driver that are used by the director in determining wage rates pursuant to Section 1773, and includes receiving the concrete at the factory or batching plant and the return trip to the factory or batching plant.

(d) For purposes of this section, the applicable prevailing wage rate shall be the current prevailing wage, as determined by the director, for the geographic area in which the factory or batching plant is located.

(e) The entity hauling or delivering ready-mixed concrete to carry out a public works contract shall enter into a written subcontract agreement with the party that engaged the entity to supply the ready-mixed concrete. The written agreement shall require compliance with the requirements of this chapter. The entity hauling or delivering ready-mixed concrete shall be considered a subcontractor solely for the purposes of this chapter. Nothing in this section shall cause any entity to be treated as a contractor or subcontractor for any purpose other than the application of this chapter.

(f) The entity hauling or delivering ready-mixed concrete to carry out a public works contract shall submit a certified copy of the payroll records required by subdivision (a) of Section 1776 to the party that engaged the entity and to the general contractor within five working days after the employee has been paid, accompanied by a written time record that shall be certified by each driver for the performance of job duties in subdivision (c).

(g) This section shall not apply to public works contracts that are advertised for bid or awarded prior to July 1, 2016.

Added Stats 2015 ch 739 § 1 (AB 219), effective January 1, 2016. Amended Stats 2016 ch 31 § 184 (SB 836), effective June 27, 2016.

§ 1730. Posting on Internet specified information related to prevailing rate of per diem wage requirements

The Director of Industrial Relations shall post a list of every California code section and the language of those sections that relate to the prevailing rate of per diem wage requirements for workers employed on a public work project on the Internet Web site of the Department of Industrial Relations on or before June 1, 2013, and shall update that list each February 1 thereafter.

Added Stats 2012 ch 280 § 1 (SB 1370), effective January 1, 2013.

§ 1742.1. Liquidated damages

(a) After 60 days following the service of a civil wage and penalty assessment under Section 1741 or a notice of withholding under subdivision (a) of Section 1771.6,, the affected contractor, subcontractor, and surety on a bond or bonds issued to secure the payment of wages covered by the assessment or notice shall be liable for liquidated damages in an amount equal to the wages, or portion thereof, that still remain unpaid. If the assessment or notice subsequently is overturned or modified after administrative or judicial review, liquidated damages shall be payable only on the wages found to be due and unpaid. Any liquidated damages shall be distributed to the employee along with the unpaid wages. Section 203.5 shall not apply to claims for prevailing wages under this chapter.

(b) Notwithstanding subdivision (a), there shall be no liability for liquidated damages if the full amount of the assessment or notice, including penalties, has been deposited with the Department of Industrial Relations, within 60 days following service of the assessment or notice, for the department to hold in escrow pending administrative and judicial review. The department shall release the funds in escrow, plus any interest earned, to the persons and entities that are found to be entitled to those funds, within 30 days following either of the specified events occurring:

(1) The conclusion of all administrative and judicial review.

(2) The department receives written notice from the Labor Commissioner or his or her designee of a settlement or other final disposition of an assessment issued pursuant to Section 1741 or from the authorized representative of the awarding body of a settlement or other final disposition of a notice issued pursuant to Section 1771.6.

(c) The Labor Commissioner shall, upon receipt of a request from the affected contractor or subcontractor within 30 days following the service of a civil wage and penalty assessment under Section 1741, afford the contractor or subcontractor the opportunity to meet with the Labor Commissioner or his or her designee to attempt to settle a dispute regarding the assessment without the need for formal proceedings. The awarding body shall, upon receipt of a request from the affected contractor or subcontractor within 30 days following the service of a notice of withholding under subdivision (a) of Section 1771.6, afford the contractor or subcontractor the opportunity to meet with the designee of the awarding body to attempt to settle a dispute regarding the notice without the need for formal proceedings. The settlement meeting may be held in person or by telephone and shall take place before the expiration of the 60-day period for seeking administrative review. No evidence of anything said or any admission made for the purpose of, in the course of, or pursuant to, the settlement meeting is admissible or subject to discovery in any administrative or civil proceeding. No writing prepared for the purpose of, in the course of, or pursuant to, the settlement meeting, other than a final settlement agreement, is admissible or subject to discovery in any administrative or civil proceeding. The assessment or notice shall advise the contractor or subcontractor of the opportunity to request a settlement meeting.

Added Stats 2000 ch 954 § 13 (AB 1646). Amended Stats 2004 ch 685 § 5 (AB 3020), operative January 1, 2007; Stats 2008 ch 402 § 3 (SB 1352), effective January 1, 2009; Stats 2016 ch 345 § 1 (AB 326), effective January 1, 2017. Stats 2017 ch 28 § 16 (SB 96), effective June 27, 2017.

Article 2

Wages

§ 1770. General prevailing wage rate; Determination; Payment of more than prevailing rate; Overtime work

The Director of the Department of Industrial Relations shall determine the general prevailing rate of per diem wages in accordance with the standards set forth in Section 1773, and the director's determination in the matter shall be final except as provided in Section 1773.4. Nothing in this article, however, shall prohibit the payment of more than the general prevailing rate of wages to any worker employed on public work. This chapter does not permit any overtime work in violation of Article 3.

Enacted 1937. Amended Stats 1953 ch 1706 § 2; Stats 1976 ch 281 § 2; Stats 2017 ch 28 § 17 (SB 96), effective June 27, 2017.

§ 1771. Requirement of prevailing local rate for work under contract

Except for public works projects of one thousand dollars ($1,000) or less, not less than the general prevailing rate of per diem wages for work of a similar character in the locality in which the public work is performed, and not less than the general prevailing rate of per diem wages for holiday and overtime work fixed as provided in this chapter, shall be paid to all workers employed on public works.

This section is applicable only to work performed under contract, and is not applicable to work carried out by a public agency with its own forces. This section is applicable to contracts let for maintenance work.

Enacted 1937. Amended Stats 1953 ch 1706 § 3; Stats 1974 ch 1202 § 1; Stats 1976 ch 861 § 2; Stats 1981 ch 449 § 1.

§ 1771.1. Registration required as qualification to bid; Notice; Internet listing; Penalties

(a) A contractor or subcontractor shall not be qualified to bid on, be listed in a bid proposal, subject to the requirements of Section 4104 of the Public Contract Code, or engage in the performance of any contract for public work, as defined in this chapter, unless currently registered and qualified to perform public work pursuant to Section 1725.5. It is not a violation of this section for an unregistered contractor to submit a bid that is authorized by Section 7029.1 of the Business and Professions Code or by Section 10164 or 20103.5 of the Public Contract Code, provided the contractor is registered to perform

Appendix

public work pursuant to Section 1725.5 at the time the contract is awarded.

(b) Notice of the requirement described in subdivision (a) shall be included in all bid invitations and public works contracts, and a bid shall not be accepted nor any contract or subcontract entered into without proof of the contractor or subcontractor's current registration to perform public work pursuant to Section 1725.5.

(c) An inadvertent error in listing a subcontractor who is not registered pursuant to Section 1725.5 in a bid proposal shall not be grounds for filing a bid protest or grounds for considering the bid nonresponsive, provided that any of the following apply:

(1) The subcontractor is registered prior to the bid opening.

(2) Within 24 hours after the bid opening, the subcontractor is registered and has paid the penalty registration fee specified in subparagraph (E) of paragraph (2) of subdivision (a) of Section 1725.5.

(3) The subcontractor is replaced by another registered subcontractor pursuant to Section 4107 of the Public Contract Code.

(d) Failure by a subcontractor to be registered to perform public work as required by subdivision (a) shall be grounds under Section 4107 of the Public Contract Code for the contractor, with the consent of the awarding authority, to substitute a subcontractor who is registered to perform public work pursuant to Section 1725.5 in place of the unregistered subcontractor.

(e) The department shall maintain on its Internet Web site a list of contractors who are currently registered to perform public work pursuant to Section 1725.5.

(f) A contract entered into with any contractor or subcontractor in violation of subdivision (a) shall be subject to cancellation, provided that a contract for public work shall not be unlawful, void, or voidable solely due to the failure of the awarding body, contractor, or any subcontractor to comply with the requirements of Section 1725.5 or this section.

(g) If the Labor Commissioner or his or her designee determines that a contractor or subcontractor engaged in the performance of any public work contract without having been registered in accordance with this section, the contractor or subcontractor shall forfeit, as a civil penalty to the state, one hundred dollars ($100) for each day of work performed in violation of the registration requirement, not to exceed an aggregate penalty of eight thousand dollars ($8,000) in addition to any penalty registration fee assessed pursuant to clause (ii) of subparagraph (E) of paragraph (2) of subdivision (a) of Section 1725.5.

(h) (1) In addition to, or in lieu of, any other penalty or sanction authorized pursuant to this chapter, a higher tiered public works contractor or subcontractor who is found to have entered into a subcontract with an unregistered lower tier subcontractor to perform any public work in violation of the requirements of Section 1725.5 or this section shall be subject to forfeiture, as a civil penalty to the state, of one hundred dollars ($100) for each day the unregistered lower tier subcontractor performs work in violation of the registration requirement, not to exceed an aggregate penalty of ten thousand dollars ($10,000).

(2) The Labor Commissioner shall use the same standards specified in subparagraph (A) of paragraph (2) of subdivision (a) of Section 1775 when determining the severity of the violation and what penalty to assess, and may waive the penalty for a first time violation that was unintentional and did not hinder the Labor Commissioner's ability to monitor and enforce compliance with the requirements of this chapter.

(3) A higher tiered public works contractor or subcontractor shall not be liable for penalties assessed pursuant to paragraph (1) if the lower tier subcontractor's performance is in violation of the requirements of Section 1725.5 due to the revocation of a previously approved registration.

(4) A subcontractor shall not be liable for any penalties assessed against a higher tiered public works contractor or subcontractor pursuant to paragraph (1). A higher tiered public works contractor or subcontractor may not require a lower tiered subcontractor to indemnify or otherwise be liable for any penalties pursuant to paragraph (1).

(i) The Labor Commissioner or his or her designee shall issue a civil wage and penalty assessment, in accordance with the provisions of Section 1741, upon determination of penalties pursuant to subdivision (g) and subparagraph (B) of paragraph (1) of subdivision (h). Review of a civil wage and penalty assessment issued under this subdivision may be requested in accordance with the provisions of Section 1742. The regulations of the Director of Industrial Relations, which govern proceedings for review of civil wage and penalty assessments and the withholding of contract payments under Article 1 (commencing with Section 1720) and Article 2 (commencing with Section 1770), shall apply.

(j) (1) Where a contractor or subcontractor engages in the performance of any public work contract without having been registered in violation of the requirements of Section 1725.5 or this section, the Labor Commissioner shall issue and serve a stop order prohibiting the use of the unregistered contractor or the unregistered subcontractor on all public works until the unregistered contractor or unregistered subcontractor is registered. The stop order shall not apply to work by registered contractors or subcontractors on the public work.

(2) A stop order may be personally served upon the contractor or subcontractor by either of the following methods:

(A) Manual delivery of the order to the contractor or subcontractor personally.

(B) Leaving signed copies of the order with the person who is apparently in charge at the site of the public work and by thereafter mailing copies of the order by first class mail, postage prepaid to the contractor or subcontractor at one of the following:

(i) The address of the contractor or subcontractor on file with either the Secretary of State or the Contractors' State License Board.

(ii) If the contractor or subcontractor has no address on file with the Secretary of State or the Contractors' State License Board, the address of the site of the public work.

(3) The stop order shall be effective immediately upon service and shall be subject to appeal by the party contracting with the unregistered contractor or subcontractor, by the unregistered contractor or subcontractor, or both. The appeal, hearing, and any further review of the hearing decision shall be governed by the procedures, time limits, and other requirements specified in subdivision (a) of Section 238.1.

(4) Any employee of an unregistered contractor or subcontractor who is affected by a work stoppage ordered by the commissioner pursuant to this subdivision shall be paid at his or her regular hourly prevailing wage rate by that employer for any hours the employee would have worked but for the work stoppage, not to exceed 10 days.

(k) Failure of a contractor or subcontractor, owner, director, officer, or managing agent of the contractor or subcontractor to observe a stop order issued and served upon him or her pursuant to subdivision (j) is guilty of a misdemeanor punishable by imprisonment in county jail not exceeding 60 days or by a fine not exceeding ten thousand dollars ($10,000), or both.

(*l*) This section shall apply to any bid proposal submitted on or after March 1, 2015, and any contract for public work entered into on or after April 1, 2015. This section shall also apply to the performance of any public work, as defined in this chapter, on or after January 1, 2018, regardless of when the contract for public work was entered.

(m) Penalties received pursuant to this section shall be deposited in the State Public Works Enforcement Fund established by Section 1771.3 and shall be used only for the purposes specified in that section.

(n) This section shall not apply to work performed on a public works project of twenty-five thousand dollars ($25,000) or less when the project is for construction, alteration, demolition, installation, or repair work or to work performed on a public works project of fifteen thousand dollars ($15,000) or less when the project is for maintenance work.

Added Stats 2014 ch 28 § 63 (SB 854), effective June 20, 2014. Amended Stats 2017 ch 28 § 18 (SB 96), effective June 27, 2017. Stats 2018 ch 455 § 2 (SB 877), effective September 17, 2018.

§ 1771.2. Action against employer that fails to pay prevailing wage; Restitution; Liquidated damages

(a) A joint labor-management committee established pursuant to the federal Labor Management Cooperation Act of 1978 (29 U.S.C. Sec. 175a) may bring an action in any court of competent jurisdiction against an employer that fails to pay the prevailing wage to its employees, as required by this article, or that fails to provide payroll records as required by Section 1776. This action shall be commenced not later than 18 months after the filing of a valid notice of completion in the office of the county recorder in each county in which the public work or some part thereof was performed, or not later than 18 months after acceptance of the public work, whichever occurs last.

(b) (1) In an action brought pursuant to this section, the court shall award restitution to an employee for unpaid wages, plus interest, under Section 3289 of the Civil Code from the date that the wages became due and payable, and liquidated damages equal to the amount of unpaid wages owed, and may impose civil penalties, only against an employer that failed to pay the prevailing wage to its employees, in accordance with Section 1775, injunctive relief, or any other appropriate form of equitable relief. The court shall follow the same standards and have the same discretion in setting the amount of penalties as are provided by subdivision (a) of Section 1775. The court shall award a prevailing joint labor-management committee its reasonable attorney's fees and costs incurred in maintaining the action, including expert witness fees.

(2) An action pursuant to this section shall not be based on the employer's misclassification of the craft of a worker in its certified payroll records.

(3) Liquidated damages shall be awarded only if the complaint alleges with specificity the wages due and unpaid to the individual workers, including how that amount was calculated, and the defendant fails to pay the wages, deposit that amount with the court to be held in escrow, or provide proof to the court of an adequate surety bond to cover the wages, within 60 days of service of the complaint. Liquidated damages shall be awarded only on the wages found to be due and unpaid. Additionally, if the defendant demonstrates to the satisfaction of the court that the defendant had substantial grounds for contesting that a portion of the allegedly unpaid wages were owed, the court may exercise its discretion to waive the payment of the liquidated damages with respect to that portion of the unpaid wages.

(4) This subdivision does not limit any other available remedies for a violation of this chapter.

Added Stats 2001 ch 804 § 1 (SB 588). Amended Stats 2013 ch 792 § 2 (AB 1336), effective January 1, 2014; Stats 2018 ch 682 § 1 (AB 3231), effective January 1, 2019.

Appendix

§ 1771.3. State Public Works Enforcement Fund created; Uses; Loans

(a) The State Public Works Enforcement Fund is hereby created as a special fund in the State Treasury to be available upon appropriation of the Legislature. All registration fees collected pursuant to Section 1725.5 and any other moneys as are designated by statute or order shall be deposited in the fund for the purposes specified in subdivision (b).

(b) Moneys in the State Public Works Enforcement Fund shall be used only for the following purposes:

(1) The reasonable costs of administering the registration of contractors and subcontractors to perform public work pursuant to Section 1725.5.

(2) The costs and obligations associated with the administration and enforcement of the requirements of this chapter by the Department of Industrial Relations.

(3) The monitoring and enforcement of any requirement of this code by the Labor Commissioner on a public works project or in connection with the performance of public work as defined pursuant to this chapter.

(c) The annual contractor registration renewal fee specified in subdivision (a) of Section 1725.5,, and any adjusted application or renewal fee, shall be set in amounts that are sufficient to support the annual appropriation approved by the Legislature for the State Public Works Enforcement Fund and not result in a fund balance greater than 25 percent of the appropriation. Any year-end balance in the fund greater than 25 percent of the appropriation shall be applied as a credit when determining any fee adjustments for the subsequent fiscal year.

(d) To provide adequate cashflow for the purposes specified in subdivision (b), the Director of Finance, with the concurrence of the Secretary of the Labor and Workforce Development Agency, may approve a short-term loan each fiscal year from the Labor Enforcement and Compliance Fund to the State Public Works Enforcement Fund.

(1) The maximum amount of the annual loan allowable may be up to, but shall not exceed 50 percent of the appropriation authority of the State Public Works Enforcement Fund in the same year in which the loan was made.

(2) For the purposes of this section, a "short-term loan" is a transfer that is made subject to both of the following conditions:

(A) Any amount loaned is to be repaid in full during the same fiscal year in which the loan was made, except that repayment may be delayed until a date not more than 30 days after the date of enactment of the annual Budget Act for the subsequent fiscal year.

(B) Loans shall be repaid whenever the funds are needed to meet cash expenditure needs in the loaning fund or account.

Added Stats 2014 ch 28 § 65 (SB 854), effective June 20, 2014. Amended Stats 2017 ch 28 § 19 (SB 96), effective June 27, 2017.

§ 1771.4. Requirements for public works projects; Compliance

(a) All of the following are applicable to all public works projects that are otherwise subject to the requirements of this chapter:

(1) The call for bids and contract documents shall specify that the project is subject to compliance monitoring and enforcement by the Department of Industrial Relations.

(2) The awarding body shall post or require the prime contractor to post job site notices, as prescribed by regulation.

(3) (A) Each contractor and subcontractor shall furnish the records specified in Section 1776 directly to the Labor Commissioner, in the following manner:

(i) At least monthly or more frequently if specified in the contract with the awarding body. For purposes of this clause, "monthly" means that a submission of records shall be made at least once every 30 days while work is being performed on the project and within 30 days after the final day of work performed on the project.

(ii) In an electronic format, in the manner prescribed by the Labor Commissioner, on the department's internet website.

(B) A contractor or subcontractor who fails to furnish records pursuant to subparagraph (A), relating to its employees, shall be subject to a penalty by the Labor Commissioner of one hundred dollars ($100) per each day in which that party was in violation of subparagraph (A), not to exceed a total penalty of five thousand dollars ($5,000) per project. Penalties received pursuant to this paragraph shall be deposited in the State Public Works Enforcement Fund established by Section 1771.3 and shall be used only for the purposes specified in that section.

(C) The Labor Commissioner shall not levy a penalty pursuant to subparagraph (B) until a contractor or subcontractor fails to furnish the records pursuant to subparagraph (A) 14 days after the requirement set forth in clause (i) of subparagraph (A).

(D) Penalties pursuant to subparagraph (B) may only accrue to the actual contractor or subcontractor that failed to furnish the records pursuant to subparagraph (A).

(4) If the contractor or subcontractor is not registered pursuant to Section 1725.5 and is performing work on a project for which registration is not required because of subdivision (f) of Section 1725.5, the unregistered contractor or subcontractor is not required to furnish the records specified in Section 1776 directly to

the Labor Commissioner but shall retain the records specified in Section 1776 for at least three years after completion of the work.

(5) The department shall undertake those activities it deems necessary to monitor and enforce compliance with prevailing wage requirements.

(b) The Labor Commissioner may exempt a public works project from compliance with all or part of the requirements of subdivision (a) if either of the following occurs:

(1) The awarding body has enforced an approved labor compliance program, as defined in Section 1771.5, on all public works projects under its authority, except those deemed exempt pursuant to subdivision (a) of Section 1771.5, continuously since December 31, 2011.

(2) The awarding body has entered into a collective bargaining agreement that binds all contractors performing work on the project and that includes a mechanism for resolving disputes about the payment of wages.

(c) The requirements of paragraph (1) of subdivision (a) shall only apply to contracts for public works projects awarded on or after January 1, 2015.

(d) The requirements of paragraph (3) of subdivision (a) shall apply to all contracts for public work, whether new or ongoing, on or after January 1, 2016.

(e) (1) No later than July 1, 2024, the department shall develop and implement an online database of electronic certified payroll records submitted pursuant to this section.

(2) The online database created pursuant to paragraph (1) shall only be accessible to multiemployer Taft-Hartley trust funds (29 U.S.C. Sec. 186(c)) and joint labor-management committees established pursuant to the federal Labor Management Cooperation Act of 1978 (29 U.S.C. Sec. 175a).

(3) Electronic certified payroll records included in the online database created pursuant to paragraph (1) shall only contain non-redacted information pursuant to subdivision (e) of Section 1776 that may be provided to multiemployer Taft-Hartley trust funds (29 U.S.C. Sec. 186(c)) and joint labor-management committees established pursuant to the federal Labor Management Cooperation Act of 1978 (29 U.S.C. Sec. 175a) under applicable law.

Added Stats 2014 ch 28 § 66 (SB 854), effective June 20, 2014. Amended Stats 2017 ch 28 § 20 (SB 96), effective June 27, 2017; Stats 2021 ch 326 § 1 (AB 1023), effective January 1, 2022; Stats 2022 ch 824 § 1 (SB 954), effective January 1, 2023.

§ 1771.5. Labor compliance program as exception to Section 1771; Requirements; Revocation

(a) Notwithstanding Section 1771, an awarding body may choose not to require the payment of the general prevailing rate of per diem wages or the general prevailing rate of per diem wages for holiday and overtime work for any public works project of twenty-five thousand dollars ($25,000) or less when the project is for construction work, or for any public works project of fifteen thousand dollars ($15,000) or less when the project is for alteration, demolition, repair, or maintenance work, if the awarding body has elected to initiate and has been approved by the Director of Industrial Relations to enforce a labor compliance program pursuant to subdivision (b) for every public works project under the authority of the awarding body.

(b) For purposes of this section, a labor compliance program shall include, but not be limited to, the following requirements:

(1) All bid invitations and public works contracts shall contain appropriate language concerning the requirements of this chapter.

(2) A prejob conference shall be conducted with the contractor and subcontractors to discuss federal and state labor law requirements applicable to the contract.

(3) Project contractors and subcontractors shall maintain and furnish, at a designated time, a certified copy of each weekly payroll containing a statement of compliance signed under penalty of perjury.

(4) The awarding body shall review, and, if appropriate, audit payroll records to verify compliance with this chapter.

(5) The awarding body shall withhold contract payments when payroll records are delinquent or inadequate.

(6) The awarding body shall withhold contract payments equal to the amount of underpayment and applicable penalties when, after investigation, it is established that underpayment has occurred.

(7) The awarding body shall comply with any other prevailing wage monitoring and enforcement activities that are required to be conducted by labor compliance programs by the Department of Industrial Relations.

(c) For purposes of this chapter, "labor compliance program" means a labor compliance program that is approved, as specified in state regulations, by the Director of Industrial Relations.

(d) For purposes of this chapter, the Director of Industrial Relations may revoke the approval of a labor compliance program in the manner specified in state regulations.

Added Stats 2011 ch 378 § 8 (AB 436), effective January 1, 2012. Amended Stats 2013 ch 28 § 41 (SB 71), effective June 27, 2013; Stats 2014 ch 28 § 67 (SB 854), effective June 20, 2014.

Appendix

§ 1771.55. [Section repealed 2012.]

Added Stats 2009-2010 2d Ex Sess ch 7 § 7 (SB 9XX), effective May 21, 2009. Repealed Stats 2011 ch 378 § 9 (AB 436), effective January 1, 2012. The repealed section related to payment of the general prevailing rate of per diem wages or the general prevailing rate of per diem wages for holiday and overtime work for any public works project of twenty-five thousand dollars ($25,000) or less, or for any public works project of fifteen thousand dollars ($15,000) or less when the project is for alteration, demolition, repair, or maintenance work.

§ 1771.6. Notice of withholding

(a) Any awarding body that enforces this chapter in accordance with Section 1726 or 1771.5 shall provide notice of the withholding of contract payments to the contractor and subcontractor, if applicable. The notice shall be in writing and shall describe the nature of the violation and the amount of wages, penalties, and forfeitures withheld. Service of the notice shall be completed pursuant to Section 1013 of the Code of Civil Procedure by first–class and certified mail to the contractor and subcontractor, if applicable. The notice shall advise the contractor and subcontractor, if applicable, of the procedure for obtaining review of the withholding of contract payments.

The awarding body shall also serve a copy of the notice by certified mail to any bonding company issuing a bond that secures the payment of wages covered by the notice and to any surety on a bond, if their identities are known to the awarding body.

(b) The withholding of contract payments in accordance with Section 1726 or 1771.5 shall be reviewable under Section 1742 in the same manner as if the notice of the withholding was a civil penalty order of the Labor Commissioner under this chapter. If review is requested, the Labor Commissioner may intervene to represent the awarding body.

(c) Pending a final order, or the expiration of the time period for seeking review of the notice of the withholding, the awarding body shall not disburse any contract payments withheld.

(d) From the amount recovered, the wage claim shall be satisfied prior to the amount being applied to penalties. If insufficient money is recovered to pay each worker in full, the money shall be prorated among all workers.

(e) Wages for workers who cannot be located shall be placed in the Industrial Relations Unpaid Wage Fund and held in trust for the workers pursuant to Section 96.7. Penalties shall be paid into the General Fund of the awarding body that has enforced this chapter pursuant to Section 1771.5.

Added Stats 2000 ch 954 § 16 (AB 1646), operative July 1, 2001.

§ 1771.7. Labor compliance program where public works project uses funds derived from Kindergarten-University Public Education Facilities Bond Act of 2002 or Kindergarten-University Public Education Facilities Bond Act of 2004; Applicability; Requirements

(a) (1) For contracts specified in subdivision (f), an awarding body that chooses to use funds derived from either the Kindergarten-University Public Education Facilities Bond Act of 2002 or the Kindergarten-University Public Education Facilities Bond Act of 2004 for a public works project, shall initiate and enforce, or contract with a third party to initiate and enforce, a labor compliance program, as described in subdivision (b) of Section 1771.5, with respect to that public works project.

(2) If an awarding body described in paragraph (1) chooses to contract with a third party to initiate and enforce a labor compliance program for a project described in paragraph (1), that third party shall not review the payroll records of its own employees or the employees of its subcontractors, and the awarding body or an independent third party shall review these payroll records for purposes of the labor compliance program.

(b) This section applies to public works that commence on or after April 1, 2003. For purposes of this subdivision, work performed during the design and preconstruction phases of construction, including, but not limited to, inspection and land surveying work, does not constitute the commencement of a public work.

(c) (1) For purposes of this section, if any campus of the California State University chooses to use the funds described in subdivision (a), then the "awarding body" is the Chancellor of the California State University. For purposes of this subdivision, if the chancellor is required by subdivision (a) to initiate and enforce, or to contract with a third party to initiate and enforce, a labor compliance program, then in addition to the requirements described in subdivision (b) of Section 1771.5, the Chancellor of the California State University shall review the payroll records on at least a monthly basis to ensure the awarding body's compliance with the labor compliance program.

(2) For purposes of this subdivision, if an awarding body described in subdivision (a) is the University of California or any campus of that university, and that awarding body is required by subdivision (a) to initiate and enforce, or to contract with a third party to initiate and enforce, a labor compliance program, then in addition to the requirements described in subdivision (b) of Section 1771.5, the payroll records shall be reviewed on at least a monthly basis to ensure the awarding body's compliance with the labor compliance program.

(d) (1) An awarding body described in subdivision (a) shall make a written finding that the awarding body has initiated and enforced, or has contracted with a third party to initiate and enforce, the labor compliance program described in subdivision (a).

(2) (A) If an awarding body described in subdivision (a) is a school district, the governing body of that district shall transmit to the State Allocation Board, in the manner determined by that board, a copy of the finding described in paragraph (1).

(B) The State Allocation Board shall not release the funds described in subdivision (a) to an awarding body that is a school district until the State Allocation Board has received the written finding described in paragraph (1).

(C) If the State Allocation Board conducts a postaward audit procedure with respect to an award of the funds described in subdivision (a) to an awarding body that is a school district, the State Allocation Board shall verify, in the manner determined by that board, that the school district has complied with the requirements of this subdivision.

(3) If an awarding body described in subdivision (a) is a community college district, the Chancellor of the California State University, or the office of the President of the University of California or any campus of the University of California, that awarding body shall transmit, in the manner determined by the Director of Industrial Relations, a copy of the finding described in paragraph (1) to the director of that department, or the director of any successor agency that is responsible for the oversight of employee wage and employee work hours laws.

(e) Because the reasonable costs directly related to monitoring and enforcing compliance with the prevailing wage requirements are necessary oversight activities, integral to the cost of construction of the public works projects, notwithstanding Section 17070.63 of the Education Code, the grant amounts as described in Chapter 12.5 (commencing with Section 17070.10) of Part 10 of Division 1 of Title 1 of the Education Code for the costs of a new construction or modernization project shall include the state's share of the reasonable and directly related costs of the labor compliance program used to monitor and enforce compliance with prevailing wage requirements.

(f) This section shall only apply to contracts awarded prior to January 1, 2012.

Added Stats 2002 ch 868 § 2 (AB 1506). Amended Stats 2003 ch 834 § 2 (AB 324); Stats 2005 ch 606 § 1 (AB 414), effective January 1, 2006; Stats 2009-2010 2d Ex Sess ch 7 § 8 (SB 9XX), effective May 21, 2009; Stats 2010 ch 719 § 49 (SB 856), effective October 19, 2010; Stats 2011 ch 378 § 10 (AB 436), effective January 1, 2012; Stats 2014 ch 28 § 68 (SB 854), effective June 20, 2014.

§ 1771.75. [Section repealed 2012.]

Added Stats 2009-2010 2d Ex Sess ch 7 § 9 (SB 9XX), effective May 21, 2009. Amended Stats 2010 ch 719 § 50 (SB 856), effective October 19, 2010. Repealed Stats 2011 ch 378 § 11 (AB 436), effective January 1, 2012. The repealed section related to the labor compliance program where public works project uses funds derived from Kindergarten-University Public Education Facilities Bond Act of 2002 or Kindergarten-University Public Education Facilities Bond Act of 2004, applicability, and requirements.

§ 1771.8. [Section repealed 2012.]

Added Stats 2002 ch 892 § 2 (SB 278). Amended Stats 2009-2010 2d Ex Sess ch 7 § 10 (SB 9XX), effective May 21, 2009; Stats 2010 ch 719 § 51 (SB 856), effective October 19, 2010. Repealed Stats 2011 ch 378 § 12 (AB 436), effective January 1, 2012. The repealed section related to adoption and enforcement of a labor compliance program by the body awarding any contract for a public works project financed in any part with funds made available by the Water Security, Clean Drinking Water, Coastal and Beach Protection Act of 2002.

§ 1771.85. [Section repealed 2012.]

Added Stats 2009-2010 2d Ex Sess ch 7 § 11 (SB 9XX), effective May 21, 2009. Repealed Stats 2011 ch 378 § 13 (AB 436), effective January 1, 2012. The repealed section related to fees to support the department's costs in ensuring compliance with and enforcing prevailing wage requirements in contracts for public works project financed in any part with funds made available by the Water Security, Clean Drinking Water, Coastal and Beach Protection Act of 2002.

§ 1771.9. [Section repealed 2012.]

Added Stats 2009-2010 2d Ex Sess ch 7 § 13 (SB 9XX), effective May 21, 2009. Repealed Stats 2011 ch 378 § 14 (AB 436), effective January 1, 2012. The repealed section related to payment of fee and adoption of labor compliance program by body awarding contract for public works under the Safe, Reliable High-Speed Passenger Train Bond Act for the 21st Century.

§ 1772. Workers deemed employed upon public work

Workers employed by contractors or subcontractors in the execution of any contract for public work are deemed to be employed upon public work.

Enacted 1937. Amended Stats 1992 ch 1342 § 7 (SB 222).

§ 1773. Ascertainment of prevailing rate; Data considered

The body awarding any contract for public work, or otherwise undertaking any public work, shall obtain the general prevailing rate of per diem wages and the general prevailing rate for holiday and overtime work in the locality in which the public work is to be performed for each craft, classification, or type of worker needed to execute the contract from the Director of Industrial Relations. The holidays upon which those rates shall be paid need not be specified by the awarding body, but shall be all holidays recognized in the applicable collective bargaining agreement. If the prevailing rate is not based on a collectively bargained rate, the holidays upon which the prevailing rate shall be paid shall be as provided in Section 6700 of the Government Code.

In determining the rates, the Director of Industrial Relations shall ascertain and consider the applicable wage rates established by collective bargaining agreements and the rates that may have been predetermined for federal public works, within the locality and in the nearest labor market area. Where the rates do not constitute the rates actually prevailing in the locality, the director shall obtain and consider further data from the labor organizations and employers or employer associations concerned, including the recognized collective bargaining representatives for the particular craft, classification, or type of work involved. The rate fixed for each craft, classification, or type of work shall be not less than the prevailing rate paid in the craft, classification, or type of work.

If the director determines that the rate of prevailing wage for any craft, classification, or type of worker is the rate established by a collective bargaining agreement, the director may adopt that rate by reference as provided for in the collective bargaining agreement and that determination shall be effective for the life of the agreement or until the director determines that another rate should be adopted.

Enacted 1937. Amended Stats 1953 ch 1706 § 4; Stats 1968 ch 699 § 1, operative July 1, 1969; Stats 1971 ch 785 § 1; Stats 1976 ch 281 § 3. Amended Stats 1999 ch 30 § 1 (SB 16).

§ 1773.1. Per diem wages; What employer payments are included therein; Credits for employer payments; Computation of credits; Filing of collective bargaining agreements

(a) Per diem wages, as the term is used in this chapter or in any other statute applicable to public works, includes employer payments for the following:

(1) Health and welfare.

(2) Pension.

(3) Vacation.

(4) Travel.

(5) Subsistence.

(6) Apprenticeship or other training programs authorized by Section 3093, to the extent that the cost of training is reasonably related to the amount of the contributions.

(7) Worker protection and assistance programs or committees established under the federal Labor Management Cooperation Act of 1978 (29 U.S.C. Sec. 175a), to the extent that the activities of the programs or committees are directed to the monitoring and enforcement of laws related to public works.

(8) Industry advancement and collective bargaining agreements administrative fees, provided that these payments are made pursuant to a collective bargaining agreement to which the employer is obligated.

(9) Other purposes similar to those specified in paragraphs (1) to (5), inclusive; or other purposes similar to those specified in paragraphs (6) to (8), inclusive, if the payments are made pursuant to a collective bargaining agreement to which the employer is obligated.

(b) Employer payments include all of the following:

(1) The rate of contribution irrevocably made by the employer to a trustee or third person pursuant to a plan, fund, or program.

(2) The rate of actual costs to the employer reasonably anticipated in providing benefits to workers pursuant to an enforceable commitment to carry out a financially responsible plan or program communicated in writing to the workers affected.

(3) Payments to the California Apprenticeship Council pursuant to Section 1777.5.

(c) Employer payments are a credit against the obligation to pay the general prevailing rate of per diem wages. However, credit shall not be granted for benefits required to be provided by other state or federal law, for payments made to monitor and enforce laws related to public works if those payments are not made to a program or committee established under the federal Labor Management Cooperation Act of 1978 (29 U.S.C. Sec. 175a), or for payments for industry advancement and collective bargaining agreement administrative fees if those payments are not made pursuant to a collective bargaining agreement to which the employer is obligated. Credits for employer payments also shall not reduce the obligation to pay the hourly straight time or overtime wages found to be prevailing. However, an increased employer payment contribution that results in a lower hourly straight time or overtime wage shall not be considered a violation of the applicable prevailing wage determination if all of the following conditions are met:

(1) The increased employer payment is made pursuant to criteria set forth in a collective bargaining agreement.

(2) The basic hourly rate and increased employer payment are no less than the general prevailing rate of per diem wages and the general prevailing rate for holiday and overtime work in the director's general prevailing wage determination.

(3) The employer payment contribution is irrevocable unless made in error.

(d) An employer may take credit for an employer payment specified in subdivision (b), even if contributions are not made, or costs are not paid, during the same pay period for which credit is taken, if the employer regularly makes the contributions, or regularly pays the costs, for the plan, fund, or program on no less than a quarterly basis.

Appendix

(e) The credit for employer payments shall be computed on an annualized basis when the employer seeks credit for employer payments that are higher for public works projects than for private construction performed by the same employer, unless one or more of the following occur:

(1) The employer has an enforceable obligation to make the higher rate of payments on future private construction performed by the employer.

(2) The higher rate of payments is required by a project labor agreement.

(3) The payments are made to the California Apprenticeship Council pursuant to Section 1777.5.

(4) The director determines that annualization would not serve the purposes of this chapter.

(f) (1) For the purpose of determining those per diem wages for contracts, the representative of any craft, classification, or type of worker needed to execute contracts shall file with the Department of Industrial Relations fully executed copies of the collective bargaining agreements for the particular craft, classification, or type of work involved. The collective bargaining agreements shall be filed after their execution and thereafter may be taken into consideration pursuant to Section 1773 whenever they are filed 30 days prior to the call for bids. If the collective bargaining agreement has not been formalized, a typescript of the final draft may be filed temporarily, accompanied by a statement under penalty of perjury as to its effective date.

(2) When a copy of the collective bargaining agreement has previously been filed, fully executed copies of all modifications and extensions of the agreement that affect per diem wages or holidays shall be filed.

(3) The failure to comply with filing requirements of this subdivision shall not be grounds for setting aside a prevailing wage determination if the information taken into consideration is correct.

Added Stats 1959 ch 2173 § 1. Amended Stats 1969 ch 1502 § 1; Stats 1976 ch 281 § 4. Amended Stats 1999 ch 30 § 2 (SB 16); Stats 2000 ch 954 § 18 (AB 1646), operative July 1, 2001; Stats 2003 ch 839 § 1 (AB 807), ch 905 § 1 (SB 868); Stats 2012 ch 827 § 1 (AB 2677), effective January 1, 2013; Stats 2013 ch 169 § 1 (SB 776), effective January 1, 2014; Stats 2014 ch 71 § 109 (SB 1304), effective January 1, 2015; Stats 2016 ch 231 § 1 (SB 954), effective January 1, 2017.

§ 1773.2. Specification of prevailing wage rates in call for bids

The body awarding any contract for public work, or otherwise undertaking any public work, shall specify in the call for bids for the contract, and in the bid specifications and in the contract itself, what the general rate of per diem wages is for each craft, classification, or type of worker needed to execute the contract.

In lieu of specifying the rate of wages in the call for bids, and in the bid specifications and in the contract itself, the awarding body may, in the call for bids, bid specifications, and contract, include a statement that copies of the prevailing rate of per diem wages are on file at its principal office, which shall be made available to any interested party on request. The awarding body shall also cause a copy of the determination of the director of the prevailing rate of per diem wages to be posted at each job site.

Added Stats 1971 ch 785 § 2. Amended Stats 1974 ch 876 § 1; Stats 1977 ch 423 § 1. Amended Stats 1992 ch 1342 § 8 (SB 222).

§ 1773.3. Notice; Required information; Penalties

(a) (1) An awarding body shall provide notice to the Department of Industrial Relations of any public works contract subject to the requirements of this chapter, within 30 days of the award, but in no event later than the first day in which a contractor has workers employed upon the public work.

(2) Notwithstanding paragraph (1) and subject to the discretion of the Labor Commissioner, an awarding body shall provide notice to the Department of Industrial Relations of any public works contract awarded pursuant to Section 10122, 20113, 20654, or 22050 of the Public Contract Code that is subject to the requirements of this chapter within 30 days after the award of the contract, but in no event later than the last day in which a contractor has workers employed upon the public work.

(3) The notice shall be transmitted electronically in a format specified by the department and shall include the name and registration number issued by the Department of Industrial Relations pursuant to Section 1725.5 of the contractor, the name and registration number issued by the Department of Industrial Relations pursuant to Section 1725.5 of any subcontractor listed on the successful bid, the bid and contract award dates, the contract amount, the estimated start and completion dates, jobsite location, and any additional information the department specifies that aids in the administration and enforcement of this chapter.

(b) In lieu of responding to any specific request for contract award information, the department may make the information provided by awarding bodies pursuant to this section available for public review on its Internet Web site.

(c) (1) An awarding body that fails to provide the notice required by subdivision (a) or that enters into a contract with or permits an unregistered contractor or subcontractor to engage in the performance of any public work in violation of the requirements of Section 1771.1, shall, in addition to any other sanction or penalty authorized by law, be subject to a civil penalty of one hundred dollars ($100) for each day

Appendix

in violation of either requirement, not to exceed an aggregate penalty of ten thousand dollars ($10,000) for each project.

(2) The Labor Commissioner shall use the same standards specified in subparagraph (A) of paragraph (2) of subdivision (a) of Section 1775 when determining the severity of the violation and what penalty to assess, and may waive the penalty for a first time violation that was unintentional and did not hinder the Labor Commissioner's ability to monitor and enforce compliance with the requirements of this chapter.

(d) An awarding body shall withhold final payment due to the contractor until at least 30 days after all of the required information in paragraph (2) of subdivision (a) has been submitted, including, but not limited to, providing a complete list of all subcontractors. If an awarding body makes a final payment to a contractor after that time and an unregistered contractor or subcontractor is found to have worked on the project, the awarding body shall be subject to a civil penalty assessed by the Labor Commissioner of one hundred dollars ($100) for each full calendar day of noncompliance, for a period of up to 100 days, for each unregistered contractor or subcontractor.

(e) The Labor Commissioner may issue a citation for civil penalties to the awarding body pursuant to subdivisions (c) and (d). The citation shall be served pursuant to Section 1013 of the Code of Civil Procedure by first-class and certified mail.

(f) The procedure for the processing and appeal of a citation or civil penalty issued by the Labor Commissioner pursuant to this section shall be the same as that prescribed in Section 1023. For these purposes, "person" as used in Section 1023 shall include an awarding body.

(g) Whenever the Labor Commissioner determines that an awarding body has willfully violated the requirements of this section or chapter with respect to two or more public works contracts or projects in any 12-month period, the awarding body shall be ineligible to receive state funding or financial assistance for any construction project undertaken by or on behalf of the awarding body for one year, as defined by subdivision (d) of Section 1782. The debarment procedures adopted by the Labor Commissioner pursuant to Section 1777.1 shall apply to any determination made under this subdivision.

(h) A contractor or subcontractor shall not be liable for any penalties assessed against an awarding body pursuant to this section. An awarding body may not require a contractor or subcontractor to indemnify or otherwise be liable for any penalties assessed against an awarding body pursuant to this section.

(i) Penalties received pursuant to this section shall be deposited in the State Public Works Enforcement Fund established by Section 1771.3 and shall be used only for the purposes specified in that section.

(j) This section shall apply only if the public works contract is for a project of greater than twenty-five thousand dollars ($25,000) when the project is for construction, alteration, demolition, installation, or repair work or if the public works contract is for a project of greater than fifteen thousand dollars ($15,000) when the project is for maintenance work.

Added Stats 2014 ch 28 § 70 (SB 854), effective June 20, 2014. Amended Stats 2017 ch 28 § 21 (SB 96), effective June 27, 2017. Stats 2018 ch 455 § 3 (SB 877), effective September 17, 2018.

§ 1773.4. Procedure for review of rates

Any prospective bidder or his representative, any representative of any craft, classification or type of workman involved, or the awarding body may, within 20 days after commencement of advertising of the call for bids by the awarding body, file with the Director of Industrial Relations a verified petition to review the determination of any such rate or rates upon the ground that they have not been determined in accordance with the provision of Section 1773 of this code. Within two days thereafter, a copy of such petition shall be filed with the awarding body. The petition shall set forth the facts upon which it is based. The Director of Industrial Relations or his authorized representative shall, upon notice to the petitioner, the awarding body and such other persons as he deems proper, including the recognized collective bargaining representatives for the particular crafts, classifications or types of work involved, institute an investigation or hold a hearing. Within 20 days after the filing of such petition, or within such longer period as agreed upon by the director, the awarding body, and all the interested parties, he shall make a determination and transmit the same in writing to the awarding body and to the interested parties.

Such determination shall be final and shall be the determination of the awarding body. Upon receipt by it of the notice of the filing of such petition the body awarding the contract or authorizing the public work shall extend the closing date for the submission of bids or the starting of work until five days after the determination of the general prevailing rates of per diem wages pursuant to this section.

Upon the filing of any such petition, notice thereof shall be set forth in the next and all subsequent publications by the awarding body of the call for bids. No other notice need be given to bidders by the awarding body by publication or otherwise. The determination of the director shall be included in the contract.

Added Stats 1953 ch 1706 § 4.5. Amended Stats 1968 ch 699 § 2, operative July 1, 1969; Stats 1969 ch 301 § 1.

§ 1773.5. Rules and regulations; Request for determination; Time limitations based on status as political subdivision; Appeal; Authority of director

(a) The Director of Industrial Relations may establish rules and regulations for the purpose of carrying out this chapter, including, but not limited to, the responsibilities and duties of awarding bodies under this chapter.

(b) When a request is made to the director for a determination of whether a specific project or type of work awarded or undertaken by a political subdivision is a public work, he or she shall make that determination within 60 days receipt of the last notice of support or opposition from any interested party relating to that project or type of work that was not unreasonably delayed, as determined by the director. If the director deems that the complexity of the request requires additional time to make that determination, the director may have up to an additional 60 days if he or she certifies in writing to the requestor, and any interested party, the reasons for the extension. If the requestor is not a political subdivision, the requester shall, within 15 days of the request, serve a copy of the request upon the political subdivision, in which event the political subdivision shall, within 30 days of its receipt, advise the director of its position regarding the request. For projects or types of work that are otherwise private development projects receiving public funds, as specified in subdivision (b) of Section 1720, the director shall determine whether a specific project or type of work is a public work within 120 days of receipt of the last notice of support or opposition relating to that project or type of work from any interested party that was not unreasonably delayed, as determined by the director.

(c) If an administrative appeal of the director's determination is made, it shall be made within 30 days of the date of the determination. The director shall issue a determination on the administrative appeal within 120 days after receipt of the last notice of support or opposition relating to that appeal from any interested party that was not unreasonably delayed, as determined by the director. The director may have up to an additional 60 days if he or she certifies in writing to the party requesting the appeal the reason for the extension.

(d) The director shall have quasi-legislative authority to determine coverage of projects or types of work under the prevailing wage laws of this chapter. A final determination on any administrative appeal is subject to judicial review pursuant to Section 1085 of the Code of Civil Procedure. These determinations, and any determinations relating to the general prevailing rate of per diem wages and the general prevailing rate for holiday, shift rate, and overtime work, shall be exempt from the Administrative Procedure Act (Chapter 3.5 (commencing with Section 11340) of Part 1 of Division 3 of Title 2 of the Government Code).

Added Stats 1953 ch 1706 § 5. Amended Stats 1989 ch 1224 § 5; Stats 2013 ch 780 § 3 (SB 377), effective January 1, 2014.

§ 1773.6. Change in prevailing per diem wage rate

If during any quarterly period the Director of Industrial Relations shall determine that there has been a change in any prevailing rate of per diem wages in any locality he or she shall make such change available to the awarding body and his or her determination shall be final. Such determination by the Director of Industrial Relations shall not be effective as to any contract for which the notice to bidders has been published.

Added Stats 1953 ch 1706 § 6. Amended Stats 1957 ch 1932 § 486; Stats 1963 ch 1786 § 68, operative October 1, 1963; Stats 1976 ch 281 § 6; Stats 2017 ch 28 § 22 (SB 96), effective June 27, 2017.

§ 1773.7. Charges for interagency services

The provisions of Section 11250 of the Government Code shall not be applicable to Sections 1773, 1773.4, and 1773.6.

Added Stats 1976 ch 281 § 8.

§ 1773.8. Increased employer contribution resulting in lower taxable wage

An increased employer payment contribution that results in a lower taxable wage shall not be considered a violation of the applicable prevailing wage determination so long as all of the following conditions are met:

(a) The increased employer payment is made pursuant to criteria set forth in a collective bargaining agreement.

(b) The increased employer payment and hourly straight time and overtime wage combined are no less than the general prevailing rate of per diem wages.

(c) The employer payment contribution is irrevocable unless made in error.

Added Stats 2012 ch 827 § 2 (AB 2677), effective January 1, 2013.

§ 1773.9. Determination of general prevailing rate of per diem wages

(a) The Director of Industrial Relations shall use the methodology set forth in subdivision (b) to determine the general prevailing rate of per diem wages in the locality in which the public work is to be performed.

(b) The general prevailing rate of per diem wages includes all of the following:

(1) The basic hourly wage rate being paid to a majority of workers engaged in the particular craft, classification, or type of work within the locality and in the nearest labor market area, if a majority of the workers is paid at a single rate. If no single rate is being paid to a majority of the workers, then the single rate being paid to the greatest number of workers, or modal rate, is prevailing. If a modal rate cannot be determined, then the director shall establish an alternative rate, consistent with the methodology for determining the modal rate, by considering the appropriate collective bargaining agreements, federal rates, rates in the nearest labor market area, or other data such as wage survey data.

(2) Other employer payments included in per diem wages pursuant to Section 1773.1 and as included as part of the total hourly wage rate from which the basic hourly wage rate was derived. In the event the total hourly wage rate does not include any employer payments, the director shall establish a prevailing employer payment rate by the same procedure set forth in paragraph (1).

(3) The rate for holiday and overtime work shall be those rates specified in the collective bargaining agreement when the basic hourly rate is based on a collective bargaining agreement rate. In the event the basic hourly rate is not based on a collective bargaining agreement, the rate for holidays and overtime work, if any, included with the prevailing basic hourly rate of pay shall be prevailing.

(c) (1) If the director determines that the general prevailing rate of per diem wages is the rate established by a collective bargaining agreement, and that the collective bargaining agreement contains definite and predetermined changes during its term that will affect the rate adopted, the director shall incorporate those changes into the determination. Predetermined changes that are rescinded prior to their effective date shall not be enforced.

(2) When the director determines that there is a definite and predetermined change in the general prevailing rate of per diem wages as described in paragraph (1), but has not published, at the time of the effective date of the predetermined change, the allocation of the predetermined change as between the basic hourly wage and other employer payments included in per diem wages pursuant to Section 1773.1, a contractor or subcontractor may allocate payments of not less than the amount of the definite and predetermined change to either the basic hourly wage or other employer payments included in per diem wages for up to 60 days following the director's publication of the specific allocation of the predetermined change.

(3) When the director determines that there is a definite and predetermined change in the general prevailing rate of per diem wages as described in paragraph (1), but the allocation of that predetermined change as between the basic hourly wage and other employer payments included in per diem wages pursuant to Section 1773.1 is subsequently altered by the parties to a collective bargaining agreement described in paragraph (1), a contractor or subcontractor may allocate payments of not less than the amount of the definite and predetermined change in accordance with either the originally published allocation or the allocation as altered in the collective bargaining agreement.

Added Stats 1999 ch 30 § 4 (SB 16). Amended Stats 2007 ch 482 § 2 (SB 929), effective January 1, 2008.

§ 1773.11. Contract with private entity for prevailing rate of per diem wages and prevailing rate for holiday and overtime work; Director to determine rates and respond to requests; Limited number of requests per calendar year

(a) Notwithstanding any other provision of law and except as otherwise provided by this section, if the state or a political subdivision thereof agrees by contract with a private entity that the private entity's employees receive, in performing that contract, the general prevailing rate of per diem wages and the general prevailing rate for holiday and overtime work, the director shall, upon a request by the state or the political subdivision, do both of the following:

(1) Determine, as otherwise provided by law, the wage rates for each craft, classification, or type of worker that are needed to execute the contract.

(2) Provide these wage rates to the state or political subdivision that requests them.

(b) This section does not apply to a contract for a public work, as defined in this chapter.

(c) The director shall determine and provide the wage rates described in this section in the order in which the requests for these wage rates were received and regardless of the calendar year in which they were received. If there are more than 20 pending requests in a calendar year, the director shall respond only to the first 20 requests in the order in which they were received. If the director determines that funding is available in any calendar year to determine and provide these wage rates in response to more than 20 requests, the director shall respond to these requests in a manner consistent with this subdivision.

Added Stats 2003 ch 343 § 1 (AB 852).

Appendix

§ 1774. Payment of not less than specified prevailing rates to workmen

The contractor to whom the contract is awarded, and any subcontractor under him, shall pay not less than the specified prevailing rates of wages to all workmen employed in the execution of the contract.

Enacted 1937.

§ 1775. Forfeiture for paying less than prevailing wage rates; Amount of penalty; Payments to workers; Liability of prime contractor; Notification of complaint

(a) (1) The contractor and any subcontractor under the contractor shall, as a penalty to the state or political subdivision on whose behalf the contract is made or awarded, forfeit not more than two hundred dollars ($200) for each calendar day, or portion thereof, for each worker paid less than the prevailing wage rates as determined by the director for the work or craft in which the worker is employed for any public work done under the contract by the contractor or, except as provided in subdivision (b), by any subcontractor under the contractor.

(2) (A) The amount of the penalty shall be determined by the Labor Commissioner based on consideration of both of the following:

(i) Whether the failure of the contractor or subcontractor to pay the correct rate of per diem wages was a good faith mistake and, if so, the error was promptly and voluntarily corrected when brought to the attention of the contractor or subcontractor.

(ii) Whether the contractor or subcontractor has a prior record of failing to meet its prevailing wage obligations.

(B) (i) The penalty may not be less than forty dollars ($40) for each calendar day, or portion thereof, for each worker paid less than the prevailing wage rate, unless the failure of the contractor or subcontractor to pay the correct rate of per diem wages was a good faith mistake and, if so, the error was promptly and voluntarily corrected when brought to the attention of the contractor or subcontractor.

(ii) The penalty may not be less than eighty dollars ($80) for each calendar day, or portion thereof, for each worker paid less than the prevailing wage rate, if the contractor or subcontractor has been assessed penalties within the previous three years for failing to meet its prevailing wage obligations on a separate contract, unless those penalties were subsequently withdrawn or overturned.

(iii) The penalty may not be less than one hundred twenty dollars ($120) for each calendar day, or portion thereof, for each worker paid less than the prevailing wage rate, if the Labor Commissioner determines that the violation was willful, as defined in subdivision (c) of Section 1777.1.

(C) If the amount due under this section is collected from the contractor or subcontractor, any outstanding wage claim under Chapter 1 (commencing with Section 1720) of Part 7 of Division 2 against that contractor or subcontractor shall be satisfied before applying that amount to the penalty imposed on that contractor or subcontractor pursuant to this section.

(D) The determination of the Labor Commissioner as to the amount of the penalty shall be reviewable only for abuse of discretion.

(E) The difference between the prevailing wage rates and the amount paid to each worker for each calendar day or portion thereof for which each worker was paid less than the prevailing wage rate shall be paid to each worker by the contractor or subcontractor, and the body awarding the contract shall cause to be inserted in the contract a stipulation that this section will be complied with.

(b) If a worker employed by a subcontractor on a public works project is not paid the general prevailing rate of per diem wages by the subcontractor, the prime contractor of the project is not liable for any penalties under subdivision (a) unless the prime contractor had knowledge of that failure of the subcontractor to pay the specified prevailing rate of wages to those workers or unless the prime contractor fails to comply with all of the following requirements:

(1) The contract executed between the contractor and the subcontractor for the performance of work on the public works project shall include a copy of the provisions of this section and Sections 1771, 1776, 1777.5, 1813, and 1815.

(2) The contractor shall monitor the payment of the specified general prevailing rate of per diem wages by the subcontractor to the employees, by periodic review of the certified payroll records of the subcontractor.

(3) Upon becoming aware of the failure of the subcontractor to pay his or her workers the specified prevailing rate of wages, the contractor shall diligently take corrective action to halt or rectify the failure, including, but not limited to, retaining sufficient funds due the subcontractor for work performed on the public works project.

(4) Prior to making final payment to the subcontractor for work performed on the public works project, the contractor shall obtain an affidavit signed under penalty of perjury from the subcontractor that the subcontractor has paid the specified general prevailing rate of per diem wages to his or her employees on the public works project and any amounts due pursuant to Section 1813.

(c) The Division of Labor Standards Enforcement shall notify the contractor on a public works project within 15 days of the receipt by the Division of Labor Standards Enforcement of a complaint of the failure of a subcontractor on that public works project to pay workers the general prevailing rate of per diem wages.

Added Stats 1997 ch 757 § 2 (SB 1328). Amended Stats 2000 ch 954 § 20 (AB 1646); Stats 2003 ch 849 § 3 (AB 1418); Stats 2011 ch 677 § 1 (AB 551), effective January 1, 2012.

§ 1776. Payroll record of wages paid; Inspection; Forms; Effect of noncompliance; Penalties

(a) Each contractor and subcontractor shall keep accurate payroll records, showing the name, address, social security number, work classification, straight time and overtime hours worked each day and week, and the actual per diem wages paid to each journeyman, apprentice, worker, or other employee employed by the contractor or subcontractor in connection with the public work. Each payroll record shall contain or be verified by a written declaration that it is made under penalty of perjury, stating both of the following:

(1) The information contained in the payroll record is true and correct.

(2) The employer has complied with the requirements of Sections 1771, 1811, and 1815 for any work performed by that person's employees on the public works project.

(b) The payroll records enumerated under subdivision (a) shall be certified and shall be available for inspection at all reasonable hours at the principal office of the contractor on the following basis:

(1) A certified copy of an employee's payroll record shall be made available for inspection or furnished to the employee or the employee's authorized representative on request.

(2) A certified copy of all payroll records enumerated in subdivision (a) shall be made available for inspection or furnished upon request to a representative of the body awarding the contract and the Division of Labor Standards Enforcement of the Department of Industrial Relations.

(3) A certified copy of all payroll records enumerated in subdivision (a) shall be made available upon request by the public for inspection or for copies thereof. However, a request by the public shall be made through either the body awarding the contract or the Division of Labor Standards Enforcement. If the requested payroll records have not been provided pursuant to paragraph (2), the requesting party shall, prior to being provided the records, reimburse the costs of preparation by the contractor, subcontractors, and the entity through which the request was made. The public may not be given access to the records at the principal office of the contractor.

(c) Unless required to be furnished directly to the Labor Commissioner in accordance with paragraph (3) of subdivision (a) of Section 1771.4, the certified payroll records shall be on forms provided by the

Division of Labor Standards Enforcement or shall contain the same information as the forms provided by the division. The payroll records may consist of printouts of payroll data that are maintained as computer records, if the printouts contain the same information as the forms provided by the division and the printouts are verified in the manner specified in subdivision (a).

(d) A contractor or subcontractor shall file a certified copy of the records enumerated in subdivision (a) with the entity that requested the records within 10 days after receipt of a written request.

(e) Except as provided in subdivision (f), any copy of records made available for inspection as copies and furnished upon request to the public or any public agency by the awarding body or the Division of Labor Standards Enforcement shall be marked or obliterated to prevent disclosure of an individual's name, address, and social security number. The name and address of the contractor awarded the contract or the subcontractor performing the contract shall not be marked or obliterated. Any copy of records made available for inspection by, or furnished to, a multiemployer Taft-Hartley trust fund (29 U.S.C. Sec. 186(c)(5)) that requests the records for the purposes of allocating contributions to participants shall be marked or obliterated only to prevent disclosure of an individual's full social security number, but shall provide the last four digits of the social security number. Any copy of records made available for inspection by, or furnished to, a joint labor-management committee established pursuant to the federal Labor Management Cooperation Act of 1978 (29 U.S.C. Sec. 175a) shall be marked or obliterated only to prevent disclosure of an individual's social security number.

(f) (1) Notwithstanding any other provision of law, agencies that are included in the Joint Enforcement Strike Force on the Underground Economy established pursuant to Section 329 of the Unemployment Insurance Code and other law enforcement agencies investigating violations of law shall, upon request, be provided nonredacted copies of certified payroll records. Any copies of records or certified payroll made available for inspection and furnished upon request to the public by an agency included in the Joint Enforcement Strike Force on the Underground Economy or to a law enforcement agency investigating a violation of law shall be marked or redacted to prevent disclosure of an individual's name, address, and social security number.

(2) An employer shall not be liable for damages in a civil action for any reasonable act or omission taken in good faith in compliance with this subdivision.

(g) The contractor shall inform the body awarding the contract of the location of the records enumerated under subdivision (a), including the street address, city, and county, and shall, within five working days, provide a notice of a change of location and address.

(h) The contractor or subcontractor has 10 days in which to comply subsequent to receipt of a written notice requesting the records enumerated in subdivision (a). In the event that the contractor or subcontractor fails to comply within the 10-day period, the contractor or subcontractor shall, as a penalty to the state or political subdivision on whose behalf the contract is made or awarded, forfeit one hundred dollars ($100) for each calendar day, or portion thereof, for each worker, until strict compliance is effectuated. Upon the request of the Division of Labor Standards Enforcement, these penalties shall be withheld from progress payments then due. A contractor is not subject to a penalty assessment pursuant to this section due to the failure of a subcontractor to comply with this section.

(i) The body awarding the contract shall cause to be inserted in the contract stipulations to effectuate this section.

(j) The director shall adopt rules consistent with the California Public Records Act (Division 10 (commencing with Section 7920.000) of Title 1 of the Government Code) and the Information Practices Act of 1977 (Title 1.8 (commencing with Section 1798) of Part 4 of Division 3 of the Civil Code) governing the release of these records, including the establishment of reasonable fees to be charged for reproducing copies of records required by this section.

Added Stats 1997 ch 757 § 4 (SB 1328). Amended Stats 2001 ch 804 § 2 (SB 588); Stats 2002 ch 28 § 1 (AB 1448) (ch 28 prevails), ch 664 § 161 (AB 3034); Stats 2003 ch 62 § 205 (SB 600); Stats 2005 ch 500 § 1 (SB 759), effective January 1, 2006; Stats 2011 ch 481 § 1 (AB 766), effective January 1, 2012, ch 677 § 2.5 (AB 551), effective January 1, 2012; Stats 2012 ch 46 § 94 (SB 1038), effective June 27, 2012; Stats 2013 ch 792 § 3 (AB 1336), effective January 1, 2014; Stats 2014 ch 28 § 71 (SB 854), effective June 20, 2014; Stats 2021 ch 615 § 321 (AB 474), effective January 1, 2022.

§ 1777.1. Penalties for violations of specified provisions; List of debarred contractors

(a) Whenever a contractor or subcontractor performing a public works project pursuant to this chapter is found by the Labor Commissioner to be in violation of this chapter with intent to defraud, the contractor or subcontractor or a firm, corporation, partnership, or association in which the contractor or subcontractor has any interest is ineligible for a period of not less than one year or more than three years to do either of the following:

(1) Bid on or be awarded a contract for a public works project.

(2) Perform work as a subcontractor on a public works project.

(b) Whenever a contractor or subcontractor performing a public works project pursuant to this chapter is found by the Labor Commissioner to have committed two or more separate willful violations of this chapter within a three-year period, the contractor or subcontractor or a firm, corporation, partnership, or association in which the contractor or subcontractor has any interest is ineligible for a period up to three years to do either of the following:

(1) Bid on or be awarded a contract for a public works project.

(2) Perform work as a subcontractor on a public works project.

(c) Whenever a contractor or subcontractor performing a public works project has failed to provide a timely response to a request by the Division of Labor Standards Enforcement, the Division of Apprenticeship Standards, or the awarding body to produce certified payroll records pursuant to Section 1776, the Labor Commissioner shall notify the contractor or subcontractor that, in addition to any other penalties provided by law, the contractor or subcontractor will be subject to debarment under this section if the certified payroll records are not produced within 30 days after receipt of the written notice. If the commissioner finds that the contractor or subcontractor has failed to comply with Section 1776 by that deadline, unless the commissioner finds that the failure to comply was due to circumstances outside the contractor's or subcontractor's control, the contractor or subcontractor or a firm, corporation, partnership, or association in which the contractor or subcontractor has any interest is ineligible for a period of not less than one year and not more than three years to do either of the following:

(1) Bid on or be awarded a contract for a public works project.

(2) Perform work as a subcontractor on a public works project.

(d) (1) In the event a contractor or subcontractor is determined by the Labor Commissioner to have knowingly committed a serious violation of any provision of Section 1777.5, the Labor Commissioner may also deny to the contractor or subcontractor, and to its responsible officers, the right to bid on or to be awarded or perform work as a subcontractor on any public works contract for a period of up to one year for the first violation and for a period of up to three years for a second or subsequent violation. Each period of debarment shall run from the date the determination of noncompliance by the Labor Commissioner becomes a final order.

(2) The Labor Commissioner shall consider, in determining whether a violation is serious, and in determining whether and for how long a party should be debarred for violating Section 1777.5, all of the following circumstances:

(A) Whether the violation was intentional.

(B) Whether the party has committed other violations of Section 1777.5.

(C) Whether, upon notice of the violation, the party took steps to voluntarily remedy the violation.

(D) Whether, and to what extent, the violation resulted in lost training opportunities for apprentices.

(E) Whether, and to what extent, the violation otherwise harmed apprentices or apprenticeship programs.

(e) A willful violation occurs when the contractor or subcontractor knew or reasonably should have known of his or her obligations under the public works law and deliberately fails or deliberately refuses to comply with its provisions.

(f) The Labor Commissioner shall publish on the commissioner's Internet Web site a list of contractors who are ineligible to bid on or be awarded a public works contract, or to perform work as a subcontractor on a public works project pursuant to this chapter. The list shall contain the name of the contractor, the Contractors' State License Board license number of the contractor, and the effective period of debarment of the contractor. Contractors shall be added to the list upon issuance of a debarment order and the commissioner shall also notify the Contractors' State License Board when the list is updated. At least annually, the commissioner shall notify awarding bodies of the availability of the list of debarred contractors. The commissioner shall also place advertisements in construction industry publications targeted to the contractors and subcontractors, chosen by the commissioner, that state the effective period of the debarment and the reason for debarment. The advertisements shall appear one time for each debarment of a contractor in each publication chosen by the commissioner. The debarred contractor or subcontractor shall be liable to the commissioner for the reasonable cost of the advertisements, not to exceed five thousand dollars ($5,000). The amount paid to the commissioner for the advertisements shall be credited against the contractor's or subcontractor's obligation to pay civil fines or penalties for the same willful violation of this chapter.

(g) For purposes of this section, "contractor or subcontractor" means a firm, corporation, partnership, or association and its responsible managing officer, as well as any supervisors, managers, and officers found by the Labor Commissioner to be personally and substantially responsible for the willful violation of this chapter.

(h) For the purposes of this section, the term "any interest" means an interest in the entity bidding or performing work on the public works project, whether as an owner, partner, officer, manager, employee, agent, consultant, or representative. "Any interest" includes, but is not limited to, all instances where the debarred contractor or subcontractor receives payments, whether cash or any other form of compensation, from any entity bidding or performing work on the public works project, or enters into any contracts or agreements with the entity bidding or performing work on the public works project for services performed or to be performed for contracts that have been or will be assigned or sublet, or for vehicles, tools, equipment, or supplies that have been or will be sold, rented, or leased during the period from the initiation of the debarment proceedings until the end of the term of the debarment period. "Any interest" does not include shares held in a publicly traded corporation if the shares were not received as compensation after the initiation of debarment from an entity bidding or performing work on a public works project.

(i) For the purposes of this section, the term "entity" is defined as a company, limited liability company, association, partnership, sole proprietorship, limited liability partnership, corporation, business trust, or organization.

(j) The Labor Commissioner shall adopt rules and regulations for the administration and enforcement of this section.

Added Stats 1989 ch 1224 § 10. Amended Stats 1998 ch 443 § 1 (AB 1569); Stats 2000 ch 970 § 1 (AB 2513); Stats 2011 ch 677 § 3 (AB 551), effective January 1, 2012; Stats 2014 ch 297 § 1 (AB 2744), effective January 1, 2015.

§ 1777.5. Employment of apprentices on public works

(a) (1) This chapter does not prevent the employment upon public works of properly registered apprentices who are active participants in an approved apprenticeship program.

(2) For purposes of this chapter, "apprenticeship program" means a program under the jurisdiction of the California Apprenticeship Council established pursuant to Section 3070.

(b) (1) Every apprentice employed upon public works shall be paid the prevailing rate of per diem wages for apprentices in the trade to which he or she is registered and shall be employed only at the work of the craft or trade to which he or she is registered.

(2) Unless otherwise provided by a collective bargaining agreement, when a contractor requests the dispatch of an apprentice pursuant to this section to perform work on a public works project and requires the apprentice to fill out an application or undergo testing, training, an examination, or other preemployment process as a condition of employment, the apprentice shall be paid for the time spent on the required preemployment activity, including travel time to and from the required activity, if any, at the prevailing rate of per diem wages for apprentices in the trade to which he or she is registered. Unless otherwise provided by a collective bargaining agreement, a contractor is not required to compensate an apprentice for the time spent on preemployment activities if the apprentice is required to take a preemployment drug or alcohol test and he or she fails to pass that test.

(c) Only apprentices, as defined in Section 3077, who are in training under apprenticeship standards that have been approved by the Chief of the Division of Apprenticeship Standards and who are parties to written apprentice agreements under Chapter 4 (commencing with Section 3070) of Division 3 are eligible to be employed at the apprentice wage rate on public works. The employment and training of each apprentice shall be in accordance with either of the following:

Appendix

(1) The apprenticeship standards and apprentice agreements under which he or she is training.

(2) The rules and regulations of the California Apprenticeship Council.

(d) If the contractor to whom the contract is awarded by the state or any political subdivision, in performing any of the work under the contract, employs workers in any apprenticeable craft or trade, the contractor shall employ apprentices in at least the ratio set forth in this section and may apply to any apprenticeship program in the craft or trade that can provide apprentices to the site of the public work for a certificate approving the contractor under the apprenticeship standards for the employment and training of apprentices in the area or industry affected. However, the decision of the apprenticeship program to approve or deny a certificate shall be subject to review by the Administrator of Apprenticeship. The apprenticeship program or programs, upon approving the contractor, shall arrange for the dispatch of apprentices to the contractor. A contractor covered by an apprenticeship program's standards shall not be required to submit any additional application in order to include additional public works contracts under that program. "Apprenticeable craft or trade," as used in this section, means a craft or trade determined as an apprenticeable occupation in accordance with rules and regulations prescribed by the California Apprenticeship Council. As used in this section, "contractor" includes any subcontractor under a contractor who performs any public works not excluded by subdivision (o).

(e) Before commencing work on a contract for public works, every contractor shall submit contract award information to an applicable apprenticeship program that can supply apprentices to the site of the public work. The information submitted shall include an estimate of journeyman hours to be performed under the contract, the number of apprentices proposed to be employed, and the approximate dates the apprentices would be employed. A copy of this information shall also be submitted to the awarding body, if requested by the awarding body. Within 60 days after concluding work on the contract, each contractor and subcontractor shall submit to the awarding body, if requested, and to the apprenticeship program a verified statement of the journeyman and apprentice hours performed on the contract. The information under this subdivision shall be public. The apprenticeship programs shall retain this information for 12 months.

(f) The apprenticeship program supplying apprentices to the area of the site of the public work shall ensure equal employment and affirmative action in apprenticeship for women and minorities.

(g) The ratio of work performed by apprentices to journeymen employed in a particular craft or trade on the public work may be no higher than the ratio stipulated in the apprenticeship standards under which the apprenticeship program operates if the contractor agrees to be bound by those standards. However, except as otherwise provided in this section, in no case shall the ratio be less than one hour of apprentice work for every five hours of journeyman work.

(h) This ratio of apprentice work to journeyman work shall apply during any day or portion of a day when any journeyman is employed at the jobsite and shall be computed on the basis of the hours worked during the day by journeymen so employed. Any work performed by a journeyman in excess of eight hours per day or 40 hours per week shall not be used to calculate the ratio. The contractor shall employ apprentices for the number of hours computed as above before the end of the contract or, in the case of a subcontractor, before the end of the subcontract. However, the contractor shall endeavor, to the greatest extent possible, to employ apprentices during the same time period that the journeymen in the same craft or trade are employed at the jobsite. When an hourly apprenticeship ratio is not feasible for a particular craft or trade, the Administrator of Apprenticeship, upon application of an apprenticeship program, may order a minimum ratio of not less than one apprentice for each five journeymen in a craft or trade classification.

(i) A contractor covered by this section who has agreed to be covered by an apprenticeship program's standards upon the issuance of the approval certificate, or who has been previously approved for an apprenticeship program in the craft or trade, shall employ the number of apprentices or the ratio of apprentices to journeymen stipulated in the applicable apprenticeship standards, but in no event less than the 1-to-5 ratio required by subdivision (g).

(j) Upon proper showing by a contractor that he or she employs apprentices in a particular craft or trade in the state on all of his or her contracts on an annual average of not less than one hour of apprentice work for every five hours of labor performed by journeymen, the Administrator of Apprenticeship may grant a certificate exempting the contractor from the 1-to-5 hourly ratio, as set forth in this section for that craft or trade.

(k) An apprenticeship program has the discretion to grant to a participating contractor or contractor association a certificate, which shall be subject to the approval of the Administrator of Apprenticeship, exempting the contractor from the 1-to-5 ratio set forth in this section when it finds that any one of the following conditions is met:

(1) Unemployment for the previous three-month period in the area exceeds an average of 15 percent.

(2) The number of apprentices in training in the area exceeds a ratio of 1 to 5.

(3) There is a showing that the apprenticeable craft or trade is replacing at least one-thirtieth of its journeymen annually through apprenticeship training, either on a statewide basis or on a local basis.

(4) Assignment of an apprentice to any work performed under a public works contract would create a condition that would jeopardize his or her life or the life, safety, or property of fellow employees or the public at large, or the specific task to which the apprentice is to be assigned is of a nature that training cannot be provided by a journeyman.

(*l*) If an exemption is granted pursuant to subdivision (k) to an organization that represents contractors in a specific trade from the 1-to-5 ratio on a local or statewide basis, the member contractors shall not be required to submit individual applications for approval to local joint apprenticeship committees, if they are already covered by the local apprenticeship standards.

(m) (1) A contractor to whom a contract is awarded, who, in performing any of the work under the contract, employs journeymen or apprentices in any apprenticeable craft or trade shall contribute to the California Apprenticeship Council the same amount that the director determines is the prevailing amount of apprenticeship training contributions in the area of the public works site. A contractor may take as a credit for payments to the council any amounts paid by the contractor to an approved apprenticeship program that can supply apprentices to the site of the public works project. The contractor may add the amount of the contributions in computing his or her bid for the contract.

(2) (A) At the conclusion of the 2002-03 fiscal year and each fiscal year thereafter, the California Apprenticeship Council shall distribute training contributions received by the council under this subdivision, less the expenses of the Department of Industrial Relations for administering this subdivision, by making grants to approved apprenticeship programs for the purpose of training apprentices. The grant funds shall be distributed as follows:

(i) If there is an approved multiemployer apprenticeship program serving the same craft or trade and geographic area for which the training contributions were made to the council, a grant to that program shall be made.

(ii) If there are two or more approved multiemployer apprenticeship programs serving the same craft or trade and county for which the training contributions were made to the council, the grant shall be divided among those programs based on the number of apprentices from that county registered in each program.

(iii) All training contributions not distributed under clauses (i) and (ii) shall be used to defray the future expenses of the Department of Industrial Relations for the administration and enforcement of apprenticeship and preapprenticeship standards and requirements under this code.

(B) An apprenticeship program shall only be eligible to receive grant funds pursuant to this subdivision if the apprenticeship program agrees, prior to the receipt of any grant funds, to keep adequate records that document the expenditure of grant funds and to make all records available to the Department of Industrial Relations so that the Department of Industrial Relations is able to verify that grant funds were used solely for training apprentices. For purposes of this subparagraph, adequate records include, but are not limited to, invoices, receipts, and canceled checks that account for the expenditure of grant funds. This subparagraph shall not be deemed to require an apprenticeship program to provide the Department of Industrial Relations with more documentation than is necessary to verify the appropriate expenditure of grant funds made pursuant to this subdivision.

(C) The Department of Industrial Relations shall verify that grants made pursuant to this subdivision are used solely to fund training apprentices. If an apprenticeship program is unable to demonstrate how grant funds are expended or if an apprenticeship program is found to be using grant funds for purposes other than training apprentices, then the apprenticeship program shall not be eligible to receive any future grant pursuant to this subdivision and the Department of Industrial Relations may initiate the process to rescind the registration of the apprenticeship program.

(3) All training contributions received pursuant to this subdivision shall be deposited in the Apprenticeship Training Contribution Fund, which is hereby created in the State Treasury. Upon appropriation by the Legislature, all moneys in the Apprenticeship Training Contribution Fund shall be used for the purpose of carrying out this subdivision and to pay the expenses of the Department of Industrial Relations.

(n) The body awarding the contract shall cause to be inserted in the contract stipulations to effectuate this section. The stipulations shall fix the responsibility of compliance with this section for all apprenticeable occupations with the prime contractor.

(o) This section does not apply to contracts of general contractors or to contracts of specialty contractors not bidding for work through a general or prime contractor when the contracts of general contractors or those specialty contractors involve less than thirty thousand dollars ($30,000).

(p) An awarding body that implements an approved labor compliance program in accordance with subdivision (b) of Section 1771.5 may, with the approval of the director, assist in the enforcement of this section under the terms and conditions prescribed by the director.

Added Stats 1937 ch 872. Amended Stats 1939 ch 971 § 1; Stats 1957 ch 699 § 1; Stats 1968 ch 1411 § 1; Stats 1969 ch 1260 § 1, effective August 31, 1969; Stats 1972 ch 1087 § 1, ch 1399 § 1; Stats 1974 ch 965 § 1; Stats 1976 ch 1179 § 2, effective September 22, 1976; Stats 1989 ch 1224 § 11; Amended Stats 1997 ch 17 § 91 (SB 947); Stats 1999

Appendix

ch 903 § 2 (AB 921); Stats 2000 ch 135 § 124 (AB 2539) (ch 875 prevails), ch 875 § 1 (AB 2481); Stats 2002 ch 1124 § 43 (AB 3000), effective September 30, 2002; Stats 2003 ch 228 § 38 (AB 1756), effective August 11, 2003; Stats 2010 ch 719 § 52 (SB 856), effective October 19, 2010; Stats 2012 ch 46 § 95 (SB 1038), effective June 27, 2012; Stats 2014 ch 890 § 1 (AB 1870), effective January 1, 2015; Stats 2016 ch 746 § 1 (AB 1926), effective January 1, 2017. Stats 2017 ch 553 § 1 (AB 581), effective January 1, 2018. Stats 2018 ch 704 § 17 (AB 235), effective September 22, 2018.

§ 1782. Receipt and use of state funding or financial assistance for a construction project by charter city

(a) A charter city shall not receive or use state funding or financial assistance for a construction project if the city has a charter provision or ordinance that authorizes a contractor to not comply with the provisions of this article on any public works contract.

(b) A charter city shall not receive or use state funding or financial assistance for a construction project if the city has awarded, within the prior two years, a public works contract without requiring the contractor to comply with all of the provisions of this article. This subdivision shall not apply if the charter city's failure to include the prevailing wage or apprenticeship requirement in a particular contract was inadvertent and contrary to a city charter provision or ordinance that otherwise requires compliance with this article.

(c) A charter city is not disqualified by subdivision (a) from receiving or using state funding or financial assistance for its construction projects if the charter city has a local prevailing wage ordinance for all its public works contracts that includes requirements that in all respects are equal to or greater than the requirements imposed by the provisions of this article and that do not authorize a contractor to not comply with this article.

(d) For purposes of this section, the following shall apply:

(1) A public works contract does not include contracts for projects of twenty-five thousand dollars ($25,000) or less when the project is for construction work, or projects of fifteen thousand dollars ($15,000) or less when the project is for alteration, demolition, repair, or maintenance work.

(2) A charter city includes any agency of a charter city and any entity controlled by a charter city whose contracts would be subject to this article.

(3) A "construction project" means a project that involves the award of a public works contract.

(4) State funding or financial assistance includes direct state funding, state loans and loan guarantees, state tax credits, and any other type of state financial support for a construction project. State funding or financial assistance does not include revenues that charter cities are entitled to receive without conditions under the California Constitution.

(e) The Director of Industrial Relations shall maintain a list of charter cities that may receive and use state funding or financial assistance for their construction projects.

(f) (1) This section does not restrict a charter city from receiving or using state funding or financial assistance that was awarded to the city prior to January 1, 2015, or from receiving or using state funding or financial assistance to complete a contract that was awarded prior to January 1, 2015.

(2) A charter city is not disqualified by subdivision (b) from receiving or using state funding or financial assistance for its construction projects based on the city's failure to require a contractor to comply with this article in performing a contract the city advertised for bid or awarded prior to January 1, 2015.

Added Stats 2013 ch 794 (SB 7), effective January 1, 2014.

§ 1784. Contractor entitled to recovery of increased costs from hiring party; Notice; Applicability

(a) Notwithstanding any other law, a contractor may bring an action in a court of competent jurisdiction to recover from the hiring party that the contractor directly contracts with, any increased costs attributable solely to the provisions of this chapter, including, but not limited to, the difference between the wages actually paid to an employee and the wages that were required to be paid to an employee under this chapter, any penalties or other sums required to be paid under this chapter, and costs and attorney's fees for the action incurred by the contractor as a result of any decision by the Department of Industrial Relations, the Labor and Workforce Development Agency, or a court that classifies, after the time at which the hiring party accepts the contractor's bid, awards the contractor a contract under circumstances when no bid is solicited, or otherwise allows construction by the contractor to proceed, the work covered by the project, or any portion thereof, as a "public work," as defined in this chapter, except to the extent that either of the following is true:

(1) The owner or developer or its agent expressly advised the contractor that the work to be covered by the contract would be a "public work," as defined in this chapter, or is otherwise subject to the payment of prevailing wages.

(2) The hiring party expressly advised the contractor that the work subject to the contract would be a "public work," as defined in this chapter, or is otherwise subject to the payment of prevailing wages.

(b) (1) To be entitled to the recovery of increased costs described in subdivision (a), the contractor shall notify the hiring party and the owner or developer within 30 days after receipt of the notice of a decision by the Department of Industrial Relations or the Labor and Workforce Development Agency, or the initiation of any action in a court alleging, that the work covered by the project, or any portion thereof, is a "public work," as defined in this chapter.

(2) The notice provided pursuant to this subdivision shall set forth the legal name, address, and telephone number of the contractor, and the name, address, and telephone number of the contractor's representative, if any, and shall be given by registered or certified mail, express mail, or overnight delivery by an express service carrier.

(c) A contractor is not required to list any prevailing wages or apprenticeship standard violations on a prequalification questionnaire that are the direct result of the failure of the owner or developer or its agent, or a hiring party, to notify the contractor that the project, or any portion thereof, was a "public work," as defined in this chapter.

(d) This section does not apply to private residential projects built on private property unless the project is built pursuant to an agreement with a state agency, redevelopment agency, or local public housing authority.

(e) This section does not apply if the conduct of the contractor caused the project to be a "public work," as defined in this chapter, or if the contractor has actual knowledge that the work is a "public work," as defined in this chapter.

(f) A contractor may seek recovery pursuant to this section only from a hiring party with whom the contractor has a direct contract.

(g) For purposes of this section, "contractor" means a person or entity licensed by the Contractors' State Licensing Board that has a direct contract with the hiring party to provide services on private property or for the benefit of a private owner or developer.

(h) For purposes of this section, "hiring party" means the party that has a direct contract for services provided by the contractor who is seeking recovery pursuant to subdivision (a) on a private works project that was subsequently determined to be a public work by the Department of Industrial Relations or the Labor and Workforce Development Agency, or by the initiation of any action in a court alleging that the work covered by the project, or any portion thereof, was a public work.

Added Stats 2014 ch 161 § 1 (AB 1939), effective January 1, 2015.

§ 1785. Strategic enforcement unit

(a) The director shall establish and maintain a strategic enforcement unit focused on construction, alteration, and repair projects. The unit shall enhance the department's enforcement of this code in construction, alteration, and repair projects, including projects funded pursuant to Section 50675.1.3 of the Health and Safety Code and other publicly funded residential construction projects. The unit shall have primary responsibility for enforcement of this code in construction projects subject to Section 50675.1.3 of the Health and Safety

Code. Any funds appropriated to the department for purposes of this section shall be administered and allocated by the director.

(b) The strategic enforcement unit described in subdivision (a) shall provide technical assistance to local public entities related to both of the following:

(1) Best practices for monitoring and enforcing requirements pertaining to construction, alteration, and repair projects paid for in whole or in part out of public funds, including, but not limited to, this chapter.

(2) Outreach and engagement with workers, employers, and state certified apprenticeship programs connected to construction, alteration, and repair projects.

Added Stats 2021 ch 111 § 26 (AB 140), effective July 19, 2021.

DIVISION 3

EMPLOYMENT RELATIONS

Chapter 2

Employer and Employee

Article 1

The Contract of Employment

§ 2750.5.   Rebuttable presumption that contractor is employee rather than independent contractor; Proof of independent contractor status

There is a rebuttable presumption affecting the burden of proof that a worker performing services for which a license is required pursuant to Chapter 9 (commencing with Section 7000) of Division 3 of the Business and Professions Code, or who is performing such services for a person who is required to obtain such a license is an employee rather than an independent contractor. Proof of independent contractor status includes satisfactory proof of these factors:

(a) That the individual has the right to control and discretion as to the manner of performance of the contract for services in that the result of the work and not the means by which it is accomplished is the primary factor bargained for.

(b) That the individual is customarily engaged in an independently established business.

(c) That the individual's independent contractor status is bona fide and not a subterfuge to avoid employee status. A bona fide independent contractor status is further evidenced by the presence of cumulative factors such as substantial investment other than personal services in the business, holding out to be in business for oneself, bargaining for a contract to complete a specific project for compensation by project rather than by time, control over the time and place the work is performed, supplying the tools or instrumentalities used in the work other than tools and instrumentalities normally and customarily provided by employees, hiring employees, performing work that is not ordinarily in the course of the principal's work, performing work that requires a particular skill, holding a license pursuant to the Business and Professions Code, the intent by the parties that the work relationship is of an independent contractor status, or that the relationship is not severable or terminable at will by the principal but gives rise to an action for breach of contract.

In addition to the factors contained in subdivisions (a), (b), and (c), any person performing any function or activity for which a license is required pursuant to Chapter 9 (commencing with Section 7000) of Division 3 of the Business and Professions Code shall hold a valid contractors' license as a condition of having independent contractor status.

For purposes of workers' compensation law, this presumption is a supplement to the existing statutory definitions of employee and independent contractor, and is not intended to lessen the coverage of employees under Division 4 and Division 5.

Added Stats 1978 ch 1246 § 1. Amended Stats 1979 ch 605 § 1.

§ 2753. Liability of person who advises employer to treat individual as independent contractor to avoid employee status

(a) A person who, for money or other valuable consideration, knowingly advises an employer to treat an individual as an independent contractor to avoid employee status for that individual shall be jointly and severally liable with the employer if the individual is found not to be an independent contractor.

(b) This section does not apply to the following persons:

(1) A person who provides advice to his or her employer.

(2) An attorney authorized to practice law in California or another United States jurisdiction who provides legal advice in the course of the practice of law.

Added Stats 2011 ch 706 § 2 (SB 459), effective January 1, 2012.

Article 2

Obligations of Employer

§ 2810.3. Definitions

(a) As used in this section:

(1) (A) "Client employer" means a business entity, regardless of its form, that obtains or is provided workers to perform labor within its usual course of business from a labor contractor.

(B) "Client employer" does not include any of the following:

(i) A business entity with a workforce of fewer than 25 workers, including those hired directly by the client employer and those obtained from, or provided by, any labor contractor.

(ii) A business entity with five or fewer workers supplied by a labor contractor or labor contractors to the client employer at any given time.

(iii) The state or any political subdivision of the state, including any city, county, city and county, or special district.

(2) "Labor" has the same meaning provided by Section 200.

(3) "Labor contractor" means an individual or entity that supplies, either with or without a contract, a client employer with workers to perform labor within the client employer's usual course of business. "Labor contractor" does not include any of the following:

(A) A bona fide nonprofit, community-based organization that provides services to workers.

(B) A bona fide labor organization or apprenticeship program or hiring hall operated pursuant to a collective bargaining agreement.

(C) A motion picture payroll services company, as defined in subparagraph (A) of paragraph (4) of subdivision (f) of Section 679 of the Unemployment Insurance Code.

(D) A third party who is a party to an employee leasing arrangement, as defined by Rule 4 of Section V of the California Workers' Compensation Experience Rating Plan-1995 (Section 2353.1 of Title 10 of the California Code of Regulations), as it read on January 1, 2014, except those arrangements described in subrule d of Rule 4 of Section V, if the employee leasing arrangement contractually obligates the client employer to assume all civil legal responsibility and civil liability under this act.

(4) "Wages" has the same meaning provided by Section 200 and all sums payable to an employee or the state based upon any failure to pay wages, as provided by law.

(5) "Worker" does not include an employee who is exempt from the payment of an overtime rate of compensation for executive, administrative, and professional employees pursuant to wage orders by the Industrial Welfare Commission described in Section 515.

(6) "Usual course of business" means the regular and customary work of a business, performed within or upon the premises or worksite of the client employer.

(b) A client employer shall share with a labor contractor all civil legal responsibility and civil liability for all workers supplied by that labor contractor for both of the following:

(1) The payment of wages.

(2) Failure to secure valid workers' compensation coverage as required by Section 3700.

(c) A client employer shall not shift to the labor contractor any legal duties or liabilities under Division 5 (commencing with Section 6300) with respect to workers supplied by the labor contractor.

(d) At least 30 days prior to filing a civil action against a client employer for violations covered by this section, a worker or the worker's representative shall notify the client employer of violations under subdivision (b).

(e) Neither the client employer nor the labor contractor may take any adverse action against any worker for providing notification of violations or filing a claim or civil action.

(f) The provisions of subdivisions (b) and (c) are in addition to, and shall be supplemental of, any other theories of liability or requirement established by statute or common law.

(g) This section does not prohibit a client employer from establishing, exercising, or enforcing by contract any otherwise lawful remedies against a labor contractor for liability created by acts of a labor contractor.

(h) This section does not prohibit a labor contractor from establishing, exercising, or enforcing by contract any otherwise lawful remedies against a client employer for liability created by acts of a client employer.

(i) Upon request by a state enforcement agency or department, a client employer or a labor contractor shall provide to the agency or department any information within its possession, custody, or control required to verify compliance with applicable state laws. Upon request, these records shall be made available promptly for inspection, and the state agency or department shall be permitted to copy them. This subdivision does not require the disclosure of information that is not otherwise required to be disclosed by employers upon request by a state enforcement agency or department.

(j) The Labor Commissioner may adopt regulations and rules of practice and procedure necessary to administer and enforce the provisions of subdivisions (b) and (i) that are under the Labor Commissioner's jurisdiction.

(k) The Division of Occupational Safety and Health may adopt regulations and rules of practice and procedure necessary to administer and enforce the provisions of subdivisions (c) and (i) that are under its jurisdiction.

(*l*) The Employment Development Department may adopt regulations and rules of practice and procedure necessary to administer and enforce the provisions of subdivisions (b) and (i) that are under its jurisdiction.

(m) A waiver of this section is contrary to public policy, and is void and unenforceable.

(n) This section does not impose individual liability on a homeowner for labor or services received at the home or the owner of a home-based business for labor or services received at the home.

(o) This section does not impose liability on a client employer for the use of an independent contractor other than a labor contractor or to change the definition of independent contractor.

(p) This section does not impose liability on the following:

(1) A client employer that is not a motor carrier of property based solely on the employer's use of a third-party motor carrier of property with interstate or intrastate operating authority to ship or receive freight.

(2) A client employer that is a motor carrier of property subcontracting with, or otherwise engaging, another motor carrier of property to provide transportation services using its own employees and commercial motor vehicles, as defined in Section 34601 of the Vehicle Code.

(3) A client employer that is not a household mover based solely on the employer's use of a third-party household mover permitted by the Bureau of Household Goods and Services pursuant to Chapter 3.1 (commencing with Section 19225) of Division 8 of the Business and Professions Code to move household goods.

(4) A client employer that is a household mover permitted by the Bureau of Household Goods and Services pursuant to Chapter 3.1 (commencing with Section 19225) of Division 8 of the Business and Professions Code subcontracting with, or otherwise engaging, another permitted household mover to provide transportation of household goods using its own employees and motor vehicles, as defined in former Section 5108 of the Public Utilities Code.

(5) A client employer that is a cable operator, as defined by Section 5830 of the Public Utilities Code, a direct-to-home satellite service provider, or a telephone corporation, as defined by Section 234 of the Public Utilities Code, based upon its contracting with a company to build, install, maintain, or perform repair work utilizing the employees and vehicles of the contractor if the name of the contractor is visible on employee uniforms and vehicles.

(6) A motor club holding a certificate of authority issued pursuant to Chapter 2 (commencing with Section 12160) of Part 5 of Division 2 of the Insurance Code when it contracts with third parties to provide

motor club services utilizing the employees and vehicles of the third-party contractor if the name of the contractor is visible on the contractor's vehicles.

Added Stats 2014 ch 728 § 1 (AB 1897), effective January 1, 2015. Amended Stats 2015 ch 792 § 3 (AB 1509), effective January 1, 2016; Stats 2019 ch 643 § 1 (SB 358), effective January 1, 2020.

Chapter 4

Apprenticeship

§ 3075. Apprenticeship program administration; Joint sponsorship; Approval of new apprenticeship program; Appeal of decision; Notice of proposed apprenticeship standards; Email updates

(a) An apprenticeship program may be administered by a joint apprenticeship committee, unilateral management or labor apprenticeship committee, or an individual employer. Programs may be approved by the chief in any trade in the state or in a city or trade area, whenever the apprentice training needs justify the establishment. Where a collective bargaining agreement exists, a program shall be jointly sponsored unless either party to the agreement waives its right to representation in writing. Joint apprenticeship committees shall be composed of an equal number of employer and employee representatives.

(b) For purposes of subdivision (a), the apprentice training needs in the building and construction trades and firefighter programs shall be deemed to justify the approval of a new apprenticeship program only if any of the following conditions are met:

(1) There is no existing apprenticeship program approved under this chapter serving the same craft or trade and geographic area.

(2) Existing apprenticeship programs approved under this chapter that serve the same craft or trade and geographic area do not have the capacity, or neglect or refuse, to dispatch sufficient apprentices to qualified employers at a public works site who have requested apprentices and are willing to abide by the applicable apprenticeship standards, as shown by a sustained pattern of unfilled requests.

(3) Existing apprenticeship programs approved under this chapter that serve the same trade and geographic area have been identified by the California Apprenticeship Council as deficient in meeting their obligations under this chapter.

(c) For purposes of subdivision (b), an existing apprenticeship program serves the "same craft or trade" as a proposed apprenticeship program when there would be substantial overlap in the work processes covered by the programs or when graduates of the existing program would be qualified to perform a substantial portion of the work that would be performed by graduates of the new program.

(d) The chief's decisions regarding applications for new apprenticeship programs in the building and construction trades and firefighters may be appealed by any interested party to the California Apprenticeship Council. For purposes of this section, an application for expansion of an existing program to include an additional occupation shall be considered an application for a "new apprenticeship program."

(e) The chief's decisions regarding applications for new apprenticeship programs outside the building and construction trades and firefighters are final and not subject to administrative appeal, except as otherwise provided in this section.

(f) The chief's decisions regarding applications for new apprenticeship programs shall be posted to the division's Internet Web site, which shall constitute the only form of notice and service. Appeals to the California Apprenticeship Council under this section must be filed within 30 days after notice of the chief's decision.

(g) The chief shall not approve a new apprenticeship program that includes a substantial number of work processes covered by a program in the building and construction trades or firefighters, or approve the amendment of apprenticeship standards to include those work processes, unless either of the following applies:

(1) The program is in the building and construction trades or a firefighter program and subject to the rules and regulations of the California Apprenticeship Council.

(2) The California Apprenticeship Council has granted consent to the approval of the program or the amendment to the apprenticeship standards. If no party files an objection with the chief to the approval of the proposed program or amendment alleging overlap of work processes under this subdivision, the chief shall not be required to seek the consent of the California Apprenticeship Council prior to approving the program or amendment.

(h) At least 30 days before approval of a new apprenticeship program, or of an amendment to the apprenticeship standards to include new work processes, the division shall post on its Internet Web site a copy of the proposed apprenticeship standards, which shall constitute the only form of notice and service that an application on the proposed program or amendment is pending. Notwithstanding subdivision (e), the chief's decision regarding any new apprenticeship program or amendment of the apprenticeship standards to include new work processes may be appealed to the California Apprenticeship Council if notice under this subdivision is not provided.

(i) The division shall create a method on its Internet Web site for members of the public to subscribe to receive email updates when

Appendix

new decisions or proposed apprenticeship standards are posted pursuant to this section.

(j) Only the following programs may dispatch apprentices to projects subject to prevailing wage or skilled and trained workforce requirements:

(1) Programs in the building and construction trades approved before July 1, 2018.

(2) Programs in the building and construction trades approved under the standard in subdivision (b).

Added Stats 1939 ch 220 § 2. Amended Stats 1976 ch 1179 § 6, effective September 22, 1976; Stats 1984 ch 330 § 3; Amended Stats 1999 ch 903 § 7 (AB 921); Stats 2015 ch 126 § 1 (AB 1308), effective January 1, 2016; Stats 2018 ch 704 § 32 (AB 235), effective September 22, 2018.

§ 3099.   [Section repealed 2012.]

Added Stats 1999 ch 781 § 1 (AB 931). Amended Stats 2000 ch 875 § 3 (AB 2481); Stats 2002 ch 48 § 1 (AB 1087); Stats 2004 ch 183 § 262 (AB 3082); Stats 2006 ch 828 § 4 (AB 2907), effective January 1, 2007; Stats 2011 ch 693 § 1 (AB 1346), effective January 1, 2012. Repealed Stats 2012 ch 46 § 102 (SB 1038), effective June 27, 2012. The repealed section related to the duties of the Division of Apprenticeship Standards and defined "electricians". For comparable provisions, see Lab C § 108.3.

§ 3099.2.   [Section repealed 2012.]

Added Stats 2002 ch 48 § 2 (AB 1087). Amended Stats 2003 ch 884 § 2 (AB 1719); Stats 2006 ch 828 § 5 (AB 2907), effective January 1, 2007; Stats 2008 ch 558 § 1 (AB 3048), effective January 1, 2009, ch 716 § 2.5 (SB 1362), effective January 1, 2009; Stats 2011 ch 432 § 36 (SB 944), effective January 1, 2012, ch 693 § 2.5 (AB 1346), effective January 1, 2012. Repealed Stats 2012 ch 46 § 103 (SB 1038), effective June 27, 2012. The repealed section related to the certification of electricians and fire/life safety technicians. For comparable provisions, see Lab C § 108.2.

DIVISION 4

WORKERS' COMPENSATION AND INSURANCE

PART 1

SCOPE AND OPERATION

Chapter 1

General Provisions

§ 3201.5. Collective bargaining agreement provisions establishing alternative dispute resolution systems

(a) Except as provided in subdivisions (b) and (c), the Department of Industrial Relations and the courts of this state shall recognize as valid and binding any provision in a collective bargaining agreement between a private employer or groups of employers engaged in construction, construction maintenance, or activities limited to rock, sand, gravel, cement and asphalt operations, heavy-duty mechanics, surveying, and construction inspection and a union that is the recognized or certified exclusive bargaining representative that establishes any of the following:

(1) An alternative dispute resolution system governing disputes between employees and employers or their insurers that supplements or replaces all or part of those dispute resolution processes contained in this division, including, but not limited to, mediation and arbitration. Any system of arbitration shall provide that the decision of the arbiter or board of arbitration is subject to review by the appeals board in the same manner as provided for reconsideration of a final order, decision, or award made and filed by a workers' compensation administrative law judge pursuant to the procedures set forth in Article 1 (commencing with Section 5900) of Chapter 7 of Part 4 of Division 4, and the court of appeals pursuant to the procedures set forth in Article 2 (commencing with Section 5950) of Chapter 7 of Part 4 of Division 4, governing orders, decisions, or awards of the appeals board. The findings of fact, award, order, or decision of the arbitrator shall have the same force and effect as an award, order, or decision of a workers' compensation administrative law judge. Any provision for arbitration established pursuant to this section shall not be subject to Sections 5270, 5270.5, 5271, 5272, 5273, 5275, and 5277.

(2) The use of an agreed list of providers of medical treatment that may be the exclusive source of all medical treatment provided under this division.

(3) The use of an agreed, limited list of qualified medical evaluators and agreed medical evaluators that may be the exclusive source of qualified medical evaluators and agreed medical evaluators under this division.

(4) Joint labor management safety committees.

(5) A light-duty, modified job or return-to-work program.

(6) A vocational rehabilitation or retraining program utilizing an agreed list of providers of rehabilitation services that may be the exclusive source of providers of rehabilitation services under this division.

(b) (1) Nothing in this section shall allow a collective bargaining agreement that diminishes the entitlement of an employee to compensation payments for total or partial disability, temporary disability, vocational rehabilitation, or medical treatment fully paid by the employer as otherwise provided in this division. The portion of any agreement that violates this paragraph shall be declared null and void.

(2) The parties may negotiate any aspect of the delivery of medical benefits and the delivery of disability compensation to employees of the employer or group of employers that are eligible for group health benefits and nonoccupational disability benefits through their employer.

(c) Subdivision (a) shall apply only to the following:

(1) An employer developing or projecting an annual workers' compensation insurance premium, in California, of two hundred fifty thousand dollars ($250,000) or more, or any employer that paid an annual workers' compensation insurance premium, in California, of two hundred fifty thousand dollars ($250,000) in at least one of the previous three years.

(2) Groups of employers engaged in a workers' compensation safety group complying with Sections 11656.6 and 11656.7 of the Insurance Code, and established pursuant to a joint labor management safety committee or committees, that develops or projects annual workers' compensation insurance premiums of two million dollars ($2,000,000) or more.

(3) Employers or groups of employers that are self-insured in compliance with Section 3700 that would have projected annual workers' compensation costs that meet the requirements of, and that meet the other requirements of, paragraph (1) in the case of employers, or paragraph (2) in the case of groups of employers.

(4) Employers covered by an owner or general contractor provided wrap-up insurance policy applicable to a single construction site that develops workers' compensation insurance premiums of two million dollars ($2,000,000) or more with respect to those employees covered by that wrap-up insurance policy.

(d) Employers and labor representatives who meet the eligibility requirements of this section shall be issued a letter by the administrative director advising each employer and labor representative that, based upon the review of all documents and materials submitted as required by the administrative director, each has met the eligibility requirements of this section.

(e) The premium rate for a policy of insurance issued pursuant to this section shall not be subject to the requirements of Section 11732 or 11732.5 of the Insurance Code.

(f) No employer may establish or continue a program established under this section until it has provided the administrative director with all of the following:

(1) Upon its original application and whenever it is renegotiated thereafter, a copy of the collective bargaining agreement and the approximate number of employees who will be covered thereby.

(2) Upon its original application and annually thereafter, a valid and active license where that license is required by law as a condition of doing business in the state within the industries set forth in subdivision (a) of Section 3201.5.

(3) Upon its original application and annually thereafter, a statement signed under penalty of perjury, that no action has been taken by any administrative agency or court of the United States to invalidate the collective bargaining agreement.

(4) The name, address, and telephone number of the contact person of the employer.

(5) Any other information that the administrative director deems necessary to further the purposes of this section.

(g) No collective bargaining representative may establish or continue to participate in a program established under this section unless all of the following requirements are met:

(1) Upon its original application and annually thereafter, it has provided to the administrative director a copy of its most recent LM-2 or LM-3 filing with the United States Department of Labor, along with a statement, signed under penalty of perjury, that the document is a true and correct copy.

(2) It has provided to the administrative director the name, address, and telephone number of the contact person or persons of the collective bargaining representative or representatives.

(h) Commencing July 1, 1995, and annually thereafter, the Division of Workers' Compensation shall report to the Director of Industrial Relations the number of collective bargaining agreements received and the number of employees covered by these agreements.

(i) The data obtained by the administrative director pursuant to this section shall be confidential and not subject to public disclosure under any law of this state. However, the Division of Workers' Compensation shall create derivative works pursuant to subdivision (h) based on the collective bargaining agreements and data. Those derivative works shall not be confidential, but shall be public. On a monthly basis the administrative director shall make available an updated list of employ-

Appendix

ers and unions entering into collective bargaining agreements containing provisions authorized by this section.

Added Stats 1993 ch 117 § 1 (SB 983), effective July 16, 1993. Amended Stats 1994 ch 963 § 1 (SB 853), effective September 27, 1994; Stats 1995 ch 886 § 3 (SB 619); Stats 2002 ch 866 § 4 (AB 486); Stats 2004 ch 34 § 6 (SB 899), effective April 19, 2004; Stats 2012 ch 363 § 8 (SB 863), effective January 1, 2013 (ch 363 prevails), ch 728 § 118 (SB 71), effective January 1, 2013.

§ 3201.7. Labor–management agreements; Requirements for recognition; Applicability; Petition to negotiate; Reporting and filing requirements; Reports to Director and Legislature; Confidentiality

(a) Except as provided in subdivision (b), the Department of Industrial Relations and the courts of this state shall recognize as valid and binding any labor-management agreement that meets all of the following requirements:

(1) The labor-management agreement has been negotiated separate and apart from any collective bargaining agreement covering affected employees.

(2) The labor-management agreement is restricted to the establishment of the terms and conditions necessary to implement this section.

(3) The labor-management agreement has been negotiated in accordance with the authorization of the administrative director pursuant to subdivision (d), between an employer or groups of employers and a union that is the recognized or certified exclusive bargaining representative that establishes any of the following:

(A) An alternative dispute resolution system governing disputes between employees and employers or their insurers that supplements or replaces all or part of those dispute resolution processes contained in this division, including, but not limited to, mediation and arbitration. Any system of arbitration shall provide that the decision of the arbiter or board of arbitration is subject to review by the appeals board in the same manner as provided for reconsideration of a final order, decision, or award made and filed by a workers' compensation administrative law judge pursuant to the procedures set forth in Article 1 (commencing with Section 5900) of Chapter 7 of Part 4 of Division 4, and the court of appeals pursuant to the procedures set forth in Article 2 (commencing with Section 5950) of Chapter 7 of Part 4 of Division 4, governing orders, decisions, or awards of the appeals board. The findings of fact, award, order, or decision of the arbitrator shall have the same force and effect as an award, order, or decision of a workers' compensation administrative law judge. Any provision for arbitration established pursuant to this section shall not be subject to Sections 5270, 5270.5, 5271, 5272, 5273, 5275, and 5277.

(B) The use of an agreed list of providers of medical treatment that may be the exclusive source of all medical treatment provided under this division.

(C) The use of an agreed, limited list of qualified medical evaluators and agreed medical evaluators that may be the exclusive source of qualified medical evaluators and agreed medical evaluators under this division.

(D) Joint labor management safety committees.

(E) A light-duty, modified job, or return-to-work program.

(F) A vocational rehabilitation or retraining program utilizing an agreed list of providers of rehabilitation services that may be the exclusive source of providers of rehabilitation services under this division.

(b) (1) Nothing in this section shall allow a labor-management agreement that diminishes the entitlement of an employee to compensation payments for total or partial disability, temporary disability, vocational rehabilitation, or medical treatment fully paid by the employer as otherwise provided in this division; nor shall any agreement authorized by this section deny to any employee the right to representation by counsel at all stages during the alternative dispute resolution process. The portion of any agreement that violates this paragraph shall be declared null and void.

(2) The parties may negotiate any aspect of the delivery of medical benefits and the delivery of disability compensation to employees of the employer or group of employers that are eligible for group health benefits and nonoccupational disability benefits through their employer.

(c) Subdivision (a) shall apply only to the following:

(1) An employer developing or projecting an annual workers' compensation insurance premium, in California, of fifty thousand dollars ($50,000) or more, and employing at least 50 employees, or any employer that paid an annual workers' compensation insurance premium, in California, of fifty thousand dollars ($50,000), and employing at least 50 employees in at least one of the previous three years.

(2) Groups of employers engaged in a workers' compensation safety group complying with Sections 11656.6 and 11656.7 of the Insurance Code, and established pursuant to a joint labor management safety committee or committees, that develops or projects annual workers' compensation insurance premiums of five hundred thousand dollars ($500,000) or more.

(3) Employers or groups of employers, including cities and counties, that are self-insured in compliance with Section 3700 that would have projected annual workers' compensation costs that meet the requirements of, and that meet the other requirements of, paragraph (1) in the case of employers, or paragraph (2) in the case of groups of employers.

(4) The State of California.

(d) Any recognized or certified exclusive bargaining representative in an industry not covered by Section 3201.5, may file a petition with the administrative director seeking permission to negotiate with an employer or group of employers to enter into a labor-management agreement pursuant to this section. The petition shall specify the bargaining unit or units to be included, the names of the employers or groups of employers, and shall be accompanied by proof of the labor union's status as the exclusive bargaining representative. The current collective bargaining agreement or agreements shall be attached to the petition. The petition shall be in the form designated by the administrative director. Upon receipt of the petition, the administrative director shall promptly verify the petitioner's status as the exclusive bargaining representative. If the petition satisfies the requirements set forth in this subdivision, the administrative director shall issue a letter advising each employer and labor representative of their eligibility to enter into negotiations, for a period not to exceed one year, for the purpose of reaching agreement on a labor-management agreement pursuant to this section. The parties may jointly request, and shall be granted, by the administrative director, an additional one-year period to negotiate an agreement.

(e) No employer may establish or continue a program established under this section until it has provided the administrative director with all of the following:

(1) Upon its original application and whenever it is renegotiated thereafter, a copy of the labor-management agreement and the approximate number of employees who will be covered thereby.

(2) Upon its original application and annually thereafter, a statement signed under penalty of perjury, that no action has been taken by any administrative agency or court of the United States to invalidate the labor-management agreement.

(3) The name, address, and telephone number of the contact person of the employer.

(4) Any other information that the administrative director deems necessary to further the purposes of this section.

(f) No collective bargaining representative may establish or continue to participate in a program established under this section unless all of the following requirements are met:

(1) Upon its original application and annually thereafter, it has provided to the administrative director a copy of its most recent LM-2 or LM-3 filing with the United States Department of Labor, where such filing is required by law, along with a statement, signed under penalty of perjury, that the document is a true and correct copy.

(2) It has provided to the administrative director the name, address, and telephone number of the contact person or persons of the collective bargaining representative or representatives.

(g) Commencing July 1, 2005, and annually thereafter, the Division of Workers' Compensation shall report to the Director of Industrial Relations the number of labor-management agreements received and the number of employees covered by these agreements.

(h) The data obtained by the administrative director pursuant to this section shall be confidential and not subject to public disclosure under any law of this state. However, the Division of Workers' Compensation shall create derivative works pursuant to subdivision (g) based on the labor-management agreements and data. Those derivative works shall not be confidential, but shall be public. On a monthly basis, the administrative director shall make available an updated list of employers and unions entering into labor-management agreements authorized by this section.

Added Stats 2003 ch 639 § 14.7 (SB 228). Amended Stats 2004 ch 34 § 7 (SB 899), effective April 19, 2004; Stats 2012 ch 363 § 9 (SB 863), effective January 1, 2013 (ch 363 prevails), ch 728 § 119 (SB 71), effective January 1, 2013.

Chapter 4

Compensation Insurance and Security

Article 1

Insurance and Security

§ 3700.1. Definitions

As used in this article:

(a) "Director" means the Director of Industrial Relations.

(b) "Private self-insurer" means a private employer which has secured the payment of compensation pursuant to Section 3701.

(c) "Trustees" means the Board of Trustees of the Self-Insurers' Security Fund.

(d) "Member" means a private self-insurer which participates in the Self-Insurers' Security Fund.

(e) "Incurred liabilities for the payment of compensation" means the sum of an estimate of future compensation, as compensation is defined by Section 3207, plus an estimate of the amount necessary to provide for the administration of claims, including legal costs.

Added Stats 1986 ch 1128 § 2, effective September 25, 1986. Amended Stats 1987 ch 169 § 1, effective July 23, 1987; Stats 2012 ch 363 § 10 (SB 863), effective January 1, 2013.

§ 3700.5. Failure to secure payment

(a) The failure to secure the payment of compensation as required by this article by one who knew, or because of his or her knowledge or experience should be reasonably expected to have known, of the obligation to secure the payment of compensation, is a misdemeanor punishable by imprisonment in the county jail for up to one year, or by a fine of up to double the amount of premium, as determined by the court, that would otherwise have been due to secure the payment of compensation during the time compensation was not secured, but not less than ten thousand dollars ($10,000), or by both that imprisonment and fine.

(b) A second or subsequent conviction shall be punished by imprisonment in the county jail for a period not to exceed one year, by a fine of triple the amount of premium, or by both that imprisonment and fine, as determined by the court, that would otherwise have been due to secure the payment of compensation during the time payment was not secured, but not less than fifty thousand dollars ($50,000).

(c) Upon a first conviction of a person under this section, the person may be charged the costs of investigation at the discretion of the court. Upon a subsequent conviction, the person shall be charged the costs of investigation in addition to any other penalties pursuant to subdivision (b). The costs of investigation shall be paid only after the payment of any benefits that may be owed to injured workers, any reimbursement that may be owed to the director for benefits provided to the injured worker pursuant to Section 3717, and any other penalty assessments that may be owed.

Added Stats 1981 ch 894 § 1. Amended Stats 1986 ch 1128 § 3, effective September 25, 1986; Amended Stats 1999 ch 553 § 1 (AB 279); Stats 2003–2004 ch 2 § 3 (SB 2XXXX), effective March 6, 2005.

§ 3701. Methods of securing private self–insuring employer's liabilities for payment of compensation

(a) Each year every private self-insuring employer shall secure incurred liabilities for the payment of compensation and the performance of the obligations of employers imposed under this chapter by renewing the prior year's security deposit or by making a new deposit of security. If a new deposit is made, it shall be posted within 60 days of the filing of the self-insured employer's annual report with the director, but in no event later than May 1.

(b) The solvency risk and security deposit amount for each private and group self-insurer shall be acceptable to the Self-Insurers' Security Fund.

(c) Unless otherwise permitted by regulation, the deposit shall be an amount equal to the self-insurer's projected losses, net of specific excess insurance coverage, if any, and inclusive of incurred but not reported (IBNR) liabilities, allocated loss adjustment expense, and unallocated loss adjustment expense, calculated as of December 31 of each year. The calculation of projected losses and expenses shall be reflected in a written actuarial report that projects ultimate liabilities of the private self-insured employer at the expected actuarial confidence level, to ensure that all claims and associated costs are recognized. The written actuarial report shall be prepared by an actuary meeting the qualifications prescribed by the director in regulation.

(d) In determining the amount of the deposit required to secure incurred liabilities for the payment of compensation and the performance of obligations of a self-insured employer imposed under this chapter, the director shall offset estimated future liabilities for the same claims covered by a self-insured plan under the federal Longshore and Harbor Workers' Compensation Act (33 U.S.C. Sec. 901 et seq.), but in no event shall the offset exceed the estimated future liabilities for the claims under this chapter.

(e) The director may only accept as security, and the employer shall deposit as security, cash, securities, surety bonds, or irrevocable letters of credit in any combination the director, in his or her discretion, deems adequate security. The current deposit shall include any amounts covered by terminated surety bonds or excess insurance policies, as shall be set forth in regulations adopted by the director pursuant to Section 3702.10.

(f) Surety bonds, irrevocable letters of credit, and documents showing issuance of any irrevocable letter of credit shall be deposited with, and be in a form approved by, the director, shall be exonerated only according to its terms and, in no event, by the posting of additional security.

(g) The director may accept as security a joint security deposit that secures an employer's obligation under this chapter and that also secures that employer's obligations under the federal Longshore and Harbor Workers' Compensation Act.

(h) The liability of the Self-Insurers' Security Fund, with respect to any claims brought under both this chapter and under the federal Longshore and Harbor Workers' Compensation Act, to pay for shortfalls in a security deposit shall be limited to the amount of claim liability owing the employee under this chapter offset by the amount of any claim liability owing under the federal Longshore and Harbor Workers' Compensation Act, but in no event shall the liability of the fund exceed the claim liability under this chapter. The employee shall be entitled to pursue recovery under either or both the state and federal programs.

(i) Securities shall be deposited on behalf of the director by the self-insured employer with the Treasurer. Securities shall be accepted by the Treasurer for deposit and shall be withdrawn only upon written order of the director.

(j) Cash shall be deposited in a financial institution approved by the director, and in the account assigned to the director. Cash shall be withdrawn only upon written order of the director.

(k) Upon the sending by the director of a request to renew, request to post, or request to increase or decrease a security deposit, a perfected security interest is created in the private self-insured's assets in favor of the director and the Self-Insurers' Security Fund to the extent of any then unsecured portion of the self-insured's incurred liabilities. That perfected security interest is transferred to any cash or securities thereafter posted by the private self-insured with the director and is released only upon either of the following:

(1) The acceptance by the director of a surety bond or irrevocable letter of credit for the full amount of the incurred liabilities for the payment of compensation.

(2) The return of cash or securities by the director.

The private self-insured employer loses all right, title, and interest in, and any right to control, all assets or obligations posted or left on deposit as security. The director may liquidate the deposit as provided in Section 3701.5 and apply it to the self-insured employer's incurred liabilities either directly or through the Self-Insurers' Security Fund.

Enacted 1937. Amended Stats 1945 ch 1431 § 64; Stats 1st Ex Sess 1946 ch 7 § 2; Stat 1959 ch 951 § 1; Stats 1971 ch 1758 § 1; Stats 1973 ch 1040 § 1; Stats 1978 ch 1379 § 3; Stats 1984 ch 252 § 1, effective June 27, 1984; Stats 1986 ch 1128 § 4, effective September 25, 1986; Stats 1987 ch 169 § 2, effective July 23, 1987. Amended Stats 1993 ch 917 § 1 (AB 424), ch 1242 § 24.5 (SB 223); Stats 1994 ch 56 § 1 (AB 968); Stats 2012 ch 363 § 11 (SB 863), effective January 1, 2013.

§ 3701.3. Return of excess individual security to private self-insured employer

The director shall return to a private self-insured employer all individual security determined, with the consent of the Self-Insurers' Security Fund, to be in excess of that needed to ensure the administration of the employer's self insuring, including legal fees, and the payment of any future claims. This section shall not apply to any security posted as part of the composite deposit, or to any security turned over to the Self-Insurers' Security Fund following an order of default under Section 3701.5.

Added Stats 1986 ch 1128 § 5, effective September 25, 1986. Amended Stats 2012 ch 363 § 12 (SB 863), effective January 1, 2013.

§ 3701.5. Use of security deposit upon failure to pay compensation; Determination; Procedure; Review

(a) If the director determines that a private self-insured employer has failed to pay workers' compensation as required by this division, the security deposit shall be utilized to administer and pay the employer's compensation obligations.

(b) If the director determines the security deposit has not been immediately made available for the payment of compensation, the director shall determine the method of payment and claims administration as appropriate, which may include, but is not limited to, payment by a surety that issued the bond, or payment by an issuer of an irrevocable letter of credit, and administration by a surety or by an adjusting agency, or through the Self-Insurers' Security Fund, or any combination thereof. If the director arranges for administration and payment by any person other than the Self-Insurers' Security Fund after a default is declared, the fund shall have no responsibility for claims administration or payment of the claims.

(c) If the director determines the payment of benefits and claims administration shall be made through the Self-Insurers' Security Fund, the fund shall commence payment of the private self-insured employer's obligations for which it is liable under Section 3743 within 30 days of notification. Payments shall be made to claimants whose entitlement to benefits can be ascertained by the fund, with or without proceedings before the appeals board. Upon the assumption of obligations by the fund pursuant to the director's determination, the fund shall have a right to immediate possession of any posted security and the custodian, surety, or issuer of any irrevocable letter of credit shall turn over the security to the fund together with the interest that has accrued since the date of the self-insured employer's default or insolvency.

(d) The payment of benefits by the Self-Insurers' Security Fund from security deposit proceeds shall release and discharge any custodian of the security deposit, surety, any issuer of a letter of credit, and the self-insured employer, from liability to fulfill obligations to provide those same benefits as compensation, but does not release any person from any liability to the fund for full reimbursement. Payment by a surety constitutes a full release of the surety's liability under the bond to the extent of that payment, and entitles the surety to full reimbursement by the principal or his or her estate. Full reimbursement includes necessary attorney fees and other costs and expenses, without prior claim or proceedings on the part of the injured employee or other beneficiaries. Any decision or determination made, or any settlement approved, by the director or by the appeals board under subdivision (f) shall conclusively be presumed valid and binding as to any and all known claims arising out of the underlying dispute, unless an appeal is made within the time limit specified in Section 5950.

(e) The director shall advise the Self-Insurers' Security Fund promptly after receipt of information indicating that a private self-insured employer may be unable to meet its compensation obligations. The director shall also advise the Self-Insurers' Security Fund of all determinations and directives made or issued pursuant to this section. All financial, actuarial, or claims information received by the director from any self-insurer may be shared by the director with the Self-Insurers' Security Fund.

(f) Disputes concerning the posting, renewal, termination, exoneration, or return of all or any portion of the security deposit, or any liability arising out of the posting or failure to post security, or adequacy of the security or reasonableness of administrative costs, including legal fees, and arising between or among a surety, the issuer of an agreement of assumption and guarantee of workers' compensation liabilities, the issuer of a letter of credit, any custodian of the security deposit, a self-insured employer, or the Self-Insurers' Security Fund shall be resolved by the director. An appeal from the director's decision or determination may be taken to the appropriate superior court by petition for writ of mandate. Payment of claims from the security deposit or by the Self-Insurers' Security Fund shall not be stayed pending the resolution of the disputes unless and until the superior court issues a determination staying a payment of claims decision or determination of the director.

Added Stats 1984 ch 252 § 2, effective June 27, 1984. Amended Stats 1986 ch 1128 § 6, effective September 25, 1986; Stats 1989 ch 1258 § 2; Stats 2012 ch 363 § 13 (SB 863), effective January 1, 2013.

§ 3701.7. Conditions to operate under certificate of consent for employer with prior unlawful uninsurance period

Where any employer requesting coverage under a new or existing certificate of consent to self-insure has had a period of unlawful uninsurance, either for an applicant in its entirety or for a subsidiary or member of a joint powers authority legally responsible for its own workers' compensation obligations, the following special conditions shall apply before the director may determine if the requesting employer can operate under a certificate of consent to self-insure:

(a) The director may require a deposit of not less than 200 percent of the outstanding liabilities remaining unpaid at the time of application, which had been incurred during the uninsurance period.

(b) At the discretion of the director, where a public or private employer has been previously totally uninsured for workers' compensation pursuant to Section 3700, the director may require an additional deposit not to exceed 100 percent of the total outstanding liabilities for the uninsured period, or the sum of two hundred fifty thousand dollars ($250,000), whichever is greater.

(c) In addition to the deposits required by subdivisions (a) and (b), a penalty shall be paid to the Uninsured Employers Fund of 10 percent per year of the remaining unpaid liabilities, for every year liabilities remain outstanding. In addition, an additional application fee, not to exceed one thousand dollars ($1,000), plus assessments, pursuant to Section 3702.5 and subdivision (b) of Section 3745, may be imposed by the director and the Self-Insurers' Security Fund, respectively, against private self-insured employers.

(d) A certificate of consent to self-insure shall not be granted to an applicant that has had a period of unlawful uninsurance without the written approval of the Self-Insurers' Security Fund.

(e) An employer may retrospectively insure the outstanding liabilities arising out of the uninsured period, either before or after an application for self-insurance has been approved. Upon proof of insurance acceptable to the director, no deposit shall be required for the period of uninsurance.

The penalties to be paid to the Uninsured Employers Fund shall consist of a one-time payment of 20 percent of the outstanding liabilities for the period of uninsurance remaining unpaid at the time of application, in lieu of any other penalty for being unlawfully uninsured pursuant to this code.

(f) In the case of a subsidiary which meets all of the following conditions, a certificate shall issue without penalty:

(1) The subsidiary has never had a certificate revoked for reasons set forth in Section 3702.

(2) Employee injuries were reported to the Office of Self-Insurance Plans in annual reports.

(3) The security deposit of the certificate holder was calculated to include the entity's compensation liabilities.

(4) Application for a separate certificate or corrected certificate is made within 90 days and completed within 180 days of notice from the Office of Self-Insurance Plans. If the requirements of this subdivision are not met, all penalties pursuant to subdivision (b) of Section 3702.9 shall apply.

(g) The director may approve an application on the date the application is substantially completed, subject to completion requirements, and may make the certificate effective on an earlier date, covering a period of uninsurance, if the employer complies with the requirements of this section.

(h) Any decision by the director may be contested by an entity in the manner provided in Section 3701.5.

(i) Nothing in this section shall abrogate the right of an employee to bring an action against an uninsured employer pursuant to Section 3706.

(j) Nothing in this statute shall abrogate the right of a self-insured employer to insure against known or unknown claims arising out of the self-insurance period.

Added Stats 1989 ch 507 § 1. Amended Stats 1990 ch 704 § 1 (AB 3853); Stats 2012 ch 363 § 14 (SB 863), effective January 1, 2013.

§ 3701.8. Alternative security system for securing aggregate liabilities of private, self–insured employers through the Self–Insurers' Security Fund

(a) As an alternative to each private self-insuring employer securing its own incurred liabilities as provided in Section 3701, the director may provide by regulation for an alternative security system whereby all private self-insureds designated for full participation by the director shall collectively secure their aggregate incurred liabilities through the

Self-Insurers' Security Fund. The regulations shall provide for the director to set a total security requirement for these participating self-insured employers based on a review of their annual reports and any other self-insurer information as may be specified by the director. The Self-Insurers' Security Fund shall propose to the director a combination of cash and securities, surety bonds, irrevocable letters of credit, insurance, or other financial instruments or guarantees satisfactory to the director sufficient to meet the security requirement set by the director. Upon approval by the director and posting by the Self-Insurers' Security Fund on or before the date set by the director, that combination shall be the composite deposit. The noncash elements of the composite deposit may be one-year or multiple-year instruments. If the Self-Insurers' Security Fund fails to post the required composite deposit by the date set by the director, then within 30 days after that date, each private self-insuring employer shall secure its incurred liabilities in the manner required by Section 3701. Self-insured employers not designated for full participation by the director shall meet all requirements as may be set by the director pursuant to subdivision (g).

(b) In order to provide for the composite deposit approved by the director, the Self-Insurers' Security Fund shall assess, in a manner approved by the director, each fully participating private self-insuring employer a deposit assessment payable within 30 days of assessment. The amount of the deposit assessment charged each fully participating self-insured employer shall be set by the Self-Insurers' Security Fund, based on its reasonable consideration of all the following factors:

(1) The total amount needed to provide the composite deposit.

(2) The self-insuring employer's paid or incurred liabilities as reflected in its annual report.

(3) The financial strength and creditworthiness of the self-insured.

(4) Any other reasonable factors as may be authorized by regulation.

(5) In order to make a composite deposit proposal to the director and set the deposit assessment to be charged each fully participating self-insured, the Self-Insurers' Security Fund shall have access to the annual reports and other information submitted by all self-insuring employers to the director, under terms and conditions as may be set by the director, to preserve the confidentiality of the self-insured's financial information.

(c) Upon payment of the deposit assessment and except as provided herein, the self-insuring employer loses all right, title, and interest in the deposit assessment. To the extent that in any one year the deposit assessment paid by self-insurers is not exhausted in the purchase of securities, surety bonds, irrevocable letters of credit, insurance, or other financial instruments to post with the director as part of the composite deposit, the surplus shall remain posted with the director, and the principal and interest earned on that surplus shall remain as part of the composite deposit in subsequent years. In the event that in any one year the Self-Insurers' Security Fund fails to post the required composite deposit by the date set the by the director, and the director requires each private self-insuring employer to secure its incurred liabilities in the manner required by Section 3701, then any deposit assessment paid in that year shall be refunded to the self-insuring employer that paid the deposit assessment.

(d) If any private self-insuring employer objects to the calculation, posting, or any other aspect of its deposit assessment, upon payment of the assessment in the time provided, the employer shall have the right to appeal the assessment to the director, who shall have exclusive jurisdiction over this dispute. If any private self-insuring employer fails to pay the deposit assessment in the time provided, the director shall order the self-insuring employer to pay a penalty of not less than 10 percent of its deposit assessment, plus interest on any unpaid amount at the prejudgment rate, and to post a separate security deposit in the manner provided by Section 3701. The penalty and interest shall be paid directly to the Self-Insurers' Security Fund. The director may also revoke the certificate of consent to self-insure of any self-insuring employer who fails to pay the deposit assessment in the time provided.

(e) Upon the posting by the Self-Insurers' Security Fund of the composite deposit with the director, the deposit shall be held until the director determines that a private self-insured employer has failed to pay workers' compensation as required by this division, and the director orders the Self-Insurers' Security Fund to commence payment. Upon ordering the Self-Insurers' Security Fund to commence payment, the director shall make available to the fund that portion of the composite deposit necessary to pay the workers' compensation benefits of the defaulting self-insuring employer. In the event additional funds are needed in subsequent years to pay the workers' compensation benefits of any self-insuring employer who defaulted in earlier years, the director shall make available to the Self-Insurers' Security Fund any portions of the composite deposit as may be needed to pay those benefits. In making the deposit available to the Self-Insurers' Security Fund, the director shall also allow any amounts as may be reasonably necessary to pay for the administrative and other activities of the fund.

(f) The cash portion of the composite deposit shall be segregated from all other funds held by the director, and shall be invested by the director for the sole benefit of the Self-Insurers' Security Fund and the injured workers of private self-insured employers, and may not be used for any other purpose by the state. Alternatively, the director, in his discretion, may allow the Self-Insurers' Security Fund to hold, invest, and draw upon the cash portion of the composite deposit as prescribed by regulation.

(g) Notwithstanding any other provision of this section, the director shall, by regulation, set minimum credit, financial, or other conditions that a private self-insured must meet in order to be a fully participating self-insurer in the alternative security system. In the event any private self-insuring employer is unable to meet the conditions set by the director, or upon application of the Self-Insurers' Security Fund to exclude an employer for credit or financial reasons, the director shall exclude the self-insuring employer from full participation in the alternative security system. In the event a self-insuring employer is excluded from full participation, the nonfully participating private self-insuring employer shall post a separate security deposit in the manner provided by Section 3701 and pay a deposit assessment set by the director. Alternatively, the director may order that the nonfully participating private self-insuring employer post a separate security deposit to secure a portion of its incurred liabilities and pay a deposit assessment set by the director.

(h) An employer who self-insures through group self-insurance and an employer whose certificate to self-insure has been revoked may fully participate in the alternative security system if both the director and the Self-Insurers' Security Fund approve the participation of the self-insurer. If not approved for full participation, or if an employer is issued a certificate to self-insure after the composite deposit is posted, the employer shall satisfy the requirements of subdivision (g) for nonfully participating private self-insurers.

(i) At all times, a self-insured employer shall have secured its incurred workers' compensation liabilities either in the manner required by Section 3701 or through the alternative security system, and there shall not be any lapse in the security.

Added Stats 2002 ch 866 § 7 (AB 486). Amended Stats 2012 ch 363 § 15 (SB 863), effective January 1, 2013.

§ 3701.9. Restriction on issuance of certificate of consent to self-insure after January 1, 2013

(a) A certificate of consent to self-insure shall not be issued after January 1, 2013, to any of the following:

(1) A professional employer organization.

(2) A leasing employer, as defined in Section 606.5 of the Unemployment Insurance Code.

(3) A temporary services employer, as defined in Section 606.5 of the Unemployment Insurance Code.

(4) Any employer, regardless of name or form of organization, which the director determines to be in the business of providing employees to other employers.

(b) A certificate of consent to self-insure that has been issued to any employer described in subdivision (a) shall be revoked by the director not later than January 1, 2015.

Added Stats 2012 ch 363 § 16 (SB 863), effective January 1, 2013.

§ 3702. Revocation of certificate of consent; Appeal; Hearing to determine good cause

(a) A certificate of consent to self-insure may be revoked by the director at any time for good cause after a hearing. Good cause includes, among other things, a recommendation by the Self-Insurers' Security Fund to revoke the certificate of consent, the impairment of the solvency of the employer to the extent that there is a marked reduction of the employer's financial strength, failure to maintain a security deposit as required by Section 3701, failure to pay assessments of the Self-Insurers' Security Fund, frequent or flagrant violations of state safety and health orders, the failure or inability of the employer to fulfill his or her obligations, or any of the following practices by the employer or his or her agent in charge of the administration of obligations under this division:

(1) Habitually and as a matter of practice and custom inducing claimants for compensation to accept less than the compensation due or making it necessary for them to resort to proceedings against the employer to secure compensation due.

(2) Where liability for temporary disability indemnity is not in dispute, intentionally failing to pay temporary disability indemnity without good cause in order to influence the amount of permanent disability benefits due.

(3) Intentionally refusing to comply with known and legally indisputable compensation obligations.

(4) Discharging or administering his or her compensation obligations in a dishonest manner.

(5) Discharging or administering his or her compensation obligations in such a manner as to cause injury to the public or those dealing with the employer.

(b) Where revocation is in part based upon the director's finding of a marked reduction of the employer's financial strength or the failure or inability of the employer to fulfill his or her obligations, or a practice of discharging obligations in a dishonest manner, it is a condition precedent to the employer's challenge or appeal of the revocation that the employer have in effect insurance against liability to pay compensation.

(c) The director may hold a hearing to determine whether good cause exists to revoke an employer's certificate of consent to self-insure if the employer is cited for a willful, or repeat serious violation of the standard adopted pursuant to Section 6401.7 and the citation has become final.

Enacted 1937. Amended Stats 1945 ch 1431 § 65; Stats 1978 ch 1379 § 4; Stats 1984 ch 252 § 3, effective June 27, 1984, ch 1521 § 1, operative July 1, 1985; Stats 1989 ch 1369 § 2, effective October 2, 1989; Stats 2012 ch 363 § 17 (SB 863), effective January 1, 2013.

Appendix

§ 3702.2. Annual report of self-insured employer; Aggregated summary of all self-insured employers' liability; Release of data

(a) All self-insured employers shall file a self-insurer's annual report in a form prescribed by the director. Public self-insured employers shall provide detailed information as the director determines necessary to evaluate the costs of administration, workers' compensation benefit expenditures, and solvency and performance of the public self-insured employer workers' compensation programs, on a schedule established by the director. The director may grant deferrals to public self-insured employers that are not yet capable of accurately reporting the information required, giving priority to bringing larger programs into compliance with the more detailed reporting.

(b) To enable the director to determine the amount of the security deposit required by subdivision (c) of Section 3701, the annual report of a self-insured employer who has self-insured both state and federal workers' compensation liability shall also set forth (1) the amount of all compensation liability incurred, paid-to-date, and estimated future liability under both this chapter and under the federal Longshore and Harbor Workers' Compensation Act (33 U.S.C. Sec. 901 et seq.), and (2) the identity and the amount of the security deposit securing the employer's liability under state and federal self-insured programs.

(c) The director shall annually prepare an aggregated summary of all self-insured employer liability to pay compensation reported on the self-insurers' employers annual reports, including a separate summary for public and private employer self-insurers. The summaries shall be in the same format as the individual self-insured employers are required to report that liability on the employer self-insurer's annual report forms prescribed by the director. The aggregated summaries shall be made available to the public on the self-insurance section of the department's Internet Web site. This subdivision does not authorize the director to release or make available information regarding private self-insured employers that is aggregated by industry or business type, that identifies individual self-insured filers, or that includes any individually identifiable claimant information. The director may publish information regarding the costs of administration, workers' compensation benefit expenditures, and solvency and performance of public self-insured employers' workers' compensation programs, including, but not limited to, information aggregated by industry or business type, and that may contain data identifying individual public self-insured filers, their third-party administrators, and their joint powers authorities, as long as the information does not include any individually identifiable claimant information. For purposes of this section, "individually identifiable claimant information" means any data concerning an injury or claim that is linked to a uniquely identifiable employee, employee's dependent, or a specific claim.

(d) The director may release a copy, or make available an electronic version, of the data contained in any public sector employer self-insurer's annual reports received from an individual public entity self-insurer or from a joint powers authority employer and its membership. However, the release of any annual report information by the director shall not include any portion of any listing of open indemnity claims that contains individually identifiable claimant information, or any portion of excess insurance coverage information that contains any individually identifiable claimant information.

Added Stats 1986 ch 1128 § 8, effective September 25, 1986. Amended Stats 1993 ch 917 § 2 (AB 424); Stats 2006 ch 115 § 1 (AB 2087), effective January 1, 2007; Stats 2012 ch 363 § 18 (SB 863), effective January 1, 2013; Stats 2018 ch 538 § 3 (AB 2334), effective January 1, 2019.

§ 3702.4. [Section repealed 2015.]

Added Stats 2012 ch 363 § 19 (SB 863), effective January 1, 2013, repealed January 1, 2015.

§ 3702.5. Cost of self–insured program; Revenues from fees and penalties

(a) (1) The cost of administration of the public self-insured program by the Director of Industrial Relations shall be borne by the Workers' Compensation Administration Revolving Fund.

(2) The cost of administration of the private self-insured program by the Director of Industrial Relations shall be borne by the private self-insurers through payment of certificate fees which shall be established by the director in broad ranges based on the comparative numbers of employees insured by the private self-insurers and the number of adjusting locations. The director may assess other fees as necessary to cover the costs of special audits or services rendered to private self-insured employers. The director may assess a civil penalty for late filing as set forth in subdivision (a) of Section 3702.9.

(b) All revenues from fees and penalties paid by private self-insured employers shall be deposited into the Self-Insurance Plans Fund, which is hereby created for the administration of the private self-insurance program. Any unencumbered balance in subdivision (a) of Item 8350-001-001 of the Budget Act of 1983 shall be transferred to the Self-Insurance Plans Fund. The director shall annually eliminate any unused surplus in the Self-Insurance Plans Fund by reducing certificate fee assessments by an appropriate amount in the subsequent year. Moneys paid into the Self-Insurance Plans Fund for administration of the private self-insured program shall not be used by any other department or agency or for any purpose other than administration of the

Appendix

private self-insurance program. Detailed accountability shall be maintained by the director for any security deposit or other funds held in trust for the Self-Insurer's Security Fund in the Self-Insurance Plans Fund.

Moneys held by the director shall be invested in the Surplus Money Investment Fund. Interest shall be paid on all moneys transferred to the General Fund in accordance with Section 16310 of the Government Code. The Treasurer's and Controller's administrative costs may be charged to the interest earnings upon approval of the director.

Added Stats 1971 ch 1758 § 2. Amended Stats 1978 ch 1379 § 7; Stats 1984 ch 1734 § 1, effective September 30, 1984, operative July 1, 1984. Amended Stats 1992 ch 532 § 2 (AB 2771); Stats 2012 ch 363 § 20 (SB 863), effective January 1, 2013.

§ 3702.8. Discharge of continuing obligations of employers who cease to be self–insured

(a) Employers who have ceased to be self-insured employers shall discharge their continuing obligations to secure the payment of workers' compensation that accrued during the period of self-insurance, for purposes of Sections 3700, 3700.5, 3706, and 3715, and shall comply with all of the following obligations of current certificate holders:

(1) Filing annual reports as deemed necessary by the director to carry out the requirements of this chapter.

(2) In the case of a private employer, depositing and maintaining a security deposit for accrued liability for the payment of any workers' compensation that may become due, pursuant to subdivision (b) of Section 3700 and Section 3701, except as provided in subdivision (c).

(3) Paying within 30 days all assessments of which notice is sent, pursuant to subdivision (b) of Section 3745, within 36 months from the last day the employer's certificate of self-insurance was in effect. Assessments shall be based on the benefits paid by the employer during the last full calendar year of self-insurance on claims incurred during that year.

(b) In addition to proceedings to establish liabilities and penalties otherwise provided, a failure to comply may be the subject of a proceeding before the director. An appeal from the director's determination shall be taken to the appropriate superior court by petition for writ of mandate.

(c) Notwithstanding subdivision (a), any employer who is currently self-insured or who has ceased to be self-insured may purchase a special excess workers' compensation policy to discharge any or all of the employer's continuing obligations as a self-insurer to pay compensation or to secure the payment of compensation.

(1) The special excess workers' compensation insurance policy shall be issued by an insurer authorized to transact workers' compensation insurance in this state.

(2) Each carrier's special excess workers' compensation policy shall be approved as to form and substance by the Insurance Commissioner, and rates for special excess workers' compensation insurance shall be subject to the filing requirements set forth in Section 11735 of the Insurance Code.

(3) Each special excess workers' compensation insurance policy shall be submitted by the employer to the director. The director shall adopt and publish minimum insurer financial rating standards for companies issuing special excess workers' compensation policies.

(4) Upon acceptance by the director, a special excess workers' compensation policy shall provide coverage for all or any portion of the purchasing employer's claims for compensation arising out of injuries occurring during the period the employer was self-insured in accordance with Sections 3755, 3756, and 3757 of the Labor Code and Sections 11651 and 11654 of the Insurance Code. The director's acceptance shall discharge the Self-Insurer's Security Fund, without recourse or liability to the Self-Insurer's Security Fund, of any continuing liability for the claims covered by the special excess workers' compensation insurance policy.

(5) For public employers, no security deposit or financial guarantee bond or other security shall be required. The director shall set minimum financial rating standards for insurers issuing special excess workers' compensation policies for public employers.

(d) (1) In order for the special excess workers' compensation insurance policy to discharge the full obligations of a private employer to maintain a security deposit with the director for the payment of self-insured claims, applicable to the period to be covered by the policy, the special excess policy shall provide coverage for all claims for compensation arising out of that liability. The employer shall maintain the required deposit for the period covered by the policy with the director for a period of three years after the issuance date of the special excess policy.

(2) If the special workers' compensation insurance policy does not provide coverage for all of the continuing obligations for which the private self-insured employer is liable, to the extent the employer's obligations are not covered by the policy a private employer shall maintain the required deposit with the director. In addition, the employer shall maintain with the director the required deposit for the period covered by the policy for a period of three years after the issuance date of the special excess policy.

(e) The director shall adopt regulations pursuant to Section 3702.10 that are reasonably necessary to implement this section in order to reasonably protect injured workers, employers, the Self-Insurers' Security Fund, and the California Insurance Guarantee Association.

(f) The posting of a special excess workers' compensation insurance policy with the director shall discharge the obligation of the Self-

Insurer's Security Fund pursuant to Section 3744 to pay claims in the event of an insolvency of a private employer to the extent of coverage of compensation liabilities under the special excess workers' compensation insurance policy. The California Insurance Guarantee Association and the Self-Insurers' Security Fund shall be advised by the director whenever a special excess workers' compensation insurance policy is posted.

Added Stats 1986 ch 1128 § 11, effective September 25, 1986. Amended Stats 1989 ch 1258 § 3; Stats 1990 ch 704 § 2 (AB 3853). Amended Stats 1999 ch 721 § 7 (AB 1309); Stats 2012 ch 363 § 21 (SB 863), effective January 1, 2013.

§ 3702.10. Rules and regulations

The director, in accordance with Chapter 3.5 (commencing with Section 11340) of Part 1 of Division 3 of Title 2 of the Government Code, may adopt, amend, and repeal rules and regulations reasonably necessary to carry out the purposes of Section 129 and Article 1 (commencing with Section 3700), Article 2 (commencing with Section 3710), and Article 2.5 (commencing with Section 3740). This authorization includes, but is not limited to, the adoption of regulations to do all of the following:

(a) Specifying what constitutes ability to self-insure and to pay any compensation which may become due under Section 3700.

(b) Specifying what constitutes a marked reduction of an employer's financial strength.

(c) Specifying what constitutes a failure or inability to fulfill the employer's obligations under Section 3702.

(d) Interpreting and defining the terms used.

(e) Establishing procedures and standards for hearing and determinations, and providing for those determinations to be appealed to the appeals board.

(f) Specifying the standards, form, and content of agreements, forms, and reports between parties who have obligations pursuant to this chapter.

(g) Providing for the combinations and relative liabilities of security deposits, assumptions, and guarantees used pursuant to this chapter.

(h) Disclosing otherwise confidential financial information concerning self-insureds to courts or the Self-Insurers' Security Fund and specifying appropriate safeguards for that information.

(i) Requiring an amount to be added to each security deposit to secure the cost of administration of claims and to pay all legal costs.

(j) Regulating the workers' compensation self-insurance obligations of self-insurance groups and professional employer organizations, leasing employers as defined in Section 606.5 of the Unemployment Insurance Code, or temporary services employers, as defined in Section 606.5 of the Unemployment Insurance Code, holding certificates of consent to self-insure.

Added Stats 1986 ch 1128 § 13, effective September 25, 1986. Amended Stats 1993 ch 121 § 26 (AB 110), effective July 16, 1993; Stats 2012 ch 363 § 22 (SB 863), effective January 1, 2013.

Article 2.5

Self–Insurers' Security Fund

§ 3742. Establishment of fund as nonprofit mutual benefit corporation; Board of Trustees; Terms; Powers

(a) The Self-Insurers' Security Fund shall be established as a Non-profit Mutual Benefit Corporation pursuant to Part 3 (commencing with Section 7110) of Division 2 of Title 1 of the Corporations Code and this article. If any provision of the Nonprofit Mutual Benefit Corporation Law conflicts with any provision of this article, the provisions of this article shall apply. Each private self-insurer shall participate as a member in the fund, unless its liabilities have been turned over to the fund pursuant to Section 3701.5, at which time its membership in the fund is relinquished.

(b) The fund shall be governed by a board of trustees with no more than eight members, as established by the bylaws of the Self-Insurers' Security Fund. The director shall hold ex officio status, with full powers equal to those of a trustee, except that the director shall not have a vote. The director, or a delegate authorized in writing to act as the director's representative on the board of trustees, shall carry out exclusively the responsibilities set forth in Division 1 (commencing with Section 50) through Division 4 (commencing with Section 3200) and shall not have the obligations of a trustee under the Nonprofit Mutual Benefit Corporation Law. The fund shall adopt bylaws to segregate the director from all matters that may involve fund litigation against the department or fund participation in legal proceedings before the director. Although not voting, the director or a delegate authorized in writing to represent the director, shall be counted toward a quorum of trustees. The remaining trustees shall be representatives of private self-insurers. The self-insurer trustees shall be elected by the members of the fund, each member having one vote. Trustees shall be elected to four-year terms, and shall serve until their successors are elected and assume office pursuant to the bylaws of the fund.

(c) The fund shall establish bylaws as are necessary to effectuate the purposes of this article and to carry out the responsibilities of the fund, including, but not limited to, any obligations imposed by the director pursuant to Section 3701.8. The fund may carry out its responsibilities directly or by contract, and may purchase services and insurance and borrow funds as it deems necessary for the protection of the members and their employees. The fund may receive confidential information concerning the financial condition of self-insured employers whose liabilities to pay compensation may devolve upon it and shall adopt bylaws to prevent dissemination of that information.

(d) The director may also require fund members to subscribe to financial instruments or guarantees to be posted with the director in order to satisfy the security requirements set by the director pursuant to Section 3701.8.

Added Stats 1984 ch 252 § 5, effective June 27, 1984. Amended Stats 1986 ch 1128 § 16, effective September 25, 1986. Amended Stats 2002 ch 866 § 8 (AB 486); Stats 2012 ch 363 § 23 (SB 863), effective January 1, 2013.

§ 3744. Reimbursement from insolvent self–insurer or security deposit

(a) (1) The fund shall have the right and obligation to obtain reimbursement from an insolvent self-insurer up to the amount of the self-insurer's workers' compensation obligations paid and assumed by the fund, including reasonable administrative and legal costs. This right includes, but is not limited to, a right to claim for wages and other necessities of life advanced to claimants as subrogee of the claimants in any action to collect against the self-insured as debtor. For purposes of this section, "insolvent self-insurer" includes the entity to which the certificate of consent to self-insure was issued, any guarantor of the entity's liabilities under the certificate, any member of a self-insurance group to which the certificate was issued, and any employer who obtained employees from a self-insured employer under subdivision (d) of Section 3602.

(2) The Legislature finds and declares that the amendments made to this subdivision by the act adding this paragraph are declaratory of existing law.

(b) The fund shall have the right and obligation to obtain from the security deposit of an insolvent self-insurer the amount of the self-insurer's compensation obligations, including reasonable administrative and legal costs, paid or assumed by the fund. Reimbursement of administrative costs, including legal costs, shall be subject to approval by a majority vote of the fund's trustees. The fund shall be a party in interest in any action to obtain the security deposit for the payment of compensation obligations of an insolvent self-insurer.

(c) The fund shall have the right to bring an action against any person to recover compensation paid and liability assumed by the fund, including, but not limited to, any excess insurance carrier of the self-insured employer, and any person whose negligence or breach of any obligation contributed to any underestimation of the self-insured employer's total accrued liability as reported to the director.

(d) The fund may be a party in interest in any action brought by any other person seeking damages resulting from the failure of an insolvent self-insurer to pay workers' compensation required pursuant to this division.

(e) At the election of the Self-Insurers' Security Fund, venue shall be in the Superior Court for the State of California, County of Sacramento, for any action under this section. All actions in which the Self-Insurers' Security Fund and two or more members or former members of one self-insurance group are parties shall be consolidated if requested by the Self-Insurers' Security Fund.

Added Stats 1984 ch 252 § 5, effective June 27, 1984. Amended Stats 1986 ch 1128 § 17, effective September 25, 1986; Stats 2012 ch 363 § 24 (SB 863), effective January 1, 2013.

§ 3745. Maintenance of liquid assets; Minimum amount; Assessment of members

(a) The fund shall maintain cash, readily marketable securities, or other assets, or a line of credit, approved by the director, sufficient to immediately continue the payment of the compensation obligations of an insolvent self-insurer pending assessment of the members. The director may establish the minimum amount to be maintained by, or immediately available to, the fund for this purpose.

(b) The fund may assess each of its members a pro rata share of the funding necessary to carry out the purposes of this article.

(c) The trustees shall certify to the director the collection and receipt of all moneys from assessments, noting any delinquencies. The trustees shall take any action deemed appropriate to collect any delinquent assessments.

Added Stats 1984 ch 252 § 5, effective June 27, 1984. Amended Stats 1986 ch 1128 § 18, effective September 25, 1986; Stats 2012 ch 363 § 25 (SB 863), effective January 1, 2013.

§ 3746. Audit and report on financial status

The fund shall annually contract for an independent certified audit of the financial activities of the fund. An annual report on the financial status of the fund as of June 30 shall be submitted to the director and to each member, or at the election of the fund, posted on the fund's Internet Web site.

Added Stats 1984 ch 252 § 5, effective June 27, 1984. Amended Stats 2012 ch 363 § 26 (SB 863), effective January 1, 2013.

Appendix

Article 4

Construction Permit

§ 3800. Certificate of consent to self-insure or of insurance

(a) Every county or city which requires the issuance of a permit as a condition precedent to the construction, alteration, improvement, demolition, or repair of any building or structure shall require that each applicant for the permit sign a declaration under penalty of perjury verifying workers' compensation coverage or exemption from coverage, as required by Section 19825 of the Health and Safety Code.

(b) At the time of permit issuance, contractors shall show their valid workers' compensation insurance certificate, or the city or county may verify the workers' compensation coverage by electronic means.

Added Stats 1941 ch 1010 § 1. Amended Stats 1945 ch 1431 § 69.5; Stats 1953 ch 552 § 1; Stats 1959 ch 361 § 1; Stats 1963 ch 1140 § 2; Stats 1988 ch 160 § 124. Amended Stats 1994 ch 178 § 2 (AB 443); Stats 1999 ch 982 § 9 (AB 1678).

Chapter 7

Medical Examinations

Article 2

Determination of Medical Issues

§ 4061. Notice of permanent disability indemnity; Comprehensive medical evaluation; Calculation of permanent disability rating; Apportionment; Reconsideration; Admissibility of evaluations in violation

This section shall not apply to the employee's dispute of a utilization review decision under Section 4610, nor to the employee's dispute of the medical provider network treating physician's diagnosis or treatment recommendations under Sections 4616.3 and 4616.4.

(a) Together with the last payment of temporary disability indemnity, the employer shall, in a form prescribed by the administrative director pursuant to Section 138.4, provide the employee one of the following:

(1) Notice either that no permanent disability indemnity will be paid because the employer alleges the employee has no permanent impairment or limitations resulting from the injury or notice of the amount of permanent disability indemnity determined by the employer to be payable. If the employer determines permanent disability indemnity is

payable, the employer shall advise the employee of the amount determined payable and the basis on which the determination was made, whether there is need for future medical care, and whether an indemnity payment will be deferred pursuant to paragraph (2) of subdivision (b) of Section 4650.

(2) Notice that permanent disability indemnity may be or is payable, but that the amount cannot be determined because the employee's medical condition is not yet permanent and stationary. The notice shall advise the employee that his or her medical condition will be monitored until it is permanent and stationary, at which time the necessary evaluation will be performed to determine the existence and extent of permanent impairment and limitations for the purpose of rating permanent disability and to determine whether there will be the need for future medical care, or at which time the employer will advise the employee of the amount of permanent disability indemnity the employer has determined to be payable.

(b) If either the employee or employer objects to a medical determination made by the treating physician concerning the existence or extent of permanent impairment and limitations or the need for future medical care, and the employee is represented by an attorney, a medical evaluation to determine permanent disability shall be obtained as provided in Section 4062.2.

(c) If either the employee or employer objects to a medical determination made by the treating physician concerning the existence or extent of permanent impairment and limitations or the need for future medical care, and if the employee is not represented by an attorney, the employer shall immediately provide the employee with a form prescribed by the medical director with which to request assignment of a panel of three qualified medical evaluators. Either party may request a comprehensive medical evaluation to determine permanent disability or the need for future medical care, and the evaluation shall be obtained only by the procedure provided in Section 4062.1.

(d) (1) Within 30 days of receipt of a report from a qualified medical evaluator who has evaluated an unrepresented employee, the unrepresented employee or the employer may each request one supplemental report seeking correction of factual errors in the report. Any of these requests shall be made in writing. A request made by the employer shall be provided to the employee, and a request made by the employee shall be provided to the employer, insurance carrier, or claims administrator at the time the request is sent to the evaluator. A request for correction that is made by the employer shall also inform the employee of the availability of information and assistance officers to assist him or her in responding to the request, if necessary.

(2) The permanent disability rating procedure set forth in subdivision (e) shall not be invoked by the unrepresented employee or the employer when a request for correction pursuant to paragraph (1) is pending.

(e) The qualified medical evaluator who has evaluated an unrepresented employee shall serve the comprehensive medical evaluation and the summary form on the employee, employer, and the administrative director. The unrepresented employee or the employer may submit the treating physician's evaluation for the calculation of a permanent disability rating. Within 20 days of receipt of the comprehensive medical evaluation, the administrative director shall calculate the permanent disability rating according to Section 4660 or 4660.1, as applicable, and serve the rating on the employee and employer.

(f) Any comprehensive medical evaluation concerning an unrepresented employee which indicates that part or all of an employee's permanent impairment or limitations may be subject to apportionment pursuant to Sections 4663 and 4664 shall first be submitted by the administrative director to a workers' compensation judge who may refer the report back to the qualified medical evaluator for correction or clarification if the judge determines the proposed apportionment is inconsistent with the law.

(g) Within 30 days of receipt of the rating, if the employee is unrepresented, the employee or employer may request that the administrative director reconsider the recommended rating or obtain additional information from the treating physician or medical evaluator to address issues not addressed or not completely addressed in the original comprehensive medical evaluation or not prepared in accord with the procedures promulgated under paragraph (2) or (3) of subdivision (j) of Section 139.2. This request shall be in writing, shall specify the reasons the rating should be reconsidered, and shall be served on the other party. If the administrative director finds the comprehensive medical evaluation is not complete or not in compliance with the required procedures, the administrative director shall return the report to the treating physician or qualified medical evaluator for appropriate action as the administrative director instructs. Upon receipt of the treating physician's or qualified medical evaluator's final comprehensive medical evaluation and summary form, the administrative director shall recalculate the permanent disability rating according to Section 4660 or 4660.1, as applicable, and serve the rating, the comprehensive medical evaluation, and the summary form on the employee and employer.

(h) (1) If a comprehensive medical evaluation from the treating physician or an agreed medical evaluator or a qualified medical evaluator selected from a three-member panel resolves any issue so as to require an employer to provide compensation, the employer shall commence the payment of compensation, except as provided pursuant to paragraph (2) of subdivision (b) of Section 4650, or promptly commence proceedings before the appeals board to resolve the dispute.

(2) If the employee and employer agree to a stipulated findings and award as provided under Section 5702 or to compromise and release the claim under Chapter 2 (commencing with Section 5000) of Part 3,

or if the employee wishes to commute the award under Chapter 3 (commencing with Section 5100) of Part 3, the appeals board shall first determine whether the agreement or commutation is in the best interests of the employee and whether the proper procedures have been followed in determining the permanent disability rating. The administrative director shall promulgate a form to notify the employee, at the time of service of any rating under this section, of the options specified in this subdivision, the potential advantages and disadvantages of each option, and the procedure for disputing the rating.

(i) No issue relating to a dispute over the existence or extent of permanent impairment and limitations resulting from the injury may be the subject of a declaration of readiness to proceed unless there has first been a medical evaluation by a treating physician and by either an agreed or qualified medical evaluator. With the exception of an evaluation or evaluations prepared by the treating physician or physicians, no evaluation of permanent impairment and limitations resulting from the injury shall be obtained, except in accordance with Section 4062.1 or 4062.2. Evaluations obtained in violation of this prohibition shall not be admissible in any proceeding before the appeals board.

Added Stats 1989 ch 892 § 28, operative January 1, 1991. Amended Stats 1990 ch 1550 § 21 (AB 2910). Amended Stats 1993 ch 121 § 30 (AB 110), effective July 16, 1993, ch 1241 § 6 (SB 147), ch 1242 § 28 (SB 223); Stats 2002 ch 6 § 51 (AB 749); Stats 2003 ch 639 § 16 (SB 228); Stats 2004 ch 34 § 13 (SB 899), effective April 19, 2004; Stats 2011 ch 544 § 4 (AB 335), effective January 1, 2012; Stats 2012 ch 363 § 27 (SB 863), effective January 1, 2013; Stats 2013 ch 287 § 4 (SB 375), effective January 1, 2014.

§ 4062. Objection to medical determination by treating physician; Notice; Medical evaluation

(a) If either the employee or employer objects to a medical determination made by the treating physician concerning any medical issues not covered by Section 4060 or 4061 and not subject to Section 4610, the objecting party shall notify the other party in writing of the objection within 20 days of receipt of the report if the employee is represented by an attorney or within 30 days of receipt of the report if the employee is not represented by an attorney. These time limits may be extended for good cause or by mutual agreement. If the employee is represented by an attorney, a medical evaluation to determine the disputed medical issue shall be obtained as provided in Section 4062.2, and no other medical evaluation shall be obtained. If the employee is not represented by an attorney, the employer shall immediately provide the employee with a form prescribed by the medical director with which to request assignment of a panel of three qualified medical evaluators, the evaluation shall be obtained as provided in Section 4062.1, and no other medical evaluation shall be obtained.

Appendix

(b) If the employee objects to a decision made pursuant to Section 4610 to modify, delay, or deny a request for authorization of a medical treatment recommendation made by a treating physician, the objection shall be resolved only in accordance with the independent medical review process established in Section 4610.5.

(c) If the employee objects to the diagnosis or recommendation for medical treatment by a physician within the employer's medical provider network established pursuant to Section 4616, the objection shall be resolved only in accordance with the independent medical review process established in Sections 4616.3 and 4616.4.

Added Stats 2003 ch 639 § 17 (SB 228). Amended Stats 2004 ch 34 § 14 (SB 899), effective April 19, 2004; Stats 2012 ch 363 § 28 (SB 863), effective January 1, 2013.

§ 4062.2. Comprehensive medical evaluation to resolve dispute over injuries on or after January 1, 2005, when employee is represented by attorney

(a) Whenever a comprehensive medical evaluation is required to resolve any dispute arising out of an injury or a claimed injury occurring on or after January 1, 2005, and the employee is represented by an attorney, the evaluation shall be obtained only as provided in this section.

(b) No earlier than the first working day that is at least 10 days after the date of mailing of a request for a medical evaluation pursuant to Section 4060 or the first working day that is at least 10 days after the date of mailing of an objection pursuant to Sections 4061 or 4062, either party may request the assignment of a three-member panel of qualified medical evaluators to conduct a comprehensive medical evaluation. The party submitting the request shall designate the specialty of the medical evaluator, the specialty of the medical evaluator requested by the other party if it has been made known to the party submitting the request, and the specialty of the treating physician. The party submitting the request form shall serve a copy of the request form on the other party.

(c) Within 10 days of assignment of the panel by the administrative director, each party may strike one name from the panel. The remaining qualified medical evaluator shall serve as the medical evaluator. If a party fails to exercise the right to strike a name from the panel within 10 days of assignment of the panel by the administrative director, the other party may select any physician who remains on the panel to serve as the medical evaluator. The administrative director may prescribe the form, the manner, or both, by which the parties shall conduct the selection process.

(d) The represented employee shall be responsible for arranging the appointment for the examination, but upon his or her failure to inform the employer of the appointment within 10 days after the medical evaluator has been selected, the employer may arrange the appointment and notify the employee of the arrangements. The employee shall not unreasonably refuse to participate in the evaluation.

(e) If an employee has received a comprehensive medical-legal evaluation under this section, and he or she later ceases to be represented, he or she shall not be entitled to an additional evaluation.

(f) The parties may agree to an agreed medical evaluator at any time, except as to issues subject to the independent medical review process established pursuant to Section 4610.5. A panel shall not be requested pursuant to subdivision (b) on any issue that has been agreed to be submitted to or has been submitted to an agreed medical evaluator unless the agreement has been canceled by mutual written consent.

Added Stats 2004 ch 34 § 18 (SB 899), effective April 19, 2004. Amended Stats 2012 ch 363 § 29 (SB 863), effective January 1, 2013.

§ 4062.3. Information provided to qualified medical evaluator; Service on opposing party; Discovery; Ex parte communications; Contempt; Evaluation and summary form; New medical issues

(a) Any party may provide to the qualified medical evaluator selected from a panel any of the following information:

(1) Records prepared or maintained by the employee's treating physician or physicians.

(2) Medical and nonmedical records relevant to determination of the medical issue.

(b) Information that a party proposes to provide to the qualified medical evaluator selected from a panel shall be served on the opposing party 20 days before the information is provided to the evaluator. If the opposing party objects to consideration of nonmedical records within 10 days thereafter, the records shall not be provided to the evaluator. Either party may use discovery to establish the accuracy or authenticity of nonmedical records prior to the evaluation.

(c) If an agreed medical evaluator is selected, as part of their agreement on an evaluator, the parties shall agree on what information is to be provided to the agreed medical evaluator.

(d) In any formal medical evaluation, the agreed or qualified medical evaluator shall identify the following:

(1) All information received from the parties.

(2) All information reviewed in preparation of the report.

(3) All information relied upon in the formulation of his or her opinion.

(e) All communications with a qualified medical evaluator selected from a panel before a medical evaluation shall be in writing and shall be served on the opposing party 20 days in advance of the evaluation. Any subsequent communication with the medical evaluator shall be in writing and shall be served on the opposing party when sent to the medical evaluator.

(f) Communications with an agreed medical evaluator shall be in writing, and shall be served on the opposing party when sent to the agreed medical evaluator. Oral or written communications with physician staff or, as applicable, with the agreed medical evaluator, relative to nonsubstantial matters such as the scheduling of appointments, missed appointments, the furnishing of records and reports, and the availability of the report, do not constitute ex parte communication in violation of this section unless the appeals board has made a specific finding of an impermissible ex parte communication.

(g) Ex parte communication with an agreed medical evaluator or a qualified medical evaluator selected from a panel is prohibited. If a party communicates with the agreed medical evaluator or the qualified medical evaluator in violation of subdivision (e), the aggrieved party may elect to terminate the medical evaluation and seek a new evaluation from another qualified medical evaluator to be selected according to Section 4062.1 or 4062.2, as applicable, or proceed with the initial evaluation.

(h) The party making the communication prohibited by this section shall be subject to being charged with contempt before the appeals board and shall be liable for the costs incurred by the aggrieved party as a result of the prohibited communication, including the cost of the medical evaluation, additional discovery costs, and attorney's fees for related discovery.

(i) Subdivisions (e) and (g) shall not apply to oral or written communications by the employee or, if the employee is deceased, the employee's dependent, in the course of the examination or at the request of the evaluator in connection with the examination.

(j) Upon completing a determination of the disputed medical issue, the medical evaluator shall summarize the medical findings on a form prescribed by the administrative director and shall serve the formal medical evaluation and the summary form on the employee and the employer. The medical evaluation shall address all contested medical issues arising from all injuries reported on one or more claim forms prior to the date of the employee's initial appointment with the medical evaluator.

(k) If, after a medical evaluation is prepared, the employer or the employee subsequently objects to any new medical issue, the parties, to the extent possible, shall utilize the same medical evaluator who prepared the previous evaluation to resolve the medical dispute.

(*l*) No disputed medical issue specified in subdivision (a) may be the subject of declaration of readiness to proceed unless there has first been an evaluation by the treating physician or an agreed or qualified medical evaluator.

Added Stats 2004 ch 34 § 19 (SB 899), effective April 19, 2004. Amended Stats 2012 ch 363 § 30 (SB 863), effective January 1, 2013.

§ 4063. Evaluation requiring employer to provide compensation

If a formal medical evaluation from an agreed medical evaluator or a qualified medical evaluator selected from a three member panel resolves any issue so as to require an employer to provide compensation, the employer shall, except as provided pursuant to paragraph (2) of subdivision (b) of Section 4650, commence the payment of compensation or file a declaration of readiness to proceed.

Added Stats 1989 ch 892 § 28, operative January 1, 1991. Amended Stats 2012 ch 363 § 31 (SB 863), effective January 1, 2013.

§ 4064. Costs and attorney fees

(a) The employer shall be liable for the cost of each reasonable and necessary comprehensive medical-legal evaluation obtained by the employee pursuant to Sections 4060, 4061, and 4062. Each comprehensive medical-legal evaluation shall address all contested medical issues arising from all injuries reported on one or more claim forms, except medical treatment recommendations, which are subject to utilization review as provided by Section 4610, and objections to utilization review determinations, which are subject to independent medical review as provided by Section 4610.5.

(b) For injuries occurring on or after January 1, 2003, if an unrepresented employee obtains an attorney after the evaluation pursuant to subdivision (d) of Section 4061 or subdivision (b) of Section 4062 has been completed, the employee shall be entitled to the same reports at employer expense as an employee who has been represented from the time the dispute arose and those reports shall be admissible in any proceeding before the appeals board.

(c) Subject to Section 4906, if an employer files a declaration of readiness to proceed and the employee is unrepresented at the time the declaration of readiness to proceed is filed, the employer shall be liable for any attorney's fees incurred by the employee in connection with the declaration of readiness to proceed.

(d) The employer shall not be liable for the cost of any comprehensive medical evaluations obtained by the employee other than those authorized pursuant to Sections 4060, 4061, and 4062. However, no party is prohibited from obtaining any medical evaluation or consultation at the party's own expense. In no event shall an employer or employee be liable for an evaluation obtained in violation of subdivision (b) of Section 4060. All comprehensive medical evaluations obtained by any party shall be admissible in any proceeding before the appeals board except as provided in Section 4060, 4061, 4062, 4062.1, or 4062.

Appendix

Added Stats 1989 ch 892 § 28, operative January 1, 1991. Amended Stats 1990 ch 1550 § 25 (AB 2910). Amended Stats 1993 ch 121 § 34 (AB 110), effective July 16, 1993, ch 1242 § 30 (SB 223); Stats 1998 ch 485 § 124 (AB 2803); Stats 2002 ch 6 § 54 (AB 749); Stats 2012 ch 363 § 32 (SB 863), effective January 1, 2013.

PART 2

COMPUTATION OF COMPENSATION

Chapter 1

Average Earnings

§ 4453. Average annual earnings; Computation

(a) In computing average annual earnings for the purposes of temporary disability indemnity and permanent total disability indemnity only, the average weekly earnings shall be taken at:

(1) Not less than one hundred twenty-six dollars ($126) nor more than two hundred ninety-four dollars ($294), for injuries occurring on or after January 1, 1983.

(2) Not less than one hundred sixty-eight dollars ($168) nor more than three hundred thirty-six dollars ($336), for injuries occurring on or after January 1, 1984.

(3) Not less than one hundred sixty-eight dollars ($168) for permanent total disability, and, for temporary disability, not less than the lesser of one hundred sixty-eight dollars ($168) or 1.5 times the employee's average weekly earnings from all employers, but in no event less than one hundred forty-seven dollars ($147), nor more than three hundred ninety-nine dollars ($399), for injuries occurring on or after January 1, 1990.

(4) Not less than one hundred sixty-eight dollars ($168) for permanent total disability, and for temporary disability, not less than the lesser of one hundred eighty-nine dollars ($189) or 1.5 times the employee's average weekly earnings from all employers, nor more than five hundred four dollars ($504), for injuries occurring on or after January 1, 1991.

(5) Not less than one hundred sixty-eight dollars ($168) for permanent total disability, and for temporary disability, not less than the lesser of one hundred eighty-nine dollars ($189) or 1.5 times the employee's average weekly earnings from all employers, nor more than six hundred nine dollars ($609), for injuries occurring on or after July 1, 1994.

(6) Not less than one hundred sixty-eight dollars ($168) for permanent total disability, and for temporary disability, not less than the

lesser of one hundred eighty-nine dollars ($189) or 1.5 times the employee's average weekly earnings from all employers, nor more than six hundred seventy-two dollars ($672), for injuries occurring on or after July 1, 1995.

(7) Not less than one hundred sixty-eight dollars ($168) for permanent total disability, and for temporary disability, not less than the lesser of one hundred eighty-nine dollars ($189) or 1.5 times the employee's average weekly earnings from all employers, nor more than seven hundred thirty-five dollars ($735), for injuries occurring on or after July 1, 1996.

(8) Not less than one hundred eighty-nine dollars ($189), nor more than nine hundred three dollars ($903), for injuries occurring on or after January 1, 2003.

(9) Not less than one hundred eighty-nine dollars ($189), nor more than one thousand ninety-two dollars ($1,092), for injuries occurring on or after January 1, 2004.

(10) Not less than one hundred eighty-nine dollars ($189), nor more than one thousand two hundred sixty dollars ($1,260), for injuries occurring on or after January 1, 2005. For injuries occurring on or after January 1, 2006, average weekly earnings shall be taken at not less than one hundred eighty-nine dollars ($189), nor more than one thousand two hundred sixty dollars ($1,260) or 1.5 times the state average weekly wage, whichever is greater. Commencing on January 1, 2007, and each January 1 thereafter, the limits specified in this paragraph shall be increased by an amount equal to the percentage increase in the state average weekly wage as compared to the prior year. For purposes of this paragraph, "state average weekly wage" means the average weekly wage paid by employers to employees covered by unemployment insurance as reported by the United States Department of Labor for California for the 12 months ending March 31 of the calendar year preceding the year in which the injury occurred.

(b) In computing average annual earnings for purposes of permanent partial disability indemnity, except as provided in Section 4659, the average weekly earnings shall be taken at:

(1) Not less than seventy-five dollars ($75), nor more than one hundred ninety-five dollars ($195), for injuries occurring on or after January 1, 1983.

(2) Not less than one hundred five dollars ($105), nor more than two hundred ten dollars ($210), for injuries occurring on or after January 1, 1984.

(3) When the final adjusted permanent disability rating of the injured employee is 15 percent or greater, but not more than 24.75 percent: (A) not less than one hundred five dollars ($105), nor more than two hundred twenty-two dollars ($222), for injuries occurring on or after July 1, 1994; (B) not less than one hundred five dollars ($105), nor more than two hundred thirty-one dollars ($231), for injuries occurring

Appendix

on or after July 1, 1995; (C) not less than one hundred five dollars ($105), nor more than two hundred forty dollars ($240), for injuries occurring on or after July 1, 1996.

(4) When the final adjusted permanent disability rating of the injured employee is 25 percent or greater, not less than one hundred five dollars ($105), nor more than two hundred twenty-two dollars ($222), for injuries occurring on or after January 1, 1991.

(5) When the final adjusted permanent disability rating of the injured employee is 25 percent or greater but not more than 69.75 percent: (A) not less than one hundred five dollars ($105), nor more than two hundred thirty-seven dollars ($237), for injuries occurring on or after July 1, 1994; (B) not less than one hundred five dollars ($105), nor more than two hundred forty-six dollars ($246), for injuries occurring on or after July 1, 1995; and (C) not less than one hundred five dollars ($105), nor more than two hundred fifty-five dollars ($255), for injuries occurring on or after July 1, 1996.

(6) When the final adjusted permanent disability rating of the injured employee is less than 70 percent: (A) not less than one hundred fifty dollars ($150), nor more than two hundred seventy-seven dollars and fifty cents ($277.50), for injuries occurring on or after January 1, 2003; (B) not less than one hundred fifty-seven dollars and fifty cents ($157.50), nor more than three hundred dollars ($300), for injuries occurring on or after January 1, 2004; (C) not less than one hundred fifty-seven dollars and fifty cents ($157.50), nor more than three hundred thirty dollars ($330), for injuries occurring on or after January 1, 2005; and (D) not less than one hundred ninety-five dollars ($195), nor more than three hundred forty-five dollars ($345), for injuries occurring on or after January 1, 2006.

(7) When the final adjusted permanent disability rating of the injured employee is 70 percent or greater, but less than 100 percent: (A) not less than one hundred five dollars ($105), nor more than two hundred fifty-two dollars ($252), for injuries occurring on or after July 1, 1994; (B) not less than one hundred five dollars ($105), nor more than two hundred ninety-seven dollars ($297), for injuries occurring on or after July 1, 1995; (C) not less than one hundred five dollars ($105), nor more than three hundred forty-five dollars ($345), for injuries occurring on or after July 1, 1996; (D) not less than one hundred fifty dollars ($150), nor more than three hundred forty-five dollars ($345), for injuries occurring on or after January 1, 2003; (E) not less than one hundred fifty-seven dollars and fifty cents ($157.50), nor more than three hundred seventy-five dollars ($375), for injuries occurring on or after January 1, 2004; (F) not less than one hundred fifty-seven dollars and fifty cents ($157.50), nor more than four hundred five dollars ($405), for injuries occurring on or after January 1, 2005; and (G) not less than one hundred ninety-five dollars ($195), nor more than four hundred five dollars ($405), for injuries occurring on or after January 1, 2006.

(8) For injuries occurring on or after January 1, 2013:

(A) When the final adjusted permanent disability rating is less than 55 percent, not less than two hundred forty dollars ($240) nor more than three hundred forty-five dollars ($345).

(B) When the final adjusted permanent disability rating is 55 percent or greater but less than 70 percent, not less than two hundred forty dollars ($240) nor more than four hundred five dollars ($405).

(C) When the final adjusted permanent disability rating is 70 percent or greater but less than 100 percent, not less than two hundred forty dollars ($240) nor more than four hundred thirty-five dollars ($435).

(9) For injuries occurring on or after January 1, 2014, not less than two hundred forty dollars ($240) nor more than four hundred thirty-five dollars ($435).

(c) Between the limits specified in subdivisions (a) and (b), the average weekly earnings, except as provided in Sections 4456 to 4459, shall be arrived at as follows:

(1) Where the employment is for 30 or more hours a week and for five or more working days a week, the average weekly earnings shall be the number of working days a week times the daily earnings at the time of the injury.

(2) Where the employee is working for two or more employers at or about the time of the injury, the average weekly earnings shall be taken as the aggregate of these earnings from all employments computed in terms of one week; but the earnings from employments other than the employment in which the injury occurred shall not be taken at a higher rate than the hourly rate paid at the time of the injury.

(3) If the earnings are at an irregular rate, such as piecework, or on a commission basis, or are specified to be by week, month, or other period, then the average weekly earnings mentioned in subdivision (a) shall be taken as the actual weekly earnings averaged for this period of time, not exceeding one year, as may conveniently be taken to determine an average weekly rate of pay.

(4) Where the employment is for less than 30 hours per week, or where for any reason the foregoing methods of arriving at the average weekly earnings cannot reasonably and fairly be applied, the average weekly earnings shall be taken at 100 percent of the sum which reasonably represents the average weekly earning capacity of the injured employee at the time of his or her injury, due consideration being given to his or her actual earnings from all sources and employments.

(d) Every computation made pursuant to this section beginning January 1, 1990, shall be made only with reference to temporary disability or the permanent disability resulting from an original injury sustained after January 1, 1990. However, all rights existing under this section on January 1, 1990, shall be continued in force. Except as provided in Section 4661.5, disability indemnity benefits shall be calculated according to the limits in this section in effect on the date of injury and shall remain in effect for the duration of any disability resulting from the injury.

Added Stats 1977 ch 17 § 26, effective March 25, 1977. Amended Stats 1977 ch 1018 § 1; Stats 1980 ch 1042 § 1; Stats 1982 ch 922 § 7; Stats 1989 ch 892 § 29, ch 893 § 3; Stats 1990 ch 1550 § 29 (AB 2910). Amended Stats 1993 ch 121 § 37 (AB 110), effective July 16, 1993; Stats 2002 ch 6 § 57 (AB 749), ch 866 § 9 (AB 486); Stats 2012 ch 363 § 34 (SB 863), effective January 1, 2013.

Chapter 2

Compensation Schedules

Article 2

Medical and Hospital Treatment

§ 4600. Medical treatment provided by employer; Liability for reasonable expense; Medical provider network; Predesignation of personal physician; Expenses incurred in submitting to examination; Qualified interpreter

(a) Medical, surgical, chiropractic, acupuncture, licensed clinical social worker, and hospital treatment, including nursing, medicines, medical and surgical supplies, crutches, and apparatuses, including orthotic and prosthetic devices and services, that is reasonably required to cure or relieve the injured worker from the effects of the worker's injury shall be provided by the employer. In the case of the employer's neglect or refusal reasonably to do so, the employer is liable for the reasonable expense incurred by or on behalf of the employee in providing treatment.

(b) As used in this division and notwithstanding any other law, medical treatment that is reasonably required to cure or relieve the injured worker from the effects of the worker's injury means treatment that is based upon the guidelines adopted by the administrative director pursuant to Section 5307.27.

(c) Unless the employer or the employer's insurer has established or contracted with a medical provider network as provided for in Section 4616, after 30 days from the date the injury is reported, the employee may be treated by a physician of the employee's own choice or at a facility of the employee's own choice within a reasonable geographic area. A chiropractor shall not be a treating physician after the employee has received the maximum number of chiropractic visits allowed by subdivision (c) of Section 4604.5.

(d) (1) If an employee has notified the employee's employer in writing prior to the date of injury that the employee has a personal physician, the employee shall have the right to be treated by that physician from the date of injury if the employee has health care coverage for nonoccupational injuries or illnesses on the date of injury in a plan, policy, or fund as described in subdivisions (b), (c), and (d) of Section 4616.7.

(2) For purposes of paragraph (1), a personal physician shall meet all of the following conditions:

(A) Be the employee's regular physician and surgeon, licensed pursuant to Chapter 5 (commencing with Section 2000) of Division 2 of the Business and Professions Code.

(B) Be the employee's primary care physician and has previously directed the medical treatment of the employee, and who retains the employee's medical records, including the employee's medical history. "Personal physician" includes a medical group, if the medical group is a single corporation or partnership composed of licensed doctors of medicine or osteopathy, which operates an integrated multispecialty medical group providing comprehensive medical services predominantly for nonoccupational illnesses and injuries.

(C) The physician agrees to be predesignated.

(3) If the employee has health care coverage for nonoccupational injuries or illnesses on the date of injury in a health care service plan licensed pursuant to Chapter 2.2 (commencing with Section 1340) of Division 2 of the Health and Safety Code, and the employer is notified pursuant to paragraph (1), all medical treatment, utilization review of medical treatment, access to medical treatment, and other medical treatment issues shall be governed by Chapter 2.2 (commencing with Section 1340) of Division 2 of the Health and Safety Code. Disputes regarding the provision of medical treatment shall be resolved pursuant to Article 5.55 (commencing with Section 1374.30) of Chapter 2.2 of Division 2 of the Health and Safety Code.

(4) If the employee has health care coverage for nonoccupational injuries or illnesses on the date of injury in a group health insurance policy as described in Section 4616.7, all medical treatment, utilization review of medical treatment, access to medical treatment, and other medical treatment issues shall be governed by the applicable provisions of the Insurance Code.

(5) The insurer may require prior authorization of any nonemergency treatment or diagnostic service and may conduct reasonably necessary utilization review pursuant to Section 4610.

(6) An employee is entitled to all medically appropriate referrals by the personal physician to other physicians or medical providers within the nonoccupational health care plan. An employee is enti-

tled to treatment by physicians or other medical providers outside of the nonoccupational health care plan pursuant to standards established in Article 5 (commencing with Section 1367) of Chapter 2.2 of Division 2 of the Health and Safety Code.

(e) (1) When at the request of the employer, the employer's insurer, the administrative director, the appeals board, or a workers' compensation administrative law judge, the employee submits to examination by a physician, the employee is entitled to receive, in addition to all other benefits herein provided, all reasonable expenses of transportation, meals, and lodging incident to reporting for the examination, together with one day of temporary disability indemnity for each day of wages lost in submitting to the examination.

(2) Regardless of the date of injury, "reasonable expenses of transportation" includes mileage fees from the employee's home to the place of the examination and back at the rate of twenty-one cents ($0.21) a mile or the mileage rate adopted by the Director of Human Resources pursuant to Section 19820 of the Government Code, whichever is higher, plus any bridge tolls. The mileage and tolls shall be paid to the employee at the time the employee is given notification of the time and place of the examination.

(f) When at the request of the employer, the employer's insurer, the administrative director, the appeals board, or a workers' compensation administrative law judge, an employee submits to examination by a physician and the employee does not proficiently speak or understand the English language, the employee shall be entitled to the services of a qualified interpreter in accordance with conditions and a fee schedule prescribed by the administrative director. These services shall be provided by the employer. For purposes of this section, "qualified interpreter" means a language interpreter certified, or deemed certified, pursuant to Article 8 (commencing with Section 11435.05) of Chapter 4.5 of Part 1 of Division 3 of Title 2 of, or Section 68566 of, the Government Code.

(g) If the injured employee cannot effectively communicate with the employee's treating physician because the employee cannot proficiently speak or understand the English language, the injured employee is entitled to the services of a qualified interpreter during medical treatment appointments. To be a qualified interpreter for purposes of medical treatment appointments, an interpreter is not required to meet the requirements of subdivision (f), but shall meet any requirements established by rule by the administrative director that are substantially similar to the requirements set forth in Section 1367.04 of the Health and Safety Code. The administrative director shall adopt a fee schedule for qualified interpreter fees in accordance with this section. Upon request of the injured employee, the employer or insurance carrier shall pay for interpreter services. An employer shall not be required to pay for the services of an interpreter who is not certified or is provisionally certified by the person conducting the medical treatment or examination unless either the employer consents in advance to the selection of the individual who provides the interpreting service or the injured worker requires interpreting service in a language other than the languages designated pursuant to Section 11435.40 of the Government Code.

(h) Home health care services shall be provided as medical treatment only if reasonably required to cure or relieve the injured employee from the effects of the employee's injury and prescribed by a physician and surgeon licensed pursuant to Chapter 5 (commencing with Section 2000) of Division 2 of the Business and Professions Code, and subject to Section 5307.1 or 5307.8. The employer is not liable for home health care services that are provided more than 14 days prior to the date of the employer's receipt of the physician's prescription.

Added Stats 2009 ch 565 § 2 (SB 186), effective January 1, 2010. See this section as modified in Governor's Reorganization Plan No. 1 § 199 of 2011. Amended Stats 2012 ch 363 § 35 (SB 863) (ch 363 prevails), effective January 1, 2013, ch. 665 § 179 (SB 1308), effective January 1, 2013; Stats 2013 ch 793 § 1 (AB 1376), effective October 13, 2013; Stats 2014 ch 71 § 111 (SB 1304), effective January 1, 2015, ch 217 § 1 (AB 2732), effective January 1, 2015 (ch 217 prevails); Stats 2019 ch 497 § 188 (AB 991), effective January 1, 2020; Stats 2022 ch 604 § 4 (SB 1002), effective January 1, 2023.

§ 4600.05. Immediate support from nurse case manager for employees injured by act of domestic terrorism; Applicability; Regulations

(a) An employer, as defined in Section 3300, shall provide immediate support from a nurse case manager for employees injured by an act of domestic terrorism, as defined in Section 2331 of Title 18 of the United States Code, whose injuries arise out of and in the course of employment, to assist injured employees in obtaining medically necessary medical treatment, as defined by the medical treatment utilization schedule adopted pursuant to Section 5307.27, and to assist providers of medical services in seeking authorization of medical treatment.

(b) (1) This section shall apply only if the Governor has declared a state of emergency pursuant to subdivision (b) of Section 8558 of the Government Code in connection with the act of domestic terrorism.

(2) Upon the issuance of a declaration pursuant to paragraph (1), an employer that has been notified of a claim for compensation arising out of the acts that resulted in the declaration shall provide a notice within three days to the claimant advising the claimant of medically necessary

services provided pursuant to subdivision (a). In the case of a claim for compensation subject to this section that is filed after the declaration, the employer shall provide the notice to the claimant within three days. The notice shall be in the form adopted by the administrative director pursuant to subdivision (d).

(c) This section shall not alter the conditions for compensability of an injury, as described in Sections 3208.3 and 3600.

(d) The administrative director shall adopt regulations to implement this section, including, but not limited to, the definition of a nurse case manager's qualifications, the scope and timing of immediate support from a nurse case manager, and the contents of the notice that employers shall provide to claimants.

Added Stats 2017 ch 736 § 2 (AB 44), effective January 1, 2018.

§ 4603.2. Notice to employer of physician's name and address; Objection to non-network physician; Reports by physician; Payment for medical treatment; Contest of itemization by employer; Interest or increase in compensation; Itemization review; Jurisdiction over disputes

(a) (1) Upon selecting a physician pursuant to Section 4600, the employee or physician shall notify the employer of the name and address, including the name of the medical group, if applicable, of the physician. The physician shall submit a report to the employer within five working days from the date of the initial examination, as required by Section 6409, and shall submit periodic reports at intervals that may be prescribed by rules and regulations adopted by the administrative director.

(2) If the employer objects to the employee's selection of the physician on the grounds that the physician is not within the medical provider network used by the employer, and there is a final determination that the employee was entitled to select the physician pursuant to Section 4600, the employee shall be entitled to continue treatment with that physician at the employer's expense in accordance with this division, notwithstanding Section 4616.2. The employer shall be required to pay from the date of the initial examination if the physician's report was submitted within five working days of the initial examination. If the physician's report was submitted more than five working days after the initial examination, the employer and the employee shall not be required to pay for any services prior to the date the physician's report was submitted.

(3) If the employer objects to the employee's selection of the physician on the grounds that the physician is not within the medical provider network used by the employer, and there is a final determination that the employee was not entitled to select a physician outside of the medical provider network, the employer is not liable for treatment provided

by or at the direction of that physician or for any consequences of the treatment obtained outside the network.

(b) (1) (A) A provider of services provided pursuant to Section 4600, including, but not limited to, physicians, hospitals, pharmacies, interpreters, copy services, transportation services, and home health care services, shall submit its request for payment with an itemization of services provided and the charge for each service, a copy of all reports showing the services performed, the prescription or referral from the primary treating physician if the services were performed by a person other than the primary treating physician, and any evidence of authorization for the services that may have been received. This section does not prohibit an employer, insurer, or third-party claims administrator from establishing, through written agreement, an alternative manual or electronic request for payment with providers for services provided pursuant to Section 4600.

(B) Effective for services provided on or after January 1, 2017, the request for payment with an itemization of services provided and the charge for each service shall be submitted to the employer within 12 months of the date of service or within 12 months of the date of discharge for inpatient facility services. The administrative director shall adopt rules to implement the 12-month limitation period. The rules shall define circumstances that constitute good cause for an exception to the 12-month period, including provisions to address the circumstances of a nonoccupational injury or illness later found to be a compensable injury or illness. The request for payment is barred unless timely submitted.

(C) The request for payment with an itemization of services provided and the charge for each service shall be submitted to the employer with the national provider identifier (NPI) number for the physician or provider who provided the service for which payment is sought in accordance with rules adopted by the administrative director pursuant to Section 4603.4. Failure to include the physician's or provider's NPI shall result in the request for payment being barred until the physician's or provider's NPI is submitted with the request for payment. This subparagraph does not preclude an employer, insurer, pharmacy benefit manager, or third-party claims administrator from requiring the physician's or provider's NPI at an earlier date. This subparagraph is declaratory of existing law.

(D) Notwithstanding the requirements of this paragraph, a copy of the prescription shall not be required with a request for payment for pharmacy services, unless the provider of services has entered into a written agreement, as provided in this paragraph, that requires a copy of a prescription for a pharmacy service.

(E) This section does not preclude an employer, insurer, pharmacy benefits manager, or third-party claims administrator from requesting

Appendix

a copy of the prescription during a review of any records of prescription drugs that were dispensed by a pharmacy.

(2) Except as provided in subdivision (d) of Section 4603.4, or under contracts authorized under Section 5307.11, payment for medical treatment provided or prescribed by the treating physician selected by the employee or designated by the employer shall be made at reasonable maximum amounts in the official medical fee schedule, pursuant to Section 5307.1, in effect on the date of service. Payments shall be made by the employer with an explanation of review pursuant to Section 4603.3 within 45 days after receipt of each separate itemization of medical services provided, together with any required reports and any written authorization for services that may have been received by the physician. If the itemization or a portion thereof is contested, denied, or considered incomplete, the physician shall be notified, in the explanation of review, that the itemization is contested, denied, or considered incomplete, within 30 days after receipt of the itemization by the employer. An explanation of review that states an itemization is incomplete shall also state all additional information required to make a decision. A properly documented list of services provided and not paid at the rates then in effect under Section 5307.1 within the 45-day period shall be paid at the rates then in effect and increased by 15 percent, together with interest at the same rate as judgments in civil actions retroactive to the date of receipt of the itemization, unless the employer does both of the following:

(A) Pays the provider at the rates in effect within the 45-day period.

(B) Advises, in an explanation of review pursuant to Section 4603.3, the physician, or another provider of the items being contested, the reasons for contesting these items, and the remedies available to the physician or the other provider if the physician or provider disagrees. In the case of an itemization that includes services provided by a hospital, outpatient surgery center, or independent diagnostic facility, advice that a request has been made for an audit of the itemization shall satisfy the requirements of this paragraph.

An employer's liability to a physician or another provider under this section for delayed payments shall not affect its liability to an employee under Section 5814 or any other provision of this division.

(3) Notwithstanding paragraph (1), if the employer is a governmental entity, payment for medical treatment provided or prescribed by the treating physician selected by the employee or designated by the employer shall be made within 60 days after receipt of each separate itemization, together with any required reports and any written authorization for services that may have been received by the physician.

(4) Duplicate submissions of medical services itemizations, for which an explanation of review was previously provided, shall require no further or additional notification or objection by the employer to the medical provider and shall not subject the employer to any additional

penalties or interest pursuant to this section for failing to respond to the duplicate submission. This paragraph applies only to duplicate submissions and does not apply to any other penalties or interest that may be applicable to the original submission.

(5) (A) An employer may defer objecting to or paying any bill submitted by, or on behalf of, a provider whose liens are stayed pursuant to Section 4615, and the time limits for taking any action prescribed by paragraphs (2) and (3) shall not commence until the stay is lifted pursuant to Section 4615.

(B) An employer may object to any bill submitted by, or on behalf of, a provider who has been suspended pursuant to Section 139.21.

(c) Interest or an increase in compensation paid by an insurer pursuant to this section shall be treated in the same manner as an increase in compensation under subdivision (d) of Section 4650 for the purposes of any classification of risks and premium rates, and any system of merit rating approved or issued pursuant to Article 2 (commencing with Section 11730) of Chapter 3 of Part 3 of Division 2 of the Insurance Code.

(d) (1) Whenever an employer or insurer employs an individual or contracts with an entity to conduct a review of an itemization submitted by a physician or medical provider, the employer or insurer shall make available to that individual or entity all documentation submitted together with that itemization by the physician or medical provider. When an individual or entity conducting an itemization review determines that additional information or documentation is necessary to review the itemization, the individual or entity shall contact the claims administrator or insurer to obtain the necessary information or documentation that was submitted by the physician or medical provider pursuant to subdivision (b).

(2) (A) An individual or entity reviewing an itemization of service submitted by a physician or medical provider, including a medical provider network, an entity that provides ancillary services, as defined in Section 4616.5, or an entity providing services for or on behalf of the medical provider network or its providers, shall not alter the procedure codes listed or recommend reduction of the amount of the payment unless the documentation submitted by the physician or medical provider with the itemization of service has been reviewed by that individual or entity. If the reviewer does not recommend payment for services as itemized by the physician or medical provider, the explanation of review shall provide the physician or medical provider with a specific explanation as to why the reviewer altered the procedure code or changed other parts of the itemization and the specific deficiency in the itemization or documentation that caused the reviewer to conclude that the altered procedure code or amount recommended for payment more accurately represents the service performed.

(B) The amendments to subparagraph (A) made by the act adding this subparagraph are declaratory of existing law.

(e) (1) If the provider disputes the amount paid, the provider may request a second review within 90 days of service of the explanation of review or an order of the appeals board resolving the threshold issue as stated in the explanation of review pursuant to paragraph (5) of subdivision (a) of Section 4603.3. The request for a second review shall be submitted to the employer on a form prescribed by the administrative director and shall include all of the following:

(A) The date of the explanation of review and the claim number or other unique identifying number provided on the explanation of review.

(B) The item and amount in dispute.

(C) The additional payment requested and the reason therefor.

(D) The additional information provided in response to a request in the first explanation of review or any other additional information provided in support of the additional payment requested.

(2) If the only dispute is the amount of payment and the provider does not request a second review within 90 days, the bill shall be deemed satisfied and neither the employer nor the employee shall be liable for any further payment.

(3) Within 14 days of a request for second review, the employer shall respond with a final written determination on each of the items or amounts in dispute. Payment of any balance not in dispute shall be made within 21 days of receipt of the request for second review. This time limit may be extended by mutual written agreement.

(4) If the provider contests the amount paid, after receipt of the second review, the provider shall request an independent bill review as provided for in Section 4603.6.

(f) Except as provided in paragraph (4) of subdivision (e), the appeals board shall have jurisdiction over disputes arising out of this section pursuant to Section 5304.

Added Stats 1975 ch 1259 § 6. Amended Stats 1984 ch 909 § 2; Stats 1990 ch 770 § 3 (SB 241); Stats 1999 ch 124 § 2 (AB 775); Stats 2000 ch 1069 § 4 (SB 1732); Stats 2001 ch 240 § 1 (AB 1179); Stats 2003 ch 639 § 25 (SB 228); Stats 2004 ch 34 § 24 (SB 899), effective April 19, 2004; Stats 2006 ch 69 § 24 (AB 1806), effective July 12, 2006; Stats 2012 ch 363 § 36 (SB 863), effective January 1, 2013; Stats 2013 ch 129 § 1 (SB 146), effective August 19, 2013; Stats 2016 ch 214 § 1 (SB 1175), effective January 1, 2017. Stats 2017 ch 300 § 2 (AB 1422), effective January 1, 2018. (ch 300 prevails); Stats 2017 ch 561 § 173 (AB 1516), effective January 1, 2018; Stats 2019 ch 647 § 5 (SB 537), effective January 1, 2020.

§ 4603.3. Explanation of review upon payment, adjustment, or denial of itemization of medical services

(a) Upon payment, adjustment, or denial of a complete or incomplete itemization of medical services, an employer shall provide an explanation of review in the manner prescribed by the administrative director that shall include all of the following:

(1) A statement of the items or procedures billed and the amounts requested by the provider to be paid.

(2) The amount paid.

(3) The basis for any adjustment, change, or denial of the item or procedure billed.

(4) The additional information required to make a decision for an incomplete itemization.

(5) If a denial of payment is for some reason other than a fee dispute, the reason for the denial.

(6) Information on whom to contact on behalf of the employer if a dispute arises over the payment of the billing. The explanation of review shall inform the medical provider of the time limit to raise any objection regarding the items or procedures paid or disputed and how to obtain an independent review of the medical bill pursuant to Section 4603.6.

(b) The administrative director may adopt regulations requiring the use of electronic explanations of review.

Added Stats 2012 ch 363 § 37 (SB 863), effective January 1, 2013.

§ 4603.4. Adoption of certain rules and regulations by administrative director; Standards

(a) The administrative director shall adopt rules and regulations to do all of the following:

(1) Ensure that all health care providers and facilities submit medical bills for payment on standardized forms.

(2) Require acceptance by employers of electronic claims for payment of medical services.

(3) Ensure confidentiality of medical information submitted on electronic claims for payment of medical services.

(4) Require the timely submission of paper or electronic bills in conformity with subparagraph (B) of paragraph (1) of subdivision (b) of Section 4603.2.

(b) To the extent feasible, standards adopted pursuant to subdivision (a) shall be consistent with existing standards under the federal Health Insurance Portability and Accountability Act of 1996.

(c) Require all employers to accept electronic claims for payment of medical services.

(d) Payment for medical treatment provided or prescribed by the treating physician selected by the employee or designated by the employer shall be made with an explanation of review by the employer within 15 working days after electronic receipt of an itemized electronic billing for services at or below the maximum fees provided in the official medical fee schedule adopted pursuant to Section 5307.1. If the billing is contested, denied, or incomplete, payment shall be made with an explanation of review of any uncontested amounts within 15 working days after electronic receipt of the billing, and payment of the balance shall be made in accordance with Section 4603.2.

Added Stats 2002 ch 6 § 62 (AB 749). Amended Stats 2003 ch 639 § 26 (SB 228); Stats 2012 ch 363 § 38 (SB 863), effective January 1, 2013; Stats 2016 ch 214 § 2 (SB 1175), effective January 1, 2017.

§ 4603.6. Request for independent review; Procedure

(a) If the only dispute is the amount of payment and the provider has received a second review that did not resolve the dispute, the provider may request an independent bill review within 30 calendar days of service of the second review pursuant to Section 4603.2 or 4622. If the provider fails to request an independent bill review within 30 days, the bill shall be deemed satisfied, and neither the employer nor the employee shall be liable for any further payment. If the employer has contested liability for any issue other than the reasonable amount payable for services, that issue shall be resolved prior to filing a request for independent bill review, and the time limit for requesting independent bill review shall not begin to run until the resolution of that issue becomes final, except as provided for in Section 4622.

(b) A request for independent review shall be made on a form prescribed by the administrative director, and shall include copies of the original billing itemization, any supporting documents that were furnished with the original billing, the explanation of review, the request for second review together with any supporting documentation submitted with that request, and the final explanation of the second review. The administrative director may require that requests for independent bill review be submitted electronically. A copy of the request, together with all required documents, shall be served on the employer. Only the request form and the proof of payment of the fee required by subdivision (c) shall be filed with the administrative director. Upon notice of assignment of the independent bill reviewer, the requesting party shall submit the documents listed in this subdivision to the independent bill reviewer within 10 days.

(c) The provider shall pay to the administrative director a fee determined by the administrative director to cover no more than the reasonable estimated cost of independent bill review and administration of the independent bill review program. The administrative director may prescribe different fees depending on the number of items in the bill or other criteria determined by regulation adopted by the administrative director. If any additional payment is found owing from the employer to the medical provider, the employer shall reimburse the provider for the fee in addition to the amount found owing.

(d) Upon receipt of a request for independent bill review and the required fee, the administrative director or the administrative director's designee shall assign the request to an independent bill reviewer within 30 days and notify the medical provider and employer of the independent reviewer assigned.

(e) The independent bill reviewer shall review the materials submitted by the parties and make a written determination of any additional amounts to be paid to the medical provider and state the reasons for the determination. If the independent bill reviewer deems necessary, the independent bill reviewer may request additional documents from the medical provider or employer. The employer shall have no obligation to serve medical reports on the provider unless the reports are requested by the independent bill reviewer. If additional documents are requested, the parties shall respond with the documents requested within 30 days and shall provide the other party with copies of any documents submitted to the independent reviewer, and the independent reviewer shall make a written determination of any additional amounts to be paid to the medical provider and state the reasons for the determination within 60 days of the receipt of the administrative director's assignment. The written determination of the independent bill reviewer shall be sent to the administrative director and provided to both the medical provider and the employer.

(f) The determination of the independent bill reviewer shall be deemed a determination and order of the administrative director. The determination is final and binding on all parties unless an aggrieved party files with the appeals board a verified appeal from the medical bill review determination of the administrative director within 20 days of the service of the determination. The medical bill review determination of the administrative director shall be presumed to be correct and shall be set aside only upon clear and convincing evidence of one or more of the following grounds for appeal:

(1) The administrative director acted without or in excess of his or her powers.

(2) The determination of the administrative director was procured by fraud.

(3) The independent bill reviewer was subject to a material conflict of interest that is in violation of Section 139.5.

(4) The determination was the result of bias on the basis of race, national origin, ethnic group identification, religion, age, sex, sexual orientation, color, or disability.

(5) The determination was the result of a plainly erroneous express or implied finding of fact, provided that the mistake of fact is a matter of ordinary knowledge based on the information submitted for review and not a matter that is subject to expert opinion.

(g) If the determination of the administrative director is reversed, the dispute shall be remanded to the administrative director to submit the dispute to independent bill review by a different independent review organization. In the event that a different independent bill review organization is not available after remand, the administrative director shall submit the dispute to the original bill review organization for review by a different reviewer within the organization. In no event shall the appeals board or any higher court make a determination of ultimate fact contrary to the determination of the bill review organization.

(h) Once the independent bill reviewer has made a determination regarding additional amounts to be paid to the medical provider, the employer shall pay the additional amounts per the timely payment requirements set forth in Sections 4603.2 and 4603.4.

Added Stats 2012 ch 363 § 39 (SB 863), effective January 1, 2013.

§ 4604. Determination of controversies by appeals board

Controversies between employer and employee arising under this chapter shall be determined by the appeals board, upon the request of either party, except as otherwise provided by Section 4610.5.

Enacted 1937. Amended Stats 1965 ch 1513 § 88, operative January 15, 1966; Stats 2012 ch 363 § 40 (SB 863), effective January 1, 2013.

§ 4604.5. Medical treatment utilization schedule and recommended guidelines; Rebuttable presumption of correctness; Limit on chiropractic, occupational and physical therapy visits

(a) The recommended guidelines set forth in the medical treatment utilization schedule adopted by the administrative director pursuant to Section 5307.27 shall be presumptively correct on the issue of extent and scope of medical treatment. The presumption is rebuttable and may be controverted by a preponderance of the scientific medical evidence establishing that a variance from the guidelines reasonably is required to cure or relieve the injured worker from the effects of his or her injury. The presumption created is one affecting the burden of proof.

(b) The recommended guidelines set forth in the schedule adopted pursuant to subdivision (a) shall reflect practices that are evidence and scientifically based, nationally recognized, and peer reviewed. The guidelines shall be designed to assist providers by offering an analytical framework for the evaluation and treatment of injured workers, and shall constitute care in accordance with Section 4600 for all injured workers diagnosed with industrial conditions.

(c) (1) Notwithstanding the medical treatment utilization schedule, for injuries occurring on and after January 1, 2004, an employee shall be entitled to no more than 24 chiropractic, 24 occupational therapy, and 24 physical therapy visits per industrial injury.

(2) (A) Paragraph (1) shall not apply when an employer authorizes, in writing, additional visits to a health care practitioner for physical medicine services. Payment or authorization for treatment beyond the limits set forth in paragraph (1) shall not be deemed a waiver of the limits set forth by paragraph (1) with respect to future requests for authorization.

(B) The Legislature finds and declares that the amendments made to subparagraph (A) by the act adding this subparagraph are declaratory of existing law.

(3) Paragraph (1) shall not apply to visits for postsurgical physical medicine and postsurgical rehabilitation services provided in compliance with a postsurgical treatment utilization schedule established by the administrative director pursuant to Section 5307.27.

(d) For all injuries not covered by the official utilization schedule adopted pursuant to Section 5307.27, authorized treatment shall be in accordance with other evidence-based medical treatment guidelines that are recognized generally by the national medical community and scientifically based.

Added Stats 2003 ch 639 § 27 (SB 228). Amended Stats 2004 ch 34 § 25 (SB 899), effective April 19, 2004; Stats 2007 ch 621 § 1 (AB 1073), effective January 1, 2008; Stats 2008 ch 179 § 175 (SB 1498), effective January 1, 2009; Stats 2012 ch 363 § 41 (SB 863), effective January 1, 2013.

§ 4605. Employee's right to provide own physicians

Nothing contained in this chapter shall limit the right of the employee to provide, at his or her own expense, a consulting physician or any attending physicians whom he or she desires. Any report prepared by consulting or attending physicians pursuant to this section shall not be the sole basis of an award of compensation. A qualified medical evaluator or authorized treating physician shall address any report procured pursuant to this section and shall indicate whether he or she agrees or disagrees with the findings or opinions stated in the report, and shall identify the bases for this opinion.

Enacted 1937. Amended Stats 2012 ch 363 § 42 (SB 863), effective January 1, 2013.

§ 4610. Employers to establish utilization review process; Criteria; Administrative penalties

(a) For purposes of this section, "utilization review" means utilization review or utilization management functions that prospectively, retrospectively, or concurrently review and approve, modify, or deny, based in whole or in part on medical necessity to cure and relieve, treatment recommendations by physicians, as defined in Section 3209.3, prior to, retrospectively, or concurrent with the provision of medical treatment services pursuant to Section 4600.

Appendix

(b) For all dates of injury occurring on or after January 1, 2018, emergency treatment services and medical treatment rendered for a body part or condition that is accepted as compensable by the employer and is addressed by the medical treatment utilization schedule adopted pursuant to Section 5307.7, by a member of the medical provider network or health care organization, or by a physician predesignated pursuant to subdivision (d) of Section 4600, within the 30 days following the initial date of injury, shall be authorized without prospective utilization review, except as provided in subdivision (c). The services rendered under this subdivision shall be consistent with the medical treatment utilization schedule. In the event that the employee is not subject to treatment with a medical provider network, health care organization, or predesignated physician pursuant to subdivision (d) of Section 4600, the employee shall be eligible for treatment under this section within 30 days following the initial date of injury if the treatment is rendered by a physician or facility selected by the employer. For treatment rendered by a medical provider network physician, health care organization physician, a physician predesignated pursuant to subdivision (d) of Section 4600, or an employer-selected physician, the report required under Section 6409 and a complete request for authorization shall be submitted by the physician within five days following the employee's initial visit and evaluation.

(c) Unless authorized by the employer or rendered as emergency medical treatment, the following medical treatment services, as defined in rules adopted by the administrative director, that are rendered through a member of the medical provider network or health care organization, a predesignated physician, an employer-selected physician, or an employer-selected facility, within the 30 days following the initial date of injury, shall be subject to prospective utilization review under this section:

(1) Pharmaceuticals, to the extent they are neither expressly exempted from prospective review nor authorized by the drug formulary adopted pursuant to Section 5307.27.

(2) Nonemergency inpatient and outpatient surgery, including all presurgical and postsurgical services.

(3) Psychological treatment services.

(4) Home health care services.

(5) Imaging and radiology services, excluding x-rays.

(6) All durable medical equipment, whose combined total value exceeds two hundred fifty dollars ($250), as determined by the official medical fee schedule.

(7) Electrodiagnostic medicine, including, but not limited to, electromyography and nerve conduction studies.

(8) Any other service designated and defined through rules adopted by the administrative director.

(d) (1) Except for emergency treatment services, any request for payment for treatment provided under subdivision (b) shall comply with Section 4603.2 and be submitted to the employer, or its insurer or claims administrator, within 30 days of the date the service was provided.

(2) (A) In the case of emergency treatment services, any request for payment for treatment provided under subdivision (b) shall comply with Section 4603.2 and be submitted to the employer, or its insurer or claims administrator, within 180 days of the date the service was provided.

(B) For the purposes of this subdivision, "emergency treatment services" means treatment for an emergency medical condition defined in subdivision (b) of Section 1317.1 of the Health and Safety Code and provided in a licensed general acute care hospital, as defined in Section 1250 of the Health and Safety Code.

(e) If a physician fails to submit the report required under Section 6409 and a complete request for authorization, as described in subdivision (b), an employer may remove the physician's ability under this subdivision to provide further medical treatment to the employee that is exempt from prospective utilization review.

(f) An employer may perform retrospective utilization review for any treatment provided pursuant to subdivision (b) solely for the purpose of determining if the physician is prescribing treatment consistent with the schedule for medical treatment utilization, including, but not limited to, the drug formulary adopted pursuant to Section 5307.27.

(1) If it is found after retrospective utilization reviews that there is a pattern and practice of the physician or provider failing to render treatment consistent with the schedule for medical treatment utilization, including the drug formulary, the employer may remove the ability of the predesignated physician, employer-selected physician, or the member of the medical provider network or health care organization under this subdivision to provide further medical treatment to any employee that is exempt from prospective utilization review. The employer shall notify the physician or provider of the results of the retrospective utilization review and the requirement for prospective utilization review for all subsequent medical treatment.

(2) The results of retrospective utilization review may constitute a showing of good cause for an employer's petition requesting a change of physician or provider pursuant to Section 4603 and may serve as grounds for termination of the physician or provider from the medical provider network or health care organization.

(g) Each employer shall establish a utilization review process in compliance with this section, either directly or through its insurer or an entity with which an employer or insurer contracts for these services.

Appendix

(1) Each utilization review process that modifies or denies requests for authorization of medical treatment shall be governed by written policies and procedures. These policies and procedures shall ensure that decisions based on the medical necessity to cure and relieve of proposed medical treatment services are consistent with the schedule for medical treatment utilization, including the drug formulary, adopted pursuant to Section 5307.27.

(2) (A) Unless otherwise indicated in this section, a physician providing treatment under Section 4600 shall send any request for authorization for medical treatment, with supporting documentation, to the claims administrator for the employer, insurer, or other entity according to rules adopted by the administrative director. The employer, insurer, or other entity shall employ or designate a medical director who holds an unrestricted license to practice medicine in this state issued pursuant to Section 2050 or 2450 of the Business and Professions Code. The medical director shall ensure that the process by which the employer or other entity reviews and approves, modifies, or denies requests by physicians prior to, retrospectively, or concurrent with the provision of medical treatment services complies with the requirements of this section. This section does not limit the existing authority of the Medical Board of California.

(B) A request for authorization, including its supporting documentation, shall not be altered or amended by any entity other than the requesting physician or provider prior to the submission of the request to the claims administrator in accordance with subparagraph (A). This subparagraph is declaratory of existing law.

(3) (A) A person other than a licensed physician who is competent to evaluate the specific clinical issues involved in the medical treatment services, if these services are within the scope of the physician's practice, requested by the physician, shall not modify or deny requests for authorization of medical treatment for reasons of medical necessity to cure and relieve or due to incomplete or insufficient information under subdivisions (i) and (j).

(B) (i) The employer, or any entity conducting utilization review on behalf of the employer, shall neither offer nor provide any financial incentive or consideration to a physician based on the number of modifications or denials made by the physician under this section.

(ii) An insurer or third-party administrator shall not refer utilization review services conducted on behalf of an employer under this section to an entity in which the insurer or third-party administrator has a financial interest as defined under Section 139.32. This prohibition does not apply if the insurer or third-party administrator provides the employer and the administrative director with prior written disclosure of both of the following:

(I) The entity conducting the utilization review services.

(II) The insurer or third-party administrator's financial interest in the entity.

(C) The administrative director has authority pursuant to this section to review any compensation agreement, payment schedule, or contract between the employer, or any entity conducting utilization review on behalf of the employer, and the utilization review physician. Any information disclosed to the administrative director pursuant to this paragraph shall be considered confidential information and not subject to disclosure pursuant to the California Public Records Act (Division 10 (commencing with Section 7920.000) of Title 1 of the Government Code). Disclosure of the information to the administrative director pursuant to this subdivision shall not waive the provisions of the Evidence Code relating to privilege.

(4) A utilization review process that modifies or denies requests for authorization of medical treatment shall be accredited on or before July 1, 2018, and shall retain active accreditation while providing utilization review services, by an independent, nonprofit organization to certify that the utilization review process meets specified criteria, including, but not limited to, timeliness in issuing a utilization review decision, the scope of medical material used in issuing a utilization review decision, peer-to-peer consultation, internal appeal procedure, and requiring a policy preventing financial incentives to doctors and other providers based on the utilization review decision. The administrative director shall adopt rules to implement the selection of an independent, nonprofit organization for those accreditation purposes. Until those rules are adopted, the administrative director shall designate URAC as the accrediting organization. The administrative director may adopt rules to do any of the following:

(A) Require additional specific criteria for measuring the quality of a utilization review process for purposes of accreditation.

(B) Exempt nonprofit, public sector internal utilization review programs from the accreditation requirement pursuant to this section, if the administrative director has adopted minimum standards applicable to nonprofit, public sector internal utilization review programs that meet or exceed the accreditation standards developed pursuant to this section.

(5) On or before July 1, 2018, each employer, either directly or through its insurer or an entity with which an employer or insurer contracts for utilization review services, shall submit a description of the utilization review process that modifies or denies requests for authorization of medical treatment and the written policies and procedures to the administrative director for approval. Approved utilization review process descriptions and the accompanying written policies and procedures shall be disclosed by the employer to employees and physicians and made available to the public by posting on the

employer's, claims administrator's, or utilization review organization's internet website.

(h) The criteria or guidelines used in the utilization review process to determine whether to approve, modify, or deny medical treatment services shall be all of the following:

(1) Developed with involvement from actively practicing physicians.

(2) Consistent with the schedule for medical treatment utilization, including the drug formulary, adopted pursuant to Section 5307.27.

(3) Evaluated at least annually, and updated if necessary.

(4) Disclosed to the physician and the employee, if used as the basis of a decision to modify or deny services in a specified case under review.

(5) Available to the public upon request. An employer shall only be required to disclose the criteria or guidelines for the specific procedures or conditions requested. An employer may charge members of the public reasonable copying and postage expenses related to disclosing criteria or guidelines pursuant to this paragraph. Criteria or guidelines may also be made available through electronic means. A charge shall not be required for an employee whose physician's request for medical treatment services is under review.

(i) In determining whether to approve, modify, or deny requests by physicians prior to, retrospectively, or concurrent with the provisions of medical treatment services to employees, all of the following requirements shall be met:

(1) Except for treatment requests made pursuant to the formulary, prospective or concurrent decisions shall be made in a timely fashion that is appropriate for the nature of the employee's condition, not to exceed five normal business days from the receipt of a request for authorization for medical treatment and supporting information reasonably necessary to make the determination, but in no event more than 14 days from the date of the medical treatment recommendation by the physician. Prospective decisions regarding requests for treatment covered by the formulary shall be made no more than five normal business days from the date of receipt of the medical treatment request. The request for authorization and supporting documentation may be submitted electronically under rules adopted by the administrative director.

(2) In cases where the review is retrospective, a decision resulting in denial of all or part of the medical treatment service shall be communicated to the individual who received services, or to the individual's designee, within 30 days of the receipt of the information that is reasonably necessary to make this determination. If payment for a medical treatment service is made within the time prescribed by Section 4603.2, a retrospective decision to approve the service need not otherwise be communicated.

(3) If the employee's condition is one in which the employee faces an imminent and serious threat to the employee's health, including, but not limited to, the potential loss of life, limb, or other major bodily function, or the normal timeframe for the decisionmaking process, as described in paragraph (1), would be detrimental to the employee's life or health or could jeopardize the employee's ability to regain maximum function, decisions to approve, modify, or deny requests by physicians prior to, or concurrent with, the provision of medical treatment services to employees shall be made in a timely fashion that is appropriate for the nature of the employee's condition, but not to exceed 72 hours after the receipt of the information reasonably necessary to make the determination.

(4) (A) Final decisions to approve, modify, or deny requests by physicians for authorization prior to, or concurrent with, the provision of medical treatment services to employees shall be communicated to the requesting physician within 24 hours of the decision by telephone, facsimile, or, if agreed to by the parties, secure email.

(B) Decisions resulting in modification or denial of all or part of the requested health care service shall be communicated in writing to the employee, and to the physician if the initial communication under subparagraph (A) was by telephone, within 24 hours for concurrent review, or within two normal business days of the decision for prospective review, as prescribed by the administrative director. If the request is modified or denied, disputes shall be resolved in accordance with Section 4610.5, if applicable, or otherwise in accordance with Section 4062.

(C) In the case of concurrent review, medical care shall not be discontinued until the employee's physician has been notified of the decision and a care plan has been agreed upon by the physician that is appropriate for the medical needs of the employee. Medical care provided during a concurrent review shall be care that is medically necessary to cure and relieve, and an insurer or self-insured employer shall only be liable for those services determined medically necessary to cure and relieve. If the insurer or self-insured employer disputes whether or not one or more services offered concurrently with a utilization review were medically necessary to cure and relieve, the dispute shall be resolved pursuant to Section 4610.5, if applicable, or otherwise pursuant to Section 4062. A compromise between the parties that an insurer or self-insured employer believes may result in payment for services that were not medically necessary to cure and relieve shall be reported by the insurer or the self-insured employer to the licensing board of the provider or providers who received the payments, in a manner set forth by the respective board and in a way that minimizes reporting costs both to the board and to the insurer or self-insured employer, for evaluation as to possible violations of the statutes governing appropriate professional practices. Fees shall not

Appendix

be levied upon insurers or self-insured employers making reports required by this section.

(5) Communications regarding decisions to approve requests by physicians shall specify the specific medical treatment service approved. Responses regarding decisions to modify or deny medical treatment services requested by physicians shall include a clear and concise explanation of the reasons for the employer's decision, a description of the criteria or guidelines used, and the clinical reasons for the decisions regarding medical necessity. If a utilization review decision to deny a medical service is due to incomplete or insufficient information, the decision shall specify all of the following:

(A) The reason for the decision.

(B) A specific description of the information that is needed.

(C) The date and time of attempts made to contact the physician to obtain the necessary information.

(D) A description of the manner in which the request was communicated.

(j) (1) Unless otherwise indicated in this section, a physician providing treatment under Section 4600 shall send any request for authorization for medical treatment, with supporting documentation, to the claims administrator for the employer, insurer, or other entity according to rules adopted by the administrative director. If an employer, insurer, or other entity subject to this section requests medical information from a physician in order to determine whether to approve, modify, or deny requests for authorization, that employer, insurer, or other entity shall request only the information reasonably necessary to make the determination.

(2) If the employer, insurer, or other entity cannot make a decision within the timeframes specified in paragraph (1), (2), or (3) of subdivision (i) because the employer or other entity is not in receipt of, or in possession of, all of the information reasonably necessary to make a determination, the employer shall immediately notify the physician and the employee, in writing, that the employer cannot make a decision within the required timeframe, and specify the information that must be provided by the physician for a determination to be made. Upon receipt of all information reasonably necessary and requested by the employer, the employer shall approve, modify, or deny the request for authorization within the timeframes specified in paragraph (1), (2), or (3) of subdivision (i).

(k) A utilization review decision to modify or deny a treatment recommendation shall remain effective for 12 months from the date of the decision without further action by the employer with regard to a further recommendation by the same physician, or another physician within the requesting physician's practice group, for the same treatment unless the further recommendation is supported by a documented change in the facts material to the basis of the utilization review decision.

(*l*) Utilization review of a treatment recommendation shall not be required while the employer is disputing liability for injury or treatment of the condition for which treatment is recommended pursuant to Section 4062.

(m) If utilization review is deferred pursuant to subdivision (*l*), and it is finally determined that the employer is liable for treatment of the condition for which treatment is recommended, the time for the employer to conduct retrospective utilization review in accordance with paragraph (2) of subdivision (i) shall begin on the date the determination of the employer's liability becomes final, and the time for the employer to conduct prospective utilization review shall commence from the date of the employer's receipt of a treatment recommendation after the determination of the employer's liability.

(n) Each employer, insurer, or other entity subject to this section shall maintain telephone access during California business hours for physicians to request authorization for health care services and to conduct peer-to-peer discussions regarding issues, including the appropriateness of a requested treatment, modification of a treatment request, or obtaining additional information needed to make a medical necessity decision.

(o) The administrative director shall develop a system for the mandatory electronic reporting of documents related to every utilization review performed by each employer, which shall be administered by the Division of Workers' Compensation. The administrative director shall adopt regulations specifying the documents to be submitted by the employer and the authorized transmission format and timeframe for their submission. For purposes of this subdivision, "employer" means the employer, the insurer of an insured employer, a claims administrator, or a utilization review organization, or other entity acting on behalf of any of them.

(p) If the administrative director determines that the employer, insurer, or other entity subject to this section has failed to meet any of the timeframes in this section, or has failed to meet any other requirement of this section, the administrative director may assess, by order, administrative penalties for each failure. A proceeding for the issuance of an order assessing administrative penalties shall be subject to appropriate notice to, and an opportunity for a hearing with regard to, the person affected. The administrative penalties shall not be deemed to be an exclusive remedy for the administrative director. These penalties shall be deposited in the Workers' Compensation Administration Revolving Fund.

(q) The administrative director shall contract with an outside, independent research organization to evaluate the impact of the provision of medical treatment within the first 30 days after a claim is filed, for a claim filed on or after January 1, 2017, and before January 1, 2021. The report shall be provided to the administrative director, the Senate Committee on Labor and Industrial Relations, and the Assembly Committee on Insurance, pursuant to Section 9795 of the Government Code, before July 1, 2023.

Added Stats 2016 ch 868 § 4.5 (SB 1160), effective January 1, 2017, operative January 1, 2018. Amended Stats 2017 ch 240 § 1 (SB 489), effective January 1, 2018; Stats 2019 ch 647 § 6 (SB 537), effective January 1, 2020; Stats 2021 ch 615 § 324 (AB 474), effective January 1, 2022; Stat 2022 ch 292 § 1 (AB 2848), effective January 1, 2023.

§ 4610.1. No entitlement to increase in compensation for unreasonable delay

An employee shall not be entitled to an increase in compensation under Section 5814 for unreasonable delay in the provision of medical treatment for periods of time necessary to complete the utilization review process in compliance with Section 4610. A determination by the appeals board or a final determination of the administrative director pursuant to independent medical review that medical treatment is appropriate shall not be conclusive evidence that medical treatment was unreasonably delayed or denied for purposes of penalties under Section 5814. In no case shall this section preclude an employee from entitlement to an increase in compensation under Section 5814 when an employer has unreasonably delayed or denied medical treatment due to an unreasonable delay in completion of the utilization review process set forth in Section 4610.

Added Stats 2003 ch 638 § 1 (AB 1557). Amended Stats 2012 ch 363 § 44 (SB 863), effective January 1, 2013.

§ 4610.5. Review of utilization review decision

(a) This section applies to the following disputes:

(1) Any dispute over a utilization review decision regarding treatment for an injury occurring on or after January 1, 2013.

(2) Any dispute over a utilization review decision if the decision is communicated to the requesting physician on or after July 1, 2013, regardless of the date of injury.

(3) Any dispute occurring on or after January 1, 2018, over medication prescribed pursuant to the drug formulary adopted pursuant to Section 5307.27.

(b) A dispute described in subdivision (a) shall be resolved only in accordance with this section.

(c) For purposes of this section and Section 4610.6, the following definitions apply:

(1) "Disputed medical treatment" means medical treatment that has been modified or denied by a utilization review decision on the basis of medical necessity.

(2) "Medically necessary" and "medical necessity" mean medical treatment that is reasonably required to cure or relieve the injured employee of the effects of his or her injury and based on the following standards, which shall be applied as set forth in the medical treatment utilization schedule, including the drug formulary, adopted by the administrative director pursuant to Section 5307.27:

(A) The guidelines, including the drug formulary, adopted by the administrative director pursuant to Section 5307.27.

(B) Peer-reviewed scientific and medical evidence regarding the effectiveness of the disputed service.

(C) Nationally recognized professional standards.

(D) Expert opinion.

(E) Generally accepted standards of medical practice.

(F) Treatments that are likely to provide a benefit to a patient for conditions for which other treatments are not clinically efficacious.

(3) "Utilization review decision" means a decision pursuant to Section 4610 to modify or deny, based in whole or in part on medical necessity to cure or relieve, a treatment recommendation or recommendations by a physician prior to, retrospectively, or concurrent with, the provision of medical treatment services pursuant to Section 4600 or subdivision (c) of Section 5402. "Utilization review decision" may also mean a determination, occurring on or after January 1, 2018, by a physician regarding the medical necessity of medication prescribed pursuant to the drug formulary adopted pursuant to Section 5307.27.

(4) Unless otherwise indicated by context, "employer" means the employer, the insurer of an insured employer, a claims administrator, or a utilization review organization, or other entity acting on behalf of any of them.

(d) If a utilization review decision denies or modifies a treatment recommendationrecommendation based on medical necessity, the employee may request an independent medical review as provided by this section.

(e) A utilization review decision may be reviewed or appealed only by independent medical review pursuant to this section. Neither the employee nor the employer shall have any liability for medical treatment furnished without the authorization of the employer if the treatment is modified or denied by a utilization review decision, unless the utilization review decision is overturned by independent medical review in accordance with this section.

(f) As part of its notification to the employee regarding an initial utilization review decision based on medical necessity that denies or modifies a treatment recommendation, the employer shall provide the employee with a one-page form prescribed by the administrative director, and an addressed envelope, which the employee may return to the administrative director or the administrative director's designee to initiate an independent medical review. The employee may also request independent medical review electronically under rules adopted by the administrative director. The employer shall include on the form any information required by the administrative director to facilitate the completion of the independent medical review. The form shall also include all of the following:

(1) Notice that the utilization review decision is final unless the employee requests independent medical review.

(2) A statement indicating the employee's consent to obtain any necessary medical records from the employer or insurer and from any medical provider the employee may have consulted on the matter, to be signed by the employee.

(3) Notice of the employee's right to provide information or documentation, either directly or through the employee's physician, regarding the following:

(A) The treating physician's recommendation indicating that the disputed medical treatment is medically necessary for the employee's medical condition.

(B) Medical information or justification that a disputed medical treatment, on an urgent care or emergency basis, was medically necessary for the employee's medical condition.

(C) Reasonable information supporting the employee's position that the disputed medical treatment is or was medically necessary for the employee's medical condition, including all information provided to the employee by the employer or by the treating physician, still in the employee's possession, concerning the employer's or the physician's decision regarding the disputed medical treatment, as well as any additional material that the employee believes is relevant.

(g) The independent medical review process may be terminated at any time upon the employer's written authorization of the disputed medical treatment. Notice of the authorization, any settlement or award that may resolve the medical treatment dispute, or the requesting physician withdrawing the request for treatment, shall be communicated to the independent medical review organization by the employer within five days.

(h) (1) The employee may submit a request for independent medical review to the division. The request may be made electronically under rules adopted by the administrative director. The request shall be made no later than as follows:

(A) For formulary disputes, 10 days after the service of the utilization review decision to the employee.

(B) For all other medical treatment disputes, 30 days after the service of the utilization review decision to the employee.

(2) If at the time of a utilization review decision the employer is also disputing liability for the treatment for any reason besides medical necessity, the time for the employee to submit a request for independent medical review to the administrative director or administrative director's designee is extended to 30 days after service of a notice to the employee showing that the other dispute of liability has been resolved.

(3) If the employer fails to comply with subdivision (f) at the time of notification of its utilization review decision, the time limitations for the employee to submit a request for independent medical review shall not begin to run until the employer provides the required notice to the employee.

(4) A provider of emergency medical treatment when the employee faced an imminent and serious threat to his or her health, including, but not limited to, the potential loss of life, limb, or other major bodily function, may submit a request for independent medical review on its own behalf. A request submitted by a provider pursuant to this paragraph shall be submitted to the administrative director or administrative director's designee within the time limitations applicable for an employee to submit a request for independent medical review.

(i) An employer shall not engage in any conduct that has the effect of delaying the independent review process. Engaging in that conduct or failure of the employer to promptly comply with this section is a violation of this section and, in addition to any other fines, penalties, and other remedies available to the administrative director, the employer shall be subject to an administrative penalty in an amount determined pursuant to regulations to be adopted by the administrative director, not to exceed five thousand dollars ($5,000) for each day that proper notification to the employee is delayed. The administrative penalties shall be paid to the Workers' Compensation Administration Revolving Fund.

(j) For purposes of this section, an employee may designate a parent, guardian, conservator, relative, or other designee of the employee as an agent to act on his or her behalf. A designation of an agent executed prior to the utilization review decision shall not be valid. The requesting physician may join with or otherwise assist the employee in seeking an independent medical review, and may advocate on behalf of the employee.

(k) The administrative director or his or her designee shall expeditiously review requests and immediately notify the employee and the employer in writing as to whether the request for an independent medical review has been approved, in whole or in part, and, if not approved, the reasons therefor. If there appears to be any medical necessity issue, the dispute shall be resolved pursuant to an independent medical review, except that, unless the employer agrees that the case is eligible for independent medical review, a request for independent medical review shall be deferred if at the time of a utilization review decision the employer is also disputing liability for the treatment for any reason besides medical necessity.

(*l*) Upon notice from the administrative director that an independent review organization has been assigned, the employer shall electronically provide to the independent medical review organization under rules adopted by the administrative director a copy and list of all of the following documents within 10 days of notice of assignment:

(1) A copy of all of the employee's medical records in the possession of the employer or under the control of the employer relevant to each of the following:

(A) The employee's current medical condition.

(B) The medical treatment being provided by the employer.

(C) The request for authorization and utilization review decision.

(2) A copy of all information provided to the employee by the employer concerning employer and provider decisions regarding the disputed treatment.

(3) A copy of any materials the employee or the employee's provider submitted to the employer in support of the employee's request for the disputed treatment.

(4) A copy of any other relevant documents or information used by the employer or its utilization review organization in determining whether the disputed treatment should have been provided, and any statements by the employer or its utilization review organization explaining the reasons for the decision to deny or modify the recommended treatment on the basis of medical necessity. The employer shall concurrently provide a copy of the documents required by this paragraph to the employee and the requesting physician, except that documents previously provided to the employee or physician need not be provided again if a list of those documents is provided.

(m) Any newly developed or discovered relevant medical records in the possession of the employer after the initial documents are provided to the independent medical review organization shall be forwarded immediately to the independent medical review organization. The employer shall concurrently provide a copy of medical records required by this subdivision to the employee or the employee's treating physician, unless the offer of medical records is declined or otherwise prohibited by law. The confidentiality of medical records shall be maintained pursuant to applicable state and federal laws.

(n) If there is an imminent and serious threat to the health of the employee, as specified in subdivision (c) of Section 1374.33 of the Health and Safety Code, all necessary information and documents required by subdivision (*l*) shall be delivered to the independent medical review organization within 24 hours of approval of the request for review.

(o) The employer shall promptly issue a notification to the employee, after submitting all of the required material to the independent medical review organization, that lists documents submitted and includes copies of material not previously provided to the employee or the employee's designee.

(p) The claims administrator who issued the utilization review decision in dispute shall notify the independent medical review organization if there is a change in the claims administrator responsible for the claim. Notice shall be given to the independent medical review organization within five working days of the change in administrator taking effect.

Added Stats 2012 ch 363 § 45 (SB 863), effective January 1, 2013. Amended Stats 2013 ch 287 § 5 (SB 375), effective January 1, 2014; Stats 2014 ch 217 § 2 (AB 2732), effective January 1, 2015; Stats 2016 ch 868 § 5 (SB 1160), effective January 1, 2017.

§ 4610.6. Independent medical review organization to conduct review of utilization review decision; Procedure upon final determination of review

(a) Upon receipt of a case pursuant to Section 4610.5, an independent medical review organization shall conduct the review in accordance with this article and any regulations or orders of the administrative director. The organization's review shall be limited to an examination of the medical necessity of the disputed medical treatment.

(b) Upon receipt of information and documents related to a case, the medical reviewer or reviewers selected to conduct the review by the independent medical review organization shall promptly review all pertinent medical records of the employee, provider reports, and any other information submitted to the organization or requested from any of the parties to the dispute by the reviewers. If the reviewers request information from any of the parties, a copy of the request and the response shall be provided to all of the parties. The reviewer or reviewers shall also review relevant information related to the criteria set forth in subdivision (c).

(c) Following its review, the reviewer or reviewers shall determine whether the disputed health care service was medically necessary based on the specific medical needs of the employee and the standards of medical necessity as defined in subdivision (c) of Section 4610.5.

(d) (1) The organization shall complete its review and make its determination in writing, and in layperson's terms to the maximum extent practicable, and the determination shall be issued, as follows:

(A) For a dispute over medication prescribed pursuant to the drug formulary submitted under subdivision (h) of Section 4610.5, within five working days from the date of receipt of the request for review and supporting documentation, or within less time as prescribed by the administrative director.

(B) For all other medical treatment disputes submitted for review under subdivision (h) of Section 4610.5, within 30 days of receipt of the

Appendix

request for review and supporting documentation, or within less time as prescribed by the administrative director.

(C) If the disputed medical treatment has not been provided and the employee's provider or the administrative director certifies in writing that an imminent and serious threat to the health of the employee may exist, including, but not limited to, serious pain, the potential loss of life, limb, or major bodily function, or the immediate and serious deterioration of the health of the employee, the analyses and determinations of the reviewers shall be expedited and rendered within three days of the receipt of the information.

(2) Subject to the approval of the administrative director, the deadlines for analyses and determinations involving both regular and expedited reviews may be extended for up to three days in extraordinary circumstances or for good cause.

(e) The medical professionals' analyses and determinations shall state whether the disputed health care service is medically necessary. Each analysis shall cite the employee's medical condition, the relevant documents in the record, and the relevant findings associated with the provisions of subdivision (c) to support the determination. If more than one medical professional reviews the case, the recommendation of the majority shall prevail. If the medical professionals reviewing the case are evenly split as to whether the disputed health care service should be provided, the decision shall be in favor of providing the service.

(f) The independent medical review organization shall provide the administrative director, the employer, the employee, and the employee's provider with the analyses and determinations of the medical professionals reviewing the case, and a description of the qualifications of the medical professionals. The independent medical review organization shall keep the names of the reviewers confidential in all communications with entities or individuals outside the independent medical review organization. If more than one medical professional reviewed the case and the result was differing determinations, the independent medical review organization shall provide each of the separate reviewer's analyses and determinations.

(g) The determination of the independent medical review organization shall be deemed to be the determination of the administrative director and shall be binding on all parties.

(h) A determination of the administrative director pursuant to this section may be reviewed only by a verified appeal from the medical review determination of the administrative director, filed with the appeals board for hearing pursuant to Chapter 3 (commencing with Section 5500) of Part 4 and served on all interested parties within 30 days of the date of mailing of the determination to the aggrieved employee or the aggrieved employer. The determination of the administrative director shall be presumed to be correct and shall be set aside only upon proof by clear and convincing evidence of one or more of the following grounds for appeal:

(1) The administrative director acted without or in excess of the administrative director's powers.

(2) The determination of the administrative director was procured by fraud.

(3) The independent medical reviewer was subject to a material conflict of interest that is in violation of Section 139.5.

(4) The determination was the result of bias on the basis of race, national origin, ethnic group identification, religion, age, sex, sexual orientation, color, or disability.

(5) The determination was the result of a plainly erroneous express or implied finding of fact, provided that the mistake of fact is a matter of ordinary knowledge based on the information submitted for review pursuant to Section 4610.5 and not a matter that is subject to expert opinion.

(i) If the determination of the administrative director is reversed, the dispute shall be remanded to the administrative director to submit the dispute to independent medical review by a different independent review organization. In the event that a different independent medical review organization is not available after remand, the administrative director shall submit the dispute to the original medical review organization for review by a different reviewer in the organization. In no event shall a workers' compensation administrative law judge, the appeals board, or any higher court make a determination of medical necessity contrary to the determination of the independent medical review organization.

(j) Upon receiving the determination of the administrative director that a disputed health care service is medically necessary, the employer shall promptly implement the decision as provided by this section unless the employer has also disputed liability for any reason besides medical necessity. In the case of reimbursement for services already rendered, the employer shall reimburse the provider or employee, whichever applies, within 20 days, subject to resolution of any remaining issue of the amount of payment pursuant to Sections 4603.2 to 4603.6, inclusive. In the case of services not yet rendered, the employer shall authorize the services within five working days of receipt of the written determination from the independent medical review organization, or sooner if appropriate for the nature of the employee's medical condition, and shall inform the employee and provider of the authorization.

(k) Failure to pay for services already provided or to authorize services not yet rendered within the time prescribed by subdivision (l) is a violation of this section and, in addition to any other fines, penalties, and other remedies available to the administrative director, the employer shall be subject to an administrative penalty in an amount determined pursuant to regulations to be adopted by the administrative director, not to exceed five thousand dollars ($5,000) for each day the decision is not implemented. The administrative penalties shall be paid to the Workers' Compensation Administration Revolving Fund.

(*l*) The costs of independent medical review and the administration of the independent medical review system shall be borne by employers through a fee system established by the administrative director. After considering any relevant information on program costs, the administrative director shall establish a reasonable, per-case reimbursement schedule to pay the costs of independent medical review organization reviews and the cost of administering the independent medical review system, which may vary depending on the type of medical condition under review and on other relevant factors.

(m) The administrative director may publish the results of independent medical review determinations after removing individually identifiable information.

(n) If any provision of this section, or the application thereof to any person or circumstances, is held invalid, the remainder of the section, and the application of its provisions to other persons or circumstances, shall not be affected thereby.

Added Stats 2012 ch 363 § 46 (SB 863), effective January 1, 2013. Amended Stats 2016 ch 868 § 6 (SB 1160), effective January 1, 2017.

Article 2.3

Medical Provider Networks

§ 4616. Establishment of medical provider network; Goal; Requirements; Regulations

(a) (1) An insurer, employer, or entity that provides physician network services may establish or modify a medical provider network for the provision of medical treatment to injured employees. The network shall include physicians primarily engaged in the treatment of occupational injuries. The administrative director shall encourage the integration of occupational and nonoccupational providers. Subject to Section 3209.11, the number of physicians in the medical provider network shall be sufficient to enable treatment for injuries or conditions to be provided in a timely manner. The provider network shall include an adequate number and type of physicians, as described in Section 3209.3, or other providers, as described in Section 3209.5, to treat common injuries experienced by injured employees based on the type of occupation or industry in which the employee is engaged, and the geographic area where the employees are employed.

(2) Medical treatment for injuries shall be readily available at reasonable times to all employees. To the extent feasible, all medical treatment for injuries shall be readily accessible to all employees. With respect to availability and accessibility of treatment, the administrative director shall consider the needs of rural areas, specifically those in which health facilities are located at least 30 miles apart and areas in which there is a health care shortage.

(3) A treating physician shall be included in the network only if, at the time of entering into or renewing an agreement by which the physician would be in the network, the physician, or an authorized employee of the physician or the physician's office, provides a separate written acknowledgment in which the physician affirmatively elects to be a member of the network. Copies of the written acknowledgment shall be provided to the administrative director upon the administrative director's request. This paragraph shall not apply to a physician who is a shareholder, partner, or employee of a medical group that elects to be part of the network.

(4) (A) (i) Commencing July 1, 2021, every medical provider network shall post on its internet website a roster of all participating providers, which includes all physicians and ancillary service providers in the medical provider network, and shall update the roster at least quarterly. Every network shall provide to the administrative director the internet website address of the network and of its roster of participating providers. The roster of participating providers shall include, at a minimum, the name of each individual provider and their office address and office telephone number. If the ancillary service is provided by an entity rather than an individual, then that entity's name, address, and telephone number shall be listed.

(ii) The administrative director shall post, on the division's internet website, the internet website address of every approved medical provider network.

(B) Every medical provider network shall post on its internet website information about how to contact the medical provider network contact and medical access assistants, and information about how to obtain a copy of any notification regarding the medical provider network that is required to be given to an employee by regulations adopted by the administrative director.

(5) Every medical provider network shall provide one or more persons within the United States to serve as medical access assistants to help an injured employee find an available physician of the employee's choice, and subsequent physicians if necessary, under Section 4616.3. Medical access assistants shall have a toll-free telephone number that injured employees may use and shall be available at least from 7 a.m. to 8 p.m. Pacific standard time, Monday through Saturday, to respond to injured employees, contact physicians' offices during regular business hours, and schedule appointments. The ad-

ministrative director shall promulgate regulations governing the provision of medical access assistants.

(b) (1) An insurer, employer, or entity that provides physician network services shall submit a plan for the medical provider network to the administrative director for approval. The administrative director shall approve the plan for a period of four years if the administrative director determines that the plan meets the requirements of this section. If the administrative director does not act on the plan within 60 days of submitting the plan, it shall be deemed approved. Commencing January 1, 2014, existing approved plans shall be deemed approved for a period of four years from the approval date of the most recent application or modification submitted prior to 2014. Plans for reapproval for medical provider networks shall be submitted at least six months before the expiration of the four-year approval period. Commencing January 1, 2016, a modification that updates an entire medical provider network plan to bring the plan into full compliance with all current statutes and regulations shall be deemed approved for a period of four years from the modification approval date. An approved modification that does not update an entire medical provider network plan to bring the plan into full compliance with all current statutes and regulations shall not alter the expiration of the medical provider network's four-year approval period. Upon a showing that the medical provider network was approved or deemed approved by the administrative director, there shall be a conclusive presumption on the part of the appeals board that the medical provider network was validly formed.

(2) Every medical provider network shall establish and follow procedures to continuously review the quality of care, performance of medical personnel, utilization of services and facilities, and costs.

(3) Every medical provider network shall submit geocoding of its network for reapproval to establish that the number and geographic location of physicians in the network meets the required access standards.

(4) Approval of a plan may be denied, revoked, or suspended if the medical provider network fails to meet the requirements of this article. Any person contending that a medical provider network is not validly constituted may petition the administrative director to suspend or revoke the approval of the medical provider network. The administrative director may adopt regulations establishing a schedule of administrative penalties not to exceed five thousand dollars ($5,000) per violation, or probation, or both, in lieu of revocation or suspension for less severe violations of the requirements of this article. Penalties, probation, suspension, or revocation shall be ordered by the administrative director only after notice and opportunity to be heard. Unless suspended or revoked by the administrative director, the administrative director's approval of a medical provider network

shall be binding on all persons and all courts. A determination of the administrative director may be reviewed only by an appeal of the determination of the administrative director filed as an original proceeding before the reconsideration unit of the workers' compensation appeals board on the same grounds and within the same time limits after issuance of the determination as would be applicable to a petition for reconsideration of a decision of a workers' compensation administrative law judge.

(c) Physician compensation may not be structured in order to achieve the goal of reducing, delaying, or denying medical treatment or restricting access to medical treatment.

(d) If the employer or insurer meets the requirements of this section, the administrative director may not withhold approval or disapprove an employer's or insurer's medical provider network based solely on the selection of providers. In developing a medical provider network, an employer or insurer shall have the exclusive right to determine the members of their network.

(e) All treatment provided shall be provided in accordance with the medical treatment utilization schedule established pursuant to Section 5307.27.

(f) Only a licensed physician who is competent to evaluate the specific clinical issues involved in the medical treatment services, when these services are within the scope of the physician's practice, may modify, delay, or deny requests for authorization of medical treatment.

(g) Every contracting agent that sells, leases, assigns, transfers, or conveys its medical provider networks and their contracted reimbursement rates to an insurer, employer, entity that provides physician network services, or another contracting agent shall, upon entering or renewing a provider contract, disclose to the provider whether the medical provider network may be sold, leased, transferred, or conveyed to other insurers, employers, entities that provide physician network services, or another contracting agent, and specify whether those insurers, employers, entities that provide physician network services, or contracting agents include workers' compensation insurers.

(h) On or before November 1, 2004, the administrative director, in consultation with the Department of Managed Health Care, shall adopt regulations implementing this article. The administrative director shall develop regulations that establish procedures for purposes of making medical provider network modifications.

(i) The administrative director has the authority and discretion to investigate complaints, conduct random reviews, and take enforcement action against medical provider networks, an entity that provides ancillary services, or an entity providing services for or on behalf of the medical provider network or its providers regarding noncompliance with the requirements of this section or Section 4603.2 or 4610.

Added Stats 2004 ch 34 § 27 (SB 899), effective April 19, 2004. Amended Stats 2012 ch 363 § 47 (SB 863), effective January 1, 2013; Stats 2015 ch 542 § 1 (SB 542), effective January 1, 2016; Stats 2019 ch 647 § 7 (SB 537), effective January 1, 2020; Stat 2022 ch 609 § 6 (SB 1002), effective January 1, 2023.

§ 4616.1. Economic profiling; Filing of policies and procedures; Disclosure to public

(a) An insurer, employer, or entity that provides physician network services that offers a medical provider network under this division and that uses economic profiling shall file with the administrative director a description of any policies and procedures related to economic profiling utilized. The filing shall describe how these policies and procedures are used in utilization review, peer review, incentive and penalty programs, and in provider retention and termination decisions. The insurer, employer, or entity that provides physician network services shall provide a copy of the filing to an individual physician, provider, medical group, or individual practice association.

(b) The administrative director shall make each approved medical provider network economic profiling policy filing available to the public upon request. The administrative director may not publicly disclose any information submitted pursuant to this section that is determined by the administrative director to be confidential pursuant to state or federal law.

(c) For the purposes of this article, "economic profiling" shall mean any evaluation of a particular physician, provider, medical group, or individual practice association based in whole or in part on the economic costs or utilization of services associated with medical care provided or authorized by the physician, provider, medical group, or individual practice association.

Added Stats 2004 ch 34 § 27 (SB 899), effective April 19, 2004. Amended Stats 2012 ch 363 § 48 (SB 863), effective January 1, 2013.

§ 4616.2. Continuity of care policy; Filing and approval; Revisions; Notice; Completion of treatment by terminated provider

(a) A medical provider network shall file a written continuity of care policy with the administrative director.

(b) If approved by the administrative director, the provisions of the written continuity of care policy shall replace all prior continuity of care policies. A medical provider network shall file a revision of the continuity of care policy with the administrative director if it makes a material change to the policy.

(c) The medical provider network shall provide all employees entering the workers' compensation system notice of the medical provider network's written continuity of care policy and information regarding the process for an employee to request a review under the policy and, upon request, a copy of the medical provider network's written continuity of care policy.

(d) (1) At the request of an injured employee, completion of treatment shall be provided by a terminated provider as set forth in this section.

(2) The completion of treatment shall be provided by a terminated provider to an injured employee who, at the time of the contract's termination, was receiving services from that provider for one of the conditions described in paragraph (3).

(3) The employer or its claims administrator shall provide for the completion of treatment for the following conditions subject to coverage through the workers' compensation system:

(A) An acute condition. An acute condition is a medical condition that involves a sudden onset of symptoms due to an illness, injury, or other medical problem that requires prompt medical attention and that has a limited duration. Completion of treatment shall be provided for the duration of the acute condition.

(B) A serious chronic condition. A serious chronic condition is a medical condition due to a disease, illness, or other medical problem or medical disorder that is serious in nature and that persists without full cure or worsens over an extended period of time or requires ongoing treatment to maintain remission or prevent deterioration. Completion of treatment shall be provided for a period of time necessary to complete a course of treatment and to arrange for a safe transfer to another provider, as determined by the employer or its claims administrator in consultation with the injured employee and the terminated provider and consistent with good professional practice. Completion of treatment under this paragraph shall not exceed 12 months from the contract termination date.

(C) A terminal illness. A terminal illness is an incurable or irreversible condition that has a high probability of causing death within one year or less. Completion of treatment shall be provided for the duration of a terminal illness.

(D) Performance of a surgery or other procedure that is authorized by the employer or its claims administrator as part of a documented course of treatment and has been recommended and documented by the provider to occur within 180 days of the contract's termination date.

(4) (A) The employer or its claims administrator may require the terminated provider whose services are continued beyond the contract termination date pursuant to this section to agree in writing to be subject to the same contractual terms and conditions that were

Appendix

imposed upon the provider prior to termination. If the terminated provider does not agree to comply or does not comply with these contractual terms and conditions, the employer or its claims administrator is not required to continue the provider's services beyond the contract termination date.

(B) Unless otherwise agreed by the terminated provider and the employer or its claims administrator, the services rendered pursuant to this section shall be compensated at rates and methods of payment similar to those used by the medical provider network for currently contracting providers providing similar services who are practicing in the same or a similar geographic area as the terminated provider. The employer or its claims administrator is not required to continue the services of a terminated provider if the provider does not accept the payment rates provided for in this paragraph.

(5) An employer or its claims administrator shall ensure that the requirements of this section are met.

(6) This section shall not require an employer or its claims administrator to provide for completion of treatment by a provider whose contract with the medical provider network has been terminated or not renewed for reasons relating to a medical disciplinary cause or reason, as defined in paragraph (6) of subdivision (a) of Section 805 of the Business and Professions Code, or fraud or other criminal activity.

(7) Nothing in this section shall preclude an employer or its claims administrator from providing continuity of care beyond the requirements of this section.

Added Stats 2004 ch 34 § 27 (SB 899), effective April 19, 2004. Amended Stats 2012 ch 363 § 49 (SB 863), effective January 1, 2013; Stats 2015 ch 542 § 2 (SB 542), effective January 1, 2016.

§ 4616.3. Initial medical evaluation; Notice of right to be treated by physician of employee's choice; Second and third opinions; Specialists

(a) If the injured employee notifies the employer of the injury or files a claim for workers' compensation with the employer, the employer shall arrange an initial medical evaluation and begin treatment as required by Section 4600.

(b) The employer shall notify the employee of the existence of the medical provider network established pursuant to this article, the employee's right to change treating physicians within the network after the first visit, and the method by which the list of participating providers may be accessed by the employee. The employer's failure to provide notice as required by this subdivision or failure to post the notice as required by Section 3550 shall not be a basis for the employee to treat outside the network unless it is shown that the failure to provide notice resulted in a denial of medical care.

(c) If an injured employee disputes either the diagnosis or the treatment prescribed by the treating physician, the employee may seek the opinion of another physician in the medical provider network. If the injured employee disputes the diagnosis or treatment prescribed by the second physician, the employee may seek the opinion of a third physician in the medical provider network.

(d) (1) Selection by the injured employee of a treating physician and any subsequent physicians shall be based on the physician's specialty or recognized expertise in treating the particular injury or condition in question.

(2) Treatment by a specialist who is not a member of the medical provider network may be permitted on a case-by-case basis if the medical provider network does not contain a physician who can provide the approved treatment and the treatment is approved by the employer or the insurer.

Added Stats 2004 ch 34 § 27 (SB 899), effective April 19, 2004. Amended Stats 2012 ch 363 § 50 (SB 863), effective January 1, 2013.

§ 4616.7. Requirements for approval; Health care organization; Health care service plan; Group disability insurance policy; Taft–Hartley health and welfare fund

(a) A health care organization certified pursuant to Section 4600.5 shall be deemed approved pursuant to this article if the requirements of this article are met, as determined by the administrative director.

(b) A health care service plan, licensed pursuant to Chapter 2.2 (commencing with Section 1340) of Division 2 of the Health and Safety Code, shall be deemed approved for purposes of this article if it has a reasonable number of physicians with competency in occupational medicine, as determined by the administrative director.

(c) A group disability insurance policy, as defined in subdivision (b) of Section 106 of the Insurance Code, that covers hospital, surgical, and medical care expenses shall be deemed approved for purposes of this article if it has a reasonable number of physicians with competency in occupational medicine, as determined by the administrative director. For the purposes of this section, a group disability insurance policy shall not include Medicare supplement, vision-only, dental-only, and Champus-supplement insurance. For purposes of this section, a group disability insurance policy shall not include hospital indemnity, accident-only, and specified disease insurance that pays benefits on a fixed benefit, cash-payment-only basis.

(d) Any Taft-Hartley health and welfare fund shall be deemed approved for purposes of this article if it has a reasonable number of physicians with competency in occupational medicine, as determined by the administrative director.

Appendix

Added Stats 2004 ch 34 § 27 (SB 899), effective April 19, 2004. Amended Stats 2012 ch 363 § 51 (SB 863), effective January 1, 2013.

Article 2.5

Medical–Legal Expenses

§ 4620. "Medical-legal expense"; "Contested claim"

(a) For purposes of this article, a medical-legal expense means any costs and expenses incurred by or on behalf of any party, the administrative director, or the board, which expenses may include X-rays, laboratory fees, other diagnostic tests, medical reports, medical records, medical testimony, and, as needed, interpreter's fees by a certified interpreter pursuant to Article 8 (commencing with Section 11435.05) of Chapter 4.5 of Part 1 of Division 3 of Title 2 of, or Section 68566 of, the Government Code, for the purpose of proving or disproving a contested claim.

(b) A contested claim exists when the employer knows or reasonably should know that the employee is claiming entitlement to any benefit arising out of a claimed industrial injury and one of the following conditions exists:

(1) The employer rejects liability for a claimed benefit.

(2) The employer fails to accept liability for benefits after the expiration of a reasonable period of time within which to decide if it will contest the claim.

(3) The employer fails to respond to a demand for payment of benefits after the expiration of any time period fixed by statute for the payment of indemnity.

(c) Costs of medical evaluations, diagnostic tests, and interpreters incidental to the production of a medical report do not constitute medical-legal expenses unless the medical report is capable of proving or disproving a disputed medical fact, the determination of which is essential to an adjudication of the employee's claim for benefits. In determining whether a report meets the requirements of this subdivision, a judge shall give full consideration to the substance as well as the form of the report, as required by applicable statutes and regulations.

(d) If the injured employee cannot effectively communicate with an examining physician because he or she cannot proficiently speak or understand the English language, the injured employee is entitled to the services of a qualified interpreter during the medical examination. Upon request of the injured employee, the employer or insurance carrier shall pay the costs of the interpreter services, as set forth in the fee schedule adopted by the administrative director pursuant to Section 5811. An employer shall not be required to pay for the services of an interpreter who is provisionally certified unless either the employer consents in advance to the selection of the individual who provides the interpreting service or the injured worker requires interpreting service in a language other than the languages designated pursuant to Section 11435.40 of the Government Code.

Added Stats 1984 ch 596 § 4, effective July 19, 1984. Amended Stats 1985 ch 428 § 1, effective July 30, 1985. Amended Stats 1993 ch 4 § 2 (SB 31), effective April 3, 1993; Stats 2012 ch 363 § 52 (SB 863), effective January 1, 2013.

§ 4622. Time limits for payment of expenses; Penalties for late payment; Notice of employer contests; Regulations

All medical-legal expenses for which the employer is liable shall, upon receipt by the employer of all reports and documents required by the administrative director incident to the services, be paid to whom the funds and expenses are due, as follows:

(a) (1) Except as provided in subdivision (b), within 60 days after receipt by the employer of each separate, written billing and report, and if payment is not made within this period, that portion of the billed sum then unreasonably unpaid shall be increased by 10 percent, together with interest thereon at the rate of 7 percent per annum retroactive to the date of receipt of the bill and report by the employer. If the employer, within the 60-day period, contests the reasonableness and necessity for incurring the fees, services, and expenses using the explanation of review required by Section 4603.3, payment shall be made within 20 days of the service of an order of the appeals board or the administrative director pursuant to Section 4603.6 directing payment.

(2) The penalty provided for in paragraph (1) shall not apply if both of the following occur:

(A) The employer pays the provider that portion of his or her charges that do not exceed the amount deemed reasonable pursuant to subdivision (e) within 60 days of receipt of the report and itemized billing.

(B) The employer prevails.

(b) (1) If the provider contests the amount paid, the provider may request a second review within 90 days of the service of the explanation of review. The request for a second review shall be submitted to the employer on a form prescribed by the administrative director and shall include all of the following:

(A) The date of the explanation of review and the claim number or other unique identifying number provided on the explanation of review.

(B) The party or parties requesting the service.

(C) Any item and amount in dispute.

(D) The additional payment requested and the reason therefor.

(E) Any additional information requested in the original explanation of review and any other information provided in support of the additional payment requested.

(2) If the provider does not request a second review within 90 days, the bill will be deemed satisfied and neither the employer nor the employee shall be liable for any further payment.

(3) Within 14 days of the request for second review, the employer shall respond with a final written determination on each of the items or amounts in dispute, including whether additional payment will be made.

(4) If the provider contests the amount paid, after receipt of the second review, the provider shall request an independent bill review as provided for in Section 4603.6.

(c) If the employer denies all or a portion of the amount billed for any reason other than the amount to be paid pursuant to the fee schedules in effect on the date of service, the provider may object to the denial within 90 days of the service of the explanation of review. If the provider does not object to the denial within 90 days, neither the employer nor the employee shall be liable for the amount that was denied. If the provider objects to the denial within 90 days of the service of the explanation of review, the employer shall file a petition and a declaration of readiness to proceed with the appeals board within 60 days of service of the objection. If the employer prevails before the appeals board, the appeals board shall order the physician to reimburse the employer for the amount of the paid charges found to be unreasonable.

(d) If requested by the employee, or the dependents of a deceased employee, within 20 days from the filing of an order of the appeals board directing payment, and where payment is not made within that period, that portion of the billed sum then unpaid shall be increased by 10 percent, together with interest thereon at the rate of 7 percent per annum retroactive to the date of the filing of the order of the board directing payment.

(e) Using the explanation of review as described in Section 4603.3, the employer shall notify the provider of the services, the employee, or if represented, his or her attorney, if the employer contests the reasonableness or necessity of incurring these expenses, and shall indicate the reasons therefor.

(1) Using the explanation of review as described in Section 4603.3, the employer shall notify the provider of the services, the employee, or if represented, his or her attorney, if the employer contests the reasonableness or necessity of incurring these expenses, and shall indicate the reasons therefor.

(2) The appeals board shall promulgate all necessary and reasonable rules and regulations to insure compliance with this section, and shall take such further steps as may be necessary to guarantee that the rules and regulations are enforced.

(3) The provisions of Sections 5800 and 5814 shall not apply to this section.

(f) Nothing contained in this section shall be construed to create a rebuttable presumption of entitlement to payment of an expense upon receipt by the employer of the required reports and documents. This section is not applicable unless there has been compliance with Sections 4620 and 4621.

Added Stats 1984 ch 596 § 4, effective July 19, 1984. Amended Stats 1993 ch 4 § 4 (SB 31), effective April 3, 1993; Stats 2012 ch 363 § 53 (SB 863), effective January 1, 2013.

Article 3

Disability Payments

§ 4650. Time of first payment for temporary or permanent disability indemnity; Increase for late payments; Reimbursement of insurer; Salary continuation plan

(a) If an injury causes temporary disability, the first payment of temporary disability indemnity shall be made not later than 14 days after knowledge of the injury and disability, on which date all indemnity then due shall be paid, unless liability for the injury is earlier denied.

(b) (1) If the injury causes permanent disability, the first payment shall be made within 14 days after the date of last payment of temporary disability indemnity, except as provided in paragraph (2). When the last payment of temporary disability indemnity has been made pursuant to subdivision (c) of Section 4656, and regardless of whether the extent of permanent disability can be determined at that date, the employer nevertheless shall commence the timely payment required by this subdivision and shall continue to make these payments until the employer's reasonable estimate of permanent disability indemnity due has been paid, and if the amount of permanent disability indemnity due has been determined, until that amount has been paid.

(2) Prior to an award of permanent disability indemnity, a permanent disability indemnity payment shall not be required if the employer has offered the employee a position that pays at least 85 percent of the wages and compensation paid to the employee at the time of injury or if the employee is employed in a position that pays at least 100 percent of the wages and compensation paid to the employee at the time of injury, provided that when an award of permanent disability indemnity is made, the amount then due shall be calculated from the last date for which temporary disability indemnity was paid, or the date the employee's disability became permanent and stationary, whichever is earlier.

(c) Payment of temporary or permanent disability indemnity subsequent to the first payment shall be made as due every two weeks on the day designated with the first payment.

(d) If any indemnity payment is not made timely as required by this section, the amount of the late payment shall be increased 10 percent and shall be paid, without application, to the employee, unless the employer continues the employee's wages under a salary continuation plan, as defined in subdivision (g). No increase shall apply to any payment due prior to or within 14 days after the date the claim form was submitted to the employer under Section 5401. No increase shall apply when, within the 14-day period specified under subdivision (a), the employer is unable to determine whether temporary disability indemnity payments are owed and advises the employee, in the manner prescribed in rules and regulations adopted pursuant to Section 138.4, why payments cannot be made within the 14-day period, what additional information is required to make the decision whether temporary disability indemnity payments are owed, and when the employer expects to have the information required to make the decision.

(e) If the employer is insured for its obligation to provide compensation, the employer shall be obligated to reimburse the insurer for the amount of increase in indemnity payments, made pursuant to subdivision (d), if the late payment which gives rise to the increase in indemnity payments, is due less than seven days after the insurer receives the completed claim form from the employer. Except as specified in this subdivision, an employer shall not be obligated to reimburse an insurer nor shall an insurer be permitted to seek reimbursement, directly or indirectly, for the amount of increase in indemnity payments specified in this section.

(f) If an employer is obligated under subdivision (e) to reimburse the insurer for the amount of increase in indemnity payments, the insurer shall notify the employer in writing, within 30 days of the payment, that the employer is obligated to reimburse the insurer and shall bill and collect the amount of the payment no later than at final audit. However, the insurer shall not be obligated to collect, and the employer shall not be obligated to reimburse, amounts paid pursuant to subdivision (d) unless the aggregate total paid in a policy year exceeds one hundred dollars ($100). The employer shall have 60 days, following notice of the obligation to reimburse, to appeal the decision of the insurer to the Department of Insurance. The notice of the obligation to reimburse shall specify that the employer has the right to appeal the decision of the insurer as provided in this subdivision.

(g) For purposes of this section, "salary continuation plan" means a plan that meets both of the following requirements:

(1) The plan is paid for by the employer pursuant to statute, collective bargaining agreement, memorandum of understanding, or established employer policy.

(2) The plan provides the employee on his or her regular payday with salary not less than the employee is entitled to receive pursuant to statute, collective bargaining agreement, memorandum of understanding, or established employer policy and not less than the employee would otherwise receive in indemnity payments.

Enacted 1937. Amended Stats 1947 ch 1033 § 5; Stats 1949 ch 408 § 1, ch 705 § 1; Stats 1959 ch 1189 § 11; Stats 1971 ch 1750 § 4, operative April 1, 1972; Stats 1973 ch 1021 § 1, operative April 1, 1974; Stats 1989 ch 892 § 34; Stats 1990 ch 1550 § 41 (AB 2910). Amended Stats 2004 ch 34 § 28 (SB 899), effective April 19, 2004; Stats 2012 ch 363 § 54 (SB 863), effective January 1, 2013.

§ 4658. Permanent disability; Computation; Benefits schedules; Increase or decrease in disability payments depending on offer or termination of regular, modified or alternative work

(a) For injuries occurring prior to January 1, 1992, if the injury causes permanent disability, the percentage of disability to total disability shall be determined, and the disability payment computed and allowed, according to paragraph (1). However, in no event shall the disability payment allowed be less than the disability payment computed according to paragraph (2).

(1)

Column 1—Range of percentage of permanent disability incurred:	Column 2—Number of weeks for which two-thirds of average weekly earnings allowed for each 1 percent of permanent disability within percentage range:
Under 10	3
10–19.75	4
20–29.75	5
30–49.75	6
50–69.75	7
70–99.75	8

The number of weeks for which payments shall be allowed set forth in column 2 above based upon the percentage of permanent disability set forth in column 1 above shall be cumulative, and the number of benefit weeks shall increase with the severity of the disability. The following schedule is illustrative of the computation of the number of benefit weeks:

Column 1—Percentage of permanent disability incurred:	Column 2—Cumulative number of benefit weeks:

Column 1—Percentage of permanent disability incurred:	Column 2—Cumulative number of benefit weeks:
5	15
10	30.25
15	50.25
20	70.50
25	95.50
30	120.75
35	150.75
40	180.75
45	210.75
50	241.00
55	276.00
60	311.00
65	346.00
70	381.25
75	421.25
80	461.25
85	501.25
90	541.25
95	581.25
100	for life

(2) Two-thirds of the average weekly earnings for four weeks for each 1 percent of disability, where, for the purposes of this subdivision, the average weekly earnings shall be taken at not more than seventy-eight dollars and seventy-five cents ($78.75).

(b) This subdivision shall apply to injuries occurring on or after January 1, 1992. If the injury causes permanent disability, the percentage of disability to total disability shall be determined, and the disability payment computed and allowed, according to paragraph (1). However, in no event shall the disability payment allowed be less than the disability payment computed according to paragraph (2).

(1)

Column 1—Range of percentage of permanent disability incurred:	Column 2—Number of weeks for which two-thirds of average weekly earnings allowed for each 1 percent of permanent disability within percentage range:

Column 1—Range of percentage of permanent disability incurred:	Column 2—Number of weeks for which two-thirds of average weekly earnings allowed for each 1 percent of permanent disability within percentage range:
Under 10	3
10-19.75	4
20-24.75	5
25-29.75	6
30-49.75	7
50-69.75	8
70-99.75	9

The numbers set forth in column 2 above are based upon the percentage of permanent disability set forth in column 1 above and shall be cumulative, and shall increase with the severity of the disability in the manner illustrated in subdivision (a).

(2) Two-thirds of the average weekly earnings for four weeks for each 1 percent of disability, where, for the purposes of this subdivision, the average weekly earnings shall be taken at not more than seventy-eight dollars and seventy-five cents ($78.75).

(c) This subdivision shall apply to injuries occurring on or after January 1, 2004. If the injury causes permanent disability, the percentage of disability to total disability shall be determined, and the disability payment computed and allowed as follows:

Column 1—Range of percentage of permanent disability incurred:	Column 2—number of weeks for which two-thirds of average weekly earnings allowed for each 1 percent of permanent disability within percentage range:
Under 10	4
10-19.75	5
20-24.75	5
25-29.75	6
30-49.75	7
50-69.75	8
70-99.75	9

The numbers set forth in column 2 above are based upon the percentage of permanent disability set forth in column 1 above and shall be cumulative, and shall increase with the severity of the disability in the manner illustrated in subdivision (a).

(d) (1) This subdivision shall apply to injuries occurring on or after January 1, 2005, and as additionally provided in paragraph (4). If the injury causes permanent disability, the percentage of disability to total disability shall be determined, and the basic disability payment computed as follows:

Column 1—Range of percentage of permanent disability incurred:	Column 2—Number of weeks for which two-thirds of average weekly earnings allowed for each 1 percent of permanent disability within percentage range:
0.25-9.75	3
10-14.75	4
15-24.75	5
25-29.75	6
30-49.75	7
50-69.75	8
70-99.75	16

The numbers set forth in column 2 above are based upon the percentage of permanent disability set forth in column 1 above and shall be cumulative, and shall increase with the severity of the disability in the manner illustrated in subdivision (a).

(2) If, within 60 days of a disability becoming permanent and stationary, an employer does not offer the injured employee regular work, modified work, or alternative work, in the form and manner prescribed by the administrative director, for a period of at least 12 months, each disability payment remaining to be paid to the injured employee from the date of the end of the 60-day period shall be paid in accordance with paragraph (1) and increased by 15 percent. This paragraph shall not apply to an employer that employs fewer than 50 employees.

(3) (A) If, within 60 days of a disability becoming permanent and stationary, an employer offers the injured employee regular work, modified work, or alternative work, in the form and manner prescribed by the administrative director, for a period of at least 12 months, and regardless of whether the injured employee accepts or rejects the offer, each disability payment remaining to be paid to the injured employee from the date the offer was made shall be paid in accordance with paragraph (1) and decreased by 15 percent.

(B) If the regular work, modified work, or alternative work is terminated by the employer before the end of the period for which disability payments are due the injured employee, the amount of each of the remaining disability payments shall be paid in accordance with paragraph (1) and increased by 15 percent. An employee who voluntarily terminates employment shall not be eligible for payment under this subparagraph. This paragraph shall not apply to an employer that employs fewer than 50 employees.

(4) For compensable claims arising before April 30, 2004, the schedule provided in this subdivision shall not apply to the determination of permanent disabilities when there has been either a comprehensive medical-legal report or a report by a treating physician, indicating the existence of permanent disability, or when the employer is required to provide the notice required by Section 4061 to the injured worker.

(e) This subdivision shall apply to injuries occurring on or after January 1, 2013. If the injury causes permanent disability, the percentage of disability to total disability shall be determined, and the disability payment computed and allowed as follows:

Column 1—Range of percentage of permanent disability incurred:	Column 2—Number of weeks for which two-thirds of average weekly earnings allowed for each 1 percent of permanent disability within percentage range:
0.25–9.75	3
10–14.75	4
15–24.75	5
25–29.75	6
30–49.75	7
50–69.75	8
70–99.75	16

(1) The numbers set forth in column 2 above are based upon the percentage of permanent disability set forth in column 1 above and shall be cumulative, and shall increase with the severity of the disability in the manner illustrated in subdivision (a).

(2) If the permanent disability directly caused by the industrial injury is total, payment shall be made as provided in Section 4659.

Enacted 1937. Amended Stats 1949 ch 1583 § 1; Stats 1959 ch 1189 § 13; Stats 1971 ch 1750 § 5, operative April 1, 1972; Stats 1973 ch 1023 § 6, operative April 1, 1974; Stats 1989 ch 892 § 37, ch 893 § 4. Amended Stats 2002 ch 6 § 66 (AB 749); Stats 2004 ch 34 § 30 (SB 899), effective April 19, 2004; Stats 2012 ch 363 § 55 (SB 863), effective January 1, 2013.

§ 4658.5. Eligibility for supplemental job displacement for injuries on or after January 1, 2004, and before January 1, 2013

(a) This section shall apply to injuries occurring on or after January 1, 2004, and before January 1, 2013.

Appendix

(b) Except as provided in Section 4658.6, if the injury causes permanent partial disability and the injured employee does not return to work for the employer within 60 days of the termination of temporary disability, the injured employee shall be eligible for a supplemental job displacement benefit in the form of a nontransferable voucher for education-related retraining or skill enhancement, or both, at state-approved or accredited schools, as follows:

(1) Up to four thousand dollars ($4,000) for permanent partial disability awards of less than 15 percent.

(2) Up to six thousand dollars ($6,000) for permanent partial disability awards between 15 and 25 percent.

(3) Up to eight thousand dollars ($8,000) for permanent partial disability awards between 26 and 49 percent.

(4) Up to ten thousand dollars ($10,000) for permanent partial disability awards between 50 and 99 percent.

(c) The voucher may be used for payment of tuition, fees, books, and other expenses required by the school for retraining or skill enhancement. No more than 10 percent of the voucher moneys may be used for vocational or return-to-work counseling. The administrative director shall adopt regulations governing the form of payment, direct reimbursement to the injured employee upon presentation to the employer of appropriate documentation and receipts, and other matters necessary to the proper administration of the supplemental job displacement benefit.

(d) A voucher issued on or after January 1, 2013, shall expire two years after the date the voucher is furnished to the employee or five years after the date of injury, whichever is later. The employee shall not be entitled to payment or reimbursement of any expenses that have not been incurred and submitted with appropriate documentation to the employer prior to the expiration date.

(e) An employer shall not be liable for compensation for injuries incurred by the employee while utilizing the voucher.

Added Stats 2003 ch 635 § 14.4 (AB 227). Amended Stats 2005 ch 22 § 144 (SB 1108), effective January 1, 2006; Stats 2008 ch 179 § 176 (SB 1498), effective January 1, 2009; Stats 2011 ch 544 § 5 (AB 335), effective January 1, 2012; Stats 2012 ch 363 § 56 (SB 863), effective January 1, 2013.

§ 4658.6. Employer liability for supplemental job displacement benefit

The employer shall not be liable for the supplemental job displacement benefit pursuant to Section 4658.5 if the employer meets either of the following conditions:

(a) Within 30 days of the termination of temporary disability indemnity payments, the employer offers, and the employee rejects, or fails to accept, in the form and manner prescribed by the administrative director, modified work, accommodating the employee's work restrictions, lasting at least 12 months.

(b) Within 30 days of the termination of temporary disability indemnity payments, the employer offers, and the employee rejects, or fails to accept, in the form and manner prescribed by the administrative director, alternative work meeting all of the following conditions:

(1) The employee has the ability to perform the essential functions of the job provided.

(2) The job provided is in a regular position lasting at least 12 months.

(3) The job provided offers wages and compensation that are within 15 percent of those paid to the employee at the time of injury.

(4) The job is located within reasonable commuting distance of the employee's residence at the time of injury.

Added Stats 2003 ch 635 § 15 (AB 227). Amended Stats 2012 ch 363 § 57 (SB 863), effective January 1, 2013.

§ 4658.7. Eligibility for supplemental job displacement for injuries occurring on or after January 1, 2013

(a) This section shall apply to injuries occurring on or after January 1, 2013.

(b) If the injury causes permanent partial disability, the injured employee shall be entitled to a supplemental job displacement benefit as provided in this section unless the employer makes an offer of regular, modified, or alternative work, as defined in Section 4658.1, that meets both of the following criteria:

(1) The offer is made no later than 60 days after receipt by the claims administrator of the first report received from either the primary treating physician, an agreed medical evaluator, or a qualified medical evaluator, in the form created by the administrative director pursuant to subdivision (h), finding that the disability from all conditions for which compensation is claimed has become permanent and stationary and that the injury has caused permanent partial disability.

(A) If the employer or claims administrator has provided the physician with a job description of the employee's regular work, proposed modified work, or proposed alternative work, the physician shall evaluate and describe in the form whether the work capacities and activity restrictions are compatible with the physical requirements set forth in that job description.

(B) The claims administrator shall forward the form to the employer for the purpose of fully informing the employer of work capacities and activity restrictions resulting from the injury that are relevant to potential regular, modified, or alternative work.

(2) The offer is for regular work, modified work, or alternative work lasting at least 12 months.

(c) The supplemental job displacement benefit shall be offered to the employee within 20 days after the expiration of the time for making an offer of regular, modified, or alternative work pursuant to paragraph (1) of subdivision (b).

(d) The supplemental job displacement benefit shall be in the form of a voucher redeemable as provided in this section up to an aggregate of six thousand dollars ($6,000).

(e) The voucher may be applied to any of the following expenses at the choice of the injured employee:

(1) Payment for education-related retraining or skill enhancement, or both, at a California public school or with a provider that is certified and on the state's Eligible Training Provider List (EPTL), as authorized by the federal Workforce Investment Act (P.L. 105-220), including payment of tuition, fees, books, and other expenses required by the school for retraining or skill enhancement.

(2) Payment for occupational licensing or professional certification fees, related examination fees, and examination preparation course fees.

(3) Payment for the services of licensed placement agencies, vocational or return-to-work counseling, and résumé preparation, all up to a combined limit of 10 percent of the amount of the voucher.

(4) Purchase of tools required by a training or educational program in which the employee is enrolled.

(5) Purchase of computer equipment, up to one thousand dollars ($1,000).

(6) Up to five hundred dollars ($500) as a miscellaneous expense reimbursement or advance, payable upon request and without need for itemized documentation or accounting. The employee shall not be entitled to any other voucher payment for transportation, travel expenses, telephone or Internet access, clothing or uniforms, or incidental expenses.

(f) The voucher shall expire two years after the date the voucher is furnished to the employee, or five years after the date of injury, whichever is later. The employee shall not be entitled to payment or reimbursement of any expenses that have not been incurred and submitted with appropriate documentation to the employer prior to the expiration date.

(g) Settlement or commutation of a claim for the supplemental job displacement benefit shall not be permitted under Chapter 2 (commencing with Section 5000) or Chapter 3 (commencing with Section 5100) of Part 3.

(h) The administrative director shall adopt regulations for the administration of this section, including, but not limited to, both of the following:

(1) The time, manner, and content of notices of rights under this section.

(2) The form of a mandatory attachment to a medical report to be forwarded to the employer pursuant to paragraph (1) of subdivision (b) for the purpose of fully informing the employer of work capacities and of activity restrictions resulting from the injury that are relevant to potential regular work, modified work, or alternative work.

(i) An employer shall not be liable for compensation for injuries incurred by the employee while utilizing the voucher.

Added Stats 2012 ch 363 § 58 (SB 863), effective January 1, 2013.

§ 4660. Percentages of permanent disability for injuries occurring before January 1, 2013; How determined; Adjusted rating schedule; Amendments and revisions to schedule

This section shall only apply to injuries occurring before January 1, 2013.

(a) In determining the percentages of permanent disability, account shall be taken of the nature of the physical injury or disfigurement, the occupation of the injured employee, and his or her age at the time of the injury, consideration being given to an employee's diminished future earning capacity.

(b) (1) For purposes of this section, the "nature of the physical injury or disfigurement" shall incorporate the descriptions and measurements of physical impairments and the corresponding percentages of impairments published in the American Medical Association (AMA) Guides to the Evaluation of Permanent Impairment (5th Edition).

(2) For purposes of this section, an employee's diminished future earning capacity shall be a numeric formula based on empirical data and findings that aggregate the average percentage of long–term loss of income resulting from each type of injury for similarly situated employees. The administrative director shall formulate the adjusted rating schedule based on empirical data and findings from the Evaluation of California's Permanent Disability Rating Schedule, Interim Report (December 2003), prepared by the RAND Institute for Civil Justice, and upon data from additional empirical studies.

(c) The administrative director shall amend the schedule for the determination of the percentage of permanent disability in accordance with this section at least once every five years. This schedule shall be available for public inspection and, without formal introduction in evidence, shall be prima facie evidence of the percentage of permanent disability to be attributed to each injury covered by the schedule.

(d) The schedule shall promote consistency, uniformity, and objectivity. The schedule and any amendment thereto or revision thereof shall apply prospectively and shall apply to and govern only those permanent disabilities that result from compensable injuries received or occurring on and after the effective date of the adoption of the schedule, amendment or revision, as the fact may be. For compensable claims arising before January 1, 2005, the schedule as revised pursuant to changes made in legislation enacted during the 2003–04 Regular and Extraordinary Sessions shall apply to the determination of permanent disabilities when there has been either no comprehensive medical–legal report or no report by a treating physician indicating the existence of permanent disability, or when the employer is not required to provide the notice required by Section 4061 to the injured worker.

(e) On or before January 1, 2005, the administrative director shall adopt regulations to implement the changes made to this section by the act that added this subdivision.

Enacted 1937. Amended Stats 1951 ch 1683 § 1; Stats 1965 ch 1513 § 91, operative January 15, 1966. Amended Stats 1993 ch 121 § 53 (AB 110), effective July 16, 1993; Stats 2004 ch 34 § 32 (SB 899), effective April 19, 2004; Stats 2012 ch 363 § 59 (SB 863), effective January 1, 2013.

§ 4660.1. Percentages of permanent disability for injuries occurring on or after January 1, 2013; How determined; Adjusted rating schedule; Amendments and revisions to schedule

This section applies to injuries occurring on or after January 1, 2013.

(a) In determining the percentages of permanent partial or permanent total disability, account shall be taken of the nature of the physical injury or disfigurement, the occupation of the injured employee, and the employee's age at the time of injury.

(b) For purposes of this section, the "nature of the physical injury or disfigurement" shall incorporate the descriptions and measurements of physical impairments and the corresponding percentages of impairments published in the American Medical Association (AMA) Guides to the Evaluation of Permanent Impairment (5th Edition) with the employee's whole person impairment, as provided in the Guides, multiplied by an adjustment factor of 1.4.

(c)

(1) Except as provided in paragraph (2), the impairment ratings for sleep dysfunction, sexual dysfunction, or psychiatric disorder, or any combination thereof, arising out of a compensable physical injury shall not increase. This section does not limit the ability of an injured employee to obtain treatment for sleep dysfunction, sexual dysfunction, or psychiatric disorder, if any, that are a consequence of an industrial injury.

(2) An increased impairment rating for psychiatric disorder is not subject to paragraph (1) if the compensable psychiatric injury resulted from either of the following:

(A) Being a victim of a violent act or direct exposure to a significant violent act within the meaning of Section 3208.3.

(B) A catastrophic injury, including, but not limited to, loss of a limb, paralysis, severe burn, or severe head injury.

(d) The administrative director may formulate a schedule of age and occupational modifiers and may amend the schedule for the determination of the age and occupational modifiers in accordance with this section. The Schedule for Rating Permanent Disabilities pursuant to the American Medical Association (AMA) Guides to the Evaluation of Permanent Impairment (5th Edition) and the schedule of age and occupational modifiers shall be available for public inspection and, without formal introduction in evidence, shall be prima facie evidence of the percentage of permanent disability to be attributed to each injury covered by the schedule. Until the schedule of age and occupational modifiers is amended, for injuries occurring on or after January 1, 2013, permanent disabilities shall be rated using the age and occupational modifiers in the permanent disability rating schedule adopted as of January 1, 2005.

(e) The schedule of age and occupational modifiers shall promote consistency, uniformity, and objectivity.

(f) The schedule of age and occupational modifiers and any amendment thereto or revision thereof shall apply prospectively and shall apply to and govern only those permanent disabilities that result from compensable injuries received or occurring on and after the effective date of the adoption of the schedule, amendment, or revision, as the case may be.

(g) This section does not preclude a finding of permanent total disability in accordance with Section 4662.

(h) In enacting the act adding this section, it is not the intent of the Legislature to overrule the holding in Milpitas Unified School District v. Workers' Comp. Appeals Bd. (Guzman)(2010) 187 Cal.App.4th 808.

(i) The Commission on Health and Safety and Workers' Compensation shall conduct a study to compare average loss of earnings for employees who sustained work-related injuries with permanent disability ratings under the schedule, and shall report the results of the study to the appropriate policy and fiscal committees of the Legislature no later than January 1, 2016.

Added Stats 2012 ch 363 § 60 (SB 863), effective January 1, 2013. Amended Stats 2019 ch 497 § 189 (AB 991), effective January 1, 2020.

Appendix

Article 4

Death Benefits

§ 4701. Liability for burial expenses and death benefit

If an injury causes death, either with or without disability, the employer shall be liable, in addition to any other benefits provided by this division, for all of the following:

(a) Reasonable expenses of the employee's burial, in accordance with the following:

(1) Up to two thousand dollars ($2,000) for injuries occurring prior to January 1, 1991.

(2) Up to five thousand dollars ($5,000) for injuries occurring on or after January 1, 1991, and prior to January 1, 2013.

(3) Up to ten thousand dollars ($10,000) for injuries occurring on or after January 1, 2013.

(b) A death benefit, to be allowed to the dependents when the employee leaves any person dependent upon him or her for support.

Enacted 1937. Amended Stats 1943 ch 678 § 1; Stats 1949 ch 321 § 1; Stats 1959 ch 1189 § 15; Stats 1st Ex Sess 1968 ch 4 § 7, operative January 1, 1969; Stats 1978 ch 487 § 1; Stats 1985 ch 1567 § 1; Stats 1988 ch 584 § 1; Stats 1989 ch 892 § 39; Stats 2012 ch 363 § 61 (SB 863), effective January 1, 2013.

PART 3

COMPENSATION CLAIMS

Chapter 1

Payment and Assignment

§ 4903. Liens against sum to be paid as compensation

The appeals board may determine, and allow as liens against any sum to be paid as compensation, any amount determined as hereinafter set forth in subdivisions (a) through (i). If more than one lien is allowed, the appeals board may determine the priorities, if any, between the liens allowed. The liens that may be allowed hereunder are as follows:

(a) A reasonable attorney's fee for legal services pertaining to any claim for compensation either before the appeals board or before any of the appellate courts, and the reasonable disbursements in connection therewith. No fee for legal services shall be awarded to any representative who is not an attorney, except with respect to those claims for compensation for which an application, pursuant to Section 5501, has been filed with the appeals board on or before December 31, 1991, or for which a disclosure form, pursuant to Section 4906, has been sent to the employer, or insurer or third-party administrator, if either is known, on or before December 31, 1991.

(b) The reasonable expense incurred by or on behalf of the injured employee, as provided by Article 2 (commencing with Section 4600), and to the extent the employee is entitled to reimbursement under Section 4621, medical-legal expenses as provided by Article 2.5 (commencing with Section 4620) of Chapter 2 of Part 2, except those disputes subject to independent medical review or independent bill review.

(c) The reasonable value of the living expenses of an injured employee or of his or her dependents, subsequent to the injury.

(d) The reasonable burial expenses of the deceased employee, not to exceed the amount provided for by Section 4701.

(e) The reasonable living expenses of the spouse or minor children of the injured employee, or both, subsequent to the date of the injury, where the employee has deserted or is neglecting his or her family. These expenses shall be allowed in the proportion that the appeals board deems proper, under application of the spouse, guardian of the minor children, or the assignee, pursuant to subdivision (a) of Section 11477 of the Welfare and Institutions Code, of the spouse, a former spouse, or minor children. A collection received as a result of a lien against a workers' compensation award imposed pursuant to this subdivision for payment of child support ordered by a court shall be credited as provided in Section 695.221 of the Code of Civil Procedure.

(f) The amount of unemployment compensation disability benefits that have been paid under or pursuant to the Unemployment Insurance Code in those cases where, pending a determination under this division there was uncertainty whether the benefits were payable under the Unemployment Insurance Code or payable hereunder; provided, however, that any lien under this subdivision shall be allowed and paid as provided in Section 4904.

(g) The amount of unemployment compensation benefits and extended duration benefits paid to the injured employee for the same day or days for which he or she receives, or is entitled to receive, temporary total disability indemnity payments under this division; provided, however, that any lien under this subdivision shall be allowed and paid as provided in Section 4904.

(h) The amount of family temporary disability insurance benefits that have been paid to the injured employee pursuant to the Unemployment Insurance Code for the same day or days for which that employee receives, or is entitled to receive, temporary total disability indemnity payments under this division, provided, however, that any lien under this subdivision shall be allowed and paid as provided in Section 4904.

(i) The amount of indemnification granted by the California Victims of Crime Program pursuant to Article 1 (commencing with Section 13959) of Chapter 5 of Part 4 of Division 3 of Title 2 of the Government Code.

Enacted 1937. Amended Stats 1945 ch 507 § 1; Stats 1947 ch 833 § 1; Stats 1949 ch 488 § 1; Stats 1957 ch 1977 § 1; Stats 1963 ch 1556 § 1; Stats 1965 ch 1513 § 103, operative January 15, 1966; Stats 1967 ch 1721 § 2; Stats 1980 ch 1041 § 2, ch 1370 § 5.1, effective October 1, 1980; Stats 1981 ch 809 § 1, effective September 25, 1981; Stats 1984 ch 1463 § 2.5, effective September 26, 1984; Stats 1987 ch 1434 § 1. Amended Stats 1991 ch 116 § 30 (SB 1218), ch 934 § 14 (AB 1673); Stats 1993 ch 876 § 28 (SB 1068), effective October 6, 1993; Stats 1994 ch 75 § 4 (AB 1702), effective May 20, 1994; Stats 1996 ch 1077 § 12 (AB 2898); Stats 2003 ch 797 § 1 (SB 727); Stats 2012 ch 363 § 62 (SB 863), effective January 1, 2013; Stats 2014 ch 217 § 3 (AB 2732), effective January 1, 2015.

§ 4903.05. Filing of written lien claim required; Form; Fee

(a) Every lien claimant shall file its lien with the appeals board in writing upon a form approved by the appeals board. The lien shall be accompanied by a full statement or itemized voucher supporting the lien and justifying the right to reimbursement and proof of service upon the injured worker or, if deceased, upon the worker's dependents, the employer, the insurer, and the respective attorneys or other agents of record. Medical records shall be filed only if they are relevant to the issues being raised by the lien.

(b) Any lien claim for expenses under subdivision (b) of Section 4903 or for claims of costs shall be filed with the appeals board electronically using the form approved by the appeals board. The lien shall be accompanied by a proof of service and any other documents that may be required by the appeals board. The service requirements for Section 4603.2 are not modified by this section.

(c) All liens filed on or after January 1, 2013, for expenses under subdivision (b) of Section 4903 or for claims of costs shall be subject to a filing fee as provided by this subdivision.

(1) The lien claimant shall pay a filing fee of one hundred fifty dollars ($150) to the Division of Workers' Compensation prior to filing a lien and shall include proof that the filing fee has been paid. The fee shall be collected through an electronic payment system that accepts major credit cards and any additional forms of electronic payment selected by the administrative director. If the administrative director contracts with a service provider for the processing of electronic payments, any processing fee shall be absorbed by the division and not added to the fee charged to the lien filer.

(2) On or after January 1, 2013, a lien submitted for filing that does not comply with paragraph (1) shall be invalid, even if lodged with

the appeals board, and shall not operate to preserve or extend any time limit for filing of the lien.

(3) The claims of two or more providers of goods or services shall not be merged into a single lien.

(4) The filing fee shall be collected by the administrative director. All fees shall be deposited in the Workers' Compensation Administration Revolving Fund and applied for the purposes of that fund.

(5) The administrative director shall adopt reasonable rules and regulations governing the procedure for the collection of the filing fee, including emergency regulations as necessary to implement this section.

(6) Any lien filed for goods or services that are not the proper subject of a lien may be dismissed upon request of a party by verified petition or on the appeals board's own motion. If the lien is dismissed, the lien claimant will not be entitled to reimbursement of the filing fee.

(7) No filing fee shall be required for a lien filed by a health care service plan licensed pursuant to Section 1349 of the Health and Safety Code, a group disability insurer under a policy issued in this state pursuant to the provisions of Section 10270.5 of the Insurance Code, a self-insured employee welfare benefit plan, as defined in Section 10121 of the Insurance Code, that is issued in this state, a Taft-Hartley health and welfare fund, or a publicly funded program providing medical benefits on a nonindustrial basis.

Added Stats 2012 ch 363 §63 (SB 863), effective January 1, 2013.

§ 4903.06. Fees for claims filed prior to January 1, 2013

(a) Any lien filed pursuant to subdivision (b) of Section 4903 prior to January 1, 2013, and any cost that was filed as a lien prior to January 1, 2013, shall be subject to a lien activation fee unless the lien claimant provides proof of having paid a filing fee as previously required by former Section 4903.05 as added by Chapter 639 of the Statutes of 2003.

(1) The lien claimant shall pay a lien activation fee of one hundred dollars ($100) to the Division of Workers' Compensation on or before January 1, 2014. The fee shall be collected through an electronic payment system that accepts major credit cards and any additional forms of electronic payment selected by the administrative director. If the administrative director contracts with a service provider for the processing of electronic payments, any processing fee shall be absorbed by the division and not added to the fee charged to the lien filer.

(2) The lien claimant shall include proof of payment of the filing fee or lien activation fee with the declaration of readiness to proceed.

(3) The lien activation fee shall be collected by the administrative director. All fees shall be deposited in the Workers' Compensation

Administration Revolving Fund and applied for the purposes of that fund. The administrative director shall adopt reasonable rules and regulations governing the procedure for the collection of the lien activation fee and to implement this section, including emergency regulations, as necessary.

(4) All lien claimants that did not file the declaration of readiness to proceed and that remain a lien claimant of record at the time of a lien conference shall submit proof of payment of the activation fee at the lien conference. If the fee has not been paid or no proof of payment is available, the lien shall be dismissed with prejudice.

(5) Any lien filed pursuant to subdivision (b) of Section 4903 prior to January 1, 2013, and any cost that was filed as a lien prior to January 1, 2013, for which the filing fee or lien activation fee has not been paid by January 1, 2014, is dismissed by operation of law.

(b) This section shall not apply to any lien filed by a health care service plan licensed pursuant to Section 1349 of the Health and Safety Code, a group disability insurer under a policy issued in this state pursuant to the provisions of Section 10270.5 of the Insurance Code, a self-insured employee welfare benefit plan, as defined in Section 10121 of the Insurance Code, that is issued in this state, a Taft-Hartley health and welfare fund, or a publicly funded program providing medical benefits on a nonindustrial basis.

Added Stats 2012 ch 363 § 64 (SB 863), effective January 1, 2013.

§ 4903.07. Conditions for entitlement to order or award for reimbursement of lien filing or activation fee

(a) A lien claimant shall be entitled to an order or award for reimbursement from the employer of a lien filing fee or lien activation fee, together with interest at the rate allowed on civil judgments, only if all of the following conditions are satisfied:

(1) Not less than 30 days before filing the lien for which the filing fee was paid or filing the declaration of readiness for which the lien activation fee was paid, the lien claimant has made written demand for settlement of the lien claim for a clearly stated sum which shall be inclusive of all claims of debt, interest, penalty, or other claims potentially recoverable on the lien.

(2) The defendant fails to accept the settlement demand in writing within 20 days of receipt of the demand for settlement, or within any additional time as may be provide by the written demand.

(3) After submission of the lien dispute to the appeals board or an arbitrator, a final award is made in favor of the lien claimant of a specified sum that is equal to or greater than the amount of the settlement demand. The amount of the interest and filing fee or lien activation fee shall not be considered in determining whether the award is equal to or greater than the demand.

(b) This section shall not preclude an order or award of reimbursement of the filing fee or activation fee pursuant to the express terms of an agreed disposition of a lien dispute.

Added Stats 2012 ch 363 § 65 (SB 863), effective January 1, 2013. Amended Stats 2014 ch 217 § 4 (AB 2732), effective January 1, 2015.

§ 4903.1. Reimbursement of certain health and welfare benefits plans

(a) The appeals board or arbitrator, before issuing an award or approval of any compromise of claim, shall determine, on the basis of liens filed with it pursuant to Section 4903.05, whether any benefits have been paid or services provided by a health care provider, a health care service plan, a group disability policy, including a loss-of-income policy or a self-insured employee welfare benefit plan, and its award or approval shall provide for reimbursement for benefits paid or services provided under these plans as follows:

(1) If the appeals board issues an award finding that an injury or illness arises out of and in the course of employment, but denies the applicant reimbursement for self-procured medical costs solely because of lack of notice to the applicant's employer of his or her need for hospital, surgical, or medical care, the appeals board shall nevertheless award a lien against the employee's recovery, to the extent of benefits paid or services provided, for the effects of the industrial injury or illness, by a health care provider, a health care service plan, a group disability policy or a self-insured employee welfare benefit plan, subject to the provisions described in subdivision (b).

(2) If the appeals board issues an award finding that an injury or illness arises out of and in the course of employment, and makes an award for reimbursement for self-procured medical costs, the appeals board shall allow a lien, to the extent of benefits paid or services provided, for the effects of the industrial injury or illness, by a health care provider, a health care service plan, a group disability policy or a self-insured employee welfare benefit plan, subject to the provisions of subdivision (b). For purposes of this paragraph, benefits paid or services provided by a self-insured employee welfare benefit plan shall be determined notwithstanding the offiial medical fee schedule adopted pursuant to Section 5307.1.

(3) (A) If the appeals board issues an award finding that an injury or illness arises out of and in the course of employment and makes an award for temporary disability indemnity, the appeals board shall allow a lien as living expense under Section 4903, for benefits paid by a group disability policy providing loss-of-time benefits and for loss-of-time benefits paid by a self-insured employee welfare benefit plan. The lien shall be allowed to the extent that benefits have been paid for the same day or days for which temporary disability indemnity is awarded and shall not exceed the award for temporary disability in-

Appendix

demnity. A lien shall not be allowed hereunder unless the group disability policy or self-insured employee welfare benefit plan provides for reduction, exclusion, or coordination of loss-of-time benefits on account of workers' compensation benefits.

(B) For purposes of this paragraph, "self-insured employee welfare benefit plan" means any plan, fund, or program that is established or maintained by an employer or by an employee organization, or by both, to the extent that the plan, fund, or program was established or is maintained for the purpose of providing for its participants or their beneficiaries, other than through the purchase of insurance, either of the following:

(i) Medical, surgical, or hospital care or benefits.

(ii) Monetary or other benefits in the event of sickness, accident, disability, death, or unemployment.

(4) If the parties propose that the case be disposed of by way of a compromise and release agreement, in the event the lien claimant, other than a health care provider, does not agree to the amount allocated to it, then the appeals board shall determine the potential recovery and reduce the amount of the lien in the ratio of the applicant's recovery to the potential recovery in full satisfaction of its lien claim.

(b) Notwithstanding subdivision (a), payment or reimbursement shall not be allowed, whether payable by the employer or payable as a lien against the employee's recovery, for any expense incurred as provided by Article 2 (commencing with Section 4600) of Chapter 2 of Part 2, nor shall the employee have any liability for the expense, if at the time the expense was incurred the provider either knew or in the exercise of reasonable diligence should have known that the condition being treated was caused by the employee's present or prior employment, unless at the time the expense was incurred at least one of the following conditions was met:

(1) The expense was incurred for services authorized by the employer.

(2) The expense was incurred for services furnished while the employer failed or refused to furnish treatment as required by subdivision (c) of Section 5402.

(3) The expense was necessarily incurred for an emergency medical condition, as defined by subdivision (b) of Section 1317.1 of the Health and Safety Code.

(c) The changes made to this section by Senate Bill 457 of the 2011-12 Regular Session do not modify in any way the rights or obligations of the following:

(1) Any health care provider to file and prosecute a lien pursuant to subdivision (b) of Section 4903.

(2) A payer to conduct utilization review pursuant to Section 4610.

(3) Any party in complying with the requirements under Section 4903.

Added Stats 1975 ch 1109 § 1. Amended Stats 1979 ch 855 § 1; Stats 1990 ch 1550 § 45 (AB 2910); Stats 2011 ch 564 § 1 (SB 457), effective January 1, 2012; Stats 2012 ch 363 § 66 (SB 863), effective January 1, 2013, ch 712 § 1.5 (SB 1105), effective January 1, 2013.

§ 4903.4. Dispute concerning lien for expenses

(a) If a dispute arises concerning a lien for expenses incurred by or on behalf of the injured employee as provided by Article 2 (commencing with Section 4600) of Chapter 2 of Part 2, the appeals board may resolve the dispute in a separate proceeding, which may include binding arbitration upon agreement of the employer, lien claimant, and the employee, if the employee remains a party to the dispute, according to the rules of practice and procedure.

(b) If the dispute is heard at a separate proceeding it shall be calendared for hearing or hearings as determined by the appeals board based upon the resources available to the appeals board and other considerations as the appeals board deems appropriate and shall not be subject to Section 5501.5.

Added Stats 1989 ch 892 § 42. Amended Stats 1990 ch 1550 § 46 (AB 2910); Stats 2012 ch 363 § 67 (SB 863), effective January 1, 2013; Stats 2013 ch 287 § 6 (SB 375), effective January 1, 2014.

§ 4903.5. Time period for filing lien for expenses; Applicability

(a) A lien claim for expenses as provided in subdivision (b) of Section 4903 shall not be filed after three years from the date the services were provided, nor more than 18 months after the date the services were provided, if the services were provided on or after July 1, 2013.

(b) Notwithstanding subdivision (a), any health care service plan licensed pursuant to Section 1349 of the Health and Safety Code, group disability insurer under a policy issued in this state pursuant to the provisions of Section 10270.5 of the Insurance Code, self-insured employee welfare benefit plan issued in this state as defined in Section 10121 of the Insurance Code, Taft-Hartley health and welfare fund, or publicly funded program providing medical benefits on a nonindustrial basis, may file a lien claim for expenses as provided in subdivision (b) of Section 4903 within 12 months after the entity first knew or in the exercise of reasonable diligence should have known that an industrial injury is being claimed, but in no event later than five years from the date the services were provided to the employee.

(c) The injured worker shall not be liable for any underlying obligation if a lien claim has not been filed and served within the allowable period. Except when the lien claimant is the applicant as provided in Section 5501 or as otherwise permitted by rules of practice and procedure adopted by the appeals board, a lien claimant shall not file a

Appendix

declaration of readiness to proceed in any case until the case-in-chief has been resolved.

(d) This section shall not apply to civil actions brought under the Cartwright Act (Chapter 2 (commencing with Section 16700) of Part 2 of Division 7 of the Business and Professions Code), the Unfair Practices Act (Chapter 4 (commencing with Section 17000) of Part 2 of Division 7 of the Business and Professions Code), or the federal Racketeer Influenced and Corrupt Organization Act (Chapter 96 (commencing with Section 1961) of Title 18 of the United States Code) based on concerted action with other insurers that are not parties to the case in which the lien or claim is filed.

Added Stats 2002 ch 6 § 70 (AB 749). Amended Stats 2012 ch 363 § 68 (SB 863), effective January 1, 2013.

§ 4903.6. Lien claim or application for adjudication; Requirements for Filing; Exemptions

(a) Except as necessary to meet the requirements of Section 4903.5, a lien claim or application for adjudication shall not be filed or served under subdivision (b) of Section 4903 until both of the following have occurred:

(1) Sixty days have elapsed after the date of acceptance or rejection of liability for the claim, or expiration of the time provided for investigation of liability pursuant to subdivision (b) of Section 5402, whichever date is earlier.

(2) Either of the following:

(A) The time provided for payment of medical treatment bills pursuant to Section 4603.2 has expired and, if the employer objected to the amount of the bill, the reasonable fee has been determined pursuant to Section 4603.6, and, if authorization for the medical treatment has been disputed pursuant to Section 4610, the medical necessity of the medical treatment has been determined pursuant to Sections 4610.5 and 4610.6.

(B) The time provided for payment of medical-legal expenses pursuant to Section 4622 has expired and, if the employer objected to the amount of the bill, the reasonable fee has been determined pursuant to Section 4603.6.

(b) All lien claimants under Section 4903 shall notify the employer and the employer's representative, if any, and the employee and the employee's representative, if any, and the appeals board within five working days of obtaining, changing, or discharging representation by an attorney or nonattorney representative. The notice shall set forth the legal name, address, and telephone number of the attorney or nonattorney representative.

(c) A declaration of readiness to proceed shall not be filed for a lien under subdivision (b) of Section 4903 until the underlying case has been resolved or where the applicant chooses not to proceed with the applicant's case.

(d) With the exception of a lien for services provided by a physician as defined in Section 3209.3, a lien claimant shall not be entitled to any medical information, as defined in subdivision (j) of Section 56.05 of the Civil Code, about an injured worker without prior written approval of the appeals board. Any order authorizing disclosure of medical information to a lien claimant other than a physician shall specify the information to be provided to the lien claimant and include a finding that the information is relevant to the proof of the matter for which the information is sought. The appeals board shall adopt reasonable regulations to ensure compliance with this section, and shall take any further steps as may be necessary to enforce the regulations, including, but not limited to, impositions of sanctions pursuant to Section 5813.

(e) The prohibitions of this section do not apply to lien claims, applications for adjudication, or declarations of readiness to proceed filed by or on behalf of the employee, or to the filings by or on behalf of the employer.

Added Stats 2006 ch 69 § 26 (AB 1806), effective July 12, 2006. Amended Stats 2012 ch 363 § 69 (SB 863), effective January 1, 2013; Stats 2013 ch 287 § 7 (SB 375), effective January 1, 2014; Stats 2019 ch 497§ 190 (AB 991), effective January 1, 2020.

§ 4903.8. Person to whom payment of lien to be made; Assignment of lien; Multiple assignments

(a) Any order or award for payment of a lien filed pursuant to subdivision (b) of Section 4903 shall be made for payment only to the person who was entitled to payment for the expenses as provided in subdivision (b) of Section 4903 at the time the expenses were incurred, and not to an assignee unless the person has ceased doing business in the capacity held at the time the expenses were incurred and has assigned all right, title, and interests in the remaining accounts receivable to the assignee.

(b) If there has been an assignment of a lien, either as an assignment of all right, title, and interest in the accounts receivable or as an assignment for collection, a true and correct copy of the assignment shall be filed and served.

(1) If the lien is filed on or after January 1, 2013, and the assignment occurs before the filing of the lien, the copy of the assignment shall be served at the time the lien is filed.

(2) If the lien is filed on or after January 1, 2013, and the assignment occurs after the filing of the lien, the copy of the assignment shall be served within 20 days of the date of the assignment.

(3) If the lien is filed before January 1, 2013, the copy of the assignment shall be served by January 1, 2014, or with the filing of a

declaration of readiness or at the time of a lien hearing, whichever is earliest.

(c) If there has been more than one assignment of the same receivable or bill, the appeals board may set the matter for hearing on whether the multiple assignments constitute bad-faith actions or tactics that are frivolous, harassing, or intended to cause unnecessary delay or expense. If so found by the appeals board, appropriate sanctions, including costs and attorney's fees, may be awarded against the assignor, assignee, and their respective attorneys.

(d) At the time of filing of a lien on or after January 1, 2013, or in the case of a lien filed before January 1, 2013, at the earliest of the filing of a declaration of readiness, a lien hearing, or January 1, 2014, supporting documentation shall be filed including one or more declarations under penalty of perjury by a natural person or persons competent to testify to the facts stated, declaring both of the following:

(1) The services or products described in the bill for services or products were actually provided to the injured employee.

(2) The billing statement attached to the lien truly and accurately describes the services or products that were provided to the injured employee.

(e) A lien submitted for filing on or after January 1, 2013, for expenses provided in subdivision (b) of Section 4903, that does not comply with the requirements of this section shall be deemed to be invalid, whether or not accepted for filing by the appeals board, and shall not operate to preserve or extend any time limit for filing of the lien.

(f) This section shall take effect without regulatory action. The appeals board and the administrative director may promulgate regulations and forms for the implementation of this section.

Added Stats 2012 ch 363 § 70 (SB 863), effective January 1, 2013.

§ 4904. Allowance and payment of liens for unemployment compensation benefits

(a) If notice is given in writing to the insurer, or to the employer if uninsured, setting forth the nature and extent of any claim that is allowable as a lien in favor of the Employment Development Department, the claim is a lien against any amount thereafter payable as temporary or permanent disability compensation, subject to the determination of the amount and approval of the lien by the appeals board. When the Employment Development Department has served an insurer or employer with a lien claim, the insurer or employer shall notify the Employment Development Department, in writing, as soon as possible, but in no event later than 15 working days after commencing disability indemnity payments. When a lien has been served on an insurer or an employer by the Employment Development Department, the insurer or employer shall notify the Employment Development Department, in writing, within 10 working days of filing an application for adjudication, a stipulated award, or a compromise and release with the appeals board.

(b) (1) In determining the amount of lien to be allowed for unemployment compensation disability benefits under subdivision (f) of Section 4903, the appeals board shall allow the lien in the amount of benefits which it finds were paid for the same day or days of disability for which an award of compensation for any permanent disability indemnity resulting solely from the same injury or illness or temporary disability indemnity, or both, is made and for which the employer has not reimbursed the Employment Development Department pursuant to Section 2629.1 of the Unemployment Insurance Code.

(2) In determining the amount of lien to be allowed for unemployment compensation benefits and extended duration benefits under subdivision (g) of Section 4903, the appeals board shall allow the lien in the amount of benefits which it finds were paid for the same day or days for which an award of compensation for temporary total disability is made.

(3) In determining the amount of lien to be allowed for family temporary disability insurance benefits under subdivision (h) of Section 4903, the appeals board shall allow the lien in the amount of benefits that it finds were paid for the same day or days for which an award of compensation for temporary total disability is made and for which the employer has not reimbursed the Employment Development Department pursuant to Section 2629.1 of the Unemployment Insurance Code.

(c) In the case of agreements for the compromise and release of a disputed claim for compensation, the applicant and defendant may propose to the appeals board, as part of the compromise and release agreement, an amount out of the settlement to be paid to any lien claimant claiming under subdivision (f), (g), or (h) of Section 4903. If the lien claimant objects to the amount proposed for payment of its lien under a compromise and release settlement or stipulation, the appeals board shall determine the extent of the lien claimant's entitlement to reimbursement on its lien and make and file findings on all facts involved in the controversy over this issue in accordance with Section 5313. The appeals board may approve a compromise and release agreement or stipulation which proposes the disallowance of a lien, in whole or in part, only where there is proof of service upon the lien claimant by the defendant, not less than 15 days prior to the appeals board action, of all medical and rehabilitation documents and a copy of the proposed compromise and release agreement or stipulation. The determination of the appeals board, subject to petition for reconsideration and to the right of judicial review, as to the amount of lien allowed under subdivision (f), (g), or (h) of Section 4903, whether in connection with an award of compensation or the approval of a compromise and release agreement, shall be binding on the lien claimant, the applicant, and the defendant, insofar as the right to benefits paid under the Unemployment Insurance Code for which the lien was claimed. The appeals board may order the amount of any lien claim, as determined and allowed by it, to be paid directly to the person entitled, either in a lump sum or in installments.

(d) Where unemployment compensation disability benefits, including family temporary disability insurance benefits, have been paid pursuant to the Unemployment Insurance Code while reconsideration of an order, decision, or award is pending, or has been granted, the appeals board shall determine and allow a final amount on the lien as of the date the board is ready to issue its decision denying a petition for reconsideration or affirming, rescinding, altering or amending the original findings, order, decision, or award.

(e) The appeals board shall not be prohibited from approving a compromise and release agreement on all other issues and deferring to subsequent proceedings the determination of a lien claimant's entitlement to reimbursement if the defendant in any of these proceedings agrees to pay the amount subsequently determined to be due under the lien claim.

(f) The amendments made to this section by the act adding this subdivision are declaratory of existing law, and shall not constitute good cause to reopen, rescind, or amend any final order, decision, or award of the appeals board.

Enacted 1937. Amended Stats 1957 ch 1977 § 2; Stats 1965 ch 157 § 6, ch 691 § 1, ch 1513 § 104, operative January 15, 1966; Stats 1967 ch 125 § 6, ch 1721 § 3; Stats 1970 ch 985 § 1; Stats 1989 ch 1280 § 2; Stats 1990 ch 1550 § 47 (AB 2910). Amended Stats 1993 ch 748 § 1 (SB 4); Stats 2003 ch 797 § 2 (SB 727); Stats 2012 ch 363 § 71 (SB 863), effective January 1, 2013.

§ 4905. Payment where lien not requested

Except with regard to liens as permitted by subdivision (b) of Section 4903, if it appears in any proceeding pending before the appeals board that a lien should be allowed if it had been duly requested by the party entitled thereto, the appeals board may, without any request for such lien having been made, order the payment of the claim to be made directly to the person entitled, in the same manner and with the same effect as though the lien had been regularly requested, and the award to such person shall constitute a lien against unpaid compensation due at the time of service of the award.

Enacted 1937. Amended Stats 1965 ch 1513 § 105, operative January 15, 1966; Stats 2012 ch 363 § 72 (SB 863), effective January 1, 2013.

§ 4907. Loss of right to appear

(a) The privilege of any person, except attorneys admitted to practice in the Supreme Court of the state, to appear in any proceeding as a representative of any party before the appeals board, or any of its workers' compensation administrative law judges, may, after a hearing, be removed, denied, or suspended by the appeals board for either of the following:

(1) For a violation of this chapter, the Rules of the Workers' Compensation Appeals Board, or the Rules of the Administrative Director.

(2) For other good cause, including, but not limited to, failure to pay final order of sanctions, attorney's fees, or costs issued under Section 5813.

(b) For purposes of this section, nonattorney representatives shall be held to the same professional standards of conduct as attorneys.

Enacted 1937. Amended Stats 1965 ch 1513 § 107, operative January 15, 1966; Stats 2012 ch 363 § 73 (SB 863), effective January 1, 2013.

PART 4

COMPENSATION PROCEEDINGS

Chapter 1

Jurisdiction

§ 5307.1. Adoption and periodic revision of official medical fee schedule; Reasonable maximum fees; Reasonable standards of service and care

(a) (1) The administrative director, after public hearings, shall adopt and revise periodically an official medical fee schedule that shall establish reasonable maximum fees paid for medical services other than physician services, drugs and pharmacy services, health care facility fees, home health care, and all other treatment, care, services, and goods described in Section 4600 and provided pursuant to this section. Except for physician services, all fees shall be in accordance with the fee-related structure and rules of the relevant Medicare and Medi-Cal payment systems, provided that employer liability for medical treatment, including issues of reasonableness, necessity, frequency, and duration, shall be determined in accordance with Section 4600. Commencing January 1, 2004, and continuing until the time the administrative director has adopted an official medical fee schedule in accordance with the fee-related structure and rules of the relevant Medicare payment systems, except for the components listed in subdivision (j), maximum reasonable fees shall be 120 percent of the estimated aggregate fees prescribed in the relevant Medicare payment system for the same class of services before application of the inflation factors provided in subdivision (g), except that for pharmacy services and drugs that are not otherwise covered by a Medicare fee schedule payment for facility services, the maximum reasonable fees shall be 100 percent of fees prescribed in the relevant Medi-Cal payment system. Upon adoption by the administrative director of an official medical fee schedule pursuant to this section, the maximum reasonable fees paid shall not exceed 120 percent of estimated aggregate fees prescribed in the Medicare payment system for the same class of services before application of the inflation factors provided in subdivision (g). Pharmacy services and drugs shall be subject to the requirements of this section, whether furnished through a pharmacy or dispensed directly by the practitioner pursuant to subdivision (b) of Section 4024 of the Business and Professions Code.

(2) (A) The administrative director, after public hearings, shall adopt and review periodically an official medical fee schedule based on the resource-based relative value scale for physician services and nonphysician practitioner services, as defined by the administrative director, provided that all of the following apply:

(i) Employer liability for medical treatment, including issues of reasonableness, necessity, frequency, and duration, shall be determined in accordance with Section 4600.

(ii) The fee schedule is updated annually to reflect changes in procedure codes, relative weights, and the adjustment factor provided in subdivision (g).

(iii) The maximum reasonable fees paid shall not exceed 120 percent of estimated annualized aggregate fees prescribed in the Medicare payment system for physician services as it appeared on July 1, 2012, before application of the adjustment factor provided in subdivision (g). For purposes of calculating maximum reasonable fees, any service provided to injured workers that is not covered under the federal Medicare program shall be included at its rate of payment established by the administrative director pursuant to subdivision (d).

(iv) There shall be a four-year transition between the estimated aggregate maximum allowable amount under the official medical fee schedule for physician services prior to January 1, 2014, and the maximum allowable amount based on the resource-based relative value scale at 120 percent of the Medicare conversion factors as adjusted pursuant to this section.

(B) The official medical fee schedule shall include payment ground rules that differ from Medicare payment ground rules, including, as appropriate, payment of consultation codes and payment evaluation and management services provided during a global period of surgery.

(C) Commencing January 1, 2014, and continuing until the time the administrative director has adopted an official medical fee schedule in accordance with the resource-based relative value scale, the maximum reasonable fees for physician services and nonphysician practitioner services, including, but not limited to, physician assistant, nurse practitioner, and physical therapist services, shall be in accordance with the fee-related structure and rules of the Medicare payment system for physician services and nonphysician practitioner services, except that an average statewide geographic adjustment factor of 1.078 shall apply in lieu of Medicare's locality-specific geographic adjustment factors, and shall incorporate the following conversion factors:

(i) For dates of service in 2014, forty-nine dollars and five thousand three hundred thirteen ten thousandths cents ($49.5313) for surgery, fifty-six dollars and two thousand three hundred twenty-nine ten thousandths cents ($56.2329) for radiology, thirty dollars and six hundred forty-seven ten thousandths cents ($30.0647) for anesthesia, and thirty-seven dollars and one thousand seven hundred twelve ten thousandths cents ($37.1712) for all other before application of the adjustment factor provided in subdivision (g).

(ii) For dates of service in 2015, forty-six dollars and six thousand three hundred fifty-nine ten thousandths cents ($46.6359) for surgery, fifty-one dollars and one thousand thirty-six ten thousandths cents ($51.1036) for radiology, twenty-eight dollars and six thousand sixty-seven ten thousandths cents ($28.6067) for anesthesia, and thirty-eight dollars and three thousand nine hundred fifty-eight ten thousandths cents ($38.3958) for all other before application of the adjustment factor provided in subdivision (g).

(iii) For dates of service in 2016, forty-three dollars and seven thousand four hundred five ten thousandths cents ($43.7405) for surgery, forty-five dollars and nine thousand seven hundred forty-four ten thousandths cents ($45.9744) for radiology, twenty-seven dollars and one thousand four hundred eighty-seven thousandths cents ($27.1487) for anesthesia, and thirty-nine dollars and six thousand two hundred five ten thousandths cents ($39.6205) for all other before application of the adjustment factor provided in subdivision (g).

(iv) For dates of service on or after January 1, 2017, 120 percent of the 2012 Medicare conversion factor as updated pursuant to subdivision (g).

(b) In order to comply with the standards specified in subdivision (f), the administrative director may adopt different conversion factors, diagnostic-related group weights, and other factors affecting payment amounts from those used in the Medicare payment system, provided estimated aggregate fees do not exceed 120 percent of the estimated aggregate fees paid for the same class of services in the relevant Medicare payment system.

(c) (1) Notwithstanding subdivisions (a) and (d), the maximum facility fee for services performed in a hospital outpatient department, shall not exceed 120 percent of the fee paid by Medicare for the same services performed in a hospital outpatient department, and the maximum facility fee for services performed in an ambulatory surgical center shall not exceed 80 percent of the fee paid by Medicare for the same services performed in a hospital outpatient department.

(2) The department shall study the feasibility of establishing a facility fee for services that are performed in an ambulatory surgical center and are not subject to a fee paid by Medicare for services performed in an outpatient department, set at 85 percent of the diagnostic-related group (DRG) fee paid by Medicare for the same services performed in a hospital inpatient department. The department shall report the finding to the Senate Labor Committee and Assembly Insurance Committee no later than July 1, 2013.

(d) If the administrative director determines that a medical treatment, facility use, product, or service is not covered by a Medicare payment system, the administrative director shall establish maximum fees for that item, provided that the maximum fee paid shall not exceed 120 percent of the fees paid by Medicare for services that require comparable resources. If the administrative director determines that a pharmacy service or drug is not covered by a Medi-Cal payment system, the administrative director shall establish maximum fees for that item. However, the maximum fee paid shall not exceed 100 percent of the fees paid by Medi-Cal for pharmacy services or drugs that require comparable resources.

(e) (1) Prior to the adoption by the administrative director of a medical fee schedule pursuant to this section, for any treatment, facility use, product, or service not covered by a Medicare payment system, including acupuncture services, the maximum reasonable fee paid shall not exceed the fee specified in the official medical fee schedule in effect on December 31, 2003, except as otherwise provided in this subdivision.

(2) Any compounded drug product shall be billed by the compounding pharmacy or dispensing physician at the ingredient level, with each ingredient identified using the applicable National Drug Code (NDC) of the ingredient and the corresponding quantity, and in accordance with regulations adopted by the California State Board of Pharmacy. Ingredients with no NDC shall not be separately reimbursable. The ingredient-level reimbursement shall be equal to 100 percent of the reimbursement allowed by the Medi-Cal payment system and payment shall be based on the sum of the allowable fee for each ingredient plus a dispensing fee equal to the dispensing fee allowed by the Medi-Cal payment systems. If the compounded drug product is dispensed by a physician, the maximum reimbursement shall not exceed 300 percent of documented paid costs, but in no case more than twenty dollars ($20) above documented paid costs.

(3) For a dangerous drug dispensed by a physician that is a finished drug product approved by the federal Food and Drug Administration, the maximum reimbursement shall be according to the official medical fee schedule adopted by the administrative director.

(4) For a dangerous device dispensed by a physician, the reimbursement to the physician shall not exceed either of the following:

(A) The amount allowed for the device pursuant to the official medical fee schedule adopted by the administrative director.

(B) One hundred twenty percent of the documented paid cost, but not less than 100 percent of the documented paid cost plus the minimum dispensing fee allowed for dispensing prescription drugs pursuant to the official medical fee schedule adopted by the administrative director, and not more than 100 percent of the documented paid cost plus two hundred fifty dollars ($250).

(5) For any pharmacy goods dispensed by a physician not subject to paragraph (2), (3), or (4), the maximum reimbursement to a physician for pharmacy goods dispensed by the physician shall not exceed any of the following:

(A) The amount allowed for the pharmacy goods pursuant to the official medical fee schedule adopted by the administrative director or pursuant to paragraph (2), as applicable.

(B) One hundred twenty percent of the documented paid cost to the physician.

(C) One hundred percent of the documented paid cost to the physician plus two hundred fifty dollars ($250).

(6) For the purposes of this subdivision, the following definitions apply:

(A) "Administer" or "administered" has the meaning defined by Section 4016 of the Business and Professions Code.

(B) "Compounded drug product" means any drug product subject to Article 4.5 (commencing with Section 1735) of Division 17 of Title 16 of the California Code of Regulations or other regulation adopted by the State Board of Pharmacy to govern the practice of compounding.

(C) "Dispensed" means furnished to or for a patient as contemplated by Section 4024 of the Business and Professions Code and does not include "administered."

(D) "Dangerous drug" and "dangerous device" have the meanings defined by Section 4022 of the Business and Professions Code.

(E) "Documented paid cost" means the unit price paid for the specific product or for each component used in the product as documented by invoices, proof of payment, and inventory records as applicable, or as documented in accordance with regulations that may be adopted by the administrative director, net of rebates, discounts, and any other immediate or anticipated cost adjustments.

(F) "Pharmacy goods" has the same meaning as set forth in Section 139.3.

(7) To the extent that any provision of paragraphs (2) to (6), inclusive, is inconsistent with any provision of the official medical fee schedule adopted by the administrative director on or after January

Appendix

1, 2012, the provision adopted by the administrative director shall govern.

(8) Notwithstanding paragraph (7), the provisions of this subdivision concerning physician-dispensed pharmacy goods shall not be superseded by any provision of the official medical fee schedule adopted by the administrative director unless the relevant official medical fee schedule provision is expressly applicable to physician-dispensed pharmacy goods.

(f) Within the limits provided by this section, the rates or fees established shall be adequate to ensure a reasonable standard of services and care for injured employees.

(g) (1) (A) Notwithstanding any other law, the official medical fee schedule shall be adjusted to conform to any relevant changes in the Medicare and Medi-Cal payment systems no later than 60 days after the effective date of those changes, subject to the following provisions:

(i) The annual inflation adjustment for facility fees for inpatient hospital services provided by acute care hospitals and for hospital outpatient services shall be determined solely by the estimated increase in the hospital market basket for the 12 months beginning October 1 of the preceding calendar year.

(ii) The annual update in the operating standardized amount and capital standard rate for inpatient hospital services provided by hospitals excluded from the Medicare prospective payment system for acute care hospitals and the conversion factor for hospital outpatient services shall be determined solely by the estimated increase in the hospital market basket for excluded hospitals for the 12 months beginning October 1 of the preceding calendar year.

(iii) The annual adjustment factor for physician services shall be based on the product of one plus the percentage change in the Medicare Economic Index and any relative value scale adjustment factor.

(B) The update factors contained in clauses (i) and (ii) of subparagraph (A) shall be applied beginning with the first update in the Medicare fee schedule payment amounts after December 31, 2003, and the adjustment factor in clause (iii) of subparagraph (A) shall be applied beginning with the first update in the Medicare fee schedule payment amounts after December 31, 2012.

(C) The maximum reasonable fees paid for pharmacy services and drugs shall not include any reductions in the relevant Medi-Cal payment system implemented pursuant to Section 14105.192 of the Welfare and Institutions Code.

(2) The administrative director shall determine the effective date of the changes, and shall issue an order, exempt from Sections 5307.3 and 5307.4 and the rulemaking provisions of the Administrative Procedure Act (Chapter 3.5 (commencing with Section 11340) of Part 1 of Division 3 of Title 2 of the Government Code), informing the public of the changes and their effective date. All orders issued pursuant to

this paragraph shall be published on the Internet Web site of the Division of Workers' Compensation.

(3) For the purposes of this subdivision, the following definitions apply:

(A) "Medicare Economic Index" means the input price index used by the federal Centers for Medicare and Medicaid Services to measure changes in the costs of a providing physician and other services paid under the resource-based relative value scale.

(B) "Hospital market basket" means the input price index used by the federal Centers for Medicare and Medicaid Services to measure changes in the costs of providing inpatient hospital services provided by acute care hospitals that are included in the Medicare prospective payment system.

(C) "Hospital market basket for excluded hospitals" means the input price index used by the federal Centers for Medicare and Medicaid Services to measure changes in the costs of providing inpatient services by hospitals that are excluded from the Medicare prospective payment system.

(D) "Relative value scale adjustment factor" means the annual factor applied by the federal Centers for Medicare and Medicaid Services to the Medicare conversion factor to make changes in relative value units for the physician fee schedule budget neutral.

(h) This section does not prohibit an employer or insurer from contracting with a medical provider for reimbursement rates different from those prescribed in the official medical fee schedule.

(i) Except as provided in Section 4626, the official medical fee schedule shall not apply to medical-legal expenses, as that term is defined by Section 4620.

(j) The following Medicare payment system components shall not become part of the official medical fee schedule until January 1, 2005:

(1) Inpatient skilled nursing facility care.

(2) Home health agency services.

(3) Inpatient services furnished by hospitals that are exempt from the prospective payment system for general acute care hospitals.

(4) Outpatient renal dialysis services.

(k) Except as revised by the administrative director, the official medical fee schedule rates for physician services in effect on December 31, 2012, shall remain in effectuntil January 1, 2014.

(*l*) Notwithstanding subdivision (a), any explicit reductions in the Medi-Cal fee schedule for pharmacy services and drugs to meet the budgetary targets provided in Section 14105.192 of the Welfare and Institutions Code shall not be reflected in the official medical fee schedule.

(m) On or before July 1, 2013, the administrative director shall adopt a regulation specifying an additional reimbursement for MS-DRGs Medicare Severity Diagnostic Related Groups (MS-DRGs) 028,

029, 030, 453, 454, 455, and 456 to ensure that the aggregate reimbursement is sufficient to cover costs, including the implantable medical device, hardware, and instrumentation. This regulation shall be repealed as of January 1, 2014, unless extended by the administrative director.

Added Stats 2003 ch 639 § 35 (SB 228). Amended Stats 2006 ch 538 § 491 (SB 1852), effective January 1, 2007; Stats 2007 ch 697 § 1 (AB 1269), effective January 1, 2008; Stats 2011 ch 545 § 4 (AB 378), effective January 1, 2012; Stats 2012 ch 363 § 74 (SB 863), effective January 1, 2013.

§ 5307.7. Vocational expert fees

(a) On or before January 1, 2013, the administrative director shall adopt, after public hearings, a fee schedule that shall establish reasonable fees paid for services provided by vocational experts, including, but not limited to, vocational evaluations and expert testimony determined to be reasonable, actual, and necessary by the appeals board.

(b) A vocational expert shall not be paid, and the appeals board shall not allow, vocational expert fees in excess of those that are reasonable, actual, and necessary, or that are not consistent with the fee schedule adopted by the administrative director.

Added Stats 2011 ch 555 § 1 (AB 1168), effective January 1, 2012. Amended Stats 2012 ch 363 § 75 (SB 863), effective January 1, 2013.

§ 5307.8. Schedule of fees for services not covered by Medicare or by Section 5307.1

Notwithstanding Section 5307.1, on or before July 1, 2013, the administrative director shall adopt, after public hearings, a schedule for payment of home health care services provided in accordance with Section 4600 that are not covered by a Medicare fee schedule and are not otherwise covered by the official medical fee schedule adopted pursuant to Section 5307.1. The schedule shall set forth fees and requirements for service providers, and shall be based on the maximum service hours and fees as set forth in regulations adopted pursuant to Article 7 (commencing with Section 12300) of Chapter 3 of Part 3 of Division 9 of the Welfare and Institutions Code. No fees shall be provided for any services, including any services provided by a member of the employee's household, to the extent the services had been regularly performed in the same manner and to the same degree prior to the date of injury. If appropriate, an attorney's fee for recovery of home health care fees under this section may be awarded in accordance with Section 4906 and any applicable rules or regulations.

Added Stats 2012 ch 363 § 76 (SB 863), effective January 1, 2013.

§ 5307.9. Schedule of fees for copy and related services

On or before December 31, 2013, the administrative director, in consultation with the Commission on Health and Safety and Workers' Compensation, shall adopt, after public hearings, a schedule of reasonable maximum fees payable for copy and related services, including, but not limited to, records or documents that have been reproduced or recorded in paper, electronic, film, digital, or other format. The schedule shall specify the services allowed and shall require specificity in billing for these services, and shall not allow for payment for services provided within 30 days of a request by an injured worker or his or her authorized representative to an employer, claims administrator, or workers' compensation insurer for copies of records in the employer's, claims administrator's, or workers' compensation insurer's possession that are relevant to the employee's claim. The schedule shall be applicable regardless of whether payments of copy service costs are claimed under the authority of Section 4600, 4620, or 5811, or any other authority except a contract between the employer and the copy service provider.

Added Stats 2012 ch 363 § 77 (SB 863), effective January 1, 2013.

Chapter 2

Limitations of Proceedings

§ 5402. Employer's knowledge of injury equivalent to service; When presumed compensable; Authorization for treatment; Liability limit

(a) Knowledge of an injury, obtained from any source, on the part of an employer, the employer's managing agent, superintendent, foreman, or other person in authority, or knowledge of the assertion of a claim of injury sufficient to afford opportunity to the employer to make an investigation into the facts, is equivalent to service under Section 5400.

(b) (1) If liability is not rejected within 90 days after the date the claim form is filed under Section 5401, the injury shall be presumed compensable under this division. The presumption of this subdivision is rebuttable only by evidence discovered subsequent to the 90-day period.

(2) Notwithstanding paragraph (1), for injuries or illnesses defined in Sections 3212 to 3212.85, inclusive, and Sections 3212.9 to 3213.2, inclusive, if the liability is not rejected within 75 days after the date the claim form is filed pursuant to Section 5401, the injury shall be presumed compensable under this division. The presumption of this

subdivision is rebuttable only by evidence discovered subsequent to the 75-day period.

(c) Within one working day after an employee files a claim form under Section 5401, the employer shall authorize the provision of all treatment, consistent with Section 5307.27, for the alleged injury and shall continue to provide the treatment until the date that liability for the claim is accepted or rejected. Until the date the claim is accepted or rejected, liability for medical treatment shall be limited to ten thousand dollars ($10,000).

(d) Treatment provided under subdivision (c) does not give rise to a presumption of liability on the part of the employer.

(e) Upon appropriation by the Legislature, the Division of Workers' Compensation shall identify and amend its existing data collection processes to include collection of the date on which the claimant is notified of acceptance, denial, or conditional denial of liability for a claim, consistent with this section.

Enacted Stats 1937 ch 90. Amended Stats 1975 ch 1099 § 2. Amended Stats 1989 ch 892 § 47; Stats 1990 ch 1550 § 57 (AB 2910); Stats 2000 ch 883 § 2 (AB 2043). Amended Stats 2004 ch 34 § 40 (SB 899), effective April 19, 2004; Stats 2012 ch 363 § 79 (SB 863), effective January 1, 2013; Stats 2022 ch 835 § 3 (SB 1127), effective January 1, 2022.

Chapter 3

Applications and Answers

§ 5502. Time for hearing; Priority calendar; Mandatory settlement conference

(a) Except as provided in subdivisions (b) and (d), the hearing shall be held not less than 10 days, and not more than 60 days, after the date a declaration of readiness to proceed, on a form prescribed by the appeals board, is filed. If a claim form has been filed for an injury occurring on or after January 1, 1990, and before January 1, 1994, an application for adjudication shall accompany the declaration of readiness to proceed.

(b) The administrative director shall establish a priority calendar for issues requiring an expedited hearing and decision. A hearing shall be held and a determination as to the rights of the parties shall be made and filed within 30 days after the declaration of readiness to proceed is filed if the issues in dispute are any of the following, provided that if an expedited hearing is requested, no other issue may be heard until the medical provider network dispute is resolved:

(1) The employee's entitlement to medical treatment pursuant to Section 4600, except for treatment issues determined pursuant to Sections 4610 and 4610.5.

(2) Whether the injured employee is required to obtain treatment within a medical provider network.

(3) A medical treatment appointment or medical-legal examination.

(4) The employee's entitlement to, or the amount of, temporary disability indemnity payments.

(5) The employee's entitlement to compensation from one or more responsible employers when two or more employers dispute liability as among themselves.

(6) Any other issues requiring an expedited hearing and determination as prescribed in rules and regulations of the administrative director.

(c) The administrative director shall establish a priority conference calendar for cases in which the employee is represented by an attorney or is or was employed by an illegally uninsured employer and the issues in dispute are employment or injury arising out of employment or in the course of employment. The conference shall be conducted by a workers' compensation administrative law judge within 30 days after the declaration of readiness to proceed. If the dispute cannot be resolved at the conference, a trial shall be set as expeditiously as possible, unless good cause is shown why discovery is not complete, in which case status conferences shall be held at regular intervals. The case shall be set for trial when discovery is complete, or when the workers' compensation administrative law judge determines that the parties have had sufficient time in which to complete reasonable discovery. A determination as to the rights of the parties shall be made and filed within 30 days after the trial.

(d) (1) In all cases, a mandatory settlement conference, except a lien conference or a mandatory settlement lien conference, shall be conducted not less than 10 days, and not more than 30 days, after the filing of a declaration of readiness to proceed. If the dispute is not resolved, the regular hearing, except a lien trial, shall be held within 75 days after the declaration of readiness to proceed is filed.

(2) The settlement conference shall be conducted by a workers' compensation administrative law judge or by a referee who is eligible to be a workers' compensation administrative law judge or eligible to be an arbitrator under Section 5270.5. At the mandatory settlement conference, the referee or workers' compensation administrative law judge shall have the authority to resolve the dispute, including the authority to approve a compromise and release or issue a stipulated finding and award, and if the dispute cannot be resolved, to frame the issues and stipulations for trial. The appeals board shall adopt any regulations needed to implement this subdivision. The presiding workers' compensation administrative law judge shall supervise settlement conference referees in the performance of their judicial functions under this subdivision.

(3) If the claim is not resolved at the mandatory settlement conference, the parties shall file a pretrial conference statement noting the specific issues in dispute, each party's proposed permanent disability rating, and listing the exhibits, and disclosing witnesses. Discovery shall close on the date of the mandatory settlement conference. Evidence not disclosed or obtained thereafter shall not be admissible unless the proponent of the evidence can demonstrate that it was not available or could not have been discovered by the exercise of due diligence prior to the settlement conference.

(e) In cases involving the Director of Industrial Relations in his or her capacity as administrator of the Uninsured Employers Fund, this section shall not apply unless proof of service, as specified in paragraph (1) of subdivision (d) of Section 3716, has been filed with the appeals board and provided to the Director of Industrial Relations, valid jurisdiction has been established over the employer, and the fund has been joined.

(f) Except as provided in subdivision (a), this section shall apply irrespective of the date of injury.

Added Stats 1989 ch 892 § 52. Amended Stats 1990 ch 1550 § 61 (AB 2910); Stats 1992 ch 1226 § 3 (AB 3758); Stats 1993 ch 121 § 64 (AB 110), effective July 16, 1993; Stats 1994 ch 1118 § 10 (SB 1768); Stats 2002 ch 6 § 80 (AB 749), ch 866 § 14 (AB 486); Stats 2011 ch 559 § 16 (AB 1426), effective October 7, 2011; Stats 2012 ch 363 § 80 (SB 863) (ch 363 prevails) effective January 1, 2013, ch 728 § 122 (SB71), effective January 1, 2013; Stats 2013 ch 76 § 144 (AB 383), effective January 1, 2014; Stats 2014 ch 71 § 122 (SB 1304), effective January 1, 2015, ch 156 § 1 (AB 1746), effective January 1, 2015 (ch 156 prevails).

Chapter 5

Hearings

§ 5703. Evidence in addition to sworn testimony

The appeals board may receive as evidence either at or subsequent to a hearing, and use as proof of any fact in dispute, the following matters, in addition to sworn testimony presented in open hearing:

(a) Reports of attending or examining physicians.

(1) Statements concerning any bill for services are admissible only if made under penalty of perjury that they are true and correct to the best knowledge of the physician.

(2) In addition, reports are admissible under this subdivision only if the physician has further stated in the body of the report that there has not been a violation of Section 139.3 and that the contents of the report are true and correct to the best knowledge of the physician. The statement shall be made under penalty of perjury.

(b) Reports of special investigators appointed by the appeals board or a workers' compensation judge to investigate and report upon any scientific or medical question.

(c) Reports of employers, containing copies of timesheets, book accounts, reports, and other records properly authenticated.

(d) Properly authenticated copies of hospital records of the case of the injured employee.

(e) All publications of the Division of Workers' Compensation.

(f) All official publications of the State of California and United States governments.

(g) Excerpts from expert testimony received by the appeals board upon similar issues of scientific fact in other cases and the prior decisions of the appeals board upon similar issues.

(h) Relevant portions of medical treatment protocols published by medical specialty societies. To be admissible, the party offering such a protocol or portion of a protocol shall concurrently enter into evidence information regarding how the protocol was developed, and to what extent the protocol is evidence-based, peer-reviewed, and nationally recognized. If a party offers into evidence a portion of a treatment protocol, any other party may offer into evidence additional portions of the protocol. The party offering a protocol, or portion thereof, into evidence shall either make a printed copy of the full protocol available for review and copying, or shall provide an Internet address at which the entire protocol may be accessed without charge.

(i) The medical treatment utilization schedule in effect pursuant to Section 5307.27 or the guidelines in effect pursuant to Section 4604.5.

(j) Reports of vocational experts. If vocational expert evidence is otherwise admissible, the evidence shall be produced in the form of written reports. Direct examination of a vocational witness shall not be received at trial except upon a showing of good cause. A continuance may be granted for rebuttal testimony if a report that was not served sufficiently in advance of the close of discovery to permit rebuttal is admitted into evidence.

(1) Statements concerning any bill for services are admissible only if they comply with the requirements applicable to statements concerning bills for services pursuant to subdivision (a).

(2) Reports are admissible under this subdivision only if the vocational expert has further stated in the body of the report that the contents of the report are true and correct to the best knowledge of the vocational expert. The statement shall be made in compliance with the requirements applicable to medical reports pursuant to subdivision (a).

Enacted Stats 1937 ch 90. Amended Stats 1965 ch 1513 § 152, operative January 15, 1966; Stats 1985 ch 326 § 24; Stats 1993 ch 120 § 7 (AB 1300), effective July 16, 1993; Stats 1994 ch 146 § 159 (AB 3601). Amended Stats 2003 ch 639 § 45 (SB 228); Stats

2004 ch 34 § 41 (SB 899), effective April 19, 2004; Stats 2012 ch 363 § 81 (SB 863), effective January 1, 2013.

§ 5710. Depositions; Expenses and fees

(a) The appeals board, a workers' compensation judge, or any party to the action or proceeding, may, in any investigation or hearing before the appeals board, cause the deposition of witnesses residing within or without the state to be taken in the manner prescribed by law for like depositions in civil actions in the superior courts of this state under Title 4 (commencing with Section 2016.010) of Part 4 of the Code of Civil Procedure. To that end the attendance of witnesses and the production of records may be required. Depositions may be taken outside the state before any officer authorized to administer oaths. The appeals board or a workers' compensation judge in any proceeding before the appeals board may cause evidence to be taken in other jurisdictions before the agency authorized to hear workers' compensation matters in those other jurisdictions.

(b) If the employer or insurance carrier requests a deposition to be taken of an injured employee, or any person claiming benefits as a dependent of an injured employee, the deponent is entitled to receive in addition to all other benefits:

(1) All reasonable expenses of transportation, meals, and lodging incident to the deposition.

(2) Reimbursement for any loss of wages incurred during attendance at the deposition.

(3) One copy of the transcript of the deposition, without cost.

(4) A reasonable allowance for attorney's fees for the deponent, if represented by an attorney licensed by the State Bar of this state. The fee shall be discretionary with, and, if allowed, shall be set by, the appeals board, but shall be paid by the employer or his or her insurer. The administrative director shall, on or before July 1, 2018, determine the range of reasonable fees to be paid.

(5) If interpretation services are required because the injured employee or deponent does not proficiently speak or understand the English language, upon a request from either, the employer shall pay for the services of a language interpreter certified or deemed certified pursuant to Article 8 (commencing with Section 11435.05) of Chapter 4.5 of Part 1 of Division 3 of Title 2 of, or Section 68566 of, the Government Code. The fee to be paid by the employer shall be in accordance with the fee schedule adopted by the administrative director and shall include any other deposition-related events as permitted by the administrative director.

Enacted Stats 1937 ch 90. Amended Stats 1945 ch 168 § 1, ch 1431 § 76; Stats 1965 ch 1513 § 157, operative January 15, 1966; Stats 1971 ch 1416 § 1; Stats 1972 ch 1316 § 1; Stats 1979 ch 603 § 1; Stats 1985 ch 326 § 26; Stats 1991 ch 116 § 32 (SB 1218); Stats 1993 ch 121 § 65 (AB 110), effective July 16, 1993; Stats 1995 ch 938 § 76

(SB 523), operative July 1, 1997. Amended Stats 1998 ch 931 § 348 (SB 2139), effective September 28, 1998; Stats 2004 ch 182 § 47 (AB 3081), operative July 1, 2005; Stats 2012 ch 363 § 82 (SB 863), effective January 1, 2013; Stats 2016 ch 868 § 11 (SB 1160), effective January 1, 2017.

Chapter 6

Findings and Awards

§ 5811. Fees and costs

(a) No fees shall be charged by the clerk of any court for the performance of any official service required by this division, except for the docketing of awards as judgments and for certified copies of transcripts thereof. In all proceedings under this division before the appeals board, costs as between the parties may be allowed by the appeals board.

(b) (1) It shall be the responsibility of any party producing a witness requiring an interpreter to arrange for the presence of a qualified interpreter.

(2) A qualified interpreter is a language interpreter who is certified, or deemed certified, pursuant to Article 8 (commencing with Section 11435.05) of Chapter 4.5 of Part 1 of Division 3 of Title 2 of, or Section 68566 of, the Government Code. The duty of an interpreter is to accurately and impartially translate oral communications and transliterate written materials, and not to act as an agent or advocate. An interpreter shall not disclose to any person who is not an immediate participant in the communications the content of the conversations or documents that the interpreter has interpreted or transliterated unless the disclosure is compelled by court order. An attempt by any party or attorney to obtain disclosure is a bad faith tactic that is subject to Section 5813.

Interpreter fees that are reasonably, actually, and necessarily incurred shall be paid by the employer under this section, provided they are in accordance with the fee schedule adopted by the administrative director.

A qualified interpreter may render services during the following:

(A) A deposition.

(B) An appeals board hearing.

(C) A medical treatment appointment or medical-legal examination.

(D) During those settings which the administrative director determines are reasonably necessary to ascertain the validity or extent of injury to an employee who does not proficiently speak or understand the English language.

(c) The administrative director shall promulgate regulations establishing criteria to verify the identity and credentials of individuals who provide interpreter services in all necessary settings and proceedings within the workers' compensation system. Those regulations shall be adopted no later than January 1, 2018.

Enacted Stats 1937 ch 90. Amended Stats 1945 ch 802 § 1; Stats 1965 ch 1513 § 168, operative January 15, 1966; Stats 1993 ch 121 § 65.5 (AB 110), effective July 16, 1993; Stats 1995 ch 938 § 77 (SB 523), operative July 1, 1997; Stats 2012 ch 363 § 83 (SB 863), effective January 1, 2013; Stats 2016 ch 868 § 12 (SB 1160), effective January 1, 2017.

DIVISION 5

SAFETY IN EMPLOYMENT

PART 1

OCCUPATIONAL SAFETY AND HEALTH

Chapter 6

Permit Requirements

§ 6501.5. Registration of persons doing asbestos–related work

Effective January 1, 1987, any employer or contractor who engages in asbestos–related work, as defined in Section 6501.8, and which involves 100 square feet or more of surface area of asbestos–containing material, shall register with the division.

The division may grant registration based on a determination that the employer has demonstrated evidence that the conditions, practices, means, methods, operations, or processes used, or proposed to be used, will provide a safe and healthful place of employment. This section is not intended to supersede existing laws and regulations under Title 8, California Administrative Code, Section 5208.

An application for registration shall contain such information and attachments, given under penalty of perjury, as the division may deem necessary to evaluate the safety and health of the proposed employment or place of employment. It shall include, but not be limited to, all of the following:

(a) Every employer shall meet each of the following criteria:

(1) If the employer is a contractor, the contractor shall be certified pursuant to Section 7058.5 of the Business and Professions Code.

(2) Provide health insurance coverage to cover the entire cost of medical examinations and monitoring required by law and be insured for workers' compensation, or provide a five hundred dollar ($500) trust account for each employee engaged in asbestos–related work.

The health insurance coverage may be provided through a union, association, or employer.

(3) Train and certify all employees in accordance with all training required by law and Title 8 of the California Administrative Code.

(4) Be proficient and have the necessary equipment to safely do asbestos–related work.

(b) Provide written notice to the division of each separate job or phase of work, where the work process used is different or the work is performed at noncontiguous locations, noting all of the following:

(1) The address of the job.

(2) The exact physical location of the job at that address.

(3) The start and projected completion date.

(4) The name of a certified supervisor with sufficient experience and authority who shall be responsible for the asbestos–related work at that job.

(5) The name of a qualified person, who shall be responsible for scheduling any air sampling, laboratory calibration of air sampling equipment, evaluation of sampling results, and conducting respirator fit testing and evaluating the results of those tests.

(6) The type of work to be performed, the work practices that will be utilized, and the potential for exposure.

Should any change be necessary, the employer or contractor shall so inform the division at or before the time of the change. Any oral notification shall be confirmed in writing.

(c) Post the location where any asbestos–related work occurs so as to be readable at 20 feet stating, "Danger—Asbestos. Cancer and Lung Hazard. Keep Out."

(d) A copy of the registration shall be provided before the start of the job to the prime contractor or other employers on the site and shall be posted on the jobsite beside the Cal–OSHA poster.

(e) The division shall obtain the services of three industrial hygienists and one clerical employee to implement and to enforce the requirements of this section unless the director makes a finding that these services are not necessary or that the services are not obtainable due to a lack of qualified hygienists applying for available positions. Funding may, at the director's discretion, be appropriated from the Asbestos Abatement Fund.

(f) Not later than January 1, 1987, the Division of Occupational Safety and Health shall propose to the Occupational Safety and Health Standards Board for review and adoption a regulation concerning asbestos–related work, as defined in Section 6501.8, which involves 100 square feet or more of surface area of asbestos–containing material. The regulation shall protect most effectively the health and safety of employees and shall include specific requirements for certification of employees, supervisors with sufficient experience and authority to be responsible for asbestos–related work, and

Appendix

a qualified person who shall be responsible for scheduling any air sampling, for arranging for calibration of the air sampling equipment and for analysis of the air samples by a NIOSH approved method, for conducting respirator fit testing, and for evaluating the results of the air sampling.

The Division of Occupational Safety and Health shall also propose a regulation to the Occupational Safety and Health Standards Board for review and adoption specifying sampling methodology for use in taking air samples.

Added Stats 1985 ch 1587 § 9, effective October 2, 1985. Amended Stats 1986 ch 1451 § 10, effective September 30, 1986.

§ 6501.7. "Asbestos"

"Asbestos" means fibrous forms of various hydrated minerals, including chrysotile (fibrous serpentine), crocidolite (fibrous riebecktite), amosite (fibrous cummingtonite—grunerite), fibrous tremolite, fibrous actinolite, and fibrous anthophyllite.

Added Stats 1985 ch 1587 § 11, effective October 2, 1985.

§ 6501.8. "Asbestos–related work;" "Asbestos containing construction material"

(a) For purposes of this chapter, "asbestos–related work" means any activity which by disturbing asbestos–containing construction materials may release asbestos fibers into the air and which is not related to its manufacture, the mining or excavation of asbestos–bearing ore or materials, or the installation or repair of automotive materials containing asbestos.

(b) For purposes of this chapter, "asbestos containing construction material" means any manufactured construction material that contains more than one–tenth of 1 percent asbestos by weight.

(c) For purposes of this chapter, "asbestos–related work" does not include the installation, repair, maintenance, or nondestructive removal of asbestos cement pipe used outside of buildings, if the installation, repair, maintenance, or nondestructive removal of asbestos cement pipe does not result in asbestos exposures to employees in excess of the action level determined in accordance with Sections 1529 and 5208 of Title 8 of the California Code of Regulations, and if the employees and supervisors involved in the operation have received training through a task–specific training program, approved pursuant to Section 9021.9, with written certification of completion of that training by the training entity responsible for the training.

Added Stats 1985 ch 1587 § 12, effective October 2, 1985. Amended Stats 1986 ch 1451 § 11, effective September 30, 1986; Stats 1993 ch 1075 § 1 (SB 877).

§ 6501.9. Duty to determine presence of asbestos before commencing work

The owner of a commercial or industrial building or structure, employer, or contractor who engages in, or contracts for, asbestos–related work shall make a good faith effort to determine if asbestos is present before the work is begun. The contractor or employer shall first inquire of the owner if asbestos is present in any building or structure built prior to 1978.

Added Stats 1985 ch 1587 § 12.5, effective October 2, 1985. Amended Stats 1986 ch 1451 § 12, effective September 30, 1986.

Appendix

PENAL CODE

PRELIMINARY PROVISIONS

§ 23. Proceeding against person holding license to engage in business or profession; Appearance of state agency

In any criminal proceeding against a person who has been issued a license to engage in a business or profession by a state agency pursuant to provisions of the Business and Professions Code or the Education Code, or the Chiropractic Initiative Act, the state agency which issued the license may voluntarily appear to furnish pertinent information, make recommendations regarding specific conditions of probation, or provide any other assistance necessary to promote the interests of justice and protect the interests of the public, or may be ordered by the court to do so, if the crime charged is substantially related to the qualifications, functions, or duties of a licensee.

For purposes of this section, the term "license" shall include a permit or a certificate issued by a state agency.

For purposes of this section, the term "state agency" shall include any state board, commission, bureau, or division created pursuant to the provisions of the Business and Professions Code, the Education Code, or the Chiropractic Initiative Act to license and regulate individuals who engage in certain businesses and professions.

Added Stats 1979 ch 1013 § 34. Amended Stats 1989 ch 388 § 6; Stats 2002 ch 545 § 3 (SB 1852).

PART 1

CRIMES AND PUNISHMENTS

TITLE 10
Crimes Against the Public Health and Safety

§ 374.3. Illegal dumping on roads, right-of-way, or private or public property; Use of own property; Mandatory fine; Removal of waste; Punishment for dumping in commercial quantities

(a) It is unlawful to dump or cause to be dumped waste matter in or upon a public or private highway or road, including any portion of the right-of-way thereof, or in or upon private property into or upon which the public is admitted by easement or license, or upon private property without the consent of the owner, or in or upon a public park or other public property other than property designated or set aside for that purpose by the governing board or body having charge of that property.

(b) It is unlawful to place, deposit, or dump, or cause to be placed, deposited, or dumped, rocks, concrete, asphalt, or dirt in or upon a private highway or road, including any portion of the right-of-way of the private highway or road, or private property, without the consent of the owner or a contractor under contract with the owner for the materials, or in or upon a public park or other public property, without the consent of the state or local agency having jurisdiction over the highway, road, or property.

(c) A person violating this section is guilty of an infraction. Each day that waste placed, deposited, or dumped in violation of subdivision (a) or (b) remains is a separate violation.

(d) This section does not restrict a private owner in the use of their own private property, unless the placing, depositing, or dumping of the waste matter on the property creates a public health and safety hazard, a public nuisance, or a fire hazard, as determined by a local health department, local fire department or district providing fire protection services, or the Department of Forestry and Fire Protection, in which case this section applies.

(e) A person convicted of a violation of this section shall be punished by a mandatory fine of not less than two hundred fifty dollars ($250) nor more than one thousand dollars ($1,000) upon a first conviction, by a mandatory fine of not less than five hundred dollars ($500) nor more than one thousand five hundred dollars ($1,500) upon a second conviction, and by a mandatory fine of not less than seven hundred fifty dollars ($750) nor more than three thousand dollars ($3,000) upon a third or subsequent conviction. If the court finds that the waste matter placed, deposited, or dumped was used tires, the fine prescribed in this subdivision shall be doubled.

(f) The court may require, in addition to any fine imposed upon a conviction, that a person convicted under this section remove, or pay the cost of removing, any waste matter which the convicted person dumped or caused to be dumped upon public or private property.

(g) The court may, in addition to the fine imposed upon a conviction, require that a person convicted of a violation of this section pick up waste matter at a time and place within the jurisdiction of the court for not less than 12 hours.

(h)(1) Except as otherwise provided in paragraph (2), a person who places, deposits, or dumps, or causes to be placed, deposited, or dumped, waste matter in violation of this section in commercial quantities shall be guilty of a misdemeanor punishable by imprisonment in a county jail for not more than six months and by a fine. The fine is mandatory and shall amount to not less than one thousand dollars ($1,000) nor more than three thousand dollars ($3,000) upon a first conviction, not less than three thousand dollars ($3,000) nor more than six thousand dollars ($6,000) upon a second conviction, and not less than six thousand dollars ($6,000) nor more than ten thousand dollars ($10,000) upon a third or subsequent conviction.

(2) If a person convicted under paragraph (1) is the owner or operator of the business involved in the illegal dumping, and that business employs more than 10 full-time employees, the fine shall amount to not less than one thousand dollars ($1,000) nor more than five thousand dollars ($5,000) upon a first conviction, not less than three thousand dollars ($3,000) nor more than ten thousand dollars ($10,000) upon a second conviction, and not less than six thousand dollars ($6,000) nor more than twenty thousand dollars ($20,000) upon a third or subsequent conviction.

(3) The court shall require, in addition to the fine imposed upon a conviction, that a person convicted under this subdivision remove, or pay the cost of removing, any waste matter which the convicted person dumped or caused to be dumped upon public or private property.

(4)(A) If a person convicted under this subdivision holds a license or permit to conduct business that is substantially related to the illegal dumping for which the person was convicted, the court shall notify the applicable licensing or permitting entity subject to the jurisdiction of the Department of Consumer Affairs as set forth in Section 101 of the Business and Professions Code, if any, of the conviction.

(B) The licensing or permitting entity shall record and post the offense on the public profile of the license or permitholder on the internet website of the entity.

(5) "Commercial quantities" means an amount of waste matter generated in the course of a trade, business, profession, or occupation, or an amount equal to or in excess of one cubic yard. This subdivision does not apply to the dumping of household waste at a person's own residence.

(i) For purposes of this section, "person" means an individual, trust, firm, partnership, joint stock company, joint venture, or corporation.

(j) When setting fines pursuant to this section, the court shall consider the defendant's ability to pay, including consideration of, without limitation, all of the following:

(1) The defendant's present financial position.

(2) The defendant's reasonably discernible future financial position, provided that the court shall not consider a period of more than one year from the date of the hearing for purposes of determining the reasonably discernible future financial position of the defendant.

(3) The likelihood that the defendant will be able to obtain employment within one year from the date of the hearing.

(4) Any other factor that may bear upon the defendant's financial capability to pay the fine.

Added Stats 1929 ch 889 § 1, as Pen C § 374b. Amended Stats 1931 ch 798 § 2; Stats 1933 ch 250 § 1; Stats 1939 ch 355 § 1; Stats 1941 ch 809 § 1; Stats 1959 ch 41 § 1; Stats 1970 ch 1548 § 1; Stats 1971 ch 1287 § 2; Stats 1973 ch 592 § 2; Stats 1980 ch 74 § 1; Stats 1983 ch 1092 § 272, effective September 27, 1983, operative January 1, 1984; Amended and renumbered by Stats 1987 ch 133 § 2; Amended Stats 1989 ch 974 § 3; Stats 1994 ch 737 § 1 (SB 1450); Stats 1998 ch 50 § 1 (AB 1799); Stats 2004 ch 137 § 1 (AB 1802); Stats 2006 ch 416 § 7 (AB 1992), effective January 1, 2007; Stats 2022 ch 784 § 1 (AB 2374), effective January 1, 2023.

§ 396. Overpricing of goods and services following state of emergency or major disaster; Penalty; Definitions

(a) The Legislature hereby finds that during a state of emergency or local emergency, including, but not limited to, an earthquake, flood, fire, riot, storm, drought, plant or animal infestation or disease, pandemic or epidemic disease outbreak, or other natural or manmade disaster, some merchants have taken unfair advantage of consumers by greatly increasing prices for essential consumer goods and services. While the pricing of consumer goods and services is generally best left to the marketplace under ordinary conditions, when a declared state of emergency or local emergency results in abnormal disruptions of the market, the public interest requires that excessive and unjustified increases in the prices of essential consumer goods and services be prohibited. It is the intent of the Legislature in enacting this act to protect citizens from excessive and unjustified increases in the prices charged during or shortly after a declared state of emergency or local emergency for goods and services that are vital and necessary for the health, safety, and welfare of consumers, whether those goods and services are offered or sold in person, in stores, or online. Further, it is the intent of the Legislature that this section be liberally construed so that its beneficial purposes may be served.

(b) Upon the proclamation of a state of emergency declared by the President of the United States or the Governor, or upon the declaration of a local emergency by an official, board, or other governing body vested with authority to make that declaration in any county, city, or city and county, and for a period of 30 days following that proclamation or declaration, it is unlawful for a person, contractor, business, or other entity to sell or offer to sell any consumer food items or goods, goods or services used for emergency cleanup, emergency supplies, medical supplies, home heating oil, building materials, housing, transportation, freight, and storage services, or gasoline or other motor fuels for a price of more than 10 percent greater than the price charged by that person for those goods or services immediately prior to the proclamation or declaration of emergency, or prior to a date set in the proclamation or declaration. However, a greater price increase is not unlawful if that person can prove that the increase in price was directly attributable to additional costs imposed on it by the supplier of the goods, or directly attributable to additional costs for labor or materials used to provide the services, during the state of emergency or local emergency, and the price is no more than 10 percent greater than the total of the cost to the seller plus the markup customarily applied by that seller for that good or service in the usual course of business immediately prior to the onset of the state of emergency or local emergency. If the person, contractor, business, or other entity did not charge a price for the goods or services immediately prior to the proclamation or declaration of emergency, it may not charge a price that is more than 50 percent greater than the cost thereof to the vendor as "cost" is defined in Section 17026 of the Business and Professions Code.

(c) Upon the proclamation of a state of emergency declared by the President of the United States or the Governor, or upon the declaration of a local emergency by an official, board, or other governing body vested with authority to make that declaration in any county, city, or city and county, and for a period of 180 days following that proclamation or declaration, it is unlawful for a contractor to sell or offer to sell any repair or reconstruction services or any services used in emergency cleanup for a price of more than 10 percent above the price charged by that person for those services immediately prior to the proclamation or declaration of emergency. However, a greater price increase is not unlawful if that person can prove that the increase in price was directly attributable to additional costs imposed on it by the supplier of the goods, or directly attributable to additional costs for labor or materials used to provide the services, during the state of emergency or local emergency, and the price represents no more than 10 percent greater than the total of the cost to the contractor plus the markup customarily applied by the contractor for that good or service in the usual course of business immediately prior to the onset of the state of emergency or local emergency.

(d) Upon the proclamation of a state of emergency declared by the President of the United States or the Governor, or upon the declaration of a local emergency by an official, board, or other governing body vested with authority to make that declaration in any county, city, or city and county, and for a period of 30 days following that proclamation or declaration, it is unlawful for an owner or operator of a hotel or motel to increase the hotel or motel's regular rates, as advertised immediately prior to the proclamation or declaration of emergency, by more than 10 percent. However, a greater price increase is not unlawful if the owner or operator can prove that the increase in price is directly attributable to additional costs imposed on it for goods or labor used in its business, to seasonal adjustments in rates that are regularly scheduled, or to previously contracted rates.

(e) Upon the proclamation of a state of emergency declared by the President of the United States or the Governor, or upon the declaration of a local emergency by an official, board, or other governing body vested with authority to make that declaration in any city, county, or city and county, and for a period of 30 days following that proclamation or declaration, or any period the proclamation or declaration is extended by the applicable authority, it is unlawful for any person, business, or other entity, to increase the rental price, as defined in paragraph (11) of subdivision (j), advertised, offered, or charged for housing, to an existing or prospective tenant, by more than 10 percent. However, a greater rental price increase is not unlawful if that person can prove that the increase is directly attributable to additional costs for repairs or additions beyond normal maintenance that were amortized over the rental term that caused the rent to be increased greater than 10 percent or that an increase was contractually agreed to by the tenant prior to the proclamation or declaration. It shall not be a defense to a prosecution under this subdivision that an increase in rental price was based on the length of the rental term, the inclusion of additional goods or services, except as provided in paragraph (11) of subdivision (j) with respect to furniture, or that the rent was offered by, or paid by, an insurance company, or other third party, on behalf of a tenant. This subdivision does not authorize a landlord to charge a price greater than the amount authorized by a local rent control ordinance.

(f) It is unlawful for a person, business, or other entity to evict any residential tenant of residential housing after the proclamation of a state of emergency declared by the President of the United States or the Governor, or upon the declaration of a local emergency by an official, board, or other governing body vested with authority to make that declaration in any city, county, or city and county, and for a period of 30 days following that proclamation or declaration, or any period that the proclamation or declaration is extended by the applicable authority and rent or offer to rent to another person at a rental price greater than the evicted tenant could be charged under this section. It shall not be a violation of this subdivision for a person, business, or other entity to continue an eviction process that was lawfully begun prior to the proclamation or declaration of emergency.

(g) The prohibitions of this section may be extended for additional periods, as needed, by a local legislative body, local official, the Governor, or the Legislature, if deemed necessary to protect the lives, property, or welfare of the citizens. Each extension by a local legislative body or local official shall not exceed 30 days. An extension may also authorize specified price increases that exceed the amount that would be permissible under this section during the initial 30 or 180 days after a proclamation or declaration of emergency.

(h) A violation of this section is a misdemeanor punishable by imprisonment in a county jail for a period not exceeding one year, by a fine of not more than ten thousand dollars ($10,000), or by both that fine and imprisonment.

(i) A violation of this section shall constitute an unlawful business practice and an act of unfair competition within the meaning of Section 17200 of the Business and Professions Code. The remedies and penalties provided by this section are cumulative to each other, the remedies under Section 17200 of the Business and Professions Code, and the remedies or penalties available under all other laws of this state.

(j) For the purposes of this section, the following terms have the following meanings:

(1) "State of emergency" means a natural or manmade emergency resulting from an earthquake, flood, fire, riot, storm, drought, plant or animal infestation or disease, pandemic or epidemic disease outbreak, or other natural or manmade disaster for which a state of emergency has been declared by the President of the United States or the Governor.

(2) "Local emergency" means a natural or manmade emergency resulting from an earthquake, flood, fire, riot, storm, drought, plant or animal infestation or disease, pandemic or epidemic disease outbreak, or other natural or manmade disaster for which a local emergency has been declared by an official, board, or other governing body vested with authority to make that declaration in any county, city, or city and county in California.

(3) "Consumer food item" means any article that is used or intended for use for food, drink, confection, or condiment by a person or animal.

(4) "Repair or reconstruction services" means services performed by any person who is required to be licensed under the Contractors' State License Law (Chapter 9 (commencing with Section 7000) of Division 3 of the Business and Professions Code), for repairs to residential or commercial property of any type that is damaged as a result of a disaster.

(5) "Emergency supplies" includes, but is not limited to, water, flashlights, radios, batteries, candles, blankets, soaps, diapers, temporary shelters, tape, toiletries, plywood, nails, and hammers.

(6) "Medical supplies" includes, but is not limited to, prescription and nonprescription medications, bandages, gauze, isopropyl alcohol, and antibacterial products.

(7) "Building materials" means lumber, construction tools, windows, and anything else used in the building or rebuilding of property.

(8) "Gasoline" means any fuel used to power any motor vehicle or power tool.

(9) "Transportation, freight, and storage services" means any service that is performed by any company that contracts to move, store, or transport personal or business property or that rents equipment for those purposes, including towing services.

(10) "Housing" means any rental housing with an initial lease term of no longer than one year, including, but not limited to, a space rented in a mobilehome park or campground.

(11) "Rental price" for housing means any of the following:

(A) For housing rented within one year prior to the time of the proclamation or declaration of emergency, the actual rental price paid by the tenant. For housing not rented at the time of the declaration or proclamation, but rented, or offered for rent, within one year prior to the proclamation or declaration of emergency, the most recent rental price offered before the proclamation or declaration of emergency. For housing rented at the time of the proclamation or declaration of emergency but which becomes vacant while the proclamation or declaration of emergency remains in effect and which is subject to any ordinance, rule, regulation, or initiative measure adopted by any local governmental entity that establishes a maximum amount that a landlord may charge a tenant for rent, the actual rental price paid by the previous tenant or the amount specified in subparagraph (B), whichever is greater. This amount may be increased by 5 percent if the housing was previously rented or offered for rent unfurnished, and it is now being offered for rent fully furnished. This amount shall not be adjusted for any other good or service, including, but not limited to, gardening or utilities currently or formerly provided in connection with the lease.

(B) For housing not rented and not offered for rent within one year prior to the proclamation or declaration of emergency, 160 percent of the fair market rent established by the United States Department of Housing and Urban Development. This amount may be increased by 5 percent if the housing is offered for rent fully furnished. This amount shall not be adjusted for any other good or service, including, but not limited to, gardening or utilities currently or formerly provided in connection with the lease.

(C) Housing advertised, offered, or charged, at a daily rate at the time of the declaration or proclamation of emergency, shall be subject to the rental price described in subparagraph (A), if the housing continues to be advertised, offered, or charged, at a daily rate. Housing advertised, offered, or charged, on a daily basis at the time of the declaration or proclamation of emergency, shall be subject to the rental price in subparagraph (B), if the housing is advertised, offered, or charged, on a periodic lease agreement after the declaration or proclamation of emergency.

(D) For mobilehome spaces rented to existing tenants at the time of the proclamation or declaration of emergency and subject to a local rent control ordinance, the amount authorized under the local rent control ordinance. For new tenants who enter into a rental agreement for a mobilehome space that is subject to rent control but not rented at the time of the proclamation or declaration of emergency, the amount of rent last charged for a space in the same mobilehome park. For mobilehome spaces not subject to a local rent control ordinance and not rented at the time of the proclamation or declaration of emergency, the amount of rent last charged for the space.

(12) "Goods" has the same meaning as defined in subdivision (c) of Section 1689.5 of the Civil Code.

(k) This section does not preempt any local ordinance prohibiting the same or similar conduct or imposing a more severe penalty for the same conduct prohibited by this section.

(*l*) A business offering an item for sale, or a service, at a reduced price immediately prior to the proclamation or declaration of the emergency may use the price it normally charges for the item or service to calculate the price pursuant to subdivision (b) or (c).

(m) This section does not prohibit an owner from evicting a tenant for any lawful reason, including pursuant to Section 1161 of the Code of Civil Procedure.

Added Stats 1st Ex Sess 1993–94 ch 52 § 2 (AB 36 X), effective November 30, 1994. Amended Stats 1995 ch 91 § 123 (SB 975); Stats 2004 ch 492 § 2 (SB 1363); Stats 2016 ch 671 § 1 (AB 2820), effective January 1, 2017. Stats 2018 ch 631 § 2 (AB 1919), effective January 1, 2019; Stats 2020 ch 339 § 1 (SB 1196), effective January 1, 2021..

TITLE 13
Crimes Against Property

Chapter 5
Larceny

Penal Code § 490a, enacted in 1927, provides that whenever any statute refers to larceny, embezzlement, or stealing, it shall be read and interpreted as if the word "theft" were substituted therefor.

§ 484b. Diversion of money received for construction of improvements

Any person who receives money for the purpose of obtaining or paying for services, labor, materials or equipment and willfully fails to apply such money for such purpose by either willfully failing to complete the improvements for which funds were provided or willfully failing to pay for services, labor, materials or equipment provided incident to such construction, and wrongfully diverts the funds to a use other than that for which the funds were received, shall be guilty of a public offense and shall be punishable by a fine not exceeding ten thousand dollars ($10,000), or by imprisonment in a county jail not exceeding one year, or by imprisonment pursuant to subdivision (h) of Section 1170, or by both that fine and that imprisonment if the amount diverted is in excess of two thousand three hundred fifty dollars ($2,350). If the amount diverted is less than or equal to two thousand three hundred fifty dollars ($2,350), the person shall be guilty of a misdemeanor.

Added Stats 1965 ch 1145 § 1. Amended Stats 1974 ch 910 § 1; Stats 1975 ch 464 § 1; Stats 1976 ch 1139 § 219, operative July 1, 1977; Stats 1983 ch 1092 § 286, effective September 27, 1983, operative January 1, 1984; Stats 2009 ch 35 § 9 (SB 174), effective January 1, 2010; Stats 2009–2010 3d Ex Sess ch 28 § 14 (SB 18XXX), effective January 25, 2010; Stats 2011 ch 15 § 367 (AB 109), effective April 4, 2011, operative October 1, 2011.

§ 484c. Submission of false voucher to obtain construction loan

Any person who submits a false voucher to obtain construction loan funds and does not use the funds for the purpose for which the claim was submitted is guilty of embezzlement.

Added Stats 1965 ch 1145 § 2.

Appendix

Chapter 8

False Personation and Cheats

§ 532e. Rebating money furnished for constructing improvements

Any person who receives money for the purpose of obtaining or paying for services, labor, materials or equipment incident to constructing improvements on real property and willfully rebates any part of the money to or on behalf of anyone contracting with such person, for provision of the services, labor, materials or equipment for which the money was given, shall be guilty of a misdemeanor; provided, however, that normal trade discount for prompt payment shall not be considered a violation of this section.

Added Stats 1965 ch 1145 § 3.

Chapter 10

Crimes Against Insured Property and Insurers

§ 551. Referral to automotive repair dealer for consideration; Discounts intended to offset deductible

(a) It is unlawful for any automotive repair dealer, contractor, or employees or agents thereof to offer to any insurance agent, broker, or adjuster any fee, commission, profit sharing, or other form of direct or indirect consideration for referring an insured to an automotive repair dealer or its employees or agents for vehicle repairs covered under a policyholder's automobile physical damage or automobile collision coverage, or to a contractor or its employees or agents for repairs to or replacement of a structure covered by a residential or commercial insurance policy.

(b) Except in cases in which the amount of the repair or replacement claim has been determined by the insurer and the repair or replacement services are performed in accordance with that determination or in accordance with provided estimates that are accepted by the insurer, it is unlawful for any automotive repair dealer, contractor, or employees or agents thereof to knowingly offer or give any discount intended to offset a deductible required by a policy of insurance covering repairs to or replacement of a motor vehicle or residential or commercial structure. This subdivision does not prohibit an advertisement for repair or replacement services at a discount as long as the amount of the repair or replacement claim has been determined by the insurer and the repair or replacement services are performed in accordance with that determination or in accordance with provided estimates that are accepted by the insurer.

(c) A violation of this section is a public offense. Where the amount at issue exceeds nine hundred fifty dollars ($950), the offense is punishable by imprisonment in the state prison for 16 months, or 2 or 3 years, by a fine of not more than ten thousand dollars ($10,000), or by both that imprisonment and fine; or by imprisonment in a county jail not to exceed one year, by a fine of not more than one thousand dollars ($1,000), or by both that imprisonment and fine. In all other cases, the offense is punishable by imprisonment in a county jail not to exceed six months, by a fine of not more than one thousand dollars ($1,000), or by both that imprisonment and fine.

(d) Every person who, having been convicted of subdivision (a) or (b), or Section 7027.3 or former Section 9884.75 of the Business and Professions Code and having served a term therefor in any penal institution or having been imprisoned therein as a condition of probation for that offense, is subsequently convicted of subdivision (a) or (b), upon a subsequent conviction of one of those offenses, shall be punished by imprisonment in the state prison for 16 months, or 2 or 3 years, by a fine of not more than ten thousand dollars ($10,000), or by both that imprisonment and fine; or by imprisonment in a county jail not to exceed one year, by a fine of not more than one thousand dollars ($1,000), or by both that imprisonment and fine.

(e) For purposes of this section:

(1) "Automotive repair dealer" means a person who, for compensation, engages in the business of repairing or diagnosing malfunctions of motor vehicles.

(2) "Contractor" has the same meaning as set forth in Section 7026 of the Business and Professions Code.

Added Stats 1992 ch 675 § 9 (AB 3067). Amended Stats 1993 ch 462 § 1 (AB 438), effective September 25, 1993; Stats 1995 ch 373 § 1 (SB 639); Stats. 2009, Ch. 28 (SBX3 18).

TITLE 16
General Provisions

§ 667.16. Enhanced sentence for fraud in repairing natural disaster damage

(a) Any person convicted of a felony violation of Section 470, 487, or 532 as part of a plan or scheme to defraud an owner of a residential or nonresidential structure, including a mobilehome or manufactured home, in connection with the offer or performance of repairs or im-

provementsto the structure or property, or by adding to, or subtracting from, grounds in connection therewith, fordamage caused by a
natural disaster, shall receive a one–year enhancement in addition
and consecutive to the penalty prescribed. The additional term shall
not be imposed unless the allegation is charged in the accusatory
pleading and admitted by the defendant or found to be true by the
trier of fact.

(b) This enhancement applies to natural disasters for which a state
of emergency is proclaimed by the Governor pursuant to Section 8625
of the Government Code or for which an emergency or major disaster
is declared by the President of the United States.

(c) Notwithstanding any other law, the court may strike the additional term provided in subdivision (a) if the court determines that
there are mitigating circumstances and states on the record the reasons for striking the additional punishment.

Added Stats 1994 ch 175 § 5 (SB 634), effective July 9, 1994. Amended Stats 2020
ch 364 § 5 (SB 1189), effective January 1, 2021.

§ 670. Scheme to defraud owner of structure regarding repairs for damage resulting from natural disaster for which state of emergency has been declared; Punishment

(a) Any person who violates Section 7158 or 7159 of, or subdivision
(b), (c), (d), or (e) of Section 7161 of, the Business and Professions
Code or Section 470, 484, 487, or 532 of this code as part of a plan or
scheme to defraud an owner or lessee of a residential or nonresidential structure in connection with the offer or performance of repairs or
improvements to the structure or property, or the adding to, or subtracting from, grounds in connection therewith, for damage or destruction caused by a natural disaster specified in subdivision (b),
shall be subject to the penalties and enhancements specified in subdivisions (c) and (d). The existence of any fact which would bring a person under this section shall be alleged in the information or indictment and either admitted by the defendant in open court, or found to
be true by the jury trying the issue of guilt or by the court where guilt
is established by a plea of guilty or nolo contendere or by trial by the
court sitting without a jury.

(b) This section applies to natural disasters for which a state of
emergency is proclaimed by the Governor pursuant to Section 8625 of
the Government Code or for which an emergency or major disaster is
declared by the President of the United States.

(c) The maximum or prescribed amounts of fines for offenses subject
to this section shall be doubled. If the person has been previously
convicted of a felony offense specified in subdivision (a), the person
shall receive a one-year enhancement in addition to, and to run con-

secutively to, the term of imprisonment for any felony otherwise prescribed by this subdivision.

(d) Additionally, the court shall order any person sentenced pursuant to this section to make full restitution to the victim or to make restitution to the victim based on the person's ability to pay, as defined in subdivision (e) of Section 1203.1b. The payment of the restitution ordered by the court pursuant to this subdivision shall be made a condition of any probation granted by the court for an offense punishable under this section. Notwithstanding any other provision of law, the period of probation shall be at least five years or until full restitution is made to the victim, whichever first occurs.

(e) Notwithstanding any other provision of law, the prosecuting agency shall be entitled to recover its costs of investigation and prosecution from any fines imposed for a conviction under this section.

Added Stats 1st Ex Sess 1989–90 ch 36 § 4 (AB 9), effective September 22, 1990. Amended Stats 2001 ch 854 § 38 (SB 205); Stats 2016 ch 86 § 226 (SB 1171), effective January 1, 2017; Stats 2020 ch 364 § 6 (SB 1189), effective January 1, 2021.

PART 2

CRIMINAL PROCEDURE

TITLE 3
Additional Provisions Regarding Criminal Procedure

Chapter 4.5

Peace Officers

§ 830.3. Investigators, inspectors, and other employees of specified agencies

The following persons are peace officers whose authority extends to any place in the state for the purpose of performing their primary duty or when making an arrest pursuant to Section 836 as to any public offense with respect to which there is immediate danger to person or property, or of the escape of the perpetrator of that offense, or pursuant to Section 8597 or 8598 of the Government Code. These peace officers may carry firearms only if authorized and under those terms and conditions as specified by their employing agencies:

(a) Persons employed by the Division of Investigation of the Department of Consumer Affairs and investigators of the Dental Board of California, who are designated by the Director of Consumer Affairs, provided that the primary duty of these peace officers shall be the enforcement of the law as that duty is set forth in Section 160 of the Business and Professions Code.

(b) Voluntary fire wardens designated by the Director of Forestry and Fire Protection pursuant to Section 4156 of the Public Resources Code, provided that the primary duty of these peace officers shall be the enforcement of the law as that duty is set forth in Section 4156 of that code.

(c) Employees of the Department of Motor Vehicles designated in Section 1655 of the Vehicle Code, provided that the primary duty of these peace officers shall be the enforcement of the law as that duty is set forth in Section 1655 of that code.

(d) Investigators of the California Horse Racing Board designated by the board, provided that the primary duty of these peace officers shall be the enforcement of Chapter 4 (commencing with Section 19400) of Division 8 of the Business and Professions Code and Chapter 10 (commencing with Section 330) of Title 9 of Part 1.

(e) The State Fire Marshal and assistant or deputy state fire marshals appointed pursuant to Section 13103 of the Health and Safety Code, provided that the primary duty of these peace officers shall be the enforcement of the law as that duty is set forth in Section 13104 of that code.

(f) Inspectors of the food and drug section designated by the chief pursuant to subdivision (a) of Section 106500 of the Health and Safety Code, provided that the primary duty of these peace officers shall be the enforcement of the law as that duty is set forth in Section 106500 of that code.

(g) All investigators of the Division of Labor Standards Enforcement designated by the Labor Commissioner, provided that the primary duty of these peace officers shall be the enforcement of the law as prescribed in Section 95 of the Labor Code.

(h) All investigators of the State Departments of Health Care Services, Public Health, and Social Services, the Department of Toxic Substances Control, the Office of Statewide Health Planning and Development, and the Public Employees' Retirement System, provided that the primary duty of these peace officers shall be the enforcement of the law relating to the duties of their department or office. Notwithstanding any other law, investigators of the Public Employees' Retirement System shall not carry firearms.

(i) Either the Deputy Commissioner, Enforcement Branch of, or the Fraud Division Chief of, the Department of Insurance and those investigators designated by the deputy or the chief, provided that the primary duty of those investigators shall be the enforcement of Section 550.

(j) Employees of the Department of Housing and Community Development designated under Section 18023 of the Health and Safety Code, provided that the primary duty of these peace officers shall be the enforcement of the law as that duty is set forth in Section 18023 of that code.

(k) Investigators of the office of the Controller, provided that the primary duty of these investigators shall be the enforcement of the law relating to the duties of that office. Notwithstanding any other law, except as authorized by the Controller, the peace officers designated pursuant to this subdivision shall not carry firearms.

(*l*) Investigators of the Department of Financial Protection and Innovation designated by the Commissioner of Financial Protection and Innovation, provided that the primary duty of these investigators shall be the enforcement of the provisions of law administered by the Department of Financial Protection and Innovation. Notwithstanding any other law, the peace officers designated pursuant to this subdivision shall not carry firearms.

(m) Persons employed by the Contractors' State License Board designated by the Director of Consumer Affairs pursuant to Section 7011.5 of the Business and Professions Code, provided that the primary duty of these persons shall be the enforcement of the law as that duty is set forth in Section 7011.5, and in Chapter 9 (commencing with Section 7000) of Division 3, of that code. The Director of Consumer Affairs may designate as peace officers not more than 12 persons who shall at the time of their designation be assigned to the special investigations unit of the board. Notwithstanding any other law, the persons designated pursuant to this subdivision shall not carry firearms.

(n) The Chief and coordinators of the Law Enforcement Branch of the Office of Emergency Services.

(o) Investigators of the office of the Secretary of State designated by the Secretary of State, provided that the primary duty of these peace officers shall be the enforcement of the law as prescribed in Chapter 3 (commencing with Section 8200) of Division 1 of Title 2 of, and Section 12172.5 of, the Government Code. Notwithstanding any other law, the peace officers designated pursuant to this subdivision shall not carry firearms.

(p) The Deputy Director for Security designated by Section 8880.38 of the Government Code, and all lottery security personnel assigned to the California State Lottery and designated by the director, provided that the primary duty of any of those peace officers shall be the enforcement of the laws related to ensuring the integrity, honesty, and fairness of the operation and administration of the California State Lottery.

(q) Investigators employed by the Investigation Division of the Employment Development Department designated by the director of the department, provided that the primary duty of those peace officers shall be the enforcement of the law as that duty is set forth in Section 317 of the Unemployment Insurance Code. Notwithstanding any other law, the peace officers designated pursuant to this subdivision shall not carry firearms.

(r) The chief, assistant chief, and all security and safety officers of museum security and safety of Exposition Park, as designated by the Exposition Park Manager pursuant to Section 4108 of the Food and Agricultural Code, provided that the primary duty of those peace officers shall be the enforcement of the law as that duty is set forth in Section 4108 of the Food and Agricultural Code.

(s) Employees of the Franchise Tax Board designated by the board, provided that the primary duty of these peace officers shall be the enforcement of the law as set forth in Chapter 9 (commencing with Section 19701) of Part 10.2 of Division 2 of the Revenue and Taxation Code.

(t) (1) Notwithstanding any other provision of this section, a peace officer authorized by this section shall not be authorized to carry firearms by their employing agency until that agency has adopted a policy on the use of deadly force by those peace officers, and until those peace officers have been instructed in the employing agency's policy on the use of deadly force.

(2) Every peace officer authorized pursuant to this section to carry firearms by their employing agency shall qualify in the use of the firearms at least every six months.

(u) Investigators of the Department of Managed Health Care designated by the Director of the Department of Managed Health Care, provided that the primary duty of these investigators shall be the enforcement of the provisions of laws administered by the Director of the Department of Managed Health Care. Notwithstanding any other law, the peace officers designated pursuant to this subdivision shall not carry firearms.

(v) The Chief, Deputy Chief, supervising investigators, and investigators of the Office of Protective Services of the State Department of Developmental Services, the Office of Protective Services of the State Department of State Hospitals, and the Office of Law Enforcement Support of the California Health and Human Services Agency, provided that the primary duty of each of those persons shall be the enforcement of the law relating to the duties of their department or office.

Added Stats 2013 ch 515 § 38 (SB 304), effective January 1, 2014, operative July 1, 2014. Amended Stats 2014 ch 26 § 13 (AB 1468), effective June 20, 2014, operative July 1, 2014 (ch 26 prevails), ch 71 § 126 (SB 1304), effective January 1, 2015; Stats 2016 ch 59 § 3 (SB 1474), effective January 1, 2017; Stats 2017 ch 561 § 182 (AB 1516), effective January 1, 2018; Stats 2021 ch 411 § 3 (AB 483), effective September 30, 2021; Stats 2022 ch 452 § 204 (SB 1498), effective January 1, 2023.

PUBLIC CONTRACT CODE

DIVISION 2
GENERAL PROVISIONS

PART 1
ADMINISTRATIVE PROVISIONS

Chapter 4
Subletting and Subcontracting

§ 4100. Citation of chapter

This chapter may be cited as the "Subletting and Subcontracting Fair Practices Act."

Added Stats 1986 ch 195 § 42.1.

§ 4101. Bid shopping and bid peddling

The Legislature finds that the practices of bid shopping and bid peddling in connection with the construction, alteration, and repair of public improvements often result in poor quality of material and workmanship to the detriment of the public, deprive the public of the full benefits of fair competition among prime contractors and subcontractors, and lead to insolvencies, loss of wages to employees, and other evils.

Added Stats 1986 ch 195 § 42.1.

§ 4103. Rights and remedies not diminished

Nothing in this chapter limits or diminishes any rights or remedies, either legal or equitable, which:

(a) An original or substituted subcontractor may have against the prime contractor, his or her successors or assigns.

(b) The state or any county, city, body politic, or public agency may have against the prime contractor, his or her successors or assigns, including the right to take over and complete the contract.

Added Stats 1986 ch 195 § 42.1.

Appendix

§ 4104. Listing of subcontractors in bid or offer

Any officer, department, board, or commission taking bids for the construction of any public work or improvement shall provide in the specifications prepared for the work or improvement or in the general conditions under which bids will be received for the doing of the work incident to the public work or improvement that any person making a bid or offer to perform the work, shall, in his or her bid or offer, set forth:

(a) (1) The name, the location of the place of business, the California contractor license number, and public works contractor registration number issued pursuant to Section 1725.5 of the Labor Code of each subcontractor who will perform work or labor or render service to the prime contractor in or about the construction of the work or improvement, or a subcontractor licensed by the State of California who, under subcontract to the prime contractor, specially fabricates and installs a portion of the work or improvement according to detailed drawings contained in the plans and specifications, in an amount in excess of one-half of 1 percent of the prime contractor's total bid or, in the case of bids or offers for the construction of streets or highways, including bridges, in excess of one-half of 1 percent of the prime contractor's total bid or ten thousand dollars ($10,000), whichever is greater.

(2) An inadvertent error in listing the California contractor license number or public works contractor registration number provided pursuant to paragraph (1) shall not be grounds for filing a bid protest or grounds for considering the bid nonresponsive if the corrected contractor's license number is submitted to the public entity by the prime contractor within 24 hours after the bid opening and provided the corrected contractor's license number corresponds to the submitted name and location for that subcontractor.

(3) (A) Subject to subparagraph (B), any information requested by the officer, department, board, or commission concerning any subcontractor who the prime contractor is required to list under this subdivision, other than the subcontractor's name, location of business, the California contractor license number, and the public works contractor registration number, may be submitted by the prime contractor up to 24 hours after the deadline established by the officer, department, board, or commission for receipt of bids by prime contractors.

(B) A state or local agency may implement subparagraph (A) at its option.

(b) The portion of the work that will be done by each subcontractor under this act. The prime contractor shall list only one subcontractor for each portion as is defined by the prime contractor in his or her bid.

Added Stats 2013 ch 258 § 2 (AB 44), effective January 1, 2014, operative July 1, 2014.
Amended Stats 2017 ch 28 § 90 (SB 96), effective June 27, 2017.

§ 4104.5. Date and time for closing of bids

(a) The officer, department, board, or commission taking bids for construction of any public work or improvement shall specify in the bid invitation and public notice the place the bids of the prime contractors are to be received and the time by which they shall be received. The date and time shall be extended by no less than 72 hours if the officer, department, board, or commission issues any material changes, additions, or deletions to the invitation later than 72 hours prior to the bid closing. Any bids received after the time specified in the notice or any extension due to material changes shall be returned unopened.

(b) As used in this section, the term "material change" means a change with a substantial cost impact on the total bid as determined by the awarding agency.

(c) As used in this section, the term "bid invitation" shall include any documents issued to prime contractors that contain descriptions of the work to be bid or the content, form, or manner of submission of bids by bidders.

Added Stats 1998 ch 1010 § 2 (AB 1092). Amended Stats 2002 ch 204 § 1 (SB 937).

§ 4105. Circumvention of subcontractor listing requirement

Circumvention by a general contractor who bids as a prime contractor of the requirement under Section 4104 for him or her to list his or her subcontractors, by the device of listing another contractor who will in turn sublet portions constituting the majority of the work covered by the prime contract, shall be considered a violation of this chapter and shall subject that prime contractor to the penalties set forth in Sections 4110 and 4111.

Added Stats 1986 ch 195 § 42.1.

§ 4106. Failure to specify subcontractor

If a prime contractor fails to specify a subcontractor or if a prime contractor specifies more than one subcontractor for the same portion of work to be performed under the contract in excess of one-half of 1 percent of the prime contractor's total bid, the prime contractor agrees that he or she is fully qualified to perform that portion himself or herself, and that the prime contractor shall perform that portion himself or herself.

If after award of contract, the prime contractor subcontracts, except as provided for in Sections 4107 or 4109, any such portion of the work, the prime contractor shall be subject to the penalties named in Section 4111.

Added Stats 1986 ch 195 § 42.1.

§ 4107. Substitution, assignment, and subletting; Notice and hearing

A prime contractor whose bid is accepted may not:

(a) Substitute a person as subcontractor in place of the subcontractor listed in the original bid, except that the awarding authority, or its duly authorized officer, may, except as otherwise provided in Section 4107.5, consent to the substitution of another person as a subcontractor in any of the following situations:

(1) When the subcontractor listed in the bid, after having had a reasonable opportunity to do so, fails or refuses to execute a written contract for the scope of work specified in the subcontractor's bid and at the price specified in the subcontractor's bid, when that written contract, based upon the general terms, conditions, plans, and specifications for the project involved or the terms of that subcontractor's written bid, is presented to the subcontractor by the prime contractor.

(2) When the listed subcontractor becomes insolvent or the subject of an order for relief in bankruptcy.

(3) When the listed subcontractor fails or refuses to perform his or her subcontract.

(4) When the listed subcontractor fails or refuses to meet the bond requirements of the prime contractor as set forth in Section 4108.

(5) When the prime contractor demonstrates to the awarding authority, or its duly authorized officer, subject to the further provisions set forth in Section 4107.5, that the name of the subcontractor was listed as the result of an inadvertent clerical error.

(6) When the listed subcontractor is not licensed pursuant to the Contractors License Law.

(7) When the awarding authority, or its duly authorized officer, determines that the work performed by the listed subcontractor is substantially unsatisfactory and not in substantial accordance with the plans and specifications, or that the subcontractor is substantially delaying or disrupting the progress of the work.

(8) When the listed subcontractor is ineligible to work on a public works project pursuant to Section 1777.1 or 1777.7 of the Labor Code.

(9) When the awarding authority determines that a listed subcontractor is not a responsible contractor.

Prior to approval of the prime contractor's request for the substitution, the awarding authority, or its duly authorized officer, shall give notice in writing to the listed subcontractor of the prime contractor's request to substitute and of the reasons for the request. The notice shall be served by certified or registered mail to the last known address of the subcontractor. The listed subcontractor who has been so notified has five working days within which to submit written objections to the substitution to the awarding authority. Failure to file these written objections constitutes the listed subcontractor's consent to the substitution.

If written objections are filed, the awarding authority shall give notice in writing of at least five working days to the listed subcontractor of a hearing by the awarding authority on the prime contractor's request for substitution.

(b) Permit a subcontract to be voluntarily assigned or transferred or allow it to be performed by anyone other than the original subcontractor listed in the original bid, without the consent of the awarding authority, or its duly authorized officer.

(c) Other than in the performance of "change orders" causing changes or deviations from the original contract, sublet or subcontract any portion of the work in excess of one-half of 1 percent of the prime contractor's total bid as to which his or her original bid did not designate a subcontractor.

Added Stats 1986 ch 195 § 42.1. Amended Stats 1998 ch 443 § 2 (AB 1569); Stats 1999 ch 972 § 3 (AB 574); Stats 2003 ch 180 § 1 (AB 902); Stats 2009 Ch. 500 (AB 1059).

§ 4107.2. Subcontracting by carpeting subcontractor

No subcontractor listed by a prime contractor under Section 4104 as furnishing and installing carpeting, shall voluntarily sublet his or her subcontract with respect to any portion of the labor to be performed unless he or she specified the subcontractor in his or her bid for that subcontract to the prime contractor.

Added Stats 1986 ch 195 § 42.1.

§ 4107.5. Clerical errors in listing of subcontractors; Procedure for substitution

The prime contractor as a condition to assert a claim of inadvertent clerical error in the listing of a subcontractor shall within two working days after the time of the prime bid opening by the awarding authority give written notice to the awarding authority and copies of that notice to both the subcontractor he or she claims to have listed in error and the intended subcontractor who had bid to the prime contractor prior to bid opening.

Any listed subcontractor who has been notified by the prime contractor in accordance with this section as to an inadvertent clerical error shall be allowed six working days from the time of the prime bid opening within which to submit to the awarding authority and to the prime contractor written objection to the prime contractor's claim of inadvertent clerical error. Failure of the listed subcontractor to file the written notice within the six working days shall be primary evidence of his or her agreement that an inadvertent clerical error was made.

Appendix

The awarding authority shall, after a public hearing as provided in Section 4107 and in the absence of compelling reasons to the contrary, consent to the substitution of the intended subcontractor:

(a) If (1) the prime contractor, (2) the subcontractor listed in error, and (3) the intended subcontractor each submit an affidavit to the awarding authority along with such additional evidence as the parties may wish to submit that an inadvertent clerical error was in fact made, provided that the affidavits from each of the three parties are filed within eight working days from the time of the prime bid opening, or

(b) If the affidavits are filed by both the prime contractor and the intended subcontractor within the specified time but the subcontractor whom the prime contractor claims to have listed in error does not submit within six working days, to the awarding authority and to the prime contractor, written objection to the prime contractor's claim of inadvertent clerical error as provided in this section.

If the affidavits are filed by both the prime contractor and the intended subcontractor but the listed subcontractor has, within six working days from the time of the prime bid opening, submitted to the awarding authority and to the prime contractor written objection to the prime contractor's claim of inadvertent clerical error, the awarding authority shall investigate the claims of the parties and shall hold a public hearing as provided in Section 4107 to determine the validity of those claims. Any determination made shall be based on the facts contained in the declarations submitted under penalty of perjury by all three parties and supported by testimony under oath and subject to cross–examination. The awarding authority may, on its own motion or that of any other party, admit testimony of other contractors, any bid registries or depositories, or any other party in possession of facts which may have a bearing on the decision of the awarding authority.

Added Stats 1986 ch 195 § 42.1.

§ 4107.7. Failure to pay hazardous waste hauler

If a contractor who enters into a contract with a public entity for investigation, removal or remedial action, or disposal relative to the release or presence of a hazardous material or hazardous waste fails to pay a subcontractor registered as a hazardous waste hauler pursuant to Section 25163 of the Health and Safety Code within 10 days after the investigation, removal or remedial action, or disposal is completed, the subcontractor may serve a stop notice upon the public entity in accordance with Chapter 4 (commencing with Section 9350) of Title 3 of Part 6 of Division 4 of the Civil Code.

Added Stats 1987 ch 746 § 2. Amended Stats 2010 ch 697 § 43 (SB 189), effective January 1, 2011, operative July 1, 2012.

§ 4108. Bonds

(a) It shall be the responsibility of each subcontractor submitting bids to a prime contractor to be prepared to submit a faithful performance and payment bond or bonds if so requested by the prime contractor.

(b) In the event any subcontractor submitting a bid to a prime contractor does not, upon the request of the prime contractor and at the expense of the prime contractor at the established charge or premium therefor, furnish to the prime contractor a bond or bonds issued by an admitted surety wherein the prime contractor shall be named the obligee, guaranteeing prompt and faithful performance of the subcontract and the payment of all claims for labor and materials furnished or used in and about the work to be done and performed under the subcontract, the prime contractor may reject the bid and make a substitution of another subcontractor subject to Section 4107.

(c)(1) The bond or bonds may be required under this section only if the prime contractor in his or her written or published request for subbids clearly specifies the amount and requirements of the bond or bonds.

(2) If the expense of the bond or bonds required under this section is to be borne by the subcontractor, that requirement shall also be specified in the prime contractor's written or published request for subbids.

(3) The prime contractor's failure to specify bond requirements, in accordance with this subdivision, in the written or published request for subbids shall preclude the prime contractor from imposing bond requirements under this section.

Added Stats 1986 ch 195 § 42.1. Amended Stats 1991 ch 754 § 1 (SB 580).

§ 4109. Subletting or subcontracting in cases of public emergency or necessity

Subletting or subcontracting of any portion of the work in excess of one–half of 1 percent of the prime contractor's total bid as to which no subcontractor was designated in the original bid shall only be permitted in cases of public emergency or necessity, and then only after a finding reduced to writing as a public record of the awarding authority setting forth the facts constituting the emergency or necessity.

Added Stats 1986 ch 195 § 42.1.

§ 4110. Options of awarding authority upon violation of chapter

A prime contractor violating any of the provisions of this chapter violates his or her contract and the awarding authority may exercise the option, in its own discretion, of (1) canceling his or her contract or (2) assessing the prime contractor a penalty in an amount of not more than 10 percent of the amount of the subcontract involved, and this penalty shall be deposited in the fund out of which the prime contract is awarded. In any proceedings under this section the prime contractor shall be entitled to a public hearing and to five days' notice of the time and place thereof.

Added Stats 1986 ch 195 § 42.1.

§ 4111. Disciplinary action by Contractors State License Board

Violation of this chapter by a licensee under Chapter 9 (commencing with Section 7000) of Division 3 of the Business and Professions Code constitutes grounds for disciplinary action by the Contractors State License Board, in addition to the penalties prescribed in Section 4110.

Added Stats 1986 ch 195 § 42.1.

§ 4112. Noncompliance by contractor on defense in action by subcontractor

The failure on the part of a contractor to comply with any provision of this chapter does not constitute a defense to the contractor in any action brought against the contractor by a subcontractor.

Added Stats 1986 ch 195 § 42.1.

§ 4113. "Subcontractor"; "Prime contractor"

As used in this chapter, the word "subcontractor" shall mean a contractor, within the meaning of the provisions of Chapter 9 (commencing with Section 7000) of Division 3 of the Business and Professions Code, who contracts directly with the prime contractor.

"Prime contractor" shall mean the contractor who contracts directly with the awarding authority.

Added Stats 1986 ch 195 § 42.1.

§ 4114. Delegation of functions by board of supervisors

The county board of supervisors, when it is the awarding authority, may delegate its functions under Sections 4107 and 4110 to any officer designated by the board.

The authorized officer shall make a written recommendation to the board of supervisors. The board of supervisors may adopt the recommendation without further notice or hearing, or may set the matter for a de novo hearing before the board.

Added Stats 1986 ch 195 § 42.1. Amended Stats 1989 ch 43 § 1.

Chapter 6

Awarding of Contracts

§ 6100. Verification of contractor's license

(a) A state agency, as defined in Section 10335.7 that is subject to this code, shall, prior to awarding a contract for work to be performed by a contractor, as defined by Section 7026 of the Business and Professions Code, verify with the Contractors State License Board that the person seeking the contract is licensed in a classification appropriate to the work to be undertaken. Verification as required by this section need only be made once every two years with respect to the same contractor.

(b) In lieu of the verification, the state entity may require the person seeking the contract to present his or her pocket license or certificate of licensure and provide a signed statement which swears, under penalty of perjury, that the pocket license or certificate of licensure presented is his or hers, is current and valid, and is in a classification appropriate to the work to be undertaken.

Added Stats 1986 ch 1230 § 2. Amended Stats 2015 ch 303 § 419 (AB 731), effective January 1, 2016.

Chapter 6.3

Construction Manager/General Contractor Authority: Department of Transportation

§ 6700. Alternative procurement procedure

(a) This chapter provides for an alternative procurement procedure for certain transportation projects performed by the Department of Transportation.

(b) The Construction Manager/General Contractor method allows the department to engage a construction manager during the design process to provide input on the design. During the design phase, the construction manager provides advice including, but not limited to, scheduling, pricing, and phasing to assist the department to design a more constructible project.

(c) The Legislature finds and declares that utilizing a Construction Manager/General Contractor method requires a clear understanding of the roles and responsibilities of each participant in the process. The

Legislature also finds and declares that cost-effective benefits are achieved by shifting the liability and risk for cost containment and project schedule to the construction manager and by permitting the coherent phasing of projects into discrete contract increments.

Added Stats 2012 ch 752 § 1 (AB 2498), effective January 1, 2013. Amended Stats 2018 ch 465 § 2 (SB 1262), effective January 1, 2019.

§ 6701. Requirements for use of Construction Manager/General Contractor method

(a) The Construction Manager/General Contractor method provided by this chapter may be used by the department, but is not limited to, when it is anticipated that the Construction Manager/General Contractor method will reduce project costs or expedite project completion in a manner that is not achievable through the design-bid-build method. Notwithstanding any other law, for projects utilizing the Construction Manager/General Contractor method provided by this chapter, the department shall advertise, award, and administer the Construction Manager/General Contractor contract. The department shall not delegate the contracting authority, except for the two projects reserved for projects in the County of Riverside as provided for in paragraph (2) of subdivision (b).

(b) (1) The department may use the Construction Manager/General Contractor method for projects that have construction costs greater than ten million dollars ($10,000,000).

(2) Consistent with Provision 2 of Item 2660-110-0042 of Section 2.00 of the Budget Act of 2016, as amended by Chapter 7 of the Statutes of 2017, two projects shall be authorized for projects in the County of Riverside and the Riverside County Transportation Commission may use the Construction Manager/General Contractor method for these projects, with the first priority for the projects listed in that budget item.

(c) On at least two-thirds of the projects delivered by the department utilizing the Construction Manager/General Contractor method provided by this chapter, the department shall use department employees or consultants under contract with the department to perform all project design and engineering services related to design required for Construction Manager/General Contractor project delivery consistent with Article XXII of the California Constitution. On all projects delivered by the department, the department shall use department employees or consultants under contract with the department to perform all construction inspection services required for Construction Manager/General Contractor project delivery consistent with Article XXII of the California Constitution. Department resources, including personnel requirements, necessary to perform all services described in this subdivision shall be included in the department's capital outlay support program for workload purposes in the annual Budget Act.

(d) (1) The department shall prepare and submit to the Legislature an interim report no later than July 1, 2021, that describes each Construction Manager/General Contractor project approved under this chapter as of January 1, 2021, and that provides relevant data, including, but not limited to, district, cost, the stage of completion, and estimated time to completion. The department shall also prepare and submit to the Legislature a final report, no later than July 1, 2025, that provides the same relevant data for projects that were approved under this chapter as of January 1, 2025. Both the interim and final reports shall also provide a comprehensive assessment on the effectiveness of the Construction Manager/General Contractor project delivery method relative to project cost and time savings.

(2) A report to be submitted pursuant to this subdivision shall be submitted in compliance with Section 9795 of the Government Code.

Added Stats 2012 ch 752 § 1 (AB 2498), effective January 1, 2013. Amended Stats 2016 ch 750 § 1 (AB 2126), effective January 1, 2017. Stats 2017 ch 20 § 5 (AB 115), effective June 27, 2017. Stats 2018 ch 465 § 3 (SB 1262), effective January 1, 2019.

§ 6702. Definitions

As used in this chapter, the following terms have the following meanings:

(a) "Construction manager" means a partnership, corporation, or other legal entity that is a licensed contractor pursuant to Chapter 9 (commencing with Section 7000) of Division 3 of the Business and Professions Code and that is able to provide, or that contracts with entities that are able to provide, appropriately licensed contracting or engineering services, or both appropriately licensed contracting and engineering services, as needed pursuant to a Construction Manager/General Contractor method contract.

(b) "Construction Manager/General Contractor method" means a project delivery method in which a construction manager is procured to provide preconstruction services during the design phase of the project and construction services during the construction phase of the project. The contract for construction services may be entered into at the same time as the contract for preconstruction services, or at a later time. The execution of the design and the construction of the project may be in sequential phases or concurrent phases.

(c) "Department" means the Department of Transportation as established under Part 5 (commencing with Section 14000) of Division 3 of Title 2 of the Government Code.

Appendix

(d) "Preconstruction services" means advice during the design phase including, but not limited to, scheduling, pricing, and phasing to assist the department to design a more constructible project.

(e) "Project" means the construction of a highway, bridge, or tunnel.

Added Stats 2012 ch 752 § 1 (AB 2498), effective January 1, 2013. Amended Stats 2019 ch 289 § 1 (AB 1475), effective January 1, 2020.

§ 6703. Evaluation and selection of Construction Manager/General Contractor

Construction Manager/General Contractor method projects shall progress as follows:

(a) (1) The department shall establish a procedure for the evaluation and selection of a construction manager through a request for qualifications (RFQ). The RFQ shall include, but not be limited to, the following:

(A) If the entity is a partnership, limited partnership, or other association, a list of all of the partners, general partners, or association members known at the time of the bid submission who will participate in the Construction Manager/General Contractor method contract, including, but not limited to, subcontractors.

(B) Evidence that the members of the entity have completed, or demonstrated the experience, competency, capability, and capacity to complete projects of similar size, scope, or complexity, and that proposed key personnel have sufficient experience and training to competently manage and complete the construction of the project, as well as a financial statement that assures the department that the entity has the capacity to complete the project, construction expertise, and an acceptable safety record.

(C) The licenses, registration, and credentials required to construct the project, including information on the revocation or suspension of any license, registration, or credential.

(D) Evidence that establishes that the entity has the capacity to obtain all required payment and performance bonding, liability insurance, and errors and omissions insurance.

(E) Any prior serious or willful violation of the California Occupational Safety and Health Act of 1973, contained in Part 1 (commencing with Section 6300) of Division 5 of the Labor Code, or the federal Occupational Safety and Health Act of 1970 (Public Law 91-596), settled against any member of the entity, and information concerning workers' compensation experience history and a worker safety program.

(F) Information concerning any debarment, disqualification, or removal from a federal, state, or local government public works project. Any instance in which an entity, its owners, officers, or managing employees submitted a bid on a public works project and were found to be nonresponsive, or were found by an awarding body not to be a responsible bidder.

(G) Any instance in which the entity, or its owners, officers, or managing employees, defaulted on a construction contract.

(H) Any violations of the Contractors' State License Law (Chapter 9 (commencing with Section 7000) of Division 3 of the Business and Professions Code), excluding alleged violations of federal or state law including the payment of wages, benefits, apprenticeship requirements, or personal income tax withholding, or of the Federal Insurance Contributions Act (26 U.S.C. Sec. 3101, et seq.) withholding requirements settled against any member of the entity.

(I) Information concerning the bankruptcy or receivership of any member of the entity, including information concerning any work completed by a surety.

(J) Information concerning all settled adverse claims, disputes, or lawsuits between the owner of a public works project and any member of the entity during the five years preceding submission of a bid pursuant to this section, in which the claim, settlement, or judgment exceeds fifty thousand dollars ($50,000). Information shall also be provided concerning any work completed by a surety during this period.

(K) In the case of a partnership or other association that is not a legal entity, a copy of the agreement creating the partnership or association and specifying that all partners or association members agree to be fully liable for the performance under the contract.

(L) For the purposes of this paragraph, a construction manager's safety record shall be deemed acceptable if the manager's experience modification rate for the most recent three-year period is an average of 1.00 or less, and the manager's average total recordable injury/illness rate and average lost work rate for the most recent three-year period does not exceed the applicable statistical standards for its business category or if the manager is a party to an alternative dispute resolution system as provided for in Section 3201.5 of the Labor Code.

(2) The information required pursuant to this subdivision shall be verified under oath by the entity and its members in the manner in which civil pleadings in civil actions are verified. Information that is not a public record pursuant to the California Public Records Act (Division 10 (commencing with Section 7920.000) of Title 1 of the Government Code) shall not be open to public inspection.

(b) For each RFQ, the department shall generate a final list of qualified persons or firms that participated in the RFQ prior to entering into negotiations on the contract or contracts to which the RFQ applies.

(c) (1) For each contract included in the RFQ, the department shall enter into separate negotiations for the contract with the highest qualified person or firm on the final list for that contract. However, if the RFQ is for multiple contracts and specifies that all of the multiple contracts will be awarded to a single construction manager, there may be a single negotiation for all of the multiple contracts. The negotiations shall include consideration of compensation and other contract terms that the department determines to be fair and reasonable to the department. In making this decision, the department shall take into account the estimated value, the scope, the complexity, and the nature of the professional services or construction services to be rendered. If the department is not able to negotiate a satisfactory contract with the highest qualified person or firm on the final list, regarding compensation and on other contract terms the department determines to be fair and reasonable, the department shall formally terminate negotiations with that person or firm. The department may undertake negotiations with the next most qualified person or firm on the final list in sequence until an agreement is reached or a determination is made to reject all persons or firms on the final list.

(2) If a contract for construction services is entered into pursuant to this chapter and includes preconstruction services by the construction manager, the department shall enter into a written contract with the construction manager for preconstruction services under which contract the department shall pay the construction manager a fee for preconstruction services in an amount agreed upon by the department and the construction manager. The preconstruction services contract may include fees for services to be performed during the contract period provided, however, the department shall not request or obtain a fixed price or a guaranteed maximum price for the construction contract from the construction manager or enter into a construction contract with the construction manager until after the department has entered into a services contract. A preconstruction services contract shall provide for the subsequent negotiation for construction of all or any discreet phase or phases of the project.

(3) A contract for construction services shall be awarded after the plans have been sufficiently developed and either a fixed price or a guaranteed maximum price has been successfully negotiated. In the event that a fixed price or a guaranteed maximum price is not negotiated, the department shall not award the contract for construction services.

(4) The department is not required to award the construction services contract.

(5) Construction shall not commence on any phase, package, or element until the department and construction manager agree in writing on either a fixed price that the department will pay for the construction to be commenced or a guaranteed maximum price for the construction to be commenced and construction schedule for the project. The construction manager shall perform not less than 30 percent

of the work covered by the fixed price or guaranteed maximum price agreement reached. Work that is not performed directly by the construction manager shall be bid to subcontractors pursuant to Section 6705.

Added Stats 2012 ch 752 § 1 (AB 2498), effective January 1, 2013; Amended Stats 2021 ch 615 § 354 (AB 474), effective January 1, 2022.

§ 6704. Construction manager to obtain bonding

(a) Any construction manager that is selected to construct a project pursuant to this chapter shall possess or obtain sufficient bonding to cover the contract amount for construction services and risk and liability insurance as the department may require.

(b) Any payment or performance bond written for the purposes of this chapter shall be written using a bond form developed by the department.

Added Stats 2012 ch 752 § 1 (AB 2498), effective January 1, 2013.

§ 6705. Subcontractors under construction manager

All subcontractors bidding on contracts pursuant to this chapter shall be afforded the protections contained in Chapter 4 (commencing with Section 4100) of Part 1. The construction manager shall do all of the following:

(a) Provide public notice of the availability of work to be subcontracted in accordance with the publication requirements applicable to the competitive bidding process of the department.

(b) Provide a fixed date and time on which the subcontracted work will be awarded in accordance with the procedure established pursuant to this chapter

(c) Comply with any subcontracting procedures adopted by the department that were included in the department's RFQ. If the department has adopted procedures to prequalify public works contractors, the construction manager may use the procedures to prequalify subcontractors.

Added Stats 2012 ch 752 § 1 (AB 2498), effective January 1, 2013.

§ 6706. Department verification of compliance

The department may retain the services of a design professional or construction project manager, or both, throughout the course of the project in order to ensure compliance with this chapter.

Added Stats 2012 ch 752 § 1 (AB 2498), effective January 1, 2013.

Appendix

§ 6707. Length of contract

Contracts awarded pursuant to this chapter shall be valid until the project is completed.

Added Stats 2012 ch 752 § 1 (AB 2498), effective January 1, 2013.

§ 6708. Effect on other rights and remedies

Nothing in this chapter is intended to affect, expand, alter, or limit any rights or remedies otherwise available at law.

Added Stats 2012 ch 752 § 1 (AB 2498), effective January 1, 2013.

Chapter 6.6

Alternative Project Delivery Program: Construction Manager/General Contractor Authority

§ 6950. Legislative findings and declarations

The Legislature finds and declares all of the following:

(a) The alternative public works project delivery methods authorized under this chapter should be evaluated for the purposes of exploring whether the potential exists for reduced project costs, expedited project completion, or design features that are not achievable through the traditional project delivery methods.

(b) The design sequencing and Construction Manager/General Contractor project delivery methods rely on existing design-bid-build and design-build procurement methods respectively and have been successfully used by both public and private sector entities in California and other states for over a decade on projects that require a quick startup as they allow construction to begin before the design plans are complete for the entire project.

(c) Both methods also have the benefit of allowing for earlier collaboration between the project owner and construction contractor.

(d) This chapter shall not be deemed to provide a preference for these project delivery methods over other delivery methodologies.

Added Stats 2012 ch 767 § 1 (SB 1549), effective January 1, 2013.

§ 6951. Definitions

For purposes of this chapter, the following definitions apply:

(a) "Alternative project delivery method" means either Construction Manager/General Contractor method or design sequencing.

(b) "Construction Manager/General Contractor method" or "CMGC" means a project delivery method using a best value procurement process in which a construction manager is procured to provide preconstruction services during the design phase of the project and construction services during the construction phase of the project. The execution of the design and the construction of the project may be in sequential phases or concurrent phases.

(c) "Construction manager" means a partnership, corporation, or other legal entity that is able to provide appropriately licensed contracting and engineering services as needed pursuant to a CMGC contract.

(d) "Design sequencing" means a method of project delivery that enables the sequencing of design activities to permit each construction phase to commence when the design for that phase is complete, instead of requiring design for the entire project to be completed before commencing construction.

(e) "Department" means the Department of Transportation as established under Part 5 (commencing with Section 14000) of Division 3 of the Government Code.

(f) "San Diego Association of Governments" means the consolidated agency created pursuant to Chapter 3 (commencing with Section 132350) of Division 12.7 of the Public Utilities Code.

Added Stats 2012 ch 767 § 1 (SB 1549), effective January 1, 2013.

§ 6952. Alternative project delivery method; Contracts; Findings

(a) Subject to the limitations of this chapter, the San Diego Association of Governments may utilize the alternative project delivery methods for public transit projects within the jurisdiction of the San Diego Association of Governments.

(b) The San Diego Association of Governments may enter into an alternative project delivery method contract pursuant to this chapter if, after evaluation of the traditional design-bid-build process of construction and of the alternative project delivery method in a public meeting, the San Diego Association of Governments makes a written finding that use of the alternative project delivery method on the specific project under consideration will accomplish one or more of the following objectives: reduce project costs, expedite the project's completion, or provide features not achievable through the design-bid-build method. This finding must be made prior to the San Diego Association of Governments entering into an alternative project delivery method contract. In the alternative project delivery method proposal, the written findings shall be included as part of any application for state funds pursuant to this chapter.

Appendix

Added Stats 2012 ch 767 § 1 (SB 1549), effective January 1, 2013.

§ 6953. Reimbursement of costs of performing prevailing wage monitoring and enforcement

(a) Except as specified in subdivision (b), the San Diego Association of Governments shall comply with subdivision (f) of Section 1771.5 of the Labor Code and shall reimburse the Department of Industrial Relations for its reasonable and directly related costs of performing prevailing wage monitoring and enforcement on public works projects pursuant to rates established by the department as set forth in subdivision (h) of that section on projects using an alternative project delivery method under this chapter. All moneys collected pursuant to this subdivision shall be deposited in the State Public Works Enforcement Fund, created by Section 1771.3 of the Labor Code, and shall be used only for enforcement of prevailing wage requirements on those projects.

(b) In lieu of complying with subdivision (a), the San Diego Association of Governments may elect to enter into a collective bargaining agreement that binds all of the contractors performing work on the project and that includes a mechanism for resolving disputes about the payment of wages.

Added Stats 2012 ch 767 § 1 (SB 1549), effective January 1, 2013.

§ 6954. Contract for preconstruction and construction services

(a) If a contract for CMGC services is entered into pursuant to this chapter and includes preconstruction services by the construction manager, the San Diego Association of Governments shall enter into a written contract with the construction manager for preconstruction services, under which the San Diego Association of Governments shall pay the construction manager a fee for preconstruction services in an amount agreed upon by the San Diego Association of Governments and the construction manager. The preconstruction services contract may include fees for services to be performed during the contract period; provided, however, the San Diego Association of Governments shall not request or obtain a fixed price or a guaranteed maximum price for the construction contract from the construction manager or enter into a construction contract with the construction manager until after the San Diego Association of Governments has entered into a services contract. A preconstruction services contract shall provide for the subsequent negotiation for construction of all or any discrete phase or phases of the project and shall provide for the San Diego Association of Governments to own the design plans and other preconstruction services work product.

(b) A contract for construction services will be awarded after the plans have been sufficiently developed and either a fixed price or a guaranteed maximum price has been successfully negotiated. In the event that a fixed price or a guaranteed maximum price is not negotiated, the San Diego Association of Governments may award the contract for construction services utilizing any other procurement method authorized by law.

(c) The construction manager shall perform not less than 30 percent of the work covered by the fixed price or guaranteed maximum price agreement reached. Work that is not performed directly by the construction manager shall be bid to subcontractors pursuant to Section 6955.

Added Stats 2012 ch 767 § 1 (SB 1549), effective January 1, 2013.

§ 6955. Protections afforded to subcontractors bidding on contracts

All subcontractors bidding on contracts pursuant to this chapter shall be afforded the protections contained in Chapter 4 (commencing with Section 4100).

Added Stats 2012 ch 767 § 1 (SB 1549), effective January 1, 2013.

§ 6956. Remedies

Nothing in this chapter affects, expands, alters, or limits any rights or remedies otherwise available at law.

Added Stats 2012 ch 767 § 1 (SB 1549), effective January 1, 2013.

§ 6957. Progress report

(a) Upon completion of a project using an alternative project delivery method, the San Diego Association of Governments shall prepare a progress report to its governing body. The progress report shall include, but shall not be limited to, all of the following information:

(1) A description of the project.

(2) The entity that was awarded the project.

(3) The estimated and actual costs of the project.

(4) The estimated and actual schedule for project completion.

(5) A description of any written protests concerning any aspect of the solicitation, bid, proposal, or award of the project, including, but not limited to, the resolution of the protests.

(6) An assessment of the prequalification process and criteria utilized under this chapter if the CMGC procurement method is used.

(7) A description of the method used to evaluate the bid or proposal, including the weighting of each factor and an assessment of the impact of this requirement on a project.

(8) A description of any challenges or unexpected problems that arose during the construction of the project and a description of the solutions that were considered and ultimately implemented to address those challenges and problems.

(9) Recommendations to improve the alternative project delivery methods authorized under this chapter.

(b) The progress report shall be made available on the San Diego Association of Governments' Internet Web site.

Added Stats 2012 ch 767 § 1 (SB 1549), effective January 1, 2013.

§ 6958. Severability of chapter provisions; Validity of contract

(a) The provisions of this chapter are severable. If any provision of this chapter or its application is held invalid, that invalidity shall not affect other provisions or applications that can be given effect without the invalid provision or application.

(b) Contracts awarded pursuant to this section shall be valid until the project is completed.

Added Stats 2012 ch 767 § 1 (SB 1549), effective January 1, 2013.

Chapter 6.7

Construction Manager/General Contractor Method: Regional Projects on Expressways

§ 6971. Definitions

(a) The Legislature finds and declares that the County of Riverside should be considered a transportation planning agency for the purposes of this chapter in order to effectuate the construction of the railroad grade separations and bridge rehabilitations and replacements specified in subparagraph (C) of paragraph (4) of subdivision (b) using Construction Manager/General Contractor authority. The passage of the Road Repair and Accountability Act of 2017 (Chapter 5 of the Statutes of 2017) provides additional transportation revenue to help close the significant funding shortfalls and address the substantial backlog of infrastructure projects that are in need of repair. The geography, topography, and location of these railroad grade separations and bridge rehabilitations and replacements projects present many potential complex challenges, and the Construction Manager/General Contractor method could reduce delays and ensure that those challenges are fully understood at the outset of construction.

(b) For purposes of this chapter, the following definitions apply:

(1) "Construction manager" means a partnership, corporation, or other legal entity that is a licensed contractor pursuant to Chapter 9 (commencing with Section 7000) of Division 3 of the Business and Professions Code and that is able to provide, or that contracts with entities that are able to provide, appropriately licensed contracting or engineering services, or both appropriately licensed contracting and engineering services, as needed pursuant to a Construction Manager/General Contractor method contract.

(2) "Construction Manager/General Contractor method" means a project delivery method in which a construction manager is procured to provide preconstruction services during the design phase of the project and construction services during the construction phase of the project. The contract for construction services may be entered into at the same time as the contract for preconstruction services, or at a later time. The execution of the design and the construction of the project may be in sequential phases or concurrent phases.

(3) "Preconstruction services" means advice during the design phase, including, but not limited to, scheduling, pricing, and phasing to assist the regional transportation agency to design a more constructible project.

(4) "Project" means any of the following:

(A) The construction of an expressway that is not on the state highway system.

(B) The construction of the following bridges that are not on the state highway system:

(i) Yerba Buena Island (YBI) West Side Bridges Seismic Retrofit Project.

(ii) Yankee Jims Road Bridge Project in the County of Placer (Replacement/Rehabilitation).

(C) The construction of railroad grade separations and bridge rehabilitations and replacements in the County of Riverside, as specified in Item 2660-110-0042 of Section 2.00 of the Budget Act of 2016, as amended by Chapter 7 of the Statutes of 2017.

(D) The construction, alteration, repair, rehabilitation, or improvement of the Golden Gate Bridge, as defined in Section 27502 of the Streets and Highways Code.

(E) A Metrolink commuter rail project.

(F) Any transportation project that is not on the state highway system.

(5) "Regional transportation agency" means any of the following:

(A) A transportation planning agency described in Section 29532 or 29532.1 of the Government Code.

(B) A county transportation commission established under Section 130050, 130050.1, or 130050.2 of the Public Utilities Code.

(C) Any other local or regional transportation entity that is designated by statute as a regional transportation agency.

Appendix

(D) A joint exercise of powers authority established pursuant to Chapter 5 (commencing with Section 6500) of Division 7 of Title 1 of the Government Code, with the consent of a transportation planning agency or a county transportation commission for the jurisdiction in which the transportation project will be developed.

(E) A local transportation authority created or designated pursuant to Division 12.5 (commencing with Section 131000) or Division 19 (commencing with Section 180000) of the Public Utilities Code.

(F) The Santa Clara Valley Transportation Authority established pursuant to Part 12 (commencing with Section 100000) of Division 10 of the Public Utilities Code.

(G) The County of Placer.

(H) The County of Riverside.

(I) The Golden Gate Bridge, Highway and Transportation District established pursuant to Chapter 18 (commencing with Section 27500) of Part 3 of Division 16 of the Streets and Highways Code.

(c) This section does not extend any other authority to the County of Riverside or the Golden Gate Bridge, Highway and Transportation District as a transportation planning agency under any other law.

Added Stats 2015 ch 413 § 1 (AB 1171), effective January 1, 2016. Amended Stats 2016 ch 753 § 2 (AB 2374), effective January 1, 2017; Stats 2017 ch 20 § 6 (AB 115), effective June 27, 2017; Stats 2018 ch 46 § 2 (SB 848), effective June 27, 2018; Stats 2018 ch 602 § 1 (SB 502), effective January 1, 2019; Stats 2019 ch 289 § 2 (AB 1475), effective January 1, 2020; Stats 2019 ch 497 § 213 (AB 991), effective January 1, 2020 (ch 289 prevails).

Chapter 6.8

High Road Jobs in Transportation-Related Public Contracts and Grants Pilot Program

§ 6980. Citation of chapter [Repealed effective January 1, 2028]

This chapter shall be known, and may be cited, as the High Road Jobs in Transportation-Related Public Contracts and Grants Pilot Program.

Added Stats 2022 ch 875 § 1 (SB 674), effective January 1, 2023, repealed January 1, 2028.

§ 6981. Legislative findings and declarations; Intent [Repealed effective January 1, 2028]

(a) The Legislature finds and declares all of the following:

(1) In a time of uncertainty with so many Americans out of work, employment stability and equity are a primary concern.

(2) Spending on green investments creates more jobs per dollar than other infrastructure investments and these jobs are accessible and well paying. Every one million dollars ($1,000,000) in spending on renewable energy creates 7.5 full-time jobs.

(3) Historically vulnerable groups have been disproportionately impacted by economic downturns. For example, for every one percentage point increase in the overall unemployment rate, there is a 1.8-percent increase in African American unemployment.

(4) It is essential that the state, in cooperation with the federal government, use all practical and commercially feasible means to promote the prompt and efficient development of energy sources that are renewable or that more efficiently use and conserve scarce energy resources.

(5) It is in the public interest to do all of the following:

(A) Prioritize reversing factors that have resulted in disproportionate health impacts and economic suffering due to the coronavirus (COVID-19) pandemic among California's low-income communities, communities of color, and immigrant communities that have historically faced underinvestment and discriminatory policies.

(B) Promote sustainable and renewable energy sources, implement measures that increase efficient energy use, advance transportation technologies that reduce the degradation of the environment, lessen the state's dependence of fossil fuels, and protect the health, welfare, and safety of the people of this state.

(C) Spend resources to avoid recreating historical patterns of injustice by allocating resources in a manner that will create a just transition to a green, regenerative economy, founded on climate, racial, and economic justice, that puts an end to extreme inequality and systemic racial injustice, and ensures all Californians have a clean and safe environment in which to live, work, and play.

(D) Support a just recovery where workers from all sectors who have lost wages or jobs as a direct result of the pandemic will be prioritized for new employment opportunities that guarantee family-sustaining incomes, pensions, benefit training, retraining, and early retirement assistance.

(E) Require recovery spending to include a mandate for a robust, fully funded public sector that includes significant investments in job creation and community development with a particular focus on a just transition for affected workers.

(F) Expend resources in a broadly inclusive economic and democratic process that ensures robust, accessible opportunities for all Californians to determine the future of our government and economy.

Appendix

(G) Allocate state funds to programs, businesses, organizations, agencies, and institutions that provide the greatest opportunities for good green jobs, strong labor provisions, and climate-based solutions in a manner that is consistent with the urgency of the climate crisis and the need to make rapid and sustained reductions in greenhouse gases and statewide emissions reduction targets and recommendations from the Intergovernmental Panel on Climate Change.

(H) Ensure that recovery funds reach communities most impacted by the coronavirus (COVID-19) pandemic and prioritize high road employers, as identified by the Labor and Workforce Development Agency, to enhance labor standards, workers' rights, career pathways, and community benefits.

(I) Restore frontline communities and rapidly accelerate achievements in environmental justice and climate goals, including, but not limited to, climate, environmental, and biodiversity protection and stimulating growth.

(b) It is therefore the intent of the Legislature to support the creation of equitable high-quality transportation and related manufacturing and infrastructure jobs in California through the enactment and implementation of this chapter.

Added Stats 2022 ch 875 § 1 (SB 674), effective January 1, 2023, repealed January 1, 2028.

§ 6982. Definitions [Repealed effective January 1, 2028]

Unless the context requires otherwise, for the purposes of this chapter, the following terms shall have the following meanings:

(a) (1) "Bidder" means a private entity that applies, bids, or seeks qualification for a covered public contract. "Bidder" may be more than a single entity.

(2) "Bidder" shall not include a firm, as defined in Section 4525 of the Government Code.

(b) "Contractor" means a private entity that has been awarded a covered public contract.

(c) (1) Except as provided in paragraph (2), "covered public contract" means, to the extent otherwise permitted by law, a public contract awarded by a relevant public agency for the acquisition of zero-emission transit vehicles or electric vehicle supply equipment valued at ten million dollars ($10,000,000) or more.

(2) (A) "Covered public contract" does not mean contracts for the construction or design of infrastructure, including, but not limited to, roads, bridges, or highways.

(B) "Covered public contract" does not mean a local agreement approved by the Labor and Workforce Development Agency that creates high road jobs.

(C) "Covered public contract" does not mean a contract relating to architecture, landscape architecture, engineering, environmental services, land surveying, or construction project management.

(D) "Covered public contract" does not include any of the following:

(i) A contract awarded before January 1, 2023.

(ii) A contract awarded based on a solicitation issued before January 1, 2023.

(iii) A grant or contract related to a grant award announced pursuant to a call for projects that occurred before January 1, 2023.

(d) "High road job standards" means a set of contract terms developed pursuant to Section 6983 that is a material part of the final contract between the bidder and the relevant public agency. Noncompliance with these commitments would violate the terms of the covered public contract.

(e) "Relevant public agency" means the Department of General Services or the Department of Transportation.

(f) "Subcontractor" means a private entity performing a portion of the work of the covered public contract through a subcontract or subgrant.

(g) "Zero-emission transit vehicle" means a vehicle, including, but not limited to, one operated on rails or tracks, which is used for public transportation service and which carries more than 20 persons, including the driver, that produces no emissions of criteria pollutants, toxic air contaminants, and greenhouse gases when stationary or operating.

Added Stats 2022 ch 875 § 1 (SB 674), effective January 1, 2023, repealed January 1, 2028.

§ 6983. Legislative intent; High road jobs standards; Development of policies, procedures, and requirements applicable to covered public contracts [Repealed effective January 1, 2028]

(a) It is the intent of the Legislature that a relevant public agency maximize economic cobenefits by conditioning eligibility to be awarded a covered public contract on a commitment to comply with the labor standards established in this section.

(b) A covered public contract shall incorporate high road job standards designed to achieve the following goals:

(1) Support the creation and retention of quality, nontemporary and full-time jobs that provide high wages, including benefits and access to training.

(2) Support the hiring of displaced workers and individuals facing barriers to employment.

(3) Encourage the development of the state's long-term, climate-sustainable transportation and related infrastructure and manufacturing sectors.

(4) Protect public health by supporting the adoption of specific protections for worker health and safety.

(c) At a minimum, the high road jobs standards shall warrant that the contractor, and any subcontractors that it may use to fulfill the covered public contract, shall satisfy the following requirements:

(1) Individuals performing work to fulfill the covered public contract shall not be misclassified as independent contractors.

(2) The contractor and any subcontractors performing work to fulfill the covered public contract shall comply with all applicable federal, state, and local laws pertaining to paid sick leave, including any antiretaliation provisions contained in those laws.

(3) The contractor and any subcontractors performing work to fulfill the covered public contract shall comply with all applicable safety and health laws and regulations, and shall comply with the employee protections set forth in Sections 6310 and 6311 of the Labor Code.

(4) The contractor shall warrant that it complies, and will continue to comply, with the federal Americans with Disabilities Act of 1990 (Public Law 101-336; 42 U.S.C. Sec. 12101 et seq.) and all regulations thereunder.

(d) A relevant public agency may incorporate additional high road factors, as defined in subdivision (r) of Section 14005 of the Unemployment Insurance Code, into its scoring criteria for covered public contracts, including, but not limited to, a consideration of job creation, wages, and benefits.

(e) The Department of General Services, in consultation with the Labor and Workforce Development Agency and the Department of Transportation, shall develop and publish policies, procedures, and requirements applicable to covered public contracts in the State Contracting Manual for the purpose of implementing this chapter. The exemption established in Section 14615.1 of the Government Code shall apply to these policies, procedures, and requirements.

(f) The programs created pursuant to this chapter shall not apply to solicitations or covered public contracts issued before January 1, 2023.

Added Stats 2022 ch 875 § 1 (SB 674), effective January 1, 2023, repealed January 1, 2028.

§ 6984. Compliance; Reporting requirements [Repealed effective January 1, 2028]

(a) Beginning 12 months after an entity is awarded a covered public contract, the contractor shall annually submit information that is necessary to demonstrate its compliance with the requirements, as specified in Sections 6983 and 6985, to the relevant public agency.

(b) Before receiving any final payment on a covered public contract, a contractor shall submit a final report to the relevant public agency that demonstrates its compliance with the requirements, as specified in Sections 6983 and 6985, for the duration of the covered public contract.

(c) If a contractor fails to comply with the reporting requirements specified in subdivision (a), for each missed report the relevant public agency shall withhold ten thousand dollars ($10,000) in payment to the contractor, or the full payment to the contractor if the amount due is less than ten thousand dollars ($10,000), until the contractor takes steps to cure the defect, pursuant to subdivision (e).

(d) If a contractor fails to comply with the final reporting requirements specified in subdivision (b), the relevant public agency shall withhold ten thousand dollars ($10,000) from the final payment, or the full final payment, if the amount due is less than ten thousand dollars ($10,000), until the contractor takes steps to cure the defect, pursuant to subdivision (e).

(e) A contractor that fails to comply with the reporting requirements established in subdivision (a) or (b) shall, after notice, be allowed to cure the defect. Notwithstanding any other law, if, after at least 15 calendar days, but not more than 30 calendar days from the date of notice, the contractor refuses to comply with the reporting requirements, the relevant public agency shall permanently deduct ten thousand dollars ($10,000) from the final payment, or the full payment if the amount due is less than ten thousand dollars ($10,000).

(f) For covered public contracts awarded pursuant to a master agreement or master contract agreement, the Department of General Services may prescribe additional or alternative mechanisms for enforcing the reporting requirements described in subdivisions (a) and (b).

(g) This section does not limit the availability of standard breach of contract remedies if a contractor fails to comply with the requirements specified in Sections 6983 and 6985, including, but not limited to, termination of the covered contract.

Added Stats 2022 ch 875 § 1 (SB 674), effective January 1, 2023, repealed January 1, 2028.

§ 6985. Legislative declarations regarding effects of climate change; Labor peace agreement [Repealed effective January 1, 2028]

(a) The Legislature declares all of the following:

(1) California will experience an increased prevalence of severe wildfires, heat, drought, and rising sea levels in the coming years as a result of climate change.

(2) The effects of climate change have already cost the state billions of dollars and will only continue to increase if we do not take immediate and decisive action to cut emissions. To name a few, these costs include all of the following:

(A) In 2018, California wildfire damages were estimated to total one hundred forty-eight billion five hundred million dollars ($148,500,000,000).

(B) The 2021 drought directly cost the California agriculture sector about one billion one hundred million dollars ($1,100,000,000) and nearly 8,750 full- and part-time jobs.

(C) The sea level along California's coasts is projected to rise by as much as 20 to 55 inches by the end of the century. A 55-inch sea level rise could put nearly half a million people at risk of flooding by 2100, and threaten one hundred billion dollars ($100,000,000,000) in costs to property and infrastructure, including roadways, buildings, hazardous waste sites, power plants, parks, and tourist destinations.

(3) The Intergovernmental Panel on Climate Change (IPCC) has found global emissions must be reduced by 43 percent by 2030 in order to limit global warming to around 1.5 degrees Celsius.

(4) The transportation sector in California accounts for 41 percent of the state's total carbon emissions.

(5) Recognizing the extreme financial threat climate change poses to the economy of California, the state has a financial interest in rolling out zero-emission transit vehicles as quickly and expeditiously as possible.

(b) To protect the state's proprietary and economic interests in performing the covered public contract without interruption due to the economic effects of a labor dispute, the contractor and any subcontractors performing work to fulfill the covered public contract, shall enter into a labor peace agreement with any organization of any kind in which its employees participate and which exists for the purpose, in whole or in part, of dealing with employers concerning grievances, labor disputes, wages, rates of pay, hours of employment, or conditions of work and which requests a labor peace agreement.

(1) The labor peace agreement shall include a binding and enforceable provision prohibiting the organization and its members from engaging in picketing, work stoppages, boycotts, or any other economic interference for the duration of the labor peace agreement, which shall include the entire term of the covered public contract.

(2) This subdivision shall not be construed as requiring a contractor or any subcontractor to change terms and conditions of employment for its employees, recognize a labor organization as the bargaining representative for its employees, adopt any particular recognition

process, or enter into a collective bargaining agreement with a labor organization.

(3) This subdivision does not abridge the rights, privileges, and benefits afforded by federal law, as applicable, including, but not limited to, Section 5333 of Title 49 of the United States Code.

Added Stats 2022 ch 875 § 1 (SB 674), effective January 1, 2023, repealed January 1, 2028.

§ 6986. Repeal of chapter [Repealed effective January 1, 2028]

This chapter shall remain in effect only until January 1, 2028, and as of that date is repealed.

Added Stats 2022 ch 875 § 1 (SB 674), effective January 1, 2023, repealed January 1, 2028.

Chapter 7

Contract Clauses

§ 7106. Form of required declaration

Every bid on every public works contract of a public entity shall include a declaration under penalty of perjury under the laws of the State of California, in the following form:
"NONCOLLUSION DECLARATION TO BE EXECUTED BY BIDDER AND SUBMITTED WITH BID

The undersigned declares:

I am the _____ of _____, the party making the foregoing bid.

The bid is not made in the interest of, or on behalf of, any undisclosed person, partnership, company, association, organization, or corporation. The bid is genuine and not collusive or sham. The bidder has not directly or indirectly induced or solicited any other bidder to put in a false or sham bid. The bidder has not directly or indirectly colluded, conspired, connived, or agreed with any bidder or anyone else to put in a sham bid, or to refrain from bidding. The bidder has not in any manner, directly or indirectly, sought by agreement, communication, or conference with anyone to fix the bid price of the bidder or any other bidder, or to fix any overhead, profit, or cost element of the bid price, or of that of any other bidder. All statements contained in the bid are true. The bidder has not, directly or indirectly, submitted his or her bid price or any breakdown thereof, or the contents thereof, or divulged information or data relative thereto, to any corporation, partnership, company association, organization, bid depository, or to any member or agent thereof to effectuate a collusive or sham bid, and has not paid, and will not pay, any person or entity for such purpose.

Any person executing this declaration on behalf of a bidder that is a corporation, partnership, joint venture, limited liability company, limited liability partnership, or any other entity, hereby represents that he or she has full power to execute, and does execute, this declaration on behalf of the bidder.

I declare under penalty of perjury under the laws of the State of California that the foregoing is true and correct and that this declaration is executed on _____ [date], at _____ [city], _____ [state]."

Added Stats 1988 ch 1548 § 1. Amended Stats 2011 ch 432 § 37 (SB 944), effective January 1, 2012.

§ 7201. Applicability to contracts entered into on or after January 1, 2012 relating to construction of public work of improvement; Retention proceeds withheld from payments; Limitations.

(a) (1) This section shall apply with respect to all contracts entered into on or after January 1, 2012, between a public entity and an original contractor, between an original contractor and a subcontractor, and between all subcontractors thereunder, relating to the construction of any public work of improvement.

(2) Under no circumstances shall any provision of this section be construed to limit the ability of any public entity to withhold 150 percent of the value of any disputed amount of work from the final payment, as provided for in subdivision (c) of Section 7107. In the event of a good faith dispute, nothing in this section shall be construed to require a public entity to pay for work that is not approved or accepted in accordance with the proper plans or specifications.

(3) For purposes of this section, "public entity" means the state, including every state agency, office, department, division, bureau, board, or commission, the California State University, the University of California, a city, county, city and county, including charter cities and charter counties, district, special district, public authority, political subdivision, public corporation, or nonprofit transit corporation wholly owned by a public agency and formed to carry out the purposes of the public agency.

(b) (1) The retention proceeds withheld from any payment by a public entity from the original contractor, by the original contractor from any subcontractor, and by a subcontractor from any subcontractor thereunder shall not exceed 5 percent of the payment. In no event shall the total retention proceeds withheld exceed 5 percent of the contract price. In a contract between the original contractor and a subcontractor, and in a contract between a subcontractor and any subcontractor thereunder, the percentage of the retention proceeds withheld shall not exceed the percentage specified in the contract between the public entity and the original contractor.

(2) This subdivision shall not apply if the contractor provides written notice to the subcontractor, pursuant to subdivision (c) of Section 4108, prior to, or at, the time that the bid is requested, that bonds shall be required, and the subcontractor subsequently is unable or refuses to furnish to the contractor a performance and payment bond issued by an admitted surety insurer.

(3) Notwithstanding any other provision of this subdivision, the retention proceeds withheld from any payment by an awarding entity set forth in paragraphs (1) to (5), inclusive, of subdivision (a) of Section 10106, from the original contractor, by the original contractor from any subcontractor, and by a subcontractor from any subcontractor thereunder, may exceed 5 percent on specific projects where the director of the department has made a finding prior to the bid that the project is substantially complex and therefore requires a higher retention amount than 5 percent and the department includes in the bid documents details explaining the basis for the finding and the actual retention amount. In a contract between the original contractor and a subcontractor, and in a contract between a subcontractor and any subcontractor thereunder, the percentage of the retention proceeds withheld shall not exceed the percentage specified in the contract between the department and the original contractor.

(4) Notwithstanding any other provision of this subdivision, the retention proceeds withheld from any payment by the awarding entity of a city, county, city and county, including charter cities and charter counties, district, special district, public authority, political subdivision, public corporation, or nonprofit transit corporation wholly owned by a public agency and formed to carry out the purposes of the public agency, from the original contractor, by the original contractor from any subcontractor, and by a subcontractor from any subcontractor thereunder, may exceed 5 percent on specific projects where the governing body of the public entity or designee, including, but not limited to, a general manager or other director of an appropriate department, has approved a finding, on a project by project basis, during a properly noticed and normally scheduled public hearing and prior to bid that the project is substantially complex and therefore requires a higher retention amount than 5 percent and the awarding entity includes in the bid documents details explaining the basis for the finding and the actual retention amount. In a contract between the origi-

nal contractor and a subcontractor, and in a contract between a subcontractor and any subcontractor thereunder, the percentage of the retention proceeds withheld shall not exceed the percentage specified in the contract between the department and the original contractor.

(5) Any finding by a public entity that a project is substantially complex shall include a description of the specific project and why it is a unique project that is not regularly, customarily, or routinely performed by the agency or licensed contractors.

(c) A party identified in subdivision (a) shall not require any other party to waive any provision of this section.

Added Stats 2011 ch 700 § 5 (SB 293), effective January 1, 2012, repealed January 1, 2016. Amended Stats 2014 ch 670 § 1 (AB 1705), effective January 1, 2015, repealed January 1, 2018; Stats 2017 ch 37 § 1 (AB 92), effective January 1, 2018, repealed January 1, 2023; Stats 2022 ch 121 § 1 (AB 2173), effective January 1, 2023.

§ 7202. Withholding retention proceeds prohibited when making progress payments to contractor for work performed on transportation project

(a) The Department of Transportation is prohibited from withholding retention proceeds when making progress payments to a contractor for work performed on a transportation project.

(b) Nothing in this section shall alter, amend, or impair the rights, duties, and obligations of an original contractor, its subcontractors, and all subcontractors thereunder, relating to the construction of any public work of improvement as set forth in Section 7200.

(c) The Department of Transportation shall promptly notify the appropriate policy committees of the Legislature if the state's best interests are compromised because retention was not withheld on a transportation project.

Added Stats 2008 ch 341 § 1 (SB 593), effective January 1, 2009, repealed January 1, 2014. Amended Stats 2012 ch 290 § 2 (AB 1671), effective January 1, 2013, repealed January 1, 2020; Stats 2019 ch 842 § 1 (SB 197), effective January 1, 2020.

§ 7203. Enforceability of delay damages clause

(a) A public works contract entered into on or after January 1, 2016, that contains a clause that expressly requires a contractor to be responsible for delay damages is not enforceable unless the delay damages have been liquidated to a set amount and identified in the public works contract.

(b) "Delay damages" as used in this section, means damages incurred by the public agency for each day after the date on which the work was to be completed by the contractor pursuant to the public works contract. Delay damages shall not include damages incurred by a public agency after the filing of a notice of completion or, in the absence of a notice of completion, the acceptance by the public agency of the public work as complete.

(c) "Public agency" shall include the state, the Regents of the University of California, a city, charter city, county, charter county, district, public authority, municipal utility, and any other political subdivision or public corporation of the state.

(d) This section shall not be construed to limit a right or remedy that the public agency has to enforce the express terms of the public works contract, except for a clause that expressly requires a contractor to be liable for delay damages.

(e) This section shall not be construed to preclude a public agency from including more than one clause for delay damages for specified portions of work when the delay damages have been liquidated to a set amount for each individual clause and identified in the public works contract.

(f) This section shall not apply to departments identified in Section 10106.

Added Stats 2015 ch 434 § 2 (AB 552), effective January 1, 2016.

PART 2

CONTRACTING BY STATE AGENCIES

Chapter 1

State Contract Act

Article 1

Scope of Chapter and General Provisions

§ 10111.2. Providing electronic copy of project's contract documents to contractor plan room

A department shall, upon request from a contractor plan room service, provide an electronic copy of a project's contract documents at no charge to the contractor plan room.

Added Stats 2010 ch 371 § 1 (AB 2036), effective January 1, 2011.

Article 4

Bids and Bidders

§ 10164. State licensing requirements where project involves federal funds

In all state projects where federal funds are involved, no bid submitted shall be invalidated by the failure of the bidder to be licensed in accordance with the laws of this state. However, at the time the contract is awarded, the contractor shall be properly licensed in accordance with the laws of this state. The contract shall not be awarded unless the state agency has verified that the contractor has a valid license in the appropriate classification for the work performed. Any bidder or contractor not so licensed shall be subject to all legal penalties imposed by law, including, but not limited to, any appropriate disciplinary action by the Contractors State License Board. The department shall include a statement to that effect in the standard form of prequalification questionnaire and financial statement. Failure of the bidder to obtain proper and adequate licensing for an award of a contract shall constitute a failure to execute the contract as provided in Section 10181 and shall result in the forfeiture of the security of the bidder.

Enacted Stats 1981 ch 306 § 2. Amended Stats 1983 ch 810 § 1; Stats 1994 ch 432 § 1 (AB 3365).

§ 10167. Sealed bids; Bidder's security

(a) All bids shall be presented under sealed cover and accompanied by one of the following forms of bidder's security:

(1) An electronic bidder's bond by an admitted surety insurer submitted using an electronic registry service approved by the department advertising the contract.

(2) A signed bidder's bond by an admitted surety insurer received by the department advertising the contract.

(3) Cash, a cashier's check, or certified check received by, and made payable to, the director of the department advertising the contract.

(b) The required bidder's security shall be in an amount equal to at least 10 percent of the amount bid. A bid shall not be considered unless one of the forms of bidder's security is enclosed with it.

(c) All bids submitted pursuant to this section shall also comply with the provisions of Section 1601 of the Public Contract Code.

Enacted Stats 1981 ch 306 § 2. Amended Stats 2012 ch 290 § 3 (AB 1671), effective January 1, 2013, operative until January 1, 2020.

Article 8

Modifications; Performance; Payment

§ 10261. [Section repealed 2023.]

Enacted Stats 1981 ch 306 § 2. Amended Stats 1998 ch 857 § 9 (AB 2084). Stats 2011 ch 700 § 6 (SB 293), effective January 1, 2012, repealed January 1, 2016; Stats 2014 ch 670 § 2 (AB 1705), effective January 1, 2015, repealed January 1, 2018. Stats 2017 ch 37 § 2 (AB 92), effective January 1, 2018, repealed January 1, 2023; repealed January 1, 2023; Stats 2022 ch 121 § 2 (AB 2173), effective January 1, 2023. Repealed Stats 2022 ch 121 § 3 (AB 2173), effective January 1, 2023.

§ 10261. Payments upon contracts; Progress payments

(a) Payments upon contracts shall be made as the department prescribes upon estimates made and approved by the department, but progress payments shall not be made in excess of 100 percent of the percentage of actual work completed plus a like percentage of the value of material delivered on the ground or stored subject to or under the control of the state, and unused, except as otherwise provided in this section. The department shall withhold not more than 5 percent of the contract price until final completion and acceptance of the project. However, at any time after 95 percent of the work has been completed, the department may reduce the funds withheld to an amount not less than 125 percent of the estimated value of the work yet to be completed, as determined by the department, if the reduction has been approved, in writing, by the surety on the performance bond and by the surety on the payment bond. The Controller shall draw their warrants upon estimates so made and approved by the department and the Treasurer shall pay them. The funds may be released by electronic transfer if that procedure is requested by the contractor, in writing, and if the department has, in place at the time of the request, the mechanism for the transfer.

(b) (1) Notwithstanding subdivision (a), when the director of the department has made a finding prior to the bid that a specified project is substantially complex and therefore requires a higher retention amount than 5 percent, and the department includes in the bid documents details explaining the basis for the finding and the actual retention amount, then payments upon contracts by the department shall be made as the department prescribes upon estimates made and approved by the department. However, progress payments shall not be made in excess of 95 percent of the percentage of actual work completed, plus a like percentage of the value of material delivered on the ground or stored, subject to, or under the control of the state, and unused, except as otherwise provided in this section. At any time after 95 percent of the work has been completed, the department may reduce the funds withheld to an amount not less than 125 percent of the estimated value of the work yet to be completed, as determined by the department, if the reduction has been approved, in writing, by the surety on the performance bond and by the surety on the payment bond. The Controller shall draw their warrants upon estimates so made and approved by the department and the Treasurer shall pay them with funds appropriated therefor. The funds may be released by electronic transfer if that procedure is requested by the contractor, in writing, and if the department has, in place at the time of the request, the mechanism for the transfer.

(2) Any finding by the director of a department that a project is substantially complex shall include a description of the specific project and why it is a unique project that is not regularly, customarily, or routinely performed by the agency or licensed contractors.

Enacted Stats 1981 ch 306 § 2. Amended Stats 1998 ch 857 § 9 (AB 2084); Stats 2011 ch 700 § 6 (SB 293), effective January 1, 2012, repealed January 1, 2016; Stats 2014 ch 670 § 2 (AB 1705), effective January 1, 2015, repealed January 1, 2018; Stats 2017 ch 37 § 2 (AB 92), effective January 1, 2018, repealed January 1, 2023; Stats 2022 ch 121 § 2 (AB 2173), effective January 1, 2023.

§ 10262. Payment to subcontractors

The contractor shall pay to his or her subcontractors, within seven days of receipt of each progress payment, the respective amounts allowed the contractor on account of the work performed by his or her subcontractors, to the extent of each subcontractor's interest therein. The payments to subcontractors shall be based on estimates made pursuant to Section 10261. Any diversion by the contractor of payments received for prosecution of a contract, or failure to reasonably account for the application or use of the payments constitutes ground for actions prescribed in Section 10253, in addition to disciplinary action by the Contractors' State License Board. The subcontractor shall notify, in writing, the Contractors' State License Board and the department of any payment less than the amount or percentage approved for the class or item of work as set forth in Section 10261.

Enacted Stats 1981 ch 306 § 2. Amended Stats 1998 ch 857 § 10 (AB 2084); Stats 2011 ch 700 § 8 (SB 293), effective January 1, 2012.

Chapter 2

State Acquisition of Goods and Services

Article 2

Approval of Contracts

§ 10295.4. State agency contracts with contractors appearing on tax delinquency list prohibited; Application

(a) Notwithstanding any other law, a state agency shall not enter into any contract for the acquisition of goods or services with a contractor whose name appears on either list of the 500 largest tax delinquencies pursuant to Section 7063 or 19195 of the Revenue and Taxation Code. Any contract entered into in violation of this subdivision is void and unenforceable.

(b) This section shall apply to any contract executed on or after July 1, 2012.

§ 10295.8. Extension or renewal of contracts awarded without competitive bidding; Report

For a contract awarded without competitive bidding for the acquisition of goods or services in the amount of seventy-five million dollars ($75,000,000) or more, entered into on or after January 1, 2023, the state agency, on or before the contract end date, shall submit to the Joint Legislative Budget Committee information regarding the terms and conditions of a proposed extension or renewal of the contract.

Added Stats 2022 ch 543 § 1 (SB 1271), effective January 1, 2023.

§ 10298.5. Use of proceeds; Contracts [Repealed effective January 1, 2028]

(a) The director may use the procedures described in Section 10298 for contracts for the installation, and contracts for the purchase and installation, of carpet, resilient flooring, synthetic turf, or lighting fixtures that will satisfy the requirements of this section. Except as specified in subdivision (b), notwithstanding any other law requiring bidding on public works projects, as defined in Section 1101, state agencies and local agencies, including school districts and any other agency subject to the Local Agency Public Construction Act (Chapter 1 (commencing with Section 20100) of Part 3), may contract with suppliers awarded those contracts, if all of the following requirements are satisfied:

(1) The installation work is not performed in connection with new construction.

(2) The contractor provides an acknowledgment to the state or local agency that the installation is a public work for purposes of Chapter 1 (commencing with Section 1720) of Part 7 of Division 2 of the Labor Code.

(3)(A) Except as otherwise provided in subparagraph (B), the contractor provides the state or local agency with an enforceable commitment that a skilled and trained workforce, as defined in Section 2601, will be used to complete the installation work.

(B) This paragraph shall not apply if the state or local agency has entered into a project labor agreement, as defined in Section 2500, that requires all contractors and subcontractors performing the installation work to use a skilled and trained workforce and the contractor agrees to be bound by that project labor agreement.

(b) A local agency shall not use the procedures authorized by this section for a contract with an award amount that exceeds the amount in an applicable requirement for the local agency to use a formal competitive bidding process for a contract that exceeds a specified amount.

(c)(1) Any state or local agency that enters into a contract for installation, or for purchase or installation, pursuant to this section shall provide notice of that contract to the Department of Industrial Relations pursuant to Section 1773.3 of the Labor Code, regardless of the size of the contract.

(2)(A) Notwithstanding Section 10231.5 of the Government Code, no later than January 1, 2027, the Department of Industrial Relations shall submit to the appropriate policy and fiscal committees of the Legislature a report on the use of the procedures authorized by this section.

(B) The report shall include, but is not limited to, the following information:

(i) A description of the contracts awarded using the procedures authorized by this section, including the state or local agency that awarded the contract.

(ii) The contract award amounts.

(iii) The contractors awarded the contracts.

(C) The report submitted pursuant to subparagraph (A) shall be submitted in compliance with Section 9795 of the Government Code.

(d) This section shall remain in effect only until January 1, 2028, and as of that date is repealed.

Added Stats 2022 ch 310 § 2 (SB 1422), effective January 1, 2023, repealed January 1, 2028.

PART 3

CONTRACTING BY LOCAL AGENCIES

Chapter 1

Local Agency Public Construction Act

Article 1

Title

§ 20103.5. Effect of license requirement on bid

In all contracts subject to this part where federal funds are involved, no bid submitted shall be invalidated by the failure of the bidder to be licensed in accordance with the laws of this state. However, at the time the contract is awarded, the contractor shall be properly licensed in accordance with the laws of this state. The first payment for work or material under any contract shall not be made unless and until the Registrar of Contractors verifies to the agency that the records of the Contractors' State License Board indicate that the contractor was properly licensed at the time the contract was awarded. Any bidder or contractor not so licensed shall be subject to all legal penalties imposed by law, including, but not limited to, any appropriate disciplinary action by the Contractors' State License Board. The agency shall include a statement to that effect in the standard form of prequalification questionnaire and financial statement. Failure of the bidder to obtain proper and adequate licensing for an award of a contract shall constitute a failure to execute the contract and shall result in the forfeiture of the security of the bidder.

Added Stats 1990 ch 321 § 2 (SB 929) as § 20104, effective July 16, 1990. Renumbered § 20103.5 by Stats 1990 ch 1414 § 1 (AB 4165).

§ 20103.7. Providing electronic copy of project's contract documents to contractor plan room

A local agency subject to this chapter taking bids for the construction of a public work or improvement shall, upon request from a contractor plan room service, provide an electronic copy of a project's contract documents at no charge to the contractor plan room.

Added Stats 2010 ch 371 § 2 (AB 2036), effective January 1, 2011.

Appendix

Article 3

School Districts

§ 20111.6. Public projects using funds from Leroy F. Greene School Facilities Act of 1998 or state school bond

(a) This section applies only to public projects, as defined in subdivision (c) of Section 22002, for which the governing board of the school district uses funds received pursuant to the Leroy F. Greene School Facilities Act of 1998 (Chapter 12.5 (commencing with Section 17070.10) of Part 10 of Division 1 of Title 1 of the Education Code) or any funds received, including funds reimbursed, from any future state school bond for a public project that involves a projected expenditure of one million dollars ($1,000,000) or more.

(b) If the governing board of the school district enters into a contract meeting the criteria of subdivision (a), then the governing board of the school district shall require that prospective bidders for a construction contract complete and submit to the governing board of the school district a standardized prequalification questionnaire and financial statement. The questionnaire and financial statement shall be verified under oath by the bidder in the manner in which civil pleadings in civil actions are verified. The questionnaires and financial statements are not public records and shall not be open to public inspection.

(c) The governing board of the school district shall adopt and apply a uniform system of rating bidders on the basis of the completed questionnaires and financial statements. This system shall also apply to a person, firm, or corporation that constructs a building described in Section 17406 or 17407 of the Education Code.

(d) The questionnaire and financial statement described in subdivision (b), and the uniform system of rating bidders described in subdivision (c), shall cover, at a minimum, the issues covered by the standardized questionnaire and model guidelines for rating bidders developed by the Department of Industrial Relations pursuant to subdivision (a) of Section 20101.

(e) Each prospective bidder shall be furnished by the school district letting the contract with a standardized proposal form that, when completed and executed, shall be submitted as his or her bid. Bids not presented on the forms so furnished shall be disregarded.

(f) A proposal form required pursuant to subdivision (e) shall not be accepted from any person or other entity that is required to submit a completed questionnaire and financial statement for prequalification pursuant to subdivision (b) or from any person or other entity that uses a subcontractor that is required to submit a completed questionnaire and financial statement for prequalification pursuant to subdivision (b), but has not done so at least 10 business days before the date fixed for the public opening of sealed bids or has not been prequalified for at least five business days before that date. The school district may require the completed questionnaire and financial statement for prequalification to be submitted more than 10 business days before the fixed date for the public opening of sealed bids. The school district may also require the prequalification more than five business days before the fixed date.

(g) (1) The governing board of the school district may establish a process for prequalifying prospective bidders pursuant to this section on a quarterly or annual basis and a prequalification pursuant to this process shall be valid for one calendar year following the date of initial prequalification.

(2) The governing board of the school district shall establish a process to prequalify a person, firm, or corporation, including, but not limited to, the prime contractor and, if used, an electrical, mechanical, and plumbing subcontractor, to construct a building described in Section 17406 or 17407 of the Education Code on a quarterly or annual basis. A prequalification pursuant to this process shall be valid for one calendar year following the date of initial prequalification.

(h) This section does not preclude the governing board of the school district from prequalifying or disqualifying a subcontractor of any specialty classification described in Section 7058 of the Business and Professions Code.

(i) For purposes of this section, bidders shall include both of the following:

(1) A prime contractor, as defined in Section 4113, that is either of the following:

(A) A general engineering contractor described in Section 7056 of the Business and Professions Code.

(B) A general building contractor described in Section 7057 of the Business and Professions Code.

(2) If utilized, each electrical, mechanical, and plumbing contractor, whether as a prime contractor or as a subcontractor, as defined in Section 4113.

(j) If a public project covered by this section includes electrical, mechanical, or plumbing components that will be performed by electrical, mechanical, or plumbing contractors, a list of prequalified general contractors and electrical, mechanical, and plumbing subcontractors shall be made available by the school district to all bidders at least five business days before the dates fixed for the public opening of sealed bids. The school district may require the list to be made available more than five business days before the fixed dates for the public opening of sealed bids.

(k) For purposes of this section, electrical, mechanical, and plumbing subcontractors are contractors licensed pursuant to Section 7058 of the Business and Professions Code, specifically contractors holding C-4, C-7, C-10, C-16, C-20, C-34, C-36, C-38, C-42, C-43, and C-46 licenses, pursuant to regulations of the Contractors' State License Board.

(*l*) This section does not apply to a school district with an average daily attendance of less than 2,500.

(m) (1) This section applies only to contracts awarded on or after January 1, 2014.

(2) The amendments made to this section by Chapter 408 of the Statutes of 2014 apply only to contracts awarded on or after January 1, 2015.

Added Stats 2012 ch 808 § 1 (AB 1565), effective January 1, 2013, inoperative January 1, 2019, repealed July 1, 2019. Amended Stats 2014 ch 408 § 5 (AB 1581), effective January 1, 2015, inoperative January 1, 2019, repealed July 1, 2019. Stats 2015 ch 214 § 4 (AB 566), effective January 1, 2016, inoperative January 1, 2019, repealed July 1, 2019. Amended Stats 2016 ch 86 § 251 (SB 1171), effective January 1, 2017, repealed July 1, 2019. Stats 2018 ch 534 § 1 (AB 2031), effective January 1, 2019.

PUBLIC RESOURCES CODE

DIVISION 15

ENERGY CONSERVATION AND DEVELOPMENT

Chapter 3

State Energy Resources Conservation and Development Commission

§ 25228. Evaluation and recommendation of policies and implementation strategies to overcome barriers to deployment and use of geothermal heat pump and geothermal ground loop technologies

(a) The commission, in consultation with the Public Utilities Commission, cities, counties, special districts, and other stakeholders, shall evaluate and recommend policies and implementation strategies to overcome barriers to the deployment and use of geothermal heat pump and geothermal ground loop technologies. In evaluating these policies and strategies, the commission shall consider all of the following:

(1) The quantitative benefits and costs to ratepayers specific to safer, more reliable, or less costly gas or electrical service and through greater energy efficiency, reduction of health and environmental impacts from air pollution, and reduction of greenhouse gas emissions related to electricity and natural gas production and use, through the use of geothermal heat pump and geothermal ground loop technologies.

(2) The existing statutory and permit requirements that impact the use of geothermal heat pumps and geothermal ground loop technologies and any other existing legal impediments to the use of geothermal heat pump and geothermal ground loop technologies.

(3) The impact of the use of the geothermal heat pump and geothermal ground loop technologies on achieving the state's goals pursuant to the California Global Warming Solutions Act of 2006 (Division 25.5 (commencing with Section 38500) of the Health and Safety Code) and achieving the state's energy efficiency goals.

(b) The commission shall include the evaluations and recommendations made pursuant to this section in the integrated energy policy report that is required to be adopted for calendar year 2013, pursuant to subdivision (a) of Section 25302.

Added Stats 2012 ch 608 § 1 (AB 2339), effective January 1, 2013.

Chapter 5

Energy Resources Conservation

§ 25402.11. Establishment of administrative enforcement process for violation of a regulation and assessment of administrative civil penalty; Considerations; Orders; Cost; Exceptions

(a) (1) The commission may adopt regulations establishing an administrative enforcement process for a violation of a regulation adopted pursuant to subdivisions (c) and (f) of Section 25402 and for the assessment of an administrative civil penalty not to exceed two thousand five hundred dollars ($2,500) for each violation. The process shall comply with the requirements of Chapter 4 (commencing with Section 11370) and Chapter 4.5 (commencing with Section 11400) of Part 1 of Division 3 of Title 2 of the Government Code.

(2) In assessing the amount of an administrative penalty, the commission shall consider all of the following factors:

(A) The nature and seriousness of the violation.

(B) The number of violations.

(C) The persistence of the violation.

(D) The length of time over which the violation occurred.

(E) The willfulness of the violation.

(F) The violator's assets, liabilities, and net worth.

(G) The harm to consumers and to the state that resulted from the amount of energy wasted due to the violation.

(b) If the commission finds that a violation of the regulations adopted pursuant to subdivisions (c) and (f) of Section 25402 has occurred or is threatening to occur, the commission may refer the matter to the Attorney General to petition a court to enjoin the violation. The court may grant prohibitory or mandatory injunctive relief as warranted by issuing a temporary restraining order, preliminary injunction, or permanent injunction, and may assess a civil penalty not to exceed two thousand five hundred dollars ($2,500) for each violation, considering the factors specified in paragraph (2) of subdivision (a).

(c) Penalties collected pursuant to this section shall be deposited into the Appliance Efficiency Enforcement Subaccount, which is hereby established in the Energy Resources Programs Account. The moneys in the Appliance Efficiency Enforcement Subaccount may be expended by the commission, upon appropriation by the Legislature, for the education of the public regarding appliance energy efficiency and for the enforcement of the regulations adopted pursuant to subdivisions (c) and (f) of Section 25402.

(d) An order imposing an administrative civil penalty shall be subject to judicial review pursuant to subdivisions (a) and (b) of Section 25534.2.

(e) A person shall not be liable for a civil penalty pursuant to subdivision (b) if that person is subject to an administrative civil penalty pursuant to subdivision (a).

(f) In a civil action brought on behalf of the commission pursuant to this section, upon granting relief, the court shall award to the commission the reasonable costs incurred by the commission in investigating and prosecuting the action.

(g) The commission shall not initiate an administrative enforcement process pursuant to the regulations adopted pursuant to this section against an entity for the unlawful sale or the unlawful offer for sale of an appliance if both of the following apply:

(1) The appliance fully complies with all of the requirements of the regulations adopted pursuant to subdivisions (c) and (f) of Section 25402.

(2) The only basis for the commission's potential enforcement action is that the appliance is not considered to be in compliance because of the commission's delay in reviewing and processing information submitted to it that demonstrates full compliance.

(h) In addition to the prohibitions specified in subdivision (g), the commission shall not initiate an administrative enforcement process pursuant to the regulations adopted pursuant to this section for a violation of a standard adopted pursuant to subdivisions (c) and (f) of Section 25402 until both of the following occur:

(1) No fewer than 60 days have elapsed since the date when the standard was published in the California Register.

(2) No fewer than 30 days have elapsed since the date when the alleged violator received written notice of the alleged violation and date when the commission provided public notice of the standard.

Added Stats 2011 ch 591 § 3 (SB 454), effective January 1, 2012. Amended Stats 2019 ch 697 § 3 (SB 49), effective January 1, 2020.

§ 25402.12. Plan to promote compliance with regulations in the installation of central air-conditioning and heat pumps

(a) On or before January 1, 2019, the commission, in consultation with the Contractors' State License Board, local building officials, and other stakeholders, shall approve a plan that will promote compliance with Part 6 of Title 24 of the California Code of Regulations in the installation of central air conditioning and heat pumps.

(b) Before approving the plan described in subdivision (a), the commission shall do all of the following:

(1) Evaluate the best available technological and economic information to ensure that data collection and its use is feasible and achievable at a reasonable cost to government, industry, and homeowners.

(2) Consider the impact of the plan on all of the following:

(A) Property owners.

(B) The heating, ventilation, and air conditioning industry, including manufacturers, distributors, and contractors.

(C) Local governments.

(D) Building officials.

(E) The Contractors' State License Board.

(3) Provide the public with the opportunity to review and comment on the proposed plan.

(c) The commission may adopt regulations to increase compliance with permitting and inspection requirements for central air conditioning and heat pumps, and associated sales and installations, consistent with the plan approved pursuant to subdivision (a).

Added Stats 2016 ch 678 § 1 (SB 1414), effective January 1, 2017. Amended Stats 2017 ch 561 § 206 (AB 1516), effective January 1, 2018.

§ 25402.13. Photovoltaic systems requirements in repair, restoration, or replacement of residential building damaged by a disaster [Effective until January 1, 2023]

(a) Notwithstanding other laws, residential construction intended to repair, restore, or replace a residential building damaged or destroyed as a result of a disaster in an area in which a state of emergency has been proclaimed by the Governor pursuant to Chapter 7 (commencing with Section 8550) of Division 1 of Title 2 of the Government Code shall comply with requirements regarding photovoltaic systems pursuant to regulations prescribed pursuant to subdivisions (a) and (b) of Section 25402, if any, that were in effect at the time the damaged or destroyed residential building was originally constructed and shall not be required to comply with any additional or conflicting photovoltaic system requirements in effect at the time of repair, restoration, or replacement.

(b) This section does not apply to emergencies proclaimed by the Governor on and after January 1, 2020.

(c) This section only applies when one or more of the following conditions are met:

(1) The income of the owner of the residential building is at or below the median income for the county in which the residential building is located as determined by the Department of Housing and Community Development state income limits.

(2) The construction does not exceed the square footage of the property at the time it was damaged.

(3) The new construction is located on the site of the home that was damaged.

(4) The owner of the residential building did not have code upgrade insurance at the time the property was damaged.

(d) This section shall remain in effect only until January 1, 2023, and as of that date is repealed.

Added Stats 2019 ch 259 § 1 (AB 178), effective January 1, 2020, repealed January 1, 2023.

Chapter 10

Enforcement and Judicial Review

§ 25900. Injunctive relief

Except as provided in Sections 25402.11 and 25531, if the commission finds that any provision of this division is violated, or a violation is threatening to take place that constitutes an emergency requiring immediate action to protect the public health, welfare, or safety, the Attorney General, upon request of the commission, shall petition a court to enjoin the violation. The court may grant prohibitory or mandatory injunctive relief as warranted by way of temporary restraining order, preliminary injunction, and permanent injunction.

Added Stats 1974 ch 276 § 2, operative January 7, 1975. Amended Stats 2011 ch 591 § 4 (SB 454), effective January 1, 2012.

PUBLIC UTILITIES CODE

DIVISION 1

REGULATION OF PUBLIC UTILITIES

PART 1

PUBLIC UTILITIES ACT

Chapter 2.3

Electrical Restructuring

Article 16

California Renewables Portfolio Standard Program

§ 399.4. Policy and intent to administer cost-effective energy efficiency programs; Rebates or incentives for energy efficiency improvement or installation; Evaluation of investments; Review of policies governing energy efficiency programs

(a) (1) In order to ensure that prudent investments in energy efficiency continue to be made that produce cost-effective energy savings, reduce customer demand, and contribute to the safe and reliable operation of the electrical distribution grid, it is the policy of this state and the intent of the Legislature that the commission shall supervise the administration of cost-effective energy efficiency programs authorized pursuant to its statutory authority, including Sections 381, 381.1, 381.2, 381.5, 382, 384.5, 400, 454.5, 454.55, 454.56, 589, 701.1, 749, and 769, Article 10 (commencing with Section 890) of Chapter 4, and Chapter 6 (commencing with Section 2781) of Part 2.

(2) As used in this section, the term "energy efficiency" includes, but is not limited to, cost-effective activities to achieve peak load reduction that improve end-use efficiency, lower customers' bills, and reduce system needs.

(b) (1) If a customer or contractor is the recipient of a rebate or incentive offered by a public utility for an energy efficiency improvement or installation of energy efficient components, equipment, or appliances in a building, the public utility shall provide the rebate or incentive only if the customer or contractor certifies that the improvement or installation has complied with any applicable permitting requirements, including any applicable specifications or requirements set forth in the California Building Standards Code (Title 24 of the California Code of Regulations), and, if a contractor performed the installation or improvement, that the contractor holds the appropriate license for the work performed.

(2) In addition to the requirements of paragraph (1), if a customer or contractor is the recipient of a rebate or incentive offered by a public utility for the purchase or installation of central air conditioning or a heat pump, and their related fans, the public utility shall provide the rebate or incentive only if the customer or contractor provides proof of permit closure. The public utility is not responsible for verifying the proof of permit closure documentation provided by the customer or contractor.

(3) This subdivision does not imply or create authority or responsibility, or expand existing authority or responsibility, of a public utility for the enforcement of the building energy and water efficiency standards adopted pursuant to subdivision (a) or (b) of Section 25402 of the Public Resources Code, or appliance efficiency standards and certification requirements adopted pursuant to subdivision (c) of Section 25402 of the Public Resources Code.

(4) This subdivision does not limit the authority of the commission to impose any additional requirements on a recipient of any rebate or incentive.

(c) The commission, in evaluating energy efficiency investments under its statutory authority, shall also ensure that local and regional interests, multifamily dwellings, and energy service industry capabilities are incorporated into program portfolio design and that local governments, community-based organizations, and energy efficiency service providers are encouraged to participate in program implementation where appropriate.

(d) The commission, in a new or existing proceeding, shall review and update its policies governing energy efficiency programs funded by utility customers to facilitate achieving the targets established pursuant to subdivision (c) of Section 25310 of the Public Resources Code. In updating its policies, the commission shall, at a minimum, do all of the following:

(1) Authorize market transformation programs with appropriate levels of funding to achieve deeper energy efficiency savings.

(2) Authorize pay for performance programs that link incentives directly to measured energy savings. As part of pay for performance programs authorized by the commission, customers should be reasonably compensated for developing and implementing an energy effi-

Appendix

ciency plan, with a portion of their incentive reserved pending post project measurement results.

(3) Authorize programs to achieve deeper savings through operational, behavioral, and retrocommissioning activities.

(4) Ensure that customers have certainty in the values and methodology used to determine energy efficiency incentives by basing the amount of any incentives provided by gas and electrical corporations on the values and methodology contained in the executed customer agreement. Incentive payments shall be based on measured results.

Added Stats 2000 ch 1050 § 4 (SB 1194). Amended Stats 2006 ch 512 § 28 (SB 1250), effective September 27, 2006; Stats 2011 ch 591 § 5 (SB 454), effective January 1, 2012; Stats 2015 ch 547 § 16 (SB 350), effective January 1, 2016; Stats 2016 ch 678 § 2 (SB 1414), effective January 1, 2017. Stats 2017 ch 561 § 210 (AB 1516), effective January 1, 2018.

PART 2

SPECIFIC PUBLIC UTILITIES

Chapter 9

Solar Energy Systems

Article 1

Solar Energy Systems

§ 2854.6. Development of standardized inputs and assumptions to be used in calculation and presentation of electricity utility bill savings

(a) On or before July 1, 2019, the commission shall develop standardized inputs and assumptions to be used in the calculation and presentation of electric utility bill savings to a consumer that can be expected by using a solar energy system by vendors, installers, or financing entities, and the commission and each electrical corporation shall post these standardized inputs and assumptions on their Internet Web sites.

(b) For purposes of this section, "solar energy system" means a solar energy device to be installed on a residential building that has the primary purpose of providing for the collection and distribution of solar energy for the generation of electricity, that produces at least one kW, and not more than five MW, alternating current rated peak electricity, and that meets or exceeds the eligibility criteria established pursuant to Section 25782 of the Public Resources Code.

Added Stats 2017 ch 662 § 3 (AB 1070), effective January 1, 2018.

DIVISION 12

COUNTY TRANSPORTATION COMMISSIONS

Chapter 2

Creation of Commissions

§ 130051.22. Establishment of prequalification program for bidders on contracts; Prequalification standardized questionnaire and financial statement

(a) The authority may establish and maintain a prequalification program for bidders on contracts not covered by subdivision (b).

(b) On public projects, as defined in subdivision (c) of Section 22002 of the Public Contract Code, the authority shall require, at a minimum, that prospective bidders for a construction contract complete and submit to the authority a prequalification standardized questionnaire and financial statement in a form specified by the authority, pursuant to subdivision (a) of Section 20101 of the Public Contract Code.

Added Stats 2012 ch 703 § 3 (AB 2440), effective January 1, 2013.

Chapter 4

Powers and Functions

Article 2

Contracts

§ 130232. Competitive bidding for contracts; Bid requirements

(a) Except as provided in subdivision (f), purchase of all supplies, equipment, and materials, and the construction of all facilities and works, when the expenditure required exceeds twenty-five thousand dollars ($25,000), shall be by contract let to the lowest responsible bidder. Notice requesting bids shall be published at least once in a newspaper of general circulation. The publication shall be made at least 10 days before the date for the receipt of the bids. The commission, at its discretion, may reject any and all bids and readvertise.

Appendix

(b) Except as provided for in subdivision (f), whenever the expected expenditure required exceeds one thousand dollars ($1,000), but not twenty-five thousand dollars ($25,000), the commission shall obtain a minimum of three quotations, either written or oral, that permit prices and terms to be compared.

(c) Where the expenditure required by the bid price is less than fifty thousand dollars ($50,000), the executive director may act for the commission.

(d) All bids for construction work submitted pursuant to this section shall be presented under sealed cover and shall be accompanied by one of the following forms of bidder's security:

(1) Cash.

(2) A cashier's check made payable to the commission.

(3) A certified check made payable to the commission.

(4) A bidder's bond executed by an admitted surety insurer, made payable to the commission.

(e) Upon an award to the lowest bidder, the security of an unsuccessful bidder shall be returned in a reasonable period of time, but in no event shall that security be held by the commission beyond 60 days from the date that the award was made.

(f) The following provisions apply only to the Los Angeles County Metropolitan Transportation Authority:

(1) The contract shall be let to the lowest responsible bidder or, in the authority's discretion, to the person who submitted a proposal that provides the best value to the commission on the basis of the factors identified in the solicitation when the purchase price of all supplies, equipment, and materials exceeds one hundred fifty thousand dollars ($150,000). "Best value" means the overall combination of quality, price, and other elements of a proposal that, when considered together, provide the greatest overall benefit in response to requirements described in the solicitation documents. The contract shall be let to the lowest responsible bidder when the purchase price of the construction of all facilities exceeds twenty-five thousand dollars ($25,000).

(2) The authority shall obtain a minimum of three quotations, either written or oral, that permit prices and terms to be compared whenever the expected expenditure required exceeds three thousand dollars ($3,000), but not one hundred fifty thousand dollars ($150,000).

(3) The authority may purchase supplies, equipment, and materials from a public auction sale, including public auctions held via the internet, using the procedures established for all other participants in the public auction.

(4) The authority may participate in a procurement agreement involving other public entities that is identified by a procuring public entity or entities as a cooperative procuring agreement from

which other public entities may make purchases or enter into contracts, and the authority may procure, and enter into contracts for, items purchased pursuant to that procurement agreement, notwithstanding that the authority may not be the procuring public entity, provided the procurement agreement is awarded or entered into by either of the following:

(A) One or more public entities or an organization of public entities, which may include the authority.

(B) A federal, state, or local public entity.

(5) (A) Notwithstanding any other provision of law requiring the authority to award contracts to the lowest responsible bidder, the authority may, except as to contracts for professional services involving private architectural, landscape architectural, engineering, environmental, land surveying, or construction management as defined in Sections 4525 and 4529.10 of the Government Code, do any of the following in facilitating contract awards with small business enterprises, medium business enterprises, local small business enterprises, and disabled veteran business enterprises:

(i) Provide for a small business enterprise preference in construction, the construction component of a design-build team, the procurement of goods, or the delivery of services. The preference to a small business enterprise shall be 5 percent of the lowest responsible bidder meeting specifications that provides for small business enterprise participation.

(ii) Provide for a local small business enterprise preference in construction, the construction component of a design-build team, the procurement of goods, or the delivery of services. The preference to a local small business enterprise shall be 5 percent of the lowest responsible bidder meeting specifications that provides for local small business enterprise participation. The authority may also offer the preference to a nonlocal business if the bid includes a 30-percent participation by local small business enterprises.

(iii) Establish a subcontracting participation goal for small business enterprises on contracts financed with nonfederal funds and grant a preference of 5 percent to the lowest responsible bidders who meet the goal.

(iv) Require bidders, prior to the time bids are opened, to comply with the small business enterprise and disabled veteran business enterprise goals and requirements established by the authority on contracts financed with nonfederal funds.

(v) In awarding contracts to the lowest responsible bidder, award the contract to the lowest responsible bidder meeting the small business enterprise and disabled veteran business enterprise goals.

(vi) Until January 1, 2028, set aside work for competition among certified small business enterprises and award each contract to the lowest responsible bidder whenever the expected expenditure required exceeds five thousand dollars ($5,000) but is less than five million dollars ($5,000,000), as long as price quotations are solicited by the authority from three or more certified small business enterprises.

(vii) Until January 1, 2028, set aside work for competition among medium business enterprises for no more than 20 contracts and award each contract to the lowest responsible bidder whenever the expected expenditure required exceeds five million dollars ($5,000,000) but is less than thirty million dollars ($30,000,000), as long as price quotations are solicited by the authority from three or more medium business enterprises.

(B) If the authority awards contracts pursuant to clause (vi) or (vii) of subparagraph (A), the authority, for purposes of legislative oversight, shall prepare and submit the reports described in this subparagraph to the Legislature regarding contracts awarded pursuant to clauses (vi) and (vii) of subparagraph (A). The reports shall be submitted in compliance with Section 9795 of the Government Code and shall be submitted in accordance with the following:

(i) By December 31, 2023, for contracts issued between January 1, 2019, and December 31, 2023.

(ii) By December 31, 2026, for contracts issued between January 1, 2019, and December 31, 2026. The report shall note the number of employees working at a medium business enterprise receiving awards pursuant to this section.

(C) A small or medium business enterprise recommended for a contract award through use of a set aside shall be performing a commercially useful function. A small business enterprise shall be presumed to be performing a commercially useful function if it performs and exercises responsibility of at least 30 percent of the total cost of the contract work with its own workforce.

(D) "Small business enterprise" as used in this paragraph, means a business enterprise that is classified as a small business under United States Small Business Administration rules and meets the current small business enterprise size standards found in Part 121 of Title 13 of the Code of Federal Regulations appropriate to the type of work the enterprise seeks to perform. The authority may establish limitations regarding the average annual grossreceipts of a small business over the previous three fiscal years and establish limitations regarding the personal net worth of the owner of the small business, exclusive of the value of the owner's personal residence.

(E) "Local small business enterprise" as used in this paragraph, means a business enterprise that is classified as a small business under United States Small Business Administration rules, meets the current small business enterprise size standards found in Part 121 of Title 13 of the Code of Federal Regulations appropriate to the type of work the enterprise seeks to perform, and is headquartered in the County of Los Angeles.

(F) "Medium business enterprise" as used in this paragraph means a company that is not a subsidiary of another company and that has a maximum of 250 employees and a maximum of two hundred fifty million dollars ($250,000,000) in gross annual receipts averaged over three years.

(G) "Disabled veteran business enterprise" as used in this paragraph has the meaning as defined in Section 999 of the Military and Veterans Code.

(H) "Goal" as used in this paragraph means a numerically expressed objective that bidders are required to achieve.

Added Stats 1986 ch 195 § 137.2. Amended Stats 1989 ch 1163 § 64; Stats 1990 ch 808 § 59 (SB 886); Stats 1999 ch 1007 § 9 (SB 532); Stats 2006 ch 814 § 2 (SB 1687), effective January 1, 2007; Stats 2007 ch 116 § 2 (AB 1326), effective January 1, 2008; Stats 2009 ch 536 § 4 (AB 1471), effective January 1, 2010; Stats 2010 ch 494 § 1 (SB 1341), effective January 1, 2011; Stats 2012 ch 703 § 4 (AB 2440), effective January 1, 2013; Stats 2016 ch 204 § 1 (AB 2690), effective January 1, 2017. Stats 2018 ch 473 § 1 (AB 1205), effective January 1, 2019; Stats 2022 ch 460 § 1 (AB 2271), effective January 1, 2023.

§ 130242. Authority to contract with private entities regarding transit systems and facilities on real property; Exceptions; Selection of subcontractors

(a) In addition to the other powers it possesses, the Los Angeles County Metropolitan Transportation Authority may enter into contracts with private entities, the scope of which may combine within a single contract all or some of the planning, design, permitting, development, joint development, construction, construction management, acquisition, leasing, installation, and warranty of all or components of (1) transit systems, including, without limitation, passenger loading or intermodal station facilities, and (2) facilities on real property owned or to be owned by the authority. The authority may solicit or award contracts pursuant to this subdivision after a majority vote of the members of the authority.

(b) A contract awarded pursuant to this section may include operation and maintenance elements, if the inclusion of those elements (1) is necessary, in the reasonable judgment of the authority, to assess vendor representations and warranties, performance guarantees, or life-cycle efficiencies, and (2) does not conflict with collective bargaining agreements to which the authority is a party. The authority may award contracts pursuant to this subdivision after a finding, by a two-thirds vote of the members of the authority, that awarding the contract will achieve for the authority a more competitive solicitation process with respect to quality, timeliness, price, and other private sector efficiencies, relevant to the integration of design, project work, and components.

Appendix

(c) Any construction, alteration, demolition, repairs, or other works of improvement performed under a contract awarded pursuant to this section shall be considered a public works project subject to Chapter 1 (commencing with Section 1720) of Part 7 of Division 2 of the Labor Code, and shall be enforced by the Department of Industrial Relations in the same way it carries out this responsibility under the Labor Code.

(d) A contract under this section shall be let to the lowest responsible bidder whose bid is responsive to the criteria set forth in the invitation for bids, or, at the authority's discretion, to a contractor chosen by a competitive bidding process that employs objective selection criteria that may include, but are not limited to, the proposed design approach, features, functions, life-cycle costs, and other criteria deemed appropriate by the authority, in addition to price. Notice requesting bids or proposals shall be published at least once in a newspaper of general circulation. For contracts estimated to exceed ten million dollars ($10,000,000), publication shall be made at least 60 days before the receipt of the bids or price proposals. For contracts estimated not to exceed ten million dollars ($10,000,000), publication shall be made at least 30 days before the receipt of the bids or price proposals. The authority, at its discretion, may reject any and all bids and proposals, and may readvertise. All bids and price proposals submitted pursuant to this section shall be presented under sealed cover and shall be accompanied by one of the following forms of bidder security: (1) cash, (2) a cashier's check made payable to the authority, (3) a certified check made payable to the authority, or (4) a bidder's bond executed by an admitted surety insurer, made payable to the authority. Upon an award, the security of each unsuccessful bidder shall be returned in a reasonable period of time, but in no event shall that security be held by the authority beyond 60 days from the time the award is made.

(e) When the design of portions of the project permits the selection of subcontractors, the contractor shall competitively bid those portions. The contractor shall provide to the authority a list of subcontractors whose work is in excess of one-half of 1 percent of the total project cost as soon as the subcontractors are identified. Once listed, the subcontractors shall have the rights provided in the Subletting and Subcontracting Fair Practices Act (Chapter 4 (commencing with Section 4100) of Part 1 of Division 2 of the Public Contract Code).

Added Stats 1993 ch 642 § 2 (SB 616). Amended Stats 1994 ch 1220 § 22 (AB 3132), effective September 30, 1994; Stats 2012 ch 703 § 5 (AB 2440), effective January 1, 2013; Stats 2021 ch 414 § 1 (AB 811), effective January 1, 2022.

REVENUE AND TAXATION CODE

DIVISION 2

OTHER TAXES

PART 1

SALES AND USE TAXES

Chapter 2

The Sales Tax

Article 2

Permits

§ 6070.5. Failure to resolve outstanding liabilities or to comply with terms of installment payment agreement as grounds for refusal to issue or revoke a seller's permit; Notice; Reconsideration

(a) The board may refuse to issue a permit to any person submitting an application for a permit as required in Section 6066 if the person desiring to engage in or conduct business as a seller within this state has an outstanding final liability with the board for any amount due under this part.

(b) In addition to the provisions of subdivision (a), the board may also refuse to issue a permit if the person desiring to engage in or conduct business as a seller within this state is not a natural person or individual and any person controlling the person desiring to engage in or conduct business as a seller within this state has an outstanding final liability with the board as provided in subdivision (a). For the purposes of this section, "controlling" has the same meaning as defined in Section 22971 of the Business and Professions Code.

(c) For purposes of this section, a liability will not be deemed to be outstanding if the person has entered into an installment payment agreement pursuant to Section 6832 for any liability and is in full compliance with the terms of the installment payment agreement.

(d) If the person submitting an application for a seller's permit has entered into an installment payment agreement as provided in subdivision (c) and fails to comply with the terms of the installment payment agreement, the board may seek revocation of the seller's permit obtained by the person pursuant to this section.

(e) (1) Whenever any person desiring to engage in or conduct business as a seller within this state is denied a permit pursuant to this section, the board shall give to the person written notice of the denial. The notice of the denial may be served personally, by mail, or by other means deemed appropriate by the board. If served by mail, the notice shall be placed in a sealed envelope, with postage paid, addressed to the person at the address as it appears in the records of the board. The giving of notice shall be deemed complete at the time of deposit of the notice at the United States Postal Service, or a mailbox, subpost office, substation or mail chute, or other facility regularly maintained or provided by the United States Postal Service, without extension of time for any reason. In lieu of mailing, a notice may be served personally by delivering to the person to be served and service shall be deemed complete at the time of the delivery. Delivery of notice by other means deemed appropriate by the board may include, but is not limited to, electronic transmission. Personal service or delivery by other means deemed appropriate by the board to a corporation may be made by delivery of a notice to any person listed on the application as an officer.

(2) Any person who is denied a seller's permit pursuant to this section may request reconsideration of the board's denial of the permit. This request shall be submitted in writing within 30 days of the date of the notice of denial. Timely submission of a written request for reconsideration shall afford the person a hearing in a manner that is consistent with a hearing provided for by Section 6070. If a request for reconsideration is not filed within the 30-day period, the denial becomes final at the end of the 30-day period.

(f) The board shall consider offers in compromise when determining whether to issue a seller's permit.

Added Stats 2011 ch 734 § 2 (AB 1307), effective January 1, 2012.

PART 10.2

ADMINISTRATION OF FRANCHISE AND INCOME TAX LAWS

Chapter 7

Administration of Tax

Article 1

Powers and Duties of Franchise Tax Board

§ 19528. Provision by various boards of information with respect to licensees; Notice to licensee failing to provide information

(a) Notwithstanding any other law, the Franchise Tax Board may require any board, as defined in Section 22 of the Business and Professions Code, and the State Bar, the Bureau of Real Estate, and the Insurance Commissioner (hereinafter referred to as licensing board) to provide to the Franchise Tax Board the following information with respect to every licensee:

(1) Name.

(2) Address or addresses of record.

(3) Federal employer identification number, if the licensee is a partnership, or the licensee's individual taxpayer identification number or social security number of all other licensees.

(4) Type of license.

(5) Effective date of license or renewal.

(6) Expiration date of license.

(7) Whether license is active or inactive, if known.

(8) Whether license is new or renewal.

(b) The Franchise Tax Board may do the following:

(1) Send a notice to any licensee failing to provide the federal employer identification number, individual taxpayer identification number, or social security number as required by subdivision (a) of Section 30 of the Business and Professions Code and subdivision (a) of Section 1666.5 of the Insurance Code, describing the information that was missing, the penalty associated with not providing it, and that failure to provide the information within 30 days will result in the assessment of the penalty.

(2) After 30 days following the issuance of the notice described in paragraph (1), assess a one-hundred-dollar ($100) penalty, due and payable upon notice and demand, for any licensee failing to provide either its federal employer identification number (if the licensee is a

partnership) or the licensee's individual taxpayer identification number or social security number (for all others) as required in Section 30 of the Business and Professions Code and Section 1666.5 of the Insurance Code.

(c) Notwithstanding Division 10 (commencing with Section 7920.000) of Title 1 of the Government Code, the information furnished to the Franchise Tax Board pursuant to Section 30 of the Business and Professions Code or Section 1666.5 of the Insurance Code shall not be deemed to be a public record and shall not be open to the public for inspection.

Added Stats 1993 ch 31 § 26 (SB 3), effective June 15, 1993, operative January 1, 1994. Amended Stats 2013 ch 352 § 514 (AB 1317), effective September 26, 2013, operative July 1, 2013; Stats 2014 ch 752 § 11 (SB 1159), effective January 1, 2015; Amended Stats 2021 ch 615 § 419 (AB 474), effective January 1, 2022.

STREETS AND HIGHWAYS CODE

DIVISION 7

THE IMPROVEMENT ACT OF 1911

PART 3

PERFORMING THE WORK

Chapter 29.1

Clean Energy Assessment Contracts

§ 5900. Applicability of article

The provisions of this article shall apply exclusively to residential real property with four or fewer units.

Added Stats 2017 ch 484 § 1 (SB 242), effective January 1, 2018.

§ 5901. Applicability of chapter

The provisions of this chapter shall not apply to any public agency that does not use a program administrator to administer a PACE program.

Added Stats 2017 ch 484 § 1 (SB 242), effective January 1, 2018.

§ 5902. Definitions [First of two; Effective until January 1, 2029; Repealed effective January 1, 2029]

For purposes of this chapter:

(a) "Assessment contract" means an agreement entered into between all property owners of record on real property and a public agency in which, for voluntary contractual assessments imposed on the real property, the public agency provides a PACE assessment for the installation of one or more efficiency improvements on the real property in accordance with a PACE program, specified in paragraph (2) of subdivision (a) of Section 5898.20 or Section 5899,5899.3 or 5899.4, or a special tax described in Section 53328.1 of the Government Code.

(b) "Authorized representative" means an attorney-in-fact, as defined in Section 4014 of the Probate Code, or conservator of the estate, as defined in Section 2400 of the Probate Code, of the property owner.

(c) "Efficiency improvement" means one or more permanent improvements fixed to real property.

(d) "PACE assessment" means a voluntary contractual assessment, voluntary special tax, or special tax, as described in subdivisions (a), (b), and (c) of Section 26054 of the Public Resources Code.

(e) "PACE program" means a program in which financing is provided for the installation of efficiency improvements on real property and funded through the use of property assessments, as well as other program components defined in this section, established pursuant to any of the following:

(1) Chapter 29 (commencing with Section 5898.10) of Part 3 of this code.

(2) The Mello-Roos Community Facilities Act of 1982 (Chapter 2.5 (commencing with Section 53311) of Part 1 of Division 2 of Title 5 of the Government Code).

(3) A charter city's constitutional authority under Section 5 of Article XI of the California Constitution.

(f) "Program administrator" means an entity administering a PACE program on behalf of, and with the written consent of, a public agency.

(g) "Property owner" means all property owners of record on the property subject to the PACE assessment.

(h) "Public agency" means a city, including a charter city, county, city and county, municipal utility district, community services district, community facilities district, joint powers authority, sanitary district, sanitation district, or water district, as defined in Section 20200 of the Water Code, that has established or participates in a PACE program, and utilizes a program administrator.

(i) This section shall remain in effect only until January 1, 2029, and as of that date is repealed.

Added Stats 2017 ch 484 § 1 (SB 242), effective January 1, 2018. Amended Stats 2018 ch 837 § 13 (SB 465), effective January 1, 2019, repealed January 1, 2029.

§ 5902. Definitions [Second of two; Operative January 1, 2029]

For purposes of this chapter:

(a) "Assessment contract" means an agreement entered into between all property owners of record on real property and a public agency in which, for voluntary contractual assessments imposed on the real property, the public agency provides a PACE assessment for the installation of one or more efficiency improvements on the real property in accordance with a PACE program, specified in paragraph (2) of subdivision (a) of Section 5898.20 or Section 5899 or 5899.3, or a special tax described in Section 53328.1 of the Government Code.

(b) "Authorized representative" means an attorney-in-fact, as defined in Section 4014 of the Probate Code, or conservator of the estate, as defined in Section 2400 of the Probate Code, of the property owner.

(c) "Efficiency improvement" means one or more permanent improvements fixed to real property.

(d) "PACE assessment" means a voluntary contractual assessment, voluntary special tax, or special tax, as described in subdivisions (a), (b), and (c) of Section 26054 of the Public Resources Code.

(e) "PACE program" means a program in which financing is provided for the installation of efficiency improvements on real property and funded through the use of property assessments, as well as other program components defined in this section, established pursuant to any of the following:

(1) Chapter 29 (commencing with Section 5898.10) of Part 3 of this code.

(2) The Mello-Roos Community Facilities Act of 1982 (Chapter 2.5 (commencing with Section 53311) of Part 1 of Division 2 of Title 5 of the Government Code).

(3) A charter city's constitutional authority under Section 5 of Article XI of the California Constitution.

(f) "Program administrator" means an entity administering a PACE program on behalf of, and with the written consent of, a public agency.

(g) "Property owner" means all property owners of record on the property subject to the PACE assessment.

(h) "Public agency" means a city, including a charter city, county, city and county, municipal utility district, community services district, community facilities district, joint powers authority, sanitary district, sanitation district, or water district, as defined in Section 20200 of the Water Code, that has established or participates in a PACE program, and utilizes a program administrator.

(i) This section shall become operative on January 1, 2029.

Added Stats 2018 ch 837 § 14 (SB 465), effective January 1, 2019, operative January 1, 2029.

§ 5913. Oral confirmation of copy of contract assessment documents and related information [Repealed effective January 1, 2029]

(a) (1) Before a property owner executes an assessment contract the program administrator shall do the following:

(A) Make an oral confirmation that at least one owner of the property has a copy of the contract assessment documents required by paragraph (2) of subdivision (a) of Section 5898.20 or Section 5899, 5899.3, or 5899.4, or Section 53328.1 of the Government Code, as applicable, with all the key terms completed, the financing estimate and disclosure form specified in Section 5898.17, and the right to cancel form specified in Section 5898.16, with hard copies available upon request.

(B) Make an oral confirmation of the key terms of the assessment contract, in plain language, with the property owner on the call or to a verified authorized representative of the owner on the call and shall obtain acknowledgment from the property owner on the call to whom the oral confirmation is given.

(2) The oral confirmation required pursuant to paragraph (1) shall include, but is not limited to, all the following information:

(A) The property owner on the call has the right to have other persons present for the call, and an inquiry as to whether the property owner would like to exercise the right to include anyone else on the call. This shall occur at the onset of the call, after the determination of the preferred language of communication.

(B) The property owner on the call is informed that they should review the assessment contract and financing estimate and disclosure form with all other owners of the property.

(C) The efficiency improvement being installed is being financed by a PACE assessment.

(D) The total estimated annual costs the property owner will have to pay under the assessment contract, including applicable fees.

(E) The total estimated average monthly amount of funds the property owner would have to save in order to pay the annual costs under the PACE assessment, including applicable fees.

(F) That the county annual secured property tax bill, which will include the installment of the PACE lien, will be mailed by the county tax collector no later than November 1 each year, and that if the lien is recorded after the fiscal year closes but before the bill is mailed, the first installment may not appear on the county tax bill until the following year.

(G) The term of the assessment contract.

(H) That payments on the assessment contract will be made through an additional annual assessment on the property and paid either directly to the county tax collector's office as part of the total annual secured property tax bill, or through the property owner's mortgage impound account, and that if the property owner pays taxes through an impound account, the property owner should notify the property owner's mortgage lender to discuss adjusting the monthly mortgage payment by the estimated monthly cost of the PACE assessment.

(I) That the property will be subject to a lien during the term of the assessment contract and that the obligations under the assessment contract may be required to be paid in full before the property owner sells or refinances the property.

(J) That the property owner has disclosed whether the property has received or is seeking additional PACE assessments and has disclosed all other PACE assessments or special taxes that are or about to be placed on the property, if known to and understood by the property owner.

(K) That any potential utility savings are not guaranteed, and will not reduce the assessment payments or total assessment amount.

(L) That the program administrator and contractor do not provide tax advice, and that the property owner should seek professional tax advice if the property owner has questions regarding tax credits, tax deductibility, or of other tax impacts on the PACE assessment or assessment contract.

(M) That if that property tax payment is delinquent within the fiscal year, the county tax collector will assess a 10-percent penalty and may assess related costs, as required by state law. A delinquent payment also subjects the property to foreclosure. If the delinquent payment continues past June 30 of a given year and defaults, the county tax collector will assess penalties at the rate of 1 1/2percent per month (18 percent per year), and the property will continue to be subject to foreclosure and may become subject to the county tax collector's right to sell the property at auction.

(N) That the property owner has a three-business day right to cancel the assessment contract pursuant to subdivision (b) of Section 5898.16, and that canceling the assessment contract may also cancel the home improvement contract under Section 5940.

(O) That it is the responsibility of the property owner to contact the property owner's home insurance provider to determine whether the efficiency improvement to be financed by the PACE assessment is covered by the property owner's insurance plan.

(P) That the property owner may repay an amount owed pursuant to an assessment contract before the date that amount is due under the contract without early repayment penalty.

(b) The program administrator shall comply with the following when giving the oral confirmation described in subdivision (a):

(1) The program administrator shall record the oral confirmation in an audio format in accordance with applicable laws.

(2) The program administrator may not comply with the requirement in subdivision (a) through the use of a prerecorded message, or other similar device or method.

(3) Recording of an oral confirmation shall be retained by the program administrator for a period of at least five years from the time of the recording.

(c) The provisions of this section shall be in addition to the documents required to be provided to the property owner under Sections 5898.16 and 5898.17.

(d) At the commencement of the oral confirmation, the program administrator shall ask if the property owner on the call would prefer to communicate during the oral confirmation primarily in a language other than English that is specified in Section 1632 of the Civil Code. If the preferred language is supported by the program administrator, the oral confirmation shall be given in that primary language, except where the property owner on the call chooses to communicate through the property owner's own interpreter. If the preferred language is not supported and an interpreter is not chosen by the property owner on the call, the PACE assessment transaction shall not proceed. For purposes of this subdivision, "the property owner's own interpreter" means a person, who is not a minor, is able to speak fluently and read with full understanding both the English language and any of the languages specified in Section 1632 of the Civil Code, and who is not employed by, and whose services are not made available through, the program administrator, the public agency, or the contractor.

(e) (1) Beginning on January 1, 2019, if the oral confirmation was conducted primarily in a language other than English that is specified in Section 1632 of the Civil Code, the program administrator shall deliver in writing the disclosures and contract or agreement required by law, including, but not limited to, the following:

(A) Assessment contract documents specified in paragraph (2) of subdivision (a) of Section 5898.20 or Section 5899, 5899.3, or 5899.4, or a special tax described in Section 53328.1 of the Government Code.

(B) The financing estimate and disclosure form specified in Section 5898.17.

(C) The right to cancel form specified in Section 5898.16.

(2) Before the execution of any contract or agreement described in paragraph (1), the program administrator shall deliver a translation of the disclosures, contract, or agreement in the language in which the oral confirmation was conducted, that includes a translation of every term and condition in that contract or agreement.

(f) This section shall remain in effect only until January 1, 2029, and as of that date is repealed.

Added Stats 2017 ch 484 § 1 (SB 242), effective January 1, 2018. Amended Stats 2018 ch 813 § 16 (AB 2063), effective January 1, 2019. Stats 2018 ch 837 § 15.5 (SB 465), effective January 1, 2019, repealed January 1, 2029 (ch 837 prevails); Stats 2020 ch 156 § 4 (AB 1551), effective January 1, 2021, repealed January 1, 2029.

§ 5913. Oral confirmation of copy of contract assessment documents and related information [Operative January 1, 2029]

(a) (1) Before a property owner executes an assessment contract the program administrator shall do the following:

(A) Make an oral confirmation that at least one owner of the property has a copy of the contract assessment documents required by paragraph (2) of subdivision (a) of Section 5898.20 or Section 5899 or 5899.3, or Section 53328.1 of the Government Code, as applicable, with all the key terms completed, the financing estimate and disclosure form specified in Section 5898.17, and the right to cancel form specified in Section 5898.16, with hard copies available upon request.

(B) Make an oral confirmation of the key terms of the assessment contract, in plain language, with the property owner on the call or to a verified authorized representative of the owner on the call and shall obtain acknowledgment from the property owner on the call to whom the oral confirmation is given.

(2) The oral confirmation required pursuant to paragraph (1) shall include, but is not limited to, all the following information:

(A) The property owner on the call has the right to have other persons present for the call, and an inquiry as to whether the property owner would like to exercise the right to include anyone else on the call. This shall occur at the onset of the call, after the determination of the preferred language of communication.

(B) The property owner on the call is informed that they should review the assessment contract and financing estimate and disclosure form with all other owners of the property.

(C) The efficiency improvement being installed is being financed by a PACE assessment.

(D) The total estimated annual costs the property owner will have to pay under the assessment contract, including applicable fees.

(E) The total estimated average monthly amount of funds the property owner would have to save in order to pay the annual costs under the PACE assessment, including applicable fees.

(F) That the county annual secured property tax bill, which will include the installment of the PACE lien, will be mailed by the county tax collector no later than November 1 each year, and that if the lien is recorded after the fiscal year closes but before the bill is mailed, the first installment may not appear on the county tax bill until the following year.

(G) The term of the assessment contract.

(H) That payments on the assessment contract will be made through an additional annual assessment on the property and paid either directly to the county tax collector's office as part of the total annual secured property tax bill, or through the property owner's mortgage impound account, and that if the property owner pays taxes through an impound account, the property owner should notify the property owner's should notify their mortgage lender to discuss adjusting the monthly mortgage payment by the estimated monthly cost of the PACE assessment.

(I) That the property will be subject to a lien during the term of the assessment contract and that the obligations under the assessment contract may be required to be paid in full before the property owner sells or refinances the property.

(J) That the property owner has disclosed whether the property has received or is seeking additional PACE assessments and has disclosed all other PACE assessments or special taxes that are or are about to be placed on the property, if known to and understood by the property owner.

(K) That any potential utility savings are not guaranteed, and will not reduce the assessment payments or total assessment amount.

(L) That the program administrator and contractor do not provide tax advice, and that the property owner should seek professional tax advice if the property owner has questions regarding tax credits, tax deductibility, or of other tax impacts on the PACE assessment or assessment contract.

(M) That if that property tax payment is delinquent within the fiscal year, the county tax collector will assess a 10-percent penalty and may assess related costs, as required by state law. A delinquent payment also subjects the property to foreclosure. If the delinquent payment continues past June 30 of a given year and defaults, the county tax collector will assess penalties at the rate of 1 ½ percent per month (18 percent per year), and the property will continue to be subject to foreclosure and may become subject to the county tax collector's right to sell the property at auction.

(N) That the property owner has a three-business day right to cancel the assessment contract pursuant to subdivision (b) of Section 5898.16, and that canceling the assessment contract may also cancel the home improvement contract under Section 5940.

(O) That it is the responsibility of the property owner to contact the property owner's home insurance provider to determine whether the efficiency improvement to be financed by the PACE assessment is covered by the property owner's insurance plan.

(P) That the property owner may repay an amount owed pursuant to an assessment contract prior to the date that amount is due under the contract without early repayment penalty.

(b) The program administrator shall comply with the following when giving the oral confirmation described in subdivision (a):

(1) The program administrator shall record the oral confirmation in an audio format in accordance with applicable laws.

(2) The program administrator may not comply with the requirement in subdivision (a) through the use of a prerecorded message, or other similar device or method.

(3) Recording of an oral confirmation shall be retained by the program administrator for a period of at least five years from the time of the recording.

(c) The provisions of this section shall be in addition to the documents required to be provided to the property owner under Sections 5898.16 and 5898.17.

(d) At the commencement of the oral confirmation, the program administrator shall ask if the property owner on the call would prefer to communicate during the oral confirmation primarily in a language other than English that is specified in Section 1632 of the Civil Code. If the preferred language is supported by the program administrator, the oral confirmation shall be given in that primary language, except where the property owner on the call chooses to communicate through the property owner's own interpreter. If the preferred language is not supported and an interpreter is not chosen by the property owner on the call, the PACE assessment transaction shall not proceed. For purposes of this subdivision, "the property owner's own interpreter" means a person, who is not a minor, is able to speak fluently and read with full understanding both the English language and any of the languages specified in Section 1632 of the Civil Code, and who is not employed by, and whose services are not made available through, the program administrator, the public agency, or the contractor.

(e) (1) Beginning on January 1, 2019, if the oral confirmation was conducted primarily in a language other than English that is specified in Section 1632 of the Civil Code, the program administrator shall deliver in writing the disclosures and contract or agreement required by law, including, but not limited to, the following:

(A) Assessment contract documents specified in paragraph (2) of subdivision (a) of Section 5898.20 or Section 5899 or 5899.3, or a special tax described in Section 53328.1 of the Government Code.

(B) The financing estimate and disclosure form specified in Section 5898.17.

(C) The right to cancel form specified in Section 5898.16.

(2) Before the execution of any contract or agreement described in paragraph (1), the program administrator shall deliver a translation of the disclosures, contract, or agreement in the language in which the oral confirmation was conducted, that includes a translation of every term and condition in that contract or agreement.

(f) This section shall become operative on January 1, 2029.

Added Stats 2018 ch 837 § 16.5 (SB 465), effective January 1, 2019, operative January 1, 2029. Amended Stats 2020 ch 156 § 5 (AB 1551), effective January 1, 2021, operative January 1, 2029.

§ 5914. Waiver or deferral of first assessment payment not permitted

A program administrator may not waive or defer the first payment on an assessment contract. A property owner's first assessment payment shall be due no later than the fiscal year following the fiscal year in which the installation of the efficiency improvement is completed.

Added Stats 2017 ch 484 § 1 (SB 242), effective January 1, 2018.

§ 5922. Advertisement of assessment contracts or solicitation of property owners

A program administrator shall not permit contractors or other third parties to advertise the availability of assessment contracts that are administered by the program administrator, or to solicit property owners on behalf of the program administrator, unless both of the following requirements are met:

(a) The contractor or third party maintains in good standing an appropriate license from the Contractors' State Licensing Board, as well as any other permits, licenses, or registrations required for engaging in its business in the jurisdiction where it operates, and maintains the required bond and insurance coverage pursuant thereto.

(b) The program administrator obtains the contractor's or third party's written agreement that the contractor or third party will act in accordance with applicable advertising and marketing laws and regulations, and all other applicable laws.

Added Stats 2017 ch 484 § 1 (SB 242), effective January 1, 2018.

§ 5923. Cash payments or other thing of material value in excess of actual price or as condition of entering into contract not permitted; Reimbursable expenses

(a) A program administrator shall not provide any direct or indirect cash payment or other thing of material value to a contractor or third party in excess of the actual price charged by that contractor or third party to the property owner for the sale and installation of one or more efficiency improvements financed by an assessment contract.

(b) A program administrator shall not reimburse a contractor or third party for expenses for advertising and marketing campaigns and collateral. A program administrator may reimburse a contractor's bona fide and reasonable training expenses related to PACE financing, provided that:

(1) The training expenses are actually incurred by the contractor.

(2) The reimbursement does not exceed one hundred dollars ($100) per each salesperson or agent of the contractor who participated in the training.

(3) The reimbursement is paid directly to the contractor, and is not paid to its salespersons or agents.

(c) A program administrator shall not provide any direct cash payment or other thing of value to a property owner explicitly conditioned upon that property owner entering into an assessment contract. Notwithstanding the above, programs or promotions that offer reduced fees or interest rates to property owners are neither a direct cash payment or "other thing of value," provided that the reduced fee or interest rate is reflected in the assessment contract and in no circumstance provided to the property owner as cash consideration.

Added Stats 2017 ch 484 § 1 (SB 242), effective January 1, 2018.

§ 5924. Tax deductibility of assessment contract

A program administrator, contractor, or a third party shall not make any representation as to the tax deductibility of an assessment contract unless that representation is consistent with representations, statements, or opinions of the Internal Revenue Service or applicable state tax agency with regard to the tax treatment of PACE assessments.

Added Stats 2017 ch 484 § 1 (SB 242), effective January 1, 2018.

§ 5925. Disclosure of amount of PACE assessment funds or property equity not permitted

A program administrator shall not provide to a contractor or third party engaged in soliciting assessment contracts on its behalf any information that discloses the amount of funds for which a property owner is eligible under a PACE assessment or the amount of equity in a property.

Added Stats 2017 ch 484 § 1 (SB 242), effective January 1, 2018.

§ 5926. Price differential for PACE assessment financed project not permitted

A contractor shall not provide a different price for a project financed by a PACE assessment than the contractor would provide if paid in cash by the property owner.

Added Stats 2017 ch 484 § 1 (SB 242), effective January 1, 2018.

§ 5940. Conditions under which home improvement contract unenforceable; Consequences of violations; Waiver of right to cancel

(a) It shall be unlawful to commence work under a home improvement contract, or deliver any property or perform any services other than obtaining building permits or other similar services preliminary to the commencement of work, and the home improvement contract shall be unenforceable, if both of the following occur:

(1) The property owner entered into the home improvement contract based on the reasonable belief that the work would be covered by the PACE program.

(2) The property owner applies for, accepts, and cancels the PACE financing within the right to cancel period set forth in subdivision (b) of Section 5898.16 or applies for but is not approved for PACE financing in the amount requested by the property owner.

(b) If work has commenced in violation of subdivision (a), then:

(1) The contractor is entitled to no compensation for that work.

(2) The contractor shall restore the property to its original condition at no cost to the property owner.

(3) The contractor shall immediately and without condition return all money, property, and other consideration given by the property owner. If the property owner gave any property as consideration and the contractor does not or cannot return it for whatever reason, the contractor shall immediately return the fair market value of the property or its value as designated in the contract, whichever is greater.

(c) (1) If the contractor has delivered any property to the property owner pursuant to a contract that is unenforceable under subdivision (a), the property owner shall make the property available to the contractor for return within 90 days of execution of the contract provided that:

(A) The provisions of subdivision (b) have been met.

Appendix

(B) The property can be practically returned to the contractor and removed, at the contractor's expense, without leaving any damage to the property owner's property.

(2) Failure of the contractor to comply with this subdivision shall allow the property owner to retain without obligation in law or equity any property provided pursuant to the unenforceable contract.

(d) The property owner may waive the requirements in subdivision (a) if all the following are met:

(1) The contract is executed in connection with the making of emergency or immediately necessary repairs to protect persons or real or personal property.

(2) The property owner initiated the contract for the emergency repair or immediately necessary repair.

(3) The property owner provides a separate statement that is handwritten in ink by a property owner and dated and signed by each property owner, describing the situation that requires immediate remedy, and expressly acknowledges that the contractor has informed them of his or her right to cancel and that he or she waive the right to cancel the sale.

(e) If the property owner waives his or her right to cancel on the home improvement contract to allow the home improvement contractor to proceed with installation, and then cancels his or her PACE financing or is not approved for PACE financing in the amount requested by the property owner, it shall not invalidate the home improvement contract.

(f) This section does not authorize the commencement of work under a home improvement contract if the commencement of work is prohibited by Sections 22684, 22686, or 22687 of the Financial Code.

Added Stats 2017 ch 484 § 1 (SB 242), effective January 1, 2018. Amended Stats 2018 ch 798 § 15 (SB 1087), effective January 1, 2019.

§ 5954. Reports; Availability of data on public agency Internet Web site [First of two; Effective until January 1, 2029; Repealed effective January 1, 2029]

(a) For each PACE program that it administers, a program administrator shall submit a report to the public agency no later than February 1 for the activity that occurred between July 1st through December 31st of the previous year, and another report no later than August 1 for the activity that occurred between January 1st through June 30th of that year. Those reports shall contain the following information, along with all methodologies and supporting assumptions or sources relied upon in preparing the report:

(1) The number of PACE assessments funded, by city, county, and ZIP Code.

(2) The aggregate dollar amount of PACE assessments funded, by city, county, and ZIP Code.

(3) The average dollar amount of PACE assessments funded, by city, county, and ZIP Code.

(4) The categories of installed efficiency improvements whether energy or water efficiency, renewable energy, wildfire safety improvements, or seismic improvements, and the percentage of PACE assessments represented by each category type, on a number and dollar basis, by city, county, and ZIP Code.

(5) The definition of default used by the program administrator.

(6) For each delinquent assessment:

(A) The total delinquent amount.

(B) The number and dates of missed payments.

(C) ZIP Code, city, and county in which the underlying property is located.

(7) For each defaulted assessment:

(A) The total defaulted amount.

(B) The number and dates of missed payments.

(C) ZIP Code, city, and county in which the underlying property is located.

(D) The percentage the defaults represent of the total assessments within each ZIP Code.

(E) The total number of parcels defaulted and the number of years in default for each property.

(8) The estimated total amount of energy saved, and the estimated total dollar amount of those savings by property owners by the efficiency improvements installed in the calendar year, by city, county, and ZIP Code. In addition, the report shall state the total number of energy savings improvements, and number of improvements installed that are qualified for the Energy Star program of the United States Environmental Protection Agency, including the overall average efficiency rating of installed units for each product type.

(9) The estimated total amount of renewable energy produced by the efficiency improvements installed in the calendar year, by city, county, and ZIP Code. In addition, the report shall state the total number of renewable energy installations, including the average and median system size.

(10) The estimated total amount of water saved, and the estimated total dollar amount of such savings by property owners, by city, county, and ZIP Code. In addition, the report shall state the total number of water savings improvements, the number of efficiency improvements that are qualified for the WaterSense program of the United States Environmental Protection Agency, including the overall average efficiency rating of installed units for each product type.

(11) The estimated amount of greenhouse gas emissions reductions.

(12) The estimated number of jobs created.

(13) The average and median amount of annual and total PACE assessments based on ZIP Code, by city, county, and ZIP Code.

(14) The number and percentage of homeowners over 60 years old by city, county, and ZIP Code.

(b) All reports submitted pursuant to this section shall include only aggregate data, and shall not include any nonpublic personal information.

(c) A public agency that receives a report pursuant to this section shall make the data publicly available on its internet website.

(d) This section does not limit another governmental or regulatory entity from establishing reporting requirements.

(e) This section shall remain in effect only until January 1, 2029, and as of that date is repealed.

Added Stats 2017 ch 484 § 1 (SB 242), effective January 1, 2018. Amended Stats 2018 ch 837 § 17 (SB 465), effective January 1, 2019, repealed January 1, 2029; Stats 2019 ch 497 § 265 (AB 991), effective January 1, 2020, repealed January 1, 2029.

§ 5954. Reports; Availability of data on public agency Internet Web site [Second of two; Operative January 1, 2029]

(a) For each PACE program that it administers, a program administrator shall submit a report to the public agency no later than February 1 for the activity that occurred between July 1st through December 31st of the previous year, and another report no later than August 1 for the activity that occurred between January 1st through June 30th of that year. Those reports shall contain the following information, along with all methodologies and supporting assumptions or sources relied upon in preparing the report:

(1) The number of PACE assessments funded, by city, county, and ZIP Code.

(2) The aggregate dollar amount of PACE assessments funded, by city, county, and ZIP Code.

(3) The average dollar amount of PACE assessments funded, by city, county, and ZIP Code.

(4) The categories of installed efficiency improvements whether energy or water efficiency, renewable energy, or seismic improvements, and the percentage of PACE assessments represented by each category type, on a number and dollar basis, by city, county, and ZIP Code.

(5) The definition of default used by the program administrator.

(6) For each delinquent assessment:

(A) The total delinquent amount.

(B) The number and dates of missed payments.

(C) ZIP Code, city, and county in which the underlying property is located.

(7) For each defaulted assessment:

(A) The total defaulted amount.

(B) The number and dates of missed payments.

(C) ZIP Code, city, and county in which the underlying property is located.

(D) The percentage the defaults represent of the total assessments within each ZIP Code.

(E) The total number of parcels defaulted and the number of years in default for each property.

(8) The estimated total amount of energy saved, and the estimated total dollar amount of those savings by property owners by the efficiency improvements installed in the calendar year, by city, county, and ZIP Code. In addition, the report shall state the total number of energy savings improvements, and number of improvements installed that are qualified for the Energy Star program of the United States Environmental Protection Agency, including the overall average efficiency rating of installed units for each product type.

(9) The estimated total amount of renewable energy produced by the efficiency improvements installed in the calendar year, by city, county, and ZIP Code. In addition, the report shall state the total number of renewable energy installations, including the average and median system size.

(10) The estimated total amount of water saved, and the estimated total dollar amount of such savings by property owners, by city, county, and ZIP Code. In addition, the report shall state the total number of water savings improvements, the number of efficiency improvements that are qualified for the WaterSense program of the United States Environmental Protection Agency, including the overall average efficiency rating of installed units for each product type.

(11) The estimated amount of greenhouse gas emissions reductions.

(12) The estimated number of jobs created.

(13) The average and median amount of annual and total PACE assessments based on ZIP Code, by city, county, and ZIP Code.

(14) The number and percentage of homeowners over 60 years old by city, county, and ZIP Code.

(b) All reports submitted pursuant to this section shall include only aggregate data, and shall not include any nonpublic personal information.

(c) A public agency that receives a report pursuant to this section shall make the data publicly available on its Internet Web site.

(d) This section does not limit another governmental or regulatory entity from establishing reporting requirements.

(e) This section shall become operative on January 1, 2029.

Added Stats 2018 ch 837 § 18 (SB 465), effective January 1, 2019, operative January 1, 2029.

Appendix

UNEMPLOYMENT INSURANCE CODE

DIVISION 1
UNEMPLOYMENT AND DISABILITY COMPENSATION

PART 1
UNEMPLOYMENT COMPENSATION

Chapter 2
Administration

Article 1

Employment Development Department

§ 329. Chairperson of Joint Enforcement Strike Force on Underground Economy; Agencies in advisory capacity; Duties of strike force; Membership of strike force; Reporting

(a) The director, or the director's designee, shall serve as Chairperson of the Joint Enforcement Strike Force on the Underground Economy provided for in Executive Order W-66-93. The strike force shall include, but not be limited to, representatives of the Employment Development Department, the Department of Justice, the Department of Consumer Affairs, the Department of Industrial Relations, the California Department of Tax and Fee Administration, the Franchise Tax Board, and the Department of Insurance.

(b) The strike force may invite the following state agencies to serve in an advisory capacity: the California Health and Human Services Agency, the Department of Motor Vehicles, the Department of Alcoholic Beverage Control, and the Department of the California Highway Patrol.

(c) The strike force shall have the following duties:

(1) (A) To facilitate and encourage the development and sharing of information by the participating agencies necessary to combat the underground economy including the enforcement activities regarding labor, tax, insurance, and licensing law violators operating in the underground economy. Duly authorized representatives of the strike

force employed by an agency listed in subdivision (a) shall exchange intelligence, data, documents, confidential information, or lead referrals pursuant to this section, to the extent permitted by state and federal laws and regulations.

(B) Any person who is involved or has been involved in the strike force pursuant to this section and at any time has obtained confidential information shall not divulge, or make known in any manner not allowed by law, any of the confidential information received by or reported to members of the strike force. Confidential information authorized to be exchanged pursuant to this section shall retain its confidential status and shall otherwise remain subject to the confidentiality provisions contained in applicable federal and state laws.

(C) Participating agencies may also cooperate and share any appropriate information with the Labor Enforcement Task Force established pursuant to Assembly Bill 1464 of the 2011-12 Regular Session (Chapter 21 of the Statutes of 2012), to the extent related to the underground economy including the enforcement activities regarding labor, tax, insurance, and licensing law violators operating in the underground economy permitted by state and federal laws and regulations. Members of the Labor Enforcement Task Force who have obtained confidential information pursuant to this section shall not divulge, or make known in any manner not allowed by law, any of the confidential information received from the strike force.

(2) To improve the coordination of activities among the participating agencies.

(3) To develop methods to pool, focus, and target the enforcement resources of the participating agencies in order to deter tax evasion and maximize recoveries from blatant tax evaders and violators of cash-pay reporting laws.

(4) To reduce enforcement costs wherever possible by eliminating duplicative audits and investigations.

(d) In addition, the strike force shall be empowered to:

(1) Form joint enforcement teams when appropriate to utilize the collective investigative and enforcement capabilities of the participating members.

(2) Establish committees and rules of procedure to carry out the activities of the strike force.

(3) To solicit the cooperation and participation of district attorneys and other state and local agencies in carrying out the objectives of the strike force.

(4) Establish procedures for soliciting referrals from the public, including, but not limited to, an advertised telephone hotline.

(5) Develop procedures for improved information sharing among the participating agencies and the Labor Enforcement Task Force, such as shared automated information database systems, the use of a common business identification number, and a centralized debt col-

lection system, to the extent permitted by state and federal laws and regulations.

(6) Develop procedures to permit the participating agencies to use civil sanctions.

(7) Provide participating agencies, including the Department of Justice, with investigative leads where collaboration opportunities exist for felony-level criminal investigations, including, but not limited to, referring leads to agencies with appropriate enforcement jurisdiction, and to pursue criminal prosecution when unscrupulous businesses violate the state's labor, employment, licensing, insurance, and tax laws with respect to the underground economy.

(8) Evaluate, based on its activities, the need for any statutory change to do any of the following:

(A) Eliminate barriers to interagency information sharing.

(B) Improve the ability of the participating agencies to audit, investigate, and prosecute tax and cash-pay violations.

(C) Deter violations and improve voluntary compliance.

(D) Eliminate duplication and improve cooperation among the participating agencies.

(E) Establish shareable information databases.

(F) Establish a common business identification number for use by participating agencies.

(G) Establish centralized, automated debt collection services for the participating agencies.

(e) The strike force shall report to the Governor and the Legislature annually during the period of its existence, by June 30, of each year, regarding its activities.

The report shall include, but not be limited to, all of the following:

(1) The number of cases of blatant violations and noncompliance with tax and cash-pay laws identified, audited, investigated, or prosecuted through civil action or referred for criminal prosecution.

(2) Actions taken by the strike force to publicize its activities.

(3) Efforts made by the strike force to establish an advertised telephone hotline for receiving referrals from the public.

(4) Procedures for improving information sharing among the agencies represented on the strike force.

(5) Steps taken by the strike force to improve cooperation among participating agencies, reduce duplication of effort, and improve voluntary compliance.

(6) Recommendations for any statutory changes needed to accomplish the goals described in paragraph (8) of subdivision (c).

Added Stats 1994 ch 1117 § 5 (SB 1490). Amended Stats 1999 ch 306 § 2 (SB 319); Stats 2001 ch 180 § 1 (AB 202); Stats 2002 ch 29 § 4 (AB 1729); Stats 2004 ch 685 § 6 (AB 3020); Stats 2017 ch 117 § 1 (AB 1695), effective January 1, 2018; Stats 2019 ch 626 § 2 (AB 1296), effective January 1, 2020.

Chapter 4

Contributions and Reports

Article 6

Records, Reports and Contribution Payments

§ 1088.5. Information to be reported relating to new employees

(a) In addition to information reported in accordance with Section 1088, effective July 1, 1998, each employer shall file, with the department, the information provided for in subdivision (b) on new employees.

(b) Each employer shall report the hiring of any employee who works in this state and to whom the employer anticipates paying wages, and also shall report the hiring of any employee who previously worked for the employer but had been separated from that prior employment for at least 60 consecutive days.

(c) (1) This section shall not apply to any department, agency, or instrumentality of the United States.

(2) State agency employers shall not be required to report employees performing intelligence or counterintelligence functions, if the head of the agency has determined that reporting pursuant to this section would endanger the safety of the employee or compromise an ongoing investigation or intelligence mission.

(d) (1) Employers shall submit a report as described in paragraph (4) within 20 days of hiring any employee whom the employer is required to report pursuant to this section.

(2) Notwithstanding subdivision (a), employers transmitting reports magnetically or electronically shall submit the report by two monthly transmissions not less than 12 days and not more than 16 days apart.

(3) For purposes of this section, an employer that has employees in two or more states and that transmits reports magnetically or electronically may designate one state in which the employer has employees to which the employer will transmit the report described in paragraph (4). Any employer that transmits reports pursuant to this paragraph shall notify the Secretary of Health and Human Services in writing as to which state the employer designates for the purpose of sending reports.

(4) The report shall contain the following:

(A) The name, address, and social security number of the employees.

(B) The employer's name, address, state employer identification number (if one has been issued), and identifying number assigned to the employer under Section 6109 of the Internal Revenue Code of 1986.

(C) The first date the employee worked.

(5) Employers may report pursuant to this section by submitting a copy of the employee's W-4 form, a form provided by the department, or any other hiring document transmitted by first-class mail, magnetically, or electronically.

(e) For each failure to report the hiring of an employee, as required and within the time required by this section, unless the failure is due to good cause, the department may assess a penalty of twenty-four dollars ($24), or four hundred ninety dollars ($490) if the failure is the result of conspiracy between the employer and employee not to supply the required report or to supply a false or incomplete report.

(f) (1) On and after January 1, 2013, and before January 1, 2019, information collected pursuant to this section may be used for the following purposes:

(A) Administration of this code, including, but not limited to, providing employer or employee information to participating members of the Joint Enforcement Strike Force on the Underground Economy pursuant to Section 329 for the purposes of auditing, investigating, and prosecuting violations of tax and cash-pay reporting laws.

(B) Locating individuals for purposes of establishing paternity and establishing, modifying, and enforcing child support obligations.

(C) Administration of employment security and workers' compensation programs.

(D) Providing employer or employee information to the Franchise Tax Board and the State Board of Equalization for the purpose of tax or fee enforcement.

(E) Verification of eligibility of applicants for, or recipients of, the public assistance programs listed in Section 1320b-7(b) of Title 42 of the United States Code.

(F) Providing employer or employee information to the Contractors' State License Board and the State Compensation Insurance Fund for the purpose of workers' compensation payroll reporting.

(G) Providing employer or employee information to the State Department of Health Care Services, the California Health Benefit Exchange, the Managed Risk Medical Insurance Board, and county departments and agencies for the purpose of:

(i) Verifying or determining the eligibility of an applicant for, or a recipient of, state health subsidy programs, limited to the Medi-Cal program, provided pursuant to Chapter 7 (commencing with Section 14000) of Part 3 of Division 9 of the Welfare and Institutions Code, the Healthy Families Program, provided pursuant to Part 6.2 (commencing with Section 12693) of Division 2 of the Insurance Code, and the Access for Infants and Mothers Program, provided pursuant to

Part 6.3 (commencing with Section 12695) of Division 2 of the Insurance Code, where the verification or determination is directly connected with, and limited to, the administration of the state health subsidy programs referenced in this clause.

(ii) Verifying or determining the eligibility of an applicant for, or a recipient of, federal subsidies offered through the California Health Benefit Exchange, provided pursuant to Title 22 (commencing with Section 100500) of the Government Code, including federal tax credits and cost-sharing assistance pursuant to the federal Patient Protection and Affordable Care Act, (Public Law 111-148), as amended by the federal Health Care and Education Reconciliation Act of 2010 (Public Law 111-152), where the verification or determination is directly connected with, and limited to, the administration of the California Health Benefit Exchange.

(iii) Verifying or determining the eligibility of employees and employers for health coverage through the Small Business Health Options Program, provided pursuant to Section 100502 of the Government Code, where the verification or determination is directly connected with, and limited to, the administration of the Small Business Health Options Program.

(2) On and after January 1, 2019, information collected pursuant to this section may be used for the following purposes:

(A) Administration of this code.

(B) Locating individuals for purposes of establishing paternity and establishing, modifying, and enforcing child support obligations.

(C) Administration of employment security and workers' compensation programs.

(D) Providing employer or employee information to the Franchise Tax Board and to the State Board of Equalization for the purposes of tax or fee enforcement.

(E) Verification of eligibility of applicants for, or recipients of, the public assistance programs listed in Section 1320b-7(b) of Title 42 of the United States Code.

(F) Providing employer or employee information to the State Department of Health Care Services, the California Health Benefit Exchange, the Managed Risk Medical Insurance Board, and county departments and agencies for the purpose of:

(i) Verifying or determining the eligibility of an applicant for, or a recipient of, state health subsidy programs, limited to the Medi-Cal program, provided pursuant to Chapter 7 (commencing with Section 14000) of Part 3 of Division 9 of the Welfare and Institutions Code, the Healthy Families Program, provided pursuant to Part 6.2 (commencing with Section 12693) of Division 2 of the Insurance Code, and the Access for Infants and Mothers Program, provided pursuant to Part 6.3 (commencing with Section 12695) of Division 2 of the Insurance Code, where the verification or determination is directly connected with, and limited to, the administration of the state health subsidy programs referenced in this clause.

(ii) Verifying or determining the eligibility of an applicant for, or a recipient of, federal subsidies offered through the California Health Benefit Exchange, provided pursuant to Title 22 (commencing with Section 100500) of the Government Code, including federal tax credits and cost-sharing assistance pursuant to the federal Patient Protection and Affordable Care Act, (Public Law 111-148), as amended by the federal Health Care and Education Reconciliation Act of 2010 (Public Law 111-152), where the verification or determination is directly connected with, and limited to, the administration of the California Health Benefit Exchange.

(iii) Verifying or determining the eligibility of employees and employers for health coverage through the Small Business Health Options Program, provided pursuant to Section 100502 of the Government Code, where the verification or determination is directly connected with, and limited to, the administration of the Small Business Health Options Program.

(g) For purposes of this section, "employer" includes a labor union hiring hall.

(h) This section shall become operative on July 1, 1998.

Added Stats 1997 ch 606 § 14 (AB 67), effective October 3, 1997, operative July 1, 1998. Amended Stats 1998 ch 858 § 8 (AB 2169); Stats 2011 ch 296 § 293 (AB 1023), effective January 1, 2012; Stats 2012 ch 783 § 7 (AB 1845), effective January 1, 2013, ch 811 § 1 (AB 1794), effective January 1, 2013, ch 815 § 3.3 (AB 174), effective January 1, 2013.

§ 1095. Purposes for which director must permit use of information in their possession

The director shall permit the use of any information in the director's possession to the extent necessary for any of the following purposes, and may require reimbursement for all direct costs incurred in providing any and all information specified in this section, except information specified in subdivisions (a) to (e), inclusive:

(a) To enable the director or the director's representative to carry out their responsibilities under this code.

(b) To properly present a claim for benefits.

(c) To acquaint a worker or their authorized agent with the worker's existing or prospective right to benefits.

(d) To furnish an employer or their authorized agent with information to enable the employer to fully discharge their obligations or safeguard their rights under this division or Division 3 (commencing with Section 9000).

(e) To enable an employer to receive a reduction in contribution rate.

(f) To enable federal, state, or local governmental departments or agencies, subject to federal law, to verify or determine the eligibility or entitlement of an applicant for, or a recipient of, public social services provided pursuant to Division 9 (commencing with Section 10000) of the Welfare and Institutions Code, or Part A of Subchapter IV of the federal Social Security Act (42 U.S.C. Sec. 601 et seq.), and state or federal subsidies offered through the California Health Benefit Exchange provided pursuant to Title 22 (commencing with Section 100500) of the Government Code, when the verification or determination is directly connected with, and limited to, the administration of public social services.

(g) To enable county administrators of general relief or assistance, or their representatives, to determine entitlement to locally provided general relief or assistance, when the determination is directly connected with, and limited to, the administration of general relief or assistance.

(h) To enable state or local governmental departments or agencies to seek criminal, civil, or administrative remedies in connection with the unlawful application for, or receipt of, relief provided under Division 9 (commencing with Section 10000) of the Welfare and Institutions Code or to enable the collection of expenditures for medical assistance services pursuant to Part 5 (commencing with Section 17000) of Division 9 of the Welfare and Institutions Code.

(i) To provide any law enforcement agency with the name, address, telephone number, birth date, social security number, physical description, and names and addresses of present and past employers, of any victim, suspect, missing person, potential witness, or person for whom a felony arrest warrant has been issued, when a request for this information is made by any investigator or peace officer as defined by Sections 830.1 and 830.2 of the Penal Code, or by any federal law enforcement officer to whom the Attorney General has delegated authority to enforce federal search warrants, as defined under Sections 60.2and 60.3 of Title 28 of the Code of Federal Regulations, as amended, and when the requesting officer has been designated by the head of the law enforcement agency and requests this information in the course of and as a part of an investigation into the commission of a crime when there is a reasonable suspicion that the crime is a felony and that the information would lead to relevant evidence. The information provided pursuant to this subdivision shall be provided to the extent permitted by federal law and regulations, and to the extent the information is available and accessible within the constraints and configurations of existing department records. Any person who receives any information under this subdivision shall make a written report of the information to the law enforcement agency that employs the person, for filing under the normal procedures of that agency.

Appendix

(1) This subdivision shall not be construed to authorize the release to any law enforcement agency of a general list identifying individuals applying for or receiving benefits.

(2) The department shall maintain records pursuant to this subdivision only for periods required under regulations or statutes enacted for the administration of its programs.

(3) This subdivision shall not be construed as limiting the information provided to law enforcement agencies to that pertaining only to applicants for, or recipients of, benefits.

(4) The department shall notify all applicants for benefits that release of confidential information from their records will not be protected should there be a felony arrest warrant issued against the applicant or in the event of an investigation by a law enforcement agency into the commission of a felony.

(j) To provide public employee retirement systems in California with information relating to the earnings of any person who has applied for or is receiving a disability income, disability allowance, or disability retirement allowance, from a public employee retirement system. The earnings information shall be released only upon written request from the governing board specifying that the person has applied for or is receiving a disability allowance or disability retirement allowance from its retirement system. The request may be made by the chief executive officer of the system or by an employee of the system so authorized and identified by name and title by the chief executive officer in writing.

(k) To enable the Division of Labor Standards Enforcement in the Department of Industrial Relations to seek criminal, civil, or administrative remedies in connection with the failure to pay, or the unlawful payment of, wages pursuant to Chapter 1 (commencing with Section 200) of Part 1 of Division 2 of, and Chapter 1 (commencing with Section 1720) of Part 7 of Division 2 of, the Labor Code.

(l) To enable federal, state, or local governmental departments or agencies to administer child support enforcement programs under Part D of Title IV of the federal Social Security Act (42 U.S.C. Sec. 651 et seq.).

(m) To provide federal, state, or local governmental departments or agencies with wage and claim information in its possession that will assist those departments and agencies in the administration of the Victims of Crime Program or in the location of victims of crime who, by state mandate or court order, are entitled to restitution that has been or can be recovered.

(n) To provide federal, state, or local governmental departments or agencies with information concerning any individuals who are or have been:

(1) Directed by state mandate or court order to pay restitution, fines, penalties, assessments, or fees as a result of a violation of law.

(2) Delinquent or in default on guaranteed student loans or who owe repayment of funds received through other financial assistance programs administered by those agencies. The information released by the director for the purposes of this paragraph shall not include unemployment insurance benefit information.

(o) To provide an authorized governmental agency with any and all relevant information that relates to any specific workers' compensation insurance fraud investigation. The information shall be provided to the extent permitted by federal law and regulations. For purposes of this subdivision, "authorized governmental agency" means the district attorney of any county, the office of the Attorney General, the Contractors State License Board, the Department of Industrial Relations, and the Department of Insurance. An authorized governmental agency may disclose this information to the State Bar of California, the Medical Board of California, or any other licensing board or department whose licensee is the subject of a workers' compensation insurance fraud investigation. This subdivision shall not prevent any authorized governmental agency from reporting to any board or department the suspected misconduct of any licensee of that body.

(p) To enable the Director of Consumer Affairs, or the director's representative, to access unemployment insurance quarterly wage data on a case-by-case basis to verify information on school administrators, school staff, and students provided by those schools who are being investigated for possible violations of Chapter 8 (commencing with Section 94800) of Part 59 of Division 10 of Title 3 of the Education Code.

(q) To provide employment tax information to the tax officials of Mexico, if a reciprocal agreement exists. For purposes of this subdivision, "reciprocal agreement" means a formal agreement to exchange information between national taxing officials of Mexico and taxing authorities of the State Board of Equalization, the Franchise Tax Board, and the Employment Development Department. Furthermore, the reciprocal agreement shall be limited to the exchange of information that is essential for tax administration purposes only. Taxing authorities of the State of California shall be granted tax information only on California residents. Taxing authorities of Mexico shall be granted tax information only on Mexican nationals.

(r) To enable city and county planning agencies to develop economic forecasts for planning purposes. The information shall be limited to businesses within the jurisdiction of the city or county whose planning agency is requesting the information, and shall not include information regarding individual employees.

(s) To provide the State Department of Developmental Services with wage and employer information that will assist in the collection of moneys owed by the recipient, parent, or any other legally liable individual for services and supports provided pursuant to Chapter 9

Appendix

(commencing with Section 4775) of Division 4.5 of, and Chapter 2 (commencing with Section 7200) and Chapter 3 (commencing with Section 7500) of Division 7 of, the Welfare and Institutions Code.

(t) To provide the State Board of Equalization with employment tax information that will assist in the administration of tax programs. The information shall be limited to the exchange of employment tax information essential for tax administration purposes to the extent permitted by federal law and regulations.

(u) This section shall not be construed to authorize or permit the use of information obtained in the administration of this code by any private collection agency.

(v) The disclosure of the name and address of an individual or business entity that was issued an assessment that included penalties under Section 1128 or 1128.1 shall not be in violation of Section 1094 if the assessment is final. The disclosure may also include any of the following:

(1) The total amount of the assessment.

(2) The amount of the penalty imposed under Section 1128 or 1128.1 that is included in the assessment.

(3) The facts that resulted in the charging of the penalty under Section 1128 or 1128.1.

(w) To enable the Contractors State License Board to verify the employment history of an individual applying for licensure pursuant to Section 7068 of the Business and Professions Code.

(x) To provide any peace officer with the Division of Investigation in the Department of Consumer Affairs information pursuant to subdivision (i) when the requesting peace officer has been designated by the chief of the Division of Investigation and requests this information in the course of and as part of an investigation into the commission of a crime or other unlawful act when there is reasonable suspicion to believe that the crime or act may be connected to the information requested and would lead to relevant information regarding the crime or unlawful act.

(y) To enable the Labor Commissioner of the Division of Labor Standards Enforcement in the Department of Industrial Relations to identify, pursuant to Section 90.3 of the Labor Code, unlawfully uninsured employers. The information shall be provided to the extent permitted by federal law and regulations.

(z) To enable the Chancellor of the California Community Colleges, in accordance with the requirements of Section 84754.5 of the Education Code, to obtain quarterly wage data, commencing January 1, 1993, on students who have attended one or more community colleges, to assess the impact of education on the employment and earnings of students, to conduct the annual evaluation of district-level and individual college performance in achieving priority educational outcomes, and to submit the required reports to the Legislature and the

Governor. The information shall be provided to the extent permitted by federal statutes and regulations.

(aa) To enable the Public Employees' Retirement System to seek criminal, civil, or administrative remedies in connection with the unlawful application for, or receipt of, benefits provided under Part 3 (commencing with Section 20000) of Division 5 of Title 2 of the Government Code.

(ab) To enable the State Department of Education, the University of California, the California State University, and the Chancellor of the California Community Colleges, pursuant to the requirements prescribed by the federal American Recovery and Reinvestment Act of 2009 (Public Law 111-5), to obtain quarterly wage data, commencing July 1, 2010, on students who have attended their respective systems to assess the impact of education on the employment and earnings of those students, to conduct the annual analysis of district-level and individual district or postsecondary education system performance in achieving priority educational outcomes, and to submit the required reports to the Legislature and the Governor. The information shall be provided to the extent permitted by federal statutes and regulations.

(ac) To provide the Agricultural Labor Relations Board with employee, wage, and employer information, for use in the investigation or enforcement of the Alatorre-Zenovich-Dunlap-Berman Agricultural Labor Relations Act of 1975 (Part 3.5 (commencing with Section 1140) of Division 2 of the Labor Code). The information shall be provided to the extent permitted by federal statutes and regulations.

(ad)

(1) To enable the State Department of Health Care Services, the California Health Benefit Exchange, the Managed Risk Medical Insurance Board, and county departments and agencies to obtain information regarding employee wages, California employer names and account numbers, employer reports of wages and number of employees, and disability insurance and unemployment insurance claim information, for the purpose of:

(A) Verifying or determining the eligibility of an applicant for, or a recipient of, state health subsidy programs, limited to the Medi-Cal program provided pursuant to Chapter 7 (commencing with Section 14000) of Part 3 of Division 9 of the Welfare and Institutions Code, and the Medi-Cal Access Program provided pursuant to Chapter 2 (commencing with Section 15810) of Part 3.3 of Division 9 of the Welfare and Institutions Code, when the verification or determination is directly connected with, and limited to, the administration of the state health subsidy programs referenced in this subparagraph.

(B) Verifying or determining the eligibility of an applicant for, or a recipient of, state or federal subsidies offered through the California Health Benefit Exchange, provided pursuant to Title 22 (commencing with Section 100500) of the Government Code, including federal tax credits and cost-sharing assistance pursuant to the federal Patient Protection and Affordable Care Act (Public Law 111-148), as amended by the federal Health Care and Education Reconciliation Act of 2010 (Public Law 111-152), when the verification or determination is directly connected with, and limited to, the administration of the California Health Benefit Exchange.

(C) Verifying or determining the eligibility of employees and employers for health coverage through the Small Business Health Options Program, provided pursuant to Section 100502 of the Government Code, when the verification or determination is directly connected with, and limited to, the administration of the Small Business Health Options Program.

(2) The information provided under this subdivision shall be subject to the requirements of, and provided to the extent permitted by, federal law and regulations, including Part 603 of Title 20 of the Code of Federal Regulations.

(ae) To provide any peace officer with the Investigations Division of the Department of Motor Vehicles with information pursuant to subdivision (i), when the requesting peace officer has been designated by the Chief of the Investigations Division and requests this information in the course of, and as part of, an investigation into identity theft, counterfeiting, document fraud, or consumer fraud, and there is reasonable suspicion that the crime is a felony and that the information would lead to relevant evidence regarding the identity theft, counterfeiting, document fraud, or consumer fraud. The information provided pursuant to this subdivision shall be provided to the extent permitted by federal law and regulations, and to the extent the information is available and accessible within the constraints and configurations of existing department records. Any person who receives any information under this subdivision shall make a written report of the information to the Investigations Division of the Department of Motor Vehicles, for filing under the normal procedures of that division.

(af) Until January 1, 2020, to enable the Department of Finance to prepare and submit the report required by Section 13084 of the Government Code that identifies all employers in California that employ 100 or more employees who receive benefits from the Medi-Cal program (Chapter 7 (commencing with Section 14000) of Part 3 of Division 9 of the Welfare and Institutions Code). The information used for this purpose shall be limited to information obtained pursuant to Section 11026.5 of the Welfare and Institutions Code and from the administration of personal income tax wage withholding pursuant to Division 6 (commencing with Section 13000) and the disability insurance program and may be disclosed to the Department of Finance only for the purpose of preparing and submitting the report and only to the extent not prohibited by federal law.

(ag) To provide, to the extent permitted by federal law and regulations, the Student Aid Commission with wage information in order to verify the employment status of an individual applying for a Cal Grant C award pursuant to subdivision (c) of Section 69439 of the Education Code.

(ah) To enable the Department of Corrections and Rehabilitation to obtain quarterly wage data of former inmates who have been incarcerated within the prison system in order to assess the impact of rehabilitation services or the lack of these services on the employment and earnings of these former inmates. Quarterly data for a former inmate's employment status and wage history shall be provided for a period of one year, three years, and five years following release. The data shall only be used for the purpose of tracking outcomes for former inmates in order to assess the effectiveness of rehabilitation strategies on the wages and employment histories of those formerly incarcerated. The information shall be provided to the department to the extent not prohibited by federal law.

(ai) To enable federal, state, or local government departments or agencies, or their contracted agencies, subject to federal law, including the confidentiality, disclosure, and other requirements set forth in Part 603 of Title 20 of the Code of Federal Regulations, to evaluate, research, or forecast the effectiveness of public social services programs administered pursuant to Division 9 (commencing with Section 10000) of the Welfare and Institutions Code, or Part A of Subchapter IV of Chapter 7 of the federal Social Security Act (42 U.S.C. Sec. 601 et seq.), when the evaluation, research, or forecast is directly connected with, and limited to, the administration of the public social services programs.

(aj)

(1) To enable the California Workforce Development Board, the Chancellor of the California Community Colleges, the Superintendent of Public Instruction, the Department of Rehabilitation, the State Department of Social Services, the Bureau for Private Postsecondary Education, the Department of Industrial Relations, the Division of Apprenticeship Standards, the Department of Corrections and Rehabilitation, the Prison Industry Authority, the Employment Training Panel, and a chief elected official, as that term is defined in Section 3102(9) of Title 29 of the United States Code, to access any relevant quarterly wage data necessary for the evaluation and reporting of their respective program performance outcomes as required and permitted by various local, state, and federal laws pertaining to performance measurement and program evaluation, including responsibilities arising under Sections 14013, 14033, and 14042 of this code and Sections 2032 and 2038 of the Streets and Highways Code; the federal Workforce Innovation and Opportunity Act (Public Law 113-128); the workforce metrics dashboard pursuant to paragraph (1) of subdi-

Appendix

vision (i) of Section 14013; the Adult Education Block Grant Program consortia performance metrics pursuant to Section 84920 of the Education Code; the economic and workforce development program performance measures pursuant to Section 88650 of the Education Code; and the California Community Colleges Economic and Workforce Development Program performance measures established in Part 52.5 (commencing with Section 88600) of Division 7 of Title 3 of the Education Code. Disclosures under this subdivision shall comply with federal and state privacy laws that require the informed consent from program participants of city and county departments or agencies that administer public workforce development programs for the evaluation, research, or forecast of their programs regardless of local, state, or federal funding source.

(2) The department shall do all of the following:

(A) Consistent with this subdivision, develop the minimum requirements for granting a request for disclosure of information authorized by this subdivision regardless of local, state, or federal funding source.

(B) Develop a standard application for submitting a request for disclosure of information authorized by this subdivision.

(C) Approve or deny a request for disclosure of information authorized by this subdivision, or request additional information, within 20 business days of receiving the standard application. The entity submitting the application shall respond to any request by the department for additional information within 20 business days of receipt of the department's request. Within 30 calendar days of receiving any additional information, the department shall provide a final approval or denial of the request for disclosure of information authorized by this subdivision. Any approval, denial, or request for additional information shall be in writing. Denials shall identify the reason or category of reasons for the denial.

(D) Make publicly available on the department's internet website all of the following:

(i) The minimum requirements for granting a request for disclosure of information authorized by this subdivision, as developed pursuant to subparagraph (A).

(ii) The standard application developed pursuant to subparagraph (B).

(iii) The timeframe for information request determinations by the department, as specified in subparagraph (C).

(iv) Contact information for assistance with requests for disclosures of information authorized by this subdivision.

(v) Any denials for requests of disclosure of information authorized by this subdivision, including the reason or category of reasons for the denial.

(ak)

(1) To provide any peace officer with the Enforcement Branch of the Department of Insurance with both of the following:

(A) Information provided pursuant to subdivision (i) that relates to a specific insurance fraud investigation involving automobile insurance fraud, life insurance and annuity fraud, property and casualty insurance fraud, and organized automobile insurance fraud. That information shall be provided when the requesting peace officer has been designated by the Chief of the Fraud Division of the Department of Insurance and requests the information in the course of, and as part of, an investigation into the commission of a crime or other unlawful act when there is reasonable suspicion to believe that the crime or act may be connected to the information requested and would lead to relevant information regarding the crime or unlawful act.

(B) Employee, wage, employer, and state disability insurance claim information that relates to a specific insurance fraud investigation involving health or disability insurance fraud when the requesting peace officer has been designated by the Chief of the Fraud Division of the Department of Insurance and requests the information in the course of, and as part of, an investigation into the commission of a crime or other unlawful act when there is reasonable suspicion to believe that the crime or act may be connected to the information requested and would lead to relevant information regarding the crime or unlawful act.

(2) To enable the State Department of Developmental Services to obtain quarterly wage data and unemployment insurance claim data of consumers served by that department for the purposes of monitoring, program operation and evaluation, and evaluating employment outcomes, of the Employment First Policy, established pursuant to Section 4869 of the Welfare and Institutions Code.

(3) The information provided pursuant to this subdivision shall be provided to the extent permitted by federal statutes and regulations.

(al) To provide the CalSavers Retirement Savings Board with employer tax information for use in the administration of, and to facilitate compliance with, the CalSavers Retirement Savings Trust Act (Title 21 (commencing with Section 100000) of the Government Code). The information should be limited to the tax information the director deems appropriate, and shall be provided to the extent permitted by federal laws and regulations.

(am)

(1) To enable the Joint Enforcement Strike Force as established by Section 329, and the Labor Enforcement Task Force, as established pursuant to Assembly Bill 1464 of the 2011-12 Regular Session (Chapter 21 of the Statutes of 2012), to carry out their duties.

(2) To provide an agency listed in subdivision (a) of Section 329 intelligence, data, including confidential tax and fee information, docu-

ments, information, complaints, or lead referrals pursuant to Section 15925 of the Government Code.

(an) To enable the Bureau for Private Postsecondary Education to access and use any relevant quarterly wage data necessary to perform the labor market outcome reporting data match pursuant to Section 94892.6 of the Education Code. The information provided pursuant to this subdivision shall be provided to the extent permitted by state and federal laws and regulations.

(ao) To enable the Civil Rights Department to carry out its duties, including ensuring compliance with Section 12999 of the Government Code. Conduct related to information provided pursuant to this subdivision shall not be subject to the criminal sanctions set forth in subdivision (f) of Section 1094.

(ap) To enable the Cradle-to-Career Data System, as established by Article 2 (commencing with Section 10860) of Chapter 8.5 of Part 7 of Division 1 of Title 1 of the Education Code, to receive employment and earnings data and, as required of the director pursuant to Section 10871 of the Education Code, to provide information to the data system, to the extent permissible by federal laws and regulations.

(aq)

(1) To enable the State Air Resources Board to receive unpaid final tax assessment information issued to a port drayage motor carrier or short-haul trucking service for misclassification of a commercial driver, for use in the administration of, and to facilitate compliance with, Chapter 3.6 (commencing with Section 39680) of Part 2 of Division 26 of the Health and Safety Code. The information shall be limited to the tax information the director deems appropriate for disclosure and shall be provided only to the extent permitted by federal laws and regulations.

(2) For purposes of this subdivision, the following definitions apply:

(A) "Commercial driver" has the same meaning as defined in Section 2810.4 of the Labor Code.

(B) "Port drayage motor carrier" has the same meaning as defined in Section 2810.4 of the Labor Code.

(C) "Short-haul trucking service" has the same meaning as defined in Section 39682 of the Health and Safety Code.

(ar) To enable the California Health Benefit Exchange to do all of the following:

(1) Notify an employer that an employee has been determined eligible for advance payments of the premium tax credit and cost-sharing reductions and has enrolled in a qualified health plan through the California Health Benefit Exchange, as required pursuant to Section 155.310(h) of Title 45 of the Code of Federal Regulations. The information shall include available employer contact information, including addresses, email addresses, and telephone numbers.

(2) Assist the California Health Benefit Exchange or the State Department of Health Care Services in determining eligibility for the insurance affordability programs administered by those state agencies. Upon the request of either the California Health Benefit Exchange or the State Department of Health Care Services, the department shall also provide to the relevant state agency information on new applicants for unemployment insurance, state disability insurance, and paid family leave. This information shall included the data points listed in paragraph (1) of subdivision (a) of Section 100503.9 of the Government Code, and shall be sent in a manner that is encrypted or otherwise complies with government data security best practices, as specified by the California Health Benefit Exchange. The determination of eligibility or entitlement shall include efforts by either the California Health Benefit Exchange or the State Department of Health Care Services to assist those individuals in obtaining that coverage, including informing those individuals potentially eligible for health coverage of the availability of that coverage.

(3) Verify if a consumer has been offered affordable comprehensive employer-sponsored health care coverage pursuant to Title 22 (commencing with Section 100500) of the Government Code and the federal Patient Protection and Affordable Care Act (Public Law 111-148). The information shall include available employer contact information, including addresses, email addresses, and telephone numbers.

(4) This subdivision shall become operative no later than September 1, 2023.

Enacted Stats 1953 ch 308. Amended Stats 1971 ch 578 § 13, effective August 13, 1971, operative October 1, 1971; Stats 1973 ch 1206 § 57, ch 1207 § 57, ch 1212 § 157, operative July 1, 1974; Stats 1977 ch 1252 § 406, operative July 1, 1978; Stats 1979 ch 288 § 2; Stats 1982 ch 1080 § 2; Stats 1983 ch 175 § 1, effective July 11, 1983; Stats 1984 ch 1127 § 5; Stats 1985 ch 543 § 4; Stats 1986 ch 331 § 1; Stats 1987 ch 855 § 3; Stats 1990 ch 1024 § 1 (AB 3092), ch 1084 § 2 (SB 2053); Stats 1991 ch 659 § 6 (AB 1137); Stats 1992 ch 1352 § 9 (AB 3660), effective September 30, 1992; Stats 1993 ch 295 § 8 (SB 774), ch 891 § 3 (AB 1881), ch 1144 § 19 (SB 857); Stats 1994 ch 146 § 216 (AB 3601), ch 1049 § 4 (AB 3086) (ch 1049 prevails); Stats 1995 ch 313 § 16 (AB 817), effective August 3, 1995, ch 701 § 1 (SB 488); Stats 1996 ch 1124 § 1 (SB 1524), effective September 30, 1996; Stats 1997 ch 78 § 4 (AB 71), ch 810 § 1.4 (SB 132); Stats 1998 ch 217 § 2 (AB 2017); Stats 1999 ch 83 § 185 (SB 966); Stats 2002 ch 744 § 11 (SB 1953); Stats 2003 ch 789 § 26 (SB 364); Stats 2007 ch 272 § 1 (AB 798), effective January 1, 2008; ch 662 § 3.5 (SB 869), effective January 1, 2008; Stats 2008 ch 369 § 8 (AB 1844), effective January 1, 2009; Stats 2009–2010 5th Ex Sess ch 2 § 22 (SBX5 1), effective April 13, 2010; Stats 2010 ch 139 § 1 (AB 2433), effective January 1, 2011; Stats 2012 ch 815 § 4 (AB 174), effective January 1, 2013, ch 832 § 2 (SB 691), effective January 1, 2013; Stats 2013 ch 553 § 1 (AB 908), effective January 1, 2014; Stats 2014 ch 692 § 2 (SB 1028), effective January 1, 2015, ch 751 § 1 (SB 1141), effective January 1, 2015, ch 889 § 3.8 (AB 1792), effective January 1, 2015; Stats 2015 ch 20 § 14 (SB 79), effective June 24, 2015; Stats 2015 ch 358 § 1 (AB 145), effective September 30, 2015; Stats 2016 ch 31 § 277 (SB 836), effective June 27, 2016; Stats 2017 ch 417 § 32 (AB 1696), effective January 1, 2018; Stats 2019 ch 25 § 53.5 (SB 94), effective

June 27, 2019; Stats 2019 ch 519 § 2 (AB 1340), effective January 1, 2020; Stats 2019 ch 611 § 1.5 (AB 593), effective January 1, 2020; Stats 2019 ch 626 § 3.7 (AB 1296), effective January 1, 2020 (ch 626 prevails); Stats 2020 ch 21 § 18 (AB 102), effective June 29, 2020; Stats 2020 ch 370 § 263 (SB 1371), effective January 1, 2021 (ch 21 prevails); Stats 2021 ch 78 § 10 (AB 138), effective July 16, 2021; Stats 2021 ch 144 § 76 (AB 132), effective July 27, 2021; Stats 2021 ch 550 § 1 (SB 753), effective January 1, 2022; Stats 2021 ch 748 § 11.5 (AB 794), effective January 1, 2022 (ch 748 prevails); Stats 2022 ch 48 § 74 (SB 189), effective June 30, 2022; Stats 2022 ch 49 § 11 (SB 188), effective June 30, 2022; Stats 2022 ch 569 § 55 (AB 156), effective September 27, 2022; Stats 2022 ch 983 § 3 (SB 644), effective January 1, 2023.

§ 1095.5. Use of information by Mental Health Services Oversight and Accountability Commission

The director shall permit the use of any information in his or her possession to the extent necessary to enable the Mental Health Services Oversight and Accountability Commission to receive quarterly wage data of mental health consumers served by the California public mental health system for the purpose of monitoring and evaluating employment outcomes to determine the effectiveness of those services, and may require reimbursement for all direct costs incurred in providing any and all information specified in this section. The information shall be provided to the extent permitted under applicable federal statute and regulation.

Added   Stats   2017   ch 403   § 1   (AB 462),   effective   January   1,   2018.

DIVISION 3

EMPLOYMENT SERVICES PROGRAMS

PART 1

EMPLOYMENT AND EMPLOYABILITY SERVICES

Chapter 4

Programs

Article 1

Eligibility

§ 10501. Exemption of assistance recipient from examination or certification fees

Any public assistance recipient who successfully completes a job training program approved under this part shall be exempted from the payment of those fees normally associated with any examination or certification required by state law if the employment opportunity is for the job for which the recipient was trained.

Added Stats 1972 ch 1281 § 1.

VEHICLE CODE

DIVISION 12
EQUIPMENT OF VEHICLES

Chapter 2
Lighting Equipment

Article 3

Rear Lighting Equipment

§ 24615. Slow moving vehicle emblem

It is unlawful to operate upon a public highway any vehicle or combination of vehicles, which is designed to be and is operated at a speed of 25 miles per hour or less, unless the rearmost vehicle displays a "slow–moving vehicle emblem," except upon vehicles used by a utility, whether publicly or privately owned, for the construction, maintenance, or repair of its own facilities or upon vehicles used by highway authorities or bridge or highway districts in highway maintenance, inspection, survey, or construction work, while such vehicle is engaged in work at the jobsite upon a highway. Any other vehicle or combination of vehicles, when operated at a speed of 25 miles per hour or less, may display such emblem. The emblem shall be mounted on the rear of the vehicle, base down, and at a height of not less than three nor more than five feet from ground to base. Such emblem shall consist of a truncated equilateral triangle having a minimum height of 14 inches with a red reflective border not less than 1¾ inches in width and a fluorescent orange center.

This emblem shall not be displayed except as permitted or required by this section.

Added Stats 1969 ch 949 § 1. Amended Stats 1971 ch 287 § 1.

Article 7

Flashing and Colored Lights

§ 25260.1. Warning lights on vehicles engaged in construction, removal, or inspection of oil or gas pipeline

Vehicles actually engaged in the construction, removal, maintenance, or inspection of any oil or gas pipeline may display flashing amber warning lights to the front, sides, or rear when necessarily parked on a highway or when necessarily moving at a speed slower than the normal flow of traffic and only in accordance with Section 25268.

Added Stats 1978 ch 120 § 1.

Article 14

Vehicles Exempted

§ 25801. Special construction and maintenance equipment

The provisions of Sections 24012, 24250, 24251, 24254, 24400 to 24404, inclusive, 24600 to 24604, inclusive, 24606 to 24610, inclusive, Section 25950, and Articles 4 (commencing with Section 24800), 5 (commencing with Section 24950), 6 (commencing with Section 25100), 9 (commencing with Section 25350), 11 (commencing with Section 25450), 12 (commencing with Section 25500), and 13 (commencing with Section 25650) shall not apply to special construction or maintenance equipment, nor to motortrucks equipped with snow removal or sanding devices, but shall apply to motortrucks and automobiles used independently of such equipment.

The provisions of Section 25803 shall be applicable to such equipment.

Enacted 1959 ch 3. Amended Stats 1961 ch 1659 § 9; Stats 1972 ch 618 § 148.

Appendix

Chapter 5

Other Equipment

Article 1

Horns, Sirens, and Amplification Devices

§ 27000. Horns; Backup device or alarm and video camera on garbage trucks

(a) A motor vehicle, when operated upon a highway, shall be equipped with a horn in good working order and capable of emitting sound audible under normal conditions from a distance of not less than 200 feet, but no horn shall emit an unreasonably loud or harsh sound. An authorized emergency vehicle may be equipped with, and use in conjunction with the siren on that vehicle, an air horn that emits sounds that do not comply with the requirements of this section.

(b) A refuse or garbage truck shall be equipped with an automatic backup audible alarm that sounds on backing and is capable of emitting sound audible under normal conditions from a distance of not less than 100 feet or shall be equipped with an automatic backup device that is in good working order, located at the rear of the vehicle and that immediately applies the service brake of the vehicle on contact by the vehicle with any obstruction to the rear. The backup device or alarm shall also be capable of operating automatically when the vehicle is in neutral or a forward gear but rolls backward.

(c) A refuse or garbage truck, except a vehicle, known as a rolloff vehicle, that is used for the express purpose of transporting waste containers such as open boxes or compactors, purchased after January 1, 2010, shall also be equipped with a functioning camera providing a video display for the driver that enhances or supplements the driver's view behind the truck for the purpose of safely maneuvering the truck.

(d) (1) A construction vehicle with a gross vehicle weight rating (GVWR) in excess of 14,000 pounds that operates at, or transports construction or industrial materials to and from, a mine or construction site, or both, shall be equipped with an automatic backup audible alarm that sounds on backing and is capable of emitting sound audible under normal conditions from a distance of not less than 200 feet.

(2) As used in this subdivision, "construction vehicle" includes, but is not limited to, all of the following:

(A) A vehicle designed to transport concrete, cement, clay, limestone, aggregate material as defined in subdivision (d) of Section 23114, or other similar construction or industrial material, including a transfer truck or a tractor trailer combination used exclusively to pull bottom dump, end dump, or side dump trailers.

(B) A vehicle that is a concrete mixer truck, a truck with a concrete placing boom, a water tank truck, a single engine crane with a load rating of 35 tons or more, or a tractor that exclusively pulls a low-boy trailer.

Enacted Stats 1959 ch 3. Amended Stats 1965 ch 1015 § 1; Stats 1982 ch 926 § 1, effective September 13, 1982; Stats 1983 ch 1144 § 8, effective September 28, 1983; Stats 1997 ch 945 § 27 (AB 1561); Stats 2005 ch 166 § 2 (AB 1637), effective January 1, 2006; Stats 2011 ch 235 § 1 (SB 341), effective January 1, 2012.

Article 3.5

Headsets and Earplugs

§ 27400. Wearing of headsets, earplugs, or earphones

A person operating a motor vehicle or bicycle may not wear a headset covering, earplugs in, or earphones covering, resting on, or inserted in, both ears. This prohibition does not apply to any of the following:

(a) A person operating authorized emergency vehicles, as defined in Section 165.

(b) A person engaged in the operation of either special construction equipment or equipment for use in the maintenance of any highway.

(c) A person engaged in the operation of refuse collection equipment who is wearing a safety headset or safety earplugs.

(d) A person wearing personal hearing protectors in the form of earplugs or molds that are specifically designed to attenuate injurious noise levels. The plugs or molds shall be designed in a manner so as to not inhibit the wearer's ability to hear a siren or horn from an emergency vehicle or a horn from another motor vehicle.

(e) A person using a prosthetic device that aids the hard of hearing.

Added Stats 1973 ch 87 § 1. Amended Stats 1975 ch 495 § 1; Stats 1977 ch 348 § 1; Stats 1980 ch 107 § 1, effective May 20, 1980; Stats 1982 ch 542 § 1, effective August 18, 1982; Stats 1985 ch 736 § 2. Amended Stats 2003 ch 594 § 45 (SB 315); Stats 2015 ch 451 § 55 (SB 491), effective January 1, 2016.

Appendix

DIVISION 14.8

SAFETY REGULATIONS

§ 34510.5. Construction transportation services; Surety bond; Violations; Penalties

(a) (1) A broker of construction trucking services, as defined in Section 3322 of the Civil Code, shall not furnish construction transportation services to any construction project unless it has secured a surety bond of not less than fifteen thousand dollars ($15,000) executed by an admitted surety insurer. The surety bond shall ensure the payment of the claims of a contracted motor carrier of property in dump truck equipment if the broker fails to pay the contracted motor carrier within the time period specified in paragraph (1) of subdivision (a) of Section 3322 of the Civil Code.

(2) (A) A broker of construction trucking services annually shall provide written evidence of the broker's valid surety bond to a third-party nonprofit organization that is related to the industry and regularly maintains a published database of bonded brokers or post a current copy of the surety bond on the broker's Internet Web site.

(B) When a copy of a surety bond is provided to a third-party nonprofit organization, the broker shall notify the third-party nonprofit organization if at any time the surety bond is cancelled or expired. When a copy of the surety bond is posted on the broker's Internet Web site, the broker shall remove the copy of the surety bond from his or her Internet Web site if at any time the surety bond is cancelled or expired.

(C) A third-party nonprofit organization shall not charge a broker for posting evidence of a valid surety bond or limit the posting of the bond only to the organization's members.

(D) A third-party nonprofit organization shall not be liable for any damages caused by the publication of any information provided pursuant to this paragraph that is erroneous or outdated.

(b) A broker of construction trucking services shall not hire, or otherwise engage the services of, a motor carrier of property to furnish construction transportation services unless the broker provides, prior to the commencement of work each calendar year, written evidence of the broker's valid surety bond to any person that hires, or otherwise engages the services of, the broker to furnish construction transportation services and also to the hired motor carrier of property.

(c) A broker of construction trucking services who furnishes construction transportation services in violation of this section is guilty of a misdemeanor and subject to a fine of up to five thousand dollars ($5,000).

(d) In any civil action brought against a broker of construction trucking services by a motor carrier of property in dump truck equipment with whom the broker contracted during any period of time in which the broker did not have a surety bond in violation of this section, the failure to have the bond shall create a rebuttable presumption that the broker failed to pay to the motor carrier the amount due and owing.

(e) For purposes of this section, "a broker of construction trucking services" does not include a facility that meets all the following requirements:

(1) Arranges for transportation services of its product.

(2) Primarily handles raw materials to produce a new product.

(3) Is a rock product operation (such as an "aggregate" operation), a hot mixing asphalt plant, or a concrete, concrete product, or Portland cement product manufacturing facility.

(4) Does not accept a fee for the arrangement.

(f) For the purposes of this section, "written evidence of the broker's valid surety bond" includes a copy of the surety bond, a certificate of insurance, a continuation certificate, or other similar documentation originally issued from the surety that includes the surety's and broker's name, the bond number, and the effective and expiration dates of the bond.

Added Stats 2010 ch 429 § 1 (AB 145), effective January 1, 2011. Amended Stats 2012 ch 490 § 1 (SB 1092), effective January 1, 2013; Stats 2013 ch 76 § 197 (AB 383), effective January 1, 2014.

WATER CODE

DIVISION 6

CONSERVATION, DEVELOPMENT, AND UTILIZATION OF STATE WATER RESOURCES

PART 2.4

RAINWATER CAPTURE ACT OF 2012

§ 10570. Citation of part

This part shall be known, and may be cited, as the Rainwater Capture Act of 2012.

Added Stats 2012 ch 537 § 2 (AB 1750), effective January 1, 2013.

§ 10571. Legislative findings and declarations

The Legislature finds and declares all of the following:

(a) As California has grown and developed, the amount of storm-water flowing off buildings, parking lots, roads, and other impervious surfaces into surface water streams, flood channels, and storm sewers has increased, thereby reducing the volume of water allowed to infiltrate into groundwater aquifers and increasing water and pollution flowing to the ocean and other surface waters. At the same time, recurring droughts and water shortages in California have made local water supply augmentation and water conservation efforts a priority.

(b) Historical patterns of precipitation are predicted to change, with two major implications for water supply. First, an increasing amount of California's water is predicted to fall not as snow in the mountains, but as rain in other areas of the state. This will likely have a profound and transforming effect on California's hydrologic cycle and much of that water will no longer be captured by California's reservoirs, many of which are located to capture snowmelt. Second, runoff resulting from snowmelt is predicted to occur progressively earlier in the year, and reservoirs operated for flood control purposes must release water early in the season to protect against later storms, thereby reducing the amount of early season snowmelt that can be stored.

(c) Rainwater and stormwater, captured and properly managed, can contribute significantly to local water supplies by infiltrating and recharging groundwater aquifers, thereby increasing available supplies of drinking water. In addition, the onsite capture, storage, and use of rainwater for nonpotable uses significantly reduces demand for potable water, contributing to the statutory objective of a 20-percent reduction in urban per capita water use in California by December 31, 2020.

(d) Expanding opportunities for rainwater capture to augment water supply will require efforts at all levels, from individual landowners to state and local agencies and watershed managers.

Added Stats 2012 ch 537 § 2 (AB 1750), effective January 1, 2013.

§ 10572. Limitations of part

Nothing in this part shall be construed to do any of the following:

(a) Alter or impair any existing rights.

(b) Change existing water rights law.

(c) Authorize a landscape contractor to engage in or perform activities that require a license pursuant to the Professional Engineers Act (Chapter 7 (commencing with Section 6700) of Division 3 of the Business and Professions Code).

(d) Impair the authority of the California Building Standards Commission to adopt and implement building standards for rainwater capture systems pursuant to existing law.

(e) Affect use of rainwater on agricultural lands.

(f) Impair the authority of a water supplier pursuant to Subchapter 1 of Chapter 5 of Division 1 of Title 17 of the California Code of Regulations.

Added Stats 2012 ch 537 § 2 (AB 1750), effective January 1, 2013.

§ 10573. Definitions

Solely for the purposes of this part, and unless the context otherwise requires, the following definitions govern the construction of this part:

(a) "Developed or developing lands" means lands that have one or more of the characteristics described in subparagraphs (A) to (C), inclusive, of paragraph (4) of subdivision (b) of Section 56375.3 of the Government Code.

(b) "Rain barrel system" is a type of rainwater capture system that does not use electricity or a water pump and is not connected to or reliant on a potable water system.

(c) "Rainwater" means precipitation on any public or private parcel that has not entered an offsite storm drain system or channel, a flood control channel, or any other stream channel, and has not previously been put to beneficial use.

Appendix

(d) "Rainwater capture system" means a facility designed to capture, retain, and store rainwater flowing off a building rooftop for subsequent onsite use.

(e) "Stormwater" has the same meaning as defined in Section 10561.5.

Added Stats 2012 ch 537 § 2 (AB 1750), effective January 1, 2013. Amended Stats 2014 ch 555 § 6 (SB 985), effective January 1, 2015.

§ 10574. Rainwater collection does not require water right permit

Use of rainwater collected from rooftops does not require a water right permit pursuant to Section 1201.

Added Stats 2012 ch 537 § 2 (AB 1750), effective January 1, 2013.

DIVISION 7

WATER QUALITY

Chapter 10

Water Wells and Cathodic Protection Wells

Article 3

Reports

§ 13750.5. Requirement of water well contractor's license

No person shall undertake to dig, bore, or drill a water well, cathodic protection well, groundwater monitoring well, or geothermal heat exchange well, to deepen or reperforate such a well, or to abandon or destroy such a well, unless the person responsible for that construction, alteration, destruction, or abandonment possesses a C–57 Water Well Contractor's License.

Added Stats 1986 ch 1373 § 2.5. Amended Stats 1996 ch 581 § 5 (AB 2334).

ADDITIONAL RESOURCES

All California codes listed below can be accessed through the
California State Legislature's Website, www.leginfo.ca.gov.

SUBJECT	RESOURCE
ACCESS FOR PERSONS WITH PHYSICAL DISABILITIES	
Disability Access Requirements	*California Code of Regulations,* Title 24 Part 2 (State Building Code) Part 3 (State Electrical Code) Part 5 (State Plumbing Code) (See also Parts 1, 8 and 12)
	Federal: The Americans with Disabilities Act (ADA) The ADA Accessibility Guidelines (ADAAG)
	California: 1988 Fair Housing Amendments Act
Publications	California:
California Access Compliance Reference Manual	Copies are available through builders bookstores throughout California or the Division of the State Architect
California Code of Regulations, Title 24	Division of the State Architect or your local technical bookstore

SUBJECT	RESOURCE
Access Guide: Survey Checklist	Disability Access Services Section, Department of Rehabilitation (916) 558-5755, Fax (916) 558-5757; TTY: (916) 558-5758
A Guide to California Multi Family Disability Access Regulations	California Building Officials 1225 8th Street, Suite 425 Sacramento, CA 95814 (916) 457-1103, Fax (916) 442-3616 *www.calbo.org*
Technical Assistance Manual on compliance	Federal: U.S. Department of Justice 950 Pennsylvania Avenue, NW Disability Rights Section – NYAV Washington, DC 20530 (800) 514-0301, (800) 514-0383 (TDD)
Americans with Disabilities Act Accessibility Guidelines (ADAAG)	U.S. Access Board 1331 F Street NW, Suite1000 Washington, DC 20004-1111 (800) 872-2253, Fax (202) 272-0081 (800) 993-2822 (TTY) *www.access-board.gov*
Telephone Assistance	
Begin by contacting	Local building department or jurisdiction

SUBJECT	RESOURCE
Code interpretations regarding all publicly funded buildings and privately funded buildings open to the general public	Division of the State Architect, Office of Universal Design Access Compliance 1102 Q Street, Suite 5100 Sacramento CA 95811 (916) 445-8100, Fax (916) 445-3521 *www.dsa.dgs.ca.gov*
Technical information or access policy, regulations and interpretations, or for information on plans approval processes for publicly funded schools, colleges, or universities	Division of the State Architect (916) 445-8100
General information regarding access requirements contained in Title 24 of the California Code of Regulations and the ADA requirements	Department of Rehabilitation, Disability Access Services Section P.O. Box 944222 Sacramento, CA 94299-9222 (916) 558-5755, Fax (916) 558-5757; TTY: (916) 558-5758 *www.dor.ca.gov*
Code interpretations relating to privately funded multifamily buildings	Department of Housing and Community Development/Codes and Standards Division 1800 3rd Street, Room 260 Sacramento CA 95814 (916) 445-9471, Fax (916) 327-4712 *www.hcd.ca.gov*
Federal accessibility requirements	Department of Justice or the Access Board, as listed above

Resources

SUBJECT	RESOURCE
ADVERTISING: ILLEGAL PRACTICES AND PENALTIES	
Advertising	Business & Professions Code Division 7, Part 3, Chapter 1
BONDS	
Bond and Undertaking Law	Code of Civil Procedure Title 14, Chapter 2
BUILDING STANDARDS	
State Housing Law, Building Standards Law	California Health and Safety Code Division 13
California Building Standards Code	California Code of Regulations Title 24
Publications	
California Building Standards Code with California Amendments (Title 24)	International Code Council 5360 Workman Mill Road Whittier, CA 90601-2298 (888) ICC-SAFE (422-7233), Fax (562) 908-5524 *www.iccsafe.org*

SUBJECT	RESOURCE
Other responsible agencies	Department of Industrial Relations
	Division of Occupational Safety and Health
	Division of the State Architect
	Department of Housing and Community Development
	Division of Housing Codes and Standards
	Department of Health Services
	California Energy Commission
	Office of State Health Planning and Development
	State Fire Marshal
EMPLOYMENT ELIGIBILITY VERIFICATION	U.S. Department of Justice, Immigration and Naturalization Service (INS), Office of Business
Responsible Agency	Liaison: Employer Information Line (800) 357-2099 National Customer Service Center (800) 375-5283, Fax (202) 305-2523 *http://uscis.gov*
EMPLOYMENT PRACTICES	
California Fair Employment and Housing Act	Government Code Title 2, Division 3, Part 2.8

SUBJECT	RESOURCE
EMPLOYMENT TAXES, FEDERAL	
Responsible Agencies	Internal Revenue Service (800) 829-1040 *www.irs.ustreas.gov*
	Social Security Administration (800) 772-1213 *www.socialsecurity.gov*
Publications	
Circular E Employer's Tax Guide	Internal Revenue Service
Employment Taxes and Information Returns	Internal Revenue Service
EMPLOYMENT TAXES, STATE	
Responsible Agencies	Employment Development Department (EDD) *www.edd.ca.gov* or contact your local office
	Franchise Tax Board (FTB) *www.ftb.ca.gov* or contact your local office

SUBJECT	RESOURCE
Publications	
California Unemployment Insurance Code	Employment Development Department Business Operations Planning and Support Division, MIC 62 P.O. Box 826880 Sacramento, CA 94280-0001 Workforce Div.: (916) 654-6856
California Employer's Tax Guide	Employment Development Department
LABOR CODE	
Department of Industrial Relations	*Labor Code,* Division 1
Employment Regulation and Supervision	*Labor Code,* Division 2 Part 1. Compensation Part 2. Working Hours Part 3. Privileges and Immunities Part 4. Employees Part 7. Public Works and Public Agencies Part 9. Health
Federal Fair Labor Standards Act of 1938	*Code of Federal Regulations,* Title 29
Employment Relations	*Labor Code,* Division 3

SUBJECT	RESOURCE
Workers' Compensation	*Labor Code*, Division 4 Part 1. Scope and Operation Part 2. Computation of Compensation Part 3. Compensation Claims Part 4. Compensation Proceedings
Safety in Employment	*Labor Code*, Division 5 Part 1. Occupational Safety and Health Part 3. Safety on Building Part 7. Volatile Flammable Liquids Part 10. Use of Carcinogens
PUBLIC INFORMATION ACCESS	
Open Meeting Act	*Government Code:* Title 2, Division 3, Part 1
California Public Records Act	*Government Code:* Title 1, Division 7, Ch. 3.5.
Information Practices Act of 1977	*Civil Code:* Title 1.8, Division 3, Part 4, Ch. 1
Business Records	*Civil Code:* Title 1.82, Division 3, Part 4, Ch. 1-3
District Attorney	*Government Code:* Title 3, Div. 2, Part 3, Ch. 1

SUBJECT	RESOURCE
SAFETY AND HEALTH *Publications* *California Occupational Safety and Health Standards— Title 8 California Code of Regulations* *Cal/OSHA Guide for the Construction Industry*	Barclay's Official Code of Regulations P.O. Box 2006 San Francisco, CA 94126 (800) 888-3600 Fax (415) 344-3906 barclaysccr@thomson.com or
Guide to Cal/OSHA	DOSH 1221 Farmers Lane, Suite 300 Santa Rosa, CA 95405 (707) 576-2388 Fax (707) 576-2598 *www.dir.ca.gov*
Guide to Developing Your Workplace Injury and Illness Prevention Program	Department of Industrial Relations P.O. Box 420603 San Francisco, CA 94142-0603 (800) 963-9424, (916) 574-2339 *www.bni-books.com*
Information concerning Occupational Safety and Health requirements	Cal/OSHA Consultation Services (see list at the end of Chapter 7)
STATE SALES AND USE TAX *Responsible Agency*	California State Board of Equalization (800) 400-7115 *www.boe.ca.gov*

Resources

Index

Index

Employer and employee.
Unfair immigration-related
practices, Appendix LC 1019,
Appendix LC 1019.1
Public works.
Prevailing wage.
Contractor recovery of increased
costs from hiring party,
Appendix LC 1784
Enforcement of requirement,
Appendix LC 1771.2
Reporting of civil actions against
licensees to registrar.
Confidential settlements or other
agreements.
Report not considered violation of
confidentiality, Ch 12 B&P
7071.22
Insurers of licensees, reporting, Ch
12 B&P 7071.21
Requirement to report, Ch 12 B&P
7071.20

ADDITIONAL RESOURCES,
Additional Resources

ADDRESS, CHANGE OF, Ch 11 B&P
135.5, Ch 12 B&P 7083 to Ch 12 B&P
7083.1

ADMINISTRATIVE REMEDIES.
Misuse of license, Ch 12 B&P 7114.2

ADVERTISING, Ch 12 B&P 7027 to
Ch 12 B&P 7027.4
Alphabetical or classified directory,
Ch 12 B&P 7099.10
Asbestos-related work, Ch 12 B&P
7099.11
Bonds, reference in, Ch 12 B&P
7071.13
Display on vehicle, Ch 12 B&P 7029.6
Drill rigs, electrical sign contractor,
plumbing contractor, Ch 12 B&P
7029.5
False or misleading, Ch 12 B&P 7160
to Ch 12 B&P 7161
Illegal practices and penalties.
Additional resources for law, rules,
etc, governing advertising,
Additional Resources
Insured or bonded.

Requirements for including terms
in advertising, Ch 12 B&P
7027.4
License number, inclusion in or
required on, Ch 11 B&P 137, Ch 12
B&P 7030.5, Ch 13 T 16 CCR 861
Minor work exemption, voided by, Ch
12 B&P 7048
Property assessed clean energy
(PACE) and clean energy financing
program.
Clean energy assessment contracts.
Advertisement of availability of
contracts, Appendix S&H 5922
Public officials, used in, Ch 12 B&P
7190
Unlicensed persons, Ch 12 B&P
7027.1, Ch 12 B&P 7027.2
In alphabetical or classified
directory, Ch 12 B&P 7099.10

**AHERA (ASBESTOS HAZARD
EMERGENCY RESPONSE ACT),
REQUIREMENTS,** p. 136

AIDING AND ABETTING, Ch 12 B&P
7114

ALARM COMPANIES.
Definitions, Appendix B&P 7590.1

**ALARM (SECURITY) COMPANY
OPERATORS, LICENSE
EXEMPTION,** Ch 12 B&P 7054

ALIENS.
Consumer affairs, department of.
Citizenship or immigration status
of applicant not to affect
licensure by entities within
department, Ch 11 B&P 135.5
Employment.
Eligibility and verification
generally.
Additional resources for law,
rules, etc, Additional Resources
Unfair immigration-related
practices, Appendix LC 1019,
Appendix LC 1019.1
Reverifying eligibility of employee
by employer when not required
by federal provision, Appendix
LC 1019.2

BOARD, DEFINED, Ch 11 B&P 22

**BOARD RULES AND
REGULATIONS,** Ch 13 T 16 CCR
810 to Ch 13 T 16 CCR 890

**BOILER, HOT-WATER HEATING
AND STEAM FITTING
CONTRACTOR (C-4),** Ch 13 T 16
CCR 832.04

BONDED STOP NOTICE, p. 112

BONDS.
Actions, bonds and undertakings,
Appendix CCP 995.010 to Appendix
CCP 995.960
Cancellation of bond or withdrawal
of sureties, Appendix CCP
996.310 to Appendix CCP
996.360
Enforcement lien, Appendix CCP
996.510 to Appendix CCP
996.560
Insufficient and excessive bonds,
Appendix CCP 996.010 to
Appendix CCP 996.030
Liability of principal and sureties,
Appendix CCP 996.410 to
Appendix CCP 996.495
New, additional and supplemental
bonds, Appendix CCP 996.210 to
Appendix CCP 996.250
Release or substitution of sureties
on bond, Appendix CCP 996.110
to Appendix CCP 996.150
Alternatives to bonds, Ch 13 T 16
CCR 856, p. 28 to 29
Blanket performance and payment
bond, Ch 13 T 16 CCR 858 to Ch 13
T 16 CCR 858.9
Bond and undertaking law generally.
Additional resources for law, rules,
etc, Additional Resources
Code of civil procedure.
Bonds and undertakings, Appendix
CCP 995.010 to Appendix CCP
996.560
Construction trucking services,
Appendix VC 34510.5
Contract bond, p. 75

Contractor bonds, p. 26, p. 27
Acceptance by registrar, Ch 12
B&P 7071.7
Action on claim against bond, Ch
12 B&P 7071.11
After suspension or revocation of
license, disciplinary bond, Ch 12
B&P 7071.8
Approved alternatives to, p. 28 to
29
Civil penalties, no payment against
bond, Ch 12 B&P 7099.7
Condition of license issuance, Ch 12
B&P 7071.6
Condition precedent to LLC license,
Ch 12 B&P 7071.6.5
Criminal convictions, report to
registrar, Ch 12 B&P 7071.18
Discrimination, Ch 12 B&P 7071.14
Failure to maintain sufficient bond,
effect, Ch 12 B&P 7071.15
Judgment bond, Ch 12 B&P 7071.6
Licensee duties, Ch 12 B&P 7071.4
LLC licenses, Ch 12 B&P 7071.6.5
Liability insurance requirement,
Ch 12 B&P 7071.19
Persons benefited, Ch 12 B&P
7071.5
Reference in advertising, Ch 12
B&P 7071.13
Release of deposit, restrictions, Ch
12 B&P 7071.4
Suspension of license, p. 30
Contractor license bonds, p. 75
Disciplinary bond, Ch 12 B&P 7071.8
General requirements, p. 28
Infrastructure financing, Appendix
GC 5956.6
Agreements between agency and
private entity, Appendix GC
5956.6
Licensing.
For revenue, by cities, Appendix
GC 5956.6
License, contractors.
Issuance of license, conditions for.
Requirements for issuance other
than exam, p. 24 to 25
Requirements, p. 3, p. 28
Where obtained, p. 26
Limited liability company surety
bond, p. 76

Index

C

Index

Index

FIRE PREVENTION AND CONTROL.
Fire protection systems, installation, Ch 12 B&P 7026.12, Ch 13 T 16 CCR 832.16

FIRE PROTECTION CONTRACTOR (C-16), Ch 13 T 16 CCR 832.16

FIRE PROTECTION SYSTEMS, Ch 12 B&P 7026.12, Ch 13 T 16 CCR 832.16

FLOORING AND FLOOR COVERING CONTRACTOR (C-15), Ch 13 T 16 CCR 832.15

FLOORING AND FLOOR COVERINGS.
Public works and public agencies.
Consolidation of needs.
Carpets, flooring, synthetic turf or lighting fixtures, installation and purchase, Appendix PCC 10298.5

FORGERY AND COUNTERFEITING.
Investigations.
Unemployment compensation records.
Access to records in aid of investigation, Appendix UIC 1095

FRAMING AND ROUGH CARPENTRY (C-5), Ch 13 T 16 CCR 832.05

FRANCHISE TAX BOARD.
Licensee information to be provided to, Appendix RTC 19528

FRAUD, Appendix PC 484b, Ch 12 B&P 7116
Insurance fraud, Appendix PC 551
Investigations.
Unemployment compensation records.
Access to records in aid of investigation of document fraud or consumer fraud, Appendix UIC 1095

Mechanics liens.
Stop payment notices, false, Appendix CC 8504
State of Emergency.
Fraud in repairing natural disaster damage, enhanced sentence, Appendix PC 667.16

FUNDS, MISUSE OF, Appendix PC 484b, Appendix PC 484c, Ch 12 B&P 7108

G

GARDENER, LICENSE EXEMPTION, Ch 12 B&P 7026.1

GENERAL BUILDING CONTRACTOR, Ch 12 B&P 7057
Addition of classification without examination, Ch 12 B&P 7065.3
Advertising.
General contractor, advertising as, Ch 12 B&P 7027.1
Asbestos work by general building contractor, Ch 13 T 16 CCR 833
Building permits.
Owner-builder of single-family residential structures.
Work done under contract with general building contractor, Appendix H&S 19825
Classification as general building contractor, Ch 12 B&P 7057, Ch 13 T 16 CCR 830
Contractors license generally. (*See* **License, Contractors**)
Contractors state license board.
Composition of board, Ch 12 B&P 7002
Landscape projects.
Work outside scope of landscape contractor classification.
Requirement of license as general building contractor, Ch 12 B&P 7002
Limitations on, Ch 12 B&P 7059, Ch 13 T 16 CCR 830, Ch 13 T 16 CCR 834
School facilities.
Bidders.

J

JOINT AND SEVERAL LIABILITY.
Independent contractor.
Advice to treat individual as,
Appendix LC 2753

JOINT CHECKS, p. 69 to 70

JOINT CONTROL.
Addendum, p. 67 to 68
Agreements, registrar-approved, p. 65
to 68
Defined, p. 65

**JOINT ENFORCEMENT STRIKE
FORCE ON UNDERGROUND
ECONOMY.**
Defined, Appendix UIC 329
Enforcement of complaints of
contractors law violations.
Division participating in strike
force, access to places of labor,
Ch 12 B&P 7011.4
Labor Commissioner authority,
Appendix LC 106
Powers and duties, Appendix UIC 329
Tax or fee administration associated
with underground economic
activities.
Information requests, Appendix GC
15925
Investigative teams to recover lost
revenue.
Collaboration of teams, Appendix
GC 15926
Unemployment compensation.
Records, reports and contribution
payments.
Use of information, Appendix UIC
1095

**JOINT SPONSORSHIP OF
APPRENTICESHIP PROGRAMS,**
Appendix LC 3075

JOINT VENTURE LICENSE.
Contracting jointly without joint
venture license, Ch 12 B&P 7029.1
Defined, Ch 12 B&P 7029
Issuance, Ch 12 B&P 7029
Suspension, Ch 12 B&P 7029

JUDGMENT BOND, Ch 12 B&P
7071.17

**JUDGMENTS AND OUTSTANDING
LIABILITIES,** p. 30 to 33

**JURISDICTION, SMALL CLAIMS
COURT,** Appendix CCP 116.220,
Appendix CCP 116.221

K

KICKBACK.
Prohibited inducements, Ch 12 B&P
7157

L

LABOR CODE.
Additional resources, Additional
Resources
Extracts from related laws, Appx
Violation, disciplinary action for, Ch
12 B&P 7110.5

LANDLORD AND TENANT.
Access by landlord to dwelling unit,
Appendix CC 1954
Rental price.
Increase during state of emergency,
Appendix PC 396

LANDSCAPE CONTRACTOR (C-27),
Ch 13 T 16 CCR 832.27
Architects, licensing and regulation.
Exemption of landscape contractor,
circumstance, Appendix B&P
5641.4
Design authority, Ch 12 B&P 7027.5
Examinations.
Revisions by board to examination,
Ch 12 B&P 7065.06

**LATHING AND PLASTERING
CONTRACTOR (C-35),** Ch 13 T 16
CCR 832.35

LAVATORIES.
Water-conserving plumbing retrofits,
Appendix CC 1101.1 to CC 1101.9

Index

Index

Index

REAL ESTATE LICENSEE, Ch 12
B&P 7044.1

REAL PROPERTY.
Residential property, transfers.
Disclosures upon transfer.
    Errors or omissions, liability,
    Appendix CC 1102.4
Water-conserving plumbing retrofits,
    Appendix CC 1101.1 to CC 1101.9
Noncompliant plumbing fixtures.
    Disclosures upon sale or transfer,
    Appendix CC 1102.155

REASONABLE ACCOMMODATION,
Appendix GC 12944, p. 19 to 20

REASONABLE DILIGENCE.
Lack of, Ch 12 B&P 7119

REBATES.
Illegal (kickbacks), Appendix PC
    532e, Ch 12 B&P 7157

**RECIPROCITY WITH OTHER
STATES,** Ch 12 B&P 7065.4, Ch 12
B&P 7103, p. 5

RECLAMATION DISTRICTS.
License exemption, Ch 12 B&P 7049

RECORDS.
Alternate dispute resolution.
    Statistical records, Ch 11 B&P
    467.6
Members of the personnel of record.
    Defined, Ch 12 B&P 7025
Preservation of, Ch 12 B&P 7111
    Consumer Affairs, Director of.
    Retention of records by providers
        of services related to treatment
        for alcohol or drug impairment,
        Ch 11 B&P 156.1
Workers' compensation insurance.
    Employer, failure to provide access
        to records, Appendix IC 11760.1

**REFRIGERATION CONTRACTOR
(C-38),** Ch 13 T 16 CCR 832.38

**REGIONAL NOTIFICATION
CENTERS,** p. 139 to 142

REGISTRAR OF CONTRACTORS,
Ch 12 B&P 7011
    Continuing jurisdiction over license
        following voluntary surrender,
        expiration or suspension of license,
        Ch 12 B&P 7106.5

REGULATIONS, Ch 13 T 16 CCR 810
    to Ch 13 T 16 CCR 890
Administrative agencies.
    Internet, publication on, Appendix
        GC 11344
Adoption of, Ch 12 B&P 7008
Americans with Disabilities Act, Ch
    11 B&P 313.2
Effective date of regulations,
    Appendix GC 11343.4
Filing and publication procedures,
    Appendix GC 11343

**REHABILITATION FOLLOWING
DENIAL, SUSPENSION, OR
REVOCATION OF LICENSE,
CRITERIA FOR,** Ch 11 B&P 482,
Ch 13 T 16 CCR 869

REINFORCING STEEL (C-50), Ch 13
T 16 CCR 832.50

**REINSTATEMENT OF SUSPENDED
OR REVOKED LICENSE,** Ch 12
B&P 7102

REMODELING.
Residential remodeling contractors,
    Ch 12 B&P 7057.5

**RENEWAL OF HOME
IMPROVEMENT
REGISTRATION,** Ch 12 B&P
7153.3, p. 65

Index

Index

Y

Z

Notes

Notes

Notes

Notes

Notes

Notes